Advances in Consumer Research
Volume XVIII

Rebecca H. Holman
Michael R. Solomon, Editors

1991 Copyright, Association for Consumer Research

All rights reserved. No part of this publication may be reproduced, stored in a retrieval system or transmitted, in any form, by any means, electronic, mechanical, photocopying, recording, or otherwise, without prior written permission of the publisher.

International Standard Book Number (ISBN): 0-915552-26-4

International Standard Serial Number (ISSN): 0098-9258

Rebecca H. Holman, Michael R. Solomon, Editors

Advances in Consumer Research, Volume 18.

(Provo, UT: Association for Consumer Research, 1991.)

ASSOCIATION FOR CONSUMER RESEARCH
1990 OFFICERS

BOARD OF DIRECTORS

President:	Elizabeth C. Hirschman, Rutgers University, New Brunswick
President Elect:	Sidney J. Levy, Northwestern University
Executive Secretary:	H. Keith Hunt, Brigham Young University
Treasurer:	Valerie S. Folkes, University of Southern California
Director:	John E. Calfee, University of Maryland
Director:	Kent B. Monroe, Virginia Tech University
Director:	Diane Schmalensee, Opinion Research

COMMITTEES

Conference:	Rebecca H. Holman, D'Arcy Masius Benton & Bowles, Inc.
	Michael R. Solomon, Rutgers University, New Brunswick
Newsletter:	Peter Bloch, University of Massachusetts
	James Muncy, Clemson University
Publications:	Michael R. Solomon (Chair), Rutgers University, New Brunswick

CONFERENCE COMMITTEE

CONFERENCE CHAIRS

Rebecca H. Holman
D'Arcy Masius Benton & Bowles, Inc.

Michael R. Solomon
Rutgers University, New Brunswick

PROGRAM COMMITTEE

Gary Bamossy, Vrije Universiteit (The Netherlands)
Joseph A. Cote, Washington State University
John Eighmey, University of Alabama
Roberto Friedmann, University of Georgia
Stephen J. Hoch, University of Chicago
Jacob Jacoby, New York University
Michael A. Kamins, University of Southern California
Trudy Kehret-Ward, University of California-Berkeley
Carole Macklin, University of Cincinnati
Paul D. Myles, Goldfarb Consultants
Michael D. Reilly, Montana State University
A. Marvin Roscoe, AT&T
Paul Schurr, State University of New York at Albany
Barbara Stern, Rutgers University, Newark
Marye Tharp, University of Texas, Austin
Gregory D. Upah, Merrill Lynch
John Wittenbraker, ARBOR, Inc.

ARRANGEMENTS COMMITTEE

Leon Schiffman, Baruch College, CUNY (Chair)
Elaine Sherman, Hofstra University
Robert F. Gilmore, Baruch College, CUNY
Rebecca H. Holman, D'Arcy Masius Benton & Bowles, Inc.
Michael R. Solomon, Rutgers University, New Brunswick

COMPETITIVE PAPER REVIEWERS

David Aaker
Joe Alba
Chris Allen
Mark Alpert
Punam Anand
Paul Anderson
Helen Anderson
Beverlee Anderson
Alan Andreasen
Craig Andrews
Charles Areni
Stephen Arnold
April Atwood
Ken Bahn
James Barnes
Rajeev Batra
Bill Bearden
George Belch
Mickey Belch
Russell Belk
Ida Berger
Peter Bloch
Paul Bloom
Ruth Bolton
Ed Bonfield
P. G. Bonner
David Burns
Julia Bristor
Merrie Brucks
Wendy Bryce
Lauranne Buchanan
Jack Calfee
Les Carlson
Dipankar Chakravarti
A. Chattopadhyay
Cathy Cobb-Walgren
Joel Cohen
Cathy Cole
Elizabeth Cooper-Martin
Kim Corfman
Dena Cox
Betsy Creyer
Mary Curren
David Currey
Scott Dawson
John Deighton
Rohit Deshpande
Bill Dillon
Ira Dolich
Cornelia Droge
Julie Edell
Basil Englis
Mike Etzel
Ron Faber
Richard Feinberg
A. Fuat Firat
Eileen Fischer
Valerie Folkes
J. D. Forbes
Gary Ford
Ellen Foxman

Jonathan Frenzen
Marian Friestad
Gary Gaeth
William Gaidis
Meryl Gardner
David Gardner
Jim Gentry
Mary Gilly
Robert Gilmore
James Ginter
Rashi Glazer
Linda Golden
Ronald Goodstein
Cathy Goodwin
Steve Gould
Donald Granbois
Paul Green
Katrin Harich
Manoj Hastak
Doug Hausknecht
William Havlena
Douglas Hawes
Scott Hawkins
Rader Hayes
Tim Heath
Susan Heckler
Deborah Heisley
Robin Higie
Ronald Hill
Elizabeth Hirschman
Susan Holak
Morris Holbrook
David Horne
John Howard
Daniel Howard
Raymond Hubbard
Joel Huber
G. David Hughes
Bruce Hutton
Francoise Jaffe
Chris Janiszewski
Bernie Jaworski
KerenAmi Johnson
Michael Johnson
Marilyn Jones
Annamma Joy
Lynn Kahle
Barbara Kahn
Wagner Kamakura
Frank Kardes
Harold Kassarjian
Carol Kaufman
James Kellaris
Kevin Keller
Robert Kelly
Jerry Kernan
Tina Kiesler
Amna Kirmani
Jolita Kiselius
Noreen Klein
Robert E. Kleine

Richard Kolbe
Robert Kopp
Shanker Krishnan
Dean Krugman
Lynn Langmeyer
Michel Laroche
John Lastovicka
Clark Leavitt
France LeClerc
James Leigh
Sidney Levy
John Liefeld
William Locander
Barbara Loken
Kenneth Lord
John Lynch
Karen Machleit
Debbie MacInnis
Scott MacKenzie
Doug MacLachlan
Tom Madden
John Mager
Jayashree Mahajan
Vijay Mahajan
D. Maheshwaran
Naresh Malhotra
Lalita Manrai
Larry Marks
Howard Marmorstein
Charlotte Mason
Michael Mayo
Michael Mazis
James McAlexander
John McCarty
Gordon McDougal
Mary Ann McGrath
James McNeal
Edward McQuarrie
Siew Meng Leong
Andrew Mitchell
Banwari Mittal
Reza Moinpour
Michele Morganosky
George Moschis
Darrel Muehling
Aydin Muderrisoglu
James Munch
James A. Muncy
Keith Murray
Kent Nakamoto
James Nelson
Thomas O'Guinn
Thomas Olney
Richard Olshavsky
Julie Ozanne
Tom Page
Connie Pechmann
Larry Percy
Steve Perkins
Susan Petroshius
Edward Popper

Ved Prakash
Ivan Preston
Robert Prus
William Qualls
S. Ratneshwar
Pradeep Rau
Peter H. Reingen
Jeff Richards
Marsha Richins
Nancy Ridgway
Debra Ringold
Scott Roberts
Deborah Roedder John
Ken Roering
Randall Rose
Ivan Ross
Michael Rothschild
Paul Sauer
Alan Sawyer
Debra Scammon
Charles Schaninger
Robert Schindler
Bernd Schmidt
Pam Scholder Ellen

John Schouten
David Schumann
Carol Scott
Subrata Sen
Elaine Sherman
John Sherry
Terry Shimp
Allen Shocker
Carolyn Simmons
S. Singh
Joe Sirgy
Ruth Smith
Susan Spiggle
George Sproles
Douglas Stayman
Brian Sternthal
David Stewart
Jeffrey Stoltman
Patricia Stout
William Strahle
Elnora Stuart
Mita Sujan
Harish Sujan
Narasimhan Srinivasan

Wayne Talarzyk
Jeff Tanner
Patriya Tansuhaj
Esther Thorson
U. N. Umesh
Joe Urbany
Meera Venkatraman
Jim Ward
Peter Webb
Barton Weitz
William Wells
John Wheatley
Josh Wiener
Bill Wilke
Liz Wilson
Russell Winer
John Wong
Arch Woodside
Richard Yalch
Youjae Yi
Valarie Zeithaml
Mary Zimmer
George Zinkhan

Preface

This volume contains papers presented at the 1990 Annual Conference of the Association for Consumer Research. The Conference was held October 4-7, 1990, at the Marriott Marquis Hotel in Manhattan. These meetings were attended by over 550 academics, practitioners, and students -- breaking previous attendance records by a wide margin.

The long-standing goal of the Conference is to provide a forum for the presentation and publication of leading-edge research in the field of consumer behavior. This volume reflects the interdisciplinary nature of this endeavor. The research presented is a healthy and diverse mixture of philosophies, literatures, and methodologies; all contribute in their own way to our understanding of consumer phenomena. The present compilation also reflects a special goal of this year's meeting -- to encourage further participation by consumer behavior practitioners. As a result, the Conference program included presentations by well over 40 representatives from business and government. Many of these papers are included herein.

Our choices of which papers to accept for presentation at the Conference and subsequent publication were certainly not easy. We received a record number of submissions, and many good papers were not able to be included due to space constraints. Three types of papers are printed in *Advances in Consumer Research*. First, papers appearing in competitive sessions were selected after undergoing a rigorous review process. Second, many papers were part of special session proposals. These proposals were reviewed by our Program Committee. Finally, since publication of these papers was optional, unfortunately many do not appear in this volume. To partially redress this void, the organizers of special sessions were invited to submit overview papers, some of which also appear in the volume.

The organization of a Conference such as ACR is a monumental task, one which certainly would never have come to fruition without the help of many people. We would like to take this opportunity to express our sincere gratitude to a few of the many colleagues and friends who made these meetings possible. Beth Hirschman, in her role as President-Elect of ACR, had sufficient faith in us to ask to take on the job (an invitation signifying a vote of confidence, an act of revenge, or both). Keith Hunt, the Executive Secretary, was constantly there with both pragmatic and moral support. Our Reviewers and members of the Program Committee did yeoman service; they are acknowledged on the following pages. Leon Schiffman, Elaine Sherman, Robert Gilmore, and Barbara Stern contributed to developing the most exciting and smoothly-run set of extra-curricular activities ever seen at an ACR meeting. In addition, Elaine, Robert, Barbara, and Jennifer Aaker joined us in contributing their time to arrange and lead field trips. Jim Muncy turned in his typically impressive performance in producing a first-rate volume.

The actual coordination of the Conference, which had the potential to be a nightmare for two compulsive folks, was made much easier with the help of some incredibly competent and conscientious people. Sharon Zydney performed the Herculean task of actually making everything work, while somehow managing to maintain a sense of humor throughout. Carol Gibson, Sakae Hata, and the staff in the Office of the Dean at Rutgers University contributed mightily to this effort. Special thanks also go to Roseann Stabile, Al Kristensen, Karen Melnick, Hank Bernstein, Carole Smargon, Joe Plummer, Jaimee Kurfirst and Peter Rosow at DMB&B for their creativity, hard work, support and patience during the months preceding the Conference. We would also like to thank the many students from Rutgers and Baruch who volunteered their time to help out at the conference.

Finally, a special word of thanks to our loved ones for putting up with us during the last year and a half.

Rebecca H. Holman
    D'Arcy Masius Benton & Bowles, Inc.

Michael R. Solomon
    Rutgers University, New Brunswick

Editors

TABLE OF CONTENTS

ACR Officers iii

ACR Conference Committee iv

Competitive Papers Reviewers v

Editor's Preface vii

Table of Contents viii

Conference Program xix

Presidential Address

    Secular Mortality and the Dark Side of Consumer Behavior: Or How Semiotics
Saved My Life 1
        Elizabeth C. Hirschman, Rutgers University

Awards

    Presentation of the Association for Consumer Research Distinguished Service Award
to H. Keith Hunt 5
        Harold H. Kassarjian, UCLA

    Distinguished Service Award Remarks 7
        H. Keith Hunt, Brigham Young University

    FELLOW'S AWARD SPEECH
One Mega and Seven Basic Principles for Consumer Research 8
        Gerald Zaltman

Session 1.1

    Children's Research: Where It's Been, Where It Is Going 11
        Judy A. Harrigan, Harrigan-Bodick, Inc.

    Qualitative and Quantitative Approaches to Child Research 18
        Langbourne Rust, Langbourne Rust Research, Inc.
        Carole Hyatt, Hyatt Associates, Inc.

    Designing Research to Assess Children's Comprehension of Marketing Messages 23
        Laura A. Peracchio, University of Wisconsin - Milwaukee
        Charise Mita, BBDO New York

Session 1.2

    Coupon Usage and the Theory of Reasoned Action 24
        Richard P. Bagozzi, University of Michigan
        Hans Baumgartner, Pennsylvania State University
        Youjae Yi, University of Michigan

    Effects of Experience on Attitude Structure (Abstract) 28
        Robert E. Burnkrant, Ohio State University
        H. Rao Unnava, Ohio State University
        Thomas J. Page, Jr., Michigan State University

On the Effectiveness of Repeated Positive Expressions as an Advertising Strategy 30
    Paul M. Herr, Indiana University
    Russell H. Fazio, Indiana University

Session 1.3

Disposition of Possessions During Role Transitions 33
    Melissa Martin Young, University of Utah

Consumption Responses to Involuntary Job Loss 40
    Scott D. Roberts, Old Dominion University

Divorce, the Disposition of the Relationship, and Everything 43
    James H. McAlexander, Oregon State University

Personal Rites of Passage and the Reconstruction of Self 49
    John W. Schouten, Iowa State University

Session 1.4

The Processing of Emotional and Cognitive Aspects of Product Usage in
Satisfaction Judgments 52
    Laurette Dubé, Université de Montréal
    Bernd H. Schmitt, Columbia University

Session 1.5

Rashomon Visits Consumer Behavior: An Interpretive Critique of Naturalistic Inquiry 57
    Douglas B. Holt, Northwestern University

May The Circle Be Unbroken: A Hermeneutic Consideration Of How Interpretive
Approaches To Consumer Research Are Understood By Consumer Researchers 63
    Craig J. Thompson, University of Tennessee

The Consumer in Postmodernity 70
    A. Fuat Fırat, Arizona State University West

Session 1.6

Some Processes in Brand Categorizing: Why One Person's Noise is Another
Person's Music 77
    Joseph Cherian, University of Illinois at Chicago

The Family Resemblance Approach to Understanding Categorization of Products:
Measurement Problems, Alternative Solutions, and Their Assessment 84
    Don Saunders, Arizona State University
    Steve Tax, Arizona State University
    James Ward, Arizona State University
    Kym Court, Arizona State University
    Barbara Loken, University of Minnesota

Consumer Expertise and the Vividness Effect: Implications for Judgment and Inference 90
    John Kim, Oakland University
    Frank R. Kardes, University of Cincinnati
    Paul M. Herr, Indiana University

Session 2.2

Effect of Ad Pacing and Optimal Level of Arousal On Attitude Toward the Ad 94
    Mark A. Pavelchak, University of Delaware
    Meryl P. Gardner, University of Delaware
    V. Carter Broach, University of Delaware

Emotions and Motivations in Advertising 100
John R. Rossiter, Australian Graduate School of Management
Larry Percy, Lintas:USA

Session 2.3

Music Television and Its Influences on Consumers, Consumer Culture, and the
Transmission of Consumption Messages 111
Basil G. Englis, Rutgers University

Session 2.4

The Cultural Meaning of Beer Commercials 115
Lance Strate, Fordham University

Youthful Drinking and Driving: Policy Implications From Mass Media Research 120
John P. Murry, Jr., University of Wisconsin-Madison

Session 2.5

Omiyage Gift Purchasing By Japanese Travelers in the U.S. 123
Terrence H. Witkowski, California State University, Long Beach
Yoshito Yamamoto, IBM Japan, Ltd.

Japan - A Culture of Consumption? 129
Laurel Anderson, Arizona State University
Marsha Wadkins, University of Virginia

The Development of Time Orientation Measures for Use in Cross-Cultural Research 135
Gary Ko, University of Nebraska-Lincoln
James W. Gentry, University of Nebraska-Lincoln

Session 2.6

In-Home Observations of Television and VCR Movie Rental Viewing 143
Dean M. Krugman, University of Georgia
Yasmin Gopal, University of Georgia

An Examination of Ethnicity Measures: Convergent Validity and Cross-Cultural
Equivalence 150
Michel Laroche, Concordia University
Annamma Joy, Concordia University
Michael Hui, Concordia University
Chankon Kim, Concordia University

The Role of Subject Awareness in Classical Conditioning: A Case of Opposing
Ontologies and Conflicting Evidence 158
Terence A. Shimp, University of South Carolina

Session 3.1

Literary Analysis of An Advertisement: The Commercial as "Soap Opera" 164
Barbara B. Stern, Rutgers University

Experiencing Ad Meanings: Crucial Aspects of Narrative/Drama Processing 172
Gregory W. Boller, Memphis State University
Jerry C. Olson, Penn State University

Session 3.3

Segmentation in Consumer and Market Research: Applications, Current Issues
and Trends 176
David W. Stewart, University of Southern California, Los Angeles
Michael A. Kamins, University of Southern California, Los Angeles

Consumer Self-Selection and Segments of One: The Growing Role of Consumers in Segmentation 179
    David W. Stewart, University of Southern California

Session 3.4

The Importance of Peripheral Cues in Attitude Formation for Enduring and Task Involved Individuals 187
    Robin A. Higie, University of Connecticut
    Lawrence F. Feick, University of Pittsburgh
    Linda L. Price, University of Colorado at Boulder

Suggestions for Manipulating and Measuring Involvement in Advertising Message Content 194
    J. Craig Andrews, Marquette University
    Srinivas Durvasula, Marquette University

Brand Familiarity and Product Involvement Effects on the Attitude Toward an Ad - Brand Attitude Relationship 202
    Joseph Phelps, University of Alabama
    Esther Thorson, University of Wisconsin-Madison

Session 3.5

Consumer Attitudes Toward Complaining And The Prediction Of Multiple Complaint Responses 210
    Diane Halstead, University of Kentucky
    Cornelia Dröge, Michigan State University

Difficulty of Pre-purchase Quality Inspection: Conceptualization and Measurement 217
    Arni Arnthorsson, University of South Carolina
    Wendall E. Berry, University of South Carolina
    Joel E. Urbany, University of South Carolina

Expert-Novice Differences in Complaint Scripts..225
    Ingrid Martin, University of Southern California

Session 4.1

Contributions from a Musical Perspective on Advertising and Consumer Behavior.....................232
    Judy I. Alpert, St. Edward's University
    Mark I. Alpert, University of Texas at Austin

Jingles in Advertisements: Can They Improve Recall?..239
    Wanda T. Wallace, Duke University

Exploring Tempo and Modality Effects On Consumer Responses to Music 243
    James J. Kellaris, University of Cincinnati
    Robert J. Kent, Drexel University

Session 4.2

The Influence of Affect on Attributions for Product Failure 249
    Lalita A. Manrai, University of Delaware
    Meryl P. Gardner, University of Delaware

Session 4.3

Historical Perspectives on Funding Opportunities in Consumer Research...............................255
    Paul N. Bloom, University of North Carolina at Chapel Hill
    George R. Milne, University of North Carolina at Chapel Hill

Session 4.4

    Qualitative Research In The Textbooks: A Review..262
        Joel Saegert, University of Texas at San Antonio
        Geraldine Fennell, Consultant

    The Role of Qualitative Research in Making What the Customer Wants to Buy..........................271
        Geraldine Fennell, Consultant

    Qualitative Research in Advertising: When To Do What..280
        J. H. "Mike" Flynn, D'Arcy Masius Benton & Bowles

Session 4.5

    It's Time To Stress *Stress*
    The Stress - Purchase/Consumption Relationship: Suggestions for Research............................284
        Kevin G. Celuch, Illinois State University
        Linda S. Showers, Illinois State University

    Consumer Guilt: Examining the Potential of a New Marketing Construct................................290
        Dana-Nicoleta Lascu, University of South Carolina

    Stress: An Ignored Situational Influence...296
        Lawrence R. Lepisto, Central Michigan University
        J. Kathleen Stuenkel, Central Michigan University
        Linda K. Anglin, Central Michigan University

Session 4.6

    Personal Relevance As Moderator of the Effect of Public Service Advertising
    on Behavior...303
        William K. Darley, University of Toledo
        Jeen-Su Lim, University of Toledo

    Consumers' Belief In Their Ability To Judge The Truthfulness of Sales Claims........................310
        Robert Baer, Bradley University
        Rustan Kosenko, Bradley University

    The Usefulness of Product Warranties for Reputable and New Brands....................................317
        Daniel E. Innis, Ohio State University
        H. Rao Unnava, Ohio State University

Session 5.3

    "The Good Old Days": Observations On Nostalgia and Its Role In Consumer Behavior.............323
        William J. Havlena, Rutgers University
        Susan L. Holak, Rutgers University

    Echoes of the Dear Departed Past: Some Work in Progress On Nostalgia...............................330
        Morris B. Holbrook, Columbia University
        Robert M. Schindler, Rutgers University - Camden

Session 5.5

    An Empirical Investigation of the Impact of Negative Public Publicity on Consumer
    Attitudes and Intentions..334
        Mitch Griffin, Bradley University
        Barry J. Babin, Louisiana State University
        Jill S. Attaway, Illinois State University

    Reconceptualizing Comparative Advertising: A Framework and Theory of Effects....................342
        Beth A. Walker, Arizona State University
        Helen H. Anderson, University of Arizona

Self Concept and Advertising Effectiveness: A Conceptual Model of Congruency,
Conspicuousness, and Response Mode 348
      George M. Zinkhan, University of Houston
      Jae W. Hong, LGAD, Inc.

Session 5.6

The Troupe: Celebrities as *Dramatis Personae* in Advertisements 355
      Linda M. Scott, University of Texas at Austin

A First Step to Identify the Meaning in Celebrity Endorsers 364
      Lynn Langmeyer, Northern Kentucky University
      Mary Walker, Xavier University

Consumers and Movies: Some Findings on Experiential Products 372
      Elizabeth Cooper-Martin, Georgetown University

Methodological Diversity in Consumer Esthetics Research 379
      Ruth Ann Smith, Virginia Polytechnic Institute and State University

Session 6.1

Toward a Theory of Sexuality and Consumption: Consumer Lovemaps 381
      Stephen J. Gould, Rutgers University - New Brunswick

Two Pornographies: A Feminist View of Sex in Advertising 384
      Barbara B. Stern, Rutgers University - New Brunswick

Session 6.2

Perceived Variability and Inferences about Brand Extensions 392
      Frank R. Kardes, University of Cincinnati
      Chris T. Allen, University of Cincinnati

The Effect of Negative Information on the Evaluations of Brand Extensions and
the Family Brand 399
      Jean B. Romeo, Boston College

Role of Product Knowledge in Evaluation of Brand Extension 407
      A. V. Muthukrishnan, University of Florida
      Barton A. Weitz, University of Florida

Session 6.3

The Effects of Advertising Context on Consumer Responses 414
      Amna Kirmani, Duke University
      Youjae Yi, The University of Michigan

The Influence of Contextual Priming on Advertising Effects 417
      Youjae Yi, University of Michigan

Session 6.4

A Brief History of the Mall 426
      Richard A. Feinberg, Purdue University
      Jennifer Meoli, Indiana University of Pennsylvania

Retail Shopping Mall Semiotics and Hedonic Consumption 428
      Frederick W. Langrehr, Valparaiso University

Shopping Choices: The Case of Mall Choice 434
      Jeffrey J. Stoltman, Wayne State University
      James W. Gentry, University of Nebraska-Lincoln
      Kenneth A. Anglin, Central Michigan University

A Reinforcement-Affect Model of Mall Patronage..441
    Jennifer Meoli, Indiana University of Pennsylvania
    Richard A. Feinberg, Purdue University
    Lori Westgate, Purdue University

Leisure and the Shopping Mall..445
    Peter H. Bloch, University of Massachusetts
    Nancy M. Ridgway, University of Colorado
    James E. Nelson, University of Colorado

Consumer Research and its Role in Shopping Center Development............................453
    Peter A. Doherty, Impact Resources, Inc.
    Judith E.P. Kulikowski, Impact Resources, Inc.

Session 6.5

The Negative Attraction Effect?
A Study of the Attraction Effect Under Judgment and Choice...................................462
    Jennifer Aaker, University of California at Berkeley

Causes of Delay in Consumer Decision Making: An Exploratory Study....................470
    Eric Greenleaf, New York University
    Donald Lehmann, Columbia University

Importance Weight Effects On Self-Explicated Preference Models: Some
Empirical Findings..476
    Paul E. Green, University of Pennsylvania
    Catherine M. Schaffer, University of Denver

Session 6.6

An Evaluation of the SERVQUAL Scales in a Retailing Setting..................................483
    David W. Finn, Texas Christian University
    Charles W. Lamb, Jr., Texas Christian University

An S-O-R Model of The Purchase of an Item in a Store..491
    Patrick G. Buckley, Queen's University

Using a Theoretical Perspective to Examine the Psychological Construct of
Coupon Proneness..501
    Donald R. Lichtenstein, University of Colorado
    Richard G. Netemeyer, Louisiana State University
    Scot Burton, Louisiana State University

Defining Impulse Purchasing..509
    Francis Piron, University of Texas at San Antonio

Session 7.2

Perspectives From Industry and Academic Research on Elderly Adults' Responses To
Advertising: Summary Of A Special Session..515
    Catherine A. Cole, University of Iowa

Approaches to the Study of Consumer Behavior in Late Life....................................517
    George P. Moschis, Georgia State University

Session 7.3

Can't Buy Me Love: Dating, Money, and Gifts..521
    Russell W. Belk, University of Utah
    Gregory S. Coon, University of Utah

When the Thought Counts: Friendship, Love, Gift Exchanges and Gift Returns..........................528
    Margaret Rucker, University of California, Davis
    L. Leckliter, University of California, Davis
    S. Kivel, University of California, Davis
    M. Dinkel, University of California, Davis
    T. Freitas, University of California, Davis
    M. Wynes, University of California, Davis
    H. Prato, University of California, Davis

Two Views of Consumption in Mating and Dating..532
    Aaron Bernard, Northwestern University
    Mara B. Adelman, Northwestern University
    Jonathan E. Schroeder, University of Rhode Island

Session 7.4

Moment By Moment Analyses of TV Commercials: Their Theoretical and Applied Roles:
Summary of the Panel...538
    Esther Thorson, University of Wisconsin-Madison

"Liking" Through Moment-To-Moment Evaluation; Identifying Key Selling...............540
Segments In Advertising
    Mark Polsfuss, Viewfacts, Inc.
    Mike Hess, Viewfacts, Inc.

The Visual Experience of New and Established Product Commercials........................545
    Charles E. Young, TLK Advertising
    Michael Robinson, TLK Advertising

Analysis Approaches to Moment by Moment Reactions to Commercials: Discussion
for Special Session on Moment by Moment Analyses of TV Commercials................550
    Linda F. Alwitt, DePaul University

Session 7.5

Clarifying the Simple Assumption of the Secondary Task Technique..........................552
    Robert S. Owen, Ohio State University

An Exploratory Investigation Of Questionnaire Pretesting With Verbal Protocol Analysis...........558
    Ruth N. Bolton, GTE Laboratories Incorporated

Respondents' Moods as a Biasing Factor in Surveys: An Experimental Study............566
    Morten Heide, Rogaland Research
    Kjell Grønhaug, Norwegian School of Economics and Business Administration

Sampled Survey Data: Quota Samples Versus Probability Samples............................576
    E. L. Melnick, New York University
    R. Colombo, New York University
    R. Tashjian, New York University
    K. R. Melnick, D'Arcy, Masius, Benton & Bowles

Some Methodological Issues in Consumer Research...583
    Naresh K. Malhotra, Georgia Institute of Technology

Session 7.6

Door-In-The-Face, That's-Not-All, and Legitimizing A Paltry Contribution:
Reciprocity, Contrast Effect and Social Judgment Theory Explanations....................586
    Ian Brennan, University of Texas at Arlington
    Kenneth D. Bahn, University of Texas at Arlington

Deal Search: An Approach for Computer-Controlled Information Processing Experiments
Involving Bargainable Attributes 591
    Paul H. Schurr, State University of New York - Albany
    Merrie Brucks, University of Arizona

To Buy or Not to Buy? That is Not the Question: Female Ritual in Home Shopping Parties 597
    Brenda Gainer, York University
    Eileen Fischer, York University

Service Satisfaction: An Exploratory Investigation of Three Models 603
    Rama Jayanti, Louisiana State University
    Anita Jackson, Louisiana State University

Session 8.1

Mutual Understanding Between Customers and Employees In Service Encounters 611
    Lois A. Mohr, Arizona State University
    Mary Jo Bitner, Arizona State University

Session 8.2

Gender Representation in Advertising 618
    Nancy Artz, University of Southern Maine
    Alladi Venkatesh, University of California, Irvine

Session 8.3

Affect and Consumer Behavior: Examining the Role of Emotions on Consumers'
Actions and Perceptions 624
    Mary T. Curren, California State University, Northridge
    Ronald C. Goodstein, University of California, Los Angeles

Session 8.4

Extending Innovation Characteristic Perception To Diffusion Channel Intermediaries
and Aesthetic Products 627
    A. Richard Petrosky, University of Arizona

The Nature of Communication Networks Between Organizations Involved in the
Diffusion of Technological Innovations 635
    David F. Midgley, Australian Graduate School of Management
    Pamela D. Morrison, Australian Graduate School of Management
    John H. Roberts, Australian Graduate School of Management

The Use of Diffusion Theory in Marketing: A Qualitative Approach to Innovative
Consumer Behavior 644
    Tina M. Lowrey, University of Illinois

Session 8.5

The Role of Love, Affection, and Intimacy in Family Decision Research 651
    Jong-Hee Park, Washington State University
    Patriya S. Tansuhaj, Washington State University
    Richard H. Kolbe, Washington State University

Financial Decision Making of Babyboomer Couples 657
    Amardeep Assar, State University of New York at Binghamton
    George S. Bobinski, Jr., State University of New York at Binghamton

An Investigation of a Role/Goal Model of Wives' Role Overload Reduction Strategies 666
    Shreekant G. Joag, St. John's University
    James W. Gentry, University of Nebraska-Lincoln
    Karin Ekstrom, University of Goteborg

Session 8.6

The Influence of Information Source on Brand Loyalty and Consumer Sex Roles
of the Elderly 673
    Ruth Belk Smith, University of Baltimore

On Golden Pond: Elderly Couples and Consumer Decision Making 681
    Louise A. Heslop, Carleton University
    Judith Marshall, Carleton University

Session 9.1

Toward a New Understanding of the Effects of Advertising: A Look at Implicit
Memorial Processes 688
    Ida E. Berger, University of Toronto

Session 9.2

Consumer Responses to Environmentally Based Product Claims 693
    T.J. Olney, Western Washington University
    Wendy Bryce, Western Washington University

The Effects of Incentives on Environment-Friendly Behaviors: A Case Study 697
    R. Bruce Hutton, University of Denver
    Frank Markley, University of Denver

Session 9.4

Recent Studies of Time in Consumer Behavior 703
    Ziv Carmon, University of California at Berkeley

Session 9.5

Evaluating the Impact of Alcohol Warning Labels 706
    Robert N. Mayer, University of Utah
    Ken R. Smith, University of Utah
    Debra L. Scammon, University of Utah

Political Advertising in the 1990s: Expected Strategies, Voter Responses, and
Public Policy Implications 715
    Ronald Paul Hill, Villanova University

An Empirical Test of a Model of Consumer Ethical Dilemmas 720
    Lawrence J. Marks, Kent State University
    Michael A. Mayo, Kent State University

Session 9.6

Elements of Experiential Consumption: An Exploratory Study 729
    Brian Lofman, University of Connecticut

A Meaning-Based Framework for the Study of Consumer-Object Relations 736
    Susan Fournier, University of Florida

Jungian Analysis and Psychological Types: An Interpretive Approach to
Consumer Choice Behavior 743
    Stephen J. Gould, Rutgers University - New Brunswick

Session 10.1

Measurement Techniques Assessing Learning Processes Across Alternative Outdoor
Advertising Executions 749
    Joan Treistman, Treistman and Stark Marketing, Inc.

Session 10.2

    "Headlines make ads work" (Caples 1979): New Evidence
Highlights of the Special Topic Session 752
        Jacqueline Hitchon, University of Wisconsin-Madison

Session 10.3

    Processes and Effects in the Construction of Normative Consumer Beliefs: The Role
of Television 755
        L. J. Shrum, University of Illinois
        Thomas C. O'Guinn, University of Illinois
        Richard J. Semenik, University of Utah
        Ronald J. Faber, University of Minnesota

    Processing Conditional Relations as Biconditionals: Some Poor Consequences
and Rich Opportunities..764
        Thomas K. Srull, University of Illinois at Urbana-Champaign

Session 10.4

    How Entrants Affect Multiple Brands: A Dual Attraction Mechanism.....................................768
        Timothy B. Heath, University of Pittsburgh
        Subimal Chatterjee, University of Pittsburgh

    An Exploratory Study Comparing Amount-of-Search Measures to Consumers'
Reliance on Each Source of Information...773
        Jeff Blodgett, Indiana University
        Donna Hill, Bradley University

    An Information Theoretic Approach to Understanding the Consideration Set/Awareness
Set Proportion..780
        Ayn E. Crowley, Washington State University
        John H. Williams, Texas Southern University

Session 10.5

    Perceived Price Fairness and Dual Entitlement..788
        Rosemary Kalapurakal, Ohio State University
        Peter R. Dickson, Ohio State University
        Joel E. Urbany, University of South Carolina

    Symbolic Meanings of a Price Ending 794
        Robert M. Schindler, Rutgers University

    Individual Differences in Latitude of Acceptable Prices...802
        Patricia Sorce, Rochester Institute of Technology
        Stanley M. Widrick, Rochester Institute of Technology

Session 10.6

    Measuring Communication-Evoked Imagery Processing 806
        Pam Scholder Ellen, Georgia State University
        Paula Fitzgerald Bone, West Virginia University

    Humor In Television Advertising: The Effects of Repetition and Social Setting.....................813
        Yong Zhang, University of Houston
        George M. Zinkhan, University of Houston

    Cue Modality: Video and Audio Effects on Recall 819
        Carolyn L. Costley, Texas A & M University
        Duane DeWald, Texas A & M University

Author Index..826

ASSOCIATION FOR CONSUMER RESEARCH

ANNUAL CONFERENCE

NEW YORK CITY
OCTOBER 4-7, 1990

ACR PROGRAM

Conference Chairs

Rebecca H. Holman
D'Arcy Masius Benton & Bowles, Inc.

Michael R. Solomon
Rutgers University, New Brunswick

THURSDAY, OCTOBER 4

10:00 am - 5:00 pm   ACR EXECUTIVE BOARD MEETING

6:00 pm - 8:00 pm   EARLY BIRD COCKTAIL PARTY

FRIDAY, OCTOBER 5

1ST SESSION: 8:30 am - 10:00 am

1.1 *Special Session*: **Measurement Issues in Children's Research**

    Co-Chairs: Carole Macklin, University of Cincinnati and Deborah Roedder John, University of Minnesota

    "Children's Research--Where It's Been, Where It Is Going"
        Judy Harrigan, Harrigan-Bodick, Inc

    "Learning About Children: Qualitative and Quantitative Approaches to Child Research"
        Carole Hyatt, Carole Hyatt Associates
        Langbourne Rust, Langbourne Rust Research, Inc.

    "Assessing Children's Comprehension of Marketing Messages"
        Laura Perracchio, University of Minnesota
        Charise Mita, BBDO

    "Behaviorally-Anchored Rating Scales: An Alternative Approach for Measuring Children's Preferences"
        Yvonne Karsten, University of Minnesota
        Deborah Roedder John, University of Minnesota

1.2 *Special Session*: **Moderators of the Attitude-Behavior Relation**

Co-Chairs: Youjae Yi, The University of Michigan, and Richard P. Bagozzi, The University of Michigan

"The Role of Action-vs. State-Orientation in the Attitude-Behavior Relation"
Richard P. Bagozzi, University of Michigan
Johann Baumgartner, Pennsylvania State University
Youjae Yi, The University of Michigan

"Effects of Experience and Thought About an Issue on Attitude Structure"
Robert E. Burnkrant, Ohio State University
H. Rao Unnava, Ohio State University

"Advertising Content and Consumer Attitude"
Paul M. Herr, Indiana University
Russell H. Fazio, Indiana University

Discussant: Terence A. Shimp, University of South Carolina

1.3 *Special Session*: **Disposition and Acquisition in Processes of Transition and Identity Reconstruction**

Chair: Russell W. Belk, University of Utah

"Disposition of Possessions During Role Transitions"
Melissa Young, University of Utah

"Consumption Responses to Involuntary Job Loss"
Scott D. Roberts, Old Dominion University

"Divorce, The Disposition of the Relationship, and Everything"
James H. MacAlexander, Oregon State University

"Personal Rites of Passage and the Reconstruction of Self"
John W. Schouten, Iowa State University

Discussant: Clinton R. Sanders, University of Connecticut

1.4 *Special Session*: **The Processing of Emotional and Cognitive Aspects of Product Usage in Satisfaction Judgments**

Co-Chairs: Laurette Dube-Rioux, University de Montreal, and Bernd H. Schmitt, Columbia University

"Emotional Response, Involvement, and Satisfaction"
Robert A. Westbrook, Rice University

"Information Processing of Satisfaction Judgments: Are Consumers Affective Misers?"
Laurette Dube-Rioux, Universite de Montreal

"The Role of Repetition and Mood in the Processing of Preference Judgments"
Punam Anand, Columbia University
Rajeev Batra, The University of Michigan

"Cognitive, Affective and Attribute Bases of Usage/Post-purchase Responses"
Richard L. Oliver, Vanderbilt University

Discussant: Alice M. Isen, Cornell University

1.5 *Competitive Papers*: **Interpretive Approaches to Consumer Behavior**

Chair: Edward F. McQuarrie, Santa Clara University

"Rashomon Visits Consumer Behavior: An Interpretive Critique of Naturalistic Inquiry"
Douglas B. Holt, Northwestern University

"May the Circle Be Unbroken: A Hermeneutic Consideration of How Interpretive Approaches to Consumer Research are Understood by Consumer Research"
Craig J. Thompson, University of Tennessee

"The Consumer in Post-modernity"
A. Fuat Firat, Arizona State University - West

Discussant: Julie Ozanne, Virginia Tech

1.6 *Competitive Papers*: **Brand Categorization**

Chair: Julia Bristor, University of Western Ontario

"Some Processes in Brand Categorizing"
Joseph Cherian, University of Illinois-Chicago
Marilyn Jones, University of Illinois-Chicago

"The Family Resemblance Approach to Understanding the Categorization of Products: Measurement Problems, Alternative Solutions, and Their Assessment"
Don Saunders, Arizona State University
Steve Tax, Arizona State University
James Ward, Arizona State University
Kym Young, Arizona State University
Barbara Loken, University of Minnesota

"Consumer Expertise and the Vividness Effect: Implications for Judgment and Inference"
John Kim, University of Cincinnati
Frank R. Kardes, University of Cincinnati
Paul Herr, Indiana University

Discussant: Srinivasan Ratneshwar, University of Florida

FRIDAY, OCTOBER 5

2ND SESSION: 10:30 am - 12:00 pm

2.1 *Special Session*: **Understanding Advertising Ideas to Do Better Advertising Research**

Chair: John Eighmey, University of Alabama

Clark Frankel, Young & Rubicam
Bob Czernysz, Young & Rubicam
Marvin Waldman, Young & Rubicam

Discussant: William L. Wilkie, University of Notre Dame

2.2 *Special Session*: **Arousal and Advertising Effectiveness**

    Co-Chairs: Meryl P. Gardner, University of Delaware, Mark A. Pavelchak, University of Delaware

    "Personal and Ad-Induced Origins of Arousal: Effects on Ad and Brand Attitudes"
        Mark A. Pavelchak, University of Delaware
        Meryl P. Gardner, University of Delaware
        V. Carter Broach, Jr., University of Delaware

    "The Link Between Emotion and Motivation in Processing Advertising"
        Larry Percy, Lintas: USA
        John Rossiter, Australian Graduate School of Management

    "Observations with Electrodermal Response in Communications Testing"
        John A. Shimell, Jr., Inner Response, Inc.
        James Fletcher,

    Discussant: William D. Wells, DDB Needham Worldwide, Inc.

2.3 *Special Session*: **Music Television and Its Influence on Consumers, Consumer Culture and the Transmission of Consumption Messages**

    Chair: Basil G. Englis, Rutgers University - New Brunswick

    "Crossing the Boundaries: A Comparison of Music Videos and Commercial Advertisements"
        Donald L. Fry, Emerson College

    "Adolescent Sexuality and Music Videos"
        Jane D. Brown, University of North Carolina

    "Music Television as a Viewing Context and its Effects on Consumer Responses to Advertising"
        Basil G. Englis, Rutgers University - New Brunswick

    "Ambiguity and Complexity in Music Video Commercials: The Role of Film Dimensions in Enhancing Commercial Recall and Persuasion"
        Esther Thorson, University of Wisconsin - Madison
        Jacqueline Hitchon, University of Wisconsin - Madison
        Peter Duckler, University of Wisconsin - Madison

2.4 *Special Session*: **Youthful Drinking and Driving: Policy Implications From Mass Media Research**

    Chair: John P. Murry, Jr., University of Wisconsin - Madison

    "The "Know When to Say When" Responsible Drinking Program of Anheuser-Busch: A Case Study in Strategy Development"
        J. H. "Mike" Flynn, D'Arcy Masius Benton & Bowles, Inc.

    "The Cultural Meaning of Beer Commercials"
        Lance Strate, Fordham University

    "Drinking and Driving Public Service Campaigns: Do You Get What You Pay For?"
        John P. Murry, Jr., University of Wisconsin - Madison
        John L. Lastovicka, University of Kansas
        Antonie Stam, University of Georgia

    Discussant: Paul N. Bloom, University of North Carolina - Chapel Hill

2.5 *Competitive Papers*: **Cross-Cultural Research**

    Chair: Gary Bamossy, Vrije Universiteit (The Netherlands)

    "*Omiyage* Gift Purchasing by Japanese Travelers in the US"
        Terrence H. Witkowski, California State University
        Yoshito Yamamoto, IBM, Japan

    "Japan - A Culture of Consumption"
        Laurel A. Anderson, Arizona State University - West
        Marsha Wadkins, University of Virginia

    "The Development of Time Orientation Measures for Use in Cross-Cultural Research"
        Gary Ko, University of Nebraska - Lincoln
        James W. Gentry, University of Nebraska - Lincoln

    Discussant: Katrin Harich, University of California - Los Angeles

2.6 *Competitive Papers*: **Measurement Issues**

    Chair: Marsha Wilcox, Decision Research

    "In-Home Observations of Traditional TV & VCR Movie Rental Viewing"
        Dean M. Krugman, The University of Georgia
        Yasmin Gobal, University of Georgia

    "An Examination of Ethnicity Measures: Convergent Validity and Cross-Cultural Equivalence"
        Michel Laroche, Concordia University
        Annamma Joy, Concordia University
        Michael Hur, Concordia University
        Chankon Kim, Concordia University

    "The Role of Subject Awareness in Classical Conditioning: A Case of Opposing Ontologies and Conflicting Evidence"
        Terence A. Shimp, University of South Carolina

    Discussant: Joseph A. Cote, Washington State University

FRIDAY, OCTOBER 5

Luncheon: 12:00 pm - 1:30 pm

3RD SESSION: 1:45 pm - 3:15 pm

3.1 *Special Session*: **Advertising and the Meaning of Meaning: Practitioner and Academic Views of the Creation, Analysis, and Measurement of an Advertisement**

    Co-Chairs: Barbara B. Stern, Rutgers University - Newark, Elizabeth C. Hirschman, Rutgers University - New Brunswick

    "Experiencing Ad Meanings: Crucial Aspects of Narrative/Drama Processing"
        Gregory W. Boller, Memphis State University
        Jerry C. Olson, Pennsylvania State University

    "What Does "Drama" Mean? Literary Analysis of an Advertisement"
        Barbara B. Stern, Rutgers University - Newark

"The GAIN Commercial: Meaning Manufacture in a Television Advertisement"
　　Grant McCracken, University of Toronto

"Creation of a Commercial"
　　Ray Hirschman, Wells, Rich, Greene, Inc.
　　Ron Hartley, Wells, Rich, Greene, Inc.

Discussant: Elizabeth C. Hirschman, Rutgers University - New Brunswick

3.2 *Special Session*: **Adaptability of Choice Strategy Selection to Environmental Conditions**

　　Chair: Joel Huber, Duke University

　　"Adapting to Correlated Attributes: Do Decision-Makers Change Strategies When Faced with Harder Choices?
　　　　Eric J. Johnson, University of Pennsylvania
　　　　James R. Bettman, Duke University
　　　　John Payne, Duke University

　　"The Environmental Determinants of Cutoff Severity"
　　　　Joel Huber, Duke University
　　　　Noreen Klein, Virginia Tech
　　　　Fred Feinberg, Duke University

　　"Effects of Information Display on Strategy Selection in Multiattribute Choice"
　　　　David A. Schkade, University of Chicago
　　　　Don N. Kleinmuntz, University of Chicago

　　"Computer Assisted Consumer Information Processing Formats: Decision Environment Effects on Actual and Perceived Effort and Accuracy in Choice"
　　　　Robert E. Widing II, Case Western Reserve University
　　　　W. Wayne Talarzyk, Ohio State University

　　Discussant: John Carroll, Massachusets Institute of Technology

3.3 *Special Session*: **Segmentation in Consumer and Market Research: Applications, Current Issues and Trends**

　　Chair: David W. Stewart, University of Southern California

　　"Case Studies on the Usage of Segmentation in Market Research"
　　　　William Heiland, Custom Research Inc.

　　"Consumer Self-Selection and Segments of One: The Growing Role of Consumers in Segmentation"
　　　　David W. Stewart, University of Southern California

　　"An Application of Segmentation Research in the Travel and Leisure Industry: The Case of Hilton Hotels"
　　　　Renee Zakoor, Hilton Hotels Corporation

　　Discussant: Michael A. Kamins, University of Southern California

3.4 *Competitive Papers*: **Involvement Issues**

    Chair: Alan Sawyer, University of Florida

    "The Importance of Peripheral Cues in Attitude Formation for Enduring and Task Involved Individuals"
        Robin Higie, University of Connecticut
        Lawrence Feick, University of Pittsburgh
        Linda Price, University of Colorado - Boulder

    "Suggestions for Manipulating and Measuring Involvement in Advertising Message Content"
        J. Craig Andrews, Marquette University
        Srinivas Durvasula, Marquette University

    "Brand Familiarity and Product Involvement Effects on the Attitude Toward an Ad-Brand Relationship"
        Joseph Phelps, University of Alabama
        Esther Thorson, University of Wisconsin - Madison

    Discussant: Clark Leavitt, Ohio State University

3.5 *Competitive Papers*: **Satisfaction and Quality Issues**

    Chair: George Belch, San Diego State University

    "Consumer Attitudes Toward Complaining and the Prediction of Multiple Complaint Responses"
        Diane Halstead, Michigan State University
        Cornelia Droge, Michigan State University

    "Difficulty of Pre-Purchase Quality Inspection: Conceptualization and Measurement"
        Arni Authorsson, University of South Carolina
        Wendal E. Berry, University of South Carolina
        Joel E. Urbany, University of South Carolina

    "The Day They Lost My Luggage: The Underlying Structure of the Complaint Script"
        Ingrid Martin, University of Southern California

    Discussant: Douglas Hausknecht, University of Akron

3.6 *Special Session*: **MEET THE EDITORS**

    Chair: Jerome Kernan, George Mason University

    Participants: To Be Announced

FRIDAY, OCTOBER 5

4TH SESSION: 3:45 pm - 5:15 pm

4.1 *Special Session*: **Music in Advertising**

    Chair: Wanda T. Wallace, Duke University

    "Contributions from a Musical Perspective on Advertising and Consumer Behavior"
        Mark I. Alpert, University of Texas at Austin
        Judy I. Alpert, St. Edwards University

"A Conceptual Framework for Considering Music in Advertising Messages"
    Patricia A. Stout, University of Texas at Austin

"Jingles in Advertisements: Can They Improve Recall?"
    Wanda T. Wallace, Duke University

"Exploring Tempo and Modality Effects on Consumer Responses to Music"
    James Kellaris, University of Cincinnati
    Bob Kent, University of Cincinnati

Discussant: Hunter Murtaugh, Young & Rubicam

4.2 *Special Session*: **The Influence of Affect on Brand-Related Cognitions**

Co-Chairs: J. Jeffrey Inman, The University of Texas at Austin, Douglas M. Stayman, Cornell University

"Some Effects of Affective State on Product Evaluations: A Categorization Perspective"
    Douglas M. Stayman, Cornell University
    Alice M. Isen, Cornell University

"The Moderating Role of Affect on Consumer Reaction to Retail Price Promotions"
    J. Jeffrey Inman, The University of Texas at Austin
    Alice M. Isen, Cornell University
    Leigh McAlister, The University of Texas at Austin
    Wayne D. Hoyer, The University of Texas at Austin

"Emotional Reactions as Mediators of the Effects of Advertisements on A_{AD} Over Time"
    Amitava Chattopadhyay, McGill University

"The Influence of Affect on Attributions for Product Failure"
    Lalita A. Manrai, University of Delaware
    Meryl P. Gardner, University of Delaware

Discussant: Stuart Agres, Lowe Marschalk Inc.

4.3 *Special Session*: **Funding Opportunities in Consumer Research**

Chair: James Shanteau, National Science Foundation

"Historical Perspectives on Funding Opportunities in Consumer Research"
    Paul N. Bloom, University of North Carolina - Chapel Hill

"Emerging Research Priorities and Research Funding at Marketing Science Institute"
    George S. Day, Marketing Science Institute

"Research Funding at NSF: Some DOs and DON'Ts"
    James Shanteau, National Science Foundation

Discussants: Peter H. Farquhar, Carnegie-Mellon University
    William L. Wilkie, University of Notre Dame

4.4 *Special Session*: **ACS and PRACS on Qualitative Research: Converging or Diverging?**

Chair: Joel Saegert, The University of Texas at San Antonio

"The Realities of Qualitative Research: A Practitioner's Report"
    Judith Lerner, Consumer Insights for Marketing

"Qualitative Research in Advertising"
    J. H. "Mike" Flynn, D'Arcy Masius Benton & Bowles, Inc.

"Qualitative Consumer Research From a Phenomenological Viewpoint"
   Scott Churchill, University of Dallas
   Frederick J. Wertz, Fordam University

"The Role of Qualitative Research in Making What the Customer Wants to Buy"
   Geraldine Fennell, Consultant

"Qualitative Research in the Textbooks: A Review"
   Joel Saegert, The University of Texas at San Antonio

4.5 *Competitive Papers*: **Stress & Guilt**

Chair: Marye Tharp, University of Texas-Austin

"It's Time to Stress Stress"
   Kevin Celuch, Illinois State University
   Linda S. Showers, Illinois State University

"Consumer Guilt: Examining the Potential of a New Marketing Construct"
   Dana-Nicoleta Lascu, University of South Carolina

"Stress: An Ignored Situational Variable"
   Lawrence R. Lepisto, Central Michigan University
   J. Kathleen Stuenkel, Central Michigan University
   Linda K. Anglin, Central Michigan University

Discussant: Melanie Wallendorf, University of Arizona

4.6 *Competitive Papers*: **Judgments in Product Evaluation**

Chair: Thomas J. Finkle, Goldfarb Consultants

"Personal Relevance as a Moderator of the Effect of Public Service Advertising on Behavior"
   William K. Darley, University of Toledo
   Jeen-Su Lim, University of Toledo

"Consumers' Belief in Their Ability to Detect the Truthfulness of Sales Claims"
   Robert Baer, Bradley University
   Rustan Kosenko, Bradley University

"The Usefulness of Product Warranties for Reputable and New Brands"
   Daniel E. Innis, Ohio State University
   Rao Unnava, Ohio State University

Discussant: Meora Venkatraman, Boston University

FRIDAY, OCTOBER 5

JCR Editorial Board Meeting: 4:30 pm - 6:00 pm

ACR PENTHOUSE COCKTAIL PARTY
THE SUMMIT HOTEL
6:00 PM - 7:30 PM

> **SATURDAY, OCTOBER 6**
>
> **5TH SESSION: 8:30 am - 10:00 am**

5.1 *Special Session*: **Health Communications: Five Intervention Programs**

    Chair: Marvin E. Goldberg, VPI, McGill University

    "The Harvard Alcohol Project: A Demonstration Project to Promote the Use of the "Designated Driver""
        Jay A. Winsten, Harvard School of Public Health

    "Persuading People to Donate Organs: An Approach Combining Social Support and Advertising Interventions"
        Marvin E. Goldberg, McGill University
        Kunal Basu, McGill University
        Amitava Chattopadhyay, McGill University

    "An Idiographic Decision Theory Approach Toward Nutrition Education"
        David Brinberg, State University of New York - Albany

    "Action on Drug Abuse - Really Me - Canada's Social Marketing Program on Alcohol and Other Drugs"
        James H. Mintz, Health and Welfare Canada

    "Prescription Drug Education: Tailoring Informational Strategies for Elderly Hypertensiveness"
        Lou Morris, Food and Drug Administration
        Ellen Tabak, Food and Drug Administration
        Nancy Olins, American Association for Retired Persons Pharmacy Service

    Discussant: Joel B. Cohen, University of Florida

5.2 *Special Session*: **Brand Extension Research - Current Studies/Future Directions**

    Chair: David A. Aaker, University of California at Berkeley

    "The Limits of Brand Stretch"
        Peter H. Farquhar, Carnegie Mellon University
        Paul M. Herr, Carnegie Mellon University

    "Diluting Brand Equity: The Negative Impact of Brand Extensions"
        Deborah Roedder-John, University of Minnesota
        Barbara Loken, University of Minnesota

    "The Name and Brand Recall"
        David A. Aaker, University of California at Berkeley
        Ziv Carmon, University of California at Berkeley

    "Brand Extensions--Some Research Priorities"
        William Wells, DDB Needham Worldwide

5.3 *Special Session*: **Going Home: Nostalgia in Consumer Behavior**

    Co-Chairs: William J. Havlena, Rutgers University - Newark, Susan L. Holak, Rutgers University - Newark

    ""The Good Old Days": Observations on Nostalgia and Its Role in Consumer Behavior"
        William J. Havlena, Rutgers University - Newark
        Susan L. Holak, Rutgers University - Newark

    "Some Propositions on the Role of Nostalgia in Shaping the Development of Consumer Tastes: An Audiovisual Preview of a Project on the Relation of Liking for the Appearances of Actors and Actresses to Individual Differences in Longing for the Dear Departed Past"
        Morris B. Holbrook, Columbia University
        Robert M. Schindler, Rutgers University - Camden

    "The Role of Nostalgia in the Development of Tastes: A Test in the Context of Fashion Advertising"
        Robert M. Schindler, Rutgers University - Camden
        Morris B. Holbrook, Columbia University

    Discussant: Elizabeth C. Hirschman, Rutgers University - New Brunswick

5.4 *Special Session*: **Global Research in Consumer Values and Perceptions of Foreign Products**

    Chair: Martin S. Roth, Boston College

    "Cross-National Consumer Values as Measured by the Rokeach Value Survey and the List of Values"
        Mary Lee Stansifer, The University of Denver

    "The Value of Country-of-Origin and Brand Name Information in Chinese and US Consumers' Decision Making: An Exploratory Analysis"
        Richard Ettenson, University of Maryland
        Gary Gaeth, University of Iowa

    "Negative Country of Origin Effects: Who Dares Buy a Soviet Tractor?"
        Michael Czinkota, Georgetown University
        Johny Johansson, Georgetown University
        Ilkka Ronkainen, Georgetown University

    "The Underlying Dimensions of Country Image and Their Relationship to Product Category Characteristics: A Cross-Cultural Investigation"
        Jean B. Romeo, Boston College
        Martin S. Roth, Boston College

    Discussant: George Faigen, Wang Laoratories, Inc.

5.5 *Competitive Papers*: **Advertising Issues**

    Chair: Roberto Friedmann, University of Georgia

    "An Empirical Investigation of the Impact of Negative Publicity on Consumer Attitudes and Intentions"
        Mitch Griffin, Bradley University
        Barry J. Babin, Louisiana State University
        Jill S. Attaway, Illinois State University

    "Reconceptualizing Comparative Advertising: A Framework and Theory of Effects"
        Beth Walker, Arizona State University
        Helen Anderson, University of Arizona

"Self-Concept and Advertising Effectiveness: The Influence of Congruency, Conspicuousness, and Response Mode"
    George M. Zinkhan, University of Houston
    Jae W. Hong, LGAD Inc.

Discussant: Michael Belch, San Diego State University

5.6 *Competitive Papers*: **Consumer Esthetics**

    Chair: Robert E. Kleine, Arizona State University

    "The Troupe: Celebrities as *Dramatis Personae* in Advertising"
        Linda M. Scott, University of Texas at Austin

    "A First Step to Identify the Meaning in Celebrity Endorsers"
        Lynn Langmeyer, Northern Kentucky University
        Mary Walker, Xavier University

    "Consumers and Movies: Some Findings on Experiential Products"
        Elizabeth Cooper-Martin, Georgetown University

    Discussant: Ruth Ann Smith, Virginia Polytechnic Institute & State University

---

SATURDAY, OCTOBER 6

6TH SESSION: 10:30 am - 12:00 pm

6.1 *Special Session*: **Sexual Significations and Consumer Lovemaps: New Directions in Improving Our Understanding of the Relationship Between Sexuality and Consumption**

    Chair: Stephen J. Gould, Rutgers University - New Brunswick

    "Toward a Theory of Sexuality and Consumption: Consumer Lovemaps"
        Stephen J. Gould, Rutgers University - New Brunswick

    "Dead Women and Other Pornographic Representations in Contemporary Advertising"
        Terry Prewitt, University of West Florida
        Karen Cox, University of West Florida

    "Two Pornographies: A Feminist View of Sex in Advertising"
        Barbara Stern, Rutgers University - Newark

    "Examples of Sexual Signification in Consumption"
        Ernest Dichter, Ernest Dichter Motivations, Inc.

    Discussant: Leon Schiffman, Baruch College/CUNY

6.2 *Competitive Papers*: **Brand Extensions**

    Chair: Connie Pechmann, University of California

    "Perceived Variability and Inferences About Brand Extensions"
        Frank Kardes, University of Cincinnati
        Chris Allen, University of Cincinnati

    "The Effect of Negative Information on the Evaluations of Brand Extensions and the Family Brand"
        Jean B. Romeo, Boston College

"Role of Product Knowledge in Evaluation of Brand Extensions"
    A.V. Muthukrishnan, University of Florida
    Bart Weitz, University of Florida

Discussant: Stephen J. Hoch, University of Chicago

6.3 *Special Session*: **The Effects of Advertising Context on Consumer Responses**

Co-Chairs: Amna Kirmani, Duke University; Youjae Yi, The University of Michigan

"The Effect of Affective Context on the Effectiveness of Advertising"
    Douglas M. Stayman, Cornell University

"Contextual Effects on Responses to Advertising: The Role of Emotion Types"
    Helen M. Anderson, University of Arizona

"Context Effects in Advertising: The Role of Other Ads in the Environment"
    Kevin Lane Keller, Stanford University
    Amna Kirmani, Duke University

"The Influence of Contextual Priming on Advertising Effects"
    Youjae Yi, The University of Michigan

Discussant: Christopher Puto, University of Arizona

6.4 *Special Session*: **The Shopping Mall as an Arena for Consumer Research**

Chair: Richard A. Feinberg, Purdue University

"A Brief History of the Mall"
    Richard Feinberg, Perdue University

"Retail Shopping Mall Semiotics and Hedonic Consumption"
    Frederick Langrehr, Valparaiso University

"Shopping Choices: The Case of Mall Choice"
    Jeffrey Stoltman, Wayne State University
    James Gentry, University of Nebraska
    Kenneth Anglin, Central Michigan University

"A Reinforcement-Affect Model of Mall Patronage"
    Jennifer Meoli, Indiana University of Pennsylvania
    Lori Westgate, Purdue University
    Richard A. Feinberg, Purdue University

"Mall Development and the Role of Consumer Research"
    Peter Dohery, Impact Resources

"Studying the Consumer in the Mall"
    Ken Wallach, Melvin Simon & Associates

"Leisure and the Shopping Mall"
    Peter Bloch, University of Massachusetts
    Nancy Ridgway, University of Colorado
    James Nelson, University of Colorado

6.5 *Competitive Papers*: **Consumer Choice**

    Chair: John Eighton, University of Chicago

    "A Negative Attraction Effect? A Story of Attraction Effect Under Judgment and Choice"
        Jennifer Aaker, University of California at Berkeley

    "Delay in Consumer Decision Making"
        Eric Greenleaf, New York University
        Donald Lehmann, Columbia University

    "Importance Weight Effects on Self-Explicated Preference Models: Some Empirical Findings"
        Paul Green, The Wharton School of the University of Pennsylvania
        Catherine M. Schaffer, Drexel University

    Discussant: Steven Perkins, Pennsylvania State University

6.6 *Competitive Papers*: **Point-of-Purchase Potpourri**

    Chair: Gregory D. Upah, Merrill Lynch Asset Management

    "An Evaluation of the SERVQUAL Scales in a Retailing Setting"
        David W. Finn, Texas Christian University
        Charles W. Lamb, Jr., Texas Christian University

    "An S-O-R Model of the Purchase of an Item in a Store"
        Patrick G. Buckley, University of Guelph

    "Using a Theoretical Perspective to Examine the Psychological Construct of Coupon Proneness"
        Donald R. Lichtenstein, University of Colorado
        Richard G. Netemeyer, Louisiana State University
        Scot Burton, Louisiana State University

    "Defining Impulse Purchasing"
        Francis Piron, The University of Texas at San Antonio

    Discussant: Marsha L. Richins, University of Massachusetts

---

SATURDAY, OCTOBER 6

Luncheon: 12:00 pm - 1:30 pm

7TH SESSION: 1:45 pm - 3:15 pm

7.1 *Special Session*: **1990 Robert Ferber Award Presentations**

    Chair: Richard J. Lutz, University of Florida

    "Choice Based on Reasons: The Case of Attraction and Compromise Effects"
        Itamar Simonson, University of California at Berkeley

    "Effects of Country-of-Origin and Product Attribute Information on Product Evaluation: An Information Processing Perspective"
        Sung-Tai Hong, Hanyang University

7.2 *Special Session*: Perspectives from Industry and Academic Research on Elderly Adults' Responses to Advertising

Chair: Catherine Cole, University of Iowa

Panel Members:
    Harlan Spotts, Northeastern University
    Joyce Wackenhut, D'Arcy Masius Benton & Bowles, Inc.
    George Moschis, Georgia State University
    Peter Bennett, Pennsylvania State University
    Seth Ginsburg, J. Walter Thompson

Concluding Comments: George Moschis, Georgia State University

7.3 *Special Session*: Can't Buy Me Love?: The Role of Consumption in Courtship

Chair: Aaron Bernard, Northwestern University

"Can't Buy Me Love: Dating, Money, and Gifts"
    Russell W. Belk, University of Utah
    Gregory Coon, University of Utah

"When the Thought Counts: Friendship, Love, Gift Exchanges and Gift Returns"
    Margret Rucker, University of California at Davis
    L. Leckliter, University of California at Davis
    S. Kivel, University of California at Davis
    M. Dinkel, University of California at Davis
    T. Freitas, University of California at Davis
    M. Wynes, University of California at Davis
    H. Prato, University of California at Davis

"Consumer Activities and Romantic Self-Presentation"
    Jonathan E. Schroeder, University of California at Berkeley

"An Empirical Test of Client Utilization Models for Social Introduction Services"
    Aaron Bernard, Northwestern University
    Mara B. Adelman, Northwestern University

7.4 *Special Session*: Moment by Moment Analyses of TV Commercials: Their Theoretical and Applied Roles

Co-Chairs: Esther Thorson, University of Wisconsin - Madison, William D. Wells, DDB Needham Worldwide

"The PEAC System: Methodology, Theory and Findings
    Mark Posfuss, Viewfacts, Inc.

"Video Rhythms in Response to Commercials for New and Established Brands"
    Charles E. Young, Tatham-Laird & Kudner

"The Game Between Advertisers and Consumers: Consumer Reactions to Advertising Tactics"
    Marian Friestad, University of Oregon
    Peter Wright, Stanford University

Discussant: Linda Alwitt, DePaul University

7.5 *Competitive Papers*: **Methodological Issues**

    Chair: Karen A. Machleit, University of Cincinnati

    "The Simple Assumption of the Secondary Task Technique"
        Robert S. Owen, The Ohio State University

    "An Exploratory Investigation of Questionnaire Pretesting with Verbal Protocol Analysis"
        Ruth N. Bolton, GTE Laboratories Incorporated

    "Respondents' Moods as a Biasing Factor in Surveys: An Experimental Study"
        Morton Heide, Norwegian School of Business & Economics Administration
        Kjell Gronhaug, Norwegian School of Business & Economics Administration

    "Sampled Survey Data: Quota Samples Versus Probability Samples"
        Edward L. Melnick, New York University
        R. Tashjian, New York University
        Richard Colombo, New York University
        K. R. Melnick, D'Arcy Masius Benton & Bowles, Inc.

    Discussant: Naresh Molhotra, Georgia Institute of Technology

7.6 *Competitive Papers*: **Buyer/Seller Interactions**

    Chair: Debbie MacInnis, University of Arizona

    "That's Not All, Door in the Face, and Legitimizing a Paltry Contribution: Reciprocity, Contrast Effect and Social Judgment Theory Explanations"
        Ian Brennan, The University of Texas at Arlington
        Kenneth Bahn, The University of Texas at Arlington

    "DEAL SEARCH: An Approach for Computer-Controlled Information Processing Experiments Involving Bargainable Attributes"
        Paul H. Schurr, The State University of New York - Albany
        Merrie Brucks, University of Arizona

    "To Buy or Not to Buy? That is Not the Question: Female Ritual in Home Shopping Parties"
        Brenda Gainer, York University
        Eileen Fischer, York University

    "Service Satisfaction: An Exploratory Investigation of Three Models"
        Rama Jayanti, Louisiana State University
        Anita Jackson, Louisiana State University

    Discussant: Harish Sujan, Pennsylvania State University

SATURDAY, OCTOBER 6

8TH SESSION: 3:45 pm - 5:15 pm

8.1 *Special Session*: **Consumer Evaluations of Service Encounters: An Interdisciplinary Perspective**

    Chair: Cathy Goodwin, University of Alaska - Fairbanks
    Moderator: Valarie Zeithaml, Duke University

    "An Equity Theory Perspective of Service Quality Evaluation"
        Cathy Goodwin, University of Alaska - Fairbanks
        Kelly L. Smith, Georgia State University

"Influence of Employee/Customer Role and Script Congruence on Evaluation of Service Encounters"
  Mary Jo Bitner, Arizona State University
  Lois Mohr, Arizona State University

"How Perceptions of Perceived Control Can Contribute to Evaluation of the Service Encounter"
  Michael Hui, Concordia University
  John Bateson, London Business School

"Perceptions of Service Systems as Determinants of Service Quality"
  G. Lynn Shostack, Joyce International, Inc.

Discussant: Kenneth L. Bernhardt, Georgia State University

8.2 *Special Session*: **Gender Representation in Advertising**

  Chair: Nancy Artz, University of Southern Maine

  "Observations on Gender Images in Advertising"
    Rena Bartos, Rena Bartos Company

  "Assessing the Effects of Spokesperson and Announcer Gender on the Communication Effectiveness of Advertisement"
    Mary K. McManamon, Cleveland State University
    Thomas Whipple, Cleveland State University

  "Authorial Perspective in Advertising: A Case Study of the Portrayal of Women"
    Nancy Artz, University of Southern Maine

  "For a Critique of the Social Construction of Gender in Advertising"
    Alladi Venkatesh, University of California, Irvine

  Discussant: Antonia Earnshaw, Young & Rubicam

8.3 *Special Session*: **Affect and Consumer Behavior: Examining the Role of Emotions on Consumers' Actions and Perceptions**

  Co-Chairs: Mary T. Curren, California State University, Northridge; Ronald C. Goodstein, University of California, Los Angeles

  "Context-Induced Mood Effects in Advertising"
    Michael A. Kamins, University of Southern California
    Henrianne Sanft, University of Southern California
    Tina Kiesler, University of Southern California

  "Emotional Intensity and Cue Type as Moderators of the Effect of Ad-Induced Emotions on Ad and Brand Evaluation"
    Julie A. Edell, Duke University
    Marian Chapman Moore, Duke University

  "Consumers' Emotional Responses to Unrealized Expectations and Variations in Temporal Distance"
    Joan Meyers-Levy, University of Chicago
    Durairaj Maheswaran, New York University

  "Effects of Positive Affect on Variety-Seeking Behavior"
    Alice M. Isen, Cornell University
    Barbara E. Kahn, University of Pennsylvania

  Discussant: Alice M. Isen, Cornell University

8.4 *Competitive Papers*: **Diffusion of Innovations**

    Chair: Peter Reingen, Arizona State University

    "Extending Innovation Characteristic Perception to Diffusion Channel Intermediaries and Aesthetic Products"
        A. Richard Petrosky, University of Arizona

    "The Nature of Communication Networks Between Organizations in Diffusion of Technological Innovations"
        David Midgley, Australian Graduate School of Management
        Pamela Morrision, Australian Graduate School of Management
        John Roberts, Australian Graduate School of Management

    "A Qualitative Exploration of Consumer Innovativeness: A New Look at Diffusion Theory"
        Tina Lowrey, University of Illinois

    Discussant: Charlotte Mason, University of North Carolina

8.5 *Competitive Papers*: **Family Issues**

    Chair: KerenAmi Johnson, Old Dominion University

    "The Role of Love, Affection, and Intimacy in Family Decision Making"
        Jong-Hee Park, Washington State University
        Patriya S. Tansuhaj, Washington State University
        Richard H. Kolbe, Washington State University

    "Financial Decision Making of Babyboomer Couples"
        Amardeep Assar, The State University of New York - Binghamton
        George S. Bobinski, Jr., The State University of New York - Binghamton

    "An Investigation of a Role/Goal Model of Wives' Role Overload Reduction Strategies"
        Shreekant G. Joag, St. John's University
        James W. Gentry, University of Nebraska - Lincoln
        Karin Ekstrom, University of Goteborg

    Discussant: Ved Prakash, Morgan State University

8.6 *Competitive Papers*: **Elderly Consumers**

    Chair: Richard Yalch, University of Washington

    "The Influence of Information Source on Brand Loyalty and Consumer Sex Roles of the Elderly"
        Ruth B. Smith, University of Baltimore

    "Frameworks for Studying Older Consumers: Present Status and Methodological Issues"
        George Moschis, Georgia State University

    "On Golden Pond: Elderly Couples and Consumer Decision Making"
        Louise A. Heslop, Carleton University
        Judith Marshall, Carleton University

    Discussant: Elaine Sherman, Hofstra University

> **SATURDAY, OCTOBER 6**
>
> Chinatown Dinner
> 6:30 pm

> **SUNDAY, OCTOBER 7**
>
> **9TH SESSION: 8:00 am - 9:30 am**

9.1 *Special Session*: **Toward a New Understanding of the Effects of Advertising: A Look at Implicit Memorial Processes**

    Chair: Ida E. Berger, University of Toronto

    "The Impact of Nonconscious Processing: Immediate vs. Time-Delayed Measurement of Automatic Processing Effects"
        Susan E. Heckler, University of Michigan
        Christopher P. Puto, University of Arizona
        Francoise Jaffe, University of Michigan

    "Automatic Processes in Consumer Response to Advertisements"
        Carol Pluzinski, New York University

    "Effects of Inference Generation and Utilization on Attitude Accessibility"
        Douglas M. Stayman, University of Texas
        Frank R. Kardes, University of Cincinnati

    "The Role of Attitude Confidence and Attitude Accessibility in the Process by Which Attitudes Guide Behavior"
        Ida E. Berger, University of Toronto

    Discussant: Larry Percy, LINTAS: USA

9.2 *Special Session*: **Environmentalism and Consumer Research: A Call to Action**

    Chair: April Atwood, University of Washington

    "Environmental Issues and Consumers' State of Mind"
        April Atwood, University of Washington

    "Teaching Environmentally Conscious Consumer Behavior"
        Carl Obermiller, Seattle University

    "Environmentally Based Product Claims and the Erosion of Consumer Trust"
        T.J. Olney, Western Washington University
        Wendy Bryce, Western Washington University

    "Effects of Incentives on Environment-Friendly Behaviors: A Field Experiment with the Public Service Company of Colorado"
        Bruce Hutton, University of Denver

    "Environment-Oriented Product and Packaging Research: Activities at P & G"
        Ron Headings, Procter & Gamble

9.3 *Special Session*: **Pattern Recognition and Consumer Behavior: Empirical Applications of an Emerging Paradigm**

    Chair: Rashi Glazer, University of California, Berkeley

    "Empirical Tests of a Holographic Theory of Pattern Recognition"
        Rashi Glazer, University of California, Berkeley

    "Pattern-Directed Processing and Consumer Choice"
        Raymond Burke, University of Pennsylvania

    "Estimation of Choice Models Using Neural Nets"
        Shahana Sen, New York University
        Richard Colombo, New York University
        Bruce Buchanan, New York University

    "Neural Networks: Learning to Associate Marketers' Behavior With Consumers' Behavior"
        Judy Bayer, Carnegie Mellon University

    Discussant: Donald Lehmann, Columbia University

9.4 *Special Session*: **New Directions in Time Research in Consumer Behavior**

    Co-Chairs: Jacob Hornik, Tel-Aviv University, Ziv Carmon, University of California at Berkeley

    "Context Effects in Consumer Preferences for Single and Multiple Queueing Systems"
        Bernd Schmitt, Columbia University
        Laurette Dube-Rioux, University of Montreal
        France Leclerc, Massachusetts Institute of Technology

    "Contextual Determinants of Consumers' Dissatisfaction with Waiting"
        Ziv Carmon, University of California at Berkeley
        Ravi Dhar, University of California at Berkeley

    "Contextual Issues in Time Perceptions and Orientation"
        Jacob Hornik, Tel-Aviv University

    "Preferences Toward Temporally Separated Outcome Sequences"
        George Lowenstein, University of Chicago
        Drazen Prelec, Harvard University

    Discussant: Eric Johnson, University of Pennsylvania

9.5 *Competitive Papers*: **Ethical Issues**

    Chair: Carol Kaufman, Rutgers University - Camden

    "Evaluating the Impact of Alcohol Warning Labels"
        Robert N. Mayer, University of Utah
        Ken R. Smith, University of Utah
        Debra Scammon, University of Utah

    "Political Advertising in the 1990's: Expected Strategies, Voter Responses, and Public Policy Implications"
        Ronald Paul Hill, Villanova University

    "An Empirical Test of a Model of Consumer Ethical Dilemmas"
        Lawrence J. Marks, Kent State University
        Michael A. Mayo, Kent State University

    Discussant: W.F. van Raaij, Erasmus University - Rotterdam

9.6 *Competitive Papers*: **Innovative Approaches to Consumption Issues**

    Chair: Elnora Stuart, Winthrop College

    "Elements of Experiential Consumption: An Exploratory Study"
        Brian Lofman, The University of Connecticut

    "The Emotional Side of Product Meaning"
        Susan Fournier, The University of Massachusetts at Amherst

    "Jungian Analysis and Psychological Types: An Interpretive Approach to Consumer Choice Behavior"
        Stephen J. Gould, Rutgers University - New Brunswick

    Discussant: Paul F. Anderson, Pennsylvania State University

---

SUNDAY, OCTOBER 7

10TH SESSION: 9:30 am - 11:00 am

10.1 *Special Session*: **"On the Road Again": Consumer Behavior Research in Outdoor Advertising**

    Chair: Andrea MacDonald, Institute of Outdoor Advertising

    "The State of Consumer Research and Future Needs in Outdoor Advertising"
        Andrea MacDonald, Institute of Outdoor Advertising

    "Defining the Research Agenda in Consumer Interactions with Outdoor Media: A Review of Published Findings"
        Joseph Cherian, University of Illinois
        Marilyn Jones, University of Illinois
        Jolita Kisielius, University of Illinois

    "Measurement Techniques Assessing Learning Processes Across Alternative Executions in Outdoor Advertising"
        Joan Treistman, Treistman and Stark Marketing Inc.

    "Recent Research on the Effectiveness of Consumers' Perceptions of Outdoor Advertised Products"
        Andy Weitzer, Gannett Publications

    Discussant: Ken Wisniewski, A. C. Nielsen

10.2 *Special Session*: **Headlines Make Ads Work: New Evidence**

    Chair: Jacqueline Hitchon, University of Wisconsin - Madison

    "Tests of Ogilvy's Conceptualization of Advertising Effectiveness for Print Headlines"
        Williams Milbrath, University of Wisconsin - Madison
        Esther Thorson, University of Wisconsin - Madison

    "Effects of Metaphorical vs. Literal Headlines on Advertising Persuasion and Recall"
        Jacqueline Hitchon, University of Wisconsin - Madison

    "How Viewer's Use News Teaser Headlines to Process Commercial Information More Efficiently"
        Joan Schluder, University of Texas at Austin

    Discussant: Martin Horn, DDB Needham Worldwide

10.3 *Special Session*: **The Construction of Consumer Social Reality: Cognitive Processes and Mass Mediated Effects**

Chair: Thomas C. O'Guinn, University of Illinois

"Counterfactuals and the Evaluation of Product Performance: What Might Have Been"
Valerie Folkes, University of Southern California
Walfried Lassar, University of Southern California

"Investigating Process in Social Reality Research: Variabilities and Uncertainties in Units of Time"
Suzanne Pingree, Stanford University
Robert Hawkins, Stanford University

"Process and Effects in the Construction of Normative Consumer Beliefs: The Role of Television
L. J. Shrum, University of Illinois
Thomas C. O'Guinn, University of Illinois
Richard Semenik, University of Utah
Ronald J. Faber, University of Minnesota

Discussants: Thomas K. Srull, University of Illinois; Andrew P. Hardy, General Motors

10.4 *Competitive Papers*: **Consideration Sets**

Chair: Paul Sauer, SUNY-Buffalo

"How Entrants Affect Multiple Brands: A Dual Attraction Mechanism"
Timothy Heath, University of Pittsburgh
Subimal Chatterjee, University of Pittsburgh

"An Exploratory Study Comparing Amount-of-Search Measures to Consumers' Reliance on Each Source of Information"
Jeff Blodgett, Indiana University
Donna Hill, Bradley University

"An Information Theoretic Approach to Understanding the Consideration Set Awareness Set Proportion"
Ayn E. Crowley, The University of Texas at Austin
John H. Williams, The University of Texas at Austin

Discussant: John Hulland, University of Western Ontario

10.5 *Competitive Papers*: **Pricing Issues**

Chair: Franklin Houston, Rutgers University - Camden

"Perceived Price Fairness and Dual Entitlement"
Rosemary Kalapurakal, The Ohio State University
Peter Dickson, The Ohio State University
Joe E. Urbany, University of South Carolina

"Symbolic Meanings of a Price Ending"
Robert M. Schindler, Rutgers University - Camden

"Individual Differences in Latitude of Acceptable Prices"
Patricia Sorce, Rochester Institute of Technology
Stanley M. Widrick, Rochester Institute of Technology

Discussant: Ivan Ross, University of Minnesota

10.6 *Competitive Papers*: **Imagery and Affect Effects**

    Chair: Kenneth R. Lord, SUNY-Buffalo

    "Measuring Communication-Evoked Imagery Processing"
        Pam Scholder Ellen, Georgia State University
        Paula Fitzgerald Bone, West Virginia University

    "Humor in Television Advertising: The Effects of Repetition and Social Setting"
        Yong Zhang, University of Houston
        George Zinkhan, University of Houston

    "Cue Modality: Video and Audio Effects on Recall"
        Carolyn L. Costley, Texas A&M University
        Duane DeWald, Texas A&M University

    Discussant: John McCarty, University of Illinois at Urbana

PRESIDENTIAL ADDRESS
Secular Mortality and the Dark Side of Consumer Behavior: Or How Semiotics Saved My Life

Elizabeth C. Hirschman, Rutgers University

INTRODUCTION

First let me say that I am really deeply honored and amazed to find myself in the position of making a presidential address today. As I looked back over the past four talks by ACR presidents, I was impressed by the depth and breadth of the topics they had covered: Russ Belk called for a revolution in theory and method; Rich Lutz declared that it had arrived (and indeed it must have, or I wouldn't be here today!) Jim Bettman provided us with an in-depth analysis of how consumers *think*; and Morris Holbrook lyrically and musically told us how they *feel*. That didn't leave much normal ground for me to cover...

And so, I decided to talk today about some strange and unusual topics similar to those for which I have become notorious. Now, as most of you know, I am a happy and upbeat person... But today I want to talk to you about some things that are not happy and upbeat, yet nevertheless have been much on my mind and have caused me to re-think much of my philosophy as a person and a researcher. I want to talk to you about some very difficult and troubling issues -- about death and life, about addiction and recovery, about poverty and racism and how they relate to consumer research. The title of my address is "Secular Mortality and the Dark Side of Consumer Behavior: or How Semiotics Saved My Life."

I became interested in these issues after two events happened to me, which I am going to relate to you in narrative form. These two events affected me very deeply, and it is my great hope that by telling them to you, they will affect you also. It is my hope that they will change the way you conduct your research and also the types of phenomena on which you choose to conduct research.

The evening of July 15, 1988 was a pretty normal one for me. It was a Friday. My husband, Ray, was in Los Angeles filming some television commercials. I had worked on some research projects during the day and then had picked the kids up from summer camp. I made them dinner and gave them a bath. I made myself a big lobster dinner and put the kids to bed. I decided to do some more work, so I drank a cup of strong coffee, took a few No Doz tablets and got busy on a paper. After a few hours, my Mom called me and we talked. Then Ray called me twice and we talked. I watched the last 15 minutes of *Predator* with Arnold Schwarzenegger on HBO, had a drink, and went to bed.

At 4:00 AM my two-year-old daughter, Annie, began calling me from her upstairs bedroom "Mommy, I want a baba" (a bottle). I got up and began walking toward the kitchen. I noticed that I was very dizzy and weak. After a few steps I was unable to walk and lay down on the floor. Annie kept screaming "I want a ba ba!" I began crawling on my stomach toward the kitchen; my heart was pounding and I was very dizzy. When I reached the refrigerator, I stood up, opened the door, and took out a carton of apple juice.

The next thing I remember is regaining consciousness on the kitchen floor in a puddle of blood and apple juice. The house was completely silent. I could not move my body. I was terrified beyond words. I realized that something had gone terribly wrong with me and that I was dying. I thought about the situation. The neighbors on both sides were on vacation; the doors were deadbolted too high up for my children to reach, and Ray was not due back from California for 5 days. I realized that if I did not get up and get help that my children would be stuck in the house for a long time with a dead mother.

And so, somehow, I crawled over to the kitchen counter, pulled myself up, and dialed 911. After telling the voice on the other end who I was and where I lived, I turned on the kitchen light so they could see me through the window. (I was afraid I would be dead or unconscious by the time the EMS people arrived, and they would drive away.) They came and helped me. I knew I *was* in bad shape when the EMS nurse would not allow me to be moved for several minutes until an IV line had been set up. She had been able to get only a weak pulse and virtually no blood pressure reading.

When I arrived at the hospital emergency room, several disgusting and frightening things were done to me, that I will not describe here -- since it is lunch time -- which revealed that I had two stomach ulcers. As the gastroenterologist told me: "One is very big, and the other is very deep." During the night, both of them had perforated my stomach wall, and I had lost between one-half to two-thirds of my entire blood supply. The doctors had no idea how I had made it to the telephone...

Why was Beth Hirschman dying of ulcers? Like most research questions, this one has a simple, direct answer and a more complex, indirect one. The simple, direct answer is that I was a caffeine junkie. I was addicted to caffeine. If you will recall the opening portion of my narrative, you'll see that the clues are there. Remember how I made myself some coffee and then took some No Doz tablets so that I could get to work after dinner? Over the past ten years of my career, that had become standard practice for me. Every morning I would consume caffeine in one form or another, every afternoon, every evening -- seven days a week, 52 weeks a year, for ten years. And every night I would have one or two drinks to bring me down from my caffeine high, so I could get some sleep. I never stopped because I couldn't. I felt too tired without it. I couldn't get anything done. I *needed* it. After a decade of consistent abuse my stomach had had enough. And that night, on July 15, it told me so.

No one starts out drinking coffee, or alcohol, or taking Valium, or smoking grass, or snorting cocaine thinking that they're going to become an addict. It just kind of creeps up on you. One day you realize that the stuff you were consuming to help you *work* better, or *sleep* better, or *feel* better has become an indispensable part of your life. You can't live without it, but as I discovered, you can die with it.

The more complex, indirect answer as to why this happened to me is harder to verbalize. I believe the roots of my problem lie beyond the simple fact of addiction, and likely relate closely to feelings and experiences you have had in your own lives. I wanted very much to succeed and do well at *everything*. I started out wanting to be a perfect daughter and did everything I could to make my parents proud of me -- often achieving many things I didn't really care about, but that I believed *they* wanted me to achieve. I carried that attitude over into my adult life. I tried to be the perfect graduate student, the perfect wife, the perfect mother, the perfect professor, the perfect researcher, the perfect committee member.

But being perfect at all those tasks was beyond what a normal human could do, so I began to use stimulant drugs -- caffeine -- to achieve them. And I was very successful at it. I became a very prolific consumer researcher, I got great teacher ratings, I was named to committee after committee, I won office after office. And then one day I ended up on the kitchen floor bleeding to death... So much for perfection.

I believe in many ways the most insidious, dangerous forms of addiction are those which make us seem successful; which are carried around by people who appear to be performing excellently and who keep receiving reinforcement after reinforcement for their achievements. Unlike the heroin junkie in the gutter, who recognizes his misery, we successful addicts are too busy basking in external affirmation until it is too late. And if we survive, as I did, we find we not only have to learn to live without our chemical dependencies, but also to drastically restructure our lives away from `being perfect' and more toward being human. Often times this means getting in touch with feelings and emotions that have been dormant for long periods of time and even rediscovering who we are.

One thing that I discovered after my collapse is that relationships with other people are much more important than secular achievements, fame, and glory. *Life* -- mine, yours and everybody's, is of supreme importance. And I wanted to do something to help other people live their lives better.

This was brought home to me in vivid fashion the second afternoon I was in the Intensive Care Unit. My two I.V. bottles were hooked up to a portable stand and, Type A personality that I am, I decided to take a walk. I wandered down the hall, past the coronary unit, past the trauma unit and on and on until I finally found myself on a strange hallway. It was full of patients. Some were languishing in their beds, some sat slumped in easy chairs in the hall. All of them looked wasted; all of them were young; all of them were men. I suddenly realized that all of them had AIDS and that they were dying... just as I had been only two days earlier. Only for them, there would be no miraculous call to 911, no EMS arrival, no life-saving transfusion in the emergency room. They were not going to make it off the kitchen floor. They were going to die. And I felt so terribly, terribly sad.

I resolved to change the course of my research toward more life-oriented forms of consumer behavior. I decided to begin examining those phenomena that can hurt and damage consumers with the thought that if I could learn about them, perhaps I could help prevent them. My first three ventures in this area dealt with the possession and commoditization of women, with prostitution and pornography, and with the diffusion of cocaine. They are nice papers, but they still weren't dealing with the real nitty-gritty issues that were out there. I had put my mind into them, but not my whole heart and soul... And then, something else happened to me...

In late May of 1989, Ray and I decided to take the kids and go on a much-needed vacation to St. Maarten, the friendly island in the Caribbean. After settling into the hotel room for a couple of days and enjoying the beautiful turquoise water and the white sand beaches, we decided to drive into the port city of Marigot. Marigot was absolutely beautiful. Yachts were docked in the harbor, there was a whole collection of excellent French restaurants, and an array of shops selling expensive and exquisite things: Lalique crystal, Cartier jewelry, Yves Saint Laurent clothing, fine wines. The stores were crowded with wealthy tourists from the U.S. and Europe.

We had a delightful lunch there and then began driving back toward our hotel. The road to our hotel passed through what you and I would view as a slum, but which comprised the normal residences of most of St. Maarten's native population: small cinder block houses with tin roofs perched on uneven, bare patches of land. Wandering from yard to yard were goats and chickens and an occasional sickly dog. In the hot sun the residents sat on their porches and watched the parade of tourist traffic drive by in rented Hyundais and Hondas.

As we pulled up at a stop light, a cream colored Mercedes convertible stopped in front of us. Inside was a beautiful blonde woman, her hair bound-up in a Hermes scarf. There were gold earrings against her neck and her wrists were covered with expensive bracelets and a diamond watch. She was wearing an elegant silk dress.

I was amazed at the contrast between her extraordinary affluence and the extreme poverty of the women sitting on the porches. The contrast was not only vivid, it was vulgar and obscene. What invisible wall, I wondered, kept the people on the porches from running forward and grabbing at her, tearing off her expensive things? What had each done to deserve their fate -- the rich and the poor?

But I put those disturbing thoughts out of my mind when we reached the hotel. That night, Ray and I were going out to dinner. We had made reservations at an excellent French restaurant, right on the water, in the town of Grand Case. It was a dinner I shall never forget. Our table overlooked the Caribbean and in the lights we could see each wave gently flowing in and spreading across the sand. The food was wonderful; we had pate' and rock lobster and champagne. There were raspberries and cream for dessert.

Driving back in the car, I realized that I had not been so at peace with myself for a long time -- for years. We were in a wonderful mood; we had the radio on to a reggae station and the windows rolled down to let in the fragrant night air.

When we were about 2 miles from our hotel, I glanced down at the clock on the dashboard to check the time so I could pay the babysitter. It was 10:45. As I looked up, I noticed the lights of another car coming up behind us. We were in no hurry, so Ray slowed down to let it pass. There was an enormous crash. Our car was thrown off the road and into a culvert. "Damn," I thought, "those people are drunk and now we've had a wreck." In the headlights of our car I saw two shadowy figures running toward us. There was a bright flash of light and an explosion BAM! on Ray's side of the car. The entire windshield on his side shattered. Ray screamed, "They're shooting at us; they're shooting at us!" I yelled to him "Drive the car! Drive the car!" There was another flash of light, and another explosion on my side of the car and the rest of the windshield fell away.

Suddenly the two men were jerking open the doors of the car. One began hitting Ray in the chest with his gun demanding his wallet. The other put his gun to my head and began grabbing my jewelry and my pocketbook. My ears strained for the sound of the gun going off for a third time. I knew it was inevitable. I knew we were dead.

But instead of shooting us, the men ordered us to get out of the car. As we were exiting, another pair of headlights appeared on the road; one man shouted to the other "Someone's coming, Mon, let's go." And they jumped back in their car and sped away, screaming, laughing, and waving their guns in the air.

I ran into the street and began waving my arms at the oncoming car. It stopped. I yelled to them "We've just been shot at; we've been robbed; our car is wrecked; please help us." It turned out to be 4 tourists from Ohio, (never have I been so glad to see tourists from Ohio) and they did help us. They gave me a ride back to the hotel, while a security man stayed with Ray and the car. Ray told the police what had happened and then was taken to the hospital. The first bullet had been fired at such close range and had passed so closely to his head that the right side of his face was covered with powder burns and glass fragments.

Why did this happen to us? Like my response to the earlier question on caffeine addiction, there is a simple, direct answer and a complex, indirect answer. The simple answer is that, as we learned from the police the next day, our attackers were crack cocaine addicts who had been rampaging around the island since February. They had stopped cars and ransacked villas, each time the wildness and viciousness of their attacks increased. We had the unique distinction, however, of being the very first people they had tried to blow the heads off of. After reflecting on this news, I realized the irony of it all. I had survived my own near-fatal addiction only to almost die, less than a year later, because of someone else's addiction. Thus, the moral of the simple answer is, if your own addiction doesn't kill you, someone else's may.

The more complex, indirect answer to the question "Why did this happen to us?", however, is bound-up in the significance of an event that had happened earlier in the day. Recall the story of the stoplight, with me watching the rich woman in the Mercedes and seeing also the hungry eyes of the poor women on the porches. The complex, indirect answer lies in the ugly structure of wealth and poverty, of white and black, of insensitivity and apathy confronted by anger and bitterness.

Although I had recognized the vulgarness and cruelty of displaying great wealth in front of people with little opportunity for achieving it, I soon put it out of my mind and continued on with my own privileged, affluent lifestyle. I'm feeling OK, so forget the rest of the world. It's too bad they're poor, but, hey, I can't/won't/needn't do anything about it... On with the party; let's go to dinner.

We never know when we will be judged. But it is usually when we least expect it, at a time when we are least prepared for it, and by those whom we most fear as judges. And so it was with me and Ray on that dark road in St. Maarten. We were judged, harshly, and terrified in the process. But we were not killed, despite our mutual certainty that we would die that night. Here were two men, our fate-designated judges, who had attempted, from a distance of about 3 or 4 feet, to shoot us in the head before robbing us. They were so wild, and reckless and high from cocaine that, remarkably, they missed their mark.

Yet when they threw open the doors to the car and their guns were up against us, and there was no margin for error, they did not shoot. They took our money, our worldly goods, but they left us the most precious of all possessions, our lives. Why? Ray and I, who think differently about nearly everything, converged on the same answer for this: It was the way we were dressed; the way we looked. For despite our affluence and despite our dinner that evening at an expensive restaurant, Ray and I were dressed the way we always are during our leisure time -- when we are really being ourselves -- or at least the selves we used to be back during our liberal, radical youths. In short, we were both wearing jeans, sneakers and T-shirts. Ray with his beard and wire-rimmed glasses; me with my long, unstyled hair and no make-up. Two middle-aged hippies. That is what the angry, addicted, poor men saw as they flung open the door of our car and that is who they decided only to rob, not to kill. Both Ray and I are sure that had we been dressed-up that night, we would be dead today. And that's how semiotics saved my life. You are what you wear, and sometimes that can make a world of difference.

Ironically, perhaps, my experience in St. Maarten convinced me that just as I could not run away from my own consumption problems, I could not run away from other people's either.

I renewed my efforts to delve into the dark side of consumer behavior. I began talking directly and openly to people who suffered from a variety of consumption-related problems -- people who are or have been heroin junkies, and alcoholics, and prostitutes; people who have smoked crack and robbed convenience stores at gunpoint. People who have lived in the street and slept in gutters. People who have gambled away their life savings. And I have found out two important things. First, they are not very different from you and me... In fact, in my case at least, they *are* me. And second, I believe that we, as consumer researchers, have much that we could do to help them, if only we would make the effort.

As we meet here today, comfortable not only in our attractive surroundings, but in our personal affluence and success, let us not ignore some uncomfortable statistics about other people's realities as consumers. At the present time, 100,000 homeless people dwell in the cities and towns of America, the wealthiest country on earth (National Coalition for the Homeless). Dispossessed and displaced, they wander aimlessly through the streets, camp in parks and live under highways. What have *we* done to help their plight?

There are currently 2 to 3 million cocaine and crack addicts in the United States (Waller 1990). 375,000 drug-addicted babies were born in 1989, alone (Kantrowicz 1990) -- consumers whose first moments of existence are distorted by the dark side of consumer behavior. What have *we* done to help them?

Every six minutes a woman is raped in the United States -- the highest incidence of this violent crime, this terrible act of personal commoditization, among the industrialized nations (Salholz 1990). Every 18 seconds a woman is beaten; 3 to 4 million women are battered every year, treated as abused possessions by husbands and lovers (Salholz 1990). What have *we* done to help them?

Every year over 10 million American consumers suffer financial losses from their addiction to gambling and over 500,000 file for personal bankruptcy as a result of credit card abuse (Brister & Brister 1987; Statistical Abstracts 1990).

There are currently 10 million alcoholics and 80 million cigarette smokers in the United States (Brister & Brister 1987). Every year, 25,000 people die as a result of alcohol-related traffic accidents; and 20,000 consumers die from the disease of alcoholism, itself (Brister & Brister 1987). On average, 360,000 consumers die every year from lung cancer, emphysema and heart disease linked to cigarette smoking -- a number greater than all the American soldiers killed in the Second World War (Brister & Brister 1987). What could *we* have done to prevent this?

All of these disturbing and disturbed behaviors result from consumption gone wrong. The dark side of consumer behavior is ugly and unhappy, but it is, perhaps, not inevitable. Consumers could likely recover from these damaging behaviors, if adequate research were conducted into their origins and treatment.

We are a bright, and talented, and productive group. How much we could accomplish if we would turn even a portion of our talents toward understanding and ameliorating the dark side of consumer behavior. I hope that through listening to my own struggle with these issues and thinking about the real people whose lives are encompassed in the statistics just presented you will be challenged to do so.

Thank you!

REFERENCES

Kantrowicz, Barbara (1990), "The Crack Children," *Newsweek*, February 12, 62-63.

Salholz, Eloise (1990), "Women Under Assault," *Newsweek*, July 16, 23-24.

Waller, Douglas (1990), "Risky Business," *Newsweek*, July 16, 16-19.

Brister, David and Phyllis Brister (1987), *The Vicious Circle Phenomenon*, Birmingham: Diadem Publishing.

Presentation of the Association for Consumer Research Distinguished Service Award to H. Keith Hunt

Harold H. Kassarjian, UCLA

I have been asked to make the first Association for Consumer Research Distinguished Service Award to a dear, wonderful friend. What a great honor! Thank you.

ACR does not give many awards, nor very often, making this award particularly special. It was created last year, during the 20th anniversary of the Association for Consumer Research, and its first recipient, whom we honor today, announced at that time. It was designed to be awarded very rarely - only at intervals representing significant anniversaries of the association - the 20 anniversary, and maybe the 25th or 35th or 50th anniversary of the founding of ACR. However, one must wonder if it will ever come to pass that another individual will meet the standards that have been set by the first recipient.

The procedures for making the award were designed to be exactly those used for the Fellow in Consumer Research award. The selection is made by the Fellows Award Nominating Committee - a chair appointed by the current president and three members consisting of the immediate past presidents. The decision of the committee must be unanimous. The candidate is then presented to the ACR elected Board of Directors for confirmation by at least 75% affirmative vote.

However, the Distinguished Service Award is completely independent of the Fellows award and rests on independent criteria - service to the association. Let me quote from the words of the award itself:

> The distinguished Service Award of the Association for Consumer Research recognizes the dedication and the devotion of a member who has served the organization with energy and generosity beyond the call of duty. This award expresses our highest gratitude to one who has helped its members in ways that have built a stronger community of scientists and scholars in consumer research.

To anyone familiar with this association, and that includes most all of us assembled here, the first recipient simply had to be, and is, Keith Hunt. The ACR Executive Secretary and the person every president and every program chair seems to publicly thank every year for doing just about everything. Keith Hunt, a very special person, but, indeed, few know the full gamut of contributions he makes to all of us.

Unlike our sister scholarly associations with professional impersonal bureaucracies, ACR is based on voluntary service. We have no paid staff. The ACR central office, the headquarters, the communications center, the mail room, the library, the publications arm, the secretariat, the accounting office, and the keeper of the checkbook is Keith Hunt. Without Keith Hunt, the Newsletter would not be mailed, the Directory would not exist, ACR programs would not be prepared, conferences would not be organized, and scholarly work would not be published and sometimes not even conceived. Keith Hunt's basement, to the everlasting distress of his family and to the gratitude of librarians and scholars, is the ACR publications warehouse. Mountains of publications - proceedings, monographs, cumulative indexes, directories, and records - extend from from floor to ceiling.

It is not a random event that for as long as Keith has been executive secretary, the association has been wealthy. Dues remain at the lowest level of any professional or scholarly association, yet ACR seems to have more money than we can spend. Somehow, everything we do, every attempt made to return value to the membership, results in even more money coming in. Let me give you one example of the Keith Hunt touch. Some years ago Keith suggested I put together a cumulative annotated index of the ACR proceedings which would be distributed free of charge to our members. It was a massive, expensive task that took several of us months to complete. But for Keith, it was one more way to give even greater value for the dues we pay. Keith published and distributed the volume. Members told nonmembers and their librarians who in turn placed orders. It went into additional printings (and even a second edition), and ended up making money for the association. Once again, our executive secretary had made a "silk purse out of a sow's ear."

Keith Hunt, his warmth and caring, is the primary cause of the wonderful esprit de corps that permeates this association, the envy of all our sister societies. But he is more than just Mister ACR. Until recently he was the subscription fulfillment arm of the *Journal of Consumer Research*. He is the publisher and organizer of the annual Satisfaction/ Disatisfaction Conference and editor of the *Journal of Consumer Satisfaction, Dissatisfaction and Complaining Behavior*. He was program chairman of the 8th annual conference of ACR (so long ago!); he was president of ACR in 1979. He is a fellow in the American Academy of Advertising, past editor of the *Journal of Advertising*, past president of the American Academy of Advertising, and its past executive secretary.

Hunt was a student of Sidney Levy, and Northwestern's representative to the very first AMA Doctoral Consortium in 1966. His early research on corrective advertising, counter advertising, and public policy is today a classic that was influential in spearheading public policy research in the decade of the seventies. His work on labeling, hoarding, and entrepreneurship is well known and his work on satisfaction/ dissatisfaction continues to be referenced in most every paper written in that field.

In 1973 Keith served a term at the FTC, among the first of us in that role. But he is still more. Few may be aware that Keith, in addition to being a professor and ACR Executive Secretary, is also a professional politician. Recently, he was reelected to the Orem City Council for a second four year term.

Keith Hunt; a gentleman and a scholar, past ACR president and past program chairman, executive secretary, editor, author, researcher, professor, a counselor in his church, a politician in his city, and a human being extraordinaire; on behalf of all of us in ACR who owe you so much, I present you with the Distinguished Service Award. Congratulations Mister ACR.

Distinguished Service Award Remarks
H. Keith Hunt, Brigham Young University

Why would I be Executive Secretary of ACR for nine years and be planning on continuing that service for the foreseeable future? There are several reasons.

The first reason is that this is the one position which puts me in regular contact with you, all my professional colleagues, some of you my close friends. What's it worth to get five to ten phone calls a week to ask a specific question but also to exchange pleasantries and keep friendships alive. You jot notes to me on your dues notices. You send me picture post cards. I even get notes jotted on the election ballots. My life is more fun living because of my regular contact with all of you.

The second reason is the people I associate with in this position. Since becoming Executive Secretary in 1982 I have had the pleasure of working with nine presidents, ten counting next year's president, Sid Levy, with whom I'm already working: Jerry Zaltman, Ken Bernhardt, Jag Sheth, Peter Wright, Russ Belk, Jim Bettman, Rich Lutz, Morris Holbrook, Beth Hirschman and Sid Levy. Add to these all the people who have served starting with 1982 as treasurer or director and members of the nine person advisory council and you get the feel for the outstanding folks with whom I work. Then add in the newsletter editors and conference program chairs with whom I work very closely. There's not a finer group of people I could associate with in the whole world.

Being an ACR member puts me in your group. Being your Executive Secretary let's me interact with you as we all give our service to ACR.

As Executive Secretary I may offer more service to ACR than any one of you, but as a percentage of the total service rendered mine is a small part of the total.

The third reason is what I can only express as a great love for ACR. ACR was the first professional group to accept me and treat me as though I had something to contribute. I presented my first paper at ACR in 1972. My ACR friends persuaded me to take the year's appointment with the Federal Trade Commission which was the turning point in my professional career.

My ACR friends have included me in their professional schemes and have responded graciously when I have invited them to be part of my professional schemes. Through all my professional activities I have always had one foot firmly anchored in ACR as my home base.

I've never gotten over the amazement of being nominated for president of ACR. That was the great wonder. And then to win that election is still so incomprehendable that I don't pretend to understand it.

Then to be selected as Executive Secretary was a further trust which has given me great satisfaction.

The fourth reason is that I appreciate opportunities to give service.

I realize some of you think I am more than a bit strange in my willingness to render such substantial service for so long,

taking so much of my time and energies. However, many of us render great service to consumer research, rendering it in different ways.

I remember discussing this with Jerry Zaltman when he was president, after he had made some comment about my service to ACR. I asked Jerry how many Ph.D. dissertations he was chairing at that time. I remember his answer being approximately ten. My point to him was that his time and excellence committed to those dissertations was far greater than the time and excellence required of me in my service as Executive Secretary.

I expect to complete my professional career at Brigham Young University. I will probably never supervise another Ph.D. dissertation or even an M.A. thesis. So my service can come in other ways.

While I get the Distinguished Service Award, and I love you for so honoring me, I openly acknowledge that many of you are spending much more time in service to the field than I spend.

Some day my service as Executive Secretary will end. It may be a political end brought on by my unwillingness to accept new directions for ACR. I may make a major mistake. Or, someone may want what I have badly enough to take it from me. Perhaps I will be fortunate enough to continue until a graceful retirement.

Until then, I cherish the opportunity for service which you give to me by letting me be your Executive Secretary.

The fifth reason is that from experience I have found that service is one of the sweet parts of life. I've found that I and you can seldom if ever give serious, substantial service without becoming happier and more satisfied with our existence. The service can be to one's community, to one's religious group, to youth, to the elderly, to the unfortunate and needy, or even to scholarship -- but all service is rewarding in ways that self-promotion and professional productivity can never be.

I love you for being scholars in the area I most like to study. I love you for your tolerance of me in my sometimes flawed service.

Thank you for honoring me today.

FELLOW'S AWARD SPEECH
One Mega and Seven Basic Principles for Consumer Research
Gerald Zaltman

INTRODUCTION

The honor of receiving this award is exceeded only by the honor of having had the opportunity to work with so many fine people in our field and of having so many others pay attention to my ideas. If the development of ideas is a researcher's primary objective, the conferral of professional recognition is the coin of the realm. This award and the honor of interacting with so many of you have made me feel very enriched today.

Just as many people have learned from me, so have I learned from others in our own and related fields. For example, during the past two years I've become interested in the use of photography as a social science research tool. As others have already demonstrated, photography has enormous potential for the study of behavior, a potential that will increase even more as digital imaging technologies applied to photography become more available to experimentalists. While photography is not the subject of my remarks today, it provides the orientation for ideas I'd like to share, particularly with newer members of the profession.

TWO LESSONS FROM GREAT PHOTOGRAPHERS

My interest in photography has brought me into contact with some important photographers who have in common two special accomplishments. First, they have mastered the same principles about their craft. Whatever these might be, they are not easily mastered. Many good photographers don't master them at all. Secondly, these photographers share a knack for bending these principles in highly individual but systematic ways.

It is important to point out that photographers who have not mastered these rules also break them but in ways which are less rich, less exciting, and which result in a much less engaging personality in their work. The same can be said of photographers who have mastered them but have not dared to break them or have not learned how.

What I have said about master photographers can probably be said of master painters, thiefs, musicians, CEOs, engineers, carpenters, chefs, and so on. I know it can be said of master consumer researchers. I have collaborated with some of them and participated with many more in numerous panels, task forces, and committees. Like the master photographers, there is a common set of principles which they seem to have learned and then distinctively altered in practice.

A MEGA PRINCIPLE

This brings me to what I would like to share with you today. I would like to say a few words about basic principles for approaching consumer research (and which apply to other endeavors as well).

There is an important mega principle: once mastered, *basic principles need to be creatively bent to reflect individuality*. Bending principles in creative and productive ways is a highly personal process which cannot be prescribed. For that matter, I have qualms about prescribing basic principles. They are more evident to me in hindsight than they ever were with foresight. I don't know that I ever really thought about them until the past few years when I began teaching a doctoral seminar on theory construction.

For what they are worth, the following principles are among the more important ones I have learned from my mentors and have subsequently bent through trial and error. My adaptation of these principles seem to have guided most of what I consider to be my best work. As just mentioned, they also seem to have been internalized and then altered in distinctive, personal ways by the consumer researchers whose work I regard most highly, however substantively and methodologically different their work is from mine.

SEVEN BASIC PRINCIPLES

Before introducing these principles I'd like to anticipate two responses and ask you to think about questions they raise. One likely response is: "They are pretty obvious". In fact, they are obvious. This prompts the question, "Why are they so frequently absent from research in our own and other disciplines?"

The second response is: "It is all well and good for a tenured full professor to espouse principles which may be dangerous for someone needing many publications in a short time for promotion and tenure". This raises the question "Why is it that leaders in our field have managed to master and adapt these principles early in their careers?" If they have, others can.

1. *Think big and do it now*, not later. By thinking big I mean tackle problems or issues where new insights have the potential of changing (a) at least some thinking on the part of many people, or (b) a great deal of thinking on the part of some people. That is, you should ask yourself a two part question, "How much thinking on the part of how many people could change if this research effort yields a new and sound insight?" If you cannot answer, "Lots!" to either part of this question, you need to seriously question whether your research is worth pursuing. There is nothing wrong with being a good carpenter. In fact, that is rather

important. But it is still more important to be an architect, too.

Moreover, if you do not engage early in your career in research which has the potential for major impact you are unlikely to do so later. The "Mental Trap of the Small Problem" is very difficult to escape once you have been ensnared. This observation goes against popular wisdom about the impact of tenure on the selection of a research program.

A corollary to this principle is that the ideas being tested should have a reasonable chance of failing. If they are quite likely to be supported, why are you wasting your time with a rather obvious idea?

2. *Think fun.* Thinking big can be risky. An impactful result may elude you. As a consolation you should at least be able to say doing the work was fun. I mean "fun" the way it is fun to read an engaging novel, participate in sports, or see an involving play. At the end you are disappointed it is over. Here, too, your motivations for doing the research should be questioned if, more evenings than not, you are not eager to get up the next morning to resume work.

Then, too, there is the issue of control. About the only thing we can control is whether most of our research is intrinsically fun. We certainly can't control research outcomes if (a) we are working on complex and messy problems, which is what important problems tend to be, and (b) we are using equal opportunity methodologies, that is, methodologies which allow equally for disconfirming evidence to show up if it is really out there. In fact, major intellectual advances often originate in disconfirming evidence. In fact, it is often the outlier in our results that are the most important phenomena.

Additionally, we really cannot control how our colleagues will respond to our work, particularly when they assume the role of journal referee. So why not at least enjoy what we are doing? It also makes for higher quality work.

3. Have the courage of your convictions when they are felt strongly. While my convictions are wrong often enough, I am wrong still more often when I act on someone else's conviction when it differs from mine. You will receive a lot of advice about what is important to research and how you should go about it. You will be especially tempted by reviewer advice and advice from senior colleagues. This advice is all the more difficult to disregard when it conflicts with your own counsel because it is well intended, comes from a respected source, and usually makes sense. But that doesn't mean it is superior to your particular stance. The more important the issue and the greater the discrepancy between your strongly felt position and someone else's, the more important it is to have the courage of your own conviction.

There is an important qualifying condition for this principle which I will discuss as a fourth principle.

4. *Use criticism as a creative tool.* Having the courage of your convictions is not the same as being stubborn. The difference lies in how one responds to criticism. When advice is received which contradicts your own position you can accept it immediately, ignore it immediately, or you can use it as a viewing lens for reexamining your own position. So long as criticism and conflicting advice are treated as an occasion to reexamine your position you won't get into too much trouble displaying the courage of your own conviction. To maintain a position without a willingness to step outside of it and question it is stubborness and, like the too ready abandonment of a conviction, no good is likely to come of it.

This brings me to a related fifth principle. But before addressing it, there is a corollary concerning criticism. Honest criticism is most readily used as a creative tool when offered with respect and care. We are dealing, after all, with someone else's valued personal property.

5. *Challenge established assumptions.* Considerable intellectual progress is a result of challenging assumptions. A look at the intellectual history of various professions and academic disciplines shows that much of what was certified knowledge in a given period was later found to be incorrect or at least substantially more inadequate than believed at the time. The current time period in consumer research is unlikely to be an exception to this observation. So, in addition to trying to conquer ignorance at the frontiers of what we know, do not be reluctant to conquer it within the context of what we think we know.

Above all else, challenge your own assumptions. This requires an ability to stop being *a part of* an idea and to be able to discard ownership in order to examine it critically. Of course, a sense of ownership and commitment to an idea are very important to its development. Overall though, *a greater commitment to the process of having a good idea than to the idea itself is required.* It is easier to detect error and to use criticism as a creative tool when you are more committed to the process of being right than to proving a particular idea.

6. *Have confidence and dedication.* Being creative, especially when developing an alternative to an established position, involves many traits. One trait is having confidence that there is a better idea and the dedication to keep working with the raw materials of that idea until an attractive form emerges. Solutions are not so much found like pebbles on a beach or potatoes in a field as they are created. Much of our educational process teaches how to find the single correct answer rather than the more robust process of creating them. I am baffled by the fact that so many exercises intended to improve creativity have predetermined correct answers. The process of creating correct answers as opposed to finding them appears to be scary for educators to address.

Creating ideas is a lot like modeling with clay; one keeps working and reworking it until the right shape emerges. Somewhere within that lump is the *creative possibility* of a perfect whatever; the task is to get as close to it as possible by strategically and continually taking some clay away and putting some back. Sometimes you do not know exactly what an idea should look like but only that what you have developed so far is not right.

7. Develop *wide cognitive peripheral vision.* It is very helpful to have exposure to a broad array of ideas via exposure to many people, diverse published works, and activities that are unrelated to any specific professional matter. For example, with respect to people, I have had and continue to have the uncommonly good fortune of working with many bright but otherwise varied mentors, colleagues, and students. And it is no surprise to me that I have learned more from my students than any other group, since they are the most diverse set of professionals one encounters.

CONCLUSION

At the outset of my comments I mentioned working with and learning from others. The principles I have shared today were presented as skills important to individual development. However, the principles are also relevant to team research and more importantly, perhaps, to establishing exciting environments for inquiry, be it at the departmental level or university and corporate levels. So, I would like to leave you with a challenge and a caveat.

The challenge is to develop and debate principles for yourself, for your own organizations, and for our profession. Do not, of course, forget to bend or alter them in your own style. But above all else, have the courage to correct or to at least ignore the many conditions that make important principles difficult to maintain and easy to forego. Perhaps that is a second mega principle.

The caveat is a kind of "Catch 22": if pursuit of these principles is motivated largely by matters of professional expediency, such as getting promotion and tenure, they are likely to backfire. Your primary motivation has to be rooted more in the intrinsic enjoyment of the Grand Waltz with these principles than in what occurs at the end of the dance.

Children's Research: Where It's Been, Where It Is Going
Judy A. Harrigan, Harrigan-Bodick, Inc.

As we launch into the 90's, it's fair to ask ourselves, as researchers, what maturational level we've reached in children's research, during the 80's.

CHILDREN'S RESEARCH -- WHERE IT'S BEEN

The ARF Children's Research Council fielded a pilot study, in 1988, to gain insight into where children's research had been during the 80's.

Two hundred questionnaires were sent to individuals in corporations and advertising agencies that market children's products. We asked them about the research they had conducted, during the preceeding year, on products for childen aged 6 to 12 years.

A total of 49 questionnaires were returned yielding a 25% response rate. Those responding represented a cross section of the industry. Approximately, three-quarters were equally divided between researching children's products for the food and toy industries. The remainder were involved in programming, candy, beverage and clothing research. Individuals answering the survey had positions of responsibility in their departments.

CHILDREN'S RESEARCH BUDGETS

A budget of 16 million dollars was spent by these respondents on children's research. About half spent $100,000 or less per year, about 30% spent $100,000 to $1/2 million, 11% spent $1/2 million to $1 million and 8% of the companies' budgets surpassed a million dollars for children's research. (Figure 1).

NATURE OF THE RESEARCH

A total of 1,138 research projects for children's products were conducted, during the preceeding year, by the 49 respondents. The majority of these were quantitative projects. (Figure 2).

RESPONDENTS INTERVIEWED

Respondents were asked among whom these research projects on children's products were conducted. For both qualitative and quantitative research, the majority of the projects were conducted only among children. Parents were researched, either alone or to complement the children's research, 42% of the time for quantitative and 38% of the time for qualitative projects. Note, these percentages were based on the total number of projects conducted, and therefore reflect the practices of companies with a larger number of projects. (Figure 3).

INTERVIEWING TECHNIQUES

The most prevalent interviewing technique used among children was the central location test. The next was mini-groups of 3 to 7 children with the rest including a variety of techniques.

When asked whether these techniques would be used "more", "less" or the "same" amount in the future, about a third of the respondents thought there would be an increase in most of the techniques. Exceptions were "self-administered in groups", "in-home interviewing" and "children's panels." The anticipated trend reflects the interest and growth in children's research. (Figure 4).

TYPES OF TESTS

Almost half of the reported tests were either product tests, concept tests or commercial tests. The remaining tests included segmentation, programming, packaging, promotion, print ads, brand name and pricing. (Figure 5).

When the number of companies conducting research, and not the number of projects was the base, it was evident that the mother continued to have an important role. Among the three most prevalent types of tests, TV commercial testing had the largest number of companies which interviewed "children only." (Figure 6).

WRITTEN SCALES

As we'll discuss today, there are diverse opinions and practices regarding the use of specific scales. Among the industry representatives in this study, the most popular written scales were "overall appeal" and "ask mom to buy." The practice of directly asking children for their purchase interest was limited. (Figure 7).

VISUAL SCALES

Visual scales were used less frequently, in general, than written scales. Given younger children's limited verbal skills, this finding was surprising. The smiley and star scales were the most commonly used scales on the aided list. (Figure 8).

SALES FORCASTING

Sales forecasting of children's products was an area of industry interest. Half of the respondents in this study had "ever tried" to forecast sales for children's products while 39% "currently" forecast sales for children's products. Most of the respondents involved in sales forecasting used a combination of child and parent input. (Figure 9).

SALES FORECASTING MODELS

Both outside suppliers and in-house proprietary sales forecasting models for children's products were used. When asked if they had "alot", "a little", or "not much" confidence in the technique they used, only about a third of the respondents said they had "alot of confidence." (Figure 10).

12 / *Children's Research: Where It's Been, Where It Is Going*

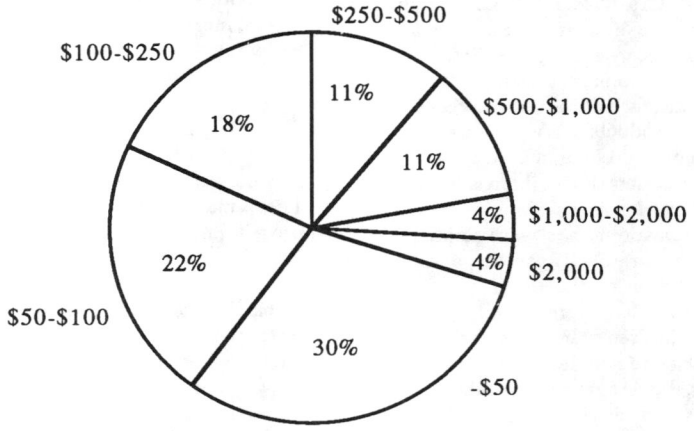

FIGURE 1
Budget for Children's Research
-- Last Year --
In Thousands ('000) of Dollars

BASE: TOTAL REPORTED CHILDREN'S RESEARCH PROJECTS ($16,100,000)

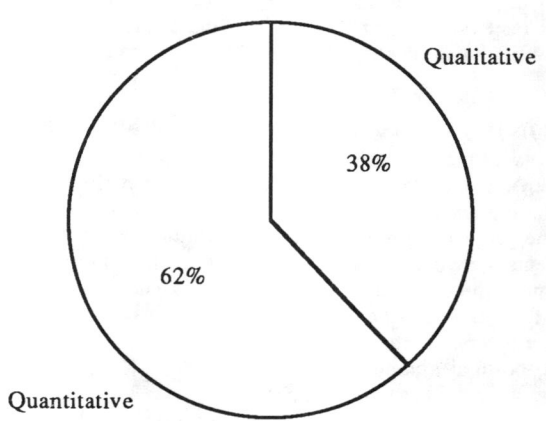

FIGURE 2
Qualitative Vs. Quantitative Research Products
Children's Products

REPORTED PROJECTS: 1138

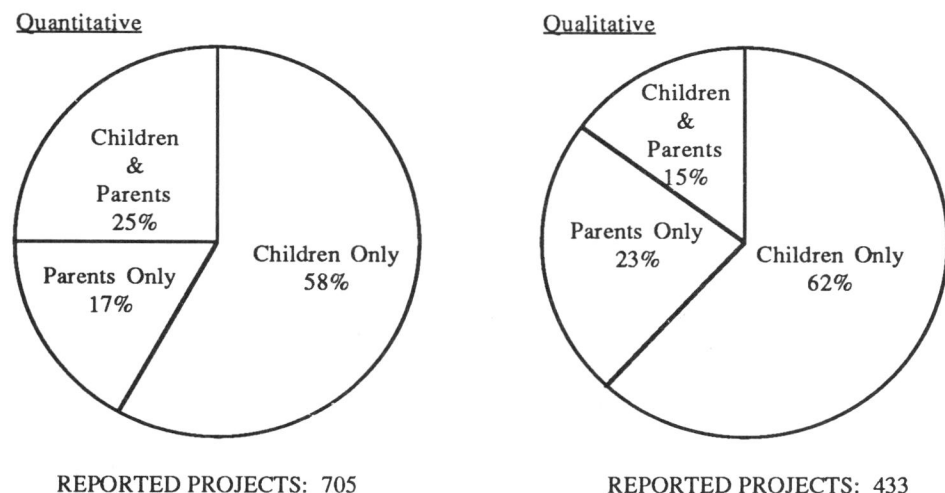

FIGURE 3
Respondents Interviewed for Children's Products
Quantitative & Qualitative

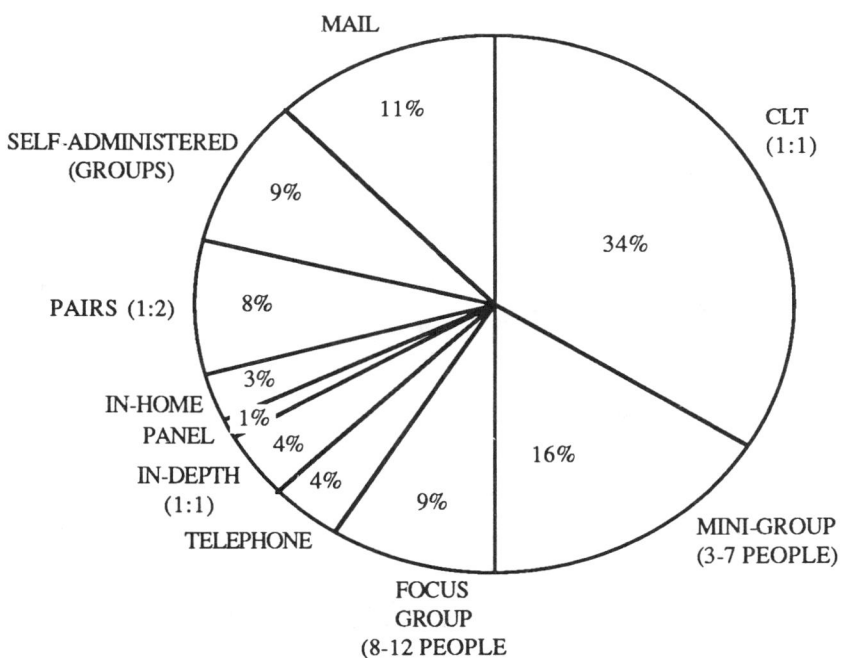

FIGURE 4
Children's Interviewing Techniques Used

14 / *Children's Research: Where It's Been, Where It Is Going*

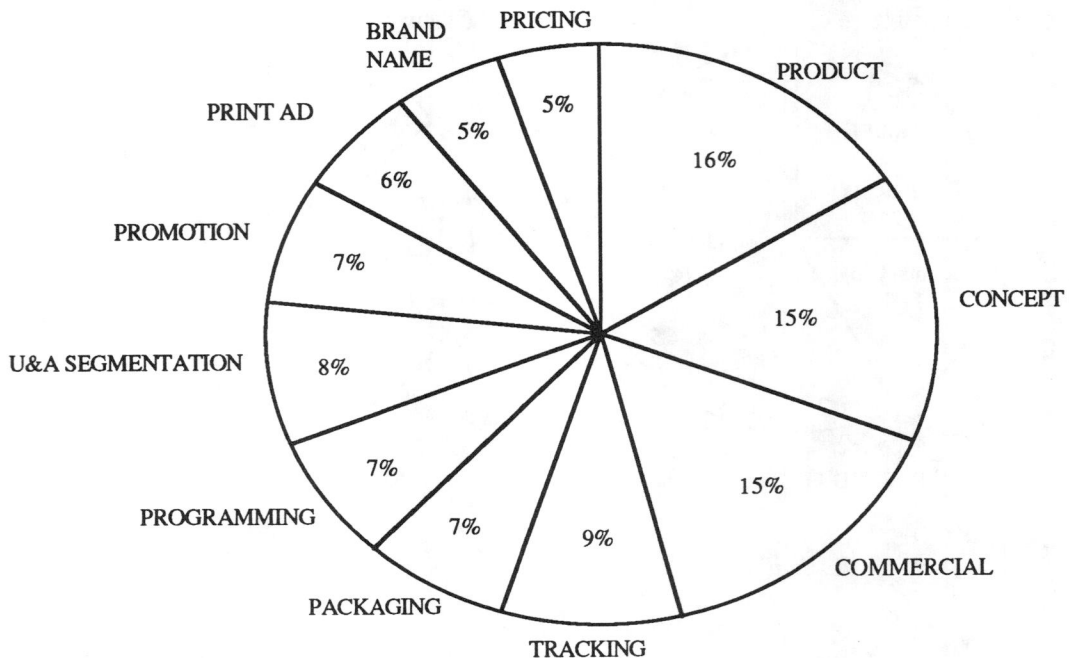

FIGURE 5
Types of Tests Conducted on Children's Products
-- Past Year --

BASE: TOTAL REPORTED TYPES OF TESTS CONDUCTED

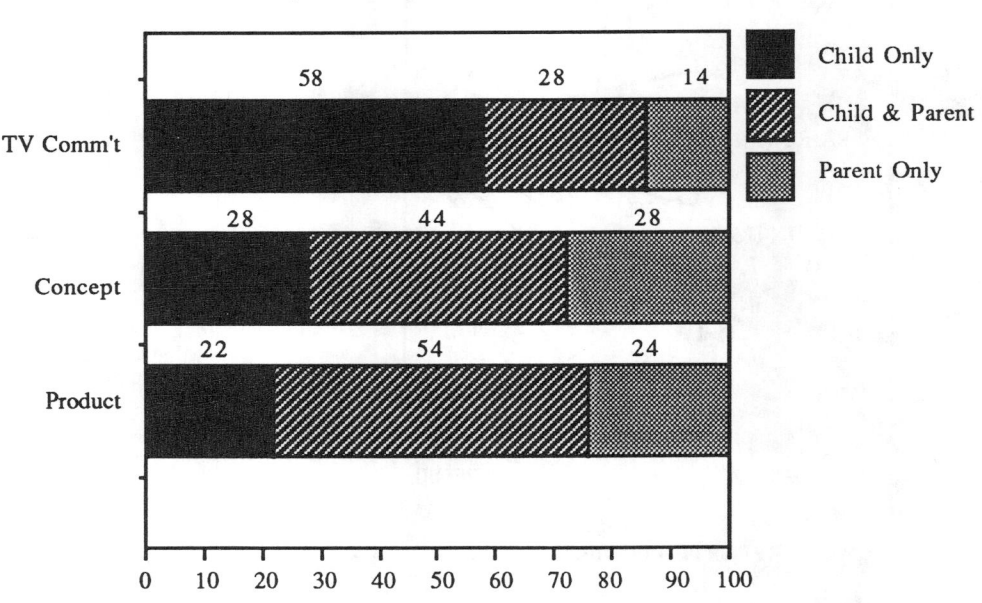

FIGURE 6
Respondents Interviewed For Different Tests

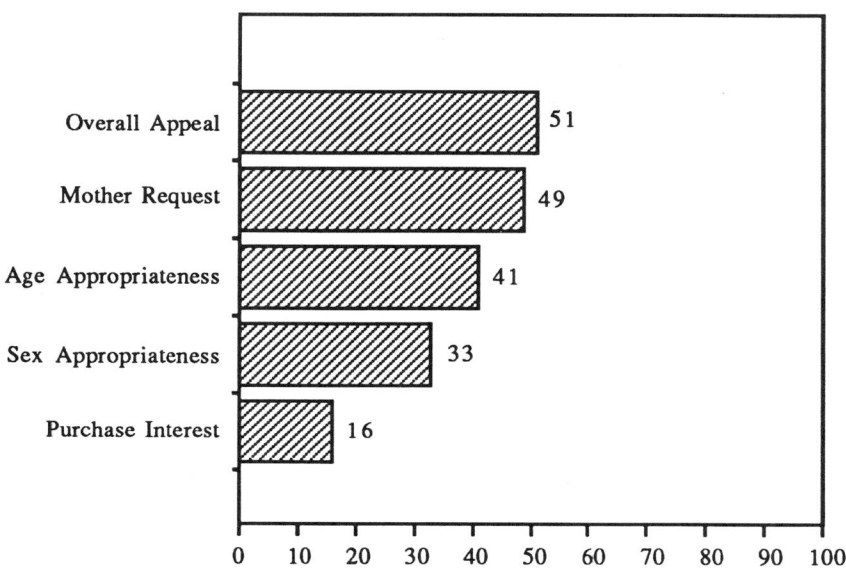

FIGURE 7
Written Scales Used Now
-- With Children --

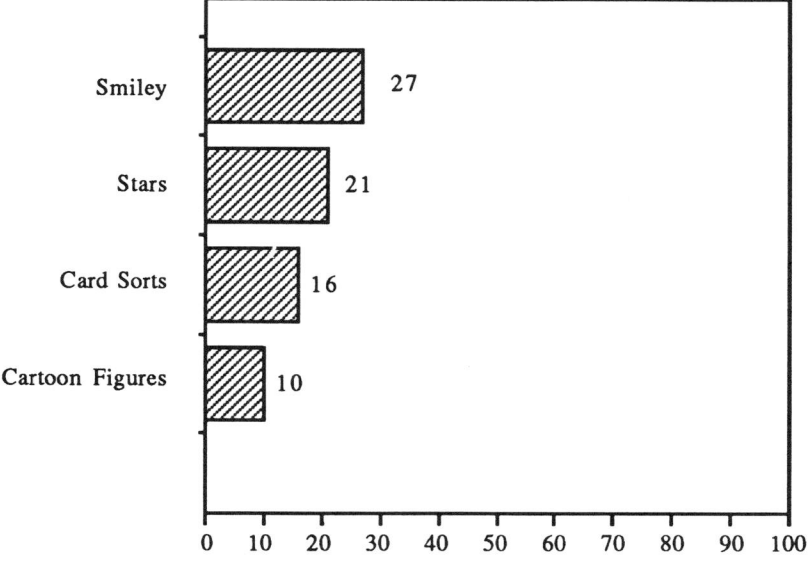

FIGURE 8
Visual Scales Used Now
-- With Children --

FIGURE 9
% of Respondents Utilizing Sales Forecasting For Children's Products

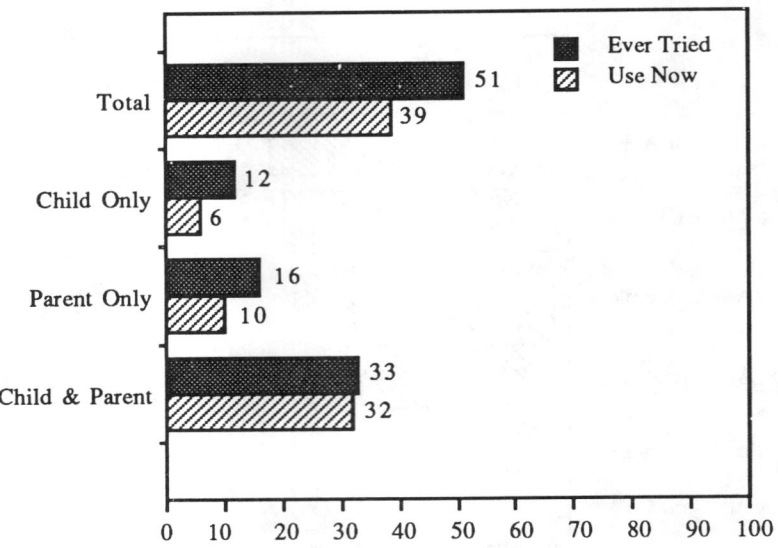

FIGURE 10
Proprietary Vs. Supplier Sales Forecasting Models
Children's Products

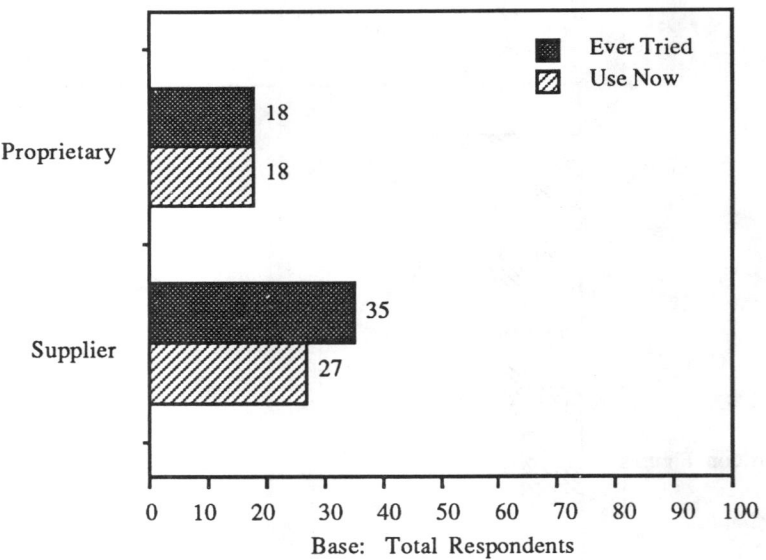

FIGURE 11
Greatest Needs For Industry-Wide Attention And Development in Children's Research
-- 1st or 2nd Mention --

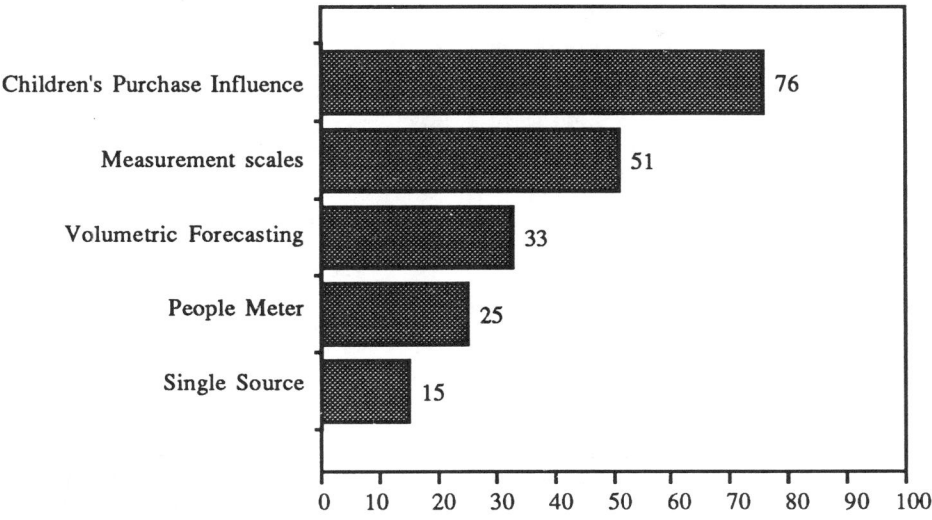

CHILDREN'S RESEARCH -- WHERE IT IS GOING

And, what were the major issues on these researchers' minds as they entered the 90's? The areas identified as having the greatest need for industry-wide attention and development in children's research were: understanding children's purchase influence, followed by measurement scales, volumetric forecasting and people meter issues. (Figure 11).

Qualitative and Quantitative Approaches to Child Research.
Langbourne Rust, Langbourne Rust Research, Inc.
Carole Hyatt, Hyatt Associates, Inc.

A TALE OF TWO SHOPPERS

Cathy and Sue are doing the week's shopping. Walking along together, pushing a half-full shopping cart, they turn down an aisle. Fruit drinks are on the right, cereals on the left. Cathy will pick out the drinks, Sue the cereals.

Each side of the aisle has 4 shelves, 40 feet long, crammed with packages on which every square inch is pushing out color, text, graphics and gimmicks. There is no way for a human mind to take in all these stimuli. Overload is reached at somewhere between 5 and 10 alternatives. Cathy and Sue are confronted with perhaps 100 times that many.

Cathy goes into a focused search. She'd made up her mind ahead of time to get the JUICY JUICE. It has 100% fruit juice, comes in aseptic boxes that are convenient to pack in a lunch bag, and Billy, the one child in the family to who takes his lunch to school, didn't complain when he took JUICY JUICE to school last week . Cathy scans the aisle, spots the section with the three-packs of aseptic boxes, and zooms in on the distinctive script-like text that identifies JUICY JUICE.

Sue takes a different approach. As she cruises down the aisle, the cereal boxes form an amorphous wall on her left. She continues along, her eye playing over the array but failing to lock securely onto anything. Then, something catches her eye. A face is looking at her: the familiar face of Tony the Tiger, with his eager, friendly, accepting smile.

As she turns her head towards Tony, locking into his gaze, her body rotates, too. She approaches him, reaches out with both hands and pulls him to her. Holding the box, this friendly familiar presence in the midst of jumbled clutter, she is pleased.

Sue is 7 years old. Cathy is 32. The moral is that children are a different kind of consumer.

A TALE OF TWO RESPONDENTS

Cathy and Sue, mother and daughter, have been recruited to participate in a market research project. Cathy is to be interviewed about fruit drinks, Sue about cereals. Cathy is interviewed first.

The interviewer shows Cathy a shelf with 5 brands of juice drinks on it and asks, "Cathy, which of these would you get for your children?" Cathy looks at each of the boxes, sees the one she's looking for and says, "JUICY JUICE." "Why?" "Well, it has 100% fruit juice, which makes me feel it's healthy, and it's real convenient, and Billy always finishes it, so he must like it."

The executive sitting behind a one-way mirror watching the interview nods and says, "Hmm, that's interesting. Makes sense to me. I think we should put more stress on the juice content of our own brand." And she goes away having learned something important.

Then it is Sue's turn -- cereals. First the shelf of boxes is revealed. There is Sugar Bear, and Fred & Barney, and Toucan Sam and Cap'n Crunch. It happens that these boxes almost never stand next to each other in the store. It also happens that Sugar Bear's box is yellow while the other three are red. And the Cap'n Crunch Box is the one closest to her. And just before Sue came to the interview she'd been watching a Smurf's re-run in which a commercial with Toucan Sam had played. "Sue, which of these cereals is your favorite?" "Cap'n Crunch." "Why?" "He's funny and I like him."

The executive sitting behind the mirror nods and says, "Hmm, that makes sense to me. We should make the character on our own brand funnier and more likeable." And he goes away with a lesson that may either be irrelevant or seriously misleading.

CHILDREN ARE DIFFERENT.

Children do not respond to things in the marketplace the way adults do, so traditional market research inquiries often miss what is going on.

TRADITIONAL MEASURES ASSUME ADULT THINKING.

* Adults can think about themselves objectively. Children can not. They are not reliable witnesses about their internal functioning. Asking children "Why" is dangerous. In focus groups, we have heard many insightful explanations of things that never, in fact, occur.
* Adults can contemplate alternatives in parallel while children are locked into serial processing. So their preferences are very unstable -- and poor predictors of future behavior.
* Adult consumers often plan their purchases. It makes sense for an advertisers to try to change adults' intentions to buy. But an intention planted in a child's mind is likely to dissolve in seconds.
* Adults size up a new product by focusing on its attributes. But kids understand product as entities. For them, familiarity and recognition are key. How they evaluate the attributes of a new product the first time they see it will not tell you how they will react in the marketplace.
* Adult marketers can understand adult consumers intuitively but they tend to read adult meanings into what they hear children say. Many wrong strategies have been hatched by unsupervised executives behind the one-way mirror.

BRINGING MARKETERS AND CHILDREN TOGETHER.

Some of our work is qualitative in the sense that we converse with children; some of it is quantitative in the sense that we use numbers. But in both our qualitative and quantitative work, our objective is the same: bringing marketers and children closer together.

Many research projects begin with narrowly framed questions. "Should we use animation or live action for this new campaign?" for example, or, "Which of these three product concepts should we carry into further development?" or, "Should we stress the wholesomeness or the wide variety of choice at our fast food restaurant?"

The questions asked by marketers tend, not surprisingly, to reflect the parameters of day to day decision-making in the life of a marketing executive. But all too often, their marketer-centric conceptualization does not mesh with the realities of children's everyday intellectual functioning in the marketplace.

ASKING BETTER QUESTIONS

On an intellectual plane, we try to help our clients ask questions that will help them understand children in the marketplace. If preferences or likability ratings or verbal recall are not appropriate, we tell them why and point out measures (like recognition, attention or in-store behaviors) that would be more valid. But some of what we do goes beyond the asking and answering of questions.

Many corporations have difficulty working on children's products. Corporate cultures get in the way. Some companies, (especially those that have been successful with adults) are wed to visions of their products' unique benefits -- and cannot accommodate to a consumer that is not benefit-oriented. At other companies (especially those that have been successful with a narrow product line for many years), habit and convention determine how things get done. In both situations, it is necessary to go beyond the narrow research question and address the corporate need to shift the focus back to where it should be -- to the kids.

FOCUSING CORPORATE ATTENTION.

In the mid 1970's, Dr. Rust, (a developmental psychologist) was hired by NBC to be Associate Producer of a children's TV program called the GO SHOW. At the insistence of the VP of Children's Programming, George Heinemann, Rust was to learn how shows were assembled, before giving any advice or counsel to the creative staff. He was to sit in on all production meetings, shoots and editing sessions and not utter a word for the first month on the job. This he did. Not a word. It was interesting to note the effect that his presence, however silent, had on the way the creative staff functioned. A typical interchange took place with Rift Fournier, one of the program producers, in the editing room.

The room was dark. The editor, a production assistant and Fournier sat in a row of seats at the computer table, their faces dimly lit by a wall of monitors in front of them. Fournier called out the time codes for the upcoming edit. The tapes rolled for the preview. When they stopped, Fournier said, "Yup, that works." He turned to the editor. "That work for you?" Editor responded, "Yup." Then Fournier noticed Rust in the back, slouching in the shadows and keeping quiet. He hesitated a beat and turned back to the editor, "Think it would work for kids?"

In addition slouching around in the shadows in the back of every room, researchers can do other things to keep corporate awareness of children high. *Periodic seminars* serve this end. *Qualitative interviews* keep executives looking at children and thinking of them as people. *Periodic testings* of products and communications help, too. Even research that is methodologically marginal helps marketers because it keeps kids top of mind.

SHAPING INTUITIONS WITH EXAMPLES.

A comedian with a good sense of timing, a storyteller with a good ear for dialogue, a teacher with a talent for finding the right book for the right child. There is a vast domain of skills that are shaped by experience but are not taught (and are probably not teachable) by books or memos or research reports. Skills like generating a good package design, creating a good commercial, formulating a good product, are as important to the success of a company as the skill of deciding whether to go with variant A or variant B. These have a large component of intuition, and although intuition is grounded on experience, it does not follow the strict rules of hypothetico deductive reasoning. Experimental designs and multivariate analyses can be extremely useful to people who make decisions about other people's creative work, but they are often irrelevant to the creative process itself. They can even be inhibiting. The following story, perhaps apocryphal, illustrates the point.

During the 1930's, in the early days of putting social science to work on marketing issues, a publisher decided to use research to find a book concept that would be assured of success. The researchers accepted the question as framed, went out to gather data, and established that the hottest topics of the day were Abraham Lincoln stories, dog stories and doctor stories. To everyone's amazement, however, the new book, *Mr. Lincoln's Doctor's Dog* proved to be a flop.

Creative enterprises need more than Mr Lincoln's Doctors Dog research. One of the problems with such mechanistic approaches to creative issues is that they are premised on a tight, a priori definition of variables. But creatives work best on a more concrete level. They are learn more from example than from theories, from anecdotes than from principles. They thrive on richness and variety of stimulus exposure, not restriction and control, which are the usual fodder for scientific abstractions.

Qualitative research done with a facility with a one-way mirror gives creatives a change to build on their store of concrete examples and stories. This kind of experience feeds into the creative needs in an especially powerful fashion.

SHAPING INTUITIONS WITH MOMENT TO MOMENT FEEDBACK.

It is no coincidence that so many of our most talented film and TV performers did their apprenticeships in media where they had direct, continuous audience feedback. Legitimate theater, music halls, the club circuit all give performers moment to moment feedback. Somehow they process that feedback. In time, the best of them develop an intuitive sense of audience perspective -- and a skill at playing to it that is uncanny.

One of the observational measures we use evolved from the distractor method that was so useful in developing SESAME STREET and THE ELECTRIC COMPANY. By videotaping children's faces while they watch TV, we calculate the percent of audience looking at the TV at each moment, and make a videotape that superimposes the attention levels over the material that the children had been watching. Attention levels give an extremely sensitive index of viewer response. To creatives, it is like playing to a live audience. Over time, as their experience base broadens, they develop an intuitive sense of how to reach and hold children's interest in the TV.

DESIGNING RESEARCH -- PART THEORY, PART INTUITION

We do not have a comprehensive theory that lets you deduce all the research tools to use in each situation. For example, although it is traditional for researchers to use qualitative research for diagnosis and quantitative for evaluation, there have been times we have used qualitative for evaluating alternative products and quantitative for diagnosing the strengths and weakness of an ad campaign. Designing a research program to help a client with a specific set of problems is not unlike creating new advertising strategy or developing a new product. Principles and theory contribute coherence and structure, but the actual creation is stimulated by examples and shaped by intuitions grounded in experience.

AN ILLUSTRATION.

Here is an example that encapsulates some of our own experience, and reflects some of our intuitions and theories about research design. To protect the proprietary interest of our clients, we have mixed the elements of several projects together, and changed the product category.

The client was a multi-national food manufacturer with minimal experience marketing to children. The product was a lunch-box snack for children.

The company came to us initially asking for a couple of focus groups with kids to explore cartoon characters in general, and to evaluate some broad concepts they had for a new character to advertise their snack. This was the first time the full team, from agency and client, had worked together on a project.

We suggested they begin instead by taking a step backwards and get their bearings. The team needed to get to know each other as people, and they needed to establish a common language for talking about their market, objectives and strategies.

SEMINAR: LEARNING ABOUT YOUNG CONSUMERS.

We began with a one-day seminar on the children as consumers, on the role of snacks in their lives, and how advertising worked -- with special emphasis on how cartoon characters functioned and what made some so much more effective than others.

CREATIVE WORKSHOP: NEW CHARACTERS, NEW WORLDS.

Day 2 took the lessons of the seminar and put the participants to work in a variety of creative tasks. Researchers, brand and account people shared in the creative work along with the writers and artists.

Some of the exercises were aimed at getting people in touch with their own childhood ("Close your eyes, and in your mind's eye, go back to a time when you were very young. Picture, if you can, your favorite toy. You are playing with it. What are you feeling...."). Bringing adults back to their own youth not only gives a tremendous release, an unshackling of their creative thinking, but it also helps them conjure up those unique properties of childhood experience -- the intensity of its focus, the purity of its feeling -- that are so important to recognize when you are trying to communicate to them.

As the day progressed, more of the creative work was done in small groups. Characters grew from loose ideas into articulate concepts with supporting casts and coherent fantasy worlds. Some concepts split and got developed in parallel tracks. Many concepts were retired, some to re-emerge in new form, others to never be seen again Ideas were passed from group to group, so people could build on the good ideas of each other, and so that ownership for each idea would be shared by all. One of the participants was new to the country -- he was an expert in international marketing who had been moved in recently from overseas. He was there only as an observer. He knew none of the other people in the room and had no authority on the project. But triggered by the recollection of his favorite childhood toy, a little dragon, he planted the seed for one of the most charming concepts of the day. No matter that the idea didn't come from a creative, we were all vested in all the concepts that came forth that day.

The next morning, the concepts that by consensus had the most potential were drawn up by the artists, and back stories were written by the writers. And that afternoon, right after school, we showed them to children

QUALITATIVE RESEARCH: GETTING TO KIDS RIGHT AWAY.

Going immediately to the field has many advantages. The lessons of the seminar, reviewed during the workshop, are still fresh and have a chance to get confirmed, rehearsed and practiced while watching real kids. The creative concepts are still plastic. No memos have been written, no reputations committed to one or the other. Ownership is still shared. All the seminar participants came to the sessions and watched through the one-way mirror. The one-way mirror brings the power of live theater to the research business. Seeing the kids and their reactions to the still-wet copy, left an indelible impression on the whole team. No one could look at any subsequent generation of those characters without remembering the looks and comments of children as they saw them for the first time.

Best friends. Children were interviewed in pairs of best friends. This makes children more relaxed, open and unselfconscious with each other and the interviewer. There is none of the "feeling each other out" or jockeying for position which is inevitable when you bring strangers together -- and which delays larger groups or one-on-ones from getting down to business. With friend pairs, the warm-up is very brief, and they get right down to work. And the interviews are not so susceptible as larger groups are to being dominated by one or two outspoken personalities.

Team-Focus interviewing. We conducted the qualitative as a team. Hyatt ran the interviews while Rust sat in the back room with the client, guiding their observations and steering them away from adult interpretation -- essentially running the session as a tutorial. In projects where theory building is a priority, the team approach is also useful. A moderator working alone must delay the analysis until the end of the day when the memories are no longer fresh and mid-course corrections impossible.

Leave the kids alone for a while. After the various characters were shown to the children, the drawings were left on the wall and the interviewer left the room. The children tended to take this private moment to chatter about the experience they'd just been through, and how they had reacted to the characters. What kids reveal when you ask them questions is not always what they reveal spontaneously in an intimate exchange with a best friend.

CONTINUED CYCLES OF TEST AND REVISION.

In the debriefing after the qualitative, the strengths and weakness of each character were discussed. Characters with least potential were dropped. The team worked up a new set of alternatives, building on what they'd learned. By the next afternoon, a new set of boards and stories were ready, and a second set of qualitative interviews were run.

At this point in time the client had three solidly grounded character concepts, filled out in considerable detail, that children were reacting very positively to and that had the support of all the key corporate players. They knew not only that these characters were working, but why they were working, so the next stages of development could capitalize upon their strengths. All this had been accomplished in 4 days.

Some weeks later, more polished presentations of three of the characters, with plots and messages closer to real commercials, were prepared and tested qualitatively. With the diagnostic feedback from that research, production of animatics was begun. The next phase of research was quantitative.

QUANTITATIVE.

Our standard copytest procedure was used. Each child was exposed to only one of the new characters. The children were 6 to 11 years old. The sample was 150 per commercial.

The purpose of the test was camouflaged. Children came in to watch a show. Viewing was done in groups of six at a time. They saw a 10-minute cartoon with two commercial breaks. The test commercial played in the middle position of both breaks. It was shown twice because we have found that children's reactions to a commercial often shift on second exposure. It was inserted in naturalistic clutter because that is the context in which commercials are viewed at home. The motivation of the home viewer is to watch the show, not a commercial. So this is the mental set we established in our test.

The layout of the room was standardized. Chair placement, set size, and set placement matched the previous copytests we have done on children's commercials. A low-level distractor (a random sequence of slides playing an adjacent screen) was provided to give the children something else to look at if their interest faded. Studies of at-home viewing has shown that most TV viewing goes on in a semi-distracted environment. Children look away and get involved in other activities. There is coming and going in the room, toys on the floor, siblings or friends to interact with. Commercials have to compete with simultaneous distractions in the real world, so we provide simultaneous distractions in our test.

While the children sat and watched the shows, a videocamera recorded their faces. Subsequent analysis of the videotapes let us calculate the percent of children actually looking at the commercials every two seconds during their first and second exposure.

After the viewing session, the children were given one-on-one interviews. A picture-based brand choice item showed them 6 different snacks and had them mark all the ones they wanted. It turned out that viewers of Commercial A were most likely to choose the test brand. Open ended questions got children to reconstruct what they remembered from the commercial, and explored what they thought it said about the product. Communications was pretty good for all the commercials. Later questions got children to rate the commercial, the various characters, and some key attributes of the product. The latter ratings all asked for binary judgments: Is it sweet? Yes/no/not sure, etc. Children do not generally perceive qualities in a dimensional fashion. A product either has a property or it does not. By concentrating on yes/no's, we find that interviewing goes much faster and more pleasurably with young children, and we feel secure that it more accurately reflects the thinking they actually do in the real world, where children are anything but slow, deliberative and measured. A general rule we follow is that if a child has to stop and think before answering, she is invoking mechanisms she probably never uses in the marketplace.

In this study, the most actionable findings came from the attention data. Comparing the executions, we were able to establish that the commercial featuring Character A significantly outpulled the others. A check of the norms showed that it did very well indeed -- and it did so by holding on to older children, who often lose interest in animated characters. By examining the attention on a moment-to-moment basis, we were able to confirm that the character was strong. There was a tendency for interest to peak every time the character was actively involved in the plot -- even on second exposure.

There were two spots where attention fell. One was where the screen portrayed one thing while the soundtrack talked about something else -- a problem that frequently afflicts animatics and would be straightened out in a finished production. The other drop-off came when the scene cut abruptly to a new setting with a new secondary character. Viewers appeared to have gotten disoriented, and some of them just turned away. This problem required some rewriting to solve.

NEXT STEPS

That is where things stand today. A final version is currently in production. The plan is to evaluate it before broadcast, using the same copytest procedures and comparing it to the full-production norms. Qualitative research will be done periodically to explore new poolouts, promotions and premiums -- and to keep the supply of fresh new stories "from the front" coming into coporate HQ. And every year or so an additional copytest will be run to see how well the copy is holding up, what parts are starting to wear out, and when it is time to come in with a new campaign.

The children will be the ultimate judges. Our job is to keep the client in touch with them. We have tried, by this example, to show how the tools we use, both qualitative and quantitative, serve this objective. They serve to keep the corporate culture focused on children, to provide a wealth of examples that can stimulate the creative process, give moment-to-moment feedback to shape intuition, and answer questions that are meaningful in the context of these unique consumers who are our children.

Designing Research to Assess Children's Comprehension of Marketing Messages
Laura A. Peracchio, University of Wisconsin - Milwaukee
Charise Mita, BBDO New York

The focus of this paper is to suggest factors a marketing researcher should consider in designing experimental procedures that are congruent with the young child's cognitive capacities. Several components of the experimental environment are identified as important in designing an age-appropriate task: familiarity with factual information, context, verbally presented information, and the goal of the experimental task.

A consideration of task components has a number of implications for how an experiment should be structured to effectively tap the emerging capacities of the young child. First, and most importantly, the task should conform to the child's understanding of the world. A task that violates this basic principle will be nearly impossible, without extensive training, for the young child to master. Secondly, the research reviewed in the paper makes salient seven specific guidelines which should be helpful to an experimenter in designing a task that assesses the child's basic abilities:

1. Ensure that the knowledge domain your task is tapping is familiar to young children. Since children process information more efficiently when they are familiar with a domain (Chi, 1976, 1977), frame your research within a topic area in which preschoolers have well developed prior knowledge. For example, ask them how they go about choosing a video game, such as Nintendo.

2. Provide the child with rich contextual support for encoding and retrieving information by employing familiar objects and pictures in your experimental task. Young children's task performance will improve if they are given external, physical support for processing information through the use of attractive child-relevant props when the experimental task is introduced and assessed. The context created by the experimental task should be congruent with the child's knowledge of objects and inter-object relationships.

3. Include only those elements essential to your task. Eliminate any unnecessary and, therefore, possibly misleading, information from your task. The experimental context should be streamlined so that all materials and information presented are relevant to the child's successful task performance. The addition of irrelevant information creates an opportunity for the child to be distracted from the main processing task, thus impairing performance.

4. Minimize the complexity of the information you present to the child. If your task requires only a simple presentation to test a child's basic ability, start with this basic format. Later you can test the child's ability to handle larger amounts of information, but first test his/her ability to perform the fundamental task.

5. Employ language that conforms to the child's conversational norms. Not only should the experimenter's vocabulary be within the child's level of understanding, but the experimenter's directives should conform to the child's use of language in everyday settings. Children often will literally interpret directives based on the meaning of words and language in their everyday world. When the experimenter violates the child's language code, performance on the task will suffer.

6. Use language that highlights the important features of your task. The experimenter can use language, as well as physical context, to direct the child's attention to the important aspects of a task. Highlighting important features of an experiment through language will improve task performance.

7. Employ a goal that will be readily apparent and meaningful to the child. The goal of an experimental task should be congruent with objectives the child may have observed or attempted to achieve in everyday environments. A goal that is clear and familiar to the child will allow the child to devise a plan for accomplishing a task and empl relatively more sophisticated strategies.

Attention to task conditions seems to reveal a young child's fledgling cognitive abilities in many areas, often minimizing developmental differences on experimental tasks. Research that incorporates a sensitivity to experimental demands and achieves congruence with the child's available processing resources, frequently reveals that the young learner is not completely lacking in the ability to perform a task and does possess some competencies in the area of interest.

REFERENCES

Chi, M. T. H. (1976). Short-term memory limitations in children: Capacity or processing deficits? *Memory and Cognition, 4,* 559-572.

Chi, M. T. H. (1977). Age differences in memory span. *Journal of Experimental Child Psychology, 23,* 266-281.

Coupon Usage and the Theory of Reasoned Action
Richard P. Bagozzi, University of Michigan
Hans Baumgartner, Pennsylvania State University
Youjae Yi, University of Michigan

INTRODUCTION

Coupon usage behavior is a widespread phenomenon in today's consumer society. According to recent statistics (Adweek's Marketing Week 1990), 273.4 billion coupons (more than 3,000 per household) were issued in 1989, at an average face value of 49.7 cents. Of these, 7.1 billion were actually redeemed, for a total of about $3.5 billion. In addition, it has been estimated that 97 percent of all households use coupons in a given month (Teinowitz 1988). Clearly, these figures indicate that it is important for consumer researchers to understand why people use coupons.

In a pioneering study, Shimp and Kavas (1984) have shown that the theory of reasoned action (Fishbein and Ajzen 1975) is useful in specifying the antecedents of coupon usage for grocery shopping. Specifically, these authors found that the cognitive (expectancy-value) structure underlying consumers' attitude toward using coupons was best represented as a multi-dimensional construct, that attitudes and subjective norms influenced behavioral intentions but had no direct effects on behavior, and that self-reported coupon usage was a function of people's intentions to use coupons.

In this paper we extend Shimp and Kavas' (1984) work on the determinants of coupon usage behavior in two ways. First, we hypothesize that a consumer's prior history of using coupons for grocery shopping will serve an important role in influencing intentions and possibly behavior. Second, we hypothesize that the individual difference variable of state- vs. action-orientation will influence the extent to which intentions are formed on the basis of attitudes or subjective norms. Each of these issues will be dealt with in turn.

PAST BEHAVIOR

The theory of reasoned action posits that attitudes and subjective norms are sufficient to predict intentions. That is, other variables are expected to influence intentions only indirectly through their impact on attitudes and/or subjective norms. Because intentions are hypothesized to mediate all of the effects of attitudes and subjective norms on behavior, the influence of other variables on behavior is also expected to be mediated by intentions. However, researchers have found that some variables have direct effects on intentions and/or behavior, unmediated by attitudes and subjective norms or intentions.

Past behavior is a case in point. Several studies have shown that the effects of past behavior on behavioral intentions are sometimes not mediated by attitudes and/or subjective norms (e.g., Bagozzi 1981; Bentler and Speckart 1979, 1981; Fredricks and Dossett 1983) and that prior behavior at times has direct effects on present behavior which are not mediated by behavioral intentions (e.g., Ajzen and Madden 1986; Bagozzi 1981; Bentler and Speckart 1979, 1981; Fredricks and Dossett 1983). Whether or not past behavior should be accommodated in the theory of reasoned action probably depends on the behavior of interest. However, particularly in the context of coupon usage past behavior would seem to be an important antecedent of behavioral intentions and possibly of behavior.

It should be noted that the inclusion of a prior behavior construct in a theory presumably dealing with reasoned behaviors is not a contradiction in terms. First, proposing a dichotomy between volitional and nonvolitional behaviors is at best an oversimplification, at worst a misrepresentation. Most behaviors contain volitional elements to a greater or lesser extent. Second, even if behavior were determined, either directly or indirectly (i.e., through behavioral intentions), by past behavior, it does not follow that such behavior is necessarily habitual (Triandis 1977, 1979), scripted (Abelson 1976, 1981), or mindless (Langer 1978). This is especially true whenever there are no direct effects of prior behavior on subsequent behavior and the intention-behavior link is significant. In this case a reasonable interpretation may be that past behavior serves as one type of informational input to the decision to act in addition to attitudes and subjective norms. For example, prior behavior may reflect an individual's assessment of the extent of perceived behavioral control, a construct suggested by Ajzen and Madden (1986). Another way to think about the inclusion of past behavior as a predictor is that it serves as a covariate controlling for the effects of omitted variables. By including past behavior in a test of the theory of reasoned action, one can discover whether attitudes and subjective norms influence intention after controlling for the effects of omitted variables. Whatever the exact mechanism may be, finding a significant effect for past behavior in the context of consumers' usage of coupons for grocery shopping would call for additional research on the nature of the underlying process.

STATE- VS. ACTION-ORIENTATION

Kuhl's (1981, 1982a, 1984, 1985, 1986) work on state- vs. action-orientation is part of his more general theory of action control. Action control refers to self-regulatory mechanisms that mediate (i.e., help overcome the difficulties inherent in) the enactment of action-related mental structures, particularly intentions (cf. Kuhl 1984, 1986). Kuhl (1982a) hypothesizes that people differ in their disposition toward, or capacity for, action control. People with low self-regulatory capacity are called state-oriented, and people with high self-regulatory capacity are called action-oriented. In a sense, state- vs. action-orientation refers to a person's general tendency to approach or avoid things in a static (passive) or dynamic (active) fashion. State-orientation reflects inertia to act; action-orientation indicates readiness to act. Kuhl (1985) developed a scale measuring decision-related action- vs. state-orientation. The scale consists of 20 forced-choice items, one response alternative in each case reflecting state-orientation (SO), the other action-orientation (AO). A representative item from the scale is, "When I want to see someone again, (a) I plan to do it some day (SO), or (b) I try to set a date for the visit right away (AO)."

Based on previous research with other individual difference variables such as locus of control (e.g., Saltzer 1978, 1981) and self-monitoring (Ajzen, Timko, and White 1982; Bearden and Rose 1989) and Kuhl's own research, it may be hypothesized that state- vs. action-orientation will (a) affect the relative weighting of attitudinal and normative considerations in the formation of behavioral intentions and/or (b) moderate the strength of the intention-behavior relationship.

One study reported by Kuhl (1982b) directly supports the latter hypothesis. Students in a German secondary school were asked for their intentions to engage in a series of after-school activities, and the next day they reported the extent to which they had actually engaged in these activities. The findings showed that the correspondence between behavioral intentions and actual behavior was significantly greater for action-oriented than for state-oriented subjects. Interestingly, the reverse result obtained for some routinized activities (e.g., cleaning one's shoes) that may be largely under situational control. Kuhl (1982a, 1982b, 1985) explains this by hypothesizing that performing socially expected behaviors may be a way for state - oriented people to overcome deficits in self-regulatory capacity. Kuhl (1982b) did not collect attitudinal or normative measures, but in the context of the theory of reasoned action the aforementioned results may suggest that state-oriented subjects form their intentions on the basis of normative expectations, while action-oriented subjects arrive at their intentions through attitudinal considerations. There are thus at least two ways in which the construct of state- vs. action-orientation may moderate the pattern of relationships in the theory of reasoned action: either in the manner in which intentions are formed and/or in how strongly behavioral intentions are related to actual behavior. Both issues were investigated in the present study.

METHOD

Female staff members at a major university participated in a study on people's "attitudes toward coupons and their redemption practices." Two questionnaires, separated by one week, were sent to potential participants. The first questionnaire contained the measures of past coupon usage, attitude toward using coupons, subjective norms, and behavioral intentions, as well as the state- vs. action-orientation scale. The second questionnaire was mailed to those people who had participated in the first wave of data collection and assessed people's coupon usage during the past week. A total of 198 subjects participated in the first wave of data collection, 163 of whom also completed the second questionnaire. After discarding cases with missing values, 149 subjects remained with complete data.

Multiple indicators were used for the attitude, subjective norm, and behavioral intention constructs so that the unreliability of measurements could be taken into account. The responses to the 20 items of the state- vs. action-orientation scale were summed up and the sample was split at the median. This resulted in sample sizes of 64 and 85 subjects, respectively, for the state- and action-oriented groups. The data were analyzed with the LISREL 7 program (Joreskog and Sorbom 1989), and both individual- and multiple-group analyses were performed to test the hypotheses stated earlier.

RESULTS AND DISCUSSION

The importance of past coupon usage behavior for subsequent decisions to use coupons for grocery shopping was confirmed. Past behavior was the most important determinant of behavioral intentions for both state- and action-oriented subjects. Furthermore, the proportion of variance in intentions accounted for by attitudes, subjective norms, and prior behavior was 63 and 68 percent, respectively, for state- and action-oriented subjects. This compares with 40 and 54 percent when prior behavior was not included as an antecedent. The latter figures are similar to the 48 percent value reported by Shimp and Kavas (1984) for one of their better-fitting models. These findings show that, even though attitudes and subjective norms (the two constructs posited as the only direct antecedents of intentions by the theory of reasoned action) explain a fair amount of the variance in behavioral intentions, past behavior adds a sizable increment, particularly in the case of state-oriented people.

Although a person's prior history of using coupons was the major determinant of behavioral intentions for both state- and action-oriented subjects, it should not be concluded that people use coupons solely out of habit or even mindlessly. The findings revealed that the effects of past behavior were primarily on intentions and not directly on future behavior, and behavioral intentions significantly influenced subsequent behavior. Thus, behavior was under volitional control. It seems more likely that people's prior experiences with coupons serve as one informational input to the decision to use coupons, reflecting in part perhaps the extent of perceived behavioral control, as suggested by Ajzen (1987).

The findings also showed that the behavioral intentions of state-oriented people were a function of subjective norms but not of attitudes, while the behavioral intentions of action-oriented people were a function of attitudes but not of subjective norms.

Thus, action-oriented people, who are characterized by a general readiness to act, seem to form their intentions on the basis of attitudinal (i.e., personal) considerations, whereas state- oriented people, who are in general not easily moved to act, appear to be influenced by normative (i.e., nonpersonal) considerations when forming intentions. For the latter group, the known expectations of significant others are apparently a strong enough influence to trigger the formation of intentions, even when personal factors are not powerful enough.

The hypothesis that state- vs. action-orientation would affect the degree of correspondence between intentions and behavior was rejected. The effects of intentions on behavior were statistically significant for both groups, confirming that coupon usage behavior is indeed under volitional control. However, the effects did not differ between the two groups.

One strength of the study is that it was not conducted with student subjects, but with female staff members, for whom the task should have been meaningful. Respondents ranged in age from 18 to 63 years, which indicates that the sample comprised a fairly broad spectrum of the population, and this contributes to the external validity of the study. Another strength might be the measurement of self-reported behavior. Subjects were presented with a table that had 21 product categories for which coupons are most commonly used as its rows (e.g., cereal, juice drinks, paper towels, snack foods, canned goods) and six sources of coupons as its columns (i.e., direct mail, newspapers, magazines, in or on packages, from store displays or flyers, from relatives or friends). By listing the product categories and incorporating alternative sources of coupons, the measurement procedure should provide more accurate estimates of coupon usage behavior than a single-item scale.

Some shortcomings of the present study should also be mentioned. One of the limitations is that the sample size in neither the state- nor action-oriented groups was very large. Fortunately, this did not lead to nonconvergence or improper solutions. In our study the most serious consequence of small sample size is probably lack of statistical power. However, the differences found between groups in the individual analyses were confirmed by multiple-group analyses, and one's confidence in the reality of the reported effects should therefore be strengthened, as a lack of statistical power works against finding significant differences. Another limitation of the study is that not everybody who filled out the first questionnaire also responded to the second questionnaire. However, the drop-out rate was fairly small at 18 percent. Most of this attrition is attributable to the time of year of the study, summer, where some respondents were absent at the second questioning due to vacations. Finally, the study relied on self-reports of coupon usage. Since reported and actual coupon usage are likely to differ, this could be another limitation of the study. However, our focus was not on how well coupon usage behavior could be explained per se, but on how state- vs. action-orientation influenced the pattern of relationships among constructs in the theory of reasoned action. From this perspective discrepancies between reported and actual coupon usage are not that important, unless state- vs. action-orientation leads to systematic over- or underreporting of actual coupon usage, which is unlikely. Furthermore, the breakdown of coupon usage by source and product category should have reduced the error in reporting actual usage.

REFERENCES

Abelson, R. P. (1976), "A Script Theory of Understanding, Attitude, and Behavior." In J. S. Carroll and J. W. Payne (eds.). *Cognition and Social Behavior*. Hillsdale, NJ: Lawrence Erlbaum Associates.

Abelson, R. P. (1981), "The Psychological Status of the Script Concept," *American Psychologist*, 26, 715-729.

Adweek's Marketing Week (1990), "Coupon Distribution Grew by 9 % in '89," *Promotion Marketing Supplement*, March 5, 5-6.

Ajzen, I. (1987), "Attitudes, Traits, and Actions: Dispositional Prediction of Behavior in Personality and Social Psychology." In L. Berkowitz (ed.). *Advances in Experimental Social Psychology*, Vol. 20, San Diego, CA: Academic Press, 1-63.

Ajzen, I. and T. Madden (1986), "Prediction of Goal-directed Behavior: Attitudes, Intentions, and Perceived Behavioral Control," *Journal of Experimental Social Psychology*, 22, 453-474.

Ajzen, I., C. Timko, and J. B. White (1982), "Self-monitoring and the Attitude-Behavior Relation," *Journal of Personality and Social Psychology*, 42, 426-435.

Bagozzi, R. P. (1981), "Attitudes, Intentions, and Behavior: A Test of Some Key Hypotheses," *Journal of Personality and Social Psychology*, 41, 607-627.

Bearden, W. O. and R. L. Rose (1990), "Attention to Social Comparison Information: An Individual Difference Factor Affecting Consumer Conformity," *Journal of Consumer Research*, 16, 461-471.

Bentler, P. M. and G. Speckart (1979), "Models of Attitude-Behavior Relations," *Psychological Review*, 86, 452-464.

Bentler, P. M. and G. Speckart (1981), "Attitudes 'Cause' Behaviors: A Structural Equation Analysis," *Journal of Personality and Social Psychology*, 40, 226-238.

Fishbein, M. and I. Ajzen (1975). *Belief, Attitude, Intention, and Behavior: An Introduction to Theory and Research*. Reading, MA: Addison-Wesley.

Fredricks, A. J. and D. J. Dossett (1983), "Attitude-Behavior Relations: A Comparison of the Fishbein-Ajzen and Bentler-Speckart Models," *Journal of Personality and Social Psychology*, 45, 501-512.

Joereskog, K. G. and D. Soerbom (1989). *LISREL 7 User's Reference Guide*. Mooresville, IN: Scientific Software.

Kuhl, J. (1981), "Motivational and Functional Helplessness: The Moderating Effect of State Versus Action Orientation," *Journal of Personality and Social Psychology*, 40, 155-170.

Kuhl, J. (1982a), "Action Vs. State Orientation as a Mediator Between Motivation and Action." In W. Hacker, W. Volpert, and M. von Cranach (Eds.), *Cognitive and Motivational Aspects of Action*. Amsterdam: North-Holland.

Kuhl, J. (1982b), "Handlungskontrolle als metakognitiver Vermittler zwischen Intention und Handeln: Freizeitaktivitaeten bei Hauptschuelern," *Zeitschrift fuer Entwicklungspsychologie und Paedagogische Psychologie*, 14, 141-148.

Kuhl, J. (1984), "Volitional Aspects of Achievement Motivation and Learned Helplessness: Toward a Comprehensive Theory of Action Control." In B. A. Maher (Ed.), *Progress in Experimental Personality Research* (Vol. 13). New York: Academic Press, 99-171.

Kuhl, J. (1985), "Volitional Mediators of Cognition-Behavior Consistency: Self-regulatory Processes and Action Versus State Orientation." In J. Kuhl and J. Beckmann (eds.), *Action Control: From Cognition to Behavior*. Berlin: Springer.

Kuhl, J. (1986), "Motivation and Information Processing: A New Look at Decision Making, Dynamic Change, and Action Control." In R. M. Sorrentino and E. T. Higgins (eds.), *The Handbook of Motivation and Cognition: Foundations of Social Behavior*, New York: Guilford Press, 404-434.

Langer, E. J. (1978), "Rethinking the Role of Thought in Social Interaction." In J. H. Harvey, W. Ickes, and R. F. Kidd (eds.). *New Directions in Attribution Research*, Vol. 2. New York: Halsted.

Saltzer, E. B. (1978), "Locus of Control and the Intention to Lose Weight," *Health Education Monographs*, 6, 118-128.

Saltzer, E. B. (1981), "Cognitive Moderators of the Relationship Between Behavioral Intentions and Behavior," *Journal of Personality and Social Psychology*, 41, 260-271.

Shimp, T. A. and A. Kavas (1984), "The Theory of Reasoned Action Applied to Coupon Usage," *Journal of Consumer Research*, 11, 795-809.

Teinowitz, I. (1988), "Coupons Gain Favor With U.S. Shoppers," *Advertising Age*, November 14, 64.

Triandis, H. C. (1977). *Interpersonal behavior*. Monterey, CA: Brooks/Cole.

Triandis, H. C. (1979), "Values, Attitudes, and Interpersonal Behavior." In M. M. Page (Ed.), *Nebraska Symposium on Motivation 1979*. Lincoln, NE: University of Nebraska Press, 195-259.

Effects of Experience on Attitude Structure
(Abstract)

Robert E. Burnkrant, Ohio State University
H. Rao Unnava, Ohio State University
Thomas J. Page, Jr., Michigan State University[1]

Traditional treatments of attitude hold that a single composite of beliefs and evaluations (hereafter called expectancy-value attitude) predicts attitude toward behavior which in turn predicts behavioral intention (e.g., Fishbein and Ajzen 1975). The creation of a single expectancy-value attitude by summing (or averaging) all belief-evaluation products assumes that these products form a unidimensional structure. However, several studies have shown that expectancy-value attitude is more adequately represented as a multidimensional rather than unidimensional structure (e.g., Bagozzi 1981, Burnkrant and Page 1988, Shimp and Kavas 1984, Oliver and Bearden 1985). Burnkrant and Page (1988) found in their study of blood donation behavior that expectancy-value attitude may be represented as a two dimensional structure with one dimension representing positive belief-evaluation products and a second dimension representing negative belief-evaluation products. These two expectancy-value dimensions were then employed as predictors of attitude toward behavior which in turn predicted BI. We expected that a similar structure would emerge in this research which examined determinants of the intention to use hearing aids.

A second objective of this research was to determine effects of experience on the structure of expectancy-value attitude and on relationships among expectancy-value attitude, attitude toward behavior and behavioral intention. This was accomplished in this research by examining hearing impaired hearing aid owners and nonowners separately and by comparing models across owners and nonowners.

There has been relatively little examination in prior research of moderators of attitude structure. However, Oliver and Bearden (1985) used a set of psychographic variables to examine moderators of structural relationships. They found differences in the predictive power of attitude dimensions between subjects who were high in familiarity with an issue and those who were low in familiarity. Bagozzi (1981) examined attitude structure separately for nondonors, past donors and current donors of blood and found support for a three dimensional structure for current and past donors. No well defined attitude structure was found for nondonors. These findings suggest that experience with an issue should be a moderator of the structure and relationships involving expectancy-value attitude.

Other relationships examined in this research include the effect of experience on whether attitude toward behavior fully mediates the relationship between expectancy-value attitude and behavioral intention and the strength of the relationship between attitude toward behavior and intention. First, it was expected that, for people who have experience with the issue, attitude toward behavior will fully mediate the relationship between expectancy-value attitude and behavioral intention; but, for subjects who do not have experience, attitude toward behavior will not fully mediate this relationship. Second, it was expected that attitude toward behavior will be a stronger predictor of intention for those who have experience than for those who do not have experience.

Hearing impaired owners and nonowners of hearing aids filled out a questionnaire in which they responded to beliefs about the consequences of using hearing aids and provided evaluations of those consequences. Exploratory research found fourteen salient consequencs and they were employed in this research. They also responded to semantic differential scales designed to measure attitude toward using hearing aids, and they provided ratings of their intention to use hearing aids within the next six months. Question wording and response scales corresponded to the procedures recommended by Ajzen and Fishbein (1980).

Results provided support for a two dimensional model of expectancy-value attitude with one dimension representing positive belief-evaluation products and a second dimension representing negative belief-evaluation products. This model held for both owners and nonowners of hearing aids. Evidence was also obtained in support of the expectation that attitude toward the behavior would fully mediate the relationship between expectancy-value attitude and behavioral intention for the experienced group but not for those lacking experience. Finally, it was found that attitude toward behavior was a stronger predictor of intention for those who had experience than it was for those who did not have experience.

REFERENCES

Ajzen, Icek and Martin Fishbein (1980), *Understanding Attitudes and Predicting Social Behavior*, Englewood Cliffs, New Jersey: Prentice-Hall.

Bagozzi, Richard P. (1981), "An Examination of the Validity of Two Models of Attitude," *Multivariate Behavioral Research*, 16 (July), 323-359.

---

[1] The authors would like to acknowledge the assistance of Philip Lewis in the early phases of data analysis and the Hearing Industries Association for making these data available.

Burnkrant, Robert E. and Thomas J. Page, Jr. (1988), "The Structure and Antecedents of the Normative and Attitudinal Components of Fishbein's Theory of Reasoned Action." *Journal of Experimental Social Psychology*, 24 (January), 66-87.

Fishbein, Martin and Icek Ajzen (1975), *Belief, Attitude, Intention and Behavior: An Introduction to Theory and Research*, Reading, Mass.: Addison-Wesley.

Oliver, Richard L. and William O. Bearden (1985), "Crossover Effects in the Theory of Reasoned Action: A Moderating Influence Attempt." *Journal of Consumer Research*, 12 (December), 324-340.

Shimp, Terence A. and Alican Kavas (1984), "The Theory of Reasoned Action Applied to Coupon Usage," *Journal of Consumer Research*, 11 (December), 795-809.

On the Effectiveness of Repeated Positive Expressions as an Advertising Strategy

Paul M. Herr, Indiana University
Russell H. Fazio, Indiana University[1]

The present research focuses upon the effectiveness of an ad that employed what appears to be a particularly interesting strategy. The ad was for a Mirage candy bar, which was both novel, and unavailable, to our subject population. Consequently, the present research examines attitude formation.

The ad itself begins with a close-up visual of Mirage candy bar and identification as such by a narrator. What ensues is a collection of endorsements by different individuals for Mirage. First, a voice is heard to say, "Incredible." This is followed by a second voice saying, "It's better than Mom's apple pie." This is followed by a third voice saying, "Exquisitely satisfying." The narrator then concludes, "It still seems to defy description; in a word, perfection."

The strategy that underlies this ad seems to be one of inducing the audience to associate the product with very positive evaluations-- in other words to build an association in memory between the brand and a positive evaluation. It seeks to do so by repeatedly pairing the brand with a positive evaluation.

We found this ad interesting because a number of different perspectives suggest that the strategy might be effective. First, from a classical conditioning perspective, a positive attitude toward the brand may be created by these repeated pairings with positive evaluative terms. Indeed, the ad is reminiscent of classic experiments on the conditioning of attitudes (e.g., Staats and Staats, 1958; Zanna, Kiesler, and Pilkonis, 1970). Second, from an attributional perspective (Kelley, 1967), it is interesting to note that the repeated pairings stem from three clearly different individuals rather than a single individual. This implies some consensus for ascribing the positive evaluation to the brand. Such assumed consensus should increase the likelihood of attributing causality for endorsements to the entity in question-- namely, the brand. Finally, from a cognitive, verbal learning perspective, the repeated pairings increase the likelihood that a viewer who is constructing a judgment of the advertised brand at some later time will recall and consider the positive descriptor as a basis for judgment. Obviously, the more such pairings, the greater the likelihood that a positive associate will be recalled and considered.

For all of these reasons, we wondered whether this ad was indeed more effective in developing positive attitudes toward Mirage than other potential ads would be. To examine this possibility, we made comparisons of this target ad (hereafter referred to as the Repeated Pairings condition) to two other commercials. One was simply an edited version of the present commercial. Editing removed the positive expressions from the three voices, leaving only the introduction and the narrator's concluding statement (hereafter referred to as the Single Pairing condition). Because this edited version is considerably shorter than the original, we also made comparisons to another Mirage commercial that did not employ the strategy of depicting positive evaluative descriptors, but was comparable in length. The ad consisted of a "striptease" of a Mirage candy bar. Little by little, accompanied by "The Stripper" and shots of excited on-lookers, the wrapping of a Mirage candy bar was provocatively removed until the candy bar inside was revealed. (This ad will be referred to as the control condition). The presence of this ad serves merely to permit a comparison of the original ad with a very different ad of comparable length. Thus, we are able to control for the amount of time that people are exposed to advertising for the product.

The major dependent variable is the subject's attitudinal rating of the Mirage Candy Bar following exposure to one of the 3 ads just described. We also considered a second possible consequence of the Repeated Pairings ad-- one that is particularly appropriate as an advertising goal when introducing a novel brand. How well, if at all, have viewers learned after a single exposure to an ad, that the brand belongs to a particular product category? In this case, have viewers learned that Mirage is a member of the candy bar category? The importance of this category to brand association has been stressed in much previous research (e.g., Baker, et al., 1986; Howard and Sheth, 1969), and is generally accepted. It is sufficient to note here that an objective of advertising is often to increase top-of-mind awareness of the advertised brand, so it will be part of a consumer's consideration set at the time of brand choice.

In the present case, why might the repeated pairings condition be especially effective in developing the candy bar-Mirage association in memory? From a purely functional perspective, any new object that has been described so positively is worth taking note of. That is, if the object really is as excellent as described, it is in the best interest of the viewer to categorize it appropriately, if for no other reason than the viewer can test the veracity of the advertising claims.

---

[1] The present work was supported by a grant from the Ogilvy Center for Research and Development and by Research Scientist Development Award MH00452 from the National Institute of Mental Health. The authors thank Alexander Biel, Director of the Ogilvy Center, for all his assistance.

METHOD

134 subjects took part in an experiment ostensibly sponsored by an ad agency. Up to 4 subjects participated in any given session. Each subject was seated in an individual booth equipped with a color monitor. Subjects in all conditions were exposed to a videotape containing 21 commercials, which were divided into 3 segments of 7 commercials each. Subjects were led to believe that each segment contained commercials prepared by a different agency (identified only as Agency A, B, and C). The subjects were asked to consider the commercials of each agency in turn. More specifically, after each agency's segment, subjects were asked to rate how unusual or distinctive the ads seemed and to describe the agency's "personality". The purpose of this "cover story" was to ensure that subjects attended to all of the ads while focusing their attention away from the true purpose of the experiment.

Among the 21 commercials presented was one Mirage commercial. Subjects saw a videotape that included one of the 3 Mirage commercials described earlier: the Repeated Pairings, the Single Pairing, or the Control version.

Following viewing of the tapes, subjects engaged in a task designed to measure whether the brand was now viewed as a member of the product category. Category membership was measured via direct inquiries about the membership of a given brand in a specified product category. The monitors in each subject's booth were now used to present stimuli for this task. First, a category label was presented (for example "KETCHUP"), remaining on the screen for 750 milliseconds. The label was replaced by a brand name which may or may not have been a member of that product category (for example "HEINZ" or "TIDE"). The subjects' task was to press, as quickly as possible, one of two buttons on a response box. If the brand was not a member of the preceding category, subjects were to press a button labelled "NO". If the brand was indeed a member of that category, then pressing the button marked "YES" was the correct response. The brand names remained on the screen until all subjects had responded (up to 6 seconds). Trials were separated by three seconds. Each of the product categories represented by the commercials just shown was presented four times; once followed by the brand featured in the commercial, once followed by another member of that category (filler brands), and twice followed by brands which were not members of that category. Included among these trials was the critical "CANDY BAR: MIRAGE" trial. In addition, fifteen other categories were included, followed by an actual category member in half the trials and by a nonmember in the other half. The order of presentation of category-brand trials was randomized by the same computer program that controlled the recording of the response latencies.

The instructions stressed both speed and accuracy in response. Given 1) the rushed nature of the response task, and 2) the limited learning that could reasonably be expected to take place following one exposure to the Mirage ad (among 20 other advertised products), how well subjects learned the category membership (if at all) might be detected by differential error rates and/or differential latencies given correct responses. So, if subjects have not learned the category membership well, they may either make an error, (respond that Mirage is not a candy bar) while attempting to respond quickly or they may take considerable time to respond correctly that it is a candy bar.

In the final segment of the experiment, subjects completed an attitude questionnaire. Subjects were asked to express their attitudes toward a list of products, including Mirage candy bars, on a 7-point scale with the lower endpoint labelled "very much dislike" and the higher endpoint labelled "very much like". Unlike the category membership measure (gathered first) Mirage was clearly noted as a candy bar. That is, the attitude object to be evaluated was "Mirage candy bar".

RESULTS

Category Membership

Analysis of category-brand responses indicated that the repeated pairings strengthened the category-brand association, relative to both the single pairing ad and the control. The proportion of subjects in each condition who correctly indicated that Mirage was a candy bar was .47, .07 and .30 for Repeated Pairings (n=47), Single Pairing (n=43), and Control (n=44) conditions, respectively. A Chi-square analysis revealed significant differences across condition, $X^2_{(2)} = 17.56$, $p<.001$. Planned comparisons revealed the Repeated Pairings condition to be significantly different from both the Single Pairing condition, $X^2(1)=17.73$, $p<.001$, and the Control condition, $X^2(1)= 2.86$, $p< .10$.

Given that so few subjects were capable of correctly identifying Mirage as a candy bar (particularly in the Single Pairing condition), analysis of the response latencies is of questionable value. In any event, for those subjects who *did* correctly identify Mirage as a candy bar, response latencies were transformed prior to being subjected to a one-way Anova with ad a between subjects factor. As response latency distributions are relatively skewed, it is necessary to first subject response latencies to a reciprocal transformation. This took the form of 1/(latency + 1). Response latencies to both the Mirage candy bar and the filler products (brands that were members of the advertised product categories, but not featured in the commercials) were subjected to this transformation. The mean transformed response latency to the filler products provide us with a baseline measure of response latency. The difference between these two transformed latencies (Mirage latency minus mean transformed filler latency) constitutes our strength of association measure.

Overall, the resulting F was marginally significant, $F(2,35)=2.86$, $p= .07$. Planned comparisons of the mean latencies revealed that subjects in the Single Pairing condition were significantly slower (M= -171 milliseconds) than those in the Control condition (M= -55 milliseconds), $t(35)$= 2.39, $p < .05$. Single Pairing subjects were also slower than those in the Repeated Pairing condition (M= -74 milliseconds), $t(35)$= 2.08, $p < .05$. The Repeated Pairing condition latencies were not reliably faster than the Control latencies. Keep in mind, however, that because of the very high error rates, this analysis is based on very few subjects. Consequently, the analysis focusing on the percent of subjects who correctly responded that Mirage is a candy bar is more valid.

Attitudes

Attitudes were significantly more favorable toward the candy bar in the Repeated Pairing condition (M= 4.02) than the Control condition (M= 3.21) and the Single Pairing Condition (M= 3.24). The one-way Anova with Ad as a between subjects factor revealed a significant effect for ad, $F(2, 123)$= 4.39, $p= .01$. Planned comparisons revealed the expected effect for the Repeated Pairings ad creating significantly more favorable attitudes than did either the Single Pairing, $t(121)$= 2.47, $p< .05$, or the Control condition, $t(121) = 2.56$, $p < .05$.

DISCUSSION

The results of an experiment in which the content of ads was systematically manipulated provide support for the notion that attitude favorability and the likelihood of correct category identification may be increased through repeated pairings of a brand and evaluations of the brand in a television ad. Although we are in no position to identify which of the processes described in the introduction was responsible for the effects, it is clear that repeated pairings can be a highly effective technique for creating favorable brand attitudes.

The data also indicate that this repeated pairings strategy is an effective technique for creating appropriate category-brand associations in memory. The increase in correct identification is intriguing, as it suggests an increased likelihood that the brand might "come to mind" when the product category is considered. Hence, not only can attitudes be made more favorable but the likelihood of a brand surfacing in an individual's consideration set can also be influenced through repeated pairings.

REFERENCES

Baker, William J., Wesley Hutchinson, Danny Moore, and Prakash Nedungadi (1986), "Brand Familiarity and Advertising: Effects on the Evoked Set and Brand Preference," in *Advances in Consumer Research*, Vol. 13, ed. Richard J. Lutz, Provo, UT: Association for Consumer Research, 637-642.

Howard, John A. and Jagdish N. Sheth (1969), *The Theory of Buyer Behavior*, New York: John Wiley.

Kelley, Harold H. (1967), "Attribution Theory in Social Psychology," In D. Levine (Ed.), *Nebraska Symposium on Motivation*. Lincoln, Neb. University of Nebraska Press.

Staats, Arthur A. and Carolyn K. Staats (1958), "Attitudes Established by Classical Conditioning," *Journal of Abnormal and Social Psychology*, 57, 37-40.

Zanna, Mark P., Charles A. Kiesler, and P. A. Pilkonis (1970), "Positive and Negative Attitudinal Affect Established by Classical Conditioning," *Journal of Personality and Social Psychology*, 14, 321-328.

Disposition of Possessions During Role Transitions
Melissa Martin Young, University of Utah

> All the world's a stage,
> And all the men and women merely players:
> They have their exits and their entrances;
> And one man in his time plays many parts,
> His acts being seven ages. At first the infant,
> Mewling and puking in the nurse's arms.
> And then the whining schoolboy, with his satchel,
> And shining morning face, creeping like snail
> Unwillingly to school. And then the lover,
> Sighing like furnace, with a woeful ballad
> Made to his Mistress' eyebrow. Then a soldier,
> Full of strange oaths, and bearded like the pard,
> Jealous in honour, sudden and quick in quarrel,
> Seeking the bubble reputation
> Even in the cannon's mouth. And then the justice,
> In fair round belly with good capon lin'd,
> With eyes severe, and beard of formal cut,
> Full of wise saws and modern instances;
> And so he plays his part. The sixth stage shifts
> Into the lean and slipper'd pantaloon,
> With spectacles on nose and pouch on side,
> His youthful hose well sav'd a world too wide
> For his shrunk shank; and his big manly voice,
> Turning again towards childish treble, pipes
> And whistles in his sound. Last scene of all,
> That ends this strange eventful history,
> Is second childishness, and mere oblivion,
> Sans teeth, sans eyes, sans taste, sans everything.
>   William Shakespeare
>   *As You Like It*

ABSTRACT

The functions of acquisition, usage, and disposition of possessions during role transitions and processes of identity reconstruction have been given little or no scrutiny in previous research either within or outside of consumer behavior literature. This study reports the effects of possession disposition preceding, during, and following role transitions. Evidence presented here indicates that possession disposition is employed to facilitate or validate both role and status changes--enhancing and solidifying new self-concepts and social role identities.

INTRODUCTION

It is commonplace when discussing role transitions to borrow dramaturgic metaphors. "Role transitions" is itself a dramaturgic metaphor; a phrase taken from theatre to describe the passage from one social status (or social role) to another (e.g., Banton 1965; Benedict 1938; Glaser and Strauss 1971; Goffman 1959; Levinson 1978; Sarbin 1954; Sarbin and Allen 1968; Sheehy 1974; von Gennep 1909/ 1965). Interpreting human behavior as theatre provides concepts that are useful in analyzing our real-life plot structures.

By using dramaturgic role concepts, one eschews mechanistic causality since roles are relevant only in the context of persons enacting multiple, reciprocal roles. Thus, a conceptual paper that begins with Shakespeare's proposition that: "All the world's a stage..." relies on a world view other than simple mechanistic causality. Instead, I emphasize contextualism, mutual shaping, change, and the functions of possessions in assisting such change. First, I discuss the variety of contexts within which human behavior occurs. These are often referred to as the social systems, or plays, we participate in. Next I consider the roles, or parts, our plays need. Then I discuss the scripts, or normative and anticipatory expectations, that our roles require. Finally, I present my core thesis: namely, that the props, or possessions, which we acquire, use, and (especially) dispose of are necessary for successful transitions from one role to another--both within and across the plays, parts, and scripts which we enact.

SOCIAL SYSTEMS
"PLAYS"

Role transitions refer to "life changes" involving social roles associated with social systems. Social systems are often referred to as social structures. However, I prefer the term "social system" to the term "social structure," since the former emphasizes our ever-changing lives, whereas the latter implies status-role invariance (e.g., Goffman 1961, 1974; Linton 1936). Using our dramaturgic metaphor, social systems are the plays we participate in. Although these social systems may justifiably be conceived as the cultures and subcultures within which we function (act), I prefer to conceptualize social systems as day-to-day social (theatrical) stages--convoluted, changing, imperfect, and dependent on symbolic communication (e.g., Buchmann 1989; Hess 1988; S_renson, Weinert, and Sherrod 1986). Consistent with my conceptualization, all social systems--plays--require social roles--parts.

SOCIAL ROLES
"PARTS"

No dramaturgic metaphor has had wider acceptance in transition literature than the metaphor of the social role, or part. A role is defined as a behavior pattern associated with a particular person in a particular social system (e.g., Linton 1945; Oswalt 1986; Spierer 1981). Concepts of self-identity (and social identity) have an important place in our theoretical framework (e.g., Mead 1934; Sarbin 1954; Young 1965). Our social roles imply action--action constrained by the associated statuses of our parts in our social system's scripts. The imagery evoked by the metaphor "role" is that of humans--actors and actresses--operating in a social system termed a theatre. To rephrase, social roles (parts) in social systems (plays) have normative and anticipatory role expectations (scripts).

ROLE EXPECTATIONS
"SCRIPTS"

In performing a social role--a part--an actor or actress follows an actual or imagined dramatic script. The script contains normative and anticipatory role expectations that define both role behavior and interactions between roles. Role expectations--scripts--are commonly presumed to offer precise formulae for role behavior. To the contrary, several variables influence the form and quality of any role enactment. First, actors and actresses freely choose between modified roles, stereotyped roles, and created roles. Next, actors and actresses possess limited artistic license to determine exactly how they will enact a script, and no two performances are ever alike. Actors and actresses perform as if all the world's a stage or, as Oliver Wendell Holmes restates:

The world's a stage--as Shakespeare said,
 one day;
The stage a world--was what he meant to
 say.

To rephrase, scripts are interactional guidelines, and actors and actresses are not merely passive participants; but instead, they are active monitors of others' reactions, and they continually modify their performances to fit each audience.

The above conceptualization is the traditional dramaturgic interpretation of role theoretic frameworks. It borrows the terms "plays," "parts," and "roles" from dramaturgy; substituting them for the abstract language of role theory that relies on terms like "social systems," "social roles," and "role expectations." Yet, role theory, as it is typically described in anthropology, psychology, and sociology fails to incorporate "props"--one of the most common dramaturgic terms. This is of particular importance to the discipline of consumer behavior because the functions of possessions, or props, are mentioned by few scholars in regard to social role transitions (e.g., Andreasen 1984; McAlexander and Schouten 1989; Schouten 1990). Thus, I propose that extant conceptualizations of role theoretic frameworks are incorrect in overlooking the importance of props and I strive to illustrate how possessions--props--affect roles and role transitions.

POSSESSIONS
"PROPS"

The term "props" literally means stage property. "Props" potentially may include virtually anything on stage, although we usually confine the term "props" to moveable, but inanimate objects. In other words, people and pets usually are not considered to be props (although they might be in a particular play). More commonly, possessions, or "props," include objects such as furniture, costumes, and decorations that facilitate, validate, and support plays, parts, and scripts.

For instance, consider the impact of the tops hats in the musical, *A Chorus Line*, written by James Kirkwood and Nicholas Dante, directed by Michael Bennett, produced by Joseph Papp in 1975, and conducted on an essentially bare stage with essentially forgettable costumes. From the opening act to the final scene, the hats, one of the few props, provide the focal point for the entire musical. Such is often the importance of possessions, or "props," in both dramaturgy and real life. The house we live in, the car we drive, and the clothes we wear have long been recognized as symbols of "who we are."

ROLE TRANSITIONS

Thus far, I have discussed plays, parts, scripts, and props as though they were permanent entities--a perspective that is relatively true within the field of dramaturgy. Yet, using a role theoretic perspective, social systems, roles, role enactments, and possessions are continually changing. The most common term for these changes is "role transitions." The four most common role transitions across all cultures are: birth, puberty, marriage, and death. However, employing a broader definition, role transitions may include: leaving parents; graduating from school; accepting a job; getting married; having children; moving; changing jobs; getting divorced; retiring; or having a spouse die. In an abstract sense, role transitions emanate from: work and financial changes; changes in home life; losses of relationships; and personal or inner changes (e.g., Bridges 1980; Fried and Fried 1980; George 1980). Von Gennep (1909/1965), in his research on rites of passage, depicts a role transition as a liminal phase--a period when a person is disconnected from a former role or status, but not yet connected to a new role or status. Turner (1974) identifies four stages in role transitions. First is a breach of custom, when the person engages in conduct that violates traditional norms. Following this breach of custom is a time of crisis or role strain; not unlike the vulnerability, profound inner conflict, and crises that are depicted by Adams, Hayes, and Hopkins (1976). Next is a period of redressive or adaptive action, during which the person strives to reduce the disharmony; similar to the findings of Hopson and Adams (1976). The last phase is either reintegration into the former role or separation into a new role. There are several classifications of role and status transitions. Holmes and Rahe (1967) developed a list of life events that pose challenges to people. Their "Schedule of Recent Events" shows the potential interface between social stress and adjustment to role transitions. The ten most stressful events--all of which represent role transitions are: (1) death of spouse; (2) divorce; (3) marital separation; (4) jail term; (5) death of close family member; (6) personal injury or illness; (7) marriage; (8) fired from work; (9) marital reconciliation; and (10) retirement. This is merely one example of a classificatory system for role and status transitions. Dohrenwend and Dohrenwend (1974) compiled the Psychiatric Epidemiology Research Interview (PERI) scale; a list of 102 life events that are potentially stressful--

many of which are role transitions--and calibrated the amount of impact entailed in each type of event. Again, this is merely another example of a classificatory system for role and status transitions and should not be perceived to be better or worse than any other classificatory system.

Now let us return to dramaturgic metaphors to detail a hypothetical example of a role transition. To refresh our memories, we claimed that "plays" (social systems) require "parts" (roles). As we attempt to enact the parts in our plays, we rely upon "scripts" (role and status expectations) and "props" (possessions) to guide our behavior and communicate social positions. Role transitions demand changes in the "plays" (social systems), the "parts" (roles), the "scripts" (role expectations), and the "props" (possessions) in our lives.

For example, a woman may participate in a "play" called "marriage." This play may require enactment of a "role" termed "wife." This "role" might involve a "script" that includes role-determined expectations such as earning an income, bearing children, and sharing in household decision-making. This "script" may be enhanced by "props" that include a house, a car, and clothes. An abrupt role transition may occur if the woman's spouse dies. The "play" is no longer called "marriage;" now it is called "widowhood," and involves enactment of a role termed "widow." This "role" might demand a new "script" that includes role-determined expectations such as earning a larger income, raising children alone, and making household decisions alone. Finally, this "script" may be accompanied by a change in the "props." The new widow may sell the family home, remove her wedding band, or donate the decedent's clothing to charity. Such possession dispositions--or prop changes--usually facilitate social and psychological adjustment to the new "play," "part," "script," and "props" (i.e., the role transition). In a detailed study of widowhood, Lopata (1973a) maintains that widowhood is a social role that represents a major role loss because the normative guidelines and role privileges of being a spouse are lost and the widow is left with few substitutes. Likewise, Rosenblatt, Walsh, and Jackson (1976) state in their discussion of tie-breaking and the death of a spouse (pp. 67-69):

> [I]n a long-term relationship such as marriage, innumerable behaviors appropriate to the relationship become associated with stimuli (sights, sounds, odors, textures) in the environment of the relationship. When death (or divorce, or migration, or some other permanent separation) makes it necessary to treat the relationship as ended and to develop new patterns of behavior, these stimuli inhibit the change, because they elicit old dispositions. To facilitate change, tie-breaking practices that eliminate or alter these stimuli seem to be of great value....In many societies, there are death customs which eliminate reminders of a deceased spouse during the bereavement period....These customs include destroying, giving away, or temporarily putting aside personal property of the deceased, observing a taboo on the name of the deceased, and changing residence. We believe...such customs serve to break ties with the deceased spouse and, as a consequence, to facilitate establishment of new patterns of living...

However, it is important to emphasize that not all life changes--even the death of a spouse--are always role transitions. The determination of what should be defined as a role transition is dependent on the emic perspective of the focal person. If a life change affects a social role, it is most appropriately termed a role transition. In contrast, if a life change has little or no impact on a social role, it does not warrant definition as a role transition--an important type of change which strongly influences behavior and social identity. In other words, some attributes of identity encompassed by roles are very central to self, and as a consequence are imbued with strong affect (e.g., Levinson 1959; Sarbin 1982; Turner 1974). Loss of such roles may have devastating consequences (e.g., Marris 1974; Parkes 1986; Stephenson 1985). For example, the centrality of the role of wife for some women is indicated by grief, mourning, or despair following the death of a spouse. In contrast, the role of wife may be peripheral to self for other women, and can be lost or abandoned with little or no distress (e.g., Dohrenwend and Dohrenwend 1974; Goffman 1959; Viorst 1986).

METHOD

The findings presented in this research are based on depth interviews with 52 student informants (ages 19 to 39, 60 percent female). All informants were requested to discuss the disposition of four possessions--yielding data for 208 dispositional experiences. The interviews were unstructured, non-directive, and guided by the informant style and the unique informant/interviewer interaction. This method was considered most appropriate for the objectives of this research since it evokes richly textured descriptions of dispositional experiences which otherwise might be dismissed or overlooked. Interviews were tape-recorded, and required from 45 minutes to over 2 hours to complete. The tape recordings were then transcribed, resulting in an accumulation of over 700 transcribed pages of data regarding the disposition of all types of possessions. Transcripts were analyzed to isolate examples of possession disposition during role transitions.

Content analysis is an excellent method to generate a "thick description" (Geertz 1973) and "thick interpretation" (Denzin 1989) because it explores the phenomenology of verbatim self-reports. This method prioritizes discovery over confirmation (e.g., Deshpande 1983; Kaplan 1964; Lincoln and Guba 1985), and is particularly appropriate because of the paucity of dispositional research. Also, this method of data analysis is consistent with the call for more naturalistic, experiential approaches to consumer behavior research (e.g., Belk 1984a; Holbrook and Hirschman 1982; Thompson, Locander, and Pollio 1989).

EXAMPLES OF POSSESSION DISPOSITION DURING ROLE TRANSITIONS

I emphasize the disposition of possessions (props) during role transitions, which is not to ignore the importance of the acquisition and usage of such props, but merely to define the bounds of this research--part of a much larger project on possession disposition. Perhaps the most fascinating aspect of this research is the fact that 100 of the 208 interviews (48 percent) concerned a possession disposition that either represented a role transition itself (e.g., quitting a job), or occurred in conjunction with a role transition (e.g., selling a house because quitting a job). This single percentage reveals the close relationship between possession disposition and role transitions. Possessions, or props, are not disposed of on whims--they are carefully calculated maneuvers that facilitate and validate role transitions. Whether such maneuvers are performed consciously or subconsciously, they allow individuals "to throw out the old to make room for the new." In contrast, when possession disposition is involuntary, it may create abrupt or uncomfortable role strain as the supporting props are removed. On the following pages, I present interview excerpts of dispositions of possessions that precede, occur in conjunction with, represent, or follow role transitions. Since most of the informants are young adults, most dispositional stories involve role transitions appropriate to this age group.

Consider the following quote from Steven (WM 20), who gave up his blanket to facilitate his role transition from "baby" to "child" (I = Interviewer):

S: [W]hen I was little I had a security blanket that I grew up with. I had had it since I was a baby and slept with it every night. Then when I was about seven or eight, I decided I had to get rid of it. None of my friends had anything like that and I knew I was too old for it....I decided I was a big boy now and it was time to get rid of childish things.

Consider the following interview quote from Liz (WF 20), who voluntarily gave her car to her brother to validate her role transition from "young rebel" to "mature adult:"

L: ...I just gave [the car] to [my brother] when he left for college.
I: You didn't care about the old car?
L: No. I associated it with a party car, so actually I was kind of glad to get rid of it. It was during my rebellious stage where I took off for weekends snow skiing and things without telling my parents, kind of just like leaving, so in a way it was to get rid of the bad things I did so it didn't bother me. I think I was relieved I got rid of those memories. I got rid of the bad things I had done. It signified that I don't do these things now. I'm older now and don't deceive my parents. That car was like a symbol of all the deceitful things I had done to my parents and to my family when I was 16 and 17. It was just a relief to get rid of the past. I was growing up and just wanted to get rid of the old baggage.

Likewise, consider the following quote from Laura (WF 21), who moved out of the family house to validate her role transition from "child" to "adult:"

L: ...I decided that I was 18 or 19 and it was time to move out. I waited until I could save up enough money. I knew I had to leave. My parents were driving me crazy. Having to be in at a certain time was driving me crazy....I wanted to be away from Mom and Dad....It felt good. I liked the freedom. I liked the responsibility.

Finally, consider Allison's (WF 21) disposition of a pair of dance shoes, a favorite remembrance of high school performances:

A: I had these shoes for years and years. I did dancing in high school. These were my favorite shoes. But then I was in West Side Story and I danced so much, I just wore them out....I had to throw them away. But I didn't throw them away until a year or two later. I put them on every once in awhile just to think about the show and stuff, but I knew they were ruined and I knew I wasn't going to dance anymore.

Steven, Liz, Laura, and Allison are all describing possession disposition related to role transitions from "childhood" to "adulthood;" a major life change in which "props" are extremely important (e.g., Bryman, Bytheway, Allatt, and Keil 1987; Mercer, Nichols, and Doyle 1989; Middleton 1970).

In contrast, consider Stephanie's (WF 25) recent divorce, a well-recognized role transition in and of itself:

S: So Dick and I weren't talking because we got in a fight...and then Dick said...I was the worst thing in his life....He moved out. I was really mad. I supported him while he finished his Master's degree here, but then he wouldn't get a job. Then, as soon as we broke up...all of a sudden he was Assistant Superintendent of the County's Budget Management Office. So he told me he couldn't get a job and he got one right after we got divorced. It was like he was pushing me to see how far he could go.

Similarly, consider Susan's (WF 23) break-up with a long-term boyfriend, and her consequential destruction of a plaque she made for him:

S: The plaque was a collage-type of plaque. I had been cutting things out of...magazines. Things that were special. Remembrances from our relationship. I even had a picture of us....I had given it to him, but later found him with another girl one time, so I took the plaque back thinking that he was not worthy of it. I was so mad over the relationship and there wasn't really anything I could do about it. The plaque really wasn't made for me, but I didn't want to give back to him because I thought it was too good for him, so I broke it, and then I gave it back to him.

Both Stephanie and Susan describe common role strain (e.g., Allatt, Keil, Bryman, and Bytheway 1987; Bryman, Bytheway, Allatt, and Keil 1987; Mercer, Nichols, and Doyle 1989) during and following transitions that required changes from wife or girlfriend to single, unattached adults.

Now consider a mid-life transition, as Teresa (BF 37) explains her decision to quit her job and return to school:

T: I worked for the telephone company for fifteen years and I was in management. It was during the time of the divestiture so there was a lot of talk that they were going to be downsizing the management team. The criteria for deciding who was going to stay and who was going to be terminated was based on education and degrees. I knew I was going to lose my job because I didn't have a degree and I decided to never lose another job because I didn't have a degree so I went to school to get a degree.

There are two particularly interesting aspects in this interview excerpt. First, Teresa provides an example to illustrate that role transitions occur throughout life (e.g., Eurich 1981; George 1980; Riley, Huber, and Hess 1988). Next, this interview quote discusses the cyclic consumption process of acquisition, usage, and disposition (Young and Wallendorf 1989) as Teresa explains how she "disposed of" her role as a manager and "acquired" the role of a student.

Thus far, all included dispositional stories related to role transitions have been voluntary. Next I list two interview excerpts related to involuntary role transitions; that is, role transitions that were forced upon the informants. Consider, for instance, how Jack's (WM 24) parents' divorce represented a role transition not only for his parents, but for himself as well:

J: Well, my parents were getting a divorce and I was 17. When my parents got divorced, my mom got the house and my dad had to move out. I wanted to live with my dad so I had to move....It was my choice to live with my dad, but I had no choice about moving out of the house. Because of the bad feelings, I felt like I had to leave. I was mad at my mom. I was mad at the fact that everything was being broke up....I guess I was rejecting her....She [was]...willing to have me stay. [I]f I had gotten over the anger, I could have stayed, but because of my emotions, I felt forced to leave....[I] felt sadness about leaving because I had lived there...my whole life.

Similarly, consider Paul's (WM 22) story of the death of his father when he was 15 years old:

P: My father....was killed by a drunk driver...
I: ...How did you feel?
P: I don't know. I was shocked. I didn't know what to think. I didn't know what was going on. It was really weird....I felt a great loss. I was still in disbelief....The thing that bugged me the most was that everyone kept saying that everything was going to be the same and I couldn't believe that....My mom changed a lot. Her attitude was really different. It wasn't like she was the same person. I don't know. It was really strange. Me and my brother did not get along with my mom....It seemed like she didn't want me to have any responsibility. I don't know. She just seemed to neglect us a lot more....It was like she was in her own little world. It was really strange. It wasn't just with her kids, it was with her friends and everything. It was this one friend of my dad's, not a really close friend, a good friend, but not one that my father would say was one of his better friends, kind of like seemed to come to my mom's aid and she kind of like took it like he was the only one that was willing to help and she was caught up in it and it seemed like he

manipulated her a lot. I felt anger toward that in particular. It seemed like he was more important that me, my brother, and my sister.

I: As a 15 year old boy who was closest to your father and having your father suddenly die like that, how do you think it influenced your life or changed your life from what it might have been?

P: ...If my father was still alive....I would probably go to school at home. I said I don't get along well with my mom. I left....I moved to California....[F]or some reason, my mom did a complete reversal after that, and from what my brother said, she totally changed. So I don't know. I don't think I would be an independent as I am.

Jack and Paul both discuss common role transitions--divorce and death--but from the perspectives of outsiders affected by uncontrollable events rather than from the viewpoints of inside participants. Nonetheless, they behave as if they were the people divorcing and dying--or perhaps even worse--due to the uncontrollable circumstances of their respective dispositional experiences.

DISCUSSION

"Who are you?" said the Caterpillar...
"I--I hardly know, Sir, just at present," Alice replied rather shyly, "at least I know who I was when I got up this morning, but I think I must have changed several times since then."
Lewis Carroll
Alice's Adventures in Wonderland

Role transitions usually have dramatic effects on self-identity and social identity: They represent changes in the plays, parts, scripts, and props in our lives. Similar to professional actors and actresses, we typically prefer certain plays, feel more comfortable with favorite parts, perform most effectively with unchanging scripts, and rely upon familiar props to guide our performances. My objective has been to provide some examples of this dramaturgic metaphor as seen in real drama, where life itself is the theatre, stage, setting, and scene, and we create the plot (or have the plot created) as we proceed.

My initial examples involve the disposition of unwanted or inappropriate "props" such as a security blanket, a car, a place of residence, and a pair of shoes. These possession dispositions facilitated movement to new plays, parts, scripts, and plots. My next examples involve the disposition of other "parts" in plays; specifically a husband, a boyfriend, and a job. Finally, I describe involuntary dispositional experiences such as parental divorce and the death of a parent, and illustrate how these events trigger disturbing changes in plays, parts, scripts, and plots.

Thus, if we--as researchers of consumer behavior--believe "All the world's a stage..." then we must study that stage if we desire to understand changes in the social systems, social roles, normative and anticipatory role expectations, and--most especially--the possessions on it. And, as implied, we will discover that the acquisition, usage, and disposition of possessions serve vital functions for the performers as they enact their roles and role transitions.

REFERENCES

Adams, John, John Hayes, and Barrie Hopson (1976), *Transition: Understanding and Managing Personal Change*, London: Martin Robinson.

Allatt, Patricia, Teresa Keil, Alan Bryman, and Bill Bytheway (1987), *Women and the Life Cycle*, eds., Patricia Allatt, Teresa Keil, Alan Bryman, and Bill Bytheway, New York: St. Martin's Press.

Andreasen, Alan R. (1984), "Life Status Changes and Changes in Consumer Preferences and Satisfaction," *Journal of Consumer Research*, 11, 784-794.

Banton, Michael P. (1965), *Roles: An Introduction to the Study of Social Relations*, New York: Basic Books.

Belk, Russell W. (1984a), "Manifesto for a Consumer Behavior of Consumer Behavior," *Scientific Method in Marketing*, eds., Paul Anderson and Michael J. Ryan, Chicago: American Marketing Association, 163-167.

Benedict, Ruth (1938), "Continuities and Discontinuities in Cultural Conditioning," *Psychiatry*, 1, 161-167.

Bridges, William (1980), *Transitions*, Reading, MA: Addison-Wesley.

Bryman, Alan, Bill Bytheway, Patricia Allatt, and Teresa Keil (1987), *Rethinking the Life Cycle*, eds., Alan Bryman, Bill Bytheway, Patricia Allatt, and Teresa Keil, London: MacMillan.

Buchmann, Marlis (1989), *The Script of Life in Modern Society*, Chicago: The University of Chicago Press.

Deshpande, Rojit (1983), "Paradigms Lost: On Theory and Method in Research and Method in Marketing," *Journal of Marketing*, 47 (Fall), 101-110.

Dohrenwend, Barbara Snell and Bruce P. Dohrenwend (1974), *Stressful Life Events: Their Nature and Effects*, New York: Wiley.

Eurich, Alvin C. (1981), *Major Transitions in the Human Life Cycle*, ed., Alvin C. Eurich, Lexington, MA: Lexington Books.

Fried, Martha Nemes and Morton H. Fried (1980), *Transitions: Four Rituals in Eight Cultures*, New York: Penguin Books.

George, Linda K. (1980), *Role Transitions in Later Life*, Monterey: Brooks/Cole.

Geertz, Clifford (1973), "Thick Description: Toward an Interpretive Theory of Culture," in *The Interpretation of Cultures*, ed., Clifford Geertz, New York: Basic Books, 231-267.

Glaser, Barney G. and Anselm L. Strauss (1971), *Status Passage*, Chicago: Aldine.

Goffman, Erving (1959), *The Presentation of Self in Everyday Life*, Garden City, New York: Doubleday.

Goffman, Erving (1961), *Encounters: Two Studies in the Sociology of Interaction*, Garden City, Indianapolis: Bobbs-Merrill.

Goffman, Erving (1974), *Frame Analysis: An Essay on the Organization of Experience*, New York: Harper & Row.

Hess, Beth B. (1988), "Social Structures and Human Lives: A Sociological Theme," *Social Structures and Human Lives*, eds., Matilda White Riley, Bettina J. Huber, and Beth B. Hess, Beverly Hills: Sage, 16-23.

Holbrook, Morris B. and Elizabeth Hirschman (1982), "The Experiential Aspects of Consumption: Consumer Fantasies, Feelings, and Fun," *Journal of Consumer Research*, 9 (2), 132-140.

Holmes, Thomas H. and Richard H. Rahe (1967), "The Social Readjustment Rating Scale," *Journal of Psychosomatic Research*, 11, 213-218.

Hopson, Barrie and John Adams (1976), "Towards an Understanding of Transition: Defining Some Boundaries of Transition Dynamics," *Transition: Understanding and Managing Personal Change*, eds., John Adams, John Hayes, and Barrie Hopson, London: Martin Robertson, 3-25.

Kaplan, Abraham (1964), *The Conduct of Inquiry*, San Francisco: Chandler.

Levinson, Daniel J. (1959), "Role, Personality, and Social Structure in the Organizational Setting," *Journal of Abnormal and Social Psychology*, 58, 170-180.

Levinson, Daniel J. (1978), *The Seasons of a Man's Life*, New York: Knopf.

Lincoln, Yvonna S. and Egon G. Guba (1985), *Naturalistic Inquiry*, Beverly Hills: Sage.

Linton, Ralph (1936), *The Study of Man*, New York: Appleton-Century-Crofts.

Linton, Ralph (1945), *The Cultural Background of Personality*, New York: Appleton-Century-Crofts.

Lopata, Znaniecka (1973a), *Widowhood in an American City*, Cambridge: Schenkman.

Marris, Peter (1974), *Loss and Change*, London: Routledge & K. Paul.

McAlexander, James H. and John W. Schouten (1989), "Transition Management Strategies: A Consumer Behavior Perspective," *Sociology and Social Research*, forthcoming.

Mead, George H. (1934), *Mind, Self, and Society*, Chicago: The University of Chicago Press.

Mercer, Ramona T., Elizabeth G. Nichols, and Glen Caspers Doyle (1989), *Transitions in a Woman's Life*, New York: Springer.

Middleton, John (1970), *From Child to Adult*, ed., John Middleton, Garden City, NY: The Natural History Press.

Oswalt, Wendell H. (1986), *Life Cycles and Lifeways*, Palo Alto, CA: Mayfield.

Parkes, Colin Murray (1986), *Bereavement*, New York: Tavistock.

Riley, Matilda White, Bettina J. Huber, and Beth B. Hess (1988), *Social Structures & Human Lives*, eds., Matilda White Riley, Bettina J. Huber, and Beth B. Hess, Beverly Hills: Sage.

Rosenblatt, Paul C., R. Patricia Walsh, and Douglas A. Jackson (1976), *Grief and Mourning in Cross-Cultural Perspective*, Human Relations Area Files.

Sarbin, Theodore R. (1954), "Role Theory," *Handbook of Social Psychology, Volume One*, ed., G. Lindzey, Reading, MA: Addison-Wesley, 223-258.

Sarbin, Theodore R. and Vernon L. Allen (1968), "Role Theory," *Handbook of Social Psychology, Volume One*, eds., G. Lindzey and E. Aronson, Reading, MA: Addison-Wesley, 448-567.

Schouten, John (1990), "Selves in Transition: The Consumption of Aesthetic Plastic Surgery," *Journal of Consumer Research*, forthcoming.

Sheehy, Gail (1974), *Passages*, New York: Dutton.

Sörenson, Aage B., Franz E. Weinert, and Lonnie R. Sherrod (1986), *Human Development and the Life Course: Multidisciplinary Perspectives*, eds., Aage B. Sörenson, Franz E. Weinhart, and Lonnie R. Sherrod, Hillsdale, NJ: Erlbaum.

Spierer, Howard (1981), "Life Cycle," *Major Transitions in the Human Life Cycle*, ed., Alvin Christian Eurich, Lexington, MA: Lexington Books.

Stephenson, John S. (1985), *Death, Grief, and Mourning*, New York: Free Press.

Thompson, Craig J., William B. Locander, and Howard R. Pollio (1989), "Putting Consumer Experience Back into Consumer Research: The Philosophy and Method of Existential Phenomenology," *Journal of Consumer Research*, 16 (September), 133-146.

Turner, Victor (1974), *Dramas, Fields, and Metaphors: Symbolic Action in Human Society*, Ithaca, NY: Cornell University Press.

Viorst, Judith (1986), *Necessary Losses*, New York: Ballantine.

von Gennep, Arnold (1909/1960), *The Rites of Passage*, trans., M. Vizedom and G. Caffee, Chicago: The University of Chicago Press.

Young, Frank W. (1965), *Initiation Ceremonies: A Cross-Cultural Study of Status Dramatization*, Indianapolis: Bobbs-Merrill.

Young, Melissa Martin and Melanie Wallendorf (1989), "Ashes to Ashes, Dust to Dust: Conceptualizing Consumer Disposition of Possessions," *Proceedings*, Educators' Conference, American Marketing Association.

Consumption Responses to Involuntary Job Loss
Scott D. Roberts, Old Dominion University

ABSTRACT
This is a case-style report of the consumption adjustments by two men as a result of the loss of their jobs and income. Emphasis is given to personal and social areas of consumption. The consumer behavior exhibited by the informants reflects both a reaction to the current context of job loss and consideration of personal, historical backgrounds.

INTRODUCTION
Sudden income loss is a phenomenon from which few are completely immune. It has been estimated that during the 1970s and 1980s nearly one-third of the population suffered a major drop (half or more) in their family income (Duncan, et al. 1986). The U.S. economy has long been shifting to a services-dominated work force, leaving in its wake large numbers of structurally unemployed workers (U.S. Congress 1986). Surprisingly little research has been done to investigate the micro consumption "fallout" of such income loss.

This paper reports on a case study of the lives of two men who were laid off for over two years from their jobs as steel workers. Data were gathered in a variety of ways, including several lengthy depth interviews with each informant and participant observation at their monthly union meetings. Additionally, naturalistic observation of the informants in their homes, including the use of photography were employed to give a more complete context to the report. These sources of evidences are recommended for conducting case studies by Yin (1984). This report is part of a larger study involving over twenty informants (Roberts 1988), which provides some backdrop for the experiences of these men. As is the standard, informant names and other identifying characteristics have been disguised for the sake of anonymity (Belk, et al. 1988).

Although it is generally accepted that the use of very small samples limits the generalizability of a study to other groups or settings, reports of small sample qualitative research projects continue to be valuable in providing insight to consumer researchers unavailable through other methodologies. For example, Pollay (1987) reported the excessive Christmas decoration activities of a single informant and Holbrook (1988) used introspective psychoanalytic techniques to explain his own consumption behavior. Each of these studies adds, in its own way, to the body of knowledge about consumer behavior.

BACKGROUND
Paul Worth (Single White Male - 34) and Mark Laydon (SWM-41) were laid off by Perry Iron Corporation after 10 and 21 years of service, respectively. Perry had been hit hard by two recessions in the early 1980s and also by low world prices for their output. They closed the doors "indefinitely" and laid off more than 8,000 workers. The economy local to Perry has a fairly low level of industrial activity, and relies instead on retailing, state government, higher education, and financial services for the bulk of it employment. This forced most laid off workers into a union-hostile and generally low-paying labor market -- usually with poor outcomes. The informants in this case were both high school dropouts, even further limiting their options.

The consumption and other responses of Paul and Mark to income and job loss were varied. The loss of jobs which paid close to $20 per hour in wages and benefits obviously necessitated some immediate adjustments. For instance, less maintenance was done on Mark's lawn, house, and automobiles and his family spent much less on clothing during the two years he was not employed by Perry. These types of adjustments are clearly functional in nature. Perhaps more interesting are the personal and social-oriented consumption reactions. The focus here is on these two major areas. The personal and social arenas are highly intertwined and overlapping where consumption is concerned. Some consumption activities fall more clearly into one or the other, whereas other consumption can be interpreted as related to both the personal and the social area.

Before going into specifics, however, it is important to note that both of these men brought to the situation a certain amount of "baggage" which is difficult to tease out of the analysis and which therefore must be provided to the reader of this type of work. Paul had been divorced a few years earlier and, the stress of this event, coupled with shift work led him to attempt suicide. He had successfully received therapy including biofeedback training before the lay off occurred. Nevertheless, the state of his mental health going into the loss of job and income certainly affected his approach to the situation. Mark reported that his entire life had been a struggle. He contracted polio as a child, which left him with one leg shorter than the other. He was put on drugs as a child to curb obesity. He learned at 38 years of age that his lifetime frustration with school and reading could be traced to dyslexia. Mark brought to the lay off a bitter perspective on life and low self esteem.

THE SELF AND OTHERS
In some ways, the loss of job is a direct threat to who a person is (unemployed refers to what you *are not*). This gap in the consumer's self identity (Belk 1988) may prompt the person to try to "complete" him or her self symbolically through consumption behavior (Wicklund and Gollwitzer 1982). Another important function of consumption is as a signal to others about who the person is and how that person is "doing" (Veblen 1899). The

inability of the individual or family to maintain such appearances is then a further problem which may be brought on by income loss (Newman 1988).

Paul

One of the most devastating losses which came as a result of the loss of income was Paul's power car, a new red Camaro with all the options. He brought it up three times in the first interview. When asked why this had been such a difficult loss, Paul stated some practical reasons for why he needed the car. Further probing yielded more interesting insights, however, as the following quote reveals: "Well, it said somethin', Perry worker, lost m'car... not because of the lay off but I lost my house and m'family, but then on top o' that, here I lose m'car, you know. Lost m'job... what next?" During the lay off, he said he felt like he wasn't the same old fun person he used to be. "I got depressed. It's really been hard, I haven't been happy. It's like I can't be happy. Can't find that old happy feeling."

Paul's deteriorating financial situation exacerbated his problems with women. He found that women were "less loyal" to him in the dating situation. He had had several female roommates who had helped him financially (three in the last three years, plus his mother). Ironically, at the same time he was relying on women for support, his perceptions of women became more distorted and grotesque. He became a collector of hard-core pornography magazines like *Asian Anal Girls* and *Swedish Erotica* and couched much of his conversation in terms of sexual needs. "I've pretty much given up women for my porn... You know, socializing's different, [pause] friends don't fill needs, [pause] it's lonely out there." Kohut (1977, p. 161) states that pornography may be used in an attempt to "stimulate [the] self erotically in order to regain the sense of aliveness and reality of [the] body-self." The consumption of pornography by Paul seems to fit Kohut's interpretation. His inability to find satisfying and appropriate social relationships was clearly related to the loss of income and status as a steel worker.

Paul had also become much more distant with his family, not seeing them much over the time of the lay off even though they live locally. Some high school buddies of his had become sufficiently concerned about him to invite him to play in their band just so he would get out more. When asked if he tried to do more social things, he replied, "for the last year I've been in my own cave, right here." While he did get out to work his interim jobs over the period of the lay off, his use of the word "cave" to describe his dwelling is apt. He lived in the basement half of a two bedroom apartment and was extremely reclusive, even hermit-like. Again, the inward turn by Paul in terms of his social network and consumption was related in great degree to his loss of status and income.

Mark

The lay off for Mark was marked in many ways by an *increase* in acquisition behavior. On the eve of the imminent lay off, he decided that he needed a new truck in order to be able to have reliable transportation so he could "follow construction." His payments throughout the lay off period were $460 per month. This purchase sets the stage for explaining Mark's approach to life. He seems to equate spending with living. At one point, he discussed the possibility of a hunting trip with his wife. She objected that this was "reckless" in light of the current financial burdens. He replied, venting anger not at her, but at the company, "Bullshit! They're not gonna break me, they're not gonna stop me from living!"

In addition to the truck, Mark bought a used Mercedes during the lay off. Again, he cited practical reasoning, that his wife needed something reliable for her commute to work. The car clearly had social benefits, as well, however. Mark reports, "We had a lot of people say 'Oh my God, you bought a Mercedes and you're laid off, you're not hurting.'" This purchase was visible enough that it sent a message to outsiders -- "The Laydons are doing just fine, thank you." Maintaining visible consumption while cutting back elsewhere to maintain "face" is a strategy reported by Newman in her study of unemployment and underemployment among the middle class in the U.S. (Newman 1988).

The Laydons did cut back in some areas. Of particular note was their almost complete cessation of outdoor family recreation. They owned a camper and a boat, both of which had received heavy use prior to the lay off. Mark and his wife also stopped their annual snow skiing trips and frequent eating out. They went from frequent golfing to almost none.

At the same time these cuts were going on, Mark reported that he smoked more marijuana, even giving vague references to small-time dealing to help supplement his income. Another consumption activity of interest was Mark's purchase of two horses while laid off. Though the price of the horses was not great, the commitment in terms of long term care was significant. He reported that feed alone amounted to several hundred dollars in the last six months. Additionally, he bought the basics of tack in order to be able to use the horses. He was looking for somewhere to store them because the owner of the land where the animals were staying for free was going to sell. This substantial allocation of resources to horses reflected his desire to return to his rural roots, he said. His family did not participate in the horse care or use at all.

CONCLUSION

The types of consumer behavior exhibited by the two informants in this case could clearly be interpreted using many theoretical angles. Mark's insistence on spending money for the truck, for example, looks a lot like denial in the Freudian sense. The angle used here is the notion of the extended self as reflected by consumption decisions.

This report has focused on some extreme reactions to income loss. But are they really so extreme? The loss of job can have devastating consequences when one's identity is diminished as a result. One's identity is important both to the self and to significant others. The consumption decisions of these men, when framed in self-protective theories such as Wicklund and Gollwitzer's "symbolic self-completion" (1982) are not so illogical as outsiders might imagine. These men took rational, thoughtful steps (admittedly forced by a difficult situation) to protect and perhaps re-define who they are and who they want to be. Were the adjustments by these men "good" or even *healthy*? That issue is best left to those who assist the unemployed most directly.

REFERENCES

Belk, Russell W. (1988), "Possessions and the Extended Self," *Journal of Consumer Research*, 15 (September), 139-168.

Belk, Russell W., John F. Sherry, Jr., and Melanie Wallendorf (1988), "A Naturalistic Inquiry into Buyer and Seller Behavior at a Swap Meet," *Journal of Consumer Research*, 14 (March), 449-470.

Duncan, Greg J., Martha Hill and Willard Rogers (1986), "The Changing Fortunes of Young and Old," *American Demographics*, 8 (August), 26-33.

Holbrook, Morris B. (1988), "Steps Toward a Psychoanalytic Interpretation of Consumption: A Meta-Meta-Meta-Analysis of Some Issues Raised by the Consumer Behavior Odyssey," in *Advances in Consumer Research* Vol. 15, Michael J. Houston, ed., Provo, UT: Association for Consumer Research, 537-542.

Kohut, Heinz (1977), *The Restoration of Self*, Oxford, England: Oxford University Press.

Newman, Katherine S. (1988), *Falling From Grace: The Experience of Downward Mobility in the American Middle Class*, New York: Free Press.

Pollay, Richard W. (1987), "It's the Thought That Counts: A Case Study in Xmas Excesses," in *Advances in Consumer Research* Vol. 14, Melanie Wallendorf and Paul Anderson, eds., Provo, UT: Association for Consumer Research, 140-143.

Roberts, Scott D. (1988), *Resource Reallocation and Other Effects of Structural Unemployment: A Naturalistic Approach*, Unpublished Dissertation, Graduate School of Business, University of Utah.

U.S. Congress Office of Technology Assessment (1986), *Technology and Structural Unemployment: Reemploying Displaced Adults*, Washington, DC: U.S. Government Printing Office.

Veblen, Thorstein (1899), *The Theory of the Leisure Class*, New York: MacMillan.

Wicklund, Robert A. and Peter M. Gollwitzer (1982), *Symbolic Self Completion*, Hillsdale, NJ: Lawrence Elrbaum Associates.

Yin, Robert K. (1984), *Case Study Research: Designs and Methods*, Newbury Park, CA: Sage.

Divorce, the Disposition of the Relationship, and Everything

James H. McAlexander, Oregon State University[1]

The disposition of possessions has been a neglected facet of consumer behavior. Yet, in some situations, the disposition of certain possessions can be more important, emotionally and symbolically, to consumers than their acquisition (Belk 1988; Belk, Wallendorf and Sherry 1989). One time that disposition may take on such a preeminent role for consumers is during times of transition (Young and Wallendorf 1989). In order to explore the relationship between the disposition of possessions and life transitions, this paper examines the disposition of possessions that accompanies divorce. This paper discusses two themes that address the disposition of marital possessions: "Disposition to Break Free", and "Disposition to Hold On." These themes have emerged from a qualitative study that more broadly examines divorce and its implications for consumer behavior.

TRANSITIONS AND CONSUMER BEHAVIOR

During the course of our lives, we encounter a never-ending series of transitions. As we go through these transitional times, such as changing jobs, getting married, or moving to a new city, we leave the comfort of our known status, experience a period of disequilibrium, and begin to assimilate into a new status and make appropriate role adaptations (Glaser and Strauss 1971; Rosow 1976; Van Gennep 1960). As recent research suggests, these times of transition can have profound implications for consumer behavior (Andreason 1984; McAlexander and Schouten 1989; Mehta and Belk 1991; Schouten 1991; Solomon 1983). For example, consumer behavior research has begun to explore how consumers modify their assortment of possessions to reflect changes in their self concept (Solomon 1983; Mehta and Belk 1991). Consumer behavior research also has explored the role possessions can play in easing or aggravating the stresses inherent to significant life transitions (McAlexander and Schouten 1989).

The Divorce Transition

There are few status transitions one can experience that are of greater personal consequence than divorce (cf. Berman and Turk 1981; Johnson 1988; Wallerstein and Kelly 1980). As the divorcing partners work out the dissolution of their marriage, the most important components of their life structure may change (Levinson 1978). For example, divorce necessitates the redefinition of one's most important relationships, including relationships with children, parents, friends, and professional colleagues (Bohannon 1970; Spanier and Casto 1979; Weingarten 1988).

Divorce is an interesting transition to study from the perspective of consumer behavior. In the midst of addressing important interpersonal problems, the divorcing partners must also accomplish other practical consumer oriented tasks, including the disposition of shared possessions. Possessions, including those that were meaningful to the couple, as well as those that were functionally necessary in running a household, must be divided and/or disposed of. While seemingly a trivial concern when compared to the interpersonal challenges facing the dissolving dyad (like redefining parent/child relationships), it would be a mistake to underestimate the importance of the disposition of marital possessions. Since possessions are integral to the definition of self, and the expression and performance of roles (Belk 1988; Solomon 1983), the disposition of them necessarily communicates important changes both to the consumer and to others (Young and Wallendorf 1989).

METHOD

This paper reports the results of depth interviews with eighteen divorced informants. Interviews were conducted by the author and three colleagues who have had training and experience in qualitative research methods. The interviews were audio-taped, and the transcription of those tapes, supplemented with field notes prepared by the interviewers, comprise the data base that was used in this study.

Data collection and analysis were guided by the constant comparative method (Glaser and Strauss 1967), and techniques specified by Miles and Huberman (1984). This iterative process of data collection and analysis was supplemented by an extensive literature review. The literature offered a number of valuable insights and emphasized the importance of purposively sampling for diversity in variables such as family composition, length of marriage, the role played in initiating the divorce, gender, and socioeconomic status (Gerstel 1988; Kaslow and Schwartz 1987; Kitson, Babri and Roach 1985; Bloom and Clement 1984; Spanier and Casto 1979; Weiss 1975).

RESULTS

Data analysis yielded a number of themes that stressed the important role that the disposition of marital possessions plays in the divorce process. Two prominent themes that emerged in the analysis will be discussed in this paper: "Disposition to Break Free" and "Disposition to Hold on." The cases of two informants are presented in order to illustrate these themes.

---

[1] The author wishes to thank Sheila Heidman, Scott D. Roberts and John W. Schouten for their assistance with this project.

Disposition to Break Free

Informants were able to use the disposition of possessions to help free themselves from their marital relationship. This was frequently a goal of informants who initiated the divorce. Initiators are those partners who claim responsibility for the divorce decision and who feel a sense of control over the process (Buehler 1987; Vaughan 1986). One way informants used disposition to help free themselves from their marital relationship was to accept a disproportionately small property settlement: keeping fewer possessions and assuming more financial obligations than their spouses. One informant, Ben Preston (pseudonym), illustrates this theme particularly well. Ben Preston (wm, 33) is a partner in a San Antonio law firm. His divorce in 1987 came after a ten year marriage. Ben had met his wife in high school and married her when he was nineteen and she was eighteen. He and his former spouse have two children: a girl, then five, and a boy, then two years old.

In recounting the events that led to his divorce, Ben reported that the inevitability of his divorce became apparent to him as he was completing his law school education. As Ben was preparing to leave law school, and begin the transition into his new professional status, he confronted a dilemma commonly encountered by upwardly mobile people (Glaser and Strauss 1971): he found many elements of his existing life structure to be incompatible with his professional and personal aspirations. As he entered his new career, Ben sought to become the archetypal "Yuppie Lawyer". Among the elements of Ben's life structure that he felt would hinder his ability to accomplish professional and personal goals were his wife and children (from S.R. field notes):

> She (his wife) was a "Yokel," he says, and when going to professional functions together "she would say things that would embarrass the hell out of me." He says he would think at those times, "God, how do I shut her up?" He says she just "didn't seem to have the skills to operate around" the kinds of people Ben needed to spend time with in his career...The kids were also a part of "the whole thing I was avoiding."

Similarly, Ben found himself surrounded by possessions from his marriage that were inconsistent with the creation of his desired status (from S.R. field notes):

> He thinks that it is incredible that in ten years of marriage they did not acquire anything he considers valuable. Blaming his former spouse, he complains, "She bought all this shit." He characterizes her as having "K-Mart taste," that people like her really thrive on getting a "blue-light special at K-Mart," rather than buying things of lasting quality.

Confronted with a life structure that was seemingly incompatible with his new aspirations, Ben chose to disassociate himself from his current situation and reconfigure his life structure. In Ben's case, the disassociation from his former life necessitated divorcing his wife, accepting limited visitation with his children, leaving his church, and giving up most of the shared possessions from his marriage. The only possessions that he reported keeping were possessions that predated his marriage or were newly acquired and a part of his professional life: an old comic book collection from his youth, professional books, and old record albums. As described by Mehta and Belk (1991), Ben "cleansed himself" of those things that constituted his former life.

While the disposition of possessions played a central part in Ben's departure from his former, now undesired, life structure, it also served an important function in easing his departure from his marriage: it eased the guilt he felt for leaving his wife and children. Even though divorce is common in our culture, divorce remains stigmatizing and frequently leaves divorcing partners with a sense of personal guilt (Gerstel 1987; Kaslow and Schwartz 1987; Berman and Turk 1981; Trafford 1982; Kessler 1975). One way that initiators can ease these feelings of guilt is by sacrificing possessions to their former spouses in the property division that accompanies the divorce (Wallerstein and Kelly 1980; Weiss 1975). That Ben's decision to relinquish his claim to most of the shared possessions from his marriage was an attempt to assuage his guilt was evident in the interview (S.R. field notes):

> He felt sorry for her, like "she was sorta helpless and kinda stupid" about the process. He says that is why she got the good car. He was also concerned that she and the kids didn't "go back to 'Butcher Holler,'" so he tried to make sure she had the things that would prevent that.

DISCUSSION

Ben's desire, in his own words, was to "check out" of his former status, and to establish a new identity. One way that he accomplished this was by disposing of those things that comprised his former life structure: his wife, children, religion, and possessions. The disposition of possessions played at least two parts in assisting Ben's departure from his former life structure. First, by leaving most shared possessions with his wife, Ben was able to leave behind artifacts that tied him to a previous, undesired identity. The void left by purging his former household goods created an opportunity for him to acquire new possessions, possessions that helped establish a new, distinctively different identity. Second, by relinquishing ownership of these possessions to his former wife, he was able to ease his conscience, facilitating his psychic break from the marriage. By granting ownership of these possessions to his wife, he felt comfort in knowing that he was able to provide her and the children a reasonable standard of living.

Ben presents one way that disposition can be used to break free from the relationship. Informants reported other strategies that assisted them in severing ties with their former spouses. One strategy that informants adopted was to cooperatively divide possessions. Informants reported cooperatively dividing possessions by distributing them evenly according to their economic value, by dividing them according to some personal identification with a specific spouse, and by taking turns selecting items from the household inventory. The cooperative division of possessions seemed to ease the divorce transition for informants. Informants who used this disposition heuristic reported that they felt fairly treated and that they received an equitable settlement in the division of marital assets.

Another method that spouses used to break themselves free of their marital relationship was to use the disposition process as a tool for communication (Young and Wallendorf 1989). By intentionally damaging or discarding valued possessions, spouses were able to communicate the unequivocal termination of the relationship. Spouses who initiate this strategy convey to their former partners the fruitlessness of reconciliation attempts, and as a result are able to overcome some of their partners' resistance to the divorce.

Disposition to Hold On

Sometimes a spouse does not seek a divorce, but would rather cling to their partner and repair the marriage. Informants were able to use the disposition process to help hold on to a partner and maintain some form of relationship. One way informants accomplished this goal was to retain control of key possessions as the partners disposed of marital assets. Rose Hillary (pseudonym) presents an interesting example of this strategy as she attempts to hold on to her marital relationship. Rose (wf, 42) is a homemaker, and undergraduate accounting student. Her divorce in 1988 came after a twenty year marriage. She and her former spouse have one child, a boy, who was thirteen years old when they divorced.

Rose's divorce was, in her own words, one of those "unshocking surprises." Her marriage had been deteriorating for the last ten years. The divorce, however, was not her idea. As a devout Catholic, Rose believes that she should have "stuck it out." Moreover, while her marriage may have had problems, Rose found the life structure that accompanied her marriage to be comfortable and secure. As a homemaker, she enjoyed being immersed in the challenges of raising her son and her many community activities.

In some ways, it appeared in the interviews, Rose does not consider herself divorced. For example, she has chosen not to date. Instead of establishing new intimate relationships through dating, Rose finds satisfaction in the good relationship she maintains with her former spouse.

To encourage this relationship, she allows her ex-husband to approach her for support and advice with even the most intimate details of his life, including details of relationships with new girlfriends. She thinks that his willingness to confide in her is due to her understanding of him: "I know him better than just about anybody else." Likewise, she seeks his advice when she has problems or makes important decisions. For example, he played a significant role in both her decision to enter school and the selection of her major.

Rose's tactics during the disposition of marital possessions further indicate a desire to maintain a close relationship with her former spouse. For example, when the couple were dividing up their possessions, Rose willingly accepted possession of the "battered" family mini-van, and allowed her husband to keep the Camaro IROC-Z. Her acquiescence to this settlement appears in part to reflect her acknowledgement that the Camaro is an important part of her ex-husband's extended self concept (Belk 1988):

> Interviewer: You are sort of attached to the Camaro, you talk about it as though you still like the car. It is really recognizable as something you identify with.
> Rose: Oh, yeah. It is a part of him because black is *the* color of a car if he has the choice. it's just him. He wants a Corvette but he can't afford it yet. It's just the kind of car he's always wanted, he likes fast cars. But the significance is it's him. (Rose transcript)

Another motive for her willingness to allow him to keep the Camaro is that its distinctive appearance makes it possible for her to monitor his life through his car:

> Rose: The way I found out he had a girlfriend was that he had to go on a business trip and I just casually asked him if he was going to leave his car at the airport. And he said, "well part of the time." Where is it going to be the rest of the time? "Well, somebody is going to pick it up." Do you have a girlfriend? He said, "yes." It's a good thing he told me because I know his license number and if I had seen her driving it I probably would have called the cops. (Rose transcript)

By allowing her ex-husband to have the car, she is able to both literally and symbolically (as part of his extended self concept) watch over him by watching out for his car.

Another way she maintains a relationship with her former spouse is that she allows her home to be a repository for her former husband's possessions. Rather than insisting that her ex-husband remove his possessions from her home, she keeps some of his furniture, clothes, and other items. Storing these possessions serves several purposes for Rose. First, by keeping some of her husband's possessions she is able to evoke memories and feelings that link Rose to her past and to her husband (Belk 1989; Csikszentmihaly and Rochberg-Halton 1981). However, Rose's selection of possessions to keep transcends the reflective qualities that they may possess. Her willingness to keep her husband's furniture, his work clothes and tools, and his broken calculator, is motivated by the unique properties that each of these possessions have that support her efforts to maintain connections with her former spouse.

When Rose's husband left her, he left most of the furniture for her. He subsequently purchased new furniture for his separate apartment. Recently, he has begun to cohabitate with a new girlfriend. As they melded their furnishings, they found that much of the newly acquired furniture was not needed. As a result, he took the furniture to Rose's house, where she now uses some of the pieces and stores others. Rose's acceptance of this warehousing role does not appear to be motivated solely by her generosity towards her spouse. When asked what possessions she would take with her when she makes an impending move from her large house to a smaller place, she offered insight into her "generosity":

> Rose: I'd like to take the couch that he bought because it's a hide-a-bed. He doesn't seem to care a whole lot, other than he said his girlfriend wants the couch he bought. She is a little bit of a fly in the ointment. She has major major hang ups with our relationship. (Rose transcript)

Apparently, by keeping the couch and other furnishings, Rose feels she is able to have some impact upon her former husband's new relationship.

Among the possessions that Rose stores are her former spouse's work clothes and tools. Keeping these articles serves Rose in two ways. First, their presence in her home dictates that her husband must visit the house in order to use these tools and clothes. Second, Rose has visions of refinishing the den, and seems to think that her ex-husband will accomplish this task. By keeping these possessions she facilitates this goal, and maintains some hope that he will make the desired modifications to the house.

Another possession Rose has kept is a calculator that was a gift that she had given to her husband. Early in the interview, when asked to describe gifts that she had given her spouse, she reminisced:

> Rose: he only had one quarter of college when we got married so he went through the rest after we got married. I was squirreling away five dollars a paycheck towards a stereo and then he needed the calculator so I gave him the money so he could buy his calculator. That's when they were a lot of money. But I didn't have the whole price, and the look on his face when I handed him the money was...(long pause). But you know the calculator doesn't work anymore and I don't know how much significance he still attaches to it..
> Interviewer: It's still around though?
> Rose: It's still in the desk. But he would never throw it away. But you see, he's not the kind that you would know what he thinks about you. (Rose transcript)

The non-functioning calculator is kept separate from other household possessions, hidden away in the desk, apparently taking on qualities of sacredness (Belk, Wallendorf and Sherry 1989). Further evidence that some of her ex-husband's possessions have assumed sacred status is suggested by her unwillingness to move one of her husband's shirts from her son's closet: the place it has occupied since he left.

DISCUSSION

Rose would prefer not to be divorced. As a result, she adopts strategies that help her to preserve her former identity and to maintain traditional spousal roles. Through selectively parting with some possessions and assenting to keep others, Rose was able to use the disposition process to aid in accomplishing this goal. By giving up the "nice car," Rose is able to continue to watch over her husband and continue to drive the "family car". By keeping her husband's tools and work clothes, she facilitates her ex-spouse's visits and accommodates performance of his traditional role as household handy-man. By keeping some of his newly acquired possessions (like the couch), Rose is able to maintain some control over her former spouse's relationships. Clearly, Rose was able to use the disposition process as an integral part of her quest to resist the divorce; to this point, she has not made the psychic break (Bohannon 1970) from her marriage.

Rose presents one way that disposition can be used to hold on to the relationship. Another strategy used by our informants to help them maintain a relationship with their former spouses can be best described as "chattel as battlefield." By quarreling over possessions, spouses are able to keep their marital relationship alive (Weiss 1979). The possessions that informants fought over were not always financially or psychically valuable. But, by fighting over these possessions, spouses were able to prolong relationships with their partners and delay the divorce transition.

CONCLUSION

This study emphasizes the important role that the disposition of possessions plays in the lives of consumers. As suggested by others (cf. Wallendorf and Young 1989; Mick 1986), the disposition of possessions has powerful symbolic properties and can convey very important meanings to consumers. By studying the division of marital assets that accompanies divorce, this study illustrates how disposition can be used to assist in the termination of existing life structures, and facilitate or impede difficult life transitions.

The two cases presented in this report provide contrasting examples of the integral role that the disposition of possessions can play in the negotiation of major life transitions. Both Ben and Rose dispose of some of their marital assets, but they do so for very different reasons. Ben uses disposition to liberate himself from his former life, and Rose uses disposition to bind herself to her former life. The possessions Ben chooses to keep either predate his marriage, or are strictly related to his career. The possessions Rose chooses to keep are designed to perpetuate her former life structure. For Ben, his former life structure represented an array of undesired constraints. Now that he is divorced, Ben feels a sense of independence that he never felt when he was married. For Rose, her former life structure represented a comfortable, secure environment, and her divorce has shaken her sense of identity. Rose continues to cling to her former life. Clearly, for these informants the disposition of marital possessions represented much more than the economic division of assets. The ordinary act of disposing of marital possessions can have very different and important meanings for consumers.

Much of the extant literature in the area of disposition has as its focus issues related to how consumers dispose of products and how the disposition of products relates to subsequent purchases (cf. Jacoby, Berning and Dietvorst 1977). While these are certainly important concerns, future research also should more fully explore the *subjective* importance of disposition to consumers. Insufficient attention has been paid to this significant facet of consumer behavior. Future research needs to better explore the symbolic, emotional, and behavioral consequences of disposition in the lives of consumers.

SELECTED REFERENCES

Adams, John, John Hayes and Barrie Hopson (1976), *Transition: Understanding and Managing Personal Change*, London: Martin Robertson.

Andreason, Alan R. (1984), "Life Status Changes and Changes in Consumer Preferences and Satisfaction," *Journal of Consumer Research*, 11 (Dec), 784-794.

Belk, Russell W. (1990), "The Role of Possessions in Constructing and Maintaining a Sense of Past," *Advances in Consumer Research*, Vol. 17, Marvin E. Goldberg, Gerald Gorn, and Richard W. Pollay, eds., Provo, UT: Association for Consumer Research, 669-676.

Belk, Russell W. (1988), "Possessions and the Extended Self," *Journal of Consumer Research*, 15, (Sept), 139-168.

Belk, Russell W., Melanie Wallendorf, and John F. Sherry, Jr. (1989), "The Sacred and the Profane in Consumer Behavior: Theodicy on the Odyssey," *Journal of Consumer Research*, 16 (June), 1-38.

Berman, William H. and Dennis C. Turk (1981), "Adaptation to Divorce: Problems and Coping Strategies," *Journal of Marriage and the Family*, (February), 179-189.

Bohannan, Paul (1970), "The Six Stations of Divorce," in *Divorce and After*, Paul Bohannan ed., New York: Doubleday

Buehler, Cheryl (1987), "Initiator Status and the Divorce Transition," *Family Relations*, 36, (January), 82-86.

Csikszentmihalyi, Mihaly and Eugene Rochberg-Halton (1981), *The Meaning of Things: Domestic Symbols and the Self*, New York: Cambridge University Press.

Gerstel, Naomi (1988), "Divorce and Kin Ties: The Importance of Gender," *Journal of Marriage and the Family*, 50, (February), 209-219.

Gerstel, Naomi (1987), "Divorce and Stigma," *Social Problems*, 34,2, (April), 172-186.

Glaser, Barney and Anselm Strauss (1971), *Status Passage*, Chicago: Aldine-Atherton.

Glaser, Barney and Anselm Strauss (1967), *The Discovery of Grounded Theory: Strategies for Qualitative Research*, Chicago: Aldine-Atherton.

Goode, William J. (1956), *After Divorce*, Glencoe: The Free Press.

Jacoby, Jacob, Carol K. Berning and Thomas F. Dietvorst (1977), "What About Disposition?," *Journal of Marketing*, (April), 22-28.

Johnson, Colleen Leahy (1988), "Socially Controlled Civility: The Functioning of Rituals in the Divorce Process," *American Behavioral Scientist*, 31 (July/August), 6, 685-701.

Kaslow, Florence W. and Lita Linzer Schwartz (1987), *The Dynamics of Divorce: A Life Cycle Perspective*, New York: Brunner/Mazel Inc.

Kessler, Sheila (1975), *The American Way of Divorce: Prescriptions for Change*, Chicago: Nelson-Hall

Kitson, Gay C., Karen Benson Babri and Mary Joan Roach (1985), "Who Divorces and Why: A Review," *Journal of Family Issues*, 6, 3 (September), 255-294.

Levinson, Daniel J. (1978), *The Seasons of a Man's Life*, New York: Ballantine.

McAlexander, James H. and John W. Schouten (1989), "Hair Style Changes as Transition Markers," *Sociology and Social Research*, 74 1 (October), 58-62.

McCracken, Grant (1988), *The Long Interview*, Beverly Hills: Sage

Mehta, Raj and Russell W. Belk (1991), "Artifacts, Identity, and Transition: Favorite Possessions of Indians and Indian Immigrants to the U.S.," *Journal of Consumer Research*, forthcoming.

Mick, David Glen (1986), "Consumer Research and Semiotics: Exploring the Morphology of Signs, Symbols and Significance," *Journal of Consumer Research*, 13 (September), 196-213.

Miles, Matthew B. and A. Michael Huberman (1984), *Qualitative Data Analysis*, Beverly Hills: Sage.

Petit, E. and B. Bloom (1984), "Whose Decision Was it? The Effects of Initiator Status on Adjustment to Marital Disruption," *Journal of Marriage and the Family*, 587-595.

Rosow, Irving (1976), "Status and Role Change Through the Life Span," in *Handbook of Aging and the Social Sciences* Robert H. Binstock and Ethel Shanas eds., New York: Van Nostrand Reinhold Co., 457-482.

Schouten, John W. (1991), "Selves in Transition: Symbolic Consumption in Personal Rites of Passage and Identity Reconstruction," *Journal of Consumer Research*, 17 (March), forthcoming.

Solomon, Michael R. (1983), "The Role of Products as Social Stimuli: A Symbolic Interactionism Perspective," *Journal of Consumer Research*, 10, 319-329.

Spanier, Graham B. and Linda Thompson (1984), *Parting: The Aftermath of Separation and Divorce*, Beverly Hills: Sage.

Spanier, Graham B. and Robert F. Casto, (1979), "Adjustment to Separation and Divorce: A Qualitative Analysis," in *Divorce and Separation*, eds. George Levinger and Oliver C. Moles, New York: Basic Books, p.211-227.

Trafford, Abigail (1982), *Crazy Time: Surviving Divorce*, New York: Harper and Row.

van Gennep, Arnold (1960), *Rites of Passage*, Chicago: University of Chicago Press.

Vaughan, Diane (1986), *Uncoupling*, New York: Vintage.

Wallerstein, Judith S. and Joan Berlin Kelly (1980), *Surviving the Breakup: How Children and Parents Cope With Divorce*, New York: Basic Books.

Weingarten, Helen R. (1988), "The Impact of Late Life Divorce: A Conceptual and Empirical Study," *Journal of Divorce*, 12, 1, 21-40.

Weiss, Robert (1979), "The Emotional Impact of Marital Separation," in *Divorce and Separation*, eds. George Levinger and Oliver C. Moles, New York: Basic Books, p.201-210.

Weiss, Robert (1975), *Marital Separation*, New York: Basic Books.

Wise, Myra J. (1980), "The Aftermath of Divorce," *The American Journal of Psychoanalysis*, 40, 2, 149-158.

Young, Melissa Martin and Melanie Wallendorf (1989), "Ashes to Ashes, Dust to Dust: Conceptualizing Consumer Disposition of Possessions" in *Proceedings 1989 AMA Winter Educators' Conference*.

Personal Rites of Passage and the Reconstruction of Self
John W. Schouten Iowa State University[1]

INTRODUCTION

Recent research has established the importance of consumption activities to the construction and maintenance of self and identity (cf. Belk 1988, Solomon 1983). However, much work is still needed if we are to understand the complex relationships between consumer behaviors and the psychosocial needs of changing, growing human beings. To the extent that the self-concept is created and comprehended through symbolic acts of consumption, the changes in self-concept that accompany human development may be wrought at least partially through the disposition and acquisition of consumer goods.

Solomon (1983), recognizing the importance of consumer goods in the learning and performance of social roles, articulated the need for further research on role transitions. Andreasen (1984) subsequently presented evidence that life status changes are linked to changes in lifestyle and the willingness to try new brands or products. Despite these intriguing beginnings, the consumer behavior literature has yet to come to grips with life transitions and self-concept change as holistic phenomena influencing and influenced by acts of disposition and acquisition.

In an in-depth, qualitative study of the consumption of cosmetic surgery (Schouten 1991) it is observed that through the surgical disposition of one physical attribute and the acquisition of another a person may symbolically shed one identity in favor of another. The process whereby this occurs is explained via van Gennep's (1960) conceptualization of rites of passage with special attention is given to the "identity play" of liminal consumers.

RITES OF PASSAGE

Van Gennep (1960) observed that important role transitions generally consist of three phases: 1) separation, in which a person disengages from a social role or status, 2) transition, in which the person adapts and changes to fit new roles, and 3) incorporation, in which the person integrates the new role or status into the self. Victor Turner (1969) described the transitional or liminal phase as a limbo between a past state and a coming one, a period of personal ambiguity, of non-status, and of unanchored identity. In primal societies, culturally prescribed rituals (rites of passage) provided individuals an experience of "communitas" or shared psychological support throughout major status passages. In the modern, secular world, however, people often experience liminoid states (cf. Turner 1974) devoid of such supportive rites. Left to their own devices to cope with difficult transitions and ambiguous self-concepts people appear to create personal rites of passage through symbolic acts of disposition and acquisition, and, in so doing, to construct new concepts of self.

SEPARATION: THE DISPOSITION OF IDENTITY

Much of the time people's self-concepts are relatively equilibrated -- they know who they are and they feel fairly stable and comfortable in their various social roles (Levinson 1978). There are times, however, when the relative stability of such states is upset by changes in the environment or from within an individual (cf. Adams, Hayes and Hopson 1976; Levinson 1978). The reconstruction of identity begins with separation from some role, relationship, or other key component of the extended self (cf. Belk 1988). Separation often occurs literally in time and space, triggered by some external force or event (e.g. the loss of a job or the death of a family member) that causes a shift in one's major roles. Separation may also be a subjective experience triggered by an internal force or psychological need (e.g. a fear of aging or a yearning for intimacy) that leads to the rejection of a particular aspect of the self. The loss or rejection of an important component of the self-concept is often finalized symbolically by the disposition of possessions that act as reminders of the former self. Such dispositional acts may serve a cleansing or stabilizing function (cf. Young 1990), thereby creating "fresh start" opportunities. However, acts of separation in and of themselves do not constitute a completed transitions. Instead they usher in the period of flux and self-concept plasticity known as a liminoid state.

TRANSITION: LIMINALITY AND IDENTITY PLAY

Liminal people face the task of reconstructing congruous, integrated self-concepts. If they have experienced unbidden separation from key roles, they must create new roles or emphasize existing roles to fill the gaps. If they have emotionally rejected traits or aspects of self with which they are dissatisfied, they may seek some way of excising them and replacing them with more desirable traits. In either case they begin to formulate possible selves (cf. Markus and Nurius 1986), i.e., they envision themselves as they might possibly become. An important characteristic of liminoid states is the tendency to play and experiment with new categories of meaning (Turner 1974). Liminal people appear to be more prone than others to engage in "identity play," that is, to formulate, elaborate, and evaluate possible selves with an eye to self-change or self-completion (cf. Wicklund and Gollwitzer 1982).

---

[1]This report is abstracted from the forthcoming paper "Selves in Transition: Symbolic Consumption in Personal Rites of Passage and Identity Reconstruction" (Schouten 1991).

Possible selves may begin as loosely articulated mental constructs or vague images. Some may be dismissed as flights of fancy, but ultimately others will be "fleshed out" through mental elaboration and then evaluated as to their desirability and the feasibility of their actualization. Identity play often involves the experimental consumption of goods and services, especially those offering symbolic or hedonic benefits. The various self-schemas that an individual "tries on" will tend to reflect personal goals, values and/or fantasies, and they may also incorporate themes and styles from popular culture, myth, and the media. Identity play, at least that which is publicly enacted, tends to be limited by one's perceptions of social constraints and shaped by social interaction (cf. Mead 1934).

The amount of time and energy a person invests in elaborating a possible self appears to vary according to such factors as the magnitude of the contemplated self-change, the level of perceived risk it entails, and the individual's imaginative tendencies. Extensive elaboration appears to give a possible self greater motivating power. The investment of psychic energy required by the elaboration process may lead to cathexis of the possible self, or the contemplated self-schema may simply become more believable as it is made more specific and detailed.

The perceived attainability of a possible self also affects its motivating power. If the likelihood of attaining a possible-self is perceived as too low, motivation to actualize it is diminished. The attainability of a particular self-state depends on such factors as one's personal resources and one's orientation to such social constraints as may exist. Perceived attainability may, therefore, change significantly during a role transition as social and financial conditions change. Failure to actualize a desired and otherwise attainable self may owe to a lack of self-efficacy (cf. Bandura 1977; Nuttin 1984), i.e., an inability to convert will to action. A possible self that is sufficiently desirable and attainable will likely become actualized.

INCORPORATION: THE ACQUISITION OF IDENTITY

People can respond to their possible selves in one of three ways: 1) with inaction, 2) with active rejection, or 3) with actualization and the incorporation of the possible self into a revised self-concept. Inaction results when possible selves are insufficiently desirable, undesirable, or plausible to motivate action, or when approach-avoidance conflicts result (cf. Lewin 1935). The short term consequence of inaction is continued liminality. Rejection occurs when a possible self is deemed unattainable, undesirable, or incongruent with other aspects of the self-concept. The rejection of a possible self leads to continued liminality and the probable formulation of yet another possible self. Failure to make a successful passage results in prolonged liminality. Painfully prolonged liminoid states have been observed in conjunction with psychological impediments to normal development (Shorter 1987), permanently debilitating or stigmatizing handicaps (Murphy 1987), and the inability to let go of past roles or statuses (Levinson 1978; Roberts 1988).

Ultimately, the more desirable and plausible a possible self seems to the individual, the more motivating power it wields and the more likely it is to be actualized (Markus and Nurius 1986). Actualization may occur via the consumption of instrumental goods and services as the individual goes about accumulating the appropriate symbols of the new self (cf. Solomon 1983). Incorporation occurs as the symbols are cathected (Belk 1988) or cultivated (Csikszentmihalyi and Rochberg-Halton 1981) as part of the new identity. Successful incorporation leads a person out of the liminoid state with a revised self-concept and an increased sense of self-congruity.

CONCLUSION

Consumption activities, including disposition and acquisition, play vital roles in the restoration of harmony to an ambiguous, incongruous, or dissatisfying self-concept. Personal rites of passage fashioned with consumer goods and services aid in the symbolic disposition of lost or rejected identities, in constructive identity play, and in the incorporation of new components of the extended self. Major role transitions are crucial times in determining the direction and quality of consumers' lives, but little is yet known about the consumption behaviors of liminal people or the importance of consumer behaviors to human growth and change. This report and the study from which it derives attempt, through a synthesis of anthropological and psychological perspectives, to move in that direction.

REFERENCES

Adams, John, John Hayes, and Barrie Hopson (1976), *Transition: Understanding & Managing Personal Change*, London: Martin Robinson & Co.

Andreasen, Alan R. (1984), "Life Status Changes and Changes in Consumer Preferences and Satisfaction," *Journal of Consumer Research*, 11 (December), 784-794.

Bandura, Albert (1977), "Self-Efficacy: Toward a Unifying Theory of Behavioral Change," *Psychological Review*, 84, 191-215.

Belk, Russell W. (1988), "Possessions and the Extended Self," *Journal of Consumer Research*, 14 (September), 139-168.

Csikszentmihalyi, Mihaly and Eugene Rochberg-Halton (1981), *The Meaning of Things: Domestic Symbols and the Self*, New York: Cambridge University Press.

Levinson, Daniel J. (1978), *The Seasons of a Man's Life*, New York: Ballantine.

Lewin, Kurt (1935), *A Dynamic Theory of Personality*, New York: McGraw-Hill.

Markus, Hazel and Paula Nurius (1986), "Possible Selves," *American Psychologist*, Vol. 41, No. 9, 954-969.

Mead, George Herbert (1934), *Mind, Self, and Society*, Chicago: University of Chicago Press.

Murphy, Robert F. (1987), *The Body Silent*, New York: Holt.

Nuttin, Joseph (1984), *Motivation, Planning, and Action: A Relational Theory of Behavior Dynamics*, Trans. R. P. Lorion and J. E. Dumas, Hillsdale, NJ: Lawrence Erlbaum.

Roberts, Scott D. (1988), *Resource Reallocation and Other Effects of Structural Unemployment*, Doctoral Dissertation, University of Utah, Department of Marketing.

Schouten, John W. (1991), "Selves in Transition: Symbolic Consumption in Personal Rites of Passage and Identity Reconstruction," *Journal of Consumer Research*, 17 (March), forthcoming.

Shorter, Bani (1987), *An Image Darkly Forming*, New York: Routledge & Kegan.

Solomon, Michael R. (1983), "The Role of Products as Social Stimuli: A Symbolic Interaction Perspective," *Journal of Consumer Research*, 10 (December), 319-329.

Turner, Victor W. (1969), *The Ritual Process: Structure and Anti-Structure*, Chicago: Aldine.

_____ (1974), "Liminal to Liminoid in Play, Flow, and Ritual: An Essay in Comparative Symbology," *Rice University Studies*, 60 (3), 53-92.

van Gennep, Arnold (1960), *The Rites of Passage*, trans. M. B. Vizedom and G. L. Caffee, Chicago: University of Chicago Press.

Wicklund, Robert A. and Peter M. Gollwitzer (1982), *Symbolic Self-Completion*, Hillsdale, NJ: Lawrence Erlbaum Associates.

Young, Melissa Martin (1990), *Possession Centrality to Self, Perceptions of Control, and the Experience of Disposition*, Master's Thesis, University of Arizona, Department of Marketing.

The Processing of Emotional and Cognitive Aspects of Product Usage in Satisfaction Judgments

Laurette Dubé, Université de Montréal
Bernd H. Schmitt, Columbia University

ABSTRACT

Consumer satisfaction is the unique construct in marketing that links consumer pre-consumption attitudes to post-consumption attitudes. Although both emotional and cognitive information may emerge from product usage, previous research has treated consumer satisfaction primarily as a cognitive process: consumers are posited to compare pre-consumption expectancies with product performances, and, as a result, derive affect from the outcome of satisfaction judgments. In the present session we propose that, in addition to cognition, a full account of post-consumption attitudes requires that we consider differentiated emotions emerging from the consumption experience as well as affective responses to the product as a whole and to its components. The session also addresses theoretical and methodological issues related to the structure and to the process involved in the influence of affect on satisfaction judgments. This paper summarizes the session by providing a brief overview of the structural and processing assumptions underlying consumer satisfaction, and by presenting abstracts of the four papers and the two discussants' comments.

How do consumers decide whether they are satisfied or dissatisfied with a product or service? According to most models, satisfaction judgments are affective outcomes of an elaborate cognitive process in which consumers compare the actual performance of a product to some internal standard. Approaches differ with respects to the nature of the internal standard and the comparison rules. Early views (e.g., the expectancy disconfirmation model, Oliver 1977; 1980) were based on multi-attribute models of attitude formation and presented internal standards as beliefs related to the probability of occurrence of a bundle of attributes. Later research provided empirical evidence for other comparison standards (e.g., best-brand norms) and for product performance beyond the effect of expectation-discrepancy (Cadotte, Woodruff and Jenkins 1987; Tse and Wilton 1988; Woodruff, Cadotte and Jenkins 1983). Only recently have researchers recognized the need to go beyond the cognitive component to provide empirical evidence for the role of emotions and feelings in the formation of satisfaction judgments (e.g., Dubé-Rioux 1989; Westbrook 1987).

Westbrook (1980; 1987) was the first to demonstrate the value of affective and emotional responses in predicting consumer satisfaction. His findings from a field study (Westbrook 1987) suggested that consumers' reports of their affective states may be complementary to measuring the cognitive evaluation of a product in predicting their satisfaction. Abelson et al. (1982), reporting a study on the formation of political preferences, also suggested that affective reports may be more accurate and a more direct assessment of satisfaction than cognitive evaluations because affective responses are less filtered than cognitive evaluations.

Progress has thus been made by introducing affective and emotional responses in the conceptualisation of consumer satisfaction. However, a detailed specification of the psychological processes involved in satisfaction judgments is still lacking. Most current models view satisfaction as a multi-stage process in which all pieces of information (expectations and performances with respects to cognitive evaluations, differentiated emotional experiences, and general affect) are combined additively. Even in the most recent views, cognitions and emotions are still hypothesized to combine with a primary affect generated by the goodness or badness of the product experience. This mental operation follows a continuous, monotonic, and linear combination of discrepancies between actual performances and past expectations, to provide the summary judgment operationally defined as satisfaction / dissatisfaction judgments. The predicted outcomes range from positive (obtained outcomes exceed expectations), to neutral (obtained outcomes exactly meet expectations), to negative (obtained outcomes fall short of expectations).

As suggested by Oliver (1989), we may need to envision more diversified types of processes in order to correctly depict the range of response states in which consumers are as they make satisfaction judgments. Although compensatory models have a good predictive validity and report a significant and robust relationship across products, situations, and methodological contexts (LaBarbera and Mazurski 1983), compensatory models may nonetheless adequately predict the outcome of non-compensatory processes (Johnson and Meyer 1984). The ability of these models to predict the outcome of satisfaction judgments at the aggregate level may be completely independent of their ability to describe the psychological processes involved in a consumer's mind. How, then, do consumers go about judging how satisfied or dissatisfied they are? It is suggested, in this session, that viewing satisfaction judgments as a categorization process may provide a more accurate description of the process involved than static, compensatory models.

Categorization is a fundamental cognitive activity involving a comparison between a target and some declarative knowledge (Mervis and Rosch 1981; Rosch and Mervis 1975). In essence, declarative knowledge stored in memory constitutes expectations which impose structure on incoming information. Memory structures are abstract cognitive representations of organized prior knowledge, derived from experience with specific instances (Brewer and Nakamura 1984; Rumelhart 1984). As expectations about product categories develop over time, the associations among related components are strengthened through experience until the entire structure can be activated in an all-or-none fashion and shift from a controlled to an automatic process (Schneider and Shiffrin 1977; Shiffrin and Dumais 1981; Shiffrin and Schneider 1977).

Though initially developed for object perception and concept identification, categorization models have recently been applied to domains such as beliefs, emotion, concepts of the self, and concepts of psychological situations (for a review see Higgins and Bargh 1987). Moreover, Barsalou (1983; 1985) has shown that in the course of engaging in goal-directed behavior, people often create specialized ad hoc categories. For example, the goal of losing weight can create the category of "food not to eat on a diet." This view may be particularly relevant to consumer behavior, because it suggests that categories do not have to be fully developed in order to be useful for judgments.

To extend this perspective to consumer satisfaction, one could argue for the operation of schematic memories of emotional and affective responses. Isen and Diamond (1989) have suggested that if the development of automaticity of affect or emotions was possible at all, it had to occur with very common, well-learned basic complexes of stimuli, or anticipated effects, responses, and outcomes. This seems to characterize most consumption experiences, at least for frequently purchased goods and services. The next question then becomes whether all emotional or affective responses emerging from product consumption are amenable to categorical processing?

The processing of low-intensity, neutral cases of satisfaction judgments seems to be accurately depicted by the schema-triggered affect models (Fiske 1982; Fiske and Pavelchak 1986), which is increasingly being used in other areas of consumer research (e.g., Sujan 1985; Sujan, Bettman and Sujan 1986). This model posits that as cognitive categories (in our case product categories) develop, affective tags are simultaneously encoded and automatically released each time an instance is recognized as descriptively consistent with a category. Affect is conceived simply as a certain state of readiness or as an affective predisposition toward the product; it does not carry any emotional intensity. In fact, consumers may be unable to report their true feelings for neutral satisfaction judgments, except for a valuation of familiarity (Mandler 1982). Therefore many consumption experiences may not involve satisfaction judgments at all but fall in a zone of indifference, as suggested a few years ago by Woodruff et al. (1983). Positive or negative affective responses occur only when perceived performances fall outside this zone.

What happens when more intense positive or negative feelings or emotions are experienced during the consumption of a new product or a new brand, or when expectations are violated? Recent evidence suggests that even intense affective responses may require less attention as they are experienced on a regular basis. For example, Wilson et al. (1989) has argued that emotional responses can be seen as theory-driven judgments because they are determined both by people's affective expectations and information about the stimulus itself. Moreover, it has been shown that affective responses to a stimulus can be automatically formed (Zajonc 1980) or may become automatically accessible (Fazio 1986).

In sum, the categorization approach to satisfaction suggests that consumers may devote attention to their responses to commercial goods or services only under some circumstance. First, more elaborate processing of both cognitive and affective reactions is likely when a product is descriptively inconsistent with the cognitive standard of the expected category, or when it triggers no existing category. Second, bottom-up processing of affective responses also may happen when positive or negative feelings generated during a consumption experience are strong enough to attract attention. Finally, consumers may proceed to elaborate affective judgments when they are motivated to do so by the importance they attach to a product category, or to specific consumption experiences.

When we talk about the development of affective categories, the intriguing question arises whether even intense affective states can become automatic? Could it be that repeated exposure to more intense emotional responses to consumption experiences lose their "attention-getting" quality? The two-factor theory introduced by Berlyne (Berlyne 1970) and extensively used in research on advertising suggests that increasing exposures initially produces a reduction in arousal due to uncertainty and conflict and thus increases liking, but, eventually, tedium and disliking.

In the present session, the first two papers by Westbrook and by Oliver illustrate the need to specify in detail the nature of affective and emotional experiences involved in product consumption and the precise role they play in satisfaction judgments. Westbrook applies a taxonomic scheme of emotions (DeRivera 1977) to a field study designed to disentangle the roles played in satisfaction judgments by valence alone (positive-negative overall affect) and by specific emotional experiences emerging during product consumption (e.g., anger, joy, pride, etc.). Based on a study of course instruction, Oliver demonstrates the value of the assessment of the affective response specifically associated with product attributes as well as the mediation role of causal attributions made with respect to these affective responses.

In the third paper, Dubé suggests that affective and emotional responses to consumption experiences can be amenable to a categorization process. Consumers are viewed as affective misers as they assess their affective or emotional responses to products that they consume regularly. The results of an experimental study show that when consumer learn to do these assessments, they develop permanent differentiated affective categories that can be later used as standards for faster satisfaction judgments. In addition, the author shows that when consumers report judgments that fall within the neutral zone previously defined, consumers may search for the absence of positively or negatively defining attributes, rather than compare expectations with product performances.

The final paper by Anand and Batra shows that affective responses, compared to cognitive responses, are less sensitive to the effect of repetition. The study was conducted in an advertising context, but raises conceptual and methodological issues with respect to the extension of this work to the domain of consumer satisfaction. For example, one could suggest that satisfaction based on the emotional experience of a product, when compared to cognitive appraisal, should be more enduring.

ABSTRACTS

Emotional Response, Involvement, and Satisfaction
Robert A. Westbrook, Rice University

Both positive and negative dimensions of affective responses to products and their associated consumption experiences have been shown to play an important role in consumers' judgments of satisfaction (Westbrook 1983, 1987). It is unclear, however, whether these relationships are attributable to valence alone, or the specific experiential basis of the emotional response (e.g., anger, pride, guilt, joy, etc.) as well. The origin of such affective response is not yet well understood, and whether they differ (if at all) from the notion of consumer involvement (Laurent and Kapferer 1985) is open to question. A limitation of previous work is the use of emotional measurement approach which focuses on basic or primary categories of emotional experience, instead of the full theoretical range of potential emotional experiences. Accordingly, this paper extends the literature by introducing the taxonomic scheme of DeRivera (1977) to research on consumption-based emotion, and empirically identifies new categories of differentiated emotional experiences within both positive and negative affective dimensions. These new emotional substrates are found to be substantially related to consumers' judgments of satisfaction. Moreover, they may be distinguished from, although also related to, the level of enduring consumer involvement with the product. Implications for future research on consumer satisfaction and emotions are discussed.

Cognitive, Affective, and Attribute Bases of Usage / Postpurchase Responses
Richard L. Oliver, Vanderbilt University

Based on recent work on the antecedents of postpurchase responses, an attempt to extend current thinking to include attribute satisfaction and dissatisfaction as separate determinants not fully reflected in either cognitive (i.e., expectancy disconfirmation) or affective paradigms is performed. In a study on satisfaction with course instruction, respondents provided the nature of emotional experiences, expectancy disconfirmation perceptions, and separate attribute satisfaction and dissatisfaction. Analysis confirmed the existence of potentially independent dimensions of positive and negative affect previously revealed by Westbrook (1987) and also suggested an additional negative affect dimension. It was also found that attribute satisfaction and dissatisfaction contributed to the variance explained in overall satisfaction beyond that of affect as did the expectancy disconfirmation variables. Extension of the analysis to intention showed that satisfaction, the expectancy disconfirmation variables, and mixed affect influences were evident. It is suggested that all dimensions tested are needed for a full accounting of postpurchase responses in usage.

Information Processing of Satisfaction Judgments: Are Consumers Affective Misers?
Laurette Dubé, Université de Montréal

Consumer satisfaction has been conceptualized as the affective summary of emotional and cognitive information emerging from the consumption of goods and services. Can we realistically assume, as previous research has done, that consumers make an elaborate and conscious judgment every time they use a product? Building on recent development in the domains of social cognition and emotions, we conducted correlational and experimental studies that showed that consumers act as affective misers as they perform (or do not perform) satisfaction judgments. The results suggest that consumers consciously process emotional and cognitive aspects of product usage only when they experience strong positive or affective responses. When consumers report neutral experiences, they may search for the absence of positively or negatively defining attributes, rather than compare expectations with product performances. Furthermore, when consumers experience positively or negatively valenced products on a repeated basis, they learn to do satisfaction judgments efficiently by developing differentiated affective categories.

The theoretical view we develop suggests that valenced information gets encoded in memory, and is juxtaposed to descriptive representations. With the development of affective categories, the processing strategy used in satisfaction judgments switches from a piecemeal processing of emotional and cognitive characteristics of consumption experiences to an increasingly automatic categorization process. This change in processing strategy is reflected in the amount of attention devoted to satisfaction judgments, and on the recall and recognition of specific consumption experiences.

We will report a study in which we empirically demonstrated the existence of affective categories in consumers' minds and experimentally tested how the development of these affective categories influences the information processing strategy used in performing satisfaction judgments. After having induced affective (valenced: positive and negative; and neutral) expectations for three different brands of restaurants, we observed facilitating effects of these expectations on subsequent satisfaction judgments for the valenced cases. As we predicted, no facilitation effects were found for the neutral cases. We discuss implication for research on the information processing of satisfaction judgments and of consumers' affective responses in general.

The Role of Repetition and Mood in the Processing of Preference Judgments
Punam Anand, Columbia University
Rajeev Batra, University of Michigan

In this paper, we will discuss the effect of repetition on cognitive and affective responses. We will report a study from the field of advertising to address theoretical and methodological issues related to the relationship between cognitive and affective responses and discuss implications of the study to satisfaction judgments. A study was designed to test the effect of repeated exposure to a stimulus on mood and affective judgments. We examined differences on the way affect and emotions are experienced after repeated exposures to two advertising executions, hard vs. soft-sell. Our findings support the notion that repetition effects on judgment occur not only because of the pattern of cognitive responses, as is typically assumed, but also because of the emotions evoked by the advertisement's executional style. Our results indicate that affective responses for products presented in soft-sell appeals may wearout more slowly than affective responses for product presented in hard-sell appeals. These effects occur because (1) positive mood evoked by soft-sell appeals does not wearout as fast as the mood evoked by hard-sell appeals, and (2) positive moods acts as a cue to retrieve positive cognitive responses. Extension of the present work to research on consumer satisfaction will be discussed.

DISCUSSANTS' COMMENTS

Bernd Schmitt, alluding in his discussion to both current movie titles and to Thomas Kuhn's work on paradigm shifts and scientific revolutions, stressed that none of presenters engaged in minor puzzle solving within the dominant expectancy-disconfirmation paradigm, which has dominated research on consumer satisfaction in the eighties and, like all paradigms, seems to "die hard." Instead, Westbrook and Oliver were characterized as "exorcists" who identified the shortcomings and limitations of the paradigm and convincingly argued for the inclusion of affect and emotions as important determinants of satisfaction judgments. Moreover, the "good fellas" Dubé, Anand and Batra were seen as introducing new concepts and methods from neighbouring disciplines, which may change the way consumer satisfaction will be conceptualized in future research. Schmitt further argued that affect may be a stronger determinant of satisfaction for services and experiences than consumer goods. In terms of practical implications, he suggested that managers identify which product features or service components are linked to which emotional experience in order to increase consumer satisfaction. Alice M. Isen, in a brief comment, welcomed the inclusion of affect and emotions in models of consumer satisfaction; she warned consumer researchers, however, not to repeat a mistake that had been committed in the psychological literature by measuring affective and emotional responses solely with verbal measures rather than seeking multiple measurements which should include behavioral responses.

BIBLIOGRAPHY

Abelson, Robert. P., Donald R. Kinder, Mark D. Peters, and Susan T. Fiske (1982), "Affective and Semantic Components in Political Person Perception," *Journal of Personality and Social Psychology*, 42, 619-630.

Barsalou, Lawrence. W. (1983), "Ad Hoc Categories," *Memory and Cognition*, 11, 211-227.

Barsalou, Lawrence. W. (1985), "Ideals, Central Tendency and Frequency of Instantiation as Determinants of Graded Structure in Categories," *Journal of Experimental Psychology: Learning, Memory, and Cognition*, 13, 629-655.

Berlyne Donald E. (1970), "Novelty, Complexity, and Hedonic Value," *Perception and Psychophysics*, 8, 279-286.

Brewer, William F. and Glenn V. Nakaruma (1984), "The Nature and Functions of Schemas" in Robert S. Wyer and Thomas K. Srull (eds.), *Handbook of Social Cognition*, vol. 1, 119-159, Hillsdale, NJ: Lawrence Erlbaum Associates.

Cadotte, Ernest R., Robert B. Woodruff and Roger L. Jenkins (1987), "Expectations and Norms in Models of Consumer Satisfaction," *Journal of Marketing Research*, 24, 305-314.

DeRivera, J. (1977), A Structural Theory of Emotions, New York: International University Press.

Dubé-Rioux, Laurette (1989), "The Power of Affective Reports in Predicting Satisfaction Judgments," in Kent B. Monroe (ed.), *Advances in Consumer Research*, vol. 17, 571-576, Ann Harbor, MI: Association for Consumer Research.

Fazio, Russell H. (1986), "How do Attitude Guide Behavior?" in Richard M. Sorrentino and E. Tory Higgins (eds.), *The Handbook of Motivation and Cognition: Foundation of Social Behavior*, 204-243, NY: Guilford Press.

Fiske, Susan T. (1982), "Schema-Triggered Affect: Application to Social Perception," in Margaret S. Clark and Susan T. Fiske (eds.), *Affect and Cognition: The 17th Annual Carnegie Symposium on Cognition*, 55-78, Hillsdale, New Jersey: Lawrence Erlbaumm Ass.

Fiske, Susan T. and Mark A. Pavelchak (1986), "Category-Based versus Piecemeal-Based Affective Responses: Develoment in Schema-Triggered Affect," in Richard M. Sorrentino and E. Tory Higgins (eds.), *The Handbook of Motivation and Cognition: Foundation of Social Behavior*, 167-203, NY: Guilford Press.

Higgins, E. Tory and John A. Bargh (1987), "Social Cognition and Social Perception," *Annual Review of Psychology*, 38, 369-425.

Isen, Alice. M. and Gregory Diamond (1989), "Affect and Automaticity," in James S. Uleman and John A. Bargh (eds.), *Unintended Thought*, 124-154, New York: The Guilford Press.

Johnson, Eric and Robert Meyer (1984), "Compensatory Choice Models of Noncompensatory Processes: The Effect of Varying Context," *Journal of Consumer Research*, 11, 528-541.

LaBarbera, Priscilla A. and David Mazurski (1983), " A Longitudinal Assessment of Consumer Satisfaction-Dissatisfaction: The Dynamic Aspect of the Cognitive Process," *Journal of Marketing Research*, 20, 393-404.

Mandler, George (1982), " The Structure of Value: Accounting for Taste," in Margaret S. Clarke and Susan T. Fiske (eds.), *Affect and Cognition: The 17th Annual Carnagee Symposium*, 3-36, Hillsdale, New Jersey: Lawrence Erlbaumm Ass.

Mervis, Carolyn B. and Eleanore Rosch (1981), "Categorization of Natural Objects," *Annual Review of Psychology*, 35, 113-135.

Oliver Richard L. (1977), "Effect of Expectations and Disconfirmation on Postexposure Product Evaluations: an Alternative Interpretation," *Journal of Applied Psychology*, 62, 480-486.

Oliver Richard L. (1980). "A Cognitive Model of Antecedents and Consequences of Satisfaction Judgments," *Journal of Marketing Research*, 17, 204-212.

Oliver, Richard L. (1989). "Processing of the Satisfaction Response in Consumption: A Suggested Framework and Research Propositions," *Journal of Consumer Satisfaction, Dissatisfaction and Complaining Behavior*, 2, 1-16.

Rosch, Eleanore and Carolyn B. Mervis (1975), "Family Resemblance: Studies in the Internal Structure of Categories," *Cognitive Psychology*, 7, 573-605.

Rumelhart, D. E. (1984), "Schemata and the Cognitive System," in Robert S. Wyer and Thomas S. Srull (eds.), *Handbook of Social Cognition*, vol. 1, 161-188, Hillsdale, NJ: Erlbaum.

Schneider, Walter and Richard M. Shiffrin (1977), "Controlled and Automatic Human Information Processing: I. Detection, Search, and Attention," *Psychological Review*, 84, 1-66.

Shiffrin, Richard M. and S. T. Dumais (1981), "The Development of Automatism," in John Anderson (ed.), *Cognitive Skills and Their Acquisition*. vol. 1, Hillsdale, NJ: Lawrence Erlbaum.

Shiffrin, Richard M. and Walter Schneider (1977), "Controlled and Automatic Human Information Processing: II. Perceptual Learning, Automatic Attending and a General Theory," *Psychological Review*, 84, 127-190.

Sujan, Mita (1985), "Consumer Knowledge: Effects on Evaluation Strategies Mediating Consumer Judgments," *Journal of Consumer Research*, 12, 31-46.

Sujan, Mita, James R. Bettman, and Harish Sujan (1986), "Effects of Consumer Expectations on Information Processing in Selling Encounters," *Journal of Marketing Research*, 23, 346-53.

Tse, David K. and Peter T. Wilton (1988), "Models of Consumer Satisfaction: An Extension," *Journal of Marketing Research*, 25, 204-212.

Westbrook, Robert A. (1980), "Interpersonal Influences on Consumer Satisfaction with Products," *Journal of Consumer Research*, 7, 49-54.

Westbrook, Robert A. (1987), "Product/Consumption-Based Affective Responses and Postpurchase Processes," *Journal of Marketing Research*, 24, 258-270.

Wilson, Timothy D., Douglas J. Lisle, Dolores Kraft and Christopher G. Wetzel (1989), "Preferences as Expectation-Driven Inferences: Effects of Affective Expectations on Affective Experience," *Journal of Personality and Social Psychology*, 56, 519-530.

Woodruff, Robert B., Ernest R. Cadotte, and Roger L. Jenkins (1983), "Modeling Consumer Satisfaction Processes using Experience-Based Norms," *Journal of Marketing Research*, 20, 296-304.

Zajonc, Robert B. (1980), "Feeling and Thinking: Preference Needs no Inference," *American Psychologist*, 35, 151-175.

Rashomon Visits Consumer Behavior: An Interpretive Critique of Naturalistic Inquiry
Douglas B. Holt, Northwestern University[1]

ABSTRACT

A body of substantive and methodological work is currently evolving within consumer behavior, drawing from Lincoln and Guba's (1985) "naturalistic inquiry" program for post-positivist research, which seeks to establish criteria to evaluate the "trustworthiness" of ethnographic-style consumer research. Applying insights from the growing body of interpretive anthropological criticism, this paper critiques the epistemological foundations of the evaluation of trustworthiness, as well as the specific techniques suggested to meet this objective. The main arguments of interpretive anthropology are summarized, the evaluation of trustworthiness as expounded by Lincoln and Guba (1985) and Wallendorf and Belk (1989) is reviewed, and then the interpretive critique is applied to this evaluative standard as it is used in consumer research.

RASHOMON AND REPRESENTATION

In the classic Japanese film *Rashomon* by Akira Kurosawa, an encounter in a forest between a newlywed couple and a bandit is described by the four individuals who observed the encounter: the husband, the wife, the bandit, and a woodchopper who was passing by. Kurosawa re-enacts each version of the incident so that each appears as reality: although the individuals are describing the same set of events from first-hand experience, the stories are startlingly different. None of the versions is given greater credence at the end of the film; each represents a "correct" interpretation for the individual participant-observer.

The *Rashomon* parable has been used in anthropology (Heider 1988) to convey the essence of the interpretive dilemma facing social scientists in seeking a "true" understanding of the phenomena under investigation. However, the implications of this dilemma have been generally avoided in the representation and evaluation of ethnographic research. Recently, though, a body of thought which travels under the covering label of "interpretive anthropology" (Marcus and Fischer 1986) has applied a Rashomon-style critique to ethnography.

The purpose of this essay is to critically examine the emerging "naturalistic inquiry" tradition in consumer research from the perspective of current interpretive anthropological thought. A brief synopsis of the nature of the interpretive anthropological critique will be presented. Then, the application of the critique to consumer research will focus on the evaluative criteria espoused by Lincoln and Guba's naturalistic inquiry framework (1985), and the extension of this framework by Belk and Wallendorf (1989). The final section will demonstrate how the interpretive critique can be brought to bear on the representation of naturalistic inquiry in consumer research.

THE INTERPRETIVE CRITIQUE OF ETHNOGRAPHIC AUTHORITY

Traditionally, anthropologists, influenced by the extended coattails of positivist science, either stated or implicitly accepted the view that their ethnographic training and method gave their interpretations a certain truth value not achievable by laymen (Clifford 1988). In participant observation, the classic ethnographic method, it was assumed that understandings were transparent, that the ethnographer as measurement instrument could reflect the informants' experiences without misshaping them. Given the (assumed) impartial, omniscient quality of the anthropologist's method, the traditional ethnography was written from an implicit position of authority derived from this "scientific" character, as evangelized by Malinowski (1922).

The critique of this authority by interpretive anthropology as misplaced was succinctly stated early-on in Geertz' (1973) famous adaptation of the constructionist view of reality (i.e., the ontological assumption that reality is constructed through ideographic social processes): that social life should be conceived as a web of negotiated meanings which, when considering the process through which one comes to understand these meanings, is analogous to a text. This metaphor is provocative because it implicates the researcher as well as the observed. Participant observation -- the communicative processes by which the anthropologist in the field gains knowledge of his or her subject's systems of cultural meaning in order to represent them in ethnographic texts (Marcus and Fischer 1986) -- could no longer be isolated from this revelation. As Clifford (1988) states:

> "Textualization" is understood as a prerequisite to interpretation...It is the process through which unwritten behavior, speech, beliefs, oral tradition, and ritual come to be marked as a corpus, a potentially meaningful ensemble separated out from an immediate discursive or performative situation...A world cannot be apprehended directly; it is always inferred on the basis of its parts, and the parts must be conceptually and perceptually cut out of the flux of experience. (p.38)

Extending the textual metaphor, culture is composed of contested codes. The ethnographer's representations of these codes can be considered

---

[1] I would like to thank John Sherry and Helen Schwartzman for their comments on an earlier draft of this paper, as well as for their sage political advice.

"partial truths" or "ethnographic fictions," in the sense (borrowed from literary criticism) that they are "something made or fashioned" in their systematic and exclusive manner of reporting (Clifford 1986). To cite Clifford (1986) again:

> Ethnographic writing is determined in at least six ways: (1) contextually (it draws from and creates meaningful social milieux); (2) rhetorically (it uses and is used by expressive conventions); (3) institutionally (one writes within, and against, specific traditions, disciplines, audiences); (4) generically (an ethnography is usually distinguishable from a novel or travel account); (5) politically (the authority to represent cultural realities is unequally shared and at times contested); (6) historically (all the above conventions and constraints are changing). (p.6)

Following Geertz' (1973, 1983) early lead, other social scientists have developed the interpretive critique to challenge the received style of ethnographic representation (Clifford 1988; Clifford and Marcus 1986; Marcus and Cushman 1982; Marcus and Fischer 1986; Van Manaan 1988) including the works of Geertz himself (Crapanzano 1986). According to these critics, ethnographic authority cannot be achieved through method. The subjective, contextual nature of the researcher's interpretive task can be no different from that of the subject. A "correct" interpretation of meaning is forever elusive because an infinite number of interpretations, based on differing "contextual assortments," are possible. When meaning is construed as a dialectic process between the object and its interpreter, rather than an immanent attribute, evaluation of the accuracy of an interpretation, based purely on the methods used, becomes impossible.

THE NATURALISTIC INQUIRY EVALUATIVE FRAMEWORK

Lincoln and Guba's *Naturalistic Inquiry*

The naturalistic inquiry framework proposed by Lincoln and Guba (1985) is a hybrid fieldwork primer -- borrowing from anthropology, sociology, educational research, and other fields -- stressing an emic, constructionist view of understanding through ethnographic and related "in situ" methods. As such, the methods reviewed in this text provide an excellent resource for guiding fieldwork. However, though espousing a constructionist view of reality, Lincoln and Guba's epistemological position fits squarely in the traditional ethnographic schools of anthropology and sociology. They advocate that the field researcher follow certain techniques that increase the trustworthiness of the research (dimensionalized as credibility, transferability, dependability, and confirmability). The reader is to judge the rigor of the research by the extent to which he or she is persuaded by its performance on these four specific evaluative criteria (which Lincoln and Guba set up as analogous to positivism's criteria of internal validity, external validity, reliability, and objectivity). The definitions of these evaluative criteria (also found in Hirschman 1986) are:

a. credibility: Does the interpretation agree with the "subject's" opinion?

b. transferability: Given sensitivity to changing context, is the interpretation generalizable?

c. dependability of measure: Is the researcher, as measurement instrument, consistent?

d. confirmability: Is the interpretation logical, nonprejudiced, nonjudgmental, supportable based on data?

The techniques that allow the researcher to meet these criteria, according to Lincoln and Guba, are: prolonged engagement/persistent observation; triangulation across sources, methods, and researchers; regular on-site team interaction; negative case analysis; debriefing by peers; member checks; seeking limiting exceptions; purposive sampling; reflexive journals; and independent audits (Wallendorf and Belk 1989). Lincoln and Guba claim that the combined evaluative dimension captured by these four criteria -- trustworthiness -- can be used:

> to make ex post facto judgments about reports or case studies as a prelude to a decision to publish or otherwise use them. Journal referees, dissertation committee members, members of other bodies called on to make judgments can use the criteria for that purpose. (p.330)

Although they warn against the constitution of a "neo-orthodoxy" in the use of the criteria (i.e., as "prescriptions of how inquiry *must* be done," p.331), they do not shy away from their argument that these are useful evaluative measures.

Wallendorf and Belk's Extension

In their contribution to *Interpretive Consumer Research* entitled "Assessing Trustworthiness in Naturalistic Consumer Research," Wallendorf and Belk (1989) propose a modified version of Lincoln and Guba's framework to be used in consumer research at the "workbench level." (Deshpande (1983) and Hirschman (1986) were the first consumer researchers to attempt to merge interpretive consumer research with positivist criteria.) Their purpose appears to be two-fold: to suggest some useful methods that have worked in their fieldwork experiences and to propose a modified version of Lincoln and Guba's evaluative criteria for consumer research. This paper only examines the techniques in their capacity to serve as evaluative criteria. (When judged as a methodological resource, the discussion of techniques provides valuable information for the naturalistic inquirer.) That Wallendorf and Belk seek to establish rigorous procedures to assess credibility in this alternative paradigm is understandable given the socio-political climate in which this research sits (i.e., the traditionally positivist turf of the *Journal of Consumer Research*). However, such normative guidelines run counter to much contemporary social thought outside the area of marketing/consumer research.

Trustworthiness, according to Wallendorf and Belk, is a "component of good research" (in addition to being interesting and insightful, p.69) that can and should be assessed as part of the evaluative process of naturalistic research. Wallendorf and Belk accept Lincoln and Guba's four evaluative criteria but somewhat modify the associated methodological techniques used to meet these criteria based on field experience. They also add a fifth criterion -- integrity (of the informant). According to Wallendorf and Belk,

> the use of these techniques enables researchers who are conducting as well as those who are reading the output of naturalistic inquiry to evaluate the completeness of the research procedures used and the human instrument employed. (p.70)

Similar to Lincoln and Guba, Wallendorf and Belk insist that they do not intend to present a "new orthodoxy" (p.70) in terms of the design and implementation of interpretive research, but they firmly adhere to the set of evaluative criteria that should be used to judge the trustworthiness of interpretive work.

In the following section, the specific techniques suggested by Wallendorf and Belk to meet these trustworthiness criteria are considered using implications derived from the interpretive critique developed earlier in the paper.

AN INTERPRETIVE CRITIQUE OF NATURALISTIC INQUIRY

Methods As Evaluative Criteria in Naturalistic Inquiry

Both Lincoln and Guba and Wallendorf and Belk insist that, through following certain methods, the naturalistic inquirer can develop more trustworthy interpretations. Wallendorf and Belk advocate that readers and reviewers should isolate, and evaluate separately, the trustworthiness component of the research (apart from the overall quality of the research, which is necessarily subjective). Trustworthiness, then, in both the Lincoln and Guba and Wallendorf and Belk conceptions, is an objective, measurable component of naturalistic research. (Wallendorf and Belk frequently mention that the measurement of trustworthiness is difficult and inherently imperfect, but this does not cause them to back away from their objectivist conception of trustworthiness as an evaluative criterion.)

Insights supplied by the interpretive critique would suggest that this evaluative enterprise is not achievable. The act of representing others (whether behaviors or beliefs) is necessarily a construction of the others' reality, one of many. This construction is shaped by many cultural and idiosyncratic forces (as the quote from Clifford (1986) above demonstrates) such that the achievement of transparent representation is not tenable. Trustworthiness -- as a criterion based on the objective, invariant, and generalizable qualities of an interpretation -- seeks to gauge transparency. The interpretive critique suggests that trustworthiness is at odds with the nature of the epistemological beast.

In addition, even if one assumes that transparent representation were tenable, it appears that its evaluation would be highly problematic. Given that in naturalistic inquiry, (1) the research instrument is a human with unique abilities and perspectives and (2) evaluation of the research rests in the hands of the (also idiosyncratic) reader/reviewer, any attempt to isolate and objectively verify the trustworthiness of researcher interpretations is fraught with epistemological problems. Thus, the trustworthiness criterion and associated techniques proposed by Lincoln and Guba and Wallendorf and Belk contradict the nature of the interpretive task, and furthermore, pose insurmountable problems in application.

Support for this critique follows by reviewing the specific list of research techniques and evaluative criteria offered for judging naturalistic inquiry. These techniques will be evaluated in four broad groups: field methods, purposive sampling and triangulation, thick description, and checks and audits.

Field Methods. The credibility criterion suggests that if the researcher follows certain field methods, the reader should have more confidence in the interpretation. For example, Wallendorf and Belk suggest a list of techniques -- prolonged engagement, persistent observation, regular on-site team interaction, negative case analysis, debriefing by peers -- that are thought to enhance the credibility of the research. Based on the argument developed above, the use of particular field methods can give no guarantee of increased credibility. The techniques certainly *may* improve the quality of the interpretation and thus attain increased credibility in the eye of the reader indirectly based on their impact on the research document; but the credibility of the interpretation cannot be inferred separate from its reading. For example, a reviewer may judge an inquiry of a phenomenon using persistent observation over three months to be more credible than an inquiry of the same phenomenon lasting a year because the first interpreter was able to coax richer or more complex information from his or her informants. Similarly, the other suggested field techniques -- negative case analysis, team interaction, and peer debriefing -- however useful in specific research applications, do not carry special status as guarantors of credibility.

Purposive Sampling and Triangulation. To meet the transferability criterion, Wallendorf and Belk and Lincoln and Guba focus on purposive sampling (which allows triangulation across sites in similar fashion to external validity). Both groups also suggest that various types of triangulation (across researchers, sources, and methods) increase the credibility, transferability, confirmability (and, in the case of Wallendorf and Belk, integrity) of the research. Neither provides an acceptable criterion for evaluating research. As Thompson (1990) cogently argues, the notion that multiple data points increase the trustworthiness of the research is inconsistent with the naturalistic inquirer's constructionist ontological position. Since each empirical source represents a unique construction of reality (i.e., the observer-observed relationship is ideographic), there is no reason to believe that a consistent result across sources is more trustworthy.

Thick Description. Lincoln and Guba also emphasize the need for "thick description" to achieve transferability. However, given the dialectic relationship between observer and observed, the thick description created in one context cannot be objectively transferred to a new context, nor could a judge objectively evaluate such a transfer. Lincoln and Guba suggest that the transfer of an interpretation must be sensitive to changing context, but who judges whose context?

Checks and Audits. Techniques meant to enhance the status of the research ex post facto are also flawed. Lincoln and Guba and Wallendorf and Belk suggest that informants review the interpretation to check for accuracy. This criterion contradicts the interpretivist's constructionist ontological assumption; a construction of a construction of a construction (a "triple hermeneutic" of sorts) does not add credibility.

Also, this criterion, as Wallendorf and Belk recognize, denies credibility to interpretive work (such as French structuralism and Marxist analysis) that takes an etic perspective. But Wallendorf and Belk are mistaken in their assertion that the member checks are appropriate techniques for ascertaining emic credibility (p.75). Emic information, while giving the appearance of transparent observation, is just as much an interpretation as the etic perspective. Informant commentary on emic interpretations does not avoid the dynamics of the "triple hermeneutic."

Both Lincoln and Guba and Wallendorf and Belk assert that confirmability can be assessed via an auditing procedure where all research materials are submitted to a peer for review of the "plausibility of the interpretations and the adequacy of the data." (Wallendorf and Belk 1989, p.79) This procedure also fails as a criterion using arguments developed above. The interpretation an auditor brings to a researcher's data is just as idiosyncratic as the researcher's original interpretation. Even if the auditors are multi-disciplinary, they still cannot capture the full range of possible interpretations. They are bounded by the social science discipline as a whole, Western ways of thinking, a time-bound theoretical position, and undoubtedly many other factors. Also, as Thompson (1990) argues, given the level of immersion characteristic of naturalistic inquiry, it is hard to believe that detached auditors could ever adequately grasp the relationship between the observer's experience and his or her interpretations.

The framework proposed by Lincoln and Guba and extended by Wallendorf and Belk serves as a valuable storehouse of naturalistic research techniques. But their belief that the successful application of these techniques leads to a more trustworthy interpretation, and that criteria exist that can be used objectively to judge this trustworthiness, cannot be supported based on arguments developed using the interpretive critique.

THE REPRESENTATION OF NATURALISTIC INQUIRY IN CONSUMER RESEARCH

At the time of this writing, three studies have been published in *The Journal of Consumer Research* using the Lincoln and Guba/Wallendorf and Belk framework (Belk, Sherry, and Wallendorf 1988; Belk, Wallendorf, and Sherry 1989; O'Guinn and Belk 1989). Again, the fact that these authors have chosen to use "naturalistic inquiry" methods is incidental to this paper. What is problematic, however, is that these articles leverage the evaluative criteria proposed by Lincoln and Guba and Wallendorf and Belk in order to represent their interpretations as more trustworthy. This "ethnographic authority," based solely on methods, is unfounded according to the interpretive critique.

For instance, in Belk et al. (1988), despite reservations expressed by an auditor, the authors assert:

> ...we are convinced that the careful use of auditing techniques and scrutiny of their outcome by reviewers and editors could prevent the publication of works that, in the final analysis, are not based on careful field methods and data collection. (p.456)

Again, regarding the audit procedure in O'Guinn and Belk (1989):

> The audit permitted careful scrutiny of our conclusions by a scholar/peer able to assess the faithfulness of our interpretations and the adequacy of our methods. (p.228)

The implication of these comments is that peer auditing should be recognized as a necessary procedure (analogous to manipulation checks in experimental science) to insure a satisfactory level of trustworthiness in naturalistic inquiry.

Unfortunately, for much the same reason that manipulation checks do not necessarily provide additional credibility to an experimental result (Sternthal, Calder, and Tybout 1987), audits do not necessarily add credibility to an interpretation. The researcher's field notes may provide an interpretation of his or her observations that is convincing enough to sway the auditor, or the auditor may just happen to draw interpretive links in similar fashion to the researcher. But both of these results are part of the constructed, idiosyncratic nature of the interpretive task; neither guarantees a more trustworthy interpretation.

Similar arguments could be drawn concerning the use of other techniques found in these articles -- such as triangulation and purposive sampling -- to the extent that their use leads to claims of ethnographic authority which lie in the method alone.

CONCLUSION

The desire to develop objective evaluative criteria for naturalistic inquiry is no-doubt seductive. Positivist-inclined researchers who pass judgement and thus participate in the legitimization of this research in the consumer behavior field are grounded in objectivist evaluation. Their most fervent concerns with post-positivist research are in regard to the "anarchy" that may result when there are no objective evaluative criteria to test theory (Calder and Tybout 1987, 1989; Hunt 1989). The Lincoln and Guba/Wallendorf and Belk evaluative framework (as well as Hirschman's (1986) original introduction of the framework to the field) can be seen as a panacea to ameliorate these positivist concerns. For instance, Cote and Foxman (1987), two positivists who participated in the Consumer Odyssey, reach a satisfactory comfort level with naturalistic inquiry because of the rigor derived from the "systematic rules for the conduct of research...[the] numerous techniques used to control the accuracy of the data...techniques used to verify "facts" after they have been recorded" (p.362), and so on, leading to such conclusions as, "the auditor plays an important role in the evaluation of naturalistic research." (p.364) In addition, Hunt (1989) comments that the Wallendorf and Belk framework is exemplary because it:

> clearly demonstrates that there are both good procedures to adopt in actually conducting naturalistic inquiry and that these procedures can be used as evaluative criteria for assessing the justificatory warrant of the knowledge-claims generated by such research. (p.187)

However successful this framework is in legitimizing naturalistic inquiry in the short-run, I can't help but feel it eventually will be self-defeating. In adopting an objectivist evaluative banner, interpretive consumer research risks displacing insightful interpretation with methodological dogma that will constrain research without yielding a balancing increase in verity.

The interpretive critique of naturalistic inquiry suggests that the research process is analogous to the reading of a text, where the observer interacts with the observed to form an ideographic, negotiated reality. Acceptance of the interpretive view gives rise to methodological and representational implications. The use of specific techniques, such as those proposed by Lincoln and Guba (1985) and Wallendorf and Belk (1989), does not necessarily lead to more trustworthy research and thus they should not be used as criteria for evaluation. Likewise, since these techniques do not insure greater trustworthiness, the researcher as author should be discouraged from using them to garner added authority in the written representation of the research.

As an alternative, I believe that interpretations should be judged on their insightfulness (for an example of this approach, see Thompson's (1990) explication of the gestalt experience) and their ability to convince the reader, no more. These criteria are by nature subjective, but do not necessarily lead to the nihilism of more solipsistic perspectives. Because interpretation is empirically grounded, the reader can confront the interpretation with his or her own experiences (including research) with the world. While it should be clear from the critique above that this empirical confrontation is an interpretive act, I believe that the subjective judgements of one's peers converge enough to allow for some interpretations to be favored over others. (Note that this convergence does not necessarily signify greater truth value, but rather shows that the interpretation is subjectively judged to be both insightful and convincing.) Cultural anthropology and interpretive sociology operate using this type of evaluative system and continue to thrive; pluralism of perspectives is dominant in these fields, not anarchy.

This "stakeholder consensus" model of knowledge differs from "contemporary social science" (Hunt 1989; or "scientific realism," Hunt 1990) only in that specific techniques cannot act as guarantors of privileged status in what is necessarily an interpretive process. Research methods are certainly pertinent to the judgement process, but they do not act as objective criteria. Like all other elements of the interpretation, research methods are judged by the reader. It is only in interaction with the reader that the interpretation can develop privileged status as a credible and insightful work.

REFERENCES

Belk, Russell W., John F. Sherry, Jr., and Melanie Wallendorf (1988), "A Naturalistic Inquiry into Buyer and Seller Behavior at a Swap Meet," *Journal of Consumer Research*, 14 (March) 449-470.

Belk, Russell W., Melanie Wallendorf, and John F. Sherry Jr. (1989), "The Sacred and the Profane in Consumer Behavior: Theodicy on the Odyssey," *Journal of Consumer Research*, 16 (June) 1-38.

Calder, Bobby J. and Alice M. Tybout (1989), "Interpretive, Qualitative, and Traditional Scientific Empirical Consumer Behavior Research," in *Interpretive Consumer Research*, ed. E. Hirschman, Provo, UT: Association for Consumer Research.

Calder, Bobby J. and Alice Tybout (1987), "What Consumer Research Is...," *Journal of Consumer Research*, 14, 136-140.

Clifford, James (1988), *The Predicament of Culture*, Cambridge, MA: Harvard University Press.

Clifford, James (1986), "Introduction: Partial Truths," in *Writing Culture: The Poetics and Politics of Ethnography*, eds. J. Clifford and G. Marcus, Berkeley: University of California Press.

Clifford, James and George E. Marcus, eds. (1986), *Writing Culture: The Poetics and Politics of Ethnography*, Berkeley: University of California Press.

Cote, Joseph A. and Ellen R. Foxman (1987), "A Positivist's Reactions To A Naturalistic Inquiry Experience," in *Advances in Consumer Research*, Vol. 14, eds. M. Wallendorf and P. Anderson, Provo, UT: Association for Consumer Research.

Crapanzano, Vincent (1986), "Hermes Dilemma: The Masking of Subversion in Ethnographic Description," *Writing Culture: The Poetics and Politics of Ethnography*, ed. J. Clifford and G. Marcus, Berkeley: University of California Press, 51-76.

Deshpande, Rohit (1983), "Paradigms Lost: On Theory and Method in Research in Marketing," *Journal of Marketing*, 47 (Fall), 101-110.

Geertz, Clifford (1983), *Local Knowledge*, New York: Basic Books.

Geertz, Clifford (1973), *The Interpretation of Cultures*, New York: Basic Books.

Heider, Karl G. (1988), "The Rashomon Effect: When Ethnographers Disagree," *American Anthropologist*, 90, 73-79.

Hirschman, Elizabeth C. (1986), "Humanistic Inquiry in Marketing Research: Philosophy, Method, and Criteria," *Journal of Marketing Research*, 23 (August), 237-249.

Hunt, Shelby D. (1989), "Naturalistic, Humanistic, and Interpretive Inquiry: Challenges and Ultimate Potential," *Interpretive Consumer Research*, ed. E. Hirschman, Provo, UT: Association for Consumer Research, 185-198.

Hunt, Shelby D. (1990), "Truth in Marketing Theory and Research," *Journal of Marketing*, 54 (July), 1-15.

Lincoln, Yvonna S. and Egon G. Guba (1985), *Naturalistic Inquiry*, Beverly Hills, CA: Sage.

Marcus, George E. and D. Cushman (1982), "Ethnographies as Texts," *Annual Review of Anthropology* 11: 25-69.

Marcus, George E. and Michael M. J. Fischer (1986), *Anthropology as Cultural Critique*, Chicago: University of Chicago Press.

Malinowski, Bronislaw (1922), *Argonauts of the Western Pacific*, London: George Routledge & Sons.

O'Guinn, Thomas C. and Russell W. Belk (1989), "Heaven on Earth: Consumption at Heritage Village, USA," *Journal of Consumer Research*, 16 (September), 227-238.

Sternthal, Brian, Alice M. Tybout and Bobby J. Calder (1987), "Confirmatory versus Comparative Approaches to Judging Theory Tests," *Journal of Consumer Research*, 14, 114-125.

Thompson, Craig (1990), "Eureka! and Other Tests of Significance: A New Look at Evaluating Interpretive Research," *Advances in Consumer Research*, Vol. 17, eds. M. Goldberg et al., Provo, UT: Association for Consumer Research, 25-30.

Van Manaan, John (1988), *Tales From the Field*, Chicago: The University of Chicago Press.

Wallendorf, Melanie and Russell W. Belk (1989), "Assessing Trustworthiness in Consumer Research," in *Interpretive Consumer Research*, ed. E. Hirschman, Provo, UT: Association for Consumer Research.

May The Circle Be Unbroken: A Hermeneutic Consideration Of How Interpretive Approaches To Consumer Research Are Understood By Consumer Researchers

Craig J. Thompson, University of Tennessee

ABSTRACT

As consumer research has broadened its methodological orientation, a question has arisen as to the epistemological status of knowledge claims ensuing from interpretivist approaches. The present paper offers a hermeneutic consideration of Calder and Tybout's classification of consumer research into the broad categories of qualitative, scientific, and interpretive. It is proposed that this typology assumes that "objective" knowledge ensues from an ahistoric, archimedean perspective. Using the Calder and Tybout typology as an illustrative vehicle, several conceptual inconsistencies are noted in this foundational view of social science. It is further proposed that these inconsistencies undermine Calder and Tybout's stated goal of encouraging methodological pluralism in consumer research. Finally, a hermeneutic perspective is offered on the role of interpretation in consumer research.

INTRODUCTION

There is little doubt that consumer research has undergone a significant broadening of its philosophical and methodological orientations. A wide array of interpretivist approaches can now be found in the consumer research literature such as ethno-methodologies (Belk, Sherry and Wallendorf 1988; McCracken 1988), literary criticism (Stern 1989), structural analysis (Hirschman 1988), semiotics (Holbrook and Grayson 1987; Mick 1986) and existential-phenomenology (Thompson, Locander and Pollio 1989). Consequent to this methodological diversity, a philosophical question has arisen concerning the role of interpretivism within consumer research and the type of knowledge such approaches provide (Hudson and Ozanne 1988).

Calder and Tybout (1987, 1989) have recently addressed this question by offering a typology which categorizes consumer research into three distinct classes: 1) *qualitative research* which seeks to describe the everyday knowledge that consumers use to understand their own behaviors; 2) *scientific research* which is guided by the research logic of *sophisticated methodological falsificationism* and subjects explanatory theories to rigorous empirical testing; and 3) *interpretive research* which seeks to gain a "subjective" insight into consumer phenomena through the imposition of an interpretive viewpoint. While this typology has engendered some critical commentary (Anderson 1989; Holbrook and O'Shaugnessy 1988), it merits serious consideration by consumer researchers because it represents a systematic attempt to incorporate qualitative/interpretive methods into the mainstream of consumer research and provides a set of criteria by which to evaluate the each class of consumer research.

One major appeal of this typology is its overt pluralistic spririt. While being philosophically aligned with the approach of the "traditional scientific enterprise," Calder and Tybout propose that no one class of knowledge is of more or less inherent value than another. Rather than being relegated to the "pre-science" role of discovering testable hypotheses, qualitative/interpretive approaches are seen as generating their own unique forms of knowledge. It is worth noting that Calder (1977) has been a long-time advocate for the utility and conceptual independence of qualitative research in marketing, noting that "focus group research must basically stand alone" (p. 361).

Despite this attractive quality, the Calder and Tybout framework is undermined by a failure to reflectively assess the implicit philosophical assumptions on which it is constructed. By being in accord with the established Western view of knowledge (Anderson 1989), this typology is easily seen as being philosophically and value neutral. This sense of value-neutral objectivity is further reinforced by the common-sense plausibility of claiming that there should be some sharp distinction between "everyday" and "scientific" knowledge. The Calder and Tybout framework, however, ensues from a network of background assumptions which have been historically prominent within the social sciences. While these background assumptions have typically been discussed under the global rubric of "positivism," the more philosophically descriptive term, *foundationalism*, will be used in the present paper (Bernstein 1986; Hekman 1986; Thompson 1990).

In proposing a typology based on foundationalist criteria, theoretical primacy is being placed on a world-view which is inconsistent with the aims of most interpretive approaches. Using such a foundationalist framework to understand the nature of qualitative/interpretive research yields several problematic conceptual inconsistencies, misrepresents the process of qualitative/interpretive research, and suggests inappropriate evaluative criteria. The present hermeneutic consideration seeks to profile this foundationalist world-view and illustrate how these background assumptions systematically subjugate Calder and Tybout's pluralistic aims. In a broader sense, the present heremeuntic assessment will also illustrate the dilemmas which confront *any* foundationalist account of the social sciences and the nature of human knowledge. Finally, some suggestions will be made as to how a hermeneutic orientation may better serve the cause of methodological pluralism within consumer research.

The two poles of foundationalism

Foundationalist philosophers, such as Francis Bacon, August Comte, and Rene Descarte, developed a highly influential distinction between beliefs which are "objective," in the sense of being unprejudiced by historical forces, and those which are "subjective" in the sense of being socially mediated and culturally contingent. For the contemporary social sciences, this distinction has served as the philosophical origin for two prominent research orientations: objectivism and subjectivism (Bernstein 1983; Rorty 1979; Thompson 1990)

"Objectivist" researchers seek lawlike principles which explain human phenomena in terms whose truth value is not contingent on cultural beliefs or personal values. With this orientation, the goal is to base knowledge claims on some "objective" foundation which allows a knowledge claim's truth value to be determined solely by degree of correspondence to actual states of the world (e.g. Bernstein 1986; Hekman 1986). The methodological approach characteristic of the natural sciences--featuring analysis, control, precision of measurement, and logical rigor--is often taken as providing these objective foundations.

Subjectivist researchers, following in the tradition of theorists such as Dithey, Mannheim, Schutz, and Weber, contend that the atemporal, acultural explanations characteristic of the natural sciences are not attainable by the social sciences and, instead, seek descriptions of the "subjective" beliefs held by the culture's participants (Hekman 1986). With a subjectivist orientation, the methodological focus is placed on attaining an empathetic understanding of the subject's experiences (Lincoln and Guba 1986).

As Rorty (1979) has noted, subjectivism and objectivism are mirror images of the same foundationalist world-view. Both adhere to a belief that scientific knowledge claims must be based on some foundation of "neutral" observation. For example, Dilthey (1926/1985) proposed that the interpreter's experience of "verstehen" (i.e. empathetic understanding) was analogous to the "objective" observation which supposedly grounded the knowldege claims of the natural sciences. In more contemporary terms, Rorty characterizes the goal of humanistic research as seeking to "crack the code" of the subject's private intentions and meanings. With both objectivist and subjectivist approaches, there is an assumption that a "perspective-free" truth can be attained through methodological procedure and their epistemological dispute between concerns which methods serve as the appropriate foundation for the social sciences.

The Calder and Tybout typology clearly follows in this foundationalist tradition. Qualitative research serves the subjectivist goal of describing the culturally contingent beliefs of consumers while scientific research uses the "objective" logic of sophisticated methodological falsificationism to develop knowledge whose truth value is not contingent on social consensus or cultural belief. Subjective and objective knowledge are easily assimilated into this foundationalist framework because both are seen as resulting from a "neutral" view of a phenomenon. Within such a framework, however, the issue of interpretive knowledge (e.g. the world as understood from some perspective) is more problematic. In this post-Kuhnian social milieu, it is difficult to maintain that any form of knowledge can be attained without some degree of interpretation. This concession, however, compromises both the distinction between objective and subjective knowledge and the related claim that interpretive knowledge is a "special case."

As an illustrative example, Calder and Tybout describe qualitative research as a case where "the data are considered to be self-reflexive [and] supply there own meaning" (p.199). This characterization of qualitative research can be seen as a projection of the objectivist dream of attaining knowledge of the world which is unmediated by human interpretation. The qualitative researcher is rendered as passive entity who simply records the phenomenon as it "really is." To be consistent with this construction, Calder and Tybout (1989) make a distinction between qualitative and interpretive approaches which even they admit is equivocal:

> The qualitative approach can obviously be viewed as version of the interpretive in which behavior is being interpreted from the standpoint of the ideas of consumers. We believe, however, that separating the two is useful (p. 199).

What this brief passage reflects is an implicit recognition that no "data" can supply their own meaning because social phenomena only have meaning within an interpretive framework. The typology's "useful" distinction between qualitative and interpretive knowledge is not only misleading but has a consequence which runs counter to Calder and Tybout's stated purpose of encouraging methodological pluralism. In presupposing a foundationalist world-view, *any* phenomenologically motivated qualitative study will be deemed invalid because such research is *necessarily* interpretive. Methodological pluralism cannot be facilitated by institutionalizing epistemological standards which are neither attainable nor paradigmatically appropriate for interpretivist research.

The presence of interpretation in the traditional scientific enterprise also poses difficulty for Calder and Tybout's framework. One paradox of their typology is that the qualitative approach is actually rendered as more "objective," in the sense of being free of interpretation, than the scientific one. Consider Calder and Tybout's (1989) comments regarding scientific knowledge:

> All we suggest is that a process of ongoing testing, and a preference at any point in time for theories that provide a better explanation than their rivals offers the possibility of scientific progress. This is the best we can

hope for, no matter what the criterion, judgment will always play a role in choosing among theories. But, if individuals share the overall goal of progress in understanding/ accounting for the phenomena, then many disputes can be resolved and general guidelines are possible (p. 202).

In these terms, the quest for scientific knowledge is a noble but flawed endeavor. This "tragic" point is further developed by reference to an earlier work by Calder, Sternthal, and Tybout (1987) which argues that no methodological procedure necessarily guarantees rigor and validity and, accordingly, the adequacy of a theory test can only be known post hoc. Thus, the best "hope" for an objective, value-free epistemological foundation is seen as the rigorous empirical comparison of rival theories.

Unfortunately for advocates of falsificationism, this comparative foundation is itself on rather shaky ground. Judging the rigor of empirical test is an interpretive act which uses a process resembling what phenomenologists refer to as "imaginative variation" (Giorgi 1986). As an example, a scientist could imagine various ways a methodological procedure, such as a manipulation check, could compromise the rigor of a comparative test and then judge if the scenario was actually played out. Sternthal et al. offer several of these imaginative scenarios to demonstrate the theoretical futility of confirmatory theory testing. This strategy, however, opens the proverbial pandora's box for the falsificationist position. Given a sufficient level of creative imagination, potential confounds can be found with any given empirical study. Thus, a supposedly "falsified" theory can always be defended on the grounds of an inadequately conducted empirical test (see Anderson 1989 for a more extensive discussion).

The history of psychology provides an excellent example of how a theory can be insulated from attempts at empirical refutation. Empirical and conceptual anomalies began to accumulate for behaviorism almost from the outset of Watson's "Little Albert" experiment (Valle and King 1978). "Mentalistic" theories such as found in the work William James (1890), gestalt psychology (Kohler 1947, and Bartlett's schema theory (1932) were available as empirically viable, theoretical alternatives. Indeed, much of the gestalt literature was devoted to demonstrating the empirical superiority of gestalt theory over the stimulus-response models of behaviorism (see Koffka 1935; Kohler 1947; Merleau-Ponty 1942/1963). The proponents of behaviorism once confronted with such anomalies, however, simply did not fold up their theoretical tents. Behaviorists avoided "falsification" in two ways. The first was by appeal to a paradigmatic value: mentalistic explanations were proclaimed as per se unscientific. The second was continually modifying behaviorist models to better account for anomalous findings (e.g. Pollio 1982). Of these two strategies, the former was by far the most central to the fifty-year hegemony of behavioristic psychology. Only when a major shift in world-view occurred within psychology (the so-called cognitive revolution) did empirical anomalies serve as evidence for falsification (Gardner 1985).

What this historical example demonstrates is that scientific theories do not exist independently of a socio-cultural context of shared metaphysical beliefs, commitments, and accepted practices (Anderson 1986). This interpretive background of the scientific enterprise is what Kuhn (1970) broadly referred to as a "paradigm." In taking a foundationalist stance, the Calder and Tybout typology has extreme difficulty in accounting for the interpretive and socio-historically contingent apsects of "scientific" knowledge.

To maintain their distinction between interpretive and scientific knowledge, Calder and Tybout are left with a demarcating criterion which misrepresents the nature of interpretive research and which poses a serious, and somewhat ironic, conceptual dilemma for the typology itself. In conceding that scientific knowledge involves some interpretation (or human judgment), Calder and Tybout propose that the difference between scientific and interpretive approaches is given by the intentions of the researchers. That is, scientists intend to challenge theories with empirical data whereas interpretivists do not. In the Calder and Tybout scheme, interpretivists use a conceptualization to give an account of the data and their intention is solely to show that their conceptualization fits the data. As Calder and Tybout (1987) phrase it, "because data may be used selectively and multiple interpretations of them may exist, there is no intention of comparing interpretations to *choose* among them....The immediate goal is support and confirmation of the conceptualization" (p. 139).

This appeal to researcher intentions, however, erroneously portrays interpretive researchers as inexorably committed to a single conceptual framework. In the conduct of interpretive research, multiple and sometimes competing interpretations are compared on the basis of which provide the more encompassing understanding of the phenomena (Belk, Sherry and Wallendorf 1988; Holbrook and O'Shaugenessy 1988). Their characterization also ignores the dialectical nature of the interpretative process. That is, precursory interpretations are continually modified to accommodate the emergent characteristics of the phenomenon (Thompson, Locander and Pollio 1989). The Calder and Tybout typlogy cannot recognize the dialectic nature of interpretative research, however, without equivocating its own critical distinction between scientific and interpretive knowledge.

Since Calder and Tybout acknowledge that scientific research involves "some" interpretation, they must reinforce their tenuous categorical distinction by denying that interpretivist research is an empirically grounded process and, instead, adhere to the problematic claim that interpretivists "escape" from the data by basing knowledge claims *exclusively* on societal consensus. Calder and Tybout (1987) wield this assumption in a pernicious fashion by asking the rhetorical question, "if relativism [which they see as a method of interpretivism] is true, then what do scientists persuade each other about (p. 138)?" Thus, the dubiousness of *their* distinction between scientific and interpretive knowledge is treated as an inconsistency confronting an alternative worldview.[1]

Another conceptual dilemma facing the Calder and Tybout framework is that researcher intentions do not serve as a workable criterion for categorizing research approaches. As Calder and Tybout (1987, 1989) astutely note, no particular method or set of quantitative procedures can guarantees scientific adequacy. Thus, "researcher intention" is not revealed by choice of method. Nor is researcher intention revealed by theoretical orientation as Calder and Tybout also note that a seemingly "unscientific" theory, such as parapsychology, could potentially meet the criteria for scientific knowledge. The situation is further complicated by the indeterminate nature of researcher intent. That is, an "interpretivist" could choose among competing accounts and, thus, have a supposedly "scientific" intention while a "scientist" (for reasons of paradigmatic commitment or "unconscious desire") might interpret the data to fit a preferred theory. As such, the Calder and Tybout typology requires an *inference* about what a given researcher "really intended." In so doing, the assessment of consumer research is removed from the domain of public discourse and becomes a matter of "cracking the code" of the researcher's private thoughts. This consequence is ironic given Calder and Tybout's (1989) view that a "troubling" feature of some interpretivist research is "the idea that one's personal intentions in submitting a paper somehow matter and that reviewers are somehow obligated to read between the lines to detect larger meanings" (p. 207). In offering researcher intentions as a demarcation criterion, however, their typology implicitly endorsers this very idea.

The legacy of the foundationalist tradition

Like other foundationalists approaches, the Calder and Tybout framework cannot adequately account for the essential role of interpretation in human knowledge. In seeing qualititative and scientific knowledge as arising from a neutral perspective, both are treated as undeniably worthwhile ways of knowing. This point is not made so incontrovertibly with respect to interpretive knowledge. While overtly endorsed as valid way of knowing, Calder and Tybout treat so-called interpretive knowledge with a great deal of suspicion. An implicit theme underlying the Calder and Tybout typology is that interpretive knowledge is a potential danger which must be carefully controlled and segregated from scientific and everyday knowledge, lest the consumer research literature become vulnerable to what they term as an "anything goes" anarchy, "weirdness," and "paroxysms of self-expression."

This concern over interpretive knowledge is not unique to Calder and Tybout's typology. The "crisis" of social science has long been discussed by foundationalist thinkers. This philosophical dissonance arises from the implicit awareness that interpretation can never be fully purged from the social sciences. As such, the knowledge generated by the social sciences is seen as more dubitable and less well-founded than that provided by the natural sciences. The normative quest has been to make the social sciences more "scientific" in terms of an idealized conception of the natural sciences. Heremeunetic philosophers see the crisis of the social sciences in entirely different terms: the crisis emerges from an unwillingness to accept that knowledge is *not* absolute and that interpretation grounds *all* knowledge claims, including those of the natural sciences (Gadamer 1975).

A HERMENEUTIC ORIENTATION TO CONSUMER RESEARCH

Hermeneutic philosophy sees the quest for a neutral perspective as significantly misrepresenting the nature of human understanding (Gadamer 1975; Habermas 1986; Heidegger 1926; Ricouer 1976). In Gadamer's terms, all social science knowledge reflects a fusion of horizons (i.e. perspectives) between the researcher and the experiencing individual. In these terms, the "neutral view" coveted by foundationalists is ontologically impossible because researchers cannot step outside of their historical context to view the world from an unsituated perspective. For hermeneutic thinkers,

---

[1] Calder and Tybout (1989) later retracted this problematic supposition:
> ....we were arguing that the possibility of appealing to nonempirical factors in evaluating theories is more an illusion than reality. How might one argue the merits of a methodology, axiology, ontology, etc., if not by appealing to some form of data or empirical observation. We did not intend to suggest that critical relativists ignore the data--just the opposite. We suggest that they are no better or worse than empiricists in their reliance on data. The primary difference lies in whether the data under consideration are limited to controlled studies or give greater emphasis to the observation of naturally occurring events (p. 203)"

This clarification, however, only further obfuscates the issue by confusing approaches to evaluating consumer research with those for conducting consumer research. Is the implication that only data from controlled studies can be "empirical" or that the merits of competing ontologies and axiologies can somehow be determined through a controlled study or, perhaps, that the observation of "naturally occurring events" is taboo for empiricist researchers?

this situatedness is not a problem to be minimized or solved but, rather, is a necessary precondition for understanding. The forefather of modern hermeneutics, Martin Heidegger (1926), pictured human knowledge as emerging from a circular process in which a preunderstanding is applied to apprehend a worldly phenomenon, which in turn gives rise to a new understanding. On this view, understanding is ongoing process rather than a final product. While a full discussion of the hermeneutic circle is beyond the scope of the present paper, one of its major implications for the "crisis" of consumer research will be addressed.

Proponents of foundationalism typically endorse the so-called *unified science hypothesis* which states that the approach characteristic of the natural sciences is *the* logic of science (e.g. Apel 1968). In adopting the logic of a natural science approach, however, a normative assumption is made about what form explanations of human phenomena should take and this implied value may be an inappropriate one with respect to social science research.

Historically, the natural sciences--especially physics--have shown that the world of everyday experience is radically different from the world as explained scientifically (Romanyshyn 1989). In seeking scientific credibility, social scientists have developed a phobia of theories which resemble a common-sense understanding (Kohler 1947; Merleau-Ponty 1962). That is, a social science approach which is closely grounded in everyday life and accounts for human phenomena in experience-near terms seems highly suspect when the standards of scientific knowledge are based on the conceptual abstraction found in the natural sciences. With such an orientation, a social scientific account of human phenomena must be rendered in terms of second-order constructs, that ideally, bear little direct resemblance to the experiential world being explained. For example, a sizable proportion of research in psychology has been devoted to explaining why the world of everyday experience is, from a scientific standpoint, illusory or epi-phenomenal (e.g. Giorgi 1986).

This normative implication of the unified science hypothesis, however, creates a dilemma for social science research. The theoretical accounts of the social sciences have not been sufficiently divorced from everyday experience to be unequivocally considered "scientific." Calder (1977) notes this problem in the following way:

> Some sociologists, mainly the ethnomethodologists, lodge a powerful criticism against conventional social science. They claim that all too often researchers confuse first-degree [everyday] constructs with second-degree ones. The explanatory constructs of everyday life are assumed implicitly to have some scientific status...The point is that much of what is considered to be scientific may belong more to everyday explanation. Phenomenological qualitative research therefore may have a stronger claim to the use of social science constructs than does scientific research (p.360).

While being truly "scientific" is commonly associated with more abstract conceptual explanations, the history of psychology shows that theoretical models which become too removed from everyday life prove sterile. The demise of Hullian behaviorism again serves as a case in point. Prior to the advent of the information processing paradigm, mainstream psychologists dismissed mentalistic accounts of human phenomena as unscientific. The Hullian paradigm accounted for psychological phenomena in a "scientific" way which was mathematically precise and used constructs removed from everyday beliefs. With the possible exception of devout behavioral psychologists, however, probably very individuals think of themselves as being mindless bundles of stimulus-response associations. Rather, the more common-sense belief is that a person is a mindful entity who actions are purposeful and goal directed. This appeal to "common-sense" understanding was a principal argument used by cognitive psychologists to assail Hullian behaviorism (e.g. Miller, Galanter and Pribram 1960). A widely shared conclusion is that the cause of psychology was greatly advanced by embracing this "everyday" view of people as mindful beings (Bower and Hilgard 1981).

In terms of a natural science model, the dialectic between the knowledge of "social science" and the whole of cultural knowledge is a sign of disciplinary immaturity. In terms of a hermeneutic world-view, social scientists do not need to somehow become detached observers of the social world. Rather, social science is seen as a *human activity* for understanding other human activities.

Rather than an idealized notion of objectivity, heremeuntic thinkers propose that social sciences should strive for an *effective historical consciousness* in which there is a reflective awareness of the background assumptions (i.e. historic tradition) from which an understanding emerges (Gadamer 1975). An effective historical consciousness is never attained "once and for all" but is ongoing effort; the explication of background assumptions requires a critical perspective which itself will be based on assumptions. In these terms, knowledge is rendered as a human practice and not a complete ahistoric product. The risk of an idealized notion of objectivity is background assumptions can become reified and their link to a historic tradition artificially severed. With a hermeneutic approach, a researcher can never become fully comfortable with a preferred world-view nor see one set of paradigmatic assumptions as objectively cutting the world at its joints. By fully embracing the interpretive nature of understanding, a heremeutic orientation cannot promise to consumer researchers absolute certainty or an aperspectival "truth." It can provide, however, a means for understanding what is perhaps the most basic and intriguing of all human phenomena: how one human being can come to understand the world of another.

REFERENCES

Anderson, Paul (1983), "Marketing, Scientific Progress, and the Scientific Method," *Journal of Marketing*, 47 (Fall), 18-31.

_____ (1986), "On Method in Consumer Research: A Critical Relativist Perspective," *Journal of Consumer Research*, 13 (September), 155-173.

_____ (1989), "On Relativism and Interpretivism--With a Prolegomenon to the Why Question" in *Interpretive Consumer Research*, ed. Elizabeth C. Hirschman, Provo, UT: Association for Consumer Research, 10-23.

Karl-Otto Apel (1985), "Scientistics, Hermeneutics, Critique of Ideology: An Outline of a Theory of Science from an Epistemological-Anthropological Point of View, in *The Hermeneutics Reader*, ed. Kurt Mueller-Vollner, New York: Continuum, 320-346.

Belk, Russell W., John F. Sherry, and Melanie Wallendorf (1988), "A Naturalistic Inquiry into Buyer and Seller Behavior at a Swap Meet," *Journal of Consumer Research*, 14 (March), 449-470.

_____, John F. Sherry, and Melanie Wallendorf (1989), "The Sacred and the Profane in Consumer Behavior: Theodicy on the Odyssey," *Journal of Consumer Research*, 16 (June), 1-38.

Berger, Peter L. and Thomas Luckmann (1967), *The Social Construction of Reality*, Garden City, NY: Anchor Books.

Bernstein, Richard (1983), *Beyond Objectivism and Relativism*,Philadelphia, University of Pennsylvania Press.

Bernstein, Richard (1986), "From Hermeneutics to Praxis," in *Hermeneutics and Modern Philosophy*, ed. Brice R. Wachterhauser, Albany, NY: State University of New York Press, 87-110.

Bleicher, Josef (1980), *Contemporary Hermenuetics*, London: Routledge & Kegan Paul.

Calder, Bobby J. (1977), "Focus Groups and the Nature of Qualitative Research in Marketing," Journal of *Marketing Research*, 14 (August), 353-364.

_____ and Alice M. Tybout (1987), "What Consumer Research Is," *Journal of Consumer Research*, 14 (June), 136-140.

_____ and Alice M. Tybout (1989), "Interpretive, Qualitative, and Traditional Scientific Empirical Consumer Research," in *Interpretive Consumer Research*, ed. Elizabeth C. Hirschman, Provo, UT: Association for Consumer Research, 199-208.

Dilthey, Wilhelm (1926/1985), "The Understanding of Other Persons and their Life-Expressions," in *The Hermeneutics Reader,* ed. Kurt Mueller-Vollner, New York: Continuum, 152-164.

Gadamer, Hans-Georg (1975), *Truth and Method*, New York: Seabury Press.

Gardner, Howard (1985), *The Mind's New Science*, New York: Basic Books.

Giorgi, Amedeo (1986), "Theoretical Justification for the Use of Descriptions in Psychological Reseach," in *Qualitative Research in Psychology*, eds. Peter D. Ashworth, Amedeo Giorgi, and Andre de Koning, Pittsburgh, PA: Dusquesne University Press, 3-22.

Habermas, Jurgen (1985), "Hermeneutics and the Social Sciences," in *The Hermeneutics Reader*, ed. Kurt Mueller-Vollner, New York: Continuum, 293-319.

Hekman, Susan (1986), *Hermeneutics and the Sociology of Knowledge*, Notre Dame IN: University of Notre Dame Press.

Heidegger, Martin (1926/1962), *Being and Time*, New York: Harper and Row.

Hirschman, Elizabeth C. (1986), "Humanistic Inquiry in Marketing Reseach: Philosophy, Method and Criteria," *Journal of Marketing Research*, 13 (August), 237-249.

_____ (1988), "The Ideology of Consumption: A Structural-Syntactical Analysis of Dallas and Dynasty," *Journal of Consumer Research*, 16 (December), 344-359.

Holbrook, Morris B. John O'Shaughnessy (1988), "On the Scientific Status of Consumer Research and the Need for an Interpretive Approach to Studying Consumption Behavior," *Journal of Consumer*, 15 (December), 398-402.

Hudson, Laurel Anderson and Julie L. Ozanne (1988), "Alternative Ways of Seeking Knowledge in Consumer Research," *Journal of Consumer Research*, 14 (March), 508-521.

Koffka, Kurt (1935), *Gestalt Psychology*, New York: Harcourt, Brace & World.

Kohler, Wolfgang (1947), *Gestalt Psychology*, New American Library Press.

McCracken, Grant (1988), *Culture and Consumption*, Bloomington, IN: Indiana University Press.

Merleau-Ponty, Maurice (1962), *The Phenomenology of Perception*, London: Routledge & Kegan Paul.

Merleau-Ponty, Maurice (1967), "The Primacy of Perception," in *Readings in Existential-Phenomenology*, eds. Nathaniel Lawrence and Daniel O'Connor, Englewood Cliffs, NJ: Prentice-Hall, 31-54.

Mick, David Glen (1986), "Consumer Research and Semiotics: Exploring the Morphology of Signs, Symbols and Signficance," *Journal of Consumer Research*, 13 (September), 196-213.

Miller, George A., Eugene Galanter, Karl H. Pribram (1960), *Plans and the Structure of Behavior*, New York: Holt Rinehart & Winston.

Pollio, Howard R. (1982), *Behavior and Existence*, Monterey, CA: Brooks/Cole.

Ricoeur, Paul (1976), *Interpretation Theory*, Fort Worth, Texas: Texas Christian University Press.

Rorty, Richard (1979), *Philosophy and The Mirror of Nature*, Princeton: Princeton University Press.

Stern, Barbara (1989), "Literary Criticism and Consumer Research: Overview and Illustrative Analysis," *Journal of Consumer Research*, 16 (December 1989), 322-334.

Sternthal, Brian, Alice M. Tybout, Bobby J. Calder (1987), "Confirmatory Versus Comparative Approaches To Judging Theory Tests," *Journal of Consumer Research*, 14 (June), 114-125.

Thompson, Craig J. (1990), "Eureka! and Other Tests of Signficance: A New Look at Evaluating Interpretive Research," in *Advances in Consumer Research* vol. XVII, eds. Richard Pollay and Gerald J. Gorn, Provo, UT: Association for Consumer Research, in press.

———, William B. Locander and Howard R. Pollio (1989), "Putting Consumer Experience Back Into Consumer Research: The Philosophy and Method of Existential-Phenomenology," *Journal of Consumer Research*, 17 (September), 133-147.

Valle, Ronald and Mark King (1978), "An Introduction to Existential-Phenomenological Thought in Psychology," in *Existential-Phenomenological Alternatives for Psychology*, eds. Ronald Valle and Mark King, New York: Oxford University Press.

The Consumer in Postmodernity
A. Fuat Fırat, Arizona State University West

ABSTRACT

Postmodern culture, which seems to be dominating advanced capitalist societies of the West, produces several major conditions which are difficult to understand and represent using modernist categories. This paper discusses some of these conditions, specifically, hyperreality, fragmentation, reversal of production and consumption, decentering of the subject, and juxtaposition of opposites. Based on these discussions, the implications of postmodernity for the consumers are considered, and the processes whereby consumers may be becoming products themselves are explored.

INTRODUCTION

A new perspective on life and the human condition is sweeping across the globe; specifically in the Western cultures. This new perspective is most often called postmodernism. According to some of its most prominent philosophers and researchers, postmodernism is a recognition of the "... complex conjuncture of cultural conditions ... [that have arisen from the] ... postwar restructuring of capitalism in the West and in the multinational global economy ..." (Ross 1988, p. x). Specifically, it is the recognition of illusions or myths in the modernist project (that of improving human life and existence by controlling nature through scientific technologies, see Angus 1989; Foster 1983; Habermas 1983) and, consequently, the liberation of a culture that unabashedly seeks different moments of being, be they fragmented and often paradoxical, that do not require a center or a central purpose. A major aspect of postmodern culture is claimed to be the transformed role of consumption in relation to premodern and modern society (Baudrillard 1975 and 1981; Ewen 1988 and 1989; Jameson 1983; Mourrain 1989). It might be argued that this new role of consumption in society is not so new, that it was present in modern society. The recognition of consumption as it is perceived in postmodernity, however, and actions taken by institutions of Western society -- specifically, marketing -- with such recognition are relatively new. These actions based on the new recognition are likely to produce and entrench the new (postmodern) consumption culture, thereby, a new type of consumer that is qualitatively different from the consumers of the past.

POSTMODERN CULTURE

Postmodern culture is specifically a phenomenon observed in the advanced capitalist countries of the First World, but its impacts are felt throughout the world due to the cultural, economic, and political influences of such countries. While discourse of postmodernity in art, architecture, literature, literary criticism, philosophy and other disciplines is very rich and many characteristics of postmodern culture are proposed, five basic traits will be discussed here. These are *hyperreality, fragmentation, reversal of production and consumption, juxtaposition of opposites,* and *decentering of the subject.*

Hyperreality

Hyperreality is a concept used to represent the power of simulation in determining reality. According to one of the most prominent philosophers of postmodernity, Baudrillard (1983a), it is the realization (becoming real) of what is (was) hype, of the simulation, or of the (romanticized) imagination of what is thought was (once) real. It is the (re)creation, as reality, of a simulated past that is imagined more so than identified. It is the (re)production, as reality, of what is presently assumed, a simulation (Massumi 1987). This reality is "hyper," it seems, for two reasons. It is a reality beyond what reality was understood to be in the scientific (modern) era, and it is composed of what originally was and is hype.

Examples of hyperreality abound (Baudrillard 1988). The more current and powerful examples of hyperreality are to be found in cultural representations in the media as well as in the transformational marketing practices of institutions which are influential in the (re)construction of reality in the image of the simulated. We continuously witness, in everyday lives of the consumers, the reproduction of human roles, relationships, and characteristics initially simulated on the screen, on television, or other media. These roles become emulated by the audience and, thus, are found in "reality," when they were imagined in soap operas, situation comedies and films. The male and female roles repeatedly proposed in advertisements, being internalized by consumers, seem to reproduce themselves as reality.

A major element that enables hyperreality is that the relation between signifiers (verbal, visual, or material signs that represent things making them intelligible) and the referents is arbitrary, as semioticians have recognized at least since Saussure (Santambrogio and Violi 1988). In postmodernity, this arbitrariness is made full use of by attaching, creatively and with the sophisticated use of form, technique and language play, any meaning (signified) to signifiers. For example, once in the advertising medium the term toothpaste is separated from its original referent -- a paste cleansing teeth -- it gets attached with new, symbolic meanings, such as sexiness, beauty, happiness, attractiveness, etc. These new meanings simulate a new reality when powerfully communicated, and therefore, accepted to be true -- that is, when a segment of consumers feel and/or attribute sexiness, attractiveness, etc., to a (special brand/kind of) toothpaste to which such meanings are attached. This simulation becomes reality for a community of believers, because, now, when the toothpaste is used, the consumer is indeed found sexy, attractive, etc. Similar examples are found with clothing items (e.g., bluejeans), cigarettes, cosmetics, and other products. They are also found in everyday life and in our material environment. Reproduction of wharf areas or boardwalks, cafes and other recreational sections in metropolitan centers that replicate only what is imagined of the past, recreation of the architecture of those past times as only pastiche (Jameson 1983), and the reproduction of imagined authenticity in tourist centers to enable a "true" experience for the tourists are only a few of such examples.

Hyperreality, then, is an "imaging" based on the signification process (imbuing signifiers with meanings) that is replicated in or into reality. It is through such images that the consumer of postmodernity builds one's own everyday life and senses the meaning of one's own existence and place in society. In postmodern culture where the fact of hyperreality is not only recognized but unabashedly practiced by the ultimate institution of postmodernity, marketing, the form of consumer literacy is transformed. The consumer becomes less literate in the modern sense, that is, in *reading* into words and signs to connect, associate and discover the essence or center of things in order to achieve an *understanding*. The new literacy is one of *watching* or exposing oneself to the innumerable images in order to develop a *recognition* of where they stand and what meanings they carry. This new literacy presents the consumer the tools for *positioning* oneself in society, in all different situations, and in (re)presenting the wanted or required images.

Fragmentation

Fragmentation is another major property of postmodern culture (Baudrillard 1981; Jameson 1983; Stephanson 1988). Fragmentation in the sense that all things are disconnected and disjointed in their representation from each other, their origins and history, and contexts. Rather, they constitute communicational instances. That is, in postmodern culture something is an entity only insofar as it presents or represents (in general, communicates) an image (as a bundle of symbols). In a culture of many competing representations there is competition to arouse interest and produce a desired effect. Lacking substantive linkages to each other or to a common content or origin, each instance of communication must be independently exciting to the senses. Interest, attention, and retention cannot be expected on the basis of relevance to other phenomena or communications due to the disconnectedness of the representations. Consequently, it is the form, the style (Ewen 1988), or the technique of each instance of communication that enables success in terms of retention of the representation or image communicated. The instances of communication acquire an intensity, specifically emotional, based on such form, style, and technique. Pace, show value, and sensationalism dominate the media (Newcomb 1979). Each instance of communication, then, becomes a spectacle (Jameson 1983; Real 1979). Television commercials and music videos which borrow many images and styles from each other, and which are increasingly imitated by other television programs and Holywood, provide excellent examples of this phenomenon of the spectacle.

Fragmentations in life and history, as well as in communicated images and representations are also reflected in consumption. This has been reinforced through the differentiation and specialization of products in the market system. Each product has an image and a communicated purpose that is specialized. In some cases, each instance of consumption of the product serves a special purpose and fulfills the acquisition of the desired image by the consumer. By consuming a microwave oven, for example, a consumer represents to oneself and to others the desired image of oneself -- which may be one of independence, of having an exciting life in the fast track, of being free from banal chores, etc. -- an image that has been produced by the interaction of the consumer's cultural context and the marketing media. On the other hand, consumption of a car may represent different images when used by the same consumer in different instances and contexts, in each instance producing the consumer's desired image -- charming, outgoing, efficient, risk-taker, cautious, lover of adventure, industrious, family-oriented, etc. -- for that context, cultivated by the same interaction (Wernick 1989).

In each instance of consumption, for example, as the consumer eats a frozen dinner, watches television, brushes his/her teeth, feeds the cat, the consumer perceives an independent, separate purpose. Each requires a different product, each fulfills a need that is fragmented and separated from others. The consumption life of the consumer is segmented, fragmented into separate moments which are not or only superficially linked. Each instance may well be cultivated to represent a different image of oneself; as a matter of fact this seems to be the rule. Thus, a schizophrenia (Deleuze and Guattari 1987; Jameson 1983) is reflected in consumption. In postmodern culture where the theme is escape from unity, cynical contempt for central authority, irreverence, difference, and segmentation (Venkatesh 1989), images represented will be different for different people. The catch in the capitalist market system is, however, that to represent the different images people will be acquiring and consuming the same products -- the microwave, the car, the television set, the designer clothing, etc. -- and adopting the same consumption pattern represented by these products (Fırat and Dholakia 1982). So, what appears to be difference at the level of symbolic culture turns out to be an underlying uniformity.

Reversal of production and consumption

The project of modernity clearly emphasized production (Aronowitz 1988) as the worthy and meaningful activity in society; one of creation and usefulness. The emphasis was on positive contribution, work, productivity, usefulness to humanity. The postmodern project has reversed the emphasis and the order of things. The central project is no longer production but consumption, no longer orderly work and contribution to society but recognition of crises in all facets of culture and society (Angus 1989; Baudrillard 1988; Lyotard 1984; Mourrain 1989).

Many thinkers of postmodernism who have been influenced by or grown within the Marxist tradition (for example, Baudrillard) are, nevertheless, critical of Marx, in that they feel he has completed and corrected classical political economy, not radically replaced it (Poster 1975). The primacy of production is very much kept in Marxist theory. Except, Marx has also recognized the unity of production and consumption (Marx 1973). While classical political economists made a clear distiction between production and consumption (productive consumption versus consumption proper; see Mill 1929; Say 1964), Marx argued that consumption is simultaneously production and production is simultaneously consumption. Within this framework, however, he emphasized that in this process the determining moment was what the classical political economists called productive consumption, the production of commodities (products for which there is market exchange). It was the relations human beings entered into during the production of commodities, which in capitalism are relations of capital, that determined class structures, dominant ideologies, and the existing social order.

Baudrillard (1975 and 1988) as well as other postmodernist thinkers reverse the priorities in the production-consumption cycle (Angus and Jhally 1989; Jameson 1983). "... Baudrillard has displaced the locus of analysis from the domain of production to the realm of consumption" (Mourrain 1989). Consumption is the moment in the process where symbolic exchanges that determine and reproduce the social code occur, where "... there is an active appropriation of signs, not the simple destruction of an object" (Poster 1975).

The implication of the reversal in postmodernism is that consumption is not the end, but a moment where much is created and produced. It is not a personal, private act of destruction by the consumer, but very much a social act where symbolic meanings, social codes, and relationships are produced and reproduced. Consumption is no longer a profane activity -- as opposed to production being sacred, for example -- and no longer is conspicuous consumption considered a folly, something not to be very proud of. On the contrary, consumption has become the means of self-realization, self-identification; a means of *producing* one's self and self-image.

Postmodernist insights lead us to conclude that production never ceases, that it is a continual process. Only, the form of production changes at different moments of the process. At the moment generally known as production, the producers are human beings, the products are the commodities. At the moment generally known as consumption, the producers are the commodities, the products are the human beings.

Decentering of the subject

In modernity, the human being as the subject, and his/her needs, were the focus, the center of attention and purpose. Improvement of the conditions of life for the subject was, as discussed earlier, the project of modernity. This project, with all its contradictions, is represented in Maslow's hiararchy (Kilbourne 1987). In postmodernity there is, what is generally called, the "death of the subject" (Jameson 1983). The subject is decentered from its position of control, and the subject-object distinctions are confused. As Baudrillard articulates discussing the automobile: "... The subject himself, suddenly transformed, becomes a computer at the wheel ... [t]he vehicle now becomes a kind of capsule, its dashboard the brain, the surrounding landscape unfolding like the televised screen (instead of a live-in projectile as it was before) ..." (Baudrillard 1983b, p. 127). Thus, the object (the product consumed) sets the parameters and the rules of the consumption process (Fırat and Dholakia 1982; Fırat 1987). The subject is not in control but controlled, becoming, in effect, an object in the consumption process. The individual subject and individualism are lost, instead we have human beings repeating and replicating the mechanics necessitated and imposed by the natures of the products they use or consume.

Maybe well aware of this loss and the frustrations it may entail, many marketing organizations continue to emphasize individuality in their promotions of mass-consumed products. Consumers are called to feel unique as they use fragrances, clothing items (designer clothes), cars, etc., that millions of others use. Postmodern culture is well reflected in this seeming contradiction. Hyperreality is evident in the representation of uniqueness through objects that are the same and mass-produced. It is further evident in the fact that many no longer feel uniqueness cannot be achieved through such mass-consumed products. Now uniqueness is attached to signifiers (in this case, brand names of products) separated from their original referents (mass-produced items initially identified by a certain brand name). But, uniqueness itself as a signifier is also detached from its original meaning and serves only as the expression of an image that excites the senses because it remotely recalls a content that it is now devoid of.

Did the independent, unique, individual subject ever exist (Jameson 1983)? Is postmodernism the death of such a subject or only the recognition that it was always a myth? Whatever our answers to these questions, they do not change our project in this paper; one of recognizing what postmodernity means for an understanding of the consumer of this era.

Juxtaposition of opposites

There is wide ranging consensus among postmodernist theoreticians that one of the major characteristics of postmodern culture is its paradoxical nature (Foster 1983; Hutcheon 1988; Wilson 1989). As anything can be juxtaposed to anything else (Gitlin 1989, p. 350), so are oppositional or contradictory emotions (love with hate, contempt with admiration) and cognitions (belief with doubt, reverence with ridicule). This phenomenon is readily observable in art, literature, advertising, as well as in other media. Consider, for example, the advertisements where the product advertised is simultaneously made fun of and promoted, or advertisements that provoke credibility by discrediting advertising. Consider talk-show hosts who propose fondness of their guests and topics through slight ridicule, and comedians who invoke reverence for institutions, political leaders, and celebrities as they offer insults. Examples of such juxtaposition of opposites also abound in art and literature (Foster 1985; Hutcheon 1988; Owens 1983).

"Postmodernism refuses to privilege any one perspective, and recognizes only difference, never inequality, only fragments, never conflict" (Wilson 1989, p. 209). This is largely the consequence of the juxtaposition of contradictory emotions and cognitions regarding perspectives, commitments, ideas, things in general. Anything is at once acceptable and suspect. On the one hand, this "... very imprecision of the concepts of postmodernism and the postmodern is exciting, even liberating" (Wilson 1989, p. 208). On the other hand, it leaves the person in a limbo, a state of never being certain where one stands, causing a continual seeking of new states and new experiences. In effect, the person becomes the ideal consumer, never finding sufficient satisfaction in who one is or what one has and continually participating in the market seeking new products for a different experience.

In advanced capitalism, this lack of commitment and consequent continual seeking in the market renders the market the dominant domain of legitimation (Amin 1982). No emotional or cognitive commitment beyond a single purchase for a trial consumption is required in the market. Anything can be tried and dropped as long as the buying power is existent. After all, in postmodernity one can simultaneously critique and make fun of oneself for one's consumption behavior (such as, being a "couch potato") and enjoy the experience. The final moral is that if a product is in the market and it is being paid for, it must be all right. In such capacity, the market in postmodern culture also becomes the great assimilator. It acculturates all kinds of rebellion and radical critique through "incorporation." By emptying the expressions (music, fashion, etc.) of rebellion (e.g., punk) of their content (original meaning) it commodifies them into money making ventures and pulls the movements into the "market economy."

THE CONSUMER IN POSTMODERNITY

A gallant effort to discuss the impact of postmodernist philosophy on consumer research has been made by Sherry (1989). His characterization of postmodernism as tolerant of incommensurable alternatives and as sensitive to differences, following Lyotard's (1984) views, however, may be an optimistic one. The cultural traits which have led to the studies of postmodernism are, at times, most unforgiving and intolerant of possible alternatives.

The consumer in postmodern culture is perplexed by the density, the intensity, and the fragmentation of the instances of communication, by hyperreality that continuously (re)creates fresh images and meanings based on the same signifiers, and by the incredible array of brands and products that impose their own rules and procedures as a way of life. The consumer in postmodern culture thus transcends the state of being the subject positioned in society to satisfy one's individual needs, and becomes positioned and identified by what one consumes, projecting (an) image(s) necessitated by the hyperreal's demands upon the role(s) assigned to one by the culture. Furthermore, the postmodern consumer is no longer only the consumer but also the consumed; produced as a product of the consumption patterns (Firat and Dholakia 1982), ready, able and willing to be effectively consumed by the reigning system in the production and reproduction of commodities of the culture that perpetuate and advance the system. The postmodern consumer is not only a consumer for one's own ends, but also an object in the cycle of production for the ends of a system. Such a consumer might be called the *metaconsumer* (Firat 1991).

Some of the implications of the entrenchment of the metaconsumer in the era of postmodernity have been recently recognized in the field of consumer research by researchers who are at the forefront of major leaps in methodological and theoretical movements in this field. The studies directly related to implications of postmodernity involve consumption experiences (Holbrook and Hirschman 1982; Holbrook 1987), materialism (Belk 1985, 1986, and 1987; Belk and Pollay 1985), meanings of possessions (Belk 1988; Wallendorf and Arnould 1988), semiotics (McCracken 1986 and 1988; Mick 1988; Sherry 1989), and consumption patterns (Firat and Dholakia 1982; Firat 1987). These studies tend to indicate that (i) consumers seek to express themselves and their relationships to others through the products they possess, (ii) they attribute value to and express feelings (such as love) through material objects, (iii) valued experiences require the presence of products, (iv) consumer self-image is dependent on the symbolic meanings culturally attached to products consumed, and (v) products widely consumed in society represent relationships and meanings that compliment each other and that are consistent with the reproduction necessities of the dominant system in society.

The implications of these findings for the roles of the consumer and marketing in society are supportive of the postmodernist conclusions. In postmodern culture the products are increasingly becoming the essence of society and consumers increasingly live as the means of reproducing the simulated images for the products. This reversal in human life is reflected in other elements of culture that postmodernist thinkers study, such as, politics, aesthetics, communication media, and the arts. In these fields, as well, the reversal is observed between the narrative and the spectacle, between the form and the substance. While in modernity the form of a film, for example, was managed to enhance its substantive message, or individual scenes of the film were used to tell the whole story (narrative) better, in postmodernity only a superficial narrative is used to provide room for the spectacle (individual scenes of great excitement and sensation) (Marchetti 1989a, 1989b). The spectacle, in the end, is the narrative. That is, the master narrative (meaning, the dominant perspective on reality, the dominant ideology) of postmodernity is (the dominance of) the spectacle. The substance of postmodernity is its form, style, and technique.

Similarly, the products of the market to be purchased and consumed are the substance of postmodern consumption culture. No longer is the master narrative of human consumption in postmodern, advanced capitalism the improvement of human lives. The new master narrative is the product (the spectacle) (Winders 1989; Wright 1989). The consumer, itself as a product, is a part of this narrative as one spectacle after another in (re)presenting the different images in one instance after another.

Marketing is the institution that facilitates, creates, and diffuses this culture. It is the ultimate social practice of postmodern culture. No longer are the production and reproduction of the images, simulations, and meanings accidental or haphazard. They are deliberate and organized through the institutions of marketing. No longer can anyone participate in the (re)production of symbols and meanings that get attached to the signifiers. They have to muster power to influence and control marketing institutions.

REFERENCES

Amin, Samir (1982), "The Disarticulation of Economy within 'Developing Societies'," in *Sociology of "Developing Societies*, H. Alavi and T. Shanin, eds., New York: Monthly Review Press, 205-209.

Angus, Ian (1989), "Circumscribing Postmodern Culture," in *Cultural Politics in Contemporary America*, I. Angus and S. Jhally, eds., New York: Routledge, 96-107.

Angus, Ian and Sut Jhally, eds. (1989), *Cultural Politics in Contemporary America*, New York: Routledge.

Aronowitz, Stanley (1988), "Postmodernism and Politics," in *Universal Abandon?* A. Ross, ed., Minneapolis, MN: University of Minnesota Press, 46-62.

Baran, Paul A. (1957), *The Political Economy of Growth*, New York: Monthly Review Press.

Baudrillard, Jean (1975), *The Mirror of Production*, St. Louis, MO: Telos.

_____ (1981), *For a Critique of the Political Economy of the Sign*, St. Louis, MO: Telos.

_____ (1983a), *Simulations*, New York: Semiotext(e).

_____ (1983b), "The Ecstasy of Communication," in *The Anti-Aesthetic: Essays on Postmodern Culture*, H. Foster, ed., Port Townsend, WA: Bay Press, 126-134.

_____ (1987), *Forget Foucault*, New York: Semiotext(e).

_____ (1988), "Consumer Society," in *Jean Baudrillard: Selected Writings*, M. Poster, ed., Stanford, CA: Stanford University Press, 29-56.

Baynes, Kenneth, James Bohman and Thomas McCarthy, eds. (1987), *After Philosophy: End or Transformation?* Cambridge, MA: MIT Press.

Belk, Russell W. (1985), "Materialism: Trait Aspects of Living in the Material World," *Journal of Consumer Research*, 12 (December), 265-280.

_____ (1986), "Art Versus Science as Ways of Generating Knowledge About Materialism," in *Methodological Innovations in Consumer Research*, D. Brinberg and R. Lutz, eds., New York: Springer-Verlag, 1-36.

_____ (1987), "Material Values in the Comics," *Journal of Consumer Research*, 14 (June), 26-42.

_____ (1988), "Possessions and the Extended Self," *Journal of Consumer Research*, 15 (September), 139-168.

_____ and Richard W. Pollay (1985), "Images of Ourselves: The Good Life in Twentieth Century Advertising," *Journal of Consumer Research*, 11 (March), 887-897.

Benton, Raymond, Jr. (1987), "Work, Consumption, and the Joyless Consumer," in *Philosophical and Radical Thought in Marketing*, A.F. Fırat, N. Dholakia and R.P. Bagozzi, eds., Lexington, MA: Lexington Books, 235-250.

Deleuze, Gilles and Felix Guattari (1987), *A Thousand Plateaus: Capitalism & Schizophrenia*, Minneapolis, MN: University of Minnesota Press.

Ewen, Stuart (1988), *All Consuming Images: The Politics of Style in Contemporary Culture*, New York: Basic Books.

_____ (1989), "Advertising and the Development of Consumer Society," in *Cultural Politics in Contemporary America*, I. Angus and S. Jhally, eds., New York: Routledge, 82-95.

Fırat, A. Fuat (1986), "Towards a Deeper Understanding of Consumption Experiences: The Underlying Dimensions," in *Advances in Consumer Research*, XIV, M. Wallendorf and P.F. Anderson, eds., Provo, UT: Association for Consumer Research.

_____ (1987), "The Social Construction of Consumption Patterns: Understanding Macro Consumption Phenomena," in *Philosophical and Radical Thought in Marketing*, A.F. Fırat, N. Dholakia and R.P. Bagozzi, eds., Lexington, MA: Lexington Books, 251-267.

_____ (1988), "Consumption as Production: The End Result of Marketing Practice," in *Marketing: A Return to the Broader Dimensions*, S.J. Shapiro and A. Walle, eds., Chicago: American Marketing Association.

_____ (1991), "Postmodern Consumption: What Do the Signs Signal?" in *Marketing Signs*, J. Umiker-Sebeok, ed., Bloomington, IN: Indiana University Press (Forthcoming).

_____ and Nikhilesh Dholakia (1977), "Consumption Patterns and Macromarketing: A Radical Perspective," *European Journal of Marketing*, 11, 291-298.

_____ and _____ (1982), "Consumption Choices at the Macro Level," *Journal of Macromarketing*, 2 (Fall), 6-15.

Foster, Hal (1983), "Postmodernism: A Preface," in *The Anti-Aesthetic: Essays on Postmodern Culture*, H. Foster, ed., Port Townsend, WA: Bay Press, ix-xvi.

Gitlin, Todd (1989), "Postmodernism: Roots and Politics," in *Cultural Politics in Contemporary America*, I. Angus and S. Jhally, eds., New York: Routledge, 347-360.

Habermas, Jürgen (1983), "Modernity - An Incomplete Project," in *The Anti-Aesthetic: Essays on Postmodern Culture*, H. Foster, ed., Port Townsend, WA: Bay Press, 3-15.

Holbrook, Morris B. (1987), "O, Consumer, How You've Changed: Some Radical Reflections on the Roots of Consumption," in *Philosophical and Radical Thought in Marketing*, A.F. Fırat, N. Dholakia and R.P. Bagozzi, eds., Lexington, MA: Lexington Books, 156-177.

_____ and Elizabeth C. Hirschman (1982), "The Experiential Aspects of Consumption: Consumer Fantasies, Feelings and Fun," *Journal of Consumer Research*, 9, 132-140.

Hutcheon, Linda (1988), *A Poetics of Postmodernism: History, Theory, Fiction*, New York: Routledge.

Jameson, Fredric (1983), "Postmodernism and Consumer Society," in *The Anti-Aesthetic: Essays on Postmodern Culture*, H. Foster, ed., Port Townsend, WA: Bay Press, 111-125.

Kilbourne, William E. (1987), "The Self Actualizing Consumer vs. the Class Cage," in *Marketing Theory*, R.W. Belk, et. al., eds., Chicago: American Marketing Association, 312-315.

Luke, Timothy (1986), "Jean Baudrillard and the Political Economy of the Sign," *Art Papers*, (January/February), 22-24.

Lyotard, Jean-François (1984), *The Postmodern Condition: A Report on Knowledge*, Minneapolis, MN: University of Minnesota Press.

Marchetti, Gina (1989a), "Action-Adventure as Ideology," in *Cultural Politics in Contemporary America*, I. Angus and S. Jhally, eds., New York: Routledge, 182-197.

_____ (1989b), "Hollywood and Its Discontents: Representa-tions of Asian American Women in *Year of the Dragon* and *Mississippi Triangle*," Paper presented at the Women in America: Legacies of Race & Ethnicity Conference, April 6-8, Washington, D.C.: Georgetown University.

Marx, Karl (1973), *Grundrisse: Foundations of the Critique of Political Economy*, New York: Vintage Books.

Massumi, Brian (1987), "Realer Than Real: The Simulacrum According to Deleuze and Guattari," *Copyright*, 1 (Fall), 90-96.

McCracken, Grant (1986), "Culture and Consumption: A Theoretical Account of the Structure and Movement of the Cultural Meaning of Consumer Goods," *Journal of Consumer Research*, 13 (June), 71-84.

_____ (1988), *Culture and Consumption: New Approaches to the Symbolic Character of Consumer Goods and Advertising*, Bloomington, IN: Indiana University Press.

Mick, David (1988), "Contributions to the Semiotics of Marketing and Consumer Behavior," in *The Semiotic Web: A Yearbook of Semiotics*, T. Sebeok and J. Umiker-Sebeok, eds., Berlin: Mouton de Gruyter.

Mill, John Stuart (1929), *Principles of Political Economy*, London: Longmons, Green and Co.

Mourrain, Jacques A.P. (1989), "The Appearance of the Hyper-Modern Commodity-form: The Case of Wine," *Proceedings of the 1989 AMA Winter Educators' Conference*, T. Childers, ed., Chicago: American Marketing Association.

Newcomb, Horace, ed. (1979), *Television: The Critival View*, Oxford: Oxford University Press (Second edition).

Owens, Craig (1983), "The Discourse of Others: Feminists and Postmodernism," in *The Anti-Aesthetic: Essays on Postmodern Culture*, H. Foster, ed., Port Townsend, WA: Bay Press, 57-82.

Poster, Mark (1981), "Technology and Culture in Habermas and Baudrillard," *Contemporary Literature*, (Fall), 41-61.

_____ (1975), "Translator's Introduction," in *The Mirror of Production*, J. Baudrillard, St. Louis, MO: Telos, 1-15.

Real, Michael R. (1979), "The Super Bowl: Mythic Spectacle," in *Television: The Critical View*, H. Newcomb, ed., Oxford: Oxford University Press (Second edition), 170-203.

Ross, Andrew, ed. (1988), *Universal Abandon?* Minneapolis, MN: University of Minnesota Press.

Santambrogio, Marco and Patrizia Violi (1988), "Introduction," in *Meaning and Mental Representations*, U. Eco, M. Santambrogio and P. Violi, eds., Bloomington, IN: Indiana University Press, 3-22.

Say, Jean-Baptiste (1964), *A Treatise on Political Economy*, New York: A.M. Kelly.

Sherry, John F., Jr. (1989), "Postmodern Alternatives: The Interpretive Turn in Consumer Research," in *Handbook of Consumer Theory and Research*, H. Kassarjian and T. Robertson, eds., Englewood Cliffs, N.J.: Prentice Hall (Forthcoming).

Stephanson, Anders (1988), "Regarding Postmodernism - A Conversation with Fredric Jameson," in *Universal Abandon?* A. Ross, ed., Minneapolis, MN: University of Minnesota Press, 3-30.

Venkatesh, Alladi (1989), "Modernity and Postmodernity: A Synthesis or Antithesis?" in *Proceedings of the 1989 AMA Winter Educators' Conference*, T. Childers, ed., Chicago: American Marketing Association.

Wallendorf Melanie and Eric J. Arnould (1988), " "My Favorite Things": A Cross-Cultural Inquiry into Object Attachment, Possessiveness, and Social Linkage," *Journal of Consumer Research*, 14 (March), 531-547.

Wernick, Andrew (1989), "Vehicles of Myth: The Shifting Image of the Modern Car," in *Cultural Politics in Contemporary America*, I. Angus and S. Jhally, eds., New York: Routledge, 198-216.

Wilson, Elizabeth (1989), *Hallucinations: Life in the Post-Modern City*, London: Hutchinson Radius.

Winders, James A. (1989), "Roland Barthes and Postmodern Visual Culture," Paper presented at the 1989 Winter Educators' Conference of the American Marketing Association, February 12-15, St. Petersburg Beach, Florida.

Wright, Talmadge (1989), "Marketing Culture: Spectacles and Simulations," in *Proceedings of the 1989 AMA Winter Educators' Conference*, T. Childers, ed., Chicago: American Marketing Association.

Some Processes in Brand Categorizing: Why One Person's Noise is Another Person's Music

Joseph Cherian, University of Illinois at Chicago
Marilyn Jones, University of Illinois at Chicago

ABSTRACT

After developing a framework for discussion, this paper proposes some new relationships in categorical processing of brands. In particular, the paper advances the thesis that (i) categorical brand information is represented in multiple and simultaneous ways, (ii) the consumer comes to the task of processing brand information with different levels of ability, motivation and opportunity, and (iii) these three levels of ability, motivation and opportunity directly affect the way in which the brand information is processed. In other words, the paper examines the question: Why does one person exposed to some sounds from a radio promptly dismiss it as 'noise', and why does another process these sounds to extract several levels of attributes such as artiste, station format, etc.?

INTRODUCTION

The importance of categorization to human functioning in general (James 1890; Bruner, Goodnow & Austin 1956) and consumer behavior in particular (Sujan, Sujan and Bettman 1988; Alba and Hutchinson 1987; Meyers-Levy and Tybout 1989) is well documented. Consumer behavior researchers have typically looked at well-defined or 'Aristotelian processes' in categorization behavior (Thompson 1989). This paper seeks to develop a framework that accounts for some relationships between the three stages: antecedents, processes and consequents of categorical processing. As such, the first major task is to identify and characterize the building blocks within each stage (Figure 1, boxes). The second major task then becomes one of specifying the relationships between these sets (Figure 1, arrows).

ANTECEDENTS TO THE CATEGORIZATION PROCESS

Following an earlier structure that was proposed to deal with the processing of information from advertisements (MacInnis and Jaworski 1989), the primary antecedents for processing of information for brand categorization are proposed to be ability, motivation and opportunity to process brand information (AMO). Each of these basic building blocks can be decomposed into components as described below.

Ability

The basic determinant of ability in a categorical perception context is expertise with relevant categories (cf Sujan 1985). There are several diverse areas in which the link between expertise and use of categorization has been demonstrated -- e.g. in chess (Chase and Simon 1973), in problem-solving (Chi, Feltovich and Glaser 1981), and in physics (Larkin et al 1980). Perhaps anything that can be coded into a Millerian 'chunk' (Miller 1956) can be called a category, and experts are able to 'chunk' more usefully than novices (Chase and Simon 1973). In consumer behavior studies it was found that consumers of low expertise tended to use category level evaluations as substitutes for brand level evaluations; it was also found that experts were more likely to go beyond such simple summary and surrogate evaluations in favor of more detailed processing (Sujan 1985). For the purposes of this framework, only expertise will be considered a relevant variable in the discussion of individual variation in ability. Future work in this particular area will have to deal with the evolution of the categories and the models of categorization used before, during and after category-formation (e.g. Cohen and Basu 1987).

Motivation

The needs, i.e. feelings of deprivation, that motivate a consumer is either utilitarian or expressive (MacInnis and Jaworski 1989). Utilitarian needs are those which require a strictly functional solution to a problem (see Rossiter and Percy 1987; Park and Young 1986). Expressive needs are those which require a socially meaningful solution (Belk 1988; Levy 1959) or an experientially satisfying solution (Holbrook and Hirschman 1982; Hirschman and Holbrook 1982). The definition of needs as feelings of deprivation is not intended to imply that motivation is essentially a 'catching-up' process; it could also be thought of as a 'moving-up' process wherein the impetus is to improve on status quo rather than to remedy a feeling of lack. The effect of chronic search to satisfy an expressive need will show up in brand categorization schemas that finely sift brand information into many shades of expressiveness. On the other hand, a self-reliant utilitarian consumer faced with the incidental problem of supply depletion would approach the very same set of brands with coarse utilitarian schema.

Opportunity

The opportunity to process the information is strongly dependent on the situation -- there are situations where there is ample time to process the information and there are situations where one is forced to 'satisfice' because of time constraints. In general, it is reasonable to expect that the more the time available for the task the greater the depth of categorical processing. Conversely, the greater the perception of time scarcity the greater the pruning of the categorical structures; this pruning is done to the extent that will satisfice the task objectives. Other situational variables are not explored in the context of this framework and is left for future

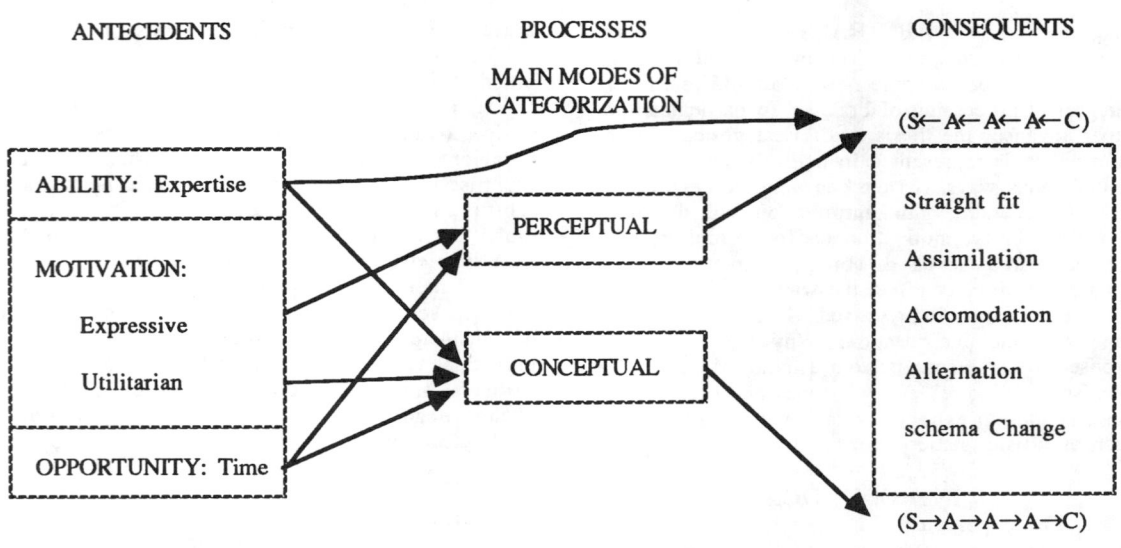

FIGURE 1
Brand Categorizing Framework
(only positive relations are shown)

theorizing and research. To summarize, the consumer approaches the brand categorization task in three basic ways: (i) either as an expert (i.e. with many, fine categories) or as a novice (with few, coarse categories); (ii) s/he is motivated primarily by utilitarian needs (which uses simple, functional categorization) or expressive needs (which uses symbolic and experiential categorization); and (iii) under severe time constraints s/he uses brand hierarchies that are pruned while under low or no time constraints s/he uses 'un-pruned' hierarchies.

PROCESSING OF BRAND INFORMATION INTO CATEGORIES

Categorization is a fundamental cognitive process (Harnad 1987). However, the basic mechanisms of categorization are still the subject of much discussion and debate (cf Thompson 1989; Ratneshwar and Shocker 1987). Some basic features of categorization processes are outlined below; then, by using an exemplar to motivate discussion, some findings of prior research and some propositions for future research are described.

The first way to divide categorization processes might be to look at what exactly is chunked or categorized -- one may ask are input data primarily perceptual or conceptual? A simple and operational definition of the differences between these two types of data follows: Perceptual data are those where the perceptual information is the sole information processed. Conceptual stimuli, on the other hand, are those where the information that is processed is far greater than what is perceptually transmitted. For example, if one is asked to categorize some boxes of detergents and if this was done only on the basis of red-packages versus blue-packages, it is categorization based on perceptual data, and therefore is called perceptual categorization (PC). On the other hand, if only brand-names were provided and then inferences were made, e.g. that some of these brands are 'experiential' brands and some are 'functional' brands, then it is categorization based on conceptual data, and therefore is called conceptual categorization (CC). It is later shown that some antecedent conditions prompt one or the other type of categorization.

The distinction between perceptual and conceptual categorization is important for four fundamental reasons --

(i) conceptual categories are necessarily fuzzier than perceptual categories because perceptual attributes can at least be perceived (Mervis and Rosch 1981); for conceptual categories, attributes range from the concrete (e.g. feathers, which can be perceived) to the abstract (e.g. flying, which can only be described) (cf. Johnson and Fornell 1987); further, categorizers use naive, implicit theories that make them select only some attributes in an ad hoc and idiosyncratic manner (Murphy and Medin 1985); for example when asked what-is-stylish a respondent may not even look at individual attributes and look instead at overall 'feel' or 'look'.

(ii) while perceptual categories are typically hierarchical and low in potential for inferences, conceptual categories can yield rich inferences (Medin and Barsalou 1987); e.g. classifying objects into the perceptual category, blue-objects, does not enable one to make too many further inferences, but classifying objects into the conceptual category, stylish cars, enables inferences about operation, upkeep, etc.

(iii) perceptual categories are probably biologically driven, conceptual categories maybe more culturally driven; when adopting the views of different cultures and subcultures categorizers perceives different prototypes for the same category (Barsalou and Sewell 1984); for example when subjects are asked to name a typical bird within the context of different cultures they typically name different species (e.g. eagles versus ostriches).

(iv) while perceptual categories are more stable, conceptual categories are more flexible across contexts (Medin and Barsalou 1987); for example what is considered typical of a category differs based on the context -- a typical animal for a milking-context is a cow, a typical animal for a riding-context is a horse (Roth and Shoben 1983).

Thus, the basic motivations and methods that drive the two types of categorization seem different. To the extent that these differences are meaningful, categorization theorists should be sensitive to this distinction. To the extent that some theories may have been developed expressly for one mode categorization, they should be used with caution or not at all for the other mode. (Medin and Barsalou, 1987, do point to several similarities between these types of categorization and attempt a reconciliation of the two perspectives).

Another way to divide categorization processes is to go beyond the input (i.e. data type) to the output (i.e. representation of the categories that are formed). It has been proposed that there is a three-level representational system for categories -- (i) an iconic representation that is an analog of the sensory input; (ii) a categorical representation that is a highly context-sensitive and consequence-dependent representation of categorical boundaries; and (iii) symbolic representations that underlie language and make it possible to learn categories by description (Harnad 1987); for the purposes of this paper Harnad's, 1987, conception of tripartite representation is adopted without explicitly refuting either Paivio's, 1986, dual encoding scheme or Pylyshyn's, 1984, monolithic approach to cognition. The implied mechanism is that whenever the categorizer encounters a sensory input, the many representations of the stimulus begin to be established if they do not already exist or become activated if they already exist. While the iconic representation is just an analog of the input, the categorical representation is essentially an analog-to-digital filter that takes the sensory input and manages to label and file the input into contextually relevant categories. The last of these, symbolic representation, is the closest in spirit to the notions of schema (cf Mandler 1982; Bettman 1979). In other words, when presented with a horse as stimulus, the iconic representation is the analog version retained in eidetic memory; the category representation is the translation of the analog-stimulus into a digital-code i.e. naming or recognizing the category relevant for the purposes of the task at hand (e.g. category: horse); and the symbolic representation activates the part of the subjects network that includes 'horse' and its relationships to other higher categories (e.g. animal) and lower categories (e.g. has four legs).

These two input-and-output views of categorization processes are highly related -- perceptual categorization (PC) depends primarily on iconic representation while conceptual categorization (CC) depends on symbolic representation. The middle stage, category representation, facilitates movement from one type of categorization to the other by acting as a translator to convert the analog information into digital output. Two basic and relevant outcomes of this perceptual-conceptual distinction must be emphasized -- (i) the perceptual categorization is essentially externally driven because of a heavy reliance on the perceptual object for information; and the conceptual categorization is essentially internally driven because of a heavy reliance on the categorizers internal schema or representational structures; and (ii) perceptual categorization is temporally localized and may have no enduring qualities, while conceptual categories simultaneously stable within simple contexts (e.g. roses are flower) and flexible across applied contexts (e.g. roses are for valentines vs. roses are thorny).

This distinction is a novel way to characterize the categorization process. Both perceptual and conceptual categorization can be done according to the three basic modes of categorization identified in the seminal article on the topic in consumer behavior literature (Cohen and Basu 1987); both perceptual and conceptual categorization can be done according to rules, prototypes or exemplars. The basic understanding still is that the information is stored in a consumers mind in hierarchical levels; these levels consist of increasingly symbolic, i.e. conceptual, representations towards the top and increasingly iconic, i.e. perceptual, representations towards the bottom.

CONSEQUENT PROCESSES OF BRAND CATEGORIZING

At the very easiest one could have just one category, 'things', into which everything is piled; at the very worst one could have one separate category for each and every thing encountered. Neither method provides any help in evaluation of categories or retrieval of data. Quite clearly, information has to be organized in some fashion; it has been suggested that information is organized categorically for any task that requires different responses to different inputs (Harnad 1987). The rationales for categorizing have been variously described as information processing efficiency

(Bruner, Goodnow and Austin 1956), cognitive stability (Lingle, Altom and Medin 1984), evaluative ease (Cohen 1982) and coherence (Cantor and Mischel 1979). These are meta-outcomes of using categorization as a preferred cognitive strategy rather than outcomes that are peculiar to a particular instance of categorization. Particular, or short-term, output processes are either (i) fitting an instance into an existing category structure with varying degrees of stress, or (ii) fitting an existing category to an instance. In other words, when trying to fit a square peg in a round hole either the peg gives in in a variety of ways or the hole gives in, depending on the rigidity of their compositions and strength of the force motivating the fit.

Any instance that a categorizer has to process either will be congruous with existing schema or incongruous with existing schema. Congruous instances fit automatically into the existing categorization. There are three ways in which an incongruous instance (II) can be made to fit into existing categorical structure or schema -- (i) assimilate, i.e. pretend II is just another instance of the category; this happens when there is a mild amount of discrepancy. (ii) accommodate, i.e. create a subcategory within to fit such IIs; this happens when there is a moderate amount of discrepancy. and (iii) alternate, i.e. go to another schema or node in the hierarchy; this happens when the stimulus cannot be either accommodated or assimilated (Rumelhart and Norman 1972). Alternately, when too many discrepant instances accrue and require too much assimilation/accommodation/alternation one can expect new categorization schemas to form. The output processes may be arrayed in increasing order of difficulty as follows, increasing from straight fit to assimilation to accommodation to alternation to changing schemas (S→A→A→A→C).

EXPLANATIONS AND PROPOSITIONS OF BRAND CATEGORIZING FRAMEWORK

After an exemplar to the task of categorizing is described and its relationships to the antecedents, processes and consequents are outlined, a simple framework is used to describe some results found by others and to propose some new ideas for future categorization research and practice.

Antecedents and Processes

Consider a person sitting at a table being given some cards from many decks one at a time and asked to sort the cards in any way that made sense. Probably, a novice would sort the cards as they came into suits, while an expert would sort the cards by the suits in a numerical order -- i.e. experts use more conceptual categorization than novices. If put under a time constraint, the performance of both experts and novices would deteriorate -- possibly, novices and experts would resort to cruder perceptual categories (e.g. reds and blacks). Finally, utilitarian needs, prompted by problem-solving situations, give lesser importance to the perceptual components of a target as long as it solves the problem; on the other hand, expressive needs depend on whether the target can perform the experiential, i.e. perceptual, function. For example, someone looking for a trump-card is less concerned about the look-and-feel of the card, and someone looking to enjoy card-playing worries about whether the cards feel smooth or look good.

Processes and Consequents

The consequent processes basically span the range from straight fit to schema change (S→A→A→A→C). The degree of adjustment and effort needed in fitting stimulus to the schema is least for straight fit and the greatest for schema change. The conceptual categorizer, dealing with fuzzier categories would be more likely and able to adjust; the perceptual categorizers, dealing with more precise categories, would find it harder to adjust. In other words, the conceptual categorizer of a stimulus would be more willing to adjust when fitting a discrepant stimulus than a perceptual categorizer.

Antecedents and Consequents

A moderately incongruent stimulus, e.g. a pink six of diamonds, would cause the novice to adjust less readily than an expert; in other words, while a novice would choose assimilation or lumping the card with other diamonds, an expert would more likely choose accommodation or creating a new sub-category for pink diamonds since the expert is capable of making/accommodating changes more easily. Similarly, the greater the time available the greater the degree of adjustment possible. Given enough time a subject would choose accommodation, or creating a sub-category for pink diamonds; increasing the time pressure would force the subject to use assimilation, or subsuming the pink diamonds within the red diamonds. Finally, no relationships between type of need and degree of adjustment is proposed.

These relationships are summarized below, and indicated by the arrows in Figure 1. The managerial relevance and implications of each set of these relationships is also discussed.

SUMMARY PROPOSITIONS AND PRACTITIONER RELEVANCE

Set One: Antecedents and Processes

(i) The greater the Expertise the greater is CC
The lower the Expertise the greater the PC

In knowing that experts are more likely to use conceptual categorization, the marketing task becomes one of finding and positioning products according to the enduring schemas used by experts. The novice, however, does not bring a well-articulated or enduring schema to the task and uses perceptual cues to do the categorizing. Thus, to woo the expert one must use the expert's categorization schema; to woo the novice one must be perceived as belonging to product category. For example, an expert buying a used car depends on his or her own categorizing schemas (which includes abstract attributes such as likely performance) to make an evaluation; a novice, however, would look more at the perceptual aspects such as how the car looks and feels, and even 'kicks the tires', to make an evaluation.

(ii) The greater the Time the greater is CC+PC
The lower the Time the greater is PC of Novices
The lower the Time the greater is CC of Experts

In general, when there is ample time to make decisions the consumer would typically use a mix of conceptual and perceptual categorization. However, when time pressures exist, the novice reverts to perceptual categorization, and the expert resorts to a pruned categorization schema, and perhaps even to perceptual categorization. The example of some consumers mistaking dishwashing liquid for lemon concentrate simply because of the picture of lemons on the package of dishwashing liquid shows that perceptual categorization is done during hurried shopping. In fact, even though grocery aisles are laid out conceptually, i.e. produce with produce etc., the perceptual cues (lemons) were sufficient to cause some consumers to miscategorize an instance.

(iii) The greater the Expressive Need the greater is PC
The greater the Utilitarian Need the greater is CC

Products that are primarily the salve for expressive needs must be very carefully positioned in the perceptual realm because perceptual categorization characterizes these products (Park, Jaworski and MacInnis 1986). Even if they are ultimately consumed and evaluated on the basis of conceptual categorization, the perceptual component is particularly important. For example, a luxury car must look good even if it does not function reliably; in fact there are numerous instances of luxury cars that continue to enjoy patronage even when the consumer suspects that they do not function reliably. This propensity for expressive needs to lead to perceptual categorizing also explains why counterfeit products emulate only the looks, and not the performance of a brand. In contrast, products that serve utilitarian needs are processed by conceptual categorization; because these attributes are fuzzier, one can expect a larger set of brands to be considered substitutes. Therefore, those driven by utilitarian needs will do more brand switching.

Set Two: Processes and Consequents

(i) The greater the PC the more the adjustment
(ii) The greater the CC the less the adjustment

When the processing is primarily through perceptual categorization there is more need to adjust to incongruous stimuli than for conceptual categorization. This follows from the rigidity of perceptual categories and fuzziness of conceptual categories. This means that perceptual categorizers will sooner perceive a stimulus as discrepant than will a conceptual categorizer. For example, perceptual categorizers would buy into the notion that a soda is an 'un-cola' sooner than would conceptual categorizers. If, after discovering the discrepancy, there is sufficient drive left to process the incongruous instance, typically, perceptual categorizers will use higher-powered adjustment -- e.g. accommodation. Conceptual categorizers will use a lower-powered adjustment, say assimilation. Thus, a differentiated product in a category will be seen as a subtype by perceptual categorizers (e.g. un-cola) and as just another category instance by conceptual categorizers (soda). The outcome of adjusting to moderate levels of incongruity has been shown to be an increase in the favorable evaluation of incongruous stimuli (Meyers-Levy and Tybout 1989). The mechanism for this is thought to be the consumers transference of a self-congratulatory feeling to the incongruous stimulus; the self-congratulation is said to follow from resolving the discrepancy between the schema and incongruous stimulus by some adjustment process (Mandler 1982). Although this phenomenon seems to indicate that it is good to have a 'moderate' level of incongruity, it must be stressed that conceptual categorizers and perceptual categorizers do not perceive incongruity in the same way. Unless these categorizers are segregated by segmentation, the level of incongruity may not be managerially manipulable.

Set Three: Antecedents and Consequents

(i) The greater the Expertise the more the adjustment
(ii) The greater the Time the more the adjustment

The experts are capable of a larger repertoire of adjustments to incongruity than are novices; therefore, introducing radical or discontinuous innovations to the expert segment will not cause quite as much consternation as it would to the novice segment. Further, the experts can recall more brand level information because of better categorization than the novices can; thus, new product introductions are more likely to be correctly assimilated by experts than by novices. Conversely, radical innovations may have to positioned as mere instances of older categories when dealing with novices. In other words, a pioneering advantage can occur only if the target segment has the desire and ability to adjust to the newness of the pioneer, like the experts do; if the target segment primarily consists of novices, a pioneering advantage may not occur. Finally, the greater the amount of time available to the categorization task, the greater will be the amount of adjustment processes considered or tried. Thus, when rushing through a grocery store a consumer is more likely to think of all sodas as substitutes for one another, but when going through the same store at a more leisurely pace the consumer sees less substitutability.

CONCLUSIONS

Allegorically, we can propose some ways to answer the question: why is one person's noise another person's music? In general, the sounds are perceived as music be somebody because (i) there is the expertise to sort the sounds into categories, (ii) the time and (iii) the motivation to process the stimuli. These stimuli could be processed into perceptual categories (e.g. loudness) or conceptual categories (e.g. melody). Typically, novices stop at the perceptual categories while experts ascend to higher conceptual levels. Finally, if the stimuli do not seem to be in accord with existing categories, i.e. if the sounds do not sound familiar, the categorization schema are preserved by creating a new category --i.e. noise. If this process is seen as valid, a marketer will find it important to identify (i) the expertise of the target segment, and (ii) the predominant mode of categorization in this segment, so that new products can be introduced in an appropriate manner and current products can be better positioned.

REFERENCES

Alba, Joseph W. and J. Wesley Hutchinson (1987), "Dimensions of Consumer Expertise," *Journal of Consumer Research*, 13 (March), 411-454.

Barsalou, L. W., and Sewell, D. R. (1984), "Constructing representations of categories from different points of view," *Cognition Project Technical Report*, Number 2, Emory University.

Belk, Russell W. (1988), "Possessions and the Extended Self," *Journal of Consumer Research*, 15 (September), 139-68.

Bettman, James R. (1979), *An Information Processing Theory of Consumer Choice*, Reading, MA: Addison-Wesley Publishing Company.

Bruner, Jerome S., Jacqueline J. Goodnow, and George A. Austin (1956), *A Study of Thinking*, New York: John Wiley & Sons.

Cantor, Nancy and Walter Mischel (1979) "Prototypes in Person Perception," *Advances in Experimental Social Psychology*, vol 12, ed: Leonard Berkowitz, New York, NY: Academic Press, 3-52.

Chase, William G. and Herbert A. Simon (1973), "Perceptions in Chess," *Cognitive Psychology*, v(4) (January), 55-81.

Chi, Michelene T. H., Paul J. Feltovich and Robert Glaser (1981), "Categorization and Representation of Physics Problems by Experts and Novices," *Cognitive Science*, 5(April), 121-152.

Cohen, Joel B. (1982), "The Role of Affect in Categorization: Towards a Reconsideration of the Concept of an Attitude," *Advances in Consumer Research*, Vol. 9, ed. Andrew A. Mitchell, Ann Arbor, MI: Association for Consumer Research, 94-100.

_____ and Kunal Basu (1987), "Alternative Models of Categorization: Toward a Contingent Processing Framework," *Journal of Consumer Research*, 13 (March), 455-472.

Harnad, Stevan (1987), "Category Induction and Representation," *Categorical Perception*, New York, NY: Cambridge University Press, 535-65.

Hirschman, Elizabeth C. and Morris B. Holbrook (1982), "Hedonic Consumption: Emerging Concepts, Methods and Propositions," *Journal of Marketing*, 46 (Summer), 92-101.

Holbrook, Morris B. and Elizabeth C. Hirschman (1982), "The Experiential Aspects of Consumption: Consumer Fantasies, Feelings, and Fun," *Journal of Consumer Research*, 9 (September), 132-40.

James, William (1890/1983), *The Principles of Psychology*, Cambridge, MA: Harvard University Press.

Johnson, M. D. and C. Fornell (1987), "The Nature and Methodological Implications of the Cognitive Representation of Products," *Journal of Consumer Research*, v(14), Sept 1987 214-223.

Larkin, Jill H., John McDermott, P. Dorothea Simon and Herbert A. Simon (1980), "Expert and Novice Performance in Solving Physics Problems," *Science*, 208 (June), 1335-1342.

Levy, Sidney (1959), "Symbols for Sale," *Harvard Business Review*, 37 (July/August), 117-24.

Lingle, John H., Mark Altom and D. L. Medin (1984), "Of Cabbages and Kings: Assessing the Extendability of Natural Object Concept Models to Social Things" *Handbook of Social Cognition* vol 1 eds. R. S. Wyer and T. K. Srull Hillsdale, NJ: Erlbaum 71-118.

MacInnis, Deborah J. and Bernard J. Jaworski (1989), "Information Processing from Advertisments: Toward an Integrative Framework," *Journal of Marketing*, 53 (October), 1-23.

Mandler, George (1982) "The Structure of Value: Accounting for Taste," *Affect and Cognition* eds: M. S. Clark and S. Fiske, Hillsdale, NJ: Erlbaum 203-230.

Medin, Douglas L. and Lawrence W. Barsalou (1987), "Categorization Processes and Categorical Perception," *Categorical Perception*, ed: Stevan Harnad, New York, NY: Cambridge University Press, 455-90.

Mervis, Carolyn B. and Eleanor Rosch (1981), "Categorization of Natural Objects," *Annual Review of Psychology*, 32, 89-115.

Meyers-Levy, Joan and Alice M. Tybout (1989), "Schema Congruity as a Basis for Product Evaluation," *Journal of Consumer Research*, 16 (June), 39-54.

Miller, G. A. (1956), "The Magical Number Seven, Plus or Minus Two: Some Limits on our Capacity for Processing Information. *Psychological Review*, 63, 81-97.

Murphy, G. L. and D. L. Medin (1985) "The Role of Theories in Conceptual Coherence," *Psychological Review*, vol 92. 289-316.

Paivio, A. (1986b), *Mental Representations: A Dual Coding Approach*. Oxford: Oxford University Press.

Park, C. Whan and S. Mark Young (1986), "Consumer Response to Television Commercials: The Impact of Involvement and Background Music on Brand Attitude Formation," *Journal of Marketing Research*, 23 (February), 11-24.

_____ , Bernard J. Jaworski and Deborah J. MacInnis (1986), "Strategic Brand Concept-Image Management," *Journal of Marketing*, 50 135-45.

Pylyshyn, Z. W. (1984), *Computation and Cognition*. Cambridge, MA: MIT/Bradford Press.

Ratneshwar, S. and A. D. Shocker (1987) "The Application of Prototypes and Categorization Theory: Some Problems and Alternative Perspectives," *Advances in Consumer Research* v(15) 280-285.

Rossiter, John and Larry Percy (1987), *Advertising and Promotion Management*, New York: McGraw-Hill Book Company.

Roth, E. M. and E. J. Shoben (1983) "The Effect of Context on the Structure of Categories," *Cognitive Psychology* v(15), 346-378

Sujan, Mita (1985), "Consumer Knowledge: Effects on Evaluation Strategies Mediating Consumer Judgements," *Journal of Consumer Research*, 12 (June), 31-46.

Sujan, Harish, Mita Sujan, and James Bettman (1988), "Knowledge Structure Differences Between More Effective and Less Effective Salespeople," *Journal of Marketing Research*, 25 (February), 81-86.

Thompson, Craig J. (1989), "The Role of Context in Consumers' Category Judgments: A Preliminary Investigation," *Advances in Consumer Research*, Editor: Thomas K. Srull, Volume 16, 542-547.

The Family Resemblance Approach to Understanding Categorization of Products: Measurement Problems, Alternative Solutions, and Their Assessment

Don Saunders, Arizona State University
Steve Tax, Arizona State University
James Ward, Arizona State University
Kym Court, Arizona State University
Barbara Loken, University of Minnesota

ABSTRACT

How consumers categorize products, and how to measure the extent to which they perceive a particular product to be a member of a category is an issue of interest to both academic and applied researchers. The study examines the family resemblance approach to measuring category membership. Although family resemblance is perhaps the most widely used and cited measure of how attribute sharing relates to typicality, scrutiny of the procedures for its computation recommended by Rosch and Mervis (1975) suggests several ways the measure might be improved or modified. Some of these alternative methods have been used in the literature, but their relative performance has not been assessed. The study compares five alternative methods of computing family resemblance, and finds similarity in results for some, but not other, measures. The results have implications for both academic and applied students of consumer behavior.

Understanding why a product will be perceived as a member of a particular category is an important issue for consumer researchers and practitioners alike. To the researcher, the question raises basic issues of how consumers perceive categories and judge whether and to what extent an item is like other category members. To the practitioner, such issues are also relevant in a variety of ways. For example, the manufacturer of a sporty looking compact car may wonder whether consumers will tend to compare the car to higher priced vehicles positioned as true sports cars or to lower priced vehicles positioned primarily as compact cars. The answer to this question could influence many aspects of marketing strategy such as market segmentation, advertising (e.g., what attributes to push, what competitors to compare to), and pricing.

One approach to understanding the determinants of product categorization that has been applied by a number of researchers (Nedgungadi and Hutchinson 1985, Sujan 1985, Ward and Loken 1986, Solomon 1988) is the family resemblance approach initially developed in psychology by Rosch and colleagues (Rosch and Mervis 1975, Mervis and Rosch 1981). Theoretically, this approach is based upon the idea that category membership is a matter of degree. In this view, most categories include more and less prototypical members. The most prototypical members are those that people tend to think of as the best, truest examples of the category. For example, people might perceive such vehicles as a Ferrari, Jaguar, or Corvette to be highly prototypical sports cars. People may also tend to call a number of other cars "sports cars," but they may tend to regard these as less good, true members of the category.

In a number of studies, Rosch and colleagues have shown that more prototypical members of a category tend to share more attributes with other members of the category than less prototypical members (Mervis and Rosch 1981). Thus, in this approach, degree of attribute sharing, or "family resemblance," determines prototypicality. Rosch and Mervis (1975) developed a procedure for measuring family resemblance that has been widely cited and used in the psychology literature.

According to Rosch and Mervis (1975), family resemblance should be measured as follows. First, the researcher develops a list of category members, perhaps by eliciting their names from subjects in a pretest. Then subjects are asked to list the attributes they believe each category member possesses. Usually, subjects are given a minute or two to list attributes for each category member. Next, the researcher develops a category member by attribute matrix. All attributes mentioned by one or more subjects are listed on the right side of the matrix, and category members are listed at the top. The researcher then goes through the matrix, and checks, for each category member, those cells that correspond to an attribute that at least one subject has noted that a category member possesses. After this task is completed, Rosch and Mervis suggest that the researcher should review the matrix, and credit any member that clearly and obviously possesses an attribute with the attribute although the attribute may not have been mentioned for the product by any subject. The researcher should also take away the credit of an attribute to any member that clearly and obviously does not possess the attribute. Upon completion of these judgements, family resemblance scores can be computed for the category members. The scores are computed by first counting the number of products that share a particular attribute in the final matrix. Each product sharing the attribute is then credited with a score equal to the number of products possessing the attribute. The larger the number sharing the attribute, the larger the score. If the attribute is unique to only one product, the product is given a score of 1. This scoring is done for every attribute listed in the matrix. Finally, the scores for each product are computed by adding the scores that were assigned for each attribute. The larger the number of attributes a member shares with other category members, and the more widely these attributes are shared with other category members, the higher the family resemblance score.

Studies that have applied the family resemblance approach to better understand the determinants of typicality in product categories suggest that the method usually produces scores that correlate highly with alternative measures of category membership, such as typicality ratings, and also yields managerially useful data on what attributes contribute more or less to an item's perception as a member of a category. For example, a study of the prototypicality of snack foods by Ward and Loken (1986) found that the consumers studied rated apples as rather prototypical snack foods. The family resemblance approach revealed that apples shared many attributes with other snack foods such as potato chips and peanuts. These included being round, crunchy, crisp, divisible into pieces, easily eaten "finger food", appropriate for many occasions, readily transportable, and liked by many people. While such attributes are not necessarily determinant in the sense of causing people to view apples as snack foods, they could prove very useful to apple marketers designing an ad to promote the use of apples as snack foods.

Despite the utility of the method, close scrutiny suggests some problems and some alternative methods of computing the measure (Loken and Ward 1987). One problem is that unique attributes increase the family resemblance score by one. This seems counterintuitive, in that a measure of attribute sharing should not increase to the extent that a member has unique attributes, not shared by any other category member. Another seeming problem in the method is that an attribute need be mentioned by only one subject to enter the matrix. Once there, judges may perceive the attribute to be shared by many other members, and credit them with the attribute. This could be a problem because the resulting scores may reflect less the attributes salient to subjects than the logic of the judges. Yet another problem is the subjectivity involved in judging whether members do or do not have attributes. For example, a subject might list the attributes "sweet," "salty," and "coated" for M&M peanut candies but not apples. Judging whether apples should be credited with these attributes seems necessarily subjective and difficult.

Perhaps as a response to these potential problems, researchers have over time tried a number of modifications to the family resemblance procedure. In the consumer behavior literature, Sujan (1985) used only attributes mentioned by two or more subjects to compute family resemblance. Loken and Ward (1987) criticized the family resemblance approach, and proposed an alternative "attribute structure" measure. In the psychology literature, Barsalou (1985) introduced a measure of family resemblance based upon the average rated similarity of category members to one another and not attribute lists. Malt and Smith (1984) examined the issue of whether attributes contribute independently to perceived typicality (as assumed by the family resemblance procedure) or whether the correlation among attributes in a category also influences judged typicality. Tversky (1977) has proposed alternative ways of computing family resemblance including giving positive weight to common features and negative weight to distinctive features, and accounting for frequency of mention. Although his work did not focus on a comparison of his methods with the Rosch et. al. approach, his data suggest that accounting for frequency of mention may improve the correlation of family resemblance with typicality.

Although a number of alternative methods of computing family resemblance have been tried in the literature, no study that we are aware of has attempted to systematically vary methods of computing family resemblance on the same data set to see if 1) the scoring of unique attributes, 2) experimenter judgment, and 3) accounting for frequency of mention produce family resemblance scores that differ in their correlations with typicality, the traditional Rosch method, and one another. The purpose of this study is to attempt to address these questions. These issues are important for two reasons. First, the family resemblance procedure is a widely used method for studying category structure in both the psychology and marketing literatures. Future researchers should be interested in whether alternative procedures yield the same or different results. Second, the results of the study will help researchers assess the comparability of past family resemblance data.

METHODOLOGY

Stimuli Development

To develop stimuli for the study, a sample of 25 undergraduate students were asked to list members of the category "types of food that people eat at their evening meal." The subjects were reminded to list types of food, not brands, and were asked to list the types in the order they were thought of. Members of other categories were also elicited as part of the pretest.

Once the data were collected, "production ranks" were computed for types of foods using the 20 types that were most frequently mentioned by subjects. A score of 20 was assigned to the first food mentioned, 19 to the second, and so on. The foods with the 20 highest production ranks were then chosen for the stimuli (shown in Table 1) for the next phase of the study.

Attribute Lists

In the next part of the study, subjects' perceptions of the attributes possessed by category members were collected. Subjects were 15 undergraduate students who volunteered to participate in the study during scheduled class periods. None of these students had participated in the first part of the study.

The procedure followed methods recommended by Rosch and Mervis (1975). Each of the 20

TABLE 1
Types of Foods Eaten at an Evening Meal

Baked Beans
Baked Potato
Chicken
Fish
Ham
Hamburger
Hotdog
Lasagna
Pizza
Rice
Ribs
Roast Beef
Salad
Shrimp
Spaghetti
Steak
Taco
Turkey
Veal
Vegetable

---

category members was printed at the top of a page. Subjects each received a packet of the 20 randomly ordered members.

Subjects were asked to list the attributes possessed by each item for a minute and a quarter. The instructions, adapted from Rosch and Mervis (1975) read, "This is a simple experiment to find out the characteristics and attributes that people feel are common to and characteristic of different kinds of ordinary, everyday objects . . . . At the top of each page is listed the name of one object. For each page, you'll have a minute and a quarter to write down all of the attributes of that object you can think of. But try not to just free associate. For example, if "bicycles" just happens to remind you of your father, don't write down "father." Each subject listed attributes for all 20 category members.

Prototypicality Ratings

The subjects were also asked to rate the prototypicality of the category members on three 0-10 point scales with endpoints very typical--very atypical, very good example--very poor example, and very representative--very unrepresentative. The instructions for the scales, once again consistent with Rosch and Mervis (1975), asked subjects to rate how good an example each category member was of the category. Subjects were cautioned not to confuse typicality with frequency of encounter or liking, using virtually the same wording as Rosch. The complete prototypicality rating instructions are shown in the Appendix. To develop an overall typicality score, the scores for each of the three scale measures (typicality, representativeness, and goodness-of-example) were summed across all subjects.

Alternative Measures of Family Resemblance

The first step in computing the alternative measures of family resemblance was to create a brand by attribute matrix showing all the attributes listed by one or more subjects for each product. Attributes were written along the right side of the matrix and products along the top. Some degree of judgment enters the creation of the matrix, because subjects often use different words that appear to mean the same attribute. Thus, the attributes that subjects list are subject to a content analysis prior to being included in the matrix. However, this analysis attempted to stay very close to what subjects said, and attempted to minimize the aggregation of disparate comments into single categories. Each alternative measure used the data in the resulting matrix as a starting point.

The first measure, FR1, computed family resemblance for the members of the category in the way recommended and used by Rosch and Mervis (1975) and most often adopted in other studies. Two of the researchers, acting as judges, first examined the applicability of each attribute to each product, as previously explained. In each case, the researchers, relying upon their own knowledge of the stimuli, decided whether the attribute might be possessed by the product or not. If the product, in their judgement, clearly possessed the attribute, the product was credited with the attribute even though no subject had actually listed the attribute for the product. If the product clearly and obviously did not possess the attribute, the attribute was deleted for the product. Although the researchers attempted to be as objective as possible, these judgements were often rather subjective. If the judges disagreed about whether a product had an attribute, a third researcher resolved the dispute.

Once the entire matrix was reviewed, family resemblance scores were computed for the products. First, the number of products possessing a particular attribute was counted, and this count was assigned as a score (weight) to each of the products. Thus, if eleven products were credited with a particular attribute, each received a score of 11. Next, the scores were summed across attributes for each product.

The second measure of family resemblance, FR2, was computed using the matrix resulting from the judges' review and the same procedure as FR1. However, this measure deleted any attributes credited to only one or two products from the computation of the family resemblance scores. As noted earlier, increasing a measure of attribute sharing for attributes unique to one or two members of a category seems to be counter to the logic of a measure that should increase to the extent that a member shares attributes with other members.

The third measure of family resemblance, FR3, was computed by relying only upon the attributes listed by the subjects. Thus the original product by attribute matrix, unchanged by experimenter judgment, was used as input data for the computation of these scores. FR3 was intended to provide insight into whether the judgments made earlier improve correlations with typicality. If they do, one might conclude that either the judges bias the measures in the expected direction, or improve the scores by in effect "reminding" subjects to accurately describe the stimuli. If judgment does not improve the correlations over the raw data, one might suggest that this time-consuming and perhaps problematic aspect of the procedure be dropped. FR4 was computed like FR3, only attributes unique to one or two products were not scored, following the procedure used for FR2.

FR5 was computed to introduce a new factor into the measure, the number of subjects who mentioned an attribute. In this procedure, the number of products that shared a particular attribute was first computed, and this score was assigned as a weight to each product having that particular attribute. The original matrix, and not the matrix modified by experimenter judgement, was used as input. For example, as explained earlier, if eleven products shared an attribute, each product possessing the attribute received a score of eleven. Next, a further weight was applied to the data. The number of subjects who mentioned the attribute was counted (e.g., nine), and then the first weight was multiplied by the number of subjects (e.g., 11 X 9 = 99). The logic for this procedure was that if more subjects mentioned an attribute, and more products shared the attribute, then it should contribute more to the perceived typicality of the category member.

RESULTS

Prior to analysis of the data, the mean typicality score for each type of food was computed across subjects (after reverse scoring so that correlations with other measures would be positive), and the median production rank was also computed across subjects. Family resemblance scores were computed for each type of food as a member of its category in the five ways described above. The n for all correlations is 20, the number of products in the category.

The resulting correlations are shown in Table 2. Supporting the validity of the typicality rating procedure, the correlation between typicality and production rank, found by past studies to be highly positive (e.g., Ward and Loken 1986, Mervis and Rosch 1981), was .63, $p < .05$.

The principle question addressed by the study is whether the five methods of computing family resemblance result in the same or different results. FR1 versus FR2, and FR3 versus FR4 compare the effect of not increasing the family resemblance score for products with attributes shared by none or only one other product. The correlation of FR1 with FR2 was .99, and the correlation of FR3 with FR4 was .98. These results strongly suggest that, at least in the present data set, increasing the family resemblance score by "1" for unique attributes is not a significant problem. Furthermore, each member of the two pairs of measures correlates about .40 with typicality. These correlations of the four resemblance measures with typicality are all in the expected positive direction and are all significant at the .10, but not the .05 level.

The correlations of FR1 versus FR3, and FR2 versus FR4 address whether experimenter judgement in adding or deleting attributes significantly influences the results. FR1 and FR3 correlated .89, and FR2 and FR4 correlated .91 with one another. Once again, using judged data versus raw data resulted in scores that correlate highly, and have comparable correlations to typicality (about .40, as noted earlier).

The family resemblance measure weighted by frequency of mention across subjects (FR5) was correlated slightly but not significantly more with typicality than the other measures (.47, significant at $p < .05$). However, this measure was poorly correlated with the other family resemblance measures ($r = .33$ to .19). This last result seemed puzzling, but may be because the measure introduces another factor into the family resemblance score, akin to familiarity or frequency of instantiation. These factors have been shown to have an influence on typicality that is independent of attribute-based measures of category structure such as family resemblance (Barsalou 1985). In other word, weighting by frequency of mention may have actually reduced the measure's relationship to family resemblance (as suggested by the low correlations with other measures) but may have added an additional factor that compensatorily raised FR5's correlation with typicality.

DISCUSSION

The family resemblance measure is a widely used method of studying categorization in both the psychology and consumer research fields. However, the approach recommended by Rosch and colleagues, although widely adopted, raises questions about

TABLE 2
Correlation Matrix

Types of Food For Evening Meal

Typicality	Typ.	PR	FR1	FR2	FR3	FR4
Prod. Rank	.82 (.00)	r prob.				
FR1	.38 (.09)	.63 (.00)				
FR2	.40 (.08)	.65 (.00)	.99 (.00)			
FR3	.42 (.06)	.63 (.00)	.89 (.00)	.88 (.00)		
FR4	.42 (.06)	.64 (.00)	.89 (.00)	.91 (.00)	.98 (.00)	
FR5	.47 (.04)	.45 (.05)	.19 (.43)	.21 (.22)	.33 (.16)	.33 (.16)

whether alternative computational procedures might yield better, or at least different, results.

The results of the present study indicate that the family resemblance measure seems to be relatively robust to scoring unique attributes or not, and using experimenter judgement or not. These findings suggest that users of the family resemblance procedure may be more confident that using the procedures recommended by Rosch does not contribute significant bias to their results. From another perspective, the results suggest that the use of judgment to decide whether products have attributes may not be an essential part of the procedure. Since this phase of the measure requires two judges to independently review the matrices and perhaps a third to resolve disagreements, its elimination might save significant amounts of time and labor, as well as alleviate whatever anxiety researchers have about introducing their own judgement into the data. This simplification might be of particular interest to practitioners who wish to use the family resemblance approach, since time may often be a more critical factor to them in choosing a method than to academic researchers.

Finally, FR5, the method that weighted for frequency of attribute mention across subjects, exhibited an interesting pattern of correlating slightly more highly with typicality than the other resemblance measures, but correlating poorly with these measures themselves. Tversky (1977) has recommended weighting by frequency of mention as a means of improving the correlation of resemblance measures with typicality. The present results do not contradict his recommendation, but it was argued that weighting by frequency of mention may create a "hybrid" measure incorporating attribute-based aspects of category structure and another factor, perhaps similar to familiarity. These suggestions are speculative, and seem worth pursuing with a larger and more varied set of measures including familiarity and other measures of category structure. Our findings are further qualified by the use of only one category for the comparison of the five measures. The category used, "types of food that people eat at their evening meal", is perhaps more ad hoc and diverse than the types of categories frequently studied by consumer researchers. Therefore, a demonstration of these same findings for other sorts of categories would be worthwhile to pursue in future research. Further confirmation of our results across a larger variety of categories would increase confidence in their generality.

REFERENCES

Barasalou, Lawrence (1985), "Ideals, Central Tendency, and Frequency of Instantiation as Determinants of Graded Structure in Categories," *Journal of Experimental Psychology: Learning, Memory, and Cognition*, 11, 629-654.

Loken, Barbara and James Ward (1987), "Measures of Attribute Structure Underlying Product Typicality," in *Advances in Consumer Research*, Vol. 14, eds. Paul Anderson and Melanie Wallendorf, Provo, UT: Association for Consumer Research, 22-26.

Malt, Barbara and Edward Smith (1984), "Correlated Properties in Natural Categories," *Journal of Verbal Learning and Verbal Behavior*, 23, 250-269.

Mervis, Carolyn and Eleanor Rosch (1981), "Categorization of Natural Objects," *Annual Review of Psychology*, 32, 89-115.

APPENDIX
Instructions for Rating Prototypicality

This part of the study is concerned with how people think about categories and their members. As an example of what I'm interested in, let's think about the category "red."

Close your eyes and imagine a very true "red."
Now imagine an orangish red.
Imagine a purple red.

Although you might still name the orangish red or the purplish red with the term "red," they are not as good examples of red as the "true" red you imagined earlier. In short, some reds are redder than others.

The same is true for other kinds of categories.

Think of dogs. You all have some notion of what a good example of a dog is, that is, a very typical dog. To some people, a retriever is a very typical dog while a poodle is a much less representative example.

Note that judgements of how typical, how representative, or how good an example something is have nothing to do with how well you like the thing. You may like and prefer to own a poodle or a Russian Wolfhound without thinking that either is the breed that best represents what people think of as a typical dog.

Note also that more typical instances of a category are not necessarily those that you encounter most often. For example, if you own a poodle or a Russian Wolfhound, you may see it every day but you still would not say that it is the breed that best represents what most people would regard as a typical dog.

In the next pages, you will find lists of items belonging to a category of types of products or brands. Your task will be to rate how typical or atypical an instance each item is of the category named on the first page of the questionnaire.

Nedungadi, Prakash and J. Wesley Hutchinson (1985), "The Prototypicality of Brands: Relationships with Brand Awareness, Preference, and Usage," in *Advances in Consumer Research*, Vol. 12, eds., Elizabeth Hirschman and Morris Holbrook, Provo, UT: Association for Consumer Research, 498-503.

Rosch, Eleanor and Carolyn Mervis (1975), "Family Resemblance: Studies in the Internal Structure of Categories," *Cognitive Psychology*, 7, 573-605.

Solomon, Michael (1988), "Mapping Product Constellations: A Social Categorization Approach to Consumption Symbolism," *Psychology and Marketing*, 5 (3), 233-258.

Sujan, Mita (1985), "Consumer Knowledge: Effects on Evaluation Strategies Mediating Consumer Judgement," *Journal of Consumer Research*, 12 (June), 31-46.

Tversky, Amos (1977), "Features of Similarity," *Psychological Review*, 84 (July), 327-352.

Ward, James and Barbara Loken (1986), "The Quintessential Snack Food: Measurement of Product Prototypes," in *Advances in Consumer Research*, Vol. 13, ed. Richard Lutz, Provo, UT: Association for Consumer Research.

Consumer Expertise and the Vividness Effect: Implications for Judgment and Inference

John Kim, Oakland University
Frank R. Kardes, University of Cincinnati
Paul M. Herr, Indiana University

ABSTRACT

Prior research has shown that product information is processed less extensively and less diligently as expertise decreases (for a review see Alba and Hutchinson 1987). This finding suggests that novices are more likely to overlook or underutilize important information (underprocessing), and, consequently, novices should be susceptible to a wide variety of inferential biases. However, the inferential biases that are likely to be exhibited by experts have been neglected in judgment and decision research. This study addresses this asymmetry by attempting to identify inferential biases that are more likely to be manifested by experts than by novices. Specifically, we suggest that novices are more likely to underprocess information, whereas experts are more likely to overprocess information. Consistent with this hypothesis, the results indicate that one type of overprocessing bias, the vividness effect, is more pronounced for experts than for novices.

CONSUMER EXPERTISE AND INFERENTIAL JUDGMENT

Consumers are frequently depicted as cognitive misers who use simplifying heuristics (e.g., Kahneman et al. 1982), peripheral cues (e.g., Petty et al. 1983), and other shortcuts designed to reduce the amount of cognitive effort required for judgment and choice tasks. Simplifying strategies are especially prevalent when issue involvement, cognitive capacity, and/or expertise is low. Under these circumstances, cognitive shortcuts enable consumers to make complex judgments and decisions on the basis of limited information. These strategies are useful because they permit consumers to make decisions quickly and easily, but they are potentially harmful because important information is often overlooked or underutilized.

Underprocessing Biases

Research on minimal information processing (underprocessing) has shown that people are susceptible to a wide variety of inferential biases when important information is overlooked or underutilized. Attributional biases (Ross and Fletcher 1985), biased assimilation (Ha and Hoch 1989, Hoch and Ha 1986, Lee et al. 1987), nonregressive judgment (Cox and Summers 1987), insensitivity to the reliability and validity of information (Kahneman et al. 1982), and other biases are common when consumers rely too heavily on simplifying strategies.

One factor that influences the extent and the intensity of information processing is expertise, which is defined as "the ability to perform product-related tasks successfully" (Alba and Hutchinson 1987, p. 411). Novices are likely to underprocess information because they lack the cognitive resources required to construe the inferential implications of a large set of product-related information. As expertise increases, however, the ability to process larger sets of information also increases. Moreover, experts are more likely to detect missing information spontaneously and to adjust their judgments accordingly (Kardes, Sanbonmatsu, and Herr 1990). Furthermore, experts are more likely to detect redundancy and to integrate information accordingly (Wallsten and Budescu 1981, 1983). Clearly, experts are able to perform much more sophisticated cognitive operations on much larger sets of information, relative to novices.

Novices -- who lack the cognitive structures and cognitive resources needed to process information extensively and diligently -- are likely to overlook or underutilize important information. Consequently, novices should be susceptible to a wide variety of inferential biases. Although it seems clear that underprocessing should lead to bias and error, it may also be possible to process information too extensively and too intensely (overprocessing). That is, there may be an optimal amount of cognitive effort required to process information (more complex information should require more effort), and when too little or too much effort is allocated to an information-processing task, bias and error results (Kardes forthcoming). We suggest that novices are likely to underprocess information, whereas experts are likely to overprocess information.

Overprocessing Biases

Most of the research that has been conducted to date has focused on underprocessing biases. However, a few studies have shown that people sometimes overutilize information that they would have been better off without. For example, judgments and decisions tend to be influenced by irrelevant analogies, if these analogies are accessible from memory (Gilovich 1981). Moreover, people tend to weigh behavioral information too heavily, without sufficiently accounting for the context in which the behavior was observed (Gilbert and Krull 1988).

In both of these cases, irrelevant information was presented in a vivid manner. Vividly presented information is inherently interesting, attention-drawing, and thought-provoking, and, consequently, vividly (as opposed to pallidly) presented information tends to be overutilized (for reviews see Kisielius and Sternthal 1986; Nisbett and Ross 1980).

However, the vividness effect is not as ubiquitous as one would expect (Taylor and Thompson 1982), and, consequently, recent research has focused on the boundary conditions of the phenomenon. For example, strong vividness effects on judgment are most likely when a large amount of information is available and when elaborative processing is likely (McGill and Anand 1989). When a relatively large set of information is available, differential attention to vivid versus pallid information is likely. Because greater amounts of attention should be allocated to vivid information, vivid information should have a greater impact on subsequent judgments.

However, recent evidence indicates that differential attention is not sufficient for producing judgmental vividness effects (Shedler and Manis 1986; Taylor and Wood 1983). This finding implies that other factors must also be important. One additional factor that appears to play a key role in the effects of vividly presented information on judgment is cognitive elaboration (Kisielius and Sternthal 1984, 1986; McGill and Anand 1989). Elaborative processing produces rich associative networks that facilitate the retrieval of target information and related information (Anderson 1983). Because vividly presented information facilitates elaborative processing, and because elaborative processing increases the amount of information that is likely to influence judgment, vividly presented information should have a greater impact on judgment.

In contrast, when elaborative processing is unlikely (due to the presence of other cognitive demands and/or due to low levels of prior knowledge in a given domain to guide processing), judgmental vividness effects should not be found. Thus, because elaboration likelihood is greater for experts than for novices (Alba and Hutchinson 1987), it was predicted that judgmental vividness effects should be more pronounced for experts than for novices.

METHOD

Subjects and Design

Eighty four undergraduates were randomly assigned to conditions in a 2 (vividly or pallidly presented information) X 2 (positive or negative valence) factorial design. Subjects were categorized as experts or as novices on the basis of their scores on an product knowledge inventory patterned after Sujan (1985). This instrument consisted of ten multiple-choice questions about the target product class, personal computers (e.g., What is the CPU? How many bits are there in a byte? What is the function of the ROM?). A median-split was performed on subjects' scores on this inventory, and experts answered more questions correctly, relative to novices (Ms = 8.22 vs. 3.52 out of a possible 10), $F(1, 78) = 3.86$, $p = .053$.

Stimuli

Subjects received a description of a new personal computer. The description was "condensed from *Consumer Reports*" and contained a summary of standard features (held constant across conditions), a rating (3rd or 17th best out of 20), and favorable or unfavorable (e.g., 640 or 512 KB) attribute information (memory, monitor, keyboard, hard drive system, printer port, graphics, and clock speed).

After exposure to the product description, subjects received a favorable or an unfavorable testimonial: "It's the best [worst] computer I've ever owned. It's really easy [hard] to use, and I haven't had a single problem [had nothing but problems] with it." The testimonial was presented either in a vivid face-to-face manner by a confederate posing as an experimental participant, or in a pallid printed transcription from *Consumer Digest*. In contrast to several previous studies (for reviews see Kisielius and Sternthal 1986, Taylor and Thompson 1982), the content of the testimonial was held constant to avoid confounding vividness with amount of information, type of information (e.g., base rate vs. case information), or other characteristics (e.g., novelty, redundancy, ambiguity) of information. Only manner of presentation (vivid or pallid) was varied. Finally, the testimonial and the product description were always evaluatively inconsistent to permit assessment of the relative impact of vivid versus pallid information.

Measures

Subjects rated the target product on three 11-point scales ranging from 0 to 10 (bad/good, favorable/unfavorable, desirable/undesirable). These ratings were averaged to form a single brand attitude index (Cronbach's alpha = .92, $p < .001$).

RESULTS

Brand attitude favorability as a function of information vividness, valence, and expertise is presented in Table 1. A 2 X 2 X 2 between-subjects analysis of variance performed on brand attitude favorability yielded a significant vividness by valence interaction, $F(1, 72) = 102.68$, $p < .001$. The predicted vividness by valence by expertise interaction was marginally significant, $F(1, 72) = 3.89$, $p = .052$. No significant main effects were obtained.

Simple effect tests were performed to interpret the interactions while controlling for the compounding of alpha. When the testimonial was favorable (and the specific attribute information was unfavorable), more favorable brand attitudes were formed when the testimonial was presented in a vivid (face-to-face) as opposed to a pallid (printed) manner ($p < .001$). In contrast, when the testimonial was unfavorable (and the specific attribute information was favorable), less favorable brand attitudes were formed when the testimonial was presented in a vivid as opposed to a pallid manner ($p < .001$). As predicted, this pattern was more pronounced for experts than for novices. As Table 1 indicates, mean differences in product evaluations following exposure to vivid versus pallid testimonials were greater for experts (Ms = 3.96 and -3.50 for positive and negative testimonials, respectively) than for novices (Ms = 2.95 and -1.90).

TABLE 1
Effects of Information Vividness, Valence, and Expertise on Product Evaluations

	Experts		Novices	
	Positive testimonial	Negative testimonial	Positive testimonial	Negative testimonial
Vivid testimonial	7.70	3.47	7.00	4.40
Pallid testimonial	3.74	6.97	4.05	6.30
Difference (vivid - pallid)	3.96	-3.50	2.95	-1.90

DISCUSSION

The manner in which information is presented has a strong effect on product evaluations, even when information content is held constant. Although vividly (as opposed to pallidly) presented information influences the judgments of both experts and novices, it has a greater impact on the judgments of experts. Of course, this effect is unwarranted because manner of presentation does not influence the reliability or validity of information. Hence, vivid information is weighed heavily in judgment, even when more important but less vivid information is available.

The present results also illustrate the paradox of the expert rather nicely. Although experts are able to learn, use, and remember more relevant information than novices (Alba and Hutchinson 1987), they are also likely to read too much into information of low or marginal probative value. Experts tend to process information more extensively and more deeply, and, consequently, experts tend to generate a richer and more elaborate associative network for a given piece of information. When experts (who are able to elaborate extensively) are exposed to vivid information (that is easy to elaborate on), a very rich associative network is formed.

What effects on memory and judgment are produced by a rich associative network? First, elaborative processing tends to increase recall (Anderson 1983). An elaborate network contains not only the target information, but also other related information. When a retrieval cue activates some related information, this information can then be used to infer the target information (Reder 1988; Walker 1986). Second, elaborative processing tends to increase judgment polarization (Tesser 1978). When missing information is correlated with presented information, presented information can be used to draw inferences about omissions. These inferences increase the amount of information that can be used as inputs for judgment, and as the amount of information available for judgment increases, judgmental extremity and confidence also increases (the set-size effect, see Anderson 1981).

Although the results are consistent with the hypothesis that novices are more susceptible to underprocessing biases, whereas experts are more likely to exhibit overprocessing biases, alternative interpretations are possible. For example, although we controlled for the amount of information presented and for information novelty, redundancy, ambiguity, coherence, etc. by holding information constant, source effects are possible. For example, a fellow undergraduate may be a more credible source, compared to an unknown individual interviewed by a consumer magazine. Furthermore, perceptions of a source may vary as a function of the level of expertise of the perceiver. Future research should control for possible source effects.

Finally, it should been emphasized that most of the research that has been conducted to date on inferential biases has focused on underprocessing biases. When too little cognitive effort is allocated to an information-processing task, important information is likely to be overlooked or underutilized and a number of systematic errors are likely to result. Novices are especially susceptible to this class of inferential errors. However, when too much effort is allocated to a cognitive task, several interesting overprocessing errors are likely to occur. Unfortunately, less is known about this class of inferential errors. The results of the present study indicate that the vividness effect is more pronounced for experts than for novices. Future research should investigate whether or not experts are more susceptible to other overprocessing errors as well. Overprocessing errors such as the correspondence bias (Gilbert and Krull 1988), the use of irrelevant analogies (Gilovich 1981), the perseverance effect (Ross et al. 1975), and the dilution effect (Nisbett et al. 1981) may also be more pronounced for experts than for novices.

REFERENCES

Alba, Joseph W. and J. Wesley Hutchinson (1987), "Dimensions of Consumer Expertise," *Journal of Consumer Research*, 13 (March), 411-454.

Anderson, John R. (1983), *The Architecture of Cognition*, Cambridge, MA: Harvard University Press.

Anderson, Norman H. (1981), *Foundations of Information Integration Theory*, New York: Academic Press.

Cox, Anthony D. and John O. Summers (1987), "Heuristics and Biases in the Intuitive Projection of Retail Sales," *Journal of Marketing Research*, 24 (August), 290-297.

Gilbert, Daniel T. and Douglas S. Krull (1988), "Seeing Less and Knowing More: The Benefits of Perceptual Ignorance," *Journal of Personality and Social Psychology*, 54 (February), 193-202.

Gilovich, Thomas (1981), "Seeing the Past in the Present: The Effect of Associations to Familiar Events on Judgments and Decisions," *Journal of Personality and Social Psychology*, 40 (May), 797-808.

Ha, Young-Won and Stephen J. Hoch (1989), "Ambiguity, Processing Strategy, and Advertising-Evidence Interactions," *Journal of Consumer Research*, 16 (December), 354-360.

Hoch, Stephen J. and Young-Won Ha (1986), "Consumer Learning: Advertising and the Ambiguity of Product Experience," *Journal of Consumer Research*, 13 (September), 221-233.

Kahneman, Daniel, Paul Slovic, and Amos Tversky (eds.) (1982), *Judgment Under Uncertainty: Heuristics and Biases*, New York: Cambridge University Press.

Kardes, Frank R. (forthcoming), "Consumer Inference: Determinants, Consequences, and Implications for Advertising," in *Advertising Exposure, Memory and Choice*, ed. Andrew A. Mitchell, Hillsdale, NJ: Lawrence Erlbaum Associates, in press.

_____, David M. Sanbonmatsu, and Paul M. Herr (1990), "Consumer Expertise and the Feature-Positive Effect: Implications for Judgment and Inference," in *Advances in Consumer Research*, Vol. 17, eds. Marvin E. Goldberg, Gerald Gorn, and Richard W. Pollay, Provo, UT: Association for Consumer Research, 351-354.

Kisielius, Jolita and Brian Sternthal (1984), "Detecting and Explaining Vividness Effects in Attitudinal Judgments," *Journal of Marketing Research*, 21 (February), 54-64.

_____ and Brian Sternthal (1986), "Examining the Vividness Controversy: An Availability-Valence Interpretation," *Journal of Consumer Research*, 12 (March), 418-431.

Lee, Hanjoon, Frank Acito, and Ralph L. Day (1987), "Evaluation and Use of Marketing Research by Decision Makers: A Behavioral Simulation," *Journal of Marketing Research*, 24 (May), 187-196.

McGill, Ann L. and Punam Anand (1989), "The Effect of Vivid Attributes on the Evaluation of Alternatives: The Role of Differential Attention and Cognitive Elaboration," *Journal of Consumer Research*, 16 (September), 188-196.

Nisbett, Richard and Lee Ross (1980), *Human Inference: Strategies and Shortcomings of Social Judgment*, Englewood Cliffs, NJ: Prentice-Hall.

_____, Henry Zukier, and Ronald E. Lemley (1981), "The Dilution Effect: Nondiagnostic Information Weakens the Implications of Diagnostic Information," *Cognitive Psychology*, 13 (April), 248-277.

Petty, Richard E., John T. Cacioppo, and David Schumann (1983), "Central and Peripheral Routes to Persuasion: Applications to Advertising," *Journal of Consumer Research*, 10 (September), 135-146.

Reder, Lynne M. (1988), "Strategic Control of Retrieval Strategies," in *The Psychology of Learning and Motivation: Advances in Research and Theory*, Vol. 22, ed. Gordon H. Bower, New York: Academic Press, 227-259.

Ross, Lee, Mark R. Lepper, and Michael Hubbard (1975), "Perseverance in Self-Perception and Social Perception: Biased Attributional Processes in the Debriefing Paradigm," *Journal of Personality and Social Psychology*, 32 (November), 880-892.

Ross, Michael and Garth J. O. Fletcher (1985), "Attribution and Social Perception," in *The Handbook of Social Psychology*, Vol. 2, eds. Gardner Lindzey and Elliot Aronson, New York: Random House, 73-122.

Shedler, Jonathan and Melvin Manis (1986), "Can the Availability Heuristic Explain Vividness Effects?" *Journal of Personality and Social Psychology*, 51 (July), 26-36.

Sujan, Mita (1985), "Consumer Knowledge: Effects on Evaluation Strategies Mediating Consumer Judgments," *Journal of Consumer Research*, 12 (June), 31-46.

Taylor, Shelley E. and Suzanne C. Thompson (1982), "Stalking the Elusive 'Vividness' Effect," *Psychological Review*, 89 (March), 155-181.

_____ and Joanne V. Wood (1983), "The Vividness Effect: Making a Mountain out of a Molehill?" in *Advances in Consumer Research*, Vol. 10, eds. Richard P. Bagozzi and Alice M. Tybout, Ann Arbor, MI: Association for Consumer Research, 540-542.

Tesser, Abraham (1978), "Self-Generated Attitude Change," in *Advances in Experimental Social Psychology*, Vol. 11, ed. Leonard Berkowitz, New York: Academic Press, 289-338.

Walker, Neff (1986), "Direct Retrieval from Elaborated Memory Traces," *Memory & Cognition*, 14 (July), 321-328.

Wallsten, Thomas S. and David V. Budescu (1981), "Additivity and Nonadditivity in Judging MMPI Profiles," *Journal of Experimental Psychology: Human Perception and Performance*, 7 (October), 1096-1109.

_____ and David V. Budescu (1983), "Encoding Subjective Probabilities: A Psychological and Psychometric Review," *Management Science*, 29 (February), 151-173.

Effect of Ad Pacing and Optimal Level of Arousal On Attitude Toward the Ad

Mark A. Pavelchak, University of Delaware
Meryl P. Gardner, University of Delaware
V. Carter Broach, University of Delaware

ABSTRACT

It was predicted that the pacing of TV advertisements would influence perceived arousal levels, and, depending on viewer's optimal level of arousal, attitudes toward the ad. Ad pacing did indeed influence arousal levels, but only for those with low optimal levels of arousal. Post hoc correlational evidence suggests that low optimals, but not high optimals, like relatively fast ads because they are emotionally arousing. Results are discussed in light of the multiply-determined nature of attitude toward the ad, and how ad pacing, through its effect of perceived levels of arousal, may increase our understanding of what makes advertisements effective.

INTRODUCTION

The concept of optimal level of arousal suggests that every organism has a preferred level of stimulation (e.g., Hebb 1955; Leuba 1955). Departures from this optimal level are aversive, which motivates (arousal seeking or avoiding) behavior intended to restore the optimum level. The concept has a long history in the study of human behavior (e.g., Berlyne 1960; Breuer and Freud 1895/1937; Driver and Streufert 1964). In consumer research, the concept has been applied to exploratory behavior (Raju 1980; Faison 1977; Venkatesan 1973), new product purchasing (Hirschman 1980; Robertson 1971), product/service satisfaction (Hanna and Wagle 1988), and reactions to television programs (Zillman and Bryant 1985). We feel that the concept has potential for enhancing our understanding of advertising effectiveness.

Two measures typically associated with advertising effectiveness are attitude toward the brand (Abrand) and purchase intent. Because attitude toward the advertisement (Aad) mediates Abrand and purchase intent (e.g., Mitchell and Olson 1981; Shimp 1981), understanding the underlying determinants of Aad is important (MacKenzie and Lutz 1989). Therefore, this study focuses on the possible effect of optimal level of arousal on Aad.

Over the years, arousal has been measured in two primary ways: physiological indices and self-report. Each approach has its advocates and detractors, and a legitimate place in research on advertising effectiveness. As our concern is with *conscious* feelings of arousal and how they are influenced by advertising, we measure arousal via self report in the current study. Consistent with previous researchers, we conceptualize arousal as a basic dimension of subjective emotional experience ranging from sleep to frantic excitement (Berlyne 1967; Mehrabian and Russell 1974). The dimension of arousal is conceptually orthogonal to pleasure/displeasure, the other primary dimension of emotional experience (Mehrabian and Russell 1974). This means that feelings of arousal per se are not inherently pleasurable or displeasurable.

It is well established that TV commercials can influence perceived levels of arousal in viewers (e.g., Pavelchak 1989, Wells 1964). However, because arousal is not inherently pleasurable, the effect of ad-induced arousal on Aad probably depends on secondary factors, such as viewers' optimal level of arousal. In general, individuals who prefer high levels of stimulation should react positively to an arousal-*inducing* ad, while those who prefer lower levels of stimulation should react positively to an arousal-*reducing* ad.

As with any stimulus, a variety of aspects of TV commercials have the potential to influence levels of arousal (e.g., humor, annoying appeals, sexually suggestive images). Many such factors, however, are only relevant to a small subset of commercials. In the present study, we selected an aspect that is relevant to *all* commercials: its activity level or pacing. Along with evaluation and potency, activity level is one of the three fundamental dimensions of stimulus meaning (Osgood, Suci, and Tannenbaum 1957). In addition, variations in ad activity level have been shown to influence perceived levels of arousal, while variations in evaluation level do not (Pavelchak 1989). Specifically, relatively "fast" ads tend to increase levels of perceived arousal, while relatively "slow" ads tend to have the opposite effect. Relating this to the construct of optimal level of arousal leads to the following hypotheses:

H1A: Individuals with relatively high optimal levels of arousal (high optimals) should like "fast" ads (given that other ad features are controlled for) more than those with relatively low optimal levels of arousal (low optimals).

H1B: Low optimals should like "slow" ads (given that other ad features are controlled for) more than high optimals.

Jointly, confirmation of these hypotheses should result in a significant interaction between self-reported optimal level (low/high) and type of ad seen (slow/fast) on Aad.

METHODOLOGY

Overview

Data for the present study were collected through a laboratory experiment with one manipulated factor, pace of the commercial (slow/fast). Upon arrival, subjects' optimal level of arousal was measured. Afterward, subjects indicated their emotional state (including level of arousal), were shown either a fast or slow-paced TV commercial, indicated their emotional state again, and then responded to measures of advertising effectiveness (including Aad). Based on their response to the optimal level of arousal measures, subjects were divided via median split into low optimals and high optimals. Therefore, the overall design of the study is 2 (fast ad/slow ad) X 2 (low optimal/high optimal), and the primary dependent measure is Aad.

Subjects

Subjects were students enrolled in an undergraduate introduction to marketing course at a major Eastern university. Subjects participated as part of a course research requirement. Of the 114 students who participated, eight were eliminated because they reported prior exposure to the ad used in their experimental session. This left a final sample of 106 subjects, 35 males and 71 females.

Advertisement Selection Procedure

The television ads used in this experiment were professionally developed by advertising agencies. Such ads generate a more "natural" emotional response than mock ads (Mitchell 1986). To minimize familiarity, the ads were videotaped from television programming in cities other than the one in which this study was conducted. Over 100 such commercials were rated by 20-30 judges on semantic differential items known to load highly on the dimensions of evaluation, activity, and potency. Each judge rated 10-20 ads (most judges rated 20). The judges, who came from the same population as those used in the main experiment, also indicated whether they had seen the ad before and whether they had purchased the product/service depicted in the ad. Based on judges' activity ratings, four ads were selected, two rated as relatively fast (ads for a bank and a coat store), and two rated as relatively slow (ads for a carpet store and a drug store). As expected, activity ratings of the fast ads were significantly higher than ratings of the slow ads ($p < .05$).

Measures

Subjective emotional states, including feelings of arousal, were measured using the Affect Grid developed by Russell, Weiss and Mendolsohn (1989). It consists of a 9 X 9 matrix of squares with two dimensions labelled as displeasure/pleasure and arousal/sleepiness. Subjects place a mark at the point on the grid that best represents their feelings at the moment. Optimal level of arousal was determined by responses to two separate scales that have some precedent in consumer research: Mehrabian and Russell's (1973) Arousal-Seeking scale, and Zuckerman, Eysenck and Eysenck's (1978) Sensation-Seeking scale. Each of these forty item scales measures the degree to which individuals tend to seek or avoid arousal-inducing situations. One primary difference between the two scales is that all of the items in the Zuckerman scale are positively worded (endorsement suggests high optimal level) whereas the Mehrabian scale contains both positively and negatively-worded items. Reliability analyses were performed on each scale and the coefficient alpha values were: Mehrabian = .86; Zuckerman = .78. These levels were deemed rather low for scales with so many items, but acceptable.

Attitude toward the ad was measured using a four-item scale developed by Mitchell (1986). Reliability for this scale was considered acceptable, as the coefficient alpha was .88.

Procedure

Prior to each session, one of the four videotaped commercials was randomly selected to be shown. Subjects were run in groups of five to ten. Upon arrival, subjects were told that the study concerned "personal characteristics and reactions to commercials." Subjects then filled out the Zuckerman scale, then the Mehrabian and Russell scale. Next, the affect grid was explained and subjects indicated on one grid their feelings at that point in time. Afterwards, the videotaped commercial was shown, and subjects filled out a second affect grid to represent how the commercial made them feel. Subjects then filled out a questionnaire that included measures of Aad, Abrand, whether or not they had seen the ad before, whether or not they had purchased the product depicted in the ad before, and other items. Finally, subjects were debriefed and thanked for their participation.

RESULTS

With the lack of control inherent in a study with self-reported factors, it important to examine the data for possible problems stemming from self-selection. Therefore, t-tests were performed on: pre-exposure arousal scores, pre-exposure pleasure scores, and Arousal and Sensation Seeking scores, with type of ad (slow/fast) as the between-subjects factor. Fortunately, none of the analyses were even close to significant (all p's > .38).

Although no ad pacing manipulation check measure was included in the post-experimental questionnaire, we sought to verify that the manipulation had the intended psychological impact by examining subjects' post-exposure arousal scores. A two-way ANOVA was performed on these scores with type of ad (slow/fast) and optimal level (low/high) as between-subjects factors. As expected, post-exposure arousal scores were significantly higher in the fast ad condition ($M = 5.31$) than in the slow ad condition ($M = 4.59$, $F(1,102) = 7.01$, $p = .009$). No other effects in this analysis were significant. Similar analyses on Aad and Abrand revealed no significant differences, indicating that there was no overall preference for the fast ads relative to the slow ads, or for the advertised brands.

TABLE 1
Aad Scores as a Function of Ad Pacing and Optimal Level of Arousal

1A: Mehrabian Scales:

Optimal Arousal Level	Ad Pacing Condition	
	Fast	Slow
Low	5.87 (n=24)	5.63 (n=28)
High	5.69 (n=31)	6.19 (n=23)

1B: Zuckerman Scales:

Optimal Arousal Level	Ad Pacing Condition	
	Fast	Slow
Low	5.99 (n=27)	5.39 (n=28)
High	5.56 (n=28)	6.48 (n=23)

Note: Aad scores could vary from 1 (Dislike Very Much) to 9 (Like Very Much).

The Pacing X Optimal level was significant for the Zuckerman scale only ($F(102) = 4.85$, $p = .03$).

Turning now to the primary analyses, the first analysis utilized Mehrabian scale scores as a measure of optimal level. An ANOVA was performed on Aad scores with type of ad (slow/fast) and optimal level (low/high) as between-subjects factors. It was predicted that high optimals would like fast ads more than low optimals, and low optimals would like slow ads more than high optimals. The predicted interaction was not significant ($p = .29$), and surprisingly, the pattern of means was *opposite* to the predicted pattern (see Table 1A). The picture was even more dramatic when the Zuckerman scale was used as a measure of optimal level, as the Optimal Level X Condition interaction was statistically significant ($F(1,102) = 4.85$, $p = .03$) (see Table 1B).

As a first step in understanding these results, the self-reported arousal data were re-examined. This time, arousal change scores, which of course take pre-exposure scores into account, were examined. It was discovered that, while the ad pacing manipulation was effective overall, the effect was due exclusively to low optimal level subjects who were shown a fast ad (See Table 2). The contrast of their arousal change scores versus the remaining subjects was statistically significant ($t(104) = 2.12$, $p < .03$).

Given that relatively fast-paced ads influenced perceived levels of arousal in low optimals but not in high optimals, it remains to be seen whether there was a subsequent effect of arousal on Aad (in the fast ad condition). As evidence that there was such an effect, the correlation between Aad and post-exposure arousal scores was $+.49$ ($p < .001$), and between Aad and arousal change scores, the correlation was $+.31$ ($p = .01$). On the surface, however, the evidence that these relationships are due to arousal seeking is weak: the correlation between Aad and arousal seeking is $-.23$ ($p < .05$) using the Zuckerman scale, and only $-.05$ (n.s.) using the Mehrabian scale.

A closer look at the data, however, is more encouraging. Responses to the Zuckerman scale were decomposed into its four sub-scales (Thrill Seeking, Experience Seeking, Disinhibition, and Boredom Avoidance). Correlations regarding the Experience Seeking scale, which basically is a measure of sensuality orientation, were intriguing: Aad and Experience seeking correlated $-.43$ ($p = .001$), while arousal change scores and Experience seeking correlated $-.44$ ($p < .001$). (Similar, although weaker results were obtained when an experience seeking scale derived from the Mehrabian scale was utilized).

Ad-induced arousal may have had an effect on Aad in the fast ad condition, but not in the slow ad condition. Neither high nor low optimals' perceived

TABLE 2
Arousal Change Scores as a Function of Ad Pacing and Optimal Level of Arousal

Optimal Arousal Level (Zuckerman Scale)	Ad Pacing Condition	
	Fast	Slow
Low	1.04 (n=24)	0.21 (n=28)
High	0.16 (n=31)	0.04 (n=23)

Note: Scores could vary from -8 (Large Decrease in Arousal) to +8 (Large Increase in Arousal).

The contrast of Low Optimals in the fast ad condition versus the remaining subjects was significant: ($t(104) = 2.12$, $p = .037$).

---

levels of arousal were influenced by the slow ads (both mean arousal change scores were close to zero; see Table 2). Nevertheless, high and low optimals differed in their liking for these ads, with high optimals (based on the Zuckerman scale) being more favorable ($t(49) = 2.06$, $p = .044$).

DISCUSSION

Ad Pacing and Arousal

One implicit objective of this study was to provide additional empirical evidence that ad pacing can influence perceived levels of arousal. To achieve this objective, subjects were shown ads that varied in activity level. We realize that the ads undoubtedly varied along many other dimensions, and that such differences may be responsible for our results. We tried to partially address this issue by using two versions of each type of ad. No doubt our results would have been more clear-cut if additional factors (such as the type of product) were held constant across the ads. In reality, however, unless time compression methodology is used, it may be impossible to vary *only* ad pacing. Our results should be interpreted in this light.

While a significant effect of ad pacing on post-exposure arousal scores was observed, a closer look at the data revealed that only the arousal levels of low optimals who saw a fast ad were influenced (increased). In contrast, the arousal levels of high optimals were unaffected by fast ads. One possible explanation for this result is that the fast ads were not fast enough. In our pretesting procedure, we encountered ads that were rated as having much higher activity levels than the ones used in the present study. Unfortunately, those ads could not be used because of an attempt to equate type of product/service across the four ads. If significantly faster ads *were* used, the arousal levels of high optimals may have been increased, although perhaps not as much as those of low optimals.

In the slow ad condition, arousal levels of both low and high optimals were virtually unaffected. It may be that 30-second television ads can be used to increase, but not decrease, levels of perceived arousal, especially when subjects have not seen the ad before. An ad's slow pacing may be counteracted by its *novelty*, which tends to increase levels of attention and perhaps arousal (Berlyne 1967). In addition, emotional states with low levels of arousal (boredom, sleepiness), may simply require a stimulus duration of longer than 30 seconds to be activated.

This study has demonstrated the usefulness of the Russell et al (1989) Affect Grid in studies of advertising and emotion. Subjects reported little difficulty using the grid, and its simplicity permits the relatively unobtrusive measurement of emotional states at multiple points during an experimental session. One flaw in our use of the scale was our failure to ask subjects to indicate their optimal level *on the grid*. Had this been done, a closer correspondence between arousal seeking and momentary perceived levels of arousal could have been made.

Arousal and Attitude Toward the Ad

The pattern of correlations in the fast ad condition among arousal change scores, Aad, and arousal (experience) seeking scores suggests that arousal change might have mediated the effect of experience seeking on Aad. The direction of the relationships suggest that low experience seekers appear to like relatively fast ads more than high experience seekers, and do so because they are emotionally arousing. High experience seekers, on the other hand, did not find the relatively fast ads emotionally arousing, and were less favorable toward them. Thus, it seems as though ad-induced arousal *can* in fact influence attitude toward the ad, although in a manner contrary to our initial expectations. These results are admittedly post hoc, but do suggest that Aad may be determined in part by ad-induced feelings of arousal *sometimes*, and that such an effect may depend on the arousal seeking or avoiding nature of the viewer.

In the slow ad condition, in contrast, the arousal levels of neither high nor low optimals were influenced by the ads, and yet the two groups differed in terms of Aad (high optimals were more favorable). This result reminds us that Aad is multiply determined; that ad-induced arousal is only one of many factors that contribute to such judgments.

It is interesting to speculate about the effect of ad pacing on Aad if "really fast" ads were used. We assume that such ads would increase the arousal levels of both low *and* high optimals, not just low optimals. Yet would extremely fast pacing be "too fast" for the so-called arousal-avoiding low optimals, and would their relatively positive reaction toward fast ads reverse? Would extremely fast pacing be to the liking of high optimals, as we originally hypothesized? If so, the pattern of means for Aad would reverse, and our hypothesis would receive support.

Ad Pacing, Arousal, and Attitude Toward the Ad

This study has shown that ad pacing may be a promising factor to manipulate in attempts to enhance advertising effectiveness. It also shows that ad pacing, or at least the small difference in ad pacing used in this study, does not influence perceived levels of arousal in all viewers. It remains to be seen what features of ads will increase levels of arousal in high optimals. It may be extremely fast pacing, or a completely different factor. Given the present results, practitioners may find it useful to develop a taxonomy of ad features that are arousing to specific segments, and manipulate those features in ads targeted toward those segments.

Directions for Future Research

Additional work is needed to understand the effects of an ad's pace or activity level, and the conditions under which pacing affects arousal. Further research is also needed to explore the relationship between arousal and attitude toward the ad. Findings indicate that attitude toward the ad is multiply determined and that arousal needs to be considered in concert with other factors. In addition, research should address the conditions under which ad pacing affects attitude toward the ad.

REFERENCES

Berlyne, Donald E. (1960), *Conflict, Arousal, and Curiosity*, New York: McGraw-Hill Book Co.
_____ (1967), "Arousal and Reinforcement," in *Nebraska Symposium on Motivation*, ed., D. Levine, Lincoln: University of Nebraska Press.
Breuer, J., and Sigmund Freud (1937), *Studies in Hysteria* (A.A. Brill, trans.), New York: Nervous and Mental Disease Publishing Company (Originally published 1895).

Driver, Michael J., and Siegfried Streufert (1965), "The 'General Incongruity Adaptation Level' (GIAL) Hypothesis: An Analysis and Integration of Cognitive Approaches to Motivation," Working Paper No. 114, Institute for Research in the Behavioral, Economic, and Management Sciences, Purdue University, Lafayette, IN.
Faison, Edmund W. (1977), "The Neglected Variety Drive: A Useful Concept for Consumer Behavior, *Journal of Consumer Research*, 4 (December), 172-175.
Hanna, Nessim and John S. Wagle (1988), "Who is Your Satisfied Customer?" *Journal of Services Marketing*, 2 (Summer), 5-13.
Hebb, D. O. (1955), "Drives and the CNS (Conceptual Nervous System)." *Psychological Review*, 62, 243-254.
Hirschman, Elizabeth C. (1980), "Innovativeness, Novelty Seeking, and Consumer Creativity," *Journal of Consumer Research*, 7 (December), 283-295.
Leuba, Clarence (1955), "Toward Some Integration of Learning Theories: THe Concept of Optimal Stimulation," *Psychological Reports*, 1, 27-33.
MacKenzie, Scott B. and Richard J. Lutz (1989), "An Empirical Examination of the Structural Antecedents of Attitude Toward the Ad in an Advertising Pretesting Context," *Journal of Marketing*, 53 (April), 48-65.
Mehrabian, Albert and James A. Russell (1973), "A Measure of Arousal Seeking Tendency," *Environment and Behavior*, 5, 315-333.
_____ (1974), *An Approach to Environmental Psychology*, Cambridge: M.I.T. Press.
Mitchell, Andrew A. (1986), "Theoretical and Methodological Issues in Developing and Individual Level Model of Advertising Effects," in *Advertising and Consumer Psychology*, eds. Jerry C. Olson and Keith Sentis, New York: Praeger Publishing Co., 172-196.
_____ and Jerry C. Olson (1981), "Are Product Attribute Beliefs the Only Mediator of Advertising Effects on Brand Attitude?" *Journal of Marketing Research*, 18, 318-332.
Osgood, Charles E., G. J. Suci, and Percy H. Tannenbaum (1957), *The Measurement of Meaning*, Urbana: University of Illinois Press.
Pavelchak, Mark A. (1989), "Dimensions of Stimulus Meaning: A Basis for Predicting Emotional Reactions to Commercials," paper presented at the meeting of the Society for Consumer Research (APA), New Orleans, LA.
Raju, P. S. (1980), "Optimum Stimulation Level: Its Relationship to Personality, Demographics, and Exploratory Behavior," *Journal of Consumer Research*, 7 (December), 272-282.
Robertson, Thomas S. (1971), *Innovative Behavior and Communication*, New York: Holt, Rinehart and Winston.
Russell, James A., Anna Weiss, and Gerald A. Mendolsohn (1989), "Affect Grid: A Single-Item Scale of Pleasure and Arousal," *Journal of Personality and Social Psychology*, 57 (March), 493-502.

Shimp, Terence A. (1981), "Attitude Toward the Ad as a Mediator of Consumer Brand Choice," *Journal of Advertising*, 10 (2), 9-15.

Venkatesan M. (1973), "Cognitive Consistency and Novelty Seeking," in *Consumer Behavior: Theoretical Sources*, eds., S. Ward and T.S. Robertson, Englewood Cliffs, N.J. pp. 354-384.

Wells, William D. (1964), "EQ, Son of EQ, and the Reaction Profile," *Journal of Marketing*, 28 (October), 45-52.

Zillman, Dolf and Jennings Bryant (1985), "Affect, Mood, and Emotions as Determinants of Selective Exposure," in *Selective Exposure to Communications*, eds., Dolf Zillman and Jennings Bryant, Hillsdale, NJ: Erlbaum, 157-190.

Zuckerman, Miron, S. Eysenck, and M. Eysenck (1978), "Sensation Seeking in England and America: Cross-Cultural, Age and Sex Comparisons," *Journal of Consulting and Clinical Psychology*, 46, 139-149.

Emotions and Motivations in Advertising

John R. Rossiter, Australian Graduate School of Management
Larry Percy, Lintas:USA

ABSTRACT

In this paper, we update Rossiter and Percy's (1987) theory of emotions and motivations in advertising, which states that: (1) a brand attitude must link the brand to a purchase motivation; (2) this linkage is effected via one or more benefit claims, which contain a cognitive component and an emotional component with the elicited emotion or emotions serving the purchase motivation; (3) informational (negative reinforcement) motives require at least a negative-to-neutral sequence of emotions whereas transformational (positive reinforcement) motives require at least a neutral-to-positive shift although the neutral part of this sequence is usually assumed as the consumer's initial exposure state; and (4) various informational and transformational motives are most effectively served by specific types of emotions. We present a pilot test of the theory. We also comment on the role of arousal and on other advertising theorists' attempts to explain the application of emotions in advertising.

INTRODUCTION

One of the most important jobs for creative people in advertising is to select the proper types of advertising stimuli that are likely to elicit appropriate emotions in the target audience. Creative people are usually *given* the benefit or benefits that they are supposed to associate with the client's brand, and their task becomes one of generating a creative idea or overall theme for the advertising as well as converting the benefits into *benefit claims* that distinguish the brand from competing brands. Whereas benefits can be conceptualized as verbal or visually implied statements linking a brand to an attribute, benefit *claims* make this verbal or visually implied statement in a way that elicits an appropriate emotion or sequence of emotions (Rossiter and Percy 1987). In short, a benefit lacks emotion, but a benefit claim depends upon emotion. Closely competing brands usually target the same benefit or set of benefits. In the detergent category, both Tide and All claim to get all the dirt out. In the world of trucks, Ford and Chevy talk about basically the same rugged performance features. And how is one to tell the difference between really good perfumes such as Obsession and Opium? More and more, what differentiates the effectiveness of advertising in most categories is not benefit selection but rather the ability of the brand's advertising agency to make benefit *claims* in an emotionally more compelling (informational) or engaging (transformational) way.

Emotional stimuli, of course, are not just inserted *ad lib* in ads. Rather, it is our contention (Rossiter and Percy 1987) that emotional stimuli are inserted, or should be inserted, to serve an underlying purchase (or usage) motivation (a motivation or motive being defined as a behavioral energizing mechanism). This emotional energizing takes place in the *brand attitude* communication effect. In the first section of this paper, we describe more fully (with some updating) our 1987 theory of emotions and motives in advertising. In the second section, we present a pilot test of the theory. In the final section, we comment on attempts by other advertising theorists and researchers to conceptualize and measure emotions in advertising.

ROSSITER AND PERCY'S THEORY

Rossiter and Percy (1987, Chapters 6-10) propose what amounts to a theory of emotions and motivations in advertising. Their theory centers on the communication effect of brand attitude (or preference, as called by marketing scientists). They define brand attitude as consisting essentially of a propositional link between a brand and a purchase motivation; the proposition can be established by, among other causes, advertising. A consumer or buyer could thus hold several attitudes (but only several) toward a brand, depending on the purchase motivation operative at the time. In defining brand attitude in terms of motivation, Rossiter and Percy (see also Katz 1960; Fennell 1975, 1978, 1989; Lutz 1978) depart from the "overall evaluation" definition of attitude popularized by Fishbein and Ajzen (1975) and argue that brand attitude must have an energizing function. "Overall evaluation" or "global affect" becomes merely a particular type of attitude where the purchase motive is sensory gratification. In our theory, there is always evaluation *for a purpose* (see especially Fennell 1989). We maintain that advertising practitioners (creatives) are much more likely to implicitly use our definition of brand attitude than to advertise a brand on "overall affect." However, a belief-evaluation or expectancy-value conceptualization is still included in the theory in that this is the way that benefit claims (the "surface structure" in ads) are hypothesized to make the propositional link between the brand and the motivation (this link, the attitude, being the "deep structure"). Figure 1 depicts this conceptualization of brand attitude, showing: the brand, as represented by the prior communication effect of brand awareness; one or more beliefs associated with the brand; an emotion associated with each belief; with the emotions tapping the purchase motivation. The standard multi-attribute formulation can be applied to this model with the addition of a subscript, m, representing the particular purchase motivation:

$$A_{bm} = \sum_{i=1}^{n} B_{bim} E_{im}$$

FIGURE 1
Rossiter and Percy's (1987) Conceptualization of Brand Attitude

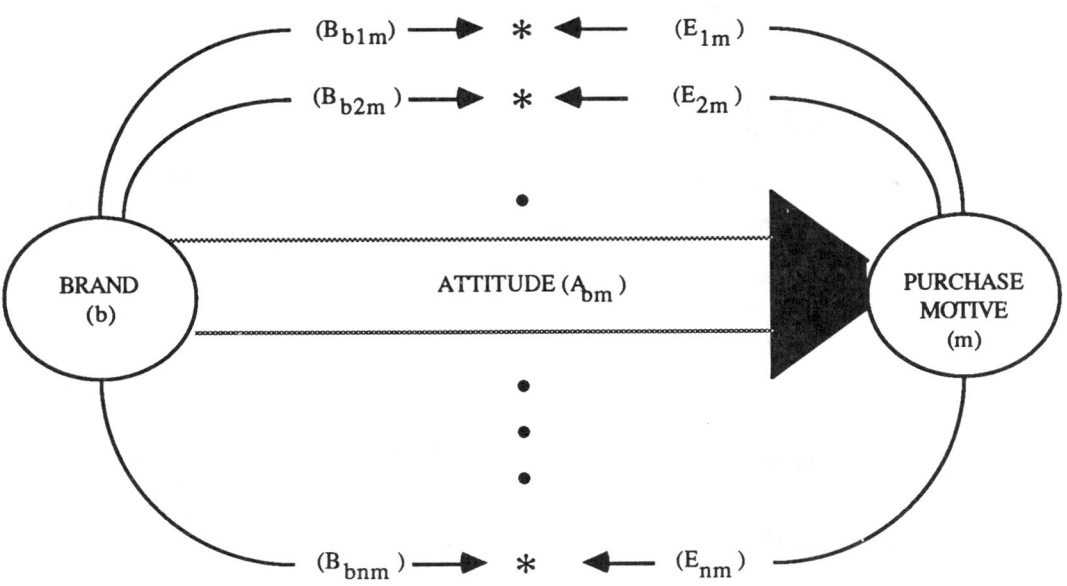

Note: B is the cognitive component (belief) and E is the affective component (emotion) of benefit claims 1...i...n. See also multi-attribute formula in text.

---

where A_{bm} = attitude toward brand b for purchase motivation m

B_{bim} = belief that brand b delivers on benefit claim i in relation to purchase motive m

E_{im} = emotional effectiveness of benefit claim i in energizing motive m

n = number of benefit claims.

Rossiter and Percy (1987) proposed eight motives (Table 1) as energizing all human behavior including purchase and consumption behavior. Their textbook was not the place to explain the theoretical basis of these motives but perhaps this paper does present an appropriate forum. Essentially we adhered to a homeostatic or equilibrium concept of motivation (Figure 2) in which there are *two* fundamental motivating mechanisms: the onset of a negative stimulus, which motivates the consumer to reduce or remove that stimulus; and the onset of a positive stimulus, which motivates the consumer to seek that stimulus until satiation sets in and the consumer returns to equilibrium. It is in the postulation of a positive (but temporary) departure from equilibrium that we differ from Fennell's ground-breaking conceptualization of motivation (most recently in her 1989 paper). Fennell postulates that all motives operate through deprivation and therefore involve negative reinforcement. Our negative motives (with her closest equivalents shown in parentheses) are as follows: problem removal (escape), problem avoidance (prevention), incomplete satisfaction (frustration), mixed approach-avoidance (conflict), and normal depletion (maintenance). Our positive motives (again with her motives' closest equivalents shown in parentheses) are as follows: sensory gratification (sensory pleasure opportunity), intellectual stimulation or mastery (exploratory interest), and social approval (*no* equivalent). Fennell's last two motives are seen as negative in that a sensory pleasure opportunity is one that the "actor is not yet enjoying," and exploratory interest is, according to her theory, due to the actor "experiencing difficulty in processing information" (1989, p. 45). Thus, Fennell sees these positive stimulus onsets as being externally-induced deprivations, a viewpoint with which we disagree (surely, the whole world is not motivated by deprivation!). It should be noted, however, that this theoretical point is somewhat moot. Arguing slightly differently from Fennell, our positive motives entail a transition from non-reward, but not necessarily punishment as Fennell implies, to reward. As Wagner (1969) points out, whereas the transition from non-reward to reward is reinforcing, it is not clear whether the reinforcement is due to

TABLE 1
Rossiter and Percy's (1987) Eight Purchase Motives

Negative Motives

1. Problem removal (solve)
2. Problem avoidance (prevent)
3. Incomplete satisfaction (search)
4. Mixed approach-avoidance (resolve)
5. Normal depletion (maintain)

"Informational"
(Drive reduction)

Positive Motives

6. Sensory gratification (enjoy)
7. Intellectual stimulation (explore, master)
8. Social approval (personal recognition)

"Transformational"
(Drive increase)

Note: Energized behaviors are shown in parentheses after each motive. The reinforcing process, drive reduction or drive increase, is shown at right, with type of advertising appeal most likely to accomplish the process shown in quotation marks.

FIGURE 2
The Two Fundamental Motivating Mechanisms, S- Onset and S+ Onset, and Their Resulting Drive and Affective Dynamics

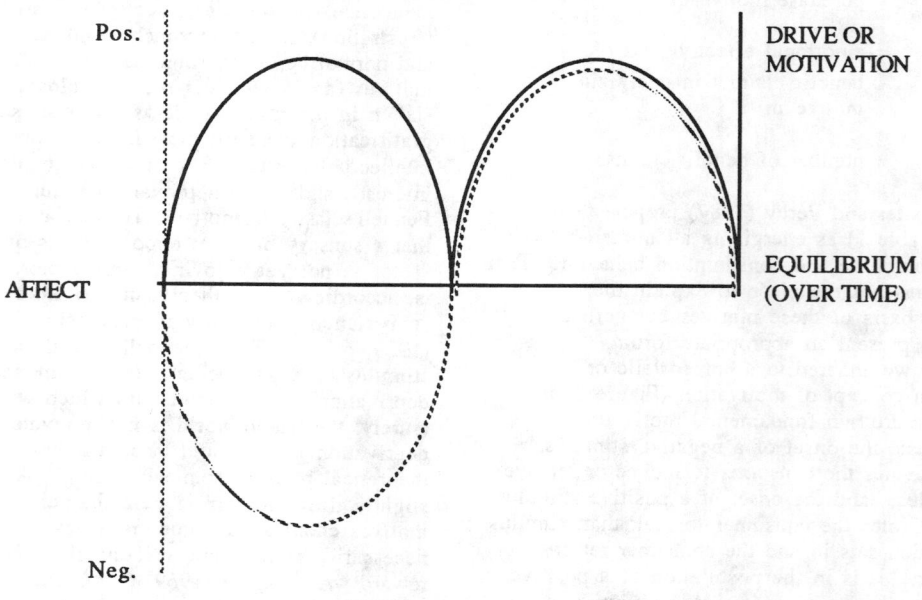

TABLE 2
Hammond's (1970) Reconceptualization of Mowrer's (1960a, b) Theory of Emotions

	ON	OFF
S-	Fear (excitatory)	Relief (inhibitory)
S+	Hope (excitatory)	Disappointment (inhibitory)

the initiation of reward or to the termination of non-reward. But we have an additional argument for our two-mechanism model of motivation over Fennell's, and this is shown in our emotional components subsequently. For positive motives, there is no necessity, and indeed rarely any advisability, in showing deprivational states in advertising prior to portraying positive stimulus onset in the form of sensory gratification, intellectual stimulation, or social approval.

Emotions enter our motivational theory by extending the innovative conceptualization proposed by Mowrer (1960a, b). To introduce Mowrer's conceptualization, we have to distinguish emotions from motivations. Motivations have as their antecedents the operations of deprivation and presentation as implied in Figure 2 earlier (see also Skinner 1938; Estes and Skinner 1941; Millenson 1967; Strongman 1987) and are usually controlled by *internal* stimulus changes. Emotions, on the other hand, have as their antecedents *abrupt external stimulus change*. Emotional responses relate to abrupt external stimulus changes, and thus to motivations, as shown in Table 2, which is a summary of Mowrer's conceptualization but with modifications proposed by Hammond (1970). For Mowrer, external stimulus changes which elicit hope and relief are postulated to produce approach behavior, whereas those that elicit fear and disappointment are postulated to elicit avoidance behavior. In Hammond's reconceptualization, hope and *fear* lead to *excitatory* behavior whereas *relief* and disappointment are *inhibitory*. Hammond's conceptualization fits precisely with our dual-mechanism homeostatic conceptualization.

Our theory of emotions and motivations in advertising gains two important advantages from its origins in Mowrer's theory. The first advantage is that, while there are numerous typologies of emotion in psychology (Davitz 1969), and now in advertising (see Batra and Holbrook 1990 for a recent typology), our *motivational* theory of emotions in advertising proposes that the *effective* emotions will be close variations of Mowrer's four, namely: fear, hope, relief and disappointment. Secondly, Mowrer's theory emphasizes stimulus *change* and thus a potential *sequence* of emotions as being motivational. Every other advertising theorist whose work we are aware of, with the possible exception of Fennell although she proposes a motivational theory without emotional specifics, has proposed a *single* emotion theory (e.g., Aaker, Stayman, and Hagerty 1986; Edell and Burke 1987; Batra and Holbrook 1990). By fitting emotions to motivations, it can be seen that, for motives that are subject to negative reinforcement, at least a two-step sequence of emotions is necessary: from some negative state (fear [S- ON] or disappointment [S+ OFF]) to relief (S- OFF). On the other hand, the motives that are subject to positive reinforcement may begin with a negative state (as Fennell suggests) *or* may simply start from neutrality and move to hope (S+ ON). In fact, recalling Charles Revson's famous comment about perfume, that "in the store we sell hope," we could turn Fennell's conceptualization around and argue that all ads make a "promise" and thereby invoke *hope*--whether this hope be for termination of a negative state (negative reinforcement) or for onset of a positive state (positive reinforcement). In this sense, although this is probably unnecessarily complicating the theory, all motives could be seen as energized, in advertising, by S+ onset, which is precisely the opposite of Fennell's view that all motives are energized by S- onset. The important point, however, is that in many brand attitude situations in advertising, *dynamic sequences* of emotions are necessary and it would be entirely misleading to look for the presence of a single emotion except in the special case of transformational advertising which we propose as being most suited to positive motives. This point will be discussed further in the applications comments at the conclusion of the paper.

A further aspect of the motivationally-relevant role of emotions in our theory is that the dual-mechanism conceptualization of "negative disequilibriation" and "temporary positive stimulus-seeking" led us to appreciate the importance not only of the two ubiquitous dimensions of emotions, unpleasantness-pleasantness (P) and intensity or arousal (A), but also the third dimension as identified by Osgood (1955; and later Mehrabian and Russell 1974; Mehrabian 1980; see also Donovan and Rossiter 1982) of dominance (D) although we prefer Osgood's term "control." Human beings are much concerned with control of their motivational states and it seems evident that any homeostatic theory of motivation that proposes a dynamic sequence of emotions would emerge with a

TABLE 3
Present Version of Rossiter and Percy's Hypothesized Relationships Linking Emotions to Motivations in Advertising

NEGATIVE (INFORMATIONAL MOTIVES)	EMOTIONAL SEQUENCE
1. Problem removal	Annoyance → relief
2. Problem avoidance	Fear → relaxation
3. Incomplete satisfaction	Disappointment → optimism
4. Mixed approach-avoidance	Conflict → peace of mind
5. Normal depletion	Mild annoyance → convenience
POSITIVE (TRANSFORMATIONAL) MOTIVES	
6. Sensory gratification	Dull (or neutral) → sensory anticipation
7. Intellectual stimulation/Mastery	Bored (or neutral) → excited/ Naive (or neutral) → competent
8. Social approval/Conformity	Apprehensive (or neutral) → flattered/ Ashamed (or neutral) → proud

dimension of control. The P-A framework that we favored was that of Russell and Pratt (1980; see also Rossiter and Percy 1987, pp. 211-212) but we also added back the dimension, D, of dominance or control.

The latest version of our hypothesized relationships linking emotions to motivations in advertising is presented in Table 3 (modified slightly from Rossiter and Percy 1987, p. 213, Table 8-4). In the theory as proposed in 1987, we stated (p. 213) that "it is possible to give a *general* indication of typical emotions that *might* be used to portray [the motives] (and thus stimulate the motivation) in advertisements": anger → relief (problem removal), fear → relaxation (problem avoidance), disappointment → optimism (incomplete satisfaction), guilt → peace of mind (mixed approach-avoidance), mild annoyance → convenience (normal depletion), neutral or dull → elated (sensory gratification), neutral or bored → excited (intellectual stimulation), neutral or apprehensive → flattered (social approval). A colleague, Robert J. Donovan, has been applying our 8-motive scheme in advertising research for a number of years now (Rossiter, Percy, and Donovan 1990) and has suggested two modifications. The first modification is that "intellectual stimulation" should be bracketed with the additional motive descriptor "mastery," so we have added the emotion sequence of neutral or naive → competent to the original intellectual stimulation motive's emotion sequence of neutral or bored → excited. The second modification is that "social approval" should be bracketed with an additional motive descriptor "conformity," so we have added the emotion sequence of neutral or ashamed → proud to the original social approval motive's emotion sequence of neutral or apprehensive → flattered; however, just as we cautioned originally (1987, p. 213) that social approval can sometimes stem from social anxiety and thus more correctly be classified as *problem avoidance*, so too can conformity, as is shown by Bearden and Rose (1990). Moreover, in the first stage of the pilot test of our theory, we employed the original emotional adjective pair anger → relief to represent problem removal but have decided, based on feedback from the respondents, to replace anger with the less emotionally intense term "annoyance," since very few ads attempt to deliberately elicit the intense emotion of anger. Similarly, the second emotion used originally for sensory gratification, "elated," seemed too intense, so we substituted the term "sensory anticipation." The final modification, also based on the pilot test, is that mixed approach-avoidance seems better characterized by the emotion pair conflict → peace of mind than by guilt → peace of mind, so the former pair is now employed. It may also be noted that we were not entirely happy with the second term in the emotion pair for normal depletion, mild annoyance → convenience. The technically correct term for "convenience," since it is not really an emotion, would be "equilibrium" but this is not very descriptive. We are still searching for a better term for this emotion.

Rossiter and Percy's (1987) theory also makes explicit predictions about the relative *contribution* of the emotional component of benefit claims according to the *type* of brand attitude that is being targeted. In 1984, we proposed a quadrant theory which is an attitudinal classification that vaguely resembles the well-known FCB grid but is much more sophisticated and operational (Rossiter, Percy, and Donovan 1984; Rossiter and Percy 1985; Rossiter and Percy 1987; Rossiter, Percy, and Donovan 1990). In the *low involvement-informational* quadrant, we predicted that the problem-solution emotional sequence would be most effective (which fits the negative motives' emotion sequences in Table 3) and that this would operate directly on brand attitude (A_b in conventional terminology). In the *low involvement-transformational* quadrant, we predicted that the (here positive) emotional portrayal would work via A_{ad} (and this is the only quadrant where we hypothesized a major mediating role for A_{ad} to subsequently affect A_b) because "emotional authenticity" (Wells 1981) of the advertising is essential to influence this type of brand attitude. In the *high involvement-informational* quadrant, we predicted that correct emotional portrayal would in general be less important in affecting A_b, except early in the product category life cycle where emotional portrayal is necessary to sell the category need, and that the cognitive component would make the dominant contribution. In the *high involvement-transformational* quadrant, we predicted that the high involvement aspect would have an arousal-like multiplicative tendency to amplify and spread "emotional authenticity" such that there would be significant individual differences in what was perceived to be an authentic emotional portrayal, leading us to postulate authenticity for "lifestyle" segments, with this authenticity operating directly on A_b, *not* on A_{ad} if A_{ad} is defined as "overall ad likability." As we will show in a forthcoming review of the empirical literature since 1987, these predictions have generally been supported.

PILOT TEST OF THE THEORY

To provide a pilot test of our theory for this conference, we decided to conduct a small-scale study with graduate students. As mentioned, Rossiter and Percy's theory has received many "real world" tests, via our applied research colleagues, but necessarily under less controlled conditions.

For this test, we omitted the normal depletion motive. The reason for this is that the normal depletion motive, in our theory, is not a motivation for purchasing a brand initially. Rather, it is a motive that applies only to a brand-loyal target audience and it motivates simple re-stocking behavior; the brand must have been purchased *originally* on the basis of one of the other seven motives. For the seven motives, we chose a pair of print ads that, in our expert judgment, utilized the respective motives. One of each pair was for a likely low purchase-risk (low involvement) brand and the other was for a likely high purchase-risk (high involvement) brand. It should be noted that we did not pay any deliberate attention to emotional stimuli in the ads; however, we recognize the possibility of some self-serving selection here, perhaps operating unconsciously, in testing our own theory.

The seven pairs of ads, 14 in total, were presented in random order in two sets of seven in two class sessions, the high involvement ads in the first session and the low involvement ads in the second session. The experimental subjects, a class of 35 MBA students, were given booklets containing a randomized list of the emotion adjective pairs (for informational motives) and single emotional adjectives (for transformational motives). They were asked to look at a color transparency version of each ad on the screen, the color being important to reproduce the emotional portrayal in the pictorial content of the ads in their original form (although several ads actually *were* black and white). Subjects also had black and white copies of the ads in their questionnaire booklets to which they could refer for the detailed copy. They were told to look at the ad and read the copy, then pick the adjective pair or adjective which "best describes how the advertiser is trying to make you feel."

The first finding was that informational and transformational ads, in general, are emotionally distinguishable. For informational ads, subjects selected informational emotions on .79 (79%) of the trials (low involvement-informational, .79; high involvement-informational, .79; chance, .44; both $Z = 2.50, p = .006$). For transformational ads, subjects selected transformational emotions on .94 (94%) of the trials (low involvement-transformational, .99; high involvement-transformational, .89; chance, .56; $Z = 6.43, p = .0001$ and $Z = 2.92, p = .002$, respectively). This finding is important because it implies that emotion *sequences* (used to represent the negative-to-neutral informational motives) are accurately detected as compared with single emotions (used to represent the positive transformational motives) as suggested by our theory.

The second finding was that "correct" emotional detection for individual informational and transformational motives ranged considerably. Given a chance level of .11 for subjects' selection of the correct (by our judgment) emotion pair or single emotion, the results, which are averaged here for convenience over low and high involvement pairs of ads, were: problem removal, .53; problem avoidance, .20; incomplete satisfaction, .10; mixed approach-avoidance, .07; sensory gratification, .69; intellectual stimulation/mastery, .29; and social approval/conformity, .50. A confusion matrix, to be reported elsewhere, revealed that the three informational motives of problem avoidance (fear → relaxation), incomplete satisfaction (disappointment → optimism) and mixed approach-avoidance (guilt → peace of mind) were often interchanged and that the transformational motive of intellectual stimulation/mastery (excited; competent) was often perceived as sensory gratification (sensory anticipation). Either we as expert judges see different motives in ads than do lay people (consumers!) or else we still have not found adequate emotional descriptors for four of the seven motives. To the extent that the latter is true, an approach in terms of *types* of emotions (Batra and Holbrook 1990), which we would have to complexly amend, for informational motives, to "sequences of types" (see discussion of their paper below), may have to be tried.

Overall, the first finding, of an informational versus transformational distinction in terms of emotional sequence types, is encouraging; but the second finding perhaps underscores the view that emotions are *extremely* discrete.

OTHER THEORETICAL AND APPLIED ISSUES

As this is a special topics forum, we take this opportunity to comment on the ideas of other theorists who are investigating the role of emotions in advertising. Also, we comment on some applications by advertising researchers.

Batra and Holbrook (1990) Study

Holbrook and Batra have been the two most productive advertising theorists working in the area of emotions in advertising. In a very important theoretical and empirical study (Batra and Holbrook 1990), they argued that, whereas conventional R-type factor analysis can be used (cf. Osgood 1955) to identify the *dimensionality* of emotions, a cluster analysis procedure (Cattell 1978) should thereafter be used to isolate *types* of emotions that then will have projections on the original R-type dimensions. A perhaps self-critical comment, since we also advocate a types-of-emotions theory, is that these investigators deleted single emotions if they did not correlate with a cluster of other emotions. It is possible that these "outliers" might be precisely the unique emotions that a creative person is seeking for a particular campaign. But our main criticism is as follows. Batra and Holbrook's theory is, of course, "motiveless." Consequently, it fails to identify *sequences* of emotions which we deem essential for informational (negatively reinforcing) motives. Moreover, in their empirical test of the typology, where the 12 emotional clusters were used to predict A_{ad}, A_b, and purchase intention (PI) with very impressive results, it is quite possible that they *inadvertently* picked up sequences of emotions since the ads in the study were rated on multiple emotion types or clusters. The use of multiple emotion ratings of ads also raises a practical issue. In their predictive regression analysis, *any* of the 12 emotion types could have contributed to prediction of the dependent variables. In the real world, creatives want to know how well their particular advertising execution has tapped a *particular* emotion or sequence of emotions. In this sense, Batra and Holbrook's theory is rather *ad hoc* in terms of its implications for advertisers. A final comment on their important work is that these investigators typically ask respondents to rate how the ads used for the study made them (the respondents) feel. In our study, in contrast, we asked respondents to rate how the advertiser is *trying* to make them feel, that is, we used a more "projective" measure that did *not* require the respondent to actually *experience* the emotion. We agree with Batra and Holbrook that ads will be more effective in terms of influencing brand attitudes to the extent that the portrayed emotion or emotion sequence is subjectively experienced by the consumer during ad processing. However, as our brand attitude quadrant predictions (outlined earlier) suggest, subjective experience is much more critical for transformational motives. Indeed, for informational motives, which are more utilitarian, "cold emotion" (to coin a term which may be the opposite of Abelson's concept of "hot cognition") may be sufficient as long as the consumer cognitively *anticipates* the emotional sequence that *would* result if he or she were to buy and use the product. This latter supposition implies the concept of *emotion memory* (Arnold 1970; Posner and Snyder 1975; Bower 1981; Bower and Cohen 1982). The concept of emotion memory, and its corollary of vicariously or not-really-experienced emotions but rather "imaged" emotions during advertising exposure (Rossiter and Percy 1980; 1983), has obvious implications for Pavelchak, Gardner, and Broach's (1990) theory presented in this session.

Pavelchak, Gardner, and Broach (1990) Study

Pavelchak, Gardner, and Broach (1990) advocate a *generalized* arousal theory that implies the concept of "unitary arousal." Evidence suggests that generalized arousal is a rather empty construct (cf. the debate between Anderson 1990 and Neiss 1990). Neiss argues that emotions are discrete psychobiological states and that generalized arousal cannot distinguish, for example, the emotions of exhilaration, fear, anger, or sexual excitement. Also, evidence for the notion of "optimal level of arousal" at the individual level is completely lacking (Strongman 1987; Neiss 1990). Arousal of the physiological kind is not in itself sufficient for an emotional state to be present, as can be exemplified by arousal during hard physical exercise (Strongman 1987). In our theory, we see arousal as representing no more than the *subjective intensity* dimension (though we label it "A") which largely distinguishes discrete emotions within the same type--for instance, happiness intensifying into joy or elation, or, as in our pilot study, annoyance being a less intense form of anger. Thus, we would direct Pavelchak *et al.* away from the generalized arousal view toward arousal as represented by the subjective intensity dimension of *discrete* emotions. We would also suggest that a more fruitful perspective on individual differences, rather than optimal level of arousal, might be Eysenck's (1981) theory of anxiety and extraversion, whereby anxiety is related to chronic levels of ANS arousal and extraversion is related to chronic levels of CNS arousal (see also Rossiter and Percy 1987; and see Cetola and Prinkey 1986 for a successful test of the introversion-extraversion dimension of Eysenck's theory in an advertising setting). Pavelchak *et al.*'s theory, while it examines the P and A dimensions of emotions, neglects the D (or control) dimension which we believe to be essential. These authors also promote the misleading generalization (in their special topic proposal) that "with pleasure reactions, if an ad makes you feel good, you like it and, via transfer, like the brand as well." The "affect transfer" notion has been overgeneralized and is far too simplistic (Allen and Shimp 1990). We remind that our theory predicts, with considerable empirical support (Rossiter and Percy 1987, p. 242), that pleasant stimuli in ads will influence brand attitude via A_{ad} only with low involvement-transformational advertising.

Yi (1990) Study

In a recent study, Yi (1990) provides evidence that supports our emotions and motivations theory even though his stated conclusions from his data imply otherwise. Yi's experiment utilized magazine ads for a new, fictitious brand of automobile which, in our framework, would be a high involvement-informational choice (informational given the attributes focused on, which were safety and gas consumption). Positive and negative affect, respectively, were induced by having subjects read positively or negatively affectively-toned magazine articles prior to ad exposure. Induced affect did significantly affect A_{ad}. But it affected A_{ad} *only*; there was no significant carryover to either attitude toward the brand (A_b) or brand purchase intention (PI). This is precisely the result that Rossiter and Percy's (1987) theory would predict, given a high involvement-informational brand attitude. As a practical implication of his study, we contended in our 1987 book that *media context* hardly ever affects advertising effectiveness except under very extreme conditions (such as might obtain in laboratory studies). To our knowledge, there is no field study evidence to support the widespread notion that media context makes a difference (Rossiter and Percy 1987; Rossiter 1988; Appel 1987). Our recommendation for advertisers is that "a good ad will work anywhere." Laboratory studies with often extreme induced affect and forced exposure do little to counter this recommendation.

Left Brain-Right Brain Theory

We are also on record (Rossiter 1980) as being entirely skeptical of the pursuit of cortical location of emotions or of ad processing in general in the right or left hemispheres of the brain. Not only are such cortical responses difficult to interpret (Olson and Ray 1983) but the whole pursuit presumes a physiological reductionism that is not adequate to explain emotions (Strongman 1987). In a practical sense, who cares where emotions may occur as long as they *do* occur? Cognitive theorists would also maintain that it is the subject's report of, and labeling of, an emotional occurrence that is determinant rather than whether there is indeed any physiological correlate (Strongman 1987). We will be very surprised if physiological measures of advertising effectiveness produce anything valid or practically worthwhile. For instance, Rothschild and Hyun's recent (1990) demonstration that EEG patterns may predict visual ad recognition is of little practical value. If you can measure visual ad recognition directly (e.g., BRC research service; Rossiter and Percy 1987, pp. 561, 587), then why bother measuring EEG?

Picture Sorts as Measures of Emotions

Based on the twin assumptions that emotions are accurately reflected through facial expression (Darwin 1878; Ekman 1965; Ekman and Oster 1979; Izard 1972) and that verbal measures are inadequate for measuring emotional experiences, several advertising agencies have developed "picture sorts" of faces representing various emotions to measure consumers' emotional responses to advertisements. For instance, FCB has developed VIP, Visual Image Profile, and ICON, Image Configurations, which show faces and situations respectively (Ratchford 1987) and BBDO has developed EPD, Emotional Photo Deck, which shows faces (Russell and Starkman 1989). In our opinion, photo sorts are another questionable pursuit. In the first place, the photo sort methodology asks consumers to pick the face that best represents how they feel *after* viewing the commercial (the photo sort method appears to have been mainly used with TV commercials rather than with ads in other media). This after-only measure would miss the emotional *sequence* that is incorporated in many ads and thus would have limited predictive validity as well as limited diagnostic value. It would, of course, be possible to ask consumers to select *several* photographs, to represent a sequence of emotions should such a sequence be intended in the commercial, but this has not been done. Secondly, there is a fundamental fallacy inherent in the picture sort methodology. The method of validating whether various pictures accurately represent various emotions has universally been to correlate picture sorts with *verbal* (adjectival) descriptions of emotions. This raises the question of: why bother switching to pictures at all? Picture sorts are more time-consuming as an applied advertising research task than merely checking off adjectives and no one has yet shown that verbal checklists of emotions are in any way inadequate. Indeed, in Rossiter and Percy (1987, pp. 209-212), we cited an extensive study by Sweeney, Tinling and Schmale (1970) demonstrating that the same emotion can be accurately portrayed and interpreted in virtually *any* medium. By "media" here we mean the types of stimuli available to creative people to elicit emotions, namely: heard words and sound effects, music, seen words, pictures, color, and movement--which are themselves obviously constrained by the actual advertising medium employed (Rossiter and Percy 1987, pp. 209-210). As we have seen in our pilot study, picking the right emotional adjective can be almost as difficult as it must be to pick accurate pictorial expressions of an emotion. However, it seems a lot easier and more practical to use verbal descriptors than to employ pictures, except perhaps when the subjects are pre-school children (Rossiter 1977). From a practitioner's standpoint, we suggest that picture sorts will turn out to be just another faddish sales gimmick used by advertising agencies under the guise of proprietary research techniques.

A-B-E Model of Benefit Claim Selection

The authors are working on a new model of benefit claim selection in advertising which was stimulated positively by an article by Moberg (1988) and negatively by our dissatisfaction with the "laddering" approach developed by Reynolds and Gutman (1984). Whereas the laddering approach probably taps emotions in relation to motives as advocated by our theory, the approach is silent as to which *level* on the "ladder" a particular benefit claim in an ad should be pitched at for maximum effect on brand attitude. We conceptualize three basic levels (assuming initially that each is tied to the same motive) which can be described as: the physical attribute (A); the subjective benefit or consequence resulting from that attribute (B); and emotional responses (E) which can be *either* the emotional consequence of perceiving the attribute (A) *or* of experiencing the benefit (B) *or* a completely independently inserted emotion as suggested by classical conditioning or by the "peripheral cue" concept (Petty and Cacioppo 1986). The current *Zeitgeist* among advertising agency practitioners, which is also implied by laddering theory, is that effective ads must focus on the emotional *consequence* (E) of benefits. This is a unitary (and therefore wrong) model for at least two reasons. Firstly, emotional consequences, and indeed emotional reactions in general, are often specific and idiosyncratic--especially under high involvement conditions (recall Rossiter and Percy's 1987 contention that high involvement amplifies emotions and leads to individuals', or individual segments', "authentic*ities*" being necessary). Only in low involvement-transformational advertising, such as for Coca-Cola, can one hope to focus on an emotional consequence that is almost universally the same for everyone in the audience. However, even Coca-Cola uses at least two emotional approaches as witnessed by the "high energy" creative idea used in the summer commercials versus the "heavy pathos" creative idea used in the Mean Joe Green commercial. An alternative benefit claim strategy would be to focus instead on the attribute (A) level and let the audience "read in" their own emotional consequences. In this way, for varied emotional "reasons," a broader audience may be targeted by the ad. Of course, there is probably a tradeoff here between audience size and persuasive effectiveness in moving from the A end of the continuum to the E end (Lautman and Percy 1984). However, we note that many low involvement-*informational* and high involvement-*informational* ads--such as retail store newspaper ads announcing sales and specials--appear to be successful with hardly any emotional content in the benefit claim other than that it tries to elicit the mildly affectively-laden belief of "That's good value." Which level, or even multiple levels, of A B or E to focus on when designing benefit claims for ads is a complicated decision that cannot be solved by any unitary theory as is popular in advertising at present and indeed may resolve to a purely empirical question that can only be answered by constructing conceptually alternative A-B-E versions of ads and subjecting them to a formal ad test with the target audience, or target audiences if a broad target with less persuasion (an A ad version) is being tested against a narrow target with more persuasion (a B or E ad version). Which "level" of benefit claim to employ in their A-B-E sense is one of the most frequent questions asked in advertising practice.

SUMMARY

We (Rossiter and Percy 1987 and this paper) have proposed a theory in which emotional stimuli, to be effective in influencing brand attitude, must serve an underlying purchase motivation. The theory proposes eight types of purchase motivations capable of energizing the consumer to act by offering either negative reinforcement or positive reinforcement. Our theory further hypothesizes that particular types of emotional sequences have to be included in the ad, with the sequence for informational (negative) motives being from negative-to-neutral and the emotional sequence for transformational (positive) motives being from neutral-to-positive. Empirical support for the two emotional sequences looks promising but the task of selecting efficient emotional descriptors for the specific motives remains challenging.

REFERENCES

Aaker, D.A., D.M. Stayman, and M.R. Hagerty (1986), "Warmth in Advertising: Measurement, Impact and Sequence Effects," *Journal of Consumer Research*, 12 (December), 365-381.

Allen, C.T. and T.A. Shimp (1990), "On Using Classical Conditioning Methods for Researching the Impact of Ad-Evoked Feelings," in *Emotion in Advertising: Theoretical and Practical Explorations*, S. Agres, J.A. Edell, and T.M. Dubitsky, eds., Westport, CT: Quorum Books.

Anderson, K.J. (1990), "Arousal and the Inverted-U Hypothesis: A Critique of Neiss's 'Reconceptualizing Arousal'," *Psychological Bulletin*, 107 (January), 96-100.

Appel, V. (1987), "Editorial Environment and Advertising Effectiveness," *Journal of Advertising Research*, 27 (August/September), 11-16.

Arnold, M.B. (1970), *Feelings and Emotions: The Loyola Symposium*, New York: Academic Press.

Batra, R. and M.B. Holbrook (1990), "Developing a Typology of Affective Responses to Advertising," *Psychology & Marketing*, 7 (Spring), 11-25.

Bearden, W.O. and R.L. Rose (1990), "Attention to Social Comparison Information: An Individual Difference Factor Affecting Consumer Conformity," *Journal of Consumer Research*, 16 (March), 461-471.

Bower, G.H. (1981), "Mood and Memory," *American Psychologist*, 36 (January), 129-148.

Bower, G.H. and P.R. Cohen (1982), "Emotional Influences in Memory and Thinking: Data and Theory," in *Affect and Cognition*, M.S. Clark and S.T. Fiske, eds., Hillsdale, NJ: Lawrence Erlbaum.

Cattell, R.B. (1978), *The Scientific Use of Factor Analysis in Behavioral and Life Sciences*, New York: Plenum.

Cetola, H. and K. Prinkey (1986), "Introversion-Extraversion and Loud Commercials," *Psychology & Marketing*, 3 (Summer), 123-132.

Darwin, C.R. (1872), *The Expression of Emotions in Man and Animals*, London: Murray.

Davitz, J.R. (1969), *The Language of Emotion*, New York: Academic Press.

Donovan, R.J. and J.R. Rossiter (1982), "Store Atmosphere: An Environmental Psychology Approach," *Journal of Retailing*, 58 (Spring), 34-57.

Edell, J. and M.C. Burke (1987), "The Power of Feelings in Understanding Advertising Effects," *Journal of Consumer Research*, 14 (March), 421-433.

Ekman, P. (1965), "Differential Communication of Affect by Head and Body Cues," *Journal of Personality and Social Psychology*, 2 (October), 726-735.

Ekman, P. and H. Oster (1979), "Facial Expression of Emotion," *Annual Review of Psychology*, 30, 527-554.

Estes, W.K. and B.F. Skinner (1941), "Some Quantitative Properties of Anxiety," *Journal of Experimental Psychology*, 29 (December), 390-400.

Eysenck, H.J. (1981), *A Model For Personality*, New York: Springer.

Fennell, G. (1975), "Motivation Research Revisited," *Journal of Advertising Research*, 15 (June), 23-28.

Fennell, G. (1978), "Consumers' Perceptions of the Product Use Situation," *Journal of Marketing*, 42 (April), 38-47.

Fennell, G. (1989), "Action Vs. Attitude: Motivation Makes the Difference," in *Proceedings: Society for Consumer Psychology*, D.W. Schumann, ed., Knoxville, TN: University of Tennessee.

Fishbein, M. and I. Ajzen, (1975), *Belief, Attitude, Intention, and Behavior: An Introduction to Theory and Research*, Reading, MA: Addison-Wesley.

Hammond, L.J. (1970), "Conditioned Emotional States," in *Physiological Correlates of Emotion*, P. Black, ed., New York: Academic Press.

Izard, C.E. (1977), *Human Emotions*, New York: Plenum.

Katz, D. (1960), "The Functional Approach to the Study of Attitudes," *Public Opinion Quarterly*, 24 (April), 163-204.

Lautman, M.R. and L. Percy (1984), "Cognitive and Affective Responses in Attribute-Based Versus End-Benefit Oriented Advertising," in *Advances in Consumer Research: Vol. 11*, T. Kinnear, ed., Ann Arbor, MI: Association for Consumer Research.

Lutz, R.J. (1978), "A Functional Approach to Consumer Attitude Research," in *Advances in Consumer Research: Vol. 5*, H.K. Hunt, ed., Ann Arbor, MI: Association for Consumer Research.

Mehrabian, A. (1980), *Basic Dimensions for a General Psychological Theory*, Cambridge, MA: Oelgeschlager, Gunn, and Hain.

Mehrabian, A. and J.R. Russell (1974), *An Approach to Environmental Psychology*, Cambridge, MA: MIT Press.

Millenson, J.R. (1967), *Principles of Behavioral Analysis*, New York: Macmillan.

Moberg, G.D. (1988), "Strategy Testing: To Execute or Not to Execute?" *Marketing News*, January 4, p. 30.

Mowrer, O.H. (1960a), *Learning Theory and Behavior*, New York: Wiley.

Mowrer, O.H. (1960b), *Learning Theory and the Symbolic Processes*, New York: Wiley.

Neiss, R. (1990), "Ending Arousal's Reign of Error: A Reply to Anderson," *Psychological Bulletin*, 107 (January), 101-105.

Olson, J.C. and W.J. Ray (1983), "Using Brain-Wave Measures to Assess Advertising Effects," Working Paper, *Marketing Science Institute*, Cambridge, MA.

Osgood, C.E. (1955), "Fidelity and Reliability," in *Information Theory in Psychology*, H. Quastler, ed., Glencoe, I.L.: Free Press.

Pavelchak, M.A., M.P. Gardner, and V.C. Broach (1990), "Ad-Induced Arousal: Effects on Ad and Brand Attitudes," Abstract of Paper for Special Topic Session, 1990 ACR Conference.

Ratchford, B.T.(1987), "New Insights About the FCB Grid," *Journal of Advertising Research*, 27 (August/September), 24-38.

Reynolds, T.J. and J. Guttman (1984), "Laddering: Extending the Repertory Grid Methodology to Construct Attribute-Consequence-Value Hierarchies," in *Personal Values in Consumer Psychology*, R. Pitts and A. Woodside, eds., Lexington, MA: Lexington Books.

Rossiter, J.R. (1977), "Reliability of a Short Test Measuring Children's Attitudes Toward TV Commercials," *Journal of Consumer Research*, 3 (March), 179-184.

Rossiter, J.R. (1980), "Point of View: Brain Hemisphere Activity," *Journal of Advertising Research*, 20 (October), 75-76.

Rossiter, J.R. (1988), "The Increase in Magazine Ad Readership," *Journal of Advertising Research*, 28 (October/November), 35-39.

Rossiter, J.R. and L. Percy (1980), "Attitude Change Through Visual Imagery in Advertising," *Journal of Advertising*, 9 (2), 10-16.

Rossiter, J.R. and L. Percy (1983), "Visual Communication in Advertising," in *Information Processing Research in Advertising*, R.J. Harris, ed., Hillsdale, NJ: Lawrence Erlbaum.

Rossiter, J.R. and L. Percy (1985), "Advertising Communication Models," in *Advances in Consumer Research*, E.C. Hirschman, and M.B. Holbrook, eds., Provo, UT: Association for Consumer Research.

Rossiter, J.R. and L. Percy (1987), *Advertising and Promotion Management*, New York: McGraw-Hill.

Rossiter, J.R., L. Percy, and R.J. Donovan (1984), "The Advertising Plan and Advertising Communication Models," *Australian Marketing Researcher*, 8 (December), 7-44.

Rossiter, J.R., L. Percy, and R.J. Donovan (1990), "A Better Advertising Planning Grid," Working Paper, Australian Graduate School of Management, University of New South Wales.

Rothschild, M.L. and Y.J. Hyun (1990), "Predicting Memory for Components of TV Commercials from EEG," *Journal of Consumer Research*, 16 (March), 472-478.

Russell, D.A. and D.L. Starkman (1989), "Measuring the Emotional Response to Advertising," *Reclame En Onderzoek*, 1 (April), 15-26.

Russell, J.A. and G. Pratt (1980), "A Description of the Affective Quality Attributed to Environments," *Journal of Personality and Social Psychology*, 38 (August), 311-322.

Skinner, B.F. (1938), *The Behavior of Organisms*, New York: Appleton-Century-Crofts.

Strongman, K.T. (1987), *The Psychology of Emotion*, 3rd edn., Chichester, UK: Wiley.

Sweeney, D.R., D.C. Tinling, and A.H. Schmale (1970), "Dimensions of Affective Expression in 4 Expressive Modes," *Behavioral Science*, 15 (5), 393-407.

Wagner, A.R. (1969), "Frustrative Nonreward: A Variety of Punishment," in *Punishment and Aversive Behavior*, B.A. Campbell and R.M. Church, eds., New York: Appleton-Century-Crofts.

Wells, W.D. (1981), "How Advertising Works," Working Paper, Needham, Harper & Steers Advertising, Chicago.

Yi, Y. (1990), "Cognitive and Affective Priming Effects of the Context for Print Advertisements," *Journal of Advertising*, 19 (2), 40-48.

Music Television and Its Influences on Consumers, Consumer Culture, and the Transmission of Consumption Messages

Basil G. Englis, Rutgers University

It is notable that little has been written in the consumer research literature concerning music television. At the same time there has been much coverage in the popular press (e.g., NYT 1988; Pareles 1989, Pendleton 1988) and in the communication literature (e.g., the winter 1986 issue of the *Journal of Communication*) about the music television revolution. What is so striking about this disparity is that one pervasive theme in what has been written concerns the impact that music television might have on the marketing of products, as well as the music. Music television has become a force which influences popular culture in ways that are important for consumer researchers to understand. It presents viewers with a new "televisual experience" (Kaplan 1987) that includes among its elements real and surreal portrayals of the "personal style" of the icons of teen popular culture -- rock stars. Thus, it has the potential to act as a consumer socializing agent especially for teenaged viewers.

Music television has also influenced advertising in several ways. Music videos are highly impactful and emotionally arousing; they provide a new viewing context within which consumers are exposed to advertising. In addition, television commercials have in some instances adopted structural and executional elements from music television. Thus the recent development and enormous popularity of music television has the potential to influence consumers via its power to shape consumer culture and also through its influence on commercial structure and positioning.

The music television cable network MTV was launched in the summer of 1981, and brought music videos to the cable television audience. MTV has rocked audiences ever since. The station was created when Robert Pittman, now executive vice president and chief operating officer of MTV Networks, came up with the idea of putting music videos on cable TV. Music videos had already existed; they were primarily used as promotional tools for the sale of albums. Today, nine years later, music videos have evolved into an art form, selling more than just the music. As a result, MTV has become an increasingly attractive medium for advertisers, especially those trying to reach the elusive teenage audience.

MTV targets audiences between the ages of twelve and thirty-four, with a median age of twenty-three; an age group which has proven highly elusive for other media. According to MTV's own research, 54% of its audience is in the 12 to 24 age group. This group watches MTV an average of a half an hour to two hours a day (Sun and Lull 1986). Although music videos originated as promotional tools for record albums, the videos themselves present the viewer with far more than music: they provide information about fashion and cosmetics, lifestyles, and social roles and behavior.

The purpose of this session was to present recent work concerning the influences of music television on the manner in which consumption messages are transmitted to and received by consumers. Because of the potential power of music television to reach young consumers, and thereby socialize consumption behavior, it is a medium that demands more research attention. The issues currently being studied by consumer researchers include the structural properties of music television, the consumption messages embedded in music videos, the effects of music video elements in advertising, and the properties of music television as a viewing context.

Crossing the Boundaries: A Comparison of Music Videos and Commercial Advertisements (Fry)

On the surface, music videos are a means for marketing music (e.g., Fry & Fry 1987; Kaplan 1987). Indeed, it is widely noted in the industry that a top hit in mainstream popular music is now unlikely without a music video as part of the promotional mix (e.g., Pareles 1989; Pendleton 1988). It is not surprising therefore that producers of music videos would initially borrow elements of executional style from television advertising (e.g., Aufderheide 1986). Indeed, Fry and Fry (1987) show that music videos are structurally very similar to television advertising, and that they also are related to televised drama. Their analysis suggests that music videos are a hybrid of the two forms; not a "hard sell" as one might expect from television advertising and yet not a linear unfolding of a story line as one might expect from a typical television drama. This hybridization of form and content has blurred the boundary between the program and the commercial message.

Although the hybridization of styles may in part be due to the intentional borrowing of form early in the history of MTV, the crossover of style may have also been due the sharing of creative personnel between advertising, hollywood, and music television (Pendleton 1988). It clearly was an approach that worked to the extent that music videos have themselves affected the structure of television commercials (e.g., NYT 1989; Pareles 1989). In addition to the crossover of production personnel the stars of music videos are often featured in commercials that run on the network. For example, Michael Jackson's and Madonna's soda commercials and Paul McCartney's ads for the Visa credit card all appeared on the network along with current videos by these stars. The close relationship between the production of advertising and music videos is also exemplified by a Louise Mandrell video, which was financed by RC Cola in return for scenes of Louise sipping the product in the video. Often both the structure and star of the television commercials seen on MTV are very similar to the videos. The viewer has a virtually seamless transition between intentional and unintentional consumption messages.

Adolescent Sexuality and Music Videos (Brown)

Music television may function to socialize consumer behavior. The research conducted by Brown and her colleagues (Brown and Campbell 1986, Brown, Campbell and Fischer 1986) suggests that socialization of adolescent sexuality may be influenced by music television. The development of sexual identity has many components, several of which involve consumption. For example, young teenagers are highly motivated to acquire a "personal style": individual and yet acceptable to the peer group. "Personal style" is often the focus of music videos and can be characterized by preferences for distinct groupings of products and types of language and behavior. Elements of personal style include clothing and fashion, make-up and hair styling, as well as patterns of values and behavior. In the development of adolescent sexuality, Brown has shown that viewing motivation varies between male and female adolescents and that the portrayal of male and female characters is markedly different and often includes highly stereotyped images (Brown and Campbell 1986). For example, this sex-role stereotypy is characterized by the portrayal of females as passive or as predatory (a sharp "virgin"/"whore" dichotomy) and by the portrayal of males as dominant and active. It is interesting that although such sex-role stereotypy is pervasive, it does not serve to turn off female members of MTV's potential audience. In fact, although music videos often present a distinctly "male"-preferred viewpoint (e.g., Kinder 1984, 1988), surveys have revealed that young girls are watching more music television than young boys. They report that their motivation in watching is to learn about the latest trends in fashion (and dance). Thus teenage audiences are aware of their own attention to the unintentional consumption messages offered by music television.

The pop-rock group New Kids On The Block provides an interesting current example of how music television may provide unintended consumption messages for its audience. The messages conveyed by this group are not linked to a particular product, but to a particular style. The clothes and lifestyles which this group represents have had such an impact on their teenage audiences, that New Kids On The Block "propaganda" is popping up everywhere. Furthermore, products which contain New Kids On The Block logos and pictures have become a big success in the marketplace. A notable feature of these products is that they are rarely, if ever, advertised: they sell themselves due to the popularity of the group and the exposure of the audience to music television.

Music Television as a Viewing Context and its Effects on Consumer Responses to Advertising (Englis)

Music videos are quite impactful for viewers (Rubin et al. 1986): they create a state of sustained tension and attention to what is likely to come next (e.g., Kaplan 1987). The visual imagery of music television is often dreamlike and highly ambiguous (Kinder 1984), which should also serve to heighten arousal and attention. The findings from one recent study show that music videos are associated with qualitatively distinct emotional responses among viewers (Englis 1989). Groups of videos were identified which evoked happiness, poignancy, disgust-anger-scorn, confusion, anxiety and disgust. The emotional responses of viewers are somewhat attenuated by previous exposure to music television such that those who have watched a great deal of music television are less emotionally aroused, butnonetheless distinct emotional reactions to the several types of music video identified were found.

It is plausible to assume that the emotions induced in viewers by the viewing context should influence their responses to the products advertised in that context. A recent experiment examined the effect of pairing product ads with music videos in an associative learning paradigm. Two products (beer, automobile) were separately paired with different types of music video (happy, poignant, or scornful feelings). Five pairings of product ad and video were presented for each condition. As expected consumer attitudes toward the high-involvement product (automobile) were not affected by viewing context. However, attitudes toward the low-involvement product (beer) became more favorable following exposure to the poignant videos and least favorable following exposure to scorn-inducting videos. There was no effect of viewing context on recall of product information. Although these findings are preliminary, they suggest that music television, as a viewing context for commercials, may have unanticipated effects on viewers' responses to commercial messages.

Ambiguity and Complexity in Music Video Commercials: The role of Film Dimensions in Enhancing Commercial Recall and Persuasion (Thorson, Hitchon and Duckler)

As noted earlier, there has been a great deal of crossover in structure between music television and television advertising. One consequence of the influence of music television on the production of television commercials is to include more ambiguous and complex visual images into television advertising. Recent research has examined the effects of including ambiguous and complex elements from music videos on consumer responses to television advertising. Both ambiguity and complexity have been identified as important dimensions in music video production (e.g., Aufderheide 1986, Kinder 1984, 1988). In this research, ambiguity was defined as the absence of a clearly understandable narrative structure with the presentation of images which are often incoherent and unrelated. Such ambiguous material has the potential for multiple interpretations (Ha and Hoch 1989). Complexity was defined as the amount of information per unit time (Thorson et al. 1987). This is exemplified in music video production by the many fast editing cuts and rapid shifts of camera angle and perspective.

In this research "music video ads" were manipulated in their levels of complexity and ambiguity by incorporating music video elements into existing television commercials. Visual material from actual music videos was used to product high and low levels of complexity and ambiguity. Six different products were included in the stimulus set. Pretest and manipulation check data indicated that viewer ratings of ambiguity and complexity reflected the intended modifications of the ads. In addition, attitudes toward the brands advertised and toward the ads were more positive following exposure to high levels of ambiguity and low levels of complexity. Recall was poorer following exposure to high levels of complexity or low levels of ambiguity as compared with low levels of complexity or high levels of ambiguity. Although the pattern of results varied somewhat across product, the findings suggest that including specific music video elements into television commercials influences consumers' responses.

Conclusion

In conclusion, these initial studies suggest that music television presents consumers with a great deal more in the form of consumption images contained in the videos themselves. Music television presents viewers with information concerning the products consumed and the lifestyles lived by highly attractive role models, especially for the teenaged audience. Music television presents consumers with powerful consumption images. Consumers view rock stars in settings other than the typical concert stage. In many instances these "rock idols" are seen using a wide array of products, ranging from clothing, to food, to entertainment products, to automobiles. This may provide information for young consumers concerning the product groups that are associated with various social roles to which they may aspire.

Music television is itself a new "televisual" experience, and is therefore a medium whose properties need to be studied apart from other forms of television programming. The short length of music videos and their ad-like executional style tend to blur the distinction between program and advertising material. The blurring of boundary between program and commercial may influence consumer receptivity to advertising messages presented within the context of music video programming. This may be particularly true for commercials which themselves contain elements of music videos. Music videos have high impact: they instigate strong emotions in viewers. These properties of music videos as a viewing context should influence how consumers respond to advertising that appears on music television.

Rather than providing any strong conclusions, it was our hope that this session would stimulate additional research and serve to focus the attention of consumer researchers on the influence of this new medium on consumption.

AUTHOR'S NOTE

This paper is a summary of a special session presented at the annual meeting of the Association for Consumer Research, New York, NY, 1990. The contributors to the session were Jane Brown, University of North Carolina, Peter Duckler, University of Wisconsin - Madison, Basil G. Englis, Rutgers University - New Brunswick, Donald L. Fry, Emerson College, Jacqueline Hitchon, University of Wisconsin - Madison, and Esther Thorson, University of Wisconsin - Madison.

REFERENCES

Aufderheide, Pat (1986). Music videos: The look of the sound. *Journal of Communication*, Winter, 57-78.

Baxter, Richard, L., Cynthia De Riemer, Ann Landini, Larry Leslie, and Michael W. Singletary (1985). A content analysis of music videos. *Journal of Broadcasting & Electronic Media*, 29, 333-340.

Brown, Jane, D. and Kenneth Campbell (1986). Race and gender in music videos: The same beat but a different drummer. *Journal of Communication*, Winter, 1-15.

Brown, Jane, D., Kenneth Campbell and Lynn Fischer (1986). American adolescents and music videos: Why do they watch? *Gazette*, 37, 19-32.

Englis, Basil G. (1989). The reinforcement properties of music videos: "I want my ... I want my ... MTV." Paper presented at the annual meeting of the Association for Consumer Research, New Orleans, LA.

Fry, Donald, L. and Virginia H. Fry (1987). Some structural characteristics of music television videos. *The Southern Speech Communication Journal*, Winter, 151-164.

Ha, Young-Won and Stephen J. Hoch (1989). Ambiguity, processing strategy, and advertising-evidence interactions. *Journal of Consumer Research*, 16, 354-359.

Kaplan, E. Ann (1987). *Rocking Around the Clock: Music Television, Postmodernism, and Consumer Culture*. New York: Methuen.

Kinder, Marsha (1984). Music video and the spectator: TV ideology and dream. *Film Quarterly*, 38, No. 1, Fall, 2-15.

Kinder, Marsha (1988). The battle of the sexes on MTV. *Media USA: Process and Effect*. Longman, Inc.: White Plains, NY.

New York Times (1989). How MTV has rocked television commercials. *The New York Times*, Oct. 9, 143.

Pareles, Jon (1989). After music videos, all the world has become a screen. *The New York Times*, Dec. 10, sec. 4, p. E6.

Pendleton, Jennifer (1988). Hollywood buys the concept. *Advertising Age*, 59, Nov. 9 158.

Rubin, Rebecca, B. Alan M. Rubin, Elizabeth M. Perse, Cameron Armstrong, Michael McHugh, and Noreen Faix (1986). Media use and meaning of music video. *Journalism Quarterly*, *63*, 353-359.

Schumann, David W., and Esther Thorson (1989). The influence of viewing context on commercial effectiveness: A selection-processing model, in J.H. Leigh and C.R. Martin (eds.), *Current Issues & research in Advertising*. Ann Arbor, MI: The University of Michigan.

Sun, Se-Wen and James Lull (1986). The adolescent audience for music videos and why they watch. *Journal of Communication*, Winter, 115-125.

Thorson, Esther, Byron Reeves and Joan Schleuder (1985). Message complexity and attention to television. *Communication Research*, *12*, 427-454.

The Cultural Meaning of Beer Commercials
Lance Strate, Fordham University

With the growing concern over the health and safety problems associated with alcohol consumption, there have been a number of studies on alcohol advertising (Atkin 1987; Finn & Strickland 1982, 1983; Hacker, Collins, & Jacobson 1987; Jacobson, Atkins, & Hacker 1983). In these studies, the tendency is to view the ads as a form of persuasion, and to focus on the strategies used, and the types of audiences targeted. My own research on beer commercials (Postman, Nystrom, Strate & Weingartner 1987; Strate 1989) takes a somewhat different approach, in that ads are seen as a form of cultural communication, and the objective is to uncover their cultural meanings. This type of approach draws on theory and research in popular culture and anthropology, semiotics and structuralism, and critical and cultural studies, and has been used to analyze many types of mass media messages, including print and broadcast advertising. (Barthes 1972; Fiske 1987; Fiske & Hartley 1984; Himmelstein 1984; Langholz Leymore 1975; McArthur 1984; McLuhan 1951; Williamson 1978) What I would like to do here is to explain my approach to analyzing beer commercials, and its implications for social problems such as youthful drinking and driving.

This approach is particularly well-suited for the analysis of modern advertising. Major advertising campaigns generally do not present logical arguments and claims for their products. Instead, they seek to associate their product with evocative images and themes. As Tony Schwartz, one of the first to use this soft-sell strategy, puts it: "The critical task is to design our package of stimuli so that it resonates with information already stored within an individual and thereby induces the desired learning or behavioral effect." (Schwartz 1974, p.24) In other words, ads are designed to evoke meaning in the minds of audience members. Ads do not need to explicitly state their meaning; they merely suggest their meaning, depending on the audience to fill in the missing pieces. The images and themes are drawn from our shared culture, and therefore tend to evoke similar meanings in many different people. To some extent, this is how any type of communication works, as educator E.D. Hirsch (1987) notes: "We know instinctively that to understand what somebody is saying, we must understand more than the surface meanings of words; we have to understand the context as well... To grasp the words on a page we have to know a lot of information that isn't set down on the page." (p.3) Advertising is merely the most extreme form of this process, as ads try to elicit the most meaning from the least amount of information.

Let me provide you with two examples. If I were to use the phrase "seventeen seventy-six," I could assume that you would associate that year with the Declaration of Independence and the Revolutionary War, with individuals such as Washington, Jefferson, and Franklin, and with values such as liberty, democracy, and patriotism. I would not need to explain the underlying meaning of "seventeen seventy-six" nor would you need to consciously summon up the associated information. I can make this assumption because we not only share the same language, but the same culture as well. I could not be so certain if I were presenting this paper at a conference in New Zealand. New Zealanders may speak the same language, but they may not be familiar with our history, and they certainly would not attach the same emotional connotations to the phrase as we would. For my second example, I would like you to consider the image of the cowboy, the "Marlboro Man" for example. This type of image is effective only because we already know what it means, because we have prior experience with the image of the cowboy as a historical type and as a fictional character in the Western genre. The advertiser does not have to explain that the image refers to masculinity, rugged individualism and self-sufficiency. We can make those associations without actively thinking about them. Now, the task of the researcher, in analyzing cultural meanings, is to fill in the missing pieces, the cultural context, to make those associations *explicit*, and to explain their implications.

The term that is used to refer to the cultural meaning of an image, theme, or any other type of sign is *myth*. (Barthes 1972; Fiske & Hartley 1984) In this sense, a myth is not a falsehood or fairytale, but an uncontested and unconscious assumption that is so widely shared within a culture that it is considered natural, instead of recognized as a social convention. Some myths take the form of recurring plotlines. For example, we have our stories about the taming of the frontier, and of individuals rising from rags to riches. Other myths may be simpler in form, but no less potent, such as when we use automobiles as symbols of status and freedom. And certain myths provide ready-made answers to universal human questions, questions about ourselves, our relationships with others, and with our environment. Myths are expressed in many different ways: in the stories we tell, the games we play, the books and newspapers we read, and in the television programs and commercials that we watch. Each individual expression of a myth is related to and depends upon other variations. And each myth itself is related to other myths in a dense web of meaning. For this reason, myths need to be analyzed through qualitative, critical methodologies. It is possible to determine the percentage of beer commercials that contain images of cars. It is possible to measure the physiological and emotional reactions of audience members to those images. But it is not possible to measure or calculate the cultural meaning of those images. What is required is the same type of in-depth study anthropologists use to understand other cultures. Moreover, the need for quantitative methodologies is reduced when you are dealing with a relatively small universe of content, as is the case with the number of different beer commercials broadcast at any given time.

I should point out to you that in analyzing the myths of beer commercials, I share at least one assumption in common with the beer industry: that advertising has the ability to influence attitudes and behavior. There is no other reasonable explanation for the fact that over one billion dollars a year is spent on alcohol ads. (Jacobs 1989) Nor would there be so much interest in consumer research unless that research could be used to influence consumer behavior through mediated messages. Therefore, the real question is not about the existence of advertising's effects, but about the nature of those effects.

It is perfectly understandable that advertisers are primarily interested in sales and market shares. But there is no reason why we must limit our concerns to those of advertisers. Just as every drug has its side-effects, and just as every innovation has its negative and unintended effects (Rogers 1983), advertisements have consequences which advertisers may not have foreseen. We all know that commercials, regardless of their intended function, can introduce new phrases into our culture, such as "Where's the beef?" and can create new celebrities, such as "Joe Isuzu." I would also argue that advertising, like any form of mass communication, performs the function of socialization, that is, the transmission of cultural values, beliefs, and attitudes, and influences the way we view our world. (Gerbner & Gross 1976; Gerbner, Gross, Jackson-Beeck, Jeffries-Fox, & Signorielli 1978; Signorielli 1987) Theory and research on social learning indicate that television programming can teach children specific behaviors, and whether those behaviors will be rewarded or punished. (Bandura 1977) In the same way, television provides instruction on social roles, and the cultural rules pertaining to them. (Meyrowitz 1985)

The effects of television content will of course vary according to individual characteristics, and television is only one of many different agents of socialization; others include the family, the community, and the school. But television commercials are a prolific source of role models, and are rarely ambiguous as to the types of behaviors that are rewarded or punished. And, aside from sleeping, children spend more time watching television that in any other single activity, which is why Neil Postman (1979) argues that television has replaced the school as the primary educational institution in America today. In other words, educational television includes not just Big Bird, but also Spuds MacKenzie. Beer commercials may be aimed for an adult audience, but their actual audience is composed of a great number of young people. And as Peter Drucker (1989, p.249) argues, "There are more hours of pedagogy in one thirty-second commercial than most teachers can pack into a month of teaching. The subject matter of the TV commercial is secondary; what matters is the skill, professionalism, and persuasive power of the presentation." The point is that beer commercials, regardless of their intended audience, have the power to reach and to influence young people.

In sum, advertisers use myths to evoke meaning in the minds of audiences. They generally do not invent those myths, but they do reinforce them and reshape them. The way in which the myths are presented, the elements that are emphasized, and the way in which they are associated with a particular product, have the potential to influence the attitudes and behavior of intended *and* unintended audiences. With this in mind, I would now like to provide you with some examples of myths commonly found in beer commercials over the last several years, based on the research reported in Postman et al. (1987) and Strate (1989).

I have already mentioned the mythic image of the cowboy, which is related to the myth of the frontier. In this myth, the frontier is seen as pure, free from the corruption of civilization. The untamed wilderness is also a scene of sudden danger, and the survival of the frontiersman depends on his ability to respond to that danger, to overcome the power of nature. And he must do so alone, without the protection that civilization provides. Unaided and unrestrained by civilization, the frontiersman is able to demonstrate, without equivocation, his mastery over nature. That is why the cowboy is seen as the archetypical man's man. This myth is used in the advertising campaign for Busch beer. In one commercial, we see a cowboy on horseback, herding cattle across a river. A small calf is overcome by the current, but the cowboy is able to withstand the force of the river and come to the rescue. The voiceover says: "Sometimes a simple river crossing isn't so simple. And when you've got him back it's your turn. Head for the beer brewed natural as a mountain stream." As this last sentence is said, we see a six-pack pulled out of clear running water, as if by magic. In this ad, the power and danger of nature takes the form of the river, but nature's gentler aspect is also present in the form of the mountain stream. The beer is presented as a form of nature, more or less identical with the stream, both in the voiceover and in the image of a hand pulling the six-pack from the water. Identity relationships between beer and water are presented in ads for a number of other beers, such as Rolling Rock, Heileman's Old Style, and Molson's Golden. Collectively, they present beer as a form of bottled nature. Drinking beer then is a relatively safe way of facing the challenge of nature. For those of us who do not wish to get our feet wet saving a calf, drinking beer is a way to symbolically re-enact the taming of the wilderness.

The symbol of Busch beer, found on its label and in its commercials, is a horse rearing on its hind legs. The stallion can be seen as a phallic symbol, but it also evokes the idea of untamed nature. And in another Busch commercial, a young rodeo rider is quickly thrown form his mount; trying to cheer him up, an older cowboy hands him a beer and says: "Here. This one don't buck so hard." In this case, the identity between nature and beer is made via the horse. Drinking beer is like rodeo-riding, only less strenuous. It is a challenge that the young rider can easily overcome, allowing him to save face. And for the less daring among us, drinking is an acceptable substitute for taming wild horses. The identification of beer with nature can also be presented through the commercial's setting. For example, the ads for Old Milwaukee beer are usually set in wilderness environments that feature water, such as the Florida Everglades and Glacier Bay, Alaska. In each ad, several men are engaged in recreational activities such as high speed airboating, boat racing, and fishing. Each commercial begins with a voiceover that says something like: "The Florida Everglades and Old Milwaukee both mean something great to these guys." And each commercial features a jingle which says: "There's nothing like the flavor of a special place and Old Milwaukee beer." The place is special because it is untouched by civilization, allowing men the freedom to engage in forms of recreation not possible in the city and its suburbs. Of course, the special place must be relatively inaccessible, otherwise it would not be special. Since beer is presented as identical to the place however, drinking beer may act as a substitute for actually visiting the place.

Associating beer with nature and the frontier is only one of a number of ways in which beer commercials use the theme of challenge. Physical challenge is implied by images of laborers and athletes, and made manifest in the depiction of work and leisure activities. The association between beer and physical challenge is problematic in and of itself, as it implies that drinking has no effect on motor coordination. But there is a more subtle problem involved, in that beer is presented as a reward for hard work or play. In the Busch and Old Milwaukee ads, beer is a reward for facing the challenge of the wilderness, not just because drinking is pleasurable, but also because drinking is a symbolic re-enactment of the taming of nature. Beer is an appropriate and meaningful reward for such activities because it is identified with rivers, wild horses, and other aspects of the natural environment. And when strength and skill are challenged in other environments, the reward of beer likewise allows for symbolic re-enactment. This can be seen in the many Budweiser commercials that use the myth of the American dream, that is, stories about economic opportunity and upward mobility.

One of Budweiser's most frequently aired commercials during the 1980s features a young Polish immigrant, and an older foreman and dispatcher. In the first scene, the dispatcher is reading names from a clipboard, giving workers their assignments. Arriving late, which earns him a look of displeasure from the foreman, the nervous young immigrant takes a seat in the back. When he is finally called, the young man walks up to the front of the room, corrects the dispatcher's mispronunciation of his name, and is given his assignment. The scene then shifts to a montage of the day's work; by the end of the day it is clear that he had earned the respect of his co-workers. The final scene is in a crowded tavern; the young man walks through the door, making his way to the bar, looking around nervously, until someone calls his name, and the foreman hands him a beer. In both the first and final scene, the immigrant begins at the back of the room, highlighting his outsider status, and moves to the front as he is given a chance to prove himself. The commercial's parallelism is not just an aesthetic device, but a mythic one as well. Having mastered the challenge of work, the reward of beer is an invitation to symbolically re-enact his feat. By working hard and well, he gains acceptance in the work world; by drinking the beer, he can also gain acceptance into the social world of the bar.

The theme of challenge is also present in a subtle way in the Bud Lite ads, where someone orders "a light," is given a substitute such as a lamp or torch, and then corrects himself, asking for "a Bud Light." Here the risk is one of social ridicule for those who are unfamiliar with the rules for ordering drinks. Particularly to a novice drinker, bars and bartenders can seem very threatening. And as one of the commercials revealed, the bartenders play these pranks because they are fed up with uninformed customers. The bizarre substitutions are a form of hazing, an initiation into proper barroom behavior. The challenge then is to know the rules and to know what you want. Challenge is also present in the ads that present beer as a medium for male-bonding, such as those for Miller Genuine Draft and Miller Lite. In these ads, men socialize in groups, tell jokes, trade insults, and even engage in shouting matches, e.g. "tastes great" vs. "less filling." Beer is shown as central to this competitive atmosphere, where the risk is losing one's poise and self-control. A similar challenge is present in the ads that depict beer as a means of facilitating interaction between the sexes, which include commercials for Michelob, Colt 45, and strangely enough, the Spuds MacKenzie ads. In these commercials, the challenge to the male is to remain cool and calm in the presence of beautiful women. Insofar as Spuds MacKenzie is treated as a human being in his ads, he fits this profile of the ladies' man as much as Billy Dee Williams does in his Colt 45 commercials. Interestingly, this same image can also be found in the Peanuts comic strip, when Snoopy puts on his "Joe cool" persona. Thus, Spuds never loses his cool while he is fawned over by women attractive enough to make the rest of us males salivate like Pavlov's dogs.

The reason why the theme of challenge, in its many forms, is all but omnipresent in beer commercials is really quite simple. Beer commercials are aimed at a male audience, and challenge is central to the myth of masculinity. According to this myth (or stereotype or social role), men demonstrate their masculinity by taking risks, facing danger, and overcoming challenges. External physical threats are supplemented and can be replaced by symbolic tests of strength, skill, and self-control. And some of these tests revolve around drinking. The challenge is to hold your liquor, to be able to drink without showing any ill effects, at least relative to your peers. Drinking can serve as a symbolic re-enactment of overcoming a challenge because in itself it is a challenge. The problem is that admitting that you are too drunk to drive would be a sign of weakness, of failure to overcome the challenge and demonstrate masculinity. And while I have no objection to the myth of masculinity in general, I would suggest to you that the association between beer and challenge in any form contributes to the problem of drinking and driving.

Driving itself presents the challenge of maintaining control over the vehicle, and allows for tests of skill and daring. That is why driving and racing are associated with the myth of masculinity. Separately, driving and drinking allow men to demonstrate their masculinity. Both provide a sense of freedom, exhiliration, and power over one's environment. And both are signs of adulthood in a culture that lacks any formal initiation rites for young males. They are linked in our myths and they all too often become linked in practice as well. And that is why the presence of cars and similar forms of transportation in beer commercials is troublesome. Automobiles and even racing cars have appeared in Budweiser's ads and promotional spots and in Michelob's commercials. Budweiser and Old Milwaukee spots have also featured powerboats, rowboats, and sailboats. Busch beer commercials show men riding on horseback, while Budweiser ads often include a horse-drawn carriage. And Coor's uses the slogan: "The Silver Bullet won't slow you down." Speed is associated with the myth of masculinity because it shortens reaction time and increases risks. The presence of the themes of speed, movement, and challenge in beer commercials is understandable given the cultural meanings of such images, but ultimately promotes drinking and driving.

In *Myths, Men, and Beer* (Postman et al. 1987) I and my coauthors recommended banning or restricting beer commercials, not as a panacea, but as one of a number of steps that need to be taken in order to alleviate problems such as youthful drinking and driving. I believe beer commercials should be banned for several reasons. First is the pervasiveness of the theme of challenge; the problem is not limited to one ad or one campaign or one brand, but is present across the board in beer advertising. Second, the presence of beer ads on television implies that the product is no different from toothpaste, candy, or soda pop. Eliminating the ads would more clearly indicate that this is an adult product, and one that is potentially dangerous. Given the ban on cigarette commercials and the voluntary abstinence of the liquor companies, a ban on the televised advertising of beer, and perhaps all alcohol products, would be a more consistent policy. And third, the sheer number of beer commercials works against any attempts at social marketing. Such campaigns can only meet with limited results when competing with the "don't worry, be happy" advertising of the beer industry. Unless equal time were provided, banning beer ads would be the only way to give social marketing a chance.

In the absence of an outright ban, restrictions on content would be helpful. At the very least, images of racing, of automobiles and similar forms of transportation, and references to speed and movement should be eliminated from beer ads. And I certainly agree with the recommendations of the Surgeon General's Workshop on Drunk Driving (United States Department of Health and Human Services 1988) that advertisers should not "portray activities that can be dangerous when combined with alcohol use," or "use celebrities with a strong appeal to youth." (p.29) Moreover, as I have tried to show in this paper, the themes of challenge and initiation should not be associated with beer. And at best, beer ads should be restricted to brand identification. Finally, I would like to point out that the same myths found in beer commercials can be used in social marketing campaigns. Public service spots could actually criticize or parody the dysfunctional elements of specific commercials, in an attempt to innoculate the consumer. Or they could deal with the broader themes of beer ads in a similar manner. Like advertising, public service campaigns are forms of cultural communication, and the goal is cultural change. Reshaping the myths of our culture should be part of any program to effect such change.

REFERENCES

Atkin, C.K. (1987), "Alcoholic-Beverage Advertising: Its Content and Impact," *Advances in Substance Abuse* Suppl. (1), 267-287.

Bandura, A. (1977), *Social Learning Theory*, Englewood Cliffs, NJ: Prentice Hall.

Barthes, R. (1972), *Mythologies* (J. Cape Ltd., Trans.), New York: Hill and Wang.

Drucker, P. (1989), *The New Realities*, New York: Harper & Row.

Finn, T.A. & D. Strickland (1982), "A Content Analysis of Beverage Alcohol Advertising, #2. Television Advertising," *Journal of Studies on Alcohol* (43), 964-989.

Finn, T.A. & D. Strickland (1983), "The Advertising and Alcohol Abuse Issue: A Cross Media Comparison of Alcohol Beverage Advertising Content," In M. Burgeon (Ed.), *Communication Yearbook* (pp. 850-872), Beverly Hills: Sage.

Fiske, J. (1987), *Television Culture*, London: Rutledge.

Fiske, J. and J. Hartley (1984), *Reading Television*, New York: Methuen.

Gerbner, G. & L. Gross (1976), "Living with Television: The Violence Profile," *Journal of Communication* (26), 182.

Gerbner, G., L. Gross, M. Jackson-Beeck, S. Jeffries-Fox, & N. Signorielli (1978), "Cultural Indicators: Violence Profile No. 9," *Journal of Communication* (28), 176-207.

Hacker, G.A., R. Collins and M. Jacobson (1987), *Marketing Booze to Blacks*, Washington, D.C.: Center for Science in the Public Interest.

Himmelstein, H. (1984), *Television Myth and the American Mind*, New York: Praeger.

Hirsch, E.D. Jr. (1987), *Cultural Literacy*, Boston: Houghton Mifflin.

Jacobs, J.B. (1989), *Drunk Driving, An American Dilemma*, Chicago: University of Chicago Press.

Jacobson, M., R. Atkins, and G. Hacker (1983), *The Booze Merchants, The Inebriating of America*, Washington, D.C.: Center for Science in the Public Interest.

Langholz Leymore, V. (1975), *Hidden Myth, Structure and Symbolism in Advertising*, New York: Basic.

McArthur, C. (1984), "TV Commercials: Moving Statues and Old Movies," In L. Masterman (Ed.), *Television Mythologies, Stars, Shows and Signs* (pp. 63-66), London: Comedia.

McLuhan, M. (1951), *The Mechanical Bride, Folklore of Industrial Man*, Boston: Beacon Press.

Meyrowitz, J. (1985), *No Sense of Place, The Impact of Electronic Media on Social Behavior*, New York: Oxford University Press.

Postman, N. (1979), *Teaching as a Conserving Activity*, New York: Delacorte Press.

Postman, N., C. Nystrom, L. Strate, & C. Weingartner (1987), *Myths, Men, & Beer: An Analysis of Beer Commercials on Broadcast Television, 1987*, Washington, D.C.: AAA Foundation for Traffic Safety.

Rogers, E.M. (1983), *Diffusion of Innovations* (3rd ed.), New York: Free Press.

Schwartz, T. (1974), *The Responsive Chord*, Garden City, NY: Anchor.

Signorielli, N. (1987), "Drinking, Sex, and Violence on Television: The Cultural Indicators Perspective," *Journal of Drug Education* (17), 245-260.

Strate, L. (1989), "The Mediation of Nature and Culture in Beer Commercials," *New Dimensions in Communications, Proceedings of the 47th Annual New York State Speech Communication Association Conference, Volume III*, 92-95.

United States Department of Health and Human Services (1988), *Surgeon General's Workshop on Drunk Driving Proceedings*, Washington, D.C.

Williamson, J. (1978), *Decoding Advertisements, Ideology and Meaning in Advertising*, London: Marion Boyars.

Youthful Drinking and Driving: Policy Implications From Mass Media Research
John P. Murry, Jr., University of Wisconsin-Madison

INTRODUCTION

By the end of this year alcohol related traffic accidents will kill over 24,000 people and inflict a half-million others with lingering trauma, spinal cord and brain injuries. This recurring tragedy is especially relevant to consumer researchers. Specifically, consumer behavior research rarely deals with dysfunctional usage problems such as those associated with alcohol and automobiles. Nevertheless, public policy officials have repeatedly emphasized the need for solid consumer research to guide the development of a comprehensive anti-drinking-driving strategy (United States Department of Health and Human Services 1988). The current lack of research on which to base drinking-driving remedies has fueled serious disagreements between the alcohol industry, government agencies, and private advocate groups. At the present time, however, these disagreements are driven more by armchair reasoning rather than research results and thus reflect little more than differences in opinion. It is clear that resolving such conflicts and advancing an effective drinking and driving policy hinges on building a strong foundation of consumer research.

Consumer researchers from a variety of backgrounds can contribute to reducing alcohol abuse problems. For example, policy research is needed in the areas of government regulation of alcohol warning labels, minimum pricing standards, alcohol distribution practices, and the targeting of disadvantaged consumer segments. It is clear, however, that the long-run solution to the drinking-driving problem requires a comprehensive public health education program that utilizes the mass media (Koop 1989). Therefore, this session focused on the potential role that the mass media can play in this education effort.

OVERVIEW

The session addressed two mass media issues previously identified as key topics requiring further consumer research (United States Department of Health and Human Services 1988). First, critics claim that beer advertising creates dangerous misconceptions about alcohol consumption. Associating beer consumption with valued end-states, such as peer respect or masculinity, and valued activities, such as athletics or work is thought to predispose young people to drink and drive. Advocates for banning lifestyle based beer advertising frequently cite the research stream of Lance Strate and his colleagues (i.e., Postman et al. 1987). Strate's presentation provided a textual analysis of the images and themes commonly found in beer ads over the past several years. Based on social learning theory, he concluded that the typically heavy exposure that youths have to these ads contributes to subsequent alcohol abuse problems such as drinking and driving. Therefore, he recommends banning beer advertising or, at a minimum, significantly restricting its content to functional product information.

The second topic concerned the effectiveness of using mass media advertising to deliver anti-drinking-driving messages. Mike Flynn discussed the developmental research and strategy upon which Anheuser-Busch's "Know When to When Campaign" is based. This highly publicized campaign is an indication of the brewing industry's efforts to curb drinking-driving. His presentation illustrated the critical linkage that should exist between consumer research in industry and both academic and government sponsored research. Similarly, the Murry, Lastovicka and Stam paper examined the effectiveness of both a "paid-media" anti-drinking-driving advertising campaign and a "donated-media" campaign (public service announcements) in curbing youthful drinking-driving fatalities. The development and implementation of these campaigns was guided by the previously published youthful male lifestyle typology (Lastovicka et al. 1987; Lastovicka, Murry and Joachimsthaler 1990). The effectiveness of the "paid-media" and "donated-media" campaigns was evaluated in three city test market that was conducted for the Department of Transportation. The study's results indicate that well-executed media campaigns can reduce youthful drinking-driving behavior. Specifically, both survey data and actual traffic accident data indicate that the incidence of youthful drinking and driving behavior decreased in the cities receiving either a "paid-media" or "donated-media" campaign treatment.

Paul N. Bloom (University of North Carolina-Chapel Hill) served as the discussant. His comments emphasized the need to focus on the "net" effect that any change in current mass media regulatory policy would have on alcohol abuse problems. He disagreed with Strate concerning the overall effect that would result from restricting beer advertising. He argued that a ban on advertising would diminish competitive pressures in the industry and stabilize current market shares. Further, Bloom noted that the ban on broadcast cigarette advertising allowed the tobacco industry to reallocate resources traditionally targeted for domestic advertising into foreign market expansion and the acquisition of new product categories such as beer. Hence, he questioned whether a similar ban on beer advertising would have a positive "net" effect on diminishing alcohol abuse problems or simply encourage brewers to invest in other types of marketing activities.

Although Bloom did not favor banning beer advertising, he acknowledge that such ads probably do contribute to alcohol abuse problems. Moreover, he did not believe that the responsible drinking media campaigns being sponsored by the brewing industry cancel out the negative effects associated their traditional advertising efforts. Therefore, he questioned whether media campaigns, such as the

Anheuser-Busch "Know When to Say When" campaign outlined by Flynn, actually provide a socially acceptable long run solution. To this end, Bloom emphasized the need for future evaluation research that examines the efficacy of wide array of policy options. He concluded by encouraging the brewing industry to sponsor consumer education evaluation research studies such as illustrated in Murry, Lastovicka and Stam's research.

ABSTRACTS

The Cultural Meanings of Beer Commercials
Lance Strate, Fordham University

Theory and research on the processes of social learning indicates that television programming and commercial advertisements, apart from their intended functions and target audiences, play an important role in socialization. Given the controversy surrounding certain products, such as alcoholic beverages, an examination of the ways in which they are advertised is in order. Modern advertising and television commercials in particular, generally do not provide logical arguments and claims for their products, but instead present associations between products and evocative images and themes. These images and themes are drawn from the set of symbols, values, and myths that make up our culture. In order to analyze the content of advertisements and understand the role that they play in socialization, it is necessary to determine the cultural meanings of the images and themes used. This type of textual analysis is commonly employed in disciplines such as semiotics, structuralism, cultural and critical studies. Applying this method to specific beer commercials aired in the last several years, this paper discusses the nature and role of beer and cultural conceptions of masculinity as presented in the ads, and their relationship with social problems such as alcoholism and drinking and driving.

The "Know When To Say When" Responsible Drinking Program of Annheuser-Busch: A Case Study in Strategy Development
J. H. "Mike" Flynn, D'Arcy, Massius, Benton and Bowles, Inc.

During 1980's the advertising and brewing industries became increasingly sensitive to alcohol abuse problems. This concern resulted in the advertising industry donating hundreds of millions of dollars in free media and contributing countless hours of creative talent. As a leader in the brewing industry, Anheuser-Busch has been in the forefront in developing programs to curb alcohol abuse problems such as drinking and driving. These programs include activities such as cooperative educational efforts with the NCAA on college campuses as well as a significant investment in the much publicized "Know When to Say When" ad campaign.

This presentation describe the research and philosophy behind Anheuser-Busch's strategy for fighting the irresponsible use of alcohol. The presentation focused on the development of the "Know When to Say When" campaign and detailed how early persuasion research concerning fear appeals was used to to develop the initial campaign strategy. The presentation went on to discuss how subsequent qualitative research was employed to refine both the strategy and creative executions. The Anheuser-Busch experience illustrates how consumer research can be used as a tool for discouraging drinking and driving as well as this company's commitment to promoting responsible alcohol consumption.

Drinking and Driving Public Service Campaigns: Do You Get What You Pay For?
John P. Murry, Jr., University of Wisconsin-Madison
John L. Lastovicka, University of Kansas
Antonie Stam, University of Georgia

A large scale field experiment tested the effects of two mass media channel policies across three cities. In the first experimental site, anti-drinking-driving messages were distributed as "paid-media" advertisements. In the second site these same anti-drinking-driving messages were distributed as public service announcements (PSA's) to be aired through donated media. A third site received no treatment and was used as a control. The relative effectiveness of the "paid-media" campaign and "PSA" campaign was evaluated by two methods. First, changes in pre- and post-test sample survey estimates of self-reported drinking-driving behavior were assessed at the PSA, paid campaign and control sites. These analyses were supplemented by time series modeling of official monthly fatal traffic accident data from each site. The sample survey and time series modeling provided converging evidence that the PSA and paid campaign channel policies were equally effective with targeted youth populations. Both media policies reduced youthful fatal and incapacitating accidents and self-reported estimates of drinking-driving incidence. These results indicate that a well planned PSA campaign can be as effective as a well planned paid media advertising campaign in reducing youthful drinking-driving problems.

SUMMARY

Drinking and driving results from the misuse of two consumer products: automobiles and alcohol. As such, it is one of the few domains in which consumer researchers can have a direct influence on either saving lives or minimizing human suffering. The goal of this session was to motivate more consumer researchers to conduct drinking-driving research. The session clearly illustrated that alcohol abuse problems and specifically drinking-driving, provide a relevant domain for testing theoretical propositions derived from numerous areas of consumer research. Although this session focused on mass media issues, it is apparent that further consumer research is needed on such diverse topics as pricing, persuasion, segmentation, distribution and information processing. Therefore, consumer researchers from a variety of backgrounds are urged to contribute their knowledge and skills to remedying this tragic social problem.

REFERENCES

Koop, C. Everett (1989), comments from a May 31 press conference as reported in the *American Association of Advertising Agencies Washington Newsletter*, Washington D. C., July/August, pg. 1.

Lastovicka, John L., John P. Murry, Jr., Erich A. Joachimsthaler, Guarav Bhalla and Jim Scheurich (1987), "A Lifestyle Typology to Model Young Male Drinking and Driving," *Journal of Consumer Research*, (14) September, 157-63.

Lastovicka, John L., John P. Murry, Jr. and Erich Joachimsthaler (1990), "Evaluating the Measurement Validity of Lifestyle Typologies With Qualitative Measures and Multiplicative Factoring," *Journal of Marketing Research*, (27) February, 11-23.

Postman, Neil, Christine Nystrom, Lance Strate and Charles Weingartner (1987), *Myths, Men and Beer: An Analysis of Beer Commercials on Broadcast Television, 1987*," AAA Foundation for Traffic Safety, Falls Church, VA.

United States Department of Health and Human Services (1988), *Surgeon General's Workshop on Drunk Driving Proceedings*, Washington D. C.

Omiyage Gift Purchasing By Japanese Travelers in the U.S.

Terrence H. Witkowski, California State University, Long Beach
Yoshito Yamamoto, IBM Japan, Ltd.[1]

ABSTRACT

This article reports an exploratory study on the purchasing behavior of Japanese travelers in the U.S. Respondents expended more effort, and nearly as much money, buying gifts to take home (*omiyage*), as they did on personal items. Price and product quality were important criteria for both types of purchases, while country-of-origin and packaging were especially important for *omiyage* gifts. These and other findings have implications for gift giving and cross-cultural consumer research.

INTRODUCTION

In 1987, 2.1 million Japanese travelers came to the U.S. for business, study, and pleasure and spent $2.1 billion, excluding airfares (Hutton 1988). The total number of foreign visitors to the U.S. that year was 29.7 million and they spent $14.8 billion (OECD 1988). Thus, the Japanese, accounting for only 7.2 percent of all foreign travelers, have expenditures amounting to 14.2 percent of the total. Since the Japanese generally take short trips when going overseas, their expenditures on a daily basis are impressive. The *Economist* (1988) reports that the average Japanese tourist spends nearly $800 on shopping on each foreign trip, "the highest spending per person by any nation's travelers" (p. 64). According to U.S. Travel and Tourism Administration (USTTA) data, the Japanese outspend the West Germans more than two to one (Go 1989).

Since the number of Japanese going abroad has been rapidly growing (over 20 percent increases in U.S. visits for both 1987 and 1988), their buyer behavior while overseas is a phenomenon of growing importance. The USTTA expects Japanese expenditures in the U.S. to rise to $3.5 billion in 1989 (Go 1989), providing potential opportunities for American retailers who serve this market. Worldwide, Japan has run a massive deficit on its balance of travel account, $5.8 billion in 1986 (Morris 1988) and $8.6 billion in 1987 (OECD 1988). The Japanese government predicts this figure will rise to $10 billion by 1991.

The high value of the yen explains part of this comparatively heavy spending, but there are other economic factors. For example, the Japanese government allows $1600 in duty free imports, a strong incentive compared to the $400 the U.S. allows. Also, the Japanese can find bargains abroad because their relatively inefficient retailing system charges high prices. According to the U.S. Commerce Department and Japan's Ministry of International Trade and Industry, 60 percent of all Japanese goods surveyed can be bought for less overseas than they can in Japan. In contrast, 90 percent of American and other foreign items cost the same or more in Japan than they do in their home countries (Pine 1989).

Finally, Japanese travel spending has an important cultural component. As Nobuo (1988) argues, "the major expedition of any trip abroad is to buy souvenirs for the folks back home, and for that there is always interest and plenty of money to burn" (p. 436). The Japanese call such gifts *omiyage*. The authors' field observations of Japanese purchasing behavior at duty-free airport shops and specialty stores in southern California support Nobuo's contention.

Omiyage purchases appear to be a major factor in the amount the Japanese spend while on trips. To investigate the extent of this form of gift buying, and to compare purchasing effort and criteria for gifts with items bought for personal use, data were collected from a convenience sample of Japanese travelers departing from Los Angeles International Airport. This article will discuss some theoretical issues that directed the study, its objectives, methodology, and findings, and its implications for gift giving research and for marketing to Japanese consumers.

GIFT EXCHANGE IN JAPAN

Gift giving has social, personal, and economic dimensions (Belk 1979). Gifts bind people together and tangibly express social relationships (Sherry 1983). The long history of ritualized gift giving in Japan began with the offerings of food and sake to supernatural beings (Befu 1968). The secular concepts of *giri* or "social obligation" and *on* or "an indebtedness" (Lebra 1969) evolved from these religious practices while the household became the basic gift giving unit. The circle of kin, friends, and acquaintances with which one has reciprocity is termed the *kosai* (Johnson 1974). During the times of *o-chugen*, in July, and *Oseibo*, near the end of the year, gifts are presented "to those persons to whom an individual or a family feels a special enduring indebtedness" (Condon 1984, p. 82).

In modern, urban Japan gift giving remains an important social custom for reinforcing a group-oriented self-concept (Green and Alden 1988). The Japanese language has over 35 different terms for gifts and households give or receive an average of 23 gifts a month (Morsbach 1977). The Japanese take reciprocity so seriously that once involved in mutual exchanges they find it difficult to opt out. Morsbach believes this resembles the Western custom of sending Christmas cards when we feel obligated to mail cards to people we do not know or care about because they have sent one first. Some educated Japanese treat this *giri*-based behavior as an

---

[1] The authors would like to thank Alan R. Andreasen, Mary Finley Wolfinbarger, and the anonymous reviewers for their helpful and encouraging comments on earlier drafts of this article.

empty formality and feel it is a nuisance (Befu 1968). However, gift packaging still matters a great deal, partly because people prefer not to open presents in front of the giver.

One of the typical Japanese gift giving occasions occurs after trips inside or outside Japan: "It is an iron rule for the Japanese that one cannot go on a trip without bringing back *omiyage*" (Isamu 1963, p. 234). The rule applies to both children and adults and for both short as well as long vacations. Japanese travel brochures emphasize shopping abroad and indicate the kinds of gifts that can be purchased (Moeran 1983). The Japanese term their "souvenir culture" *omiyage bunka*. Like picture postcards, gifts brought back from trips reaffirm social relationships.

The cultural basis for giving *omiyage* is partly an egalitarian attempt to share an outside experience with the people left at home, but also a status marker that shows the person has been abroad. The concepts of *kinen* or "souvenir" and *meibutsu* or "a specialty of the area visited" are very important in Japanese culture (Graburn 1987). Thus, *omiyage* should properly be obtained from the tourist site. The act of giving also represents thoughtfulness and is much more important than the actual contents of the gift. The presentation of gifts to fellow workers "is often accompanied by deep apologies for the long absence" (Nobuo 1988, p. 433). Japanese norms dictate that these gifts should cost approximately half of any *senbetsu*, farewell gifts given to those going on a trip, and be tailored to the age and sex of the donor (Graburn 1987). *Omiyage* should also be the monetary equivalent of previously received *omiyage* in order to keep the relationship in balance. Gifts that are too cheap or too expensive disrupt balance.

In Japan, railway stations and numerous souvenir shops carry a wide variety of inexpensive, cleverly packaged *omiyage* products. Department stores display gifts by price and advertise mid-year gift sales in newspapers. Japanese traveling abroad, on the other hand, must look hard to find suitable *omiyage*. Purchasing such gifts "usually causes a great last-minute rush among Japanese during their final days overseas" (Morsbach 1977, 110). This suggests potential marketing opportunities for retailers in the U.S. and other countries who wish to better serve Japanese travelers.

RESEARCH OBJECTIVES

The first priority was to discover how much a typical Japanese traveler in the U.S. was spending on *omiyage* and what kinds of products were being purchased. The study also investigated the motivational components of giving *omiyage*. While the Japanese are guided by traditionally strong norms of social obligation, they also buy gifts to express personal affection for the receiver. Such individual-to-individual gift giving, a relatively modern, urban trend (Befu 1968), compares to Western gift giving, as well as some traditional non-Western practices (Gregory 1980), where exact reciprocation is not that essential. It is motivated by *ninjo* or a person's "natural feelings and desires."

To place these findings within a larger context, the study examined expenditures on items bought for personal use and on differences in purchasing effort (time spent, stores shopped) between these items and *omiyage*. Condon (1984) believes that the Japanese spend more money on gifts than on items for themselves. Although some prior research has found that purchasing gifts requires more effort (Clarke and Belk 1979), other studies find more effort expended on buying for own use (Heeler, et. al. 1979). Belk (1982) reconciles these conflicting findings by observing that some gift giving occasions are simply much more involving than others. Rucker *et. al.* (1986) suggest that, in terms of timing, personal items are given priority over gifts.

Exploring the absolute as well as relative importance of eleven product purchasing criteria was another major objective. One important criterion was country-of-origin (Japan, other Asian country, Europe, or U.S.). The increasing globalization of business has stimulated research on country-of-origin effects (see, for example, Han and Terpstra 1988). Since custom dictates that *omiyage* gifts should be made in and representative of the area where they are purchased, Japanese consumers in the U.S. should value American manufacture highly when buying these items.

Hutton (1988) and Moeran (1983) have noted that the Japanese love to accumulate status symbols abroad by shopping for name brands in prestigious stores. Therefore, they should view product quality, fashionableness, and brand image as important purchase criteria. Other criteria of interest included comparative price (Japan vs. U.S.), product appearance and packaging, and the availability of a Japanese-speaking salesperson. Because of the importance of gift appearance and packaging in Japanese culture, travelers should rate this criterion as more important for *omiyage* than for other purchases.

Finally, the research examined the effect selected demographic and behavioral variables, such as gender, age, and purpose and duration of trip, have on the amount expended and on purchasing attitudes and criteria. For example, it was hypothesized that compared to older tourists who are probably more supportive of tradition, younger travelers would find gift purchasing to be a less pleasant experience and would be more likely to buy gifts to express individuality and personal feelings.

METHODOLOGY

This exploratory study used survey research methods to gather several kinds of descriptive data. The survey instrument consisted of a cover letter on university stationary and a five page, self-administered questionnaire. The authors first developed an English language version and then two translators, whose native language is Japanese, translated the English version into Japanese. Both translators hold masters degrees from American universities. No attempt was made to back translate the questions.

An instrument pretest was conducted to ensure that all questions were simple and understandable and that the answering time was less than ten minutes. The pretest sample consisted of a group of Japanese students attending a large southern California university. Like all modern Japanese, the final version of the questionnaire was printed using a combination of *kanji, hiragana*, and *katakana* characters.

Over several days in July, 1989, sixty Japanese travelers about to depart Los Angeles International Airport completed the questionnaire. Although children sometimes buy *omiyage* for their friends, and are even given an allowance to do so, the sample did not include anyone under the age of fifteen. Both members of a married couple were asked to fill out the questionnaire only if they had separate obligations to, say, different bosses and coworkers. Otherwise, couples were regarded as an individual, as they are in Japan.

Although a convenience sample, the authors believe that the airport location yielded a reasonably representative mix of Japanese travelers since virtually all come and go by air and southern California is their most frequent destination in the continental U.S. The terminal seemed a good place at which to approach these busy people since they were relaxed and waiting for boarding. Also, many Japanese travelers appear to make a final purchase at duty-free shops and, hence, product purchasing should still be fresh on their minds.

RESULTS

Demographic and Behavioral Findings

The Japanese travelers in the sample tended to be young (two-thirds were 34 or younger), educated (over 60 percent attended junior college or better), and affluent (nearly half of the full-time workers earned over $35,000). Sixty percent were male and slightly more than half (53%) were married. Our field observations of Japanese travelers, their comportment, and their dress support these findings.

The primary purposes for visiting the U.S. were sightseeing (41.7%), study (20.0%), and business (16.7%). Trip duration broke into two major groups: shortstay travelers here less than two weeks (55.0% of the sample) and longer-stay travelers, usually students here for more than six months (28.3%). Only 16.6 percent stayed from two weeks to six months. For seventy-five percent of the respondents, the appreciated yen had at least some impact upon their decision to make a U.S. trip.

Product Purchasing

Over eighty-three percent of the sample (83.3%) purchased *omiyage*, spending an average of $566 per person. Asked to "please list the main product items you purchased as *omiyage*," the respondents most frequently named alcohol, cigarettes, beef jerky, chocolate, clothing, and perfume. The data did not reveal whether the respondents considered these specific items to be distinctly American or simply purchased them because they were convenient and in the appropriate price range. Many of these items seem to have been purchased at the airport's duty-free shop.

In comparison, slightly more than 78 percent (47 out of 60) of the sample purchased products for their own use. Typical items in this category included clothing, jewelry and accessories, bags and wallets, alcohol, shoes, and cosmetics. Excluding those who purchased houses and automobiles (one traveler spent $450,000 and four spent $15,000 or more), the travelers spent an average of $581 on personal items. However, nearly half of the respondents (46.7%) spent more on *omiyage* than on products for themselves.

The extent of *omiyage* purchasing was also indicated by the number of people for whom gifts were intended. Of those respondents who purchased *omiyage* gifts, 11.8% bought for 5 people or less, 25.5% bought for 6 to 10 people, 17.6% bought for 11 to 15 people, and 45.1% bought omiyage for *15 or more people*, a sizeable gift giving network. Although the questionnaire did not address the issue of uniqueness, the second author's personal experience suggests that the Japanese buy the same gifts for many different people. In Japan, equal treatment is a critical factor in maintaining good relationships with others. Only very close friends can expect a special gift.

The most frequent recipients were friends: 66.7 percent of those who purchased *omiyage* gifts said they were buying for friends. Other recipients and percentages were parents (60.0%), siblings (58.3%), other relatives (41.7%), co-workers (38.3%), neighbors (31.7%), bosses (23.3%), and spouses (18.3%). The comparatively low figure for "bosses" seems reasonable because over one-third of the respondents were self-employed or nonworking students or retired. The low figure for "spouses" can be attributed to the fact that 41.7 percent of the respondents were single and some others were traveling as couples.

Neither age, gender, nor education were significantly associated with the amount spent on gifts or on oneself. As one might expect, however, trip duration was positively correlated with purchasing for oneself ($r = .43$, $p < .01$). Sooner or later personal items need to be replaced and longer trips offer more shopping opportunities for specialty goods. Trip duration was unrelated to *omiyage* expenditures ($r = -.005$). Whether away for a week or for six months, Japanese travelers must fulfull their gift giving obligations.

Exchange rates had somewhat less influence on product purchasing than they had on choosing to travel. While sixty percent said that the yen had a fair to significant impact on buying *omiyage* (56.6% on buying for own use), 75 percent thought it had this effect on the decision to make the trip. Thus, the demand for gifts seems slightly more inelastic than the demand for overseas travel.

TABLE 1
IMPORTANCE OF PURCHASE CRITERIA

Respondents who rated criterion as important or very important in buying for:	Personal Use (percent)	*Omiyage* (percent)
Product quality	93.6	88.2
Only available in the U.S.	80.9	80.4
Cheaper than buying in Japan	78.7	78.4
Made in U.S.A.	55.3	76.5
Well-known brand	44.7	56.9
Fashionable item	29.8	33.3
Product appearance & packaging	21.3	43.1
Made in Japan	12.8	3.9
Made in Europe	10.7	23.5
Japanese-speaking salesperson	8.5	13.7
Made in other Asian countries	4.2	2.0

Motivational Components of *Omiyage*

The data suggest that two different kinds of motives influence *omiyage* purchasing. The first involves reciprocal obligations: 43.3 percent of the respondents said they purchased in return for *sembetsu*, bon-voyage gifts or money, and 35 percent said they purchased in return for previously received *omiyage*. Eighty percent of the sample said they regarded the buying of souvenirs to be the traditional social norm in Japan.

The other type of motive reflects individuation and the expression of personal feelings. Respondents said they purchased *omiyage* to express appreciation (46.7% said this), to express friendship and love (40%), and to give pleasure to the recipient (21.7%). Although these reasons might always have accompanied souvenir gift giving in Japan (in the sense that they appear to be socially desirable responses), their strong showing supports Befu's notion of a modern, urban culture adding new ideas to its traditional norms of reciprocity. Compared to respondents over 30 and to those who had not finished college, younger and better educated respondents more frequently said they bought *omiyage* to express appreciation or friendship and love. However, none of these predicted differences were statistically significant.

Purchase Effort

For many Japanese travelers, buying *omiyage* is, at best, a necessary chore. Less than 7 percent of the respondents said that they obtained any pleasure out of buying *omiyage*. In answer to another question, only 20 percent of the respondents felt positive or very positive about buying these gifts. Nearly 42 percent (41.7%) were indifferent and slightly more than 38 percent (38.4%) felt that this buying was bothersome or very bothersome. Respondents over age 30 were somewhat more likely than the rest to say gift buying was bothersome or very bothersome (46.7% vs. 30.0%), but this finding was not statistically significant.

These attitudes may be related to the amount of effort expended on buying *omiyage*. In terms of time spent and stores shopped, 66.7 percent of those who bought both products for own use and gifts answered that selecting gifts took more work. Only 13.7 percent said they spent more effort on their own purchases. These findings might be due to the fact that 88.2 percent of the gift purchasers selected products for more than five people, a seemingly demanding bit of shopping. Even if gifts were purchased several at a time, suitable *omiyage* are probably harder to find in U.S. retail establishments than they are in Japan. Since many *omiyage* purchases are convenience goods like cigarettes and beef jerky, they would seem to be low involvement gifts. However, shopping difficulties actually may make them high in involvement for the travelers.

Purchase Criteria

Table 1 shows the importance of eleven different purchase criteria. A high percentage of respondents rated several criteria as being either important or very important when purchasing for personal use. These criteria were "product quality" (93.6%), "only available in the U.S." (80.9%), "cheaper than buying in Japan" (78.7%), "made in U.S.A." (55.3%), and "well-known brand" (44.7%). The relatively low figures for "well-known brand," "fashionable item" (29.8%), and "product appearance & packaging" (21.3%) indicate that status is not of overwhelming importance as a purchase criterion when buying for personal use.

The same criteria were rated similarly for *omiyage* purchases: "product quality" (88.2%), "only available in U.S." (80.4%), "cheaper than buying in Japan" (78.4%), "made in U.S.A." (76.5%), and "well-known brand" (56.9%). As expected, the "made in U.S.A." criterion was more important for *omiyage* purchases. Recall that these gifts are supposed to be a specialty of the area visited. Another criterion rated more highly for *omiyage* than for own use purchasing was "product appearance and packaging." While only 21.3 percent of the respondents rated this important or very important for own use, 43.1 percent gave this rating for *omiyage* purchases. Since the Japanese usually do not open their gifts in front of the giver, the packaging is relatively more important.

Purchase criteria ratings varied somewhat when cross tabulated with age, gender, and education. For example, respondents over 30 were more likely than younger travelers to rate *omiyage* "product appearance and packaging" as important or very important (Chi-square = 7.32, p <.01). Interestingly, more males rated "fashionable item" important for *omiyage* than did females (Chi-square = 5.85, p <.02). They also rated personal use "fashionable item" and both personal use and *omiyage* "well-known brand" as important criteria more often than females, but rated personal use "made in U.S.A." as important less frequently. None of these differences were statistically significant. Finally, respondents without a college degree rated the "made in U.S.A." criterion for both personal and gift purchases as important *more* frequently than the others, but this finding too was not significant.

CONCLUSION AND IMPLICATIONS

This research supports most of the theory and anecdotal observations of the buying behavior of Japanese travelers abroad. The respondents surveyed did expend a good deal of time, money, and effort choosing gifts for their friends and relatives back home. Compared to the items they bought for themselves, the respondents attached more importance to the country-of-origin and to the appearance and packaging of *omiyage*. For both types of goods, however, product quality, place of manufacture, and prices lower than in Japan were important purchase criteria.

The respondents showed very few differences in either buyer behavior or attitudes that could be explained by age, gender, or education. Only two out of approximately one-hundred chi-square tests showed statistical significance. This lack of variation, which may be caused by some unknown response bias, does support the oft-mentioned description of the Japanese as a very homogeneous culture. Future investigations of Japanese consumers should aim for larger sample sizes and try other forms of questioning to tease out more response variance. Such research should produce more clearly defined buyer segments than has the present effort.

The study also contributes to the literature on gift-giving. Clearly, *omiyage* are purchased for the sake of reciprocity, but they do express other, perhaps deeper and more personal feelings. Personal motives seem to be more prevalent among the young and better educated travelers as predicted, but the evidence is far from conclusive. These gifts also require more purchase effort than items bought for personal use. This might result from the large number of such purchases made by respondents and, perhaps, from the lack of readily available *omiyage* gifts in U.S. retail stores. These situational factors seem to explain differences in purchase effort, but level of involvement remains an alternative explanation in need of empirical test.

The findings suggest that Japanese travelers comprise a distinct segment of consumers willing and able to spend. Thus, U.S. and other retailers who serve this market should evaluate the suitability of their product line for *omiyage* purchases. Specifically, they need to consider whether they offer a sufficient breadth of merchandise in the price ranges and packaging most desired by the Japanese. Because the Japanese buy a number of these items, ease of purchase should not be overlooked. Place of manufacture is also a very important purchase criterion and, consequently, a good assortment of clearly labeled, regionally-made products should be quite saleable to the Japanese traveler. For example, Darrel F. Corti, a Sacramento wine merchant, sells a private brand called "Poppy" that features the California state flower on the label. Through a special gift program set up by Yoshiya Co., a Tokyo supermarket chain, Japanese tourists can purchase the wine during their California visit but take delivery in Japan (Yoshihara 1989).

Retailers should consider contacting potential buyers before they leave Japan, while enroute, and at their destination. Since most Japanese travel and, according to Green and Alden (1988), shop for gifts in groups, promotions to or through tour operators should be especially productive. Promotional material should stress the availability of brand name merchandise and the prestige of the store. Perhaps manufacturers should augment these campaigns by providing cooperative advertising funds for use in reaching the Japanese tourist market.

REFERENCES

Befu, Harumi (1968), "Gift-Giving in a Modernizing Japan," *Monumenta Nipponica*, 23, 445-456.

Belk, Russell W. (1979), "Gift-Giving Behavior," in *Research in Marketing*, Vol. 2, ed. Jagdish Sheth, Greenwich, CT: JAI Press, 95-126.

_____ (1982), "Effects of Gift-Giving Involvement on Gift Selection Strategies," in *Advances in Consumer Research*, Vol. 9, ed. Andrew Mitchell, Ann Arbor, MI: Association for Consumer Research, 408-412.

Clarke, Keith and Russell W. Belk (1979), "The Effects of Product Involvement and Task Definition on Anticipated Consumer Effort," in *Advances in Consumer Research*, Vol. 6, ed. William Wilkie, Ann Arbor, MI: Association for Consumer Research, 313-318.

Condon, John C. (1984), *With Resect to the Japanese: A Guide for Americans*, Yarmouth, ME: Intercultural Press, Inc.

Economist (1988), "Japanese Tourism: Broadening the Mind," 307 (May 7), 64-65.

Go, Frank (1989), "United States of America," in *International Tourism Report, No. 2*, London: The Economist Intelligence Unit Limited, 42-60.

Graburn, Nelson H.H. (1987), "Material Symbols in Japanese Domestic Tourism," in *Mirror and Metaphor: Material and Social Constructions of Reality*, eds. Daniel W. Ingersoll, Jr. and Gordon Bronitsky, Lanham, MD: University Press of America, 17-27.

Green, Robert T. and Dana L. Alden (1988), "Functional Equivalence in Cross-Cultural Consumer Behavior: Gift Giving in Japan and the United States," *Psychology and Marketing*, 5 (Summer), 155-168.

Gregory, C.A. (1980), "Gifts to Men and Gifts to God: Gift Exchange and Capital Accumulation in Contemporary Papua," *Man*, 15, 626-652.

Han, C. Min and Vern Terpstra (1988), "Country-of-Origin Effects for Uni-national and Bi-national Products," *Journal of International Business Studies*, 19 (Summer), 235-255.

Heeler, Roger, June Francis, Chike Okechuku, and Stanley Reid (1979), "Gift Versus Personal Use Brand Selection," in *Advances in Consumer Research*, Vol. 6, ed. William Wilkie, Ann Arbor, MI: Association for Consumer Research, 325-328.

Hutton, Cynthia (1988), "Born to Shop," *Fortune* 117 (June 6), 14.

Isamu, Nishimura (1963), "Doing Things Differently," *Japan Quarterly*, 10 (April-June), 232-239.

Johnson, Colleen L. (1974), "Gift Giving and Reciprocity Among the Japanese Americans in Honolulu," *American Ethnologist*, 1, 295-308.

Lebra, Taki Sugiyama (1969), "Reciprocity and the Asymetric Principle: An Analytical Reappraisal of the Japanese Concept of On," *Psychologia*, 12, 129-138.

Moeran, Brian (1983), "The Language of Japanese Tourism," *Annals of Tourism Research*, 10, 93-108.

Morris, Stephen (1988), "Japan: National Report No. 147," in *International Tourism Reports*, London: The Economist Intelligence Unit Limited, 29-45.

Morsbach, Helmut (1977), "The Psychological Importance of Ritual-Gift Exchange in Modern Japan," *Annals of the New York Academy of Sciences*, 293, 98-113.

Nobuo, Takagi (1988), "Japanese Abroad: Armed With Slippers and Soy Sauce," *Japan Quarterly*, 35 (October-December), 432-436.

Organisation for Economic Cooperation and Development (1988), *Tourism Policy and International Tourism in OECD Member Countries*, Paris: OECD.

Pine, Art (1989), "Japanese Pay More When the Label Reads 'Made in Japan,'" *Los Angeles Times*, (November 8), D1.

Rucker, Margaret, Susan Kaiser, Mary Barry, Debra Brummett, Carla Freeman, and Alice Peters (1986), "The Imported Export Market: An Investigation of Foreign Visitors' Gift and Personal Purchases," in *Developments in Marketing Science*, Vol. 9, ed. Naresh K. Malhotra, Atlanta: Academy of Marketing Science, 120-124.

Sherry, John F. (1983), "Gift Giving in Anthropological Perspective," *Journal of Consumer Research*, 10 (September), 157-168.

Yoshihara, Nancy (1989), "California Style Strikes Gold in Japan," *Los Angeles Times* (September 24), Part IV, 1, 5.

Japan - A Culture of Consumption?

Laurel Anderson, Arizona State University
Marsha Wadkins, University of Virginia

ABSTRACT

The *shinjinrui* or "new breed" in Japan has many parallel characteristics to consumers in the United States when it became a culture of consumption. Two structural aspects of Japanese culture - the "synthetic ideal" and the "sacred nothing" have components that seem to both facilitate and inhibit Japan's becoming a culture of consumption. These two structural aspects are examined with regard to their impact on Japan's development into a culture of consumption.

INTRODUCTION

A number of observers have noted a major socio-economic shift which is occurring in Japan. Most of the attention has focused on a phenomenon known as the *shinjinrui* (translation, "new human beings" or "new breed"). This generation of young Japanese appears to constitute a major break with the past. The shinjinrui are characterized by personal ambition, an appreciation for the "good life", and an emphasis on individuality and self-actualization (see Nakano 1988a, 1988b; Fuchino 1988, Iwao 1988). They represent the first class of modern consumers in Japan. This description of the shinjinrui has many interesting parallels to consumers in the United States at the turn of the century. Many factors contributed to the transformation of the United States into a consumer culture at the turn of the century. Technological innovations precipitated vastly increased production capabilities. A rising level of affluence expanded buying power. But perhaps most significant was the development of limitless demand. Insatiability became a vital component of economic expansion. A major factor in the proliferation of wants was the linkage of consumer goods with selfhood. A characteristic of a culture of consumption is that one's sense of personal identity and one's relationship to others become increasingly mediated by commodities. An individual's identity is tied to what one consumes rather than in a production culture where an individual's identity is more tied to what one produces. Advertising both reflected and enabled this phenomenon, by associating goods with love, happiness, social status, and independence (see Leiss, Kline and Jhally 1986; Fox and Lears 1983; Marchand 1985; Ewen 1976; Belk and Pollay 1985; McCracken 1986; and Anderson and Wadkins 1989a on the development of a consumer culture in the United States and the role of advertising.

Japan is undergoing a similar expansion in buying power and a shift toward more emphasis on consumption by individuals. As mentioned, there are striking parallels between the shinjinrui and the first modern consumers in the United States (Anderson and Wadkins 1989b). However, what is questionable is the way and degree to which Japan will complete the transformation to a consumer culture. Despite economic pressures which favor the shift, there are mitigating factors. As will be discussed, in some ways, Japan is uniquely adapted to the linking of commodities and self definition. But other aspects exert a countervailing force. Both tendencies are functions of two structural principles which characterize Japanese culture: "the synthetic ideal" (Buruma 1984) and "the sacred nothing" (Barthes 1982). These principles deal with the traditional constitution of "self" and society.

We will first explore the socio-economic changes which point to a shift toward a consumer culture, including the trend toward a service economy and the rise of the shinjinrui. We will then explicate the two structural principles and explore their manifestations in traditional and modern cultural elements; we will argue that the absence of moral absolutes and the construction of multiple selves which characterize Japanese culture predispose it to the adoption of a consumer mentality. However, the dichotomy between real and ideal and the relationship between visual representation and fantasy oppose the development, because they limit the effectiveness of advertising in promoting demand. Through their contradictory influences "the synthetic ideal" and "the sacred nothing" make the shift to a consumer culture uniquely Japanese. They also serve as the means by which indigenous cultural values may persist despite a surface "Westernization".

SOCIO-ECONOMIC CHANGES

Japan's economic growth in the post-WWII years has been an astonishing success story. Through hard work, sacrifice, and a strong emphasis on cooperative effort, the Japanese have transformed themselves into a modern industrial power. But observers agree that a certain phase has ended and another has begun. The present period is referred to as the "post-recovery" era, and appears to mark the end of rapid economic growth. The slowing began in the mid-1970s, and coincided with the oil crisis of 1973-74. Since then, a restructuring of Japan's economy has gradually taken hold. Noda (1988) notes that the number of smaller retail companies is declining, while the proportion of information and service industries is increasing. These shifts have begun to alter the nature of work in Japan. Fuchino (1988) points out that the ratio of highly educated individuals is increasing while the value of a college education in the work force is declining. Job obsolescence is a reality for many workers. While they are guaranteed employment, they face being transferred to another company. They may find themselves doing unfamiliar work, and many have to relocate away from their families. The possibility of promotion, once an almost certain reward for seniority, is now more often based on merit. The result is an erosion of the strong corporate loyalty which has characterized the work force during the last 40 years. As Fuchino writes, work in Japan is becoming a "private affair" (1988, p.17). Workers are less concerned with group cohesiveness and more concerned with personal advancement. "Job-hopping", once socially unacceptable, is becoming more commonplace. Thus the emotional satisfaction derived from feeling a part of a corporate "family" producing, is diminishing. At the same time, work itself is becoming less absorbing, as highly skilled positions are replaced by service-sector jobs requiring less training. Rather than a source of fulfillment, work is becoming a means to an end.

Despite a slowing of growth and job restructuring, Japan is still a relatively affluent society. Over 90% of the Japanese characterize themselves as "middle-class" (Noda 1988, p. 27). In the past, much of what workers earned was saved, accounting for Japan's traditionally high rate of savings and its low interest rates. This frugality was in part nominative, and in part the result of a dearth of consumer goods. Both aspects are changing. With work less fulfilling, workers are turning to leisure pursuits for satisfaction, and displaying a willingness to spend, not save. Lifestyles are diversifying, and self-definition is becoming a matter of consumption patterns. Just as the United States did at the turn of the century, Japan is becoming a society where one's identity is a function of how one consumes, not what one produces. The shinjinrui represent the vanguard of this transformation. Observers have noted their need for instant gratification, reflected in the proliferation of credit cards (Iwao 1988). The "new breed" is associated with a preoccupation with fashion, hobbies, and the mass media. Rather than conforming to traditional patterns of consumption, which involved never living above one's station, or place in the corporate hierarchy, they seek higher status *through* consumption.

Along with a shift in the nature of work, Japan has also seen a transformation in the make-up of the family. The traditional emphasis on the extended family has been replaced by the nuclear family structure common to the West. The "average Japanese household" now consists of 3 members (Iwao, 1988, p.4). This atomization of the social collectivity has reinforced the tendency toward individuality and diversity.

The changes in work and family structure are functions of the larger economic shift occurring in Japan. It is now national policy in Japan to decrease the number of working hours in an effort to stimulate domestic demand and perhaps reduce international criticism on the large trade surplus (Fields, 1988). These changes have created a climate receptive to the proliferation of consumer goods. This tendency is reinforced by the demands of the new economic order. An economy built upon consumer goods is one where novelty and variety are preeminent values. Iwao notes that between 1975 and 1985, the number of different labels of beer increased by 500%, while overall production only rose by 20% (1988, p 2). Mass-lot production is being replaced by smaller lots, creating greater opportunities for people to individuate themselves through commodities.

The socio-economic changes occurring in Japan seem to support the conclusion that it is being transformed into a true consumer culture. The rise to prominence of the *shinjinrui* lends added support. But, if this is true and if the changes occurring in Japan merely replicate the transformation which occurred earlier in the United States, then a larger question looms. What is the significance of indigenous Japanese values and institutions? If they are inconsequential, then the consolidation into a culture of consumption similar to the United States is a foregone conclusion. But the evidence suggests otherwise. In some respects, Japanese culture is highly compatible with the values of a consumer culture. In other respects, it is not, and raises questions in particular about the potential effectiveness of advertising. The constellation of values with which we are concerned may be grouped into two general categories: the "synthetic ideal" and the "sacred nothing".

STRUCTURAL PRINCIPLES

The "synthetic ideal"

In Japan...people are not interested so much in 'real selves' and no attempts are made to hide the fake. On the contrary, artificiality is appreciated for its own sake (Buruma 1984, p.69).

The value placed on artifice is perhaps the dominant aesthetic principle underlying the arts in Japan. The great Kabuki actor Yoshisawa Ayame (1673-1729) referred to this as "the synthetic ideal", a term which is as viable today as it was over two centuries ago (Buruma 1984, p.116). The logic behind the synthetic ideal involves a dichotomy between "real" and "ideal". Roland Barthes characterizes artistic expression in Japan as where "reality . . . [is] signified but not represented" (1982, p.91). Art in Japan deals almost wholly with a world removed from everyday experience. Beauty is found not in that which is natural, but in that which is skillfully cultivated. Buruma sees at the heart of the synthetic ideal a "principle of depersonalization" (1984, p.115). The individuating qualities which characterize the particular are subordinated to stylized representations of the universal. This can be seen behind such manifestations as the geisha (where make-up obliterates individual differences); No theatre (masks) and even Sumo wrestlers (where fat is used as a "costume"). Clearly the purpose in such artistry is not to capture or expose that which *is*, but to create that which *is not*. Since representing "real life" is not the goal, the subterfuge is explicit. Indeed, to emphasize the unreality is to emphasize the degree of skill necessary to create the illusion. In Japan, there is a long-standing tradition of puppet theatre, which predates Kabuki. Unlike marionettes (or muppets) in the West, in Japan little attempt is made to conceal the puppeteers. They share the stage with the large puppets. Kabuki evolved in part out of this tradition. The stylized movements of Kabuki actors were intended to mimic the puppets; not, as Buruma notes "life" (1984). The synthetic ideal is perhaps best expressed by the *omagata*, the male actors who specialize in female roles in Kabuki. The collective rationale for this clearly demonstrates the synthetic ideal at work: it is believed that men playing women are more beautiful than any woman could be. As Buruma writes,

> people do not pretend the ideal has anything to do with reality. They enjoy seeing Lady MacBeth played by a famous Kabuki star, precisely because it is more artificial, thus more skillful, in a word, more beautiful (1984, p.117).

The *illusion* is thus valued so highly because it is so difficult to achieve. This can be seen in *bonsai* cultivation, where painstaking training and shaping are employed to create a stylized, miniaturized version of "nature". An additional demonstration of the synthetic ideal lies in the re-creation of Hawaii in Kagoshima, Japan. An artificial microcosm of Hawaii was built complete with a staff made up of Hawaiian dancers in hula skirts, palm-tree motifs, "alohas," a Hawaiian restaurant, a quasi-Hawaiian jungle, etc. As Buruma (1989) wonders:

> "One suspects that many people prefer this artificial paradise to the real thing. The synthetic is traditionally favored over the organic, the miniature considered more beautiful than the original model." (23)

Artists in the West have traditionally sought to convey some sense of the authentic nature of their subjects. Portraiture, novels, theatre and landscape painting have been perceived as vehicles through which reality could be transmitted. To borrow from the semioticians, in the artistic tradition of the West, specific works *signify* specific aspects of reality; they strive to individuate their subjects. In Japan, works of art signify the ideal; they strive to represent an abstraction. Barthes (1982) notes that Japanese grammar distinguishes animate from inanimate objects; and that fictional characters are classified as inanimate.

As Buruma (1984) points out, focusing artistic expression on the presentation of an ideal abstraction from reality imbues the work of art with an inevitable sense of pathos. Beauty is only possible through illusion; it is not a given in the real world. The ideal can never be attained; only symbolized.

The gulf between real and ideal in Japan reveals itself in a number of ways. One not yet dealt with here is the imagery of *masks*, traditionally associated with No theatre. Barthes refers to the practice of masking or painting the face in Japan as "the written face"; turning the face into a canvas devoid of real expression (1982, p.36). As a metaphor, masking transcends No, and pervades Japanese social life. Buruma points to the "striking gap" between public and private personas in Japan (1984, p.69). Outside the home, roles are rigidly prescribed. It is not considered appropriate to express one's true feelings publicly. The ease with which the Japanese may switch roles can be disconcerting to Westerners, particularly Americans, who stress openness and "being themselves". Of course, role playing is a feature of all cultures. In many, however, the *illusion* of authenticity is maintained. In Japan, no attempt is made to conceal the subterfuge. Thus, for Japanese society, the synthetic ideal greatly impresses through its artificiality and the beauty of this which is unattainable in reality.

The "sacred nothing"

Besides the synthetic ideal, another related structural principle mediates the relationship between artistic expression and life in Japan; it is what Barthes called "the sacred nothing" (1982, p.32). Traditionally, the Emperor was a role almost without an inhabitant, unseen, unheard, and essentially lacking in political power. Buruma describes this system as a hierarchy with a void at the top (1984). Barthes notes that the spatial layout of Tokyo reflects this principle, since unlike most Western cities its center is not densely populated - it is "empty". It is there that the Emperor resides, his palace hidden from view. Lacking a "self"; an individual identity, the Emperor is instead whatever his subjects perceive his as being. This carries over to the individual Japanese also. In fact, the Japanese have a phrase to express the shallow and fragile concepts of themselves as individual entities. The phrase *jibun ga mai* means "I have no self." Sociologists say this concept is probably unique to the Japanese. Given the "Japanese Way" of giving precedence to the group, it is understandable why this feeling became a significant aspect of the Japanese character. (DeMente, 1989).

The ambiguity which characterizes the image of the Emperor is the primary political manifestation of the "sacred nothing". But the ideological repercussions are much broader. Buruma, writing about the indigenous religion of Japan, argues that "Shinto has many rituals but no dogma" (1984, p.4). Shintoism is a moral system devoid of absolutes. Good and bad are seen as relative terms dependent on the particular social context. Given this relativism, as Buruma notes, the concept of evil, or "original sin", is absent. Instead, the ultimate transgression involves "pollution", or the violation of boundaries (Buruma 1984). The key elements in this system are the hierarchy of relationships, and proper conduct. One is dependent on the other. This is a contextual system. How people act toward each other is a function of their relative status. The emphasis is on adherence to a code of behavior that depends on the context one is in. *Form* takes precedence over substance; that one acts correctly for the situation.

Many Japanese scholars have identified the seeming ease by which the Japanese accept change and are adaptable to situations (c.f. Christopher, 1983). Political ideologies and religious philosophies do not provide the same absolute basis for most Japanese as they do for many Westerners. There is an indifference to any settled foundations. This perplexes many Westerners who have different ideas of integrity and trust, (Maruyama, 1969). Robert Christopher believes that because of this remarkable degree of flexibility, "there is no nation whose social and political course over the long term is as chancy to predict as Japan's." (55).

Three manifestations of this sacred nothing structure are in packaging, (Sherry and Camargo 1987) in the Japanese language and in the format of advertising. Barthes (1982) discusses the semantic purpose of Japanese packages. Here the careful design, geometric lines, and interplay of materials create a package that is a temporary accessory meant to transport an object, but itself becomes the precious object. The box becomes the object, not what it contains. In fact, Japanese packaging specializes in presenting the triviality of the object inside as disproportionate to the luxury of the envelope. Thus, the inside is, in essence, emptied and contains nothing. This is evidenced in the care and attention that marketers in Japan need to take in packaging.

With regard to language, this "nothingness" of the self except with dependence on the context, is vividly demonstrated. Two fundamental characteristics of the Japanese language may reflect the conception of the self held by speakers of the language. The first characteristic is *keigo*, which translates as "respect language." Japanese is a language that is close to devoid of vocabulary that is neutral with respect to status differences. *Keigo* expresses status differences, respect, deference and intimacy. It is necessary to know another person's status relative to one's self before the correct language can be used. This presents a challenge to advertising copywriters who want to appeal to masses. Secondly, in the Japanese language, the personal pronoun, "I", is always relational and thus, constantly shifting in Japanese (Miyoshi, 1979).

Mood advertising identified as the prototype of Japanese advertising is consistent with the "sacred nothing" also. The "packaging," the contextual or mood aspect, is the foreground of the ads. The center or product itself often receives little explicit emphasis. The extensive contextual cues allow Japanese consumers to determine the appropriateness of the product for them and its appropriate use.

EFFECTS ON A CULTURE OF CONSUMPTION

Facilitating a culture of consumption

The dual principles of the synthetic ideal and the sacred nothing both reinforce and hinder the development of a consumer culture. They promote consumption through the fostering of multiple identities and the emphasis on form over substance. The synthetic ideal and the sacred nothing are principles of personal identity based on the assumption of multiple roles. The "self" is compartmentalized and contextual. Buruma (1984) notes the "theatricality" which the Japanese bring to daily life, the care with which different professions dress and act to differentiate themselves. This construction of selfhood through appearance and behavior would seem to mesh with a developing consumer culture. One principle which drives an economy based on the production of consumer goods is the assumption one can create an identity through what one purchases. (see Lears 1983 on the creation of the "self"). The notion of "lifestyle" is a function of this belief. if one's self-identity is a matter of acting a role, then linking that with consumption would seem to be a logical progression.

This focus on the superficial aspects of the self is one way in which the synthetic ideal could reinforce consumption. Another is its preoccupation with fantasy. The ceaseless demand for new products in consumer cultures is fueled by the implicit linkage of those products with one's aspirations. By associating commodities with emotional gratification, wealth, power, and/or fame, consumption is endowed with the ability to transform lives.

In Japanese popular culture today, fantasy is the predominant idiom. Particularly in the visual arts-film and *manga*, the setting is almost always someplace else in place or time. Science fiction is featured prominently, as are samurai epics set in feudal Japan. Buruma (1984) suggests that the escapist nature of mass entertainment in Japan is in part a response to the repressive, conformist nature of the social order. The synthetic ideal's association of beauty with artifice reinforces this aspect, because it posits an aesthetic sense grounded in unreality. Since their visual arts are so preoccupied with fantasy, the Japanese would appear to be predisposed to accept advertising claims which link products with aspirations.

The "sacred nothing" also could be seen to promote a consumer culture. Like the synthetic ideal, it favors form over content, rules over dogma. As noted before, this tendency is compatible with consumerism, because it links identity with role playing and surface appearance. The sacred nothing also pertains to the lack of an overall paradigm. Buruma notes the ease with which the Japanese tolerate contradictions. This is, in part, a function of morality in Shintoism. One may be violent in one context and gentle in another. Ruth Benedict focuses on this phenomenon in *The Chrysanthemum and the Sword* (1946). This aspect also could favor consumption, because at times the implicit claims about commodities ability to provide self-fulfillment and emotional gratification are contradictory. The very notion that one can individuate oneself by the purchase of mass-produced goods is paradoxical.

Inhibiting a culture of consumption

Despite the ways in which the synthetic ideal and the sacred nothing would seem to make Japan uniquely receptive to the development of a consumption ethic, the transformation to a consumer culture cannot be conceded. This is because both these structural principles also contain elements which work *against* consumption. In the case of the sacred nothing, there is the contextual notion of hierarchy. Implicit in the relationship between self-identity and consumer goods is the concept of individualism. In a culture dominated by an ethic of consumption, social status is seen as a function of how one consumes. "Keeping up with the Jones'" suggests the possibility of social mobility through selective purchasing. This wisdom can be seen in the popular adage that to succeed in business one should dress like those in the next tier of management. The belief that commodities can enhance individualism runs counter to the traditional Japanese emphasis on hierarchy and the collectivity. One writer notes that there are strong norms which dictate proper buying behavior among corporate wives in Japan. Women are careful to select items which reflect their husband's status in the company. Care is taken not to appear ostentatious. The writer compares this approach to the "Western" mode of consumption, which is competitive and seeks to alter the status quo (Masatsuga 1982, pp. 59-60).

The potential limiting effect of the synthetic ideal on the development of a consumer culture in Japan is even greater because it raises doubts about the efficacy of consumption. The synthetic ideal posits a dichotomy between reality and the ideal. The latter is "ideal" by virtue of *not being real*. Hence depictions of courage, beauty, or love in Japanese popular culture are set somewhere other than the here and now. As noted previously, a preoccupation with fantasy could work in favor of a consumption ethic. The difference in Japan is that fantasy is viewed as unattainable. Implicitly, the message is that attempts to satisfy one's deepest longings are futile. Buruma (1984) notes how evocative a metaphor the cherry tree is in Japan - its beauty is heightened by its brief period of bloom. So much of drama in Japan is tragic; happy endings are very rare, even in manga. This aspect of artistic representation would seem to work against the efficacy of some types of advertising. Ads often promise the attainment of one's fantasies through their products. But for ads to successfully link goods with an image and then translate that into sales, some suspension of disbelief is required. In opposing fantasy to everyday life, the synthetic ideal would seem to make this difficult.

CONCLUSIONS

Because these elements of Japanese culture can work for and against an ethic of consumption, they pose a real dilemma for those attempting to predict whether a Western-style consumer culture will take hold. Attempting to analyze the effects of a social structure predicated on internal contradictions is a complex process. Structural anthropology has noted the apparently universal co-existence of structural principles which constitute opposing forces in society. Levi-Strauss (1969) laid the groundwork theoretically in his writings on *myth*. Myths, he believes, are vehicles for an ongoing collective dialogue about social structure. Levi-Strauss posits that all such systems are built upon internal contradictions. Myths act to mitigate such contradictions by elucidating them symbolically and then through a series of transformations, resolving them. Other anthropologists have considered the social consequences of structural contradictions. Victor Turner spent years studying Notembu society and the ways in which rituals serve to redress imbalances. In *Schism and Continuity* (1957), Turner analyzes the regularities in form and process which constitute social structure. From those, he derives certain contradictions. Social roles and norms are seen as making conflicting demands on individuals. The result is that norms are violated and tensions ensue. Through rituals, which Turner likened to social dramas, contradictions are acknowledged, and society is reintegrated.

Turner's work suggests that contradictory structural principles operate a kind of collective energy. But his work (and that of other symbolic anthropologists) raises the possibility of social change, as well. Contradictions may require mechanisms for maintaining equilibrium, or they may transform the system. That is the issue which is raised by current developments in Japan.

The issues raised by the interaction of macro-economic change and traditional structural principles in Japan are both theoretical and practical. In terms of the former, we would argue that assumptions about economic development based on a Western model need to take into account the effects of indigenous cultural elements. Whether the combined influence of the synthetic ideal and the sacred nothing works to promote or hinder the conversion of Japan into a consumer culture is problematic. As we have demonstrated, some of the "modern" qualities which are associated with the shinjinrui may instead be the influence of traditional values and structures. We would argue that despite "Westernization", the indigenous culture is still enormously influential. It may be that its strong representation in the visual arts and popular culture is a means of preserving structures which are uniquely Japanese in spite of socio-economic change.

In practical terms, the efficacy of advertising is brought into question. Given the balance of trade, the United States is pursuing Japan as an expanding market. But given the questions raised by the synthetic ideal, it is not possible to assume that ads will stimulate buying. If the dichotomy between reality and fantasy is strongly held, then consumption as a means to fulfill aspirations is discounted. Advertising may, as just another kind of visual representation, be seen as unrelated to real life. Observers, including Buruma (1984), have noted that the extreme violence which characterizes much of popular culture in Japan is in sharp contrast to what is essentially a non-violent society. This ability to compartmentalize cultural elements reflects the influence of the sacred nothing, and suggests that the value transmuted by ads may not effect behavior. Questions about the effectiveness of advertising in Japan need to be answered. The outcome is of crucial importance to the Japanese as well. Their economy is attempting to make the switch to one dominated by the service sector and predicated on consumer goods. Whether demand can achieve the necessary levels is crucial. The consequences for indigenous cultural values if the transformation to a consumer culture is completed, could be dramatic. The consequences for Japan's economic survival if the transformation is not completed could also be dramatic.

REFERENCES

Anderson, Laurel and Marsha Wadkins, (1989a), "Social Unrest and the Resulting Consumer Culture," Advertising as an Artifact, working paper, University of Virginia.

_____ (1989b), "New Breed in Japan," working paper, Arizona State University - West.

Barthes, Roland, 1982, *Empire of Signs*, New York: Hill and Wang.

Belk, Russell W. and Richard Pollay (1985), "Images of Ourselves: the Good Life in Twentieth Century Advertising," *Journal of Consumer Research*, 2 (March), 887-894.

Benedict, Ruth (1946), *The Chrysanthemum and the Sword*, Boston: Houghton Mifflin Company.

Buruma, Ian, (1984), *Behind the Mask*, London: Jonathan Cape.

Buruma, Ian, (1989), *God's Dust*, London: Jonathan Cape.

Christopher, Robert C., (1983), *The Japanese Mind*, New York: Fawcett Columbine.

DeMente, Boye, (1989), *Japanese Etiquette and Ethics in Business*, Lincolnwood, Illinois: NTC Business Books.

Ewen, Stuart, (1976), *Captains of Consciousness*, New York: McGraw-Hill Book Company.

Fields, George, (1988), "The Year 'of the Shinjinrui' and 'Kokusaika'," *Dentsu Japan Marketing Advertising Yearbook*, 58-68.

Fox, Richard and T. Jackson Lears, (1983), *The Culture of Consumption*, New York: Pantheon Books.

Fuchino, Koichi, (1988), "Wage Earners Changing Attitudes," *Japan Echo*, 15, 17-23.

Iwao, Sumiko, (1988), "The Japanese: Portrait of Change," *Japan Echo*, 15, 2-6.

Kariel, Henry S., (1989), *The Desperate Politics of Postmodernism*, Amherst: The University of Massachusetts Press.

Lears, T. Jackson, (1983), "From Salvation to Self-Realization: Advertising and the Therapeutic Roots of the Consumer Culture," in *The Culture of Consumption*, Richard W. Fox and T. Jackson Lears, eds., New York: Pantheon Books.

Leiss, William, Stephen Kline, and Sut Jhally, (1986), *Social Communication in Advertising*, Toronto: Metheun.

Levi-Strauss, Claude, (1969), *The Elementary Structure of Kinship*, Boston: Beacon Press.

Marchand, Roland, (1985), *Advertising the American Dream*, Berkeley: University of California Press.

Maruyama, Masao, (1969), *Thought and Behavior in Modern Japanese Politics*, London: Oxford University Press.

Masatsuga, Mitsuyuki, (1982), *The Modern Samurai Society*, New York: Amacom

McCracken, Grant, (1987), "The History of Consumption: A Literature Review and Consumer Guide," *Journal of Consumer Policy*, 10, 139-166.

Miyoshi, Masao, (1979), *As We Saw Them: The First Japanese Embassy in the United States*, (1860), Berkeley and Los Angeles: University of California Press.

Nakano, Osamu, (1988a), "A Sociological Analysis of the New Breed," *Japan Echo*, 12-16.

_____ (1988b), "The Surrogate Family," *Japan Echo*, 15, 48-52.

Noda, Masaaki, (1988), "Why Are Middle-aged Men Killing Themselves?", *Japan Echo*, 15, 24-27.

Pollay, Richard W., (1985), "The Subsiding Sizzle: A Descriptive History of Print Advertising, 1900-1980," *Journal of Marketing* 49 (Summer), 24-37.

Richie, Donald, (1984), as quoted in Christopher Lasch, *The Minimal Self*, New York: W.W. Norton.

Sherry, John and Eduardo Carmargu (1987), " 'May Your Life Be Marvelous:' English Language Labeling and the Semiotics of Japanese Promotion," *Journal of Consumer Research*, 14 (September), 174-188.

Turner, Victor, (1957), *Schism and Continuity in an African Society: A Study of Ndembu Village Life*. Manchester University Press.

The Development of Time Orientation Measures for Use in Cross-Cultural Research

Gary Ko, University of Nebraska-Lincoln
James W. Gentry, University of Nebraska-Lincoln

ABSTRACT

We argue that concern for one's time orientation in studies of cross-cultural consumer behavior is needed, and then discuss the development of measures for the construct. Although the reliability of the measures is weak even for exploratory purposes, the pattern of relationships between time orientation and other variables used in cross-cultural research (acculturation and locus of control) is what should be expected on a theoretical basis. Thus, the study concludes that more work in the scale development area concerning time orientation may well be a contribution to the area of cross-cultural consumer research.

Time is a multi-dimensional cognitive-motivational-cultural construct (Trommsdorf 1983). Due to its complexity, Fraisse (1984) suggests that time should be viewed as a notion rather as a construct. Lehmann (1967) classified time into four categories: external time (clock time), internal time estimation (internalized clock time), subjective time awareness (duration), and subjective time perspective. The first two conceptions refer to our objective understanding of time, while the last two refer to our subjective experience of time. To the extent that human behaviors are in response to what is perceived, and not what exists in reality, subjective time is of particular relevance to the study of consumer behavior. Subjective time duration, which refers to our subjective experience of time passage as influenced by our affect, emotion, and/or other situational and structural variables, has received a great deal of coverage in the psychology literature (see Fraisse 1984 for a review). Consumer researchers have also shown a growing interest in time (Feldman and Hornik 1981; Graham 1981; Hirschman 1987; Hornik 1982, 1984; Jacoby, Szybillo, and Berning 1976).

Relatively less attention has been paid to subjective time perspective, which is related to our subjective experience of the past, present, and future (Edlund 1987). However, some researchers (Doob 1971; Graham 1981; Kluckhohn and Strodtbeck 1961; Hall 1976, 1987) have recognized distinctive cultural differences in subjective time perspectives. This paper explores the possibility of developing valid measures for some dimensions (time orientation and time extension) of the cross-cultural time perspective.

Time orientation refers to the emphasis of the past and tradition as opposed to living for today or investing in tomorrow (Henry 1976). Evidence suggests that some people are more prone to a past-orientation, whereas others are prone to a future-orientation, depending on their cultural backgrounds. Kluckhohn and Strodtbeck (1961) included time orientation as one of the four fundamental value orientations of different cultures. One's time orientation may help explain one's rate of conducting negotiations, one's rate of adopting product innovations, and one's expected payback period for new products. This study will discuss the development of a time orientation scale, and will then contrast it with measures of time extension and with other cultural variables (locus of control and acculturation) frequently found in cross-cultural research.

A secondary purpose of the research is to investigate further the Tan and McCullough (1985) Chineseness scale as a possible measure of acculturation for use with students from the Pacific Rim (coming from countries with a strong Confucian background) now in the United States. Much cross-cultural research originates in the West and researchers frequently use international students in the pilot study stage of instrument development. A frequently raised question concerns the extent to which international students have become Westernized and no longer maintain their former cultural identity. The Tan and McCullough scale offers an attitudinal measure of one's maintenance of traditional Confucian values, and it is also flexible enough to use with non-Asian samples, as was done in the Ellis, McCullough, Wallendorf, and Tan (1985) study.

Before delving into the measure issues, we will first review briefly the constructs to be investigated.

TIME ORIENTATION

As Kluckhohn and Strodtbeck (1961) noted, one's time orientation is largely a product of his/her culture, e.g., a person may be encouraged through a complex socialization process to have a past or future orientation. Doob (1971) argues forcefully that traditional societies favor a past time orientation, while modern Western societies favor a future time orientation. In general, people from Far-Eastern countries such as China, Japan, and Korea tend to have past time orientations, while Latin-Americans are more present-oriented, and Westerners (Americans and Northern Europeans) have more of a future time orientation (Benedict 1946; Graham 1981; Hall 1959, 1976; Meade 1971; Kluckhohn and Strodtbeck 1961; Yau 1988).

Hall (1959, 1976) dichotomizes time-orientations into monochronic (m-time) and polychronic (p-time). M-time people tend to prefer to do one thing at a time, resulting in a greater reliance on schedules, segmentation, and promptness. Time can be saved or wasted, notions frequently foreign to p-time people. P-time systems are characterized by several things happening at once, and they stress involvement of people and completion of transactions rather than adherence to preset schedules. Hall asserts that Westerners are likely to be monochronic, while p-time systems are more common in Latin American and in the Mediterranean countries.

Graham (1981) offers a slightly different categorization of time orientations, those of linear-separable, circular-traditional, and procedural-traditional. The linear-separable time perception, which is characteristics of Anglos, favors a strong future time orientation. If time is perceived as flowing from the past to the future in an irreversible fashion, it should be properly spent so as to achieve a future goal. The circular-traditional time perception, on the other hand, fosters a present time orientation, which is often described as the manana spirit in the cultures with Spanish backgrounds. The procedural-traditional time perception is common among those influenced by Confucian values; the reliance on strong traditional values tends to favor a strong past orientation (Kluckhohn and Strodtbeck 1961; Yau 1988). It should be noted that Hall's (1976) notion of monochronic time relates to a strong future orientation, whereas the notion of polychronic time implies present and past orientations.

Having a specific time orientation does not necessarily mean that one's cognitions and behaviors are completely dictated by a single dominant orientation. As Cottle and Klineberg (1974) noted, one's being past oriented does not mean that s/he is totally unaffected by future time; it may be that s/he differs from others in his/her preferential ordering of past-, present-, and future-oriented activities. Relying on the concept of operating culture, Graham (1981) also maintains that a person is able to operate within a variety of different sets of beliefs and time perceptions.

Future Extension. For some individuals, the future seems to be perceived as something dynamically changing and for others it is perceived as somewhat more static but extending farther, again depending upon culture. Smith (1952), for instance, maintained that American egos tended to extend forward to the somewhat curtailed future with little attention paid to the past, whereas both Hindu and Chinese egos tended to extend far backward to the past and far forward to the future. According to Wallace (1956), extension refers to the conceptualization of the length of future time. He measured time extension as the range of years between the subject's actual age and the most distant event envisioned by him/her. Cottle (1976) proposed the experiential inventory method in which the subjects were asked to list the ten most important experiences of their lives and to locate each experience in a particular time zone. People may have a more extended but less structured time perspective or have a less extended but more structured future time. However, the combination of an extended and structured future is not likely, due to limitations in cognitive capacity.

As suggested earlier, having a past time orientation does not necessarily mean that the future cannot be anticipated or envisioned. In fact, there is some evidence that Easterners have a longer future time span. Cottle and Klineberg (1974) argued that humans make of themselves a bridge between past and future; thus, the deeper their ties with the past, the longer their perspectives on the future. Japanese businessmen are reputed to have a longer time horizon than their American counterparts and to emphasize increases in market share rather than the maximization of short term profits. West (1989) relates Asians' longer view of time to longer histories, a greater sense of the past, and a group-orientation. Hall (1959, p. 30) describes an important characteristic of American time:

> The future to us is the foreseeable future, not the future of the South Asian that may involve centuries ....Anyone who has worked in industry or in the government of the United States has heard the following: "Gentlemen, this is for the long term! Five or ten years."...The South Asian, however, feels that it is perfectly realistic to think of a long time in term of thousands of years or even an endless period....The Americans view of the future is linked to a view of the past, for tradition plays an equally limited part in American culture. As a whole, we push it aside.

Asians have an intergenerational time perspective that considers both current and future generations (Tse, Lee, Vertinsky, and Wehrung 1988). While Americans have a less extended future time orientation, they are more likely to have a better structured and more dynamic future. A monochronic perception of time (Hall 1976; Hall and Hall 1987; McClelland 1961) forces Americans to plan ahead with accuracy. The polychronic time perception characteristic of Arabic, Asian, and Spanish cultures is less conducive to a coherent structuring of the future. In sum, regarding future time perspectives, American consumers experience a less extended but dynamically changing future, while Asians experience a more extended but stable future.

ACCULTURATION

Acculturation has been found to be a very strong factor altering one's time perspective. Melikian (1969) investigated differences in future orientation for Saudi-born Moslem male college students, finding that the students exposed to foreign cultures were more future-oriented than the students who were not exposed to foreign cultures.

A common proxy measure of acculturation has been the length of stay in the United States, but there is not always a one-to-one correspondence between time here and the change in one's cultural values. We are interested in psychological acculturation, a term coined by Graves (1967) to refer to the changes that an individual experiences as a result of being in contact with other cultures, and as a result of participating in the process of acculturation that one's cultural or ethnic group is undergoing. As Berry and Kim (1988) note, the acculturation process will vary according to type of group membership. Immigrants may want to accept the norms of the dominant culture, whereas refugees and sojourners do so at a much slower pace. Berry (1990) concludes that the assumption that acculturation is a linear process over time is probably true for those in the "assimilation mode" (as are immigrants), but not those who have not adopted that mode (refugees and sojourners). International students intending to stay in the United States would be similar to immigrants, while those planning to return to their own country (as is the case of the Korean students included in this study) are more properly labeled sojourners, as they are more likely to seek cultural maintenance (Berry, Trimble, and Olmedo 1986).

Thus, we sought a scale which captures traditional Confucian values. Tan and McCullough (1985) developed such a scale which reflected traditional value orientations (Hsu 1948; Kingston 1976; Levy 1949). Their original scale (alternately called the Ethnic Attitude Inventory and the Chineseness Index) had ten items, but it was expanded to 12 items when it was used with an American sample (Ellis et al. 1985). One advantage of the scale is that it can be used with American as well as Asian respondents (Ellis et al. 1985); years in the United States is usually quite meaningless when used with U. S. respondents, as it is the same as one's age in most instances.

TIME ORIENTATION AND TIME EXTENSION MEASURES

To measure time orientation, a Likert-type 22-item scale was developed. Kluckhohn and Strodtbeck's measure of time orientation was used as a basis for some of the items.

Time extension was tested using Cottle's (1976) approach, which asked subjects to list the ten most important experiences of their lives and to locate each experience in a particular time zone. Additionally, in order to measure time perspective in the consumer domain, subjects were asked to list their ten most important purchases made during their life time and to locate them in a particular time zone. Subjects were also asked in what year other than the current year they would most like to live in the future and in the past.

OTHER MEASURES

In addition to the time measures, the subjects completed the 12-item Tan and McCullough scale measuring adherence to traditional Confucian values and Levenson's (1974) shortened (and improved) version (24 items) of the Rotter (1966) Locus of Control scale.

SAMPLE

The survey questionnaire was written in English and translated and backtranslated into Korean for Korean subjects. Data were collected from 102 American students and 65 Korean students. All were seniors or graduate students attending a state university in the Midwest. The average age of the American subjects was 26.4 years and the average age of the Koreans was 30.2. Considering the tradition that Koreans count their ages starting from the year of birth, their reported ages are one or two years higher than their ages in the American sense.

RESULTS

Evaluation of the Scales

Factor analysis of the 22 time orientation items indicated that the future and past dimensions were distinct. Accordingly, two separate scales were developed for future and past orientations. After removing items due to low item to total correlations for respondents from both countries, the scales shown in Figure 1 were obtained. As indicated there, the Cronbach alpha levels for both the past and future orientation scales are unacceptable even for exploratory research (past: Korean .59, U. S. .51; future: Korean .38, U. S. .55). However, the pattern of results confirms our expectations. That is, Korean respondents were more consistent in their measures for the past items, but less so for the future items as would be expected according to the earlier conclusion that the Korean culture is past oriented. On the other hand, the U. S. respondents were slightly more consistent in their responses for future items, consistent with the conclusion that the U. S. culture is future oriented.

Two of the items in the second version of the Tan and McCullough (1985) Ethnic Attitude Scale were deleted due to low item to total correlations. The remaining ten items can also be seen in Figure 1. No alphas or factor structures were reported in Tan and McCullough (1985) or in Ellis et al. (1985), so the marginally acceptable alphas reported here (.63 for the U. S. subsample and .65 for the Korean subsample) have no basis for comparison.

The 24-item Locus of Control scale, as modified by Levenson (1974), exhibited good reliability (Cronbach alphas: U. S. subsample .87; Korean subsample .81). Further, the three subscales (Powerful Others, Internal Control, Chance Control) also exhibited good reliability (U. S.: .75, .76, .76, respectively; Korea: .77, .51, .75, respectively) except for the Internal Control construct for Koreans. At least two possible explanations exist for the low Cronbach alpha for Internal Control among the Korean students. First, the general finding (McGinnies et al. 1974; Reitz and Grof 1974) is that Asians are more externally controlled than are U. S. respondents. Consequently, the low alpha might indicate that Koreans view the internal control items as being confusing. Second, there is evidence that the internal control subscale is less reliable than the other two subscales, as its reliabilities as reported by Levenson (1974) were consistently lower (in the range .62 to .64 as compared to reliabilities in the .70's for the other two sub-scales). The pattern of correlations among the three subscales differed across subsamples. For both subsamples, the Powerful Others and Chance

FIGURE 1
SCALE ITEMS

PAST TIME ORIENTATION
Cronbach Alphas: U. S. Subsample .51   Korean Subsample .59

Children should be taught well the traditions of the past.
When conversing with my friends, I would like them to know of my past accomplishments.
The best way to do new tasks well is to rely on what has been done in similar instances in the past.
I like to hear my elders talk about the "old days."
It is important to know one's family history.
The longer a person works at the same place, the more he or she should be paid.
The future is very uncertain.
It is very important to understand what has happened in the past.

FUTURE TIME ORIENTATION
Cronbach Alphas: U. S. Subsample .55   Korean Subsample .38

I usually use a calendar to schedule events well ahead of time.
Things which you do now will affect how you are treated later.
I like to read about how others see the future.
I like science fiction.
When talking with friends, our interests tend to anchor around what we are going to do.
If we work hard and plan right, things in our country will improve for those people who really try.
If a new young member has more potential to contribute to an organization, he or she should be paid more than other members in the organization.
The future is dynamic, but we can anticipate most outcomes beforehand.
I like to think about what I am going to do in the future.

TAN AND MC CULLOUGH'S (1985) ETHNIC ATTITUDE SCALE
Cronbach Alphas: U. S. Subsample .63   Korean Subsample .65

Women's place is in the home.
When making important decisions, consideration of family comes first.
Caring for one's aged parents is the duty of everyone.
I often do the right things so as not to lose face.
Every family should have a son.
My relationship with my parents is formalized.
I feel strongly about returning favors to others.
One should not go to extremes in one's behaviors.
Marriage is a life-long commitment.
I consider myself a traditional person.

Control subscales had a correlation of .57 (p<.001) in each case. For the Korean subsample, the Internal Control subscale was negatively correlated with the Powerful Others subscale (r=-.41, p<.001) and Chance Control (r=-.13, p>.1). However, for the U. S. subsample, the Internal Control subscale was positively correlated with the Powerful Others (r=.16, p>.1) and the Chance Control (r=.40, p<.001) subscales. Thus, the Levenson (1974) revised Locus of Control instrument seems to be capturing different patterns of relationships in the two subsamples.

The time extension measures were operationalized as follows. The ten life events were categorized as occurring in the past, the current time (near past, now, near future), or in the future. The ten product purchases were categorized in a similar method. Then the number of events (purchases) in each time period was summed and used in the analyses. The second time extension measure was operationalized by obtaining the difference between the current year and the years in the future and the past which the respondents listed; these measures will be labeled future and past extension.

Relationships among the Constructs

The correlations among the various constructs are shown in Tables 1 and 2. In the U. S.

TABLE 1
CORRELATIONS AMONG THE TIME CONSTRUCTS AND ACCULTURATION

KOREA

n=60	TIMEPAST	TIMEFUT	ACCULT	LOC
EXTEND FUT	-.13	.12	.13	.02
EXTEND PAST	-.21	.22	-.18	-.05
NUMBER BACK LIFE EVENTS	.14	.04	.02	.14
NUMBER BACK PURCHASES	.21 (.1)	-.10	.23 (.1)	.19
NUMBER FUT LIFE EVENTS	.01	-.01	.10	.19
NUMBER FUT PURCHASES	-.08	.27 (.03)	-.07	-.18
TIMEPAST	1.00			
TIMEFUT	-.20	1.00		
ACCULT	.54 (.001)	-.03	1.00	
LOC	.33 (.01)	-.13	.32 (.02)	1.00
YEARS IN U S	-.09	.05	-.06	.04

UNITED STATES

n=100	TIMEPAST	TIMEFUT	ACCULT	LOC
EXTEND FUT	-.04	.21 (.05)	.01	-.16
EXTEND PAST	-.14	.09	.00	-.09
NUMBER BACK LIFE EVENTS	.30 (.01)	.06	.05	.14
NUMBER BACK PURCHASES	.18 (.1)	-.07	.00	-.09
NUMBER FUT LIFE EVENTS	-.17 (.1)	.07	.00	.00
NUMBER FUT PURCHASES	-.13	.02	-.09	-.08
TIMEPAST	1.00			
TIMEFUT	-.28 (.001)	1.00		
ACCULT	.45 (.001)	-.41 (.001)	1.00	
LOC	.25 (.01)	-.01	.17 (.1)	1.00

The numbers in parentheses are p-values indicating the level of significance if less than .1.

TIMEPAST is past time orientation, TIMEFUT is future time orientation, ACCULT is the Ethnic Attitude Scale, LOC is Locus of Control, EXTEND FUT is the difference between the current year and the year selected in the future, EXTEND PAST is the difference for the year selected in the past, the LIFE EVENTS measures are Cottle (1976) measures of time extension, and the PRODUCTS measures are our adaptation of the Cottle measures to the consumer domain.

---

subsample, past time orientation (TIMEPAST) is not related to the year-based time extension measures, but is related to the relative likelihood of mentioning past life events (p<.01) and of past purchases (p<.1). In addition, there is some indication that those in the U. S. sample with a past time orientation were less likely to list future life events (p<.1). For the Korean subsample, there was a marginally significant tendency (p<.1) for those with past time orientations to list more past purchases. Future time orientation has fewer relationships to time extension. In the U. S. subsample, it is correlated (p<.05) to the year in the future in which one would like to live, but is not related to any of the other extension measures (future or past). In the Korean subsample, future time orientation is related (p<.05) to the number of expected future purchases, but not to any of the other time extension measures.

In both subsamples, past time orientation is related strongly to locus of control (coded so that a higher score indicates an external locus of control). As indicated in Table 2, this relationship is explained by the positive correlations found between past time orientation and two of the three locus of control subscales (Powerful Others and Chance Control). Also, future time orientation is not related to locus of control in either culture. Those who emphasize the past tend to have an external locus of control, but those who think more about

TABLE 2
CORRELATIONS BETWEEN TIME CONSTRUCTS AND LOCUS OF CONTROL

KOREA

n=60

	TOTAL LOC	POWERFUL OTHERS	INTERNAL	LOC SUBSCALES CHANCE
EXTEND FUT	.02	-.05	-.05	.06
EXTEND PAST	-.05	-.11	.09	-.01
NUMBER BACK LIFE EVENTS	.14	.07	.02	.18
NUMBER BACK PURCHASES	.19	.09	.08	.21
NUMBER FUT LIFE EVENTS	.19	.12	.01	.20
NUMBER FUT PURCHASES	-.18	-.18	.10	-.17
TIMEPAST	.33 (.001)	.41 (.001)	-.20	.33 (.01)
TIMEFUT	-.03	-.10	.03	-.11
ACCULT	.32 (.02)	.40 (.001)	-.22 (.08)	.33 (.01)
YEARS IN U S	.04	.01	.01	.11

UNITED STATES

n=100

	TOTAL LOC	POWERFUL OTHERS	INTERNAL	LOC SUBSCALES CHANCE
EXTEND FUT	-.16	-.03	-.28 (.01)	-.11
EXTEND PAST	-.09	-.07	-.21	.02
NUMBER BACK LIFE EVENTS	.14	.06	.05	.22 (.03)
NUMBER BACK PURCHASES	-.09	-.09	-.14	.01
NUMBER FUT LIFE EVENTS	.00	-.16	.03	.05
NUMBER FUT PURCHASES	-.08	-.11	-.01	-.11
TIMEPAST	.25 (.01)	.26 (.01)	-.01	.31 (.003)
TIMEFUT	-.01	-.21	.15	.01
ACCULT	.17 (.1)	.13	.01	.14

The numbers in parentheses are p-values indicating the level of significance if less than .1.

TIMEPAST is past time orientation, TIMEFUT is future time orientation, ACCULT is the Ethnic Attitude Scale, LOC is Locus of Control, EXTEND FUT is the difference between the current year and the year selected in the future, EXTEND PAST is the difference for the year selected in the past, the LIFE EVENTS measures are Cottle (1976) measures of time extension, and the PRODUCTS measures are our adaptation of the Cottle measures to the consumer domain.

the future do not necessarily have a strong internal locus of control.

Past time orientation is related very strongly (p<.001) to the traditional Confucian values expressed in the Tan and McCullough (1985) Ethnic Attitude Scale in both cultures. Given that the Tan and McCullough scale represents traditional values in both cultures, the relationships are to be expected. Interestingly, the similarity in patterns breaks down when we investigate future time orientation, which is negatively correlated (p<.001) in the U. S. subsample but unrelated in the Korean subsample. In the U. S., an orientation to the future requires a break with traditional values, while no such separation is required for Koreans.

The relationship between the traditional Confucian values and locus of control varies across the subsamples, as might be expected since the relationship among the locus of control subscales varies across the subsamples. In the U. S. subsample, the relationship is only marginally significant (r=.17, p<.1) for the total scale, and none of the subscales are significantly related. In the Korean subsample, the total scale (r=.32, p<.02) and two of the subscales (Powerful Others: r=.40, p<.001; Chance Control: r=.33, p<.01) are positively correlated with the Tan and McCullough scale, while the internal control subscale is negatively correlated (r=-.22, p<.08).

The number of years spent in the United States by the Korean respondents is not related to differences in past or future time orientations. Given the low levels of reliability for these scales, one cannot conclude that time in the culture and attitudinal changes are unrelated. However, years in the U. S. is similarly unrelated to one's maintenance of Confucian values or to Locus of Control. In total, these results do not provide much substantiation for the use of years in another culture as a proxy for psychological changes taking place, especially when one is using international students not in the "assimilation mode" as subjects.

CONCLUSIONS AND DISCUSSION

Our results present some evidence that there are cross-cultural differences in time orientation and that these differences may be useful to consumer researchers in terms of explaining differences in terms of consumption. While we believe strongly that the development of reliable time orientation measures is greatly needed, we also have evidence that our current scales are in great need of improvement. A more systematic development of past and future time measures is needed, and we advocate the use of international samples in the purification process and the simultaneous use of emic and etic measures as discussed by Triandis (1972; Triandis and Marin 1983). This study has supported the notion that past-oriented cultures can deal with the future, but they view it differently (as being more stable) than do future oriented cultures (who view it as being more dynamic but also more structured in the short run). Our findings indicated that future-oriented U. S. respondents disagreed strongly with traditional Confucian values (whereas past-oriented Americans agreed strongly with them). On the other hand, more future-oriented Koreans saw no reason to disagree with the traditional values.

The use of a student sample has obvious limitations in terms of generalizing the results to the cultures as a whole. Yang (1986) reviewed a series of studies investigating the values of Chinese young people in Taiwan and Hong Kong, and found that there has been a drastic movement away form the traditional Chinese pattern. Further, he concluded that Chinese students now tend to have value orientations fairly similar to those of rural American students as reported in a study by Green (1979). Assuming that a similar transition is occurring among Korean youth, the differing patterns of time perceptions found in this study are probably only the tip of the iceberg in terms of the differences in time perceptions held by older adults in the two cultures.

A secondary purpose of this study was to make a preliminary investigation of the Tan and McCullough (1985) Ethnic Attitude Scale as a possible covariate to represent the level of psychological acculturation. Commonly, years of residence in the new culture is used as a proxy; our findings indicate that time spent in the U. S. was unrelated to one's time orientation, one's adherence to Confucian values, or to one's Locus of Control.

The Tan and McCullough scale has marginally acceptable reliability in both the U. S. and Korean cultures and can be used as a co-variate in analyses in which data from both subsamples are combined. Thus we recommend that the scale be considered for use in pilot studies conducted in the U. S. which look at cross-cultural issues involving Pacific Rim cultures.

SELECTED REFERENCES
[The remaining references are available from the authors.]

Berry, John W. (1990), "Psychology of Acculturation," in John Berman (Ed.), *Nebraska Symposium on Motivation*, 38, Lincoln, NE: University of Nebraska Press, Forthcoming.

Cottle, Thomas J. (1976), *Perceiving Time*, New York: John Wiley & Sons.

_____ and Stephen L. Klineberg (1974), *The Present of Things' Future*, New York: The Free Press.

Doob, Leonard W. (1971), *Patterning of Time*, New Haven: Yale University Press.

Ellis, S., James McCullough, Melanie Wallendorf, and C. T. Tan (1985), "Cultural Values and Behavior: Chineseness Within Geographic Boundaries," in *Advances in Consumer Research*, 12, eds. Elizabeth C. Hirschman and Morris B. Holbrook, Provo, UT: Association for Consumer Research, 126-128.

Feldman, Laurence P. and Jacob Hornik (1981), "The Use of Time: An Integrated Conceptual Model," *Journal of Consumer Research*, 7 (March), 407-419.

Graham, Robert J. (1981), "The Role of Perception of Time in Consumer Research," *Journal of Consumer Research*, 7 (March), 335-342.

Hall, Edward T. (1959), *The Silent Language*, Garden City, NY: Doubleday & Company, Inc.

_____ (1976), *Beyond Culture*, Garden City, NY: Doubleday & Company, Inc.

_____ (1987), *Hidden Differences: Doing Business with the Japanese*, Garden City, NY: Anchor Press/Doubleday.

Hirschman, Elizabeth C. (1987), "Theoretical Perspectives of Time Use: Implications for Consumer Behavior Research," in Jagdish N. Sheth and Elizabeth C. Hirschman (Eds.), *Research in Consumer Behavior*, Greenwich, CT: JAI Press, Vol. 2, 55-81.

Hornik, Jacob (1984), "Subjective versus Objective Time Measures: A Note on the Perception of Time in Consumer Behavior," *Journal of Consumer Research*, 11 (June), 615-618.

Jacoby, Jacob, George J. Szybillo, and Carol Kohn Berning (1976), "Time and Consumer Behavior: An Interdisciplinary Overview," *Journal of Consumer Research*, 2 (March), 320-338.

Kluckhohn, F. and F. L. Strodtbeck (1961), *Variations in Value Orientations*, Evanston, IL: Row and Peterson.

Levenson, Hanna (1974), "Activism and Powerful Others: Distinctions Within the Concept of Internal-External Control," *Journal of Personal Assessment*, 38, 377-383.

Melikian, Levon H. (1969), "Acculturation, Time Perspective, and Feeling Tone: A Cross-Cultural Study in the Perception of the Days," *Journal of Social Psychology*, 79, 273-275.

Rotter, J. B. (1966), "Generalized Expectancies for Internal vs. External Control of Reinforcement," *Psychological Monographs*, 80 (entire no. 609).

Tan, Chin Tiong and James McCullough (1985), "Relating Ethnic Attitudes and Consumption Values in an Asian Context," in *Advances in Consumer Research*, 12, eds. Elizabeth C. Hirschman and Morris B. Holbrook, Provo, UT: Association for Consumer Research, 122-125.

Triandis, Harry C. (1972), *The Analysis of Subjective Culture*, New York: Wiley.

_____ and Gerardo Marin (1983), "Etic Plus Emic Versus Pseudoetic; A Test of a Basic Assumption of Contemporary Cross-Cultural Psychology," *Journal of Cross Cultural Psychology*, 14 (December), 489-500.

Trommsdorff, Gisela (1983), "Future Orientation and Socialization," *International Journal of Psychology*, 18, 381-406.

Tse, David K., Kam-Hon Lee, Ilan Vertinsky, and Donald A. Wehrung (1988), "Does Culture Matter? A Cross-Cultural Study of Executives' Choice, decisiveness, and Risk Adjustment in International Marketing," *Journal of Marketing*, 52 (October), 81-95.

Wallace, M. (1956), "Future Time Perspective in Schizophrenia," *Journal of Abnormal and Social Psychology*, 52, 240-245.

West, Philip (1989), "Cross-Cultural Literacy and the Pacific Rim," *Business Horizons*, (March/April), 3-17.

Yang, Kuo-Shu (1986), "Chinese Personality and its Change," in Michael Harris Bond (Ed.), *The Psychology of the Chinese People*, Oxford: Oxford University Press, 106-170.

Yau, Oliver H. M. (1988), "Chinese Cultural Values: Their Dimensions and Marketing Implications," *European Journal of Marketing*, 22 (No. 5), 44-57.

In-Home Observations of Television and VCR Movie Rental Viewing

Dean M. Krugman, University of Georgia
Yasmin Gopal, University of Georgia[1]

In-home observations were conducted for both traditional broadcast viewing and VCR movie rental viewing. Results show that television consumption changes as VCR movie rentals enter the home. VCR movie rental viewers pay more attention to the screen and are less apt to participate in other social or individual activities.

The purpose of this study is to investigate television consumption in order to determine if VCR movie rentals differ from traditional broadcast viewing. The study provides a framework for defining viewing, a technique for assessing viewing and the implications of viewing change. Focus groups were used to generate relevant characteristics of both preparation and viewing. Following the focus groups, in-home observations were employed to measure both the preparation for and the actual viewing of traditional broadcast programming and VCR movie rentals.

DEFINING TELEVISION VIEWING

The major commercial measurement of television viewing has been the rating system. People meters, in use by Nielsen since 1987, automatically record the channel to which a set is tuned, and rely on viewers to punch in when they start watching a program and punch out when they stop. People meters as a measurement system leave the concept of "viewing" open to interpretation. Viewing is a multifaceted process that is not all or nothing. It is clear that mechanical or diary measures will not be able to capture the total viewing experience.

Activities and Attention to the Set

One research strategy has been to define television viewing as an activity that takes place within a range of other individual and family activities. Earlier work, using both surveys and observations, concluded that television viewing is not a singular behavior but, one that encompasses many other activities, individual as well as group (Bechtel, Achelphol and Akins 1972). Morely (1988) stated that watching television cannot be assumed to be a one-dimensional activity. He argued that more investigation is needed to understand what the act of television viewing entails. Lindlof, Shatzer and Wilkinson (1988), used personal interviews and in-home observations to research different viewing styles. In addition to focused viewing, they found "monitoring"--when a separate activity is pursued in the viewing vicinity with the television engaged as a secondary source of interest. They also found "idling," which is regarded as a temporary use of television between other activities.

The second strategy has defined television viewing by measuring attention to the screen or the length of time audience members look at the set. Laboratory and in-home studies are used to measure visual orientation to the screen. Thorson, Zhao and Friestad (1987) used a viewing room, structured to create a natural or realistic viewing environment, to film eyes-on-screen. Calvert and Scott (1989) used a hidden video camera in a viewing room to measure the number of times children had their eyes directed to the screen. Anderson et.al. (1986) used video recordings in the home to measure visual orientation or how long individuals look at the set. Collet and Lamb (1986) also used video recordings in the home to measure the amount of looking at the screen and other activities which occurred during both commercial breaks and programming.

It is clear that two of the main strategies used to study viewing are social and individual activities taking place during viewing and the time spent looking at or being visually oriented towards the screen. Recent work has argued that further definitions of television viewing need to account for a fuller explanation of viewing behavior, including both activities during viewing, and visual orientation to the set. Krugman (1989b) argued that more explanation was needed regarding how audiences look, listen, and talk during television viewing. He noted the need for better explanations regarding the viewing environment, making a careful distinction between monitoring and watching.

VCR Viewing and VCR Movie Rental Viewing

VCR movie rental viewing is of growing importance. In 1988, an estimated $5.7 billion were spent on video rentals. The estimated number of movie rentals for the first 6 months of 1989 was 2.7 billion. Almost all VCR homes (91%) rent at least one tape per year and half rent from once a week to twice a month, according to Simmons Market Research Bureau (AAAA Media Newsletter, June, 1989). VCR users indicate that the number one benefit of having a VCR is movie rentals (National Demographics and Lifestyles, 1986). VCR owners have been found to be heavy movie viewers of both pay cable and rental movies (Murray and White 1987).

Compared to other kinds of viewing, VCRs provide greater control over both program selection and scheduling (Krugman and Childers 1989; Kim, Baran and Massey 1988; Murray and White 1987). It is quite possible that VCR rentals have created a genre' of viewing that is different from traditional broadcast or standard cable viewing. Studies indicate that viewing of VCR rental movies can provide a qualitatively different viewing experience than that of traditional broadcast programming. Lull (1988)

---

[1] The authors would like to thank the National Association of Broadcasters for partially funding this research.

concluded that a VCR movie has much greater status as a viewing event than does regular television. VCR movie viewing has been associated with socializing or getting together with family and friends (Morgan et.al. 1989, Rubin and Bantz 1987). The opportunity for greater socializing is confirmed by the fact that more individuals are in the room for a movie rental than for traditional television or home-recorded (time-shifted) VCR tapes (Sims 1989).

RESEARCH QUESTIONS

The central issue of the study is to investigate the viewing process for VCR movie rentals and traditional television viewing. "Viewing" is broken down into the in-home preparation to view, activities during viewing and, visual orientation during viewing.

The overarching research question is: Do individuals alter or structure their viewing environment for VCR movie rentals differently than they structure the viewing environment for traditional television? Scholars have argued that we need a broader understanding of the television viewing environment and a better definition of how individuals actually view (Krugman 1989b; Lull 1988). In an era marked by changing media services and viewing habits, understanding the viewing process is becoming increasingly important. The following gives a brief rationale and states each research question.

Research indicates that VCR viewing is more control and selection oriented than traditional broadcast fare (Kim, Barren and Massey 1988; Rubin and Bantz 1987). Therefore, once the programming has been obtained the viewing process will become more active and focused. In order to get ready to view, audience members should take more directed action.

> *R1.* Do VCR movie rentals require viewers to spend more time preparing to view when compared with traditional television viewing?

Because VCR movie rentals are more directed and goal oriented, viewers should participate in fewer activities that compete for their attention. Prior research indicates that television viewing styles can be either focused viewing, idling between activities or monitoring when engaging in a competitive activity (Lindlof, Shatzer and Wilkenson 1988; Lull 1988).

> *R2.* Will fewer competitive activities take place during VCR movie rental viewing than during traditional television viewing?

It is logical to assume that viewers of such programming will be more visually oriented to the set and not as easily distracted as when watching traditional television. Lin (1988) suggested that VCR rentals are akin to a home video theatre. Under such circumstances viewers may adopt behaviors that are similar to going to a movie theatre, paying closer attention to the programming.

> *R3.* Will viewers will be more visually oriented to the screen during VCR movie viewing than during traditional television viewing. Will viewers have their eyes on the screen a greater proportion of the time during VCR rental viewing when compared to traditional television viewing.

METHOD

The research plan included: 1) five focus groups, and 2) eighteen in-home observations followed by a final focus group to assess reactivity.

Focus groups

Five focus groups were conducted. Subjects were recruited from a list purchased from a video rental business with two locations. The business had been in operation since 1982 and was the first such enterprise in the area. Both stores were located in a two county area with a population of 125,000 residents in the Southeastern United States.

Subjects were recruited by telephone and paid $15 to participate. All groups lasted between 1 1/2 and 2 hours. Group discussions allowed for an understanding of viewing characteristics and preparation to view.

The groups were phenomenological because they provided a basic familiarity with the language, phrases and terms that individuals use to describe the viewing process (Goldman and McDonald 1987). The descriptions were extremely valuable in determining the in-home observation formats and coding sheets. Characteristics were generated for: 1) activities and behaviors occurring in preparation for and during traditional television viewing, 2) activities and behaviors occurring in preparation for VCR movie rental viewing, 3) activities and behaviors that take place during traditional television viewing and 4) activities and behavior that take place during VCR movie rental viewing.

Two final focus groups were conducted to determine if specific characteristics and items previously generated were appropriate for both the in-home observations and mail questionnaire. Group sizes were 15 and 9 respectively.

In-home Observations

In-home observations provided measures of (1) preparation to view both traditional television and VCR movie rentals, (2) activities during viewing for both traditional television and VCR movie rentals, and (3) visual orientation represented by a timed measure of eyes-on-screen.

Eighteen homes in the Southeastern area described in the previous sections, participated in the study. Each home was visited twice by the same observer. One observation took place during VCR movie rental viewing and one observation took place during traditional television viewing. Three different types of observations were collected, activities prior to viewing, activities during viewing and eyes-on-screen during viewing.

A convenience sample of homes which met the following criteria was used: owned a VCR, were on the list of a video rental store and lived in a neighborhood deemed safe to send an observer. Families were paid a fee of $40.00 to participate. Families were asked to select two periods when an observer could enter the home. During one period, participants were asked to select a time when they would normally view a VCR movie rental of their choice and sent a coupon for a free rental. During another period, participants were asked to select a time when they normally viewed traditional television. Observation periods lasted between 1-2 hours.

Coding sheets developed from the focus groups, listed and categorized anticipated in-home preparation and viewing activities. The formats were pretested over a two-night period in one of the homes. Four doctoral students served as observers and were used to collect the data. Training sessions included reviewing the coding sheets and observational formats from the pretest.

Observers visited the participant's home, approximately fifteen minutes before the program began or the rental was to be played. During the initial visit this time was used for introductions answering any questions regarding the study and for filling out subject consent forms. It also gave the subjects time to settle down or get ready to view and allowed the observer the chance to make a mental note of any in-home preparations for viewing.

Observers were instructed to wait until offered a seat in the viewing room and if possible to avoid sitting on a couch with another individual. In all cases the observer was offered a seat and allowed to sit in a place that was not in the center of the room. If others in the room were snacking, observers accepted refreshments, when offered. This allowed the observer to appear more natural or consistent with the group.

Observers had a small clipboard that contained the coding sheets and two small chronometers. Coding sheets were used to record viewing behavior - one set for traditional television and one for VCR movie rentals. Observers also had a pre-viewing activity sheet.

As noted earlier, the recruited contact person usually served as the principal subject to be observed. Activities related to the viewing behavior of this individual and up to two others were recorded. However, for the analysis of viewing activities and eyes-on-screen, only the principal subject was taken into account.

An eyes-on-screen measure was also conducted. Three five-minute segments during the viewing of traditional television programming and VCR rental movies were used to measure if the subject was visually orientated to the set. These uninterrupted episodes were predetermined and set approximately thirty minutes apart. The five minute periods began at least five minutes into the program. The small chronometers were used to take these measures. The first was used as a running clock to determine when the five minute periods were to start and stop. The second served as a stop watch that was started at the beginning of the five minutes, stopped when the subject looked away from the set, and restarted when the subject's attention was back on the set. The timing chronometers were sensitive, responded to the slightest touch, and did not require the observer to constantly look down at the clipboard.

Following the second observation period, the principal subject was asked to fill out a short questionnaire pertaining to demographics and media ownership. Subjects were also asked to describe if and how the presence of an observer altered their viewing behavior.

A final focus group with four of the principal subjects was held after the observations were collected. The purpose of the group was to assess the amount and type of reactivity to the in-home observers. Participants were paid $20.

IN-HOME OBSERVATION RESULTS

Demographics

Out of the 18 principal viewers who participated in the study, only one was single. Eleven of the subjects were females and seven were male. Of the 17 married subjects, most were in the mid 30's to mid 40's age group (mean age was 38). All subjects had attended undergraduate college and seven had completed graduate education. Five of the subjects were homemakers, two were students and the remaining were professionals. Seventeen of the households had children. The number of children ranged from 1-3. Subjects were generally upscale in terms of income and lifestyle, with fifteen of the families reporting a total household income of over $45,000. In addition to owning a VCR, all households owned at least one color television. Fourteen of the households subscribed to a basic cable service, and six subscribed to at least one premium cable service.

Preparation

Only a limited amount of preparation activity was observed prior to either traditional television or VCR movie rentals. Therefore, few differences between the two types of viewing were observed. During traditional television viewing, there was no visible preparation for viewing traditional television in five of the homes. In four homes subjects prepared something to drink. Other activities were either household chores including: tidying up or doing dishes, preparing kids for bed or putting them to bed, setting up the VCR to tape a show.

Five homes showed no overt signs of activity before the VCR movie rental. In six of the homes, subjects prepared either a drink or a snack. Three homes turned down the room lights.

TABLE 1
IN-HOME OBSERVATIONS
ACTIVITIES DURING TELEVISION PROGRAM AND VCR VIEWING

ACTIVITIES		PERCENT ENGAGING IN ACTIVITY	
		TV PROGRAM	VCR MOVIE RENTAL
Household chores[1]	:	28(5)	11(2)
Reading[1]	:	39(7)	6(1)
Writing[1]	:	11(2)	--
Eating[1]	:	39(7)	22(4)
Drinking[1]	:	56(10)	72(13)
Interaction with children[1]	:	56(10)	50(9)
Hobbies[1]	:	11(2)	6(1)

		NUMBER OF CONVERSATIONS	
		TV PROGRAM	VCR MOVIE RENTAL
Conversation (non- program)[2]	:	5.00	3.44
Conversation (program)[2]	:	5.33	9.94
Talk aloud to set[2]	:	1.78	3.06

[1] Indicate the percent of principal subjects who engaged in the activity at least once during the TV program or the VCR movie. Numbers in parenthesis indicate the number of subjects who participated in the activity.

[2] Represents the average number of conversations taking place during the TV program or the VCR movie.

Activities

Table 1 compares activities taking place during VCR movie rental and television program viewing. To be included as occurring, an activity had to take place at least once during the program. Percentages indicate the proportions of subjects who engaged in the activity; while the number in parenthesis indicates the actual count of subjects.

During the TV program, 28 percent performed a household chore, 39 percent read (mostly newspaper). Fifty-six percent had something to drink, and 39 percent ate a snack or candy. The average number of conversations related to the television program was 5.3, while the average number on topics other than the program was 5. It should be noted that a conversation was attributed to an individual only when it was initiated by that individual. Also, one conversation was differentiated from another only if there was at least a one-minute pause between the two. In other words, even if conversations between individuals continued for a long period without a one-minute break, it was counted as a single conversation. Conversations or questions directed to the observer that related to the project were not counted.

During VCR viewing, fewer household chores were taking place. Activities such as reading and writing were also at a minimum. More subjects snacked or ate their meal during VCR viewing than during TV viewing (56% for VCR, 39% for TV). The number of conversations during VCR viewing was limited for non-movie topics (3.44), but it was very high for those related to the movie (an average of

TABLE 2
IN-HOME OBSERVATIONS
FIVE-MINUTE VIEWING TIME MEASURE FOR TV AND VCR
PERCENT OF THE TIME SUBJECTS EYES WERE ON SCREEN

SUBJECT	PERCENT TIME EYES-ON-SCREEN	
	TELEVISION PROGRAM*	VCR MOVIE RENTAL*
1	84.00	91.33
2	23.50	36.44
3	8.44	16.79
4	96.44	92.56
5	44.67	88.78
6	54.89	75.44
7	37.67	87.89
8	24.56	95.78
9	42.00[a]	93.33
10	73.44	75.11
11	77.78	90.11
12	65.11	86.17[a]
13	93.33[a]	91.00
14	25.33[b]	88.89
15	59.56	77.33
16	90.67	90.89
17	99.33[a]	97.44
18	92.11	95.89
MEAN	60.71	81.73

* Represent the percent of time each of the 18 subjects were visually oriented and had their eyes on the screen. Unless otherwise indicated the percent represents the total of three different five minute view times.

[a] Averages calculated over two five-minute viewing time measures.
[b] Averages calculated over one five-minute viewing time measure.

9.94). Interaction with children was the same for both types of viewing.

Five Minute View Times of Eyes-on-Screen

Table 2 shows the eyes-on-screen or visual orientation for the 18 principal subjects. As noted earlier, the measure determines the percentage of time a subject was looking at the set. The percentage is usually based on three separate five-minute viewing segments.

Percentages of visual orientation were calculated for each viewer for both television programming and VCR movies. Summing these percentages over all viewers, a composite figure based on the mean was derived for both television and VCR viewing. The mean eyes-on-screen for VCR viewing was 81.73 percent and for TV viewing was 60.71 percent. Moreover, there is a large difference in the amount eyes-on-screen varies across subjects. Six of the respondents have roughly equal view times. Five of the subjects have VCR view times that indicate 10 to 30 percent more eyes on screen. Seven of the subjects show 50 to 100 percent more eyes on screen for VCR movie rentals.

Measuring Reactivity

Following the second observation, respondents were asked to answer open-ended questions related to the presence of an observer. Respondents were asked, has my being here altered the way you view TV? If so, how? Eleven of the responses indicated no changes were made. Six responses stated that a limited amount of change took place. These respondents said they may have done more channel changing or would have been interrupted by their children more often had the observer not been present. One respondent noted a great deal of reaction to the observer. She stated that she was conscious of remaining in the same room due to the presence of the observer.

Respondents were asked the same question for VCR movie rental viewing. Eleven responses indicated no viewing change. One respondent mentioned that the family would have stopped the movie more often. Three indicated that they would not have watched with their children. Two of the respondents indicated that they would have rented the movie on a Saturday (the observation took place on a weekday). One stated that they would not have rented the tape at all.

Final Focus Group

A final focus group was held in order to assess reactivity to the in-home observers. The group consisted of four respondents who had been principal subjects during the in-home observations.

Respondents noted they "felt comfortable" with the observer and for the most part did not alter their behavior. One respondent noted that her son was made to stay in the television viewing room because the study was being conducted. Generally, the subjects were comfortable by the middle of the first night. Respondents knew they were being observed, but indicated they did not feel a need to alter their behavior. To a limited degree, the respondents felt the need to stay in the room.

Respondents could not tell what the observer was recording. Respondents were then shown the clipboard and the chronometers. No respondents had an idea they were being timed during the five-minute view periods.

DISCUSSION OF RESEARCH QUESTIONS/IMPLICATIONS

In-home observation results indicate that more activities take place during the viewing of traditional television viewing than VCR movie rentals. Activities such as reading, housework and hobbycraft, which require attention and at least partially divert viewing from the screen, are much more likely to take place when viewing traditional television. Activities such as eating, drinking, or talking, which do not necessarily require as much visual attention, do not greatly differ between traditional television and VCR movie rental viewing.

In-home observations using timed measures of eyes-on-screen for the eighteen subjects indicate a greater visual orientation to VCR movie rentals than to traditional television. Across all subjects the mean eyes-on-screen was 82 percent for VCR movie rentals and 61 percent for traditional television. However, the viewing differences did not remain consistent for all subjects. One third of the subjects indicated no differences, approximately one third indicated differences of 10 - 30 percent and approximately one third indicated differences between 50 - 100 percent.

Results indicate that the way audience members view television varies dramatically in relation to the type of service consumed. Audience members structure their environment differently with respect to traditional television and VCR movie rentals. The viewing process for VCR rental movies is more active and consuming.

The eyes-on-screen measure shows that in the majority of cases VCR movie rental viewing is a more engaging process, whereby consumers pay more attention to the screen. Because fewer competing activities are taking place, there is more opportunity to pay closer attention to VCR movie rentals. This is confirmed by the in-home observations. When compared to VCR movie rental viewing, traditional television viewing has more monitoring than focused viewing.

DISCUSSION OF METHOD

The sample frame is a limiting factor. Respondents were middle class and well educated. The ability to observe families from other socio-economic groups is a continual problem for in-home observations. A review of other television observations studies also reveals this bias (Stoneman and Brody 1983; Anderson 1986, and Lull 1982).

Meaningful differences in preparation activities were not found. A follow-up group meeting with observers revealed that subjects get ready *before* the observer arrives; therefore, there is less opportunity to observe such activities as housework, snack preparation or putting the kids to bed.

In-home observations provided a method for measuring eyes-on-screen or visual orientation. It is important to note that subjects stated they could not tell what the observers were doing during the observations. Respondents noted that at times they felt the observer was making an occasional note but did not know they were being timed.

A problem associated with having only one observer is coder reliability. Other methods using video tape provide an opportunity to calculate intercoder reliability. The one coder technique does not allow for such a determination.

Although others have limited in-home observations to either one or two separate periods (Lull 1980, 1983; Stoneman and Brody 1983), it would no doubt be better to have been in each subject's home for more than two observation periods. During the focus group devoted to discussing reactivity to observers, subjects noted they began to get comfortable during the first observation and were even more comfortable during the second observation.

REFERENCES

AAAA Media Newsletter, June, 1989, 10-11.

Anderson, Dan R., Elizabeth P. Lorch, Diane E. Field, Patricia Collins and John Nathan (1986), "Television Viewing at Home: Age Trends in Visual Attention Time with TV," Child Development, 57, 1024-1033.

Becthtel, R.B., C. Achelpohl, and R. Akins (1972), "Correlates Between Observed Behavior and Questionnaire Responses on Television Viewing," *Television and Social Behavior, Reports and Paper, Volume IV: Television in Day-to-Day Life: Patterns of Use, A Technical Report to the Surgeon General's Scientific Advisory Committee on Television and Social Behavior*, Rubinstein, E.A., George A. Comstock, and John P. Murray, eds., U.S. Department of Mental Health Administration, National Institute of Mental Health, Rockville, MD. Washington, D.C.: U.S. Government Printing Office.

Calvert, Sandra L. and M. Catherine Scott (1989), " Sound Effects for Children's Temporal Integration of Fast Paced Content," Journal of Broadcasting and Electronic Media, 33 (Summer), 233 - 246.

Childers, Terry L. and Dean Krugman (1987), "The Competitive Environment of Pay-per-view," Journal of Broadcasting and Electronic Media, 31 (Summer), 335-342.

Collet, P. and R. Lamb. (1986), "Watching People Watch TV," presented in a report to the Independent Broadcasting Authority, London.

Goldman, Alfred E. and Susan McDonald (1987), *The Group Depth Interview*, Englewood Cliffs, NJ: Prentice Hall, 13-21.

Harvey, Michael G. and James T. Rothe (1986), "Videocassette Recorders: Their Impact on Viewers and Advertisers," Journal of Advertising Research, 25 (December 1985/January 1986), 19-27.

Kim, Wong K., Stanley J. Baran and Kimberly Massey (1988), "Impact of the VCR on Control of Television Viewing," Journalism Quarterly, 32 (Summer), 351-358.

Krugman, Dean M. and Terry Childers (1989), "The Pay-per-view Experience, Insights from a Field Experiment," *Cable TV Advertising*, Rajeev Batra and Rashi Glazer, eds., New York: Quorum Books, 153-169.

Krugman, Herbert E. (1989b), "Point of View: Limits of Attention to Advertising," Journal of Advertising Research, 28 (October/November), 47-50.

Levy, Mark R. (1987), "Some Problems of VCR Research," American Behavioral Scientist, 30 (May/June), 461-470.

Lin, Carolyn A. (1988), "Assessing the Impact of the Evolution of Home Video Culture," presented at the Association for Education in Journalism and Mass Communication, Portland, Oregon.

Lindlof, Thomas R., Milton J. Shatzer, and Daniel Wilkinson (1988), "Accommodation of Video and Television in the American Family," *World Families Watch Television*, James Lull, ed., Newbury Park, CA: Sage Publications, 158-192.

Lull, James (1988), "Constructing Rituals of Extension Through Family Television Viewing," *World Families Watch Television*, James Lull, ed., Newbury Park, California: Sage Publications, 237-259.

Morgan Michael, Alison Alexander, James Shanahan and Cheryl Harris (1989), "Adolescents, VCRs, and the Changing Media Environment of the Family," a paper presented to Broadcast Educators Association, Las Vegas, Nevada.

Morley, David (1988), "Domestic Relations: The Framework of Family Viewing in Great Britain," *World Families Watch Television*, James Lull, ed., Newbury Park, CA: Sage Publications, 22-48.

Murray, Michael J. and Sylvia E. White (1987), "VCR owner's Use of Pay Cable Services," Journalism Quarterly, 64 (Spring), 193-195.

National Demographics and Lifestyles (1986), "The VCR User Report," in research report no. 2, Denver, CO: author.

Poltrack, David (1987), "People Meters," *New Yorker*, March 2nd, 25.

Rubin, Alan M. and C.R. Bantz (1987), "Utility of Videocassette Recorders," American Behavioral Scientist, 30 (May/June), 471-485.

Sims, Jonathan (1989), "Viewing Patterns: An Electonic and Passive Investigation," Journal of Advertising Research, 29 (April/May), 11-17.

Stoneman, Zolinda and Gene H. Brody (1983), " Family Interactions During Three Programs: Contextualist Observations," Journal of Family Issues, 4 (June), 349.

Thorson, Esther, Xinshu Zhau and Marian Friestad (1987), "Attention to Program Context in a Natural Viewing Environment: Effects on Memory and Attitudes Toward Commercials," paper presented at the Association for Consumer Research, Boston, MA.

An Examination of Ethnicity Measures: Convergent Validity and Cross-Cultural Equivalence

Michel Laroche, Concordia University
Annamma Joy, Concordia University
Michael Hui, Concordia University
Chankon Kim, Concordia University[1]

ABSTRACT

With its focus on English-Canadian and French-Canadian ethnicity, this study examines five measures of ethnicity with respect to their convergent validity and cross-cultural equivalence. Results show that the five measures including four unidimensional measures and self-identification do converge in capturing both French-Canadian and English-Canadian ethnicity. The assumption of cross-cultural equivalence of the five measures was unsubstantiated. However, three of the measures showed equivalent estimates of measurement parameters as indicators of English-Canadian and French-Canadian ethnicity.

INTRODUCTION

Studies of ethnicity as a correlate or cause of consumption patterns have emerged as a major stream of consumer research. Studies to date have focused on such diverse ethnic markets as black consumers (Sexton 1972; Sturdivant 1973), Hispanics (Deshpande, Hoyer, and Donthu 1986; Wallendorf and Reilly 1983), Jewish Americans (Hirschman 1981), Asian Americans (Lee 1989), and French Canadians (Schaninger, Bourgeois, and Buss 1985). Despite the proliferation of findings in the area, the fundamental issues concerning the conceptualization and operationalization of the concept of ethnicity are in need of clarification and refinement. Criticisms have been directed at the overly simplistic treatment of the concept and the operationalization inadequately reflecting the complex domain of ethnicity (O'Guinn and Faber 1985; Valencia 1985). This study has the following purposes: the first is to examine more closely the concept of ethnicity itself and the diverse operational practices as shown in the current consumer behavior literature; the second is to examine the convergent validity of several measures of ethnicity that are found in the past studies of consumer behavior; and finally, the cross-cultural equivalence of these measures of ethnicity is investigated in the bi-cultural environment of Quebec.

LITERATURE REVIEW

Definition of Ethnicity

The concept of ethnicity, as depicted in the anthropological and sociological literature, in a loose sense, refers to the character or quality encompassing several cultural identifiers which is used to assign people to groupings. According to Cohen (1978), ethnicity is defined as a series of "nesting dichotomizations of inclusiveness and exclusiveness." The process of assigning persons to groups is both subjective and objective, carried out by self and others, and depends on what diacritics are used to define membership. Yinger's (1985) definition of an ethnic group encompasses a similar conception. He defines it as "a segment of a larger society whose members are thought, by themselves and/or others, to have a common origin and to share important segments of a common culture and who, in addition, participate in shared activities in which the common origin and culture are significant." (p. 159) Four elements often cited in the existing definitions of ethnicity are: 1. a self-perpetuating population; 2. sharing of cultural values; 3. a field of communication and interaction; and 4. a membership which identifies itself, and is identified by others as constituting a distinguishable category (Barth 1969). The important point is that the concept characterizes solidarity and loyalty among the group members generated by sharing of common cultural traits. Such traits, according to Weber (1961), may be as diverse as to include common customs, language, religion, values, morality, and etiquette.

Measurement of Ethnicity

While most researchers tend to share a similar conception of ethnicity, with respect to its operationalization, there are two schools of thought whose perspectives are in disagreement. They are labeled as "subjective" and "objective" approaches. The difference between the two is significant for the reason that the groupings resulting from each approach do not coincide (Nagata 1974; Anderson and Frideres 1981). In the subjective approach, ethnicity is viewed as a matter of personal belief and its operational definition reflects the individual's own psychological identification based on internal beliefs relating to his/her cultural attributes that are perceived to be relevant (Barth 1969; Shibutani and Kwan 1965).

In contrast, the objective approach dictates that researchers measure ethnicity with a set of objective cultural attributes such as religion, language, and cultural tradition which they perceive are relevant. While the subjective approach is sometimes criticized for its extreme subjectivism, the objective approach has drawn criticisms for the imprecision inherent in determining the "objective criteria". Some researchers (c.f., Van den Berghe

---

[1] The authors gratefully acknowledge the financial support of the Social Sciences and Humanities Research Council of Canada.

1975) propose a combination of the both approaches in conceptual and operational definitions to overcome the limitations in each.

Much of the traditional marketing research of consumer ethnicity relied on a single objective indicator in identifying ethnic membership. Hirschman (1981) points out that this practice may have been largely due to the lack of well-conceived *a priori* conceptual and operational scheme. Rather, classification of subjects into the ethnic group of interest was frequently *post hoc* in design.

A more elaborate multi-dimensional operationalization is found in the study of Hispanic ethnicity by Valencia (1985). The author in developing an "Hispanicness" index, combines six indicators: self-identification, English language ability, the extent of Spanish language use at home, language preference, relative length of residence in the U.S., and miscegenation. Similarly, the general acculturation scale proposed by O'Guinn and Faber (1985) for Hispanics incorporate multiple dimensions tapping national origin, a general language preference, and demographics.

With respect to the issue of subjective/objective operationalization of ethnicity, the tendency in the current consumer behavior literature has been to emphasize the subject's self-perception in the ethnic identification process. Except for a few studies which incorporate both subjective as well as objective measures (Valencia 1985; Bergier 1986), self-identification has become a prevalent approach in operationalizing ethnicity (Deshpande, Hoyer, and Donthu 1986; Hoyer and Deshpande 1982; Hirschman 1981).

Multidimensionality of Ethnicity

Ethnicity is commonly conceived as a multidimensional concept. Without reference to one specific ethnic identity, the existing literature reveals, among others, the following facets of ethnicity: language use (Tzu 1984; Kim 1985); religion (Yinger 1985; Segalman 1967); social interaction (Driedger 1975); endogamy (Sanua 1965; Driedger 1975); media communication (Kim 1985; Shibutani and Kwan 1965).

However, the various cultural traits of individuals take on different magnitude of importance as ethnicity indicators, depending upon which ethnic group is under consideration. For instance, in studying Jewish ethnicity, the language dimension plays a less important role than in the case of studying Hispanic ethnicity in the U.S. or the French-Canadian ethnicity in Canada. While there is little disagreement regarding the multidimensionality of the concept, delineation of essential elements in measuring a particular ethnic identity remains a challenge primarily faced by those researchers who rely on the objective operational approach. Their objective assessment of one's ethnic identity requires that one or more of important dimensions be identified and used in the measurement process. On the other hand, in the subjective measurement approach, the individual's self-identification of ethnicity is presumed to be based on a set of ethnicity attributes that the individual perceives to be important.

It follows then, the diversity in the current operational definitions of ethnicity is largely a result of differences among the various objective measures in the selected set of ethnicity attributes. One can suspect, however, that various dimensions of ethnicity are not independent of one another. For instance, an individual's language preference (or use) is highly likely to be correlated with his/her ethnic mode of social interaction as well as media communication. Similarly, a certain degree of overlap should exist between self-perception of ethnic identity and the various objective criteria of ethnicity.

RESEARCH OBJECTIVES

As can be summarized from the above review, the past measures of ethnicity found in the consumer behavior literature fall in to one of the following categories: those with a single or multiple objective indicators; those with a subjective indicator using self-identification; and those with objective indicators and self-identification. The past operational practices raise several issues worth examining. Among these are the extent of convergence between the various unidimensional, single objective item measures of ethnicity, the extent of convergence between self-identification and single or multidimensional objective measures of ethnicity, and the stability of various unidimensional ethnicity indicators in a measurement situation involving more than one ethnic identity.

The focus of this study is on the convergent validity of five measures of English-Canadian and French-Canadian ethnic identification in the context of Quebec's bi-cultural environment. The five selected measures include self-identification and four unidimensional indicators, namely, language use in various social communication settings, religious beliefs, social interaction, and upbringing. Also investigated is the stability of these measures in the identification the two different ethnic identities of Quebec, i.e., English-Canadian and French-Canadian ethnicity.

METHODS

Data

Data for this come from a survey of residents in various districts of the Greater Montreal area conducted in 1988. The population consisted of only those people who identified themselves as French or English Canadian. The area sampling method employed in this study involved first numbering of the 1986 census tracts of the Greater Montreal area and drawing fifteen tracts randomly with the use of a table of random numbers. As the census tracts were drawn, some judgments were exercised to eliminate those with large concentrations of industrial/commercial activities and/or other ethnic minorities. Within each of the chosen census tracts, a number of streets were further picked at random and efforts were made to survey as many households on these streets as possible. Interviewers, after the initial introduction, used a filter question to screen out those who identified themselves as belonging to neither group. Those who qualified were asked whether they preferred a French or English questionnaire. The self-administered questionnaire was then left with the consenting individual to be picked up at a later time. The sample analyzed in this study consists of 810 respondents.

Measurement

The questionnaire first measured respondents' language use in eleven interpersonal and mass-communication contexts. They were asked to estimate the percentage of times they used French, English or other languages (adding up to 100) in the following contexts: 1. with spouse; 2. with children; 3. with relatives; 4. at work; 5. when watching television; 6. when listening to radio; 7. when reading newspapers; 8. when reading magazines or books; 9. when shopping; 10. with close friends; 11. when in school.

The ethnic mode of social interaction, as all other measures to follow, was measured in two parts; French-Canadian social interaction and English-Canadian social interaction. The primary reason for this was that the degree of French-Canadian interaction may not mirror that of English-Canadian social interaction, i.e., a respondent may interact with other ethnic cultures, just as s/he may use languages other than French or English in various communication contexts. The following questions using 10-point Likert scales (1=Strongly Disagree; 10=Strongly Agree) were used to measure the degree of English-Canadian (French-Canadian) social interaction:

1. All my closest friends are Anglophones (Francophones).

2. All my neighbors are Anglophones (Francophones).

3. I am very comfortable dealing with Anglophones (Francophones).

4. I go to places where I can be with Anglophones (Francophones).

5. I often participate in the activities of Anglophone (Francophone) community or political organizations.

For the measure of self-identification, respondents were asked to indicate the degree of agreement (1=Strongly Disagree; 10=Strongly Agree) with the statement, "I consider myself to be Anglophone (Francophone)." Again, instead of assuming the unidimensionality which would have required one measurement scale, individuals' self-identification with English-Canadian ethnicity as well as that with French-Canadian ethnicity were measured separately.

The respondent's religious beliefs were measured using three 10-point Likert statements:

1. I consider myself to be a strong Protestant (Catholic) believer.

2. I had a strong Protestant (Catholic) childhood upbringing.

3. Protestant (Catholic) beliefs are important part of my life.

Finally, the measure of upbringing contained two Likert statements:

1. My parents were Anglophones (Francophones).

2. I grew up in mostly Anglophone (Francophone) neighborhood.

ANALYSIS AND RESULTS

Prior to conducting the analysis to examine the convergence of these measures in capturing English-Canadian and French-Canadian ethnicity as well as their cross-cultural equivalence, items in each of the ten measures (five English-Canadian and five French-Canadian ethnicity measures) were analyzed for their internal consistency. This analysis was aimed at testing the feasibility of combining the items in each measure into a simple index. Toward this end, ten correlation matrices and Cronbach's reliability coefficients were computed and examined. The average correlation among the items in a measure ranged from .40 for French-Canadian social interaction to .83 for English-Canadian religious beliefs. The Cronbach's reliability coefficients, which ranged between .77 and .97, similarly indicate a high level of internal consistency among the items in all of the ten measures. Subsequently, the items in each measure were averaged for the ensuing analysis.

The investigation of convergence among the five measures (for each ethnic identity) and their cross-cultural equivalence employed the multi-sample LISREL analysis (Joreskog and Sorbom 1983). The original sample was divided randomly into two split-half subsamples. In one, only the items which measure E-C ethnicity were considered while in the other subsample, only the items which measure F-C ethnicity were considered. The examination of convergence involved testing a confirmatory factor model which specifies that the five index measures are indicators of E-C ethnicity for the first split-half subsample and F-C ethnicity for the other subsample (see Figure A). The goodness of fit of the model will thus indicate if each set of five indicators converge in measuring their respective ethnicity (E-C ethnicity and F-C ethnicity). The multi-sample LISREL also allows for testing the equivalence of these measures in capturing E-C ethnicity and F-C ethnicity, to be discussed later.

Advances in Consumer Research (Volume 18) / 153

FIGURE A
Multi-Sample LISREL Model

Subsample A (n=402)

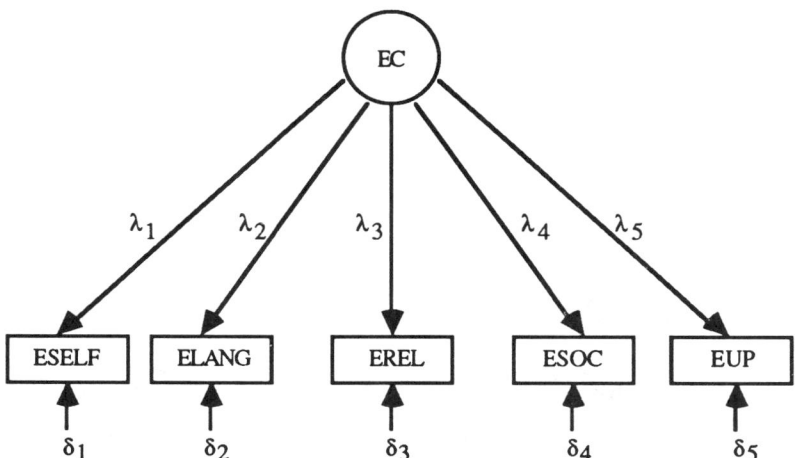

EC = English-Canadian ethnicity
ESELF = Measure of English self-identification
ELANG = Measure of English language use
EREL = Measure of Protestant belief
ESOC = Measure of social interaction with anglophones
EUP = Measure of English upbringing

Subsample B (n=408)

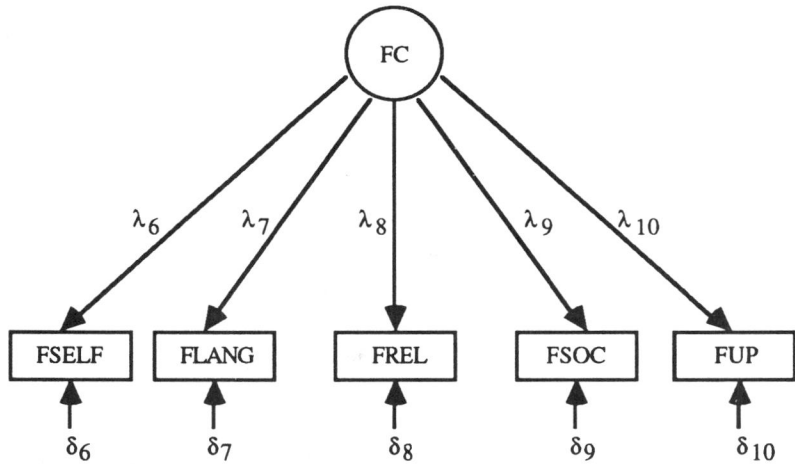

FC = French-Canadian ethnicity
FSELF = Measure of French self-identification
FLANG = Measure of French language use
FREL = Measure of Catholic belief
FSOC = Measure of social interaction with francophones
FUP = Measure of French upbringing

TABLE 1
Goodness-of-Fit of Various Competing Models

Model	Chi-square	d.f.	p	GFI1[a]	GFI2[a]	RMR1[a]	RMR2[a]
M-1	20.05	10	.029	.994	.987	.007	.014
M-2	14.46	9	.107	.999	.987	.003	.014
M-3	28.27	14	.013	.993	.981	.050	.059
M-4	35.44	14	.001	.989	.977	.028	.031
M-5	47.19	19	.000	.983	.973	.048	.044
M-6	33.48	17	.010	.990	.978	.047	.044
M-7	16.77	15	.333	.998	.986	.006	.017

[a] GFI1 and GFI2 refer to the Goodness of Fit Indices obtained for the E-C ethnicity and the F-C ethnicity sample respectively. RMR1 and RMR2 refer to the Root Mean Square Residual obtained for the E-C ethnicity and the F-C ethnicity sample respectively.

Convergent Validity of the Five Measures

If these five measures have convergent validity, they should all load on the same common factor. The model testing the convergent validity of the measures as shown in Figure A (M-1) produces a chi-square value of 20.05 with 10 degrees of freedom. The probability level of this chi-square value (p=.029) indicates that the goodness-of-fit of the model is below the common .05 acceptable level.

The undesirable goodness-of-fit level can be attributed to a number of factors related to LISREL itself such as large sample size (N=810) and violation of the multi-normal distribution assumption. A review of the modification indices obtained from the LISREL analysis also suggests that for the E-C ethnicity sample, a correlation may exist between the error terms of two of the indicators, language and social interactions. The possibility of a pair of correlated errors provides an alternative explanation to why M-1 does not produce a good fit. This latter argument is confirmed when the parameter (δ_{42}) representing the correlation between the two error terms is set free in another multi-sample LISREL analysis. The respecified model (M-2) gives a chi-square of 11.17 with 9 degrees of freedom (p=.107) implies an excellent fit. Two other goodness-of-fit indicators, Goodness-of-Fit Index (GFI1 and GFI2) and Root Mean Square Residual (RMR1 and RMR2), also suggest that the respecified model (M-2) has a better fit than the original model (M-1, see Table 1).

Conceptually speaking, a correlation between the two error terms in the E-C sample is deemed possible as the language indicator actually refers to the respondents' language use in various types of social interactions (e.g. at work, with friends, ...). On the other hand, the two error terms are found to be independent in the F-C ethnicity sample. The finding may be due to the fact that in Quebec, French is the dominant language and therefore, the use of French does not necessarily imply positive attitudes in dealing with francophones.

Factorial Congruence between E-C Ethnicity and F-C Ethnicity

The findings obtained from the first part of our analysis provide strong evidence for convergence validity for the five measures. Moreover, the one-factor structure is found to hold when the five indicators are employed to operationalize either E-C ethnicity or F-C ethnicity. The finding also provides preliminary evidence to the cross-cultural equivalence of the five variables as measures of ethnicity or what Olmedo (1979) has labelled as derived etics - "the development of explanatory constructs that are applicable to all cultures" (p. 1064). A more stringent test of cross-cultural equivalence, however, involves both the factor structure as well as the estimated parameters (i.e. the λ's and the δ's). The equivalence of the factor structure has already been confirmed, the second part of our analysis therefore deals with the equivalence of the estimated parameters.

Three multi-sample LISREL analyses are conducted to test (a) the equivalence of the λ's (the λ elements are set to be invariant between the two samples), (b) the equivalence of the δ's (the δ elements are set to be invariant between the two samples), and (c) the equivalence of both the λ's and the δ's (both the λ and the δ elements are set to be invariant between the two samples). Chi-square values of 28.27 (d.f.=14, p=.013), 35.44 (d.f.=14, p=.001), and 47.19 (d.f.=19, p=.000) are obtained from the three models, labelled as M-3, M-4, and M-5 respectively (Table 1). Since all the three constrained models are nested with M-2, the chi-square difference between M-2 and M-3 (or M-4 or M-5) also has a chi-square distribution. All the three incremental chi-square values, 13.81 (d.f.=5) for M-3, 20.98 (d.f.=5) for M-4, and 32.73 (d.f.=10) for M-5 are significant.

Accordingly, the hypothesis that the λ or the δ matrix (or both) is equivalent between the two samples is therefore rejected. However, the finding

TABLE 2
LISREL Estimates for M-7

Parameters	Estimated Values (E-C)	Estimated Values (F-C)
Self-identification:		
λ_1 & λ_6	.941 (35.38)[a]	.941 (35.38)
δ_1 & δ_6	.115 (12.08)	.115 (12.08)
Language:		
λ_2 & λ_7	.962 (36.85)	.962 (36.85)
δ_2 & δ_7	.074 (8.54)	.074 (8.54)
Religious Beliefs:		
λ_3 & λ_8	.591 (13.43)	.388 (8.14)
δ_3 & δ_8	.652 (13.83)	.849 (14.17)
Social Interaction:		
λ_4 & λ_9	.828 (23.25)	.890 (27.22)
δ_4 & δ_9	.315 (11.75)	.208 (12.10)
Upbringing:		
λ_5 & λ_{10}	.820 (28.27)	.820 (28.27)
δ_5 & δ_{10}	.327 (18.33)	.327 (18.33)

[a] Numbers inside the parentheses are the t-values of the estimates.

does not deny the possibility that some of the parameters may be identical between the two samples. In fact, the modification indices obtained from the most constrained model (M-5) suggest that different estimates are required only for some of the parameters. Multi-sample LISREL analysis gives (a) a chi-square value of 33.48 (d.f.=17, p=.010) when the constraints on the λ and the δ of social interaction are relaxed (labelled as M-6 in Table 1), and (b) a chi-square value of 16.77 (d.f.=15, p=.333) when the constraints on the λ's and the δ's of social interaction and religion are relaxed (labelled as M-7 in Table 1).

The three models, M-5, M-6 and M-7, are nested and therefore the chi-square difference can be used as an indicator of relative fit between M-5, M-6 and M-7. Compared between M-5 and M-6, the latter model has 2 degrees of freedom less but its chi-square value is also 13.71 smaller. This shows that M-6 has a significantly better fit than M-5 (p<.001). By the same token, M-7 can also be proved to have a significantly better fit than either of the two more constrained models, M-5 and M-6 (p<.001 in either case). On the other hand, the chi-square difference between M-2 (the least constrained model) and M-7 (2.31, d.f.=6, p>.10) is non-significant. This last finding suggests that further relaxation of constraints on M-7 will not produce any significant improvement in terms of goodness-of-fit. It is therefore concluded that M-7 is the model which exhibits the optimal fit. The following discussion will therefore be based on this optimal model.

An examination of the LISREL estimates for M-7 reveals that among the five indicators included in this study, "religion" is the least valid measure of either E-C ethnicity or F-C ethnicity. Compared with the other four indicators, "religion" produces the smallest (though significant) λ value and the greatest δ value in both the E-C and F-C ethnicity subsamples (Table 2). Nonetheless, the estimated value of λ is greater and the estimated value of δ is smaller in the E-C sample than in the F-C sample. The finding suggests that Protestanism as an indicator of E-C ethnicity shows greater validity than Catholicism as an indicator of F-C ethnicity.

"Self-identification" and "language" have a similar factor loading (λ) and measurement error (δ) and their estimated values show that as a single indicator of ethnicity, either variable is considerably better than the other three indicators (Table 2). Moreover, the estimated values are found to be identical across the E-C ethnicity and the F-C ethnicity subsample and this suggests that either "self-identification" or "language use" has satisfied the most stringent requirement as an "etic" (vs "emic") measure of ethnicity. The above findings in part corroborate Hirschman's (1981) argument that the subjective self-labeling method of measuring ethnicity is the most appropriate approach. More recently, language use has also been employed to operationalize ethnicity in the study of cultural impact on consumption patterns (Kim, Laroche, and Joy 1990). The findings obtained from this study provide strong support to the employment of language use as an alternative operationalization of ethnicity.

Finally, as in the case of "religion", different estimated values of λ and δ were obtained for "social interaction" between the E-C ethnicity and the F-C ethnicity subsample. Our findings indicate that "social interaction" is a better measure when it is used to operationalize F-C ethnicity (a higher estimated λ and a lower estimated δ are obtained) than when it is used to operationalize E-C ethnicity (see Table 2). Since francophones consist of the majority of the Quebec population, it is not surprising that even for anglophones, interactions with francophones may be inevitable in many occasions. An alternative explanation is that when one is uncertain about the ethnic origin of the people one interacts with, one will likely regard them as francophones who may be in fact English, Italians, Greeks or others. These arguments may explain why "interactions with francophones" as an indicator of F-C ethnicity shows greater validity than "interactions with anglophones" as an indicator of E-C ethnicity.

Reliability of Findings

Since all the above findings are derived from two random split-half samples, there is a possibility that the findings are an outcome of capitalization on chance. To examine the reliability of the findings, we ran all the tests again with five other sets of random split-half samples. In general, the findings are consistent with that obtained from the original analysis.

CONCLUSIONS

With its focus on English-Canadian and French-Canadian ethnicity in Quebec, this study examined five measures of ethnicity in terms of their convergent validity and cross-cultural equivalence. The five measures including four unidimensional objective measures and self-identification did show convergence in capturing both French-Canadian and English-Canadian ethnicity. These measures, however, displayed varying degrees of validity. In both cases involving E-C and F-C ethnicity, measures of language use and self-identification proved to be the most valid indicators. Language and self-identification separately or in conjunction have recently been the two most frequently used elements of Hispanic and English- or French-Canadian ethnicity measures seen in consumer behavior research. Findings of this study provide support for those measures.

Findings from the test of cross-cultural equivalence of the five measures are also worth reiterating. The assumption of equivalence of the overall variable structure was unsubstantiated in this research. However, it was shown that three of the measures (self-identification, language use, and upbringing) have equivalent values of measurement parameters as indicators of E-C and F-C ethnicity. Thus, using the "emic-etic distinction" (Price-Williams 1975; Olmedo 1979), these three measures meet the requirement of etic measures of ethnicity, i.e., they are equally valid measures of two ethnic identities. The search for equivalent measurement for many consumer behavior constructs including ethnicity in cross-cultural settings is a difficult but important task for researchers. Most of the traditional measurement instruments were developed within narrow cultural perspectives. The increasing level of importance attached to the cross-cultural and cross-national investigations of consumer behavior may subsequently require a reexamination and reorientation of measurement practices.

REFERENCES

Anderson, Alan B. and James Frideres (1981), *Ethnicity in Canada: Theoretical Perspectives*, Toronto: Butterworths.

Barth, Frederik (1969), *Ethnic Groups and Boundaries: The Social Organization of Culture Difference*, London: Allen and Unwin.

Bergier, Michel J. (1986), "Predictive Validity of Ethnic Identification Measures: An Illustration of the English/French Classification Dilemma in Canada," *Journal of the Academy of Marketing Science*, 14 (Summer), 37-42.

Cohen, Ronald (1978), "Ethnicity: Problems and Focus in Anthropology" *Annual Review of Anthropology*, Vol 7, 379-403.

Deshpande, Rohit, Wayne D. Hoyer and Naveen Donthu (1986), "The Intensity of Ethnic Affiliation: A Study of the Sociology of Hispanic Consumption," *Journal of Consumer Research*, 13 (September), 214-220.

Driedger, Leo (1975), "In Search of Cultural Identity Factors: A Comparison of Ethnic Students," *Canadian Review of Sociology and Anthropology*, 12 (2), 150-162.

Hirschman, Elizabeth C. (1981), "American Jewish Ethnicity: Its Relationship to Some Selected Aspects of Consumer Behavior," *Journal of Marketing*, 45 (Summer), 102-110.

Hoyer, Wayne D. and Rohit Deshpande (1982), "Cross-Cultural Influences on Buyer Behavior: The Impact of Hispanic Ethnicity," in *Assessment of Marketing Thought and Practice*, eds., Orville C. Walker et al., Chicago: American Marketing Association, 89-92.

Joreskog, Karl G. and Dag Sorbom (1983), *LISREL VI*, Chicago: National Educational Resources, Inc.

Kim, Chankon, Michel Laroche, and Annamma Joy (1990), "An Empirical Study of Ethnicity on Consumption Patterns in a Bi-Cultural Environment," *Advances in Consumer Research*, Vol. 17, eds., Marvin E. Goldberg, Gerald Gorn and Richard W. Pollay, Provo, UT: Association for Consumer Research, 839-846.

Kim, Young Yun (1985), "Communication and Acculturation," in *Intercultural Communication: A Reader*, eds., Samovar, Larry A. and Richard E. Porter, Belmont, California: Wadsworth Publishing Company, 379-386.

Lee, Wei-Na (1989), "Acculturation and Consumption-Related Adjustments: The Chinese Subculture," in *Proceedings of the Society for Consumer Psychology*, ed. D.W. Schumann, American Psychological Association, 127-134.

Nagata, Judith A. (1974), "What is a Malay? Situational Selection of Ethnic Identity in a Plural Society," *American Ethnologist*, 1(2): 331-350.

O'Guinn, Thomas C. and Ronald J. Faber (1985), "New Perspectives on Acculturation: The Relationship of General and Role Specific Acculturation with Hispanics' Consumer Attitudes," in *Advances in Consumer Research*, Vol. 12, eds., Elizabeth C. Hirschman and Morris B. Holbrook, Provo, UT: Association for Consumer Research, 113-117.

Olmedo, Esteban L., "Acculturation: A Psychometric Perspective," *American Psychologist*, Vol. 34, No. 11 (November), 1061-1070.

Price-Williams, D.R. (1975), *Explorations in Cross-Cultural Psychology*, San Francisco: Chandler and Sharp.

Sanua, Victor D. (1965), "A Study of Adolescents Attending Jewish Community Centers in New York," *Journal of Jewish Communal Service*, 41, 401-424.

Schaninger, Charles M., Jacques B. Bourgeois and W. Christian Buss (1985), "French-English Canadian Subcultural Consumption Differences," *Journal of Marketing*, 49 (Spring), 82-92.

Segalman, Ralph (1967), "Jewish Identity Scale: A Report," *Jewish Social Studies*, 29.

Sexton, Donald E. (1972), "Black Buyer Behavior," *Journal of Marketing*, 36 (October), 36-39.

Shibutani, T. and K.M. Kwan (1965), *Ethnic Stratification: A Comparative Approach*, New York: MacMillan Co.

Sturdivant, F.D. (1973), "Subculture Theory: Poverty, Minorities, and Marketing," in *Consumer Behavior: Theoretical Sources*, eds., S.F. Ward and T.S. Robertson, Englewood Cliffs, NJ: Prentice Hall, 469-520.

Tzu, Lao (1984), "Strangers' Adaptation to New Cultures," in *Communicating with Strangers: An Approach to Intercultural Communication*, eds., Gudykunst, W.B. and Y.Y. Kim, Addison-Wesley Publishing Company, Inc., 205-222.

Valencia, Humberto (1985), "Developing an Index to Measure Hispanicness," in *Advances in Consumer Research*, Vol. 12, eds., E.C. Hirschman and Morris B. Holbrook, Provo, UT: Association for Consumer Research, 118-121.

Van den Berghe, Pierre L. (1975), "Ethnicity and Class in Highland Peru," in *Ethnicity and Resource Competition in a Plural Society*, ed., Leo A. Despres, The Hague: Mouton Publishers, 71-85.

Wallendorf, Melanie and Michael Reilly (1983), "Ethnic Migration, Assimilation, and Consumption," *Journal of Consumer Research*, 10 (December), 293-302.

Weber, Max (1961), "Ethnic Groups," in *Theory of Society*, eds., Talcott Parsons et al., New York: Free Press, 301-309.

Yinger, Milton J. (1985), "Ethnicity," *Annual Review of Sociology*, 11, 151-180.

The Role of Subject Awareness in Classical Conditioning: A Case of Opposing Ontologies and Conflicting Evidence

Terence A. Shimp, University of South Carolina

ABSTRACT

The role of subject awareness has been prominent in discussions of classical conditioning of human subjects for over three decades. Skeptics of classical conditioning contend, on the one hand, that the presence of subject awareness violates the conditioning model's ontological premises, and, on the other, that the presence of subject awareness implies the likelihood that putative conditioning effects are actually attributable to demand artifacts. This paper confronts both of these challenges.

INTRODUCTION

The past decade in consumer research has witnessed both increased activity and greater sophistication in the empirical study and theoretical/critical examination of classically conditioned learning (e.g., Allen and Janiszewski 1989; Allen and Madden 1985; Bierley, McSweeney, and Vannieukerk 1985; Gorn 1982; Gorn, Jacobs, and Mana 1987; Kahle, Beatty, and Kennedy 1987; Kellaris and Cox 1989; Macklin 1986; McSweeney and Bierley 1984; Nord and Peter 1980; Stuart, Shimp, and Engle 1987). However, empirical results claiming to demonstrate the classical conditioning of consumer attitudes have been challenged by skeptics on grounds they violate conditioning theory's ontological premises (Kahle, Beatty, and Kennedy 1987) or reflect little more than demand artifacts (Kellaris and Cox 1989).

The present paper seeks to illuminate the issues by (1) evaluating opposing ontologies on the role of subject awareness, and (2) reviewing relevant empirical work that provides commentary on demand artifacts and related issues. Before pursuing these objectives, it is worth noting that the role of subject awareness has long been controversial in the study of classical conditioning of human subjects (e.g., Insko and Oakes 1966; Page 1969; Staats and Staats 1957, 1958; Zanna, Kiesler, and Pilkonis 1970). The Staatses (1957, 1958) prompted the awareness-issue debate by asserting their results evidenced classical conditioning without awareness. Subsequent researchers (e.g., Insko and Oakes 1966; Page 1969) challenged this claim; most notably, Page (1969) asserted that there is no conditioning without awareness and implicated demand artifact as the villain (cf. Staats 1969). Insko and Oakes (1966) presented data showing that contingency awareness mediates the effect of conditioning but that demand artifacts is not a necessary precondition. Other studies (e.g., Zanna, Kiesler, and Pilkonis 1970; Frcka, Beyts, Levey, and Martin 1983; Baeyens, Crombez, Van den Bergh, and Eelen 1989) have demonstrated conditioning effects in the absence of subject awareness of the CS-US contingency. (See for further literature citations Kahle 1984; Kahle et al. 1987; and Allen and Janiszewski 1989.)

COMPETING ONTOLOGIES: PRISTINE AND COGNITIVE POSITIONS

As suggested above, the philosophical issue involved is whether subject awareness violates the ontological premises of the classical conditioning model. Two competing stances on this matter are termed here the Pristine and Cognitive positions.

The Pristine Position

This philosophical position extends from classical conditioning's historical roots in behaviorism. Because behaviorist ontology rejects mentalistic constructs, it follows that subject awareness of the CS-US contingency (itself a mentalistic phenomenon) cannot be accomodated by a theory of classical conditioning. Hence, according to this philosophical stance, to acknowledge contingency awareness is to disavow classical conditioning as a theoretical account for observed effects.

In an especially well-articulated position, Kahle et al. (1987) argue that conditioning theory's ontological premises require that conditioning occur without awareness. Kahle and colleagues favor complete separation of behaviorist and cognitive traditions and claim that cognitive classical conditioning is an inherently contradictory phrase. They go so far as to conclude that, since the evidence shows the widespread presence of subject awareness in conditioning experiments, "perhaps researchers should study new topics" (p. 413).

Cognitive Position

In contrast to the pristine position, modern Pavlovian theory warmly embraces cognitive concepts as elements of classical conditioning's ontology. This fully cognitive position rejects the view that classical conditioning is simply reflexive, passive, low-involvement learning, and views it, instead, as cognitive associative learning, that is, the learning of relations among events in the environment (cf. Dawson, Schell, Beers, and Kelly 1982; Furedy, Riley, and Fredrikson 1983, p. 126; Holland 1984; Holyoak, Koh, and Nisbett 1989; Rescorla 1988). Modern conditioning theorists contend that the presence of contingency awareness is indeed a necessary condition for classical conditioning: "the acquisition of autonomic CRs is not an automatic process, but rather requires conscious cognitive processing of the stimulus contingency" (Dawson and Schell 1987, p. 33).

Brewer (1974), whose brilliant essay claimed there is no convincing evidence of classical (or operant) conditioning in adult humans, is often cited as evidence that classical conditioning is nonexistent. In actuality, Brewer had simply anticipated the cognitive revolution in Pavlovian theory and was saying essentially what others since have recognized: "all the results of the traditional conditioning literature are due to the operation of higher mental processes, as assumed in cognitive theory, and that there is not and never has been any convincing evidence for unconscious, automatic mechanisms in the conditioning of adult human beings" (p. 27). This argument did *not* deny conditioning, it rather required that cognitive notions such as awareness and expectations be incorporated within conditioning's purview if the theory were to represent an accurate account of human learning.

Neo-Pavlovians are clear in pointing out that awareness of the CS-US relationship is a necessary condition for classical conditioning. Indeed, survival (especially for animals) and goal achievement (especially for humans) require awareness of the many critically informative relations that exist between environmental events. For example, animals learn and probably are fully aware that smoke precedes fire, that the odor of a predator indicates the likelihood of a life-threatening attack, and that the sight of another animal's tracks implies the possibility of food. Brewer (1974) himself, in arguing that conditioning in human subjects involves cognitive processes, acknowledged that this leaves open the possibility, a possibility he was fully willing to accept, that cognitive operations are also present in the conditioning of lower animals.

Awareness of the temporal or spatial relation between environmental events is the sine qua non for conditioned learning in the natural world. There is no reason to expect it should be otherwise in laboratory experiments with human subjects. In fact, awareness is absolutely essential because consequences of behavioral responses in the laboratory are so relatively trivial in comparison to real-world consequences. That is, assignment of subjects to a conditioning group does *not* assure all will be conditioned, because some will not devote the level of attention necessary to become aware of the CS-US contingency (cf. Staats 1969; Gormezano in Petty and Cacioppo 1981, p. 46). It is only by paying attention and becoming aware of the CS-US contingency that an experiment stands a chance of conditioning a response. Maltzman (1987, p. 230) perhaps said it best:

> Conditioning does not occur in a black box, an empty shell, or a buffer. We do not condition a disembodied response. We condition an organism, usually an inquiring, suspicious, curious, bored--all of these and more, or none--college sophomore. The conditioned response is a small sample of the complex behavioural, physiological, and neurochemical changes occurring at the moment. It is produced in a person with a variety of cortical sets, dominant foci, interests, attitudes, etc., present at the moment the CS and US are presented which influence and direct the nature of the CR.

Recapitulation

Modern theorists of classical conditioning (the Neo-Pavlovians cited above) have taken a fully cognitive position in formulating their view of how Pavlovian conditioning operates. These theorists readily accept subject awareness of CS-US relations as a fundamental property of conditioning. Hence, the opposing, pristine position that subject awareness violates conditioning's ontological premises is based on an obsolete view of classical conditioning theory. Robert Rescorla, a noted conditioning scholar, recently chastised this anachronistic view in a self-descriptive review article titled "Pavlovian Conditioning: It's Not What You Think It Is" (Rescorla 1988).

EMPIRICAL EVIDENCE ON THE ROLE OF SUBJECT AWARENESS

When discussing the awareness issue at the empirical level, it is important to make clear distinctions between contingency awareness and demand bias (cf. Allen and Janiszewski 1989; Insko and Oakes 1966; Petty and Cacioppo 1981; Stuart, Shimp, and Engle 1987). Specifically, it is necessary to delineate four constructs: contingency awareness, demand awareness, demand bias, and conditioned effect. The Figure presents the relations among these constructs and their corresponding necessity and sufficiency conditions.

Contingency awareness (CA) exists when experimental subjects know that CS and US have been related temporally in an experiment's sequencing of these two events. For example, subjects were judged to be contingency aware in Allen and Janiszewski's (1989) study when they knew that certain Norwegian words (the CS) were more likely than others to be followed by positive feedback (the US).

Demand awareness (DA) means that a subject has some idea about his or her expected role in a conditioning experiment. She or he thinks (conjectures, infers) that the experimenter expects him or her to emit a particular response, such as reflecting a favorable attitude on a response scale.

Demand bias (DB), also called demand artifacts, means that subjects, because they are demand aware, alter their natural (i.e., unbiased) response in a direction either intended to support or counter their assumption of what the experimenter expects them to do. The important point, though typically neglected (Allen and Janiszewski provide an exception), is that DB does not necessarily follow from DA. Because a subject has some idea of what the experimenter expects does not necessarily mean that s(he) will adjust her(his) behavior accordingly. Moreover, individual subjects may sometimes alter their behavior, but because different subjects likely alter their behavior in different directions, the effect of such random deviations is that individual data values may vary from true scores, but aggregate statistics are not necessarily systematically biased.

Conditioned effect (CE) is an individual- or aggregate-level measure of conditioned response. At

FIGURE
CONCEPTUAL FRAMEWORK FOR AWARENESS ISSUE

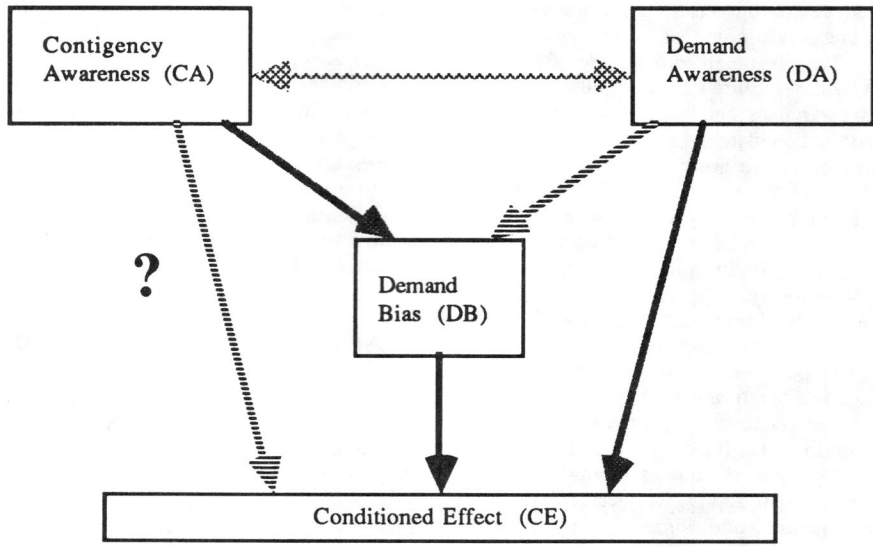

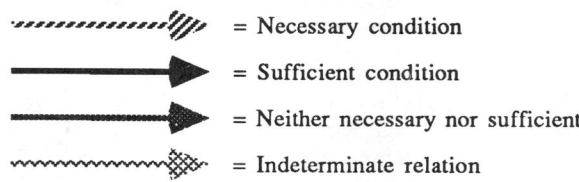
= Necessary condition

→ = Sufficient condition

→ = Neither necessary nor sufficient

⌇⌇⌇⌇ = Indeterminate relation

---

the individual-subject level, the effect is a conditioned response which an experiment attempts to bring as close to asymptote as possible. When studying autonomic (e.g., GSR) or skeletal (e.g., eyeblink) responses, it is possible to test whether an individual subject has in fact been conditioned. This is done by comparing a baseline measure of response to the US (e.g., the heart rate when the US is present) with a postmeasure of response to the CS alone. However, when studying attitudinal conditioning, which is the type of learning most relevant for consumer behavior, individual-level measurement is virtually impossible because unambiguous baseline measures are unavailable. Thus, with attitudinal conditioning, the CE is measured at an aggregate-level; i.e., the CE represents the statistical difference between conditioning and control groups' average attitudinal responses. CE will be used in this aggregate-effect sense throughout the remaining discussion.

Returning to the Figure, the arguments can be summarized as follows:

1. Contingency awareness (CA) *may be* necessary for a conditioned effect (CE) to materialize. (Empirical evidence is inconsistent on this point, hence justifying the equivocal statement.)

2. But CA is *not* necessary nor sufficient for demand bias.

3. The relationship between CA and demand awareness (DA) is indeterminate; i.e., either type of awareness may alert the subject to the other, but whether it does or not is entirely contingent on the conditions in a particular experiment.

4. DA *is* necessary but *not* sufficient for demand bias (DB). Indeed, heroic assumptions must be made to assume that (aggregate-level) demand artifacts exists just because subjects may be aware of the experimenter's expectations.

5. Demand awareness is neither necessary nor sufficient for a conditioned effect (CE) to materialize.

6. Demand bias *is* sufficient for CE but is *not* necessary.

This rather protracted, though necessary, prelude makes it possible now to meaningfully discuss the various awareness issues and the challenges they pose for classical conditioning. The discussion is restricted to recent research evidence and is divided into two sections, contingency-awareness and demand-bias evidence.

Contingency-Awareness Evidence

The issue of contingency awareness can be summarized in this question: Is contingency awareness necessary for conditioning, or can conditioning occur without cognition?[1] As discussed below, the evidence is mixed.

Evidence Supporting Cognitive Mediation. Allen and Janiszewski (1989) performed two experiments employing a creative computerized word game to condition attitudes to five neutral Norwegian words. Experimental results (especially Experiment 1) evidenced attitudinal conditioning; however, the most important facet of this research is the showing in both experiments that contingency awareness is a *necessary precondition* for attitudinal conditioning. Allen and Janiszewski do not assert that their results disprove noncognitive conditioning (i.e., conditioning without subject awareness), but they present an impressive argument that it is difficult to demonstrate conditioning without awareness.

Evidence Challenging Cognitive Mediation. Some influential recent European conditioning research has yielded results in conflict with Allen and Janiszewski's (1989) findings. Baeyens and his colleagues' (Baeyens, Crombez, Van den Bergh, and Eelen 1989; Baeyens, Eelen, and Van den Bergh 1989; Baeyens, Eelen, Van den Bergh, and Crombez 1989) experiments have demonstrated attitudinal conditioning without subject awareness. The significance of this finding is in the suggestion that affect for an initially neutral object can be formed automatically without the subject necessarily being aware of the CS-US contingency.

The disagreement between Allen and Janiszewski's findings and those from Europe is perplexing, but not necessarily inexplicable. Whereas Allen and Janiszewski conditioned attitudes toward neutral Norwegian words using verbal feedback as unconditioned stimuli, Baeyens and his colleagues conditioned attitudes toward human faces using other human faces (either liked or disliked) as unconditioned stimuli. Baeyens and colleagues contend that their experimental paradigm yields evaluative conditioning (i.e., affective learning), which is fundamentally different than the type of signal learning that is probably more typical of Allen and Janiszewski's paradigm as well as that employed by Stuart et al. (1987). Further research is certainly in order to confront this incongruity.

Demand-Bias Evidence

While acknowledging the presence of contingency awareness as necessary for conditioned effects, Allen and Janiszewski (1989) and Stuart et al. (1987) deny their results are due to demand bias. However, in an impressive recent challenge, Kellaris and Cox (1989) raise the possibility that the seminal consumer behavior demonstration of classical conditioning by Gorn (1982) may be attributable to demand bias. Briefly, Kellaris and Cox performed two true experiments (one a slight modification of Gorn's procedures, and the other a close replication) that failed to replicate Gorn's findings (that subjects exposed to a pen paired with liked music were more likely to prefer that pen compared to subjects exposed to a pen paired with disliked music). However, a third study (a nonexperiment that reenacted Gorn's procedure by merely describing rather than administering treatments to subjects) yielded results similar to Gorn's original findings.

Kellaris and Cox's (1989) overall results would appear to suggest that Gorn's findings (and, by implication, findings from other conditioning experiments) are purely artifactual. However, Kellaris and Cox provide no concrete evidence to show that specific features of Gorn's study would have rendered its findings artifact-laden. Moreover, Kellaris and Cox's experiments, although conscientious and close replications of Gorn's work, differ in the music used as US, which may account for why they were unable to replicate Gorn's findings. Finally, the fact that Kellaris and Cox's nonexperiment supports Gorn's findings is not itself convincing evidence that Gorn's results were due to demand artifacts inasmuch as this procedure has been criticized on grounds that it tends to produce a special mental set that is unique to role-playing subjects (Kruglanski 1975).

In sum, although it is difficult to ever entirely discount a demand-artifacts challenge-- especially in view of the fact that efforts to measure the presence of demand artifacts are themselves subject to demand artifacts (Gorn, Jacobs, and Mana 1987)--it would seem that the logic chain necessary to suggest that Gorn's results were artifact laden is based on considerable speculation. The fact is that contingency awareness is not tantamount to guessing the experimental hypothesis; furthermore, subjects who do correctly guess the hypothesis may or may not alter their behavior in the direction called for by the hypothesis.

CONCLUSION

Consumer researchers during the past decade displayed considerable interest in classical conditioning. To sustain this momentum will require (1) examining various heretofore untested issues (e.g., the role of CS-US similarity), (2) possibly pitting the conditioning model against alternative accounts of attitude formation/change in

---

[1] Readers will note an obvious similarity with the more general issue of whether affect is formed independently of cognition or whether it is cognitively mediated (Anand, Holbrook, and Stephens 1988; Zajonc 1980; Zajonc and Marcus 1984).

a comparative-testing sense (Sternthal, Tybout, and Calder 1987), and (3) safeguarding against alternative explanations that threaten the internal validity of experimental evidence. In the spirit of this last desideratum, the purpose of this paper has been to evaluate whether the empirical presence of subject awareness (of the contingent relation between conditioned and unconditioned stimuli) poses a pernicious blow to the classical conditioning paradigm.

This possibility was examined first by evaluating the philosophical argument which contends that mentalistic constructs are inherently incompatible with classical conditioning's ontological premises. This so-called pristine position was discounted on grounds that it is out of step with the modern, fully cognitive position on the nature of Pavlovian conditioning, a position that warmly embraces cognitive constructs.

The paper also examined the related issues of contingency awareness and demand bias. Regarding the latter, it was concluded that the evidence favoring a demand-bias challenge to claimed classical conditioning results (particularly Kellaris and Cox's (1989) challenge to Gorn's (1982) findings) is more speculative than definitive. With respect to the role of contingency awareness, the paper amplifies Allen and Janiszewski's (1989) position that conditioned learning is cognitively mediated by subject awareness of the temporal relation between CS and US. However, this position was taken with some degree of equivocation in view of the recent evidence from Europe by Baeyens and his colleagues, who have presented evidence of classical conditioning without contingency awareness. No definitive conclusion is possible at this point, but it would appear that the conditioning paradigm used by the European researchers may better evidence evaluative learning in comparison to the serial-learning procedure more characteristic of recent consumer behavior conditioning studies (especially Allen and Janiszewski 1989; Bierley et al. 1985; and Stuart et al. 1987). This provocative possibility demands future examination in view of Baeyens et al.'s claim that evaluative conditioning is possible without cognitive mediation, and, even more interestingly, that such conditioning is nonextinguishable.

REFERENCES

Allen, Chris T. and Chris A. Janiszewski (1989), "Assessing the Role of Contingency Awareness in Attitudinal Conditioning with Implications for Advertising Research," *Journal of Marketing Research*, 26 (February), 30-43.

Allen, Chris T. and Thomas J. Madden (1985), "A Closer Look at Classical Conditioning," *Journal of Consumer Research*, 12 (December), 301-315.

Anand, Punam, Morris B. Holbrook, and Debra Stephens (1988), "The Formation of Affective Judgments: The Cognitive-Affective Model Versus the Independence Hypothesis," *Journal of Consumer Research*, 15 (December), 386-391.

Baeyens, Frank, Geert Crombez, Omer Van den Bergh, and Paul Eelen (1988), "Once in Contact Always in Contact: Evaluative Conditioning Is Resistant to Extinction," *Advances in Behavioural Research and Therapy*, 10, 179-199.

Baeyens, Frank, Paul Eelen, and Omer Van den Bergh (1989), "Contingency Awareness in Evaluative Conditioning: A Case for Unaware Affective-Evaluative Learning," *Cognition and Emotion*, 3.

Baeyens, Frank, Paul Eelen, Omer Van den Bergh, and Geert Crombez (1988), "Acquired Affective-Evaluative Value: Conservative But Not Unchangeable," *Behavioural Research and Therapy*, 27 (3), 279-287.

Bierley, Calvin, Frances K. McSweeney, and Renee Vannieuwkerk (1985), "Classical Conditioning of Preferences for Stimuli," *Journal of Consumer Research*, 12 (December), 316-323.

Brewer, William F. (1974), "There Is No Convincing Evidence for Operant Or Classical Conditioning in Adult Humans," in W. Weimer and D. Palermo (eds.), *Cognition and the Symbolic Processes*, Lawrence Erlbaum, Hillsdale, NJ., 1-42.

Dawson, Michael F. and Anne M. Schell (1987), "Human Autonomic and Skeletal Classical Conditioning: The Role of Conscious Cognitive Factors," in G. Davey (ed.), *Cognitive Processes and Pavlovian Conditioning in Humans*, Chichester: John Wiley & Sons Ltd., 27-55.

Dawson, Michael E., Annel M. Schell, James R. Beers, and Andrew Kelly (1982), "Allocation of Cognitive Processing Capacity During Human Autonomic Classical Conditioning," *Journal of Experimental Psychology: General*, III (September), 273-295.

Frcka, Gertrude, Johanna Beyts, A. B. Levey, and Irene Martin (1983), "The Role of Awareness in Human Conditioning," *Pavlovian Journal of Biological Sciences*, 18 (April-June), 69-76.

Furedy, John J., Diane M. Riley, and Mats Fredrikson (1983), "Pavlovian Extinction, Phobias, and the Limits of the Cognitive Paradigm," *Pavlovian Journal of Biological Science*, 17 (July-September), 126-135.

Gorn, Gerald J. (1982), "The Effects of Music in Advertising on Choice Behavior: A Classical Conditioning Approach," *Journal of Marketing*, 46 (Winter), 94-101.

Gorn, Gerald J., W. J. Jacobs, and Michael J. Mana (1987), "Observations on Awareness and Conditioning," in Melanie Wallendorf and Paul F. Anderson (eds.), *Advances in Consumer Research*, 14, Provo, UT: Association for Consumer Research, 415-416.

Holland, Peter C. (1984), "Origins of Behavior in Pavlovian Conditioning," G. H. Bower (ed.), *The Psychology of Learning and Motivation*, 18, 129-174.

Holyoak, Keith J., Kyunghee Koh, and Richard E. Nisbett (1989), "A Theory of Conditioning: Inductive Learning Within Rule-Based Default Hierarchies," *Psychological Review*, 96 (No. 2), 315-340.

Insko, Chester A. and William F. Oakes (1966), "Awareness and the 'Conditioning' of Attitudes," *Journal of Personality and Social Psychology*, 4, No. 3, 487-496.

Kahle, Lynn R. (1984), *Attitudes and Social Adaptation: A Person-Situation Interaction Approach*, Oxford, U.K.: Pergamon Press.

Kahle, Lynn R., Sharon E. Beatty, and Patricia Kennedy (1987), "Comment on Classically Conditioning Human Consumers," in Melanie Wallendorf and Paul F. Anderson (eds.), *Advances in Consumer Research*, 14, Provo, UT: Association for Consumer Research, 411-414.

Kellaris, James J. and Anthony D. Cox (1989), "The Effects of Background Music in Advertising: A Reassessment," *Journal of Consumer Research*, 16 (June), 113-118.

Kruglanski, A. W. (1975), "The Human Subject in the Psychology Experiment: Fact and Artifact," in L. Berkowitz (ed.), *Advances in Experimental Social Psychology*, 8, Orlando: Academic Press, 101-147.

Macklin, M. Carole (1986), "Classical Conditioning Effects in Product/Character Pairings Presented to Children," in Richard J. Lutz (ed.), *Advances in Consumer Research*, 13, Provo, UT: Association for Consumer Research, 198-203.

Maltzman, Irving (1987), "A Neo-Pavlovian Interpretation of the OR and Classical Conditioning in Humans: With Comments on Alcoholism and the Poverty of Cognitive Psychology," in G. Davey (ed.), *Cognitive Processes and Pavlovian Conditioning in Humans*, Chichester: John Wiley & Sons Ltd., 211-250.

McSweeney, Frances K. and Calvin Bierley (1984), "Recent Developments in Classical Conditioning," *Journal of Consumer Research*, 11 (September), 619-631.

Nord, Walter R. and J. Paul Peter (1980), "A Behavior Modification Perspective on Marketing," *Journal of Marketing*, 44 (Spring), 36-47.

Page, Monte M. (1969), "Social Psychology of a Classical Conditioning of Attitudes Experiment," *Journal of Personality and Social Psychology*, 11, No. 2, 177-186.

Petty, Richard E. and John T. Cacioppo (1981), *Attitudes and Persuasion: Classic and Contemporary Approaches*, Dubuque, Iowa: Wm. C. Brown.

Rescorla, Robert A. (1988), "Pavlovian Conditioning: It's Not What You Think It Is," *American Psychologist*, 43 (March), 151-160.

Staats, Arthur W. (1969), "Experimental Demand Characteristics and the Classical Conditioning of Attitudes," *Journal of Personality and Social Psychology*, 11, No. 2, 187-192.

Staats, Carolyn K. and Arthur W. Staats (1957), "Meaning Established by Classical Conditioning," *Journal of Experimental Psychology*, 54, 74-80.

Staats, Arthur W. and Carolyn K. Staats (1958), "Attitudes Established by Classical Conditioning," *Journal of Abnormal and Social Psychology*, 57, 37-40.

Sternthal, Brian, Alice M. Tybout, and Bobby J. Calder (1987), "Confirmatory Versus Comparative Approaches to Judging Theory Tests," *Journal of Consumer Research*, 14 (June), 114-125.

Stuart, Elnora W., Terence A. Shimp, and Randall W. Engle (1987), "Classical Conditioning of Consumer Attitudes: Four Experiments in an Advertising Context," *Journal of Consumer Research*, 14 (December), 334-349.

Zanna, Mark P., Charles A. Kiesler, and Paul A. Pilkonis (1970), "Positive and Negative Attitudinal Affect Established by Classical Conditioning," *Journal of Personality and Social Psychology*, 14, No. 4, 321-328.

Zajonc, Robert B. (1980), "Feeling and Thinking: Preferences Need No Inferences," *American Psychologist*, 35, 151-175.

Zajonc, Robert B. and Hazel Markus (1982), "Affective and Cognitive Factors in Preferences," *Journal of Consumer Research*, 9 (September), 123-131.

Literary Analysis of An Advertisement: The Commercial as "Soap Opera"
Barbara B. Stern, Rutgers University

ABSTRACT

The paper analyzes the meaning of a television commercial for Procter & Gamble's GAIN detergent from a literary perspective. Three questions are posed: "What kind of commercial is it?" "How is it constructed?" and "What responses is it likely to elicit?" The analysis begins with identification of the advertisement's *genre* -- a miniature soap opera -- to examine the typical subject matter, structure, style, and emotional effects associated with its literary family. The commercial itself is then analyzed in detail to illustrate what the soap elements are and how they function. Since the soap opera genre has been associated with viewer responses, the paper will end by suggesting anticipated consumer responses of identification, involvement, and word-of-mouth communication.

INTRODUCTION

Lively debate swirls around varied approaches to the "meaning" of advertising. The central question is, "Who or what determines an ad's meaning?" Does it emanate from the creator's (copywriter's, art director's) mind? Does it reside in the text (verbal and visual) and the media/vehicle (print, television, and so forth)? Is it governed by the socio-cultural context that, like amniotic fluid, surrounds an ad? Or is it a consumer-based construct, in the mind of the perceiver? Controversy as to whether advertising is an art, a science, or a business hinges on different approaches to meaning.

The panel presentation on "Advertising and the Meaning of Meaning" (see Boller and Olson, McCracken, and Hirschman, following) was designed to bring together advertising researchers *and* creators for the first time to take advantage of their varied perspectives. First, each researcher used his/her perspective to analyze an advertising specimen: a 30-second television commercial for Procter & Gamble's GAIN detergent. Next, the commercial's creators -- Ray Hirschman and Ron Hartley, Senior Vice-Presidents and Creative Directors at Wells, Rich, Greene, Inc. -- revealed their ideas about how the commercial came into being. Last, a discussant (Elizabeth Hirschman) explored the concept of multiple meanings and its value in consumer research.

This first paper proposes literary criticism as a research approach to meaning that may help integrate our understanding of why consumers respond the way they do. The purpose of the following analysis -- based on the methodology of "close reading" or explication (Stern 1989) -- is to provide a systematic framework for consideration of three questions: "What kind of commercial is it?" "How is it constructed?" and "What responses is it likely to elicit?" The response to the first question identifies the advertisement's *genre* -- it is a soap opera -- in order to ascertain its distinctive subject matter, structure, style, and emotional effects (Abrams 1988). In answer to the second question, the paper describes generic soap elements and then illustrates how they function in the GAIN commercial. To deal with the last question, the paper proposes that consumer responses to the soap commercial may resemble reader responses (Stern and Gallagher 1990) of identification, involvement, and word-of-mouth said to be associated with televised soap programs.

THE SOAP OPERA: A GENRE UNTO ITSELF

Genre criticism is a useful way to enter text, for an advertisement's family provides information about the conventions or codes that govern form and content (Abrams 1988). The name "soap opera" testifies to the blending of advertising and programming that characterized the first radio serials created for women audiences in the 1930s. These programs were developed by detergent companies, notably Procter & Gamble, as "tie-ins" with their products (Ensign and Knapton 1985). When soaps moved to television in the 1950s (Leiss, Kline, and Jhally 1986), the close connection between programming and advertising continued. Nonetheless, despite this linkage, little attention has been paid to similarities between the programs and the commercials (Cantor and Pingree 1983), and the genre has not yet been analyzed as an *advertising* format. Thus, this paper turns to genre studies to address a research gap in our understanding of what a soap opera commercial looks like and how it works.

In order to analyze the genre, some historical background is required, for the soaps' typical (see Cantor and Pingree 1983; Fiske 1987) subject matter, setting, form, structure, characters, and values can best be viewed as modern reworkings of older material. While contemporary soaps are specific to the electronic media, their peculiar blend of realism and fantasy stems from roots in older literary antecedents -- family sagas, domestic novels, romance literature, and realistic drama.

Subject and Setting

Soap opera *subjects* -- their typical topics -- reveal ancestral ties to the eighteenth century sentimental novel (see Cantor and Pingree 1983), the nineteenth century domestic novel (Bridgewood 1986), and the early twentieth century romance novel (Baym 1981). Domestic novels were frequently serialized, and were primarily written by, for, and about women. They generally dealt with the problems of courtship, marriage, and family life. When soaps moved from radio to television, the topic of pre-marital romance was supplanted by that of the post-marital family. Whereas "romances" traditionally end at the altar, the "family sagas" (Bridgewood 1986, p. 172) from which soaps descend begin there.

The most frequently encountered subject of television soaps is real-life family relationships (Edmundson and Rounds 1976; Ensign and Knapton 1985; La Guardia 1983), including but not limited to spousal love. Even though soaps deal with a broad array of relationships, their focus on the domestic world shuts out many other important subjects -- among others, work, religion, political passions, moral causes, intellectual pursuits, and current affairs. Notwithstanding this constricted world, the genre aims at verisimilitude, here defined as the achievement of an illusion of reality (Abrams 1988). Soap realism is manifested in the *setting's* fidelity to the details of dailyness (Ensign and Knapton 1985; La Guardia 1983). "Setting" includes all of the physical details that locate a story in time and space (Abrams 1988): geographical location, costumes, hairstyles, food, interior decor, architecture, and so forth. The most important soap locale is the home and neighboring environs (Fiske 1987), and its realism -- like the naturalistic drama to which it is distantly related (Hatlen 1962) -- consists of representation of the minutia of ordinary life.

Form and Structure

While the soap setting aims at verisimilitude, both its structure and form depart from the conventions of realistic drama. The soap opera *form* -- its principles of organization -- and *structure* -- its plot or series of actions -- represent an amalgam of stylized elements drawn from earlier domestic novels (Edmundson and Rounds 1976; Ensign and Knapton 1985; Hirschman 1988), modified to suit electronic media. Soaps are, first of all, *serials* -- that is, their structure is episodic and their narrative is ongoing. Each episode presents a more or less coherent set of events (Hirschman 1988), but lacks definitive narrative closure. For this reason, soaps have been called "cliché cliffhangers" (Ensign and Knapton 1985), designed to end with an unresolved problem so that viewers will tune in to the next installment.

Serialization entails an unusual plot structure, in that soaps have no clear beginning or end. They are, instead, "an *infinitely extended middle*" (Fiske 1987, p. 180). Action often begins in the middle, leaving viewers to unravel complex scenarios on their own. Announcers whose function is to help the audience figure out what is going on are not ordinarily present in television soaps (Cantor and Pingree 1983). In their place, other contextual cues are provided, the most important of which is *music* (Scott 1990). This is both a first cue to the genre (the opening bars) and an ongoing one signifying change (transitions in time, space, and action) (Ensign and Knapton 1985).

Although changes in milieu occur frequently, soap plots do not develop momentum in order to achieve a climax. On the contrary, a key aspect of their middle-heaviness is that the overall structure is infinite: soaps *never end*. One sub-plot leads to another, and semi-resolved conflicts in one set of actions are incorporated into later ones (Cantor and Pingree 1983). Just as the traditional dramatic unity of beginning-middle-end is not a value, neither is dramatic continuity. Instead, *disjunction* is the rule, for numerous stories are interwoven by means of abrupt jump-cuts from one to another (Fiske 1987). Rapid shifts in action with neither causal transitions nor narrative guidance are features of open-ended plots, structural oddities in that they are capable of infinite extension because they can go off in any direction at will.

This open-ended structure determines the soaps' unusual treatment of *time* as well: it is the only genre in which time passage within the story parallels the actual passage of time in real life. This accounts for the *slow pace* and *paucity of action*. Techniques such as flashbacks and repetitious dialogue needed for recapitulation of vital information add to an atmosphere of stasis. Soaps seem to be going nowhere, for while *endless talk* swirls around trivial events (Edmundson and Rounds 1976), nothing much happens. Lengthy conversations require the camera to linger on the characters, and *close-up* shots enable audiences to "read" facial expressions and body language. Television soaps, in fact, rely on dialogue and portraiture to such an extent that they have been called "radio with pictures" (Cantor and Pingree 1983, p. 24).

Characters and Values

The prototypical soap characters behave like cardboard pictures because they are simplistic and unidimensional stereotypes rather than fully-rounded individuals (Buckman 1984; Ensign and Knapton 1985). Their personalities are bounded by family roles, for the family is construed as a "universal form" or "everyfamily" as a result of common role-requirements that over-ride situational differences in social, economic, or national status (Bridgewood 1986). Motherhood, especially, is the same everywhere, and soap women show even less individuality than do men as a result of ubiquitous female roles in child bearing and rearing. Soap heroines are identified by family roles such as "mother," "wife," "helpmate," and so forth, because the nature of a character is defined by her relationships to others: husband, children, parents, and outsiders who interact with the family.

The domestic orientation of soap characters is rooted in the middle class ethos, for they "are supposed to be average, just like their audience" (Edmundson and Rounds 1976, p. 15). They represent middle America: white Anglo-Saxon Protestants who live in the suburbs, who are not too poor or too rich, too proud or too humble, too ignorant or too educated. Generally, the men have professional careers and the women are housewives, but even when the women work outside the home, they are expected to view household chores as "women's work."

Despite the characters' averageness, however, their lives are anything but dull. On the contrary, they revel in rich emotionality, often displaying intense reactions to mundane events. Melodramatic plot devices (Ensign and Knapton 1985) and habitual sentimentality (La Guardia 1983) are the rule, for the characters' spin out exhaustive analyses of their feelings and tend to react to ordinary events more strongly than one would expect of people in real-life situations (Abrams 1988). Indeed, heightened emotionality is the hallmark of two popular stereotypical "good" characters: the "decent husband" (Fiske 1987) and the "devoted wife" (Buckman 1984).

"The Decent Husband"

The sensitive hero is a soap convention that distinguishes it from other types of "women's literature." A "decent husband" is the pillar of the soap family, one whose moral fibre is made visible by his physical attractiveness. He may be young or young-looking, but he is never jejeune, for he reveals sufficient traces of weariness to let viewers know that he is struggling under the weight of a heroic burden. The burden is one of family obligations: this hero is a law-abiding citizen who obeys the Ten Commandments, loves his wife, honors his parents, and nurtures his children. Most notably, the soap husband is portrayed as dependable, persevering in the "hardest, dullest, and least rewarding task of all" -- that of providing emotional security to those who depend on him (Buckman 1984).

Notwithstanding his noble nature, the hero is not a goody-goody, too perfect to be believable. The reason is that his sensitivity to others -- especially women -- legitimizes the "caring, nurturing, and verbal" aspects of his nature (Fiske 1987, p. 186). He is a man who likes women, who is interested in the things that interest them, and who is attuned to their needs. Unlike other romance heroes, the soap husband is emotionally accessible: he is "usually open and supportive, interested in children and clothes, feelings, and cooking" (Bridgewood 1986, p. 193). While he may wield power in his own "place" -- the external world -- he becomes tender and vulnerable in private life (Bridgewood 1986). The "decent husband" presents a picture of what soap heroines want in a man: commitment, fidelity, and open articulation of feelings.

"The Devoted Wife"

Because the soap hero is the kind of man who causes his "wife's eyes to shine when she hears his key in the latch" (Buckman 1984, pp. 40-41), she responds with devotion. The "devoted wife" is at once good *and* strong, a role-model who maintains marital happiness by performing necessary household chores to perfection. Her most important job is to keep the domestic machinery running smoothly and efficiently (Buckman 1984). She is expected to cope with family crises (not to create them), and to dispense the balm of love and nurturance needed to heal inevitable domestic wounds.

The heroine's role demands qualities such as patience, good humour, tact, and common sense, all associated with traditional values of "home" as woman's "place" (Welter 1966). The soap wife's patience shows that old-fashioned simplicity and the work ethic are superior to the modern world's insistence on instant gratification. Her good humor permits her to respond cheerfully to the crises of motherhood, jollying the family into civility when tempers flare. These wifely virtues -- parodied in *The Stepford Wives* -- are "the stuff of nostalgia" (Buckman 1984, p. 48), for although the devoted wife is a modern woman, her morality is rooted in traditional virtues. These ties to the past permit women to pass the torch of civilization from one generation to the next.

Soap Values: Traditionalism, Marriage, and Matriarchy

Passing the torch involves women's role in the preservation of traditional American social and moral values (Fiske 1987), a role that is fundamental to the concept of matriarchal power. Soap values -- defined as abstract ideals representing beliefs about ideal modes of behavior and outcomes of life decisions (Rokeach 1973) -- look backwards to a mythical golden age of old-fashioned family togetherness. These bygone values are presented as superior to those governing the chaotic modern world (Buckman 1984), for the soaps' long view of time favors the supremacy of history, respect for one's cultural heritage, and belief in family continuity. This is the reigning ideology of the status quo, where history repeats itself, what goes around comes around, and eternal verities remain constant. At best, the values laud female bonding (mothers/daughters) in generational cycles ultimately responsible for perpetuating the human race (Bridgewood 1986).

In the soap world, the value of family security rests on the centrality of marriage as an institution that guarantees happiness in human life. Family continuity stems from a cardinal tenet of bourgeois morality -- marriage for love (Bridgewood 1986, p. 183) -- and the most salient soap belief is that everyone can attain happiness in marriage. As Edmundson and Rounds say, "The central tenet of soap opera is that personal happiness is possible, right here on this earth....The vision of supreme happiness that is held out -- and demonstrably available to the ordinary, quite average person -- is that of a happy marriage" (1976, p. 16).

However, the family can never rest in a state of stable equilibrium, for perpetual disturbance is what keeps the soap world in motion (Fiske 1987). Even happy marriages require an ongoing set of problems to push the action forward. These problems serve more than a structural purpose, however, for their existence highlights the source of matriarchal power. The feminine value most idealized in the soap world is women's power to control relationships. But since the concept of feminine power is complex, soap values are often paradoxical. While women do have a great deal of power in relationships, the domain itself is a limited one, for it is men who have power everywhere else. In this view, repetitious soap themes are the structural equivalent of a housewife's confinement to a life of domestic monotony routinized by the multiplicity and endlessness of housework tasks (Fiske 1987). The heroine's series of small victories afford her minor pleasures rather than big societal rewards, and for this reason they have been judged negatively as emblems of a social system that "buys" consent to full-time domesticity with small sops.

In fairness, however, soaps have also been said to present a more positive valuation of feminine power by emphasizing process rather than product, by depicting pleasure as ongoing rather than finite, and by displaying domestic life rather than business or politics or war as a source of gratification. Thus, soaps can be said to validate feminine principles as sources of legitimate pleasure within a society that tends to value whatever is masculine more highly. The affirmation of relationship-power is said to raise the level of feminine self-esteem by depicting a feminized culture (Modlewski 1982). In this respect, soaps are interpreted as empowering women by approving their ability to influence men to marry them, father their children, and take responsibility for the family (Fiske 1987). While validation of motherhood as the pre-eminent female role (Modlewski 1982) does limit women's power to the home, it nevertheless presents at least one positive stereotype to counterbalance the misogynistic figures often found in other media offerings. In sum, typical soap characters, values, subjects, and structural elements define the genre and set it apart from most others on television.

THE GAIN COMMERCIAL

The GAIN commercial derives much of its meaning as a specimen within this genre, for it is indebted to the historical association between detergent manufacturers, soap programs, and advertisements. While it conforms for the most part to genre conventions, some elements have been modified to reflect the detergent's regional market: the south-eastern United States. The opening bars of music provide a first genre clue, for this innocuous "needledrop" melody (Scott 1990) tells viewers that what they are about to see can be categorized as a soap opera. The familiar subject of family love here concerns the relationship between Bobby (husband), Mary Lou (wife), and Laura (little girl).

The topic of post-marital domesticity is worked out by means of the pattern of hugs designed to move the action forward. Bobby hugs Laura; Mary Lou hugs her laundry; but -- we note this now (see below) -- Bobby and Mary Lou do not hug each other. The hugs create a structural link between the plot's domestic problem and the product's role as a problem-solver. Laura's problem is that in her quest for successful housewifery, she must see to it that laundry not only *looks* clean, but also *smells* clean. Her problem is solved by GAIN, a detergent whose main benefit is "that huggable smell" -- the package slogan is "the sunshine scent -- for great smelling laundry." The pattern of successive hugs moves towards a successful resolution of the laundry problem, and at the same time demonstrates Laura's success in creating family intimacy.

This intimacy takes on heightened importance within the ad's closed system of reference. Although Bobby's uniform signals the presence of the non-domestic external world (see below), he has exited from this external reality by the time we meet him. Bobby's passage through the door of the home into the yard -- like Alice in Wonderland's descent underground -- symbolizes crossing a barrier from the world outside the family (war and work) to the world within (home and hearth). Domestic setting details build up verisimilitude for the viewers, whom we recall are southerners. The commercial's two locales -- a "family get together" at a barbeque and a laundry room -- are filled with appropriate regional visibilia. The food sizzling on a grill is cut-up skin-on chicken parts, an inexpensive staple popular in the south, one also indicative of the family's lower middle class socio-economic status. If, hypothetically, the commercial were instead targeted to northern upscale city dwellers, the barbeque might feature grilled chicken kebobs or fish.

Verisimilitude is further enhanced by the characters' attire, appropriate to the southern lifestyle and weather conditions. The day is hot and humid, and the gathering is an informal one where people might be expected to wear cool and comfortable clothing rather than their party best. Mary Lou wears a sleeveless flowered loose shift, and Laura wears a t-shirt and denim rompers. Only Bobby's full military uniform is inappropriately formal. On a hot day, a soldier who leaves base seems more likely to fold his soft hat (note that he is not wearing a brimmed cap) and tuck it under his epaulet. However, this formality may serve as a narrative aid to the audience, in need of definitional clues to facilitate accurate identification of characters. It is interesting to speculate that perhaps Bobby wears the soft rather than the brimmed cap because only the former is distinctively military, and hence Bobby is not likely to be mistaken for a policeman or a parcel post driver.

Just as the commercial's setting displays salient soap characteristics as genre cues, so too does its treatment of time. The episode is, firstly, complete in itself, the story of a husband's return home and the reunification of a family. However, it is also part of an ongoing tale, for it seems to be a skewed middle, showing no clear-cut beginning, but (unlike soap programs) a clear-cut end. The lack of background about events preceding Bobby's entry through the door raises several questions: where was he? why was he away? what did he do when he was away? was he away for a long time? Recall that the commercial is dated 9/1/89, before the Iraq crisis, so we cannot assume that Bobby's absence is war-related. Nor can we make a similar assumption about his homecoming, and additional mystery surrounds the connection (if any) between his return and the family get-together. As expected, the passage of time is disjunctive, in that quick camera

168 / *Literary Analysis of An Advertisment: The Commercial as "Soap Opera"*

FIGURE A
PROCTER & GAMBLE: GAIN DETERGENT -- 30 SECOND SPOT: "BOBBY"

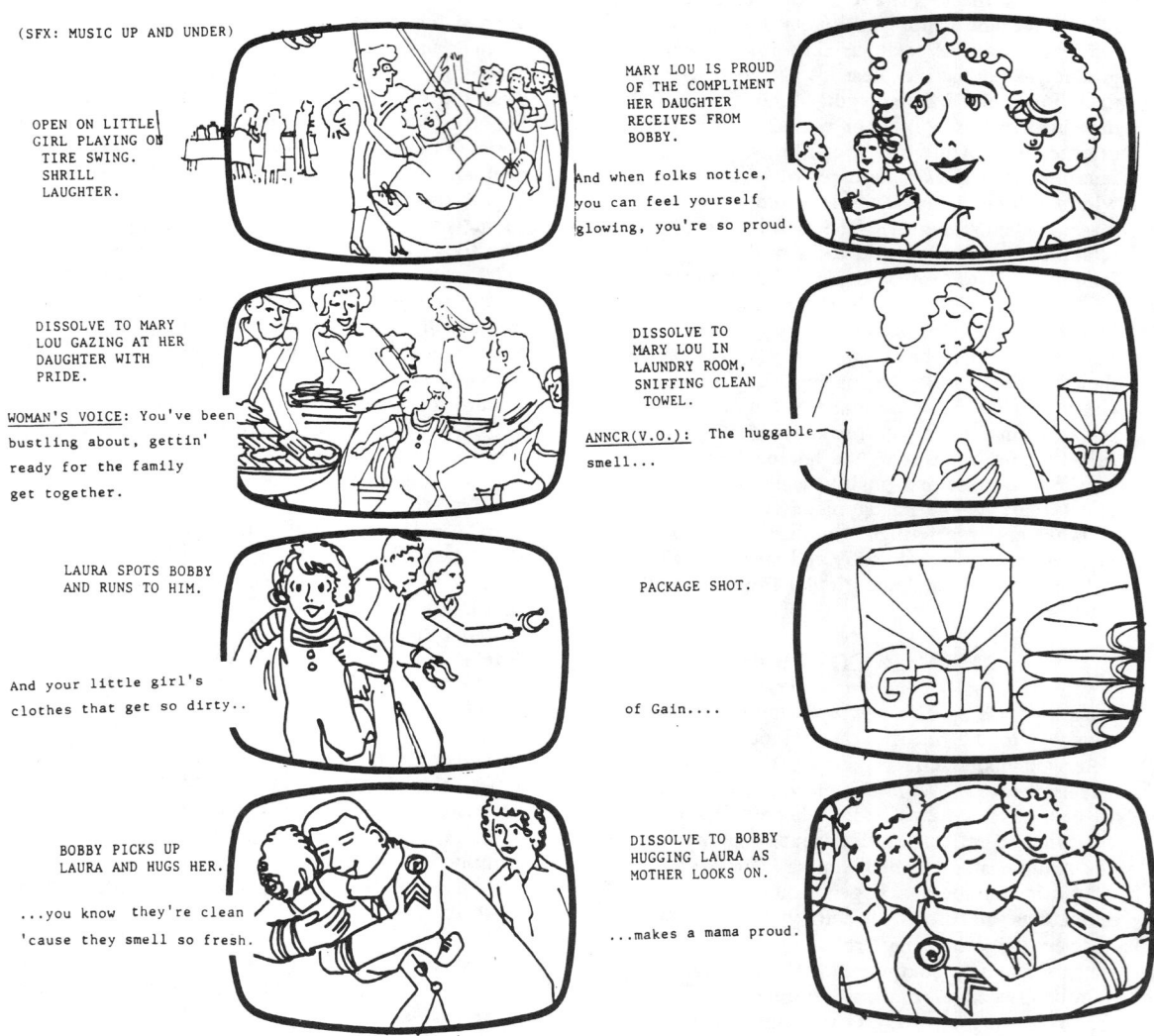

cuts jump from the chickens on the grill, to Laura, to Bobby and Mary Lou outdoors, to Mary Lou alone in the laundry room, and to all three together at last in the final frame. The dissolve to the laundry room is a flashback, drawing an event prior to the commercial's opening into the middle of the plot.

The middle is not extended indefinitely, however, for a flash-forward to a climax suggests that the soap commercial superimposes a structured problem-solving plot on the more usual serialized program format. The reason is that while a program has infinite tomorrows in which action can be continued, an advertisement does not. Both a narrator and a climax have been introduced to meet advertising's need for closure. The commercial ends with a narrative message lest the audience miss the point of the product's benefit. The next-to-the last shot (detergent package) is followed by the final spoken line -- "makes a mama proud" -- in a metonymic association of clean-smelling laundry with good motherhood. This narrative closure can probably be understood in light of the difference between an advertisement's persuasive goal (buy the product now), and a program's entertainment goal (tune in tomorrow).

The message seeks to persuade with an emotional (rather than a rational) appeal, for it taps into feelings associated with clean-smelling laundry. Bobby and Mary Lou are stereotypes, unidimensional in their fixation on laundry, and individuated only insofar as required by the southern milieu. Their identity is defined primarily by family roles, for sexual expressivity is limited not only to product-related attributes, but also to requirements of family decorum. In light of the focus on clean-smelling clothes, we notice that Bobby not only hugs Laura, but also sniffs her clothing. This fleeting hint of sexuality is emboldened in the laundry room scene, where Mary Lou is seen embracing her laundry. She glows with pride, face upwards, and seems to be ecstatically relating to the laundry as if it were her lover's body. However, Bobby and Mary Lou do not make physical contact, for both male and female sexuality must be sublimated. In the soap world, individual sexual gratification has to be kept in its place, for it may not threaten family unity.

The supremacy of family unity ensures that Bobby's sexy good looks -- he is tall, dark, and handsome -- delineate him as a "decent husband" rather than as a romantic suitor. His demeanor bears tribute to dedication to God and country in both public and private life. Bobby's career symbolizes honor, for a current American cultural value is respect for military service (as distinct from other cultures, which may associate soldiering with violence or subversion). The ironic tension between Bobby's career and his emotional openness keeps his character from being too good to be true. Bobby is able to leave militaristic detachment at the office and move into a more loving mode at home. In the soap lexicon, his ability to articulate feelings defines him as a sensitive man. He not only notices that Laura's clothes smell good, but also has the capacity to express his pleasure openly by hugging her. His demonstrativeness in displaying affection makes both mother and daughter happy: Mary Lou says she is "that proud" of Bobby's compliment.

Mary Lou's pride in her family demarcates her as the "devoted wife." Her job is running the home, for she is intent on making sure that every domestic detail is "just right." She bears primary responsibility for special events (the family gathering) as well as for daily chores. Her investment of self-esteem in proper performance of domestic roles is indicated by the glow of pride she feels as a result of complements on the way her laundry smells. Mary Lou is a testimonial to soap heroine qualities such as patience (she waits at home while Bobby is away), nurturance (if "food = love," she is the one who cooks the chickens), and caring for others (she braids Laura's hair). Her happiness stems from small domestic successes: she enjoys seeing her stack of perfectly folded towels, and she smiles with pleasure while hugging clean linen. In the final frame, she beams when Bobby hugs Laura, even though Bobby has not noticed her in any way unconnected with motherhood. This spells out the foundation of her identity: Mary Lou is a proud "mama."

The commercial thus enshrines the values of motherhood, America, and apple pie in a nostalgic evocation of an ideal past. Celebration of a traditional family ritual in this insulated world suggests the cyclical bonding between mothers and daughters that links present generations with the American heritage. The family's values rest on mature love encompassed by the institution of marriage, and Bobby and Mary Lou seem to have found happiness in their relationship. Laura is the beneficiary of their joy, hinting at the perpetuation of this value system into the next generation.

Indeed, Bobby and Mary Lou seem like quintessentially average parents in many ways, except for one: they express a degree of emotionality in excess of what the occasion seems to require. This display of emotional excess in reference to clean-smelling clothes is an expected genre idiosyncracy, however, here related to the product being advertised. The product functions as a problem-solver, for the implicit -- but small -- disturbance in family equilibrium is the problem of getting laundry to smell good. Mary Lou solves the problem, for she is in charge of relationship maintenance, displaying her power by showing her love. Like the women in *Steel Magnolias*, Mary Lou's strength is gentled by a fragile exterior (sweet voice, slow drawl, light touch). She willingly accedes to her daughter in receiving open acknowledgement of Bobby's affection, and articulates pride in selfless sacrifices. However, her joy need not be interpreted as being either trivial or demeaning to women, for it is Mary Lou who guides her family to an appreciation of life's small pleasures. While the commercial's values do appear conservative, they also seem likely to match those of the target market -- lower middle class southern women living outside of big cities -- a substantial group of American women.

CONSUMER RESPONSES: IDENTIFICATION, INVOLVEMENT, ESCAPE

This paper suggests that consumers are likely to respond to soap advertisements as they do to the programs themselves, for prior experience with the genre may acculturate the viewer both in terms of expectations and responses (see Scott 1990). That is, a consumer may be said to watch this kind of commercial "successfully" if s/he possesses the requisite "degree of cultural capital constituted by knowledge of the conventions of the genre" (Brusdon in Fiske, 1987, p. 193). Three previously identified viewer responses -- identification, involvement, and word-of-mouth discussion (Buckman 1984) -- are summarized very briefly, for Boller and Olson (ff.) deal fully with consumer processing.

Identification

The majority of the soap audience (adult women) is said to identify (Buckman 1984) with the heroine, the most important character in our GAIN commercial as well as in most programs. Women have been found to identify with female characters on television (Fiske 1987) when the characters are recognizable human beings to whom the audience can relate as being in some way like themselves. The soaps' complete fidelity to setting details appears likely to lend a surface verisimilitude that is mimetic of real life, inviting the viewer to see her/himself in the "social tableau" (Marchand 1985). The tendency of theatre audiences to participate vicariously in the lives of characters on stage suggests that imaginative identification may be a response to dramatic advertisements as well (see Boller and Olson, ff.).

Involvement

Soap audiences from the outset have evidenced so high a level of identification with the characters that it is often termed "involvement" (Fiske 1987; La Guardia 1983). This is defined as a viewer's ongoing and active response to programs that become so much a part of his or her daily life that no barrier is erected between fact and fiction. Because soap characters live on from day to day in viewers' living rooms, they hold a special place in "the memory and gossip of viewers" (Fiske 1987, p. 180). High involvement is expressed by viewer failure to distinguish between the performance and the performer, and the tendency to confuse real actors and actresses with the characters they portray. Many viewers try to contact the characters, and television networks, producers, and writers often receive mail, phone calls, cards, and gifts from fans. In addition, viewers support a wide array of soap publications, especially fan magazines, a phenomenon not encountered in other television genres. Thus, viewers not only participate vicariously in soap characters' lives in the process of identification, but also endow these characters with status in their own personal lives by means of a process that seems more akin to involvement.

Social Gratification: Word-of-Mouth

High involvement has stimulated word-of-mouth activity, especially in light of the new soap audience in the 1970s: college students. Students engage in mass viewing of daytime soaps -- especially "General Hospital" -- unlike the lone listening or viewing habits of housewives tuned in to radio or television (La Guardia 1983). Physical proximity has been found to increase product-related conversations (Price and Feick 1984), and the habit of group television watching suggests that viewers' discussions of soap stories may spill over to discussions of products. If advertisements in soap formats inspire viewers to talk about the products shown, they may stimulate word-of-mouth responses, and thus acquire marketplace as well as social utility.

CONCLUSION

Advertising and soaps have remained closely linked for half a century, despite criticism on the part of "media snobs" who poke fun at the fantastically unrealistic soap world (bizarre events, exotic diseases, incredible coincidences), and condemnation on the part of early feminists who damned the heroines as caricatures (Fowles 1983). However, a re-valuation of soaps has led more recent critics to a deeper understanding of the genre. Now soaps are said to affirm a "feminine aesthetic" by offering positive views of feminine culture that empower rather than oppress women. They may even serve a useful social purpose by teaching men how women would like them to behave. Even if the soap problems seem far removed from everyday reality, the programs may convey the supportive message that individuals are capable of solving problems through their own efforts. While this revaluation may be an optimistic argument for the social desirability of soap programs, much further research on soap advertisements is needed to determine whether they reflect reality, shape it, or do a bit of both.

REFERENCES

Abrams, M.H. (1988), *A Glossary of Literary Terms*, Fifth Edition. New York: Holt, Rinehart and Winston, Inc.

Baym, Nina (1981),"Melodramas of Beset Manhood: How Theories of American Fiction Exclude Women Authors," *American Quarterly* 33 (Summer), 125-139.

Bridgewood, Christine (1986), "Family Romances: The Contemporary Popular Family Saga," in *The Progress of Romance: The Politics of Popular Fiction*, ed. Jean Radford, London: Routledge & Kegan Paul, 167-193.

Buckman, Peter (1984), *All for Love: A Study in Soap Opera*, London: Secker and Warburg.

Cantor, Muriel and Suzanne Pingree (1983), *The Soap Opera*, Beverly Hills: Sage Publications.

Edmundson, Madeleine and David Rounds (1976), *From Mary Noble to Mary Hartman: The Complete Soap Opera Book*, New York: Stein and Day Publishers.

Ensign, Lynne Naylor and Robyn Eileen Knapton (1985), *The Complete Dictionary of Television and Film*, New York: Stein and Day Publishers.

Fiske, John (1987), *Television Culture*, London: Methuen.

Fowles, Jib (1982), *Television Viewers vs. Media Snobs: What TV Does for People*, New York: Stein and Day Publishers.

Hatlen, Theodore W. (1962), *Orientation to the Theater*. New York: Appleton-Century-Crofts.

Hirschman, Elizabeth C. (1988), "The Ideology of Consumption: A Structural-Syntactical Analysis of *Dallas* and *Dynasty*," *Journal of Consumer Research*, 15 (December), 344-359.

La Guardia, Robert (1983), *Soap World*, New York: Arbor House.

Leiss, William, Stephen Kline, and Sut Jhally (1986), *Social Communication Through Advertising: Persons, Products, and Images of Well-Being*, Toronto, CAN: Methuen.

Price, Linda L. and Lawrence F. Feick, "The Role of Interpersonal Sources in External Search: An Informational Perspective," in *Advances in Consumer Research*, Vol. 9, ed. Thomas C. Kinnear, Ann Arbor: Association for Consumer Research, 250-255.

Rokeach, Milton (1973), *The Nature of Human Values*, New York: Free Press.

Stern, Barbara B. (1989), "Literary Explication: A Methodology for Consumer Research," in *Interpretive Consumer Research*, ed. Elizabeth C. Hirschman, Provo, UT: Association for Consumer Research, 48-59.

_____ and Katherine Gallagher (1990), "Advertising Form, Content, and Values: Lyric, Ballad, and Epic," in *Current Issues in Research and Advertising*, Volume 13, eds. James H. Leigh and Claude R. Martin, Jr., Ann Arbor, MI: The University of Michigan, in press.

Welter, Barbara (1966), "The Cult of True Womanhood: 1820-1860," *American Quarterly*, 18 (Summer), 151-174.

Experiencing Ad Meanings: Crucial Aspects of Narrative/Drama Processing
Gregory W. Boller, Memphis State University
Jerry C. Olson, Penn State University

How should consumer and advertising researchers study ad meaning? We can think of four viable approaches to the study of ad meaning. First, researchers can examine the manner in which the rhetorical structures in an ad present meaning (see Stern, this session). Second, researchers can examine the specific affective and cognitive processes by which consumers create and experience ad meanings. Third, researchers can examine how consumers use ad-influenced meanings in ordinary social contexts (see McCracken, this session). And finally, researchers can assemble the "findings" from all three approaches, compare them to the meanings intended by the ad creators, and explore the meta-meaning of the resulting gestalt (see Laing 1982 for a tantalizing discussion on the value of meta-meanings). We hope that the fourth approach (the intended purpose of this session) will yield provocative insights into the meaning of ad meaning. Our contribution to this session consists of a discussion of "experiencing ad meanings" (the second approach).

Rather than identifying many of the specific meanings consumers may create in response to a commercial, we discuss a process through which consumers experience the meanings portrayed in a commercial. The process we discuss is known as empathy, and is particularly appropriate to consider when studying the effects of narrative advertisements.

AD FORMS

An Initial Description of the GAIN Commercial

As evident from the title of this paper, we believe that the GAIN commercial is best described as a narrative form. By this we mean, the content and structure of this commercial is that of a story. In terms of content, the GAIN commercial contains *events* (e.g., preparations for a family get-together, arrival of a spouse, parental greeting of a child) as well as *characters* (e.g., a young momma, a husband/father home from the military, an excited young daughter) who react to and experience these events. The temporal sequence of lead character reactions to story events defines the structure or *plot* of the narrative commercial--in this case, a folklore-ish portrayal of maternal triumph in the context of family relationships.

In terms of narrative exposition, the GAIN commercial is an example of a "narrated drama" (cf. Deighton, Romer and McQueen 1989). That is, the experiences of the ad characters are communicated to the viewing audience through *dramatic enactment* (as evident in the visual sequence), as well as through *overt narration* (as evident in the ongoing and tag voice-overs). The dramatic component of the GAIN commercial narrative is clearly the dominant mode of exposition. The enactments portray the characters' experiences with and about the advertised brand. The overt narration embellishes and elaborates these experiences by providing the viewing audience with "key insights" into the lead character's thoughts and feelings related to the brand.

Although the above description is admittedly cryptic (see Stern, this volume, for a more thorough description), establishing the GAIN commercial as a narrative is critical because the processes by which consumers create and experience meanings during exposure to an advertisement largely depends upon the form of advertisement they are given (Boller 1990). We argue that theoretical accounts of ad processing should be contingent upon the form of the ad in question.

Important Assumptions about Narrative Advertisements

Until recently (see Boller 1990; Deighton, Romer and McQueen 1989: Wells 1989), consumer researchers have devoted little attention to narrative forms of advertising. Information processing and advertising response models implicitly assume that advertisements have an argumentative form (see, for example, the Elaboration Likelihood Model-- Petty, Cacioppo and Schumann 1983). That is, advertisements are treated as the purveyors of objective brand meanings that contain structured systems of attribute-benefit logic designed to convince audiences of the validity of specific brand claims. There are undoubtedly many reasons for this particular view of advertisements, not the least of which is that the archetypal language of science, the social system that studies the effects of advertisements, happens to be argument (cf. Bruner 1986).

Of course, many advertisements (especially those in the U.S.) have an agumentative form, and therefore, traditional models of advertising response are generally helpful. However, these models have a rather limited ability to account for the effects of narrative ads (Wells 1989). And given the burgeoning number of narrative advertisements, new theories of ad processing will be needed.

Unlike argumentative advertisements, narrative ads tend to portray experiential brand meaning (i.e., meanings about the self-relevant consequences associated with brand use) by telling stories about one or more character's experiences with the advertised brand. In these stories, characters generally interact with or consume the advertised brand, and thereby provide overt indications about their feelings toward the brand (e.g., through emotional displays). Through their actions with and reactions to the advertised brand, narrative ad characters can provide viewers with a "taste" of the psychosocial consequences associated with brand use (Boller 1990).

The importance of character in a narrative cannot be overstated. Events, though crucial components of any narrative, cannot convey experiential meaning. Only characters, as they respond to events in a story, can convey experiential meaning. As each character brings a particular emotional and cognitive point-of-view to bear during his or her interactions with story events, multiple "windows of experience" are opened to the viewing audience. Herein lies the power of narrative advertising--it can convey a multiplicity of brand meaning from the varying perspectives of consumer-characters.

We contend that any theoretical account of narrative ad processing must start by describing how viewers "process" the ad characters. In short, we believe that viewers generally process narrative ads by building empathic relationships with the ad characters. Through their empathy with ad characters, viewers can vicariously experience the personal relevance of the advertised brand. The key dimensions of this process (empathy) and its effects are described next.

EMPATHY AND NARRATIVE AD PROCESSING

Since Aristotle's *Poetics* (Trans. 1987), literary theorists have long recognized that compelling narratives (those capable of influencing social action) move an audience to empathize with their characters (Booth 1961; Martin 1986). These theorists suggest that the experiential perspectives provided by story characters virtually demand imaginative processes of "participation" to be fully appreciated and understood. To effectively grasp the meanings portrayed in a story, audience members must, in a sense, partially assume the experiential identity of a character (Katz 1963).

Within the context of narrative advertising, empathy can be conceptualized as a dynamic process whereby consumers imaginatively project themselves into the experiences of featured ad characters (cf. Booth 1961; Katz 1963). This process involves consumers' 1) *identification* with a character (their experience of sharing core aspects of self-identity with a character) and 2) *vicarious participation* in that character's experiences (their apprehension of the story events from the cognitive and affective perspectives of a character).

Character Identification

During exposure to a narrative ad, consumers' empathy with a featured character typically begins with identification. That is, consumers begin to perceive similarities between aspects of their own self identity and that depicted by the character. Initially, these similarites may include simple expressions of self such as style of dress, speech and posture. However, as the commercial unfolds, consumers' initial identification with a character may deepen to include similarities in terms of interests, values and goals (Burke 1969). In some instances, consumers may feel as if their self-identity is indistinguishable from that of the character with whom they are empathizing.

Turning to the GAIN ad, it is clearly evident that the lead character is the "young momma." If consumers strongly identify with this character, they may feel similar interests and goals pertaining to "motherly responsiblities," which in this case might include 'please thy husband' and 'deliver unto him a daughter with clean, fresh smelling clothes'). And, like this "young momma," empathizing consumers should perceive GAIN as a means to satisfy these interests and goals.

Vicarious Participation

During their identification with an ad character, empathizing consumers also begin to feel as if they are participating in that character's experiences (Katz 1963). That is, consumers imaginatively experience the story events from the affective and cognitive perspectives of the character with whom they identify. Initially, consumers' vicarious participation may be limited to simple thoughts and perceptions. As their identification with a character deepens however, their vicarious participation will generally intensify to include emotional reactions and sometimes physical reactions. In rare instances, strongly empathizing consumers may feel as though they have actually "lived through" the story events.

Returing to the GAIN ad, what would empathizing consumers experience if they vicariously participated with the "young momma" character? Perhaps these consumers would, in part, experience the ambivalence of the homecoming event (e.g., anxiousness about her husband's return, worry about how 'perfect' the party appears to others, joy in seeing her husband hug their daughter, pride in being a good mother). Ideally though, these consumers would experience satisfaction with GAIN detergent since it made this significant family event "perfect" and momma feel "proud."

The Persuasive Impact of Empathy

In essence, empathy is a process of "participating consciousness" whereby consumers "try on" another's identity and obtain vicarious experiences with the brand in question. In advertising, identification with a character should lead to the activation and consideration of consumption-related interests and goals. Vicarious participation with this character provides consumers with means to experience the partial fulfillment of these interests and goals.

We argue that consumers' empathy, in response to a narrative ad, can be persuasive in that they *learn* about the *self-relevance* of the advertised brand. Empathizing consumers indirectly experience the self-relevant consequences associated with using or consuming the brand from the perspective of a character with whom they "share" similar interests and goals. Thus, they learn how the brand is instrumental in attaining desired goals.

Persuasion via "learned self-relevance" of course presupposes that consumers empathize with characters who are featured interacting with the brand in self-relevant ways. Consumers who empathize with "peripheral characters" (i.e., those with little stake in the advertised brand) will not likely *experience* brand consequences (Boller 1990). We suggest that one step toward evaluating the potential effectiveness of a narrative advertisement should involve assessing the execution in terms of its ability to generate empathy with characters whose experiences are "central" to the advertised brand.

EMPATHY, PERSUASION AND THE GAIN AD

In this section, we offer an informal procedure for thinking about the relationship between narrative ad execution and its potential ability to communicate self-relevant brand experiences. Although this "procedure" is presently sketchy, we believe it can provide a fundamental basis for developing testable hypotheses concerning an ad's effectiveness. Therefore, our comments about the GAIN commercial itself are intended as "points for subsequent testing."

Empathic Potential

As conceptualized in this paper, empathy is a natural process through which people attempt to understand the experiences of others. During exposure to a narrative ad however, there are numerous factors that might hinder the development of this process. For instance, we believe most would agree that factors such as casting, acting, direction and editing all influence the development of empathy. Slip-shod execution is highly distracting, and renders imaginative participation in the portrayed experiences difficult, if not impossible. The detrimental effects of poor technical execution are rather obvious, and we will not belabor them further. Instead, we consider the potential empathy-hindering effects of 1) narration, 2) weak character development, and 3) questionable verisimilitude.

Narration. Many narrative advertisements, including the GAIN commercial, use overt narration to embellish character thoughts and feelings and thus elaborate their experiences. Unfortunately, narration tends to interfer with the development of empathy by distancing consumers from the characters (cf. Aristotle's *Poetics*). When narrators provide verbal interpretations of character thoughts and feelings, consumer empathy is tantamount to redundancy--there is no need for vicarious participation if interpretations of experience have already been provided. More importantly though, narration can often prove to be distracting, particularly if the narrator's interpretations of character thoughts and feelings are inconsistent with consumers' vicarious experience of the same. In all fairness though, there is a good argument for the use of narration. Specifically, consumers rarely give narrative *advertisements* the same level of attention they give to cinema, novels or theater. Thus, narration ensures that consumers will at least be exposed to a verbal rendering of the characters' experiences, losses in empathy notwithstanding.

Weak character development. Before consumers can empathize with an ad character, they must be given an opportunity to "know" that character. Identification, in particular, will be difficult if little information about a character's identity is provided. Narrative advertisements that are short in length, those that contain many different characters, and/or those that spend a great deal of time on setting and action may contain character development inadequate for the development of empathy. The GAIN commercial is a mere 30 seconds--sufficient length by conventional, argumentative ad standards, but relatively short by narrative standards. Very little time exists to fully develop the character of the "young momma." As such, consumer empathy with this character may be rather shallow.

Questionable verisimilitude. Broadly defined, verisimilitude refers to the believability of character actions and dialogue, within the context of the story (Todorov 1977). The portrayed experiences must be consistent with consumers' own general understanding of human experience for the story to possess verisimilitude. If consumers perceive a narrative ad to be contrived or hokey (i.e., lacking in verisimilitude), empathy will probably fail to develop (Wells 1989).

The GAIN commercial contains at several areas of concern regarding verisimilitude. First, the chicken barbeque (opening scene) may possess verisimilitude problems. The intended target audience for this commercial is clearly Southern women. Unfortunately, many areas in the South consider chicken barbeque an act of heresy, particularly for an event as significant as a family homecoming--pork is the favored meat for barbeques. Although some may find this concern somewhat trite, we believe that it is possible for some Southern consumers to note the oversight, assume that the characters in the commercial are pretending to be Southern and view subsequent actions and dialogue as unbelievable. A second area of concern can be noted in the "young momma's" emotional reaction to the reunion between her husband and their daughter. Given the story context, consumers are asked to believe that her "joyful gasp" is more a function of her pride in her daughter's clean smelling clothes than the excitement of the reunion itself. This inference may be too difficult for even the most imaginative of consumers to accept.

Communication of Brand Experience

At this point, we will assume that the GAIN execution provides sufficient empathic potential, and move to the next step in our assessment procedure. Here, we ask two questions. First, with which of the featured characters will the intended target audience likely empathize? Second, is the advertised brand an integral component of this character's depicted experiences?

Three characters are featured in the GAIN commercial--the young momma, the returning husband, and the young daughter. If the intended target audience is narrowly defined as working-class Southern women, these consumers will most likely empathize with the "young momma" character. Their identification with this character may be especially strong if 1) they are married to soldier, 2) have young children, and 3) do not take offense to being called a "momma." If, however, the target audience is more broadly defined to include professional Southern women, it is unclear with which of the three characters they may empathize-- the "momma" characterization is very restrictive.

Assuming that the "young momma" character is the likely target for consumer empathy, we now need to examine whether this character's interactions with the brand are sufficient to convey meaningful brand experiences. Apart from a "quick-edit visual" of "young momma" finishing her laundry with GAIN detergent in the foreground, this character's interaction with the brand is primarily limited to her "joyful gasp" reaction to the father/daughter reunion. If the previously mentioned concern regarding verisimilitude does not arise, empathizing consumers may experience a powerful, self-relevant consequence associated with consuming GAIN detergent--pride. If the verisimilitude concern does arise, it is not clear what sort of brand experience these empathizing consumers may obtain.

Concluding Remarks

In this paper, we have outlined a conceptual framework for understanding the potential effects of narrative ads. Our conceptualization of empathy, coupled with discussions about its antecedents and effects, is intended to provide an informed basis for rethinking the manner in which consumers can experience ad meanings. We hope that our analysis of the GAIN commercial (tentative as it is) demonstrates the critical need for research on empathy and narrative ad processing.

REFERENCES

Aristotle (1987), *Poetics I: with The Tractatus Coislinianus, A Hypothetical Reconstruction of Poetics II, and The Fragments of the On Poets*, trans., R. Janko, Indianapolis: Hackett Publishing Company.

Boller, Gregory W. (1990), "The Vicissitudes of Product Experience: 'Songs of Our Consuming Selves' in Drama Ads," in *Advances in Consumer Research*, eds., M. Goldberg, G. Gorn and R. Pollay, Association for Consumer Research, 621-626.

Booth, Wayne C. (1961), *The Rhetoric of Fiction*, Chicago: The University of Chicago Press.

Bruner, Jerome (1986), *Actual Minds, Possible Worlds*, Cambridge, MA: Harvard University Press.

Burke, Kenneth (1969), *A Rhetoric of Motives*, Berkeley, CA: University of California Press.

Deighton, John, Daniel Romer and Josh McQueen (1989), "Using Drama to Persuade," *Journal of Consumer Research*, 16 (December), 335-343.

Katz, Robert L. (1963), *Empathy: Its Nature and Uses*, London: The Free Press of Glencoe.

Laing, R. D. (1982), *The Voice of Experience*, New York: Pantheon Books.

Martin, Wallace (1986), *Recent Theories of Narrative*, Ithaca, NY: Cornell University Press.

Petty, Richard E., John T. Cacioppo and David Schumann (1983), "Central and Peripheral Routes to Advertising Effectiveness: The Moderating Role of Involvement," *Journal of Consumer Research*, 10 (September), 135-146.

Todorov, Tzvetan (1977), *The Poetics of Prose*, trans., R. Howard, Ithaca, NY: Cornell University Press.

Wells, William D. (1989), "Lectures and Dramas," in *Cognitive and Affective Responses to Advertising*, eds., P. Cafferata and A. Tybout, Lexington, MA: Lexington Books, 13-20.

Segmentation in Consumer and Market Research: Applications, Current Issues and Trends
David W. Stewart, University of Southern California, Los Angeles
Michael A. Kamins, University of Southern California, Los Angeles

AN APPLICATION OF SEGMENTATION RESEARCH IN THE TRAVEL AND LEISURE INDUSTRY: THE CASE OF HILTON HOTELS (A SYNOPSIS)

Renee' Zakoor, Hilton Hotels Corporation
(Condensed by Dr. Michael A. Kamins)

The focus of this presentation examined how Hilton Hotels Corporation uses segmentation research in the development of successful marketing programs. Consistent with her objective, Ms. Zakoor discussed two specific examples relating to the business traveler and the weekend leisure traveler at Hilton.

In the development of marketing strategy, it was noted that Hilton closely monitors industry trends. Specifically, according to recent information (1988) from the U.S. travel data center, it was noted that while overall travel has increased recently, the average number of nights spent away from home has decreased. The inference made was that while people travel more often, their trips are of shorter duration. When this information was examined in more depth through sub-classification, some interesting trends appeared. Specifically, the data was found to show that business travel volume has remained relatively flat over the past few years whereas leisure travel volume has increased. Moreover, both business and leisure trips have been shortened. Therefore, it can be concluded that vacation travel has increased in frequency and declined in duration, whereas business trips, while relatively stable in frequency, have shortened in duration.

While three quarters of all travel in the United States in 1988 was for leisure purposes, at Hilton, the majority of travel was for business (approximately 60%). This fact, coupled with the information above, had specific implications for Hilton's marketing efforts for both the business *and* the leisure traveler.

Taking the business traveler first, it was noted that internal tracking studies at Hilton revealed that the business traveler who stays at Hilton can be classified into four (4) distinct categories or segments which differ demographically as follows:

- "no surprises" - (25% of frequent business travelers). These individuals typically look for a hotel which anticipates problems. They prefer chain hotels to avoid the unfamiliar.

- "shoppers" - (24% of frequent business travelers). These individuals represent a growing segment of individuals who are typically looking for the best accommodations at any price.

- "best of everything" - (31% of frequent business travelers). These individuals are prestige-oriented and wish to be recognized and valued as frequent guests. They wish to receive personal and attentive service. They are the wealthiest segment (average income is $72,000).

- "games players" - (20% of frequent business travelers). These individuals are very loyal to hotels and airlines that offer frequency programs. They are the youngest segment (average age is 41).

It was noted that the "best of everything" and "games players" segments account for almost two-thirds of business travelers' hotel stays and, hence, these segments are of particular interest to Hilton. Specifically, to address the needs of the "best of everything" segment, Hilton reportedly introduced Towers Floors to cater to the needs of this traveler. They continually refine this product as the needs of this segment change. Regarding the "games players," Hilton introduced the Hilton Honors Frequent Guest Program which is currently reported to be the second largest program in the industry in terms of membership.

Regarding the leisure traveler, the trend noted earlier was for shorter trips. This has contributed to the weekend get-away becoming a growing market in the travel industry. Hilton strategy was to take advantage of this phenomenon by expanding its weekend discount strategy to a consumer "end benefit" marketing strategy that focuses on the needs of tired couples and families to "bounce back" from the stress of hectic schedules and work week. Therefore, the concept of the bounceback weekend was created.

It was reported that the bounceback strategy was developed with the reliance on some key emerging consumer lifestyle trends such as--more people working, busier schedules, less time for relaxation and fun. The underlying premise guiding the strategy was that Americans have allowed their leisure time to be regulated to the narrow time frame known as "the weekend" and, as such, do not seem to be getting as much relaxation/refreshment from the time as they should. Research conducted for Hilton using a telephone omnibus survey through R.H. Bruskin Associates and involving 1,024 interviews supported this premise. That is, it was found that most people start their weekends tired and by the end of the weekend, very few feel any more energetic than when the weekend began. Specifically, on average during weekends, people spend about eight hours less than they would like on relaxing activities and about six-and-a-half more hours than they want to doing chores.

According to Hilton research, the solution to the dilemma of a non-relaxing weekend with too many chores is to get away. To address this need, Hilton designed the bounceback weekend, a get-away break which allows the guest to relax and recharge from a stressful week. Hilton also prepared a "guide to bouncing back" which provides helpful hints on how to manage the week so that one can get away and get the *most* relaxation from the weekend.

A multi-million dollar advertising campaign was developed to support the program. The advertising is targeted toward younger audiences since they lead the trend toward get-away weekends, and they're an audience which Hilton wants to attract. It was reported that the results from the bounceback campaign have been very positive since February of this year. Bounceback generated more than twice the number of bookings relative to Hilton's previous weekend product.

The paper concludes by noting that "finding a need and filling it is the core of the marketing process. Research is the catalytic force that enables Hilton to identify these needs and once identified, to build a product that successfully fills these needs."

CASE STUDIES ON THE USAGE OF SEGMENTATION IN MARKET RESEARCH. (A SYNOPSIS)

Bill Heiland, Custom Research Inc.
(Condensed by Dr. Michael A. Kamins)

Three different case studies on the use of segmentation in market research were discussed. These studies illustrated the use of different techniques in segmentation research as well as different types of data.

Mr. Heiland made the point that everyone segments in virtually every quantitative study since the banners in a cross tabulation are really a priori segment definitions. Specifically, the concept is that the researcher has chosen the segments to examine, and the tabs (hopefully) indicate whether or not there are any differences between or among the columns of interest.

According to Mr. Heiland, the difference with statistical/mathematical clustering, is that first you find segments that are different, and then (hopefully) identify the segments by other variables or attributes. The presentation was limited to this case using as illustration three different techniques or applications in segmentation differing in purpose, data collected, and statistical technique.

(1) "Classic" Attitude Segmentation:

The Objective of this study was to determine groups of people who have common attitudes about eye glasses. The first stage of the study involved the collection of attitudinal statements about eye glasses from focus groups, marketing and marketing research personnel. The statements were first edited into a reduced set of 70. Then, through the use of a multi-stage Q sort procedure, each statement for each individual was categorized along an eleven point agree/disagree scale ranging from "most agree" (5) through "neutral" (0) to "most disagree" (-5). This procedure was designed to result in a rescaled data set in the shape of an inverted triangle (pseudo normal) distribution such that for a particular individual, the bulk of statements are rated within a narrow range of neutrality.

The analytical task then undertaken was a Q-factor analysis with the output (factor-scores) indicating the degree to which subjects agreed (+) or disagreed (-) with these statements. Results revealed three specific segments regarding attitudes towards eyeglasses: those consumers identified as "medically oriented," "style conscious," and "I can't be bothered." To further round out the analyses undertaken, the segments were cross-tabulated with other demographic/usage data to help in their identification. As noted by Mr. Heiland, one side benefit of this procedure is that the statements are often good starters for an ad agency's creatives.

(2) Regression Trees:

The task of this technique was described as the classification of respondents on a particular (dependent) variable (e.g., purchase intention, overall satisfaction, or sales volume) into segments determined by other (independent) variables (e.g., product characteristics such as appearance) such that the distance between the segments is maximized while each group's variance is minimized. It was noted that the advantages of this technique involve its stability, easy use of categorical data, use of surrogate variables when data for splitting variables is missing, and a lot of competitive variables (those which compete to be the splitting variable) for each split that the tree generates. It should be noted, however, that the procedure requires a sample of approximately 300 respondents to be stable.

A case study was presented to illustrate the use of this technique. It involved a dinner entree which had two forms, with no significant difference in overall purchase intent between them. Using the regression tree technique, the sample of 294 individuals was first split on the overall hedonic characteristics of the product with a sub-split regarding the appeal of product appearance. When these factors were considered it was evident that appearance of one product form was detracting from the buying intent.

(3) Importance Ratings, A Post Analysis Use of Segmentation

It was noted that when subjects are asked to evaluate the importance of product/service performance attributes prior to evaluating a competitive set of brands on performance, there is no easy way to remove the potential presence of a high/low rater effect. According to Mr. Heiland, since performance is affected by the products while importance ratings are not, a two-stage procedure was proposed and illustrated to uncover such an effect.

First, a cluster analysis was undertaken and reported on attribute importance ratings for a given product. The first break was into two segments which were high versus low raters. A Standardized Thurstone scale was then run to determine if the rank order of attribute importance ratings varied between the segments. In the example presented, they did not and the conclusion presented was that "while there are high and low raters, they don't differ in the order of importance of the attributes."

Mr. Heiland also noted that this segmentation procedure can be used as one of the effects in a general linear model (the other being the brands) to look for interactions.

Consumer Self-Selection and Segments of One: The Growing Role of Consumers in Segmentation

David W. Stewart, University of Southern California

ABSTRACT

Variance in consumer behavior is increasing and the source of this variance is increasingly under the control of the consumer. This increase in variance and the degree of control exercised by consumers poses new challenges for segmentation research. Increasingly, consumers are segmenting themselves through a process of self-selection guided by idiosyncratic purposes. The present paper suggests that segmentation strategies should begin with identification of the purposes that consumers seek to achieve through the purchase and use of products. These purposes ultimately lead consumers to place themselves in particular situations in which they seek specific benefits. This view is consistent with control theories of human behavior and recent work on consumer self-selection. The paper offers an approach to segmentation that constructs segments from building blocks defined by the individual consumer in a specific usage context.

INTRODUCTION

Consumer researchers, like most social scientists are keen observers of behavior. They may differ is what they choose to observe and the method of observation, but observation is the most basic of the research tools used by researchers interested in consumer behavior. Researchers observe responses to paper and pencil tasks such as attitude measurement scales. They observe actual purchase behavior via scanner panels. They observe behavior of individuals who are shopping and who are engaged in various consumption experiences. They even observe consumers observing themselves and reporting on the results of these observations.

Observations, of whatever types, are used to make inferences about behavior in the context in which it occurred. Sometimes the observed behavior can be easily interpreted; sometimes it appears purposeless and random. The latter types of behavior have led to the suggestion that behavior, at least at the individual level, should be treated as a stochastic process (Bass 1974) since no explanation can be discerned. Other researchers have suggested that certain types of behavior are governed by automated processes that involve no conscious thought or decision making (Olshavsky and Granbois 1979) and is, thus, in some sense without explanation. Still others (Belk 1987, Lincoln and Guba 1985) have suggested that explanation should not even be an objective of consumer research. Rather, consumer researchers should be content to describe behavior in great detail. These views of consumer behavior are not comforting for researchers seeking to build deterministic models. These views are outright discouraging for marketing managers seeking some means for influencing the behavior of consumers in the market place.

Even among those researchers who seek deterministic explanations for consumer behavior the results of observation and inferences have been disappointing. Although behavior can often be predicted well, it is seldom explained very well. Even the most controlled of experiments tend to produce results that account for ten percent or less of the variance in observed behavior. Such disappointing outcomes have led to a certain disillusionment with consumer research. This disillusionment, while not universal, has resulted in significant reductions in research staffs and expenditures on marketing research in many organizations.

Among the many tools used by consumer researchers and marketing managers alike, no tool has received as much attention and use as market segmentation. Despite this attention and frequency of use (or perhaps because of it), segmentation has been the object of frequent criticism. Davis (1987) has suggested that segments are almost always too few and too heterogeneous to be of practical value. McDonald (1985) has questioned whether any segmentation system, including recent approaches based on the availability of substantial databases, is useful for developing persuasive marketing programs. There has long been a debate about the best basis for segmentation (Dickson and Ginter 1987, Wind 1978, Wilkie and Cohen, 1977, Frank, Massy, and Wind 1972, Haley 1968), but recent criticism is directed at the concept of segmentation as a marketing strategy. This raises the question of whether segmentation has ceased to be viable as a marketing strategy, and if so, why? To answer this question a brief discussion of the relationship between variance and segmentation is required.

SEGMENTATION AND VARIANCE IN CONSUMER BEHAVIOR

It is axiomatic that any behavior, including consumer behavior, is interesting only to the extent that it exhibits variance. Indeed, it is only because variations in behavior exist among individuals and within the same individual over time that causal mechanisms can be identified. To a large extent, the very recent origin of the science of consumer behavior may be attributed to the general paucity of variance in behavior among most consumers. When most consumers have little money to spend and few options for spending it, consumer behavior is decidedly uninteresting.

Variance in consumer behavior grew perceptibly after the Second World War as a result of the increase in the affluence of consumers and the increase in the number of alternative products and services available to consumers. During the first forty years after the Second World War, students of consumer behavior and marketing tended to view consumer behavior as a *response* to marketing stimuli. The variance in consumer behavior tended to be viewed as stemming from variations in the environments of consumers. Over time, marketers came to recognize that systematic differences in the variance of consumers could be identified and market segmentation was born (Smith 1956).

Market segments have traditionally been defined in terms of the differential response (variance) of consumers to marketing stimuli- product, price, market communications. For many products, a relatively small number of segments appeared to capture most of the variance in consumer response. This did not mean that researchers failed to recognize that consumers exercised some judgment in the selection of their response, or that researchers regarded consumers as purposeless respondents to marketing stimuli. Nevertheless, when the alternatives from which consumers may choose are limited in number, it is easy to view consumers as passive respondents to marketing actions. After all, until very recently consumers had a choice of only three television networks, a modest selection of conveniently located shopping outlets, and a limited number of options with respect to product or service offerings.

In situations characterized by small variance as a result of limited options for response, the number of groupings of homogeneous consumers will, by definition, be small. In fact, in the extreme, there will exist but one group or segment. The latter circumstance may arise because consumers are actually homogeneous, but it is just as likely to arise because consumers do not have alternatives for expressing the very real differences that exist. It follows that as more alternatives are available to the consumer, more groups (segments) may emerge as expressions of the differences that exist among consumers. It is the thesis of the present paper that current dissatisfaction with segmentation reflects the growth in the number of options available to consumers and the concomitant increase in the number of segments that exist. In fact, the case can be made that the number of options available to the consumer is increasing exponentially. In the limit, the number of potential segments will equal the number of consumers when the options available to the consumer becomes very large. Segments of one are a natural consequence of the growth in alternatives available to consumers.

Segments of one may sound impractical to the marketing manager, and there will certainly be many circumstances where some aggregation is required if efficient marketing programs are to be designed and implemented. Thus, efficiency alone will force managers to look for segments of some type. Nevertheless, the approach to segmentation will need to change in order to accommodate the increase in the variation in consumer behavior. The remainder of this paper will discuss the reasons for the increase in the variance in consumer behavior, and suggest a conceptual outline for a segmentation approach that can accommodate this increase in variance.

CONSUMER ALTERNATIVES, SELF-SELECTION AND CONTROL THEORY

Recent years have seen a proliferation of alternatives from which the consumer may choose. Media options, both in broadcast and print, have grown exponentially over the past several years as cable television penetration has expanded. This proliferation of media is continuing with the advent of international television via satellite and cable, interactive computer networks such as Compuserve and Prodigy, and telephone information services. At the same time, the number of options for obtaining many products and services, the number of points of distribution, has also expanded. Catalogs, direct response, telephone, and interactive computers have taken their place as competitors to the more traditional retail outlets.

Product and service options have also proliferated as firms have made use of computer assisted-manufacturing to provide more variations of basic designs. For example, R. R. Donnelly has been a pioneer in "selective-binding" whereby magazines are "customized" for individual consumers in terms of both editorial material and advertising. Automobile manufacturers are experimenting with the production of customized option packages that will be available for delivery within 72-hours. Insurance companies now offer "cafeteria" plans that allow consumers to construct their own benefits from an extensive menu of offerings. Davis (1987) has refered to the proliferation of product and service options as mass customization. Such mass customization has been made possible by the merger of information, manufacturing, and service delivery technologies.

As noted above, one important outcome of these increasing options is that the variance in consumer behavior is increasing and an increase in variance carries with it an increase in the number of potential segments within the market. More important, a significant increase in the variance of consumer behavior may require a change in the philosophical orientation of segmentation research. It may no longer be sufficient to ask how consumers may differ in their response to marketing stimuli. It may be more important to ask to which marketing stimuli consumers will attend. Another way of saying this is that it may no longer be sufficient to ask what marketing stimuli do to consumers. Rather, it may be more appropriate to ask what consumers do to marketing stimuli. Segments of consumers will no longer be defined by marketing stimuli to which they respond. Consumers will segment themselves based on their own self-selected behaviors. This change in philosophical orientation is consistent with the growing body of literature on consumer self-selection (Zimmer and Dorfman 1985). This literature makes it very clear that consumers scan their environments for personally relevant stimuli to which they then respond (Cotton, 1985, Pechmann and Stewart 1990, Tolley 1991). Self-selection is, itself, a process. This process, while clearly an empirically demonstrable phenomenon, is not well understood.

It is obvious that an individual will selectively attend to personally relevant stimuli. The more important questions are how this process of self-selection works and how this process might be captured in segmentation research. A potentially useful framework for understanding the process of self-selection is found in a psychological theory called control theory (Powers 1973, 1978).

Control theory suggests that it is inappropriate to make inferences about human behavior solely on the basis of the observation of behavior. Rather, it is important to understand the purpose behavior serves for the actor, or consumer. Control theory suggests that the observation of behavior, without an understanding of purpose is meaningless. Indeed, behavior may appear meaningless, even random, without an understanding of purpose. Control theory suggests that human behavior is purposeful and that consumers attend to personally relevant stimuli and engage in strategic behaviors that are designed to realize specific goals. Further, it suggests that behavior, in and of itself, is of no importance. Behavior occurs only for the purpose of controlling consequences that affect the actor (Powers 1978). Note that this is a very different view from the Skinnerian view that behavior is controlled by its consequences (Skinner 1938).

Control theory suggests that an explanation of behavior must include definition of the purpose of the actor. Two identical behaviors may, in fact, be carried out for very different purposes. Two highly dissimilar behaviors may, in actuality, be designed to achieve the same outcome. The interpretation of the meaning of the behavior is not possible without knowledge of the purpose of the behavior, which serves as a kind of reference signal. Marketers and consumer behavior researchers have not ignored the purposefulness of consumer behavior or the self-selection that characterizes much of consumer response to marketing stimuli. Recognition of the purposes that provide the foundation of consumer behavior has led to the use of means-ends analyses (laddering) (Gutman 1982, Reynolds and Gutman 1988) as an approach for linking behavior to consumer purposes. Nevertheless, such analyses are infrequent and have seldom been systematically linked to market segmentation. More often than not, purpose is inferred from the point of view of the observer, rather than from the point of view of the actor. This has tended to be the case regardless of whether experimental observation or more naturalistic observation served as the basis for the inference.

AN ILLUSTRATIVE TALE

Imagine an individual sitting in front of a computer screen and at apparently random intervals moving a control stick in some direction. The probability of moving the control stick increases with the amount of time since the last movement, and the direction of movement, measured in degrees, follows a uniform distribution. Now assume a whole room of such individuals sitting at a computer screen and moving a control stick. Using models that are quite familiar to mathematical modelers of consumer behavior, it would be possible to predict accurately the number of individuals at any given point in time who will move the control stick and the direction of that movement. Missing from this analysis are the reasons the individuals are sitting at a computer screen and moving a control stick. Neither is there any information about how the probability of movement or the direction of movement might be influenced. Dissatisfied with mere prediction, a researcher observing this situation may decide to construct an experiment. He obtains his own computer and control stick. He brings in respondents and instructs them that their task is to keep a pointer on the computer screen within a circle that is moving about the screen. After forty respondents have participated in the task, the researcher observes that there is a direct correspondence, subject to some error perturbation, between the movement of the circle on the screen and the frequency and direction of a respondent's movement of the control stick. The researcher shouts "Eureka!" and races out to observe the circles to which all of the earlier subjects were responding. Much to the researcher's chagrin, he finds no circles moving about the computer screens. He *knows* that moving circles influence the movement of a control stick; he has empirical evidence from the laboratory. But wait, this is a clever and creative researcher. Upon pondering the situation he concludes that the circle does not have to be physically present on the screen. He posits a "latent circle" that exists in the mind of the actor. He reasons that this latent circle guides the behavior of the control stick.

The clever researcher sets out to test his new theory of latent circles. Being well trained at a leading research university he knows that he will need to carry out several studies employing different methodologies if he is to establish the credibility of his theory. He designs two studies. In the first, he observes behavior and asks a representative group of respondents where they would place a circle that would guide the movements he has observed. With the exception of a couple of troublemakers who insisted they did not use circles, all of the respondents place the circle in the expected location. The data from the two troublemakers cannot be included in the analysis, and they are dropped from the sample. A retrospective study is subject to various confounding effects, however, so the researcher conducts a second study.

In the second study, respondents are asked to imagine that a circle exists on the screen. The task of the respondents is to use a control stick to keep the cursor within the imagined circle on the screen. The researcher finds that there is a direct relationship between the location respondents reported for their latent circles and their movement of a control stick. The researcher concludes that his theory is supported, writes an award winning journal article, receives a chaired professorship, and spends the rest of his days training students to do research on latent circles and pondering the metaphysical implications of latent circle theory.

Unfortunately, all is not well. Latent circle theory just does not help predict how the average person sitting at a computer will move a control stick. If respondents are asked about circles, the theory seems to work retrospectively. If respondents are asked to specify the location of a circle immediately prior to moving a control stick, the theory works well too. But, when measures of latent circles are obtained several days prior to the interaction with the computer they do not predict very well, even when the respondent claims to be using them. Even more troubling is the finding that distractor tasks, like computer games, seem to eliminate the influence of latent circles.

A second researcher, after years of work on latent circles, decides it is time for a new paradigm. This second researcher hypothesizes that latent circle theory is little more than the stage management of behavior. This researcher sets out to visit people who interact with computers and use control sticks. He obtains a large grant from a well known institute, solicits the cooperation of a number of other social scientists who are disillusioned with latent circle theory, and sets out to find users of computers. As he and his band of researchers cross the country, they interview numerous users of computers; some are interviewed even as they use the computer.

The outcome of the second researcher's odyssey produces a remarkable variety of human responses. One respondent used the control stick to play a computer game that demanded considerable eye-hand coordination. This respondent reported an affinity for the game that bordered on the religious. A second respondent, an accountant, reported use of the control stick to access menu commands on a spreadsheet program. This respondent suggested that he only engaged in such behavior because he was paid to complete a particular task, a decidedly secular motivation. Other respondents were interviewed, and each offered his or her own idiosyncratic response.

The second researcher, upon pondering all that he has learned, concludes that latent circle theory is vacuous; it does not capture the richness of responses he has discovered. More important, there are such interesting idiosyncrasies among respondents. Each has his or her own unique interpretation of behavior. Even the same behavior, using a computer and a control stick, can be explained in numerous ways. There is no single explanation, no single reality. He declares the old paradigm dead; long live the GO Observe Demonstrable Verbal Interactive Boundary Expanding Solutions (GOOD VIBES) Paradigm.

The second researcher writes several widely acclaimed papers, develops a cult following in the field, receives a chaired professorship from his university, and spends the remainder of his days enjoying conversations with interesting individuals who are not university professors, have no aspirations to be university professors, and have found meaning in life outside the confines of a university campus.

Alas, there is still discontent in the land. A middle-aged (in years only. Psychologically he/she is in her/his late 20's) marketing researcher sits reading a series of memoranda from corporate management. One informs him/her of the downsizing of the marketing research department (she/he has been spared, for the moment). A second memorandum asks the researcher whether she/he might be interested in a transfer to sales management at a substantial increase in compensation. A third memorandum is from an obviously peeved vice president of marketing who has just caught grief from other members of the corporate operating committee for a decline in sales and an increase in marketing costs. This vice president suggests that the problem is the current segmentation system, which appears no better and perhaps worse than the last two. She is particularly peeved that the advertising designed to attract new users of the corporation's services seems to have high recall among only current users, and on the persuasion measure the current strategy seems to produce a net switch to competitors. On the other hand, the price promotion designed to hold current users in the face of competitive price promotions seems to have attracted some new customers, but has caused some existing customers to complain about reductions in the quality of service delivery and, in some cases, actually switch to a competitor.

This industry researcher is dismayed by the frequency with which the firm has changed segmentation strategies. She is also dismayed by the lack of direction provided by academic researchers. She is a student of researcher one, the founder of latent circle theory. She helped obtain support from her corporation for the work of professor two, who founded the GOOD VIBES movement. She appreciates the contributions or both researchers, but she finds no solution to her firm's segmentation and marketing problems in their work. She wonders if there is a way to combine elements of the two approaches, so she visits some users of computers in her own firm. She asks each in turn what they are doing. Like professor two, she receives a variety of responses. Each user seems to have some unique reason for using the computer. Even those individuals who claim similar purposes have selected different computers, different control devices, and different software. On the other hand, several users who report very different purposes are using identical control sticks, identical computers, and even identical software. She also observes that all individuals use a control stick. Apparently, the control stick is used to move a pointer around the screen.

The corporate researcher decides to ask a few more questions. After asking the more general question about purpose, the researcher probes. An interesting pattern begins to emerge. The type of computer, control stick, and software selected appear to be related to each individual's general purpose. Each individual can explain the purpose behind their use of the computer. Individual variations in equipment and software used for the same or similar purposes are explained as the outcome of slight differences in what the individual users are trying to accomplish and by differences in the characteristics of the users.

The industry researcher continues to ask questions. She observes each individual moving the control device and asks what the movement is designed to accomplish. Each respondent indicates that the benefit they are seeking from the movement of the control stick is the placement of the cursor at a certain point on the computer screen (could this validate latent circle theory?). The placement of the cursor is not random, however. It is related to particular outcomes that the individual user is seeking, and constraints that are imposed by the software, hardware, and control stick. For example, one individual frequently moves the control stick forward because, he explains, this is the way to move the cursor to a set of menus located at the top of the computer screen. The pattern was complete. The individual behaviors of individual respondents were the outcome of a complex process. The process was guided by the self-selection of specific purposes. These purposes in turn, guided the selection of tools with specific characteristics. The characteristics of the tools, in turn, constrained the nature of specific observable behaviors.

The industry researcher now knows how to segment markets. She rushes to explain her insights to the vice president for marketing. After listening patiently, the vice president of marketing dismissed the plan as too expensive and time consuming. The industry researcher also shared her insights with her mentor, the founder of latent circle theory. He listened patiently and complimented the researcher for her insights. He also suggested that the behavioral process she had identified could never be submitted to empirical test; there were too many variables to control and subjects would have too much latitude for influencing outcomes. The industry researcher also shared her insights with the founder of the GOOD VIBES movement. He also listened patiently and complimented the researcher's insight. He told her that her view was certainly one of many possible truths, but he found that the process she described lost too much of the rich artistic component of behavior for him to find it useful.

The disappointed industry researcher left her job and founded a consulting firm that applied her insights to the analysis of markets. She grew wealthy and traveled throughout the world (since most of her clients are European and Japanese). At last report she was splitting her time between her Beverly Hills home and her chalet outside Geneva.

What is the point of these stories? It is quite simple. Consumer behavior is complex and it is largely under the control of the consumer. Even the constraints on behavior that may be present are frequently the result of a process of self-selection. Consumers choose situations that suit particular purposes and use products and services that are appropriate for achieving these purposes in given situations. Consumers behave in order to achieve specific consequences that are consistent with specific purposes. This view of consumer behavior has some important implications for segmentation research.

SOME NORMATIVE IMPLICATIONS OF CONTROL THEORY AND CONSUMER SELF-SELECTION FOR MARKET SEGMENTATION

Consumer purposefulness and self-selection suggest that individuals interact with their environment to achieve specific consequences. This means that genuinely useful market segmentation must explicitly incorporate consumer purposefulness and the interaction of the individual consumer and his/her environment. The importance of the interaction of person and environment for segmentation research has been discussed elsewhere (Dickson 1982, Punj and Stewart 1983). Rather than repeat this discussion, the remainder of the present paper outlines a conceptual approach for segmentation research.

1. *Segmentation should begin with discovery of the purpose(s) for which consumers acquire and use individual products and services.* It is the consumer's purpose that drives the processes of information search and acquisition, weighting of information, formation of impressions and attitudes, decision making, and post-purchase evaluation. Research designed to discover consumer purposes is inherently qualitative in is early stages, but in its latter stages, it can also include the construction of taxonomies of purposes, benefits, and use occasions. Consumers self-select from an array of purposes those which require action over the short, intermediate, and long term. Understanding of any particular behavior will be incomplete without an understanding of purpose and the consumer's process of self-selection.

2. *Purposes occur within the context of situations.* These situations include potential use occasions, benefits sought, and consequences to be avoided. Consumers engage in a conscious process of selecting situations that are consistent with a particular purpose and avoiding those situations that are inconsistent with a particular purpose. A mapping of situations (usage and purchase situations) into purposes can provide insight into the consumer's process of self-selection.

3. *Benefits sought from products and services grow directly from purposes and usage contexts.* Specific product benefits are, except at the most abstract level, insufficient for determining the purposes of consumers. Benefits (consequences) that are desirable for some purposes and for particular situational contexts may be undesirable and actively avoided for other purposes and in different situations. A mapping of benefits into purposes and use occasions is necessary if consumer behavior is to be predicted over the long term. Benefit segmentation (Haley 1968), is a necessary, but insufficient basis for segmentation, particularly over the long term.

4. *The relative importance of product features and attributes are key determinants of consumer preference and choices. The importance of product features and attributes will vary both across and within individual consumers as a function of benefits sought, usage situation, and purpose.* Thus, the importance of product features and attributes should be measured for each benefit and use occasion for which the product is appropriate (in the view of the consumer). These importance ratings should ultimately be mapped into consumer purposes.

5. *The set of products that the consumer considers appropriate for providing particular benefits and for realizing specific purposes will vary as a function, of purpose, use occasion, and benefits sought.* Thus, for *each* identifiable use occasion, a set of products the consumer views as substitutes should be identified. This set of products should include those that the consumer produces for himself or herself.

6. *The consumer's evaluation (or expectations) of product performance will vary across purposes, use occasions, and benefits sought.* Evaluations of the relative performance of products will also vary by purpose, use occasion, and benefit sought. Thus, performance evaluation cannot be measured in an absolute sense; it can only be obtained relative to the use of other products or services that the consumer considers appropriate for a given purpose, benefit, and use occasion.

7. *A frequent assumption of many choice modeling exercises is that relative ratings of product performance may be combined with consumer's importance weighting to describe and ultimately predict choice. There is a general recognition in the literature that this type of exercise must be done at the individual level (Shocker, Stewart, and Zahorik 1990a&b) because importance weights may differ from individual to individual.* On the other hand, most choice modeling exercises make an important simplifying assumption. This assumption is that all consumers use the same decision rule, namely, a compensatory rule. Research on consumer decision making is quite clear, however, that single-stage compensatory rules are used by consumers less frequently than other rules.

Consumers often use multi-stage decision strategies, screening out many alternatives on the basis of one or a few attributes. Simple heuristics, brand based or not, are among the more common decision rules used by consumers. For example, research has shown the lexicographic rule to be one of the more common rules employed by consumers (Reilly and Holman 1977). Screening strategies and heuristics used by consumers tend to be highly idiosyncratic and are driven by both the consumer's purpose and situational constraints such as budgets, time, and product availability. Individual difference characteristics, factors such as expertise, need for cognition, and involvement, have figured prominently in research on consumer decision making. *An important implication of consumers' use of idiosyncratic decision rules for market segmentation is that modeling of choice behavior must be at the level of the individual and must provide a means for capturing idiosyncratic choice rules used by consumers.* This is a far more complex and formidable task than modeling choice based on a uniform decision rule. Nevertheless, it is an approach that is consistent with the purposeful self-selection of consumers-consumers select alternatives for comparison, they select attributes on which to base their decisions, and they select decision rules which suit their purposes, their circumstances, and their individual characteristics.

Identification of individual choice rules is the last stage in the segmentation process. Note that choice rules are specific to individuals and are context bound, that is, the rules apply only for choices among a specific set of alternatives that are evaluated within a specific usage or purchase situation in order to acquire specific benefits for a specific purpose. The results of this operation are occasion specific market segments consisting of a single consumer. In fact, each consumer may represent multiple segments, one segment for each occasion. This represents the most basic unit for segmentation research.

Obviously, for most products and services, individual by use occasion segments are impractical as units to which marketing actions can be targeted. Some type of aggregation will be necessary to provide a smaller number of segments for which marketing plans can be formulated and implemented. The issue is not whether aggregation should occur, but what the building block for such aggregation should be. The foregoing discussion suggests that the building block for segmentation should be the individual within use of occasion.

SOME ADVANTAGES OF INDIVIDUAL BY OCCASION BUILDING BLOCKS

For many products and services, those with single and simple uses, the individual by occasion building block will reduce to the simple, individual level approach to segmentation that has been typical of past research. Aggregation may be quite straight-forward in these circumstances. More complex products and services, that offer multiple benefits and have the potential to serve multiple purposes, will offer more interesting opportunities for complex segmentation typologies based on individual by occasion building blocks. Such segmentation offers a number of potential advantages for the marketer and the consumer:

1. The approach provides a basis for offering individually customized products and services where it is economically justifiable (and this is increasingly the case in numerous product categories);

2. It directly maps product attributes, benefits, and use occasions into one another and links them to purposive consumer behavior;

3. It explicitly recognizes that consumers may use information in different ways. Consumers selectively attend to information and frequently adopt idiosyncratic decision rules. Knowledge of this selectivity and idiosyncrasy provides a better understanding of consumer behavior and a foundation for more effective marketing programs;

4. It shifts the focus of segmentation away from marketing actions and stimuli, and to the consumer and his or her purposes. As such, the approach is more consistent with the concept of consumer sovereignty. It also explicitly recognizes that consumers segment themselves through a process of self-selection. Marketers and consumer researchers merely discover these segments.

The question may arise as to whether the approach to segmentation outlined above can be implemented in any practical and economical fashion. The experience of a number of firms suggests the answer is yes despite the greater demands for data collection and analysis the procedure imposes.

CONCLUSION

The increasing number of options available to consumers has resulted in an exponential increase in the variance of consumer behavior. This increased variance is at least partially the result of consumers' exercising greater self-selection. This self-selection, in turn, has moved the locus of segmentation from the marketer to the consumer. Discovery of these consumer defined segments requires a more complex approach to segmentation that recognizes the purposefulness of consumer behavior and uses individual by use occasion as the basic building block for segmentation.

REFERENCES

Bass, F. (1974), "The Theory of Stochastic Preference and Brand Switching," *Journal of Marketing Research*, 11 (February), 1-20.

Belk, R. (1987), "The Role of the Odyssey in Consumer Behavior and in Consumer Research," *Advances in Consumer Research*, Vol. 14, (Provo, Utah: Association for Consumer Research), pp. 357-361.

Cotton, John L. (1985), "Cognitive Dissonance in Selective Exposure," in D. Zillman and J. Bryant (Eds.), *Selective Exposure to Communication*, (Hillsdale, NJ: Lawrence Erlbaum Associates, Inc.), 11-34.

Davis, S. M. (1987), *Future Perfect*, (New York: Addison Wesley).

Dickson, P. P. (1982), "Person-Situation: Segmentation's Missing Link," *Journal of Marketing*, 46 (Fall), 56-64.

Dickson, P. P. and J. L. Ginter (1987), "Market Segmentation, Product Differentiation, and Marketing Strategy," *Journal of Marketing*, 51 (April), 1-10.

Frank, R. E., W. F. Massy, and Y. Wind (1972), *Market Segmentation*, (Englewood Cliffs, N.J.: Prentice-Hall).

Gutman, J. (1982), "A Means-End Chain Model Based on Customer Categorization Processes," *Journal of Marketing*, 46 (Spring), 60-72.

Haley, R.I. (1968), "Benefit Segmentation: A Decision-Oriented Research Tool," *Journal of Marketing*, 32 (July), 30-35.

Y. S. Lincoln and E. G. Guba (1985), *Naturalistic Inquiry*, (Beverly Hills, Calif.: Sage).

F. P. McDonald (1985), "Whither the New Segmentation Systems," *Marketing and Media Decisions*, 20 (6), 94, 96.

Olshavsky, R. W. and D. H. Granbois (1979), "Consumer Decision Making - Fact or Fiction," *Journal of Consumer Research*, 6 (September), 98-100.

Pechmann, C. and D.W. Stewart (1990), "The Role of Comparative Advertising: Documenting Its Effects on Attention, Recall, and Purchase Intentions," *Journal of Consumer Research*, 17 (September), 180-191.

Powers, W. T. (1973), "Feedback: Beyond Behaviorism," *Science*, 179, (Jan. 26), 351-356.

Powers, W. T. (1978), "Quantitative Analysis of Purposive Systems: Some Spadework at the Foundations of Scientific Psychology," *Psychological Review*, 85, 417-435.

Punj, G. N. and D. W. Stewart (1983), "An Interaction Framework of Consumer Decision Processes," *Journal of Consumer Research*, 10 (September), 181-196.

Reilly, M. and R. Holman (1977), "Does Task Complexity or Cue Intercorrelation Affect Choice of an Information Processing Strategy: An Empirical Investigation," in W. D. Perreault, Jr. (Ed.), *Advances in Consumer Research*, Vol. 4 (Chicago: Association for Consumer Research), 185-190.

Reynolds, T. J. and J. Gutman (1988), "Laddering Theory, Method, Analysis, and Interpretation," *Journal of Advertising Research*, 28 (February/March), 10-31.

Shocker, A. D., D. W. Stewart, and A. J. Zahorik (1990a), "Mapping Customer Perceptions of Markets," *Journal of Management Issues*, 2 (Summer), 127-159.

Shocker, A. D., D. W. Stewart, and A. J. Zahorik (1990b), "Mapping Competitive Relationships: Practice, Problems, and Promises," in G. Day, B. Weitz, and R. Wensley (Eds.), *The Interfaces of Marketing and Strategy*, (Greenwich, CT: JAI Press).

Skinner, B. F. (1938), *The Behavior of Organisms*, (New York: Appleton-Century-Crofts).

Smith, W.R. (1956), "Product Differentiation and Market Segmentation as Alternative Marketing Strategies," *Journal of Marketing*, 21 (July), 3-8.

Tolley, R.S. (1991), "The Search: Patterns of Newspaper Readership," in E. Clark, T. Brock, and D.W. Stewart (Eds.), *Advertising and Consumer Psychology*, (Hillsdale, NJ: Lawrence Erlbaum Associates, Inc.).

Wilkie, W. L. and J. B. Cohen (1977), "An Overview of Market Segmentation: Behavioral Concepts and Research Approaches," Working Paper, (Cambridge, Mass.: Marketing Science Institute).

Wind, Yoram (1978), "Issues and Advances in Segmentation Research," *Journal of Marketing Research*, 15 (August), 317.

Zimmer, D. and J. Bryant (1985), *Selective Exposure to Communication*, (Hillsdale, NJ: Lawrence Erlbaum Associates, Inc.).

The Importance of Peripheral Cues in Attitude Formation for Enduring and Task Involved Individuals

Robin A. Higie, University of Connecticut
Lawrence F. Feick, University of Pittsburgh
Linda L. Price, University of Colorado at Boulder

ABSTRACT

This research examines the importance of a communication's peripheral cues to consumers with enduring and task involvement. In particular, the study experimentally manipulated subjects' task involvement and the spokesperson's product category expertise. Subjects' enduring involvement with the product category was measured. Our results indicate that both enduring and task involvement increase attention to product-related information, but suggest that there are other important processing differences between the two types of involvement. Specifically, consumers with enduring involvement focus more on the spokesperson in the ad, and their attitudes are more dependent on spokesperson expertise.

INTRODUCTION

Over the years, researchers have examined the effects of numerous consumer characteristics on processing style and ad persuasiveness. One characteristic of considerable interest has been consumer involvement. Although pioneers in involvement used the concept more generally, recent research distinguishes among types of involvement. In this study, we focus on the distinction between task involvement which is transitory and due to particular situations, and enduring involvement which is lasting and independent of situations (Celsi and Olson 1988; Houston and Rothschild 1978; Richins and Bloch 1986).

The present research examines the differential importance of peripheral cues for people with different levels of enduring and task involvement. We test the proposition that consumers with varying levels of enduring and task involvement differentially attend to a peripheral cue: spokesperson expertise. In addition, we examine the effects of these two types of involvement on various measures of persuasion, including individuals' attitudes toward the ad and brand, and intention to buy.

THEORY

Involvement has been a focus of much research in advertising and marketing. Over the years, the involvement construct has been conceptualized and operationalized in many ways (Houston and Rothschild 1978; Laurent and Kapferer 1985). Therefore, before discussing specific hypotheses, it is important to carefully define and distinguish between enduring and task involvement.

Enduring Involvement

Research in marketing on enduring involvement dates to Houston and Rothschild (1978). Enduring involvement is an intrinsically motivated individual difference variable that is relatively long-lasting, and the focus of an individual's enduring involvement may be either a product or an activity. Enduring involvement varies with the degree to which the product is related to the individual's self-image or the pleasure received from thoughts about or the use of the product (Higie and Feick 1989). Research dealing with various product categories supports the hedonic and self-expression components of enduring involvement (Bloch 1981,1982; Richins and Bloch 1986). In other words, people not only find pleasure in products, but also use objects to help develop and project self-image (Belk 1988; Csikszentmihalyi and Rochberg-Halton 1981).

Task Involvement

Researchers have also examined involvement that is externally motivated, referred to as situational sources of personal relevance (Celsi and Olson 1988), issue involvement (Chaiken 1980; Petty and Cacioppo 1979), and situational involvement (Richins and Bloch 1986; Houston and Rothschild 1978). In such cases, factors or consequences associated with a particular task or situation result in some level of personal relevance. We refer to this type of involvement as task involvement. Researchers have examined naturally occurring task involvement, e.g., consumers considering product alternatives to purchase (Richins and Bloch 1986), but more commonly have used experimental manipulations to approximate the effects of naturally occurring task involvement (Celsi and Olson 1988; Park and Young 1986; Petty, Cacioppo and Schumann 1983).

Amount of Information Processing

Research has documented that consumers who have enduring involvement attend to product-related ads and magazines and think more about product-relevant information (Bloch, Sherrell and Ridgway 1986; Celsi and Olson 1988; Richins and Bloch 1986). Similarly, research demonstrates that people who have naturally occurring (Richins and Bloch 1986) or experimentally manipulated (Celsi and Olson 1988; Park and Young 1986; Petty, Cacioppo and Schumann 1983) task involvement attend to and process product-relevant information more than people who are not task involved. Thus, individuals should generate more thoughts the greater is either their enduring or task involvement.

Focus of Information Processing

Because people with task and enduring involvement are driven by different motivations, the focus of their thoughts is expected to differ. The

Elaboration Likelihood Model and its supporting research (Petty, Cacioppo and Schumann 1983) suggest that individuals with high task involvement focus more on brand attribute information and less on peripheral cues (information other than brand attribute information) in deriving overall attitudes and impressions about a brand. Empirical tests of this theory have found that peripheral cues, such as source expertise, celebrity status, and attractiveness, are less important determinants of attitudes for subjects in high rather than in low task involvement conditions (Park and Young 1986; Petty, Cacioppo and Schumann 1983; Rhine and Severance 1970; Swasy and Munch 1985). Additionally, Celsi and Olson (1988) found that consumers with greater task involvement and greater product knowledge generated a greater proportion of product-related thoughts. Thus, as individuals' task involvement increases, they are expected to focus more thoughts on brand attribute information.

On the other hand, individuals with enduring involvement have an ongoing interest in the product category, pay close attention to product-related ads, magazines and other information (Celsi and Olson 1988; Richins and Bloch 1986; Higie and Feick 1989). Because people with enduring involvement have internally generated interest, and perceive the product to be part of their self-image and fun, we expect them to pay attention to all aspects of advertisements. Thus, whereas people with task involvement are attentive to brand attribute information, we expect that people with enduring involvement will attend not only to brand attribute information (Bloch, Sherrell and Ridgway 1986), but also to peripheral cues. Therefore, we expect that as individuals' level of enduring involvement increase, they will focus more of their total thoughts on the peripheral cues in an advertisement.

Persuasiveness of Advertisements

Because individuals with high enduring involvement are expected to attend to peripheral cues, we expect that these individuals will translate more positive peripheral cues into more positive brand and advertisement-related opinions.

For individuals with low enduring involvement, task involvement is important in determining their focus of processing and attitudes. As we have noted, subjects in experimentally manipulated high task involvement conditions rely on brand attribute information, whereas subjects in experimentally manipulated low task involvement conditions are more likely to rely on peripheral cues to derive attitudes and impressions. Hence, we expect individuals with low enduring involvement under conditions of high task involvement to focus primarily on the message. For these individuals, peripheral cues should not affect brand and advertisement-related opinions. Alternatively, we expect, individuals with low enduring involvement under conditions of low task involvement to focus primarily on peripheral cues. As individuals perceive the peripheral cues to be more positive, their brand and advertisement-related opinions will become more positive.

HYPOTHESES

Based on this theoretical development, we offer the following hypotheses. Because our study manipulated the peripheral cue of spokesperson expertise, our hypotheses are set in those terms.

Amount of Information Processing

H1A: As enduring involvement increases, more thoughts related to the product-relevant information will be generated.

H1B: As task involvement increases, more thoughts related to the product-relevant information will be generated.

Focus of Information Processing

H2A: As task involvement increases, a smaller proportion of the generated thoughts will focus on the spokesperson in the ad.

H2B: As enduring involvement increases, a larger proportion of the generated thoughts will focus on the spokesperson in the ad.

Persuasiveness of Advertisements

H3A: Individuals with high enduring involvement will focus on both the source and the message. As individuals perceive the spokesperson to have more expertise, their brand/advertisement-related opinions will be more positive.

H3B: Individuals with low enduring involvement under conditions of high task involvement will focus primarily on the message. For these individuals, perceived spokesperson expertise should not affect brand/advertisement-related opinions.

H3C: Individuals with low enduring involvement under conditions of low task involvement will focus primarily on the spokesperson. As individuals perceive the spokesperson to have more expertise, brand/advertisement-related opinions will be more positive.

METHOD

The present study examined hypotheses about processing and persuasion reactions using an experiment in which subjects responded to print ads. Enduring involvement with personal computers (EI) is measured and subjects are classified as high (HEI) or low (LEI). Subjects' task involvement with personal computers (TI) and the spokesperson's expertise with personal computers (EX) are manipulated at high (HTI and HEX) and low (LTI and LEX) levels, respectively. The experiment is a balanced full factorial 2^3 design with seven male MBA students per cell. The 56 students were enrolled at three eastern universities.

Procedure

Subjects attended two sessions, held two weeks apart, for this "New Product Introduction Study." In Session 1, we collected measures of enduring product involvement, and product-related information search and transmission for four products: air conditioners, personal computers, dehumidifiers, and lawn mowers. The presentation order of the set of questions for the four products was randomized within questionnaires. In addition, subjects were informed that to limit the number of questions, each subject would be required to answer technical questions about only one product. The questionnaire had all four products listed as possible options, but all subjects answered questions about the personal computer.

During the week between Session 1 and Session 2, the scale measuring enduring involvement (EIS) was analyzed. Subjects whose personal computer EIS score was below the median were categorized as having LEI with personal computers, those above the median were classified as having HEI. Next, subjects were assigned randomly to one of the four task involvement/spokesperson expertise conditions.

Upon reporting to Session 2, subjects examined an ad booklet and completed dependent measures and manipulation and confound checks. A note debriefing the subjects was distributed after all subjects had completed Session 2.

Ad Booklet. Each ad booklet contained an instruction page with the task involvement manipulation and one advertisement for each of the four products. Five advertisements were used in the experiment -- two for the personal computer (expert/non-expert spokesperson, varied between subjects) and one for each of the other three products. Each of the advertisements contained a 3 by 5 inch black and white photograph of the spokesperson, a brief description of the spokesperson's background and qualifications, and the spokesperson's description of the product's attributes. The ads were of comparable quality.

Task Involvement Manipulation. Task involvement was manipulated using a distraction technique (Kahle and Homer 1985; Park and Young 1986). Subjects assigned to the high task involvement with personal computers condition read:

> When examining this booklet, please ASSUME that you have decided to purchase a personal computer (or upgrade your present system). In addition, you have just received a telephone call from a close friend who just decided to purchase a personal computer, and would like for you to give him some advice. Please examine the booklet of advertisements for new products that will be introduced later this year, keeping in mind that you and your close friend are planning to purchase a personal computer in the next few months. After examining the booklet you will be taken through a simulated shopping experience in which you will be asked to identify the personal computer described in the advertisement from among several displayed brands.

The attention of subjects assigned to the low task involvement with personal computers condition was focused on the dehumidifier. These subjects read the message above, except that dehumidifier was substituted for personal computer.

Spokesperson Expertise Manipulation. The description of the expert and non-expert, respectively, were:

> John Matthews is a Harvard-trained computer programmer. He has extensive business experience with IBM and WANG and is a recognized expert on personal computers. In addition, he writes a column for a major computer magazine.

> John Matthews is an elementary school teacher. Two weeks ago, he began a part-time evening job as a sales clerk at a computer store. He has little hands-on experience with personal computers, but plans to take a computer course in the near future.

Personal Computer Advertisement Message. The message included relevant product attribute information, and was derived using 1987 *Consumer Reports* product ratings (the study was conducted in June 1987) to identify important product attributes. The personal computer advertisement read:

> The new personal computer is IBM compatible. It runs word processing and statistical software packages, and other popular game and educational software. This personal computer has six full-sized expansion slots, and its memory can be expanded to one megabyte. The personal computer is speed switchable (4.77 and 8 MHz), and has built-in high resolution text plus CGA, EGA and Hercules graphics compatibility. Moreover, this personal computer is less expensive than any IBM model, and it has a one-year warranty.

MEASUREMENT

Independent Variables

Enduring Involvement Measurement. Several researchers have developed scales to measure the general construct of involvement (Laurent and Kapferer 1985; McQuarrie and Munson 1987; Zaichkowsky 1985). Higie and Feick (1989), focusing on the self-expression and hedonic components, developed and validated the Enduring

Involvement Scale (EIS), an elaboration of Zaichkowsky's Personal Involvement Inventory (1985). In this research, we used the EIS which includes ten seven-point semantic differential items, five measuring the self-expression component and five measuring the hedonic component. Cronbach's alpha for EIS was .91. The range of responses was 25 to 67, and the means on the EIS for the LEI and HEI groups were 37.6 and 55.1, respectively.

Product Knowledge Covariate

The hypotheses in this study are based on the effects of motivation to process information, not ability to process. Hence, it was necessary to control for product knowledge. Because objective product knowledge seems to better control for ability to process than subjective product knowledge (Brucks 1985), three people knowledgeable of personal computers developed a fourteen item multiple choice objective product knowledge test on personal computer software, hardware and operation. The test was culled to five items after pilot testing. Subjects received a 0 to 5 score, depending on the number of correct answers.

Manipulation Checks

Task Involvement. Three seven-point Likert scale items (involved in reading; concerned with understanding; careful in evaluating the personal computer advertisement), with endpoints labeled "not at all" and "very", were used to measure task involvement with the personal computer advertisement (Chaiken 1980). The scale formed by an unweighted sum of the items had a Cronbach's alpha of .93.

Spokesperson Expertise. Subjects responded to three seven-point Likert scale items (expert/not an expert; very/not at all knowledgeable; very/not at all experienced using personal computers) regarding their impression of the spokesperson's level of expertise (Petty and Cacioppo 1981). The scale formed by an unweighted sum of the items had a Cronbach's alpha of .94.

Dependent Measures

To examine processing and persuasion, we used two types of measures: an open-end cognitive response measure and closed-end attitude and intention measures.

Cognitive Responses. After examining the ad booklet, subjects recorded their cognitions about the personal computer ad. The instructions read:

> We would like to know what you were thinking about while you looked at the personal computer advertisement in the booklet. Please list, on the lines below, any thoughts you had about the personal computer advertisement. Phrases are okay. Don't worry about spelling, grammar or punctuation. Write down only the ideas you were thinking about while examining the personal computer advertisement.

Three judges familiar with the coding categories, but not with the experimental hypotheses, independently coded the cognitive responses as related to either 1) brand attributes, 2) spokesperson attributes, 3) ad execution comments or 4) other, and as either 1) positive, 2) negative or 3) neutral (MacKenzie, Lutz and Belch 1986). A modal scoring convention was used. If at least two of the three judges agreed on the category for the response, it was assigned to that category. This scoring convention successfully coded 100 percent of the cognitions. Cognitive response data were used to derive total cognitions, percentage of spokesperson cognitions, and net valence of cognitions, i.e., the number of positive minus the number of negative brand, spokesperson and ad execution cognitions (MacKenzie, Lutz and Belch 1986).

A_{ad}. The subject's attitude toward the personal computer advertisement was measured using a seven-point semantic differential item, "What is your overall opinion of the personal computer advertisement?" The endpoints were "unfavorable" and "favorable".

A_{br}. The subject's attitude toward the personal computer described in the ad was evaluated using three seven-point semantic differential items: bad/good; unsatisfactory/satisfactory; unfavorable/favorable. The scale formed by an unweighted sum of the items had Cronbach's alpha of .90.

I_{buy}. Intention to purchase the personal computer in the ad was measured by two seven-point Likert scale items: "Suppose you were seriously considering purchasing a personal computer. Would you...1) seriously/not seriously consider the personal computer in the booklet, and 2) be not at all/very interested in the personal computer described in the booklet." The correlation between the items was .72.

RESULTS

Manipulation Checks

Task Involvement. Results of the three-way (EI x TI x EX) ANOVA indicated the successful manipulation of task involvement ($F=17.43$; d.f.=1,48; $p<.001$). The mean in the HTI condition was 5.21 compared to 3.81 in the LTI condition. (The average of the component items for all manipulation checks and dependent variables generated from closed-end scales are reported. The base for each was a seven point scale.) In addition, there was a significant TI x EX interaction ($F=11.06$; d.f.=1,48; $p<.05$). The TI manipulation was more effective when the spokesperson was not an expert ($\bar{x}_{LTI}=3.07$, $\bar{x}_{HTI}=5.59$) than when the spokesperson was an expert ($\bar{x}_{LTI}=4.54$, $\bar{x}_{HTI}=4.83$). However, in both the expert and non-expert conditions, subjects in the HTI condition reported greater involvement than those in the LTI condition. No other main or interaction effects were significant.

Spokesperson Expertise. The three-way ANOVA results indicated a successful manipulation of spokesperson expertise (F=91.37; d.f.=1,48; p<.001). The personal computer spokesman in the expert condition was perceived as having significantly more expertise ($\bar{x}$=5.48) than the spokesman in the non-expert condition ($\bar{x}$=2.23). No other main or interaction effects were significant.

Product Knowledge Covariate

The objective product knowledge score was included as a covariate in a three-way ANCOVA for each dependent variable. It was a significant covariate only for total number of cognitions generated, and is discussed in those results only.

Dependent Measures

Amount of Information Processing. H1A and H1B predicted that as EI and TI increased, the total number of cognitions generated would increase. The three-way ANCOVA results indicated that product knowledge was a significant covariate in the analysis of total number of cognitions generated (F=4.20; d.f.=1,47; p=.05). The adjusted marginal means for EI are $\bar{x}_{HEI}$=2.47 and $\bar{x}_{LEI}$=2.07 and TI are $\bar{x}_{HTI}$=2.43 and $\bar{x}_{LTI}$=2.11. Although the total number of cognitions generated increased with higher involvement, the effects were not statistically significant (H1A: F=.82; d.f.=1,47, p=.37; H1B: F=.54, d.f.=1,47, p=.47).

There was, however, a significant TI x EX interaction (F=7.57; d.f.=1,47; p<.01). When the spokesperson was a non-expert, the result was as expected: HTI subjects ($\bar{x}$=2.93) listed more cognitions than LTI subjects ($\bar{x}$=1.36). On the other hand, when the spokesperson was an expert, LTI subjects ($\bar{x}$=2.86) listed more cognitions than HTI subjects ($\bar{x}$=1.98). This finding might be explained, in part, by the greater than expected task involvement of subjects in the LTI/HEX condition, as reported in the TI manipulation check results. No other main or interaction effects were significant.

Focus of Information Processing. H2A predicted that as task involvement increased, a smaller proportion of thoughts would focus on the spokesperson. Alternatively, H2B predicted that as enduring involvement increased, a larger proportion of thoughts would focus on the spokesperson. Testing these hypotheses in a three-way ANOVA implies main effects of EI and TI. As predicted, HEI subjects ($\bar{x}$=.37) reported a higher proportion of spokesperson cognitions than LEI subjects ($\bar{x}$=.16; F=3.81, d.f.=1,48, p=.06). Also, as expected, LTI subjects ($\bar{x}$=.31) generated a larger proportion of spokesperson cognitions than HTI subjects ($\bar{x}$=.22; F=.99, d.f.=1,48, p=.33). Other main and interaction effects were not significant. The lack of a significant main effect of TI may have been due to the greater than expected task involvement in the LTI/HEX cells.

Persuasiveness of Advertisements. To determine the effects of EI, TI and EX on attitude formation, we analyzed four persuasion measures: net valence of cognitive responses (NETCOG), A_{ad}, A_{br} and I_{buy}. The *a priori* hypotheses about particular comparisons were examined using 1 degree of freedom tests of simple effects (Keppel 1982; Rosenthal and Rosnow 1985). The Table reports the means and tests of significance for H3A, H3B and H3C.

H3A hypothesized that HEI individuals would have more favorable impressions of the product when they perceived the spokesperson to have more rather than less expertise. The results are directionally consistent with the hypotheses for all four measures of persuasion and statistically significant for NETCOG and A_{br}.

H3B hypothesized that the impressions of LEI individuals in HTI conditions would not differ across conditions of spokesperson expertise. The results for NETCOG, A_{ad} and A_{br} support H3B. However, the expert created a significantly greater I_{buy} than did the non-expert.

Finally, H3C hypothesized that LEI individuals in LTI conditions would have more favorable impressions of the product when they perceived the spokesperson to have more rather than less expertise. The results for the four measures of persuasiveness are directionally consistent with the hypotheses, but not statistically significant.

DISCUSSION

The concept of consumer involvement has interested marketers for years. This research, along with that of Richins and Bloch (1986) and Celsi and Olson (1988), emphasize the need to distinguish between intrinsically and extrinsically motivated involvement. Our study examines the importance of peripheral cues, in particular, spokesperson expertise, in creating positive ad and brand impressions for people with varying levels of enduring and task involvement. The results discussed below are conservative in the sense that the study was based on a small sample size per cell and a median split used to categorize subjects' level of enduring involvement.

Involvement and Processing

Consistent with the findings of Celsi and Olson (1988), our results indicate that individuals who have greater involvement with a product (either task or enduring involvement) generate more cognitions. We found, however, that the focus of these cognitions varied with levels of enduring and task involvement. Specifically, as predicted, individuals with high enduring involvement (who were expected to focus more on peripheral cues) reported a greater proportion of source cognitions than did individuals with low enduring involvement. Individuals with low task involvement, as expected, relied on simple cues in information processing and generated a larger proportion of thoughts about the spokesperson than individuals with high task involvement.

TABLE
Hypotheses and Results For H3A, H3B, H3C

Hypothesized Relationship	Results			
	HEX	LEX	$F(1,48)$	p
High Enduring Involvement (H3A: HEX > LEX)				
NETCOG	.29	> −.79	10.07	.01
A_{ad}	4.64	> 3.79	3.74	.06
A_{br}	5.07	> 3.93	6.14	.02
I_{buy}	5.21	≅ 4.60	1.14	>.25
Low Enduring Involvement and High Task Involvement (H3B: HEX = LEX)				
NETCOG	.43	≅ .57	0.90	>.25
A_{ad}	4.29	≅ 4.57	0.20	>.25
A_{br}	5.19	≅ 4.07	2.82	.10
I_{buy}	5.85	> 4.07	4.91	.03
Low Enduring Involvement and Low Task Involvement (H3C: HEX > LEX)				
NETCOG	.00	≅ −.86	3.22	.08
A_{ad}	3.71	≅ 2.71	2.55	.13
A_{br}	4.42	≅ 4.04	0.34	>.25
I_{buy}	4.50	≅ 3.78	0.79	>.25

Involvement, Spokesperson Expertise and Persuasion

Consistent with past research (Petty, Cacioppo and Goldman 1981; Rhine and Severance 1970), our ad effectiveness results, in general, indicate that a more knowledgeable spokesperson is more persuasive. However, our findings are of particular importance because they indicate that the effects of spokesperson expertise on ad persuasiveness depend on the individual's levels of enduring and task involvement. Both the spokesperson cognition results and the persuasion results suggest that the expertise of the spokesperson is particularly important to individuals with high enduring involvement, and those who have both low enduring and low task involvement. One explanation for the importance of the expert spokesperson to high enduring involvement consumers is that their self-image is tied to the product category. Hence, it may be important to consumers with high enduring involvement that the spokesperson be someone they can respect and relate to. For consumers with low enduring and low task involvement, an expert spokesperson provides an attention-getting means for relaying credible information.

IMPLICATIONS

Marketers are faced with developing advertising strategies and campaigns targeted to consumers with varying profiles. The results from our research emphasize the need to distinguish between enduring and task involvement when making marketing and advertising decisions. Individuals with high enduring involvement are a critical target audience for many companies (Bloch 1986). These individuals are likely to be opinion leaders. As such, they communicate product information to others, and can be instrumental in generating product adoption (Richins and Bloch 1986). Advertisers take care in selecting appropriate product-related media vehicles to reach these audiences. For example, Bose and Coustic brands of stereo equipment are advertised in *Stereo Review* and Salomon brand ski equipment and

Obermeyer brand skiwear are advertised in *Ski*. Our research indicates that consumers with high enduring involvement attend to both brand attribute information and the peripheral cue of spokesperson expertise. Moreover, the results indicate the importance of a credible spokesperson. These findings provide insights about ad copy. In particular, when targeting high enduring involvement consumers, it appears necessary to not only provide information about product attributes and quality, but also attend to characteristics of the spokesperson. Moreover, given high enduring involved consumers' attention to all facets of the ad, ad managers also may need to be attentive to executional cues and commercial production.

Our study also provides insights regarding consumers with low involvement. Consider the case when the company's target market is identified as having low enduring and low task involvement. These consumers tend to minimize expenditure of cognitive resources in processing and may use spokesperson expertise as a cue about the advertised brand's quality and attributes. Thus, for consumers with low enduring and low task involvement, spokesperson effects may be the result of cognitive economizing (Kahle and Homer 1985). As such, it is important that advertisers communicate the spokesperson's qualifications immediately in an advertisement, thereby increasing brand awareness and recall among consumers with low involvement.

Finally, our results support past research that suggests that consumers with high task involvement focus more on brand attribute information than on peripheral cues in an advertisement. These findings suggest that marketers who are designing ads for consumers intent on buying a particular product, i.e., consumers who have high task involvement, provide comprehensible brand attribute information. For these consumers, the advocation of the brand by a knowledgeable spokesperson will serve only to complement the brand attribute information in creating positive attitudes and impressions about the brand.

REFERENCES

Belk, Russell W. (1988), "Possessions of the Extended Self," *Journal of Consumer Research*, 15 (September), 139-168.

Bloch, Peter H. (1981), "An Exploration into the Scaling of Consumers' Involvement with a Product Class," in *Advances in Consumer Research*, Vol. 8, ed. Kent B. Monroe, Ann Arbor, MI: Association for Consumer Research, 61-65.

_____ (1982), "Involvement Beyond the Purchase Process: Conceptual Issues and Empirical Investigation," in *Advances in Consumer Research*, Vol. 9, ed. Andrew A. Mitchell, Ann Arbor, MI: Association for Consumer Research, 412-417.

_____ (1986), "The Product Enthusiast: Implications for Marketing Strategy," *Journal of Consumer Marketing*, 3 (Summer), 51-62.

_____, Daniel L. Sherrell and Nancy Ridgway (1986), "Consumer Search: An Extended Framework," *Journal of Consumer Research*, 13 (June), 119-126.

Brucks, Merrie (1985), "The Effects of Product Class Knowledge on Information Search Behavior," *Journal of Consumer Research*, 12 (June), 1-16.

Celsi, Richard L. and Jerry C. Olson (1988), "The Role of Involvement in Attention and Comprehension Processes," *Journal of Consumer Research*, 15 (September), 210-224.

A complete list of the references for this paper is available from the first author at 368 Fairfield Road, U41-M Department of Marketing, Storrs, CT 10626-2041.

Suggestions for Manipulating and Measuring Involvement in Advertising Message Content
J. Craig Andrews, Marquette University
Srinivas Durvasula, Marquette University

ABSTRACT

Given the recent interest in the theoretical predictions of many involvement-driven frameworks applied in advertising (e.g., the ELM, the Aad model), successfully manipulating and measuring involvement in advertising content is of great importance. Our paper seeks to aid researchers developing their own manipulations and measures of advertising involvement by providing an operational example of manipulated involvement in advertising content. Direct manipulation checks of the manipulated ad involvement condition are provided that successfully meet the requirements of a unidimensional, reliable, and valid measure of advertising content involvement. Implications for those attempting to measure involvement in advertising research are provided.

INTRODUCTION

Adequately manipulating and measuring a person's involvement in advertising message content is becoming an increasingly important issue in experimental research today. This is because of the recent advancement and testing of many involvement-driven models in advertising that have an important bearing on knowledge development in the advertising and consumer research fields (e.g., the Elaboration Likelihood Model (Petty and Cacioppo 1981a; 1986), the Attitude-Toward-the-Ad Model (Lutz 1985; Mitchell and Olson 1981; Shimp 1981) and the Integrated Information Response Model (Smith and Swinyard 1982; 1983)).

To best examine the moderating effects of involvement in advertising content, the *manipulation* of involvement levels is recommended (cf., Petty, Cacioppo, and Schumann 1983). A sound manipulation of involvement will help to enhance *internal validity* (i.e., the ability to draw cause and effect inferences) and rule out confounding extraneous variable explanations (Carlsmith, Ellsworth, and Aronson 1976; Cook and Campbell 1979). However, manipulations of involvement in advertising message content vary greatly, including instructions for the memorization of ad content, expectations of purchase decisions, implications of purchases influenced by brand differences, expectations of local product availability, and distraction to reduce involvement (cf., Gardner 1985; Gardner, Mitchell, and Russo 1978; Laczniak, Muehling, and Grossbart 1989; Leigh and Menon 1987; Park and Young 1986; Petty, Cacioppo, and Schumann 1983). To be successful, however, researchers must manipulate differing levels of involvement in ad content, while holding all other factors constant (Andrews 1988; Apsler and Sears 1968).

Perhaps more troubling is the need for psychometrically-sound measures (i.e., manipulation checks) of manipulated advertising involvement. The development of psychometrically-sound measures begins with an explication of the construct for which the measures are to be derived (Cook and Campbell 1979). Some would agree that involvement can be defined as an internal, individual state of arousal with intensity and direction properties (Mitchell 1979; 1981). Others define involvement as personal relevance (Greenwald and Leavitt 1984; Petty and Cacioppo 1986; Zaichkowsky 1985; 1986). Still others have linked the two definitions arguing that a motivational state of arousal or activation can emanate from the personal relevance of the stimulus in question (Andrews 1988; Cohen 1983).

From this point, however, a multitude of options face the researcher attempting to measure manipulations of involvement in advertising content. A first choice for some may be the use of Zaichkowsky's (1985) 20-item personal involvement inventory (PII) used to assess one's personal involvement in a product category. However, questions have arisen regarding the PII's unidimensionality (McQuarrie and Munson 1987; Mittal 1989); that it is somewhat cumbersome to use with other important advertising effect variables (e.g., ad cognitive responses, Aad, brand attitude); and that it remains validated only for product categories (as opposed to advertising message content).

A second choice for many researchers is to use ad hoc measures to determine if they have successfully manipulated involvement in ad content. A wide array of measures have been used, including recall of ad content, recall of involvement instructions, and message cognitive responses (see Laczniak, Muehling, and Grossbart 1989 for a review). However, as indicated by Cohen (1983), cognitive responses and recall can be viewed as *consequences* of involvement, as opposed to more direct measures of whether or not a person is involved in the ad's message content.

One alternative choice is a six-item measure of advertising content involvement proposed by Andrews (1985; 1988). As suggested by Andrews (1985), the state of involvement in an advertising message can be checked via multiple items assessing the degree to which subjects attend to, concentrate on, think about, focus on, spend effort in looking at, and carefully read the advertising message. These proposed items are consistent with the definition of involvement as an internal, individual state of arousal with intensity and direction properties and would be less cumbersome to apply than the 20-item PII in an experiment. However, the unidimensionality (via confirmatory factor analysis; Gerbing and Anderson 1988), reliability, and validity (Fornell and Larcker 1981) of this six-item, advertising message involvement scale remain to be explored.

Therefore, the purpose of our paper is to provide an operational example of manipulated involvement in advertising message content in order to offer guidance to researchers attempting to manipulate and/or measure advertising message involvement. Included in this example are: direct manipulation checks (i.e., Andrews' six proposed measures) of the advertising content involvement condition; assessments of the measure's unidimensionality, reliability, and validity; its impact on predicted consequences; and how it differs from other related constructs of advertising content involvement. Implications for those attempting to manipulate and/or measure involvement in experimental advertising research are also provided.

INVOLVEMENT AND YOU: 1000 GREAT IDEAS

As indicated in Cohen's (1983) provocative article on the conceptualization of involvement, there may very well be "1000 great ideas" on the concept of involvement (cf., Andrews 1988; Antil 1984; Batra and Ray 1983; Cohen 1983; Gardner, Mitchell, and Russo 1978; 1985; Greenwald and Leavitt 1984; Houston and Rothschild 1978; Krugman 1966-1967; Lastovicka and Gardner 1979; Mitchell 1979; 1981; Park and Young 1986; Petty and Cacioppo 1986; Wright 1973; Zaichkowsky 1986; see Andrews, Durvasula and Akhter, 1990 for a comparison of involvement conceptualizations). Various "types" or targets of involvement have been outlined, such as task involvement (i.e., the importance of adopting a position - or performing a task - that will maximize immediate rewards; Sherif and Hovland 1961; Zimbardo 1960), personal involvement (Apsler and Sears 1968; Petty and Cacioppo 1981b; 1986), product involvement (Bloch 1981; Day 1970; Zaichkowsky 1985), and advertising message (content) involvement (Andrews 1988; Laczniak, Muehling, and Grossbart 1989; Wright 1973).

Typology labels, however, may give the wrong impression since it is the *individual* who is involved, not products, tasks, or advertising content. Some involvement theorists have gone beyond involvement types and focused on the underlying properties of those in the state of involvement. For example, one view that is emerging is that involvement represents an individual, internal state of arousal with intensity and direction properties (Mitchell 1979; 1981).[1] In this sense, involvement is more than simply "arousal," because it not only is characterized by a variety of intensity levels, but is *directed* toward a particular stimulus object or situation. As proposed by Mitchell (1979), *intensity* refers to the level (or degree) of arousal, interest, or drive in a stimulus object or situation. For example, in the case of involvement in advertising message content, one can measure the *degree* of focus, concentration, attention, thought, effort, etc. expended (on scrutinizing the content of a target advertisement). *Direction*, on the other hand, concerns the actual evoking stimulus object and/or situation. With advertising involvement, involvement direction can refer to different levels of specificity; that is, toward the ad in general, its executional features, or its message content (Baker and Lutz 1987). For the purposes of our paper, we will focus on the manipulation and measurement of involvement in advertising message content.

As suggested by Andrews (1988, p. 220), "...indicators tapping the involvement *state* (vs. antecedents or consequences of this state) should be used as a measure (i.e., manipulation check) of involvement." For example, numerous antecedents to advertising message involvement exist, such as the personal relevance of a product, prior product experience, risk, decision factors (e.g., time and magnitude), and personality traits (e.g., need for cognition) (Andrews 1988; Petty and Cacioppo 1986; Zaichkowsky 1986). Similarly, numerous consequences of involvement also exist, including one's degree of search behavior, information processing (e.g., cognitive response activity, message recall), and persuasion (Cohen 1983). These distinctions are important because there may be a temptation to simply *infer* from antecedents or consequences that one's advertising involvement manipulation has "taken" without assessing more direct measures of the involvement state. Certainly, however, involvement state measures should also be related to their antecedents and consequences in the experiment.

MEASURING MANIPULATED INVOLVEMENT IN ADVERTISING MESSAGE CONTENT: SOME SUGGESTIONS

In experimentation, researchers face the difficult challenge of providing a close correspondence between their constructs (and proposed manipulations) at a conceptual level and their measures (e.g., manipulation checks) at the operational level. While correspondence rules between the conceptual and operational levels can be assessed through the content validity of the measures, it is clear that more rigor is needed in subjecting our measures of manipulated advertising involvement to accepted procedures of unidimensionality, reliability, and validity assessment (Churchill 1979; Fornell and Larcker 1981; Gerbing and Anderson 1988; Perdue and Summers 1986; Peter 1981). For example, internal consistency and exploratory factor analysis are argued *not* to be explicit tests of the predicted dimensionality of a construct (Gerbing and Anderson 1988, p. 189, 190). Rather, in order to confirm whether the number of predicted dimensions can be verified empirically, a confirmatory factor analysis is strongly suggested in scale construction (Churchill 1979; Gerbing and Anderson 1988). Also, in order to enhance the researcher's confidence in the causal explanations of the experiment, the potential confounding of involvement manipulations

---

[1] See Greenwald and Leavitt (1984) for the conceptualization of involvement as a process.

should be avoided (Perdue and Summers 1986). Confounding occurs when a manipulation of one theoretical construct (e.g., involvement) is found to represent more than one construct (e.g., involvement and opportunity to respond due to distraction instructions). Therefore, confounding checks (Perdue and Summers 1986) are needed to determine if related constructs (e.g., opportunity to respond) have been inadvertently affected by the involvement manipulation. Also, manipulations of other variables in the experiment (e.g., ELM-related variables, such as source credibility and argument strength) should not have an influence on involvement manipulation checks. With this in mind, we now present an overview of our experiment manipulating involvement in advertising message content. Theoretical predictions and results for measures of the manipulated involvement condition are then discussed.

AN OPERATIONAL EXAMPLE OF MANIPULATING INVOLVEMENT IN ADVERTISING MESSAGE CONTENT

Experiment Overview

Consistent with involvement antecedents suggested by Petty and Cacioppo (1986), subjects' involvement in the content of a target, mock advertisement was manipulated by varying the personal relevance of a low alcohol beer brand. The targeted mock ad appeared in a booklet of nine mock and real ads presented to 186 undergraduate students of legal drinking age. The overall purpose of the experiment was to examine the persuasive effects of advertising content involvement, source characteristics, and argument strength treatments. These variables represent important elements in ELM-related research (see Petty, Cacioppo, and Schumann 1983 for similar manipulations). A series of four pretests were first conducted varying involvement procedures suggested by Petty, Cacioppo, and Schumann (1983), number of booklet ads (0-9 ads), and viewing time constraints (1-7 minutes). The last pretest was successful and a final manipulation was developed in which both high and low involvement subjects were given five minutes to view the nine ads in the booklet. High involvement subjects expected the target advertised brand to be test marketed in their city, expected a gift choice in the advertised brand's product category, and the possibility of an interview to determine if they carefully read the target ad's claims. Low involvement subjects, on the other hand, only expected the target advertised brand to be test marketed in a distant region and a product gift choice in an unrelated product class.

Theoretical Predictions

Consistent with our conceptualization of involvement, the theoretical predictions regarding the advertising content involvement manipulation and manipulation checks are as follows. First, an immediate check on the personal relevance instructions should indicate, for example, that high involvement subjects did indeed expect the low alcohol beer brand to be test marketed in their own city to a greater extent than low involvement subjects (see Petty, Cacioppo, and Schumann 1983). However, these types of checks do *not* indicate whether or not high involvement subjects were indeed more involved in the content of the advertisement than low involvement subjects. To accomplish this, the summation of six, 9-point items (coefficient alpha = .95) was used as a check to measure the intensity of manipulated involvement in the message content of the target advertisement. Subjects indicated their level of agreement/disagreement to whether they were paying attention to, concentrating on, thinking about, focusing on, spending effort looking at, and carefully reading the content of the target advertisement (Andrews 1985). These items were originally developed and purified following Churchill's (1979) first four steps in scale development. For example, regarding content validity, an attempt was made to sample items that tapped the involvement state definition of an individual's internal state of arousal in advertising content. Coefficient alphas during scale purification ranged from .89 to .95. The focus of the present study is on the evaluation of the resulting six-item measure on the basis of Churchill's: step #5 (collection of data on the proposed measure), an assessment of dimensionality, step #6 (reliability assessment) and step #7 (validity assessment).

To begin, because the six-item advertising involvement check was developed to measure the intensity of the involvement state, it is expected that the check be *unidimensional* in nature. In order to verify the check's undimensionality, data was collected and subjected to a confirmatory factor analysis using LISREL VI (Joreskog and Sorbom 1983). The specific assessment of undimensionality can then be examined through fit indices (e.g., χ^2; goodness-of-fit index; adjusted goodness-of-fit index; and root mean square residual), normalized residuals, and significance of the t-values of each manipulation check item from the confirmatory factor analysis results (Gerbing and Anderson 1988). Next, the measurement properties and predicted structure of the advertising involvement check items can also be examined through the results of the confirmatory factor analysis. In particular, the *reliability* of the measures can be evaluated via item and construct reliability estimates, with a desired minimum standard of .50 (Fornell and Larcker 1981, p. 45).

It was also expected that the check of the advertising involvement state be *construct valid* (Peter 1981). That is, the six-item measure should demonstrate content validity (as previously discussed), convergent validity, discriminant validity, and predictive validity within its nomological network of relationships (see Peter 1981; Zaltman, Pinson, and Angelmar 1973, p. 44 for validity definitions). The proportion of variance extracted (i.e., shared variance, Fornell and Larcker 1981, p. 46) from the multiple items provides an estimate of the convergent validity of the advertising involvement construct. Again, the minimum cutoff is to explain at least 50 percent of the variance. The convergence between the advertising involvement manipulation and the advertising involvement check can be assessed by the degree to which high involvement subjects do, in fact, indicate higher levels of involvement on the check than low involvement subjects (Perdue and Summers 1986). Discriminant validity can be estimated by showing that the shared variance estimates within two related constructs (e.g., advertising involvement and argument strength) are greater than the squared correlation between the two constructs (Fornell and Larcker 1981, p. 46). In addition, the predictive validity of the advertising involvement manipulation can be established if important theoretical predictions regarding the influence of the manipulation on criterion variables (e.g., message-oriented thoughts, message argument recall) are confirmed. For example, the ELM (Petty and Cacioppo 1986, pp. 36, 37) predicts that greater message-oriented thoughts and message argument recall should occur under high versus low involvement.

Consistent with our previous conceptualization of involvement, the directionality (i.e., toward the content, as opposed to the sources) of the advertising involvement manipulation can be assessed through a nine-point measure of relative concentration, anchored by "I concentrated most on the claims in the ad" versus "I concentrated most on the people in the ad" (Wright 1973). It is expected that the relative concentration on claims (vs. people) in the ad will be greater for high versus low involvement subjects in the experiment. Finally, the argument strength and source manipulations should not influence (i.e., confound) the involvement manipulation check. An example of a confound check (Perdue and Summers 1986) is also provided in a second advertising involvement experiment to determine if a related construct (i.e., opportunity to process) had been inadvertently influenced by the involvement manipulation.

Results

First, a check on the personal relevance instructions was made by asking subjects, on a nine-point measure, the likelihood that the low alcohol beer described in the advertisement will soon be available in their region. As expected, high involvement subjects (M = 7.71, SD = 1.73) expressed a stronger likelihood of the product's availability than low involvement subjects (M = 5.85; SD = 2.34; F(1,184) = 34.67, p < .001). However, as previously indicated, in order to assess whether subjects were then more involved in the content of the ad, the six-item measure of advertising involvement intensity was examined.

To help examine the unidimensionality of the manipulation check of advertising involvement intensity, overall model fit statistics (e.g., χ^2, GFI, AGFI, and RMSR) are estimated from the confirmatory factor analysis and provided in Table 1. However, due to the sensitivity of χ^2 to sample size, it is generally agreed that χ^2 should only be used as a guide rather than an absolute assessment of fit (Bagozzi and Yi 1988; Bearden, Sharma, and Teel 1982; Fornell and Larcker 1981; Hayduk 1987; Shimp and Kavas 1984). The goodness-of-fit and adjusted goodness-of-fit indices, as well as the root mean square residual, indicate a relatively good fit of the predicted one-factor model for the advertising involvement check (see Table 1).[2] Furthermore, all normalized residuals are less than .61 indicating an appropriate specification of the model. (Normalized residuals greater than 2 indicate a need for respecification; cf., Gerbing and Anderson 1988). Finally, each indicator t-value exceeded 12.30 (p < .001). Therefore, the confirmatory factor analysis results provided support for the predicted unidimensionality of the manipulation check of advertising involvement intensity in the experiment.

Regarding the measurement properties of this six-item measure of advertising content involvement, results of the confirmatory factor analysis in Table 1 indicate that all item and construct reliabilities, as well as the shared variance estimate, exceed the minimum standard of .50 for the scale. This manipulation check also revealed that high involvement subjects were significantly more involved in the target advertisement (M = 45.13; SD = 8.35) than low involvement subjects (M = 35.67; SD = 12.28; F(1,184) = 33.99; p < .001), thereby providing evidence for the convergence between the advertising involvement manipulation and its associated check of the manipulation. The discriminant validity of the advertising involvement check was evaluated through its comparison with checks of the two other manipulations in the experiment: source characteristics (the sum of ten, 9-point items; α = .96) and argument strength (the sum of four, 9-point items; α = .91). The shared variance of the advertising involvement (.749) and source characteristics (.661) constructs were both greater than the squared correlation between the two constructs (.062). In turn, the shared variance estimates of the advertising involvement (.749) and argument strength (.695) constructs were also greater than the squared correlation between the two respective constructs (.180), thereby demonstrating

---

[2] For comparison purposes, a principal components analysis of the six-item, advertising content involvement measure indicated that one factor accounted for 78.9 percent of the total variance. All factor loadings were .82 or greater on this single factor.

TABLE 1
Measurement Model and Fit Statistics for the Advertising Content Involvement Scale

Construct and indicators	Construct and item reliabilities	Item error variance	Proportion of variance extracted
Advertising content involvement	.947		.749
paying attention to	.709	.291	
concentrating on	.819	.181	
thinking about	.736	.264	
focusing on	.837	.163	
spending effort in looking at	.794	.206	
carefully reading	.598	.402	
Chi-square:	28.91		
Degrees of Freedom:	9		
Probability:	.001		
Goodness-of-Fit:	.954		
Adjusted Goodness-of-Fit:	.892		
Root mean square residual:	.021		

the discriminant validity of the advertising involvement check versus the checks of the other two related manipulations in the experiment. In addition, the source and argument strength manipulations did not have a confounding effect (i.e., a significant influence) on the advertising involvement check, as desired. In support of the predictive validity of the advertising involvement manipulation and consistent with central route predictions of the ELM, high involvement subjects recalled a significantly greater number of message arguments from the advertisement (M = 2.01; SD = 1.19) than did low involvement subjects (M = 1.32; SD = 1.02; $F(1,184) = 17.89$; $p < .001$). In addition, high involvement subjects generated significantly greater message-oriented thoughts (M = 1.70; SD = 1.18) than low involvement subjects (M = 1.05; SD = 1.04; $F(1,184) = 15.41$; $p < .001$), as predicted.

To examine the predicted directionality (i.e., toward the content) of the involvement in the target ad, subjects' relative concentration in the ad was measured (Wright 1973). As expected, the relative concentration on "claims in the advertisement" (as opposed to "people in the advertisement") was significantly greater for high (M = 6.54; SD = 2.46) versus low involvement subjects (M = 5.50; SD = 2.52; $F(1,184) = 7.95$, $p < .005$). In conjunction with previous results indicating greater *message-*oriented thoughts (i.e., support and counterarguments regarding the message content of the ad) under high (vs. low) involvement, this finding provides support for the intended directionality of the involvement manipulation.

Confound Checks

In addition to providing valid manipulation checks that successfully measure the degree to which subjects are involved in the goal-related object, it is important to also include *confounding checks* as well. A confounding check is a special type of manipulation check that tests for a divergence of measures and manipulations of related, but distinct "things" (Perdue and Summers 1986). Related, but distinct "things" that may be inadvertently manipulated or found operating in an advertising involvement study include one's opportunity and/or ability to process information (Andrews 1988; Batra and Ray 1986). For example, Wright (1974) found important interactions between ad content involvement and media conditions, serving to limit one's opportunity to process the advertised message.

A second advertising experiment can be used as an example of the use of this type of confound check for involvement. This experiment manipulated both the involvement in ad content, as well as the distinctiveness of the ad (via color). An opportunity to process confound check was included ("The study coordinator gave me enough time/opportunity to look at the _____ advertisement" on a 7-point, Likert-type scale) to determine whether or not the manipulations had inadvertently limited the subjects' processing of the target ad. The results indicated that neither manipulation had impacted the opportunity to process confound check, as hoped. However, if they were to have an effect, it is suggested that one look at the relative size of the confound effect (e.g., via omega-squared for ANOVA) to determine if it is greater in magnitude than the predicted effects for the study's dependent variables (cf., Perdue and Summers 1986).

CONCLUSION

The primary objective of our paper is to assist researchers in the development and validation of advertising involvement manipulation checks by providing an example of an advertising involvement manipulation and corresponding checks of the induced involvement state. Specifically, we experimentally manipulated advertising content involvement through personal relevance instructions for an advertised brand (an antecedent); measured the intensity and direction of the involvement manipulation; and examined the impact of the involvement manipulation on cognitive response and message argument recall activity (consequences). The use of an advertising involvement confound check (i.e., opportunity to process) is also demonstrated in an example from a second experiment.

Our study provides advertising involvement researchers with another option in the form of a unidimensional, reliable, and valid scale of advertising content involvement. The scale can be of assistance to those examining theoretical predictions of advertising involvement, such as those based on the ELM's central and peripheral routes to persuasion (Petty and Cacioppo 1986). For example, under high message content involvement, subjects are expected to scrutinize the content of the advertising message (Petty and Cacioppo 1981b). Therefore, it is important to first determine if these subjects are involved in the message content before any interpretation of predictions regarding their cognitive and affective responses to the ad. This understanding also holds true for advertisers and public policy officials. The design of relatively strong ad copy and the effectiveness of message arguments in alcohol and drug awareness campaigns may depend upon whether message recipients are involved in the examination of message content (cf., DePaulo, Rubin, and Miller 1987). However, if it can't be determined whether or not the target audience is actually involved in the content of the message, otherwise persuasive and believable arguments may simply turn out to be ineffective ones.

Future research should also examine the reliability, validity, and dimensionality of other advertising involvement manipulations and manipulation checks. For example, it is quite possible that physiological measures of involvement arousal (e.g., EEG patterns--Alwitt 1985; voice-pitch analysis; eye cameras, etc.) can be used in conjunction with the measures reported in our study to strengthen the insight into underlying properties of involvement. Also, manipulation check measures of advertising execution (vs. content) involvement could be developed and assessed using the techniques employed in our study. Efforts in this regard will help to enhance our understanding of the role that involvement plays in advertising research.

REFERENCES

Alwitt, Linda F. (1985), "EEG Activity Reflects the Content of Commercials," in *Psychological Processes and Advertising Effects: Theory, Research, and Application*, Linda F. Alwitt and Andrew A. Mitchell, eds., Hillsdale, NJ: Lawrence Erlbaum Associates, 201-217.

Andrews, J. Craig (1985), *Tests of the Elaboration Likelihood Model Involving Persuasive Marketing Communication*, unpublished doctoral dissertation, University of South Carolina, Columbia, SC.

_____ (1988), "Motivation, Ability, and Opportunity to Process Information: Conceptual and Experimental Manipulation Issues," in *Advances in Consumer Research*, XV, Michael J. Houston, ed., Provo, UT: Association for Consumer Research, 219-225.

_____, Srinivas Durvasula, and Syed Akhter (1990), "A Framework for Conceptualizing and Measuring the Involvement Construct in Advertising Research," *Journal of Advertising*, 19(4).

Antil, John H. (1984), "Conceptualization and Operationalization of Involvement," in *Advances in Consumer Research*, XI, Thomas C. Kinnear, ed., Ann Arbor, MI: Association for Consumer Research, 203-209.

Apsler, Robert and David O. Sears (1968), "Warning, Personal Involvement, and Attitude Change," *Journal of Personality and Social Psychology*, 9, 162-166.

Bagozzi, Richard P. and Youjae Yi (1988), "On The Evaluation of Structural Equation Models," *Journal of the Academy of Marketing Science*, 16 (Spring), 74-94.

Baker, William E. and Richard J. Lutz (1987), "The Relevance-Accessibility Model of Advertising Effectiveness," in *Nonverbal Communication in Advertising*, S. Hecker and D.W. Stewart, eds., Lexington, MA: Lexington Books, 59-84.

Batra, Rajeev and Michael L. Ray (1983), "Operationalizing Involvement as Depth and Quality of Cognitive Response," in *Advances in Consumer Research*, X, Richard P. Bagozzi and Alice M. Tybout, eds., Ann Arbor, MI: Association for Consumer Research, 309-313.

_____ and _____ (1986), "Situational Effects of Advertising Repetition: The Moderating Influence of Motivation, Ability, and Opportunity to Respond," *Journal of Consumer Research*, 12 (March), 432-445.

Bearden, William A., Subhash Sharma, and Jesse E. Teel (1982), "Sample Size Effects on Chi Square and Other Statistics Used in Evaluating Causal Models," *Journal of Marketing Research*, 19 (November), 425-430.

Bloch, Peter H. (1981), "An Exploration into the Scaling of Consumers' Involvement with a Product Class," in *Advances in Consumer Research*, VI, Kent R. Monroe, ed., Ann Arbor, MI: Association for Consumer Research, 61-65.

Carlsmith, J. Merrill, Phoebe C. Ellsworth, and Elliot Aronson (1976), *Methods of Research in Social Psychology*, Reading, MA: Addison-Wesley.

Churchill, Gilbert A., Jr. (1979), "A Paradigm for Developing Better Measures of Marketing Constructs," *Journal of Marketing Research*, 16 (February), 64-73.

Cohen, Joel C. (1983), "Involvement and You: 1000 Great Ideas," in *Advances in Consumer Research*, X, Richard P. Bagozzi and Alice M. Tybout, eds., Ann Arbor, MI: Association for Consumer Research, 325-328.

Cook, Thomas D. and Donald T. Campbell, *Quasi-Experimentation: Design and Analysis Issues for Field Settings*, Boston: Houghton Mifflin.

Day, George (1970), *Buyer Attitudes and Brand Choice Behavior*, New York: Free Press.

DePaulo, Peter J., Mary Rubin, and Brenton Milner (1987), "Stages of Involvement with Alcohol and Heroin: Analysis of the Effects of Marketing on Addiction," in *Advances in Consumer Research*, Vol. XIV, Melanie Wallendorf and Paul Anderson, eds., Provo, UT: Association for Consumer Research, 521-525.

Fornell, Claes and D.F. Larcker (1981), "Structural Equation Models with Unobservable Variables and Measurement Error," *Journal of Marketing Research*, 18 (February), 39-50.

Gardner, Meryl Paula (1985), "Does Attitude Toward the Ad Affect Brand Attitude Under a Brand Evaluation Set?" *Journal of Marketing Research*, 22 (May), 192-198.

_____, Andrew A. Mitchell, and J. Edward Russo (1978), "Chronometric Analysis: An Introduction and an Application to Low Involvement Perception of Advertisements," in *Advances in Consumer Research*, V, H. Keith Hunt, ed., Ann Arbor, MI: Association for Consumer Research, 581-589.

_____, _____, and _____ (1985), "Low Involvement Strategies for Processing Advertisements," *Journal of Advertising*, 14 (2), 4-12, 56.

Gerbing, David W. and James C. Anderson (1988), "An Updated Paradigm for Scale Development Incorporating Unidimensionality and Its Assessment," *Journal of Marketing Research*, 25 (May), 186-192.

Greenwald, Anthony G. and Clark Leavitt (1984), "Audience Involvement in Advertising: Four Levels," *Journal of Consumer Research*, 11 (June), 581-592.

Hayduk, Leslie A. (1987), *Structural Equation Modeling with LISREL: Essentials and Advances*, Baltimore, MD: Johns Hopkins University Press.

Houston, Michael J. and Michael L. Rothschild (1978), "Conceptual and Methodological Perspectives in Involvement," in *Research Frontiers in Marketing: Dialogues and Directions*, S. Jain, ed., Chicago: American Marketing Association, 184-187.

Joreskog, Karl G. and Dag Sorbom (1983), *LISREL VI: Analysis of Linear Structural Relationships by Maximum Likelihood and Least Squares Methods*, Mooresville, IN: International Educational Services.

Krugman, Herbert E. (1966-1967), "The Measurement of Advertising Involvement," *Public Opinion Quarterly*, 30 (Winter), 583-596.

Laczniak, Russell N., Darrel D. Muehling, and Sanford Grossbart (1989), "Manipulating Message Involvement in Advertising Research," *Journal of Advertising*, 18 (2), 28-38.

Lastovicka, John L. and David M. Gardner (1979), "Components of Involvement," in *Attitude Research Plays for High Stakes*, John C. Maloney and Bernard Silverman, eds., Chicago, IL: American Marketing Association, 53-73.

Leigh, James H. and Anil Menon (1987), "Audience Involvement Effects on the Information Processing of Umbrella Print Advertisements," *Journal of Advertising*, 16 (3), 3-12.

Lutz, Richard J. (1985), "Affective and Cognitive Antecedents of Attitude Toward the Ad: A Conceptual Framework," in *Psychological Processes and Advertising Effects: Theory, Research, and Application*, Linda F. Alwitt and Andrew A. Mitchell, eds., Hillsdale, NJ: Lawrence Erlbaum, 45-63.

McQuarrie, Edward F. and J. Michael Munson (1987), "The Zaichkowsky Personal Involvement Inventory: Modification and Extension," in *Advances in Consumer Research*, XIV, Melanie Wallendorf and Paul Anderson, eds., Provo, UT: Association for Consumer Research, 36-40.

Mitchell, Andrew A. (1979), "Involvement: A Potentially Important Mediator of Consumer Behavior," in *Advances in Consumer Research*, VI, William Wilkie, ed., Ann Arbor, MI: Association for Consumer Research, 191-196.

_____ (1981), "Dimensions of Advertising Involvement," in *Advances in Consumer Research*, VIII, Kent B. Monroe, ed., Ann Arbor, MI: Association for Consumer Research, 25-30.

_____ and Jerry C. Olson (1981), "Are Product Attribute Beliefs the Only Mediators of Advertising Effects on Brand Attitudes?" *Journal of Marketing Research*, 18 (August), 318-332.

Mittal, Banwari (1989), "A Theoretical Analysis of Two Recent Measures of Involvement," in *Advances in Consumer Research*, XVI, Thomas K. Srull, ed., Provo, UT: Association for Consumer Research, 697-702.

Park, C. Whan and S. Mark Young (1986), "Consumer Response to Television Commercials: The Impact of Involvement and Background Music on Brand Attitude Formation," *Journal of Marketing Research*, 23 (February), 11-24.

Perdue, Barbara C. and John O. Summers (1986), "Checking the Success of Manipulations in Marketing Experiments," *Journal of Marketing Research*, 23 (November), 317-326.

Peter, J. Paul (1981), "Construct Validity: A Review of Basic Issues and Marketing Practices," *Journal of Marketing Research*, 28 (May), 133-145.

Petty, Richard E. and John T. Cacioppo (1981a), *Attitudes and Persuasion: Classic and Contemporary Approaches*, Dubuque, IA: William C. Brown.

_____ and _____ (1981b), "Issue Involvement as a Moderator of the Effects on Attitude of Advertising Content and Context," in *Advances in Consumer Research*, VIII, Kent B. Monroe, ed., Ann Arbor, MI: Association for Consumer Research, 20-24.

_____ and _____ (1986), *Communication and Persuasion: Central and Peripheral Routes to Attitude Change*, New York: Springer-Verlag.

_____ , _____ , and David Schumann (1983), "Central and Peripheral Routes to Advertising Effectiveness: The Moderating Role of Involvement," *Journal of Consumer Research*, 10 (September), 135-146.

Sherif, Muzafir and Hadley Cantril (1947), *The Psychology of Ego-Involvements, Social Attitudes and Identifications*, New York: John Wiley & Sons, Inc.

Shimp, Terence A. (1981), "Attitude Toward the Ad as a Mediator of Consumer Brand Choice," *Journal of Advertising*, 10 (2), 9-15, 48.

_____ and Alican Kavas (1984), "The Theory of Reasoned Action Applied to Coupon Usage," *Journal of Consumer Research*, 11 (December), 795-809.

Smith, Robert E. and William R. Swinyard (1982), "Information Response Models: An Integrated Approach," *Journal of Marketing*, 46 (Winter), 81-93.

_____ and _____ (1983), "Attitude-Behavior Consistency: The Impact of Product Trial Versus Advertising," *Journal of Marketing Research*, 20 (August), 257-267.

Wright, Peter (1973), "The Cognitive Processes Mediating Acceptance of Advertising," *Journal of Marketing Research*, 10 (February), 53-62.

_____ (1974), "Analyzing Media Effects on Advertising Responses," *Public Opinion Quarterly*, 38, 192-205.

_____ (1980), "Message-Evoked Thoughts: Persuasion Research Using Thought Verbalizations," *Journal of Consumer Research*, 7 (September), 151-175.

Zaichkowsky, Judith Lynne (1985), "Measuring the Involvement Construct," *Journal of Consumer Research*, 12 (December), 341-352.

_____ (1986), "Conceptualizing Involvement," *Journal of Advertising*, 15 (2), 4-14, 34.

Zaltman, Gerald, C.R.A. Pinson, and R. Angelmar (1973), *Metatheory and Consumer Research*, New York: Holt, Rinehart, and Winston.

Zimbardo, Philip G. (1960), "Involvement and Communication Discrepancy as Determinants of Opinion Conformity," *Journal of Abnormal and Social Psychology*, 60 (1), 86-94.

Brand Familiarity and Product Involvement Effects on the Attitude Toward an Ad - Brand Attitude Relationship

Joseph Phelps, University of Alabama
Esther Thorson, University of Wisconsin-Madison

ABSTRACT

This study builds upon earlier Attitude-toward-an-ad (Aad) research. It adds empirical evidence to the current debates about the effects of brand familiarity and product involvement on the Aad-Ab (brand attitude) relationship and makes suggestions for future research.

The results indicate that Aad significantly affects Ab for unfamiliar brands. More important for theory development, Aad affects Ab for familiar brands, even after controlling for prior brand attitude. However, product involvement does not seem to affect the Aad-Ab relationship. It is suggested that product involvement's influence should be reexamined in a more natural viewing environment.

INTRODUCTION

Attitude toward an ad (Aad) can be thought of as a viewer's general liking or disliking of an advertisement. Recently Aad has become a topic of considerable research interest (e.g. Mitchell and Olson, 1981; Shimp, 1981; Shimp and Yokum, 1982; Moore and Hutchinson, 1983; Lutz and Belch, 1983; Gardner, 1985; Batra and Ray, 1986; Muehling, 1987).

One reason these researchers are interested in Aad is the evidence that suggests Aad is one of the factors that influences brand attitude (Ab) and intent to purchase (PI) (Gresham and Shimp, 1985; Cox and Locander, 1987; Moore and Hutchinson, 1983).

Along with these theoretical relationships come some very practical consequences. With the ever increasing cost of media, more effort has been put into the development of commercial pretesting methodology. Pragmatically, understanding the role of Aad may increase the efficiency of designing and pretesting advertisements (MacKenzie, Lutz and Belch, 1986; Gardner, 1985).

Please note that given the limitations of space, this discussion will limit itself to the empirical question that asks: What effects do product involvement and brand familiarity have on the Aad-Ab relationship. For a discussion of the theoretical underpinnings see Thorson and Page (1990).

Product Involvement and the Aad-Ab Relationship

In the complex world of a viewer processing an advertisement, many variables may intervene in the Aad-Ab relationship. Two such variables are product class involvement and brand familiarity.

Although the effects of product involvement and brand familiarity in Aad-Ab relationship have been studied, the effect these variables have is still under debate. In Aad-Ab research, Thorson and Page (1989); Rossiter and Percy (1984); and others have studied product involvement. These studies suggest conflicting observations of product involvement's role in the Aad-Ab relationship. Before discussing the product involvement studies, it is important that a distinction be made between product involvement and message response involvement. Although the two involvement constructs are related they are not the same.

Recently a number of studies have examined message response involvement's role in the Aad-Ab-PI relationship. (Batra and Ray, 1985; Muehling and Laczniak, 1988; Park and Young, 1986), to name just a few. Batra and Ray (1985) define message response involvement as that which:

> refers conceptually to the "depth" of processing for a particular message, by a particular recipient, at a particular time. ... this construct is not purely motivational in origin. Such processing "depth," however operationalized, would be a function not just of the viewer's motivation to respond "deeply," but also his/her ability to do so, as a function of prior usage and knowledge, and of the opportunity to do so, caused by message pace and distraction, for instance.

Laczniak, Muehling, and Grossbart (1989) defined message involvement as the motivational state of an individual induced by a particular advertising stimulus or situation.

Product involvement has also been conceptualized as a motivational construct (Batra and Ray, 1985), where the amount of motivation may depend on the relevance of the product (Zaichowsky, 1985). Thus, previous research has conceptualized product involvement as more purely a motivational construct, while including motivation, ability, and opportunity in the conceptualization of message involvement.

Product involvement was included in this study to examine its potential as a mediator in the Aad-Ab relationship. Message response involvement was not examined in this study. Given the distinctions noted above it is time to return to the product involvement studies. These studies suggest competing observations of product involvement's role in the Aad-Ab relationship.

Rossiter and Percy (1984) reported that most of the published studies where Aad had been found to contribute significantly to Ab used low involvement products, and hence they suggest the Aad-Ab relationship may be stronger for low involvement products than it is for high involvement products. Nevertheless, Thorson and Page (1989) report that the level of product involvement had no impact on the Aad-Ab relationship. This study will examine these conflicting observations.

Brand Familiarity and the Aad-Ab Relationship

The role brand familiarity plays in the Aad-Ab relationship is also controversial. Although there is general agreement that Aad affects Ab when unfamiliar brands are tested, there is conflicting evidence on whether this Aad-Ab relationship occurs with familiar brands.

In theory, if a person is unfamiliar with a brand, the information they get from the ad and their Aad should have a relatively strong influence on their Ab. However, if the person is familiar with the brand, they may have already formed an Ab and their Aad should not have as strong of an effect.

Most of the early studies that found a relationship between Aad-Ab used either unfamiliar or hypothetical brands. However, studies using familiar brands have also found Aad-Ab effects (Thorson and Page, 1989; Batra and Ray, 1986; Edell and Burke, 1984, 1986; Messmer, 1979; Gresham and Shimp, 1985).

In contrast, Machleit and Wilson (1988), hypothesized there is no Aad-Ab relationship for familiar brands and suggested the studies that showed a direct effect of Aad on Ab for familiar brands were flawed because of the researchers' failure to account for prior brand attitude.

In their study, Machleit and Wilson controlled for prior brand attitude. Without such a control, the Aad-Ab relationship, under familiar brands, may be inflated. They indicate that Aad did not significantly affect Ab for familiar brands.

However, Edell and Burke's (1986) results conflict with what Machleit and Wilson found. Edell and Burke reported that both prior brand attitude and Aad affected Ab even when brands were familiar. The present study also controlled for prior brand attitude. Given the conflicting results noted above, this study has a unique opportunity to test the competing hypotheses.

In light of the literature on brand familiarity and product involvement, four hypotheses were articulated. Because the preponderance of studies support Aad influence on Ab for both unfamiliar and familiar brands (Thorson and Page, 1989; Batra and Ray, 1986; Edell and Burke, 1984; Messmer, 1979; Gresham and Shimp, 1985) it was hypothesized that this will be true even when prior brand attitude is controlled. In accordance with these assumptions, the following hypotheses were made:

H1: Prior brand attitude will significantly affect (explain a significant portion of the within-subjects variance) Ab under the familiar brands condition.

H2: After controlling for prior brand attitude, Aad will significantly affect Ab under the familiar condition.

H3: Aad will significantly affect Ab under the unfamiliar brands condition.

Given the conflicting evidence reviewed above, it is harder to predict product involvement's role in the Aad-Ab relationship. However, it seems likely that as motivation (product involvement) increases, Aad's influence should decrease.

H4: The Aad-Ab relationship under high product involvement will be significantly weaker (Aad will explain less of the Ab variance) than under low product involvement.

METHOD

Pretest

A pretest was designed to determine which product categories were high or low-involvement for college students and which brands were familiar and unfamiliar to them. The pretest was also designed to measure a subject's prior brand attitude.

The pretest was administered four weeks prior to the main experiment. Undergraduate students in an introductory marketing course were told that the test was designed to find out how they felt about various products. The respondents filled out the questionnaire in class. Sixty-five questionnaires were distributed and 63 were returned in useable condition.

Product Involvement

The construct of involvement has been conceptualized and operationalized in many different ways. These discrepancies have led to much confusion when trying to interpret results across studies. Salmon (1986) examined the various conceptualizations of involvement in consumer and communication research. He states:

> Differences in perspectives on involvement reflect the extent to which involvement is seen primarily as a characteristic of the individual or of the stimulus.

In this study product involvement is viewed as an interaction between the individual and the stimulus. It includes the salience or relevance of a product and the individuals interest in a product.

To operationalize product involvement, a modified version of the Personal Involvement Inventory developed by Zaichowsky (1985) was used to differentiate high and low-involvement products. The Personal Involvement Inventory is a 20-item seven-point semantic differential scale designed to measure the involvement construct. The modified version used in this study is a 10-item seven-point semantic differential scale (important-unimportant, of no concern for me-of concern to me, irrelevant-relevant, very meaningful to me-means nothing to me, trivial-fundamental, matters to me-doesn't matter, interesting-not interesting, significant-insignificant, vital-superfluous, boring-exciting). This modified version was selected after studies by Nowak (1986) and Nowak and Salmon (1987) found that the chosen 10 items still produced a reliable

TABLE 1

High Involvement	Mean	Low Involvement	Mean
Automobiles	57.33	Candy Bars	29.67
Computers	56.64	Hot Dogs	28.67
Airlines	51.71	Dog Food	25.33
Gasoline	48.29	Furniture Polish	23.40

measure of involvement and had a higher coefficient alpha that the original instrument.

Using the scale, a product that was of no interest to a respondent would theoretically have a total score of 10 points. Each scale item representing the low extreme receives one point, while items rated at the high extreme receive seven points. The total score for a product can range from 10 to 70. The mean scores for the product categories used in the pretest are given in Table 1. High involvement products were products that had an average score between 48 and 57; and low involvement products had an average score between 23 and 29. Based on this pretest, 8 product categories were chosen for use in the main experiment.

A repeated measures anova indicated that the lowest high involvement mean (for gasoline) was significantly higher than the highest low involvement mean (for candy bars). [$F(1,56)=49.28$].

Brand Familiarity

The most straightforward conceptualization of brand familiarity is used here. Baker, Hutchinson, Moore and Nedungai (1986) define brand familiarity as a unidimensional construct that is directly related to the amount of time that has been spent processing information about the brand, regardless of the type or content of the processing that was involved.

The respondents indicated on a single bipolar scale whether they were familiar or unfamiliar with the brand. The brands were selected for the pretest based on the following criteria: There would be at least two brands for each of the product categories in the survey. Brands that did not advertise in this area of the country were included to increase the likelihood that at least one brand in each product category would be unfamiliar the respondents.

Thus the pretest designated eight product categories, four each for high and low involvement products. It also designated two brands for each of the products, producing a total of 16 brands for which ads would be shown in the main experiment.

Prior Brand Attitude

The pretest was also designed to measure the respondent's prior brand attitude. The respondents were asked to complete a four-item seven-point scale (dislike very much - like very much, bad - good, unpleasant - pleasant, worthless - valuable).

Main Experiment

A 2 (product involvement level) X 2 (brand familiarity) factorial design was used to test the hypotheses. Each subject saw 24 commercials; 16 of which were test commercials.

Stimulus Materials

The stimulus materials consisted of 24 television commercials, 21 of which were 30-seconds long. All the test ads were 30-seconds long. Of the filler ads, two ran 60 seconds and one ran 15 seconds.

Three stimulus tape orders were prepared to randomize the effects of order. The only deviation from randomization was that brands from the same product category were separated to minimize interference. Each commercial was followed by 10 seconds of black to provide the moderator time to pause the VCR between ads.

Methodology

Subjects: The subjects were undergraduate students enrolled in an introductory marketing course at the University of Wisconsin-Madison. A total of 63 students participated in the pretest and 58 of these same students also participated in the main experiment. Seven questionnaires were not useable. This left a total of 51 completed questionnaires. Students taking part in the pretest and the main experiment received extra credit points for their participation.

The moderator told the subjects they would be watching commercials and answering questions about them. The first ad was shown, the tape stopped, and the moderator went through the questionnaire instructions with the respondents. After each ad was shown, 90 seconds were allotted for answering the relevant questions and then the next ad was shown. No subject had difficulty responding in this time. The experiment took approximately 50 minutes.

After watching an ad, the subjects completed the section of the questionnaire for the specific ad and brand. The questions involved three categories: questions regarding Aad; Ab; and a manipulation check concerning brand familiarity.

Attitude Toward an Ad

To operationalize Aad, the mean of a 5-item seven-point semantic differential scale was used. The 5-item scale (favorable-unfavorable, boring-interesting, dislike very much-like very much, not irritating-irritating, holds attention-does not hold attention) was based on the work of many

TABLE 2 REGRESSIONS

Predicting Ab under familiar brands condition

Independent Variables	sr^2	pr^2	F
Subjects Variance	.1361		
Prior Brand Attitude	.1936	.2241	21.35
Attitude Toward Ad	.1046	.1211	11.54

Predicting Ab under unfamiliar brands condition.

Independent Variables	sr^2	pr^2	F
Subjects Variance	.0945		
Attitude Toward Ad	.2463	.272	23.497

Predicting Ab under high product involvement condition.

Independent Variables	sr^2	pr^2	F
Subjects Variance	.0364		
Prior Brand Attitude	.1770	.1837	17.99
Attitude Toward Ad	.1791	.1859	18.21

Predicting Ab under low product involvement condition.

Independent Variables	sr^2	pr^2	F
Subjects Variance	.0423		
Prior Brand Attitude	.1675	.1749	16.75
Attitude Toward Ad	.1737	.1814	17.37

researchers (e.g. Lutz, MacKenzie and Belch, 1983; Mitchell and Olson, 1981; Gardner, 1985; MacKenzie, Lutz and Belch, 1986). A check on the reliability of the items indicated a Chronbach's alpha =.91

Brand Attitude

The operationalization of Ab in this study is based on past research (Shimp, 1981; Park and Young, 1986; Gardner, 1985; Gardner, Mitchell and Russo, 1985; Muehling, 1987). Ab is defined as the mean of four seven-point bipolar scales (dislike very much - like very much, bad - good, unpleasant - pleasant, worthless - valuable). A check on the reliability of the items indicated a Chronbach's alpha =.82

RESULTS

To test the hypotheses, separate within-subjects repeated measures hierarchial regressions were run for high product involvement, low product involvement, familiar brands, and unfamiliar brands. These four regressions were run using Ab as the dependent variable. The basis for this statistical technique can be found in Cohen and Cohen (1983) and Pedhazur (1977,1982).

The design used here involved multiple observations from each subject. With a repeated measures design it is necessary to partition out the variance attributable to a subject's unique bias on the dependent variable (subject effect). To remove this subjects variance, in each regression reported below the mean for each subject was first calculated and then entered as the first independent variable. After the subjects variance was removed it was possible to examine the residual effects of the other variables. Variance attributable to subjects is referred to below as bmean. Therefore, for the regressions with Ab as the dependent variable, the independent variables were bmean, prior brand attitude, and Aad.

Table 2 shows the semipartial (sr^2) and partial (pr^2) regression coefficients. The semipartial and the partial coefficients indicate the contribution of each independent variable to the multiple correlation (see Cohen and Cohen, 1983). Figures 1 and 2 show the significant paths demonstrated by the regression results.

Effects of Brand Familiarity

In the pretest, subjects indicated whether they were familiar or unfamiliar with each brand. As a manipulation check subjects were also asked to indicate whether the brand was familiar or unfamiliar in the main experiment. A comparison of the responses indicated that the brands which were identified as unfamiliar/familiar in the pretest were also identified as unfamiliar/familiar in the main experiment.

FIGURE 1
Amount of Within Subjects Variance Explained

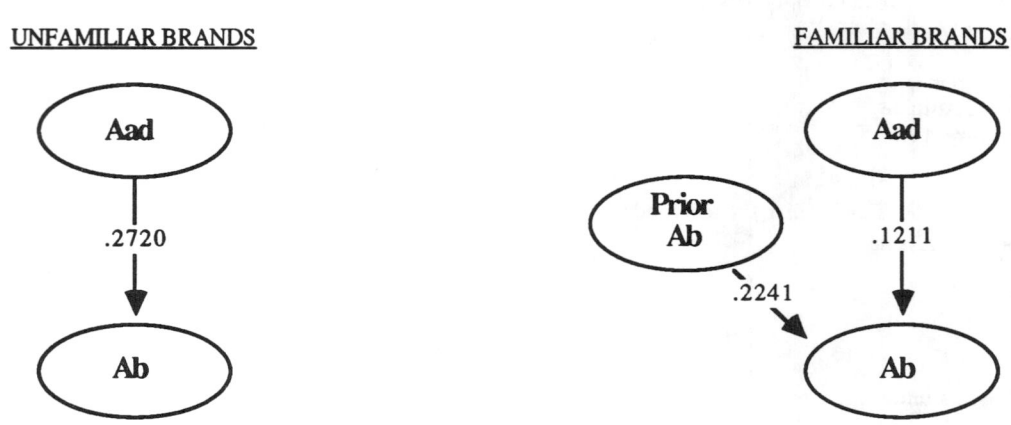

UNFAMILIAR BRANDS — FAMILIAR BRANDS

FIGURE 2
Amount of Within Subjects Variance Explained

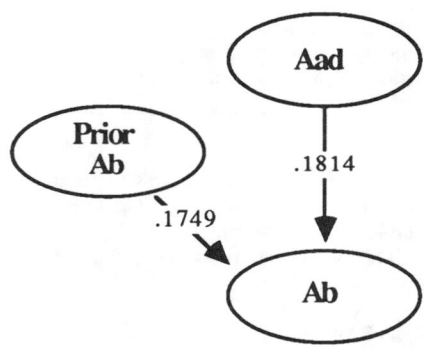

HIGH PRODUCT INVOLVEMENT — LOW PRODUCT INVOLVEMENT

Hypothesis 1 suggested that prior brand attitude would significantly affect Ab when brands were familiar. After subjects variance was removed, prior brand attitude explained over 22 percent of the Ab variance. [$F(1,168)=21.35$, $p<.05$]. Hypothesis 1 was therefore supported. Not only was prior brand attitude significant, it was also the best predictor of Ab under the familiar brands condition.

Hypothesis 2 suggested that after controlling for prior brand attitude, Aad will significantly affect Ab under the familiar brand condition. This hypothesis was also supported. After controlling for prior brand attitude, Aad still explained over 12 percent of the remaining Ab variance. [$F(1,168)=11.54$, $p<.05$].

Hypothesis 3 suggested that Aad will significantly affect Ab under the unfamiliar brands condition. As expected, Hypothesis 3 was supported. After removing the between subjects variance, Aad explained over 27 percent of the remaining Ab variance for unfamiliar brands. [$F(1,168)=23.50$, $p<.05$].

Effects of Product Involvement
Hypothesis 4 suggested the Aad-Ab relationship under high product involvement will be significantly weaker than under low product involvement. Hypothesis 4 was not supported. Under both high and low product involvement, Aad explains just over 18 percent of the Ab variance. There is not a significant difference. See Figure 2.

DISCUSSION
The results of this study provide a better understanding of the Aad-Ab relationship under various conditions of brand familiarity and product involvement. This study suggests that Aad can influence Ab for unfamiliar and familiar brands. It

also suggests that the Aad's affect on Ab is significant even when one controls for prior brand attitude.

The results also suggest that the level of product involvement does not influence the Aad-Ab relationship.

Brand Familiarity

As the results indicate, Aad affects Ab for familiar and unfamiliar brands. Finding Aad explains a significant portion of the Ab variance for unfamiliar brands is not surprising. This result has been shown often in the literature. However, finding Aad explains a significant portion of the Ab variance for familiar brands, after controlling for prior brand attitude is important. This result contradicts the Machleit and Wilson (1988) study which reported Aad did not significantly affect Ab if prior brand attitude was controlled, and supports the Edell and Burke (1986) results. This result is also consistent with other studies (Batra and Ray, 1986; Edell and Burke, 1984) that found Aad significantly affected Ab for familiar brands, but did not control for prior brand attitude.

Although the results show that Aad affects Ab for familiar and unfamiliar brands, it must be noted that the strength of the Aad-Ab relationship is influenced by brand familiarity. The Aad-Ab relationship was much stronger for unfamiliar brands than for familiar brands. In fact, for familiar brands, prior brand attitude explained more of the Ab variance than did Aad. This makes sense considering that people have more information on which to base their Ab than just the ad when the brand is familiar.

Product Involvement

Product involvement did not significantly affect the Aad-Ab relationship. Aad explains approximately an equal amount of the Ab variance for low and high involvement products. This is consistent with the results of Thorson and Page (1989). However, it is inconsistent with reports that the Aad-Ab relationship is stronger for low involvement products than for high involvement products (Rossiter and Percy, 1984).

Limitations of the Study

As with all studies, aspects of the design may limit its generalizability. A first concern is the ecological validity of the viewing situation. Subjects viewed commercials in a large room, with one group as large as 25. Subjects knew they would be answering questions after each commercial they viewed. Obviously the unnatural viewing environment may have altered the way the subjects processed the commercials, perhaps increasing the individual involvement with watching the ads.

Artificially heightened involvement is likely most serious in looking at the effects of product involvement on the Aad-Ab relationship. The laboratory setting may force a deeper processing of commercials for low involvement products than would otherwise be found. If this is the case, then a difference in the Aad-Ab relationship might actually exist for low and high involvement products, but that difference would not be apparent. It is therefore suggested that future research use a more natural viewing environment when examining product involvement role in the Aad-Ab relationship.

Several measurement issues must be addressed. Subjects completed the Aad measures just prior to the Ab measures. Edell and Burke (1984, 1986) speculate that taking similar measures of attitudes proximally may overstate their actual correlation. Future research should separate the measures.

Researchers have found that both brand beliefs and Aad are mediators of Ab (Mitchell and Olson, 1981; Mittal, 1990). Brand beliefs were not investigated in this study. According to Mittal (1990) the size of the Aad-Ab relationship may be overestimated when brand beliefs (both utilitarian and image beliefs) are not included. Future research should include brand beliefs. However, it should be noted that Mittal's results show that the Aad is still a significant predictor of Ab even after controlling for the contribution of brand beliefs.

Another measurement issue concerns the measure of brand familiarity used here. Brand familiarity can be conceptualized and operationalized in many different ways. The most straightforward conceptualization of brand familiarity is used here. Brand familiarity was conceptualized to be unidimensional, and therefore a single-item bipolar scale (unfamiliar - familiar) was used as the index of the concept. However, brand familiarity has also been conceptualized as a more complex concept. Questions have been raised about when someone is truly familiar with an object and whether it may be more useful to conceptualize familiarity as a continuous rather than a dichotomous variable. Using a single-item scale to measure a construct always increases the possibility of not tapping into all the facets of the construct. Although the potential problem is lessened for unidimensional constructs, if familiarity is conceptualized as multidimensional, then the risk involved in using a single-item scale increases tremendously. Therefore, future research should explore the use of multiple-item measures of brand familiarity.

Conclusions and Practical Implications

The results of this study may be particularly important for introducing a new brand to the market. For brand introductions, the ad is often the first information about the brand for the consumer, and is very important to help insure the consumer will form a favorable Ab. This study suggests that one way to increase the probability of obtaining a favorable Ab is by having ads that elicit a favorable Aad. Therefore, measures of Aad should be included when pretesting commercials.

Although the study indicates that the Aad-Ab relationship is considerably weaker for familiar brands than unfamiliar brands, it is still a significant relationship. That is important because most of the advertisements which consumers are exposed to are for existing brands (Edell and Burke, 1987).

REFERENCES

Baker, W., J. W. Hutchinson, D. Moore and P. Nedungadi (1986) Brand Familiarity and Advertising: Effects on the Evoked Set and Brand Preference. *Advances in Consumer Research*, Vol. 9, Ann Arbor: Association for Consumer Research, pp. 637-642.

Batra, R. & Ray, M.L. (1985) How Advertising Works on Contact. In *Psychological Processes and Advertising Effects: Theory and Research Applications*, L.F. Alwitt & A.A. Mitchell (Eds.), Hillsdale, N.J.: Erlbaum, pp. 13-44.

Batra, R. & Ray, M.L. (1986) Affective Responses Mediating Acceptance of Advertising. *Journal of Consumer Research*, Vol.13, pp. 234-249.

Cohen, J. & Cohen, P. (1983) *Applied Multiple Regression/Correlation Analysis for the Behavioral Sciences*. 2nd edition. Hillsdale, New Jersey: Lawrence Erlbaum Associates

Cox, D.S. & Locander, W.B. (1987) Product Novelty: Does it Moderate the Relationship Between Ad Attitudes and Brand Attitudes? *Journal of Advertising*, Vol. 16(3), pp. 39-44.

Edell, J.A. & Burke, M.C. (1984) The Moderating Effect of Attitude Toward an Ad on Ad Effectiveness Under Different Processing Conditions. *Advances in Consumer Research*, Vol. 11, Ann Arbor: Association for Consumer Research pp. 644-649.

Edell, J.A. & Burke, M.C. (1986) The Relative Impact of Prior Brand Attitude and Attitude Toward the Ad on Brand Attitude After Ad Exposure. In *Advertising and Consumer Psychology*, Jerry Olson & Keith Stentis, (eds), Vol. 3, pp. 93-107.

Gardner, M.P. (1985) Does Attitude Toward the Ad Affect Brand Attitude Under a Brand Evaluation Set? *Journal of Marketing Research*, Vol. XXII, pp.192-198.

Gardner, M.P., Mitchell, A.A., & Russo, J.E. (1985) Low Involvement Strategies for Processing Advertisements. *Journal of Advertising*, Vol. 14(2), pp. 4-12.

Gresham, L.G. & Shimp, T.A. (1985) Attitude Toward the Advertisement and Brand Attitudes: A Classical Conditioning Perspective. *Journal of Advertising*, Vol. 14(1), pp. 10-17.

Laczniak, R.N., Muehling, D.D. and Grossbart, S. (1989) Manipulating Message Involvement in Advertising Research. *Journal of Advertising*, Vol. 18(2), pp. 28-38.

Lutz, R.J. & Belch, G.E. (1983) Attitude Toward the Ad as a Mediator of Advertising Effectiveness: Determinants and Consequences. *Advances in Consumer Research*, Vol. 10, Ann Arbor: Association for Consumer Research pp. 532-539.

Machleit, K.A. and Wilson, R.D. (1988) Emotional Feelings and Attitude Toward the Advertisement: The Roles of Brand Familiarity and Repetition. *Journal of Advertising*, Vol. 17(3), pp. 27-35.

MacKenzie, S.B., Lutz, R.J., & Belch, G.E. (1986) The Role of Attitude Toward the Ad as a Mediator of Advertising Effectiveness: A Test of Competing Explanations. *Journal of Marketing Research*, Vol. XXIII, pp. 130-143.

Messmer, D.J. (1979) Repetition and Attitudinal Discrepancy Effects on the Affective Response to Television Advertising. *Journal of Business Research*, Vol.7, pp. 75-93.

Mitchell, A.A. & Olson, J.C. (1981) Are Product Attribute Beliefs the Only Mediator of Advertising Effects on Brand Attitude? *Journal of Marketing Research*, Vol. XVIII, pp. 318-332.

Mittal, B. (1990) The Relative Roles of Brand Beliefs and Attitude Toward the Ad as Mediators of Brand Attitude: A Second Look. *Journal of Marketing Research*, Vol. XXVII, pp. 209-219.

Moore, D.L. & Hutchinson, J.W. (1983) The Effects of Ad Affect on Advertising Effectiveness. *Advances in Consumer Research*, Vol. 10, Ann Arbor: Association for Consumer Research pp. 526-531.

Muehling, D.D. (1987) An Investigation of Factors Underlying Attitude-Toward-Advertising-In-General. *Journal of Advertising*, Vol. 16(1) pp. 32-40.

Muehling, D.D. (1987) Comparative Advertising: The Influence of Attitude-Toward-The-Ad on Brand Evaluation. *Journal of Advertising*, Vol. 16(4), pp. 43-49.

Muehling, D.D. & Laczniak, R.N. (1988) Advertising's Immediate and Delayed Influence on Brand Attitudes: Considerations Across Message-Involvement Levels. *Journal of Advertising*, Vol. 17(4), pp. 23-34.

Nowak, G. (1986) The Effects of Product Involvement, Message Appeal, and Viewing Condition on Memory and Evaluation of Television Commercials. Unpublished Masters Thesis at the University of Wisconsin-Madison.

Nowak, G. & Salmon, C. (1987) Measuring Involvement with Social Issues. Paper presented at the Association for Education in Journalism and Mass Communication, San Antonio.

Park, C.W. & Young, S.M. (1983) Types and Levels of Involvement and Brand Attitude Formation. *Advances in Consumer Research*, Vol. 10, Ann Arbor: Association for Consumer Research pp. 320-323.

Park, C.W. & Young, S.M. (1986) Consumer Response to Television Commercials: The Impact of Involvement and Background Music on Brand Attitude Formation. *Journal of Marketing Research*, Vol. XXIII, pp. 11-24.

Pedhazur, E.J. (1977) Coding Subjects in Repeated Measures Designs. *Psychological Bulletin*, Vol. 84, pp. 298-305.

Pedhazur, E.J. (1982) *Multiple Regression in Behavioral Research: Explanation and Prediction*. Second edition. New York: CBS College Publishing.

Rossiter, J.R. & Percy, L. (1984) Advertising Communication Models. *Advances in Consumer Research*, Vol. 12, Ann Arbor: Association for Consumer Research, pp. 510-524.

Salmon, C.T. (1986) Perspectives on Involvement in Consumer and Communication Research. In *Progress in Communication Sciences*, Brenda Dervin & Melvin J. Voight (eds). Ablex Publishing Corporation, Norwood, New Jersey. pp. 243-269.

Shimp, T. (1981) Attitude Toward the Ad as a Mediator of Consumer Brand Choice. *Journal of Advertising*, Vol. 10(2), pp. 9-15.

Shimp, T. & Yokum, J.T. (1982) Advertising Inputs and Psychophysical Judgments in Vending-Machine Retailing. *Journal of Retailing*, Vol. 58(1), pp. 95-113.

Thorson, E. and Page, T.J. (1990) On the Ubiquity of Aad-->Ab Effects. Paper presented at the Annual Meeting of the American Academy of Advertising, Orlando, Florida.

Zaichowsky, J.L. (1985) Measuring the Involvement Construct. *Journal of Consumer Research*, Vol.12(3) pp. 341-352.

Consumer Attitudes Toward Complaining And The Prediction Of Multiple Complaint Responses

Diane Halstead, University of Kentucky
Cornelia Dröge, Michigan State University

ABSTRACT

This paper investigates the role of consumer attitudes toward complaining as predictors of complaining behavior. In addition to satisfaction, several attitude factors significantly influenced five consumer complaint responses: word-of-mouth behavior, word-of-mouth favorability, repurchase intentions, complaining intentions, and seller-directed complaint actions. Consumer attitudes about channel members' responsiveness to complaints demonstrated the greatest ability to predict multiple complaint behaviors.

INTRODUCTION

It is a commonly held view in consumer behavior theory that attitudes precede intentions and behavior, particularly in high involvement situations. Fishbein and Ajzen (1975) have argued that an individual's attitude toward a concept or object may influence their overall *pattern of responses* even though it may not predict a particular action. This research investigates whether consumer attitudes toward complaining predict *patterns of consumer complaining responses*.

Several consumer complaining behavior (CCB) studies have examined *formal* complaint actions or intentions as a function of consumer attitudes toward complaining (Bearden and Crockett 1981; Richins 1982; Singh 1989). However, conceptualizing CCB as only complaints directed to a seller or third party (i.e., formal complaints) is generally viewed as overly restrictive (Best and Andreasen 1977; Day et al. 1981; Richins 1983; Singh 1988). Singh (1988) in particular argues that CCB should be defined as "a set of multiple (behavioral and nonbehavioral) responses, some or all of which are triggered by perceived dissatisfaction with a purchase episode" (p. 94). Doing nothing about an unsatisfactory consumption experience is a legitimate CCB response, as is a decision not to repurchase, or telling friends (Day 1984; Day et al. 1981; Richins 1983).

With the exception of Folkes (1984), few studies have investigated *multiple* complaint responses, particularly in conjunction with consumer attitudes toward complaining. In addition, many studies have focused on consumer dissatisfaction as a primary determinant of complaining behavior (e.g., Singh 1988). While theoretical and empirical support exists for an inverse satisfaction - complaining relationship (Bearden and Teel 1983; Day and Landon 1977; Oliver 1987), only about 15 percent of the variation in formal complaining is explained by satisfaction level (Oliver 1987). Thus, additional variables beyond satisfaction are needed to fully explain CCB.

Consumer attitudes toward complaining are likely to contribute to the prediction of several complaining behaviors. This paper, therefore, addresses the following research questions. First, what is the role of consumer attitudes toward complaining in the prediction of complaint behavior? Once consumer (dis)satisfaction is accounted for, can these attitudes provide *additional* explanatory power? Finally, will the effects of satisfaction and attitudes toward complaining be the same across a *variety* of CCB responses? Five CCB responses are considered: 1) extent of word-of-mouth (WOM) behavior, 2) favorability of WOM transmissions, 3) intentions to repurchase, 4) future complaint intentions, and 5) seller-directed complaint actions.

The paper is organized as follows. First, background on consumer complaining attitudes and behaviors is provided. Next, a conceptual model is proposed which presents CCB as a function of both satisfaction and attitudes toward complaining. Finally, multiple regression and discriminant analysis results are discussed and implications provided.

THEORETICAL BACKGROUND

The traditional focus of complaint behavior studies has been on *behavioral* responses, i.e., those consumer actions that directly convey expressions of dissatisfaction (Landon 1980; Singh 1988). These actions include complaints directed to manufacturers and retailers, complaints to third parties or consumer agencies (e.g., Better Business Bureaus), and telling friends and family members (negative WOM). Numerous studies, however, have documented that a common response to consumer dissatisfaction is to "do nothing" or decide not to repurchase (Andreasen and Best 1977; Best and Andreasen 1977; Day and Bodur 1978; Day and Landon 1976; A.C. Nielsen 1981; TARP 1979; Warland, Herrmann, and Willits 1975). These *nonbehavioral* responses should be considered forms of consumer complaining, despite the passive nature of these responses (Singh 1988).

With only a few exceptions, however (e.g., Folkes 1984; Singh 1988), research on CCB has either failed to recognize the multidimensionality of the CCB construct, or has focused on only *one* CCB action. For example, Richins (1983) investigated negative WOM, Singh (1989) and Ursic (1985) examined consumers' decisions to seek third party or legal redress, and Gilly and Gelb (1982) addressed brand repurchase issues. Thus, studies investigating a *variety* of CCB responses, with explicit recognition that CCB encompasses numerous behavioral and nonbehavioral actions, are needed.

Predictors of Consumer Complaining Behavior

A considerable amount of CCB literature has focused on the theoretical antecedents of complaining. A commonly accepted view in CCB research is that a certain level of consumer dissatisfaction must exist for complaining to occur (Day 1984; Day and Landon 1977). Complaining by satisfied consumers is considered outside the realm of CCB (Singh 1988), although Jacoby and Jaccard (1981) cite instances when this may occur. Empirical support for an inverse satisfaction - complaining relationship is found in Bearden and Teel (1983), Oliver (1987), and Westbrook (1987).

Even when dissatisfaction occurs, a consumer's propensity to complain may still be low under certain conditions. Day and Landon (1977) and others have proposed that characteristics of the *product* may affect complaint propensity (e.g., cost, durability, importance). In addition, *marketing channel* factors may influence whether a consumer complains. Firms with well-known reputations for providing fair redress often encourage consumers to complain. *Consumer-related factors* such as personality, motives, sociodemographic status, and attitudes are also likely to affect complaining behavior (Jacoby and Jaccard 1981). Consumers' attitudes toward business, government, consumer organizations, and complaining have been studied in order to predict complaining behavior, but the results have been mixed (Barnes and Kelloway 1980; Moyer 1985).

Several researchers have focused on consumer attitudes toward *complaining* in particular. Given Ajzen and Fishbein's (1977) contention that strong attitude-behavior relationships are obtained "only under high correspondence between at least the target and action elements of the attitudinal and behavioral entities" (p. 888), it seems likely that attitudes toward the *action* of complaining should be more strongly related to complaining behaviors than attitudes toward either business or government.

The importance of attitudes toward complaining in the determination of a variety of CCB responses has empirical support. For example, in his study of the antecedents of third party actions by dissatisfied patients, Singh (1989) found that the normative dimension of attitude (e.g., "I should complain") positively and significantly influenced consumers' intentions *to seek redress*. In fact, a person's attitude toward complaining was the most influential factor when compared to two other consumer-related variables: 1) the consumer's subjective probability of third party success in obtaining a desirable outcome, and 2) the consumer's evaluation of the cost-benefit tradeoffs of complaining. Several other studies support the role of attitudes toward complaining as direct positive antecedents of either complaining *intentions* (Bearden and Crockett 1981; Richins 1982) or complaining *behavior* (Day 1984; Richins 1982). Whether attitudes toward complaining directly impact *other* CCB responses such as WOM behavior (the number of people told about a product experience), WOM favorability (the valence of WOM communications), or repurchase intentions is one of the research questions to be addressed here.

The Proposed Model

Given the demonstrated roles of satisfaction and attitudes toward complaining in the determination of CCB, the following conceptual model is proposed (Figure A).

The attitude dimensions proposed were selected based on the following. Day and Landon's (1977) and Jacoby and Jaccard's (1981) conceptualizations of additional factors (i.e., beyond satisfaction) leading to complaint behavior included consumer-specific, market-specific, and product-specific variables. The personal norms and negative affect dimensions are consumer-related variables. The channel responsiveness dimension relates to market-related variables, and the product-specific dimension of attitude is the third category.

Personal norms refers to the individual's feeling that complaining is/is not an appropriate activity. Richins (1982) noted that some consumers don't like to be seen as nuisances or troublemakers, and this could inhibit them. Both Richins and Singh (1989) found empirical support for the role of normative complaining attitudes.

Negative affect refers to the unpleasant feelings experienced by some consumers during the complaining process (e.g., embarrassment, annoyance, intimidation). Bearden, Crockett, and Teel (1979) used psychosocial risk and Richins (1982) found affective responses spread across two significant factors. In addition, Wesbrook (1987) provides empirical support for the role of negative affect in seller-directed complaint behavior.

Channel responsiveness refers to the consumer's attitude that sellers are willing/unwilling to provide a remedy for complaints. Granbois, Summers, and Frazier (1977) found that the perception of a store's willingness to provide redress was the most significant correlate of complaining behavior.

The *product-specific* dimension relates to consumers' attitudes about the product category and whether or not complaints about this particular product are typical and/or appropriate. Day and Landon (1977) have argued that consumers often fail to complain when dissatisfied because of the nature or cost of the product category (e.g., defective ball-point pens versus defective automobile brakes).

METHOD

The sampling frame consisted of new owners of a nationally advertised carpet brand. The household members most responsible for the selection of the carpet were interviewed by telephone by an independent marketing research firm. Stratified random sampling was conducted within three distinct customer segments. Segment I (n=208) consisted of customers who reported no problems with their new carpet (Noncomplainers). Segment II (n=90) consisted of those customers who complained about a problem with their carpet and

FIGURE A
The Proposed Model of Consumer Complaint Responses

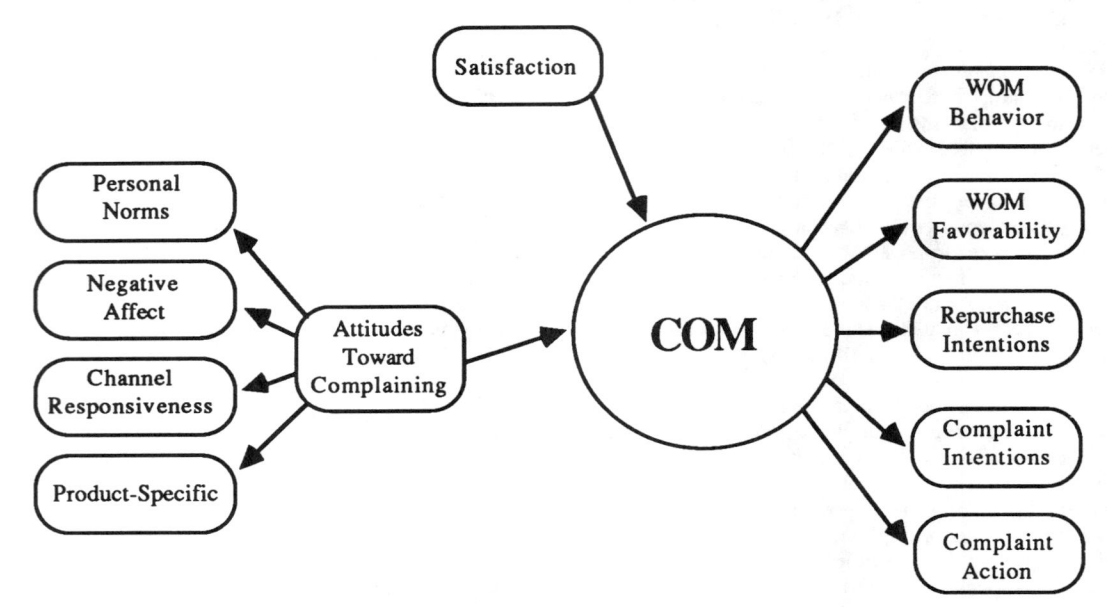

had the problem resolved (Complainers). Segment III (n=103) was comprised of customers who complained and eventually had their new carpets replaced under warranty due to quality defects (Replacements). These three segments were identified by the research sponsor as customer groups needing research attention.

After a series of focus groups among carpet consumers, 16 attitude statements tapping several dimensions were developed. Two double-barrelled items were later deleted to increase factor interpretability. The remaining 14 items, scaled on a five-point Likert scale from "strongly disagree" to "strongly agree", were: (1) Carpet manufacturers don't care about problems people have with their carpeting once it's installed; (2) Most people are stuck with their carpet if it gets stained; (3) Carpet warranties protect manufacturers more than consumers; (4) People who complain about products or services are wasting their time; (5) I'm uncomfortable when returning a product; (6) I dislike making any kind of complaint; (7) I would probably not complain about a product if I thought I'd made a poor choice to begin with; (8) I think people who complain about poor service are nuisances; (9) I don't think complaining is an appropriate activity under any circumstances; (10) Most people will complain about their carpet right after purchase rather than later; (11) My carpet retailer will provide help if I complain; (12) I would feel justified to complain about carpet problems even without a warranty; (13) Fewer people complain about carpet purchases than about other household items; and (14) I believe I should complain and have my problem resolved.

The attitude statements were factor analyzed using principal components and were subjected to a varimax rotation. An orthogonal rotation was used in order to maintain independent attitude factors since they would later be used in multiple regression and discriminant analyses. Four factors were initially specified as the model proposes. Due to an uninterpretable four factor solution and an eigenvalue greater than one in the five factor solution, five rather than four factors were retained in the final pattern.

The attitude factors were then used as independent variables (with satisfaction) in four multiple regression analyses with the following dependent variables: 1) *extent of WOM behavior* (the number of people told about the consumption experience), 2) *WOM favorability* (measured on a five-point scale from "very negative" to "very positive"), 3) *repurchase intention* (measured on a four-point scale ranging from "definitely would not buy (this brand) again" to "definitely would buy again", and 4) *future complaint intentions* (the sum of consumers' responses to six yes - no statements which queried them about their intentions to complain at various points in time if a problem developed). *Consumer satisfaction* levels were determined using a four-point "very dissatisfied" to "very satisfied" scale which measured consumers' satisfaction with their (original) carpet.

The fifth dependent variable was *complaint action*, i.e., Noncomplainer, Complainer, Replacement. The same independent variables were

TABLE 1
Factor Analysis Of Attitudes Toward Complaining

Item	Factor 1	Factor 2	Factor 3	Factor 4	Factor 5
1	.68	-.13	.15	-.24	-.07
2	.71	.21	-.19	.13	.10
3	.64	.06	.11	.17	-.02
4	.42	.21	.29	-.20	.14
5	.08	.64	.25	-.30	-.13
6	-.01	.73	.10	-.13	-.04
7	.13	.70	-.06	.20	.21
8	.03	.26	.67	.17	.11
9	.11	-.02	.76	-.05	.09
10	.01	-.03	.23	.55	-.32
11	-.37	.13	-.17	.53	.15
12	.11	-.17	.02	.63	-.05
13	.09	-.02	.03	.05	.74
14	.09	-.05	.23	.23	-.61
Eigenvalue	2.32	1.50	1.32	1.13	1.05

therefore subjected to a stepwise multiple discriminant analysis in order to: 1) determine which variables were *significant* in the classification of the three sample segments, and 2) classify each consumer into one of the three groups. For the discriminant analysis only, the total sample was split randomly into an analysis (n=201) and a holdout sample (n=200). This prevents the upward bias that would occur in the prediction accuracy of the discriminant function if the individuals used in developing the classification matrix were the same as those used to compute the function (Hair, Anderson, and Tatham 1987).

RESULTS

The factor analysis solution is presented in Table 1. The five factors bear resemblance, but not complete similarity, to the expected attitude dimensions. Factor One clearly reflects consumers' negative perceptions of channel members' (especially manufacturers') responsiveness to consumer complaints. Factor Two corresponds to the negative affect consumers associate with the complaining experience (discomfort, dislike). Both Factor One and Factor Two clearly reflect the expected facets discussed previously. Factor Three appears to relate to personal norms, but normative items also loaded on Factors Four and Five (see Item 12 loading on Factor Four and Item 14 loading on Factor Five). Thus, the normative aspects of consumer complaining attitudes were spread across three factors. As a result, Factors Four and Five are less easily interpreted, both reflecting a combination of normative and product-specific items. Factor Five appears to reflect a negative attitude toward carpet complaining specifically, while Factor Four reflects a response to problems within the product category.

The results of the regression analyses are shown in Table 2. As the table indicates, satisfaction significantly predicted all complaint responses except complaint intentions. In *addition to* satisfaction effects, however, four of the five attitude factors significantly predicted at least one of the four complaint responses shown in Table 2. Two factors, Factor Two and Factor Four, significantly predicted two complaining behaviors, and Factor One was significant in the prediction of WOM extent, WOM favorability, and repurchase intentions. Thus, even when satisfaction level is accounted for, consumer attitudes toward complaining contribute to the prediction of multiple CCB responses.

Of the four CCB responses shown in Table 2, complaint intentions and extent of WOM behavior were the least likely to be explained by the six independent variables. This holds both in terms of the number of significant coefficients (two out of six possible in each case) and in terms of variance explained (R^2 = .06 and .07, respectively, for complaint intentions and WOM extent).

The stepwise discriminant analysis and classification results are both given in Table 3. Only satisfaction and Factor One (channel responsiveness) were retained in the final discriminant analysis. Both were able to significantly predict group membership (i.e., Noncomplainers, Complainers, and Replacements). Results of the three-group discriminant analysis classifying consumers into complaint action groups are shown in part (B) of Table 3. The rows of the classification table relate to actual group membership, whereas the columns give predicted group membership. Thus, "hits" (i.e., correct classifications) appear on the main diagonal and "misses" (i.e., incorrect classifications) appear off the diagonal.

Noncomplainers and Replacement customers were very well classified with hit ratios of 86 percent and 73 percent, respectively. The overall hit ratio for the sample was only 72 percent, however, due to the low classification rate of Segment II - the Complainers. Only 40 percent of these consumers were correctly placed into Segment

TABLE 2
Multiple Regression Results

Independent Variables	Dependent Variables			
	WOM Extent	WOM Valence	Repurchase Intentions	Complaint Intentions
Satisfaction	-0.13 (0.0001)	0.72 (0.0001)	0.52 (0.0001)	-0.05 (0.43)
Factor 1	-0.08 (0.04)	-0.13 (0.01)	-0.13 (0.009)	-0.05 (0.49)
Factor 2	0.04 (0.24)	-0.03 (0.54)	-0.13 (0.006)	0.30 (0.0001)
Factor 3	-0.06 (0.11)	-0.04 (0.47)	-0.04 (0.36)	-0.10 (0.17)
Factor 4	0.03 (0.46)	0.10 (0.06)	0.06 (0.20)	-0.13 (0.08)
Factor 5	0.03 (0.40)	0.08 (0.10)	0.02 (0.59)	-0.09 (0.25)
Model R^2	0.07 (0.0002)	0.51 (0.0001)	0.36 (0.0001)	0.06 (0.001)

Note: Significance levels are in parentheses.

TABLE 3
Discriminant Analysis Results With Complaint Action As The Dependent Variable

(A) Stepwise Discriminant Analysis Results

Independent Variable	F (prob.)	Wilks' Lambda (prob.)
Satisfaction	224.3 (0.0001)	0.47 (0.0001)
Factor 1	13.6 (0.0001)	0.44 (0.0001)
Factor 2	NS	NS
Factor 3	NS	NS
Factor 4	NS	NS
Factor 5	NS	NS

(B) Classification Results

Actual Group	Number of Cases	Predicted Group Membership		
		Noncomplainers	Complainers	Replacements
Noncomplainers	104	89 (85.6%)	14 (13.5%)	1 (.9%)
Complainers	45	13 (28.9%)	18 (40%)	14 (31.1%)
Replacements	51	8 (15.7%)	6 (11.8%)	37 (72.5%)

Percentage correctly classified = 72.3 (weighted to reflect unequal group sizes)

II. The misclassifications of Complainers were split fairly evenly between the other two groups (29 and 31 percent), further complicating this finding. A 72 percent hit ratio is still a significant improvement over that which could be expected by chance (51.7 percent) or by arbitrarily classifying all consumers into the largest group. Thus, the discriminant function using satisfaction and attitudes toward complaining to predict *actual* complaint behavior is valid for Factor One only. Factors Two through Five did not contribute significantly to the discriminant classification.

DISCUSSION

Several conclusions can be drawn from the results of this study. First, sufficient evidence exists to suggest that the conceptual model warrants further research. Consumers' attitudes toward complaining significantly influence whether or not they will engage in seller-directed complaint behavior. They also affect WOM behavior, repurchase intentions, and likelihood of future complaining. Attitudes play a significant role in the prediction of CCB responses even when the effects of satisfaction are accounted for, underscoring the need for inclusion of attitudinal variables in comprehensive models of CCB. Although Day (1984) conceptualized attitude toward complaining as a mediating variable in the complaining/noncomplaining decision process, the results show that satisfaction and attitude are both direct predictors of CCB.

Second, although four of the five attitude dimensions which emerged were significant in the prediction of *at least one* CCB response, Factor Three (personal norms) was not significant. This result appears counterintuitive and contradicts the empirical findings of Richins (1982) and Singh (1989). This may indicate that the normative aspect of consumers' attitudes toward complaining is product and/or situation specific. For example, Singh's study was on third-party complaints which differ substantially from the seller-directed complaints studied here. While Richins' study sampled both third party and other complainers, consumers could respond about complaints in *any* product category. Since several of the normative items in this study spread across the product-specific factors (although a separate normative dimension did emerge), consumers' perceptions about the appropriateness of complaining may depend on the specific situation encountered, especially the nature of the product. Carpeting may not be viewed as a product for which complaining is either appropriate or natural. Everyone complains about auto repairs, but once carpeting is installed, the consumer may think no recourse is available. It is relatively simple to return unwanted clothing items, but returning unwanted carpeting involves considerable upheaval (*if* the seller even agreed to it). The normative aspect of complaining clearly needs additional investigation.

Finally, the attitude factor that most consistently predicted CCB response was the consumer's perception of the responsiveness/caring of channel members (manufacturers especially) regarding problems and redress. This attitude dimension significantly predicted four of five CCB responses. The implications of this for customer service and complaint-handling managers are three-fold. First, being more responsive to consumers' complaints should increase the number of complaints *articulated* to an organization. Thus, rather than having a group of silent but disgruntled customers who may eventually exit rather than voice a complaint, a firm may increase the probability of satisfying customers because it gets a second chance when a consumer complains. Second, creating perceptions of responsiveness will directly affect other post-purchase behaviors such as WOM and repurchase intention *even if actual complaints remain unchanged* (responsive attitudes significantly predicted WOM extent, valence of WOM, and repurchase intention in addition to complaint behavior). Third, creating a perception of willingness to respond to complaints may also lead consumers to believe that the original product/service offering is of higher quality than the competition since few firms would "back up" a poor product.

Further research on the nature and role of attitudes toward complaining is needed. It may be that additional dimensions exist which were not discovered here. Additional research on the normative dimension of attitude toward complaining (in particular its possible relation to product category) is also warranted.

REFERENCES

A.C. Nielsen Co. (1981), *The Consumer's View of Product and Package Performance*, Northbrook, IL: A.C. Nielsen Co.

Ajzen, Icek and Martin Fishbein (1977), "Attitude-Behavior Relations: A Theoretical Analysis and Review of Empirical Research," *Psychological Bulletin*, 84:5, 888-918.

Andreasen, Alan R. and Arthur Best (1977), "Consumers Complain - Does Business Respond," *Harvard Business Review*, 55 (July-August), 93-101.

Barnes, James G. and Karen R. Kelloway (1980), "Consumerists: Complaining Behavior and Attitudes Toward Social and Consumer Issues," in *Advances in Consumer Research*, Vol. 7, Jerry C. Olson (ed.), Ann Arbor, MI: ACR, 329-34.

Bearden, William O. and Jesse E. Teel (1983), "Selected Determinants of Consumer Satisfaction and Complaint Reports," *Journal of Marketing Research*, 20 (February), 21-8.

_____ and Melissa Crockett (1981), "Self-Monitoring, Norms, and Attitudes as Influences on Consumer Complaining," *Journal of Business Research*, 9 (June), 255-66.

———, Melissa Crockett, and Jesse E. Teel (1979), "Alternative Framework for Predicting Consumer Complaining," in *Proceedings of the American Marketing Association Educators' Conference*, Neil Beckwith (ed.), Chicago, IL: AMA, 239-43.

Best, Arthur and Alan R. Andreason (1977), "Consumer Responses to Unsatisfactory Purchases: A Survey of Perceived Defects, Voicing Complaints, and Obtaining Redress", *Law and Society Review*," 11(Spring), 701-42.

Day, Ralph L. (1984), "Modeling Choices Among Alternative Responses to Dissatisfaction," in *Advances in Consumer Research*, Vol. 11, Thomas C. Kinnear (ed.), Ann Arbor, MI: ACR, 496-9.

Day, Ralph L. and E. Laird Landon, Jr. (1976), "Collecting Comprehensive Consumer Complaint Data by Survey Research," in *Advances in Consumer Research*, Vol. 3, Beverlee B. Anderson (ed.), Ann Arbor, MI: ACR, 263-8.

——— (1977), "Towards a Theory of Consumer Complaining Behavior," in *Consumer and Industrial Buying Behavior*, Arch Woodside, Jagdish Sheth, and Peter Bennett (eds.), Amsterdam: North-Holland Publishing Company, 425-37.

Day, Ralph L. and Muzaffer Bodur (1978), "Consumer Response to Dissatisfaction with Services and Intangibles," in *Advances in Consumer Research*, Vol. 5, H. Keith Hunt (ed.), Ann Arbor, MI: ACR, 263-72.

Day, Ralph L., K. Grabicke, T. Schaetzle, and F. Staubach (1981), "The Hidden Agenda of Consumer Complaining," *Journal of Retailing*, 57 (Fall), 86-106.

Fishbein, Martin and Icek Ajzen (1975), *Belief, Attitude, Intention, and Behavior*, Reading, MA: Addison-Wesley.

Folkes, Valerie S. (1984), "An Attributional Approach to Postpurchase Conflict Between Buyers and Sellers," in *Advances in Consumer Research*, Vol. 11, Thomas C. Kinnear (ed.), Ann Arbor, MI: ACR, 500-503.

Gilly, Mary C. and Betsy D. Gelb (1982), "Post-Purchase Consumer Processes and the Complaining Consumer," *Journal of Consumer Research*, 9 (December), 323-8.

Granbois, Donald, John O. Summers, and Gary L. Frazier (1977), "Correlates of Consumer Expectation and Complaining Behavior," in *Consumer Satisfaction, Dissatisfaction and Complaining Behavior*, Ralph L. Day (ed.), Bloomington, IN: Indiana University, 18-25.

Hair, Joseph F., Jr., Rolph E. Anderson, and Ronald L. Tatham (1987), *Multivariate Data Analysis with Readings*, New York: Macmillan Publishing Company.

Jacoby, Jacob and James J. Jaccard (1981), "The Sources, Meaning and Validity of Consumer Complaining Behavior: A Psychological Review," *Journal of Retailing*, 57 (Fall), 4-24.

Landon, E. Laird, Jr. (1980), "The Direction of Consumer Complaint Research," in *Advances in Consumer Research*, Vol. 7, Jerry C. Olson (ed.), Ann Arbor, MI: ACR, 335-8.

Moyer, Mel S. (1985), "Characteristics of Consumer Complainants: Implications for Marketing and Public Policy," *Journal of Public Policy and Marketing*, Vol. 3, 67-84.

Oliver, Richard L. (1987), "An Investigation of the Interrelationship Between Consumer Dis(satisfaction) and Complaint Reports," in *Advances in Consumer Research*, Vol. 14, Melanie Wallendorf and Paul Anderson (eds.), Ann Arbor, MI: ACR, 218-22.

Richins, Marsha L. (1982), "An Investigation of Consumers' Attitudes Toward Complaining," in *Advances for Consumer Research*, Vol. 9, Andrew A. Mitchell (ed.), Ann Arbor, MI: ACR, 502-506.

——— (1983), "Negative Word-of-Mouth by Dissatisfied Consumers: A Pilot Study," *Journal of Marketing*, 47 (Winter), 68-78.

Singh, Jagdip (1988), "Consumer Complaint Intentions and Behavior: Definitional and Taxonomical Issues," *Journal of Marketing*, 52 (January), 93-107.

——— (1989), "Determinants of Consumers' Decisions to Seek Third Party Redress: An Empirical Study of Dissatisfied Patients," *Journal of Consumer Affairs*, 23 (Winter), 329-63.

TARP, Inc. (1979), *Consumer Complaint Handling in America: Final Report*, Washington, D.C.: White House Office of Consumer Affairs.

Ursic, Michael L. (1985), "A Model of the Consumer Decision to Seek Legal Redress," *Journal of Consumer Affairs*, 19 (Summer), 20-36.

Warland, Rex H., Robert D. Herrmann, and Jane Willits (1975), "Dissatisfied Consumers: Who Gets Upset and Who Takes Action," *Journal of Consumer Affairs*, 9 (Winter), 148-63.

Westbrook, Robert A. (1987), "Product/Consumption-Based Affective Responses and Postpurchase Processes," *Journal of Marketing Research*, 24 (August), 258-70.

Difficulty of Pre-purchase Quality Inspection: Conceptualization and Measurement

Arni Arnthorsson, University of South Carolina
Wendall E. Berry, University of South Carolina
Joel E. Urbany, University of South Carolina

ABSTRACT

In this paper, we conceptualize and develop a measurement approach for assessing "difficulty of pre-purchase quality inspection," a key construct in information economics. After reviewing the need for empirically defining this construct, we present a conceptual model to lay the foundation for our measurement procedure. Reliability of the measurement approach is acceptable. Evidence of convergent validity is provided by comparing rankings based on the DPQI measure with rankings provided by independent sources. Further, the measurement technique produces significantly higher scores (i.e., indicating easier pre-purchase quality inspection) for durables than for nondurables, as expected. Applications of such a measurement approach in examining predictions from information economics are considered.

Marketing researchers make frequent reference to Phillip Nelson's work on information and consumer behavior (see Nelson 1970; 1974). These references focus on the useful distinction between "search" and "experience" goods (e.g., Huber and Elrod 1981; Bettman 1982) and the key construct underlying the difference between them: difficulty of pre-purchase quality inspection (DPQI).

DPQI is a search cost fundamental to Nelson's research and subsequent work in the information economics area (Schmalensee 1978; Wilde 1980; 1981) and in the marketing literature (Hauser and Wernerfelt 1990). We develop a measurement procedure for DPQI here with the goal of facilitating tests of the propositions from these rich theories. Before detailing the measurement procedure, we consider the roots of the construct and a conceptual definition for it.

The Original Theory

In his widely cited theoretical and empirical research, Nelson proposed that consumer search differs quantitatively and qualitatively for products which differ in the ease/difficulty with which quality can be inspected prior to purchase. Search goods are easier to inspect prior to purchase than are experience good -- therefore consumers will sample more offerings, be better informed in general about quality, and will less likely use external cues for quality (like amount of advertising) for search goods.

This has wide implications for how sellers of search goods behave. According to the theory (Nelson 1970; 1974), they will tend to be more clustered in retail locations, will provide more informative advertising, and their industries will be less heavily concentrated than those of experience goods sellers (goods for which quality is more difficult to discern prior to purchase). In the marketing literature, concepts related to DPQI have been incorporated recently in Hauser and Wernerfelt's (1990) model of evoked set size, Tellis and Fornell's (1988) model of the advertising-quality relationship, and Zeithaml's (1988) discussion of price, quality, and perceived value. In spite of the importance of the construct in testing predictions from the theoretical work, only limited effort has been spent attempting to conceptualize and measure it.

Nelson's Empirical Operationalization

In Nelson's (1970) often-cited original paper, he empirically categorizes durable goods as either experience or search based upon aggregate ratios of nonmerchandise receipts-to-sales with the following logic: assuming that nonmerchandise receipts reflect in large part post-purchase repairs, then goods with higher ratios have a higher incidence of repairs and, therefore, a larger predominance of characteristics which could not be inspected prior to purchase. Durables with higher nonmerchandise receipts-to-sales ratios, then, were classified by Nelson as experience goods. This empirical definition suffers from (1) some leaping assumptions about the interpretation of nonmerchandise receipts and (2) the use of aggregate statistics to define a concept that effectively depends upon consumer perception. With the exception of Albion and Farris (1979), few researchers in marketing have questioned Nelson's empirical work.

A Conceptual Model of DPQI

DPQI is defined here as the difficulty of assessing or verifying the quality of a product prior to purchasing it. This definition requires specifying what is meant by "inspection" and what is meant by "quality." Inspection is defined as the consumer's effort to physically examine, assess, and verify the quality of the product at the point of purchase. Following Zeithaml (1988), quality is defined as the value or payoff that the consumer obtains from purchase and consumption of the product. Pre-purchase quality inspection, then, involves examining the product in an effort to determine (before purchasing) how well the product will deliver on the benefits the consumer expects from it.

Q for Quality = Whether the Product is Expected to Deliver the Benefits Desired. One could alternatively define quality in terms of the technical characteristics of a product or the more abstract dimensions -- i.e., the benefits (value or payoff) one derives from using the product. We focus on the latter under the assumption that, at the point of purchase, the consumer's primary objective in examining quality is to assess the product's value-in-use. We assume that the pre-purchase assessment of

FIGURE A
CONCEPTUAL MODEL OF "DIFFICULTY OF PRE-PURCHASE QUALITY INSPECTION"

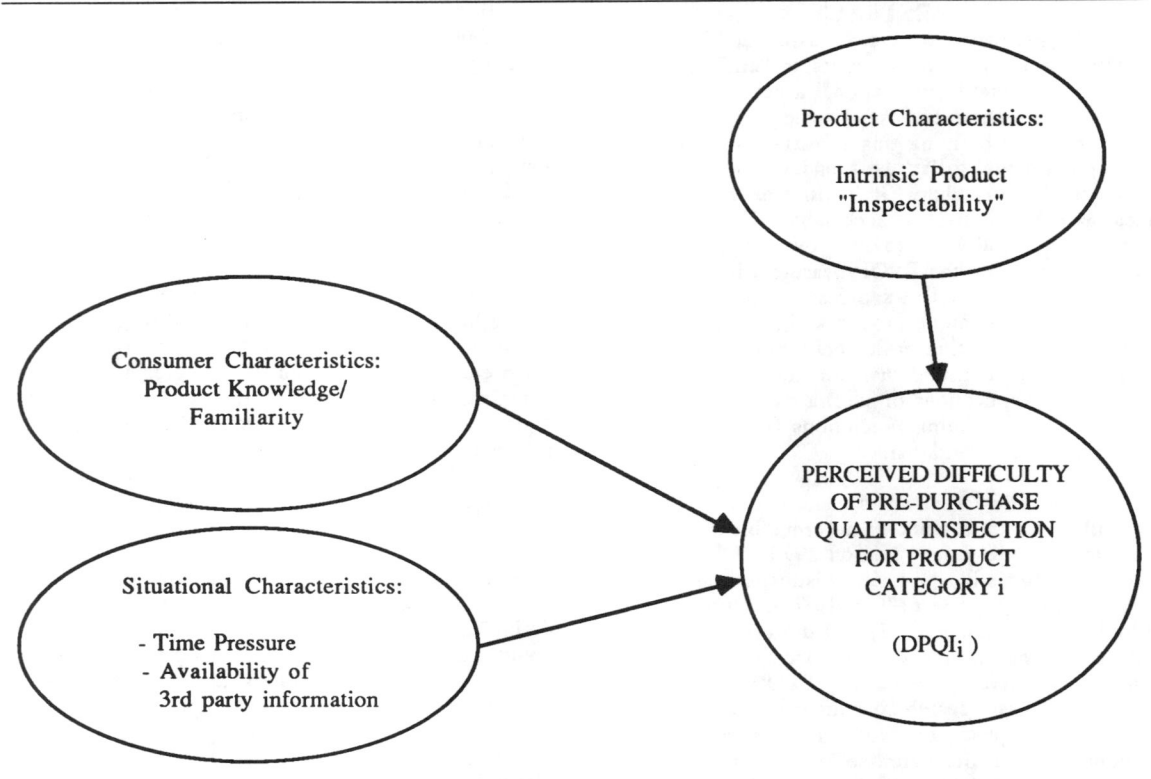

value-in-use involves the evaluation of lower level "intrinsic" attributes as a step, but the ultimate judgment relates to whether the product will deliver the benefits the consumer expects. For example, a consumer may consider an intrinsic or lower level attribute of cola (e.g., whether or not it has caffeine) as a step in assessing whether or not the product delivers a desired benefit (e.g., "helps me to stay awake"). The consumer uses the information about the intrinsic attribute to judge the product's "quality" -- i.e., whether it will deliver the desired end benefit.

D for "Difficulty" of Inspecting Quality without the Help of Extrinsic Cues. As Zeithaml (1988) notes, consumers judge product quality prior to purchase via *extrinsic* attributes (e.g., brand reputation, price) as well as via physical inspection of the product's intrinsic attributes. However, we contend that the "difficulty of inspection" measure must ignore the use of extrinsic attributes because such cues are search attributes, are generally available across product categories and, therefore, provide little help in attempting to distinguish product categories based upon DPQI. Further, many of the predictions from the information economics theories to be tested argue that consumers use extrinsic cues to judge quality more *for products which are higher in DPQI*. To test this proposition,

researchers must first have a way of separating lower DPQI products from higher DPQI products independent of the extrinsic cues attached to those products. Consistent with Nelson's original intention, then, our approach to defining DPQI focuses on the natural "inspectability" of a product's intrinsic characteristics at the point of purchase.

The Determinants of DPQI: A Simple Model

The measure of DPQI is, in essence, an empirical indicator of the "inspectability" of a product's intrinsic characteristics, stripped of brand name and price information. This is depicted in Figure A. Independent of the product's inspectability, however, DPQI may vary across consumers and even within consumers across different situations. Prior familiarity with the product should, all else equal, reduce DPQI, as experienced consumers who have gone through the consumption process may be able to more confidently estimate prior to purchase the chance that a product will perform adequately in the consumption setting (Tellis and Fornell 1988).

Further, characteristics of the purchase situation may influence the difficulty that a consumer has in inspecting a product's quality prior to purchase. For example, time pressure will generally have the effect of making pre-purchase quality assessment more difficult, potentially even for an experienced consumer evaluating a product which tends to have predominantly search characteristics. Finally, the availability of external information sources naturally influences DPQI. A salesperson or *Consumer Reports* can provide useful product information even (or, perhaps, *especially*) for the most difficult to evaluate products. Consistent with this, Nelson (1974) proposes that advertising to sales ratios will be greater for experience goods industries.

The survey procedure for measuring DPQI described below also incorporates the measurement of individual respondent familiarity with the product, as we naturally want to examine the influence of familiarity on DPQI. We either ignore or hold constant the other determinants of product category "inspectability" described in the Figure A model. We ignore situational characteristics given the random nature with which they are likely to occur in the marketplace (i.e., it is not clear that time pressure would be associated systematically with certain product categories and not others). We hold constant the external information sources (e.g., sales people, where relevant) by instructing respondents to assume that no such source is available as they are evaluating the product prior to purchasing it.

Predictions. While the major purpose of this paper is to develop and evaluate a scale to measure DPQI, two predictions are also assessed. The predictions simply provide a basis for determining whether the scale produces face valid results. The first is based upon Nelson's (1970) contention that durables have more "searchable" qualities than do nondurables. The second is based on the intuition from our model that familiarity should be negatively related to DPQI. Formally stated:

P1: Durables should have lower DPQI scores than nondurables.

P2: DPQI scores for low familiarity respondents should be higher than those for high familiarity respondents.

METHOD

DPQI Scale Development

Our procedure for measuring DPQI evolved over a series of attempts to ask consumers how easy/difficult it was to judge a given product's quality before purchase. The failures led to a procedure which focused on *end benefits*. In this final procedure, questions were framed in terms of how sure respondents could be (prior to purchase) that a specific end benefit would be obtained if they purchased a new brand X after evaluating it only at the point of purchase. Sureness was measured on a 10 point scale ranging from "I'm UNSURE before I buy" to "I'm SURE before I buy." To illustrate, the Appendix provides the page from the questionnaire which asked respondents to evaluate a new brand of VCR.

Pilot Study. A pilot study was done for the purposes of (1) determining product categories with which students would be most familiar and (2) determining what attributes/end benefits should be included in the measures for each product category. The pilot study involved a paper and pencil survey of 80 undergraduate business majors. The survey asked respondents to rate their familiarity with 29 durable and nondurable product categories and to list the important considerations in evaluating the quality of the five product categories with which they were most familiar. Based upon the familiarity ratings and the five most familiar products identified, ten products were selected for the study -- NONDURABLES: beer, soda (2 litre, plastic bottle), toothpaste, cold cereal (flakes), deodorant; DURABLES: a VCR, a television set, a head stereo set (Walkman), jeans, and a wrist watch.

As the pre-purchase assessment of quality ultimately relates to the expected benefits, a list of benefits was generated for each of the ten products. The pilot study responses, along with Garvin's (1987) eight general dimensions of product quality (performance, features, reliability, conformance, durability, serviceability, aesthetics, and perceived quality) provided a framework for enumerating end benefits for each product category. In evaluating each product category, we attempted to generate statements of benefits/attributes for the relevant dimensions from Garvin's framework, making sure to address all the issues mentioned by the pilot study respondents. Five to eight questions were generated for each product.

Survey Administration

One hundred and four undergraduate business students each responded to the final questionnaire, which included the following measures for each of ten product categories: (1) the sureness measures for each of several benefits/attributes, (2) three measures of product familiarity (see the Appendix), and (3) rankings of several brands on quality, advertising, and price (not reported in this paper). Four respondents were eliminated from the sample for providing incomplete or incoherent responses. For half the questionnaires, a random ordering of the products was used. This ordering was reversed for the other half. It was found that product ordering had no effect on any of the key measures in the study.

The survey was administered in a classroom setting, with all respondents present at once. Prior to beginning the questionnaire, respondents were given explicit instruction on the use of the measures in the questionnaire. Overhead transparencies were used to explain the measures and their meaning. The questionnaire took from between 25 and 45 minutes to complete.

RESULTS

The questionnaire administration involved having respondents judge their "sureness" in

TABLE 1
SURENESS ABOUT JUDGING QUALITY[a] PRIOR TO PURCHASE

PRODUCT CATEGORY	Low sureness about benefits delivered		Moderate sureness about benefits delivered		High sureness about benefits delivered	
1. Deodorant	rash proof	(3.3)	smells good	(5.8)	easy to apply	(6.8)
	stops wetness	(4.1)				
	stops bad odor	(4.4)				
2. Cold Cereal (Flakes)	tastes good	(4.1)	stays fresh	(5.2)	satisfies hunger	(6.3)
			not too sweet	(5.3)	nutritious	(7.3)
3. 2 Litre Soft Drink (plastic bottle)	not too sweet	(4.0)	keeps you awake	(5.0)	quenches thirst	(6.2)
	stays fizzy	(4.0)	not fattening	(6.1)		
	tastes good	(4.0)				
4. Toothpaste	won't irritate	(3.9)	removes tartar	(5.1)	easy container	(6.8)
	tastes good	(4.6)	no bad breath	(5.5)		
	whitens teeth	(4.7)	no cavities	(5.6)		
5. Beer (six pack cans)	tastes good	(3.9)	too fattening	(5.4)		
	keeps taste	(4.1)	quenches thirst	(6.0)		
	too filling	(4.6)				
6. Jeans	will (won't fade)	(4.6)	comfortable	(5.9)	will fit	(6.4)
			will last	(5.9)	style appealing	(8.3)
					color match	(8.6)
7. Head Stereo Set (Walkman)	will last	(4.2)	clear sound	(5.4)	has features	(7.9)
	will be reliable	(4.3)	volume	(6.0)	style appealing	(8.2)
	good reception	(4.9)			right size	(8.4)
8. VCR	rewinds quickly	(4.0)	compatible	(5.6)	has features	(7.0)
	searches quickly	(4.3)			right size	(7.9)
	will be reliable	(4.3)				
	will last	(4.3)				
9. Wrist Watch	will last	(4.7)	accurate	(5.4)	has features	(7.6)
					color match	(8.6)
					style appealing	(8.8)
10. Television Set	will last	(4.7)	good reception	(5.7)	compatible	(6.7)
					clear picture	(7.0)
					quick channel change	(7.1)
					good sound	(7.1)
					has features	(7.6)
					right size	(8.6)

[a]The survey questions asked respondents how sure they were about judging prior to purchase whether the product would deliver the specific end benefits listed in the table.

evaluating a new brand's quality prior to purchase on several benefits/attributes. Reliability is evaluated via a test-retest procedure for four of the ten products used. Convergent validity is evaluated by comparing the ranking of the 10 products produced by four "experts" (based upon a separate measurement procedure) with the ranking produced by our respondents (based upon their average "sureness" ratings). We then assessed the general a priori expectation that the five durables in the product list would be easier to evaluate prior to purchase than the nondurables and that respondents more familiar with the product category would report being more sure about pre-purchase quality evaluation than respondents less familiar.

TABLE 2
OVERALL RANKINGS OF THE 10 PRODUCT CATEGORIES ON DPQI

	Rank Order (mean sureness score in parentheses: lower sureness = higher DPQI)		
Product Category	Low Familiarity	High Familiarity	Experts[a]
NONDURABLES:			
Deodorant	4 (4.90)	1 (4.99)	3
2 litre soft drink	2 (4.41)	2 (5.25)[b]	1.5
Toothpaste	5 (5.17)	3 (5.27)	5
Beer	1 (3.97)	4 (5.70)[b]	1.5
Cold cereal	6 (5.34)	5 (5.83)	4
DURABLES:			
VCR	3 (4.52)	6 (6.13)[b]	7
Head Stereo Set	7 (5.76)	7 (6.70)[b]	9
Jeans	8 (6.41)	8 (6.99)	10
Television Set	9 (6.67)	9 (7.07)	8
Wrist Watch	10 (6.71)	10 (7.42)[b]	6

[a] Experts were four teaching faculty colleagues. They provided a global ranking of the products (i.e., they did not respond to the DPQI measures).

[b] Difference between mean sureness scores for low and high familiarity subjects is significant.

Reliability

DPQI for the ith consumer and the jth product was empirically determined by calculating the average sureness for that consumer across the attributes for that product category. To evaluate the reliability of this indicator of DPQI, a second administration of the questionnaire including four of the original product categories was undertaken with 88 of the original respondents. Just four product categories were chosen to reduce the required time for answering the second questionnaire. The product categories most familiar to pilot test respondents were selected (toothpaste, wrist watch, soft drink, jeans). The overall test-retest correlation for the average sureness measure (aggregating the data across the 4 products) was .67, an acceptable level for basic research (Nunnally 1967).

Convergent Validity

Three faculty members and one doctoral student were asked to provide an overall ranking of the 10 product categories based upon their general perceptions of the ease/difficulty of inspecting the product's quality at the point of purchase (with no brand name or price information available). The experts' aggregate ranking (based upon the average ranking of each product category across the four experts) is presented in the last column in Table 2, next to the rankings provided by the low and high familiarity respondents based upon their average sureness measures (to be discussed later). The Spearman rank order correlations between the experts' and respondents' rankings are .72 for low familiarity respondents (t=2.92, p<.05) and .75 for high familiarity respondents (t=3.19, p<.05). In short, there was strong agreement between the independent product rankings provided by the experts and the rankings produced by the DPQI scale, providing evidence of convergent validity.

Descriptive Results

For each product category, each respondent rated their perceived "sureness" in judging (prior to purchase) whether a new brand would deliver on five to eight end benefits. The overall mean position of each attribute (or end benefit) for each product category on the sureness scale is presented in Table 1. In the table, nondurables are presented first and durables second. The attributes of each product are categorized based upon the sample's mean sureness ratings on the 10 point scale. Each attribute is categorized as either in the middle of the scale (not significantly different from the middle point 5.5), or toward the low/high end of the scale (significantly different from the middle point). In Nelson's terminology, the attributes on the lower end of the scale would tend to be experience attributes (i.e., respondents less sure about their ability to evaluate the benefits prior to purchase) while the attributes on the higher end would tend to be search attributes.

In examining the attributes falling in the column marked "low sureness," it is clear that they tend to relate to such unobservable (prior to purchase) characteristics as performance, taste, reliability, and durability. The attributes falling in the third column, "high sureness" tend to be more observable, relating to available product features, product color, style, size, and benefits delivered via packaging. Just two of the ten products failed to support our general expectation that the nondurables' attributes would tend toward low sureness and that the durables' attributes would tend toward the high sureness end of the scale. For cereal, only taste falls into the low sureness category, while judgments of nutrition and hunger satisfaction were on the higher sureness end of the scale. This latter finding could be a result of package information and/or respondents' confidence in generalizing from experience with other brands. The other exception is the VCR category, which predominantly has features which are difficult to evaluate outside of the consumption context. In hindsight, the key attributes of a VCR do tend to be more difficult to observe (or more difficult for a salesperson to demonstrate) than, say, the key attributes of a TV.

Explaining the Variance in DPQI

An ANOVA model was run which examined differences in DPQI across the ten product categories and two familiarity groups. The three measures of familiarity for each product category ("familiar," "experienced in using," "experienced in shopping for") had an overall alpha of .87 across the 10 product categories. For each product category, these three measures were summed to form an index, and respondents were split into low and high familiarity groups for each product category based upon a median split.

The 10 X 2 ANOVA model explained 23 percent of the variance in DPQI. Both the product and familiarity factors had significant main effects ($F(9, 1006) = 28.37$, $p < .001$ for product; $F(1, 1006) = 53.41$, $p < .001$ for familiarity) and, unexpectedly, the interaction was significant as well ($F(9, 1006) = 2.65$, $p < .01$). The significant product effect appears due to the lower average sureness scores received by nondurables.[1] The interaction occurs because familiarity increased sureness for some product categories (beer, soda, wrist watch, vcr, head stereo set) but not others. The reason for this is not entirely clear. In sum, the scale passes our test of face validity in detecting differences in DPQI between durables and nondurables. The results are consistent for half of the product categories with the expectation that DPQI would be lower for consumers more familiar with the product category.[2]

DISCUSSION

A limitation of the proposed procedure for measuring DPQI is that respondents are asked to answer questions which require them to "pretend" that they are evaluating a new brand at the point of purchase. Further, they are asked to assume that they have no external information available (other than packaging). This approach asks a lot of respondents' ability to imagine the situation. In spite of this potential shortcoming, however, the DPQI measure showed reasonable reliability and convergent validity and, further, was sensitive enough to identify differences between durables and nondurables. Future development of the measurement approach will focus on identifying aspects of the questioning approach that are not entirely clear to respondents. While there appeared to be no confusion among our respondents during administration, the test-retest reliability suggests that improvements can be made in making the questions more concrete.

Why does one care to measure DPQI? We contend that DPQI is one of a class of costs facing consumers which may affect consumer behavior in important ways (Hauser and Wernerfelt 1990; Zeithaml 1988). Further, the empirical identification of how product classes vary in DPQI holds the potential of examining many propositions regarding how sellers behave under varying conditions of consumer search/evaluation cost.

REFERENCES

Albion, Mark S. and Paul W. Farris (1979), "Appraising Research on Advertising's Economic Impact," Marketing Science Institute Working Paper 79-115, Cambridge, MA.

---

[1] A separate 2 X 2 ANOVA substituting a two level durability factor for the product factor indicated that nondurables had significantly lower sureness scores than did durables ($p < .001$), and found no interaction between durability and familiarity.

[2] A reviewer has noted correctly that the relationship between familiarity and DPQI may be driven in part by the fact that the constructs were measured on the same page of the questionnaire.

APPENDIX
ILLUSTRATION OF DPQI SCALE QUESTIONS: VCR

VIDEO CASSETTE RECORDER (VCR)

ASSUME: You're in the store, examining a NEW brand of VCR. There's no price on the VCR. There's no salesperson available to help you.

BY JUST INSPECTING THE VCR
IN THE STORE (before you buy)
HOW SURE CAN YOU BE THAT:

	I'm UNSURE before I buy									I'm SURE before I buy
it will rewind tapes quickly?	1	2	3	4	5	6	7	8	9	10
it will allow you to "search" uickly?	1	2	3	4	5	6	7	8	9	10
it will be compatible with your television set?	1	2	3	4	5	6	7	8	9	10
it has all the features that you'll need?	1	2	3	4	5	6	7	8	9	10
it is the right size for you?	1	2	3	4	5	6	7	8	9	10
it will be reliable?	1	2	3	4	5	6	7	8	9	10
it will keep working for a reasonable time?	1	2	3	4	5	6	7	8	9	10
it will generally meet your expectations?	1	2	3	4	5	6	7	8	9	10

Please rate yourself on the following scales:

Familiar with VCRs	____:____:____:____:____:____:____	Unfamiliar with VCRs
Experienced in using VCRs	____:____:____:____:____:____:____	Inexperienced in using VCRs
Experienced in shopping for VCRs	____:____:____:____:____:____:____	Inexperienced in shopping for VCRs

Bettman, James R. (1982), "A Functional Analysis of the Role of Overall Evaluation of Alternatives in Choice Processes," in Andrew Mitchell (ed.), *Advances in Consumer Research*, Vol. 9, Chicago: Association for Consumer Research.

Hauser, John R. and Birger Wernerfelt (1990), "An Evaluation Cost Model of Evoked Sets," *Journal of Consumer Research*, 16 (March), 393-408.

Huber, Joel, and Terry Elrod (1981), "Consumer Learning through Experience: A Study and Experimental Paradigm," in Kent Monroe (ed.), *Advances in Consumer Research*, Vol. 8, Chicago: Association for Consumer Research.

Nelson, Philip (1980), "Advertising and Ethics," in Tom L. Beauchamp and Norman E. Bowie (eds.), *Ethical Theory and Business*, Englewood Cliffs, NJ: Prentice-Hall, 343-7.

_____ (1978), "Advertising as Information Once More," in David Tuerck (ed.), *Issues in Advertising*, Washington, D.C.: American Enterprise Institute, 133-60.

_____ (1975), "The Economic Consequences of Advertising," *Journal of Business*, 48 (April), 213-41.

_____ (1974), "Advertising as Information," *Journal of Political Economy*, 81 (July/August), 729-54.

_____ (1970), "Information and Consumer Behavior," *Journal of Political Economy*, 78 (March/April), 311-29.

Nunnally, Jum C. (1967), *Psychometric Methods*, New York: McGraw-Hill.

Parasuraman, A., Valerie A. Zeithaml, and Leonard L. Berry (1985), "A Conceptual Model of Service Quality and Its Implications for Future Research," *Journal of Marketing*, 49 (Fall), 41-50.

Tellis, Gerard J. and Claes Fornell (1988), "The Relationship between Advertising and Product Quality over the Product Life Cycle: A Contingency Theory," *Journal of Marketing Research*, 25 (February), 64-71.

Zeithaml, Valerie A. (1988), "Consumer Perceptions of Price, Quality, and Value: A Means-End Model and Synthesis of Evidence," *Journal of Marketing*, 52 (July), 2-22.

Expert-novice Differences in Complaint Scripts
Ingrid Martin, University of Southern California[1]

ABSTRACT

Script theory is the theoretical framework used to investigate expert/novice differences in a complaint domain. This exploratory study investigated the differences in content knowledge between experts and novices as well as the differences in the ability to generalize to novel complaint situations. Three hypotheses were examined. H1 found that there is a significant difference between experts and novices based on prior knowledge, certainty and effort expended on the complaint process. H2 and H3 found that experts are better able to generalize their knowledge to a novel problem.

INTRODUCTION

We all know what it is like to discover that your luggage hasn't arrived or that your flight will be delayed for several hours. But, do we all know how to resolve these problems? Typically, these problems are resolved by complaining. However, not all people know how to complain, and those that do, may not know how to complain effectively. For example in a recent article in the Wall Street Journal, it was found that "... many fliers don't know that most airlines will put them on another carrier - if asked to - when a flight is canceled". It was concluded that "... you've got to know to ask" and many consumers just don't have the appropriate knowledge base to deal effectively with complaint situations.

When representative groups of consumers were examined in various studies, it was found that a large number of consumers do not complain or complain ineffectively when confronted with problems concerning products, services or issues (e.g. Best & Andreasen 1977). Some of the factors that have been consistently found to influence propensity to complain include the economic and psychological costs and benefits of seeking redress as well as various demographic characteristics. The critical issue that has not been addressed in the complaint literature is whether this large group of consumers has the awareness and knowledge required to effectively complain.

It is important to understand why some people are more effective at complaining than others. This requires determining the content of the knowledge base for complaining and understanding how an effective complainer differs from an ineffective complainer or a noncomplainer in a complaint domain.

This exploratory study categorizes effective complainers as experts and ineffective complainers as novices. This differentiation of complainers is based on the premise that experts have more complete representations of a task domain (Chi, et al. 1982). The appropriate organization of knowledge should allow experts to perform the complaint task more effectively than novices.

Using scripts as the theoretical framework to investigate consumers' knowledge in the complaint domain addresses the call for theoretical constructs to better understand consumer complaint behavior (Fornell & Didow 1980). This type of knowledge structure stores a set of standard event sequences that guide behavior in a routine situation. The objective of this study is to investigate the content of scripts for experts and novices in a specific complaint domain. For example, expert complainers should have elaborate scripts which contribute to more effective complaint outcomes, whereas novices in a similar complaint situation, will have a much simpler script resulting in less effective complaining.

What follows is an exploratory study designed to address the differences in content knowledge of experts and novices in a complaint domain. Previous research has established the need for further study regarding the complaint process to better understand the phenomenon (e.g. Day, et al., 1978). The critical differentiating factors in the content of scripts for expert and novice complainers are the amount of prior knowledge in the complaint process, the certainty they have in the complaint outcome, and the overall effort expended on complaining.

LITERATURE REVIEW

Script Content

A script is defined as a "... coherent sequence of events expected by the individual, involving him either as a participant or as an observer" (Abelson 1976, 1981). It consists of knowledge stored in longterm memory as sets of well structured cognitions that have been learned over time as experience accumulates. Specifically, these mental representations contain a series of actions causally linked in hierarchical order involving props and participants in common activities.

The expectations that an individual has in a particular situation act as a cue to automatically trigger the appropriate script. For example, if you order a hamburger and the waitperson brings you a ham and cheese sandwich instead, the expectation that you were to get a hamburger acts as a cue to trigger the complaint script. At this point, you will tell the waitperson a mistake has been made and to bring the correct order. The usefulness of a script is related to its ability to conserve limited processing capacity. Since a script retains the action sequences of prior situations, the individual doesn't have to re-learn the steps every time this sequence of actions is needed. She can use that processing capacity to

---

[1] The author gratefully acknowledges the guidance and helpful comments of Henrianne Sanft as well as three referees.

better develop her script to include new steps needed to more effectively complain.

This implies that once a person has a well developed script for some sequence of actions such as eating in a restaurant or complaining about poor service on an airline flight, the expert's script will result in routine response behavior. The novice, in contrast, will have to seek out information and put more effort into learning the appropriate complaint process.

Experts and Novices

The literature on expert/novice differences addresses several important factors that are relevant to this study. First, novices and experts have consistently been found to differ on the complexity and size of their knowledge base. Experts have larger and more complex knowledge bases from which to draw on when "... mapping new problems in terms of familiar patterns" (Charness, 1983). This is extended to the problem solving situation that experts and novices face when a problem arises concerning consumer products or services. The expert's complaint script should have the knowledge to allow her to generalize from one familiar complaint situation to a new complaint situation in a given domain. For example, an expert complainer in poor service at a restaurant, when faced with a new problem of a broken toaster, will have the knowledge to effectively complain.

Following from above, the literature shows that experts in domains such as chess, and other problem solving situations, have been found to produce more accurate solutions than novices (e.g. Larkin, et al. 1980). This would imply that expert complainers are also more effective complainers than novice complainers. Chase and Simon (1973) found that skill level in chess players varies by the number of move generations. In other words, less skilled players (novices) might run out of potential moves before the more skilled players (experts). The solution to these problem solving situations (i.e. chess) is mediated by the level of knowledge, potential moves, and other variables encountered by the player. This is similar to the mediating factors (e.g. who is receiving the complaint, what type of day they are having) encountered by the complainant. This implies that novice complainers either give up or resort to "sabotage" behavior unlike an expert complainer.

Charness (1981) conducted a study on age and skill differences in chess playing and found that expert chess players search more extensively and deeply for a solution. This can be extended to the complaint arena where an expert complainer would expend more overall effort to pursue a problem than would a novice. This increase in effort to solve the problem is a result of a knowledge structure with a larger, more complex content.

Underlying Dimensions Of Scripts

The study of expert-novice differences in schematic and category structures has resulted in several common underlying dimensions (e.g. Galambos & Rips, 1982). The underlying factors used to differentiate the content of the knowledge base of the expert and novice include centrality, contingency and hypotheticality measures. These three dimensions play a critical role in the different complaining results found between experts and novices.[2] Centrality is a "... measure of how important an action is to its activity" (Galambos, 1986). These actions are the major goals or subgoals of the activity. For example, in the restaurant script the central actions would be "look at a menu, order meal, eat food, pay bill, leave" (Bower, et al.,1979). An individual who has little experience in a given domain will have the major goals and subgoals relevant to a particular domain-related task. Galambos (1986) found that subjects' centrality information tended to be coordinated with subgoal information in activities. The above implies that as prior experience, certainty in the outcome and overall complaining effort increase, based on many single experiences in a particular domain, so will the number of possible central actions within the complaint script.

Contingency is the hierarchical structure of well developed scripts among experienced subjects which includes conditional statements to cover more variations. These conditional statements serve as decision trees containing alternative sets of subgoals when obstacles are encountered in a complaint situation. For example, *if* a store clerk is unable to help with a defective toaster, *then* a expert complainer would ask to speak to the store manager. This would continue until a satisfactory outcome was obtained much the same as the expert bridge player who revises his bid given added information from his partner. This also shows that subjects with less expertise are more constrained in how they are able to deal with variations in the script. For example, a novice bridge player may not realize the need to revise her bid.

The last dimension, hypotheticality, refers to the level of abstraction of the knowledge structure. Greater expertise allows individuals to generalize from previous experiences to a new experience. Individuals with less expertise have scripts with more concrete representations and display less successful behavior when confronted with a novel situation. For example, an expert should be able to effectively complain in a new complaint situation in the same domain. This does not hold for a novice who has less general knowledge about complaining due to less prior experience, less certainty in the complaint outcome, and less effort expended on the complaining process.

---

[2] A fourth dimension, distinctiveness, has been identified as a factor in cognitive scripts. This dimension refers to the extent to which an action is unique to a particular track of a script. Subjects were asked for a specific complaint situation rather than a general complaint script. There were little, if any, listings of distinctive actions in the written protocols of either experts or novices.

Determinants of Script Dimensions

The three independent variables believed to determine the level of centrality, contingency, and hypotheticality of the knowledge structure are prior knowledge in the specific domain of interest, certainty in the complaint outcome, and the overall effort that subjects will devote to the complaint process. This is based on the concept that learning involves any process that "... modifies a system so as to improve, more or less irreversibly, its subsequent performance of the same task or of tasks drawn from the same population" (Langley & Simon, 1981). This implies that as expertise increases subjects should be able to go from using a situation specific knowledge structure to a more general knowledge structure.

The independent variable, prior knowledge, is based on the direct and vicarious experience that a person has with the complaint process. Alba and Hutchinson (1987) found that the ability to solve a problem is partially determined by one's prior experience and knowledge in that domain. In familiar complaint situations, prior experience may lead to the direct retrieval of a prior solution outlined in an elaborate, routinized script. Another aspect of prior knowledge is the simple repetition of the task performance resulting in a more elaborate knowledge base.

The next independent variable is certainty in the successful complaint outcome. In other words, the amount of confidence that a person has in the resulting outcome of a problem has a positive effect on knowledge (Fischoff & MacGregor, 1982). This implies that lack of expertise in an area tends to increase perceived risk and decrease certainty in the knowledge a person has about an issue. Hence, a person is more likely to cease complaining when confronted with an unresponsive complainee. The resulting uncertainty tends to invoke heuristics (Folkes, 1986). For example, if the ticket agent doesn't help you with your problem then you conclude that airlines are unresponsive to customer needs and you cease to complain. This means that certainty in a successful complaint outcome can lead to an increase in expertise. Therefore, experts are believed to have a higher certainty measure than novices when involved in a complaint situation.

The independent variable, overall effort, is based on the attribution theory of motivation. This theory suggests that when people make behavioral attributions concerning a problem they are motivated to act (Weiner 1980). People want to maximize the probability of a successful complaint, therefore, putting more effort into complaining can increase the certainty that they will be successful. The increased effort involved in ensuring a successful outcome furthers the mastery of the complaint process. Thus, to ensure a successful outcome, an expert will expend more effort to pursue all the required subgoals. This is in contrast to the novice, who lacking the elaborate script structure, will display minimal effort in complaining. Instead the novice may expend more effort in such action as negative word of mouth, boycotting stores and switching brands. This is be discussed further in the supplemental analysis section.

HYPOTHESES

The content of the knowledge base that expert and novice complainers have is organized in terms of central actions, contingency sub-branches, and hypotheticality measures. The central actions are the goals and subgoals of the script whereas the contingency statements lead the subjects to the relevant subgoals. The hypotheticality information determines the level of abstraction that the knowledge is organized in memory. This content base is shaped by the different levels of prior experience, certainty, and effort that experts and novices attach to the complaint process. The research hypotheses of interest are:

H_1: As prior knowledge, certainty, and overall effort increase, subjects' scripts will provide more central actions, contingency statements, and hypotheticality measures.

H_2: An expert's script will not differ significantly across familiar and unfamiliar complaint situations for centrality, contingency and hypotheticality measures.

H_3: A novice's scripts will be significantly different across familiar and unfamiliar complaint situations for centrality, contingency, and hypotheticality measures.

The first hypothesis tests the content of the knowledge between experts and novices whereas the remaining two hypotheses investigate the differences in the ability of experts and novices to generalize to domain tasks in which they have no experience. It is expected that novices should not be able to generalize across new complaint tasks whereas experts should have no problem generalizing to new complaint situation.

MEASURES

Dependent Measures

The dependent variables in this study are centrality, contingency, and hypotheticality. Centrality is operationalized as the total number of central or basic actions reported in the written protocols. The centrality measure was determined by comparing both scripts for common statements. These basic actions were determined to be critical to all complaint situations. An example would be "... complain about problem to appropriate person".

Contingency was measured by counting the number of conditional clauses in the elicited scripts. The methodology developed by Martin, et al. (1980) was used to code statements in each protocol that included such clauses as "either, or; neither, nor; if-then; depending on; unless; etc".

Hypotheticality was determined also using the Martin, et al. (1980) methodology of summary totals of the number of general statements made, roles mentioned, and frequency indicators. The approach was based on the premise that "... increased ability for abstraction requires more general statements, frequency indicators, and roles to summarize multiple incidents whereas describing isolated episodes does not" (Leong, et al. 1989).[3]

The hypotheticality measure, was coded for four different categories of statements. The first was the number of times that frequency words were used such as "frequently, some, many, and other synonyms. The second coded group was the number of general statements that subjects made about the complaint process. This included statements such as "the waitress will usually..." or other statements which refer to all events. The third group of codes related to the number of job or role titles that were mentioned in each protocol. For example, "... I reported the problem to the clerk ... then I asked to speak to the manager...". The final code was tallied for the number of examples or incidental events included in each protocol.

Independent Measures

The independent variables for this experiment were prior knowledge, certainty, and effort. Prior knowledge was a composite measure of frequency of complaint experiences and familiarity with the complaint process. Certainty and overall effort were measured using likert scales. The certainty measure looked at the likelihood that experts would have a higher level of confidence in the complaint outcome. Overall effort measured the likelihood of pursuing all possible complaint options.

METHODOLOGY

The students in this study were 35 undergraduate students in an advertising course in a major university. The dependent constructs for this study were operationalized in the form of two script elicitations. The subjects were asked to report the types of complaint situations they had been involved in from a comprehensive list of possible complaint situations. This list included such complaint situations as poor service in a restaurant, defective merchandise, lost baggage, and so on. They indicated the approximate number of times they had complained about a problem over the last year. Next, half of the subjects were asked to select a complaint situation in which they had no experience from this list and to write down all the possible steps they would take to complain until all avenues were exhausted. The other half of the group was asked to do the same task for the complaint situation in which they had the most experience. Then the next task was reversed for both groups so that all subjects provided two script elicitations, one for an experienced complaint situation and one for a novel complaint situation. The students were given as much time as they wished to finish the task. After completing the questionnaire, the students were debriefed concerning the study.

RESULTS

Due to the exploratory nature of this study, expertise was measured, not manipulated, resulting in the need to conduct a median split on the three independent variables. This approach was used so that subjects could be categorized into either expert or novice groups. The median value of the prior knowledge was five complaint experiences in one year reported by the subject. The second independent variable was a five point certainty scale with a median value of three. This was midway between being very certain and very uncertain of a successful resolution to the complaint. The last independent variable was the likelihood that a person would make the effort to complain about the problem. A median split resulted in a value of three, midway between very unlikely and very likely that someone would make this effort. The next step categorized subjects into expert and novice groups if they scored either above or below the median value on *all* the independent variables. The result was a sample size of 10 novices and 9 experts.

The first hypothesis (H1) was concerned with the difference between experts and novices in measures of centrality, contingency, and hypotheticality. Three separate repeated measures ANOVAs were run with one within-subjects factor (familiar and novel experience) and one between-subjects factor (expert-novice). The result of the analysis found that expert complainers had a significantly higher number of central actions, contingency statements and hypotheticality measures. (See Table One.) This implies that experts may have a more abstract and elaborate script content. The interaction effects were not significant for centrality and contingency measures. There was a significant interaction effect between expertise and familiar and novel experience situation in the hypotheticality measure. This significant interaction points to the possibility that an increase in hypotheticality measures (i.e. roles, general statements, incidental events) may be critical to making a novice an expert. That is, increasing people's knowledge about various roles when complaining may point to the alternatives available to the complainer. In the airline complaint script, learning that other people (i.e. customer relations personnel, ticket agents, pilots, travel agents) are

---

[3] The preceding measures were evaluated by two coders who were blind to the objectives of the study. The judges were required to code separately each sentence of the written protocol. For each sentence the judges coded the centrality, contingency and hypotheticality measures. The results of each protocol were compared and descrepancies were discussed between the judges until an agreement was made as to the appropriate code.

TABLE ONE
RESULTS FROM REPEATED MEASURES ANALYSIS OF VARIANCE FOR EXPERTISE AND FREQUENCY

Source	Mean Square	F-value	Probability
Centrality Measures:			
Expertise	26.2278	11.96	.003
Familiar vs. Novel Experience	11.4631	11.46	.001
Interaction	.0947	.13	.727
Contingency Measures:			
Expertise	19.7661	7.08	.016
Familiar vs. Novel Experience	5.0947	5.48	.031
Interaction	.0421	.05	.834
Hypotheticality Measures:			
Expertise	24.0845	10.92	.004
Familiar vs. Novel Experience	165.7921	80.41	.000
Interaction	20.8446	10.11	.005

TABLE TWO
MEANS AND STANDARD DEVIATIONS FOR DEPENDENT MEASURES

	Novice	Expert
Centrality: Familiar Experience	2.200 (1.22)	3.778 (1.20)
Centrality: Novel Experience	1.00 (0.67)	2.778 (1.64)
Contingency: Familiar Experience	1.400 (1.42)	2.778 (1.39)
Contingency: Novel Experience	0.600 (.084)	2.111 (1.69)
Hypothetical: Familiar Experience	2.700 (1.63)	5.778 (2.43)
Hypothetical: Novel Experience	1.300 (1.05)	5.333 (4.00)

possible outlets for complaining is critical to a successful complaint outcome. This means they are not confined to stop the process at the first person with whom they complain. The knowledge that other functional roles are available to move their complaint forward will increase expertise in the process.

The second hypothesis predicted that experts would have no problem generalizing their script knowledge to a new complaint situation. This was tested in a difference of means test for the three dependent measures. The results show that experts were not significantly different in centrality, contingency and hypotheticality measures when asked to relate a complaint script for a complaint task in which they had no experience (t=1.47, p=.09; t=.92, p=.19; t=.288, p=.71, respectively). The results indicate that experts have the knowledge base needed to generalize their complaint script to a novel situation. This implies that an expert should be able to successfully complain about a new problem. This is similar to the expert chess player, who encounters a new chess move made by an opponent and is able to counter that move due to his ability to generalize from past experiences.

The third hypothesis (H3) stated that novices would not be able to generalize their script knowledge to a new complaint situation. The difference of means test for centrality and hypotheticality were highly significant (t=2.72, p=.008; t=2.30, p=.0175, respectively) and the contingency measure was marginally significant (t=1.54, p=.065). This means that a novice complainer, however capable of handling a specific problem, will not be able to generalize that knowledge to a new situation. Much the same occurs with the novice chess player who must concede the game when a new move is made by her opponent.

Supplemental Analysis

Earlier it was argued that novices would put less overall effort into the complaint process and instead, turn to such actions as boycotting the store, switching brands, warning friends and family to avoid the firm and so on. A directional difference of means test was conducted on the number of "sabotage" statements made by both experts and novices. The results show that novices did tend to include more "sabotage" statements in their scripts than experts (t=2.02, p=.03).

DISCUSSION AND CONCLUSIONS

Theoretical Implications

This exploratory study was designed to address two specific questions about the content of the knowledge base in a given domain. This was accomplished through the comparison of the knowledge base of an expert with that of a novice. The first critical finding is associated with the content of the knowledge base in memory between these two groups. Experts have significantly more central actions, contingent actions, and hypothetical information stored in their scripts. This allows them the flexibility to deal with many different obstacles that could be encountered in the complaint process.

The second critical finding is the difference between the ability of an expert to abstract to new complaint situations whereas a novice is more restricted in her/his ability to generalize. This restriction in the novice's knowledge is what a columnist for the Wall Street Journal referred to when he said that "... many travelers say complaints don't bring the results they used to, but speaking up still can have rewards with airlines". It goes back to the basics; you have to know how to complain effectively.

By understanding the content of the knowledge structure one uses to guide behavior, we are one step closer to understanding the process by which a novice becomes an expert. An important theoretical implication from this study is that this lays the foundation for further research in understanding how novices become experts. Understanding the differences between the two knowledge bases can provide some insight into how knowledge for routine event sequences develop in adults.

Managerial Implications

Understanding the complaint process that consumers use is not only critical to a firm's customer relations but intrinsic to intraorganizational relationships as well. If a firm has a good grasp of what consumers' perceive as the sequential set of complaint actions, then a firm can develop a responsive set of policies that will portray them as customer-oriented. An example of this is Nordstrom's liberal policy of allowing their customers to exchange any product purchased at their stores no matter how worn or old it may be. The issue is that firms should use knowledge of consumer complaining as an insight into customer needs.

LIMITATIONS AND FUTURE RESEARCH

The methodology used to elicit the written protocols was established by Bower, et al. (1979). It was found that using this method of script elicitation, distinctive actions are not part of the subjects' explicit knowledge structure. Had the verbal protocol method been used, through direct probing by interviewers, the subject could also provide more of the implicit knowledge in memory related to distinctive actions. This is based on the argument that Ericsson and Simon (1980) make for the use of verbal reports, which if "... elicited with care and interpreted with full understanding of the circumstances under which they were obtained, are a valuable and thoroughly reliable source of information about cognitive processes". This limitation can also be viewed as an contribution to the methodological aspect of script elicitation.

A second limitation was the need to measure rather than manipulate the independent variables resulting in a loss of half the subjects. Since this was an exploratory study, however, it allowed the determination of which independent variables may be critical for complaint expertise.

The next step in this research should be to investigate the same variables in an experimental setting using the verbal protocol methodology while manipulating the independent variables to determine how a novice becomes an expert. Based on the work in the learning literature on analogical learning, learning through doing, learning through reminding, etc. a plausible approach would be to develop three or four learning contexts. Then randomly assign subjects to one of the learning contexts and manipulate expertise based on the three independent measures used in this exploratory study. This should lead to interesting and relevant findings based on this exploratory study.

REFERENCES

Abelson, R. P., (1976), "Script Processing in Attitude Formation and Decision Making", in *Cognition and Social Behavior*, John S. Carroll & John W. Payne (eds.), LEA, Hillsdale, NJ, 33-45.

Abelson, R. P., (1981), "Psychological Status of the Script Concept", *American Psychologist*, 37(7), 715-29.

Alba, J. W. & W. J. Hutchinson (1987), *Journal of Consumer Research*, 13(1), 411-54.

Best, A. & A. Andreasen (1977), "Consumer Response to Unsatisfactory Purchases: A Survey of Perceiving Defects, Voice Complaints, and Obtaining Redress", *Law and Society*, 701-37.

Bower, G. H., et al. (1979), "Scripts in Memory for Text", *Cognitive Psychology*, 11, 177-220.

Charness, N. (1983), "Age, Skill, and Bridge Bidding: A Chronometric Analysis", *Journal of Verbal Learning and Verbal Behavior*, 406-16.

Charness, N. (1981), "Search in Chess: Age and Skill Differences", *Journal of Experimental Psychology: Human Perception and Performance*, 7(2), 467-76.

Chi, M.T.H., et al. (1980), "Representation of Physics Knowledge by Experts and Novices", Technical Report No. 2, Learning Research and Development Center, University of Pittsburgh.

Day, R. et al. (1981), "The Hidden Agenda of Consumer Complaining", *Journal of Retailing*, 57(3), 86-105.

Fischoff, B. & D. MacGregor (1982), "Subjective Confidence in Forecasts", *Journal of Forecasting*, 1, 155-72.

Folkes, V. (1986), "The Availability Heuristic and Perceived Risk", *Journal of Consumer Research*, 15(June), 13-23.

Galambos, J.A., (1986), "Knowledge Structures for Common Activities", *Knowledge Structures*, James A. Galambos, et al. (eds), LEA, Hillsdale, NJ.

Galambos, J.A. & Lance J.R. (1982), "Memory for Routines", *Journal of Verbal Learning and Verbal Behavior*, 260-81.

Langley, P. & H.A. Simon (1981), "The Central Role of Learning in Cognition", *Cognitive Skills and Their Acquisition*, J.R. Anderson (ed), LEA, Hillsdale, NJ, 361-81.

Larkin, J.H., et al. (1980), "Expert and Novice Performance in Solving Physics Problems", *Science*, June, 1335-42.

Leong, M., et al. "Knowledge Bases and Salesperson Effectiveness: A Script-Theoretic Analysis", *Journal of Marketing Research*, 26(2), 164-78.

Martin, J. et al. (1980), "The Development of Knowledge Structures", *Research Paper No. 557*, Stanford University.

Schank, R. (1982), *Dynamic Memory*, Cambridge University Press, Cambridge, MA.

Weiner, B. (1980), *Human Motivation*, Holt, Rinehart, and Winston.

Contributions from a Musical Perspective on Advertising and Consumer Behavior

Judy I. Alpert, St. Edward's University
Mark I. Alpert, University of Texas at Austin

ABSTRACT

The role of music in advertising has recently attracted considerable interest in marketing and consumer psychology. This paper will discuss the role of formal analysis of musical structure in advertising, noting that music's effects must also consider key elements of the culture, the ad and what preceded it, consumer perceptions, moods, and involvement, and the fit between the music and the theme of the ad. A tentative musical hierarchy presence model is suggested, which describes the salience of music in different advertisements, and a framework which integrates the key moderators of musical influence in advertising is advocated.

INTRODUCTION

The role of music in marketing and consumer behavior research has been addressed in education, psychology, communication, and other fields to determine its effects on behavior, mood, and preferences. As a result of this body of work, we know that in some instances music appears to increase communication effectiveness in the context of advertisements. In other circumstances, music may decrease effectiveness, for reasons that are not self-evident (e.g, "When is `popular' music an inappropriate background?") Discussing how, when, and why music works seems to be appropriate to understanding the role of music in communications.

In an effort to provide possible explanations, this paper will discuss the structural elements of music in the surrounding context of an advertisement and its interaction with the consumer. However, although knowledge of formal musical analysis can assist in drawing inferences regarding how listeners may be affected by particular musical passages, it is also necessary to consider the context in which the musical and advertising "communication" takes place. Although it is beyond the scope of this paper to detail the links between musical elements and specific processing effects, we shall provide reasons why music seems to work in certain situations and not in others. This is not intended to be an all inclusive review, but one based on some of the research done so far in the area. Accordingly, we shall consider musical structure, its interactions with important moderators such as involvement, processing, sociological factors, (e.g., peer pressures and preferences in music), familiarity and prior associations, and the like.

Musical structure consists of elements such as sound, harmony, melody, and rhythm. Key factors in how these musical elements impact on the ad and the product are: 1) the consumer, through different levels of involvement and cognitive or affective processing; 2) the consumer's subjective perception of the appropriateness of the music as it relates to the central idea of the ad ("fit" as defined by MacGinnis and Park, 1990), and, 3) the organization of musical elements. There has been interest in examining how musical elements influence affect and processing (Alpert and Alpert, 1990; Bruner, forthcoming). These relationships are moderated by the level of consumer involvement, processing, and perceived "fit" of the music to the ad. Knowledge of cultural and social conditioning in forming musical taste as well as products can help in this prediction (Farnsworth, 1976; and Holbrook and Schindler, 1989). Given a target market's demographics, we can predict with some accuracy its musical and product preferences and tastes. Although level of involvement and processing may vary across individuals, we may know with some degree of certainty how they might perceive the appropriateness of certain musical selections with the overall message of an ad. An examination of these elements may offer some explanation of how, when, and why they contribute to the effectiveness of music within an ad. Applying relevant research to this problem is hampered by the fact that many studies do not isolate variables dealing with levels of involvement and processing. Others focus on particular issues in isolation. We shall attempt to bridge the gaps and build an integrative framework for understanding music in advertising.

Within an ad there are many messages. They are musical, verbal, non-verbal, and visual messages which interact and impact each other and the viewer. The consumer brings with him or her an existing set of conditions, which impact on how the music and the ad will be perceived. At some point, the music, along with the other stimuli in the ad, will change these existing conditions. This produces constant feedback between the stimuli and the viewer's perceptions and responses to them.

Which set of conditions the consumer brings to an advertisement and which ones will be evoked during the ad can vary in viewing situations. So, whether and how a consumer will respond to the musical aspects of an ad may depend on some of the following variables which researchers have isolated for investigation: 1) whether there is high, low, or affective involvement concerning the product and the ad (Park and Young 1986), and whether there is central or peripheral processing (Petty, Cacioppo, and Schumann, 1983), 2) whether the music evokes a receptive mood (Fried and Berkowitz, 1979). Receptivity may depend upon the following factors: a) familiarity and liking of the music (Russell, 1987), b) whether the music brings forth pleasant thoughts and associations, memories, and imagery (MacInnis and Park, 1990; Dowling and Harwood 1986), c) how musical structure is organized (Milliman, 1982; Smith and Curnow, 1966; Holbrook, 1981; Alpert and Alpert, 1990; Infante and Berg, 1979), d) what effect the program content has in which the ad is seen (Goldberg and Gorn, 1987), e) whether positive or negative association with the brand are "conditioned" by the music (Gorn, 1982), f) whether the ad's musical content is perceived to be consistent (fit) with the meaning of the advertisement (Park and Young 1986), and g) how important a role music has been assigned within the ad (Stout and Leckenby, 1988). Hence it is clear that the effects of music are dependent upon a host of personal, environmental, and musical factors. The following discussion will elaborate on these factors, citing examples of research relevant to different areas within consumer information processing.

Music Exists In A Context

Music does not work alone. It exists within an advertisement with complex visual, verbal, and other nonverbal stimuli. How all of these are perceived depends on the complex interaction of internal (biological) and external (social, cultural influences) factors which also affect when and how musical taste is developed (Holbrook and Schindler, 1989; Farnsworth, 1976). This paper takes the view that music is primarily a cultural and social phenomenon and reflects the values and attitudes of a subculture (Radocy and Boyle, 1988). Sociological forces affect images and preferences about products that are desirable, and music, if it fits with those images, may enhance the following variables: 1) persuasion through prior learning and verbal association, (Farnsworth, 1976), 2) recall, (Stewart, Farmer and Stannard, 1990), 3) overall ad effectiveness, (Evans, 1975), 4) preference for the product (MacInnis and Park, 1990), and 5) facilitation of mental images (Bae, 1985; Bilotta and Lindauer, 1978). The following discussion will elaborate further on the topic of music as a facilitator of mental images, and its role in advertising, education, communication, psychology, and marketing.

The Importance Of The Role Assigned To Music In An Ad

How music is actually used in an ad, and under what conditions music will assume a salient role in advertising executions influences communication effectiveness. Stewart and Furse (1986) examined the relationship of many executional variables, and performance measures of recall, comprehension and persuasion scores. They found that the brand-differentiating message was the single most important executional factor for explaining both ad recall and persuasion for an established product. Stout and Leckenby (1988) studied the relationship of emotional and cognitive viewer responses to specific musical variables. They found that the roles music plays in ads can influence information retrieved by consumers from the ads. Also, purchase intent was higher with ads that had music in it, and generally, subjects had more negative attitudes toward ads without music.

It seems that the salience of music in an ad will depend on whether the ad is primarily affective or cognitive based (Park and Young, 1986; and Holbrook and Hirschman, 1982), who the target market is, and how well the message communication goal (meaning) of the ad will fit with the music. Consequently, we suggest a tentative hierarchy of musical presence model, to define the role assigned to music in communicating the advertising message. Basically, the degree to which music is assigned a dominant role is revealed by the degree to which it will be in the foreground, be distinctive, will be noticed, and will be more likely to be part of an affect-based ad. The degree to which music is assigned a less dominant role is the degree to which it will recede into the background, be less distinctive, be less attention-getting, and the ad will be less likely to be affect-based.

This model is based on observation of about 60 advertisements on day-time T.V., and is presented here as way of summarizing the role music plays going from a most dominant and distinctive to a barely noticeable presence, to no presence. Since many ads have a combination of cognitive and affective components, with degrees of emphasis on one or the other, the role of music will tend to follow this degree of emphasis in the advertisement. That is, all things being equal, the more salient the role music has in the ad, the more affect-based the ad is likely to be, and the less salient role music has, the more cognitive-based the ad will be.

The hierarchy of musical presence model is suggested as follows, going from most to least salient:

A. in ads where music primarily carries the entire message and meaning, music will be used in the following ways:
   1. when music with lyrics carries the ad's verbal message and meaning, it has been assigned a dominant role in also providing an atmosphere, creating an image, setting a mood, and influencing affect throughout the ad. The ad will be primarily affective-based, appealing to feelings. In this case, music will always be in the foreground, with very little voice-over, if any. Sometimes music composed especially for the purpose of the ad, or a fairly well-known song for example, such as "April in Paris" (for rich French roast coffee by Maxwell House), can be used primarily to carry the message of the ad. The use of "April in Paris" reflects the age of the target market, desire for foreign travel, and its taste in style of music;
   2. when the lyrics of the song do not carry the ad's message directly (the words are about things other than the product and do not contribute to the atmosphere or mood), but the music is in the foreground throughout the ad, and is the primary form of communication;
   3. when instrumental or electronic music (without lyrics) is in the foreground, there is almost no voice-over, and the verbal message is brief and in written form,

music has also been assigned a dominant role and will provide the above-mentioned attributes;

B. in ads where the message is carried primarily by a voice-over, music is used in the following ways:
1. music is in the background, very quiet, generally not distinctive, resembles "elevator music," and the voice-over continues throughout the ad;
2. the music background lasts for the duration of one or two short verbal phrases, usually at the end of the ad. It is used to emphasize a phrase as in a key brand attribute, or logo;
3. no music.

Although most commercials use music (Stewart and Furse, 1986), some research has indicated that music may distract from message processing (Park and Young, 1986; and Stout and Leckenby, 1988), and other research supports the facilitating effect of music (Hecker, 1984). While musical characteristics or elements do shape overall musical meaning, a musical selection can distract or enhance message processing, if placed in an inappropriate advertising context, where the ad's intended meaning and the music are not a good fit (MacInnis and Park, 1990). While music may enhance processing in one setting, it may distract in another. It's impact largely depends on how well it fits with the advertisement's meaning, and the audience's level and type of ad involvement. *In trying to determine what musical selection fits with what advertisement, a clear communication goal of the ad is required (cognitive, affective), along with knowledge of the intended target market's musical taste, preferences, and if possible, the meanings and feelings associated with particular musical selections.* Finally, it is useful to possess an understanding of the musical characteristics or elements of the designated musical selection, as these often affect the above variables. From the musical presence hierarchy model, we note through preliminary observation that the more salient music is in an ad, the more affect-based the ad is. In general, advertising practitioners have used music which was familiar with their target market, and which fit with the ad's meaning. Note that under conditions of high cognitive involvement, music is seldom used, and when used, seldom effective.

How, When, Why Music Works In Imagery Production

A number of studies find that music is considered a valid facilitator of mental images (Bilotta and Lindauer, 1978). Music also has been used as a stimulus to evoke images in educational and therapeutic settings (Kaser, 1986). Music used simultaneously with words and sounds was found to increase image production (Bae, 1985; and Bilotta and Lindauer, 1978).

Farnsworth (1976) reports that music evokes very little universally similar mental imagery beyond what appears in all cultures, such as the use of soft melodies for mothers' lullabies. He also states that in western culture most people of the same subculture have similar imagery stimulated when presented with a descriptive narrative with specific imagery using concrete words. These words used to accompany music make for powerful, learned associations, so that when we hear the "Star Spangled Banner," we hear the words that go with it and we all tend to have similar visual imagery (Farnsworth, 1976).

Since the same music may not evoke uniform imagery among listeners, there is uncertainty regarding whether or not high and low imagery music can be 1) agreed upon, and 2) distinguished by the type of music represented. Although the designative meaning of music is made up of individual images, thoughts, and memories associated with a particular musical piece (Meyer, 1956), and is therefore frequently individualistic, musicians have often written programmatic music with titles which encourage similar imagery. For example, Mussorgsky used pizzicato strings to represent what he labeled "chicken clucking" in his "Pictures at an Exhibition." Advertisers of course supply "labels" with verbal statements about the product (emphasized by music) and/or lyrics of jingles. *It appears that prior learning and verbal associations, when paired repeatedly with certain pieces of music, are likely to evoke more nearly uniform mental imagery among listeners.*

In a marketing and advertising context, imagery impacts consumers' knowledge in many important ways (MacInnis and Price, 1987). Imagery systems contribute to a definition of product imagery and affect how a brand "communicates" with the consumer. Imagery is a process through which sensory information is stored in working memory (MacInnis and Price, 1987). Since memory imagery involves sensory and concrete representations of ideas, feelings, and memories, it can allow a visual reconstruction of an event in one's mind which has been experienced before and stored in memory.

Among the variables that can produce imagery in an advertisement are words, imagery instructions, and music. Stewart, Farmer, and Stannard (forthcoming) note that in those situations where image advertising uses music, the use of a musical cue provides the opportunity to elicit images, beliefs, and associations. Their forthcoming study's results indicate that music with lyrics is statistically significant in eliciting more image types of responses referring to people, actions, or setting than verbal cues. Findings in this study suggest that the musical cue is a more sensitive measure of memory than verbal product and brand cues. Another example where imagery plays a part in the degree of fit between the music and the meaning of the advertisement is in the romantic, nostalgic song "I"ll Be Seeing You." Used as background for a FTD florist ad, this song may prove effective. However, if paired with the packing up of a seasonal, everyday item like a portable fan, the effect will be somewhat comical. The organization of musical elements remain the same in the song, but the context surrounding the music has changed from a romantic, nostalgic setting (a good fit in terms of imagery) to a more mundane one. *Therefore imagery of the product and the ad can be affected by the fit between musical meaning and the meaning of the ad.*

Music Also Affects Important Mood States

Music not only enhances recall for a product or an ad through an evoked image, but it may evoke a mood, feelings, emotions, and behaviors. Consumer behavior theorists have conceptualized how consumers' attitudes, affective states, and behaviors have been impacted by moods under central and peripheral processing, as well as affect and behavior conditioning.

In a recent paper (Gardner, 1985), mood was defined as a fleeting, temporary feeling state, usually not intense, and not tied to a specifiable behavior. Moods can be positive or negative, such as cheeriness, peacefulness, or guilt and depression. According to Clark and Isen (1982), feeling states are general, pervasive, and occur frequently, and do not usually interrupt on-going behavior. In fact, the impact of feeling states on behavior is not immediately obvious. Feeling states or moods are distinguished from emotions, which are usually more intense, obvious, and are said to involve a cognitive component.

A number of studies have shown that mood has an impact on attitudes and behavior. We shall summarize major works in this stream. Given that mood is relevant and of increasing interest in consumer behavior, its sensitivity to the influence of music in commercials is worth examining. Research has shown that mood states have an important influence on behavior, evaluation, and recall (Gardner, 1985). While this general conclusion may not hold in all cases, Gardner notes that mood states appear to bias evaluations and judgments in similar directions to mood, and she reviews studies detailing this process (1985).

The association between mood states and affective responses, judgments, and behavior can be seen as both direct and indirect. A direct affective reaction may be viewed as a conditioned response when there are direct linkages in associations in memory between mood states and affective reactions (Griffitt and Guay, 1969), and mood states and behavior (see Gardner, 1985 for additional references). Indirect associations between feeling states and affective responses and/or behavior include the influence of information processing, or cognitive activity. Mood may affect evaluations by evoking mood-congruent thoughts and affect the performance of the behavior by increasing the accessibility of positive associations to the behavior (Clark and Isen, 1982; Goldberg and Gorn, 1987). To the extent that associations are direct and involve little conscious information processing, mood's effects may be seen as via the peripheral route. Indirect associations may operate via the central route when other salient cues are processed to yield attitudes in a manner affected by mood.

The likelihood that a host of behaviors may be performed appear to be enhanced by positive moods (Gardner, 1985). Negative moods' effects on behavior may be more complex than the effects of positive moods (Isen, 1984; Cialdini and Kenrick, 1976). For example, helping may be enhanced by some negative mood states such as sadness (Baumann, Cialdini, and Kenrick, 1981) and not by others such as frustration. This may be due to some evidence that negative mood states are not as homogeneous as positive ones (Isen, 1984), and that behaviors seen to reverse unpleasant mood states (e.g., helping) may overcome tendencies to enact mood-congruent behavior (e.g., withdrawal).

Variables Affecting Mood

Moods can be affected by many different variables. Gardner (1985) discusses studies of independent variables found to induce mood states, such as weather and temperature variation, positive test feedback, finding a dime in a phone booth, winning a computer game, receiving a free gift, getting cookies, and receiving good news and bad news. Participation in activities such as smiling or frowning, reading stories, and recalling or imagining emotional experiences may also induce mood changes.

In view of the fact that music is a common element in commercials, and one which has a long history of mood inducement in a variety of contexts, the next section will focus on how music has been used as an independent variable to affect moods, as well as other dependent variables of interest to marketers. For brevity, this section will highlight key studies. Details on these and other studies are in Alpert and Alpert (1990) and Bruner (forthcoming).

Music Effects

Gorn (1982) suggests that peripheral influences such as background music used in commercials may become associated with the advertised product (in memory, even if not consciously), and influence product choice through classical conditioning. Mere exposure did not lead to liking, which apparently depended on whether the target product, a pen, was presented with liked vs. disliked music.

The second experiment by Gorn (1982) provided support for his hypothesis that when subjects were not in a decision-making mode, the commercial's impact appeared to be more influential in its appeal when presented with musical background as opposed to product information. He concluded that through classical conditioning, the product becomes associated with the positive feelings of liked music.

Bierley, McSweeney, and Vannieuwkerk (1985) extended Gorn's studies. Preference ratings for stimuli that "predicted" (preceded) pleasant music were significantly greater than preference ratings for stimuli that predicted the absence of music. In another extension of Gorn's work, researchers questioned the theory of affective-conditioning and suggested the mood position theory of Bower (1981) and Isen (1984) as a possible explanation (Allen and Madden, 1985). Results indicated that there was an interaction between subjects' thought processes and the moods invoked by the "background" stimulus in the ad (in their case, liked vs. disliked humor). Music in advertising's possible effects on audience moods may thus complicate the effects of "simple" conditioning by the music. A recent replication of the Gorn study (1982) by Kellaris and Cox (1989) failed to reproduce the positive effect of liked vs. disliked music, after controlling for musical structural elements and possible demand effects. They call for research on the influence of music's structural characteristics on cognitive and affective responses (such as consumer mood) toward the ad and the product.

Park and Young (1986) extended Gorn's work by examining the impact of music on attitude toward the brand, the ad, and behavioral intention under conditions of high cognitive, high affective, and low involvement towards the advertising situation. Under high-cognitive involvement, they found music to be a distraction, lowering these dependent variable scores, because it was unrelated to attribute-based message contents. In the low-involvement condition, they found that music (which had been preselected as popular and liked) was associated with more positive attitudes towards the brand than was no music. Under high-affective involvement, the expected positive effect of music on brand attitude was not found, probably because the music selected did not really fit the image of the product and affective theme. As Park and Young note, the music, "The Tide is High" by "Blondie" may have been incongruent with the stylish classic beauty of Ingrid Bergman and the consumers' intended self-concept stressed in the hair shampoo commercials for which this music appeared as background. Subsequently MacInnis and Park (1990) supported this notion. They found that music which aroused emotion-laden memories which were congruent with the ad's primary message created positive feelings and ad attitudes. Music which aroused emotions and memories not congruent with the key ad message distracted from message processing and lowered advertising attitudes and feelings.

Since many commercials are viewed by consumers who are interested in the programs, and not in the commercials, the audience may be largely comprised of potentially uninvolved, nondecision-making consumers rather than cognitively active problem solvers. In this context, emotionally arousing components such as music, colors, or lighting may exert strong but subtle influence on viewers' product attitudes and choices. Some of this impact may come via associations conditioned and linked to the advertised products. Others may come through an indirect route resulting from music's influence on mood and other emotional responses, which in turn affect information processing.

An illustration of music's power to affect subjects' emotional responses was reported in a study by Rohner and Miller (1980), where sedative music showed a trend to decrease anxiety. Another study dealt with persuasion, among other variables. Subjects had greater affective arousal, persuasion affect, and attitudinal acceptance of the song's message with guitar accompaniment than without guitar accompaniment (Galizio and Hendrick, 1972). Thus changes in the presentation of music influenced subjects' responses.

The key basic research relating musical elements to emotional responses was reported by Hevner (1935), who presented subjects with identical pieces, controlling for all elements but major and minor modes. She concluded that all of the historically affirmed characteristics of the two modes were confirmed in her study. In later research, she also reported associations between musical elements such as fast tempo, loud dynamics, lively and varied rhythm, and high register with perceptions of the music as happy, merry, graceful, playful. Musical elements such as slower tempo, quiet dynamics, unvaried rhythm, and low register were reported to be sad, dreamy, and sentimental (Hevner, 1935, 1936). She noted that, although mode is never the sole factor which determines the way music is perceived, it is the most stable, generally understood, and influential of any of the elements in expressing the affective mood of music.

Recently, Alpert and Alpert (1990) replicated Hevner's findings, concluding that equally liked but unfamiliar music produced emotional responses predictable from analysis of its structural profile of musical elements. Interestingly, music affected mood and buying intention for greeting cards, without affecting central route processing of card attributes.

Summary - Toward An Integrative Framework

Music is a powerful language, and it interacts with other nonverbal and verbal advertising elements. The extent and effectiveness of its use in advertising depend on many factors, including amount and type of audience involvement, familiarity and associations of the music with the target audience and culture, product and advertising messages attempted, and the "fit" among these elements and the musical meanings communicated.

A number of studies have looked at elements of this process in isolation, or occasionally in pairs. Further research that examines multiple factors discussed here, preferably experimentally, should prove to be productive in aiding the understanding about music's roles in advertising. To this end, initial cooperative efforts between academic researchers and industry practitioners applying musical theories to advertising executions should be pursued, so that hypotheses about how, when and why music works in advertising can be subjected to empirical testing.

REFERENCES

Allen, Chris T. and Madden, Thomas J., (1985), "A Closer Look At Classical Conditioning," *Journal of Consumer Research*, 12 (December), 301-315.

Alpert, Judy I. and Mark I. (1990), "Music Influences on Mood and Purchase Intentions," *Psychology & Marketing*, 7 (Summer), 109-134.

Bae, Chungsook (1985), "Effects of Time Press, Music Type, and Presentation Order of Music on Original Verbal Images," in *Dissertation Abstracts International*, March, Vol. 45 (9-A) 2800.

Baumann, Donald J., Robert B. Cialdini, and Douglas T. Kenrick, (1981), "Altruism as Hedonism: Helping and Self-Gratification as Equivalent Responses," *Journal of Personality and Social Psychology*, 40 (6), 1039-1046.

Bierley, Calvin, Frances K. McSweeney, and Renee Vannieuwkerk (1985), "Classical Conditioning of Preferences for Stimuli," *Journal of Consumer Research*, 12 (December), 316-323.

Bilotta, J., and Lindauer, M.S., "Imagery Arousal as a Function of Exposure to Artistic Stimuli." Paper presented at the 5th Annual Convention, Genesee Valley Psychological Association, Rochester, N.Y. 1978.

Bower, Gordon H. (1981), "Mood and Memory," *American Psychologist*, 36, 129-148.

Bruner, Gordon C. (forthcoming), "Music, Mood, and Marketing: A Review of Their Interrelationship, *Journal of Marketing*.

Cialdini, Robert and Douglas Kenrick (1976), "Altruism as Hedonism: A Social Development of Negative Mood State and Helping," *Journal of Personality and Social Psychology*, 34 (5), 907-914.

Clark, Margaret and Alice Isen (1982), "Toward Understanding the Relationship Between Feeling States and Social Behavior," in *Cognitive Social Psychology*, eds. Albert Hastorf and Alice Isen, New York: Elsevier/North-Holland, 73-108.

Dowling, W. Hay and Dane L. Harwood (1986), *Music Cognition*, New York: Academic Press.

Evans, M. *Soundtrack: The Music of the Movies.* New York: Hopkinson and Blake, 1975.

Farnsworth, Paul R. (1969), *The Social Psychology of Music*, Ames, Iowa: Iowa State University Press.

Fried, Rona and Leonard Berkowitz (1979), "Music Hath Charms...And Can Influence Helpfulness," *Journal of Applied Social Psychology*, 9 (2), 199-208.

Galizio, Mark and Clyde Hendrick (1972), "Effect of Musical Accompaniment on Attitude: The Guitar as a Prop for Persuasion," *Journal of Applied Social Psychology*, 2 (October/December), 350-59.

Gardner, Meryl Paula (1986), "Mood States and Consumer Behavior: A Critical Review," *Journal of Consumer Research*, 12 (December), 281-300.

Goldberg, Marvin E. and Gerald J. Gorn (1987), "Happy and Sad TV Programs: How They Affect Reactions to Commercials," *Journal of Consumer Research*, 14 (December), 387-403.

Gorn, Gerald J. (1982), "The Effects of Music in Advertising on Choice Behavior: A Classical Conditioning Approach," *Journal of Marketing*, 46 (Winter), 94-101.

Griffitt, William and Peter Guay (1969), "'Object' Evaluation and Conditioned Affect," *Journal of Experimental Research in Personality*, 4 (July), 1-8.

Hecker, S. (1984), "Music For Advertising Effect," *Psychology and Marketing*, 1 (Fall/Winter), 3-8.

Hevner, Kate (1935), The Affective Character of the Major and Minor Modes in Music, *American Journal of Psychology*, 47, 103-118.

Hevner, Kate (1936), "Experimental Studies in the Elements of Expression in Music," *American Journal of Psychology*, 48, 246-268.

Holbrook, Morris B. (1981), "Integrating Compositional and Decompositional Analyses to Represent the Intervening Role of Perceptions in Evaluative Judgments," *Journal of Marketing Research*, 18 (February), 13-28.

Holbrook, Morris B. and Elizabeth C. Hirschman, (1982), "The Experiential Aspects of Consumption: Consumer Fantasies, Feelings, and Fun," *Journal of Consumer Research*, Vol. 9, September 1982, pp.132-140.

Holbrook, Morris B. and Robert M. Schindler, (1989), "Some Exploratory Findings on the Development of Musical Tastes," *Journal of Consumer Research*, 16 (1), 119-124.

Infante, Dominic A. and Charles M. Berg, (1979), "The Impact of Music Modality on the Perception of Communication Situations in Video Sequences," *Communication Monographs*, 46 (June), 135-148.

Isen, Alice M. (1984), "The Influence of Positive Affect on Decision Making and Cognitive Organization," in *Advances in Consumer Research*, Vol. 11, ed. Thomas C. Kinnear, Provo, UT: Association for Consumer Research, 534-537.

Kaser, Vaughn A. (1986), "The Effects of an Auditory Subliminal Message Upon the Production of Images and Dreams," *Journal of Nervous and Mental Disease*, 174 (7), 397-407."

Kellaris, James J. and Anthony D. Cox (1989), "The Effects of Background Music in Advertising: A Reassessment," *Journal of Consumer Research*, 16 (June), 118-118.

MacInnis, Deborah J. and C. Whan Park (1990), "The Differential Role of Music on Consumers' Processing of and Reactions to Ads," Working Paper #5, Department of Marketing, University of Arizona.

MacInnis, Deborah J. and Linda L. Price (1987), "The Role of Imagery in Information Processing: Review and Extensions," *Journal of Consumer Research*, 13 (March), 1-19.

McSweeney, Frances K. and Calvin Bierley (1984), "Recent Developments in Classical Conditioning," *Journal of Consumer Research*, 11 (September), 619-631.

Meyer, Leonard B. (1956), Emotion and Meaning in Music. Chicago: The University of Chicago Press.

Milliman, Ronald E. (1982), "Using Background Music to Affect the Behavior of Supermarket Shoppers," *Journal of Marketing*, 46 (Summer), 86-91.

Paivio, Allan (1971), Imagery and Verbal Processes, New York: Holt, Rinehart and Winston.

Park, C. Whan and Mark S. Young (1986), "Consumer Response to Television Commercials: The Impact of Involvement and Background Music on Brand Attitude Formation," *Journal of Marketing Research*, 23 (February), 11-24.

Petty, Richard E., John T. Cacioppo, and David Schumann (1983), "Central and Peripheral Routes to Advertising Effectiveness: The Moderating Role of Involvement," *Journal of Consumer Research*, 10 (September), 135-146.

Radocy, Rudolf E. and Boyle, J. David (1988), *Psychological Foundations of Musical Behavior*, Springfield, Illinois: Charles C. Thomas Publisher.

Rohner, Stephen J. and Richard Miller (1980), "Degrees of Familiar and Affective Music and Their Effects of State Anxiety," *Journal of Music Therapy*, 17, (Spring), 2-15.

Russell, Philip A. (1987), "Effects of Repetition on the Familiarity and Likability of Popular Music Recordings," *Psychology of Music*, 15 (2), 187-197.

Smith, Patricia Cane and Ross Curnow (1966), "Arousal Hypotheses and the Effects of Music on Purchasing Behavior," *Journal of Applied Psychology*, 50, 3, 255-56.

Stout Patricia A. and John D. Leckenby (1988), "Let the Music Play: Music as a Nonverbal Element in Television Commercials," in *Nonverbal Communication in Advertising*, Sidney Hecker and David Stewart (eds.), Lexington, MA: Lexington Books, 207-223.

Stewart, David W., Kenneth M. Farmer, and Charles I. Stannard (forthcoming), "Music As a Recognition Cue in Advertising Tracking Studies," *Journal of Advertising Research*.

Stewart, David W., and David H. Furse (1986), *Effective Television Advertising: A Study of 1000 Commercials*. Lexington, Mass.: Lexington Books.

Jingles in Advertisements: Can They Improve Recall?
Wanda T. Wallace, Duke University

The traditional approach to studying music in advertising has focused on the effect of music on attitudes towards the advertised product (Gorn 1982; Kellaris and Cox 1989; MacInnis and Park 1990), the consumer's mood (Alpert and Alpert 1990), and the consumer perception of an ad containing music of any form such as the perception of an ad being upbeat, informative, etc. (Stout and Leckenby 1988). Music has also been shown to influence the consumer's pace while shopping and eating (Milliman 1982, 1986). All of these papers address more of the affective side of the consumer response as opposed to the cognitive side. Within a more cognitive perspective, music has been viewed as a distraction (Park and Young 1986).

In contrast to the above approaches, the current paper takes a strong cognitive approach and considers how and when music might serve as a recall aid. Some experiments supporting this view are presented.

Music in this paper will be primarily lyrical music rather than background or nonvocal music. Although some of the ideas can apply to nonvocal music, that is not the focus of the investigations. Also, the paper considers unique, novel lyrics written for a particular ad rather than old songs imported to or adapted for an ad. Although again, some of the ideas have a direct application to the use of well-known music.

Why might music aid or improve memory for an ad? First, consider how difficult it can be to get a jingle out of your head when you have heard it several times. Whether or not you like the jingle is irrelevant; you just can't seem to stop humming it. One well worn example is the Oscar Mayer song. Just saying the brand name is usually enough to start part of the jingle playing through your mind. Second, jingles seem to be easily recalled even if they have not been heard for years. For example, the Mounds/Almond Joy "sometimes you feel like a nut" jingle was just recently revived for a Mounds ad campaign because consumers consistently reported remembering those lines even though they had not been aired for years (Dagnoli 1989).

There is some experimental evidence to support the notion that music can improve recall (Wallace 1990). This experiment involves ballads rather than advertisements. The advantage of using ballads is that they are novel melodies which are mostly unknown and the texts describe simple events and ideas. Since these stimuli are purely auditory any potential interaction with or interference from a visual display is eliminated.

In this experiment, subjects either heard three verses of a ballad spoken or the same three verses sung and then recalled in writing the text they had heard. Subjects knew in advance that they would be asked to recall the text. In addition, subjects were instructed to recall the text as close as possible to the exact, original wording. Subjects listened to one of the two ballads five times and recalled the words of that ballad in writing after the first, second, and fifth repetitions. After learning an additional song, subjects were asked to recall the song they had learned once more in a delayed recall task. The time between the last recall and the delayed recall is about 15 minutes; however, learning the additional song is somewhat disruptive.

The subjects in this experiment are undergraduates with no particular expertise although most subjects had a few years of choral experience. According to pretest measures, no participants were familiar with the ballads to be learned.

Two different ballads were used in the experiment; however, since there were no differences between the ballads this factor will be ignored here. The set of three verses from each ballad contained 80 or 85 words. Both the sung and spoken versions of each ballad were equally understandable and were performed by the same person.

The percentage of words recalled verbatim was calculated for each subject. The basic results are presented in Figure 1. A repeated measures analysis of variance (ANOVA) with condition and ballad as between subjects factors and trial as a within subjects factor compared verbatim recall for sung and spoken conditions. As expected, performance improves across trials ($F(2,120) = 598.96$, $p < .0001$). More importantly, both overall ($F(1,60) = 19.95$, $p < .0001$) and at every trial, verbatim recall is significantly better for the sung condition than for the spoken condition. After five trials, recall is very good, averaging about 86% of the words recalled verbatim in the sung condition and 76% in the spoken condition. Even with such high recalls on the last trial, there is still a significant advantage for the sung condition in the delayed recall task ($F(1,63) = 12.49$, $p < .001$). Mean verbatim recall for the sung and spoken conditions at the delayed recall task are 81% and 67% words correctly recalled, respectively.

Music however does not always result in improved recall. One such limitation involves the repetition of the melody and how easy it is to learn the melody. In a follow-up experiment (Wallace 1990) to the one described above, the first verse from each three-verse ballad segment was excerpted from the original tape. Subjects received the same instructions and the same procedure as in the three-verse case. That is, subjects heard either the sung or spoken version for one of the two ballad segments and were asked to recall the verse as close to verbatim as possible after the first, second, and fifth repetitions. After learning additional material, subjects were asked to recall the verse again in a delayed recall task. However, in this experiment the results differ dramatically from those in the prior experiment.

The advantage of hearing the ballad sung that is found in the three-verse case reverses when

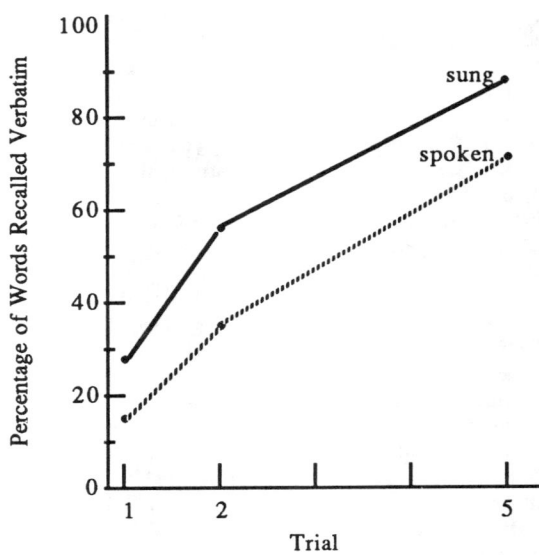

FIGURE 1
Recalls for Three Verse Segment

subjects heard only one verse. The spoken condition results in better verbatim recall than the sung condition ($F(1,35) = 4.29$, $p < .05$). At the first and fifth trials, the difference between the sung and spoken conditions is only marginally significant ($F(1,35) = 3.79$, $p < .06$ and $F(1,35) = 3.86$, $p < .06$, respectively). On the second trial, the difference between conditions is significant ($F(1,35) = 5.26$, $p < .03$). Finally, in the delayed recall task, no effects or interactions are significant. Thus, once the verse is well learned, there appears to be very little long term difference between verbal recall of material that was sung and material that was spoken. Perhaps over a very long period between learning and recall, such as months or years, a difference could emerge.

Even though the differences between conditions are borderline on the first and last trials and nonexistent in the delayed task, the results clearly indicate that music is not a facilitator as in the prior experiment and that music can serve as a distractor. It is important to keep in mind that the verse heard in this experiment is identical to the first of the three verses heard in the prior experiment. The only difference between the experiments is that the first group of subjects heard and recalled two additional verses which the second group of subjects did not hear.

Part of the difference between the one-verse and the three verse experiments could result from a decreased cognitive load. For recalls of the common verse between the two experiments, subjects in the one-verse spoken condition have better recall than those in the three-verse spoken condition because of the reduced cognitive load. Nevertheless, that same advantage of reduced cognitive load is not found in the sung condition. Here, subjects recall the one common verse between the two experiments equally as well, regardless whether they must learn two additional verses or no additional verses. Therefore, those subjects hearing three verses sung have a definite advantage at recall even if they do have more material to remember. In addition, the music appears to be a distractor when subjects hear only one verse. Perhaps this occurs because subjects have not yet had sufficient rehearsals of the melody to make it salient or clear. Even though subjects hear the melody five times in the one-verse experiment, they should not learn the melody as well as when they hear it in a multi-verse context. In the three-verse context, encoding variability should facilitate learning (see Hintzman 1976 for a review). Since the music is not sufficiently learned to facilitate recall, it becomes a distractor. In the three-verse experiment, subjects must learn the melody better and/or be better able to use that melody as a retrieval aid.

Music provides a very powerful retrieval cue. Music is more than just an additional piece of information, it is an integrated cue that provides information about the nature of the text. The music defines the length of lines, chunks words and phrases, identifies the number of syllables, sets the pattern of stressed and unstressed syllables within the text. Thus, the music acts as a frame within which the text is tightly fit. That frame can connect words at encoding, limit retrieval search, as well as constrain guessing or recreation at retrieval.

For example, the melody could assist subjects in distinguishing one verse from the other by making each verse a coherent unit. In addition, the melody could cue subjects to search for lines to fit

FIGURE 2
Recalls for One Verse Segment

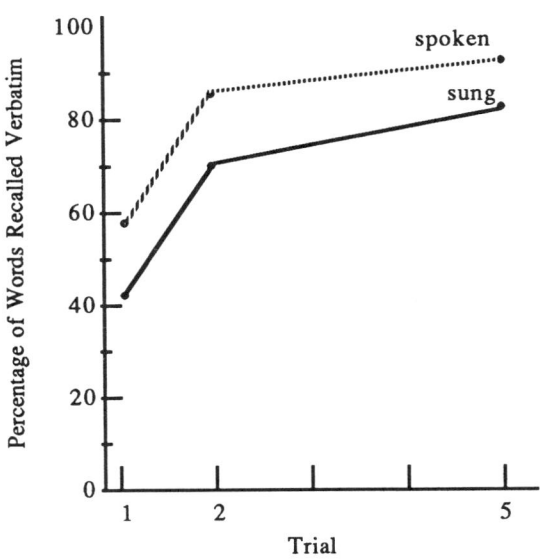

points within the melody thus reducing the chances of a subject omitting a line. Furthermore, the structure of the music, that is the rises and falls in the melody, the accents, et cetera; accentuate particular components of each verse and thus may make it more memorable. At this stage in the experimental work, these mechanisms are not mutually exclusive and cannot be distinguished.

There are some limitations to interpreting these results for advertising. For one, subjects in this experiment were attempting to learn the song whereas consumers watching an ad are not likely to give as much attention or effort to the ad nor are they likely to try to recall the ad, although, on occasion, consumers may make an effort to recall the brand name or perhaps a new brand claim. Second, these recalls are reported as verbatim recalls which again is an unlikely scenario for advertising. However, gist recall and verbatim recall are correlated. Given the emphasis on learning the material, a verbatim recall measure is a reasonably stringent measure. In conditions for which consumers are not intentionally learning material, recognition or gist measures should be comparable in difficulty to the verbatim measure used here. However, if you want consumers to sing a jingle over and over to themselves, you expect them to learn the words accurately and not alter the words. One of the points of the above experiments is that it is easier for subjects to learn words verbatim when they are sung.

Obviously, music should only aid recall when the lyrics are as clearly understood when they are sung as when they are spoken. In addition, it is important that the text match the music in terms of rhythmical structure, stress patterns, phrasing and points of emphasis. In order to be memorable, the music should also have a simple form with a basic pattern of ascents and descents, and a clear rhythmical pattern. These musical factors should facilitate learning of the musical score as a frame or retrieval cue. English and Scottish ballads that are still sung in North Carolina contain these musical properties (Wallace forthcoming). Since this is a tradition that has been passed from generation to generation by word of mouth for two hundred years, it is reasonable to assume that they are in a good form to facilitate memory. Thus they provide one example of memorable melodic structures.

By considering music's effect on recall, I certainly do not intend to imply that all music does is improve recall. Certainly there are emotional reactions to music which may spread to attitudes about the product. Music also probably serves many additional functions as well.

In conclusion, there is evidence that music can improve recall of a text and there is reason to expect that this will hold for jingles as they occur within an advertisement.

REFERENCES

Alpert, Judy I. and Mark I. Alpert (1990), "Music Influences on Mood and Purchase Intentions," *Psychology and Marketing*, 7 (Summer) 109-133.

Dagnoli, Judann (1989), "Best-loved Themes Get Sweet Reprise," *Advertising Age*, (September), 32.

Gorn, Gerald J. (1982), "The Effects of Music in Advertising on Choice Behavior: A Classical Conditioning Approach," *Journal of Marketing*, 46 (Winter) 94-101.

Hintzman, Douglas L. (1976), "Repetition and Memory," in *The Psychology of Learning and Motivation*, Vol. 10, ed. Gordon H. Bower, New York: Academic Press.

Kellaris, James J. and Anthony D. Cox (1989), "The Effects of Background Music in Advertising: A Reassessment," *Journal of Consumer Research*, 16 (June) 113-118.

MacInnis, Deborah J. and C. Whan Park (1990), "The Differential Role of Music on Consumers' Processing of and Reactions to Ads," Working Paper No. 5, Karl Eller Graduate School of Management, Tucson, AZ.

Milliman, Ronald E. (1986), "The Influence of Background Music on the Behavior of Restaurant Patrons," *Journal of Consumer Research*, 13 (September) 286-289.

_____ (1982), "Using Background Music to Affect the Behavior of Supermarket Shoppers," *Journal of Marketing*, 46 (Summer) 86-91.

Park, C. Whan and S. Mark Young (1986), "Consumer Response to Television Commercials: The Impact of Involvement and Background Music on Brand Attitude Formation," *Journal of Marketing Research*, XXIII (February) 11-24.

Stout, Patricia A. and John D. Leckenby (1988), "Let the Music Play: Music as a Nonverbal Element in Television Commercials," in *Nonverbal Communication in Advertising*, eds. Sidney Hecker, and David W. Stewart, Lexington, Massachusetts/Toronto, Canada: D.C. Heath and Company, 207-223.

Wallace, Wanda T. (1990), "Memory for Melodies: The Effect of Learning Music and Text Together," Working Paper.

_____ (forthcoming), "Characteristics and Constraints in Ballads and Their Effects on Memory," *Discourse Processes: A Multidisciplinary Journal*.

Exploring Tempo and Modality Effects, On Consumer Responses to Music

James J. Kellaris, University of Cincinnati
Robert J. Kent, Drexel University

ABSTRACT

Music plays a pervasive role in consumers' lives and is often used in marketing communication. Several sources have recommended "dissecting" music to isolate component properties responsible for various effects on consumers. Recent advances in electronic music technology facilitate such research. Two experiments were conducted to explore tempo and modality effects on listeners' responses to music. Experiment I used computer technology to create music containing orthogonal manipulations of tempo and mode. To assess the generality of effects observed in Experiment I, Experiment II used commercially recorded music to manipulate tempo and mode. A consistent pattern of main and interaction effects was found across the two experiments.

BACKGROUND

Consumers are exposed to music in many contexts, yet relatively little is understood concerning music's effects. Thus it is not surprising to see the recent emergence of interest in music among consumer researchers. Musical studies have recently appeared in consumer esthetics (e.g. Holbrook and Anand 1988), hedonic consumption (e.g. Lasher 1988), mood research (e.g. Bruner 1990), advertising (e.g. Alpert and Alpert 1988; Kellaris and Cox 1989) and retail atmospherics (e.g. Milliman 1982, 1986).

Music is a complex composite of structural elements such as tempo, pitch, and timbre (Bruner 1990), yet it is frequently treated by researchers as a unidimensional stimulus. For example, advertising studies have examined the effects of music's presence or absence (e.g. Park and Young 1986) and the effects of pleasant vs. aversive music (e.g. Gorn 1982). Few studies in our discipline have attempted to isolate the individual components of music responsible for observed effects. If our understanding of music's influence on consumers is to progress, we must recognize the multidimensional nature of music and "dissect" it experimentally.

This approach was advocated by Hevner in the 1930's, but difficulties of stimulus construction were an impediment until recently. Advances in electronic music technology facilitate the construction of musical stimuli necessary for such an experimental approach. For example, music stored as digital information in a computer may be reproduced at various speeds without affecting the pitch. This digital information can be edited to manipulate any dimension of music while keeping all other dimensions constant.

Music has been characterized in terms of three dimensions: time, pitch, and texture (Bruner 1990). The present study explores the effects of two major structural elements of music: tempo and modality. Tempo is an important time-related variable since it controls the pace or "spacing" of sounds. It is a particularly important predictor of human response to music (Hevner 1937; Rigg 1940). Previous studies (e.g. Milliman 1982, 1986) have tended to ignore potential nonlinear and interactive effects of tempo with other musical variables. Modality is an important pitch-related variable since it provides the basic framework within which pitches are organized to form melodies and harmonies. Modality refers to the configuration of intervals between notes in a scale, the most common examples being the "major" and "minor" modes (Apel 1973). Modality is a well-established antecedent of affective response to music (e.g. Heinlein 1928; Hevner 1935a). In general, major keys tend to be associated with positive thoughts and feelings, and minor keys with negative thoughts and feelings. There are also many "atonal" modalities which are neither major nor minor, each with its own aesthetic character. A recent study by Stout and Leckenby (1988) found mode to have the greatest impact of the musical components examined.

Bruner (1990) proposed that the components of music are capable of producing main and interactive effects on affective, cognitive, and behavioral responses of consumers. He states that "although attempts have been made over the years to understand the main effects of musical components. . . interaction effects have received much less attention" (p. 11). It is important to consider interactive effects since single-variable studies can lead to erroneous conclusions if undetected interactions exist.

The present study tests Bruner's interaction proposition by manipulating two important dimensions of music and measuring multiple outcomes in two experiments. This study extends previous research on tempo and modality effects by exploring nonlinear and interactive effects, and by considering unconventional "atonal" modalities in addition to major and minor keys. The first experiment used original computer-generated music to provide maximally "clean" manipulations of tempo and modality. Experiment I focuses strongly on internal validity to establish the existence of effects. The second experiment assessed the generality of the effects observed in the first experiment. Experiment II used multiple examples of commercially recorded music to represent orthogonal combinations of tempo and modality.

EXPERIMENT I

A 3 X 3 factorial experiment using a between-Ss design was conducted. Treatments included three levels each of musical tempo (fast = 180 BPM, moderate = 120 BPM, slow = 60 BPM) and modality (major, minor, atonal). Outcome measures included multi-item evaluative and behavioral intent scales. The procedure involved randomly assigning Ss to treatment conditions, exposing them to music via headphones, and having them fill out a questionnaire.

Subjects

One hundred eighty (n = 180) volunteers were recruited from a large introductory class at the University of Cincinnati (U.C.). The sample was 54.2 % male. Ages ranged from 20 to 40 with a median age of 21 years.

Stimuli

The stimuli were audio cassette recordings of original "classical" style instrumental music produced by the authors in a digital sound studio at U.C. Nine versions of one musical composition were produced: one in each of three modes (C major, C minor, and an "atonal" version based on a wholetone scale); with each played at fast (180 BPM), moderate (120 BPM), and slow (60 BPM) speeds. These tempo levels were based on musical convention and precedent. Three levels were chosen because of the possibility of non-linear effects.

To create the stimuli, one of the authors composed a four-part instrumental fugue in eighteenth century contrapuntal style, based on thematic material taken from an unpublished transcription of a Byzantine chant. The composition was scored for woodwinds and cello, and recorded using digitally sampled sounds. The score was input through an electronic keyboard and stored in digital form using ProPerformer midi sequencer software and a MacIntosh computer. This allowed the authors to edit and output multiple versions of the score representing orthogonal combinations of tempo and mode, while holding all other dimensions of the music constant. The digital information was sent through a polyphonic synthesizer to produce the sound signal.

Procedure

At the time of recruitment, Ss were told that their participation was sought for a "music study," and offered course credit for participation. As individuals arrived at the lab, they were issued a set of headphones, a randomly assigned numbered audio cassette tape, and a (matching) numbered questionnaire. An attendant directed each S to an audio carrel, where printed instructions guided them through the procedure. After listening to a tape and completing a questionnaire, Ss returned the materials to a lab attendant. Responses were anonymous; Ss signed a separate form to receive course credit. The entire procedure took about twelve minutes.

Measures

Dependent variables included multi-item evaluative and behavioral intent scales. Other items were included on the questionnaire but not analyzed in this study.

The evaluative measures consisted of sixteen seven-point semantic differential scales preceded by the prompt "The Music I Heard Was:" The specific items were compiled from Berlyne (1974) and other sources. Half of the items were reverse scored. Two composite scales were formed from these items: the first scale consisted of "appealing, beautiful, likeable, and pleasant" (Cronbach's alpha = .93). We labeled this construct "appealingness." The second scale consisted of "arousing, stimulating, energetic, exciting, and loud" (alpha = .68), which we labeled "arousingness."

The behavioral intent scale consisted of four five-point agreement items relating to intention to listen to the music again if given the opportunity, intention to choose the music over an alternative choice, and intention to purchase the music if it were commercially available. The alpha reliability of the composite scale based on these items was .91.

Other items on the questionnaire included open-ended debriefing items, some standard demographic items, three scales relating to level of interest in music, listening habits, and extent of formal training, and a question on musical preferences.

Results and Discussion

Analyses of variance (ANOVAs) assessed group differences on each outcome measure. (See Table 1.) The analysis revealed significant main effects of mode (F = 36.85; p < .0005) and tempo (F = 9.02; p < .0005), as well as a two-way interactive effect (F = 3.00; p < .02) on appealingness. The magnitude of the interaction was estimated at omega-squared = .03. Figure 1 illustrates this interaction.

The "major" mode was generally evaluated as more appealing than the "minor" mode. This finding is consistent with previous work (Hevner 1935a). As one might expect, the "atonal" versions were the least appealing. This could be due to the greater dissonance, or the unfamiliar sound of this mode.

Consistent with previous work by Holbrook and Anand (1988), the response pattern for the major mode follows an inverted U shape across tempi -- the classic "Wundt curve." The moderate tempo is evaluated as more appealing than slower or faster tempi, even within the fairly restricted range of speeds examined in this study. This is not the case, however, for music pitched in other modes. Both minor and atonal versions were rated as more appealing (or perhaps less unappealing) at faster tempi. The notion of harmonic dissonance (Helmholtz 1862) may explain this finding. The sustained dissonances heard at slower tempi should be perceived as harsher than the relatively briefer dissonances experienced at faster tempi.

An ANOVA on the five-item arousingness scale found only a tenuous positive main effect of tempo (F = 2.73; P < .068), and no other main or interactive effects. Musical tempo, as a psychophysical stimulus property, should be expected to produce greater arousal at higher intensity levels (Berlyne 1974). While this effect is somewhat evident in the data, the range of tempi in this experiment may be too narrow to allow the effect to manifest itself strongly.

TABLE 1
OVERVIEW OF EXPERIMENT I RESULTS

DEPENDENT MEASURE	MAIN EFFECTS				INTERACTION	
	TEMPO		MODALITY		TEMPO-MODE	
	F	p<	F	p<	F	p<
APPEALINGNESS	9.02	.0005	36.85	.0005	3.00	.02
AROUSINGNESS	2.73	.068	2.10	.12	.63	n.s.
BEHAVIORAL INTENT	5.16	.007	8.71	.0005	1.71	.15

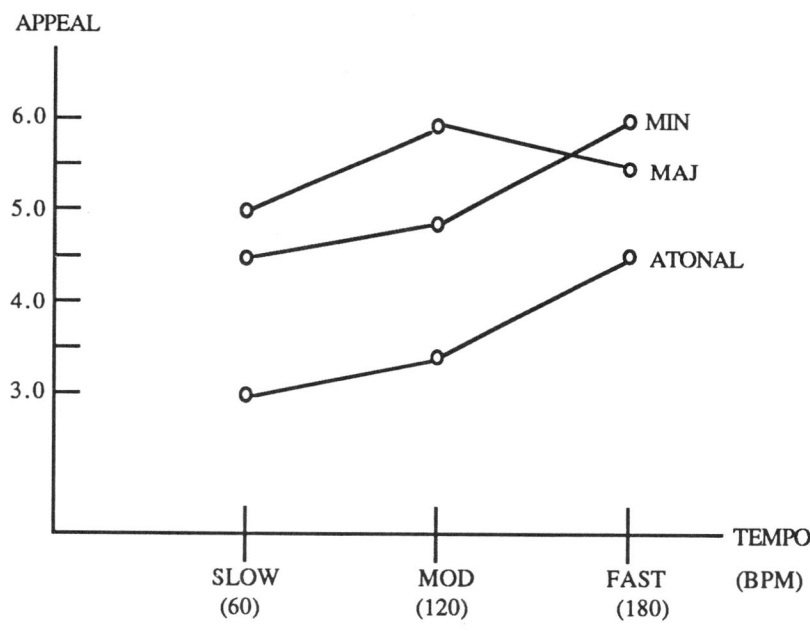

FIGURE 1
TWO-WAY INTERACTION OF TEMPO AND MODE ON EVALUATIONS OF MUSIC'S APPEALINGNESS (EXPERIMENT I)

Analysis of the behavioral intent scale found significant main effects of both mode (F = 8.71; p < .0005; omega^2 = .075) and tempo (F = 5.16; p < .007; omega^2 = .04), and a statistically marginal interaction of the two (F = 1.71; p < .15). The effect of tempo on behavioral intent was almost monotonically positive. The modal effect followed a pattern typical of most of the analyses: major keys produced the most positive intent, followed by minor keys, with the atonal versions producing the least positive intent.

To summarize, tempo and modality appear to be important influences on responses to music. Consistent with Bruner's proposition, tempo and modality operated through main effects and interactively. Tempo appears to operate as a psychophysical property of sound -- its influence seems to stem simply from its intensity. Modality effects are more complex. They may stem from the relative consonance/dissonance associated with different modes, or, in the case of atonal modalities, from the relative novelty of the sound.

To explore the generality of the effects observed in Experiment I, a second experiment was conducted using multiple examples of commercially recorded music.

EXPERIMENT II

Experiment II is a replication of Experiment I with different musical stimuli. Unfamiliar commercially recorded music was substituted for the computer-generated stimuli used in Experiment I. Three musical selections represented mode and tempo within each cell. The basic design (3 X 3 between-Ss factorial), procedure, and measures remained the same. Composite scale reliabilities (Cronbach's alpha) were .91 and .85 for the appealingness and arousingness scales, and .91 for behavioral intent.

Method

One hundred sixty-two (n = 162) students were recruited for Experiment II. None had participated in Experiment I. Ss were given course credit for their participation and were naive to the purpose of the study. The sample was 53.7% male. Ages ranged from 19 to 35 with a median age of 21 years.

The stimulus materials were audio cassette recordings of instrumental musical excerpts selected to manipulate three levels each of tempo and modality orthogonally. Each excerpt faded to silence after three minutes. Three pieces of music were selected for each cell of the 3 X 3 design to avoid confounding treatment groups with any given piece of music. In each cell, one selection was an obscure classical orchestral piece, one an Indian raga, and one a Chinese piece. The use of obscure classical and non-western instrumental music was intended to avoid problems associated with prior exposure. An attempt was made to minimize confounding treatments with composer, instrumentation, or other musical variables to the extent possible. Of course, using commercial recordings in place of the artificial "perfect" operations in Experiment I is likely to introduce noise in the manipulations; but, the purpose of Experiment II is to see if the effects survive the "imperfect" operations of tempo and modality.

Two important changes were made in the operations of tempo and modality. First, a broader range of tempi was used. Because of the rather weak effect of tempo on arousingness found in Experiment I, tempo levels were set at 60 or *fewer* BPM (slow), 120 BPM (moderate), and 180 or *more* BPM (fast). Second, the "atonal" mode in Experiment I was based on a whole-tone scale, which is neither major nor minor. There are numerous other atonal modes: polytonal, serialistic, and minimalistic music are examples from western traditions; non-western music is often based on microtonal systems which are also neither major nor minor. Whereas only one specific type of "atonal" mode was used in Experiment I, a broader range of unconventional tonalities were represented in Experiment II.

Results and Discussion

ANOVA results are summarized in Table 2. The appealingness analysis suggested a pattern of main and interactive effects directionally similar to those in Experiment I; however, the effects were weaker. There are weak main effects of tempo (F = 2.72; p < .069) and mode (F = 2.18; p < .12), as well as a tenuous interactive effect (F = 1.94; p < .106). (See Figure 2.)

The inverted U-shaped "Wundt curve" remains evident among the major mode groups. The positive effect of tempo on evaluations of atonal music is also evident.

An ANOVA on the arousingness scale revealed significant main effects of both tempo (F = 22.09; p < .0005) and modality (F = 2.97; p < .05). As in Experiment I, no interactive effect was found. The effect of tempo was positive, i.e., faster music was evaluated as more arousing. The modality effect was slightly different from that observed in Experiment I. In both experiments music pitched in major keys was evaluated as least arousing and atonal music was more arousing; however, in Experiment II minor modalities produced higher arousal ratings than atonal music.

Finally, the ANOVA on behavioral intent found significant main effects of tempo (F = 3.19; p < .044; omega^2 = .025) and modality (F = 3.99; p < .021; omega^2 = .034), and a tenuous tempo-mode interaction (F = 2.01; p < .095). The statistical results are similar to those found in Experiment I. Again, slower tempos and atonal modalities produced the least positive behavioral intent.

In sum, the pattern of main and interactive effects of tempo and modality in Experiment II was very consistent with Experiment I. In the case of appealingness ratings, the tempo-mode interaction effect was weaker in Experiment II. This is what one might expect given the less pure (but more realistic) manipulations in Experiment II. The arousal effect of tempo was more pronounced given the expanded range of tempi represented in Experiment II. The effects on behavioral intent were fairly consistent across the experiments, with atonal music producing the least positive intent.

CONCLUSION

This study has explored the effects of two important objective stimulus properties of music (tempo and modality) on consumers' responses to music. Findings were generally supportive of Bruner's (1990) proposition concerning interactive effects of music's components. A consistent pattern of effects was found across two experiments using different operations. Tempo was found to have positive main effects on evaluations of music's arousingness and on behavioral intent. Modality also influenced arousal and intent, with atonal modalities producing the least positive responses. Tempo and mode were found to operate interactively on evaluations of music's appealingness, and, to some extent, on behavioral intent.

Some limitations of the study should be recognized. First, the instrumental music examined

TABLE 2
OVERVIEW OF EXPERIMENT II RESULTS

DEPENDENT MEASURE	MAIN EFFECTS				INTERACTION	
	TEMPO		MODALITY		TEMPO-MODE	
	F	p<	F	p<	F	p<
APPEALINGNESS	2.72	.069	2.18	.12	1.94	.106
AROUSINGNESS	22.09	.0005	2.97	.05	1.14	n.s.
BEHAVIORAL INTENT	3.19	.044	3.99	.021	2.01	.095

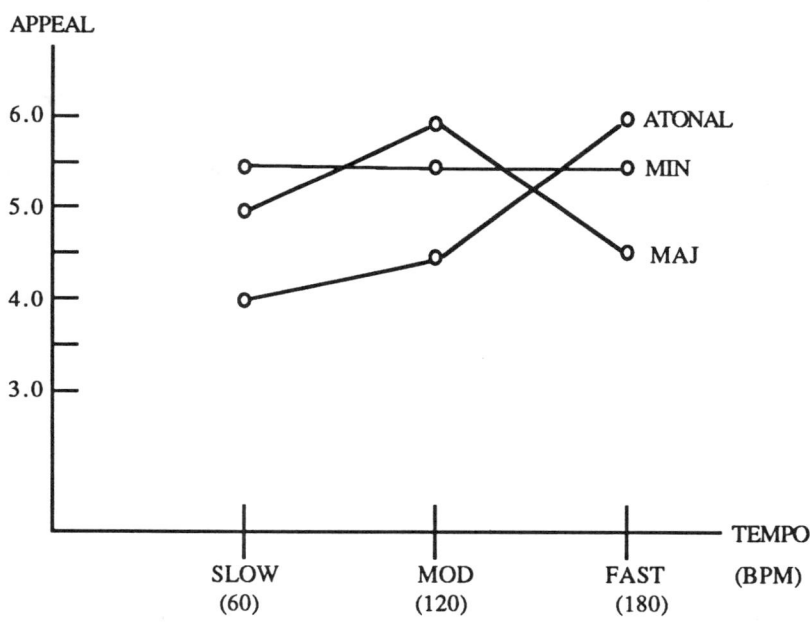

FIGURE 2
EVALUATIONS OF MUSIC'S APPEALINGNESS (EXPERIMENT II)

in this study was drawn from classical sources. Thus, the findings might be more characteristic of "art music" as opposed to popular/commercial forms of music. Second, the duration of exposure to the musical stimuli was relatively brief (three minutes). It is possible that different responses to music could develop after more prolonged exposures, such as in a store, restaurant, or concert setting. Third, the sample has both advantages and disadvantages. The use of student subjects offers statistical advantages of homogeneity, but may impose limitations on generality. College students spend more time listening to music than the general adult population, and their musical tastes lean strongly toward current Rock/Pop. (68.5% of the sample across the two experiments reported preference for this listening category.) On the other hand, this may be an advantage of the sample because treatment effects of classical and non-western music would be *less* likely to show themselves among Ss who generally lack knowledge and interest in these musical genres. The use of less familiar, less preferred music constitutes a stronger test for treatment effects.

This study yields a number of preliminary implications. First, it is clear that music's structural components (at least tempo and mode) can work interactively as influences on listeners. This implies that individual components of music should not be treated in isolation in research or practical applications. Second, music pitched in major keys seems to generate the most positive responses; however, given the "Wundt curve" effect, tempi which are either too fast or slow are likely to mitigate this influence. Marketers or other parties wishing to take advantage of music's positive influences should search for optimal tempi at which hedonic response is maximized. Third, under certain circumstances it may be desirable to use minor or atonal music because it provides variety or is more aesthetically congruent with an advertised product or message (e.g. dissonant music in anti-drug abuse ads). In such cases, faster tempi might mitigate negative thoughts and feelings, and slower tempi might intensify negative effects. Finally, the findings on behavioral intent toward music may generalize to behavioral intent toward products via an associative process when music is used in ads or in retail environments. This could be explored in future research.

Several other directions for future research are suggested by this study. For example, effects of other musical components such as sound texture could be examined. Objective stimulus properties of music such as tempo and modality might operate through "subjective" stimulus properties such as novelty or complexity (Berlyne 1974). It would be interesting to explore the mediating role of such variables, and perhaps to assess the relative predictive power of objective vs. subjective stimulus properties of music. Finally, this research could be extended by studying the effects of musical components on the processing of verbal material (e.g. song lyrics, advertising messages). The aesthetic congruency of music with words may influence the reception and interpretation of verbal material.

SELECTED REFERENCES

Alpert, Judy I. and Mark I. Alpert (1988), "Background Music as an Influence in Consumer Mood and Advertising Responses," in Thomas K. Srull, ed., *Advances in Consumer Research*, Vol. 16, Association for Consumer Research, Provo, UT, 485-491.

Bruner, Gordon C., III (1990), "Music, Mood, and Marketing," *Journal of Marketing*, 54, 4 (October), 94-104.

Gorn, Gerald J. (1982), "The Effects of Music in Advertising on Choice Behavior: A Classical Conditioning Approach," *Journal of Marketing*, 46, (Winter), 94-101.

Hevner, Kate (1935a), "The Affective Character of the Major and Minor Modes in Music," *American Journal of Psychology*, 47, 103-118.

Hevner, Kate (1935b), "Expression in Music: A Discussion of Experimental Studies and Theories," *Psychological Review*, 42, 186-204.

Hevner, Kate (1937), "The Affective Value of Pitch and Tempo in Music," *American Journal of Psychology*, 49, 621-630.

Holbrook, Morris B. and Punam Anand (1988), "Aims, Concepts, and Methods in Marketing Research on Consumer Esthetics: The Effects of Tempo on Perceptual and Affective Responses to Music," unpublished working paper, Columbia University.

Kellaris, James J. and Anthony D. Cox (1989), "The Effects of Background Music in Advertising: A Reassessment," *Journal of Consumer Research*, 16 (June), 113-118.

Lasher, Kathleen T. (1989), "Hedonic Consumption: Music as a Product," in Thomas K. Srull, ed., *Advances in Consumer Research*, Vol. 16, Association for Consumer Research, Provo, UT, 367-373.

Milliman, Ronald E. (1982), "Using Background Music to Affect the Behavior of Supermarket Shoppers," *Journal of Marketing*, 46 (Summer), 86-91.

Milliman, Ronald E. (1986), "The Influence of Background Music on the Behavior of Restaurant Patrons," *Journal of Consumer Research*, 13 (September), 286-289.

Park, C. Whan and S. Mark Young (1986), "Consumer Response to Television Commercials: The Impact of Involvement and Background Music on Brand Attitude Formation," *Journal of Marketing Research*, 23(February), 11-24.

Stout, Patricia A. and John D. Leckenby (1988), "Let the Music Play: Music as a Nonverbal Element in Television Commercials," in S. Hecker and D.W. Stewart, eds., *Nonverbal Communication in Advertising*, Lexington, MA, D.C. Heath, 207-223.

A complete reference list is available from the first author on request.

The Influence of Affect on Attributions for Product Failure
Lalita A. Manrai, University of Delaware
Meryl P. Gardner, University of Delaware

Consumers' cognitive and affective reactions to product failure are central to understanding post-purchase behavior. The extant research has provided many insights into the nature of these reactions and their mediating role on such post-purchase behaviors as complaining and word of mouth (e.g., Curren and Folkes 1987; Day and Ash 1979; Day and Bodur 1978; Folkes 1984, 1988; Folkes, Koletsky and Graham 1987; Folkes and Kotsos 1986; Krishnan and Valle 1979; Landon 1977; Valle and Wallendorf 1977). In all this research, disconfirmation of expectations is considered as the force that generates affective and cognitive reactions. In contrast, there is a dearth of research examining the impact of the emotional context of product failure on subsequent cognitive and emotional reactions. The term "emotional context" is used here to refer to the consumer's feeling state prior to product failure. The purpose of this paper is to provide a conceptual model which addresses the issue of how emotional context affects attributions for product failure. Before presenting our model, we will provide an overview of the satisfaction literature. This review is meant to be representative rather than inclusive and provides a historical context for the model.

PRODUCT FAILURE AND SATISFACTION

The area of consumer satisfaction/dissatisfaction has particularly captured the interest of researchers in the last decade. Most of the early research in this area is based on the expectancy disconfirmation paradigm (Churchill and Surprenant 1982; LaBarbera and Mazursky 1983; Oliver 1980; Oliver and Linda 1981). This conceptualization of satisfaction is based on the proposition that satisfaction is a function of prior expectancies and actual product performance. If performance exceeds expectations, consumers will be satisfied; if performance falls below expectations, consumers will be dissatisfied. In the context of product failure, this suggests that disconfirmation is the primary determinant of (dis)satisfaction and is depicted in Model-A of Figure A.

Weiner's (1980) work extends this paradigm. It suggests that disconfirmation does not lead directly to satisfaction, and that the effects of disconfirmation are mediated by attributional processing. In marketing, Folkes and her colleagues (Curren and Folkes 1987; Folkes 1984; Folkes, Koletsky and Graham 1987; Folkes and Kotsos 1986) have extensively studied product failure, using attribution theory to predict consumers' post-purchase behavior. Using the categorization system suggested by Weiner (1980), Folkes (1984) studied how the three dimensions of attributions - i.e., stability, locus and controllability - affect consumer reactions. Her findings support the prediction that stable attributions lead to certainty about product failure and preference for a refund rather than an exchange. In addition, she found that locus, is related to market equity reactions: Consumers felt that the firm owes them an apology and refund when product failure was firm-related. Finally, she found that controllability, in conjunction with locus, influences "anger" reactions: Consumers felt angry and wanted to hurt the firms' business when they felt that the firm could have controlled the failure. In another study, Curren and Folkes (1987) found these three dimensions were related to both positive and negative consumer reactions. These reactions were studied in terms of communications such as complaining/complementing and negative/positive word of mouth. The results indicated that the desire to communicate was greater for seller-controlled causes, with seller-related stable causes leading to more positive communications and stable causes (irrespective of locus) leading to more negative word of mouth than unstable causes. Thus the work of Folkes and her colleagues (Curren and Folkes 1987; Folkes 1984; Folkes Koletsky and Graham 1987; Folkes and Kotsos 1986) clearly establishes the utility of Weiner's (1980) attribution framework in the context of product failure and satisfaction. A simplified conceptualization of this work is represented by Model B in Figure A.

Folkes' (1984) finding that the controllability dimension, in conjunction with locus, influences "anger" reactions suggests that attributions can lead to specific types of emotional reactions. This link between attributions and emotions is amply researched and supported in psychology. In particular, the work of Weiner and his colleagues (Weiner 1985; Weiner, Russell and Lerman 1978, 1979) investigates the link between many specific attributions and resulting specific emotions. Westbrook (1987) suggests that emotions affect consumer satisfaction. Thus the next development in consumer researchers' conceptualizations of satisfaction includes emotions as mediating between attributions and satisfaction. This is depicted in Model C in Figure A.

Oliver (1989) provides a comprehensive conceptual framework which integrates the cognitive consequences of disconfirmation (attributions) and the affective consequences of disconfirmation (emotions) enabling both to mediate the effects of disconfirmation on consumer satisfaction. In his model, disconfirmation is viewed as having both a direct effect on attributions and an indirect effect - i.e., through primary evaluation (success/failure) processing. Consistent with Weiner (1985), attribution processing is viewed as affecting satisfaction/dissatisfaction through distinct emotions (guilt/anger). In addition, primary evaluations also affect satisfaction/dissatisfaction (through primary affect - i.e., happy/sad). Basic

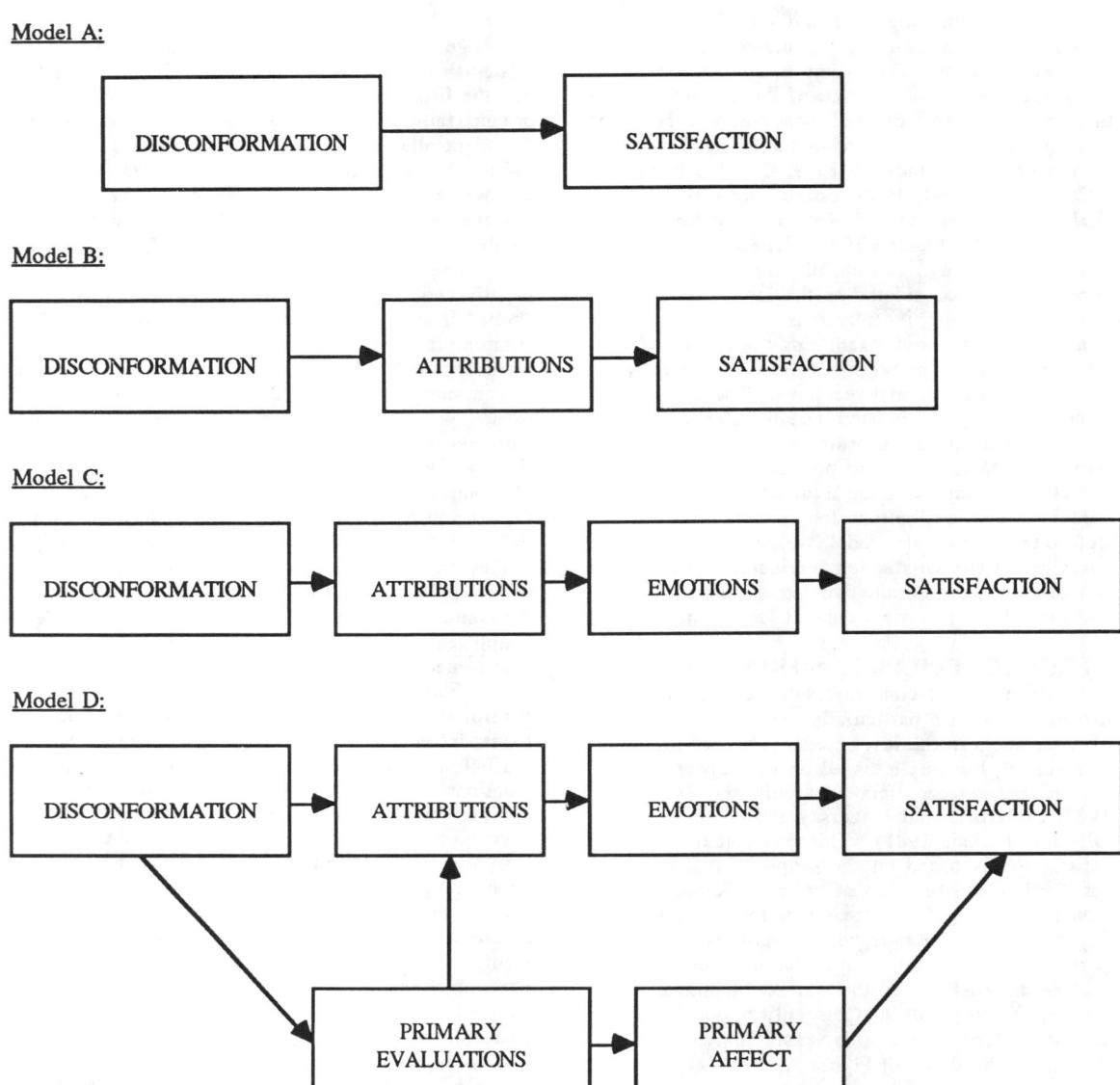

FIGURE A
Current Models of Product Failure and Consumer Satisfaction*

*Note: These are simplified conceptualizations of the work by the researchers. The objective is to show gradual progression of conceptualization and integration of cognitive and effective reactions into the satisfaction framework.

---

conceptualization of Oliver's (1989) work is depicted in Model D in Figure A.

Note that models A - D in Figure A all posit disconfirmation as the major determinant of attributional processing. It is possible that factors other than disconfirmation may account for the extent and content of attributional processing. For example, a cycle-recycle pattern of emotion-attribution-emotion may mediate the effects of disconfirmation on consumer satisfaction. Such a multistage model of the relationship between achievement outcomes, outcome related affect, attribution and emotion was supported in two studies conducted by Stephan and Gollwitzer (1981). These studies showed that achievement outcome created an affect which caused attributions, and attributions in turn resulted in emotions. Thus, emotions may precede attributions instead of (or in addition to) resulting from attributions. It is also possible that emotions prior to an outcome may affect reactions to the outcome. Thus in the context of product failure, prior mood or emotional context of product failure may affect subsequent cognitive and affective reactions. Differential emotion theory suggests that emotion is constantly present in consciousness and influences attribution processes (Izard 1982). One possible way in which the effects of differential emotions on attributions can be captured is as an individual difference. Consider two individuals: one in a happy mood and the other in a sad mood. When confronted with a product failure situation, they may react differently. The work of Beck and his colleagues studying depression (Beck 1967; Kovacs and Beck 1977) suggests that depressed individuals tend to negatively view outcomes.

Further evidence for the conjecture that emotions affect cognitions is offered in the area of memory research. Findings indicate that prior affective states influence memory processes (Bower 1981; Clark & Isen 1982; Isen and Daubman 1984; Isen, Shalker, Clark and Karp 1978). While quite a few of these studies are based on mood congruency effects, two other possible influences of mood states were suggested by Wyer and Carlston (1979). One was the informational function of mood - i.e., an individual may treat a mood as an informational input for making judgments. The other was the directive function of mood - i.e., an individual's attention may be directed towards specific information to explain a mood. These effects of prior mood states suggest that the emotional context in which product failure takes place may affect subsequent information processing. For example, a consumer may blame a restaurant for poor service not only because his/her soup was cold but also due to the fact that s/he had a bad day at work or was stuck in the traffic jam. The emotional context of product usage situations thus may influence attributional processing.

CONCEPTUAL MODEL AND HYPOTHESES

With this in mind, we propose a two-stage model in which emotional context affects satisfaction and other post-purchase processes in the context of product failure. The basic conceptual model is given in Figure B. Its first stage relates the emotional context of product failure to resulting attributions, and its second stage examines the effects of these attributions on satisfaction and other post purchase behavior. The model integrates four issues: 1) how different mood states affect the number of attributions, 2) how different mood states affect the type of attributions, 3) how quantity of attributions affects post purchase behavior and 4) how type of attributions affects post purchase behavior. Before these issues are discussed, we need to define some terminology for examining emotional context and provide a framework for discussing types of attributions.

Oliver (1989) integrates research on emotion typologies in his conceptual model. Three typologies discussed by Oliver (1989) are those of Russell (1978, 1979, 1980), Plutchick (1980) and Watson and Tellegen (1985). While these typologies differ, they suggest a common underlying dimensional structure for emotions. Two orthogonal dimensions most commonly accepted by these and other researchers (Mehrabian and Russell 1974) are pleasure and arousal. We believe these two dimensions provide a staring point for exploring the effects of emotional context on attribution processing. Russell, Weiss and Mendelsohn (1989) describe the specific mood states on a two-dimensional affect grid with pleasure and arousal as the two dimensions. Depression/gloominess is characterized as a low arousal-negative mood state, anger/stress as high arousal-negative, excitement/ecstacy as high arousal-positive and relaxation/serenity as low arousal-positive. Each of these mood states is a specific one differing from each other along either or both of the dimensions of emotions, i.e., arousal and pleasure. Against these specific moods, an "average, every day, normal" mood is depicted as the very center of the affect grid - i.e., moderate arousal and neither pleasure nor displeasure.

As regards the attributional framework, Weiner's (1980) three-dimensional taxonomy provides a conceptual framework of proven value in consumer behavior (Curren and Folkes 1987; Folkes 1984; Folkes, Koletsky and Graham 1987; Folkes and Kotsos 1986; Oliver 1989). We believe this three dimensional framework will also prove useful in examining the effects of emotional context on attribution processing. The first causal dimension is locus of control, where causes such as ability, effort, mood and patience are identified as internal causes and task difficulty and luck are identified as external causes. The second dimension suggested by Weiner is variance of causes, where causes such as ability, task difficulty and patience are considered to be relative invariant or stable and causes such as luck, effort and mood are considered as variant or unstable. Finally the third dimension deals with controllability, where causes such as effort are considered as intentional or controllable and causes such as ability, task difficulty or mood are considered unintentional or uncontrollable.

Turning back to the four issues in our model, we now develop hypotheses pertaining to the first issue - i.e., how different emotional states affect the extent or quantity of attributional processing. Specific mood states may lead to more attributional processing than normal, less distinct mood states because the former are likely to have more readily identifiable, elaborate associative networks than the latter. Work of Clark and Isen (1982) suggests that when something positive or negative happens to a person, the affective tone associated with that experience may be stored in memory with other things associated with that experience. Things that produce a given feeling tone may be linked together in memory as a category. If this is so, the associative network for an event that takes place in a specific emotional context would include both

FIGURE B
Proposed Modified Model of Product Failure and Consumer Satisfaction

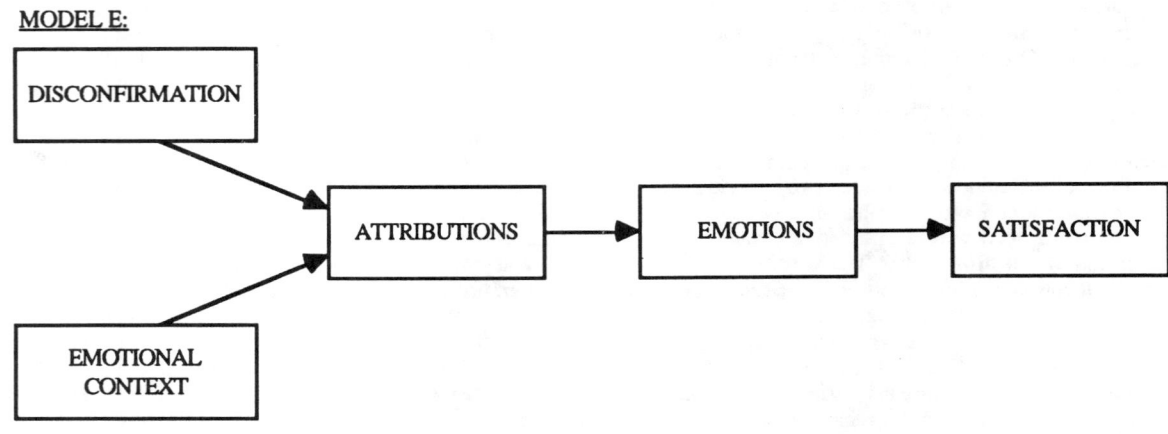

those things *directly* linked to the particular experience and those things *indirectly* related through their sharing of a common affective tone. For example, if one is in an angry mood and has a bad experience in a restaurant, both one's restaurant schema and set of experiences related to anger may be triggered. In contrast, a person in a normal mood having a bad experience in the restaurant will have a smaller activated network consisting primarily of restaurant-related things.

The elaborate network activated by product failure in an emotional context is expected to lead to greater attributional processing. More specifically, the four mood states discussed earlier - i.e., depression, anger, excitement, and relaxation are expected to have more elaborate networks and thus lead to greater attributional processing than a normal mood state. Thus we hypothesize that:

H_1: Attributional processing is higher when product failure is experienced in an emotional context than when no emotional context is present.

Next we examine the two dimensions of emotions, i.e., pleasure and arousal as they relate to the extent of attributional processing. Existing research in psychology and related areas suggests that negative affect results in more attributional processing. Schwartz and Clove (1983) studied how judgments of happiness and satisfaction with one's life are influenced by mood at the time of judgment. Unpleasant affective states led to greater search for and greater use of information to explain the emotional state than pleasant affective states. In another study by Gilovich (1983), gamblers were found to spend more time explaining their losses than their wins. These findings suggest that negative affective states are associated with more attributions than positive affective states. We propose that this would apply in case of product failure and hypothesize that:

H_2: Attributional processing in response to product failure is higher when the emotional context is negative than when it is positive.

As regards the second dimension of emotions, i.e., arousal, work by Pyszczynski and Greenberg (1981) suggests that individuals engage in more thorough attributional processing for unexpected events than they do for expected events. Since unexpected or unusual events are likely to be high in arousal, this suggests that high arousal may be associate with greater attributional processing than low arousal. This conjecture is also consistent with the work of Oliver (1989). A comparison of the five different types of satisfaction response models suggested by Oliver (1989) indicates that a specific satisfaction response such as surprise, which is high in arousal, has very active attributional processing in contrast to contentment, which is low in arousal. We, therefore, hypothesize that:

H_3: Attributional processing in response to product failure is higher when the emotional context is high in arousal than when it is low in arousal.

Research to test these hypotheses and the proposed models is underway. We hope the findings will contribute to our understanding of consumer satisfaction processes by adding the effects of affective state prior to product failure.

REFERENCES

Beck, A. T. (1967), *Depression: Clinical, Experimental, and Theoretical Aspects*, New York: Harper & Row.

Bower, Gordon H. (1981), "Mood and Memory," *American Psychologist*, 36, 129-148.

Churchill, Gilbert A., Jr. and Carol Surprenant (1982), "An Investigation into the Determinants of Customer Satisfaction," *Journal of Marketing Research*, 19 (November), 491-504.

Clark, Margaret S. (1982), "A Role for Arousal in the Link Between Feeling States, Judgments, and Behavior," in *Affect and Cognition*, The Seventeenth Annual Carnegie Symposium on Cognition, Margaret S. Clark and Susan T. Fiske, eds., Hillsdale, NJ: Lawrence Erlbaum Associates, 263-290.

_____ and Alice M. Isen (1982), "Toward Understanding the Relationship Between Feeling States and Social Behavior," in *Cognitive Social Psychology*, A. H. Hastorf and A. M. Isen, eds., Elsevier, NY, 73-108.

Curren, Mary T. and Valerie S. Folkes (1987), "Attributional Influences on Consumer's Desire to Communicate About Products," *Psychology & Marketing*, 4, 31-45.

Day, Ralph L. and Stephen B. Ash (1979), "Consumer Response to Dissatisfaction with Durable Products," in *Advances in Consumer Research*, Vol. 6, ed. William L. Wilkie, Ann Arbor, MI: Association for Consumer Research, 438-440.

_____ and Muzaffer Bodur (1978), "Consumer Response to Dissatisfaction with Services and Intangibles," in *Advances in Consumer Research*, Vol. 5, ed. H. Keith Hunt, Ann Arbor, MI: Association for Consumer Research, 263-272.

Folkes, Valerie S. (1984), "Consumer Reactions to Product Failure: An Attributional Approach," *Journal of Consumer Research*, 10 (March), 398-409.

_____ (1988), "The Availability Heuristic and Perceived Risk," *Journal of Consumer Research*, 15 (June), 13-23.

_____ , Susan Koletsky and John Graham (1987), "A Field Study of Causal Inference and consumer Reaction: The View from the Airport," *Journal of Consumer Research*, 13 (March), 534-539.

_____ and Barbara Kotsos (1986), "Buyers' and Sellers' Explanations for Product Failure: Who Done It?" *Journal of Marketing*, 50 (April), 74-80.

Gilovich, Thomas (1983), "Biased Evaluation and Persistence in Gambling," *Journal of Personality and Social Psychology*, 44, 6, 1110-1126.

Isen, Alice M. and K. A. Daubman (1984), "The Influence of Affect on Categorization," *Journal of Personality and Social Psychology*, 47, 1207-1217.

_____ , T. Shalker, M. Clark and L. Karp (1978), "Affect, Accessibility of Material in Memory, and Behavior: A Cognitive Loop?," in *Journal of Personality and Social Psychology*, 36, 1-12.

Izard, Charles E. (1982), "Comments on Emotion and Cognition: Can There be a Working Relationship" in *Affect and Cognition*, The Seventeenth Annual Carnegie Symposium on Cognition, Margaret S. Clark and Susan T. Fiske, eds., Hillsdale, NJ: Lawrence Erlbaum Associates, 229-242.

_____ (1984), "Attributional Processing Style Differences in Depressed and Non-depressed Individuals," *Motivation and Emotion*, 8, 211-220.

Kovacs, M. and A. T. Beck (1977), "Empirical-Clinical Approach Toward a Definition of Childhood Depression," in *Depression in Childhood: Diagnosis, Treatment and Conceptual Models*, eds. J. G. Schulterbrandt & A. Raskin, New York: Raven Press.

Krishnan, S. and Valerie A. Valle (1979), "Dissatisfaction Attributions and Consumer Complaint Behavior," in *Advances in Consumer Research*, Vol. 6, ed. William L. Wilkie, Ann Arbor, MI: Association for Consumer Research, 445-449.

LaBarbera, Priscilla A. and David Mazursky (1983), "A Longitudinal Assessment of Consumer Satisfaction/Dissatisfaction: The Dynamic Aspect of the Cognitive Process," *Journal of Marketing Research*, 20 (November), 393-404.

Landon, E. Laird (1977), "A Model of Consumer Complaint Behavior," *Consumer Satisfaction, Dissatisfaction and Complaining Behavior*, ed. Ralph L. Day, Bloomington, IN: Indiana University School of Business.

Mehrabian, Albert and James A. Russell (1974), *An Approach to Environmental Psychology*, Cambridge, MA: MIT Press.

Oliver Richard L. (1980), "A Cognitive Model of the Antecedents and Consequences of Satisfaction Decisions," *Journal of Marketing Research*, 17 (November), 460-469.

_____ and Gerald Linda (1981), "Effect of Satisfaction and its Antecedents on Consumer Preference and Intention," in *Advances in Consumer Research*, Vol. VIII, Kent B. Monroe, ed., Ann Arbor, MI: Association for Consumer Research, 88-93.

_____ (1989), "Processing of the Satisfaction Response in Consumption: A Suggested Framework and Research Propositions," *Journal of Satisfaction, Dissatisfaction and Complaining Behavior*, Vol. II, 1-16.

Pyszczynski, Thomas A. and Jeff Greenberg (1981), "Role of Disconfirmed Expectancies in the Instigation of Attributional Processing," *Journal of Personality and Social Psychology*, 40, 1, 31-38.

Russell, James A. (1978), "Evidence of Convergent Validity on the Dimensions of Affect," *Journal of Personality and Social Psychology*, 36, 1152-1168.

_____ (1979), "Affective Space is Bipolar," *Journal of Personality and Social Psychology*, 37, 345-356.

_____ (1980), "A Circumplex Model of Affect," *Journal of Personality and Social Psychology*, 39, 1161-1178.

_____, Anna Weiss and Gerald A. Mendelsohn (1989), "Affect Grid: A Single Item Scale for Pleasure and Arousal," *Journal of Personality and Social Psychology*, 57, 3, 493-502.

Schwartz, Norbert and Gerald L. Clove (1983), "Mood, Misattributions and Judgments of Well-being: Informative and Directive Functions of Affective States," *Journal of Personality and Social Psychology*, 45, 513-523.

Stephan, Walter G. and Peter M. Gollwitzer (1981), "Affect as a Mediator of Attributional Egotism," *Journal of Experimental Social Psychology*, 17, 443-458.

Valle, Valerie A. and Melanie Wallendorf (1977), "Consumers' Attributions of the Cause of their Product Satisfaction and Dissatisfaction," *Consumer Satisfaction, Dissatisfaction and Complaining Behavior*, ed. Ralph L. Day, Bloomington, IN: Indiana University School of Business.

Watson, David and Auke Tellegen (1985), "Toward a Consensual Structure of Mood," *Psychological Bulletin*, 98 (September), 219-235.

Weiner, Bernard (1980), *Human Motivation*, New York: Holt, Rinehart & Winston.

_____ (1985), "An Attributional Theory of Achievement Motivation and Emotion," *Psychological Review*, 92 (October), 548-573.

_____, Dan Russell and David Lerman (1978), "Affective Consequences of Causal Ascriptions," in *New Directions in Attribution Research*, Vol. 2, John M. Harvey, William Ackes, and Robert F. Kidd, eds., Hillsdale, NJ: Lawrence Erlbaum Associates, 59-90.

_____, _____, and _____ (1979), "The Cognition-Emotion Process in Achievement-Related Contexts," *Journal of Personality and Social Psychology*, 37 (July), 1211-1220.

Westbrook, Robert A. (1980), Product/Consumption-Based Affective Responses and Post Purchase Processes," *Journal of Marketing Research*, 24 (August), 258-270.

Wyer, R. S. and D. Carlston (1979), *Social Cognition Influence and Attribution*, Hillsdale, NJ: Erlbaum.

Historical Perspectives on Funding Opportunities in Consumer Research

Paul N. Bloom, University of North Carolina at Chapel Hill
George R. Milne, University of North Carolina at Chapel Hill

ABSTRACT

The history of how consumer research has been funded is examined. Data are presented that show the sources of financial support for published articles over the last twenty-five years, and additional thoughts about research funding are offered based on the authors' personal observations. Several ideas for improving the availability of funds to consumer researchers are also presented.

INTRODUCTION

The relatively young discipline of consumer research has grown and advanced without the benefit of significant amounts of funding to support research activity. The vast majority of the studies in the field have been paid for out of either researchers' own pockets or their school's limited research funds. Big government or foundation grants to support programmatic research efforts have played a minor role.

This paper attempts to document this situation, drawing primarily on the results of a small empirical study. Specifically, the following questions are addressed here:

1. Where have the funds come from to support consumer research?

2. How has funding influenced the types of studies that have been done?

3. What are the historical reasons for low levels of funding for consumer research?

4. What can we learn from the past to improve the situation in the future?

The empirical study completed to address these questions consisted of a content analysis of the funding acknowledgements provided by authors at the beginning of articles appearing in four different outlets. In addition to this study, answers to the questions were formulated by drawing on the lead author's experience as (1) a long-time member of ACR (since 1972), (2) the author of a book that recounts the history of the Marketing Science Institute (Bloom 1987), and (3) a member of the American Marketing Association's "Development of Marketing Thought" Task Force, which spent considerable time addressing the topic of obtaining more funds for basic research in marketing (Monroe et al. 1988).

SOURCES OF FUNDS

In order to make a more accurate assessment of where funds have come from to support consumer research, a content analysis was conducted of the footnotes or acknowledgements found at the beginning of the following articles:

1. All of the articles that have appeared in *Advances in Consumer Research* from 1973 through 1989.

2. All of the articles that have appeared in the *Journal of Consumer Research* from 1974 through 1989.

3. All of the articles that were indexed under the headings "Consumer Behavior" and "Consumer Analysis" in the *Journal of Marketing* from 1964 through 1989.

4. All of the articles that were indexed under the headings "Buyer Behavior" and "Information Processing" in the *Journal of Marketing Research* from 1964 through 1989.

The information found in these acknowledgments was used to place each article in one or more of the following categories:

1. No funding source acknowledged.

2. Funding acknowledged from the school(s) of the author(s).

3. Funding acknowledged from the National Science Foundation.

4. Funding acknowledged from another Federal government agency (e.g., the Federal Trade Commission or Food and Drug Administration).

5. Funding acknowledged from the Canadian government.

6. Funding acknowledged from other governments.

7. Funding acknowledged from the Marketing Science Institute.

8. Funding acknowledged from another private, nonprofit organization.

9. Funding acknowledged from a private corporation.

No attempt was made to record anything about an article other than its source of funding. Clearly, future research could look at additional information such as the types of methods employed in the research, the topics studied, or the citations a work received from other researchers. In addition, while we attempted to be thorough in our content

TABLE 1
TOTAL CONSUMER RESEARCH FUNDING IN ALL OUTLETS
1964-1989

Year	N	B	%B	Sch	NSF	USG	Can	OG	MSI	NP	PC
1964	5	45	11	1	3	1	0	0	0	0	0
1965	2	15	13	1	1	0	0	0	0	1	0
1966	0	8	0	0	0	0	0	0	0	0	0
1967	6	10	60	2	1	0	0	0	0	3	3
1968	4	16	25	2	1	1	0	0	0	0	1
1969	8	23	35	4	0	0	0	0	0	0	5
1970	6	37	16	2	0	0	0	0	0	2	2
1971	5	31	16	3	0	1	0	0	1	0	1
1972	12	40	30	8	0	2	0	0	0	0	2
1973	19	79	24	9	2	4	0	0	1	6	1
1974	38	134	28	20	7	3	0	1	2	10	3
1975	28	132	21	16	5	3	0	2	4	2	6
1976	24	116	21	14	5	2	0	0	1	3	4
1977	32	171	19	16	7	2	2	0	1	6	3
1978	27	134	20	7	6	6	2	0	1	4	3
1979	21	104	20	13	3	4	0	0	2	2	1
1980	45	196	23	15	3	8	3	5	1	9	5
1981	34	160	21	13	3	10	1	2	3	8	2
1982	43	176	24	28	2	4	2	0	5	8	1
1983	29	181	16	20	1	2	1	1	0	8	0
1984	37	153	24	22	6	3	2	1	2	2	3
1985	32	133	24	19	2	2	4	0	1	4	3
1986	28	182	15	22	2	2	1	0	3	3	2
1987	32	163	20	23	2	2	0	1	5	2	3
1988	38	179	21	25	2	4	0	0	6	5	7
1989	47	187	25	26	1	7	3	1	3	4	9
Total	602	2805	21	331	65	73	21	14	42	92	70

Key: N=Number of articles that reported funding. B=Base number of articles examined. %B=N as a percent of B. Sch = School Sources. NSF=National Science Foundation. USG=Another Federal agency. Can=Canadian government. OG=Other governments. MSI=Marketing Science Institute. NP=Non profit organizations. PC=Private corporation.

analysis, we recognize it is possible that some research efforts might not have acknowledged funding in a footnote.

The results of the content analysis are reported in Tables 1 through 5. Table 1 shows how many articles in all four outlets received one of the eight types of funding. Tables 2 through 5 show how many funded articles appeared in each outlet, starting with *Advances in Consumer Research*.

The most notable result in Table 1 is the low percentage of articles that contained any type of acknowledgement of funding. Over the examined time period in all four outlets, only 602 of the 2,805 published articles (21%) contained an acknowledgement of having received funding from at least one source. The table also shows who was acknowledged for providing funding, and this indicates that the most common acknowledgements cited the authors' schools. Among the 708 sources acknowledged -- which is higher than the 602 articles containing funding acknowledgements, since several articles acknowledged multiple funding sources -- 331 were school sources (47%). The next most frequently mentioned sources were "Nonprofit organizations" (13%), "Another Federal agency" (10%), "private corporations" (10%), the National Science Foundation (9%), and the Marketing Science Institute (6%). The Canadian and other foreign governments were the least represented of the funding sources.

It should be stressed that none of these non-school sources of funds were acknowledged in more than ten articles in all the outlets in any given year. It should also be noted that several of the funding sources are not known for giving out very large awards. For example, the typical MSI award has only been a few thousand dollars.

TABLE 2
CONSUMER RESEARCH FUNDING FOR *ADVANCES* 1973-1989

Year	N	B	%B	Sources of Funding							
				Sch	NSF	USG	Can	OG	MSI	NP	PC
1973	15	61	25	5	2	4	0	0	1	6	0
1974	21	83	25	12	4	0	0	1	1	6	0
1975	12	79	15	3	4	1	0	1	3	0	3
1976	8	66	12	5	2	0	0	0	0	1	0
1977	13	121	11	9	3	0	1	0	0	1	0
1978	7	81	9	3	0	3	1	0	1	0	0
1979	9	54	17	7	0	2	0	0	0	1	0
1980	17	130	13	6	2	3	1	4	0	1	1
1981	7	86	8	2	0	3	0	1	1	0	1
1982	12	117	10	9	0	1	0	0	1	1	1
1983	13	129	10	10	0	2	0	1	0	2	0
1984	16	110	15	10	1	1	1	1	1	0	1
1985	7	75	9	5	1	0	0	0	0	0	1
1986	6	129	5	4	0	2	0	0	0	0	0
1987	6	103	6	5	0	0	0	1	1	0	1
1988	7	124	6	3	1	2	0	0	1	0	1
1989	15	127	12	4	1	5	3	0	0	1	2
Total	191	1675	11	102	21	29	7	10	11	20	12

Key: N=Number of articles that reported funding. B=Base number of articles examined. %B=N as a percent of B. Sch = School Sources. NSF=National Science Foundation. USG=Another Federal agency. Can=Canadian government. OG=Other governments. MSI=Marketing Science Institute. NP=Non profit organizations. PC=Private corporation.

Looking at the data in Table 1 over time, a few patterns seem to emerge. It appears that NSF funding was much more prevalent in the 1970s than the 1980s, with the exception of the year 1984. Funding from other Federal government agencies also seemed more prevalent in the 1970s, with acknowledgements peaking in articles appearing in 1980 and 1981 (although 1989 was a relatively high year with 7 acknowledgements). Similarly, the funding from other private nonprofits seemed to peak in the late 1970s and early 1980s. Some of the slack in funding opportunities during the late 1980s seemed to be picked up by MSI and private corporations, as their number of acknowledgements increased over the last few years.

Table 2 shows the history of acknowledgements in *Advances in Consumer Research*. Overall, only 11% of the articles contained acknowledgements of funding from at least one source, and 48% of the sources mentioned were school-related. There were too few mentions of any individual non-school source to detect any interesting patterns.

In contrast, the *Journal of Consumer Research*, as shown in Table 3, did have 43% of its articles containing acknowledgements to one or more funding sources. Still, 47% of the acknowledgements mentioned the authors' schools. Additionally, the historical pattern for the non-school funding was essentially the same as that described in discussing Table 1. Indeed, *JCR* articles produced a high proportion of all the non-school acknowledgements that were identified.

The fact that *JCR* articles seemed to receive more funding raises a provocative cause-and-effect question: Did funding play a major role in creating the higher quality work -- that *JCR* articles tend to represent -- or did the higher quality work (or the promise of it) attract more funding? Although we cannot answer this question definitively, we have some thoughts to share about this issue in the next section of this paper.

The most noteworthy pieces of information in Tables 4 and 5 are the larger relative numbers for acknowledgements of private corporations. Otherwise, there are no discernible patterns to the support given to a portion of the consumer research articles that appeared in *JM* and *JMR*.

FUNDING'S INFLUENCE ON STUDIES

Since we did not code anything about the content of articles, we cannot use empirical results to guide our comments about how funding has influenced the types of studies that have been done. Our views on this subject are based on our personal observations and on what we gleaned as a by-product of coding the acknowledgements. Our comments are focused on how the availability of funding has influenced (1) the topics that have been studied, (2)

TABLE 3
CONSUMER RESEARCH FUNDING FOR JCR 1974-1989

Year	N	B	%B	Sources of Funding							
				Sch	NSF	USG	Can	OG	MSI	NP	PC
1974	11	26	42	4	2	3	0	0	0	2	2
1975	9	31	29	7	1	2	0	0	0	1	2
1976	8	23	35	4	2	2	0	0	1	1	2
1977	11	25	44	4	3	1	1	0	0	3	1
1978	10	25	40	2	3	2	1	0	0	2	1
1979	8	32	25	4	3	2	0	0	1	1	0
1980	19	37	51	6	1	4	2	1	1	6	1
1981	16	45	36	6	2	3	1	1	1	5	0
1982	23	36	64	14	2	3	2	0	3	4	0
1983	10	34	29	5	1	0	1	0	0	5	0
1984	15	34	44	9	5	2	1	0	0	1	0
1985	16	37	43	9	0	2	3	0	0	2	1
1986	16	34	47	13	2	0	1	0	2	2	2
1987	17	36	47	12	2	2	0	0	2	1	0
1988	23	45	51	18	1	2	0	0	4	4	2
1989	19	40	48	16	0	1	0	1	3	1	2
Total	231	540	43	133	30	31	13	3	18	41	16

Key: N=Number of articles that reported funding. B=Base number of articles examined. %B=N as a percent of B. Sch = School Sources. NSF=National Science Foundation. USG=Another Federal agency. Can=Canadian government. OG=Other governments. MSI=Marketing Science Institute. NP=Non profit organizations. PC=Private corporation.

the methods and scope of projects, and (3) the quality of the research.

We do think it is possible for funding to influence the types of topics that are studied in a discipline. In the interviews conducted by Bloom (1987) with researchers who had received funding from MSI, the availability of funding was one of the five most frequently offered explanations -- in responses to both unprompted and prompted questions -- of what first sparked their interest in a particular topic. The availability of funding was also one of the six most frequently mentioned reasons why they chose to invest time studying a topic. Indeed, the recent impressive response MSI received for its Brand Equity Competition illustrates how funding can lure researchers to investigate a given topic.

However, we do not feel that enough funding has been available in the consumer research field to have had a significant influence on what topics have been studied in the past. In a sense, the discipline has remained "pure," with the researchers deciding for themselves what are the important topics to investigate, avoiding being even slightly "corrupted" by the lure of money to study topics that they probably would not have studied otherwise.

On the other hand, we feel that the methods and scope of consumer research projects have definitely been influenced by funding. Overall low funding levels clearly deserve some of the blame for frequently-lamented shortcomings such as the overuse of student subjects, the tendency to do "quick-and-dirty" small experiments or surveys, the limited use of multi-disciplinary perspectives, and the failure to sustain programmatic research efforts.

When funding has been available, we think that it has facilitated the completion of higher quality research studies, such as those that have appeared in JCR. But we do not feel that the causation runs primarily from funding to higher quality. Instead, we think the stronger effect has been in the other direction, with higher quality research stimulating higher levels of funding. We think more accomplished, higher quality researchers, who formulate and propose higher quality studies, have shown greater ability to persuade their schools (primarily) and other funding agencies to support their research endeavors. Thus, we feel this entrepreneurial activity of researchers has had much more to do with advancing funding, quality, and knowledge in consumer research than any enlightened generosity of funding agencies.

REASONS FOR LIMITED FUNDING

Consistent with what we have just said about the value of entrepreneurial activity by researchers, we must place much of the blame for the limited amount of funding of consumer research on the researchers in the field themselves. We feel that systematic, sustained, and well-packaged efforts by consumer researchers to "sell" their research ideas to funding agencies have been infrequent. Frankly,

TABLE 4
CONSUMER RESEARCH FUNDING FOR JM 1964-1989

Year	N	B	%B	Sch	NSF	USG	Can	OG	MSI	NP	PC
1964	0	8	0	0	0	0	0	0	0	0	0
1965	0	3	0	0	0	0	0	0	0	0	0
1966	0	4	0	0	0	0	0	0	0	0	0
1967	2	2	100	1	0	0	0	0	0	1	0
1968	2	7	29	0	1	1	0	0	0	0	0
1969	2	12	17	0	0	0	0	0	0	0	2
1970	2	12	17	0	0	0	0	0	0	0	2
1971	0	11	0	0	0	0	0	0	0	0	0
1972	0	12	0	0	0	0	0	0	0	0	0
1973	0	8	0	0	0	0	0	0	0	0	0
1974	2	13	15	2	0	0	0	0	0	0	0
1975	1	7	14	1	0	0	0	0	0	0	1
1976	0	4	0	0	0	0	0	0	0	0	0
1977	1	10	10	1	0	0	0	0	0	1	0
1978	1	5	20	0	0	1	0	0	0	0	0
1979	3	6	50	2	0	0	0	0	1	0	0
1980	0	2	0	0	0	0	0	0	0	0	0
1981	7	18	39	2	1	4	0	0	1	2	0
1982	3	12	25	2	0	0	0	0	0	1	0
1983	1	5	20	1	0	0	0	0	0	0	0
1984	3	5	60	2	0	0	0	0	0	0	1
1985	3	6	50	2	0	0	0	0	0	1	0
1986	2	7	29	2	0	0	0	0	0	1	0
1987	3	7	43	1	0	0	0	0	0	0	2
1988	2	3	67	0	0	0	0	0	1	0	2
1989	3	5	60	1	0	0	0	0	0	1	1
Total	43	194	22	20	2	6	0	0	3	8	11

Key: N=Number of articles that reported funding. B=Base number of articles examined. %B=N as a percent of B. Sch = School Sources. NSF=National Science Foundation. USG=Another Federal agency. Can=Canadian government. OG=Other governments. MSI=Marketing Science Institute. NP=Non profit organizations. PC=Private corporation.

business school professors -- who still make up the bulk of the ACR membership -- do not have the set of incentives and pressures that researchers in other disciplines have for going out and "getting money." The market value of professors in business schools is not as affected by their "grant-winning" ability as it is for professors in the hard sciences or some of the social sciences. Moreover, business school professors can frequently turn to consulting to provide them with added wealth, travel opportunities, and feelings of being influential -- things that professors in other disciplines may only be able to acquire by building little "empires" for themselves through their grant-winning prowess.

With lower incentives and pressures to "get money," even many of those business-school-based consumer researchers who have had some success in obtaining grants have failed to sustain their grant-getting activities. Therefore, the opportunity to pass on some of their know-how about grant-getting to younger colleagues or students has often not been capitalized upon. Moreover, these experienced grant-getters have frequently not stayed visible with the funding agencies, missing the chance to pave the way for other consumer researchers through being "gray-haired," credible spokespersons for the merits of funding consumer research.

It might also be possible to blame consumer researchers for being too "in-between" in their approach to research problems. It could be argued that the field tends to be too basic to appeal to the business community -- which wants results that can be easily and quickly applied to real-life problems -- and too applied to appeal to the basic research advocates in some of the government agencies and foundations.

Other factors that we feel have contributed to a shortage in research funds include the relative youth of the field of consumer research and the overall decline in funding of research of any type during the Reagan Administration (which spanned a major portion of the history of consumer research).

TABLE 5
CONSUMER RESEARCH FUNDING FOR JMR 1964-1989

Year	N	B	%B	Sch	NSF	USG	Can	OG	MSI	NP	PC
1964	5	37	14	1	3	1	0	0	0	0	0
1965	2	12	17	1	1	0	0	0	0	1	0
1966	0	4	0	0	0	0	0	0	0	0	0
1967	4	8	50	1	1	0	0	0	0	2	3
1968	2	9	22	2	0	0	0	0	0	0	1
1969	6	11	55	4	0	0	0	0	0	0	3
1970	4	25	16	2	0	0	0	0	0	2	0
1971	5	20	25	3	0	1	0	0	1	0	1
1972	12	28	43	8	0	2	0	0	0	0	2
1973	4	10	40	4	0	0	0	0	0	0	1
1974	4	12	33	2	1	0	0	0	1	2	1
1975	6	15	40	5	0	0	0	1	1	1	0
1976	8	23	35	5	1	0	0	0	0	1	2
1977	7	15	47	2	1	1	0	0	1	1	2
1978	9	23	39	2	3	0	0	0	0	2	2
1979	1	12	8	0	0	0	0	0	0	0	1
1980	9	27	33	3	0	1	0	0	0	2	3
1981	4	11	36	3	0	0	0	0	0	1	1
1982	5	11	45	3	0	0	0	0	1	2	0
1983	5	13	38	4	0	0	0	0	0	1	0
1984	3	4	75	1	0	0	0	0	1	1	1
1985	6	15	40	3	1	0	1	0	1	1	1
1986	4	12	33	3	0	0	0	0	1	0	0
1987	6	17	35	5	0	0	0	0	2	1	0
1988	6	7	86	4	0	0	0	0	0	1	2
1989	10	15	67	5	0	1	0	0	0	1	4
Total	137	396	35	76	12	7	1	1	10	23	31

Key: N=Number of articles that reported funding. B=Base number of articles examined. %B=N as a percent of B. Sch = School Sources. NSF=National Science Foundation. USG=Another Federal agency. Can=Canadian government. OG=Other governments. MSI=Marketing Science Institute. NP=Non profit organizations. PC=Private corporation.

In a sense, the field is starting to gain the respectability to fight for funding against the other mature disciplines, only to find that the absolute size of funding is smaller.

LESSONS FOR THE FUTURE

Our examination of the past leads us to believe that a few actions and developments might serve to increase the amount of funding made available for consumer research. First and foremost, we think that consumer researchers need to develop the skills and the will needed to become more successful at marketing their studies to funding agencies. Additional conference sessions like the one at which this paper was presented can help to develop the necessary skills, but developing the will to seek funding is much more problematical. Leadership of ACR officers and thought-leaders (e.g., Fellows) could help to popularize grant-seeking, as could leadership from Deans and department chairs. However, changes in the performance appraisal and compensation systems of academic departments might be the most needed development.

Additional conference sessions encouraging joint research between consumer-research academics and practitioners could help, as could sessions encouraging more multi-disciplinary research efforts. The former could lead to projects that are viewed as more applied, making them potentially more acceptable to private corporations and MSI. The latter could lead to projects that are viewed as more basic and interdisciplinary, making them potentially more acceptable to NSF and certain foundations. At the same time, we think it would be helpful if ACR officers and thought-leaders engaged in a systematic effort to educate and inform funding agencies about the merits and value of consumer research.

ACR could go a step further and actually organize a foundation to fund high-quality, programmatic research efforts. Financing might be provided from a number of sources, including membership dues, ACR commercial ventures, donations from publishers, and corporate donations. We recognize that ACR has resisted getting in the funding business for a variety of reasons, including a short-lived bad experience with having a dissertation proposal contest. We are especially concerned about the problems of avoiding too much donor influence over what projects get supported. But we think that it is possible to create appropriate safeguards to avoid ethical conflicts and compromises, and we would like to see a foundation receive serious discussion. We feel that continued reliance on the sources of funding currently available to consumer researchers may not be adequate for advancing knowledge in this field at a desirable rate.

REFERENCES

Bloom, Paul N. (1987), *Knowledge Development in Marketing: The MSI Experience*, Lexington, MA: Lexington Books.

Monroe, Kent et al. (1988), "Developing, Disseminating, and Utilizing Marketing Knowledge," *Journal of Marketing*, 52(October), 1-25.

Qualitative Research In The Textbooks: A Review
Joel Saegert, University of Texas at San Antonio
Geraldine Fennell, Consultant

ABSTRACT

Fifteen currently available marketing research textbooks were reviewed for their depiction of qualitative research, especially in the context of the marketing concept. Although most of the texts mention the marketing concept as a rationale for marketing research, they fail to present, through theoretical discussions and/or by presentation of examples, the role of qualitative research as a means of investigating the state of want-satisfaction in prospective markets. In this respect, textbooks fail to communicate to students the role that qualitative research plays in implementing the marketing concept.

Marketing research can be said to be the primary means by which the marketing concept is implemented. That is, marketing research is a set of procedures by which the state of want satisfaction, the *sine qua non* of marketing practice, is revealed to producers. Fennell (1987) has discussed the marketing concept as required by the nature of the marketer's task, namely to provide the interface between customers and the firm's productive capability. In implementing the marketing concept's dictum, "Don't sell what you happen to make; make what the customer wants to buy," marketers turn to research to describe the state of want satisfaction. Moreover, qualitative research has provided researchers with a method of studying customer wants *as found*, starting with unstructured interviews. For example, in attempting to describe customer circumstances to facilitate choosing attributes with which to imbue brand offerings, "qualitative research, in particular the focus group interview, is the well-trodden ground by which marketing research generates its attribute set" (Fennell 1980a).

This paper is concerned with how qualitative research is presented to students in marketing research textbooks, chiefly those that are used by instructors of introductory marketing research courses in business education. Of particular interest is the presentation of qualitative research as a method of identifying wants and assessing the state of want satisfaction. Because of space limitations, the scope of this review focuses on how marketing research textbook authors present:

- the theoretical/philosophical basis for the practice of marketing research

- the role of qualitative research in the practice of marketing research

- the methods of qualitative research, as they follow from the theoretical/philosophical basis

The data base for this investigation consists of 15 marketing research textbooks made available by publishers to instructors in marketing research courses. Only texts published in the past five years were included. While this selection may not be exhaustive, these books are likely those most popularly adopted by research faculty at US business colleges and departments, thus reflecting the collective portrayal of qualitative research to marketing students. Since our concern is the overall presentation of research concepts to business students in general, we have chosen not to attribute specific quotations to their authors. The texts reviewed are listed at the end of the paper.

PHILOSOPHICAL UNDERPINNINGS

The marketing concept, as a philosophy of business enterprise, is almost universally included in the introductory chapters of textbooks in marketing. Similarly, in their introductory chapters, authors of textbooks in customer behavior and marketing research typically invoke the marketing concept as the justification for studying their respective subject matters. As illustrated in Fig. 1, in all of the marketing research textbooks reviewed for this paper, explicitly or implicitly authors have referred to the marketing concept when stating a rationale for marketing research.

Given its apparently central place as a statement of the discipline's philosophy, it is reasonable to expect that the marketing concept has profound implications for business strategy, namely, in advising organizations that their success lies in responding to wants as found. Surprisingly, however, authors have not made systematic use of the marketing concept in discussing the role of marketing research in business decision-making processes, nor in presenting the many examples used to instruct students in research practice. In fact, following its initial presentation, it is difficult to discern that the marketing concept's implications are considered at all. Specifically, authors do not make a connection between marketing's fundamental philosophy and the techniques required to relate human wants to business opportunity.

In various writings over the past 15 years, Fennell, (e.g. 1978, 1979, 1980b, 1985a, 1989) is one of the few authors to have been interested in developing the implications of the marketing concept as a philosophy of business, and as a theory of marketing and human behavior (readers may welcome being reminded of early statements of the marketing concept such as those of Borch 1957, Mortimer 1959, and Keith 1960; see also Fennell, 1991). Figure 2 presents some implications of the marketing concept for marketing research, as discussed in Fennell's work.

Perhaps the aspect of the marketing concept that has the most far-reaching implications for

FIGURE 1
Marketing Research Textbook Quotations: The Marketing Concept as the Rationale for Marketing Research

A. Research is one of the prime tools enabling firms to implement the philosophical idea of the marketing concept.
B. With increased acceptance of the marketing concept, it became evident that more information about customers and potential markets was needed. The desire for such information gave impetus to marketing research.
C. Another reason for the increase in marketing research relates to widespread endorsement of the marketing concept.
D. Organizations which embrace the marketing concept tend to view marketing research as a research system...focused on the needs and wants of the consumer as opposed to the needs and wants of the organization.
E. The marketing concept suggests that the central focus of the firm should be the customer's satisfaction...Marketing research is the firm's formal communication link with the environment.
F. To the extent that a firm practices the marketing concept, marketing research serves the role of finding out what the consumer wants and evaluating how well the firm's current or proposed offerings meet these desires. Thus, in the marketing concept, marketing research finds itself in the role of a feedback mechanism for management guidance.
G. In today's hotly competitive marketplace, (the) marketing concept has been gaining in importance. In a management context the marketing concept states that the principal task of the marketing function is to serve the interests of the customer rather than the interests of the business.
H. The role of marketing research...is steadily increasing as more and more firms embrace the *marketing concept*--the philosophy of customer orientation urging firms to uncover customer needs first and then coordinate all their activities to satisfy those needs. The marketing concept, by emphasizing the need to gain a good understanding of customers, is also stressing the importance of marketing research.
I. An essential ingredient in developing effective marketing strategy is a thorough understanding of consumers' needs and wants. An important role of marketing research is to provide such information...
J. An ever increasing premium has been placed on making sound marketing decisions, and companies are becoming more *market-driven* in their strategic decision making. In response to this requirement a formalized means of acquiring information to assist inthe making of such decisions has emerged... This means is *marketing research*...
K. ...why is it even necessary for companies to use something called "marketing research? ...managers...find themselves becoming more separated from the final consumers of their products......organizations...need certain kinds of information in order to be able to satisfy their customers' wants and needs...
L. ...the most ambitious types of marketing research attempt to assess future markets in terms of customer preferences and competitive actions. ...Moreover, it also is appropriate...to be involved in longer run and hence, in some sense, more important decisions (e.g., providing input to R & D).
M. ...Marketing managers of consumer goods are particularly active in monitoring their competitors and their customers. "The more you know about the customer the better," says R. Stephen Fountaine, the vice-president of market research at Kimberly- Clark Corp. "You never know when a small fact might lead to a better product."
N. ...Think for a minute about the marketing manager's job. He or she must make decisions concerning which consumers to serve (market segmentation), and what product features, price levels, promotional strategies, and distribution channels to use. ...the research process help(s)...management select a market segment, design a product, and develop an advertising campaign.
O. Understanding the customers--who they are, how they behave, why they behave as they do, and how they are likely to respond in the future--is at the heart of marketing research. It is the responsibility of this function to be experts on how to learn about customers.

Note: Many of these quotations, as well as others in later Figures, contain statements which bear discussion beyond the specific reason for their being included in the Figure. Space limitations do not permit full treatment of each quotation here.

FIGURE 2
The Marketing Concept as Discussed by Fennell

A. Marketing's first law, "*Don't sell what you happen to make; make what the consumer wants to buy,*" is implemented through the identification of consumer wants and the formulation of brand positionings to respond to these wants. In a competitive environment, this means, in particular, the identification of consumer wants *that are not being addressed or adequately satisfied by the brands currently available.* (Fennell 1978, p. 38) ...consumer wants exist independently of, and are logically prior to, the brands that are created to satisfy them. (Fennell 1978, p. 39)

B. At base, the marketer's task is not to assess perceived value in objects that already exist but to identify the antecedents of perceived value so that valuable offerings can be fashioned, produced and made available for sale. (Fennell 1985b, pp. 65-66)
Marketing and selling both involve exchange but differ in that marketing, as distinct from selling, embraces decisions about what shall be produced, mandating that productive decisions are guided by customer wants. (Fennell 1985b, p. 65)
(My theoretical formulation) has been presented as illustrative of the broad outline of an integrating framework for...various facets of marketing's coordination of the firm's resources and specialized activities in response to consumer wants... (providing) the basis for marketing's guidance of advertising, on the one hand, and of R&D product development on the other. (Fennell 1978, p. 47)

C. I consider separately the determinants of the consumer's perception of the product- use situation and of brands. (Fennell 1978, p. 39)
We begin to have some understanding of what the consumer is asking for only when we refuse to be satisfied with answers expressed in the form of product benefits and inquire further into the conditions that lead the consumer to ask for (e.g.) *power* and *complexion care*. When we shift focus from what consumers ask for to the conditions that lead them to want what they ask for, we become better able to understand their wants... (Fennell 1978, p. 39)
...marketing researchers ask respondents to talk about a focal behavioral domain. Reactions to existing products and brands, and suggested modifications thereof are elicited only toward the end of the interview, which is largely devoted to exploringrespondents' beliefs, feelings, desires, expectations, information, and routines in regard to activities of interest. Practitioners are likely to take the position that it is the job, not of respondents, but of marketing in conjunction with R&D to translate information about the context of use into the attributes of instrumental goods/services. (Fennell 1985b, p.67)

D. No producer is interested in all the wants of all the people, so the question arises of identifying prospects in a naturally-occurring population. Most usually, prospects are identified as individuals who perform some activity, such as buying/using a particular kind of good/service (e.g., using dog food), or engaging in some life activity (e.g., taking care of a pet), or who own some item (e.g., pet owners). Note that an important aspect of the task of identifying prospects is stating a focal behavioral domain. Strictly speaking, the universe that is of interest to a producer is not a universe of individuals but of person-activity occasions (Fennell 1982b), i.e., actions extended in space and time, for example, all dog feedings in the United States in a twelve month period. (Fennell 1985b, p. 67)

E. For my purposes here, the choice of situational units corresponds to the activities and conditions for which products are created and marketed, such as doing the laundry, feeding the dog, having a headache. The marketing concept implies that the meaning of such product-use situations differs in important ways across consumers, and calls for an approach stated in terms of participants' perceptions. Accordingly, *a product-use situation as perceived* is my unit of analysis. (Fennell 1978, p. 39)
A moment's thought makes it clear that words such as power,...complexion care,...while referring to product benefits that may satisfy wants, do not in themselves tell us anything about the situations in which consumers find themselves--the situations that make power, complexion care, and the like desirable to them. In fact, such expressions can be motivationally ambiguous. (Fennell 1978, p. 39)
...it is not enough to assess audience members' degrees of favorability to a proposed message or to bundles of attributes. Among other requirements, audience members (consumers) must be characterized in terms that predict what they will perceive as valuable... (Fennell 1985b, p. 66)
We must then find ways to represent the fact that individual producers do not try to respond to all the circumstances that allocate human resources. A first cut through a universe of activity-occasions is needed in order to exclude the portion for which a producer's domain of expertise is likely to be irrelevant (nonprospects). Within the remainder (prospects), circumstances are likely to be varied (Behavioral demand is segmented.). From the totality of the producer's domain of expertise, only a portion may be deployed in producing an offering, which likely responds to a subset of the circumstances of prospective users (targeted circumstances). (Fennell 1978, p. 302)

FIGURE 2 (CONTINUED)

F. The marketing concept is unambiguous on the point that, before producers enter the picture, people have wants i.e., their energies are already allocated to certain pursuits and they think about, seek information relating to, and engage in action that is intended to achieve certain environmental impacts and states of their being. Society assigns to the producer the task of helping users to bring about their desired external and internal states. (Fennell 1985b, p. 66)

We must model an individual doing something or trying to do something or wishing things were different and a producer offering to help. (Fennell 1985b, p. 67)

---

marketing research is the notion that customer wants take precedence over goods/services (See Fig. 2A for the opening paragraph, and a later statement, of Fennell 1978). Responding to wants as found implies:

1. Marketers cannot be satisfied merely to investigate customer reactions to arbitrarily-given existing or candidate goods/services or attributes (Fig. 2B);

2. Marketers must distinguish and investigate both (a) the conditions that lead to customer wants and (b) what the customer knows and believes about brands (Fig. 2C);

3. At any one time, marketers are interested in only a fraction of the total population and of the scope of human action (Fig. 2D);

4. Since wants are heterogeneous within a focal universe as defined and since product attributes and benefits are motivationally ambiguous, it is necessary to characterize respondents in terms that predict their kind of desired outcome (Fig. 2E);

5. Since the producer's job is to offer goods/services that help users to do what they are already trying to do, the marketer's task includes modeling and then describing the (heterogeneous) context in which individuals try to act (Fig. 2F). In fact Fennell (1980) has developed such a general model of action, and later (e.g. 1982a, 1985a) has shown how the classic tasks of marketing practice (e.g. the 4 P's) as well as the major kinds of marketing research in common business use, may be coordinated to the terms of that model.

THE MARKETING CONCEPT IN MARKETING RESEARCH TEXTS

As noted, most of the texts reviewed mention the marketing concept to students in their introduction of the rationale underlying marketing research. Following this, they give numerous examples to show the many ways in which research is used--those in Fig. 3 are typical of the hundreds of examples included in the texts' introductory chapters.

These examples, all of which appear in the initial chapters of the reviewed texts, say surprisingly little about the marketing concept's mandate to respond to wants as found. In fact, only two (i.e., Fig. 3E and I) refer to obtaining information about possible wants. Wants may have been investigated in two others (Fig. 3H and J), but since the marketing concept implies developing the offering from information obtained initially about the customer's circumstances, both H and J seem to fly in the face of sound marketing practice. Further, none of the examples of Fig. 3 illustrates marketing research undertaken for the express purpose of describing wants as found, e.g., the conditions that affect people in their daily lives, that lead them to want to use some good/service. Moreover, even when the chosen examples quite legitimately illustrate projects whose primary objectives are other than identifying wants, no reference is made to the fact that investigations of, e.g., price, marketing communications and other considerations, were conducted in the context of respondents' wants.

In sum, when the examples of Fig. 3 are presented--without critical commentary--to illustrate the use of marketing research, they convey to students a misinterpretation of one of the most important implications of the marketing concept, namely, production efforts proceed from finding out what customers want and tailoring the offering accordingly. Strictly speaking, the kind of examples used to introduce marketing research illustrate what Principles of Marketing texts label the "selling concept," i.e., considering ways to make a brand acceptable only after the brand is in existence. The point is an important one, fundamental to understanding the marketer's task and research's contribution to marketing: the role of marketing is to respond to wants as found. Such examples, and the accompanying discussion, fail to teach the marketing concept. At the very least, this constitutes a missed opportunity in the marketing research textbooks in that they provide no model or technique for proactively discovering customer wants across heterogeneous prospects and contexts for action.

FIGURE 3
Marketing Research Textbook Quotations: Examples to Illustrate the Use of Marketing Research

A. When Columbia Pictures Industries, Inc., was planning the promotion for its new movie *Starman*, it had to decide how much to spend for advertising the movie and when the advertising should occur.
B. For evidence that could be used to convince bottlers to switch to Nutra-Sweet, G.D. Searle's NutraSweet division interviewed 5,000 users of low-calorie soft drinks. The company found that given a choice between a saccharine-NutraSweet blend and 100% NutraSweet, 70% of them chose NutraSweet.
C. The Chevrolet Division of General Motors is increasingly turning to computer interviewing at trade shows to assess attendees' reactions to its new models.
D. Marketing research played a key role in Mercedes-Benz's 1983 introduction of the 190 class--the "Baby Benz"...(As a result of the research)...ads for Mercedes-Benz discussed its engineering and design, and were without flash copy or gimmicks. These ads were extremely successful.
E. United Airlines surveyed 1000 passengers to determine what factors they deemed most important in choosing an airline...United's "friendly skies" were perceived as less friendly than either Delta's or American's, but friendly personnel were relatively unimportant factors in a customer's selection of a carrier.
F. Product X's sales have fallen drastically because its price is too high. We need data that will shed light on what is a more effective price.
G. In a study conducted by the author, focus group interviews were used in helping to determine the strengths and weaknesses of the Defensive Driving Course of the National Safety Council.
H. The following example...demonstrates how marketing research can help identify and pursue opportunities in the marketplace. Clairol...found...there was no portable manicure device to fill the nail care needs of (the) market. The company did additional research to pinpoint and understand the marketing for such a device.
I. Johnson Wax did extensive marketing research in the late 1970s prior to the national launch of Agree Shampoo. Research helped to identify the opportunity, define the target user, define the positioning and strategy, and define the attributes and features the product should have.
J. A few years ago Seagram was marketing a new wine and the vice-president of marketing requested a survey of the U.S. wine market. Discussion between "management" and the research department led to the decision that the survey should produce advertising copy strategy, target groups, an image of the brand compared with that of other wines, and a media mix.

QUALITATIVE RESEARCH IN THE TEXTBOOKS

Rationale for Doing Qualitative Research

As Fennell has pointed out (e.g., 1980a, 1985c), qualitative research is a primary and widely-used approach to implementing the marketing concept in business practice. The attitude toward qualitative research in marketing research texts, however, is overwhelmingly one of reservation. Across this group of texts, the authors assign qualitative research to a secondary role, one that is to be considered guardedly (see Fig. 4).

Sometimes, qualitative research is discussed for situations where cost or time are the researcher's primary concern (Fig. 4A, D), thereby furthering the notion that qualitative research is somehow a substitute for, although less respectable than, quantitative research, a deficit for which its low price ticket relative to quantitative research seems to compensate. In specific references cited here, it is left unclear how "acting as a group" and "dynamic communication" (Fig. 4F) as reasons for conducting qualitative research flow from or, even, are consistent with marketing's task of responding to wants as found. While caution is certainly to be recommended with qualitative research, as it is with any technique, and while quantification of discoveries made by qualitative research is typically appropriate, the degree to which authors dwell on the shortcomings and limitations of qualitative research probably reflects their failure to appreciate a systematic role for such an approach in applied settings (see Fennell 1991).

Examples of Qualitative Projects

Some examples provided in the textbooks to illustrate the use of qualitative research are shown in Fig. 5.

Searching these examples for footprints of the marketing concept, one comes away disappointed. Three obvious problems are that in most cases (1) the particular qualitative project seems to have been conducted only after an offering has already been conceived; (2) there is no clear indication (e.g., in the promising case of Fig. 5G) that customer wants in the focal domain of activity had been investigated earlier--before the firm embarked upon brand or new product development; (3) there is no indication that information on the conditions that formed the context of use was obtained from respondents so that such reactions as they provided to the presented stimuli/concepts could be understood in light of the individual's perspective. Again, when presented without critical discussion, these examples communicate the role of

FIGURE 4
Marketing Research Textbook Quotations: Rationale for Using Qualitative Research

A. At one time, the author as well as many other researchers treated qualitative research as an interesting anachronism but somehow less pure and useful than quantitative studies of large samples. Recently, due to cost considerations... qualitative research has reemerged as an important part of marketing research.
B. They are relatively easy to conduct and so intriguing that they are misused for conclusive purposes. It is said that clients too often fail to use them to understand consumers, but instead interpret them as showing how consumers behave.
C. Critics of focus groups argue that the results obtained are little more than the creative ideas of the researcher and should not be considered research.
D. Why is it that methodology with so many limitations is so popular? The answer is that focus groups can be conducted quickly and cheaply and almost always results in some new ideas.
E. Focus groups, although widely used, remain controversial. Chrysler Corporation conducts over 13 thousand interviews a year, "many" of which are focus groups interviews. In contrast, a research manager of Ford discounts focus groups, claiming that they "generate random, top-of-the-head remarks instead of substantive suggestions and ideas."
F. ...The rationale underlying a focus group interview is that study participants, after an introductory discussion period, act as a group rather than as simply a collection of separate individuals. ...To attain the status of a group, study participants need to have common interests with respect to the research subject. Without such commonality, dynamic communication is unlikely, and the interview will fail to provide meaningful data.
G. Exploratory research is an essential step in the development of a successful research study. In essence, this kind of research is insurance that major elements of the problem or important competing hypotheses will not be overlooked.

FIGURE 5
Marketing Research Textbook Quotations: Examples of the Use of Qualitative Research

A. Eleven people (including the moderator) participated in a focus group to evaluate a new restaurant menu in El Paso, Texas.
B. For example, a company hires outside consultants to assist in marketing a new product. In such instances, a focus group interview with a sample of product-class users furnishes a nonmanagerial background on the product class, as well as information and perceptions about the company itself.
C. (Applications...best...for Qualitative Research): The brand manager in charge of Rise baking soda wishes to develop an understanding of how, when, where, and why consumers use Rise.
D. The Johnson company developed a new filter to be used in car air conditioning systems. Management wanted to find out the feasibility of the new product and develop a workable marketing plan...Focus groups interviews were used...to help develop hypotheses to identify potential markets.
E. The marketing department of Curlee Clothing undertook a major marketing research effort to help management evaluate current advertising and product strategy. As part of this effort, it brought together various groups of 6 or 7 young men...(who were) placed in comfortable surroundings... (and) asked to discuss clothing in terms of why and how they purchased it, their likes and dislikes, and so forth.
F. US WEST used (focus groups) in an analysis of demand for a new property maintenance service for "technologically sophisticated" buildings.
G. According to Neil DeClark, associate marketing research manager of Johnson Wax, "Using focus groups to further our understanding of users' problems and perceptions--and also to get early reactions to some product concepts--we found that we were on the right path. The oiliness problems were major, and our ideas were regarded as important by the potential users.
H. Pilsbury, for example, held focus-group discussions around the United States...to find out what consumers did not like about frozen pizza.
I. Just prior to the introduction of the new glass radial tires, Owens-Corning Fiberglas conducted a series of 15 focus-group interviews with mass merchandise, oil company, and private-label dealers to see what the dealers perceived as being the key benefits and merchandising aids that would best help them sell the new type of tires. J. General Motors uses consumer and dealer focus groups--as well as extensive questionnaires--to identify the best features of their own and of competitors' automobiles. These give insight on "world class" elements they want to meet or exceed.

qualitative research as merely that of obtaining reactions: (1) to offerings or candidate offerings that have originated "elsewhere," whose origin is, from a marketing perspective, unsystematic; (2) from individuals details of whose *relevant personal and environmental circumstances* are not available to elucidate the information they provide.

Interesting questions arise. Do the examples that authors selected fairly represent actual qualitative research projects? Did authors express personal biases by excluding some examples available to them, perhaps because they deemed the research "nonmanagerial?" In this connection, Fig. 5B is provocative. What could a "nonmanagerial" background on the product class mean? Perchance could it mean that respondents were asked to speak about aspects of their lives outside the marketplace, i.e., the everyday context in which marketplace offerings may be used? If so, why should such information be regarded as nonmanagerial?

From the perspective of implementing the marketing concept, it is troubling that the authors failed to reflect on and discuss the plain disparity between such examples and the marketing concept's emphasis on responding to wants as found with which marketing research had been introduced in early chapters.

RECOMMENDED METHODS OF QUALITATIVE RESEARCH

Since marketing research textbooks are unashamedly methodological handbooks, their treatment of qualitative research includes a great deal of attention to method. Some of the methodological discussion provides insights into the view of qualitative research held by the textbook authors and illustrates the attitudes that they may impart to students. Topics discussed include the selection of the participants of group studies and the composition of groups regarding homogeneity or heterogeneity of participants.

Screening

One critical aspect of qualitative research concerns screening of participants. If qualitative research is to investigate the "focal behavioral domain," researchers must insure that subjects in qualitative studies have tendencies to engage in the focal activities. Fennell has discussed this critical aspect of qualitative research as follows:

"Even when selecting people to study for strategic development, marketers typically do not proceed by recruiting people at random from the population at large. They first identify for study potential buyers, broadly defined. What marketers want at this point is to be able to talk with people...who have action tendencies that are favorable to their proposed offering category.

"Typically, qualifiers are stated in terms of (1) actual or planned product use or ownership...or (2) activities or conditions that do or may involve the use of a marketplace offering...

"In addition to the fact that questions about product use/ownership are usually well understood by survey respondents, they serve as surrogates for the focal behavioral domain." (Fennell 1985a)

Screening of participants is discussed in fewer than half of the texts (see Fig. 6), but sometimes the treatment focuses on demographic characteristics of participants, and whether or not they have participated in qualitative studies (focus groups) before (to avoid "professional" respondents). Overall, in only about a third of the texts, readers are exhorted to screen for "use of certain products, and frequency of product use" (Fig. 6B through H) a practice that is standard procedure among practitioners of qualitative research; however, none of the 15 texts reviewed discusses the screening of participants in terms of prior focal activities.

Heterogeneity/homogeneity of participants.

There is much discussion in the texts of whether qualitative group research should be conducted with homogeneous or heterogeneous groups. The resolution suggested is usually that homogeneity is required, since heterogeneity is thought to open the door to distractions to the purpose at hand. Thus, researchers are advised "to maintain as much homogeneity or commonality among group members as possible." Here again, authors typically refer to homogeneity in terms of the demographic characteristics of the participants, rather than in terms of their prior interest in the activity that is focal for the producer/researcher. This discussion seems to miss an important point of qualitative research, that customers are naturally heterogeneous regarding their motivations to participate in the focal activity.

"A universal finding (in qualitative research) is heterogeneity, a diversity of orientations to the focal activity, not only among individuals but, within individuals, over occasions for the activity. Accordingly, in regard to any proposed intervention, the nature of demand, as a producer finds it, is heterogeneous--the conditions that form the context for doing the laundry are varied. The market for laundry detergent--or toothpaste, dog food, Mexican food, denture cleanser/adhesive, razors--comprises various segments of demand" (Fennell and Saegert 1988).

Thus, if the primary purpose of conducting qualitative research is to gain insight into the private worlds of customers regarding a particular focal activity, a universal expectation of researchers

FIGURE 6
Marketing Research Textbook Quotations: Comments on Screening

A. Respondents for groups are generally selected so that they are relatively homogeneous, minimizing both conflicts among group members on issues not relevant to the study objectives... Most firms conducting focus groups use screening interviews to determine the individuals that will compose a particular group. One type they try to avoid is the individual who has participated before in a focus group...

B. ...screening is essential to the success of the focus group interview...the members must have adequate experience with the object or issue being discussed...

C. ...recruited participants must have had some experience related to the product or the issue to be discussed. The reason should be obvious: Respondents lacking relevant experience are not likely to make any valuable contribution to the group discussion. To the contrary, they may adversely affect the discussion by making meaningless remarks just for the sake of participating.

D. The composition of the group varies according to the needs of the client, especially the "problem" under study.

E. In almost all cases it is desirable to have individuals who have had experience with the product in question and are articulate. Therefore, product and brand usage and frequency of purchase are often the basis for selection to the group.

F. Focus groups usually involve anywhere from 6 to 12 people, prerecruited to meet defined characteristics-- for example, age, gender, use of certain products, and frequency of product use...

G. When Toyota wanted to learn what Americans preferred in small, imported cars, they asked groups of Volkswagen Beetle owners what they liked and disliked about that particular car.

H. Within an otherwise homogeneous group it may be helpful to provide for a spark to be occasionally struck by introducing contrasting opinions. One way to do this is to include both users and nonusers of the product or service or brand.

---

is that customers will be heterogeneous as to their motivations for performing the activity. In fact, this heterogeneity is the basis for competitive advantage in marketing: heterogeneous motivations among a firm's prospects provide opportunity for brand differentiation that is responsive to the characteristics of demand as found. Failing to discuss expected heterogeneity within groups denies the fundamental purpose of qualitative research, namely to uncover heterogeneous bases for customer demand (Fennell 1985c).

CONCLUSION

This paper is but a first, brief excursion into the enterprise of reviewing the extent to which textbooks relate the principles of marketing research to the marketing concept. Space limitations prevent us from more than skimming the surface of possible topics that might have been addressed in this regard. An extension of the present review, for example, would include a look at new product and/or attitude measurement chapters to see what the texts say about how attributes for goods/services are to be generated.

At this stage, we can conclude as follows:

1) The textbooks reviewed acknowledge the marketing concept as providing the philosophical rationale for marketing research.

2) Many discussions of business examples that the texts have used to illustrate research in marketing practice do not point out that, as follows from the marketing concept, the state of want satisfaction must have been investigated prior to the development of brands of goods/services.

3) When speaking of qualitative research, the texts largely imply that its role is relatively unimportant and secondary, compared to that of quantitative research.

4) The texts often portray the role of qualitative research as obtaining reactions to existing goods/services rather than exploring the state of want satisfaction in advance of brand formulation.

5) Authors' treatments of the methodological aspects of qualitative research often fail to alert readers to the necessity for screening participants in qualitative studies for predispositions favorable to the product category of interest. In addition, many authors overlook the fact that exploring heterogeneous motivations is a primary objective of qualitative research.

In conclusion, after initial affirmation, marketing research texts fail to give expression to the marketing concept's dictum, "Make what the customer wants to buy," as they develop the theory and practice of marketing research. Moreover, they do not discuss qualitative research as a means of investigating the circumstances that give rise to human wants, which marketers use as a basis for generating attributes. Those who would teach marketing research serve the discipline well by reminding students that the marketer's task is not simply to dispose of brands whose attributes were conceived "elsewhere," but rather to determine the attributes that will be attractive to customers whose wants marketers have researched.

TEXTS REVIEWED

Aaker, David A., and George S. Day (1990), *Marketing Research*, Fourth Edition, New York: John Wiley & Sons.

Boyd, Harper W., Ralph Westfall, and Stanley F. Stasch (1989), *Marketing Research: Text and Cases*, Seventh Edition, Homewood, IL: Irwin.

Churchill, Gilbert A., Jr. (1987), *Marketing Research: Methodological Foundations*, Fourth Edition, Chicago: The Dryden Press.

_____ (1988), *Basic Marketing Research*, Chicago: The Dryden Press.

Dillon, William R., Thomas J. Madden, and Neil H. Firtle (1987), *Marketing Research in a Marketing Environment*, Second Edition, Homewood, IL: Irwin.

Green, Paul E., Donald S. Tull, and Gerald Albaum (1988), *Research for Marketing Decisions*, Fifth Edition, Englewood Cliffs, NJ: Prentice Hall.

Kinnear, Thomas C. and James R. Taylor (1987), *Marketing Research: An Applied Approach*, Third Edition, New York: McGraw-Hill Book Company.

Kress, George (1988), *Marketing Research*, Third Edition, Englewood Cliffs, NJ: Prentice Hall, Inc.

Lehmann, Donald R. (1989), *Market Research and Analysis*, Third Edition, Homewood, IL: Irwin.

Luck, David J., and Ronald S. Rubin (1987), *Marketing Research*, Seventh Edition, Englewood Cliffs, NJ: Prentice-Hall, Inc.

Parasuraman, A. (1986), *Marketing Research*, Reading, MA: Addison-Wesley Publishing Company.

Peterson, Robert A. (1988), *Marketing Research*, Second Edition, Plano, TX: Business Publications, Inc.

Tull, Donald S. and Del I. Hawkins (1987), *Marketing Research: Measurement and Method*, Fifth Edition. New York: Macmillan Publishing Company.

Weiers, Ronald M. (1988), *Marketing Research*, Second Edition, Englewood Cliffs, NJ: Prentice Hall, Inc.

Zikmund, William G. (1989), *Exploring Marketing Research*, Third Edition, Chicago: The Dryden Press.

REFERENCES

Borch, F. J. (1957), "The Marketing Philosophy as a Way of Business Life," in *The Marketing Concept: Its Meaning to Management*, Marketing Series No. 99, New York: American Management Association.

Fennell, Geraldine (1978), "Consumers' Perceptions of the Product-Use Situation." *Journal of Marketing*, (April), 38-47.

_____ (1979), "Attention Engagement." In J.H. Leigh and C.R. Martin, Jr. (Eds.), *Current Issues and Research in Advertising*, Ann Arbor: University of Michigan.

_____ (1980a), "Attitude, Motivation, and Marketing or, Where Do the Attributes Come From?" In R.C. Olshavsky (Ed.), *Attitude Research Enters the Eighties*. Chicago: American Marketing Association.

_____ (1980b), "The Situation," *Motivation and Emotion*, Vol. 4 (December), 299-322.

_____ (1982a), "Terms vs. Concepts: Market Segmentation, Brand Positioning, and Other Aspects of the Academic-Practitioner Gap." In R. Bush and S. Hunt (Eds.) *Marketing Theory: Philosophy of Science Perspectives*, Chicago: American Marketing Association.

_____ (1982b), "The Unit to be Classified: Persons v. Behaviors. In *Consumer Classification: A need to Rethink*, Brugge, Belgium: ESOMAR.

_____ (1985a), "Persuasion: Marketing as Behavioral Science in Business and Nonbusiness Contexts." In R. Belk (Ed.), *Advances in Nonprofit Marketing*, Greenwich: JAI.

_____ (1985b), "Finally, Let's Model Marketing Communications." In M. Houston and R. Lutz, eds., *Marketing Communications Theory and Research*. Chicago: American Marketing Association.

_____ (1985c), "Things of Heaven and Earth: Marketing, Phenomenology, and Consumer Research." In E. Hirschman and M. Holbrook (Eds.), *Advances in Consumer Research*, XII.

_____ (1987), "A Radical Agenda for Marketing Science: Represent the Marketing Concept!" In F. Furat, N. Dholakia, and JR. Baggozzi (Eds.), *Philosophical and Radical Thought in Marketing*, Lexington: Lexington Books.

_____ (1989), "Aspects of a Dynamic View of Marketing-As-Exchange: Realworld Repercussions of a Model in the Mind." In Terry L. Childers, et al. (Eds.), *Marketing Theory and Practice*, Chicago: American Marketing Association.

_____ (1991), "The Role of Qualitative Research in Making what the Customer Wants to Buy." In R. Holman and M. Soloman (Eds.), *Advances in Consumer Research*, XVIII.

_____ and Joel Saegert (1988), "Marketing: In Loco Parentis?," *Proceedings* of the American Marketing Association Winter Educators' Conference, San Diego.

Keith, R. J. (1960), "The Marketing Revolution," *Journal of Marketing*, 24 (January), 35-8.

Mortimer, C. G. (1959), "The Creative Factor in Marketing," Fifteenth Annual Parlin Memorial Lecture, Philadelphia Chapter, American Marketing Association.

The Role of Qualitative Research in Making What the Customer Wants to Buy

Geraldine Fennell, Consultant

ABSTRACT

Qualitative research has become an active topic in publications within and outside the field of marketing. Recent work overlooks its special role in implementing top management's charge to marketers to proactively tailor the firm's output to customer wants. Reasons for such an oversight are considered and aspects of qualitative research that have been neglected, or misunderstood, are discussed. Emphasized here is the *exploratory* function of qualitative research in obtaining information on the realworld conditions for which goods/services are designed.

INTRODUCTION

The number of monographs and articles published in the past few years that discuss qualitative research in marketing and in the social sciences generally attests to a growing interest in qualitative investigations (e.g., Advertising Research Foundation 1985, Cox and Higginbotham 1979, Durgee 1986, Fennell 1985, Goldman and McDonald 1987, Greenbaum 1988, Merton 1987, Wertz and Greenhut 1985, Yoell 1979). Moreover, the academic community's neglect of qualitative research, to which Calder (1977) drew attention, is beginning to be repaired and the status of qualitative research in the broader context of the scientific enterprise has been receiving attention in the work of consumer researchers (e.g., Hirschman 1989).

As yet, however, authors have neglected to consider marketers' *essential* reason for doing qualitative work. Authors, even those who write for the marketing literature, draw on mainstream social and behavioral science without screening constructs and formulations for relevance to a marketing application. In consequence, misunderstandings and misdirections for future managers have entered the literature, which, remaining uncorrected, may harm professional practice and impede developing an authentic marketing science. A statement of marketing's function and the place of qualitative research in implementing that function is necessary as a platform from which to evaluate not only concepts and formulations found readymade in the mainstream but guidelines for professional practice that the literature may suggest.

This paper describes the systematic contribution of qualitative research to implementing marketers' role as society's provisioners, whether the customer is a consumer or a business.[1] In the immediately following section, I consider why authors have so far overlooked the essential *marketing* grounds for conducting qualitative research. A section then follows in which the *exploratory* function of qualitative research is described. Finally, I consider a number of commonly discussed issues that may now appear in a new light, including (a) the notion that hypotheses may be tested by means of qualitative research, (b) using qualitative studies to "test" brand concepts/advertising messages, (c) the desirability of similarity/consensus among respondents when qualitative research uses group interviews, and (d) the point in the course of brand development when qualitative research should be undertaken.

TWO VIEWS OF MARKETING'S ROLE

The literature of the past couple of decades shows two contrasting views of marketers' responsibility for what is produced.[2] In the introductory chapters of textbooks, authors describe marketers' responsibility for ensuring that goods/services are responsive to customers' wants and desires *as found*. In the body of those same textbooks, and in new research and theorizing generally, investigators and theorists proceed as though marketers' point of entry occurs *after* the attributes of goods/services are largely in place, i.e., at a time when the task is to gain acceptance for an

---

[1] As the following three excerpts show, early statements of the "marketing concept" leave no doubt that top management intended marketers to lead the firm in deciding the nature of its output (original emphases): (1) "It will be only after identification of (customer) needs that marketing people can take the lead for the business in determining what each function of the business should do by way of product and service to satisfy them" (Borch 1957, p. 387); (2) Mortimer (1959, pp. 3, 18) speaks to the behavioral implications of making what people are willing to buy: "Projecting our imaginations into the lives of our fellow human beings, challenging every product we are presently offering them, and every characteristic of that product, as to its suitability and worth...we must apply our creativeness more intelligently to *people* and their wants.., rather than to *products*;" (3) "Our attention has shifted from problems of production to problems of marketing, from the product we *can* make to the product the consumer *wants* us to make...(p. 35) and "Marketing plans and executes the sale--all the way from the inception of the product idea, through its development and distribution, to the customer purchase. Marketing begins and ends with the consumer. New product ideas are conceived after careful study of her wants and needs, her likes and dislikes. Then marketing takes the idea and marshalls all the forces of the corporation to translate the idea into product and the product into sales" (Keith 1960, p. 37).

[2] As I am discussing views found widely in the literature, it seems inappropriate to cite particular authors. Specific references are available in my files.

output that producers want to sell. It is particularly in connection with the former view, i.e., marketing as an activity that *generates* candidate attributes of goods/services from analysis of the world of prospective users, that a *systematic* need for conducting qualitative research arises. Accordingly, absence of an authentically *marketing* perspective on qualitative research may be seen as part of a wider issue within the discipline namely, two mutually exclusive views of marketing's role existing side-by-side, one of which receives lip service while the other pervades the mainstream. As background to the present treatment of qualitative research in marketing, I now briefly discuss the origin and implications of marketers' assignment to ensure that what producers offer reflects users' wants *as found*.

MAKING WHAT THE CUSTOMER WANTS TO BUY

For simplicity here, consider that the producer's decision about what to make may proceed according to one of two models (e.g., Smith 1956). Producers may offer variants of a particular kind of output (1) without regard to or, (2) in response to, the heterogeneous (segmented) nature of preexisting demand. As discussed in the "marketing revolution" writings of the 1950s when marketing was distinguished from selling, top management and professional marketers regarded the second alternative as the essence of the marketing concept. As Keith put it: "Our attention has shifted from the product we *can* make to the product the consumer *wants* us to make" (footnote 1.3).

Operationally, this means that the marketer starts with the user's world, selects a behavioral domain for study and, within that domain, identifies characteristics of contexts for action, which s/he then employs to generate candidate attributes for a brand. For example, a producer of laundry detergent, dog food, or office equipment, needs to know about the circumstances--psychological and nonpsychological--in which laundering, feeding the dog, and performing office tasks, respectively, occur. Here, the requirement is for a differentiated understanding of prospective contexts for action *within* activity domains. There is a widely-repeated mistaken belief that the marketing concept implies that marketers should ask people to state the kind of goods/services that they want (e.g., Belk and Zhou 1987, Bennett and Cooper 1979, Hayes and Abernathy 1980, Oxenfeld and Moore 1978, Park and Zaltman 1987). One or two experiences of asking prospective users to describe the kind of soap, dog food, or office equipment that they want are enough to banish the idea of using such an approach. In fact, as early statements of the marketing concept show (see footnote 1), top management was aware that marketers would have to obtain information about the *context* for the activities in conjunction with which people may use goods/services, from which marketers would then generate desirable attributes to be designed into brands.

RESEARCH OPERATIONS TO IMPLEMENT THE MARKETING CONCEPT

To lay the ground here for later discussion of the role of qualitative research, let me outline the research approach that top management's charge to marketers implies. In a naturally-occurring population e.g., US residents, (Figure 1[a]), a marketer distinguishes prospects and nonprospects (Figure 1[b]). Prospects are individuals who engage in a focal activity, e.g., "do laundering," "communicate findings of a study to a large audience within the firm." To allow for variation within an individual over time in the context in which an activity takes place, it is advisable to think of the focal universe as consisting of occasions, rather than individuals, and to specify the time frame. Accordingly, the outer limit of a market-as-defined may be stated as, e.g., occasions for engaging in the focal activity, in the US, in calendar 1990 (Figure 1[c]). Within such an arena, the marketer identifies the naturally-occurring segments of demand (Figure 1[d]), and selects one or more for targeting (Figure 1[e]). For these purposes, business has used the two-stage, qualitative-quantitative, research approach known as market segmentation analysis. In qualitative investigations, marketers start by asking prospects to speak, not directly about their wants, or about their reactions to existing goods/services, but about what they know at first hand namely, their experiences of engaging in a focal behavioral domain. Respondents supply information about the psychological and nonpsychological context in which they engage in the focal activity. Marketers use such information to write items for large-scale surveys that quantify incidence, in some relevant universe, of the elements thus identified. Subsequently, the findings are used to select a segment of demand for targeting, including designing a brand with segment-appropriate attributes (the positioning decision).[3]

---

[3]Inasmuch as they recurrently allocate resources to keeping their brands in existence, producers address the positioning decision on an ongoing basis for all their brands. The essential structure of the producer's task is unchanged whether s/he is considering allocating resources to a new brand, or to continuing an existing brand in its present or modified form. Typically, producers are aware of, or actively considering, candidate variants of their current strategy, including candidate alternative formulations. Accordingly, with alternative uses for their resources, even maintaining last year's program unchanged implies a decision that the current brand in its current formulation is the producer's best strategy for securing a share of exchanges.

FIGURE 1
Core Marketing Tasks: Market Definition, Market Segmentation Analysis, and Brand Positioning

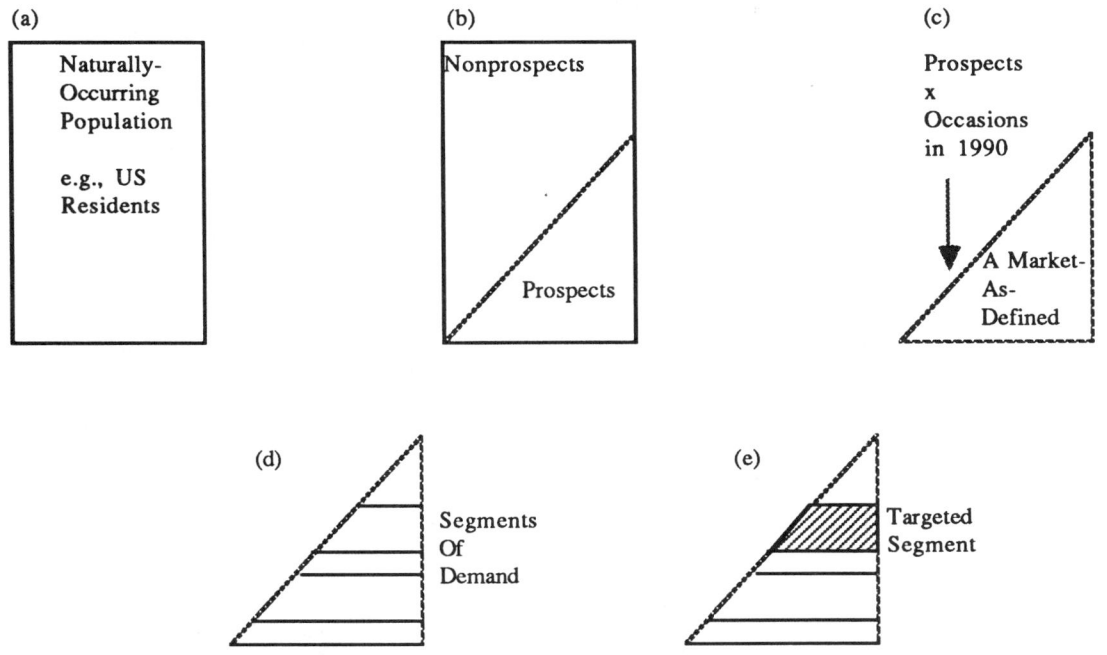

To summarize to this point: In the decade of the 1950s, top management distinguished *what* and *how* aspects of producing goods/services, and assigned to marketers the responsibility for answering the question: What shall we make? Specifically, marketers were to obtain information on the state of want-satisfaction in order to lead production management (e.g., manufacturing and R&D) in tailoring output accordingly. It soon became clear that to implement this assignment, marketers would need to ask prospective users to describe the characteristics of contexts for action corresponding to a particular class of output (e.g., laundry detergent, office equipment), some version of which the firm offers (or plans to offer).

ESSENTIALS OF MARKETING'S QUALITATIVE RESEARCH

Qualitative research has a role in marketing that arises directly from the behavioral implications of the marketing concept. Perhaps because the marketing concept itself has been largely misunderstood in the literature, authors have overlooked qualitative research's role in implementing it: To bring into the firm information about the actual elements that give rise to wants in relevant behavioral domains (e.g., corresponding to the firm's product categories). With regard to this exploratory function,[4]

qualitative work has had to proceed purely empirically. Its potential contribution is enhanced and its role is better understood when considered in conjunction with a model of the terrain that is being explored. Immediately following, I discuss its exploratory function, followed by its behavioral implications.

1. *Exploring Focal Aspects of the User's World*. Since a good/service relates to a particular, small, region of the total range of an individual's activities, it follows that a qualitative investigation is limited in scope to one or a few domains of activity. Typically, the analyst defines a behavioral domain that is broader than the focal activity. If the focal activity is "communicating findings of a study to a large group," the moderator/interviewer may initially place on the table the topic of "doing one's job in a corporate environment." The reason is, insofar as possible, to allow the respondent's categories and frames of reference to emerge without their being influenced by a framework that the researcher imposes (Fennell 1985a). The objective of the investigation is to elicit the concrete psychological and nonpsychological--personal and environmental--elements that are present in the context for engaging in the focal activity. The status of each element that respondents contribute is unchanged by the frequency with which the element is mentioned. At this stage, an element that is

---

[4] As noted elsewhere (Fennell 1985b, p. 547 note), researchers are exploring, not for constructs (Calder 1977), but for specific information about the real world.

mentioned once has status equal to one that is mentioned more often. Later, quantitative work ascertains the incidence in a focal universe of the elements that the qualitative phase has uncovered. Note that in qualitative work, the researcher seeks to identify relevant realworld facts. In quantitative work, the researcher seeks quantified information about (presumably) relevant realworld facts.

The exploratory objective of qualitative research is hard to realize in the absence of a model of the terrain that is being described. While it has been a useful tool, purely empirical qualitative research is a hazardous undertaking. Researchers lack guidelines relating both to the content and the form of the information that they seek. Regarding *content*, they find it hard to judge the comprehensiveness and possible redundancy of information that they obtain. A qualitative researcher may well ask: When have I fully explored a focal behavioral domain? How do I know that some vital element in the context for the focal activity has not been omitted--for any number of reasons: Its absence in the experience of the particular individuals who were my respondents, or their neglecting to mention it despite its actual presence in their experience --through forgetfulness, or some inhibitory event that occurred during the interview? Trying to guard against such eventualities, qualitative investigations sometimes grow in physical volume to unwieldy proportions, as indeed do the questionnaires for the subsequent quantitative phase, which are based on the qualitative findings. As to *form*, researchers must rely on the naive understanding of participants, project designer, and moderator, supplemented in the case of the professionals by on-the-job learning. In contrast, taking a position on what the relevant classes of entities are (e.g., occasions for action), a model articulates issues for researchers.

2. *Behavioral Implications*. Even when it proceeds on a purely empirical basis, qualitative research in fact explores some region of behavior, presumably guided by common sense ideas about the information that is helpful to a producer in deciding which kind of demand to respond to. Such implicit ideas may be articulated as follows. "*Making* what the customer wants to buy," or "responding to user wants *as found*," means the following: At the moment when a producer considers allocating resources to producing and offering some output,[5] people are proceeding with their lives outside the marketplace. They are engaged in certain kinds of activities that they attempt to perform whether or not the producer's offering is available. Already-existing conditions have allocated people's resources in certain ways, specifying the tasks and interests that occupy them. Looking for a return on investment, producers and the marketers who guide them seek profitable opportunities to invest productive resources in order to participate in (some of) these activities that are already ongoing. They ask: Is it possible to identify some output, which a producer can profitably offer, that customers (on some occasions) will find competitive with their present options--enough that they are ready to spend resources for the right to use it? Information about the context in which people engage in relevant activities helps producers to formulate the kinds of output that would be appropriate, in light of prospects' views of available options, and the producer's ability to profitably offer a competing option.

A GENERAL MODEL OF ACTION

Accordingly, as a systematic framework to use in conjunction with a qualitative study, what is needed is a general model of the context for action-- a model that is applicable across all substantive domains of human instrumental action. Cutting across product categories, the common element that needs to be modeled is one occasion on which an individual may consider acting. This is because a producer's eventual offering is a brand of good/service that succeeds or fails depending on how it performs on the individual occasions when people try to make environmental impacts, e.g., try to remove soil from clothes, communicate study findings to a group. An appropriate model is one that represents personal and environmental elements of the context in which people try to act. For illustrative purposes here, let me use an abbreviated version of a model of action discussed at greater length elsewhere (e.g., Fennell 1988). Three components of the context for acting are shown in Figure 2. Personal and environmental elements combine to allocate an individual's resources in a particular way (Figure 2[a]), specifying both the domain (e.g., providing information for an upcoming decision) for instrumental acts/objects, and the criterion for a desired outcome; from the internal and external environment, the individual generates candidate acts/objects (Figure 2[b]), orders them (if more than one) and judges costworthiness, possibly selecting one to try to enact; upon acting, the individual evaluates the outcomes (Figure 2[c]) against the criterion that the resource-allocating conditions specify.

HETEROGENEOUS RESOURCE-ALLOCATING CONDITIONS

With such categories in mind, a researcher may direct a qualitative investigation systematically, to obtain information on the concrete-- psychological and nonpsychological--elements that are present in the context for a focal activity in some spacetime region of the real world. A more differentiated version of the model gives a qualitative investigator more finely grained guidance. For example, Fennell (1978) describes seven classes of resource-allocating condition, reflecting qualitatively different kinds of motivating conditions that experimental psychologists have

---

[5]Or, at the moment when a marketer begins to investigate an aspect of the real world in order to recommend how productive resources should be allocated.

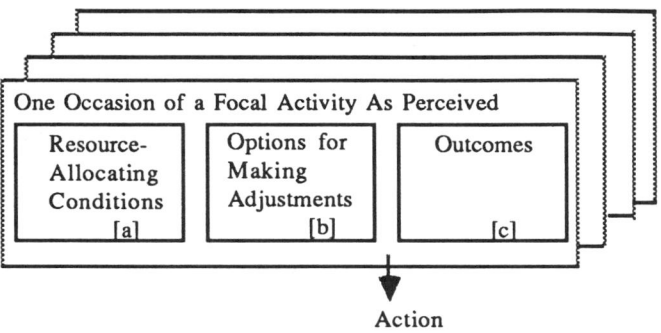

FIGURE 2
Universe of Activity-Occasions & Main Components

used. In the case of a focal activity such as "communicating findings of a study to a group," the general classes of Figure 3 may manifest themselves along lines such as the following:

Is the prospect working under extreme pressures of time? Amount of material? Facing a mixed audience of generalists and technical types? [1].[6] Is the prospect concerned to be viewed as: Favoring substance over form? Being at the frontier of communicative technology? Knowing that appearance is more than half the battle? [2]. Does the prospect perform this task as a routine matter, viewing it as requiring minimal investment of time and thought?[3]. Is the prospect a student of inner workings? A technology-freak in thrall to bells and whistles? [4]. Is the prospect an aesthete, who sees an opportunity to create beauty in every task undertaken? [5]. In addition to experiencing one or more elements such as the preceding in the context for performing the focal activity, is the prospect: Concerned about cost? Waste? Intimidated by machines? [6]. Familiar with all available aids to presentation, yet dissatisfied in that none helps achieve certain important effects? [7]. In keeping with long-standing marketing research practice, a qualitative investigator does not introduce examples that the classes of Figure 3 suggest until respondents have an opportunity to articulate their individual perspectives.

A set of motivation classes helps researchers to probe neglected topics and to identify among respondents' utterances those that are alternative ways of stating the same underlying motivational perspective. More generally, a model of the behavioral terrain that a qualitative investigator explores makes the task more orderly, easing concerns about comprehensiveness and redundancy. Experienced managers may be heard to say: "There's never a shortage of ideas about customer orientations, but knowing which ideas are similar and different in some fundamental way is a problem." It is a problem that only theory can help solve.

ESSENTIAL FUNCTION OF QUALITATIVE RESEARCH

The idea of conducting qualitative research guided by a conceptual model helps to clarify the systematic role of qualitative research. Assume there exists a comprehensive, optimally differentiated, general model of human instrumental action. By definition, such a model comprises concepts that abstract across disparate realworld psychological and nonpsychological elements and events. As such, the model is not immediately meaningful to a producer whose offering must respond to conditions that exist (on at least some occasions) in one particular behavioral domain. To be useful to a producer, the model's constructs must be rendered concrete for a specific realworld application. For example, the formal components of a single occasion of an activity (Figure 2[a,b,c]) are equally applicable to the following activities: "doing the laundry," "feeding the dog," "communicating the findings of a study to a large group," yet different substantive elements--psychological and nonpsychological--are implicated in each case. At present, using qualitative research to search for these elements, marketers proceed in a purely empirical manner.

We may understand the systematic role of qualitative research as follows. Science makes natural processes available for human use by representing those processes in a manner that reflects their inherent order. To do so, it creates constructs that abstract across apparently disparate elements and events. If order has been found in human instrumental action, a general model represents the context for acting by showing relationships among theoretically distinct *classes* of elements. Its classes (e.g., the components of Figure 2 or more finely-grained versions) apply equally to all instances of action, regardless of substantive domain. However, the model's abstractions are not immediately useful to a producer who plans to participate with a user in his/her

---

[6]Numbers in square brackets refer to the classes of Figure 3.

FIGURE 3
Classes of Resource-Allocating Condition

Simple Cases
1. Escape. (Believed) presence of grave, unpleasant circumstances whose occurrence is outside the actor's control in the short run. The actor must deal with them. Among others, "grave" may refer to intensity, speed of onset, or frequency, of something an individual dislikes.
Essential idea: Unpleasantness will continue, unless I act.

2. Prevention. (Believed) future presence of unpleasant circumstances whose occurrence, being contingent on the actor's behavior, may be prevented. Negative evaluations are significant here--whether the source is oneself or another, and whether the other is a human being, infant, or some nonhuman entity whom the actor regards as significant.
Essential idea: Future unpleasantness is assured unless I act (appropriately).

3. Maintenance. (Believed) presence of a state of affairs that requires action--maintenance of some sort--to keep it functioning. Deterioration is outside the actor's control in the short run, and all the actor can do is periodically make good whatever deficit has occurred.
Essential idea: Unpleasantness will worsen, unless I act.

4. Exploratory Interest. Experienced difficulty in processing information. The actor becomes aware that insufficient, too much, contradictory, unexpected, data impede his/her ability to process information and that steps must be taken to remove this impediment.
Essential idea: Impediment to information processing must be removed.

5. Sensory Pleasure Opportunity. (Actual or imagined) opportunity for sensory pleasure is (believed) available.
Essential idea: Deficiency will continue, until I experience these sensations.

More than one of the above classes may coexist. Moreover, any one may become a complex case should the indicated action entail added resource-allocating elements, such as:

Complex Cases
6. Resolve Conflict. Effecting the adjustment that the resource-allocating condition calls for entails new resource-allocating elements, implicating undue cost.

7. Restructure. Adjustment is called for but no way to effect it is available.

---

realworld acts in some focal domain. A producer's task is to help a user achieve an environmental impact in the particular realworld conditions that constitute the occasion for a single act (e.g., getting a particular load of laundry clean, given the clothes' particular kind of use and soil, fabric construction, kind of water supply, water temperature, washing equipment, the launderer's subjective understanding of the act and available options). For a producer's purposes, the process of abstracting, which gives science its generality and power, must be *reversed* to retrieve the concrete, realworld properties of the individual occasions on which a producer's offering may or may not deliver satisfaction. Accordingly, whether implemented by analysts working at their desks and/or by researchers using respondents as a source of information, qualitative work identifies the particular elements present in the context for realworld events. As such, it is an essential component of any realworld intervention. It answers questions of *what*--what are the specific, concrete elements that must be taken into account if a particular realworld intervention is to be successful?

It remains to be seen whether it will always be necessary to use individuals who engage in a focal activity as a source of qualitative information, or whether a marketing analyst may rely totally on his/her ability to generate likely realworld elements using only a conceptual model. At present, in advance of conducting qualitative research, it is advisable for a marketing analyst to use a conceptual model to generate such likely realworld elements. Moreover, a marketer may use a general model of action in the same way, prior to discussing brand strategy with production management (e.g., manufacturing and R&D). The model permits the marketer (i) to specify the different kinds of contexts in which the focal activity may arise, and (ii) to ask the production people to discuss in each instance, (a) the kinds of productive responses that are feasible with present and foreseen technology, and (b) the likely competitive environment. Such preliminary interfaces with production management may narrow the scope of subsequent qualitative investigations, in the event that technological or other considerations enable a producer to rule out, up front, responding to certain *classes* of user-circumstances within a focal activity domain.

In sum, qualitative research is conducted to identify concrete psychological and nonpsychological elements that exist in a particular behavioral region of the real world. Producers need such information if they are to tailor output for actual conditions in which it could be used. Although qualitative research may proceed in a purely empirical manner, it is unsatisfactory that it should have to. Marketing scientists must construct formal representations of the behavioral terrain that managers use qualitative research to explore. They must also have regard to unpacking an abstract model of that terrain to help managers systematically investigate the personal and environmental contexts in which people pursue their tasks and interests.

SOME MISPERCEPTIONS

Let me discuss briefly some common misperceptions relating to: (a) the contrasting roles of qualitative and quantitative research, e.g., using qualitative research (i) for hypothesis-testing, (ii) to identify hypotheses for testing in a subsequent survey, and (iii) to "test" (i.e., select) brand or advertising concepts or messages; (b) intragroup similarity and consensus when group interviews are used for qualitative research; (c) what constitutes meaningful information, including implications for the appropriate timing of qualitative investigations in brand development, and marketers' professional role.

(a) *Qualitative/Quantitative*. It is often said that researchers use qualitative research to (i) test hypotheses, or (ii) formulate hypotheses for testing in subsequent quantitative work: (i) Considering the exploratory function of a qualitative investigation, the question of hypothesis-testing does not arise: The research is conducted to identify qualitatively different elements that constitute the context for a focal activity in some realworld region of space and time. If the researcher knows, going in, of some element that occurs in the context for the focal activity, which no respondent mentions in a particular investigation, it is not appropriate to say that the findings failed to confirm a hypothesis that the particular element occurs in the context for the focal activity. Moreover, if a question arises whether or not that element is to be included in a subsequent quantitative phase, the answer will likely depend on considerations other than its failing to emerge in a qualitative study. (ii) The role of subsequent quantification is not to "test hypotheses identified in the qualitative phase" but, in some focal universe, to establish the incidence of elements identified in the qualitative phase. (iii) Similarly, a qualitative investigation is not properly used to select a brand or advertising concept. By definition, qualitative research is not intended to ascertain degree of liking for candidate brand or advertising concepts. In sum, qualitative (what?) and quantitative (how many?) research do not lend themselves to interchangeable use.

(b) *Intragroup Similarity/Consensus*. A couple of issues need to be disentangled regarding the *similarity* of members selected for a group interview. A universally necessary element of similarity among respondents assembled for an exploratory group interview is the recruiting qualification--usually stated as engaging in the focal activity as defined (Figure 1[c]). As the need arises and common sense dictates, it may be advisable to conduct separate sessions of qualified respondents, should the researcher believe that the presence, in the same group, of individuals with certain (perceived) characteristics or attitudes may impede disclosing personal perspectives. It would not be in keeping with the exploratory function of qualitative research to expect, or to try to secure, *consensus* or common voice among group members. A comprehensive description of the circumstances in which individuals perform the focal activity is the research goal. If qualified respondents are interviewed in a group, rather than individually, it is mainly due to the belief that the informational objective is furthered because the presence of others helps each respondent to recall his/her own experience of engaging in the focal activity, thus resulting in a higher yield of information per interview hour, compared with individual interviews.[7] With the qualifying characteristic, i.e., engaging in the focal activity, as the main feature in common among group members, heterogeneity as regards contextual features of the focal activity is expected and consistently obtained. From such heterogeneity, as quantified later, the analyst may define homogeneous segments of naturally-occurring demand. It would be inappropriate to try to find homogeneity while conducting a group interview, if only because the investigator's information is incomplete, until the exploratory task is finished.

Moreover, in some writing on focused group research, it seems that authors envisage group interviews being conducted among respondents who are similar on features additional to the screening qualification of performing the focal activity. Perhaps authors have in mind groups who share demographic characteristics such as age (teens, seniors), or race (blacks, hispanics). For whatever reason, a decision has presumably been made to *define* the producer's focal universe as consisting of such a demographic class. For example, considering Figure 1, the marketer starts at 1[a] by considering a population of black US residents. Moving to 1[b], the marketer defines prospects as blacks who engage in the focal activity. Once again, as regards characteristics of the context in which respondents experience the focal activity, heterogeneity rather than homogeneity is expected and consistently obtained. There is no reason to expect that teens,

---

[7]Note, in contrast to Fern (1982), I am discussing qualitative research that is used, not to "generate ideas," but to provide information on concrete elements--psychological and nonpsychological--in the context for engaging in the focal action.

or seniors, or blacks, or hispanics, are homogeneous in regard to their experience of "doing the laundry," "feeding the dog," "communicating the findings of a study to a group." At our present stage of social enlightenment, it goes without saying that members of demographic groups are not clones of each other. The objective of qualitative work is to uncover the concrete elements of individual experience in regard to a domain of activity. Trying to impose or to find homogeneity in an exploratory investigation defeats its purpose.

(c) *Meaningful Information*. Textbook examples often describe "qualitative" research that seems to have been conducted to obtain reactions to existing or candidate goods/services, brand concepts, advertising messages, executions, in a word to some *stimulus* that an analyst/researcher presents to weakly characterized subjects or respondents. If the study fails to articulate the characteristics of the circumstances that respondents have in mind as they react to the test stimulus, it is impossible to retrieve information about the qualitatively different kinds of contexts, within and across individuals, for such reactions as the respondents provide. Failing to characterize respondents independently (e.g., in terms of Figure 2[a]) of the attributes of the test stimulus, its content is, essentially, uninterpretable.

Marketers use the focal activity as a basis for defining prospects and qualifying respondents. But, knowing only that the customer engages in the activity of "communicating the findings of a study to a group," a producer lacks information that can guide designing output for a prospect's particular circumstances. Similarly, hearing that a respondent wants audio/visual equipment that can "do many different things" leaves a producer without useful information. Such a remark may be offered by respondents speaking from a variety of perspectives (e.g., considering the seven motivation classes, minimally, from the perspectives of classes 1, 2, 4, and 5--see discussion accompanying Figure 3), with differing implications for brand strategy. Elsewhere I have noted that the problem here traces to the *motivational ambiguity* of product benefits/attributes (Fennell 1978).

In this connection, consider Axelrod's (1975 p. 6) characterizing qualitative research as a chance for clients to put themselves: "in the position of the consumer and to be able to look at his product and category from her vantage point." Authors have failed to appreciate that tapping the customer's "vantage point" in a way that is useful to a producer requires first ascertaining the characteristics of that vantage point, i.e., the substantive elements that are present in the context(s) in which the prospective user engages in the focal activity.

Appreciating the customer's "vantage point" means obtaining information about the various kinds of resource-allocating conditions that prospective users experience (Figure 2[a]), and the options (Figure 2[b]) and outcomes (Figure 2[c]) that prospective users consider as they try to perform their tasks and pursue their interests. A study that obtains reactions to candidate offerings, without also obtaining information on the kinds of resource-allocating conditions that may be present in a respondent's mind while reacting to the test stimulus, provides a producer with information that is systematically flawed.

Stage of Brand Development. Closely related to the previous point, the mistaken idea seems to be widely accepted in the literature that the time to design a qualitative investigation is following management's decision to introduce a good/service, when the objective is to obtain information to help sell the item. Over the occasions for performing a focal act such as "communicating the findings of a study to a group," whether within one individual or across individuals, the context may vary to include one or more orientations such as those mentioned earlier, or indeed others. In such elements are found the criteria for a brand's successful performance. In order to *make* what the customer wants to buy, it is imperative that, as the first step in brand development, a producer have good information about behavioral contexts. That is the simple managerial wisdom with which top management intended to inaugurate a new era of professional marketing when it formulated the marketing concept in the 1950s. From top management's perspective, it makes no sense for production management to design some version of a product just because the capability exists, without first becoming informed of the characteristics of the contexts in which that class of output may be used, and customer perceptions of their currently available options. Nevertheless, statements such as the following appearing in the marketing literature suggest what is being taught to future managers:

> "Management has determined the ideas which are most attractive from a business standpoint, and now has to understand how a given idea should be positioned so as to appeal to prospective buyers."

Quite simply, management does not know that its ideas are "attractive from a business standpoint" until it knows if its ideas "appeal to prospective buyers." *Before* production management commits to a particular direction for brand development, it makes sense to acquire the requisite information about prospective users' worlds, since the conditions pertaining there ultimately determine the fate of management's investment. Exploratory qualitative research is professional marketers' method of opening the door to the necessary information.

Organizational issues. Moreover, *marketers*, not production management, were to be responsible for selecting the *kind of demand* that the firm's output would respond to. Asking marketers to explore ways to gain acceptance for an offering to whose existence they had no input is directly at variance with top management's charge to marketers to lead the firm in choosing the kind of demand to respond to. Acquiescing, marketers abdicate their essential *professional* contribution. Accordingly, authors should not leave the impression that it is appropriate for marketers to conduct qualitative research in order to learn how to sell a good/service in whose conception they had no part.

CONCLUSION

When they articulated the marketing concept in the decade of the 1950s, top management nominated marketers to be the inhouse source of information on the customer's perspective. It became marketers' job to obtain information on the concrete conditions--psychological and nonpsychological--in which people find their resources allocated to making adjustments. The systematic role of exploratory research in implementing the marketing concept has been neglected for too long in the literature, an oversight that the present paper begins to repair.

REFERENCES

Advertising Research Foundation (1985). *Focus Groups: Issues and Approaches.* New York: Advertising Research Foundation.

Axelrod, M. D. (1975), "Marketers Get an Eyeful When Focus Groups Expose Products, Ideas, Images, Ad Copy, Etc., to Consumers." *Marketing News* (February 28), 6-7.

Belk, R. and N. Zhou (1987), "Learning to Want Things," *Advances in Consumer Research*, 14, P. Anderson and M. Wallendorf, eds., Provo: Association of Consumer Research, 478-481.

Bellenger, D., K. Bernhardt, and J. Goldstucker (1976), *Qualitative Research in Marketing.* Chicago: American Marketing Association.

Bennett, R. C. and G. G. Cooper (1981), "The Misuses of Marketing: An American Tragedy," *Business Horizons*, (November-December) 51-61.

Borch, F. J. (1957), "The Marketing Philosophy as a Way of Business Life," in *The Marketing Concept: Its Meaning to Management*, Marketing Series No. 99, New York: American Management Assoc.

Calder, B. (1977), "Focus Groups and the Nature of Qualitative Marketing Research," *J. of Marketing Research*, 14 (August, 353-64.

Durgee, J. (1986), "Depth Interview Techniques for Creative Advertising," *J. of Advertising Research*, 25 (6), 29-37.

Fennell, G. (1978), "Consumers' Perceptions of the Product-use Situation," *J. of Marketing*,

_____ (1985a), "Persuasion: Marketing as Behavioral Science in Business and Nonbusiness Contexts," in *Advances in Nonprofit Marketing*, 1, R. Belk, ed., Greenwich, CT: JAI Press.

_____ (1985b), "Things of Heaven and Earth: Phenomenology, Marketing and Consumer Research," in *Advances in Consumer Research*, 12, eds. E. Hirschman and M. Holbrook, Provo, UT: Association for Consumer Research, 544-49.

_____ (1988), "Action as Counterchange: Identifying the Antecedents of the Domain and Goal of Action," in *Proceedings, Division 23 (Consumer Psychology)*, 95th Annual Convention of the American Psychological Association, L. Alwitt, ed.

Fern, E. (1982), "The use of focus groups for idea generation: The effects of group size, acquaintanceship, and moderator on response quantity and quality." *J. of Marketing Research*, 19, (February), 1-13.

Goldman, A. (1962), "The Group Depth Interview," *J. of Marketing*, 26, 61-8.

_____ and S. McDonald (1987), *The Group Depth Interview.* Englewood Cliffs, NJ: Prentice Hall.

Greenbaum, T. (1988), *The Practical Handbook and Guide to Focus Group Research*, Boston: Heath.

Hayes and Abernathy (1980), "Managing Our Way to Economic Decline," *Harvard Business Review*, 58 (July-August), 67-77.

Hollander, S. (1986), "The Marketing Concept--A Deja View," in G. Fisk, ed., *Marketing Management Technology as Social Process*, New York: Praeger.

Lazarsfeld, P. (1944), "The Controversy over Detailed Interviews--An Offer for Negotiation," *Public Opinion Quarterly*, 8, 38-80

Merton, R. (1987), "The Focused Interview and Focus Groups: Continuities and Discontinuities," *Public Opinion Quarterly*, 51, 550-6.

_____ and P. Kendall (1946), "The Focused Interview," *American J. of Sociology*, 51, 541-57

Oxenfeld, A. R. and W. L. Moore (1978), "Customer or Competitor: Which Guideline for Marketing?" *Management Review*, (August), 43-48.

Park, C. W. and G. Zaltman (1987). *Marketing Management.* Hinsdale: Dryden.

Wells, W. (1974), "Group Interviews," in *Handbook of Marketing Research*, ed. R. Ferber, NY: McGraw-Hill.

Wertz, F. and J. Greenhut (1985), "A Psychology of Buying: Demonstration of a Phenomenological Approach to Consumer Research," in *Advances in Consumer Research*, 12, eds., E. Hirschman and M. Holbrook, Provo, UT: Association for Consumer Research.

Yoell, W. (1979), "How Useful is Focus Group Interviewing?" in *Focus Group Interviews*, eds., K. Cox and J. Higginbotham, Chicago: American Marketing Association.

Qualitative Research in Advertising: When To Do What
J. H. "Mike" Flynn, D'Arcy Masius Benton & Bowles

Qualitative research as a way of understanding consumer reactions was born when sociologist Robert K. Merton developed the "focussed interview."[1] as a way to measure reactions to radio morale programs during World War II. Since that time, a variety of forms of qualitative research have been developed by marketing research practitioners, including:

- Focus groups
- In-depth one-on-one interviews
- Mini-groups
- Dyadic interviews

This paper addresses qualitative research in advertising: when to do what. To the author's knowledge, this topic has not been addressed in the academic literature. Neither the area of qualitative research in advertising nor the appropriateness of the different forms of qualitative research has received much attention.

Relative to forms of quantitative research, little has been published in academic journals on qualitative research, although the trade press frequently publishes articles by practitioners on the "do's" and "don'ts" of focus groups. Seldom is qualitative research in advertising treated as a special topic. An exception is an article published recently by Durgee (1990) in which he discusses qualitative methods for developing creative strategies in advertising.

Moreover, almost no quantitative research has been published regarding the effectiveness of the different forms of qualitative research because the problem is somewhat tautological. Qualitative research is designed to investigate that which cannot be measured by quantitative research. Thus, we have no "proof" that some forms of qualitative research work better than others, but we can rely on experience of well-qualified professional judgement and experience.

The current paper summarizes the experience of the author and many conversations the author has had with other professionals in the field of advertising research, both moderators and clients, over the last twelve years, concentrating on how to match methods with tasks.

Before that, however, we need to clarify the role of qualitative research, especially as it relates to advertising. Only by delineating the role of qualitative research can we understand how roles and forms of research can match.

---

[1] For an interesting retrospective by Merton on the evolution of qualitative research since that time, see Merton, R.K. "The Focused Interview and Focus Groups: Continuities and Discontinuities." Public Opinion Quarterly, winter, 1987.

THE ROLE OF QUALITATIVE RESEARCH
The role of qualitative research can be defined both by purpose -- how the research will be used -- and by the variables appropriately observed by qualitative research.

Purposes
Qualitative research has a unique place in the mix of the research analyst's tools. It has its own purposes.

The primary purpose is *to develop in-depth understanding and insight into how consumers think and feel*. This understanding is used to guide decisions regarding modifications to advertising and advertising strategy development, including target and message.

For advertising agencies, qualitative research has another purpose as well: to allow the creative personnel an opportunity to hear people who represent their target talk about themselves and their attitudes toward the product of interest as well as toward advertising for the product or advertising in general. This opportunity is used as a reminder of who the target is and frequently will spark ideas for advertising.

Qualitative research can also be used as an exploratory tool to find out what questions to ask in a later study. In copy research, for example, we sometimes conduct research to identify items which can later be used in a quantitative copy test.

Variables
A number of variables are appropriately observed by qualitative research. Some can also be measured quantitatively, but generally not to the same depth.

Communication. Qualitative research is used to ascertain advertising communication. In an unstructured interview, advertising communication can be identified at several levels, from the most obvious and direct to understanding associations with the communication to identifying personal relevance.

For example, the following dialogue might occur in an interview:

Direct
    INTERVIEWER: What did that ad say to you?
    RESPONDENT: Budweiser is a good beer.
    I: How did it say that?
    R: It showed people enjoying beer.
    I: How were they enjoying the beer?
    R: They were drinking it and it looked like they were having a good time and enjoying the beer.

Association: I: What do you mean by that?
R: Well, you couldn't look like you were enjoying yourself if
Beer with the beer was no good. They
Good times looked like they were really enjoying the taste of the beer. Like it tasted really good and that they were enjoying themselves, too.

I: Does that make sense to you?
Relevance: R: Yes. I like having a good time and I enjoy beer.

Involvement. We define involvement as having two dimensions: identification and emotional reaction.

Identification can be with people in the ads or with the situation portrayed in the ads. Qualitative research can be used to identify what an individual respondent identifies with and to gauge the strength of identification.

We are discovering that emotional reaction to the ad itself is an important variable in copy research (Batra and Ray, 1986; Burke and Edell, 1989; Edell and Burke, 1987). If the ad engages a viewer emotionally, the viewer is more likely to evaluate positively both the ad and the brand. That does not mean that every ad should be a "tear jerker," but most emotions other than anger or repulsion seem to involve the viewer in the ad. Qualitative research provides an opportunity to observe whether an ad produces an emotional response.

The following reconstructed excerpt from an interview illustrates how involvement can be ascertained:

I: What did you think (of the commercial)?
Emotional R: I liked it. It made me hungry!
reaction I could eat a Cancun Special right now.

I: What did you think of the people in the ad?
R: It looked like they were relaxed and having fun. The music made it sound like a fun place to be.
I: Can you picture yourself in that commercial?
Identifi- R: Definitely. We go to Chi-
cation Chi's quite often, mostly because of the casual atmosphere. You don't feel like an idiot if you drop your fork. You can really relax and let your hair down there.
I: Is that the kind of atmosphere you saw in the commercial?
R: Yeah. It seemed like a fun place to go.

Appeal. Qualitative research can be used to understand what is appealing about the advertising and to obtain a rough measure of overall appeal. This is generally a very straightforward variable to measure. The interviewer simply asks for an overall rating of the ad and probes for likes and dislikes. For that reason, appeal can be in some ways better measured using quantitative methods. Quantitative research can provide a more reliable overall measure of appeal and likes and dislikes can be probed, although not in as much depth.

METHODS

Qualitative methodological parameters are defined by the number of people in an interview and the kinds of questions the interviewer asks. We shall refer to the number of people as the form and the kinds of questions as the technique.

Forms

Many variations of qualitative research exist. We will discuss the three most popular: focus groups, mini-groups, and one-on-one interviews.

Focus Groups. Focus groups are the form most often associated with qualitative research. In fact, some marketers use focus groups as a generic term for qualitative research.

Focus groups should be used for two purposes:

1. Idea generation for creatives.
2. As an aid to designing a quantitative study.

In both instances, the interaction of a large group promotes discussion of a wide range of issues. The interaction of the group also is more likely to stimulate ideas for the creatives.

Mini-Groups. As we use the term, mini-groups refer to a group discussion with four to five respondents. In most instances, a mini-group will last about half the duration of a regular focus group discussion, about 45 minutes to an hour. Occasionally, the discussion will last an hour and a half to two hours.

Mini-groups provide the optimum forum for discovering beliefs respondents have about products. These beliefs can be about our brand, competitive brands, the product category, or even about the advertising. When advertising is targeted to people who are likely to talk about it - young adults, for example - mini-groups come closest to simulating the kind of discussion the target might have about the advertising. This form of qualitative research can provide valuable information on how the target believes about things external to himself.

We have found that the small group environment of mini-groups can generate discussion of a wider range of issues while still getting at some deeper issues through the use of projective techniques (to be discussed later).

FIGURE 1
A SUMMARY OF QUALITATIVE METHODS IN ADVERTISING RESEARCH

PURPOSE	VARIABLES	FORM	TECHNIQUE	RATIONALE
Gain insight into consumer reaction to advertising	1. Communication 2. Involvement 3. Appeal	One-on-one interviews	Projective, using advertising as stimulus	One-on-ones allow respondents to provide in-depth responses in a relatively risk-free environment, uncontaminated by group influence.
Allow creatives to hear consumers talk	1. Attitudes toward product 2. General lifestyle statements	Focus groups	Straightforward	Interaction of the large group discussion is more likely to stimulate ideas and to generate a broad range of issues.
Guide strategy development	1. Beliefs about self	One-on-one interviews	Projective	One-on-ones allow respondents to be more open in a relatively risk-free environment and allow for individual responses to projective techniques.
	2. Beliefs about product*	Mini-groups	Straightforward and projective	The small group environment can generate discussion of a wider ranger of issues than one-on-ones while also allowing for the use of projective techniques.
Develop input into quantitative study	Exploratory	Focus groups	Straightforward	Large group discussion can generate a wide range of issues.

*Product can include category, brands, and advertising

One-on-One Interviews. One-on-one interviews (also called In-Depth Interviews) have burgeoned in popularity as a tool for advertising research in recent years.[2]

One-on-one interviews are the form of choice to meet two research purposes:

1. to aid in strategy development by helping to discover beliefs about self.
2. to gain insight into consumer reaction to advertising.

The relatively risk-free environment and the opportunity for more in-depth probing and responses will provide greater insight into how a consumer sees himself/herself and into how the consumer reacts to the advertising. Projective techniques can be used more successfully in one-on-one interviews than with any other form of qualitative research.

---

[2] A variation of one-on-one interviews, the dyad, is appropriate where the purchase decision is a joint one, or where the one-on-one situation might be intimidating.

Additional Considerations

This section has suggested some guidelines for using forms of qualitative research in advertising. They are only guidelines. Occasions will occur when exceptions to these suggestions will be advisable.

One overriding consideration should be taken into account when deciding upon a form of qualitative research to use in obtaining consumer reaction to advertising: the form should parallel as closely as possible the way advertising is consumed in "real life." For the most part, advertising is consumed by individuals, not groups.

Techniques

Two basic interviewing techniques are used in qualitative research for advertising: straightforward and projective.

Straightforward is simple. The interviewer asks a question and the respondent answers. The answer is pretty much taken at face value.

Projective techniques are somewhat more subtle and a greater emphasis is placed on interpretation of responses. A respondent is shown some sort of stimulus to encourage talking about himself/herself, not to evaluate the stimulus. Thematic Apperception Tests, sentence completion exercises, photo sorts, even advertising can be used as projective devices.

As a general rule, projective techniques are appropriate when we want to learn more in-depth responses, whereas straightforward techniques are adequate when more superficial responses will suffice.

CONCLUSION

This paper has set out to provide some guidelines for when to use what kinds of qualitative research as tools to improve advertising. These guidelines have been summarized in Figure 1.

REFERENCES

Batra, Rajeev and Michael L. Ray (1986), "Affective Responses Mediating Acceptance of Advertising," *Journal of Consumer Research*, 13 (September), 234-49.

Burke, Marian Chapman and Julie A. Edell (1989), "The Impact of Feelings on Ad-Based Affect and Cognition," *Journal of Marketing Research*, 26 (February), 69-93.

Durgee, Jeffrey (1990), "Qualitative Methods for Developing Advertising That Makes Consumers Feel, 'Hey, That's Right for Me,'" *Journal of Consumer Marketing*, 7 (Winter), 15-21.

Edell, Julie A. and Marian Chapman Burke (1987), "The Power of Feelings in Understanding Advertising Effects," *Journal of Consumer Research*, 14 (December), 421-33.

Merton, Robert K. (1987), "The Focussed Interview and Focus Groups: Continuities and Discontinuities," *Public Opinion Quarterly*, 51 (Winter), 550-66

It's Time To Stress *Stress*
The Stress - Purchase/Consumption Relationship: Suggestions for Research

Kevin G. Celuch, Illinois State University
Linda S. Showers, Illinois State University

ABSTRACT

This paper is in line with recent calls to broaden the research agenda in the consumer behavior discipline (Belk 1987; Holbrook 1987). As such, it highlights a topic which has been practically ignored by consumer researchers - the relationship of stress to purchase/consumption. Further, the paper uses Andreasen's (1984) benchmark study as a springboard from which to offer conceptual and methodological suggestions for research in the area. Stress research stands to increase our understanding of consumer behavior in contemporary society as well as offer insights for marketing and public policy decision makers.

INTRODUCTION

The intent of this paper is twofold: First, we hope to call attention to a virtually ignored yet potentially significant topic for consumer research - the relationship of stress to purchase/consumption. Second, we offer several conceptual and methodological suggestions regarding future research in this area.

In his 1986 presidential address to the Association for Consumer Research, Russell Belk (1987) observed that consumer researchers have been guilty of studying purchase and consumption in isolation from other aspects of human life. He suggested that the mission of consumer researchers should be to "...examine the relationship between consumer behavior and the rest of life" (p.1). Holbrook (1987) echoes this perspective when he points out that a recent trend in the *Journal of Consumer Research* has been to expand the consumer research realm, and he argues that consumer research "...encompasses almost all human activities," (p. 131).

It is our contention that there is a component of contemporary western lifestyles which has the potential to impact behavior across many purchase and consumption situations, but which has not received adequate attention by researchers. In tracking current consumer lifestyle patterns, a recurring descriptor of households in the U.S. is the hectic pace and resulting stress associated with "living" today. Stress and its antecedents may be one of those aspects of human activity that Holbrook (1987) refers to which should be more closely examined for its influence on purchase and consumption behavior.

During the 1980's, much has been written in the popular press about stress in contemporary lifestyles. A general shift in values emphasizing career and success, coupled with changing household structures and characteristics (e.g., dual income families and single-parent households), have certainly contributed to the interest in stress and its effects on individuals. Stress "management" or "reduction" seminars have become commonplace. Books on managing or reducing stress are eagerly sought by consumers (e.g., Selye 1974; Tubesing 1981), and the topic of stress in modern life has been a recurring theme in the media.

Despite the recent wave of interest in and popularity of the topic of stress in contemporary lifestyles, it has been virtually ignored among consumer researchers. Practitioners and textbook authors frequently refer to the potential for stress in dual income households, etc., but published data on the effects of stress on purchasing and consumption patterns is markedly absent.

One exception is Andreasen's (1984) study which included a measure of stress within a larger framework relating life status changes to consumer behavior. However, in his model stress was characterized as having no direct influence on consumption.

If, as Belk (1987) and Holbrook (1987) propose, consumer researchers should be expanding the realm of investigation of consumer research, a factor which has become an increasingly common element in contemporary lifestyles, i.e., stress, should be a topic of current investigations of consumer behavior. It is our contention that certain antecedents (daily hassles related to family, work, household activities, etc.) lead to stress (operationalized via physiological and psychological symptoms) which have a *direct* influence on a variety of daily purchase and consumption behaviors (e.g., patronizing convenience outlets, consuming services and convenience-oriented products, and purchasing and consuming hedonic goods). It is this *daily* pattern of antecedents and stress symptoms which may provide valuable insight into contemporary consumer behavior. (Refer to Figure 1)

Stress Research

Research on stress, its antecedents and its effects has spanned many disciplines. Empirical work on stress has examined issues including, 1) the measurement of stress via psychological versus physiological operationalizations (e.g., Derogatis, Lipman, Rickels, Uhlenhuth, and Covi 1974; Lazarus, Speisman, and Mordkoff 1963), 2) the impact of "daily" stress on health and mood (e.g., DeLongis, Folkman, and Lazarus 1988), 3) the use of alcohol as a stress-reducer (e.g., Steele, Southwick and Pagano 1986), 4) behavioral changes, and illness resulting from stressful life events or life change (e.g., Dohrenwend and Dohrenwend 1978; Kiecolt-Glaser and Glaser 1987), and 5) the effects of occupational stress on

FIGURE 1
Stress-Purchase/Consumption Relationship

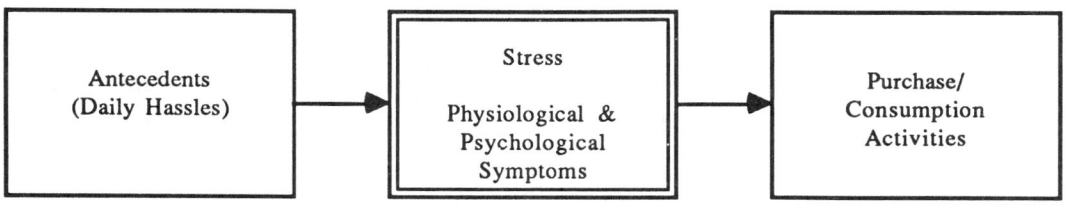

productivity (Hoiberg 1982). Investigations across disciplines reveal the scope of human existence affected by stress. By extension, it seems plausible that stress might, in some situations, directly affect purchase and consumption.

Despite the abundance of work done on stress across many related disciplines, consumer and marketing researchers have ignored the question of whether stress has a direct influence on purchase and consumption behavior. It is our contention that purchase/consumption can be viewed as a means of *coping* with stress. Cohen and Lazarus (1979) broadly define coping as "efforts, both action-oriented and intrapsychic, to manage (that is, master, tolerate, reduce, minimize) environmental and internal demands, and conflicts among them, which tax or exceed a person's resources." (p. 219) As such, coping can occur in anticipation of stress or in reaction to present or past stress.

According to Hamburg, Coelho, and Adams (1974), the two functions of coping are problem-solving and/or emotion-regulation. *Problem-solving* consists of addressing internal or environmental demands that create threat (e.g., taking the car to the car wash because you are too busy this week to wash it yourself). *Emotion-regulation* consists of efforts to modify the distress associated with threat (e.g., consuming sweets or alcoholic beverages to make you feel better). It is possible that a behavior can serve both problem-solving and emotion-regulation functions (e.g., going out to eat because you worked late). Given that purchase/consumption might serve as a means of coping with stress, the study of stress (i.e., antecedents, symptoms, outcomes) would, therefore, appear to offer a promising research area for consumer researchers.

Research Relating Stress to Consumer Behavior

As indicated earlier, the marketing and consumer behavior literature has generally ignored the effects of stress on purchase and/or consumption activities. One notable exception is a pioneering study by Andreasen (1984). Andreasen included the concept of stress in an attempt to model the effects of changes in consumer life status or life events (e.g., death of a spouse, changed employer) on consumer behavior. Specifically, Andreasen proposed that the number of life status changes influences consumption behavior (operationalized as brand preference changes). He further proposed that the number of life status changes and the quantity of life status change (operationalized as weighted life status changes) influence lifestyle which in turn influences consumption behavior. Lastly, Andreasen posited that the average evaluation of consequences of life status changes influences stress which in turn influences purchase satisfaction. Note that Andreasen's model implicates stress in the postpurchase process (satisfaction/dissatisfaction) only.

Andreasen employed a cross-sectional (across-subject) survey design. Regarding the key exogenous variable, life status changes, respondents were asked to indicate the major life events that had occurred within the last six months. The intervening variable, lifestyle change, was measured by asking individuals to indicate changes in twelve activities (e.g., increased/decreased the number of times eating out, consumed more/less medicine) over the previous six months. With respect to the key dependent variable, brand preference change, respondents were asked if they had changed brands in thirteen selected product (service) categories in the last six months, as compared to the prior six months. Lastly, the intervening variable stress was assessed via a six-item measure with five of the items relating to psychological symptoms (e.g., worrying about things, feeling unsettled) and one item relating to a behavior (not sleeping soundly). Overall, bivariate and multiple equation analyses supported relationships proposed in the model.

Suggestions for Future Research Relating Stress to Consumer Behavior

Andreasen should be credited with explicitly recognizing and introducing stress into consumer research. However, as Andreasen himself noted, several limitations are extant in his study. Further, recent conceptual and empirical work in related disciplines has provided insights for research relating stress to consumer behavior. In this section of the paper we use the Andreasen study as a springboard from which to offer suggestions for future research in this area.

Recall that a key exogenous variable in the Andreasen study was life status change. However, the focus on "major" life events, which occur relatively infrequently, as antecedents of stress limits our ability to examine *daily* antecedents of stress which may provide insight into many contemporary purchase/consumption activities. Although life events, such as the birth of a child, certainly result in dramatic and immediate changes in consumer behavior, they are not as useful in understanding day-to-day purchase/consumption as are daily antecedents and symptoms of stress. Given that daily "hassles" resulting from work, family, etc. are more prevalent than life events, it is not surprising that Kanner, Coyne, Schaefer, and Lazarus (1981) found that daily hassles were a "considerably better predictor" of psychological symptoms of stress than life events. It is our contention that *daily* antecedents of stress (e.g., daily hassles) will reveal considerable insight into daily consumption behavior. Therefore, in addition to studying life events or life status changes, future research should examine daily patterns of stress, its antecedents and resulting changes in purchase/consumption behavior.

The Andreasen model also does not specify a *direct* relationship between level of stress and changes in consumption patterns (operationalized by changes in brand preference during the previous six months). However, examples of the direct effects of stress on purchase/consumption are relatively easy to imagine: perception of too little time to cook dinner, so one stops at a fast food drive-through window; a feeling of anxiety which prompts the purchase of an hedonic good such as chocolate or cheese cake to make oneself feel better; or using shopping as a means of easing tension.

Interestingly, Andreasen did find a significant relationship between stress and changes in lifestyle. In fact, since his "lifestyle" measure could be viewed as a measure of consumption behavior (e.g., the number of times eating out, consumed more/less medicine, the number of sporting events, movies, and concerts attended), it would appear that stress can have a *direct* influence on purchase/consumption. However, Andreasen's focus on changes in brand preferences as the dependent variable reflects a very restricted view of consumption behavior. Future research could more thoroughly monitor selected purchase/consumption episodes through the use of daily diaries which have been used extensively in consumer/marketing research (Sudman and Ferber 1974; Walsh 1977).

As noted by Andreasen, another limitation of the study relates to the use of a cross-sectional design with subjects providing self-reports of life status, lifestyle, stress, and brand preference changes over the previous six months. In fact, this limitation goes beyond the Andreasen study and is applicable to the body of research which has examined the relationship between stress and health (Kasl and Cooper 1987). Even when such studies have employed longitudinal designs, the time between measurement of a life event and health status is often too long making it extremely difficult if not impossible to sort out what has occurred between the variables of interest (Kasl and Cooper 1987; DeLongis, Folkman, and Lazarus 1988).

The limitations noted above hold important methodological implications for consumer researchers interested in examining the relationship between stress and purchase/consumption. First, the assessment of antecedents, stress, and purchase/consumption on a *daily* basis over several days in a multiple week period would prove valuable in examining relationships, and would result in more reliable data as memory loss would be minimized. DeLongis et al. (1988) have demonstrated the effectiveness of daily assessments in their investigation of relationships between hassles, health, and mood.

Further, it would be fruitful to monitor relationships between antecedents, stress, and purchase/consumption using within-subject approaches in addition to across-subject approaches. Several researchers have successfully employed within-subject designs to investigate the relationship between daily stressors and mood (Eckenrode 1984; Stone and Neale 1984; Caspi, Bolger, and Eckenrode 1987).

The work of Lazarus, Speisman, and Mordkoff (1963) and Rehm (1978) demonstrate the utility of a within-subject approach. In both studies, an across-subject approach yielded small correlations between the variables of interest (autonomic nervous system indicators of arousal for Lazarus et al. and daily events and mood for Rehm). However, with a within-subject approach, substantial correlations were found between the variables of interest. In both instances, individual differences introduced by the across-subject method masked relationships between variables. In contrast, individual differences were controlled through the within-subject method as each subject acts as his or her own control thus eliminating the influence of across-subject differences.

As Delongis et al. (1988) point out, across-subject and within-subject methods approach a problem from somewhat different perspectives. In contrast to the across-subject approach which does not allow for an adequate assessment of changes in variables over time, a within-subject approach would address the conceptually relevant issue of whether *changes* in antecedents covary with *changes* in stress which, in turn, covary with *changes* in purchase/consumption. By examining relationships among changes in variables over time, the within-subject approach allows for a more *dynamic* exploration of the stress - purchase/consumption relationship than does the more *static* across-subject approach.

Finally, Andreasen used a very limited self-report measure of stress. The measure consisted of five items relating to psychological symptoms and one item relating to a physiological symptom. Recognizing this limitation, Andreasen called upon consumer researchers to develop better measures of stress. Prior stress-health research has also been found to employ simplistic measures of stress (Gruen, Folkman, and Lazarus 1988). Derogatis, Lipman, Rickels, Uhlenhuth, and Covi (1974) argue that a comprehensive assessment of stress should incorporate physiological as well as psychological dimensions.

Future research examining the relationship between stress and purchase/consumption must attempt to thoroughly assess physiological and psychological dimensions of stress. For example, health diaries could be used to assess physiological indicants of stress on a daily basis (e.g., headaches, backaches, nausea, etc.). Verbrugge (1980) discusses advantages of this approach with respect to levels of reporting symptoms, reduction of recall error, validity, and utility for analysis of individual health and health dynamics.

In addition to physiological indicants of stress, psychological indicants should also be assessed. For instance, mood could be measured on a daily basis through the use of an adjective check list (Nowlis 1965). Another possible alternative relates to the use of an activation check list in order to monitor daily arousal (Thayer 1967). Such measures have been dependably used in psychological research. In fact, Thayer reports that self-reports of activation may be more representative of arousal than individual peripheral physiological indicants. Yet another example of a psychological indicant of stress could be sense of time urgency (Rizkalla 1989). Originally conceived as a personality trait, this concept could be adapted to reflect a more situationally dependent psychological state and assessed on a daily basis.

A related measurement issue worthy of mention concerns overlapping items between antecedent and stress measures. For instance, prior studies examining the relationship between antecedent events and health status have used physiological items in antecedent measures and also included similar items in the health assessments. As a consequence, antecedents (physical stressors) were confounded with stress (physical symptoms) (Kasl and Cooper 1987). Thus, care must be taken in order to avoid confounds of content between antecedent and stress measures.

SUMMARY

Belk (1987) noted that consumer researchers have tended to study purchase/consumption in isolation from other aspects of human existence. In response to this situation, Belk advocated studying consumer behavior "within the broader tableau of human behavior." (p. 3) In advocating the study of the stress-purchase/consumption relationship, this paper is very much in line with Belk's call to broaden the research agenda in consumer behavior. Further, using Andreasen's (1984) ground-breaking study as a point of departure, we have offered conceptual and methodological suggestions for future research in this area. Specifically, it was suggested that our understanding of the stress - purchase/consumption relationship could be enhanced through: 1) examining *antecedents*, *stress*, and *purchase/consumption* over short time intervals (i.e., on a *daily* basis); 2) the use of longitudinal designs; 3) the use of within-subject methods; and 4) the assessment of multiple dimensions of stress.

IMPLICATIONS

It is widely recognized that the success of a marketing strategy is dependent on knowing and influencing the consumer. It is the thesis of this paper that future research which incorporates comprehensive daily assessments of antecedents of stress, symptoms of stress, and purchase/ consumption will help increase our understanding of consumer behavior in contemporary society. For instance, stress might influence end-goals - the needs or objectives that consumers want to satisfy or achieve. In response to stressful situations, some decisions might become more oriented toward the avoidance of aversive states. Further, Fennell (1975) has distiguished between optimizing end-goals and satisficing end-goals. In reaction to stress, consumers may opt for satisficing as opposed to optimizing end-goals.

In addition, stress may influence the specific consequences used to evaluate alternatives. Functional choice criteria (product/service performance) as well as psychosocial choice criteria (affective) could be impacted depending upon whether purchase/consumption coping is intended to serve problem-solving or emotion-regulation functions. Beyond influencing choice criteria used in decision making, stress might also affect the evaluation of choice criteria. Some choice criteria may be evaluated a certain way in a given situation but may be evaluated differently in a more stressful context.

According to Bettman and Park (1980) and Hoyer (1984), consumers are prone to use a combination of integration strategies in decision making. Stress might contribute to the use of simpler non-compensatory strategies in order to screen alternatives to a manageable number so that more complex compensatory strategies can be used. Further, stress might also be implicated in search, evaluation, and choice heuristics given that such processes are constructed to meet the needs of particular situations (Hoyer 1984).

Stress research would offer insights for marketing strategy in the profit-making as well as the not-for-profit realms. For instance, by merging stress research with traditional demographic and lifestyle research, marketers may be able to more thoroughly segment markets for selected products and services.

Further, given agency research agendas within the Department of Health and Human Services, research examining the relationship between stress and purchase/consumption could have important public policy implications. For example, the National Institute of Child Health and Human Development has encouraged researchers to investigate family and household dynamics. Future research in this area could explore the influence of stress on household decision making, influence strategies, and conflict within purchase/consumption contexts.

Another Department of Health and Human Services agency, the National Institute on Alcohol Abuse and Alcoholism has encouraged researchers to investigate the impact of advertising and media on alcohol consumption. The susceptibility of consumer segments to persuasive communications (e.g., advertisements and public service anouncements) when experiencing stress would be a logical avenue of research in this area. Research questions relating stress to other harmful consumption realms such as drug abuse, smoking, and eating disorders could also be of interest to relevant Health and Human Service Agencies.

The stress - purchase/consumption relationship would appear to warrant the attention of consumer researchers. Research in this area holds the potential for broadening our understanding of consumer behavior as well as offering valuable insights to the marketing and public policy realms.

REFERENCES

Andreasen, A. (1984), "Life Status Changes and Changes in Consumer Preferences and Satisfaction," *Journal of Consumer Research*, 11, 784-794.

Belk, R. (1987), "ACR Presidential Address: Happy Thought," in *Advances in Consumer Research*, Vol. 14, eds. M. Wallendorf and P. Anderson, Provo, UT: Association for Consumer Research, 1-4.

Bettman, J. and C. W. Park (1980), "Effects of Prior Knowledge and Experience and Phase of the Choice Process on Consumer Decision Processes: A Protocol Analysis," *Journal of Consumer Research*, (December), 234-248.

Caspi, A., N. Bolger and J. Eckenrode (1987), "Linking Person and Context in the Daily Stress Process," *Journal of Personality and Social Psychology*, 52, 184-195.

Cohen, F. and R. Lazarus (1979), "Coping with the Stresses of Illness," in *Health Psychology-A Handbook: Theories, Applications,and Challenges of a Psychological Approach to the Health Care System*, eds. G. Stone et al., San Fransisco: Jossey-Bass, 217-254.

Delongis, A., S. Folkman and S. Lazarus (1988), "The Impact of Daily Stress on Health and Mood: Psychological and Social Resources as Mediators," *Journal of Personality and Social Psychology*, 54, 486-495.

Derogatis, L., R. Lipman, K. Rickels, E. Uhlenhuth and L. Covi (1974), "The Hopkins Symptom Checklist (HSCL): A Self-Report Symptom Inventory," *Behavioral Science*, 19, 1-15.

Dohrenwend, B. and B. P. Dohrenwend (1978), "Some Issues in Research on Stressful Life Events," *The Journal of Nervous and Mental Disease*, 166, 1, 7-15.

Eckenrode, J. (1984) "Impact of Chronic and Acute Stressors on Daily Reports of Mood," *Journal of Personality and Social Psychology*, 46, 907-918.

Fennell, G. (1975), "Motivation Research Revisited," *Journal of Advertising Research*, (June), 23-28.

Hamburg, D., G. Coelho and J. Adams (1974), "Coping and Adaptation: Steps Toward a Synthesis of Biological and Social Perspectives," in *Coping and Adaptation*, eds. G. Coelho et al., New York: Basic Books, 403-440.

Hoiberg, A. (1982), "Occupational Stress and Illness Incidence," *Journal of Occupational Medicine*, 24, 445-451.

Holbrook, M. (1987) "What is Consumer Research," *Journal of Consumer Research*, 14, 1, 128-132.

Hoyer, W. (1984), "An Examination of Consumer Decision Making for a Common Repeat Purchase Product," *Journal of Consumer Research*, (December), 822-829.

Kanner, A., J. Coyne, C. Schaefer, and R. Lazarus (1981), "Comparison of Two Modes of Stress Measurement: Daily Hassles and Uplifts Versus Major Life Events," *Journal of Behavioral Medicine*, 4, 1, 1-39.

Kasl, S. and C. Cooper (1987), *Stress and Health: Issues in Research and Methodology*, London: John Wiley and Sons.

Kiecolt-Glaser, J. and R. Glaser (1987), "Psychosocial Moderators of Immune Function," *Annals of Behavioral Medicine*, 9, 2, 16-20.

Lazarus, R., J. Speisman and J. Mordkoff (1963), "The Relationship Between Autonomic Indicators of Psychological Stress: Heart Rate and Skin Conductance," *Psychological Monographs*, 76 (34, No. 553).

Nowlis, V. (1965), "Research with the Mood Adjective Check List," in *Affect: Measurement of Awareness and Performance*, eds. S. Tomkins and C. Izard, New York: Springer, 352-389.

Rehm, L. (1978), "Mood, Pleasant Events, and Unpleasant Events: TwoPilot Studies," *Journal of Consulting and Clinical Psychology*, 46, 854-859.

Rizkalla, A. (1989), "Sense of Time Urgency and Consumer Well-Being: Testing Alternative Causal Models," in *Advances in Consumer Research*, Vol. 16, ed. T. Srull, Provo, UT: Association for Consumer Research, 180-188.

Selye, H. (1974), *Stress Without Distress*, Philadelphia: Lippincott.

Steele, C., L. Southwick, and R. Pagano (1986), "Drinking Your Troubles Away: The Role of Activity in Mediating Alcohol's Reduction of Psychological Stress," *Journal of Abnormal Psychology*, 95, 2, 173-180.

Stone, A. and J. Neale (1984), "The Effects of Severe Daily Events on Mood," *Journal of Personality and Social Psychology*, 46, 137-144.

Sudman, S. and R. Ferber (1974), "A Comparison of Alternative Procedures for Collecting Consumer Expenditure Data for Frequently Purchased Products," *Journal of Market Research*, 11, 128-135.

Thayer, R. (1967), "Measurement of Activation Through Self-Report," *Psychological Reports*, 20, 663-678.

Tubesing, D. (1981), *Kicking Your Stress Habits*, N.Y., N.Y.: New American Library.

Verbrugge, L. (1980), "Health Diaries," *Medical Care*, 18, 73-95.

Walsh, T. (1977), "Selected Results From the 1972-73 Diary Surveys," *Journal of Market Research*, 14, 344-359.

Consumer Guilt: Examining the Potential of a New Marketing Construct
Dana-Nicoleta Lascu, University of South Carolina

ABSTRACT

A negative emotion frequently employed by marketing practitioners in designing advertising appeals, yet afforded little attention in the consumer behavior literature is guilt. This paper presents a review of past research on the topic of guilt and it describes how guilt can be used in a persuasion context. It then offers a propositional inventory directed at fostering research toward the understanding of the effects of guilt as a message variable on the target consumer.

INTRODUCTION

Numerous marketing studies have demonstrated that inducing negative emotions can have desirable effects on consumers' attitude change and behavior (Ghingold 1981). These studies have focused mostly on fear and have not kept abreast with marketing practitioners' attempts to appeal to consumer anxieties in advertisements by arousing other negative emotions such as guilt, shame, or anger. A "guilt market" (Edmondson 1986) has been identified, but optimal appeals to consumer guilt have yet to be determined. The objective of this manuscript is to describe how guilt can be effectively used in a persuasion context. We define the concept of consumer guilt, review past research relevant to its psychometric properties, and conclude with a propositional inventory directed at fostering research toward the understanding of guilt as a message variable.

Guilt as a Psychological Construct

The principle of differential emotions (Izard 1977) states that there are a number of discrete emotions which can be differentiated in terms of their neurophysiological manifestations, the facial patterns they elicit, and their experiential motivational characteristics. Guilt as an affect, according to this principle, is an unlearned, fundamental emotion which took shape through evolutionary-biological processes (Izard 1977).

Guilt is a multidimensional, a posteriori, affective-cognitive concept designating both a personality disposition and an episodic emotion (Izard 1977; Mosher 1980). Guilt as a personality disposition -- the guilt trait -- has been defined by Mosher (1980, p. 602) as a "generalized expectancy for self mediated punishment for violating, anticipating violating, or failing to attain an internalized moral standard." When experienced as an emotion -- guilt state, -- guilt refers to the painful experience of regret, remorse, self blame, and self-punishment experienced upon committing or contemplating committing a transgression (Izard 1977; Mosher 1980). While guilt weighs heavily on one's mind, it also stimulates one's preoccupation with the transgression and with schemes for setting things right. Upon experiencing guilt, one also experiences the need to make retributions in order to reduce guilt to a tolerable level (Wolman 1973; Izard 1977; Ghingold 1981).

Guilt is defined differently depending on the situation in which it occurs. If experienced in response to an overt act contradicting one's moral standards, it is known as reactive guilt (Rawlings 1970). If experienced as one contemplates a transgression, it is known as reflective (Janis 1969) or anticipatory (Rawlings 1970) guilt. Guilt may also be experienced simply due to the discrepancy in well-being between oneself and others (existential guilt) (Izard 1977; Hoffman 1982; Ruth and Faber 1988). Unlike most negative emotions, guilt applies to both negative and positive outcomes. A condemnable act may have positive or a negative consequences; guilt generated by either situation will manifest itself behaviorally in the same manner (Ghingold 1981).

CONSUMER GUILT: A NEW MARKETING CONSTRUCT

Based on the conceptualization of guilt discussed in the previous section, we define consumer guilt as an affect triggered by the anxiety a consumer experiences upon the cognition that he is transgressing a moral, societal, or ethical principle. The transgression can be purchasing a product, service, idea, or experience (i.e., a brand that does not abide by quality standards), or not purchasing a product prescribed by moral, societal, or ethical principles.

Is Consumer Guilt a Valid Construct?

Ghingold and Bozinoff (1982) assessed the construct validity of guilt using the Campbell and Fiske (1959) multitrait multimethod matrix. As yet another test of construct validity, the matrix was factor analyzed and additional evidence of construct validity was provided. A similar experiment was conducted by Bozinoff and Ghingold (1983) which once again confirmed that the guilt construct had both convergent and discriminant validity.

P1 Consumer guilt is measurable, unique, and distinguishable from other emotion constructs.

GUILT -- AN IMPORTANT DRIVER OF CONSUMER BEHAVIOR

The purpose of this section is to draw upon behavioral and marketing research in order to demonstrate how guilt interacts with other emotions and, as a consequence, is amplified, and how guilt will persuade or motivate consumers to engage in a desired behavior. This section will also examine the possibility of identifying market segments that will be more responsive to guilt inducement.

Guilt Interacting with Other Negative Emotional Appeals

Izard (1977) states that emotions interact with each other: one emotion may activate, amplify, or attenuate another. A frequently mentioned interaction in the behavioral literature is that between guilt and shame. Both guilt and shame create anxiety in the affected individual and both assume a fundamental orientation towards someone else. The two emotions differ in that shame stems from a goal not reached, while guilt arises from an exceeded boundary (Wicker, Payne, and Morgan 1983). Shame results from the negative judgment of others about actions not immoral in the eyes of the offender (Izard 1977).

Guilt also interacts with fear. While guilt is an a posteriori emotional response following a particular action or thought, fear is an a priori emotional response generated by anticipated consequences to particular actions or cognitions (Ghingold 1981). Feelings of guilt prompt one to atone for the offense while fear leads to avoidance or prevention of the outcome (Ghingold 1981). There are situations where the two emotions overlap: it is sometimes difficult to identify which of the two emotions is actually operating, such as, for instance, when an individual senses a fear of guilt or experiences guilt from fear (Ghingold 1981). For example, the "ring around the collar" ad represents both a fear appeal, causing one to attempt to avoid or prevent the situation, and a guilt appeal prompting one to rectify the situation (Ghingold 1981). In both situations, the goal directed behavior is the same: the launderer will avoid the ring around the collar and rectify the situation by using the appropriate detergent when the shirt is washed again.

Consumer Guilt and Persuasion

As opposed to positive appeals which stress the positive gain to the person from complying with the persuasive message, guilt, a negative appeal, raises anxiety by stressing loss if one fails to comply in order then to allay it (McGuire 1974). Since guilt as a negative emotion is an anxiety arouser, we can use the two-factor theory of anxiety, applying McGuire's (1974) information processing approach to provide guidelines for advertising practice. The theory states that the relationship between the amount of anxiety involved in the reception of a message and the effectiveness of the message in producing learning and influencing behavior involves two opposing forces. On one hand, associating guilt-induced anxiety with a message impairs attention and comprehension as it evokes responses such as withdrawal of attention and dislike of the source (cf. McGuire 1974, p.176). On the other hand, anxiety increases yielding to the message, and, as a result of the two opposing forces, the net relationship between guilt-induced anxiety and persuasive effectiveness is nonmonotonic. The effect of guilt inducement is thus, paradoxically, negative on comprehension and positive on yielding. Therefore, to maximize the persuasive effect of the message, the level of anxiety induced should be at an intermediate level (McGuire 1974).

Mediators of Guilt Appeal Effectiveness

There are a number of individual difference variables that mediate the effectiveness of a guilt appeal; one such variable is self-esteem (Ghingold 1981). High self-esteem individuals think highly of themselves, are more likely to spend lavishly on themselves than individuals low in self-esteem, and, in general, spend more on products and services that make them feel good, such as beauty products, entertainment, and fragrances (Giges 1987). However, this very desirable market segment is not likely to be responsive to guilt appeals. Research studying the interaction between guilt and self-esteem indicates that people who rate high in self-esteem use avoidance defense mechanisms which lead them to reject threatening communications such as guilt appeals and to be more receptive to optimistic messages (Ghingold 1981). Low self-esteem individuals, on the other hand, tend to use defenses which lead them to accept threatening appeals (Leventhal and Perloe 1962).

> P2 Individuals who have high self-esteem are less susceptible to guilt appeals than individuals low in self-esteem.

Another individual difference variable which mediates the effects of guilt inducement on persuasion is locus of control (Rotter 1966; Ghingold 1981). Individuals with an external locus of control, believing that external forces control one's destiny, are more likely to adhere to the recommendations contained in the advertisement prescribing modalities of reducing guilt than individuals with an internal locus of control (Ghingold 1981).

> P3 Suggestions embodied in guilt appeals are more likely to be followed by individuals with an external locus of control than by individuals with an internal locus of control.

Similarly, copers, individuals who respond to stimuli of significance to them, and avoiders, individuals who avoid responding to such stimuli, react differently to persuasive appeals. Copers are more susceptible to tension-producing persuasion than avoiders (Goldstein 1959; Ghingold 1981). Ghingold (1981) indicates that copers are more likely to display susceptibility to high levels of aroused guilt. Low-guilt persuasive appeals, however, are believed to be effective when targeted at avoiders. In addition, susceptibility to guilt also affects individuals' drive to resolve guilt, and the likelihood that they will abide by the recommendations of the persuasive ad (Ghingold 1981).

P4 The higher one's susceptibility to guilt, the higher the drive to reduce guilt and the more likely it is that the consumer will follow the recommendations of the ad to reduce guilt.

P5 Consumers fitting an avoider's profile are more likely to yield to low-guilt persuasion and to follow the recommendations of a low guilt appeal ad.

P6 Consumers fitting a coper's profile are more likely to yield to high-guilt persuasion and to follow the recommendations of a high guilt appeal ad.

In the same manner, individuals who manifest a strong personality disposition of guilt -- a high "generalized expectancy for self-mediated punishment for violating, anticipating violating, or failing to attain an internalized moral standard" (Mosher 1980, p. 602) -- are more susceptible to guilt-induced persuasion and more likely to follow the recommendations of the persuasive message (Ghingold 1981).

P7 Consumers who have a strong guilt personality disposition are more susceptible to persuasive attempts inducing guilt and tend follow the recommendations of a guilt-inducing ad.

Motivation and Consumer Guilt

Tomkins' (1962) theory of differential affects considers emotions the primary motivational system in humans (Izard 1977; Mosher 1980). The motivational aspect of guilt pertains to the fact that, when one feels guilty, one also feels the urge to make some form of reparation (Hoffman 1982). As such, guilt is the principal motivational factor in the mature conscience (Izard 1977, 1979). Numerous behavioral studies attempt to demonstrate subjects' motivation to comply with requests after committing a transgression. McMillen (1971) found that compliance increases following transgression as it restores the self-esteem lost as a result of the transgression. Carlsmith and Gross (1969) show that individuals are motivated to comply with a request after transgressing, since the transgression is inconsistent with an individual's self image. By complying, he regains his self image. Carlsmith and Gross (1969) and Darlington and Macker (1966) suggest that using guilt to motivate an individual to comply is most effective when the request to comply is made by someone other than the person transgressed against.

P8 Guilt is more effective in motivating a consumer to comply with a donation or purchase request when the request is made by someone other than the individual inducing the guilt.

Variations in the level of motivation were noted in Deci's (1975) cognitive evaluation theory which describes the conditions that influence individual affect-determined motivation. He finds that motivation is decreased when an individual perceives a change in the locus of control from internal to external. If one perceives that the reason for his experiencing guilt is no longer attributed to him alone, but it is attributed externally, to factors beyond his control, his motivation to reduce guilt will decrease.

P9 A consumer's motivation to comply with a marketer's request decreases as a function of the extent to which the consumer believes that he no longer controls the situation created by the marketer to induce guilt.

Motivation is increased as an individual's feelings of competence and self-determination are increased (Deci 1975; Izard 1977). If one feels capable and is willing to undertake the reparations necessary to reduce guilt, one is more likely to be motivated to do so. Therefore, the efforts of the marketer should concentrate on reassuring the consumer that he is easily capable of making the reparation by providing immediate solutions to atoning for the transgression. In this manner, the consumer is certain that he can reduce guilt and his motivation to do so increases.

P10 A consumer's motivation to comply with a request increases as a function of the immediacy with which a marketer suggests solutions for reparations.

Consumer Guilt as a Segmentation Criterion

According to Ray and Wilkie (1970), personality-based segmentation is frequently used in marketing. Marketers need to understand how personality influences consumption; armed with such knowledge, they can use marketing strategies that will effectively appeal to target segments. Personality, as previously discussed, plays a key role in determining one's susceptibility to guilt, the anxiety level aroused by guilt, and the likelihood that one would follow the recommendations of the guilt inducer or of another party on how to atone for one's transgression.

A number of individual difference variables that mediate the effect of guilt inducement have been mentioned: self esteem, locus of control, the strength of an individual's personality guilt disposition, whether one is a coper or an avoider, all affect the subject's drive to reduce guilt. Although personality variables have not been used in strategic applications as frequently as, for instance, life-styles and demographics, the mentioned personality characteristics can be effectively used in segmenting markets and positioning products by identifying those groups of individuals most likely to respond in a desired manner to guilt inducement.

THE OTHER SIDE OF GUILT

When a consumer is experiencing guilt, he or she is not enjoying the experience; guilt is a painful affective experience of regret, remorse, self-blame, and self-punishment (Mosher 1980). It is an emotion that individuals would attempt to avoid. A simple avoidance technique would be to tune out a guilt appeal, or, if one has been exposed to the appeal, one could simply repress the negative feelings that the guilt-inducing effort has caused to surface. Thus, even individuals susceptible to guilt inducement could show immunity to guilt in the same fashion that individuals not susceptible to guilt would. Even if they admit to guilt feelings, they may prefer not to allow themselves to be tormented by unpleasant, related thoughts.

Marketers have recently started capitalizing on the consumers' desire not to be tormented by guilt feelings by diminishing the importance of guilt. For example, an ice cream ad flashed the words "Enjoy your guilt!" on the television screen -- a woman was shown as being apologetic for having finished the ice cream in a jar (Edmondson 1986). And, children, husbands, and politicians have more recently been portrayed as tactfully avoiding guilt after eating the entire content of someone else's cereal box.

What marketers are in fact telling consumers is that the guilt they experience due to overindulgence in a product should not be a cause for torment: pleasure is more important than guilt. The sensory pleasure derived from the ice cream's good taste should have precedence over one's conscience and preoccupation with the transgression. Consumers seek hedonic experiences, using products to create fantasies, feelings, and fun (Holbrook and Hirschman 1982). They seek to gain pleasure through the senses (taste, in this case).

Guilt, however, could set in after the consumption takes place and end the hedonic experience, replacing it with remorse. To keep guilt in check, marketers must address it in order to diminish its impact. One method of addressing guilt is to show that it is inappropriate to experience it and that the consumer should instead focus on the pleasure afforded by the product consumption. The marketer would thus create a state of "guiltless hedonism" in the consumer who will then delight in the enjoyment or anticipation of enjoyment of the product, neither of which will be slighted by subsequent guilt.

MEASURING THE GUILT CONSTRUCT

When measuring the guilt construct, it is recommended that several methods be used, since empirical tests should not rely on a single measure (Ghingold 1981). A scale that can be used to this purpose is Izard's (1977) Differential Emotions Scale which assumes that emotions are separate and distinct and that each emotion has measurable experiential and motivational properties. The scale is a self-report instrument that measures the state or trait of emotional experiences. Affect adjectives are used to assess the emotion of guilt, among which are "guilty," "blameworthy," and "repentant" (Izard 1972, 1977). Mosher (1980) also offers an affect adjective measure of guilt using adjectives to assess a variety of affective states, one of which is guilt. Adjectives used to describe guilt are "guilty," "sinful," "blameworthy," "conscience-stricken," "repentant," and "remorseful."

The Gottschalk and Glesser (1969) measure of guilt anxiety is based on an analysis of comments on an interesting or dramatic personal life experience. It assumes that the thematic content of phrases containing adverse criticism, abuse, condemnation, moral disapproval, guilt, or threat implies the underlying presence of the guilt emotion (Mosher 1980). Otterbacher and Munz (1973) developed the Perceived Guilt Index (a state-trait measure of guilt) using the adjectives "innocent," "undisturbed," "restrained," "pent-up," "fretful," "chagrined," "reproachable," "marred," "degraded," "disgraceful," and "unforgivable" to assess guilt as an affective state.

Measures of guilt as a personality disposition that are more extensively validated are Mosher's (1966, 1968) guilt inventories (Mosher 1980). Mosher uses sentence completion, true-false statements, and forced-choice inventories to measure guilt. The inventories have been reported to be high in reliability and construct validity (Mosher 1980). Ghingold (1981) suggests using attitudinal measures of guilt by appealing to one's existential guilt by arousing guilt over the plight of the world's underprivileged, requesting contributions to charity, and, subsequently, measuring the extent to which respondents experience guilt. In order to have a more precise measure of the extent to which marketing efforts are successful in inducing guilt, both the guilt trait and the guilt state should be measured before and after guilt inducement to determine the success of marketing efforts alone in inducing guilt.

CONCLUSION

The purpose of this paper was to provide a review of the behavioral and marketing literature on the subject of guilt and to argue for the use of guilt in a number of marketing situations. Considerable research shows that guilt inducement could have favorable effects in directing consumer purchase. Marketing practitioners should identify those consumers who are more susceptible to guilt -- the "guilt market" (Edmondson 1986). Upon inducing guilt, marketers should alleviate the anxiety of the guilt-exposed consumers by promptly offering atonement suggestions that would direct them to purchase the appropriate product or service. In doing so, however, marketers should exercise care and responsibility. Merely taking advantage of consumers susceptible to guilt inducement in order to turn a profit will be transparent and will most likely damage the image of the company and the advertised product or service.

The propositions offered herein, with the purpose of guiding future theory construction and empirical consumer guilt research, constitute a starting point in addressing the unlimited possibilities that this affect construct offers to marketing practitioners. Further research should be undertaken to explore the consumer guilt construct. This study relied heavily on the findings of the psychology literature on guilt. Time has come that marketing research endeavors explore the possibilities that consumer guilt offers to the field of marketing and develop a self-standing body of consumer guilt theories.

REFERENCES

Bozinoff, Lorne and Morry Ghingold (1983), "Evaluating Guilt Arousing Marketing Communications," *Journal of Business Research*, 11, 243-55.

Campbell, D.T. and D. W. Fiske (1959), "Convergent and Discriminant Validation by the Multitrait-Multimethod Matrix," *Psychological Bulletin*, 56, 81-105.

Carlsmith, J. Merril and Allan E. Gross (1969), "Some Effects of Guilt on Compliance," *Journal of Personality and Social Psychology*, 11, 3, 232-239.

Darlington, Richard B. and Clifford E. Macker (1966), "Displacement of Guilt-Produced Altruistic Behavior," *Journal of Personality and Social Psychology*, 4, 4, 442-443.

Deci, E. (1975), *Intrinsic Motivation*, New York: Plenum Press.

Edmondson, Brad (1986), "The Demographics of Guilt," *American Demographics*, March, 33-35.

Ghingold, Morry (1981), "Guilt Arousing Communications: An Unexplored Variable," in *Advances in Consumer Research*, Vol. VIII, ed. Kent Monroe, Ann Arbor, MI: Association for Consumer Research, 442-448.

_____ and Lorne Bozinoff (1982), "Construct Validation and Empirical Testing of Guilt Arousing Marketing Communications," in *Advances in Consumer Research*, Vol. IX, ed. Andrew Mitchell, Ann Arbor, MI: Association of Consumer Research, 210-14.

Giges, Nancy (1987), "Buying Linked to Self Esteem," *Advertising Age*, April 13, p. 68.

Goldstein, M. J. (1959), "The Relationship Between Coping and Avoiding Behavior and Response to Fear Arousing Propaganda," *Journal of Abnormal and Social Psychology*, 58 (March), 247-52.

Gottschalk, L. and G. Glesser (1969), *The Measurement of Psychological States Through the Content Analysis of Verbal Behavior*, Berkeley, CA: University of California Press.

Hoffman, Martin L. (1982), "The Development of Prosocial Motivation: Empathy and Guilt," in *The Development of Prosocial Behavior*, Nancy Eisenberg ed., New York: Academic Press.

Holbrook, Morris B. and Elizabeth Hirschman (1982), "The Experiential Aspects of Consumption: Consumer Fantasies, Feelings, and Fun," *Journal of Consumer Research*, 9 (September), 132-40.

Izard, Carroll E. (1972), *Patterns of Emotions*, New York: Academic Press.

_____ (1977), *Human Emotions*, New York: Plenum Press.

Janis, Irving L., George F. Mall, Jerome Kagan, Robert R. Holt, (1969) *Personality: Dynamics, Development, and Assessment*, New York: Harcourt, Brace and World, Inc..

LaCroix, Jean (1977), *Philosophie de la Culpabilite*, Presses Universitaires de France: Philosophie d'aujourd'hui.

Leventhal, S. and S. Perloe (1962), "A Relationship Between Self-Esteem and Persuasibility," *Journal of Abnormal and Social Psychology*, 64 (June), 385-88.

McGuire, William (1974), "An Information Processing Model of Advertising Effectiveness," in *Behavioral and Management Science in Marketing*, H. Davis and A. Silk eds., New York: Ronald Press, 156-80.

McMillen, David L. (1971), Transgression, Self-Image and Compliant Behavior," *Journal of Personality and Social Psychology*, 20, 2, 176-179.

Mosher, Donald L. (1965), "Interaction of Fear and Guilt in Inhibiting Unacceptable Behavior," *Journal of Consulting Psychology*, 29, 161-7.

_____ (1966), "The Development and Multitrait-Multimethod Matrix Analysis of Three Measures of Three Aspects of Guilt," *Journal of Consulting Psychology*, 30, 1, 25-29.

_____ (1968), "Measurement of Guilt in Females by Self-Report Inventories," *Journal of Consulting and Clinical Psychology*, 32, 6, 690-95.

_____ (1980), "Guilt," in R. H. Woody ed., *Encyclopaedia of Clinical Assessment*, Washington, D.C.: Bass, 602-13.

Otterbacher, John R. and David C. Munz (1973), "State-Trait Measure of Experiential Guilt," *Journal of Consulting and Clinical Psychology*, 40 (1), 115-21.

Rawlings, Edna I. (1970), "Reactive Guilt and Anticipatory Guilt in Altruistic Behavior," in *Altruism and Helping Behavior*, J. Macaulay and L. Berkowitz eds., New York: Academic Press, 163-77.

Ray, Michael L. and William L. Wilkie (1970), "Fear: The Potential of an Appeal Neglected by Marketing," *Journal of Marketing*, 34 (January) 54-62.

Rotter, J. B. (1966), "General Expectancies for Internal Versus External Control of Reinforcement," *Psychological Monographs*, 609, 1-28.

Ruth T. and R. Faber (1988), "Guilt: An Overlooked Advertising Appeal," in *The American Academy of Advertising Proceedings*, Austin, Texas: American Academy of Advertising, 83-89.

Tomkins, S.S. (1962), "Affect, Imagery and Consciousness," in *The Positive Affects*, Vol. 1, New York: Springer.

Viney, L. (1971), "Anxiety as a Function of Self-Evaluation and Related Feedback, *Personality*, 2, 205-17.

Wicker, Frank W., Glen C. Payne, and Randall D. Morgan (1983), "Participant Description of Guilt and Shame," *Motivation and Emotion*, 7 (1), 25-39.

Wolman, B. B. (1973), *Dictionary of Behavioral Science*, New York: Van Nostrand Reinhold Company.

Stress: An Ignored Situational Influence

Lawrence R. Lepisto, Central Michigan University
J. Kathleen Stuenkel, Central Michigan University
Linda K. Anglin, Central Michigan University

Abstract

Although a factor in the lives of many consumers, stress has had little attention paid to it in consumer research. This paper introduces the concept of stress, suggests dimensions of buyer behavior potentially affected by stress, and proposes future research issues.

Introduction

The concept of stress has generated an enormous amount of research. In a review of two literature bases, MEDLARS and Psychological Abstracts, Vingerhoets and Marcelissen (1988) found more than 1,000 articles a year that deal, in part, with stress, which is the body's reaction to a stimulus that generally is appraised as aversive or unpleasant. Given the salience and broad application of this concept, it would seem appropriate for marketers to explore the role of stress in buyer behavior.

Existing research on stress covers a bewildering variety of issues and approaches as described by Goldberger and Breznitz (1982, p. xi), "The stress field is a sprawling one, characterized by unevenness and lack of coordination. . . with pockets of substantial development separated by faddish, superficial, or one-time forays." This lack of precision is, in part, a function of the conceptualization of stress. In their discussion of the definition of stress, Morse and Furst (1979) point out that Selye's 1950 adaptation of the physics concept "stress" was inadvertently applied to the reaction of the body (referred to as strain in physics) rather than to the causative factors (referred to as stress in physics). While Selye coined the term "stressor" for the causative factors, other researchers failed to differentiate between factors and reactions thus leading us to the current situation where both the cause and the result are called "stress" by different researchers.

Furthermore, Maes, Vingerhoets and Van Heck (1987, p. 567) define stress as a "state of imbalance within a person, elicited by an actual or perceived disparity between environmental demands and the person's capacity to cope with these demands." When stress is viewed as the result of the interaction between the stressor (causative factor) and the individual, modified by the person's state at the time (Morse and Furst 1979), it is unreasonable to expect stress to take only one form. This variability is further described by Schafer (1978, p. 27):

> "Stressors vary in many ways or along many dimensions. They may originate inside or outside the person. They may be pleasant or unpleasant. They may be few in number or many. They may be mild or intense; chronic or acute; new or familiar. And they may be easily changed or difficult or impossible to change."

Kinds of Stress

Morse and Furst (1979) identify three kinds of stressors: physical, social and psychological. *Physical stressors* are external factors such as drugs, foods, noise, temperature, and trauma. *Social stressors* or life-change events are externally induced and result from the interaction of the individual with his/her environment, for example, death of a loved one, divorce, job loss, a move to a new city, or financial difficulty. *Psychological stressors* (intense emotions) may be brought on by physical or social stressors and include frustration, worry, anger, happiness, sadness, fear, anxiety, etc. This conceptualization further reflects the confusion of the concept of stress as both the causative factor (physical or social stressors) and the result/reaction (psychological stressor).

Stress Intensity and Duration

Adding to the confusion, stressors can be further categorized in terms of intensity (micro- and macro-stressors) and duration (Schafer 1978). *Micro-stressors* tend to be more localized to limited situations (Monroe 1983) and reflect those little hassles that are a part of everyday life (e.g., returning home from work and attempting to cook a meal with children demanding the parent's time). *Macro-stressors* are more intense pressures such as death, divorce, or a complex task. The *duration* of a stressor (acute or chronic) refers to how long the pressure exists. Stressors which last a relatively short time (last-minute Christmas shopping or relocation) are acute stressors while those lasting over a longer period are chronic stressors (e.g., managing career and household, income conditions, or family strains) (Pearlin 1983). Both acute and chronic stressors can vary by intensity.

STRESS AS A SITUATIONAL VARIABLE

Even though a common definition of stress still eludes researchers, some definitions are offered here that correspond closely to the orientation of situational influences. It is interesting to note the similarity between the disparity in definitions of stress and the disparity existing in the definition of situations (see Magnusson 1981). Keane (1985) summarized the definitions of stress as follows:

> "While some researchers have defined stress by the individual's response to environmental events, others have defined stress as an environmental event (e.g., rape, combat) or a procedural variable (e.g., food deprivation, sleep deprivation). Still others have preferred

to define stress as a person/environment interaction, a definition that has become increasingly well accepted in the psychological literature."

Harel (1988) feels these definitions are in line with socioecological theory which "stipulates that factors external to the individual and the individual's reaction to these factors influence behavior, adjustment, and well-being" (p. 576). In view of this definition and the previously presented conceptualization for stressors, life situations and episodes can be linked directly to types of stress/stressors. Sjoberg (1981) examined life situations and episodes as the basis for situational influence on behavior. He defined the individual's life situation as a relatively stable set of needs, abilities, conceptual structures and external conditions. Episodes were defined in terms of time, from very brief to very long. These definitions parallel those for micro-, macro-, chronic, and acute stressors. This clearly puts stress in the domain of a situational influence. As a situational influence, stress can be applied to each of the three definitional viewpoints of a situation: objective, subjective, and person/environment (Leigh and Martin 1981).

The Objective Situation

For those theorists who view situations as objective in nature (Belk 1975), stress can be examined in relation to the five situational characteristics: physical and social surroundings, task definition, temporal perspective, and antecedent states. These characteristics can be considered as stressors or causative factors creating a stressful situation. For example, *physical stressors* might include a crowded mall (Harrell, Hutt, and Anderson 1980), a dirty supermarket, lack of parking or product assortment. A person encountering any one of these factors may consider it a stressful situation. *Social stressors* could include salespeople, shopping with children, shopping alone, or shopping with an indifferent friend or spouse. The intent to select, shop for or obtain information about a purchase refers to *task definition*. Such tasks as gift-giving, last-minute Christmas shopping, or failure to obtain the needed information to make an optimal decision may serve as stressors.

Time constraints, a *temporal perspective*, have been addressed in both the stress and situational influence literature. The definition of stress (see p. 2) offered by Maes, Vingerhoets and Van Heck (1987) points out the disparity between environmental demands (e.g., shopping, household chores, or job-related demands) and a person's capacity to cope with these demands (i.e., handle these tasks within the limited time available). This disparity of demands and available time is common in two-income households (Burke 1986; Lewis and Cooper 1987) and in persons experiencing job-related stress (Pavett 1986). It might be even more applicable to single parents who have no one with whom to share responsibilities. In contrast, for older consumers, the excess of available time associated with retirement is often found to be stressful (Palmore, Cleveland, Nowlin, Ramm and Siegler 1979).

In the consumer behavior literature, time pressure has been reported to influence store choice and store attribute saliencies (Mattson 1982). The increased importance of immediate salesperson attention, broad product selection, and store familiarity were revealed as factors important to time-pressured shoppers. Park, Iyer, and Smith (1989) maintain that store knowledge and available time for shopping affected unplanned buying, brand switching, and level of purchase volume deliberation. Under time pressure, the frequency of failure to make intended purchases increased.

Finally, stress can be related to the fifth characteristic of objective situations, *antecedent states* (i.e., moods and/or momentary conditions). These conditions are stipulated to be immediately antecedent to the current situation in order to distinguish between those states which the individual brings to the situation and those which result from the situation. Research in psychology and medicine suggests stress can lead to such emotional states as anxiety and panic (Schafer 1978), depression (Brown and Siegel 1988), guilt and distress (Janis and Mann 1977), a variety of diseases (Cooper 1983; Hendrix, Steel and Schultz 1987), alcohol abuse (Palmore et al. 1979), and marital difficulties (Plummer and Koch-Hattem 1986). Further evidence is offered by consumer behavior researchers. Gardner and Vandersteel (1984, p. 525), suggest "mild, transient, pervasive feeling states or 'moods' may influence one's ongoing behavior."

It is important, however, to recognize that stress does not always have a negative impact. Kahn, Wolfe, Quinn, Snock and Rosenthal (1964) report that in some situations stress can be an energizer resulting in increased motivation. Janis and Mann (1977) suggest that stress can be an incentive in the "work of worrying" that forces a person to be more thorough and complete. In Sjoberg's 1981 life situation study, "instrumental actions" (toward a goal) tended to be deeper in intention, and also tended to be carried out in somewhat more tense and unpleasant moods.

The Subjective Situation

Theorists supporting the subjective definition of situations [whether and how the subject perceives, processes, and responds to the situation (Kakkar and Lutz 1981)], can view stress as suggested by Lazarus, DeLongis, Folkman, and Gruen (1985, p. 770):

"...our view is that stress lies not in the environmental input but in the person's appraisal of the relationship between that input and its demands and the person's agendas (e.g., beliefs, commitments, goals) and capabilities to meet, mitigate, and alter these demands in the interests of well-being."

It is conceivable that two persons encountering the same environmental situation will react quite differently. For example, two drivers may react differently to rush hour traffic (a stressor) even though both encounter it on a daily basis. One may find it to be very stressful while the other has little reaction.

Lazarus et al. (1985, p. 770), however, expressed concern with the subjective approach to defining stress: "The searching question...is whether and how relational, cognitive approaches to psychological stress, which draw on subjectively defined assessments of stress, can overcome the dangers of confounding and circularity." Cote (1985, p.40) shares the same concerns in discussing the subjective definition of situations, "This definition, in fact, contains two separate issues, what is a situation, and what is the subject's response to the situation. Taken to the extreme, the subjective definition of situations is actually a type of behavior because it is concerned with response." If a consumer's stress level increases because they are not able to find "just the right gift for Uncle Lou" the resulting stress can be viewed as a predisposition taken to the next situation. This circularity issue can be limited by examining relational definitions.

The Person/Environment Situation

Finally, for those theorists adopting the interactionist approach to situations (Magnusson 1981; Snyder 1981), a view that encompasses both the actual and perceptual dimensions, stress can be included as a person-bound variable. It can be both a predisposition brought to the situation and a response to the interaction between the person and the environment (e.g., a chronically stressed consumer may experience acute stress when encountering a crowded shopping mall with only one hour to complete their purchasing). In this situation, the crowded shopping mall and time constraints can be viewed as acute or episodic stressors, that in interaction with the predisposition "stress," could result in a situation described as stressful.

While much of the psychology and marketing literature suggests that situations represent an understandable and predictable source of consumer behavior variance, Cote (1985) proposes that situation research should not focus on explaining variability, but rather on why and how situations affect behavior. Having established that stress is a plausible situational influence, the discussion will now turn to how consumers might respond to stress in their buying behavior.

RESPONSES TO STRESS

Coping Behavior

Situational stimuli that influence behavior may be processed either consciously or unconsciously. Conscious behavior may then be determined, in part, by those cognitive processes which govern the encoding and categorization of incoming stimuli. As a result, the individual can attend to salient environmental features, and respond with an appropriate problem solving or learned behavioral strategy (Snyder 1981). In a stressful situation, individuals react through the invocation of coping patterns, with coping defined herein as "the use of cognitive processes and problem-solving behaviors that are invoked to reduce or manage anxiety and other distressing emotion states" (Folkman and Lazarus 1988). Janis and Mann (1977) identified five coping patterns that affect decision-making: (1) unconflicted adherence; (2) unconflicted change; (3) defensive avoidance; (4) hypervigilance; and (5) vigilance. *Unconflicted adherence* would occur when a person perceives no serious threat from his/her current course of action and no change in behavior is warranted. *Unconflicted change* occurs when a stressor is perceived and the appropriate reaction is readily apparent, such as looking for a gas station when the gas gauge approaches empty. Generally, unconflicted adherence and unconflicted change would occur in low stress situations.

When stress is higher, a person may practice *defensive avoidance*. A person may avoid making any decision when a stressor is perceived and no acceptable alternative is readily apparent. *Hypervigilance* occurs when potential risks are high, little decision-making time is available, and behavior is automatic, e.g., in situations such as when a tornado is present and heading to the basement is the obvious decision. A less excited state is *vigilance*. In this situation the threat is serious but potential alternatives are still considered. Unlike a person in a paniclike (hypervigilant) state, a person in a vigilant state can still gather information and consider alternatives. In these situations, improvement in decision-making could result from training, e.g., teaching pilots to deal with emergencies.

THE EFFECTS OF COPING ON CONSUMER BEHAVIOR

It is not the intent of this paper to provide an exhaustive review of the stress literature but rather to illustrate the potential links between stress, the coping patterns employed, and consumer behavior. Research in both psychology and management indicates that the type of coping pattern adopted in response to stress can affect an individual's ability to process information and identify and consider alternative solutions. It is proposed that these phenomena are rich in implications for understanding consumer information processing and identification of alternatives.

Information Processing

Stress literature suggests that high levels of stress can impair information processing by narrowing perceptual attention and limiting the ability to assimilate available information (Janis 1982). The effects of stress on information processing depend, in part, on the amount of time available to make the decision. Janis and Mann (1977) maintain that given the belief that an acceptable course of action in a stressful situation exists, and that there is a sufficient amount of time to discover that action, an individual will engage in a vigilant coping pattern. In this case, stress may be perceived as positive because it could result in heightened information processing (i.e., individuals would search actively for all relevant information regarding the problem). Alternatively, if the individual perceives that an appropriate course of action exists but does not believe an appropriate amount of time can be allocated to its discovery, a hypervigilant coping pattern may emerge, and information processing could be impaired because of high emotional arousal. Individuals in this state will be overly reactive to the MOST AVAILABLE types of information. However, when no real alternative is believed to exist, individuals may cope by using a defensive avoidance pattern. This individual may suffer from impaired information processing because of the tendency to either exaggerate positive consequences, or minimize the negative.

Other researchers also propose that high levels of stress effect information processing. Beach (1982, p. 190) states that "if time constraints are imposed under high stress, the result is a frantic search for a way out, shortsightedness, impulsive selection of an action without seeking or appraising relevant information or consideration of consequences." Others report that stressed individuals are more likely to weigh negative information most heavily (Wright 1974), cope by suppressing thoughts and feelings about the stressful event, and "selectively ignore" certain information (Parkes 1984). Gray and Calsyn (1989) report that stress causes some people to seek out information and advice, as well as, moral support.

From a consumer behavior perspective, information processing is thought to be fundamental to the assimilation and utilization of information used in making consumption-related decisions. Since stress does appear to have an influence on information processing, it is proposed that this phenomenon could be, in part, a determinant of patterns of consumer behavior. It can be inferred that consumers in stress situations would attempt to selectively process information. In a study examining role overload for husbands and wives, Foxman and Burns (1987) argue that when one spouse is underloaded and one overloaded, information acquisition activities will be carried out by the underloaded spouse. In contrast, when both spouses experience role overload, shortened information acquisition activities, minimal joint decision-making, and extensive use of convenience items will prevail.

In some stressful situations, consumers will engage in vigilant coping behavior. Locander and Hermann (1979) found higher levels of anxiety were related to social information seeking. In an earlier study, Bell (1967) found automobile shoppers with low psychosocial certainty and high performance certainty, were more likely to take friends with them on shopping trips for social support.

Other consumers will employ defensive avoidance when faced with a stressful situation. Sjoberg (1981, p. 272) states, "Perhaps people strive less for the satisfaction of needs or the fulfillment of value-based commitments than they strive to avoid unpleasant actions and situations." In family purchase decisions, when stress results from conflict among family members Peter and Olson (1990, p. 388) state, "Some consumers might procrastinate, ignoring the problem and hoping that the situation will improve by itself." This suggests that, where possible, consumers may seek to avoid a purchase decision in a stressful situation.

A major component of the stress management literature offers techniques to provide escape or diversion from chronic stress (Morse and Furst 1979). These techniques allow a person to become involved in an activity to change his/her focus away from stressors or to find activities that have a rejuvenating effect. The objective is a change in mood. Gardner (1985) outlined the literature on mood and describes how mood can affect buyer behavior. Consumers participate in activities such as hobbies, sports, meditation, and exercise to alter moods. Products like liquor, books, and music also provide escape from stressors.

Identification and Consideration of Alternatives

As noted previously, decision-makers experiencing high levels of stress may suffer from impaired information processing. Stress can also result as decision-makers attempt to find ways to simplify their decision by ignoring long-term implications (Simon 1987), practicing premature closure (Keinan 1987), and utilizing fewer data dimensions (Wright 1974). Premature closure occurs when a decision is made before all available alternatives have been considered. This is a result of reduced perceptual attention and limited ability to assimilate available information. In "restraint coping" behavior, consumers might intentionally hold off on a decision so as not to act prematurely (Carver, Scheier and Weintraub 1989).

A related facet of decision-making is an individuals' ability to evaluate information systematically. Keinan (1987) defines the inability of a decision-maker under stress to evaluate information systematically as nonsystematic scanning. Nonsystematic scanning is the consideration of alternatives in a nonsystematic and disorganized fashion. Isenberg (1981) found that time-induced stress resulted in more emphasis being placed on the speed with which the decision was made rather than the accuracy of the decision. From a consumer behavior perspective, Park, Iyer, and Smith (1989) suggest that this is more likely to occur when consumers cannot rely on memory or routine to assist in their decision-making.

Janis (1982) suggests that stressed decision makers are likely to experience reduced problem-solving capabilities and consider only a narrow range of alternatives. These decision-makers will also have a tendency to overlook long-term consequences, engage in inefficient search, erroneously assess expected outcomes, and use oversimplified decision rules. When confronted by a stressful situation, Janis suggests the more common types of decision rules invoked: (1) a minimally satisfactory criterion of choice (satisficing); (2) confining the alternative choices to small incremental changes when gross changes are needed; (3) deciding on the basis of what people seem to want without considering the outcomes; (4) giving undue weight to historical analogies; and (5) relying on either a general formula based on ideological principles or an operational code as a guide to action without carrying out detailed analysis of the specific issue at hand.

In some situations, stress can act as an incentive. Stress may lead to heightened vigilance, and hence, motivate decision makers to anticipate the situation, to engage in efficient and systematic search, and to employ appropriate choice heuristics (Arthur 1987; Beach 1982; Janis and Mann 1977; Kahn et al. 1964). Use of heuristics to make product choices results from efforts by consumers to compensate for impaired information processing. Bettman (1979, p. 188) states, "there may be strong impacts of task or situational factors on use of heuristics, so that the same individual may use different heuristics in different choice situations." When facing a purchase decision under stress, the consumer can utilize a heuristic to simplify decision-making. Bettman suggests consumers may use a type of hybrid heuristic (phased strategy) to help reduce the number of alternatives that need to be evaluated and to simplify a complex choice. When using a phased strategy, the consumer first eliminates some alternatives from consideration and then makes comparisons among the reduced set. Miller and Ginter (1979) found consumers when making restaurant decisions under time pressure increased the salience of service quickness. Price served as a basis for eliminating alternatives in a study concerning women's clothing (Haines 1974 cited by Bettman 1979).

In summary, decision makers experiencing high levels of stress will not only engage in inefficient search activity, but also may use a simplified decision heuristic. When levels of stress become more moderate, however, decision makers may be more likely to engage in a rational problem solving process -- engaging in higher levels of systematic search, and employing appropriate choice heuristics.

FUTURE RESEARCH AND IMPLICATIONS

While the links have been theorized, little is understood about the role of stress in consumer behavior. Although this paper suggests more questions and issues than answers, future research can take direction from those examined. First and foremost, studies should be limited in scope. Eulberg, Weekley and Bhagat (1988) suggest models including stress as a situational variable need to be clear, specific and conceptually tight as opposed to comprehensive and trying to account for too many related themes. Only by limiting their focus can findings be integrated and mid-range theories made more meaningful. Second, methods of measuring stress in a consumer behavior context need to be developed. While a variety of measurement approaches are available (psychological scale - Campbell, Converse and Rogers 1976; daily hassles scale - Folkman and Lazarus 1982; and Life Events Scale - Holmes and Rahe 1967), it is not clear which scales are appropriate for consumer research.

Third, once scales have been adapted, the role of stress in consumer behavior can be explored. The roles of chronic stress and acute stress must be differentiated. Each type of stress might expect different coping behaviors with differing degrees of urgency. Other literature, such as the medical literature, can be explored to identify potential relationships with consumer behavior. Chronic stress, while perhaps more intensive than that generally experienced by most consumers, may lead to insights for consumer research. While the existing stress literature has placed substantial importance on the role of temporal factors, most studies have looked at stress as a static variable and ignored its dynamic nature (Eulberg, Weekley and Bhagat 1988). This presumes stress is an enduring characteristic and overlooks the adaptive capacities of consumers. Work is needed to provide likely theoretical linkages to guide future research.

Fourth, an understanding of the impact of stress necessitates an examination of mediating variables. More emphasis is needed on process theories rather than variance theories. Examining the relationships between a person and the environment seem to befit a process approach. It might be that furthering the understanding of coping strategies and behaviors may be more beneficial than the measurement of stress.

Finally, while these issues have not yet been resolved, this exploration of the effects of stress on consumer behavior does have some managerial implications. First, marketers must be sensitive to the existence of stress in consumer's lives, whether it be their lifestyle or some episodic encounter. For proponents of the marketing concept, this recognition may lead to strategy changes that try to accommodate and/or relieve some of the "daily hassles" faced by today's consumers. For a retailer, these strategies might include extended hours, increased customer service, better trained salespeople, home delivery, soothing atmospherics, increased usage of point-of-purchase displays and consistent merchandising. The periodic changing of product location within a store may increase stress as consumers spend more time trying to find the new location, leaving less time for other purchases which may result in failure to make intended purchases. Manufacturer's strategies could include active marketing research efforts to identify stressors, development of more convenience products and/or more direct marketing through catalogs.

REFERENCES

Arthur, A. Z. (1987), "Stress as a State of Anticipatory Vigilance," *Perceptual and Motor Skills*, 64, 75-85.

Beach, L. (1982), "Decision Making: Diagnosis, Action Selection, and Implementation," in *Choice Models for Buyer Behavior Research in Marketing*, JAI Press, 185-200.

Belk, R. W. (1975), "Situational Variables and Consumer Behavior," *Journal of Consumer Research*, 2 (December), 157-164.

Bell, G. (1967), "Self-Confidence, Persuasability and Cognitive Dissonance Among Automobile Buyers," in *Risk Taking and Information Handling in Consumer Behavior*, ed. D. Cox, Boston: Harvard University, 442-468.

Bettman, J. (1977), *An Information Processing Theory of Consumer Choice*, Reading, MA: Addison-Wesley.

Brown, J. and J. Siegel (1988), "Attributions for Negative Life Events and Depression: The Role of Perceived Control," *Journal of Personality and Social Psychology*, 54, 316-322.

Burke, R. J. (1986), "Occupational and life stress and the family: conceptual frameworks and research findings," *International Review of Applied Psychology*, 35, 347-369.

Campbell, A., P. Converse, and W. Rodgers (1976), *The Quality of American Life*, New York: Sage.

Carver, C., M. Scheier, and J. Weintraub (1989), "Assessing Coping Strategies: A Theoretically Based Approach," *Journal of Personality and Social Psychology*, 56, 267-283.

Cooper, C. (1983), *Stress Research: Issues for the Eighties*, New York: John Wiley & Sons.

Cote, J. A. (1985), "The Person by Situation Interaction Myth: Implications for the Definition of Situations," in *Advances in Consumer Research*, Vol. 13, ed. Richard Lutz, Provo, UT: Association for Consumer Research, 37-41.

Eulberg. J., J. Weekley, and S. Bhagat (1988), "Models of Stress in Organizational Research: A Metatheoretical Perspective," *Human Relations*, 41, 331-350.

Folkman, S. and R. Lazarus (1980), "An Analysis of Coping in a Middle-aged Community Sample," *Journal of Health and Social Behavior*, 21, 219-239.

Foxman, E. and A. Burns (1987), "Role Load in the Household," in *Advances in Consumer Research*, XIV, eds., Melanie Wallendorf and Paul Anderson, Provo, Utah: Association for Consumer Research, 458-462.

Gardner, M. (1985), "Mood States and Consumer Behavior: A Critical Review," *Journal of Consumer Research*, 12, 281-300.

Gardner, M. and M. Vandersteel (1983), "The Consumer's Mood An Important Situational Variable," in *Advances in Consumer Research*, Vol. 11, ed. Thomas Kinnear, Provo, UT: Association for Consumer Research, 525-529.

Goldberger, L. and Breznitz (1982), *Handbook of Stress: Theoretical and Clinical Aspects*, New York: The Free Press.

Gray, D. and R. Calsyn (1989), "The Relationship of Stress and Social Support to Life Satisfaction: Age Effects," *Journal of Community Psychology*, 17, 214-219.

Harel, Z. (1988), "Coping with Extreme Stress and Aging," *Social Casework: The Journal of Contemporary Social Work*, 575-583.

Harrell, G., M. Hutt, and J. Anderson (1980), "Path Analysis of Buyer Behavior Under Conditions of Crowding," *Journal of Marketing Research*, 17 (Feb), 45-51.

Hendrix, W. H., R. P. Steel and S. A. Schultz (1987), "Job Stress and Life Stress: Their Causes and Consequences," *Journal of Social Behavior and Personality*, 2 (3), 291-302.

Holmes, R. and R. Rahe (1967), "The Social Readjustment Rating Scale," *Journal of Psychosomatic Research*, 11, 213-218.

Isenberg, D. (1981), "Some Effects of Time-Pressure on Vertical Structure and Decision Making in Small Groups," *Organizational Behavior and Human Performance*, 27, 119-134.

Janis, I. (1982), "Decision Making Under Stress," in Handbook of Stress: Theoretical and Clinical Aspects, eds., L. Goldberger and S. Breznitz, New York: Free Press, 69-80.

Janis, I. and L. Mann (1977), *Decision Making: A Psychological Analysis of Conflict, Choice, and Commitment*, New York: Free Press.

Kahn, R. L., D. M. Wolfe, R. P. Quinn, J. D. Snock, and R. A. Rosenthal (1964), *Organizational Stress*, New York: Wiley.

Kakkar, P. and R. J. Lutz (1981), "Situational Influence on Consumer Behavior: A Review," in *Perspectives in Consumer Behavior*, eds., H. H. Kassarjian and T. S. Robertson, Scott Foresman.

Keane, T. (1985), "Defining Traumatic Stress: Some Comments on the Current Terminological Confusion," *Behavior Therapy*, 16, (September), 419-423.

Keinan, G. (1987), "Decision Making Under Stress: Scanning of Alternatives Under Controllable and Uncontrollable Threats," *Journal of Personality and Social Psychology*, 52, 639-644.

Lazarus, R. S., A. DeLongis, S. Folkman, and R. Gruen (1985), "Stress and Adaptational Outcomes," *American Psychologist*, 40 (7), 770-779.

Leigh, J. and C. Martin (1981), "A Review of Situational Influence Paradigms and Research," in *Review of Marketing, 1981*, eds., Enis, B. and K. Roering, Chicago: American Marketing Association, 57-74.

Lewis, S. N. C. and C. L. Cooper (1987), "Stress in Two-Earner Couples and Stage in the Life-Cycle," *Journal of Occupational Psychology*, 60, 289-303.

Locander, W. and P. Hermann (1979), "The effect of Self-Confidence and Anxiety on Information Seeking in Consumer Risk Reduction," *Journal of Marketing Research*, 16, 268-274.

Maes, S., A. Vingerhoets, and E. Van Heck (1987), "The Study of Stress and Disease: Some Developments and Requirements," *Social Science Medicine*, 25, 567-578.

Magnusson, D. (1981), "Wanted: A Psychology of Situations," in *Toward a Psychology of Situations: An Interactional Perspective*, ed., D. Magnusson, Hillsdale, NJ: Lawrence Erlbaum Associates, 9-36.

Mattson, B. (1982), "Situational Influences on Store Choice," *Journal of Retailing*, 58 (Fall), 46-58.

Miller, K. and J. Ginter (1979), "An Investigation of Situational Variation in Brand Choice Behavior and Attitude," *Journal of Marketing Research*, 16, 111-123.

Monroe, S. (1983), "Major and Minor Life Events as Predictors of Psychological Distress: Further Issues and Findings," *Journal of Behavioral Medicine*, 6, 189-205.

Morse, D. R. and M. L. Furst (1979), *Stress for Success*, New York: Van Nostrand Reinhold.

Olson, J. and J. P. Peter (1990), *Consumer Behavior and Marketing Strategy*, Homewood, IL: Irwin.

Palmore, E., W. P. Cleveland, J. B. Nowlin, D. Ramm, and I. C. Siegler (1979), *Journal of Gerontology*, 34 (6), 841-851.

Park, C. W., E. S. Iyer, and D. C. Smith (1989), "The Effects of Situational Factors on In-Store Grocery Shopping Behavior: The Role of Store Environment and Time Available for Shopping," *Journal of Consumer Research*, 15 (March), 422-433.

Parkes, K. (1986), "Locus of control, Cognitive Appraisal and Coping in Stressful Episodes," Journal of Personality and Social Psychology, 46, 655-668.

Pavett, C. M. (1986), "High Stress Professions: Satisfaction, Stress, and Well-Being of Spouses of Professionals," *Human Relations*, 39 (12), 1141-1154.

Pearlin, L. I. and C. Schooler (1978), "The Structure of Coping," *Journal of Health and Social Behavior*, 2, 21.

Plummer, L. P. and A. Koch-Hattem (1986), "Family Stress and Adjustment to Divorce," *Family Relations*, 35, 523-529.

Schafer, W. (1978), *Stress, Distress and Growth*, Davis, CA: Responsible Action.

Simon, H. (1987), "Making Management Decisions: The Role of Intuition and Emotion," *Academy of Management Executive*, (February), 57-63.

Sjoberg, L. (1981), "Life Situations and Episodes as a Basis for Situational Influence on Action," in *Toward a Psychology of Situations: An Interactional Approach*, ed., David Magnusson, New Jersey: Lawrence Erlbaum Associates, 259-274.

Snyder, M. (1981), "On the Influence of Individuals on Situations," in *Personality, Cognition and Social Interaction*, eds., N. Cantor and R. Kihlstrom, New Jersey: Lawrence Erlbaum Associates, 309-329.

Vingerhoets, A. J. J. M. and F. H. G. Marcelissen (1988), "Stress Research: Its Present Status and Issues for Future Developments," *Social Science Medical*, 26 (3), 279-291.

Wright, P. (1974), "The Harassed Decision Maker: Time Pressures, Distractions, and the Use of Evidence," *Journal of Applied Psychology*, 59, 555-561.

Personal Relevance As Moderator of the Effect of Public Service Advertising on Behavior

William K. Darley, University of Toledo
Jeen-Su Lim, University of Toledo

ABSTRACT

This paper examines the interaction of personal relevance and feelings toward a public service advertisement (Aad) and feelings toward the "drunk driving" issue (Aissue) on behavioral intention (BI). The results show that personal relevance significantly moderates the Aad-BI relationship as well as the Aissue-BI relationship. Directions for future research and public policy implications are discussed.

INTRODUCTION

Despite the recent increase in research efforts aimed at a greater understanding of attitude toward the advertisement and its role in the persuasion process (Shimp 1981; Burton and Lichtenstein 1988; MacKenzie, Lutz, and Belch 1986; Gorn 1982), many aspects of this complex phenomenon remain that have yet to receive proper theoretical and empirical consideration (Lutz 1985). The bulk of advertising research has been oriented toward what is said or felt about the advertisement that affects choice processes (Cushing and Douglas-Tate 1985). Previous studies have focused on the attitude toward the advertisement (Aad)-behavioral intention (BI) relationship with little interest in the possible moderating influence of other factors.

It is widely believed that ad effectiveness is moderated by audience involvement (Greenwald and Leavitt 1984). Although the data base regarding the behavioral consequences of persuasion has been growing, many questions remain unanswered. While past studies have focused on commercial or product advertising, the relevance to an applied and important realm of public service advertising has been ignored.

This study extends our understanding of individuals' affective reactions to a persuasive message. It examines the overall moderating effect of personal relevance upon the relationship between feelings toward a public service advertisement (Aad) and behavioral intention as well as between feelings toward an issue (Aissue) and behavioral intentions.

Attitude-behavior consistency has been the subject of much study. However, the affective reactions to an advertisement as they relate to intentions have received little attention, particularly in the context of the moderating role of personal relevance. In this study, consumers' reactions to a public service announcement introduce a new dimension in the subject matter as compared with previous studies.

HYPOTHESIS

Two types of involvement can affect message acceptance. One type concerns the extent to which the attitude issue under consideration is personally important to the recipient. The other type concerns the extent to which the particular attitudinal response adopted is of personal importance to the individual (Petty and Cacioppo 1979). This study focuses on the extent to which the attitude issue under consideration is of personal importance.

Personal relevance of an issue is one determinant of the route to persuasion that an individual is liable to follow while selecting between the alternatives of "central" versus "peripheral" routes to persuasion. Petty, Cacioppo, and Schumann (1983) contend that under the central route, attitude change is based on the careful and diligent consideration of the message claims or content. In contrast, under the peripheral route, attitude change is based on peripheral cues such as source attractiveness, quantity of arguments presented, and musical background. High personal relevance is expected to enhance thoughtful evaluation of message content. Low personal relevance is expected to lead to less thoughtful evaluation of the message content (Petty and Cacioppo 1979, 1981; Petty, Cacioppo, and Goldman 1981). Subjects involved with an issue are more likely to process message arguments in a systematic manner, employing the central route, than are less-involved subjects (Chaiken 1980). Borgida and Harvard-Pitney (1983) also found that more-involved subjects are more responsive to the message content, whereas less-involved subjects are more susceptible to perceptual salience effects.

High personal relevance leads to high attitude-behavior consistency. Sivacek and Crano (1982) found that the degree to which an individual perceives an attitude as hedonistically relevant affects the relationship between attitude and behavior. Leippe and Elkin (1987) found that issue-involved subjects were more likely to engage in attitude-behavior consistency. Thus, high personal relevance leads to high attitude-behavior consistency.

Attitude change induced via the peripheral route tends to be weak compared to attitude change resulting from central route processing. Individuals who are deeply involved with a product are more likely to behave in accordance with their deeply held attitudes and feelings. Strong affect or high order affect will tend to lead to strong behavioral intention. Conversely, weak affect or low order affect will tend to lead to weak behavioral intention (Smith and Swinyard 1988). The foregoing discussions suggest the following hypotheses concerning feelings toward the advertisement (Aad) and behavioral intention (BI) relationship as well as feelings toward the drunk driving issue (Aissue) and behavior intention (BI).

H1(a): The relationship between Aad and BI will be moderated by the level of personal relevance.

H1(b): For high personal relevance condition, the relationship between Aad-BI will be stronger than for low personal relevance condition.

H2(a): The relationship between attitude toward the issue (Aissue) and BI will be moderated by the level of personal relevance.

H2(b): For high personal relevance condition, the relationship between Aissue-BI will be stronger than for low personal relevance condition.

METHODOLOGY

Subjects, Research Design and Exposure Conditions

Subjects were undergraduate business students enrolled at an urban midwestern university. They were all above 21 years of age, were juniors and seniors, were working part or full time, and held driver's licenses. Eighty-seven subjects participated in the study and were randomly assigned to one of the three conditions (high personal relevance, low personal relevance, and control group). Accordingly, there were twenty-nine subjects per cell or condition.

The stimulus for the present study was an actual public service announcement put together by a State Governor's Task Force on Drunk Driving. It was a professionally produced sixty-second commercial. None of the respondents had been previously exposed to this public service announcement. Appendix 1 presents the actual wording of the public service announcement.

To operationalize personal relevance, subjects in the high personal relevance condition were told that an identical "get-tough" drunk-driving campaign was to be initiated in their own state starting on a specified date (see Appendix 1). Thus, the message would affect all subjects personally. In the low personal relevance condition, subjects were told that the campaign was currently going on in another state. The message, therefore, would personally affect none of the subjects. The foregoing procedure is similar to the approach of Petty and Cacioppo (1981), and Petty, Cacioppo, and Schumann (1983).

Subjects listened to the radio ad. The same version was presented to the two personal relevance groups. Written instructions were provided before and after the radio ad. After listening to the radio ad, subjects responded to the primary or dependent variables. Responses were also elicited concerning manipulation check items and ancillary items such as demographic variables.

Dependent Variables

The dependent measures collected in this study were (a) feelings toward the public service advertisement, Aad, (b) feelings toward the drunk driving issue, Aissue, and (c) Behavioral Intention, BI. Following the presentation of the ad stimulus, subjects reported their reactions to the aforementioned measures.

(a) Feelings toward the advertisement (Aad)

This was measured by asking subjects to complete the statement: "I feel the advertisement I just heard is ...." Responses were to be made in terms of four evaluative semantic differentials. This part of the questionnaire was designed to assess relevant affect toward the commercial. The scales were bipolar (bad/good, irritating/non-irritating, uninteresting/interesting, unpleasant/pleasant) and were anchored -3 to +3. This measure was consistent with the current conceptualization and operationalization of this construct (see for examples Edell and Staelin 1983; Gardner 1983). A positive score indicates a positive feeling toward the advertisement.

(b) Feelings toward the drunk-driving issue (Aissue)

Aissue was measured using a 3-item semantic differential scale. Subjects were asked to indicate their general feelings about "drunk-driving" as a pressing issue by completing the statement: "I feel concern about drunk-driving is... (useless/useful, unimportant/important, meaningless/meaningful)." The scales were bipolar and anchored -3 to +3. A positive score in this scale indicates the subject perceives the drunk-driving issue as a pressing one.

(c) Behavioral Intention (BI)

To measure behavioral intention, each subject was asked to indicate on a 7-point scale personal likelihood of (a) driving under the influence of alcohol when a "get tough" with drivers who drive under such influence is introduced in the individual's state, and (b) trying to stop a friend who wanted to drive under the influence of alcohol when a "get tough" with drivers under the influence of alcohol is introduced in the individual's state. These conative measures were coded 1 to 7, anchored by "unlikely" and "likely." The second measure was reverse-scored to maintain consistency so that the higher the score on the BI, the more likely the subject would drive under the influence of alcohol.

ANALYSIS

Moderated Multiple Regression (MMR) analysis was used to assess the statistical significance of personal relevance as a moderator variable. MMR examines the hypothesized interaction and main effects by model comparisons of the full- and restricted-regression models (Pedhazur 1982; Saunders 1956; Zedeck 1971).

An F test was performed to determine whether the addition of interaction terms significantly increases the variance explained in the dependent variable. Differences in the R^2 were tested using a procedure recommended by Saunders (1956). The significant F test on R^2 difference indicates the slopes of the regression equation for the subgroups are statistically different. Subgroup analysis was

TABLE 1
Cell Means and Reliability of Aad, Aissue and Behavior Intention

Variables	Low PR Condition	High PR Condition	Control Group	Reliability
Attitude toward Advertisement (Aad)	2.00 (5.56)	3.14 (5.54)	N.A.	.82
Attitude toward Issue (Aissue)	5.55 (4.57)	6.52 (4.06)	4.86 (4.51)	.88
Behavioral Intention	3.86 (3.22)	3.07[a] (2.27)	4.17 (2.79)	.76

PR: Personal Relevance.
[a] cell mean is significantly different from the control group mean at the .1 level.
N.A.; Not Applicable.
Standard deviations are in parentheses.

employed to investigate the directionality of the significant moderating effects (see for examples, Cohen and Cohen 1975; Anderson 1986). Graphs of the regression lines for each subgroup were evaluated to determine the nature of the interactions.

RESULTS

To assess personal relevance manipulation effectiveness, subjects were asked to tell how well they thought each of three phrases ("important to me," "meaningful to me," and "worth remembering") described the "get tough on drunk-driving campaign." Each scale was anchored by "not well at all" (1) and "extremely well" (7). These three phrases were abstracted from the "personal relevance" factor in Wells, Leavitt, and McConville (1971). In addition, this scaling parallels that employed in the latter study.

The manipulation checks for the personal relevance condition indicated this manipulation had been successful. Subjects in the high personal relevance condition scored higher than the subjects in the low personal relevance condition. For "important to me," "meaningful to me," and "worth remembering," means were 3.41, 3.55 and 2.62 respectively for the low personal relevance condition and were 4.00, 4.57 and 4.40 for the high personal relevance conditions. The differences between the respective high and low condition means were in the right direction and significant at $p < .05$.

Primary Variables

Table 1 presents the reliability measures of and the summated scores for the 4-item attitude toward the advertisement (Aad) scale, the 3-item attitude toward the drunk-driving issue (Aissue) scale, and the 2-item behavioral intention (BI) scale. The reliability measures were .82, .88, and .76 for Aad, Aissue and BI respectively.

For both Aad and Aissue, the high personal relevance condition elicited stronger feelings than the low personal relevance condition. The high personal relevance condition revealed a tendency of a more positive Aad (3.14) than the low personal relevance condition (2.0). The high personal relevance group also tended to consider the drunk driving issue (Aissue) as a more pressing issue (6.52) than did the low personal relevance subjects (5.55). In addition, for behavioral intentions (BI), the high personal relevance condition generated a lower level of intentions (3.07 versus 3.86). Thus, for the foregoing, subjects were less likely to drive under the influence of alcohol. Also, the control group means were in the right direction.

The prediction of Hypothesis 1a was that the relationship between Aad and BI would be moderated by personal relevance. Table 2 shows the results of the moderated regression analysis with personal relevance as moderator. The results show significant moderating effect of personal relevance on the relationship between Aad and behavioral intention. The change in R^2 from .074 of the restricted model to .187 of the full model for Aad is statistically significant at the 0.05 level. The foregoing provides support for Hypothesis 1a.

The partial regression coefficients are reported in Table 2. The partial regression

TABLE 2
Moderated Regression Analysis on Behavioral Intention with Personal Relevance (PR) as Moderator

Independent
Variables

Attitude toward Advertising (Aad)

Regression Model	R^2	ΔR^2	$F(\Delta R^2)$	d.f.
Full (Aad+PR+Aad*PR)	.187			
Restricted (Aad+PR)	.074	.113	4.49*	(1,56)

	B	SEB	t
Aad	.23	.19	1.19
PR	1.65	.75	2.19*
Aad*PR	-.26	.12	-2.12*

Attitude toward Issue (Aissue)

Regression Model	R^2	ΔR^2	$F(\Delta R^2)$	d.f.
Full (Aissue+PR+Aissue*PR)	.286			
Restricted (Aissue+PR)	.141	.145	10.93**	(1,56)

	B	SEB	t
Aissue	.49	.23	2.14*
PR	4.05	1.12	3.62**
Aissue*PR	-.50	.15	-3.31**

**P < .01, * P < .05

coefficient for Aad by personal relevance interaction is significant at the .05 level(t = -2.12). The partial regression coefficient for the interaction term is -.26, indicating a negative moderating effect of personal relevance on behavioral intention (BI). To further examine the directionality of this interaction, subgroup analysis was performed. In this procedure, subgroup regression lines were graphed by plotting scores of BI for the high (mean plus 1 standard deviation) and the low (mean minus 1 standard deviation) Aad and Aissue. For example, the BI score for the high Aad is calculated from the regression equation by substituting "Aad" with mean plus one standard deviation for the Aad value. For a detailed discussion of the procedure, see Pedhazur (1982), Cohen and Cohen (1975), and Anderson (1986). The slope of the subgroup regression line for the high PR group is steeper than that for the low PR condition (see Figure 1). The high PR group showed a significantly stronger Aad-BI relationship than did the low PR group. The results in Table 2 and Figure 2 provide support for Hypothesis 1b. Therefore, the hypothesis that the relationship between Aad-BI would be stronger for the high personal relevance condition than for the low personal relevance condition is supported.

Hypothesis 2a stated that the relationship between attitude toward drunk-driving issue (Aissue) and behavioral intentions is moderated by personal relevance. The results presented in Table 2 show that the R^2 change from the restricted (.141) to the full model (.286) for Aissue is statistically significant at the .01 level. This provides support for Hypothesis 2a.

The partial regression coefficient for Aissue by personal relevance interaction is significant at the .01 level with a t value of -3.31 (see Table 2). The partial regression coefficient for the interaction

FIGURE 1
Interactions Between Personal Relevance and Independent Variables

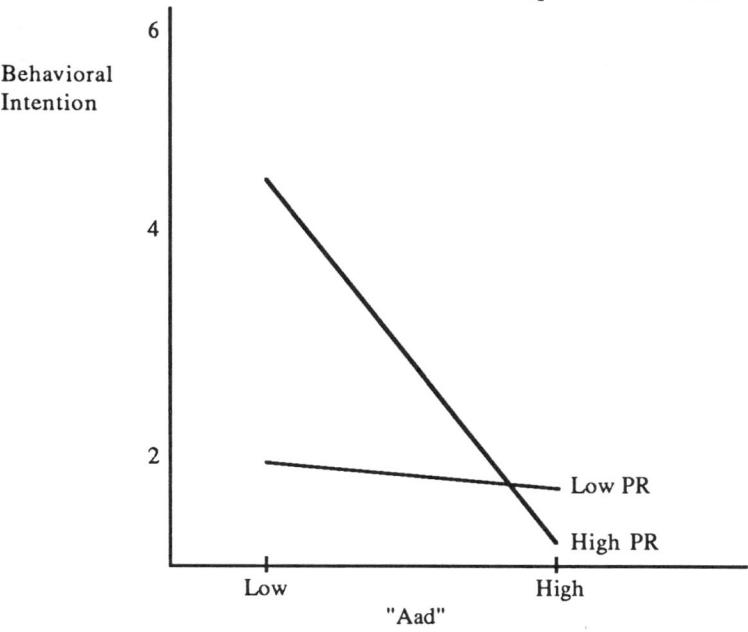

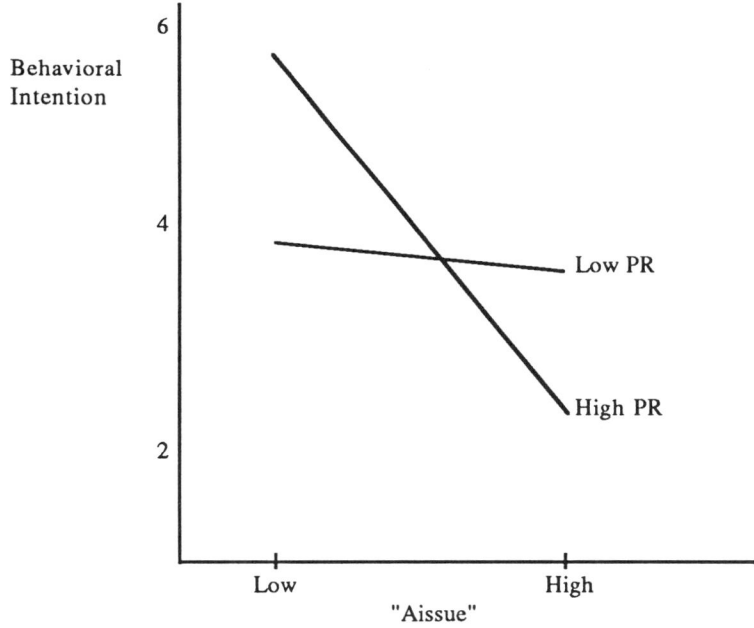

term is -.50 which suggests a negative moderating effect of personal relevance on behavioral intention. Subgroup analysis was performed to further examine the directionality of this interaction. The slope is steeper for the high personal relevance condition than for the low personal relevance condition (see Figure 1). Thus, the hypothesis that the relationship between Aissue-BI would be stronger for the high personal relevance condition than for the low personal relevance condition is supported (see Table 2 and Figure 1).

CONCLUSION AND DISCUSSION

The focus of this paper was to test the moderating role of personal relevance. The moderating hypothesis of personal relevance in the Aad-BI relationship (Hypothesis 1) was supported. Also, the evidence showed that the strength of the relationship between Aad-BI was significantly stronger for the high personal relevance group than for the low personal relevance group. The subgroup regression slope for the Aad was steeper for the high personal relevance group than for the low personal relevance group.

The moderating hypothesis of personal relevance in the Aissue-BI relationship was supported (Hypothesis 2). The evidence provided in Table 2 and Figure 1 showed that the strength of the relationship between Aissue-BI was significantly stronger for the high personal relevance condition than for the low personal relevance condition.

The foregoing results show that high personal relevance enhances the relationship between attitude toward the ad and intentions as well as between attitude toward the issue and intentions. Thus, the findings are consistent with the Elaboration Likelihood Model (Petty, Cacioppo, and Schumann 1983). Past studies have found that attitude change via the central route tends to be persistent and predictive of subsequent behavior for the central route. Consequently, for the high personal relevance condition, stronger relationships were found for the two types of feelings and behavioral intentions.

The results suggest some public policy implications, at least for the design of advertisements concerning social causes or issues. Public service advertising has generally focused on the content and source characteristics and has ignored the potential consequences of subjects' reactions toward the message and issue involvement. These results would suggest that elicited feelings toward the public service advertisement need to be carefully considered.

The personal relevance of an advertisement, with some creative ingenuity, is manipulatable in real world situations. Thus, public service announcements should be presented in such a way as to make them personally relevant to consumers. It is also important in public service advertising to stress a link between the issue in question and the self. Such personal connection should add to the effectiveness of public service advertising.

While this study adds to the growing but still uncertain research data base regarding the behavioral consequences of persuasion under differing involvement conditions, further research is needed. Investigations of the reactions in the context of actual product advertisements involving different types of content and consideration of overt behavioral measures may provide useful insights. Differences among individuals' personal relevance links to brands or products and the possible impact of this variable on the Aad-behavioral intention relationship should be studied.

Research has shown that in some cases, the consumer's feelings toward the advertisement mediates the consumer's feelings toward the object. However, while the exact nature of the relationship between feelings toward the advertisement (Aad) and toward the object (Ao) is still under investigation (see for example Mackenzie et al. 1986), it has been shown that feelings toward the advertisement (Aad) can make a significant contribution toward feelings toward the advertised product or issue and behavioral intention. Thus, the incorporation of feelings regarding the advertised issue should extend our understanding of the role of feelings evoked by an advertisement in the persuasion process.

This study is not without its limitations. Although the results are interesting, care should be exercised in the interpretation and generalization of the findings. The study utilized a single ad design with a single exposure. Thus, it is possible that the results might have been influenced by impression management biases. This may be true in the behavioral intention (BI) results in that when subjects are asked sensitive questions like the "likelihood of drunk driving" they might give socially desirable answers. An alternative operationalization of the BI measure which does not entail the potentially sensitive "driving under the influence" wording is, for example, to measure the likelihood of driving after a specific number of drinks/body weight are consumed in a specific time period (Lastovicka, Murry, Joachimstaller, Bhalla, and Scheurich 1987). These authors found greater agreement with this objective measure than with the measure of driving drunk. Future research should therefore investigate this measurement issue together with the possible "subject effects" and the influence of personal relevance on "subject effects" or demand artifacts.

APPENDIX 1
CONTENT OF PUBLIC SERVICE ANNOUNCEMENT

In 19--, (STATE) adopted new tougher drunk driving laws, and we told you that if we pulled you over you'd better be sober. Some of you listened, but a lot of you did not. Those of you who still drink and drive, despite all the warnings, are at a terrible risk, a risk of killing yourself, or worse killing someone else, and the risk you're taking is unacceptable. We are going to do everything in our power to stop you. As a consequence of the death and destruction caused by drunk drivers, the combined police forces of (STATE) are coming out in force. There will be more officers, more cars, more sobriety checkpoints. If you drive drunk we want you to remember this, that you are on a collision course with every law enforcement officer in (STATE). The heat is on this summer. Don't drink and drive! This is a message from the Governor's task force to reduce drunk driving.

REFERENCES
Anderson, Carol H. (1986), "Hierarchical Moderated Regression Analysis: A Useful Tool For Retail Management Decisions," *Journal of Retailing*, 62, 186-203.

Borgida, E. and B. Howard-Pitney (1983), "Personal Involvement and the Robustness of Perceptual Salience Effects," *Journal of Personality and Social Psychology*, 45, 560-570.

Burton, Scot and Donald R. Lichtenstein (1988), "The Effect of Ad Claims and Ad Context on Attitude Toward the Advertisement," *Journal of Advertising*, 17, 3-11.

Chaiken, Shelly (1980), "Heuristic Versus Systematic Information Processing and the Use of Source Versus Message Cues in Persuasion," *Journal of Personality and Social Psychology*, 39, 752-766.

Cohen, Jacob and Patricia Cohen (1975), *Applied Multiple Regression/Correlation Analysis for the Behavioral Sciences*, Hillsdale, N.J.: Lawrence Erlbaum Associates, Publishers.

Cushing, Peter and Melody Douglas-Tate (1985), "The Effect of People/Product Relationships on Advertising Processing," in *Psychological Processes and Advertising Effects*, Linda A. Alwitt and Andrew A. Mitchell, eds. Hillsdale, NJ: Lawrence Erlbaum Associates, Publishers, 241-259.

Edell, Julie A. and Richard Staelin (1983), "The Information Processing of Pictures in Print Advertisements," *Journal of Consumer Research*, 10, 45-61.

Gardner, Meryl P. (1983), "Advertising Effects on Attributes Recalled and Criteria Used for Brand Evaluations," *Journal of Consumer Research*, 10, 310-318.

Gorn, Gerald J. (1982), "The Effects of Music in Advertising on Choice Behavior: A Classical Conditioning Approach," *Journal of Marketing*, 46, 94-101.

Lastovicka, John L., John P. Murry, Jr., Erich A. Joachimstaller, Gaurav Bhalla and Jim Scheurich (1987), "A Lifestyle Typology to Model Young Male Drinking and Driving," *Journal of Consumer Research*, 14, 257-263.

Leippe, Michael R. and Roger A. Elkin (1987), "When Motives Clash: Issue Involvement and Response Involvement as Determinants of Persuasion," *Journal of Personality and Social Psychology*, 52, 269-278.

Lutz, Richard J. (1985), "Affective and Cognitive Antecedents of Attitude Toward the Ad: A Conceptual Framework," in *Psychological Processes and Advertising Effects*, Linda A. Alwitt and Andrew A. Mitchell, eds. Hillsdale, N.J.: Lawrence Erlbaum Associates, Publishers, 45-63.

Mackenzie, Scott B., Richard J. Lutz and G. Belch (1986), "The Role of Attitude Toward the Ad As A Mediator of Advertising Effectiveness: A Test of Competing Explanations," *Journal of Marketing Research*, 23, 130-143.

Pedhazur, Elazar J. (1982), *Multiple Regression in Behavioral Research*, New York: Holt, Rinehart and Winston, Inc.

Peter, Paul J. and Jerry C. Olson (1987), *Consumer Behavior: Marketing Strategy Perspectives*, Homewood, IL: Richard Irwin, Inc.

Petty, Richard E., John T. Cacioppo and David Schumann (1983), "Central and Peripheral Routes to Advertising Effectiveness: The Moderating Role of Involvement," *Journal of Consumer Research*, 10, 135-146.

Petty, Richard E. and John T. Cacioppo (1981), "Issue Involvement As A Moderator of the Effects on Attitude of Advertising Content and Context," in *Advances in Consumer Research*, Vol. 8, Ken Monroe, ed. Ann Arbor, MI: Association for Consumer Research, 20-24.

Petty, Richard E., John T. Cacioppo and Rachel Goldman (1981), "Personal Involvement As A Determinant of Argument-Based Persuasion," *Journal of Personality and Social Psychology*, 41, 847-855.

Petty, Richard E. and John T. Cacioppo (1979), "Issue Involvement Can Increase or Decrease Persuasion by Enhancing Message-Relevant Cognitive Responses," *Journal of Personality and Social Psychology*, 37, 1915-1926.

Richins, Marsha L. and Peter H. Bloch (1986), "After the News Wears Off: The Temporal Context of Product Involvement," *Journal of Consumer Research*, 13, 280-285.

Saunders, David R. (1956), "Moderator Variables in Prediction," *Educational and Psychological Measurement*, 16, 209-222.

Shimp, Terence A. (1981), "Attitude Toward the Ad As a Mediator of Consumer Brand Choice," *Journal of Advertising*, 10, 9-15.

Sivacek, John and William D. Crano (1982), "Vested Interest As A Moderator of Attitude-Behavior Consistency," *Journal of Personality and Social Psychology*, 43, 210-221.

Smith, Robert E. and William R. Swinyard (1988), "Cognitive Responses to Advertising and Trial: Belief Strength, Belief Confidence and Product Curiosity," *Journal of Advertising*, 17, 3-14.

Wells, William D., Clark Leavitt and Maureen Mcconville (1971), "A Reaction Profile for TV Commercials," *Journal of Advertising Research*, 11, 11-17.

Zedeck, Sheldon (1971), "Problems With the Use of Moderator Variables," *Psychological Bulletin*, 76, 295-310.

Consumers' Belief In Their Ability To Judge The Truthfulness of Sales Claims
Robert Baer, Bradley University
Rustan Kosenko, Bradley University

ABSTRACT

The present paper reports that consumers have confidence in their ability to detect whether or not a salesperson is telling the truth. They believe that they can guage salesperson truthfulness by the persuasiveness and quality of the sales message. In an experimental setting, we found that subjects' tendency to believe the salesperson was influenced by whether or not experimental conditions reinforced or challenged their belief in the relationship between sales message persuasiveness and salesperson truthfulness.

INTRODUCTION

Discerning whether or not an advertiser or salesperson is telling the truth is a pervasive problem encountered by consumers and is a concern of governmental regulatory bodies. Although our economic system generally has faith in the individual as a consumer, critics contend that many products and services are so complex that even a reasonably well-informed buyer would need the aid of an expert to make a wise decision. The situation is complicated by the fact that some marketers consciously attempt to deceive their customers. Establishing the credibility of promotional claim is becoming a pressing problem. Investigators have reported that feelings about advertising have grown less favorable over time (Anderson and Engledow, 1978; Bauer and Greyser, 1968). A recent poll (USA Today, 1989) indicated that 24% of the public believe that marketing claims have become less honest in recent years while Krugman and Ferrell (1981) reported that advertising practitioners said that the second most difficult problem they faced was creating honest, nonmisleading advertisements.

Marketing trustworthiness can be considered from an attributional perspective (Settle and Golden, 1974; Hansen and Scott, 1976; Calder and Burnkrant, 1977; Smith and Hunt, 1978. Attribution theory is a collection of theories (Bem, 1965; Kelley 1967, 1971, 1972; Jones and Davis, 1965) that seek to explain the cognitive processes involved when an individual infers the causes of their own or another person's behavior. Mizerski, Golden and Keenan (1979) and Folkes (1988) have provided two excellent reviews that describe the applicability of attribution theory to a wide range of consumer behavior. A theme that runs throughout attributional work is the perceiver's tendency to characterize behavior as caused by either inner traits, beliefs or dispositions (internal attribution) or by prevailing social and environmental concerns (external attribution). This dichotomy is especially useful for considering consumer perceptions of truthfulness. For example, given an opinion expressed by a salesperson, the customer must decide whether the stated opinion was caused by (1) the salesperson's true beliefs about the product (internal attribution) or (2) variable situational contingencies such as the salesperson's vested interest in the making of the sale or simply the normal expectations of the job (external attribution). Through this attributional process, a person judges whether a salesperson's verbal statements are trustworthy, i.e., a reflection of their genuine beliefs about the product (Hansen and Scott, 1976).

The principle importance of the attributional process stems from the relationship between attribution and behavior. Often we react not so much as to the mere fact of another's behavior as to the perceived causes and intentions underlying that behavior. Knowing *why* a salesperson said what he or she said is more useful than merely knowing what was said. Thus, if a sales message was attributed to the salesperson's vested interest in the sale, the consumer would be less certain about the actual characteristics of the product and would be less inclined to buy than if the message was considered to be an indication of the salesperson's true beliefs.

Despite a propensity to mistrust marketing claims, there is evidence to suggest, that to some extent, consumers may take the salesperson's word at face value and that consumers are perhaps less skeptical than they realize. Baer (1990) reported that subjects tended to believe salespeople even when there was little reason to have confidence in the truthfulness of their claims. Subjects in his experiment were asked to judge an automobile salesperson's genuine belief toward the product he or she was selling. Some subjects had been told that due to many choices of available brands from which to choose (long product line), the salesperson could be considered to have little stake in the sale of any single product item and was therefore free to express his or her genuine beliefs about the product (choice). Other subjects had been told that there was only one product available (short product line) and that the salesperson was forced to sell that one car (no choice). The salesperson then gave a sales message that was either favorable or unfavorable towards the product. The results indicated that in both the choice and no-choice condition, subjects attributed a product attitude toward the salesperson that was consistent with the direction of the sales message. That is, in the long product line condition, salespersons who spoke favorably about the product were perceived as having more favorable attitudes than those who spoke unfavorably. More importantly, even in the short product line condition, subjects still tended to infer attitudes that were consistent with the direction of the sales message. Thus, subjects made attributions that indicated that they thought salespersons held attitudes toward the product that were consistent with their verbal statements about the product. This is a rather surprising finding that runs counter to intuitive notions that depict consumers as highly skeptical of marketing claims.

Why would consumers infer that the sales message is a reflection of the salesperson's true beliefs about the product? After all, a sales environment is one in which there are powerful plausible external causes for the salesperson's behavior. As a result, consumers should approach this situation with caution and be skeptical about salesperson motives.

The purpose of the present study was to examine an explanation for this tendency to regard the sales message as a reflection of the salesperson's genuine product attitudes. One possible explanation is that even though consumers know that some marketing claims are not truthful, they nonetheless believe in their ability to detect which claims are truthful and which ones are not. The problem for the customer is that even though there are powerful external forces that may account for the salesperson's behavior, many salespeople may still actually believe what they say. The customer must somehow use the available information to make an inference regarding a particular salesperson's truthfulness.

Miller and Rorer (1982) and Miller, Baer and Schonberg (1979) theorized that people in this situation adopt a diagnostic judgment set and invest the person's behavior with diagnosticity under the assumption of a strong correlation between the quality, extremity and persuasiveness of the person's behavior and their true beliefs. Thus, consumers have confidence in their ability to detect the salesperson's beliefs. They perceive that salespeople will produce strong, unequivocal and persuasive sales messages if, and only if, they personally endorse the product. Conversely, salespeople will perform relatively poorly if, and only if, they are forced to argue against their true product beliefs. Thus, if a salesperson gives a convincing sales presentation, consumers will infer that he or she believes in what they say. Similarly, Reeder and his colleagues (Reeder, 1985; Reeder and Brewer, 1979; Reeder, Fletcher and Furman, 1989) have shown that people expect others to behave consistently with their attitudes such that a person who possesses a certain attitude would not be expected to be able to act in a way that deviates from that attitude to any great extent. Thus, a salesperson forced to take a position about a product with which they do not agree, would be expected to do a relatively poor job (i.e., would be rather unconvincing), while those who had to defend a product in which they did believe would make a rather convincing presentation. Under the assumption of a strong correlation between message quality and persuasiveness and the salesperson's true beliefs, consumers believe that they can detect the salesperson's true beliefs from the quality and persuasiveness of their sales presentations.

If this line of reasoning is correct, then one should be able to either diminish or heighten the tendency for perceivers to regard the salesperson as truthful by providing them with information that either challenges (disconfirms) or reinforces (confirms) their belief in a strong correlation between sales message quality and persuasiveness and the salesperson's product attitude. The present study created experimental conditions that either challenged or supported subjects' belief in their ability to detect salesperson truthfulness. Subjects in our experiment received information that showed that there was either a strong or weak relationship between a salesperson's product attitude and the kind of sales message they gave when required to sell a product in which they did not believe. If judgments about message truthfulness are based upon the persuasiveness and strength of the message, then one should be able to diminish consumer faith in the sales message by providing subjects with information that shows the message persuasiveness is not a good predictor of salesperson product beliefs. Similarly, faith in the message can be enhanced by providing information that confirms people's belief that sales message persuasiveness is a good predictor of the salesperson's product beliefs. On the basis of this analysis, the following predictions can be made:

H1: In the absence of any information regarding the predictability of salesperson belief by message persuasiveness, subjects will tend to regard a persuasive sales message as truthful and attribute an attitude to the salesperson that is consistent with the position taken in the sales message.

H2: When information is provided to subjects that confirms their belief that message persuasiveness and salesperson beliefs are related, subjects' tendency to attribute an attitude to the salesperson that is consistent with their position taken in the sales message will be strengthened.

H3: When information is provided to subjects which disconfirms the predictability of salesperson product belief by message persuasiveness, subjects will regard the sales message with caution and should not attribute attitudes to the salesperson that are consistent with the position taken in the sales message.

METHOD

Overview

The design was a 2 x 3 factorial. The independent variables were the salesperson's expressed beliefs toward the product (favorable versus unfavorable) and the extent to which the sales message confirmed or disconfirmed subjects' assumptions regarding message strength as a predictor of salesperson beliefs (confirm versus disconfirm versus no information). The major dependent variable was the subjects' estimation of the salesperson's genuine beliefs about the product.

Participants

The participants were 129 male and female undergraduate business students who volunteered to participate in the study. Participants were run in small groups ranging in size from four to twelve. Participants were randomly assigned to one of the six cells in the experimental design.

Construction of Stimulus Materials

Persuasive messages pertaining to the sale of an automobile were developed. The messages were adopted from sets of persuasive messages reported by Pratkanis, Greenwald, Ronis, Leippe and Baumgardner (1983). The sales message consisted of a fictitious brand name and a description of the product's attributes. To create a description, paragraphs based on articles appearing in *Consumer Reports* were composed. Three attributes (durability, safety and handling) were chosen because different automobiles should vary among these characteristics. Fifteen different sales messages were created to reflect widely varying degrees of persuasiveness and quality. The sales messages were pre-tested by a convenience sample of twenty students who, on four separate 9-point semantic differential scales, rated each sales message in terms of its persuasiveness, quality, strength and extremity. These ratings confirmed that the fifteen messages did indeed vary in terms of these four characteristics.

Procedure

Stimulus materials were presented in booklet form. The cover page of the booklet described the experiment as an investigation of the way in which people make judgments about products and salespeople based upon limited information. Subjects read written scenarios portraying automobile sales transactions. Each subject was given a sales message to read. Subjects were told that there was a short product line, i.e., only one model available. Because of the short product line, the instructions emphasized that the salesperson may not have been free to express his or her real opinion to the customer. Subjects were shown a 9-point semantic differential rating scale (1 = extremely unfavorable, 9 = extremely favorable) upon which the salesperson's genuine attitude toward the product had been checked. Subjects received fourteen additional sales messages. The instructions to each one emphasized the potential inability of the salesperson to express his or her true beliefs because of a short product line. Also, for each sales message, the salesperson's genuine attitude was indicated by a circle on the rating scale. For all fifteen sales messages, the salesperson expressed either a favorable attitude toward the product (7, 8 or 9 on the 9-point scale) or an unfavorable attitude (1, 2 or 3 on the 9-point scale). In some cases, the salesperson's real attitude conflicted with what they stated in their sales presentation, while in other cases it was consistent.

Manipulation of Confirmation-Disconfirmation of Assumptions

In the *confirmation condition*, we intended to lead subjects to believe that the persuasiveness and quality of the sales message was indicative of a salesperson's beliefs. The sales messages and corresponding salesperson product attitudes that were provided showed that salespersons with attitudes strongly in favor of the product (7, 8 or 9 on the 9-point scale) gave sales messages that supported the product that were strong, persuasive, extreme and of high quality (rated 7, 8 or 9 on a 9-point scales during the pre-test). Those who did not believe in the product (1, 2 or 3 on the 9-point scale) gave sales messages that supported the product that were weak, unpersuasive, mild and of low quality (rated 1, 2 or 3 on 9-point scales during the pre-test). Thus, for subjects in the confirmation condition, sales messages were used that correlated highly ($r = .82$) with the salesperson's attitude.

In the *disconfirm condition*, we intended to lead subjects to believe that the strength and quality of the sales message was not related to how the salesperson felt about the product. As in the confirmation condition, each subject read fifteen sales messages ostensibly given by fifteen different salespeople who, because of a short product line, were not necessarily free to express their true beliefs about the product. However, in the disconfirmation condition, salespersons who were either strongly in favor or strongly against the product gave sales messages that varied in terms of quality, strength, extremity and persuasiveness. That is, regardless of their personal feelings toward the product, some salespeople gave weak sales messages while others gave either ambivalent or convincing presentations (ratings of 1-9 on 9-point scales). In the disconfirmation condition, sales message strength and quality correlated poorly ($r = .10$) with salesperson product attitude and could therefore not be used to guage the salesperson's product attitude.

Subjects in the *no-information condition* did not receive any information regarding the extent to which salesperson attitudes could be predicted from sales message strength. That is, subjects in this condition did not receive the fifteen different sales messages and they did not receive any information about the product attitudes of any previous salespeople.

Manipulation of Salesperson's Expressed Beliefs

Following the fifteen different sales messages, subjects received one final sales message. This message omitted the attitude scale that had been used to indicate the salesperson's genuine attitude in the fifteen previous cases. Subjects were instructed once again that there was only one brand of car currently available. Consequently, it was emphasized that salespersons were not free to sell the models in which they most believed. If the

TABLE 1
Attitude Attribution[a]

Salesperson's Expressed Beliefs	Sales Message Strength - Salesperson Belief Relationship		
	Confirm	No-Information	Disconfirm
Favorable	7.55	6.68	6.05
Unfavorable	3.82	4.85	5.80

[a]"What do you think is the salesperson's deepest and most genuine belief about the product?" (1 = extremely poor car, 9 = extremely good car).

---

salesperson thought that the one car was not a good car, they were not free to express their opinion to the customer.

Salespersons expressed beliefs toward the car that were favorable or unfavorable. The belief consisted of one sentence for three different product attributes that were described that assigned a value of either "poor" (unfavorable) or "excellent" (favorable) to each of three attributes. In addition, salespeople in the favorable condition began their sales message with an overall excellent assessment of the car and concluded by recommending its sale. Salespersons in the unfavorable condition began with a poor evaluation and concluded by not recommending its sale.

Dependent Measures

As the major dependent measure, subjects attributed an attitude toward the salesperson. Subjects were asked, "What do you think is the salesperson's deepest and most genuine belief about the car?" (1 = extremely poor car, 9 = extremely good car). Additional questions asked subjects to rate the quality, strength, persuasiveness and extremity of the sales message (all on 9-point scales).

RESULTS

Results were analyzed by a 2 x 3 ANOVA. Manipulated variables were the salesperson's expressed beliefs toward the product (favorable versus unfavorable) and the extent to which subjects' assumptions about the sales message strength-salesperson belief relationship were confirmed (confirmed versus disconfirmed versus no information).

Attitude Attribution

A significant main effect for expressed beliefs, $F(1,123) = 31.22$, $p < .01$ was obtained. These results indicated that salespeople who spoke favorably about the product were perceived as having more favorable attitudes ($\bar{x} = 6.76$) towards the product than those who spoke unfavorably ($\bar{x} = 4.85$). In terms of the central questions of this research, however, the data are best understood in terms of expressed beliefs x confirmation of assumptions interaction, $F(1,123) = 8.59$, $p < .01$. The means are shown in Table 1. These results indicated that in the no-information control group, attitudes were attributed to salespeople in line with the direction of the sales message, i.e., salespersons who spoke favorably about the product were perceived as having more favorable attitudes ($\bar{x} = 6.68$) than those who spoke unfavorably ($\bar{x} = 4.85$), $F(1,44) = 9.89$, $p < .01$. Data from the no-information condition support the first hypothesis and replicate those of Baer (1990) by showing that even under no-choice conditions (short product line), people are prone toward internal attributions and tend to take the salesperson's word at face value.

The second hypothesis was also supported. Subjects in the confirmation condition attributed attitudes that were even more extreme in the direction of the sales message $\bar{x}$ favorable = 7.55, $\bar{x}$ unfavorable = 3.82, $F(1,40) = 37.84$, $P < .01$. The third hypothesis was also supported. Under disconfirmation conditions, there was no statistically significant difference in the attitudes attributed to salespersons who spoke favorably ($\bar{x} = 6.05$) and unfavorably ($\bar{x} = 5.80$), $F < 1$.

Sales Message Ratings

Subjects rated the quality, extremity and persuasiveness of the sales message. These sales message characteristics were rated on 9-point rating scales (1 = very low, 9 = very high). A main effect for direction was obtained for both the persuasive, $F(1,123) = 6.10$, $p < .01$, and quality measure, $F(1,123) = 11.96$, $p < .01$. Sales messages in favor of the product were seen as more persuasive ($\bar{x} = 5.31$) and of higher quality ($\bar{x} = 5.61$) than sales messages against the product ($\bar{x} = 4.48$ and 4.49 respectively). Also a significant main effect for confirmation of subjects' assumptions was obtained for all three measures. Subjects in the confirmation condition reported that the sales message was more persuasive ($\bar{x} = 5.50$) than subjects in either the disconfirmation ($\bar{x} = 4.46$) or no-information condition ($\bar{x} = 4.67$), F (1,123) 3.41, p < .05. They also thought the message was of higher quality in the confirmation ($\bar{x} = 5.93$) than disconfirmation ($\bar{x} = 4.78$) or no-information condition ($\bar{x} = 4.44$), F (1,123) = 7.92, p < .01, and was more extreme in the confirmation ($\bar{x} = 6.0$) than disconfirmation ($\bar{x} = 4.78$) and no- information condition ($\bar{x} = 5.09$), F (1,123) = 5.19, p < .01. No interactions were obtained between the salesperson's attitude (favorable/unfavorable) and the confirmation/no confirmation/disconfirmation manipulation for either the quality, extremity or persuasiveness measure.

DISCUSSION

Consumers' perceptions of salesperson truthfulness were examined from an attributional perspective. Given an opinion about a product expressed by a salesperson, the customer must decide whether those statements accurately reflect the salesperson's true beliefs (trustworthy), or whether they are merely the result of the salesperson's vested interest in making the sale. The present paper contends that consumers have confidence in their ability to detect the salesperson's true beliefs even when they know that there is ample reason to doubt the veracity of the claim. A study was designed to test the proposition that consumers hold implicit expectations about the kinds of behaviors that are likely to be emitted by salespeople who hold particular beliefs toward the products they sell. People expect salespeople to compose sales messages in such a way that their personal beliefs can be inferred. They assume a correlation between the salesperson's attitude and the persuasiveness, strength and quality of the sales presentation. They believe that a salesperson who tries to sell a product in which they do not believe will give themselves away by doing a relatively poor job, while those who truly believe in what they say will do a good job. These expectations are held to play a key role in the attributional process.

If perceptions of salesperson beliefs are based on the presumed correlation between salesperson belief and sales message persuasiveness and quality, then one should be able to influence perceptions of salesperson belief by strengthening or diminishing consumer confidence in this presumed correlation. We created experimental conditions that showed that the presumed correlation was either accurate or inaccurate and observed the corresponding effect on subjects' tendency to believe a persuasive sales message. We found that subjects were less likely to regard the persuasive message as indicative of the salesperson's beliefs when we diminished rather than strengthened confidence in the presumed correlation. These results add further support for the contention that customer inferences about salesperson truthfulness are based upon the perceived persuasiveness and quality of the sales message.

We also reported that subjects in the confirmation condition thought that the sales message was more persuasive, extreme and of higher quality than subjects in the disconfirmation and control conditions. It appears that not only did subjects use the persuasiveness and quality of the sales presentation to gauge the salesperson's attitude, but that the reverse was also true., i.e., they used the salesperson's attitude to make judgments about sales presentation persuasiveness. Having presumed a correlation between message persuasiveness and salesperson attitude and having read a persuasive sales message, subjects elevated their perceptions of persuasiveness, quality and strength relative to the subjects in the other conditions.

The results of this study highlight the importance of message quality, strength and persuasiveness as a basis for consumer perception of a salesperson's truthfulness. However, these intuitive beliefs may often mislead a consumer into believing a salesperson just because they make a convincing presentation. Reeder et al. 1989 reported that people often underestimate the extent to which someone can do an effective job despite not believing in what they say. Miller et al. 1979 reported that students forced to perform a task that contradicted their personal beliefs often did a reasonably good job. Students in their experiment were assigned to write essays defending political positions in which they did not believe. Yet, these essays were rated just as persuasive and of the same quality as essays written by students who believed in what they wrote. Since salespeople should be particularly adept at making convincing presentations regardless of their personal beliefs, the consumer may often be mislead by this presumed correlation.

The results from the no-information control group replicate those of Baer (1990). Surprisingly, these data show that rather than being skeptical about the veracity of sales claim, subjects tended to take the salesperson's word at face value and attribute an attitude that was consistent with the position taken in the sales message. Although surprising for a marketing context, these results are consistent with what Ross (1977) claims is a rather pervasive tendency in the perception of other people. He claims that people are generally biased toward making *internal* attributions. People tend to infer that an individual's actions are compatible with their beliefs even when that individual *clearly* had no choice in his or her actions. Logically, one should discount the behavior as an indication of the person's underlying beliefs when the individual had little or no control over their behavior. This bias toward internal attributions has been termed the "fundamental attribution error." While some (e.g., Harvey, Town and Trope, 1981; Monson and Snyder, 1977) have questioned whether or not the error is "fundamental", the evidence suggests that in many situations people are prone to make internal attributions. Attributional studies (e.g., Jones and Harris, 1967; Miller, 1976; Miller, Baer and Schonberg, 1979) have gone to great lengths to minimize the tendency to make internal attributions by exaggerating the salience of the external pressure on the actor. These studies do not successfully reduce the error because they do not challenge or negate subjects' belief in their ability to detect the truth despite the external pressure. This study suggests that the error is based on the presumed belief-persuasiveness correlation rather than the reduced salience of the external pressure.

How can we rectify the apparent contradiction between attributional research that indicates a tendency to accept the salesperson's word and the more commonly held view that consumers have widespread mistrust for sales claims. Two suggestions are posed. First, by considering trustworthiness from an attributional perspective, we have measured trustworthiness differently. In the traditional approach, subjects rate trustworthiness or credibility on a semantic differential scale. However, this is a rather leading question which is liable to prompt responses indicating a lack of trust for the message. Attributional studies, on the other hand, ask subjects to attribute a product attitude to the salesperson. That is, subjects try to estimate the salesperson's genuine product attitude, i.e., the degree to which they hold a certain attitude. These measures also show that the message is regarded with caution, i.e., subjects do not attribute very strong attitudes to the salesperson. Nevertheless, they do attribute product attitudes in the direction of the sales message. A second possible reason for the apparent contradiction may revolve around differences in mass media versus personal presentations. Perhaps the dishonesty that is perceived in advertising can be subsumed by a personal touch, i.e., a salesperson who appears to believe what they say. People just seem to trust other people. This underscores once again the importance of the sales message in determining perceived truthfulness.

These findings are somewhat distressing. With the propensity of consumers to believe in salespeople's veracity, the potential for consumers to be taken advantage of by unscrupulous salespersons evoking sincerity and confidence in their sales presentations could serve to undermine the integrity of boni fide sales professionals. Given the potential spill-over effect (a dissatisfactory purchase experience that carries over to the next purchase situation), there is a potential for pronounced public policy implications.

REFERENCES

Anderson, R.D., J.L. Engledow and H. Becker (1978), "How Consumer Reports Subscribers See Advertising," *Journal of Advertising Research*, 18, 29-34.

Baer, Robert (1990) "Overestimating Salesperson Truthfulness: The Fundamental Attribution Error," in *Advances in Consumer Research*, in press.

Bauer, Raymond and Stephen A. Greyser (1968), *Advertising in America: The Consumer's View*, Boston: Harvard University Press.

Bem, Daryl (1972), "Self Perception Theory" in *Advances in Experimental Social Psychology*, Vol. 6 ed. Leonard Berkowitz, New York: Academic Press.

Calder, Bobby J., and Burnkrant, Robert E. (1977), "Interpersonal Influence on Consumer Behavior: An Attribution Theory Approach," *Journal of Consumer Research*, 4, 29-38.

Folkes, Valerie, S., (1988), "Recent Attribution Research in Consumer Behavior: A Review and New Directions," *Journal of Consumer Research*, 14, 548-565.

Hansen, Robert A., and Scott, Carol A. (1976), "Comments on 'Attribution Theory and Advertiser Credibility'," *Journal of Marketing Research*, 13, 193-197.

Harvey, John, J.P. Town and K.L. Yarkin (1981), "How Fundamental is the "Fundamental Attribution Error?", *Journal of Personality and Social Psychology*, 40, 346-349.

Jones, Edward E., and Davis, Keith E. (1965). "From Acts to Dispositions: The Attribution Process in Person Perception," in *Advances in Experimental Social Psychology* Vol. 2 ed L. Berkowitz, New York: Academic Press.

_____ and V.A. Harris (1967), "The Attribution of Attitudes," *Journal of Experimental Social Psychology*, 3, 1-24.

Kelley, Harold (1967), "Attribution Theory in Social Psychology," in *Nebraska Symposium on Motivation*, ed. David Levine, Lincoln, NB: University of Nebraska Press.

_____ (1971). *Attribution in Social Interaction*. Morristown, NJ: General Learning Press.

_____ (1972), *Causal Schemata and the Attribution Process*, Morristown, NJ: General Learning Press.

Krugman, Dean M. and O.C. Ferrell (1981), "The Organizational Ethics of Advertising: Corporate and Agency Views," *Journal of Advertising*, 10, 21-30.

Miller, Arthur G. (1976), "Constraint and Target Effects in the Attribution of Attitudes," *Journal of Experimental Social Psychology* 12, 325-339.

_____ and Len Rorer (1982), "Toward an Understanding of the Fundamental Attribution Error: Essay Diagnosticity in the Attitude Attribution Paradigm," *Journal of Research in Personality*, 16, 41-59.

_____, Robert Baer and Pete Schonberg (1979), "The Bias Phenomena in Attitude Attribution: Actor and Observer Perspectives," *Journal of Personality and Social Psychology*, 37, 1421-1431.

Mizerski, Richard, Linda L. Golden and Jerome B. Kernan (1979), "The Attribution Process in Consumer Decision-Making," *Journal of Consumer Research*, 6, 123-140.

Monson, T.C. and Melvin Snyder (1977), "Actors, Observers and the Attributional Process: Toward a Reconceptualization," *Journal of Experimental Social Psychology*, 13, 89-111.

Pratkanis, Anthony, R., Anthony G. Greenwald, David L. Ronis, Michael R. Leippe and Michael H. Baumgardner, (1987) "Consumer-Product and Socio- Politcal Messages for Use in Studies of Persuasion," unpublished paper, Graduate School of Industrial Administration, Carnegie-Mellon University, Pittsburgh, PA 15213.

Reeder, Glenn D. and Maryln B. Brewer (1979), "A Schematic Model of Dispositional Attribution in Interpersonal Perception," *Psychological Review*, 86, 61-79.

―――― (1985), "Implicit Relations between Dispositions and Behaviors: Effects on Dispositional Attribution," In J.H. Harvey and G. Weary (Eds) *Attribution: Basic Issues and Applications*. New York: Academic Press.

―――― , Garth J.O. Fletcher, and Kenneth Furman (1989), "The Role of Observers' Expectations in Attitude Attribution," *Journal of Experimental Social Psychology*, 25, 168-188.

Ross, Lee (1977), "The Intuitive Psychologist and His Shortcomings: Distortion in the Attribution Process," in ed. *Advances in Experimental Social Psychology*, Vol. 10, New York: Academic Press.

Settle, Robert B., and Golden, Linda L. (1974), "Attribution Theory and Advertiser Credibility," *Journal of Marketing Research*, 11, 181-185.

Smith, Robert E., and Hunt, Shelby (1978), "The Effectiveness of Personal Selling over Advertising," in *Research Frontiers in Marketing: Dialogueand Directions*, ed Subhash C. Jain, Chicago: American Marketing Association, 158-163.

The Usefulness of Product Warranties for Reputable and New Brands

Daniel E. Innis, Ohio State University
H. Rao Unnava, Ohio State University[1]

This paper investigates the impact that product warranties have on consumer product evaluations for new and established high-performance brands. Results indicate that strong warranties affect product evaluations positively for new brands but have little effect for established reputable brands.

The role of product warranties in the marketing of products has undergone a significant change in the past several years. Used initially as an indicator of the limit of a manufacturer's liability in the event of product failure, warranty information is presently being used as a competitive weapon to differentiate one's product from competition. Contemporary examples include the 7/70 protection plan offered by Chrysler Corporation, and the now well-known claim by Victor Kiam that Remington shaving system "shaves as close as a blade or your money back."

Despite the increased importance attained by warranty information in the marketing of products, literature is sparse on the effects of warranty information on consumers' evaluations of products. Several studies have, in the past, examined the importance of warranty information to consumers (e.g., Olson and Jacoby 1972; Ross 1975; Lehmann and Ostlund 1973), and how product warranties affect consumers' perceptions of risk (Ross 1975; Bearden and Shimp 1982; Shimp and Bearden 1982). The conditions under which warranty information may or may not be effective, however, have received little attention. Specifically, if a relatively unknown manufacturer launches a new brand in the market, and provides attractive warranties that are superior to those provided by existing brands, should the existing brands match these warranties? In other words, does brand image interact with warranty information? The objective of the research reported here is to examine the interaction between brand image and warranty information. It is proposed that warranty information will be more effective in influencing evaluations of new brands than it will be in influencing evaluations of brands that hold positive images in consumers' minds.

BRAND NAME AS A MODERATOR OF WARRANTY INFORMATION

Consumers appear to be very sensitive to brand names and use them as risk relievers in their product choices (Shimp and Bearden 1982; Levitt 1967, Montgomery 1975). Research has shown that warranty information is not considered as important as brand name information (Olson and Jacoby 1972; Roselius 1971). However, consumers do seem to rely on warranty information to reduce risk and form product evaluations (Bearden and Shimp 1982). The positive effects of both brand name and warranty information on consumers' product evaluations should not be interpreted to mean that these effects are additive, however (cf. Olson and Jacoby 1972). These cues may interact with each other such that warranty information is effective only under certain conditions.

The influence of brand name on consumers' attitudes has received unequivocal support in the literature. In a classic study, Simon (1970) had subjects evaluate three brands in the home furnishings product category, based on advertisements for the three brands with their names masked. It was found that the evaluations given the three brands by the subjects were completely reversed when the brand names were revealed. The market leader, which was rated third in the masked condition, was rated highest when the brand names were available. Simon concluded that brand leaders, based on their reputation, will elicit more favorable response to their advertising than less-known manufacturers.

In a somewhat similar study, Jacoby, Olson and Haddock (1971) found that the evaluations given various brands of beer by their subjects were influenced by the presence of brand name information. Specifically, the difference between subjects' ratings of an ultra-premium brand and an inexpensive brand with brand names withheld widened when the brand names were revealed. The idea that an established brand name reduces perceived risk and enhances product evaluations has been supported by a number of other researchers as well (e.g., Shimp and Bearden 1982; Levitt 1967; Montgomery 1975; see also Rao and Monroe 1989).

Some of the earlier research on product warranties sought to assess the importance consumers attach to warranty information in their evaluation of products. For example, in one study, Olson and Jacoby (1972) asked housewives to indicate the factors they consider most important when they were contemplating the purchase of five different products (hairdryers, living room rug, ground coffee, shampoo and aspirin tablets). A list of over 12 factors was made available for each product. It was found that except in the case of hair dryers, housewives did not consider warranty information to be an important factor in the purchase of the experimental products. Brand name, on the other hand, was consistently indicated to be an important consideration in buying four of the five products.

Olson and Jacoby (1972), in discussing these results, proposed the distinction between intrinsic and extrinsic product quality cues. Intrinsic cues are

---

[1] The authors thank Paul Miniard and Peter Dickson for their valuable comments on an earlier version of this manuscript.

those product attributes that, when changed, will result in a change in the composition of the product itself. Extrinsic cues, on the other hand, can be changed without affecting the composition of the product (e.g., warranties, brand name). In the Olson and Jacoby study, subjects were found to use intrinsic cues more often than extrinsic cues to infer product quality. Based on this result, Olson and Jacoby suggested that when intrinsic cues are available to consumers, the effect of extrinsic cues on product quality perceptions will be reduced. More important, Olson and Jacoby argued that the effect of multiple cues will not be additive, but interactive (e.g., Jacoby, Olson and Haddock 1971). The limited use of warranty information by consumers as an aid to reduce their perceived risk has also been reported by Roselius (1971).

More recently, however, Bearden and Shimp (1982) varied the quality of warranty information, the reputation of the manufacturer offering the warranty, and the price of the product, in a 2 X 2 X 2 experimental design. Two products - plastic tires and an exercise jogging system - were used. Unlike prior research, Bearden and Shimp provided subjects with other information on the products, apart from the warranty, brand name and price information. Thus, the effect of these extrinsic cues was examined when they were embedded in other intrinsic cues. Perceived quality of and attitudes toward the products were used as the dependent measures. It was found that both warranty information and manufacturer reputation had significant effects on reducing consumers' perceived risk, and enhancing their attitude toward the products. The interaction between these two variables, however, was not examined.

The positive impact of warranty information on perceived product quality has also been reported by Perry and Perry (1976) and Shimp and Bearden (1982). It appears, therefore, that even in the presence of other intrinsic cues, consumers rely on warranty information to make inferences about product quality and form attitudes.

In terms of the possible interaction between brand name information and warranty information, Shimp and Bearden (1982) hypothesized an interaction between reputation of the warrantor and the quality of warranty. They argued that for reputable manufacturers, perceived risk should monotonically decrease with an increase in the quality of warranty. For an unknown manufacturer, however, Shimp and Bearden (1982) proposed a boomerang effect with better warranties actually resulting in negative attitudes. This argument was based on their assumption that when warranties that are very attractive are offered by unknown manufacturers, consumers will respond negatively because they think the warranty is 'too-good-to-be-true." In the Shimp and Bearden (1982) study, however, this interaction hypothesis was not supported.

Past research, however, indicates that both warranty information and brand name are used as risk reducers by consumers (Roselius 1971; Bearden and Shimp 1982; Shimp and Bearden 1982). Between brand name and warranty information, the former appears to be a more reliable risk reducer (Roselius 1971; Olson and Jacoby 1972). This suggests that an established brand name, by virtue of its record of good performance, is warrantying its performance to a prospective consumer. That is, consumers appear to be inferring a high probability of performance of an established brand based on its record of good performance in the past. In such conditions, the role of warranty information should be minimal, because a brand's past performance is acting as an implied warranty or as a signal of reliability. Thus, when a brand is well established in its product class, the role of warranty information in affecting consumers' evaluations of the brand should be minimal.

On the other hand, when a new brand is launched by a relatively unknown manufacturer, brand name can no longer act as a risk reliever. Consumers, in this case, should rely on warranty information to reduce their perceived risk about the possibility of product failure, assuming that warranty information is available. Therefore, for an unknown brand, warranty should affect consumer evaluations positively. In fact, consumer evaluations should increase monotonically with the quality of the warranty.

In sum, when consumers have available positive information about a brand's performance history, their reliance on warranty information in forming an evaluation of a new product under the same brand name would be limited. On the other hand, when no information is available to consumers about a brand's performance history, consumers will tend to rely on warranty information to form evaluations of that brand.

EXPERIMENT

The moderating effect of brand name on the effect of warranty information was tested in a 2 (brand name: established vs. unknown) X 3 (warranty quality: warranty information absent, three-month warranty, 10-year warranty) between-subjects design. A total of 120 subjects, recruited from undergraduate marketing classes, participated in the study for extra credit. Subjects were randomly assigned to treatment conditions.

Target Advertisement

A new brand of bicycle was used as the target product in this study. The choice of the target product was based on two considerations: 1) that the subjects in the sample will find the product relevant, and 2) that some degree of performance risk is associated with the product so that subjects will rely on warranty information in their product evaluations.

The information about the bicycle was presented in the form of an advertisement. The copy for the ad was derived from several existing bicycle ads in a cycling-enthusiast magazine. Seven strong and positive product claims (e.g, gel saddle to ease road shock) were presented along with a picture of the bicycle. The inclusion of these arguments rendered the test of the efficacy of warranty claims more conservative because it has been argued that the effect of extrinsic cues will be minimized in the presence of intrinsic cues (Olson and Jacoby 1972). The detection of effects of warranty information in these conditions would increase our confidence in the role of warranty information in consumer product evaluations.

Warranty Quality

The information about warranty was included as the eighth argument in the bicycle ad. In the condition where no warranty information was available, the eighth argument was not included. Thus, this condition acted as a control condition. An alternative would have been to include a phrase in the ad that there was no warranty for the bicycle. However, the presence of such a phrase was deemed to make subjects sensitive to warranty information, when in fact, they may be not. Thus, the effect of warranty information was gauged in a situation where subjects either processed it in conjunction with a substantial amount of other product-related information, or were not even primed to the existence of warranty information.

Brand Name

Two versions of the bicycle ad were developed to achieve the brand name manipulation. The first version promoted the bicycle as a new model in the Schwinn line of bicycles. Pretests revealed that the brand name Schwinn was associated with high performance and reliability. Thus, the use of the name 'Schwinn' was expected to arouse favorable impressions in subjects' minds. The second version of the target ad promoted the bicycle as a new model with a fictitious name Monarch. Pretests revealed that students were unfamiliar with Monarch bicycle. Thus, students could not rely on this brand name for performance assurance.

Procedure

The study was conducted with small groups of four to eight subjects each. Upon entering the experiment room, subjects were told that their task was to examine an ad for a new product and answer some questions about their impressions of the product. They were then given a booklet that contained some procedural instructions, the target ad, and the questionnaire.

The first question measured subjects' attitude toward the target product using five seven-point bi-polar scales (anchored by "very good- very bad", "very desirable-very undesirable", "very negative-very positive", "very superior-very inferior", and "very awful-very nice"). Following that, subjects indicated their likelihood of buying the advertised brand if they were in the market for a bicycle. Two seven-point scale were used to measure buying intention (anchored by "very likely-very unlikely" and "very probable-very improbable"). Finally, subjects responded to a series of eight questions that measured their product attribute beliefs. These questions were included to see if the warranty information had any effects on subjects' beliefs about the product attributes. The eight questions were derived from the eight arguments presented in the bicycle ad. Subjects indicated their agreement with each of the eight statements on a seven-point scale anchored by "strongly disagree" and "strongly agree". After completing the questionnaire, subjects were dismissed and debriefed the following day.

RESULTS

The data were coded so that higher scores meant more positive attitudes, higher buying intentions, and more positive beliefs about the product.

Manipulation checks

The awareness of the two experimental brands was first examined by comparing the number of subjects who indicated that they were aware of Schwinn and Monarch brands. All the respondents in the established brand category indicated that they had heard the Schwinn brand name before. Only three subjects (<6%) in the new brand condition indicated that they were aware of the Monarch brand name. In addition, more than 75% of the subjects rated Schwinn brand bicycles 'good'. Based on these data, the brand name manipulation was deemed successful.

Next, the rating provided by all the subjects on the quality of warranty offered by the target brand was submitted to an ANOVA with brand name reputation and warranty quality as the independent variables. The analysis revealed only a warranty main effect ($p<0.001$). As the quality of warranty increased, subjects indicated more agreement with the statement that the warranty offered by the target brand was good. This finding supported the warranty quality manipulation. The mean warranty rating scores are presented in Table 1. It is interesting to note from the mean warranty quality ratings that subjects perceived the difference between the 10-year warranty and no warranty to be greater for the unknown brand ($\Delta=2.31$) than for the established brand ($\Delta=1.36$). This may be viewed as preliminary support for the idea that warranty information has more impact for unknown brands than for established brands.

Attitude

The five scales composing the attitude measure were found to be highly reliable (Cronbach's $A = 0.95$). Therefore, the mean of these scales was computed and used in the analysis. The mean attitude scores are presented in table 1.

It was hypothesized that the quality of warranty information will interact with the brand name reputation. To test for this hypothesized interaction, an ANOVA was performed on the attitude score with warranty quality and brand name reputation as the independent variables. The ANOVA revealed no main effects ($p > 0.5$) for either the brand name or the warranty quality. There was, however, a significant interaction ($p < 0.03$)

TABLE 1
Mean Attitude, Buying Intention and Product Attribute Belief Scores By Experimental Condition

Measure	Established Brand			New Brand		
	No Warranty	3-month Warranty	10-year Warranty	No Warranty	3-month Warranty	10-year Warranty
Warranty rating	4.24	4.57	5.60	3.74	4.58	6.05
Attitude	5.79	5.56	5.57	5.35	5.68	5.89
Buying intention	5.26	4.79	4.72	4.79	5.11	5.40
Product belief index	5.54	5.33	5.54	5.23	5.52	5.73
n	21	21	20	19	19	20

between brand name and warranty quality and the direction of mean attitude scores were in the expected direction.

Given the nature of the hypothesis, a series of a-priori multiple t-tests were conducted (Kirk 1982, p.95). First, the mean attitude score for the established brand in the no warranty condition was contrasted with the mean attitude scores for the established brand when warranty information was available. The analyses revealed no significant differences between these conditions (p > 0.2 for both t-tests) which was supportive of the hypothesis. Similar t-tests were then conducted for the new brand. The analyses revealed that the mean attitude score for the new brand was significantly higher (p < 0.01) when it was accompanied by a ten-year warranty (M = 5.89) than when it was not (M=5.35). The difference between the attitude scores when the warranty was only three months (M=5.68) and the other experimental conditions, however, was not significant.

Because it was hypothesized that the attitude scores for the new brand will monotonically increase with the quality of warranty offered by it, a linear trend analysis was performed on those attitude scores. The analysis revealed that the attitude scores exhibited a linear trend as expected (F=4.8, p < 0.03). Thus, the hypothesis that warranty quality affects only new brands, but will not affect established brands was supported.

Buying Intention

The two scales used to measure buying intention correlated highly (r=0.9). Therefore, their mean was computed and used in an ANOVA with warranty quality and brand name reputation as the independent variables. Although the direction of means mirrored the attitude data, the interaction between warranty quality and brand name reputation was not significant (p<0.1).

A series of a-priori contrasts was then performed on the mean buying intention scores. Once again, no reliable differences between buying intentions were found between the various warranty quality conditions for the established brand (all p-values > 0.2). Surprisingly, no differences were exhibited by subjects in their likelihood of buying the target brand in the unknown brand condition, as a function of warranty quality. Thus, the attitude results did not extend to buying intention, although the direction of the means was in the expected direction.

Product attribute beliefs

The responses to the eight product attribute belief statements were submitted to a reliability analysis. The average inter-correlation between the responses was moderate (A=0.64). Therefore, the average of the responses to the belief questions was computed and used as an index of subjects' product attribute beliefs.

The belief index was then analyzed using ANOVA with warranty quality and brand name reputation as the independent variables. No main effects emerged (p > 0.5 for both main effects). The interaction between warranty quality and brand name reputation was, however, marginally significant (p < 0.1).

A priori pairwise contrasts were performed on the mean scores within each brand name condition. The contrasts revealed that the belief scores of the subjects were unaffected by the warranty quality manipulation when the brand name was well known (all p-values were > 0.2). For the unknown brand condition, however, subjects exhibited significantly more positive product attribute beliefs (p<0.01) when they were exposed to the 10-year warranty brand (M = 5.73) than when they were exposed to the no warranty brand (M = 5.23). The difference between the three-month warranty condition and the other two conditions was not significant (p>0.1). Thus, the belief index scores exhibited the same pattern as the attitude scores.

DISCUSSION

Previous research on warranty information has not examined how it interacts with the reputation of the warrantor. Our research examined the moderating effect of the reputation of the warrantor on the effect of warranty information on subjects' brand evaluations. It was hypothesized that warranty information exerts greater impact when it is offered by an unknown brand than when it is offered by a relatively established brand. This differential impact of warranty information was argued to be due to the risk-alleviating ability of an established brand name. The reduction of perceived risk by consumers that results from brand name reputation makes the role of warranty information for established brand names of minimal importance. For unknown brands, consumers do not have any past performance statistics to rely on for perceived risk reduction. Therefore, warranty information achieves greater importance when presented for an unknown brand because it performs the task of risk reduction. The perception of reduced risk, in turn, results in more positive attitudes toward the product (Bearden and Shimp 1982). This hypothesis was generally supported in our research. Subjects exhibited more favorable attitudes toward an unknown brand when a strong warranty was offered than when no warranty was offered. The attitude of subjects, however, was not influenced by the warranty offered by an established brand.

It is interesting that the direction of the interaction hypothesized in our research is opposite of what was hypothesized by Shimp and Bearden (1982). In the Shimp and Bearden study, warranty information was hypothesized to be more effective for established brands than for unknown brands. Their reasoning behind this expectation was that when outstanding warranties are offered with unknown brands, consumers may feel that these warranties are 'too-good-to-be-true'. The resulting counterargumentation was expected to reduce consumers' evaluations of unknown products that are coupled with good warranties. This pattern of interaction was not supported in the Shimp and Bearden (1982) study.

We believe that the 'too-good-to-be-true' perception of consumers is plausible but only under certain limited conditions. Specifically, for consumers to conclude that the warranty offered by an unknown manufacturer is too good to be true, the warranty should diverge from the industry standard significantly so that consumers would notice the disparity. This appears to be the case in the Shimp and Bearden study, especially for the plastic tire product. The positive warranty condition offered a full money-back guarantee if the tire did not perform as promised for 5 years or 50,000 miles. Warranties for tires are normally pro-rated. Consequently, a warranty that is not pro-rated appears suspicious. Second, for a consumer to discount warranty information based on a company's reputation, the consumer must hold a negative impression about the company. In the Shimp and Bearden study, the low reputation company was portrayed as a company that did *not have any experience* in manufacturing tires, but only in the manufacture of plastic products (p. 231-232 of Bearden and Shimp (1982)). An unknown manufacturer who advertises its product would not make consumers aware of its inexperience. Therefore, in reality, unless consumers hold negative attitudes toward a company or the warranty offered is incongruous with competitive warranties, warranty information more likely will evoke positive response from consumers.

In our research, differences in warranty quality were found to cause statistically significant, but only small differences in subjects' evaluations of the target product. Specifically, for an unknown brand, the difference in evaluations between the no warranty condition and the 10-year warranty condition was only 0.54 on a seven-point scale. The low sensitivity to warranty quality changes may indicate that warranty information may not be very important in consumers' product evaluations (Olson and Jacoby 1972; Roselius 1971). Another possible reason for the small differences in evaluations with changes in warranty quality may be the presence of strong product attribute information which might have overwhelmed the relatively less important warranty information. This explanation is consistent with the finding of Olson and Jacoby (1972) that people rely more on intrinsic cues than extrinsic cues to arrive at product evaluations.

When a new brand enters a market, it has to overcome steep barriers imposed by the brand images associated with existing high-performance brands. An important implication of our research is that a useful strategy in this situation is for the new brand to differentiate itself from the competition through the use of warranties. This is because it was found that the evaluations given by subjects to the new brand with a strong warranty were equivalent to the evaluations given to an established brand with a strong reputation but no warranty. Warranty information, however, did not affect subjects' evaluations of a well-known high performance brand. Therefore, in a competitive market where consumers have well-defined images of the existing brands, our results indicate that the use of warranty by a market leader as a means of differentiation may not be as effective.

Several other extrinsic cues that have been researched in the past include price, country of origin, and store image. Future research should examine the interactive nature of these cues. However, as Rao and Monroe (1989) suggest, "...Further, the interactive effect of brand name, store name, and price on quality perceptions should be investigated." (p.356). Our research underscores the interactive nature of extrinsic cues, as pointed out by Olson and Jacoby (1972), by examining the interaction between warranty quality and brand name. Future research should examine the interactive nature of other cues.

REFERENCES

Bearden, William O. and Terence A. Shimp (1982), "The Use of Extrinsic Cues to Facilitate Product Adoption," *Journal of Marketing Research*, 19 (May), 229-239.

Bilkey, Warren J. and Nes, Erik (1982), Country of Origin Effects on Product Evaluations," *Journal of International Business Studies*, Spring/Summer, 89-99.

Jacoby, Jacob, Jerry Olson and Rafael Haddock (1971), "Price, Brand Name, and Product Composition Characteristics as Determinants of Perceived Quality," *Journal of Applied Psychology*, 55 (6), 570-579.

Kirk, Roger E. (1982), *Experimental Design: Procedures for Behavioral Sciences*, Monterey, CA: Brooks/Cole.

Lehmann, Donald and Lyman Ostlund (1972), "Consumer Perceptions of Product Warranties: An Exploratory Study," in *Proceedings, Third Annual Conference of Association for Consumer Research*, ed. M. Venkatesan, Chicago: Association for Consumer Research, 51-65.

Levitt, Theodore (1967), "Communications and Industrial Selling," *Journal of Marketing*, Vol. 31, 15-21.

Montgomery, David B. (1975), "New Product Distribution: An Analysis of Supermarket Buyer Decisions," *Journal of Marketing Research*, Vol. 12, 255-264.

Olson, Jerry and Jacob Jacoby (1972), "Cue Utilization in the Quality Perception Process," in *Proceedings of the Third Annual Conference of the Association for Consumer Research*, ed. M. Venkatesan, Iowa City: Association for Consumer Research, 167-179.

Perry, Michael and Arnon Perry (1976), "Service Contract Compared to Warranty as a Means to Reduce Consumer's Risk," *Journal of Retailing*, 52 (Summer), 33-40.

Rao, Akshay and Kent Monroe (1989), "The Effect of Price, Brand Name, and Store Name on Buyers' Perceptions of Product Quality: An Integrative Review," *Journal of Marketing Research*, 26 (August), 351-357.

Roselius, Ted (1971), "Consumer Rankings of Risk Reduction Methods," *Journal of Marketing*, 35 (January), 56-61.

Ross, Ivan (1975), "Perceived Risk and Consumer Behavior: A Critical Review," in *Advances in Consumer Research, Vol. 2*, ed. M. Schlinger, Cincinnati: Association for Consumer Research, 1-19.

Shimp, Terence and William Bearden (1982), "Warranty and Other Extrinsic Cue Effects on Consumers' Risk Perceptions," *Journal of Consumer Research*, 9 (June), 38-46.

Simon, Marji (1970), "Influence of Brand Names on Attitudes," *Journal of Advertising Research*, 3 (June), 28-30.

Wiener, Joshua (1985), "Are Warranties Accurate Signals of Product Reliability?," *Journal of Consumer Research*, 12 (September), 245-250.

"The Good Old Days": Observations On Nostalgia and Its Role In Consumer Behavior

William J. Havlena, Rutgers University
Susan L. Holak, Rutgers University

ABSTRACT

Nostalgia--a longing to return home--was first described by Johannes Hofer in 1688. Recently it has received increased attention from marketers and advertisers. The literature on nostalgia from psychology and sociology is used to introduce a brief survey and description of the use of nostalgia in marketing and its impact on consumer behavior. Products and advertisements aimed at two broad market segments--"baby boomers" and senior citizens--are examined. Two types of nostalgic products and advertisements are noted: (1) products or messages drawn directly from the past and (2) new products and messages that create a "period" feeling. Based on these observations, the paper offers some suggestions for future research.

INTRODUCTION

One notable trend as we leave the 1980's and enter the decade of the 90's is the increasing visibility of nostalgia--"a painful yearning to return home"--in marketing, advertising, and entertainment media. Despite the popularity of nostalgic products and messages, little research has studied nostalgia within the context of consumer behavior.

Nostalgia as an emotion contains both pleasant and unpleasant components. This "bittersweet" quality of the emotion is a distinguishing characteristic of nostalgia. It refers back to an earlier period in the individual's life and draws on biased or selective recall of past experiences.

This paper will review the concept of nostalgia and its history from its first appearance in 1688 in a paper by Johannes Hofer. It will then present some observations concerning nostalgia and illustrate them using current advertising and marketing examples.

DEFINITIONS OF AND PAST RESEARCH CONCERNING NOSTALGIA

What is Nostalgia?

The word "nostalgia" has a Greek derivation with two roots: "nostos" meaning to "return home or to one's native land" and "algos" referring to "pain, suffering, or grief" (Hofer 1688; Daniels 1985). This condition was first discussed by Johannes Hofer in his thesis which was presented to Johannes Harder, a Doctor of Philosophy and Medicine and Professor of Anatomy and Botany at the University of Alsace in 1688. Hofer's contribution was considered a key work in psychological and psychosomatic medicine for at least two reasons: (1) he was the first individual to describe nostalgia as a clinical condition, and (2) in his writing he gave credence to the effects of mind over body (Martin 1954).

Symptoms. Throughout history, nostalgia has been associated with a myriad of physiological and psychological symptoms. According to Hofer's dissertation (1688), sufferers "wander about sad," experience insomnia, suffer from fever, hunger, thirst, diminished senses, and a loss of strength. Given the medical paradigm involving humors popular at the time, Hofer contended that nostalgia resulted from thoughts of home due to animal spirits in the innermost parts of the brain. These spirits caused the blood to thicken and the heart to slow. It was thought that death could result unless the sufferer were somehow transported back to his or her home (Hofer 1688; Martin 1954). McCann (1941) wrote of physiological symptoms affecting the respiratory and circulatory systems as well as other bodily functions. Psychological suffering was thought to take the form of loss of appetite, nausea, listlessness, fainting, and varied additional symptoms.

History. Although perhaps not documented in such an explicit manner as in Hofer's work, nostalgia has appeared in literature and poetry through the ages in references to homesickness. From Biblical psalms to the writings of Homer, Hippocrates, and Caesar, the yearning for one's home is a reoccurring motif (Martin 1954). Throughout history, nostalgia was known to adversely affect troops from Caesar's centurions of Helvetian Gaul, where the condition was called "la Maladie du Pays" (Hofer 1688), to soldiers in the more recent world wars (Martin 1954; Nawas and Platt 1965). All sorts of maladies and behaviors, including pyromania, were diagnosed as resulting from a nostalgic condition (Martin 1954). In more recent times, nostalgia or homesickness was listed among the standard medical diagnoses by the Surgeon General (Martin 1954). As Fodor (1950, p. 25) writes, "Nostalgia is not a mental disease but it may develop into a monomaniacal, obsessive mental state causing intense unhappiness and leading to a complete uprooting of a settled existence. It usually manifests itself in an intense desire to return to the country or town from where we came, or --- on more acute analysis --- to return to the home which we had left behind." It is no wonder then that the nostalgic condition is a major cause of freshman dropouts on the college campus (Nawas and Platt 1965). As noted by Beardsley Ruml [cited by Martin (1954)], "Nostalgia is older and more fundamental than human nature itself and all people of the world, all ages and all temperaments, weak and strong, are more or less susceptible to it." Authorities have even noted that symptoms which resemble those experienced by nostalgic humans are exhibited by animals (Martin 1954).

Despite its prevalence in history, however, relatively little formal study has been made of the condition. It is interesting to note that the few early cases and writings concerned displaced Swiss soldiers as discussed by Swiss authors almost exclusively, giving the early impression that this specific nationality was particularly nostalgia-prone (Martin 1954). According to Martin (1954, p. 94), "...We should note that although it had gone beyond the province of medicine, nostalgia never attracted the degree of scientific interest warranted by its universal occurrence." Nawas and Platt (1965, p. 51) corroborate this observation as follows, "It is rather curious that a phenomenon as pressing, as ubiquitous, and as little understood as nostalgia has received only passing attention from psychologists; in the last quarter century no more than six empirical studies have appeared on the subject."

Research in Clinical Psychology

Researchers in the clinical psychology field trace the cause of nostalgia to a human desire to return to the womb. Even Hofer contended that those stricken "do not know how to forget their mother's milk" (Martin 1954, p.94). In his psychoanalytic analysis, Fodor (1950) noted that humans sense that they had a safe, comfortable existence in their pre-natal state. This perfect happiness appears symbolically in many forms and outlets, including Biblical teachings. According to Fodor (1950, p. 35), "The Biblical concept of Heaven is a projection of organismic memories of a Canaan flowing with milk and honey, where wants were satisfied without wanting, and where we reigned as kings and were the absolute center of the universe because nothing else seemed to exist, the post-natal world being as yet beyond comprehension." Freud maintained that nostalgia had a basis in adorned memories and dreams as noted by Daniels (1985, p. 379) who wrote, "Freud (1906) illustrates perhaps more simply the 'message of nostalgia': the desire to return to a hidden home, to monuments concocted of our wanderings through the half-forgotten memories of another time, festooned and elaborated by our present fantasies."

Recent Perspectives on Nostalgia

A more recent interpretation of nostalgia has altered considerably from its medical, often pathological, base to connote more of a sociological phenomenon. According to Davis (1979, p. 4), "Not only does the word *nostalgia* appear to have been fully 'demilitarized' and 'demedicalized' by now but, with its rapid assimilation into American popular speech since roughly the nineteen-fifties, it appears to be undergoing a process of 'depsychologization' as well." Given the meteoric increase in mobility in today's society, individuals are less attached to a country, town, or particular house than in the past. As a result, "homesickness" no longer applies in the same way when describing nostalgic emotion. Rather, from the sociological perspective, nostalgia allows human beings to maintain their identity in the face of major transitions which serve as discontinuities in the life cycle (e.g., the identity change from childhood to pubescence, from adolescence to adulthood, from single to married life, from spouse to parent, etc.). Not all past experiences or eras are equally likely to evoke nostalgic feelings. Nostalgia for adolescence and early adulthood appears to be stronger than for any other period. In addition, this tendency to engage in nostalgic feelings varies over the course of the individual's lifetime. "Nostalgia-proneness" has been hypothesized to peak as individuals move into middle age and during the "retirement" years.

Men have been deemed to be more nostalgic than women, given that in western culture they have until very recently experienced more life cycle discontinuities (Davis 1979). Other research implies that the character and subject matter of nostalgia for men and women may differ as well. Csikszentmihalyi and Rochberg-Halton (1981), in their study of "special" objects, found that older subjects and women were more likely than men and children to cherish objects as a source of memories. While men tended to mention objects of action (such as sports equipment, televisions, and vehicles), women tended to mention objects of contemplation (such as photographs, artwork, plates, and textiles). Although not examined by the authors, one might expect similar gender differences in the types of stimuli that evoke nostalgic feelings.

Aggregation. Given these universal yet individual transitions, there exist personal or private and collective or societal realms of nostalgic experience (Davis 1979). The intersubjectivity element associated with nostalgia is noted by Daniels (1985, p. 372) who wrote, "An inquiry concerning nostalgia is difficult -- more than some experiences, it can be peculiarly private: what is nostalgic for me may leave another indifferent." Given the structure of society, its values, and conventions, we experience life's discontinuities along with others who are our contemporaries. As a result, there is a "collective identity" among members of the same generation in terms of their nostalgic experiences (Davis 1979, p. 101). It is possible for these two levels to overlap and be intertwined as evidenced in the following example (Davis 1979, p. 124), "Thus, a nostalgic summoning of 'everybody's favorite song of 1943' (essentially a collectively oriented symbol) may inwardly shade off into some very private reminiscences of a particular romance in a particular place on a particular day, replete with special fragrances, sounds and visual traces."

Relevant Past. A key element defining nostalgia according to Davis (1979) is that while experiences undoubtedly draw from the past, they must draw from *one's own* personal history rather than from books, stories, publications, etc. An individual cannot be nostalgic for a period, event, etc., during which he or she has not lived. As noted earlier, because of the preponderance of key life cycle discontinuities during adolescence and early adulthood, this has been observed to be a particularly potent period from which to draw nostalgic experiences (Davis 1979). Memories tend to be filtered and recalled sans negative elements.

Generations. Although nostalgic experience is defined to draw from one's lived past, there is an important intergenerational phenomenon. As one generation both privately and collectively reminisces about its adolescence, these memories become, in essence, a new experience for the next generation. As Davis (1979, p. 61) noted, "...when today's adolescents reach middle age it is probable that their nostalgic revivals will include symbolic fragments and residues of what had been the nostalgia of their parents."

Orders of Nostalgia. An important distinction has been made by Davis (1979) among three orders or levels of nostalgic experience. *First order* or *simple nostalgia* is associated with the base belief that "things were better in the past." According to Davis (1979, p. 21), "The emotional posture is that of a yearning for return, albeit accompanied often by an ambivalent recognition that such is not possible." In *second order* or *reflexive nostalgia*, individuals question or analyze the past rather than sentimentalize it. The posture is much more a sense of "was it really that way?" (Davis 1979). Finally, in *third order* or *interpreted nostalgia*, the individual analyzes to a much greater extent his or her nostalgic experience. Davis (1979, p. 24) writes, "The actor here seeks in some fashion to objectify the nostalgia he feels. He directs at it (again with varying diligence and to varying degree) *analytically oriented* questions concerning its sources, typical character, significance, and psychological purpose. Why am I feeling nostalgic?" While second order nostalgia attempts to analyze the past critically, third order nostalgia analyzes the nostalgic response itself.

Consumer Research and Nostalgia

Two related papers examine the role of the past in determining current preferences and perceptions. Holbrook (1990) has developed an index for the measurement of nostalgia-proneness and nostalgic feelings that appears to have satisfactory reliability and some degree of face and predictive validity. This index supplements the empirical work done by McCann (1943) on the measurement of nostalgia and extends this research into a consumption-oriented setting. More research in this area is necessary to refine the index and test it in a broader range of situations. Holbrook and Schindler (1989) found that respondents favored music popular during their late adolescence or early adulthood, with the peak in preferences occurring between 23 and 24 years of age. This finding supports Davis's (1979) hypothesis concerning the most fertile period(s) for nostalgic reflection.

THE USE OF NOSTALGIA IN MARKETING AND ADVERTISING

References to the past in the marketplace reach back to periods within the consumer's own experience--possibly ranging from perhaps ten to seventy years--and to eras that predate the consumer's lifespan. They may evoke memories of peaceful, pleasant times or of times of tension and turmoil. The current boom of nostalgia-based products, advertising and promotional messages, magazines, and radio and television programming is targeted primarily to two large groups of consumers: the baby-boomers (now in their late 30s and 40s) and senior citizens.

To reach these consumers, the current wave of nostalgia-related marketing looks back primarily to the 1960s and to the 1930s and 40s. These are periods consistent with the adolescence or early adulthood of members of the "baby boom" generation, now in their late 30s or early 40s, and the senior citizen market. The following section will discuss several examples of the use of nostalgia in television and print advertising, examining both the subjects of nostalgia and the means used to encourage nostalgic feelings.

A parallel trend has been the increase in interest in the more distant past, as reflected in the success of magazines and books dealing with the 19th century and the early 20th century. The contrast between the evocation of nostalgia for the recent past and the elicitation of feelings for the more distant past will also be discussed. While interest in the 1800s or early 1900s may reflect a longing for a "golden age," it is not identical with true nostalgia (as narrowly defined in the research reviewed earlier), which relies primarily on individual memories and experience. However, the feelings of warmth, happiness, and security that may be evoked by these messages are likely to be similar enough to those evoked by true "nostalgic" messages to warrant classifying these magazines, books, and advertisements as "nostalgia-based" stimuli. Therefore, we feel that a broader definition of nostalgia may be appropriate in the context of consumer behavior.

Products and Advertising Appeals

Advertising for products may consciously evoke past associations and memories to create or recall positive affective responses. The products themselves may also engender nostalgic emotions during consumption, allowing consumers to "re-experience" aspects of their past or to experience the collective past of the society vicariously through fantasy in much the same manner as Disney's Main Street U.S.A. allows visitors to "experience" as small town America that never really existed.

Numerous products and packages from the past or inspired by the past have been (re)introduced or (re)positioned to appeal explicitly to consumers' nostalgic feelings. Many of the products evoke a distant past beyond the direct experience of most consumers. For example, General Foods recently introduced Maxwell House 1892 Slow-Roasted Coffee. The can is a copy of a 19th-century design (Rothenberg 1989). Print advertising for the product claims that "1892 was a very good year for coffee" and evokes images of an era when merchants "did things a little differently" and "with something of a reverence for the old way of making things." Television advertising for 1892 coffee is filled with images of small-town activities and patriotism from a not-too-clearly-defined time in the past. Kellogg's celebrated the sixtieth anniversary of Rice Krispies with advertising images from the 1920s. In a similar manner, Hershey recreated a "Vintage Edition" package design from 1912 for its milk chocolate bars and the Dial Corporation packaged 20 Mule Team Borax in an "period"-design box. Although these products are either new or have been available continuously since their introduction, the packaging and/or messages clearly conjure up impressions of a bygone era when "things were better."

The past evoked by these products and packages is an idealized image of a period in our cultural history. This nostalgia for a past era in our nation's history crosses ethnic and subcultural boundaries. When Lord & Taylor chose a Victorian theme for the store's Christmas decorations last year a vice president of the store noted that "it gives everyone a warm, cozy feeling and brings back memories" (Fabricant 1989). It did not matter that many consumers' own personal memories may have had little in common with Victorian decoration, horse-drawn sleighs, and plum pudding. Similarly, the scenes of small town life depicted in the Maxwell House ads for 1892 coffee are designed to evoke a warm feeling of nostalgia, even among consumers for whom home is the Upper West Side of Manhattan and whose ancestors never directly experienced small-town America.

The non-literal nature of many of the images associated with nostalgia is illustrated by the new plazas being constructed along the [New York] Gov. Thomas E. Dewey Thruway (*The New York Times* 1990a). Designed in a turn-of-the-century Adirondack style, they are intended to "bring up images of holidays and vacations." However, despite the stone or brick 19th-century exteriors and slate roofs, the interiors will be modern, with brightly colored synthetic materials, and will contain such familiar names as Burger King and Bob's Big Boy. Consumers will be able to fantasize about a lost era of travel without having to forgo a Whopper for lunch.

Other products evoke a period more directly related to the consumer's own past, more closely allied to the original meaning of nostalgia. For most baby boomers, this means a past and a home heavily influenced by television programming and advertising. One group of products and advertising messages attempts to evoke strong childhood memories. Thus, Leaf Inc. is using television commercials featuring "Frankie and the Switzers," a parody of 1960s-style singing groups, to advertise Switzer's licorice and is bringing back Choo-Choo Charlie to promote Good and Plenty candy (Scott 1989). Parents of young children will be transported back to their own childhood when Punchy asks "How about a nice Hawaiian Punch?" (Schiller 1990). Jiffy Pop popcorn combats the trend to microwave popcorn by reminding consumers that "Some things are even better than you remember," a strong claim considering the filtering and positive halo typically attached to nostalgic memories. Sonic, a chain of drive-in restaurants, has grown by targeting aging baby boomers, adopting a 50s image and using Frankie Avalon as the company spokesperson (Diamond 1989).

Other products and themes targeted to baby boomers may be more strongly associated with adolescence or early adulthood, a particularly fertile period for nostalgic reminiscence (Davis 1979; Holbrook and Schindler 1989). Coca-Cola directly evokes its advertising of twenty years ago with its remake of "I'd Like to Teach the World to Sing" (Mabry 1990). In the mid '80s Rhino Records reissued the 20-year-old recordings of the Monkees as "Original Classics" (Morris 1986). (Shortly thereafter the television series was itself rebroadcast on Nickelodeon, a cable network specializing in "nostalgia" programming from the 1960s and '70s.) As we move into the 90s, the interval of about twenty years noted by Davis (1979) between an individual's first major nostalgic period and his/her strongest memories is clearly illustrated by the return of the ubiquitous Happy Face on new clothing styles (Hirsch 1989), beehive hairstyles, and the release of such recorded compilations as "Have a Nice Day: Super Hits of the '70s" (Pareles 1990).

Other marketers have targeted an older market. Joe Franklin Productions plans to introduce such products as a "Nostalgicize" exercise video (complete with 1940's music, a period of adolescence for many of those exercising to the tape) and the Memory Lane Club of America, a service aimed at collectors of old records and movies (Viuker 1987). Warner-Lambert is once again selling Beeman's, Clove, and Blackjack chewing gum, brands likely to be recognized by older consumers.

A retail industry has emerged to satisfy the desire of consumers for products from their past (Smith n.d.). The purchasers of these objects are more apt to be men than women. As Alan Dershowitz notes (1987, p. 46),

> Salesmen at the nostalgia shops tell me that men in their 40's and 50's experience the need to "collect" their adolescence more than women do. "When I see a guy with a goofy looking grin dragging a couple of teen-age kids through my door on a weekend, I know my summer vacation will be paid for," one shop owner told me. "But if he's got his wife with him, he'll probably buy just one sensible memento for his office."

While products such as Maxwell House 1892 coffee may "safely" construct a past with carefully-controlled images, products and images directly related to the consumer's own past may evoke a host of memories both good and bad. Certainly, the 1960s (for baby boomers) and the 1940s (for their parents) were periods in history of great turmoil and are as likely to evoke negative emotions as positive ones. While "I'd like to teach the world to sing" may be fondly remembered by a generation of Coca-

Cola consumers, the memories it evokes may not all be pleasant. However, the vividness of these memories may result in consumers quickly noticing and remembering the new commercial. In addition, first order (or simple) nostalgia tends to filter information, leaving the consumer with the impression that life (or a product) was better in the past that it (perhaps) really was.

Media

The recent appearance of magazines like Memories: *The Magazine of Then and Now*, *Nostalgia Magazine*, and *Joe Franklin's Nostalgia* contain page after page of articles discussing the 1940s, '50s, and '60s and represent a direct appeal to nostalgic sentiments (Malanga 1990). Memories has proved so successful that NBC is producing a television spinoff based on the magazine (Rothenberg 1990). By 1984, close to 200 radio stations had adopted a "nostalgia" format, programming popular music of the '30s and '40s (McGuigan 1984). The "Music of Your Life" syndicated format has extended this approach forward to the 1960s, targeting the 35-and-older audience ignored by many popular music stations. Television programs such as *The Wonder Years* and the programming on "Nick at Nite" put the viewer in the context of the 1960s. Targeting a different audience, the Nostalgia Channel specializes in older movies aimed at the "over 49 market" (*Broadcasting* 1987). These magazines and programs provide an obvious outlet for nostalgia-based marketing messages; some of the magazines encourage reproduction of period advertising. As in the case of recent products (i.e., those remembered from childhood or adulthood) the articles and programs evoke specific associations in the minds of consumers. For example, The *Wonder Years* uses visual images, products, music, fashions, and news reports to clearly evoke the late 1960s.

Not only is there a boom in current programming and advertising that turns to the past for inspiration, but there is also a sizable market for old programs and advertisements themselves. For example, Video Resources produces a 16-page newsletter advertising twenty-four one-hour video volumes of "Classic Commercials," as well as more specialized videos of beer commercials, car commercials, and kids commercials (*The New York Times* 1990b).

The success of *Victoria* magazine illustrates the strong appeal of a past that is well beyond the direct experience of its readership and that in many instances has little to do with the reality of the period being evoked (Foltz 1990). These "manufactured memories" are quite similar to the messages used in advertising such as the Maxwell House 1892 coffee ads discussed above.

DISCUSSION

Nostalgia--the longing to return to home, whether real or fantasized, whether in the recent or distant past--exerts an influence in varied aspects of consumer and consumption behavior. Although first described as a pathological phenomenon, current research views nostalgia as a milder, "normal" condition that contains both personal and universal characteristics. The apparent tendency of individuals to feel nostalgic emotions more strongly during transitional periods in the life cycle has not gone unrecognized by advertisers and marketers. The simultaneous passage from one life stage to another by two large, important consumer market segments-- the baby boomers and the senior market--has provided marketers with an unusual opportunity to capitalize on this inclination.

Nostalgic messages targeted toward baby boomers have focused on the 1960s and early 1970s, an interval of approximately twenty years. This mirrors neatly the difference between the generation's period of adolescence and the present. It is interesting to note that "period" television programs of a decade ago (e.g., *Happy Days*, *Laverne and Shirley*) were often set in the 1950s, preserving the twenty-year gap between the subject matter and the current time period. This decade seems much less evident in current advertising and television programming aimed at a young adult audience. Similarly, media and messages aimed at senior citizens tend to concentrate on the 1930s and 1940s, when those now in their sixties and early seventies were adolescents and young adults.

The products and messages used by advertisers seem designed to elicit first order (or simple) nostalgia (Davis 1979). There is little attempt to critically examine the past. In fact, such an analysis would tend to negate much of the power of nostalgia in marketing situations, since the appeals seem to be designed to produce positive affective responses with a minimum of cognitive processing of negative information. One interesting example is the Jiffy Pop slogan ("Some things are even better than you remember"), which explicitly argues against the tendency (characteristic of second order nostalgia) to examine the past objectively.

One clear distinction may be drawn between (1) nostalgia-based marketing messages for new brands or products and (2) inherently nostalgic products or services. Sonic restaurants may evoke the 1950s through decor, music, and commercial spokesmen, but the restaurants themselves remain basically a new experience for most consumers. Products such as Good and Plenty, Jiffy Pop popcorn, Coca-Cola, and Ovaltine are themselves likely to evoke memories of past times and to inspire nostalgic reflection, not only through advertising appeals but through the consumption of the products themselves. The advertising may explicitly encourage the retrieval of these memories through cues such as music, jingles, slogans, and visual images. In these cases, the consumer already has a potentially complex network of associations built up around the product and the marketer only needs to facilitate access. As mentioned earlier, there is some risk of recalling negative associations, but one important characteristic of nostalgia is the filtering of negative information--

the past is almost always remembered as better or happier than it probably was (Davis 1979).

CURRENT CONSUMER RESEARCH IN NOSTALGIA AND DIRECTIONS FOR FUTURE RESEARCH

Two papers presented at the 1990 Conference of the Association for Consumer Research examine the impact of age on the formation of preferences for different stimuli. Holbrook and Schindler (1990) extend their research concerning musical tastes to relate the shape of the preference curve for actors and actresses to nostalgia, using the Nostalgia Index described above. Schindler and Holbrook (1990) use the Nostalgia Index to examine the relationship of nostalgic tendencies to fashion tastes.

An exploratory empirical examination of nostalgia in the domain of consumer behavior is currently underway and is designed to address the following issues:

1] perceptions of nostalgia as related to consumption,
2] the characteristics of "nostalgic experience,"
3] the identification of the types of products and messages most suited to the use of nostalgia, and
4] the relationship of individual characteristics to nostalgia-proneness.

This study will assist in identifying the range of nostalgic experiences in a consumer framework and help to develop a working definition of nostalgia in an advertising and consumption context.

Additional research is needed to refine measures of consumption-specific nostalgic reactions and nostalgia-proneness across a wider variety of products, services, and consumption situations and for diverse groups of consumers. In addition, research concerning the impact of various stimuli (music, images, objects, smells) on the evocation of nostalgic feelings, and the effectiveness of alternative modalities in evoking nostalgia is needed.

REFERENCES

Broadcasting (1987), "Nostalgia Channel's Weisberg Predicts Bright Future for Cable", July 27, 104-105.

Csikszentmihalyi, Mihaly and Eugene Rochberg-Halton (1981), *The Meaning of Things: Domestic Symbols and the Self*, Cambridge: Cambridge University Press.

Daniels, Eugene B. (1985), "Nostalgia and Hidden Meaning," *American Image*, 42, 371-383.

Davis, Fred (1979), *Yearning for Yesterday: A Sociology of Nostalgia*, New York: The Free Press.

Dershowitz, Alan M. (1987), "Collectible Adolescence," *The New York Times Magazine*, May 31, 46.

Diamond, Helene (1989), "Marketing By Nostalgia: Looking Back Pays Off For Restaurant Industry," *Marketing News*, August 14, 6.

Fabricant, Florence (1989), "Victorian Era: Holiday Images For All Times," *The New York Times*, November 29, C1, C6.

Fodor, Nandor (1950), "Varieties of Nostalgia," *Psychoanalytic Review*, 37, 25-38.

Foltz, Kim (1990), "Victoria Uses Old Charms On Readers," *The New York Times*, July 31, D17.

Hirsch, James (1989), "Happy Face Has a Nice New Day," *The New York Times*, February 15, 13, 21.

Hofer, Johannes [trans. Carolyn Kiser Anspach] (1934), "Medical Dissertation on Nostalgia by Johannes Hofer, 1688," *Bulletin of the History of Medicine*, 2, 376-391.

Holbrook, Morris B. (1990), "Nostalgic Consumption: On the Reliability and Validity of a New Nostalgia Index," Working paper.

Holbrook, Morris B. and Robert M. Schindler (1989), "Some Exploratory Findings on the Development of Musical Tastes," *Journal of Consumer Research*, 16 (June), 119-124.

Holbrook, Morris B. and Robert M. Schindler (1990), "Some Propositions on the Role of Nostalgia in Shaping the Development of Consumer Tastes: An Audiovisual Preview of a Project on the Relation of Liking for the Appearances of Actors and Actresses to Individual Differences in Longing for the Dear Departed Past," Paper presented at the 1990 Conference of the Association for Consumer Research, New York, New York, October 4-7.

Jacobson, Mark (1987), "The Way We Weren't," *Esquire*, October, 65-68.

Mabry, Marcus (1990), "Remembrance of Ads Past," *Newsweek*, July 30, 42.

Malanga, Steve (1990), "How Sweet It Is On Memory Lane," *Crain's New York Business*, March 19, 1, 37.

Martin, Alexander R. (1954), "Nostalgia," *The American Journal of Psychoanalysis*, 14, 93-104.

McCann, Willis H. (1941), "Nostalgia: A Review of the Literature," *Psychological Bulletin*, 38 (3), 165-182.

McCann, Willis H. (1943), "Nostalgia: A Comparative and Descriptive Study," *Journal of Genetic Psychology*, 62, 97-104.

McGuigan, Cathleen (1984), "Memories Are Made of This," *Newsweek*, February 27, 69.

Morris, Chris (1986), "Monkeemania Reaps $$ for Rhino," *Billboard*, July 12, 46.

Nawas, M. Mike and Jerome J. Platt (1965), "A Future-Oriented Theory of Nostalgia," *Journal of Individual Psychology*, 21, 51-57.

New York Times, The (1990a), "Nostalgia and a Burger For Thruway Motorists", April 5, C3.

New York Times, The (1990b), "One Man's Obsession With Past Creates Wave of TV Nostalgia," August 2, C1, C10.

Pareles, John (1990), "The 70's Revisited: The Nostalgia Trail Hits Rock Bottom," *The New York Times*, April 15, 28.

Rothenberg, Randall (1989), "The Past Is Now the Latest Craze," *The New York Times*, November 29, D1, D19.

Rothenberg, Randall (1990), "NBC Planning Nostalgia Show," *The New York Times*, May 9, D17.

Schiller, Zachary (1990), "The Punch P&G Will Put Behind Hawaiian Punch," *Business Week*, March 26, 42.

Schindler, Robert M. and Morris B. Holbrook (1990), "The Role of Nostalgia in the Development of Tastes: A Test in the Context of Fashion Advertising," Paper presented at the 1990 Conference of the Association for Consumer Research, New York, New York, October 4-7.

Scott, Carlee R. (1989), "For Candy Maker, Recipe for Success Includes Nostalgia," *The Wall Street Journal*, June 16.

Smith, Robert L. (n.d.), *The Nostalgia Merchants*, Audio recording, Kalamazoo, MI: Western Michigan University.

Viuker, Steven J. (1987), "Television's Master of Memory Lane Goes Public," *The New York Times*, November 22, F7.

Echoes of the Dear Departed Past: Some Work in Progress On Nostalgia

Morris B. Holbrook, Columbia University[1]
Robert M. Schindler, Rutgers University - Camden

ABSTRACT

This paper provides a brief preview of some work in progress on the phenomenon of nostalgia in consumer behavior. It begins by introducing some background considerations and key definitions. It then reviews an initial finding on what appears to be a nostalgia-related preference peak in musical tastes. Three limitations in this study suggest directions for further research. The resulting work in progress involves three studies designed to address various aspects of these three limitations.

NOSTALGIA IS OLD

The phenomenon of nostalgia is almost as old as life itself.

Metaphorically, when God banished Adam and Eve from the Garden of Eden, they very soon had reason to look back with longing to how nice things had been in the good old days. Since then, a wistful desire to recapture the dear departed past has haunted humankind.

Many agree with M. H. Abrams (1971) that this impulse to regain Paradise - to achieve a reconciliation with Lost Innocence and a reunification with the Prelapsarian Beauty of the World - is the essence of romanticism. Thus, Homer's Odysseus struggles to return home, and the hero of Joyce's *Ulysses* repeats a comparable journey. Poets like Milton in *Paradise Lost*, novelists like Proust in *Remembrance of Things Past*, songwriters like Lennon and McCartney in "Yesterday," and screenwriters like George Lucas in "American Graffiti" have constantly reiterated similar themes. And, as Bart Giamatti (1989) never tired of reminding us, our National Pastime replays the urge to come home at least 52 times per game, weather permitting.

In sum, then, it seems fair to say that the sense of nostalgia has always inextricably infused our consciousness of the basic human condition.

NOSTALGIA IS NEW

Nevertheless, nostalgia has recently received renewed attention from popular journalists and marketing practitioners observing the contemporary scene in America. Many commentators feel that the role of nostalgia in modern society is increasing, perhaps because the multitudinous Baby-Boom Generation has now started to reach an age at which nostalgia begins to matter in a Big Way.

Thus, for example, Becky Holman recently told a columnist for the Minneapolis Star Tribune that "people are studying nostalgia today the way they studied sex in advertising three years ago" (Meyers 1990, p. 1D). We see evidence of this nostalgia boom everywhere we look - in reruns of the old Jackie Gleason programs and the formation of the Royal Association for the Longevity and Preservation of the Honeymooners (R.A.L.P.H.); in the reassessment of Richard Nixon and a new willingness to reconsider him as something more human(e) than he seemed at the time of Viet Nam and Watergate; in the emergence of Victorian and Country-Kitchen fashion trends and the introduction of such fad-oriented magazines as *Victoria*, *Memories*, and Joe Franklin's *Nostalgia*; in the resurgence of 1950s Rock 'n' Roll and the insistence among many true believers that Elvis is still alive.

Perhaps most conspicuously for consumer researchers, nostalgia-related themes have begun to permeate the clutter of advertising that fills our daily exposure to the mass media. Thus, once again, Campbell soups are "M'm, M'm, Good." Once again, Timex watches can claim to "take a licking and keep on ticking." Once again, Coke can want "to teach the world to sing in perfect harmony." And, once again, Clairol can pose the profound problem, "Does She or Doesn't She?"

NOSTALGIA IS NEGLECTED

Yet, somewhat surprisingly, nostalgia has received relatively little attention from academicians in general and from scholars devoted to the study of consumer research in particular. Appropriately enough, some members of the Consumer-Behavior Odyssey - who identify so strongly with the quest described by Homer and by Joyce - have explored such nostalgia-related themes as collecting, the sacredness of ancestral objects, leaving home, or possessions and the sense of past (Belk 1990). But, to our knowledge, the present Special Topic Session at ACR is the first forum to address the phenomenon of consumer nostalgia in an explicit and systematic way.

NOSTALGIA IS DEFINABLE

Fred Davis (1979), the one sociologist who has pursued the theme of nostalgia at considerable length, views nostalgia as a longing for the past or a "yearning for yesterday." We might expand or extend this view by defining nostalgia more broadly as a preference (general liking, positive attitude, or favorable affect) toward objects (people, places, or things) that were more common (popular, fashionable, or widely circulated) when one was younger (in early adulthood, in adolescence, in childhood, or even before birth).

Notice that, in this definition, we consider nostalgia to include far more than just those poignant, bittersweet impulses associated with early life events in a way often characterized as "sentimental" or "sappy." Rather, our view of nostalgia covers any and all liking for past objects

---

[1] The first author gratefully acknowledges the support of the Columbia Business School's Faculty Research Fund.

that, for whatever reason, are no longer commonly experienced. For example, someone who used to eat Oreo cookies as a child but who now avoids sweets altogether for reasons of weight control could harbor a nostalgic longing for Oreos even though they are still widely available to others. Notice also that some controversy exists concerning whether one can feel nostalgia toward objects from history, but we shall not enter this debate beyond saying that it does seem possible to identify psychologically with figures, experiences, or cultural moments dating from before one's own birth - as, for example, in the case of movie Westerns that evoke reminiscences of a bygone era in 19th Century America.

Davis (1979) goes further to distinguish three levels or "orders" of nostalgia. As with other phenomena related to consumer behavior, these have been anticipated and brilliantly illustrated in songs by David Frishberg.

Level III is analytic and involves an interpretive exploration of questions about nostalgia. Thus, for example, one of Frishberg's songs presents a sensitive probing of his own homesickness after moving from the Big Apple to Los Angeles. It asks the titular question, "Do You Miss New York?," but couches this in a tone of ironic ambivalence: "Do you miss the thrill, the subways, the schlepping?/And is it second nature, still, to watch where you are stepping?" (Frishberg 1981).

Level II is reflexive and involves the self-conscious investigation of themes that characterize the nostalgic impulse. For example, as Holbrook (1989) argued is one of his columns for the *ACR Newsletter*, Frishberg's song entitled "The Dear Departed Past" is the definitive masterpiece in this genre. It explicitly raises such issues as, "Can one feel a real nostalgia for a time and place one never even knew?" (Frishberg 1985).

Level I is expressive and simply conveys the desire to return to the good old days or even the potentially unconscious belief that things used to be better than they are now. As a quintessential manifestation of this feeling (one intimately connected to the ethos of baseball), we would offer one of Frishberg's old songs newly recorded on compact disc (Frishberg 1990). The song is entitled "Matty" and presents Frishberg's tribute to the great right-handed pitcher, Christy Mathewson, who played for the New York Giants from 1900 to 1916 and who won 373 games (tied for third best in history). This song merits our consideration because it carries the spirit of nostalgia to exalted heights that achieve nearly messianic proportions (cf. O'Guinn 1990).

Specifically, the song connects the name of "Matty" to a series of terms associated with the spiritual or the sacrosanct -- words like "great," "soul," "true," "trust," "faith," "hallowed," "mightiest," "miracle," "swear," and "God." Moreover, the musical line emphasizes these connections by repeating a dramatic fall in the melody that coincides with the words "soul," "down to do or die," "miracle," and "God Himself." Then, at the song's climax, a key change from F-natural to A-flat entails a transformation and thereby reflects a metaphoric transubstantiation of Matty the baseball player into a kind of heroic Christ-like figure: "I'd swear that God Himself had sent His Right-Hand Man to see us through./And it was you, Matty, it was you." In this context, the phrase "Right-Hand Man" carries at least three salient and multiply-charged meanings. First, Matty was a right-handed pitcher. Second, he won a lot of ball games - more than almost anyone else, ever - and was certainly a handy guy to have around. Third, at the level of nostalgic hero worship, he bears some resemblance to Christ - who, in the words of the Nicene Creed, "ascended into Heaven and is seated at the right hand of God, the Father Almighty." Lest we doubt this association, we should recall Matty's real name - which is never explicitly mentioned in the song itself - Christy Mathewson.

This minor masterpiece lasts just three minutes but will boundlessly repay the investment in time and energy of anyone who chooses to track it down and to listen with care.

NOSTALGIA IS DEMONSTRABLE

If we define nostalgia as a longing for or favorable affect toward things from the past, it bears a clear relation to a phenomenon demonstrated by Holbrook and Schindler (1989) for the case of popular music. Very briefly, we proposed that esthetic tastes might reflect a tendency analogous to imprinting in which certain species form irreversible attachments to objects encountered during certain critical periods in their early lives (Lorenz 1951). In the movie *The Big Chill*, for example, former classmates from the University of Michigan reconvene for a funeral and spend the weekend eating the same foods, wearing the same clothes, talking the same talk, and listening to the same music that they enjoyed when they were in college. We suggested that this tendency, if generalizable, might cause preferences to reach their peak for music that was popular when a consumer entered the stage of late adolescence or early adulthood.

To test this hypothesis, we played popular songs from the years from 1932 to 1986 for a sample of 108 respondents ranging in age from 16 to 86 years old. Affective responses were aggregated not by songs, but rather by song-specific ages. This way of analyzing the data showed a clear and strong nonmonotonic tendency for respondents to prefer music that was popular when they were young adults. Peak preference occurred at 23.5 years of age, with a multiple correlation coefficient of R = 0.84.

Colloquially, this finding suggests that whatever music you liked when you first reached maturity will continue to please you best for the rest of your life. If so, depending on your point of view, you are the victim or the beneficiary of musical nostalgia.

NOSTALGIA IS DEEPER THAN THAT

But nothing is ever that simple. Thus, the study on musical tastes entails at least three limitations that invite further investigation.

First, the study applies primarily to preferences for popular music. Questions arise concerning whether the findings will generalize to esthetic tastes in other areas of music (jazz, classical), other art objects (films, novels), and other types of consumer products (clothing, grooming aids, food).

Second, the study suffered from one potential methodological flaw. Subjects listened to the musical selections in small groups varying in size from 14 to 61 people. This aspect of the design raises the possibility of alternative hypotheses based on potential sequence effects and/or possible biases due to social contagion. For example, in a worst-case scenario, if respondents watched the faces and body language of similarly aged people in their groups, some potential biasing effects could possibly have occurred. Further, conceivable artifacts due to order effects could not be definitively ruled out.

Third, the study neglected the possibility that different people might experience different degrees or different age-related peaks of preference toward the same objects. For example, the preferences for college graduates might peak later than those for high-school dropouts; those who lived in a dormitory or a sorority/fraternity house in college might experience the nostalgic effect more strongly than those who lived at home; women might display nostalgic reactions more strongly than men - or vice versa. Most saliently in the present context, people might differ in their levels of nostalgia proneness.

Subsequent research, still in progress, has begun to focus on the questions raised by these three limitations. For ease of exposition, we shall begin by considering the third.

THE NOSTALGIA INDEX

Work in progress by Holbrook (1990) has developed a Nostalgia Index intended to assess individual differences in the tendency to feel nostalgic impulses. This index of nostalgia proneness consists of 20 statements related to the general theme that "things were better in the good old days," each accompanied by a nine-point numerical scale of agreement/disagreement. Half of the items are scored in the positive, half in the negative direction: e.g., "They don't make 'em like they used to" (+) versus "Newer is almost always better" (-). After the appropriate scale reversals, the summative score of these ratings forms a 20-item Nostalgia Index that can be assessed for reliability and tested for validity.

Such assessments appear to support the reliability and validity of the Nostalgia Index. A recently completed study on 72 marketing students showed good reliability (alpha = 0.80) and promising predictive validity in explaining general preferences (e.g., musicians, singers, songs, TV shows, baseball stars, automobiles - $r = .37$) and specific preferences for films (e.g., musicals versus war stories - $r = .61$). Such results give us some confidence that the Nostalgia Index may capture some of the individual differences of importance in further accounting for the formation of preference peaks (Holbrook 1990).

THE GENERALIZABILITY OF NOSTALGIC PEAKS

A second study in progress addresses the question of whether the phenomenon of peak preferences in consumer tastes for music can be generalized to other areas of esthetic experience and, if so, whether it reflects the kinds of individual differences just described. Here, the relevant stimuli are models in fashion advertisements selected from issues of *Vogue* and *Esquire* published during the period from 1932 to 1988. Groups of respondents view slides of these ads and evaluate their responses to the fashion styles of the models on nine-point scales of general liking. As an extension of the earlier findings for musical tastes, we expect fashion preferences to show a nonmonotonic relation with ad-specific age, peaking somewhere in late adolescence or early adulthood. Further, we would expect the degree of peaking (the extent of nonmonotonicity or, in other words, the strength of the quadratic term) to increase with nostalgia proneness (as measured by the aforementioned Nostalgia Index) or possibly to shift to the left for the high- versus low-nostalgia respondents (as reflected by a nostalgia-moderated change in the slope for the linear term).

INDIVIDUAL-LEVEL DATA TO TEST THE NOSTALGIA HYPOTHESES

A third study, currently beginning the phase of data analysis, addresses all three of the limitations mentioned earlier. Specifically, it examines affective responses toward the visual appearance of movie actors and actresses and how these do or do not reflect preference peaks moderated by individual differences in nostalgia proneness.

The key stimuli for this third study are 64 photographs of film stars dated from the 1920s to the 1980s. In individually administered questionnaires, respondents have rated their degrees of liking for the appearances of the stars in these photos on nine-point preference scales, with the pictures presented in a different randomized order to each respondent. Each student in two marketing classes administered these questionnaires to two respondents drawn from the general population and differing in age by at least 30 years. This procedure provides roughly 200 sets of responses, collected in randomized orders at the individual level, from real people (not business students) covering a wide range of ages. Also, each respondent completed the aforementioned 20-item index of nostalgia proneness.

Briefly, other than the important difference in methods for collecting the data (intended to rule out alternative hypotheses concerning possible methods artifacts), the hypotheses to be tested in this third study resemble those under investigation in the work on fashion preferences described earlier. Thus, we expect preferences for photos of the stars to peak at a star-specific age somewhere in late adolescence or early adulthood. Further, we expect this preference peak to become more exaggerated (a stronger quadratic term) or to move to the left (a downward shift in the linear term) at higher levels of the Nostalgia Index.

CONCLUSION

If individual differences in the Nostalgia Index moderate the degree or position of preference peaks for tastes toward fashion models and movie stars in the manner just envisioned, we believe that we shall have progressed some distance in the direction of generalizing the effect found for musical tastes and tying it to personality characteristics related to nostalgia proneness.

Thus, we believe that the research previewed here is important because it fits into a programmatic stream that focuses on the nostalgia-related development of consumer tastes in such areas as music, movies, literature, television, fashion, food, and other aspects of esthetic consumption experiences. It extends a focus that has already produced highly suggestive results in the area of popular music. Moreover, it addresses questions concerning the role of nostalgia - the subject of the present Special Topic Session at ACR - that must remain close to the heart and mind of any consumer researcher who maintains both a scientific interest and a human fondness toward issues connected with the Dear Departed Past.

REFERENCES

Abrams, M. H. (1971), *Natural Supernaturalism: Tradition and Revolution in Romantic Literature*, New York: W. W. Norton.

Belk, Russell W. (1990), "The Role of Possessions In Constructing and Maintaining a Sense of Past," in *Advances in Consumer Research*, Vol. 17, ed. M. Goldberg, J. Gorn, and R. Pollay, Provo, UT: Association for Consumer Research.

Davis, Fred (1979), *Yearning for Yesterday: A Sociology of Nostalgia*, New York: The Free Press.

Frishberg, David (1981), "Do You Miss New York?" *The Dave Frishberg Songbook*, Vol. 1, Omnisound N-1040.

Frishberg, David (1985), "The Dear Departed Past," *Live At Vine Street*, Fantasy F-9638.

Frishberg, David (1990), "Matty," *Let's Eat Home*, Concord Jazz CCD-4402.

Giamatti, A. Bartlett (1989), *Take Time For Paradise: Americans and Their Games*, New York: Summit Books.

Holbrook, Morris B. (1989), "'These Foolish Things,' 'The Dear Departed Past,' and the Songs of David Frishberg: A Commentary and Critique," *ACR Newsletter*, (June), 1-8.

Holbrook, Morris B. (1990), "Nostalgic Consumption: On the Reliability and Validity of a New Nostalgia Index," working paper, Columbia University, Graduate School of Business.

Holbrook, Morris B. and Robert M. Schindler (1989), "Some Exploratory Findings on the Development of Musical Tastes," *Journal of Consumer Research*, 16 (June), 119-124.

Lorenz, Konrad Z. (1951), "The Role of Gestalt Perception in Animal and Human Behavior," in *Aspects of Form*, ed. Lancelot Law Whyte, Bloomington: Indiana University Press, 157-178.

Meyers, Mike (1990), "Ads Seek Loudest Blasts from the Past," *Minneapolis Star Tribune*, (August 12), 1D-3D.

O'Guinn, Thomas C. (1990), "Touching Greatness," in *Highways and Buyways*, ed. Russell W. Belk, Provo, UT: Association for Consumer Research, forthcoming.

An Empirical Investigation of the Impact of Negative Public Publicity on Consumer Attitudes and Intentions

Mitch Griffin, Bradley University
Barry J. Babin, Louisiana State University
Jill S. Attaway, Illinois State University

ABSTRACT

Negative publicity episodes have become increasingly common over the past several years. To a marketing practitioner, such incidents represent a serious threat to a firm's well being. A better understanding of consumer reactions to negative publicity may enable marketers to more effectively deal with these threats. Limited academic research, however, has investigated the strategic impact of negative publicity. This paper reports an experimental study intended to explore the influence of various negative publicity scenarios and target firm responses on consumer attitudes and purchase intentions.

Each year billions of dollars are spent on promotional activities in the United States in an attempt to influence consumer attitudes. Favorable publicity, coming from an uncompensated source lending a high level of credibility, is a very effective element of the promotional mix. Nearly everyone, from television evangelists to political candidates, neighborhood restaurants to the largest industrial manufacturers, uses various forms of publicity to secure donations, votes, or customers. Each of these organizations, however, is also vulnerable to the potentially devastating impact of negative publicity.

The influence of negative publicity is difficult to overstate. Empirical studies have found that negative information is capable of significantly affecting consumers' consumption related beliefs and attitudes. In fact, it has been shown that a single item of negative information is capable of neutralizing five similar pieces of positive information (Richey, Koenigs, Richey and Fortin 1975). Other research has found negative information results in more strongly held attributions regarding product beliefs than does positive information (Mizerski 1982) and the effect of negative information is more enduring than positive information (Cusumano and Richey 1970; Richins 1983). Researchers have also shown that negative information more strongly influences attitudes and purchase intention than does positive information, particularly in the service sector (Weinberger and Dillon 1980). In addition to empirical findings, even casual observation of recent events (i.e. Perrier contamination, Exxon's Valdez accident, and the ongoing saga of the PTL Club) clearly illustrate the damaging impact of negative publicity.

The questions "How do negative publicity events influence consumer attitudes and purchase intentions?" and "What actions can the target firm take to minimize the impact of negative publicity?" are of relevance to both marketing academicians and practitioners. Addressing these questions requires a better understanding of the relationship among the various elements pertaining to negative publicity, and their impact on consumer attitudes. In addition, how the target's response affects consumer attitudes requires investigation. Academic research in general, however, and empirical investigations in particular, regarding consumer's perceptions of negative publicity episodes are scarce. Similarly, little attention has been focused on the strategic importance of the target firm's response to such incidents.

One notable exception is the study by Tybout, Calder and Sternthal (1981) investigating the application of information processing to the design of marketing strategies. This research provided the essential first step in the examination of negative publicity. Tybout et al. used an experimental setting to evaluate the effectiveness of different response strategies to a negative publicity rumor. The results suggest the traditional strategy of directly refuting the rumor was not effective. However, this study did not include manipulation of any situational variables, nor investigate situations where negative publicity resulted from an actual incident rather than rumor. As a future research issue, Scott and Tybout (1981) called for the investigation of "situational qualifiers" (p. 408) which influence the impact of negative information and are therefore of particular relevance to managers.

This study attempts to help fill the informational void regarding negative publicity situational qualifiers. First, the impact that three characteristics have on consumer attitudes will be measured. The three dimensions, previously posited as classification dimensions of negative publicity (Sherrell and Reidenbach 1986), are *locus of responsibility*, *credibility of the reporting source*, and the target's *performance history*. Second, the influence of the target's potential response strategies will be assessed for their influence on consumer attitudes. Third, respondent suggestions for response strategies will be analyzed and discussed.

BACKGROUND AND HYPOTHESES

A study was designed to provide information on the impact of the experimental manipulations on the consumer's general attitude toward the target firm and future purchase intentions. Subjects' ability to make causal attributions provides the conceptual framework for the hypothesized relationships.

Locus of Responsibility

Locus of responsibility has a theoretical foundation in attribution theory. Specifically, the "discounter principle" provides insight into the hypothesized impact of internal and external locus of responsibility. Kelley stated "The role of a given cause in producing a given effect is discounted if other plausible causes are present" (1973, p. 113). In negative publicity situations lacking plausible alternative causes, the consumer is likely to make a stronger firm-related attribution, placing the blame on the target company and lowering the consumer's attitude toward the firm. Conversely, if alternative plausible causes are present the firm attribution will be less strong and not affect the subject's attitude as severely.

Previous empirical work partially supports the theoretical propositions. Mowen, Jolly and Nickell (1981) used regression analysis to determine the situational variables influencing consumer response to recalled products. One of the variables studied was the company's responsibility for the defect. In one of four recall cases responsibility for the defect did have a significant negative influence on consumers' impression of the company. However, in the other three situations no significant relationship was discovered. In another study regarding consumer reactions to product failure, Folkes (1984) found locus to be a significant predictor of both the consumer's future expectations and type of redress preferred. In summary, there exists intuitive, theoretical and limited empirical support for:

H_1: External locus of responsibility will result in more positive attitude ratings toward the firm and greater intention to purchase.

Source Credibility

Marketers have long assumed that a more credible source is more influential (see McGuire 1968; Sternthal, Phillips and Dholakia 1978). Conceptual support for this assumption is provided by traditional attitude theory and attribution theory. Attitude theory suggests that attitude change occurs when an individual is exposed to a persuasive message which alters the individual's beliefs. Source credibility is a central variable to the formulation of such a message.

In attribution theory, the receiver of a message attempts to determine the reason for that message. The credibility of the source is one factor affecting the receiver's inference (Eagly, Wood and Chaiken 1978). A highly credible source draws the receiver into making a stronger attribution regarding the message, yielding a more significant impact on attitudes. Conversely, a source low in credibility may be "discounted" and result in little attitude change. Richins (1984) suggests that positive information is expected and has little impact, while negative information is unexpected and is more likely to be believed. Richins' position is consistent with the literature regarding the impact of negative information (Kanouse and Hanson 1972; Mizerski 1982; Richey et al. 1975; Weinberger and Dillon 1980).

Empirical research on the impact of source credibility in negative information scenarios is contradictory. As an example, Weiner and Mowen (1986) investigated the influence of source expertise and trustworthiness on consumer attitude formation. They found that in situations where the source was expected to be biased, the subjects did indeed discount the message. (For other examples see Dholakia and Sternthal 1977; Sternthal, Phillips and Dholakia 1978).

Other research has resulted in opposing conclusions. Wegner, Wenzlaff, Kerker and Beattie (1981) manipulated media source credibility to detect the influence on innuendo. The results show that regardless of the source (*New York Times* versus *National Enquirer*) the innuendo was equally effective. Similarly, Rosenbaum and Levin (1969) discovered credibility of source does not influence the impact of negative information as it does positive information. In spite of the conflicting empirical findings, the preponderance of theoretical and empirical literature supports:

H_2: Less credible sources will result in more positive attitude ratings toward the firm and greater intention to purchase.

Performance History

When attributors are exposed to multiple observations, substantially more information is available to apply in an individual's causal attribution process. These circumstances give rise to Kelley's (1973) "principles of covariance". Kelley suggests that, given multiple observations of the same effect, an "effect is attributed to the one of its possible causes with which, over time it covaries" (1973, p. 108). In a negative publicity setting, a firm with multiple occurrences of a problem is more likely to be perceived as the cause of that problem. Conversely, if the episode is an isolated incident, the consumer's ability to attribute the responsibility solely to the firm is less powerful.

Empirical evidence regarding the impact of performance history has shown conflicting results. In one study the number of previous product recalls by a manufacturer was found to influence consumer perceptions of the firm and replacement products (Mowen 1979). Similarly, Folkes (1984), using Weiner's (1980) attribution categories to study product failure, found the stability dimension significantly related to consumer expectations and preferred redress. Two other studies, however, failed to reveal a significant relationship between comparable previous problems and consumer perception of the firm (Mowen 1980; Mowen, Jolly and Nickell 1981). Again, the intuitive logic and theoretical foundation, in light of inconclusive empirical evidence, led us to hypothesize:

H_3: Target firms with no history of product failure will receive more positive attitude ratings and higher intention to purchase.

Response Tactic

The target responses used in the study are similar to those investigated by Tybout, Calder and Sternthal (1981). These researchers discovered, contrary to previous attitude theory and intuition, simply refuting a negative rumor was an ineffective response tactic. Based on information processing theory, an explanation for the failure of the denial strategy was offered. In brief, consumers' attitudes are affected simply by processing information they receive, even if they do not actually believe it. As plausible alternative response tactics, Tybout, Calder and Sternthal (1981, p. 74) propose utilizing a "storage strategy", whereby a second positive piece of information is interjected when the negative information is being stored, or a "retrieval strategy", through which additional stimuli are introduced as a means of diluting the association between rumor and target. Basically, these strategies involve providing additional informational cues which associate the firm with positive information or inhibit the retrieval of the negative information. Both strategies avoid repeating the rumor which is necessary in a denial strategy. Results of the Tybout et al. study supported the use of both storage and retrieval strategies.

Based on the work of Tybout, Calder and Sternthal, we believe that consumers exposed to a denial of the incident will react strongly to the scenario, reporting lower attitude ratings and purchase intentions than consumers receiving no response from the firm. Subjects receiving a redress response, a form of storage strategy, will report more positive attitudes and purchase intentions than those in the no response category. Thus, we propose:

H_4: A denial response will result in the lowest attitude and purchase intention ratings, no response a neutral rating, and a redress response the most favorable attitude and purchase intention ratings.

METHODOLOGY

Subjects

One hundred and ninety-six students attending a major state university voluntarily participated in the study. The subjects were recruited from those enrolled in various undergraduate business classes and were assigned randomly to one of the treatment groups in a 2 X 2 X 2 X 3 full factorial experimental design. After editing, 188 subjects were retained for analysis.

Experimental Context

Prior to developing the scenarios and designing the questionnaires, an appropriate context had to be determined. The context had to be relevant to the experimental subjects, but yet not so personal as to limit the range of attitudes. After reviewing several possible options, the fast food industry was selected as an appropriate experimental context. Fast food franchises have experienced their share of negative publicity (i.e. McDonalds massacre; reports of ground worms in hamburger meat; kangaroo meat passed off as beef) and hold high personal relevance to the test subjects. In addition, the subjects (college-age consumers) represent an important market segment to the fast food industry. One of the recent negative publicity episodes focused on the presence of salmonella bacteria in poultry products. Applying this to the fast food industry was simply a matter of reporting that a restaurant had allegedly sold chicken that resulted in several cases of salmonella poisoning.

Scenario Development

Scenarios were constructed around the fried chicken franchise/salmonella poisoning context. The three situational manipulations were developed in all possible combinations and then matched with three response strategies. The scenarios are as similar as possible in all other respects.

Locus of responsibility was manipulated by reporting that salmonella poisoning could result from (1) improper storage and preparation of the chicken or by (2) failure to refrigerate the chicken following preparation. Under the internal (firm-responsible) locus condition, it was reported that high levels of bacteria were detected in chicken tested on the premises of the target firm. The franchise was then charged with failure to properly store or prepare the product. The external locus condition reported no bacteria was found in the chicken at the store and the poisoning was attributed to the consumer's failure to refrigerate leftover chicken.

The credibility manipulation was operationalized by either (1) "city public health officials" or (2) "unconfirmed reports" as the source of the information. The high credibility construct was written in a manner suggesting that the scenario was *fact*, whereas the low credibility suggested that the report was an unsubstantiated *rumor*.

Historical performance was defined as (1) the presence or (2) an absence of similar incidents having occurred to the target firm. The manipulation was operationalized in the "isolated" scenario by reporting the poisoning was "an isolated incident"; in the "chronic" scenario by stating "similar incidents have been reported in other cities".

Target firm responses fell into three categories: (1) no response from the firm, (2) a denial response, and (3) a redress response. In the denial response tactic the target firm refused to accept any responsibility for the incident, to the point of implying that the reported sicknesses might not have even occurred. Under the redress response tactic the target firm made a concerted effort to remedy any potential problems and provided informational brochures to consumers regarding the safe handling of poultry products.

Operational Measures

Scales were developed to measure subjects' attitudes toward the chicken franchise's locations, promotional efforts and an overall evaluation. In addition, an intent to purchase measure was developed. The measures for franchise locations and promotional efforts were included as checks for demand artifacts. The overall evaluation and purchase intention measures were utilized as dependent variables in subsequent analysis.

The attitude measures consisted of seven point semantic differential scales using polar terms germane to the individual construct. The polar adjectives were adopted from previous research (Osgood, Suci, and Tannenbaum 1957) and have been found to display high levels of reliability. An effort was made to select terms relevant to the construct being measured as well as covering the three dimensions of attitude - activity, evaluation, and potency. Intent to purchase was assessed directly, but phrased in a context suited to the sample. After purification in pretesting, the scales utilized in the present study displayed coefficient alpha estimates ranging from 0.78 to 0.90.

Procedure

The experiment was administered in classrooms on the university campus. The subjects were introduced to a research assistant who provided general information regarding the task they were about to perform, but not the particular issue under investigation. The subjects were instructed to read the questions and information carefully, proceed through the test instrument in the sequence in which it was presented and to answer each question as accurately as possible at that time.

Questionnaires were constructed to gather the subject's attitude assessments and intent to purchase at two different points - before and after exposure to the experimental stimuli. The pretest measures used for analysis were embedded in a number of questions regarding fast food franchises. All subjects initially responded to identical instruments. Each subject then read a one page negative publicity/firm response scenario determined by experimental group membership. Following the suggestion of Wetzel (1977, p. 89), subjects responded to the dependents measures directly after exposure to the experimental scenarios. After completion of the attitude measures, suggestions of what the firm should have done to address the incident were solicited.

After completion of testing, the subjects were debriefed. Of primary concern was insuring that the subjects recognized the hypothetical nature of the scenarios and that the particular franchise selected was utilized solely because it was a well known franchise capable of providing a base of reference for the study. To accomplish this, both a written disclaimer and a verbal explanation were provided.

Manipulation/Confounding Checks

In experimental designs, subjects are exposed to various conditions and expected to react differently to those conditions. To insure the internal validity of this experiment, manipulations were tested and revised during pretesting (Wetzel 1977). In addition, as a strong test of manipulations, checks were included as the last questions in the main experiment (Perdue and Summers 1986, p. 320). The measures asked the respondents if: (1) the target firm was solely responsible for the incident (locus of responsibility); (2) the incident was reported by a reliable source (source credibility); and (3) the target firm had experienced similar problems (historical performance).

To examine the manipulations the subjects were classified into high and low groups for each of the manipulations and then tested for a difference in the mean response on the three check questions. With this approach, both the effectiveness of the manipulations and any potential confounding effects between manipulations can be tested (Wetzel 1977, p.88). In each case, a significant difference was found between mean scores on the appropriate measure, but not the others, suggesting that the manipulations were effective and independent. The results are presented in Table 1.

A second concern in consumer research is the impact of demand artifacts on the validity of the experiment (Sawyer 1975). In the present study, the possibility of subjects attempting to respond in a "socially desireable" manner is particularly relevant. While no fool proof method exists for detecting or eliminating demand artifacts, two specific steps were taken to minimize the occurrence in the study. First, relevant measures taken before exposure to the experimental stimuli were disguised by their inclusion with several distracter items. Second, two firm-related measures were included that were not expected to be changed by the manipulations in an attempt to detect yea saying. Analysis of these measures, reported in Table 2, suggests demand artifacts are not a major problem. The only significant effect found in this analysis pertains to the impact of response type on attitude toward a firm's promotion (p=.03). Although this could be attributed to a demand effect, it is quite plausible that this effect is due to subject perceptions of response style as part of a firm's promotional mix.

ANALYSIS AND RESULTS

Given the nature of the data, in particular that the desired subject responses were measured both before and after exposure to the experimental scenario, the general form of the model required to test the research hypotheses is given by Neter, Wasserman and Kutner (1985) as:[1]

$$Y_{ijklmn} = \mu + \alpha_i + \beta_j + \delta_k + \pi_l + \sigma_n + \varepsilon_{ijklmn} \quad (1)$$

---

[1] Interaction temrs are omitted for simplicity in the equation, but were, of course, included in the analysis.

TABLE 1
Results of Manipulation Checks

Experimental Element	Manipulation Check Variable					
	Locus		Credibility		History	
	T Value	Prob.	T Value	Prob.	T Value	Prob.
Locus of Responsibility	**2.77**	**.006**	0.59	.553	0.48	.633
Source Credibility	1.29	.199	**6.24**	**.000**	1.44	.152
Performance History	1.00	.318	0.42	.672	**4.34**	**.000**

TABLE 2
Results of Analysis of Variance for Demand Artifacts

Dependent Variable Factor	Partial F	p-value
Attitude Toward Firm's Location		
Within Subjects Factor	.24	.622
Locus	.00	.950
History	1.28	.260
Credibility	.07	.795
Response	.51	.599
Attitude Toward Firm's Promotion		
Within Subjects Factor	.35	.555
Locus	1.86	.175
History	.04	.833
Credibility	.83	.364
Response	3.59	.030

where l represents the grand mean, a_i represents the ith level of locus, b_j the jth level of history, d_k the kth level of credibility, p_l the lth level of response, and s_n a blocking (within-subject) factor accounting for the two responses on each subject. The results of this analysis are shown in Table 3.

As shown in Table 3, the partial F statistics for the within subject factor are highly significant for both response measures (attitude and purchase intention). This result supports the ability of the experimental scenario to affect the dependent variables. In terms of the present study, this result, along with analysis of the group means, is interpreted as evidence of a tendency among respondents to lower their attitudes and purchase intentions toward the target firm. Furthermore, this effect holds regardless of the combination of experimental treatments they were exposed to.

In addition, Table 3 shows partial F values for each experimental treatment while controlling for both the within-subject factor and all possible two and three-way interactions. Since no interaction effects were hypothesized or found significant at a p-level of .10, they were omitted from the table. Each hypothesis was examined by analyzing these partial F values.

TABLE 3
Results of Analysis of Variance for Dependent Measures

Dependent Variable Factor	Partial F	p-value
Attitude Toward Firm		
Within Subject Factor	49.63	.000
Locus	6.70	.011
Credibility	18.08	.000
History	5.56	.020
Response	3.69	.027
Purchase Intentions		
Within Subject Factor	17.61	.000
Locus	3.20	.075
Credibility	1.10	.296
History	.41	.524
Response	1.46	.236

Locus of Responsibility. H_1 predicted that both attitudes and purchase intentions toward the firm would be relatively lower when the locus of responsibility was directed toward the store rather than the customer. The partial F values shown in Table 3 support this hypothesis for the attitude measure ($p \leq .011$) while showing only marginal support when using intentions as a response ($p \leq .075$).

Source Credibility. H_2 predicted lower source credibility would be associated with relatively higher attitudes and purchase intentions. The partial F values for this effect support H_2 for attitudes ($p \leq .0001$), but fail to support it using intentions as a dependent measure ($p \leq .296$).

Performance History. H_3 predicted that attitudes and intentions would be significantly effected when a firm is portrayed as having chronic problems with product failures as opposed to having no such previous record. Again, the F-value supports the hypothesis with regard to lower attitudes under conditions of chronic product failures ($p \leq .02$); however, no significant effect is shown on purchase intentions ($p \leq .524$).

Response Tactic. H_4 hypothesized attitudes and purchase intentions would vary according to which response level a subject was exposed (no response, redress, denial). Again, the partial F values support this hypothesis for the attitude measure ($p \leq .027$) while failing to support it for purchase intentions ($p \leq .236$). Analysis of the cell means indicates the significant effect observed on respondent attitudes was due mainly to higher mean scores on the redress response category compared to both denial and no response conditions, which displayed virtually identical scores.

In sum, each of the research hypotheses were clearly supported with respect to the impact of experimental factors on attitudes toward a firm suffering from exposure to negative public publicity. The picture is not as clear with regard to the impact of locus, credibility, history, and response on purchase intentions. While only the hypothesized effect of locus on intentions reached even a marginal level of significance, a comparison of cell means of purchase intentions showed that all observed effects were in the hypothesized direction. This is consistent with a significant reduction in overall purchase intention scores between the pre-exposure and post-exposure conditions mentioned above (within-subjects). However, despite evidence demonstrating lower purchase intentions based on exposure to negative public publicity, the individual effects of each experimental factor on intentions cannot be confidently supported based on these data.

Qualitative Data. Respondents were given an opportunity to comment on the incident reported after completing the questionnaire. The majority of subjects offered suggestions on how the target firm should have handled the negative publicity episode.

Honesty was the most common term utilized by subjects who read the denial and no response scenarios. Over half of the respondents in these conditions (56%) included some suggestion that the target deal with the situation honestly. In general, subjects wanted the target firm to face the problem rather than avoid it, and several suggested that an independent agency should investigate the incident.

Offering information to consumers on proper handling of poultry products was also suggested by eight respondents. In addition, six subjects wanted punitive action taken against the firm or employee responsible (five subjects recommended publicly announcing that an employee of the firm was fired over the incident). Only two respondents stated the incident was handled properly by a denial tactic.

Subjects exposed to the redress response tactic displayed overall satisfaction with the target's actions. Many respondents (63%) stated the firm had "handled the situation well". In particular, subjects cited the target's willingness to provide informational brochures as a very positive action. No mention was made of punitive action, suggesting a more positive approach to the incident satisfies consumers' "call for blood" to rectify the problem.

DISCUSSION AND CONCLUSIONS

The results of this experiment indicate source credibility and firm responsibility, history, and response tactic are important situational factors leading to changes in consumer attitudes based on a negative publicity episode. In addition, while purchase intentions were significantly lowered by experimental stimuli, individual relationships hypothesized between situational factors and purchase intentions were not confirmed.

Although not hypothesized, a significant interaction among situational variables would not have been surprising. In particular, a locus by history interaction would correspond to the locus by stability interaction found in Folkes' (1984) study of consumer reactions to product failure. The differing results between Folkes' work and this study may be attributed to slightly different dependent measures, experimental settings and operationalization of manipulations. The main effects, however, do further corroborate findings reported by Folkes.

From a pragmatic viewpoint, it appears target firms have little to lose by taking a proactive approach toward negative publicity. One could argue denial of a rumor might have either a positive effect by persuading consumers that it is indeed untrue, or a negative impact be serving to legitimatize the charges. The results of the study, however, indicate denial produces similar results to ignoring the event entirely. On the other hand, a redress approach to negative publicity appears to help restore firm image regardless of the situational factors. An admission of responsibility may not be necessary, but taking a proactive consumer oriented approach pays dividends.

While certainly no surprise, the significance of the history manipulation reinforces the importance of maintaining a strong corporate image. Knowledge of previous problems or a poor reputation will negatively influence consumer reactions to current incidents. Therefore confronting today's negative publicity in a positive and timely manner should not only benefit accused firms immediately, but also provide insulation against whatever tomorrow might bring.

This area of academic research holds substantial future promise. While this study is somewhat limited by the wide arrange of phenomena addressed, it does provide an impetus for further, and more in-depth, investigations of each of the effects operationalized through experimental manipulations. Although further theoretical development and empirical verification are needed, the present study illustrates these manipulations are capable of significantly altering consumers' attitude ratings. The findings compliment and support the earlier work of Tybout, Calder and Sternthal (1981). Additional experimental studies with larger and more generalizable samples would also be valuable. In addition, a "vulture approach" (laying in wait for a negative publicity episode to occur) seems a useful, if not efficient, approach to conducting field studies of negative publicity which may provide effects applications of relationships explored here.

REFERENCES

Cusumano, Donald R. and Marjorie H. Richey (1970), "A Negative Salience in Impressions of Character: Effects of Extremeness of Stimulus Information," *Psychometric Science*, 20, 81-83.

Dholakia, Ruby and Brian Sternthal (1977), "Highly Credible Sources: Persuasive Facilitators or Persuasive Liabilities?," *Journal of Consumer Research*, 3, 223-232.

Eagly, Alice H., W. Wood and S. Chaiken (1978), "Causal Inferences About Communicators and Their Effect on Opinion Change," *Journal of Personality and Social Psychology*, 36, 424-435.

Folkes, Valerie S. (1984), "Consumer Reactions to Product Failure: An Attributional Approach," *Journal of Consumer Research*, 10, 398-409.

Kanouse, David E. and L. Reid Hanson Jr. (1972), "Negativity in Evaluations," in *Attribution: Perceiving the Causes of Behavior*, Edward E. Jones et al., editors, Morristown, NJ: General Learning Press, 47-62.

Kelley, Harold (1973), "Processes of Causal Attribution," *American Psychologist*, 28, 107-128.

McGuire, W. J. (1968), "The Nature of Attitudes and Attitude Change," in G. Linzey and E. Aronson, eds., *Handbook of Social Psychology*, Reading, MA: Addison-Wesley.

Mizerski, Richard W. (1982), "An Attribution Explanation of the Disproportionate Influence of Unfavorable Information," *Journal of Consumer Research*, 9, 301-310.

Mowen, John C. (1979), "Consumer Reactions to Product Recalls: An Empirical and Theoretical Examination," unpublished working paper, Department of Marketing, Oklahoma State University.

_____ (1980), "Further Information on Consumer Perceptions of Product Recalls," *Advances in Consumer Research*, Jerry C. Olson, ed., Ann Arbor: Association for Consumer Research, 7, 519-523.

———, David Jolly and Gary S. Nickell (1981), "Factors Influencing Consumer Responses to Product Recalls: A Regression Analysis Approach," *Advances in Consumer Research*, Kent B. Monroe, ed., Ann Arbor: Association for Consumer Research, 8, 405-407.

Neter, John, William Wasserman and Michael H. Kutner (1985), *Applied Linear Statistical Models*, Homewood, IL: Richard D. Irwin, Inc.

Osgood, Charles E., George J. Suci and Percy H. Tannenbaum (1957), *The Measurement of Meaning*, Champaign, IL: University of Illinois Press.

Perdue, Barbara C. and John O. Summers (1986), "Checking the Success of Manipulations in Marketing Experiments," *Journal of Marketing Research*, 23, 317-326.

Richey, Marjorie H., Robert J. Koenigs, Harold W. Richey and Richard Fortin (1975), "Negative Salience in Impressions of Character: Effects of Unequal Proportions of Positive and Negative Information," *Journal of Social Psychology*, 97, 233-241.

Richins, Marsha L. (1983), "Negative Word-of-Mouth by Dissatisfied Consumers: A Pilot Study," *Journal of Marketing*, 47, 68-78.

——— (1984), "Word of Mouth Communication as Negative Information," *Advances in Consumer Research*, Thomas C. Kinnear, ed., Provo UT: Association for Consumer Research, 11, 697-702.

Rosenbaum, Milton E. and Irwin P. Levin (1969), "Impression Formation as a Function of Source Credibility and the Polarity of Information," *Journal of Personality and Social Psychology*, 12, 34-37.

Sawyer, Alan G. (1975), "Demand Artifacts in Laboratory Experiments in Consumer Research," *Journal of Consumer Research*, 1, 20-30.

Scott, Carol A. and Alice M. Tybout (1981), "Theoretical Perspectives on the Impact of Negative Information in Impression Formation: Does Valence Matter?," *Advances in Consumer Research*, Kent B. Monroe, ed., Ann Arbor: Association for Consumer Research, 8, 408-409.

Sherrell, Daniel L. and R. Eric Reidenbach (1986), "A Consumer Response Framework for Negative Publicity: Suggestions for Response Strategies," *Akron Business and Economic Review*, 17, 37-44.

Sternthal, Brian, Lynne Phillips and Ruby Dholakia (1978), "The Persuasive Effects of Source Credibility: A Situational Analysis," *Public Opinion Quarterly*, 285-314.

Tybout, Alice M., Bobby J. Calder and Brian Sternthal (1981), "Using Information Processing Theory to Design Marketing Strategies," *Journal of Marketing Research*, 18, 73-79.

Wegner, D. M., R. Wenzlaff, R. M. Kerker and A. E. Beattie (1981), Incrimination Through Innuendo: Can Media Questions Become Public Answers?," *Journal of Personality and Social Psychology*, 40, 822-832.

Wetzel, Christopher G. (1977), "Manipulation Checks: A Reply to Kidd," *Representative Research in Social Psychology*, 8, 88-93.

Weinberger, Marc C. and William R. Dillon (1980), "The Effects of Unfavorable Product Rating Information," in *Advances in Consumer Research*, Jerry C. Olson, ed., Ann Arbor: Association for Consumer Research, 7, 528-532.

Weiner, Bernard (1980), *Human Motivation*, New York: Holt, Rinehart & Winston.

Weiner, Joshua L. and John C. Mowen (1986), "Source Credibility: On the Independent Effects of Trust and Expertise," *Advances in Consumer Research*, Richard J. Lutz, ed., Provo UT: Association for Consumer Research, 13, 306-310.

Reconceptualizing Comparative Advertising: A Framework and Theory of Effects

Beth A. Walker, Arizona State University
Helen H. Anderson, University of Arizona

ABSTRACT

Although most researchers have studied comparative ads that explicitly compare two or more brands, we believe that ads need not be explicit or limited to brand-level comparisons before they are considered comparative. In this paper, we identify (1) the level of the comparison object and (2) the explicitness of the comparative claim as dimensions on which comparative ads may vary. We present a conceptual framework and develop propositions, based on the concepts of memory schemata and category knowledge, that explain how differences along these dimensions may affect inferences and claim believability. We conclude by discussing the research and public policy implications of our approach.

INTRODUCTION

Advertisers are making increasing use of comparative advertising both in the print (Jackson, et al., 1979) and television media (Muehling and Kangun 1985). This trend is particularly interesting given the often conflicting and generally negative empirical evidence regarding its effectiveness (Johnson and Horne 1987). We believe that this apparent discrepancy may, in part, be explained by differences in the *types* of comparative ads that are used by practitioners and those whose effects are typically studied by advertising researchers.

The FTC defined a comparative advertisement as one which "compares alternative brands on objectively measurable attributes or price, and identifies the alternative brand by name, illustration, or other distinctive information (Federal Register 1979, p. 47328). In most studies, researchers have examined comparative ads in which explicit reference is made to one or more brands that are compared on one or more mentioned attributes. Researchers then compare the effects of "comparative advertising" to noncomparative advertising, making conclusions which are presumably generalizable to all comparative ads.

Most empirical evidence suggests that "comparative ads" are no more effective and sometimes less effective than conventional advertising (Turgeon and Barnaby 1989; Walker, et al. 1986). To get more positive results and to avoid a lawsuit that sometimes challenges explicit comparative claims, marketers seem to be resorting to other forms of comparative advertising to persuade consumers. For example, ads may use comparative adjectives without mentioning a competitor ("highest quality"), compare their brand to to "other brands," or make a comparison visually without an explicit mention of it in the copy. In addition, ads often compare the sponsored brand to objects other than a competing brand (i.e. the product class in general, noncomparable product classes).

Given these variations in comparative advertising, it seems unlikely that we can make generalizable conclusions about something called "comparative advertising." Thus, we are faced with a more interesting question about how differences in comparative advertising affect information processing and resulting outcomes. In this paper, we propose two dimensions on which comparative ads may vary: (1) the degree of the comparison (implicitness/explicitness of the comparative claim) and the (2) nature of the comparison object (the concreteness/abstractness of the comparison object). We present a conceptual framework, based on the concepts of memory schemata and category knowledge, to explain how differences along these dimensions may affect inferences and claim believability. We develop propositions regarding key relationships, and conclude by discussing relevant research and public policy implications.

A TYPOLOGY OF COMPARATIVE ADVERTISEMENTS

There are probably hundreds of subtle variations in comparative advertisements that have emerged to produce more positive results. To find the dimensions that are most meaningful, we more closely examined the FTC's original definition. This definition rigidly delineates comparative ads on two basic dimensions: (1) the nature of the comparison object (i.e. traditionally, competing brands), and (2) the explicitness of the comparative claim. We propose the nature of the comparison object and the explicitness of the comparative claim not as defining features, but as dimensions on which comparative ads may vary. Specifically, we conceptualize ads as varying in terms of the level of abstractness of of the comparison object and the implicitness/explicitness of the comparative claim.

The Level of the Comparison Object

Casual observation of the types of comparative ads featured on television and in magazines reveals that advertisers often compare the sponsored product to a wide variety of other objects, not just to competing brands. For example, a "Saab Turbo" has been compared to "European Sports Cars," "Borden's Cottage Cheese" has been compared to cottage cheeses, "Skippy Peanut Butter" has been compared to other sandwich foods, and "Cadillac" has been compared to a Ming Vase and string of pearls.

A critical issue is how best to conceptualize these differences between comparison objects. Muehling and Kangun (1985) suggested that comparison objects be classified in terms of their similarity to the sponsored product, where comparison objects range from very similar products (i.e. Chevas Regal Scotch comparing itself to Johnny Walker Red) to very dissimilar products (i.e. Chevas Regal Scotch comparing itself to a Rolls-Royce). We adopt a similar approach by differentiating comparison objects in terms of their level of abstraction or generality.

It is widely held that knowledge of any object, including products, is organized hierarchically in memory in terms of its level of abstraction (Lingle, Altom and Medin 1984; Mervis and Rosch 1981). Categorization theorists differentiated these levels in terms of categories of knowledge, with superordinate categories being the most abstract, followed by basic categories, and finally, subordinate categories at the most concrete or specific level. Sujan and Dekleva (1987) substantiated that product classes, product types, and brands correspond to each of these three levels, respectively, and suggest that any given product could be grouped according to any one of these levels.

However, comparison objects are often more abstract than even the product class level (Bettman and Sujan 1987). Sponsored brands are often compared to noncomparable alternatives (i.e. a camera to a computer) or even to a noncomparable non-alternative (Muehling and Kangun 1985) such as a wallet to a pair of jeans. Beginning with the most concrete level, we propose the following five levels of comparison objects: brands, product types, product classes, alternative product classes, and non-alternative product classes.

Implicitness/Explicitness of the Comparative Claim

According to the FTC, explicitness is a function of naming your competitors and specifically identifying the attributes on which the brands are compared. However, claims need not be so explicit. For example, a comparative claim may assert that the sponsored brand is "better than the leading brand" (Jackson, et al. 1979). Jackson, et al. (1979) reported that the use of these implicit comparative claims far exceeds that of the more traditional explicit comparisons which names or showed two or more competing brands.

Other ads may simply describe the sponsored brand as the "freshest" or "highest quality" (Levy 1983; Shimp 1978; Shimp and Preston 1982; Wyckham 1987). Shimp (1978) and Wyckham (1987) studied the effects of these "indirect" comparisons, defined as ads which use a comparative adjectival form (bigger, better, etc.) to compare a brand with an implicit competitive brand on the basis of an implicit attribute (i.e. "Mennen E goes on warmer and dryer"). Both researchers found that, after exposure to an indirect comparison, individuals made comparative inferences about the sponsored brand beyond the manifest content of the incomplete statement, leading them to suggest that indirect comparisons could lead to miscomprehension and/or deception.

Given the wide variety of comparative ads, it may be an oversimplification to categorize ads as either explicit and implicit. We agree with Levy (1983), who suggested that the explicit/implicit dimension be treated as a continuum, so that we may recognize and study the varying degrees of implicit and explicit comparison.

To establish a continuum of explicitness, we have identified specific aspects of advertisements that may contribute to an overall degree of explicitness. After reviewing the ways in which explicitness has been defined in previous research, and analyzing the results of a pilot study where subjects' sorting of comparative ads in terms of their perceived explicitness, we have developed a coding scheme for ad content and structure based on two factors leading to perceived explicitness: (1) the *clarity* of the claim statement, and (2) the *obviousness* that the comparison is made. These distinctions are consistent with what Keller (1986) identified as factors of an ad critical to processing (i.e. structure and content).

The clarity of the claim statement refers to the degree of attribute support for the comparative claim. For example, a claim may not mention a specific attribute at all (e.g. "we're the best"), may mention an attribute in a more vague fashion (e.g. "number one in quality"), or may feature explicitly stated, measurable attributes (e.g. Hyundai costs $2999 less than Toyota"). The number of attributes that are presented may also increase the perceived clarity of the comparative ad. As the number and specificity of comparison attributes increase, so does the clarity of comparison.

The obviousness of the claim relates to the location of the claim within the advertisement. Claims made in the headline or in the visual portion of the advertisement are more obvious than those hidden somewhere in the copy. Based on these distinctions, advertisements could be coded according to factors contributing to obviousness and clarity. This score treated as continuous, or used to divide comparative ads into distinct groups according to the explicitness/implicitness of the ad.

In the next section, we consider how the level of the comparison object and the explicitness of the comparative claim may influence consumer's inference processes.

CONCEPTUAL FRAMEWORK

The inferences that consumers make while processing advertisements is increasingly being recognized as fundamental in explaining an advertisement's effects (cf. Ford and Smith 1987; Kardes 1990). Inferences are particularly useful in distinguishing the effects of comparative and noncomparative advertisements (Sujan and Dekleva 1987), and are being used more frequently to identify deceptive advertising claims (Shimp 1978; Shimp and Preston 1982). We identified the concepts of memory schemata and category knowledge to help predict how the level of the comparison object and the explicitness of the comparative claim may affect the source (e.g. memory-based or ad-based) and type of inferences that consumers generate.

Memory Schemata and Inferential Belief Formation

A schema is defined as an associative network of interrelated meanings that represent a person's declarative knowledge about a concept (Alba and Hasher 1983). Schemas about brands and products contain previously learned knowledge about the concept plus the interrelationships between these items of knowledge, stored in an organized, logical framework (Olson 1978). For any product, consumers may have several interrelated schemas which may be organized hierarchically in memory in terms of its level of specificity or abstraction.

There are important differences in the content of the schemas at different levels of abstraction (Lingle, Altom and Medin 1984; Myers-Levy and Tybout 1989; Rosch 1975) which are likely to affect the number and type of inferences that consumers use to frame evaluations (Sujan and Dekleva 1987). Members of *superordinate* categories, such as product class categories, are distinguished from each other on key attributes, but they share few features. According to Sujan and Dekleva (1987), only a few inferences can be drawn at this level. At the next level are *basic*, or product type categories. These categories are called basic because they tend to be used most frequently to categorize both natural and social objects. Basic level categories have a greater number of shared attributes than at the superordinate level, as well as attributes that distinguish one basic level category from another. Categorization at this level also allows many more inferences to be drawn which tend to be more evaluative in nature (Sujan and Dekleva 1987). *Subordinate* categories are at the most concrete level which share only a few attributes in common. Subordinate categories, such as brand-level categories, are have a few more beliefs than basic level categories but the increase in the number of beliefs is small. However, beliefs and attributes at this level tend to be very concrete and specific.

Schema Activation and the Level of Comparison Object

Categorization of an object, such as the sponsored brand, depends on the schema that is activated or evoked from memory (i.e. made available for conscious processing). We propose that the level of the comparison object used in the advertisement will cue or trigger the "matching" schema in memory. For example, an ad that compares a new brand of beer to "Lowenbrau" may activate a person's schema for "Lowenbrau." Once activated, this schema controls what informational cues are selected for processing and how they are encoded in memory (e.g. the ad information is processed relevant to the stored knowledge relevant to "Lowenbrau"). That is, the information in the ad will then be processed "in light of" the activated schema. These activated beliefs will serve as the basis for framing processing and evaluations.

However, this proposition assumes that consumers have acquired schemas at different levels of abstraction for the advertised brand or product and that these relevant schemas are available in memory.

This is clearly not the case for all consumers for all brands and products. If a specific schema is not available in memory, the advertisement may activate a more general or abstract schema in memory. For example, if the comparative advertisement compares a new brand of beer to "Lowenbrau," and the consumer is unfamiliar with Lowenbrau beer, the advertisement may then activate a more general schema for imported beers, or beer in general. Alternatively, the consumer could rely primarily on the information available in the advertisement, and form beliefs based on this information as opposed to that which is stored in memory (cf. Bettman and Sujan 1987).

Based on these ideas, we assert that the level of the comparison object will serve as a cue to activate the corresponding or matching schema in memory. If the schema is available in memory, the formation of inferential beliefs will primarily be a function of the contents of that schema. In other words, it will serve as a basis for framing processing and evaluations. When the corresponding schema has not been acquired by the consumer and is not available in memory, processing will be guided by either a schema at a higher level of abstraction and/or primarily by the information available in the advertisement.

If we examine the conditions under which schemas would most likely be available in memory, we may make more specific predictions about when evaluations are more likely to be framed in terms of inferences generated primarily from ad information versus inferences generated from memory, as well as for the types of memory-based inferences depending on the level of the schema that is activated (e.g. brand, product type, product class, etc.).

Categorization theory suggests that the availability of schema in memory is likely to be a function of the (1) level of the category and (2) the knowledge level of the consumer.

Category Level. Categorization theory suggests that there is one basic level of inclusiveness at which individuals naturally categorize and spontaneously name objects. Since most individuals have acquired knowledge and communicate at the basic category level, this schema should be fairly large for most consumers. Therefore, basic level categories should be available in memory for processing advertisement information. For products, Sujan and Dekleva (1987) and Myers-Levy and Tybout (1989) found that the product type level constitutes the basic level of categorization.

Because schemas at the basic category level (product class) are generally available in memory, we propose the following:

P1A: When the comparison object is at the basic category level, processing will more likely be framed primarily in terms of inferences generated from the corresponding memory schemata than by ad-based inferences.

Also,

P1B: When the comparison object is at more specific levels (e.g. brand) or more abstract levels (e.g. non-alternative products), processing and evaluations are more likely to be framed in terms of inferences generated from the ad versus memory based inferences.

Knowledge Level of the Consumer. The second factor that should affect the availability of schemas in memory is the knowledge level of the consumer. Although in general, the basic category level is the one which is most likely to be developed and available for processing, categorization theory also suggests that as consumers' knowledge increases in a domain, so does the specificity of their knowledge structure (Mervis and Rosch 1981). Indeed, the research of Bettman and Sujan (1987) and Walker, et al. (1987) supports the notion that more knowledgeable consumers have access to more specific knowledge. Therefore, we would expect that more knowledgeable consumers would have acquired more specific category schemas (at brand and product type levels) with which to process information, and that this information may be more useful to them than more general, basic category knowledge.

However, although more and less knowledgeable consumers may differ in terms of their knowledge at the brand, product type, and product class levels, they are likely to have equal access to schemas for noncomparable alternatives and non-alternative products. Even for experts, these schemas are often unique and newly formed, and may not have ever considered the particular combination of alternatives (Bettman and Sujan 1987). Therefore, schemas for these alternatives are not likely to be cognitively related to the schema for the sponsored brand in memory. Bettman and Sujan (1987) found that experts and novices did not differ in terms of their ability to evaluate non-comparable alternatives, suggesting that they had equal access to these category structures. Based on their research, we propose the following:

P2A: For less knowledgeable consumers, processing and evaluations are more likely to be framed in terms of inferences generated primarily from the advertisement versus from memory for all levels of the comparison object except when the is at the basic category level.

P2B: For more knowledgeable consumers, processing and evaluations are more likely to be framed in terms of inferences generated primarily from the advertisement versus from memory only when the level of the comparison object is very abstract (e.g.noncomparable alternatives, non-alternative products). Otherwise, memory based inferences will predominate.

P2C: Processing differences between more and less knowledgeable consumers will increase as the level of the comparison object becomes more specific.

The above propositions suggest to what extent category schemata versus advertisement information direct or control the inferences used to frame processing and evaluations. Basically, the level of the comparison object serves as a trigger to activate the corresponding schema in memory. If this schema has been acquired by the consumer, the activated schema will serve as a basis for generating inferences that frame evaluations. Although we did not offer predictions here, the specific nature of inferences generated will likely depend on the particular level of category schema that is activated (see Sujan and Dekleva 1987). If the schema is unavailable in memory, the inferences used to frame processing will be closely related to the information available in the advertisement. The availability of memory schemata is a function of the level of the category and the knowledge level of the consumer.

INFERENTIAL BELIEF FORMATION AND INFORMATION ACCEPTANCE

In addition to having differential effects on the source and types of inferences that consumers make, different types of comparative ads may also effect the believability of the comparative claim. The degree of brand comprehension depends on the degree of information acceptance by the consumer (Droge and Darmon 1987) which has been of central concern to comparative advertising researchers. Although comparative ads have been reported to be less believable than noncomparative advertising (cf. Wilson 1976; Levine 1976; Shimp and Dyer 1978; Golden 1979; Swinyard 1981; Wilson and Muderrisolglu 1979), an examination of the inferential belief formation process suggests that this may depend on the explicitness of the comparative ad.

Inferential Belief Formation

According to Olson (1978), the inferential process itself can be likened to an attributional process in which incoming encoded information from the advertisement environment is matched or fitted into the established beliefs that are stored in memory schemata. Inferences may then be drawn about other concepts not present in the immediate environment. For example, if an advertisement describes a winter coat as "down-filled," this descriptive belief will be compared to the schema for winter coats, and will enable the consumer to then infer certain other qualities of the coat (i.e. light weight, very warm).

However, what happens if the information in the ad does not match or "fit" the belief that is already stored in the existing schemata? For example, a comparative advertisement that states that "Skippy Peanut Butter has more protein than any other sandwich food," may generate the inference that "Skippy" is the best sandwich food. Represented in the consumer's activated schema for peanut butter, however, are the strongly held beliefs that peanut butter is high in fat, high in calories, and is a food to be avoided. Since the information in the advertisement may not "fit" with the schema that is activated in memory, we may expect the information in the ad to be rejected, affecting the acceptance and believability of the comparative claim.

Given these ideas, the explicitness of the comparative claim may determine when information in a comparative advertisement is more or less likely to be accepted. While processing comparative advertisements that are implicit and ambiguous, (i.e. "Mennen goes on warmer and dryer" or "Ragu beats all other brands"), it is likely that the basic level category is automatically activated. Since the implicit claim does not contain specific points with which to conflict with the general or basic level category schema, the ad will be processed naturally and automatically, with minimal conflict. Researchers have found that consumers believe their own inferences after exposure to an implicit comparative advertisement as if they were stated in the advertisement itself (Shimp 1978; Wyckham 1987).

On the other hand, more explicit comparative advertisements that name the competitor and compare the objects based on explicitly named attributes, more opportunity exists for the presence of assertions in the ad that do not fit with the beliefs already stored in the activated memory structure. This situation would lead to the generation of more negative inferences, and stimulate processing as mismatches of ad and memory information have been shown to do (cf. Sujan 1985). Thus, we assert that:

P3: As comparative advertisements become more explicit, the likelihood that the advertisement information will not fit with beliefs that are stored in the activated schemata increases.

Consequently, we are likely see a greater number of total inferences, and more negative inferences, than if the advertisement is more implicit.

Finally, the explicitness of the comparative advertisement will interact with the level of knowledge of the consumer. Because more knowledgeable consumers have more complex and well-defined schemata, they are more likely to conflict with the advertisement than less knowledgeable consumers who do not have schemata available in memory with which to compare the incoming information, whether the comparison is explicit or implicit. Consequently, we propose the following:

P4: Category knowledge will moderate the effects of the explicitness of the comparative ad. Specifically, the explicitness of the comparative claim will have a greater effect on the inferences of more versus less knowledgeable consumers.

RESEARCH IMPLICATIONS

We hope that our "reconceptualization" of comparative advertising will give a new direction to comparative research. Although understanding the effects of explicit brand to brand comparisons that has predominated research is important, there are likely to be dozens of different types of comparative ads, the effects of which are virtually unexplored. Indeed, expanding our view of comparative advertising offers an almost endless prospect of research exploring comparative ads in their numerous degrees, conditions, and outcomes.

We hope that our typology and framework will provide a useful theoretical foundation for future research on comparative advertising. The concepts of memory schemata and category knowledge provide a very useful theoretical foundation, particularly for predicting the inferences that consumers use to frame processing. Inferential beliefs are a powerful indicator of how ads are processed and may provide great insight into understanding the differences between types of comparative ads.

Finally, we believe that our conceptualization may have important implications for public policy. First, our conceptualization suggests that the FTC broaden its definition of comparative advertising, so that all forms of comparative ads be subject to their regulations. Second, it suggests that inferences generated after processing a comparative ad may be an excellent indicator of the deceptive nature of an ad. Recent research suggests that many ads subtly deceive consumers by encouraging them to make inferences about the sponsored brand which may be misleading or completely untrue (Shimp and Preston 1982). We believe that deception through inference or implication may be especially likely to occur with implicit advertisements and ads that compare the sponsored brand to objects with which the consumer is relatively unfamiliar. In these cases, inferences are likely to be generated automatically, without much conscious awareness because they do not conflict with information stored in memory. Understanding and measuring this subtle form of deception and identifying what ads are most likely to mislead is a challenge for future research.

REFERENCES

Bettman, J. R. and M. Sujan (1987), "Effects of Framing of Evaluation of Comparable and Noncomparable Alternatives by Expert and Novice Consumers," *Journal of Consumer Research*, 14, 141-154.

Droge, C. and R.Y. Darmon (1987), "Associative Positioning Strategies Through Comparative Advertising: Attribute vs. Overall Similarity Approaches," *Journal of Marketing Research*, 24, 377-389.

Federal Register (1979), "Comparative Advertising: Issuance of a Policy Statement," 4, no.157 (August 13), 47328-29.

Jackson, D., S. Brown and R. Harmon (1979), "Comparative Magazine Advertisements," *Journal of Advertising Research*, 19(Dec), 21-26.

Johnson, Michael and David Horne (1987), "Subject/Referent Positioning in Comparative Advertising: A Pilot Study," in *Advances in Consumer Research*, vol. 14, eds. Paul Anderson and Melanie Wallendorf, Ann Arbor, MI: Association for Consumer Research, 164-167.

Keller, K. L. (1986), "Memory in Advertising: The Effect of Advertising Memory Cues and Brand Evaluations, " unpublished doctoral dissertation, Duke University, Durham, NC.

Levy, Sidney (1983), "How Comparative is Comparative Advertising?," in Richard P. Bagozzi and Alice M. Tybout, eds., *Advances in Consumer Research*, 381-382.

Lingle, John, M. Altom, and D. Medin (1984), "Of Cabbages and Kings: Assessing the Extendability of Natural Object Concept Models to Social Things," in *Handbook of Social Cognition*, eds. Robert S. Wyer and Thomas K. Srull, Hillsdale, NJ: Lawrence Erlbaum Associates, 71-118.

Mervis, C. B. and E. Rosch (1981), "Categorization of Natural Objects," *Annual Review of Psychology*, 12, 89-115.

Muehling, D. and N. Kangun (1985), "The Multidimensionality of Comparative Advertising: Implications for the FTC," *Journal of Public Policy and Marketing*, 112-128.

Myers-Levy, J. and A. M. Tybout (1989), "Schema Congruity as a Basis for Product Evaluation," *Journal of Consumer Research*, 16, 39-54.

Olson, Jerry (1978), "Inferential Belief Formation in the Cue Utilization Process," in *Advances in Consumer Research*, vol. 5, H. Keith Hunt, ed., Ann Arbor, Michigan: Association for Consumer Research, pp. 706-713.

Rosch, Eleanor (1978), "Principles of Categorization," in *Cognition and Categorization*, eds. Eleanor Rosch and Barbara B. Lloyd, Hillsdale, NJ: Lawrence Erlbaum Associates, 27-48.

Shimp, T. A. (1978), "Do Incomplete Comparisons Mislead?," *Journal of Advertising Research*, 18(December), 21-27.

Shimp, T. A. and Ivan Preston (1982), "Deceptive and Nondeceptive Consequences of Evaluative Advertising," *Journal of Marketing*, 45, 22-32.

Sujan, Mita and C. Dekleva (1987), "Product Categorization and Inference Making: Some Implications for Comparative Advertising," *Journal of Consumer Research*, 14, 372-378.

Turgeon, N. and D. J. Barnaby (1989), "Comparative Advertising: Two Decades of Practice and Research," in J.H. Leigh and C. R. Martin (eds), *Current Issues and Research in Advertising*, vol 11., Ann Arbor, MI: University of Michigan, Graduate School of Business, 41-45.

Walker, Beth, John Swasy, and Arno Rethans (1986), "The Impact of Comparative Advertising on Perception Formation in New Product Introductions," in *Advances in Consumer Research*, vol. 13, ed. Richard Lutz, Ann Arbor, MI: Association for Consumer Research, 121-125.

Walker, Beth, R. Celsi and J. Olson (1987), "Exploring the Structural Characteristics of Consumers' Knowledge," in *Advances in Consumer Research*, Vol. 14, eds. M. Wallendorf and P. Anderson, Provo, UT: Association for Consumer Research, 17-21.

Wyckham, R. G. (1987), "Implied Superiority Claims," *Journal of Advertising Research*, February/March, 54-63.

Self Concept and Advertising Effectiveness: A Conceptual Model of Congruency, Conspicuousness, and Response Mode

George M. Zinkhan, University of Houston
Jae W. Hong, LGAD, Inc.

ABSTRACT

The purpose of this paper is to develop a theoretical model to explain the relationship between self concept and advertising effectiveness. In brief, it is hypothesized that advertising appeals congruent with viewers' self-concept would be superior to incongruent appeals in terms of enhancing advertising effectiveness. Advertising effectiveness is conceptualized as: brand memory, brand attitude, and purchase intentions. It is further expected that various types of self-concept would result in differential impacts under different response measures. A theoretical model is constructed to predict the varying effects of self-concept congruency. The major moderating variables include product conspicuousness and response mode.

INTRODUCTION

Behavioral researchers are increasingly interested in examining symbolic consumer behavior. The impact of the symbolic meaning of a product, however, hinges on the association between the product symbol (a subjective meaning assigned to an object) and consumers' self image (a mental picture representing an entity). If the symbol of a product does not tie in closely with one's self-image, it may have little influence on purchasing behavior, irrespective of its potential symbolic richness. Thus, the impact of product symbolism depends upon the interrelationship between a product's perceived image and the buyer's self-image. In this respect, symbolic purchasing behavior should be studied within the context of the buyer's self-concept, which denotes the way a person perceives her/himself.

Since symbolism is such an important tool in advertising and affects purchase primarily when it connotes an association with self, self-concept can be expected to play a central role in influencing advertising effectiveness (Sirgy 1986). However, there has been relatively little conceptual or empirical work completed to determine under what circumstances advertising appeals congruent with one's self-concept would be superior to incongruent appeals. Congruence here refers to the degree to which advertising expressions coincide with self-concept. In addition, it is not clear which self-concept (actual vs. ideal) would generate the greatest effect on various advertising effectiveness measures (i.e., cognition vs. affect vs. conation).

The purpose of this paper is to construct a theoretical model to predict the effects of advertising expressions (both congruent and incongruent with self-concept) on the dependent variables: memory, preference and purchase intention. A conceptual model (consisting of 7 hypotheses) is proposed to predict the relative importance of various types of self-concept.

SELF-CONCEPT: DEFINITIONS AND DISTINCTIONS

Despite the fact that there is not necessarily agreement concerning the precise conceptualization of self-concept, a basic definition of this term is: "the totality of the individual's thoughts and feelings having reference to himself as an object" (Rosenberg 1979: 7). Self-concept does not refer to the real or existential self (isolated from one's perception). In other words, it is not an objective entity independent of the perceiver. Instead the term denotes individuals' subjective thoughts toward themselves. In this sense, self-concept is a unique sort of attitude. Unlike other attitudes which are perceptual products of an external object, self-concept is an image shaped by the very person holding the image.

Recently, cognitive psychologists have considered self-concept as a set of self-schemata, which are organized cognitive structures in certain domains of the self (Markus, Smith and Moreland 1985). As other schemata, these structures are activated when a person encounters a situation involving personally-relevant information, and they function as mnemonic devices in remembering external stimuli.

Although self-concept can be conceptualized as a cognitive structure, self-concept does not refer to mere knowledge of facts. Rather, self-concept is a cognitive structure which is associated with strong feelings or motivations. That is, self-concept is the knowledge of oneself which includes the driving thrust of other behaviors.

Self-concept is composed of multidimensional characteristics. For instance, a single individual may be a father, a manager, a part-time evening student, a Catholic and a Democrat; a person may be an extrovert, a liberal and an intellectual all at the same time. Nonetheless, self-concept is not a mere conglomeration or addition of isolated concepts of self, but a patterned interrelationship or Gestalt of all these.

Self-concept was defined above as the way a person looks at herself; this is the definition of "actual self-concept". An individual is cognizant of not only what s/he is, but also what s/he wishes to be. The ideal state of imaginative self is termed ideal self-concept. Ideal self-concept is distinguished from actual self-concept in that the former is based on the perceptual reality of oneself, while the latter is shaped by imagination of the ideal self state.

In general, ideal self-concept is the reference point with which actual self is compared. If there is a gap between them, an individual strives to achieve the ideal state. In this respect, ideal self is a motive force driving an individual upward (self-esteem motive). Actual and ideal self-concepts both have social dimensions; however, due to space limitations, no specific hypotheses are developed concerning this social aspect of self concept.

ADVERTISING APPEALS AND SELF-CONCEPT: A MODEL

Self-concept has become accepted as an important psychological construct and the majority of applications which have been completed in a consumer behavior context have been concerned with the self-concept/product (or store) image congruence effect on some criterion variables. From this perspective, self-concept is a promising variable for explaining the effectiveness of various promotional strategies. Specifically, promotional efforts may be more effective if they are directed toward establishing a product image congruent with the consumer's own self-concept. A matching advertising appeal, compared to non-matching appeals, may lead consumers to subsequent behaviors favorable to the product advertised.

Self-concept involves an integrated conceptual system composed of information about oneself. It is concerned with individuals' fundamental frame of reference, and it plays a pivotal role in human behavior. In advertising settings, viewers are presumed to go through a process of comparing ad contents with self-concept when they are exposed to advertising messages. Advertising effectiveness, then, varies depending upon the degree of match between the two entities.

Self-Concept Effects on Memory

Self-concept contains self-related prototypes or self-schemata. As a form of schema, self-schema denotes a knowledge structure composed of conceptually related information about oneself. Markus (1977) defined this concept as "cognitive generalizations about the self, derived from past experience, that organize and guide the processing of self-related information contained in the individual's social experience."

Self-schema contains various types of information about the self. It includes not only verbal information, but also other forms of information such as images, representations and feelings. But as an individual grows up, s/he tends to describe her/himself by more traits, which thus become more significant components of self-concept.

An individual uses this self-schema in processing a variety of other incoming information about the self. It carries out all the functions that schema usually does: selection, abstraction, interpretation, and integration. It directs special attention to, and encodes, only the information which is relevant to an individual. It affects the abstraction process in which the semantic content of the stimulus is extracted from the information selected, and the surface form is lost. The semantic content is then interpreted in such a way as to be consistent with the present self-schema. Finally, the information that remains is integrated with previously acquired, related self-schemata and then stored. Thus, self-schema guides the processes of self-related information in memory, including encoding, organizing, and retrieval.

Like other schemata, self-schema functions as a memory aid. It is self-schema that is active when processing self-related information. External stimuli compatible with self-schema would be readily attended, encoded, comprehended and retained, in comparison with those stimuli which do not fit with it. In other words, individuals with well-developed self-schema process self-related information with relative certainty and resist counter-schematic information. These functions of self-schema lead to a better memory of self-relevant stimuli.

Some suggestive evidence comes from a series of judgment studies by Markus and her associates (Markus 1977; Markus, Crane and Siladi 1978). They provided subjects with a set of trait adjectives, congruent or incongruent with the respondents' own self-concepts, and asked them to judge whether each adjective described the subjects themselves or not. The results consistently revealed that subjects were much faster at endorsing the trait adjectives when the adjectives were congruent with their self-concept than when they were not. Moreover, aschematics who did not have a self-schema with regard to the study domain (i.e., independence/dependence or masculinity/femininity) did not show any systematic differences in their processing times for different trait adjectives.

Other studies conducted in the context of self-reference have shown more direct influence of self-schema on memory. For instance, Rogers, Kuiper and Kirker (1977) utilized the depth of processing paradigm in their study and had subjects make four different judgments on forty adjectives presented: a structural decision (whether the word had big letters), a phonemic decision (whether the word rhymed with another word), a semantic decision (whether the word meant the same as another word), and self-reference decision (whether the word described the subject him/herself). An incidental recall test after the word presentation revealed that the self-reference task resulted in superior recall performance, followed by semantic, phonemic and structural tasks in this order. These results imply that the self-reference tasks generated the deepest memory trace, which, in turn, brought about superior incidental recall. In this respect, self-reference is a more powerful encoding device than a semantic task which is usually found to produce the deepest encoding traces in levels of processing research.

These studies outlined above suggest that people have a well-organized knowledge structure or self-schema about themselves, and if external stimuli are congruent with this self-schema, information processing is facilitated, leading to better memory. Self in this case serves as an encoding device or as a retrieval cue during the recall phase.

Projecting the research results of self-schema into an advertising setting leads to the general prediction that advertisements whose expressions are congruent with a viewer's self-concept should be remembered better than those which are self-incongruent. Memory superiority of self-relevant expressions is expected in terms of the recall and recognition of the brand names delivered in ads.

In addition to the congruency effect of actual self-concept, we may expect similar effects from the congruency between advertising expressions and ideal self-concept. Although our conception of ideal self-image may not be as well developed as that of actual self-concept, we still have ideas about what we want to be like. It is, therefore, foreseeable that ideal self-concept also exerts influences on the recall of the brand names advertised.

The above discussion of memory effect leads to the following set of hypotheses:

H1a: Advertising expressions congruent with one's self-concept produce better memory of advertised brands than self-concept-incongruent ads.

H1b: Advertising expressions congruent with one's ideal self-concept produce better memory of advertised brands than ideal self-concept-incongruent ads.

Self-Concept Effects on Evaluation

In advertising settings, no studies have specifically examined the effects of self-concept on product evaluation. However, data amassed in closely related areas lead to the notion that advertising expressions congruent with the audience's self-concept would be easily accepted and result in a favorable attitude toward the advertised brand.

The research outcome of the self-concept/product image congruency effect might be projected here as the most relevant evidence. Self-concept studies have typically made the following assumptions about buyer behavior. Consumers desire to express themselves in brand choices. Products, services, and/or stores convey certain images or personalities beyond their functional characteristics. Consumers prefer or search for products (or stores) which have images compatible with their perception of self. In other words, consumers buy or prefer those products which possess images most similar to the images they either perceive or wish of themselves. They prefer those products which match their self-concept, since purchases provide a vehicle for self expression. Extending these findings into advertising settings, it is predicted that advertising appeals which match the viewer's self-concept would bring forth preference toward the advertised brand.

Another theoretical basis is derived from social psychology researchers who have studied similarity effects on liking/ attraction in inter-personal relationships. According to research results in this area, similarity among people has a pervasive influence on liking or attraction (Freedman et al. 1974). Thus, there is a strong tendency for people to like others who are similar to themselves in terms of demographics, culture, personality, attitudes, beliefs, hobbies, religion, social class, nationality, and so on.

Empirical research found this tendency when people had similarities in attitude, and even in the description of attitude, opinions and other characteristics (see Byrne 1971 for a review). Although subsequent studies revealed that similarity effects were not unanimous in all conditions, it is generally accepted that similarity is a determining factor in evaluating other people or objects favorably or unfavorably (Berscheid 1985).

The findings of these works both in product/consumer congruity effects and the similarity effects on person/object liking can be logically projected to advertising settings. Thus, ads which depict the product to be similar in its image or characteristics to the target audience's perception of themselves are expected to produce more favorable attitudes toward the product advertised than those which are not similar in this regard.

This contention can be extended to ideal self-concept too. Ideal self-concept is also important to an individual and has high emotional valences. Moreover, it is substantially correlated with actual self-concept (Landon 1974). As such, advertising appeals which are congruent with ideal self-concept are also expected to generate higher preference toward the product than the appeals which are not compatible.

Thus the following effects are expected with respect to attitude formation toward the advertised brand:

H2a: Advertising expressions congruent with one's self-concept produce more favorable attitude toward the product advertised than self-concept-incongruent ads.

H2b: Advertising expressions congruent with one's ideal self-concept produce more favorable attitude toward the product advertised than ideal self-concept-incongruent ads.

Self-Concept Effects on Purchase Intention

Although research pertaining to the effect of self-concept on purchase intention is rare, Landon (1974) and Belch (1978) found that both actual and ideal self-concept influence purchase intention (though their degree of relative impact is different). That is, the more closely a product's image matches the buyers' self-concept, the higher the purchase intention is for that product. The projection of these findings into an advertising setting leads to the prediction that a product described as being congruent with viewers' self-concept would elicit higher purchase intention than a similar product which does not match viewers' self-concept quite so well.

Moreover, studies of the attitude-behavior relationship suggest that purchase intentions are highly related with product attitudes (Ryan and Bonfield 1975). As such, advertising expression congruent with one's self-concept is expected to elicit both a positive attitude toward the advertised product and a favorable purchase intention.

Thus, the arguments developed concerning self-concept effects and attitudes are expected to apply in much the same way to purchase intentions:

H3a: Advertising expressions congruent with one's self-concept produce stronger buying intentions for the product advertised than self-concept-incongruent ads.

H3b: Advertising expressions congruent with one's ideal self-concept produce stronger buying intentions for the product advertised than ideal self-concept-incongruent ads.

Response Modes and the Relative Influences of Self-Concepts

The next question concerns the relative importance of various types of self-concept. For example, is self-concept congruency more influential in terms of purchase intention effect than ideal self-congruency, or is the reverse true? The answer to this question is not straight-forward; however, the basic position is that it depends upon the situation.

Memory or Evaluation? One factor which is presumably critical in determining which self-concept would be most influential is response mode. Specifically, when the task is to remember the information given in an advertisement (i.e., brand name and product information), actual self-concept is expected to play a more significant role than ideal self-concept. In contrast, when the task is to evaluate the advertised product, ideal self-concept is expected to become prominent, compared to actual self-concept (Sirgy 1986).

The rationale underlying this contention is inherent in self-concept motivation. Since self-concept is a central system to everyone, a person tends to maintain or protect self-concept on the one hand, and enhance it on the other hand. These two competing motives are referred to as the self-consistency motive and self-esteem motive, respectively. They co-exist within an individual, providing differing implications; human behavior is influenced by these two fundamental driving forces.

Rosenberg (1979) defined self-consistency motive as "the motive to act in accordance with the self-concept and to maintain it intact in the face of potentially challenging evidence." Although self-concept may change gradually, people have a tendency to preserve or maintain a consistent cognitive state of self. Any external stimuli which threaten the stability of internal conceptual unity produce anxiety or cognitive dissonance between one's own self-perception and incoming stimuli. Consequently, people make attempts to reduce conflict arising from inconsistencies. That is, those stimuli which are incompatible with existing self-concept meet resistance, and only the information which is in accordance with the self-concept is accepted.

Another motive related to self-concept is self-esteem motive (Sirgy 1987). It is the tendency to raise oneself to an aspired state or standard. This motive induces people to engage in activities that may lead them to be seen more positively. This motive is so fundamental that it may not be educeable to further elementary drives (James 1890).

These two motivations -- self-consistency and self-esteem -- may be in accordance with each other in some cases (i.e., when the discrepancy between actual and ideal components of self-concept is minimal), but they may be in conflict in other cases (i.e., actual-ideal discrepancy is extreme). Thus, people may encounter a situation in which they have to choose between enhancing and maintaining their self-concept. Then the relevant question is which motive dominates the other when they are in discord.

The question of whether self-esteem or self-consistency motive is more powerful may depend on the response tasks required. More specifically, it is likely that self-consistency dominates self-esteem if the response mode is memory. Conversely, if one is required to evaluate the given object, it is highly probable that the brand which is likely to enhance one's self-image in the direction of the ideal self will be preferred.

If an individual's task is to remember given information, s/he is more likely to remember information consistent with her/his actual self-concept, compared to information consistent with ideal self-concept. A person possesses a well-developed (actual) schema about her/himself and this constitutes a rich self-oriented information base. Hence s/he would better attend to, encode and retrieve the information congruent with the schema, leading to a deeper memory trace, as long as it is consistent with the actual self-schema developed. The desire to enhance self-image is not particularly relevant for memory processes. What matters is the maintenance of unity within the construal system. One way to do this is to accept the information compatible with one's existing knowledge structure or schema. Henceforth, one would better remember the information congruent with one's self-concept, which has been organized as a form of well-developed self-schema. This is one way to secure a state of cognitive consonance. Therefore the congruence between given information and the actual self gets priority, regardless of the valence (degree of desirability) of the actual self-concept (positive or negative). The effect of ideal self congruency may exist, but its impact is expected to be secondary, only moderating the actual self-concept congruency effect. The primary operative motive here is the self consistency motive, the motive to keep one's actual self-concept intact.

The situation becomes different with evaluation, however. Since evaluation is an affective activity, through which the desirability of an object is determined, the self-esteem motive has a greater impact than the self-consistency motive.

Unlike remembering, evaluating a given object is highly affected by whether or not it is likely to enhance one's self-image toward an ideal state. Accordingly, the brand congruent with one's ideal self will be evaluated more favorably than that which is congruent with actual self. (This is particularly true when the actual self is negative.) That is, the congruity sought more is between product image and ideal self-concept. The product in this case vicariously satisfies the desire to approach the ideal state of self-image. And the brand preference would be decided by the degree to which the brand is described as similar to one's ideal self. This is a way to gratify the self-esteem motive. An example may demonstrate this contention more vividly. A Porsche automobile may be perceived as being consistent with the following set of traits: dynamic, young, wealthy, and powerful. If an individual has an ideal self-concept of "I want to be dynamic, young, wealthy, and powerful," this ideal self-concept coincides with the car image, and preference for the car will be high, irrespective of whether actual self-concept matches with the car image or not.

Summarizing the above discussion from an advertising perspective, advertising information congruent with actual self-concept would be better remembered than that congruent with ideal self-concept; whereas advertising expressions congruent with ideal self would elicit more favorable attitude toward the brand advertised than those congruent with actual self-concept.

These arguments lead to the following hypotheses:

H4: When individuals are required to remember the brand name, those brands with images consistent with their actual self-concept are better remembered than those consistent with ideal self-concept.

H5: When individuals are required to evaluate advertised brands, brands with images consistent with their ideal self-concept are preferred to those with images consistent with actual self-concept.

Product Conspicuousness and Self-Concept Congruity The next issue concerns the relationship between ideal self-concept and ideal social self-concept. That is, which one of these two self-concepts has a greater impact on product evaluation?

One moderating factor which is assumed to be critical in this regard is product conspicuousness. Specifically, when the consumption of a product takes place mainly in public, the consumer will be more concerned with others' responses regarding their consumption. Thus, ideal social self-concept, the image one wants others to hold, is likely to be more relevant than ideal self-concept (the image one would ideally like to be, regardless of others). This is because people have a basic need to receive approval from society or they try to create positive impressions of themselves in others' minds. Some label this the "social approval motive" (Crowne and Marlowe 1964) while others term it "self-presentation motive" (Baumeister 1982). This is the public dimension of the self-esteem motive which operates more in private situations. Accordingly, when consumption of a product is relatively visible to others, social approval motive substitutes for self-esteem motive.

On the other hand, when a product is consumed primarily in private, the consumer will be less concerned about what others think about the consumption of that specific product. The main consideration here is the degree to which the product is satisfactory from the individual's point of view. Under these circumstances, self-esteem motive prevails and the product matching with one's ideal self-concept would be preferred to that compatible with ideal social self-concept.

In summary, when product consumption is mainly private, self-esteem motive is more important than a social approval motive, and consumers are expected to be guided by their ideal self-concept. Thus, the brand most similar to their ideal self is preferred to that consistent with ideal social self. In contrast, when the consumption takes place in public, social approval motive prevails, and the reverse holds true. These arguments lead to the following hypotheses:

H6a: If an advertised product is mainly consumed in private, the brand most consistent with a consumer's ideal self-concept is preferred to that consistent with ideal social self-concept.

H6b: If an advertised product is mainly consumed in public, the brand most consistent with a consumer's ideal social self-concept is preferred to that consistent with ideal self-concept.

Purchase Intention and Differential Impact of Self-Concept It is expected that purchase intention will be affected more by ideal self-concept than actual self-concept. Self-esteem is the prime motive here as consumers strive to reduce the actual-ideal gap by choosing a product with a similar image to their ideal self.

However, this argument holds true only when the discrepancy between actual self-concept and product image is moderate. As long as the discrepancy is low or moderate, one's motivation to enhance oneself (self-esteem motive) would prevail, thus increasing buying intention of the brand with images consistent with ideal self. If the discrepancy is extreme, on the other hand, one's buying intention would be no more in line with ideal self. The product image deviates too much from actual self-concept so that the consumer would realize that the product image is too far from his/her actual image, and buying intention would diminish. Thus, products congruent with ideal self would evoke low buying intention when the gap between product image and the present state of self is excessive. The relevant hypotheses for purchase intentions are extracted from this contention.

> H7a: If the discrepancy between product image and actual self-concept is low or moderate, advertised brands consistent with ideal self-concept elicit higher purchasing intention than those consistent with actual self-concept.
>
> H7b: If the discrepancy between product image and actual self-concept is extreme, advertised brands consistent with actual self-concept elicit higher purchasing intention than those consistent with ideal self-concepts.

Sirgy (1980) found partial support for the hypothesis 7. However, his hypotheses were not specified in terms of the degree of gap between product image and actual self-concept as is the case in H7a and H7b.

The above discussion has centered on the notion that the congruity between advertising expression and self-concept plays an important role in ad effectiveness. The relative impact of the various types of self-concept is expected to vary depending on response modes and product conspicuousness. The resulting conceptual model specifies 7 hypotheses to organize and summarize the extant literature on self-concept and advertising effects.

DISCUSSION

The conceptual model developed in this paper is designed to predict the various influences which self concept have on advertising effectiveness. To date, this has been a relatively under-investigated area in consumer behavior research. We know a fair amount about the notion of self concept and how it applies to consumer bahvior in general. However, we know comparatively less about how self concept relates to advertising principles and strategies. It may be that self concept exerts some of its strongest effects on consumer behavior by acting through promotional vehicles and images. In this regard, the notions of self-congruency and product conspicuousness may be especially useful for understanding and predicting these promotional effects.

Past research has also been somewhat unclear in specifying the roles which various sorts of self concept play in guiding behavior. For example, which is more important for predicting attitude formation: actual self concept or ideal self concept? We don't always have very precise answers to these kinds of questions, and there is some reason to suspect that situational influences may play an important role. One of the goals of this paper has been to shed some light on this issue by specifying the circumstances under which one variety of self concept may be dominant over another.

Measurement is another potentially delicate issue. As pointed out by Sirgy (1982), the scales typically used for the measurement of self-concept and brand image are susceptable to halo effects. In this respect, it is important for self-concept researchers to employ alternative methodologies, such as protocol measures, which are less prone to halo effects. In addition, it might prove fruitful to employ multiple indicators for memory in order to provide more specific insights about the role which self-schema plays at each stage of information processing.

Particular emphasis should be placed on investigating the theoretical foundations of the self-concept effect. Most self-concept studies to date have merely shown that self-concept/ brand image congruency and brand preference (or purchase intention) are correlated. No plausible explanations were provided regarding the underlying, conceptual rationale.

Here, a conceptual model has been developed to explain various self-concept effects. However, there may be many other relevant perspectives not yet developed. Alternatively, such conceptual schemes may have been developed, but not specifically applied to the context of self-concept research.

REFERENCES

Baumeister, Roy F. (1982), "A Self-Presentation View of Social Phenomena," *Psychological Bulletin*, 91, 3-26.

Belch, George E. (1978), "Belief Systems and the Differential Role of the Self-Concept," in *Advances in Consumer Research*, Vol. 5, ed. H. Keith Hunt, Ann Arbor, MI: Association for Consumer Research, 320-325.

Berscheid, Ellen (1985), "Interpersonal Attraction," in *Handbook of Social Psychology*, Vol. 2, eds. Gardner Lindzey and Elliot Aronson, New York: Random House, 413-484.

Byrne, Don (1971), *The Attraction Paradigm*, New York: Academic Press.

Crowne, Douglas P. and David Marlowe (1964), *The Approval Motive: Studies in Evaluative Dependence*, New York: Wiley.

Freedman, Jonathan L., J. Merrill Carlsmith, and David O. Sears (1974), *Social Psychology*, Englewood Cliffs, NJ: Prentice-Hall.

James, William (1890), *Principles of Psychology*, New York: Holt.

Landon, E. Laird, Jr. (1974), "Self Concept, Ideal Self Concept, and Consumer Purchase Intentions," *Journal of Consumer Research*, 1 (September), 44-51.

Markus, Hazel (1977), "Self-Schemata and Processing Information about the Self," *Journal of Personality and Social Psychology*, 35 (2), 63-78.

_____, Marie Crane, and Michael Siladi (1978), "Cognitive Consequences of Androgyny," paper presented at the meeting of the Midwestern Psychological Association, Chicago.

———, Jeanne Smith, and Richard Moreland (1985), "Role of the Self-Concept in the Perception of Others," *Journal of Personality and Social Psychology*, 49 (6), 1494-1512.

Rosenberg, Morris (1979) *Conceiving the Self*, New York: Basic Books, Inc.

Rogers, T.B., N. A. Kuiper, and W. S. Kirker (1977), "Self-Reference and the Encoding of Personal Information," *Journal of Personality and Social Psychology*, 35 (9), 677-688.

Ryan, Michael J. and E.H. Bonfield (1975), "The Fishbein Extended Model and Consumer Behavior," *Journal of Consumer Research*, 2 (September), 118-136.

Sirgy, M. Joseph (1980), "Self-Concept in Relation to Product Preference and Purchase Intention," in *Developments in Marketing Science*, Vol. 3, ed. V. V. Bellur, Marquette, MI: Academy of Marketing Science, 350-354.

——— (1982), "Self-Concept in Consumer Behavior: A Critical Review," *Journal of Consumer Research*, 9 (December), 287-300.

——— (1986), *Self-Congruity*, New York: Praeger.

——— (1987), "The Moderating Role of Response Mode in Consumer Self-Esteem/Self-Consistency Effects," *AMA Winter Educators' Conference*, 50-55.

The Troupe: Celebrities as *Dramatis Personae* in Advertisements
Linda M. Scott, University of Texas at Austin

The theater of advertising plays on a stage where the curtain never falls. Plots range from farce to melodrama, from pathos to parody, requiring a range of actors to fill the roles. Because ads depend on quick characterization, their *dramatis personae* often come from the repertory troupe of popular culture. Public characters appear in ads in all their variety: heroes and harlots, villains and virgins, paupers and pop stars make up the ever-assembling ensemble. The typical, the ideal, the notorious, the famous, and the fictive jostle each other as the cast rushes from television to film to sports to politics to art--stopping here and there to act in a commercial *mise èn scene*. Easily, like a film star slips into a soap spot, advertising creatures creep into the discourses of art or politics. The interconnections between players and texts become increasingly labyrinthine.

The commercial stage is large, the cast is huge, and the plays various, yet scholarly study of celebrity advertising reduces it to ahistorical, untheatrical formulae. The purpose here is to broaden the scope of inquiry by elaborating on Grant McCracken's argument (1989) that celebrity advertising is a culturally-grounded phenomenon. I will argue that these ads combine the power of *two* cultural constructs: the celebrity persona and the advertising text itself. My intention is to refine McCracken's notion of "meaning transfer," providing articulation between his concept of celebrity and the suggestion, made by Wells (1988), Stern (1989), McCracken himself (1987), and others, that ads be viewed as a cultural form, specifically as literary or dramatic texts. In the process, several means by which consumers invoke cultural frameworks and perform interpretive moves within the genre of celebrity advertising will be described.

I also wish to address here McCracken's concern that current cultural critiques of celebrity are reductive of the market system and the public mind:

> There is indeed a delicate and thoroughgoing relationship between the culture, the entertainment industry, and the marketing system in modern North America. We are beginning to understand what this relationship is and how it works. We must hope that the first victims of this emerging understanding will be the glib assertions that characterize North American consumers as the narcissistic, simple-minded, manipulated playthings of the market place.... As we begin to render a more sophisticated account of how these systems work, we will begin to see that North American culture and commerce are more interesting and more sophisticated than its critics have guessed (McCracken 1989, 318-319).

In broaching this issue, I intend to bring the discourse of cultural criticism further into the collective knowledge of consumer research, adding to the process begun by Rogers (1987).

CULTURAL CRITICISM AND CELEBRITY: A QUICK SKETCH

The study of popular culture in industrial society currently comes under the rubric of "cultural studies." Because departments of literature, music, and art have historically shunned the scholarly analysis of popular artifacts, the serious study of "mass" forms has been a fairly recent phenomenon--one that still retains the stigma of dilettantism in more traditional circles. But a certain intellectual status has been attained by cultural study employing the neomarxian perspective known as "critical theory." This work on popular culture is increasingly known preemptively as "cultural criticism."

Cultural criticism is rooted in the work of the Frankfurt School, a group of German Marxists who began to write about capitalist culture shortly before World War II. The School sought to reestablish the Hegelian dialectic as the analytical template for Marxist thought and applied the theory to culture as well as to economy. The emphasis was on identifying negations in cultural forms as symptoms of dialectical antinomies at work--proof of the process of an idealized History (Jay 1973). Cultural criticism, as practiced by Adorno, Horkheimer, Marcuse, and Benjamin, tended to favor theory over empirical observation and historical research. Their essays on popular culture thus often convey a disturbing sense of presentism, elitism, ethnocentrism, and even a limited familiarity with the object. Further, the School's theory of the culture industry conceptualizes culture as ideological form imposed on the populace by an economic monolith (Arato and Gebhart 1988). Today's cultural critics are influenced by other theorists, such as Althusser, Barthes, and Bakhtin, but despite efforts of later marxians, especially Raymond Williams and Fredric Jameson, there is still a marked tendency to look for contradictions as a basis for theoretical speculation, to ignore the "us-ness" of culture, to avoid empirical study in favor of abstractions, and to shut out consideration of historical continuities.

Celebrity fascinates cultural critics. However, their assumptions about the nature and conditions of celebrity reflect the motivations of theory. These critics assert that celebrity:

(1) is unique to capitalism, existing to perpetuate a consumption ethic through emulative desire (Dyer 1982)

(2) is unique to the twentieth century, a product of technologies that reproduce

images (Schickel 1985, Dyer 1982, and others)

(3) depends on audiences given to trance-like adoration/emulation (Tudor 1974)

(4) requires large-scale, bureaucratic societies (Alberoni 1972)

(5) occurs only in societies that produce a surplus and have a "culture industry" charged with perpetuating dominant ideologies (King qtd. in Dyer 1982, p. 8, Marcuse 1964).

Cultural criticism characterizes the theatrical roles of stars as a deceptive ideological device, rather than as interpreted experience grounded in dramatic tradition. The difference between the "real" celebrity and the playing of a character is seen as evidence of "inauthenticity" or "contradiction" (Braudy 1986, p. 580; Dyer 1982, pp. 22-24). To appear in a commercial renders the celebrity "meaningless" (Boorstin 1961; Dyer 1982, p. 14). Ads themselves are given only superficial ideological critiques, poorly researched, without a sense of cultural or historical links between forms, between political economies, or even between the ad and the object it fetishizes (see especially Miller 1979; Williamson 1978). Cultural critics cast the audience in remarkably denigrative terms, particularly given their social sympathies. Mass communications audiences are seen as ideologically blinded, helpless at the mercy of their industrial controllers, easily led into slavishly emulating capitalist idols (Dyer 1982, Braudy 1986, Schiekel 1985). Mass communications "speakers" are presented as prime movers in a "top down" ideological apparatus, collaborating to control the passive populace.

Although the opposites engaged in dialectical process can be correctly seen as intermingled and transformative, cultural criticism generally insists on treating the market society and all its attributes as an anomaly. This is apparently due to an overemphasis on the oppositions of the dialectic, as opposed to its processual aspect. Thus, in current cultural criticism, forms produced by capitalism are presented in opposition to both a past and a future moment in History. The finding that something approximating celebrity occurred in a previous period would fundamentally challenge the overriding grand theory. Further, the possibility that celebrity occurs in nonindustrial culture, or that it serves some cultural purpose, would violate the negative hermeneutic that has driven cultural criticism since Adorno and Horkheimer (Arato and Gebhart 1988). It should not be surprising, therefore, that past foundations of celebrity are never explored in such works. Celebrity in all its forms becomes a contemporary phenomenon that has no forebears in pre-industrial history and no commonality of experience within the sociology of the human.

ADVERTISING RESEARCH

Advertising researchers have seen themselves as applied scholars, serving the needs of the marketing community with objective, generalizable, and commercially-useful findings. Thus, the historically intertwined axes of science and instrumentality are everywhere present. The hallmarks of scientific method control for the particular, accidental, and problematic in pursuit of the universal. Thus, in its desire for universality, the prevailing practice of advertising research has tended to ahistorical and culture-blind.

As McCracken argues, studies of the commercial use of celebrities search for the quintessential elements in a public personality that result in persuasion and purchase (recent examples are Akin and Block 1983; Homer and Kahle 1990; Kahle and Homer 1985; Kamins 1990; Kamen, Azhair, Kragh 1985; Klebba and Unger 1983). Celebrities are rated for "likeability," "credibility," and "attractiveness" in a process that smoothes over individuated meanings. Results are correlated with reported viewers' responses, suggesting that the celebrity insinuates desire for the product in the viewer directly through his/her personal attributes. So, any highly likeable celebrity could sell any product to any viewer in any format at any point in time. This leaves little room for a discriminating viewer. Furthermore, none of this literature studies textual mediation of the meaning of the celebrity appearance. The cultural tradition, stylistic particularities, or historical grounding of the celebrity endorsement are merely extraneous sources of variation.

THE ALTERNATIVE APPROACH

McCracken calls attention to the anomalies existing both within the literature and in the experience of celebrity advertising. He proposes that celebrities have specific, highly-refined meanings that are culturally-derived and brought to the advertisement. He argues that these meanings are transferred to the product by the ad. Consumers then choose those meanings and products that best fit their "production of self" project.

McCracken's article constitutes a challenge to both models outlined above. It insists on the specificity of celebrities and of products, and cites culture as the source and ground for making their meaning (see also McCracken 1988). Yet in proposing such a straightforward model of meaning transfer, he implies a certain sameness of advertising forms. While emulation is frequently suggested by celebrity advertising, it is not the only stance that ads take with regard to the famous. A model of celebrity advertising should accomodate many stories and many voices, not just those we wish to emulate. For example, as McCracken points out, the characters previously played by a celebrity impinge on the ads in which that person appears. But this is true whether the referred character is a hero, a clown, or a villain--and the ad may use that character theatrically without intending or effecting a transfer of that meaning to the product. In this way, the narrative, poetic, or rhetorical text in which a celebrity persona appears has an impact on the meaning ultimately conveyed. Modern advertisements bend, refract, even parody the meanings of the celebrities they employ. The relationship between character and meaning is far from direct. Finally, celebrity advertising is a genre with traditions that frame the viewer's interpretation. So, advertising history and conventions are themselves germane. The practice of linking a celebrity to an object has a long past. Today's celebrity ads are part of that tradition, making each present instance but the latest one.

A POSSIBLE HISTORY OF CELEBRITIES AND PRODUCTS

Despite the desires of the scientific and cultural critical schools to separate the modern market from more "primitive" or "communal" societies, an illuminating avenue for understanding the modern marketplace is to look for its roots in preindustrial culture (Hirschman 1985). In his classic analysis of gift systems, Marcel Mauss outlined the practices of tribal cultures of North America, Asia, and the Pacific, as well as archaic cultures from Greek to Hindu (1954). Among other similarities was a consistent tendency to imbue goods with personified meanings, generally associated with the giver of the item, but also elaborated by stories of trading and ownership. Exchanges were accomplished through the tribal chieftains, who often played a shamanistic role in which ancestors or mythical characters were invoked in the gift transfer. Objects thus became both profoundly storied and thoroughly personified.

More recent anthropologists have contrasted these practices with modern commodity distribution, arguing that the homogeneity of things in modern capitalist society is fundamentally anticultural, working against a basic need to singularize goods (Appadurai and Kopytoff 1986). Yet even a cursory acknowledgement of modern advertisements must admit their effort to singularize commodities. Particularly in celebrity advertising, there appears an intention similar to preindustrial rituals for personifying material objects.

In archaic societies, goods were often personified by association with gods, military heroes, or athletes. The mythologies of Roman, Greek, Egyptian, and Teutonic cultures are supported by arcane systems of attribution between goods and gods. Decorative artifacts frequently depict the lives of gods, heroic battles, or athletic contests. Among cultural critics, Dyer dismissed similarities between ancient gods and current celebrities by insisting that gods were ideal, unlike the depressingly "typical" heroes of today (1982, p. 24). Yet we can easily recall myths that depict gods with human foibles, such as vanity, greed, and forgetfulness, and tell stories of gods participating in such unidealized acts as treachery and rape. Further, the current angst over criminal acts by athletes could be explained as cultural disappointment in idealized heroes.

In Western medieval society, goods were no longer decorated with images of the gods. The transition to a monotheistic, abstract notion of god--as well as to a religion that denied the material--made this practice both narratively limited and blasphemous. However, the institution of a Christian pantheon of saints finds expression in household artifacts decorated with and dedicated to personages of Christian celebrity (Csikszentmihalyi and Rochberg-Halton 1981). Today's penchant for Elvis plates and Lucy figurines suggests the continuity between the saints of the Dark Ages and the celebrities of these dark ages. Ultimately, the rise of the secular state provided another basis for artifactual celebrity--that of the royal patronage. The insignia of the sovereign on a commodity testified to its quality and social acceptability. Even today, royal endorsement of goods is a significant gesture in Great Britain.

Just before industrialization, the public "arbiter of taste" emerged. These worthies were often royalty (Empress Eugenie, Josephine, Princess Borghese) or aristocracy (Mme. Pompadour), but sometimes warriors (Napoleon) or just self-proclaimed connoisseurs (Beau Brummel). They affected the distribution of goods of all sorts: permission to associate their names with a fragrance or type of cloth was considered a guarantee of success (Morris 1984).

Mass distribution of print media and goods, as well as the aristocracy's decline, eventually supported another source of celebrity, the arts. The cultural critics' notion that there were no stars before television or film is, of course, nonsense. It is hard to argue that Caruso, Bernhardt, and Njinsky were not stars simply because we have no tapes of them. And, even in those times, creating an association with the people, characters, and works of the arts was thought to bring an "aesthetic appeal" to goods and to retail establishments (Wicke 1989). Showing Shakespeare on a brochure, putting a Rudyard Kipling story in a pack of tobacco, or caricaturing Oscar Wilde in an advertisement represent common practices during this period (Wicke 1989).

During the period from about 1850 to 1920, we also see a growing incidence of fictive characters in advertising: characters portrayed on stage, characters of literature and myth, and characters designed specifically for ads. For example, the characters of the *Pickwick Papers* appeared right away in the names and ads for goods and services in Dicken's London (Wicke 1989). In 1920s magazines, actresses endorsing products are often pictured in costume. Many "celebrities" were developed specifically for advertising: the Campbell's Soup Kids, Betty Crocker, Lydia E. Pinkham. In the early industrial public mind, as in ancient and preindustrial cultures, the meanings of celebrities and objects were tied up in the fictive and storied.

It appears plausible that a cultural trajectory goes from the personification of gifts and the material attributes of gods to the royal patronage to the modern celebrity endorsement. All give

"I lost 30 pounds in three months and never felt better in my life."
— *Tommy Lasorda*

"Everybody knows I love to eat and it really showed. For years I tried to lose weight but all my diets failed because they made me feel hungry, tired and irritable...

Then I Discovered Ultra Slim-Fast® The Safe, Healthy Way to Lose Weight Fast.

I was amazed by how incredibly good Ultra Slim-Fast tastes. I had a shake for breakfast, one for lunch and then a healthy dinner—even pasta. I felt so nourished and satisfied, I was never hungry. And the pounds just dropped away.

I Expected to Lose Weight. I Didn't Expect This Incredible Feeling of Energy.

These days I can pitch an hour of batting practice after my regular workout. My coaches are so impressed that they've put many of the players on Ultra Slim-Fast. They love it too.

Today I'm Keeping the Weight Off the Same Way I Took It Off —with Ultra Slim-Fast.

Now I enjoy an Ultra Slim-Fast shake for breakfast, and as a high-energy snack every day. I never felt better in my life. With thick, cold and delicious Ultra Slim-Fast shakes, losing weight and keeping it off is easy. Take my word for it and get yourself Ultra Slim-Fast. It works."

Enjoy a sensible, well-balanced meal for dinner.

Ultra Slim-Fast is a healthy, well-balanced weight-loss program, complete with 18 essential vitamins and minerals, plus fiber, protein and carbohydrates.

Give us a week, we'll take off the weight.

NOTE: Tommy Lasorda may not be typical of the average Slim-Fast user. Most users need to lose less weight. Weight loss varies with the individual depending on a variety of factors

© 1989 Thompson Medical Company.

THE FRESHNESS SHOULD NOT LEAVE ONE'S MOUTH AS SOON AS ONE'S TOOTHBRUSH DOES.

—The Colgate Wisdom Tooth

Ahh, the clean sensation of brushing your teeth. Wouldn't it be great if that feeling could last longer than the few moments it took to achieve it?

With Colgate Tartar Control toothpaste, it can. Colgate is the wise choice because it helps you fight tartar and feel it. Colgate helps to keep your teeth cleaner and smoother, and gives your mouth an incredibly fresh tingle. It's a breathtaking feeling, noticeably fresher than you may be used to. And best of all, it lasts even after you brush.

So make the wise choice. Fight tartar with Colgate. And freshness will be more than just a memory.

The Wise Choice.

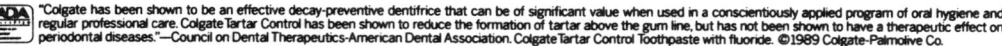

"Colgate has been shown to be an effective decay-preventive dentifrice that can be of significant value when used in a conscientiously applied program of oral hygiene and regular professional care. Colgate Tartar Control has been shown to reduce the formation of tartar above the gum line, but has not been shown to have a therapeutic effect on periodontal diseases."—Council on Dental Therapeutics-American Dental Association. Colgate Tartar Control Toothpaste with fluoride. ©1989 Colgate-Palmolive Co.

meaning to goods through association with people that have a shared status in the public mind.

ADVERTISING, READING, AND CULTURAL TRADITION

Advertisements themselves are cultural artifacts. As such, they reflect both the traditions of the past and the styles of the moment: they are unavoidably situated in history and society. Ads have formal conventions of their own. But they also reflect the formal conventions of other, related forms such as literature, drama, and art, as part of the historical path in which the mass media have developed. In turn, if the style of the moment is for irony or parody, we can be sure that some ads will be parodic or ironic. In each case, the viewer must correctly assemble the meaning of the ad by invoking the norms of both past and present. So, we learn to interpret the actor in an ad in much the same way that we interpret an actor in a play--within the framework of that particular theatrical instance. In sum, actual advertisements are complex cultural constructions that require real reading, as opposed to mere "decoding" or "response."

Cultural critiques of advertising advance rapidly to the systemic level of analysis, leaving behind the empirical study of specific ads (Simon 1980, Wicke 1989). Similarly, the scientific approach to advertising, in its penchant for isolating executional elements or aggregating large numbers of commercials for testing, *also* advances to the systemic level without first building an appreciation for the specificity of the texts. In both cases, generalizations thus reached are often in basic conflict with the particulars. Notions of stimulus/response, direct meaning transfer, or blind ideological manipulation are all contradicted by the complexity of the forms themselves, as the following examples will demonstrate.

THE ETHOS AND THE READER

In the Slimfast ad in Figure 1, Tommy Lasorda makes the kind of straightforward, exhortative pitch that is clearly paradigmatic for both the cultural critical and scientific studies of celebrity advertising. As readers living in twentieth-century Western culture, we know that a corporation is, in fact, the real speaker behind this advertisement. But as an organizational abstraction, the company has, in actuality, no voice. Instead, it has hired or otherwise persuaded Lasorda to endorse its product and represent it as a speaker to the community. So, Lasorda's function is fundamentally one of representation. As a speaker chosen by the company, he represents its character. He is thus suggestive of what rhetoricans call the *ethos* or what reader-response theorists call the *implied author* (Gibson 1980). The ethos/implied author is a fictive construct that exists between the characters in the piece (including direct speakers like Lasorda) and the author/speaker who is responsible for the work itself.

The ethos is suggested by actions and words, and by the style and choice of visual and sound cues. The entire system of cues that describes the ethos--the deixis--constitutes a description of the implied author. Characters in any symbolic form are considered deictic, especially first-person narrators or direct addressors. In this ad, the picture(s) of Lasorda, the exhortative tone of the copy, the excess of verbiage, and the overuse of bold-face, italics, and call-outs all suggest a particular, perhaps rather overbearing, ethos.

The construction of the implied author directly describes a corresponding fictive reader, known in reader-response theory as the "*mock reader*" (Gibson 1980). The deictic cues, designed to appeal in a certain way to a certain sort of reader by describing a certain ethos, suggests the desired relationship between speaker, reader, and object (Bakhtin 1989), and thus are a major basis for building the ground of mutual confidence necessary to persuasion. Importantly, the reader, in order to be persuaded, must *choose* to step into this triangle. Texts are rejected by readers who don't want to become the implied reader suggested by the deixis (Booth 1961). Thus, we can see that the foundation for celebrity advertising is the dialogic relationship between speaker and viewer that the celebrity alone merely suggests.

INTERPRETING THE DEIXIS

The deixis in a celebrity ad may point to an ethos in a veiled, indirect, or playful way. In the recent commercials for Oldsmobile, the children of famous stars of television and film are shown driving under circumstances that allude to the fictive characters played by their parents. In one spot, Deborah Moore, daughter of Roger Moore, drives an Oldsmobile through a car chase scene that is full of James Bond conventions: gadgetry, fancy driving, sudden explosions, an attack by a helicopter, close calls, shadowy bad guys dressed like cat burglars, and so on. These formal features point *not* to Roger Moore as a person, but to the fictive character of James Bond--who has been played by other actors. But the ethos being constructed, despite the preponderance of Bond/Moore references, is neither Bond nor Moore. We know this because the theatrical circumstances, the appearance and cool demeanor of Deborah Moore, and the campaign tagline actually play *against* the fictive character so carefully evoked: "This is not your father's Oldsmobile." Taken together, these spots suggest an ethos that is the progeny of fast car drivers and spaceship captains of yesterday--yet a progeny that is marked by an assertive insouciance. Clearly, this campaign, which is self-referential and intertextual at many levels, is far more complex than a transfer of the meaning of Roger Moore--who doesn't even appear in the spot. Instead, the meaning must be understood as a youthful, rebellious challenge to that celebrity insofar as he may be seen to allegorize the authority of fathers.

Just as constituting the ethos suggested by a celebrity often requires complex interpretive moves by the viewer, so may finding the mock reader. In the Colgate toothpaste ad in Figure 2, we see the image of the quintessential Chinese wise man. The headline, written like a Confucian proverb, and the "wisdom tooth" pun all play on a conventional picture of Oriental wisdom. Yet this not just any spiritual teacher, but Pat Morita, who effected the most recent popularization of the Chinese wise man in the "Karate Kid" film series. Morita himself is not identified anywhere in the ad--his meaning is confined to the narrative character being evoked. In the case of Morita, two potential narrative characters could be evoked: the wise teacher of the "Karate Kid" and Arnold, the comical malt shop owner of "Happy Days." The other formal elements constrain the choice of the character. The reader must correctly interpret the cues and make the choice in order to "get" the message. This is the reader's portion of the narrowing and selection of formal cues alluded to by McCracken (1989, p. 316). Even so, the meaning transfer is not between Pat Morita and the actual reader, because there is a mock reader involved with a strong narrative character of his own: the neophyte who is always the counterpart to the Chinese wise man. Thus, the reader is not being asked to identify with Pat Morita, but with his implied student. Entering into the relationship of this persuasion thus requires stepping into the role of the neophyte--not the emulation of the speaker.

In situations like these, we are dealing not just with dialogue, but with theater. Thus, we can't assume that celebrities function only as emulative models in advertising, or even that they always appear as "positive stimuli." In a Mastercard commercial made about five years ago, Vincent Price appears gleefully watching insects die in a bug light he bought with the card. Is emulation the purpose? Or laughter based on parody? Clearly, the circumstances of appearance direct the interpretation of the celebrity by the viewer.

THEATRICALITY AND DRAMATIC FORM

As in the production of a Broadway play, the choice of casting a "star" in an ad is available to those who can pay the price. But, as in the case of a play, the meaning of the star is both *brought to* and *altered by* the drama itself. Think about the famous Joe Namath ads for Beautymist pantyhose. In these mid-1970s ads, the camera pans slowly up a pair of sleek, pantyhosed legs to register their owner (surprise!), a famous football player. Now, surely, the potential buyer of the pantyhose is not supposed to be attributing the meaning of Joe Namath to the pantyhose and thus to herself. And, surely, to interpret this ad as an example of perverted gender contradictions in late capitalist society entirely misses the point.

Here we have a time-honored dramatic form of entertainment--the farce. Farce dates to medieval France and is typified by ridiculous situations and burlesqued characters. The ancestor of the farce, the fabliaux, brought ribaldry to the tradition--cross-dressing is endemic to the genre. The choice of Joe Namath in this farcical construct is not coincidental. When these advertisements appeared, Namath had established a strong national persona who was flippant, bawdy, arrogant, and vain. He was also aggressively virile and heterosexual. Yet he was repeatedly characterized in the popular press as someone who could "get away with it," whether "it" was a swinging singles lifestyle or an unabashed vanity--or wearing a pair of pantyhose. The meaning of Joe Namath is part of the farce. It could not have been Dick Butkus in these pantyhose. Nor Truman Capote. Nor Richard Nixon. We read this commercial *as farce* and not as a mean perversion precisely because it *is* Broadway Joe and no one else on the other end of those sleek legs.

The theatrical form of the spot is important not only to its interpretation, but to its evaluation as felt experience. In the American Express credit card campaign of the 1980s, various celebrities who were well known by their names, but not their faces, talk about the problems they have when they are not recognized at a restaurant or on the road. From the beginning of the spot, the actual identity of the "celebrity" is held in secret. It becomes part of the game of watching these commercials to guess who the celebrity is. At the end, we are told by the now-familiar punching of their name on the American Express credit card.

This campaign mirrors the form of the masque, in which masked players enacted a drama without revealing their identities. That is, until the end. The pleasure of the entertainment, usually conducted among friends, was to guess who was playing behind the mask prior to the revelation. In this case, a similar kind of pleasurable suspense is being recreated. It can occur only by using celebrities because these are the "friends" that we as the culture of viewers would recognize. Notice also that the suspense can only take place because there is that category of celebrities, even in the electronic age, *who are known by their names, but not their images.*

CELEBRITY AND SUBVERSION

Cultural critics and advertising researchers tend to overlook uses of advertising that are not consumption-related. Yet in this area we see an increasingly important use of celebrities--the "subversive" celebrity as social spokesman. This kind of celebrity, usually a rock star, (1) challenges the dominant order artistically or politically, (2) becomes famous, and (3) does not become famous or successful enough to be considered "coopted." These celebrities differ substantively from the implicit celebrity in traditional advertising research--a celebrity who is likeable, credible, and unequivocally mainsteam. But it is this very difference that gives subversive celebrities their rhetorical power, particularly in the ads where we now find them.

On an average evening with MTV, there are many commercials for goods, but there are also a noticeable number of ads telling viewers not to take drugs, not to drive drunk, not to have sex carelessly, not to litter, not to smoke, not to drop out of school, and so on. In many cases, the speakers in these spots will be scruffy celebrities dressed in black leather, affecting a rebellious stance, and wearing earrings in unlikely places. The subversive celebrity has become a crucial tool in an advertising genre that attempts to prevent socially destructive behaviors. These speakers do not fit the traditional advertising model of celebrity likeability. In fact, their apparent persuasiveness on such sensitive topics is that they decidedly do not represent the dominant order--in the form of parents or teachers. Thus, their credibility lies in subcultural standing, rather than mainstream appeal. In light of this genre, the ethnocentricity of the scientific model's notions of "credibility" and "likeability" is made starkly visible.

THE PROBLEM OF DOUBLENESS

As in stylistics or linguistics in literature (see Hirsch 1976), the texts that disprove simple models of meaning in advertising have meanings that are "doubled," as in parody, irony, satire, puns. Such forms are becoming frequent in advertising, as an outgrowth of postmodern style.

In a Tony Lama boot ad appearing currently, a full-length photograph of an old cowboy is identified as "Calvin Klein--Horsebreeder, Klein, Texas." The picture of this old cowboy is purposefully juxtaposed with the name of a famous designer. The small copy block explains, "We're told our boots are preferred by rockers, celebrities, movie stars, even presidents. That notion always brings a chuckle to Calvin." A rural working man-- with the ironic, but fortuitous, coincidence that his name is Calvin Klein-- is thus invoked to make the preferences of the rich and famous look ridiculous. The point here isn't that the boots are endorsed by Calvin Klein, but precisely that they are not. This ad reverses the conventional roles of celebrity advertising, and so employs one of the classic strategies of satire, in which the pretensions of the high and mighty are reduced metaphorically and effectively to the absurd. Yet this ad cannot exist except within a *recognizable tradition* of celebrity endorsements.

An eleven-page ad for Nike features photographs of five famous athletes with corresponding athletic shoes. The copy, however, is a stream-of-consciousness rambling that is clearly parodic of celebrity endorsements: "Israel Paskowitz after considering long and hard the technical superiorities of Nike Aqua Socks and how they've helped his surfing career --'Huh?'" All of these interludes are introduced by a picture of Michael Jordan with the headline: "Things they might have said but never did." This ad is a far cry from the old Vitalis ads where athletes would nuzzle the bottle and grin for the camera. In fact, it is clearly a spoof of *all such ads*. So, reading it requires a culturally-sophisticated, self-conscious, and historically-grounded reader. Not an organism giving an automatic response. And not an ideologically-manipulated marionette.

In such parodic/ironic/satirical constructions, the reader must be able to stand apart from the discourse of advertising and laugh at it. This requires a cultural knowledge and awareness of ideology that would defy the viewer construct of either the cultural critic or the advertising scientist. Further, if the reader were simply seeking a role-model, he/she would be thoroughly confused by these ads. Interpretive distance is required: by the authors, by the celebrities, and by the readers. The joke is on them all and between them all. This is hardly the capitalist-as-cultural-puppeteer model of a communication at work. It is a shared, negotiated, and transformed meaning, one that recognizes the traditions of the genre, the purpose of the ideology, and the intelligence and independence of both reader and celebrity.

CONCLUSIONS

Celebrity advertising is a historically-continuous phenomenon grounded in pre-capitalist, pre-electronic media cultures. The continuity of celebrity has been seen in the geneology of gods, saints, royals, actors, athletes, statesmen. The continuity of product personification in the tradition of the potlatch, of divine attributes, of royal patronage, of modern celebrity advertising. The continuity of advertising forms in the narrative myth, the proverb, the farce, the satire, the masque, the parody. Thus, to understand celebrity advertising as a phenomenon is to understand it as being culturally and historically linked to other times, other forms, other practices--yet reinterpreted in the styles and norms of the present. This requires historical scholarship, both of consumption and advertisements, as well as the use of both anthropological and textual interpretive concepts. Finally, a theory of celebrity advertising thus cast introduces us to a most reassuring figure--the selective, participating, and, ultimately, empowered viewer.

REFERENCES

Alberoni, Francesco (1972), "The Powerless Elite: Theory and Sociological Research on the Phenomenon of the Stars,"in *Sociology of Mass Communications*, ed. and trans, D. McQuaid, London: Penguin, 75-98.

Arato, Andrew and Eike Gebhart (1988), eds. *The Essential Frankfurt School Reader*, New York: Continuum.

Appadurai, Arjun and Igor Kopytoff (1986), eds., *The Social Biography of Things*, New York: Cambridge Unversity Press.

Akin, Charles and Martin Block (1983), "Effectiveness of Celebrity Endorsers," *Journal of Advertising Research*, 23 (Feburary/March), 57-61.

Boorstin, Daniel (1961), *The Image*, New York: Harper & Rowe.

Booth, Wayne (1961), *The Rhetoric of Fiction*, Chicago: University of Chicago Press.

Braudy, Leo (1986), "Hostages of the Eye: The Body as Commodity," *The Frenzy of Renown: Fame and Its History*, Oxford University Press, New York and Oxford.

Csikszentmihalyi, Mihaly and Eugene Rochberg-Halton (1981), *The Meaning of Things: Domestic Symbols and the Self*. Cambridge: Cambridge University Press.

Dyer, Richard (1982), *Stars*, London: BFI.

Finn, David W. (1980), "The Validity of Using Consumer Input to Choose Advertising Spokesmen," *Advances in Consumer Research*, 7, 776-779.

Friedman, Hershey H. and Linda Friedman (1979), "Endorser Effectiveness by Product Type," *Journal of Advertising Research*, 19, (October), 63-71.

Friedman, Hershey H., Salvatore Termini, and Robert Washington (1976), "The Effectiveness of Advertisements Utilizing Four Types of Endorsers," *Journal of Advertising*, 5 (Summer), 22-24.

Gibson, Walker (1980), "Authors, Speakers, Readers, and Mock Readers," *Reader-Response Criticism: From Formalism to Post-Structuralism*, Ed., Jane P. Tompkins, Baltimore: Johns Hopkins University Press, 1-6.

Hirsch, E.D. Jr. (1976), *The Aims of Interpretation*, Chicago: University of Chicago Press.

Hirschman, Elizabeth C. (1985), "Primitive Aspects of Consumption in Modern American Society," *Journal of Consumer Research*, 12, 142-154.

Homer, Pamela M. and Lynn R. Kahle (1990), "Source Expertise, Time of Source Identification, and Involvement in Persusuasion: An Elaborative Processing Perspective," *Journal of Advertising*, 19, 30-39.

Jay, Martin (1973), *The Dialectical Imagination: A History of the Frankfurt School and the Institute of Social Research, 1923-1950*, Boston: Little, Brown.

Kahle, Lynn R. and Pamela M. Homer (1985), "Physical Attractiveness of the Celebrity Endorser: A Social Adaptation Perspective," *Journal of Consumer Research*, 11 (March), 954-961.

Kaikati, Jack G. (1987), "Celebrity Advertising: A Review and Synthesis," *International Journal of Advertising*, 6(2), 93-105.

Kamins, Michael A. (1990), "An Investigation into the 'Match-Up' Hypothesis in Celebrity Advertising: When Beauty May Be Only Skin Deep," *Journal of Advertising*, 19, 4-13.

Kamen, Joseph M., Abdul C. Azhair, and Judith R. Kragh (1985), "What a Spokesman Does for a Sponsor," *Journal of Advertising Research*, 15 (April), 17-24.

Klapp, Orrin E. (1964), *Symbolic Leaders: Public Dramas and Public Men*, Aldine Publishing Co.: Chicago.

Klebba, Joanne M. and Lynette S. Unger (1983), "The Impact of Negative and Positive Information on Source Credibility in a Field Setting," *Advances in Consumer Research*, 10, 11-16.

Marcuse, Herbert (1964), *One-Dimensional Man: Studies in the Ideology of Advanced Industrial Society*, Boston: Beacon Press.

Mauss, Marcel (1954), *The Gift*, trabs., Ian Cunnison, Glencoe, Ill.: Free Press.

McCracken, Grant (1989), "Who is the Celebrity Endorser?" *Journal of Consumer Research*, December, 310.

McCracken, Grant (1988), *Culture and Consumption: New Approaches to the Symbolic Character of Consumer Goods and Activities*, Bloomington: Indiana University Press.

McCracken, Grant (1987), "Advertising: Meaning or Information?" *Advances in Consumer Research*, 14, 121-124.

Miller, Mark (1979), *Boxed In*, Chicago: Northwestern.

Morris, Edwin T. (1984), *Fragrance: The Story of Perfume from Cleopatra to Chanel*, New York: Charles Scribner's Sons.

Rogers, Everett (1987), ""The Critical School and Consumer Research," *Advances in Consumer Research*, Ed. Melanie Wallendorf and Paul Anderson, 14, 7-11.

Schickel, Richard (1985), *Intimate Strangers: The Culture of Celebrity*, Garden City, NY: Doubleday.

Stern, Barbara (1989), "Literary Criticism and Consumer Research: Overview and Illustrative Analysis," *Journal of Consumer Research*, 16, 322-334.

Tudor, Andrew (1974), *Images and Influence*, London: Allen and Unwin.

Wells, William D. (1988), "Lectures and Dramas," in *Cognitive and Affective Responses to Advertising*, ed. Pat Cafferata and Alice Tybout, Lexington, MA: D.C. Heath.

Wicke, Jennifer (1989), *Advertising Fictions*, New York: Columbia University Press.

Williamson, Judith (1978), *Decoding Advertisements*, Boston: Marion Boyars.

A First Step to Identify the Meaning in Celebrity Endorsers

Lynn Langmeyer, Northern Kentucky University
Mary Walker, Xavier University

ABSTRACT

Typical studies on celebrity endorsement have focused on source credibility and source attractiveness rather than symbolic properties of the celebrity endorser or associated "meaning movement." This study uses a response elicitation format, with a celebrity endorser, Cher, a celebrity endorsed product, Scandinavian Health Spas, and a non-endorsed product, bath towels, as stimuli to identify the meaning in celebrity endorsers and to document the transfer of meaning from endorser to product. Although a "first step," the results are encouraging.

INTRODUCTION

It has been proposed by McCracken (1986, 1988, 1989) and other (e.g., Atkin and Block 1983; Holman 1980; Levy 1959; Mick 1986; O'Guinn et. al. 1989; Sherry and McGrath 1989; Stern 1988; Umiker-Sebeok 1981), that celebrity endorsers embody symbolic meanings; meanings elicited by a person, place or thing that go beyond those directly contained in themselves. Celebrity endorsers pass on their symbolic meanings and acquired associations to the products they endorse. Over time, the cultivation analysis proponents hypothesize (e.g., Gerbner et. al. 1977), the symbolic meanings are passed on to the consumer; the product is uniquely differentiated and its perceived value is infinitely enhanced. If the actual process operates as the model proposes, then the increase in the use of celebrity endorsers (Levin 1988; Sherman 1985) makes sense. It has been difficult, however, to test and support the celebrity endorser effect; what have been tested are "pieces" of the process and what has been found leaves important questions still unanswered. This investigation was undertaken to address the most basic question in the endorsement process: can symbolic meanings embodied in a celebrity be identified and once identified can they be classified and categorized? Second, if meanings can be classified and categorized, then can such classifications and categorizations be used to understand the process by which symbolic meaning is transferred?

Typical studies on celebrity endorsement have focused on two social psychological aspect of the process: source credibility and source attractiveness. The source models, as McCracken (1989) labels them, trace their history to the early Yale communication studies of Hovland and Weiss (1951-52) and the early studies on source attractiveness reported by McGuire in his 1985 review article. The models rest on the assumption that the effectiveness of a message depends on certain characteristics of the message source and past studies have identified characteristics, such as physical attractiveness and credibility, that tend to increase the persuasiveness of a message.

McCracken (1989) notes that, although these models are important to our understanding the endorsement process, the "research itself is littered with puzzles and peculiarities the source models cannot explain" (McCracken 1989, p. 311). Furthermore, the endorsement process depends upon the symbolic properties of the celebrity endorser and therefore an understanding of "meaning movement" is essential. Traditional approaches tend not to provide such direction.

For example, a puzzle identified by Kamins (1990) is that "physical attractiveness of the sources does not always enhance measures of attitudes change toward issues, products, and ad-based evaluations." He proposes the "match-up" hypothesis as the solution (Kahle and Homer 1985) and then using a self-report multiple choice-type scale, demonstrates that Tom Selleck, as a celebrity endorser for an "attractiveness-related product" (luxury car), compared to Telly Savalas as a celebrity endorser for the same product, enhanced measures of spokesperson credibility and attitude toward an ad. No differences in those measures were found for the attractiveness-unrelated product (home computer). Kamins' study (1990), although technically more than adequate and appropriate, does not increase our understanding the "meaning movement" of Selleck's physical attractiveness -- one of his symbolic meanings as a celebrity endorser. What meanings are passed on to the product, enhance spokesperson measures, and thereby make Selleck a better "match-up" than Savalas with a luxury car? That seems to be the underlying puzzle needing a solution.

McCracken (1989) states "we know that each role, event, or accomplishment in the career of the celebrity changes the meanings of the celebrity, but we do not know precisely how this takes place ... Nor do we know how meanings transfer from one to the other ... We need an instrument that allows us to determine methodologically the meanings that adhere in celebrities. We know that the meanings that exist in celebrities are various, but we have yet to devise an instrument that allows us to detect and survey these meanings" (p. 319). This study is an exploratory step in devising that instrument. We chose to emphasize a "qualitative" rather than "quantitative" direction in our study because it seems a better match for investigating symbolic meanings.

WHAT DO CELEBRITY ENDORSERS MEAN

Because a celebrity endorser is defined as "an individual who enjoys public recognition and who uses this recognition on behalf of a consumer good by appearing with it in an advertisement" (McCracken 1989, p. 310), our first step was to determine if celebrity/product associations are easily recalled. Rather than present our respondents with a recognition check-list which would not reveal easily remembered associations, we asked our respondents, undergraduate business students (most of whom were 18 to 34 year-olds) to "please give us as many celebrity/product pairs as you can recall." The free elicitation approach has been used successfully in similar studies.

The first step generated 93 celebrity/product pairs with frequencies ranging from a high of 29 for Boomer Esiason and Diet Coke or Hanes and 28 for Bill Cosby and Jello, to lows of single mentions for Santa Claus and Oreo Cookies and Jay Leno and Doritos. From this list of 93 pairs, we selected three frequently mentioned pairs to use in our pilot test for the working of the instrument. It was difficult to identify specific appropriate and effective open-ended question rhetoric from previous studies that would give us the desired quality of responses in terms of content; not many studies have investigated this topic other than on a conceptual level (McCracken 1989) or using "positivist" rather than "interpretive" approaches (e.g., Kamins 1990). We considered and discarded phrases such as "symbolic meanings" and symbolic properties" as jargonized and unnecessarily obtuse. We eventually settled on the following directions to question respondents on already existing celebrity/endorser pairs:

> "Please describe the meaning each celebrity has for you when he/she advertises the indicated product."

The pairs used were Cher and Scandinavian Health Spas, Boomer Esiason and Hanes Underwear for Men, and Bill Cosby and Jello Pudding.

In the review of literature and research, it became apparent that, conceptually, endorsed products elicit associations that go beyond those directly contained in the stimuli per se -- they acquire conscious or unconscious associations that are linked to the endorser. If this assumption is true, then what about non-endorsed products? The quality and quantity of symbolic meanings in non-endorsed products should be identifiably different than that in endorsed products. Therefore, in addition to identifying the symbolic meanings in products that are currently associated with celebrity endorsers, we wanted to determine if respondents could describe the symbolic meanings they would want a celebrity endorser to possess to "pass on" to a non-endorsed product. For this purpose, we asked the following"

> "Please describe the celebrity that you would want to see advertising bath towels."

The results of the pilot indicated that the directions were insufficient and unclear; we had to "interview" the respondents to obtain responses we could use because they had trouble knowing what we were asking. We determined from our interviews that the words "communicate" and "associate" seemed to be the best elicitors of symbolic meanings. We also determined from our interviews that some "priming of the pump" was helpful in getting respondents to think about the advertisements.

For the third step, then, we developed an introduction and instructions for the instrument to "set the stage" for the questions and tested the effectiveness of "communicate" and "associate" for response generation. The two parts of the instrument and the test of two elicitors created four versions of the instrument. The Cher/Scandinavian Health Spa pairing was the most successful of the three pairings in generating responses in the pilot, and so we continued to use it in all four versions. The bath towel category elicited high content responses and was also continued in all four versions. The four versions of the instrument had the same instructions for the paired meanings sections and the un-endorsed meanings section. For the paired meanings section introduction respondents were told: "We are interested in how celebrities who advertise particular products are perceived by the audience. There are no right or wrong answers. Ignore for the purpose of this study what you think the advertiser may have intended. We are interested in your personal opinions and feelings and ideas. Please read the directions carefully and respond in as much detail as you can."

For the un-endorsed meanings section introduction, the same directions were used except respondents were informed that we were "interested in what types of celebrities would be good endorsers for certain types of products."

The specific question for the paired meanings was as follows: "Think about the last time you saw Cher advertise Scandinavian health Spas. In your own words, please describe what you associate with Cher advertising Scandinavian Health Spas (what you think is being communicated when Cher advertises SHSs)." The specific question for the unpaired meanings was as follows: "Think about bath towels. In your own words, please describe what associations you would want to be created by a celebrity advertising bath towels (the kind of celebrity you would want to advertise bath towels)." Gender as well as responses to a few filler questions were also requested. Again, respondents were undergraduate business students. The results of this step indicated that "associate" and "communicate" elicited similar symbolic meanings; "associate" was chosen for use in the final phase of the study.

The final phase of the study asked respondents who had not previously participated in the study to think about the last time they saw Scandinavian Health Spa advertised. The purpose of this phase was to elicit responses that could be used to assess the consistency of associations between a product/celebrity endorser pair.

ANALYSIS

Cher and Scandinavian

Fifty-one undergraduate business students completed the survey: 29 male respondents and 22 female respondents. Eight themes emerged from the

TABLE 1
Summary Findings Cher and Scandinavian

Responses Made	Number of Responses Made By Gender	
	Male	Female
Attractive/Great Body Like Cher's	15	17
Health/Fitness	12	6
Hard Work	5	11
Sexy	11	5
Lacks Credibility	10	4
Any Age	5	3
Independence/Confidence	4	3
Place to Meet Opposite Sex	6	-
Total Number of Respondents	29	22

analysis of the pairing of Cher and Scandinavian Health Spas. A summary of the findings, which is presented below, are shown in Table 1.

You can have an attractive, great body Like Cher's was most frequently associated with Cher endorsing Scandinavian provided by 63% of the respondents. It is interested to note that males tended to respond that "working out at Scandinavian will produce an attractive or great body" whereas females were more likely to indicate this association by responding "a workout at Scandinavian will produce a body like Cher's."

Typical male responses included in this category were the following: "Cher is one well put together woman (attractive)," and "Working out will give you a great body." Typically female responses were : "Cher's body is being advertised. They want women to perceive that going to Scandinavian can give you a shapely figure like Cher's," and "If you go to Scandinavian you can have a body like Cher's."

You can be healthier or more fit as the result of working out at Scandinavian was the second most frequent association with Cher's endorsing Scandinavian provided by 35% of the respondents however, as Table 1 indicates, males mentioned this two times more frequently than females. Typical responses were the following: "I associate Cher with physical fitness," and "Healthiness is definitely being promoted. Staying physically fit is a better way of life."

It's hard work to get into shape was elicited from 31% of the respondents. It is interesting to note that although 50% of the female respondents included this response in their association, only 17% of the males did so. The hard work theme was represented by statements such as "Great bodies are hard work but the results are worth it," and "Cher communicates will and determination."

Sexiness is also associated with Cher and Scandinavian Health Spas according to 31% of the respondents -- the high percentage generated to a large degree by the male respondents. Of the 16 mentions, 11 or almost 70% were from males. Example of responses that best reflect this dimension include: "In a word SEX! Cher has been a sex symbol since the days when she and Sonny Bono were a team," and "It's dark and smokey, she's pumping iron ... some kind of sex goddess."

Cher's lack credibility was frequently mentioned; 27% of the respondents included this comment. Reports of plastic surgery on various parts of her body was the most frequently cited reason for her lack of credibility. Examples include: "Although Cher is supposedly showing that hard work in the gym will give you a great body its ironic that Scandinavian would use her since she has had plastic surgery on various parts of her body," and"I associate Cher with getting paid alot of money to show off a body which I'm sure didn't come from Scandinavian."

A person of any age can benefit from working out at Scandinavian was indicated by 16% of the respondents and the responses typically include a reference to Cher's age (which is now closer to 50 than to 40). Representative responses

TABLE 2
Summary Findings Associations With Scandinavian

Responses Made	Number of Responses Made By Gender	
	Male	Female
Attractive/Great Body Like Cher's	9	9
Work Related	6	5
Cher	6	7
Negative Attitude/ Lack Credibility	6	4
Sexy	4	4
Health/Fitness	2	6
Celebrity Endorsers Other Than Cher	2	3
Total Number of Respondents	15	17

include: "That even though she is an older woman (my guess is 40's) you can still remain physically fit (good body)," and "I think of a slightly older woman who seems to be in good shape because she works out regularly."

You can become more independent and self confident by working out at Scandinavian was mentioned by 14% of the respondents and associated with Cher's endorsement. Responses include ones such as: "Better self image!" and "What I associate with Cher is `get tough' with yourself and get yourself in shape."

Finally, *Scandinavian is a good place to meet members of the opposite sex* was an association for 12% of the respondents all of whom were male. Excerpts from typical responses are: "A place to go if you want to meet members of the opposite sex," "If I go to this gym maybe I'll hook up with someone like Cher," and "It's more of a social club than a gym."

No additional themes were identified from responses provided by approximately 10% of the respondents because they lacked unifying dimensions.

The second phase of the study, as mentioned in the previous section was designed to elicit responses that could be used to assess the consistency of associations between a product/endorser pair (e.g., Scandinavian and Cher) and the product itself. Thirty-two respondents, 15 males and 17 females, completed this version of the survey. Seven major themes emerged based on the elicited responses. A summary of the findings, which are presented below, are shown in Table 2.

You can have an attractive or great body like Cher's was given by 56% of the respondents and was the most frequent association. Statements were given such as: "I associate the good looks and a good body with Scandinavian. They seem to advertise that rather than health," and "Beautiful women with very well shaped bodies." It is interesting to note than 41% of the respondents made a specific reference to Cher in their associations; the comments generally focused on her body.

The equipment on which the workout take place or the physical workout itself was mentioned by 34% of the respondents. Typical comments centered on lifting weights and nautilus machines.

Scandinavian's advertising lacks credibility was mentioned by 31% of the respondents and this was associated with a negative perception of Scandinavian. Negative comments revolved around Cher as well as the lack of reality of the advertising representations and questionable marketing tactics: "I associate Cher with Scandinavian. I don't have a good image of Scandinavian because of Cher and her many tummy tucks, etc.," "I associate rich snobs working out. The typical people who make fun of fat people," "Beautiful bodies for a cheap price ... a line of crap," and "Beautiful women. Rip off. Too good to be true."

Sexiness was also associated for 31% of the respondents with Scandinavian Health Spas. Typical responses included: "When I think of this spa I

TABLE 3
Summary Findings For Bath Towels

	Number of Responses Made By Gender			
	Kind of Celebrity		Associations	
Responses Made	Male	Female	Male	Female
Bath Towel/Celebrity Attributes	3	2	12	11
Traditional Role	6	7	5	-
Athletic	5	5	3	2
Attractive	3	2	6	2
Sexy	2	1	3	1
Total Number of Respondents	12	12	17	10

automatically think of a sexual emphasis. The ads depict women as sexy which implies fitness," "Scandinavian promotes sex appeal," and "Sexy women with very little clothing."

A workout at Scandinavian can make you more healthy or fit according to 25% of the respondents although there were significant gender differences with females being nearly three times as likely to make this association than males.

Celebrity endorsers other than Cher were mentioned by 16% of the respondents with Sheena Easton being the endorser mentioned most frequently other than Cher.

Bath Towels

One objective of the study was to assess differences in associations for endorsed products and unendorsed products. Therefore, in an initial version of the instrument respondents were asked to either "describe the *kind* of celebrity you would want to advertise bath towels" or "describe what *associations* you would want to be created by a celebrity advertising bath towels." This instrument was completed by 29 male and 22 female undergraduate business students. A summary of the findings are presented in Table 3. Responses centered around five basic themes and although types of responses were similar across versions, there were differences in the magnitude of responses with respect to certain themes. The similarities and differences will be reported in this section.

A celebrity endorser who exemplifies personality characteristics that could also be applied to the inanimate characteristics of a "good" towel was the first theme to emerge from responses given by 53% of the respondents; however respondents who were asked "what associations would you want to be created by a celebrity advertising bath towels" were nearly four times more likely to give this response compared to respondents who were asked to "describe the kind of celebrity you would want to advertise bath towels." Respondents used words such as "soft," "gentle," "clean," "quality," "luxurious," "warm," and "comfortable," to describe the desired person and associations. Specific examples include: "A clean cut celebrity who looks clean, refreshed and renewed by a shower ... than dries off with a supple towel," "Soft warmth -- a good one might be Michael J. Fox," and "Softness and clean bright colors. I feel someone like Christy Brinkley or maybe a baby could advertise towels."

Use of an "average" person was the second theme identified. Respondents described this type of celebrity as "average," "motherly/ grandmotherly," "simple," "family-minded," and "down-to-earth." These terms were used by 35% of the respondents; however, respondents who were asked the "kind of celebrity" question were nearly three times as likely to give a response in this category compared to "association" respondents. A celebrity in this category was, on occasion, contrasted to the glamorous, aloof or media conscious celebrity in the following ways: "I would want a female but it's not necessary. Mid 40's, motherly type. Barbara Billingsley 20 years ago is a perfect example," and "I would want a popular woman actress to advertise. One who plays a mom or grandma. Someone with strong traditional morals."

An athletic celebrity was identified as the third theme and respondents in this category indicated that athletes were believed to be good endorsers of bath towels because they are "heavy" towel users. Some respondents mentioned particular celebrities by name. Twenty-five percent of the respondents mentioned an athletic celebrity as a potential endorser. Typical responses included: "The kind of celebrity I would want to advertise bath towels is a professional athlete. This is someone who showers often and is a person I can admire," and "I don't think glamour can sell towels. When thinking of towels, I think of athletes.

An attractive or good looking celebrity was listed as a potential endorser by 25% of the respondents. Examples of responses that were categorized in this theme are: "Someone who is good looking," "I think bath towels should be advertised by a good looking woman wearing nothing but a towel. Perhaps a *Sports Illustrated* model," and "Good-looking, very feminine."

Sexy endorser was the final identified theme and responses in this category indicated clearly that bath towels should be advertised in a sexy situation such as the following: "Associate sex with the bath towels by using Christy Brinkley, Heather Locklear or Paula Abdul. All three are sexy and I would love to see any of them in a towel."

DISCUSSION

The Instrument

The results of this study suggest that additional work needs to be done on the data collection instrument if we are to continue to use it to investigate the meanings that "adhere" in celebrities. Some of the responses elicited by the exploratory instrument were disappointing although it is apparent that the "tell us what you think" approach can be successful. We are able to demonstrate that celebrities possess symbolic meanings and we were able to demonstrate that celebrities pass on these symbolic meanings to the products they endorse. We were also able to demonstrate that unendorsed products tend to have symbolic meanings that are diffuse and undifferentiated compared to the more dimensionalized and unique symbolic meanings of endorsed products. The instrument did give us insights into the product/celebrity endorser relationship.

It was our experience, however, that the abstract nature of symbolic associations may make it difficult for respondents to be sure they are responding appropriately; this was particularly true in the pilot study. There are two possible solutions to this problem: one, the instrument might fare better used with an interview; and two, the use of visual stimuli rather than language might be more effective (especially since our data indicate that many associations do depend on what is seen as well as what is heard or read) once the meanings of celebrities are established. It might be easier for respondents to associate visual representations of celebrities and products rather than describe them. This is an approach that has been suggested (in private correspondence) by McCracken. It was out intention to establish meanings, empirically, before attempting to investigate matches and we turn our attention now to that issue.

Cher and Scandinavian

It appears that celebrities do contain symbolic meanings, these meanings can be articulated and, to some degree, they are consistent and interconnected. To begin, despite the problems with the instrument, our study was able to verify empirically the meanings that McCracken suggests (1989, p. 313) are embodied in Cher and, as he suspected, her meanings take on a power of their own and are "transferred" to the product she endorses. There was a not-surprising consistency between the language used to describe associations of Cher and Scandinavia Health Spas and the language used to describe Scandinavian Health Spas alone.

Cher as an endorser of Scandinavian represents at least eight different themes which include her physical appearance, her age, her "personality," and her life style; she is "more than" Cher. She represents attractiveness, fitness, hard work, sex, independence, confidence and "good" middle age. When Cher endorses Scandinavian Health Spas she brings these qualities with her and although the advertisement places an emphasis on certain qualities (e.g., physical appearance) the meanings elicited by her presence go far beyond the emphasized qualities (e.g., independence, confidence, hard work).

Two finding somewhat surprised us: the extent to which respondents mentioned reports of plastic surgery on various part of Cher's body and gender differences in comments on the meanings of the endorsement. The plastic surgery reports had a direct effect on Cher's endorsement and the product: it discredited her as a credible source for the product and "passed on" the discrediting to the product. This is, most certainly, an unintended symbolic meaning transfer and we wonder if the company is aware of the situation. As an aside, males mentioned the plastic surgery considerably more frequently than females; we are at a loss to explain this difference.

Other gender differences are also interesting. For instance, females were much more likely than males to indicate that Cher's body resulted from hard work (it does seem more difficult for women than men to maintain a good body image); however, only males indicated that Scandinavian was a good place to meet members of the opposite sex (perhaps spas fulfill different needs for men and women). Are these intended or unintended meanings in the endorsement? Regardless, it is apparent that celebrities contain powerful and multi-dimensional meanings that they "deliver" along with their persona (McCracken 1989, p. 315). Therefore, despite problems with the instrument, our data supports Stage 1 of McCracken's endorsement process -- individuals charged with detailed and powerful meanings.

Bath Towels

What about unendorsed products? Our objective in examining unendorsed products was to determine if the associations for endorsed products (Cher and Scandinavian as the representative of this category) are different in qualitative and quantitative respects than those of unendorsed products (bath towels representing this category). We expected a wider range of associations for an unendorsed product than for an endorsed product because it seems likely that the presence of a celebrity endorser, whose meanings are relatively limited, passes on his/her reduced range of associations.

The results indicate that our expectations were correct; a broad and unfocused sample of mostly inanimate attributes were elicited by bath towels -- from ordinary and clean to luxurious and comfortable. Bath towels do not have a celebrity endorser to reduce the thematic dimensions and so they are perceived by some as ordinary, others as athletic, and still others sexy and so on. The celebrity endorser appears to focus attention on a narrow range of associations with the product which are consistent with his/her presence. These associations may tend to create the more human or animated descriptions of endorsed products or product attributes as opposed to the more inanimate descriptions of unendorsed products.

FUTURE DIRECTIONS AND CONCLUDING COMMENTS

The broad range of attributes elicited by the unendorsed bath towels suggests that an additional pairing study should be conducted. The responses indicated a wider range of celebrity types, from attractive to motherly to sexy, might make suitable endorsers. Bath towels should be paired with a celebrity in each of these categories. If meaning is transferred then the bath towels should assume the symbolic meanings associated with the endorser. This type of study could be useful in two ways: it could determine first if different types of endorsers can transfer different types of meaning and second, it could determine if the pairing of an endorser and a product narrows the meanings associated with a product.

Further studies could be undertaken, then, to assess whether a celebrity can be used to change the meaning of a product or if a mismatch between a celebrity and a product results in an inconsistent image. We have taken a first step to identify the meaning in celebrity endorsers and a first step to document the transfer of meaning from endorser to product. We are encouraged by our results while recognizing that they are a "first step."

REFERENCES

Atkin, Charles and Martin Block (1983), "Effectiveness of Celebrity Endorsers," *Journal of Advertising Research*, 23 (February/March), 57-61.

Gerbner, George, Larry Gross, Michael Elley, Marilyn Jackson-Beeck, Suzanne Jeffries-Fox and Nancy Signorielli (1977), "TV Violence Profile #8," *Journal of Communications*, 27, 171-180.

Holman, Rebecca (1980), "Product Use as Communication: A Fresh Appraisal of a Venerable Topic," in *Review of Marketing*, eds. Ben M. Enis and Kenneth J. Roering, Chicago: American Marketing Association, 25-272.

Hovland, Carl I. and Walter Weiss (1951-1952), "The Influence of Source Credibility on Communication Effectiveness," *Public Opinion Quarterly*, 15 (Winter), 635-650.

Kamins, Michael A. (1990), "An Investigation of the 'Match-Up Hypothesis in Celebrity Advertising: When Beauty May be Only Skin Deep," *Journal of Advertising*, 19 (1), 4-13.

Kahle, Lynn R. and Pamela M. Homer (1985), "Physical Attractiveness of the Celebrity Endorser: A Social Adaptation Perspective," *Journal of Consumer Research*, 11 (March), 954-961.

Levin, Gary (1988), "Celebrity Licensing Gets Tougher," *Advertising Age*, 59 (February 1), 63.

Levy, Sidney (1959), "Symbols for Sale," *Harvard Business Review*, 37, 117-124.

Levy, Sidney (1981), "Interpreting Consumer Mythology: A Structural Approach to Consumer Behavior," *Journal of Marketing*, 45, 117-124.

McCracken, Grant (1986), "Culture and Consumption: A Theoretical Account of the Structure and Movement of the Cultural Meaning of Consumer Goods," *Journal of Consumer Research*, 13 (June), 71-84.

McCracken, Grant (1989), "Who Is the Celebrity Endorser? Cultural Foundations of the Endorsement Process," *Journal of Consumer Research*, 16 (December), 310-321.

McCracken, Grant (1988), *Culture and Consumption: New Approaches to the Symbolic Character of Consumer Goods and Activities*, Bloomington, IN: Indiana University Press.

McGuire, William J. (1985), "Attitudes and Attitude Change," in *Handbook of Social Psychology*, Vol. 2, eds. Gardner Lindzey and Elliot Aronson, New York: Random House, 233-346.

Mick, David (1986), "Consumer Research and Semiotics: Exploring the Morphology of Signs, Symbols, and Significance," *Journal of Consumer Research*, 13 (September), 196-213.

O'Guinn, Thomas C., Ronald J. Faber, Nadine J.S. Curias and Kay Schmitt, "The Cultivation of Consumer Norms," in *Advances in Consumer Research*, ed. Thomas K. Srull, Vol. 16, Provo: UT Association for Consumer Research, 779-785.

Sherman, Stratford P. (1985), "When you Wish Upon A Star," *Fortune*, 138 (August 9), 66-73.

Sherry, John F., Jr. and Mary Ann McGrath (1989), "Unpacking the Holiday Presence: A Comparative Ethnography of Two Gift Stores," in *Interpretive Consumer Research*, ed. Elizabeth C. Hirschman, Provo: UT Association for Consumer Research, 148-167.

Stern, Barbara (1988), "Medieval Allegory: Roots of Advertising Strategy for the Mass Market," *Journal of Marketing*, 52 (July), 89-94.

Umliker-Sebeok, Jean, ed. (1988), *Marketing and Semiotics*, Bloomington, IN.

Consumers and Movies: Some Findings on Experiential Products
Elizabeth Cooper-Martin, Georgetown University

ABSTRACT

This paper studies movies as an example of experiential products, defined as those products which consumers choose, buy and use solely to experience and enjoy. The consumption experience, especially its hedonic and aesthetic aspects, is key for understanding experiential products. The results of a survey confirm that involvement with movies is dominantly hedonic. When selecting a movie, subjects consider more alternatives that consume time than ones that consume only money and also consider more subjective than objective features and more global than unidimensional features.

All goods and services are consumed, but for some products, like the performing arts, wine, and vacations, the consumption experience is an end in itself. This paper identifies and studies this type of product and labels them *experiential* products. Consumers choose, acquire and use experiential products solely to experience them and enjoy them. Experiential products include both physical goods, such as wine and recreational drugs, and services, such as sporting events and restaurant meals. The dominant benefit of these products is hedonic consumption, that is the feelings, emotions and sensations experienced during product usage (Hirschman and Holbrook 1982).

Given the special nature of experiential products, consumer behavior for them is likely to differ from that for other types of products. The purpose of this paper is to demonstrate some of the unique aspects of consumer behavior for these special products. Its contribution is to build on the experiential or hedonic perspective (Hirschman and Holbrook 1982; Holbrook and Hirschman 1982) to describe and identify a specific type of product and to begin to understand consumer behavior for it.

Specifically, this paper focuses on movies as an example of the class of experiential products. Movies are a good example because they appeal to a wide range of consumers, compared to the arts (see summary in Capon and Cooper-Martin 1990) or wine (Jobson 1989). Further, movies are purely experiential, as compared to television and radio which may accompany other activities. For example, broadcast music can serve as a background for shopping (Milliman 1982) or a restaurant meal (Milliman 1986). In particular, this study researches two aspects of consumer behavior for movies: alternatives and choice features. Predictions for both aspects are based on the consumption experience, which differentiates experiential products from others.

The next section discusses experiential products in more detail and develops the hypotheses on what types of alternatives and choice features consumers use for movies. The following two sections describe the methodology and results. The discussion section includes suggestions for additional research on experiential products. The final section describes potential implications for managers interested in marketing movies.

EXPERIENTIAL PRODUCTS

Experiential products are defined by their dominant emphasis on the consumption experience. The main benefit from these products is the pleasure or hedonic value in consumption. Experiential products contrast with goods and services that primarily fulfill utilitarian functions. For example, the major benefit of shampoo is to leave hair clean and shiny, blankets keep one warm, a visit to the dentist protects one's teeth. Clearly, there may be hedonic aspects of consuming non-experiential products; for example, the lovely fragrance of a peach-scented shampoo or the fondness for a blanket received from a dear relative. But the primary reason for consuming these products is not to experience them.

Just as utilitarian products may have some hedonic value, experiential products may have some utilitarian functions. For instance, food clearly has the utilitarian benefit of keeping one alive. Thus under certain circumstances, for example grabbing a quick snack to stave off hunger pangs, food is more of a utilitarian product. But under certain circumstances, food can be an experiential product; for example, in a first-class restaurant. The emphasis then is clearly hedonic; to enjoy the sight, aroma, texture and taste of the food. A restaurant meal can be hedonic in other ways: savoring a fine wine, soaking in the elegant surroundings, enjoying the luxury of excellent service.

To savor the feelings, emotions and sensations of using an experiential product requires the expenditure of time. Likewise, the experiential perspective argues that the key resource which consumers expend in a transaction is time, rather than money (Holbrook and Hirschman 1982). Thus one intrinsic quality of experiential products is that they demand the consumption of time. Another useful way to describe products is to distinguish between those directed to people and those directed to their possessions (Lovelock 1983). Products directed at possessions include laundry detergent which cleans clothes and banking services which protect money. Experiential products, such as movies, restaurant meals, and vacations, are directed towards people, not towards their possessions. This description again suggests that consuming an experiential product involves allocating time.

Because experiential products require expenditures of time, the alternatives for them are likely to be other products that utilize the same resource. To consume such products, consumers must actively devote some level of cognitive or physical effort, as when reading a book or playing basketball. Some products do not require the consumer's time or attention during consumption but are consumed passively, for example wearing clothes or sitting on a couch. For a movie, alternatives that require expenditures of time would include other movies, as well as other product classes, as in the following hypothesis:

> H1: As alternatives to a movie, consumers will consider more alternatives that require expenditures of time than alternatives that only require expenditures of money.

If consumers do consider other product classes as alternatives to movies, what types of features do they use for comparisons? Research using other types of products reveals that as consumers choose from alternatives in increasingly dissimilar product classes, the abstractness of product comparisons used increases (Johnson 1984). More abstract features describe a greater number of alternatives than concrete features (Johnson and Kiselius 1985). For instance, exclusivity is an abstract feature which could be applied to alternatives in several product classes: wine, performing arts, sporting events, restaurant meals. Thus it is likely that consumers use features that are abstract to select experiential products.

Because the benefit from experiential products is pleasure in consumption, consumers should choose movies and similar products based on what they like and enjoy, on what pleases them, in other words, based on intrinsic preference (O'Shaughnessy 1987). Therefore, consumers use subjective features, such as "funny", "suspenseful", "scary", "romantic", to select movies. ("Feature" is used here to refer to a product characteristic as defined by consumers. It is not used in the sense that such characteristics are dichotomous.) Subjective features reflect the consumer's viewpoint, i.e., the personal nature of the experience, and describe the consumption experience, for example, what it is like to see and hear the movie. The subjective features of products are important from an experiential perspective (Holbrook and Hirschman 1982) and by extension are important for experiential products. In fact, such features can be described as aspects of consumption (Holbrook and Hirschman 1982).

Consumers also consider objective features of experiential products; such features can be externally verified. Examples for a movie are the director, theatre location, admission price or schedule convenience. Objective features are often tangible and utilitarian (Holbrook and Hirschman 1982). They should be less important for experiential products than subjective features because such products, by definition, do not fulfill utilitarian functions.

Subjective features are more generalizable and more abstract than objective ones. Similarly, Johnson and Kiselius (1985) argue that experiential (i.e., subjective) versus tangible (i.e., objective) features reflect differences in the dimension of abstractness-concreteness. Subjective features can be used to describe different types of products. For example, subjective features such as fun, relaxing, and exciting are appropriate for comparing one movie to another, as well as to several other product classes that require an expenditure of time: watching TV or a video, or going to a restaurant or club. By contrast, leading actor and the director are objective features of a movie. Though useful for comparisons with other movies, they are less so with non-movie alternatives. Thus to choose a movie, subjective features will be more useful due to their abstractness and their reflection of the hedonic experience, as per the following hypothesis.

> H2a: Consumers will consider more subjective features than objective ones when choosing movies.

The experiential view of consumption emphasizes both the hedonic and aesthetic nature of products (Holbrook and Hirschman 1982). For the aesthetic qualities of products, there appears to be a relationship between stimulus complexity and hedonic value (Berlyne 1971). More specifically, for aesthetic products, consumer evaluations seem to depend on cue configuralities or interactions among product features (Holbrook 1983). While exploring aesthetic alternatives, consumers are more likely to consider global features, which refer to the entire product, not just one dimension. Global features reflect the entire product and thus capture the product's complexity or interactions. Global features should be more useful than unidimensional features which apply only to a single, specific characteristic of a product. For instance, plot/storyline and genre (e.g., action, comedy, science fiction) seem to be the two most important considerations in deciding what movie to see (Austin 1981; Variety 1981). These are complex descriptors which capture the interactions among features such as setting, character development, pacing, special effects.

Global features refer to the entire product, and so may not be product-specific; for example, good, awful, moving. If a consumer applies such terms to a movie, it is not clear which facet of the film portrayed each of these features. Further, these descriptors could be used to describe other products, such as a play or novel. Thus global features tend to be abstract and for this reason, along with their ability to capture complexity and feature interactions, should be useful when selecting experiential products. This leads to the following hypothesis.

> H2b: Consumers will consider more global features than unidimensional features when choosing movies.

The next section describes the research conducted to test these hypotheses.

METHODOLOGY

The study had two phases. Phase one was conducted to confirm the hedonic nature of experiential products, such as movies. Phase two tested the hypotheses on alternatives and choice features for movies.

Phase 1

The importance of hedonic value for movies and other experiential products was assumed by definition and used to develop the hypotheses on alternatives and choice features. Thus, it seemed important to test this assumption before testing the hypotheses.

To confirm the importance of the hedonic consumption for experiential products, it seemed appropriate to use existing measures of hedonic or pleasure value. These measures are part of a well-researched and tested scale that measures product class involvement, i.e. the consumer's concern for a product class (Kapferer and Laurent 1985; Laurent and Kapferer 1985). The scale includes pleasure/hedonic as one of five antecedents to or facets of involvement. The remaining four facets of involvement are: perceived importance of the product, perceived importance of the consequences of a mispurchase, subjective probability of a mispurchase, and symbolic value. For movies, and other experiential products, involvement should primarily be hedonic and should be the dominant one of these five facets.

This paper asserts that experiential products are unique because of their emphasis on consumption and therefore differ from other products. To test this assumption for movies, it would be most appropriate to compare them to similar, but utilitarian, products. Recall that experiential products, including movies, are directed to people, not their possessions. Another important distinction between types of products is physical goods versus services; a movie is a service. Examples of utilitarian, people-directed, services are health care, transportation, haircuts, exercise clinics and education. The experience of consuming these products is not necessarily pleasant and so the consumption experience is not the dominant benefit. Compared to an experiential product, the result of consuming these utilitarian ones is more permanent and long-term, for example, a cured illness, a new hair style, an educated mind. For utilitarian, people-directed services, the involvement facet reflecting the consequences of a mispurchase should be very high. Also hedonic involvement should be greater for experiential, people-directed services than for these similar, but utilitarian, ones.

Subjects. The subjects were 160 undergraduate business students from a major university in the Mid-Atlantic region. The sample was 49% male and 51% female; mean age was 20.5. This age group is very appropriate for a study about movies, because 15-24 years old accounted for 48% of movie admissions in 1983 (Newspaper Advertising Bureau 1984).

Procedure Each subject answered a written questionnaire and so provided self-reports on hedonic/pleasure value and the other four facets of product class involvement: product class importance, symbolic value, risk consequences of purchase, and subjective risk probability of a bad purchase. The questionnaire was based on existing scales (Laurent and Kapferer 1985) and had been used reliably previously (Cooper-Martin 1989); it included four items on risk probability and three items on each other facet of involvement. Each item had a 5-point Likert-type response format (fully disagree to fully agree). Each facet's scale was the mean of its items and ranged from 1-5. The hedonic scale consisted of the following three questions (using movies as an example): For me, a movie is a real pleasure; When you go to the movies, it's a way to reward yourself; and I don't particularly like movies. The score on the latter item was reversed to form the hedonic scale. The involvement questionnaire concerned four product classes: movies; another experiential product, wine; and two utilitarian, people-oriented services: haircuts and dentists. Subjects who never used a product class (e.g., wine) did not answer items on it.

For the hedonic involvement scale, the mean Cronbach's alpha over all products was .71. For the other scales related to movies, Cronbach's alpha was .78 for importance, .68 for symbolic, .77 for risk consequences, and .41 for risk probability. Except for the latter, reliability coefficients of all scales analyzed exceeded .6, and so their reliability was judged acceptable (Peter 1979).

Results. Mean values for all facets of involvement for each product class are in the Table. The importance of pleasure and hedonic responses for experiential products is supported. For movies, subjects report a higher level of involvement on the hedonic facet than on any of the other four facets of involvement: importance ($t(160) = 6.60$, $p < .0001$), symbolic ($t(160) = 6.20$, $p < .0001$), risk consequences ($t(160) = 16.96$, $p < .0001$), and risk probability ($t(159) = 15.59$, $p < .0001$). (Although these different mean values are interpreted as significant differences across facet of involvement, they may possibly be due to item differences across the five scales.)

The importance of hedonic value was also supported when tested with wine, a second experiential product included on the questionnaire. For wines, subjects report a higher level of involvement on the hedonic facet than on any of the other four facets of involvement: importance ($t(145) = 9.14$, $p < .0001$), symbolic ($t(145) = 6.65$, $p < .0001$), risk consequences ($t(145) = 8.94$, $p < .0001$), and risk probability ($t(144) = 3.29$, $p < .005$).

The findings also support and confirm the greater importance of hedonic responses for movies, than for similar (i.e., people-directed services) but non-experiential products. Subjects report higher hedonic involvement for movies than for either of the two, people-oriented services: haircuts ($t(160) = 11.15$, $p < .0001$) and visits to the dentist (t

TABLE
Mean Values of Involvement Facets for Four Product Classes

Facet of Involvement	Product Class			
	Movies	Wines	Haircuts	Dentist
Hedonic	4.22	3.68	3.22	2.04
Product class importance	3.92	3.08	3.81	3.54
Symbolic value	3.79	3.06	4.06	1.97
Risk consequences of purchase	2.80	2.89	4.35	4.16
Risk probability of a bad purchase	2.94	3.32	3.50	3.08

(159) = 24.47, p < .0001). The analysis with wines confirms this result; hedonic involvement is greater for wine than for haircuts (t (145) = 3.66, p < .0005) or visits to the dentist (t (144) = 16.37, p < .0001).

Because of these confirmatory results on the hedonic nature of movies, further study on consumer behavior for these products seemed justified.

Phase 2

This study tested the hypotheses on alternatives and choice features for movies.

Subjects. The subjects were 181 undergraduate business students. This sample was 56% women and 44% men; mean age was 20.4 years. The sample was taken from the same university as that used for the questionnaire on involvement and so was from the same population.

Procedure. Subjects responded to a written survey; they were tested in groups but each filled out the survey individually. Each subject answered the following question: What alternatives to this movie did you consider? Each subject also gave a written report on whatever he/she could remember about choosing the last movie attended. The directions asked the subjects to include all thoughts, observations and feelings. Since these protocols are retrospective, they are not as reliable as concurrent ones. However, it seems unlikely that the subjects altered their responses in favor of the hypotheses (i.e., by increasing the number of subjective and global features reported).

A judge who was unaware of the hypotheses coded each alternative as either one that requires expenditure of time or one that only requires expenditure of money. Features in the written protocol were identified; features were broadly defined as any characteristic of the movie itself (e.g., actress) or of going to the movies (e.g., theatre location) or any criteria used in the choice process (e.g., my companion wanted to see the movie). The same judge then coded each feature in every written protocol as subjective or objective. An objective feature was defined as one that is externally verifiable. In other words, people would agree on whether or not a particular product has this feature; for example, whether a particular actor is in a movie. The most frequently mentioned objective features of movies were location, not seen before, price, schedule convenience, setting, and a particular actor. By contrast, subjective features were defined as those for which each consumer is likely to have his/her own opinion about whether a product has this feature. The most common examples were good, liked the actors, funny, others wanted to see it, and I wanted to see it.

The same judge also coded each feature as global or unidimensional. Global descriptors refer to the entire product, not to just one part that can be delineated. For example, one subject described the latest remake of "The Fly" as "1 1/2 hours of a gross and stupid movie"; "gross" and "stupid" are global descriptors. The most frequent examples were descriptions like "I heard it would be good", comedy, "I wanted to see this movie", and "I hadn't seen it before". Unidimensional features refer to one specific part of a product. Subjects most frequently mentioned specific actors or producers, theatre location, price, show time, and the movie's setting.

Analysis Because every hypothesis involved a comparison between two measures for the same subject, each hypothesis was analyzed by paired t-tests.

RESULTS

H1 is supported; when choosing a movie, subjects consider more alternatives that consume time than alternatives that only consume money. There is a significant difference between the number of alternatives that consume time (mean = 1.2) and those that only consume money (mean =0.1) t (181) = 16.94, p < .0001.

Of the 181 subjects, 80% (145) listed an alternative to the last movie attended. Of this group, 41% (59) considered only other movies, 36% (52) considered non-movie alternatives, and 23% (34) considered both other movies and non-movie alternative. They mentioned 140 alternatives that consume time. The majority (67%) of these alternatives involved other experiential products, for example, watching TV or a video, drinking, going to a restaurant or to a club. The rest (33%) were other activities, like staying home, studying or partying.

As predicted by H2a, subjects use more subjective features (mean =1.77) than objective ones (mean = 1.08) in selecting movies, t (181) = 4.96, p < .0001. Also, as hypothesized by H2b, the subjects use more global (mean = 1.77) than unidimensional features (mean = 1.04) in choosing a movie, t (181) = 5.17, p < .0001.

DISCUSSION

As expected, tests for both movies and wines confirmed the importance of hedonic value for experiential products and its greater importance for these products compared to more utilitarian ones. The importance of hedonic and pleasure value was used for predictions on alternatives and choice features for movies, as examples of experiential products. The results of a study on these aspects of choice behavior support the predictions; when choosing a movie, subjects predominantly considered alternatives that require time allocations and examined subjective and global product features. These two findings are consistent, as follows. Both these types of features are abstract. As such, they facilitate comparisons with other product classes (as shown by Johnson 1984). Because consumers consider as alternatives products that require expenditures of time, they are likely to compare movies to other product classes (e.g., TV shows, restaurants).

Of the four product classes researched, the two experiential products, wine and movies, had the highest levels of hedonic involvement. This suggests that the consumer's relationship with these products is largely hedonic. This confirms a study on movies which tested the relationship of 30 lifestyle characteristics to filmgoing; only four were related but one of those was hedonism/optimism (Knapp and Sherman 1986). Another study found very high levels of hedonic involvement for champagne, which is similar to wine (Laurent and Kapferer 1985). Laurent and Kapferer did not focus on experiential products but did include three products which could be so classified: champagne, chocolate, and TV sets (assuming that consumers rated TV shows not simply the sets). These three products (plus dresses) clearly had the highest scores for hedonic/pleasure value of the products studied (no tests for significant differences between products were reported).

Laurent and Kapferer (1985) also found that hedonic involvement was not related to the reported extensiveness of the choice process. Extensiveness reflected time, effort and number of features used. Thus, given the importance of hedonic value for experiential products, the choice process for such products is likely to involve less time and less effort than the process for people-directed, non-experiential products. Future research using decision time and/or concurrent protocols of the choice process for various products (experiential and utilitarian) could be used to test this hypothesis.

Despite the evidence for the importance of hedonic value for experiential products, including movies, there is one way in which movies can be utilitarian. In American society, movie-going is a social activity; 96% of movie-goers attend with at least one other person (Johnson 1981). Likewise, of the 181 subjects who answered questionnaires on features and alternatives, 97% went with someone else to the last movie attended. It is possible that a consumer would attend a movie simply to join friends or take someone else on a date and so has little interest in the movie itself; the movie might thus be utilitarian in the sense of furthering or enhancing a social relationship. (Eight of the 181 subjects reported in their protocols that they went along due to an invitation by friends.) Given the social nature of movies, joint decision-making, in which the final selection must be acceptable to all those involved, is very likely. (Of the 181 subjects, 68 or 38% had evidence of joint decision-making in their protocols.) Also, the interaction between consumers who go together, as well as among all consumers in a movie theatre, may well be an important dimension of the consumption process for this product. Thus another topic for future research is to go beyond the individual consumer to understand both choice and consumption behavior for movies and other experiential products that are also leisure activities.

The current results suggest that consumers rely more on subjective than objective features to select a movie. Consumers may search different sources for these two types of features. Faber and O'Guinn's (1984) survey of movie consumers included information sources; their subjects rated previews and friends' comments as more useful and more credible for evaluating movies than advertisements or critics' reviews. Thus, to learn about movies, it appears that consumers may turn to experiential sources of information; these sources are distinguished by their ability to convey a sense of the consumption experience, that is, of what it is like to see the movie. Previews are a chance to try the movie; friends who have seen the movie can describe it. Non-experiential sources, such as ads are less useful because they don't concern the consumption experience. Although reviews should be an experiential source, the subjects found them less useful.

These different types of information sources, experiential versus non-experiential, relate to subjective and objective features as follows. The usefulness and credibility of the information source may depend on what information it provides. Specifically, a non-experiential source (e.g., a magazine ad) should be just as credible and useful as a friend to determine an objective features (e.g., the movie's director). However, for subjective features (e.g., how funny the movie is), experiential sources (e.g., a friend) should be more credible and useful. Building on the findings from the current study, I am developing another to address whether experiential information sources are more credible and useful than non-experiential sources for both objective and subjective features.

CONCLUSIONS

This paper focused on the special nature of experiential products and began the process of understanding consumer behavior for them. The results confirm the hedonic nature of these products and show that as alternatives to movies, subjects considered more products that require expenditure of time than ones that only require expenditures of money. Further, they examined more subjective than objective features and more global than unidimensional ones.

The current findings are limited by a non-random, relatively small sample that focuses on the most important age group for movie-goers but neglects other age groups, including teenagers. If a study with a bigger, projectable sample confirms the current findings, then certain managerial implications would result. For example, communication efforts for movies and others types of experiential products should include subjective features, visually or verbally, and not simply focus on objective ones, such as the star. The results concerning alternatives to movies indicate that competition for movies includes other activities or products, as well as movies. This information may help to better position movies relative to the competition or to direct management's efforts on information gathering about competition. For example, if drinking and eating out are popular alternatives (as in this study), then there may be a ready market for movie theatres that serve alcoholic beverages or meals. Likewise, it seems reasonable that movie theatres locate in malls where consumers can have a meal and/or a drink before or after seeing a film.

The results of this study are encouraging and give us the courage to go on to do the future research described above. They show that experiential products have specific patterns of consumer behavior. It appears that hedonic consumption can define a category of products and further, is key for understanding them. This emphasis thus contributed towards the need in the field of consumer behavior to address the experiential aspects of consumption.

REFERENCES

Austin, Bruce A. (1981), "Film Attendance: Why College Students Chose to See Their Most Recent Film," *The Journal of Popular Film and Television*, 9 (Spring), 43-49.

Capon, Noel and Elizabeth Cooper-Martin (1990), "Public and Nonprofit Marketing: A Review and Directions for Research," in *Annual Review of Marketing 1990*, ed. Valarie Zeithaml, Chicago: American Marketing Association.

Cooper-Martin, Elizabeth (1989), "The Effect of Three Contingency Factors on Consumer Choice Strategies: A Test of Awareness of Costs and Benefit," in *Advances in Consumer Research*, Vol. 16, ed. Thomas Srull, Provo, UT: Association for Consumer Research.

Faber, Ronald J. and Thomas C. O'Guinn (1984), "Effect of Media Advertising and Other Sources on Movie Selection," *Journalism Quarterly*, 61 (Summer), 371-377.

Holbrook, Morris B. and Elizabeth C. Hirschman (1982), "The Experiential Aspects of Consumption: Consumer Fantasies, Feelings, and Fun," *Journal of Consumer Research*, 9 (September), 132-140.

Jobson (1989), *Jobson's Wine Marketing Handbook*, New York: Jobson Publishing.

Johnson, Keith F. (1981), "Cinema Advertising," *Journal of Advertising*, 10 (4), 11-19.

Johnson, Michael D. (1984), "Consumer Choice Strategies for Comparing Noncomparable Alternatives," *Journal of Consumer Research*, 11 (December), 741-753.

_____ and Jolita Kiselius (1985), "Concreteness-Abstractness and the Feature-Dimension Distinction," in *Advances in Consumer Research*, Vol. 12, eds. Morris Holbrook and Elizabeth C. Hirschman, Provo, UT: Association for Consumer Research, 325-328.

Kapferer, Jean-Noel and Gilles Laurent (1985), "Consumers' Involvement Profiles: New Empirical Results," in *Advances in Consumer Research*, Vol. 12, eds. Morris Holbrook and Elizabeth C. Hirschman, Provo, UT: Association for Consumer Research, 290-295.

Knapp, Steven, and Barry L. Sherman (1986), "Motion Picture Attendance: A Market Segmentation Approach," in *Current Research in Film: Audiences, Economics, and Law*, , Volume 2, ed. Bruce A. Austin, Norwood, NJ: Ablex Publishing Corporation, 35-46.

Laurent, Gilles and Jean-Noel Kapferer (1985), "Measuring Consumer Involvement Profiles," *Journal of Marketing Research*, 22 (February), 41-53.

Lovelock, Christopher H. (1983), "Classifying Services to Gain Strategic Marketing Insights," *Journal of Marketing*, 47 (Summer), 9-20.

Milliman, Ronald E. (1982), "Using Background Music to Affect the Behavior of Supermarket Shoppers," *Journal of Marketing*, 46 (Summer), 86-91.

_____ (1986), "The Influence of Background Music on the Behavior of Restaurant Patrons," *Journal of Consumer Research*, 13 (September), 286-289.

Newspaper Advertising Bureau (1984), *Demographic Characteristics of Frequent Movie-goers*, New York: Newspaper Advertising Bureau.

O'Shaughnessy, John (1987), *Why People Buy*, New York: Oxford University Press.

Peter, J. Paul (1979), "Reliability: A Review of Psychometric Basics and Recent Marketing Practice," *Journal of Marketing Research*, 16 (February), 6-17.

Variety (1981), "Film Subject Matter Looms Large in Stay-Away; Ticket prices are Related to Age; Income Strata," *Variety*, 305 (November 18), 5 and 32.

Methodological Diversity in Consumer Esthetics Research
Ruth Ann Smith, Virginia Polytechnic Institute and State University

My initial inclination as discussant for this session was to try to make some summary statements about the collective implications of the papers by Scott, Langmeyer and Walker, and Cooper-Martin for consumer esthetics, which is the topic of the session. Perhaps reflecting my own limited creativity, however, I found the papers to be only peripherally related to that subject. Consequently, I am unable to offer any stunning insights about their meaning in that context.

What I did find striking about the work of these authors, however, was the relationship between the research questions that were posed and the research methods used to address these questions. Although pertaining to two diverse subjects (meaning transfer and experiential products), the research questions seem to me to be largely interpretive. That is, the process by which meaning becomes associated with celebrity endorsers and transferred to products appears to be one that is highly idiosyncratic and likely to defy precise quantification. Similarly, consumers' selection and evaluation of experiential products like movies, music, or art also seems to require interpretation rather than quantification. I was impressed by the authors' creativity in developing these questions, and believe their interest in these subjects is evidence of a substantial broadening in our perceptions about the domain of consumer research.

The research methods used to address these questions, however, seem to me to be more in the positivist tradition of empirical hypothesis testing. Langmeyer and Walker (1991), for example, describe the process of developing a measure of meaning transfer and use it to test hypotheses about the meanings of celebrity endorsers and the products they promote. Cooper-Martin's (1991) study is designed to test hypotheses about the attributes used to select experiential products. The objective of both studies seems to be to discover generalizations about the phenomena under investigation.

Scott (1991) did employ an interpretive method, historical analysis, in developing part of her argument about celebrity endorsements as an active, rather than a passive, process. Her use of this method, however, was to demonstrate that the transfer of meaning from people to objects is a phenomenon that has persisted across a variety of cultures and time periods. I suspect this application of history to demonstrate continuity would be surprising to an historian who would likely view the strength of historical analysis as its ability to explain the causes of change, or discontinuity, rather than continuity.

Given this interesting match between interpretive questions and traditional methodologies (or interpretive methods used conservatively in the case of Scott), I would suggest that the major contribution of these papers is conceptual. That is, these authors have posed for our consideration some very unique and unusual issues about consumer behavior that force us to stretch our definitions about the domain of the discipline. I believe the methodological contribution of the papers is smaller in that the authors seem to have been less innovative in their choices of research approaches to address these questions. Consequently, I would like to focus my remarks on the subject of methodological diversity in consumer research.

METHODOLOGICAL DIVERSITY

Broadening our research horizons with respect to the kinds of questions we ask about consumer behavior is, I believe, certainly a sign of maturity in our discipline and I applaud these authors for their creativity in this regard. It is, however, equally important to broaden our methodological repertoire so we can select the methods most appropriate to the research questions we address. I cannot claim to be the first to suggest the benefits of methodological diversity in consumer research, and I doubt that I will be the last. In his 1988 ACR Presidential Address, for example, Lutz (1989) argued that:

> At *minimum*, each of us needs to understand the current dominant paradigm in consumer research. Then, we need to learn more about the alternatives to positivism. Just as consumers search for information in order to make informed purchases, we owe it to ourselves to make informed choices about how we seek knowledge (p. 6, emphasis added).

Failure to diversify our methodological bag of tricks risks imposing two limitations on our research. First is the risk that we will restrict our attention only to those questions that are compatible with the methods with which we are comfortable. Second is the risk that even if we ask innovative questions, we may develop incomplete or even misleading answers if we select methods that are poorly suited to these questions. I would like to suggest that in addition to the unique research questions posed in these papers, there is a multitude of other fascinating questions about meaning transfer and experiential products that might be investigated. And, to do so will require using some methods that are unconventional, at least in the context of consumer research. However, in order to fully understand these phenomena, we need to ask the questions and we need to master these, and other methods.

WHAT QUESTIONS AND WHAT METHODS?

Meaning Transfer
A variety of issues pertaining to meaning transfer seem to focus on questions of change

through time. For instance, Scott (1991) suggests that the source of the meaning transferred to goods has changed over time from the giver of the goods, to gods and military heroes, to film and rock stars. Why and how did this change come about? Another question pertains to the change in the meanings embodied by currently popular celebrity endorsers. Cher, who was the focus of the study by Langmeyer and Walker (1991), began her career in the 1960's as a counter-culture singer. After her initial success with Sonny Bono, she became essentially a co-opted rocker when she "sold out" for the security and material benefits of a prime time TV variety show and an aggressively sexual Bob Mackie wardrobe. How and why did the (probably negative) meanings associated with her at that time change to the tough-minded, tough-bodied, independent woman who now functions so successfully as a health spa endorser?

Investigating processes of change such as these is difficult using the positivist methods that have dominated consumer behavior research in the past. Historical method, however, is uniquely suited to explaining the causes of change through time, and is therefore an ideal tool to examine questions pertaining to changing meanings, or changes in the sources of those meanings.

Experiential Products

Consumption of products that are experienced, as opposed to used in a utilitarian sense, also poses some intriguing research questions. How and why consumers' tastes for experiential products like movies and music change through time is one example. Although it is tempting to suggest that such changes are dictated by marketers, one only has to think about product failures like the Edsel and the midi-skirt to realize that consumers' tastes are not easily dictated or simply explained. Historical analysis is an ideal approach to explain the complex causes underlying these changes.

Other questions pertaining to experiential products concern consumers' feelings and evaluations during and after consumption. For example, is one's satisfaction with an experiential product a function of the type of feeling it evokes (e.g. happiness, fear, satiation) or the intensity of the feeling? Also, what is the effect of others' presence when an experiential product is consumed? Is the experience better or worse if shared with others as opposed to experiencing the product alone? Questions such as these could potentially be examined through an ethnographic study in which a descriptive anthropology of consumers of experiential products (like movie buffs or wine connoisseurs) is developed.

CONCLUSIONS

As a discipline, consumer behavior has made enormous progress toward recognizing that the research questions deserving our attention go far beyond those suggested by the traditional paradigms of information processing, economics, and behaviorism. The research presented by Scott, Langmeyer and Walker, and Cooper-Martin are tangible evidence of this progress. Asking these questions, however, is only the first step. The next, and perhaps more difficult, step is to acquire the methodological tools that are best suited to examining these new questions.

REFERENCES

Cooper-Martin, Elizabeth (1991), "Consumers and Movies: Some Findings on Experiential Products," in *Advances in Consumer Research*, Vol. 18, Rebecca H. Holman and Michael R. Solomon, eds., Provo, UT: Association for Consumer Research, in press.

Langmeyer, Lynn and Mary Walker (1991), "A First Step to Identify the Meaning in Celebrity Endorsers," in *Advances in Consumer Research*, Vol. 18, Rebecca H. Holman and Michael R. Solomon, eds., Provo, UT: Association for Consumer Research, in press.

Lutz, Richard J. (1989), "Positivism, Naturalism and Pluralism in Consumer Research: Paradigms in Paradise," in *Advances in Consumer Research*, Vol. 16, Thomas K. Srull, ed., Provo, UT: Association for Consumer Research, p. 1-8.

Scott, Linda M. (1991), "The Troupe: Celebrities as *Dramatis Personae* in Advertisments, in *Advances in Consumer Research*, Vol. 18, Rebecca H. Holman and Michael R. Solomon, eds., Provo, UT: Association for Consumer Research, in press.

Toward a Theory of Sexuality and Consumption: Consumer Lovemaps
Stephen J. Gould, Rutgers University

I always find that wearing Robert Lee Morris jewelry causes men to gather around me as if I'm emitting a powerful aphrodisiac. I like this.
(*Robert Lee Morris Jewelry and Accessories* undated, p. 13)

He was our group's guide on a trip to Israel and we immediately *hated* each other (I was the Snob, he the Corporate Clone)...After a few days, though, we began to soften enough so that when he invited me to his room for a nightcap, I went...I was wearing a bodysuit with snaps up the back, and he very gently unfastened them, one by one. We made love twice - not the typical fumbling kind of way - and were so much in sync in terms of speed, pressure, and our needs. Before I went back to my room the next morning, he carefully fastened all the snaps back up again. (*New Woman* 1990, p. 76).

Golden Lotus took his silken gown. Something dropped out of the sleeve and fell tinkling to the ground. She picked it up and weighed it in her hand. It was like a little ball, but very heavy. She looked at it for a long time, but could not imagine what it was for.
"What is it?" she said. "And why does it seem so heavy?"
"Don't you know?" he said, laughing. "They call it the Bell of Fecundity...A good one is worth four or five measures of silver."
"Where is it to be put?" the woman asked.
"First put it inside you, and then get on with what has to be done. The results are quite indescribable."
(Chin P'ing Mein in Douglas and Slinger 1989, p. 365)

INTRODUCTION

As the above quotes indicate there is a broad spectrum of omnipresent sexuality present in everyday life which is directly involved with consumption, much as two bodies become entwined in the sex act. Although we as consumer researchers recognize this pervasive influence, we nonetheless appear to have gone to great pains to ignore it as a research topic, except perhaps in the advertising context, and to act as if consumer behavior were devoid of sexuality - sometimes I think life as phenomenologically felt experience has been just as ignored, as well, though it's certainly more fashionable to bemoan such conditions these days. Both this session and this paper are designed to fertilize our barren and dry our research womb with the seminal fluid of the vital essence of living, libidinous consumer behavior.

THE SEXUALITY-CONSUMPTION CONNECTION AND CONSUMER LOVEMAPS

We may view the sexuality-consumption connection in terms of various levels of phenomenological manifestation: (1) the sex act itself and consumption objects involved (e.g. sexual toys) as well as the exchange terms between sexual partners (e.g. prostitution; forming a relationship with a sexual partner), (2) the consumption surrounding the act both directly (e.g. the acquisition and use of boudoir accompaniments) and indirectly (e.g. the ritualistic use of consumption objects to attract sexual partners), and (3) investments of sexual libido in symbolic reenactments or simulacra of the sex act (e.g. dancing suggestively).

How should we view such seemingly disparate phenomena as well as the vast individual differences that manifest in sexual behavior? The perspective I wish to offer here is informed by the field of sex research, one which has been overlooked by consumer research, in spite of our seeming obsession with sex. This field offers rich potential for consumer researchers which I want to call attention to. Here in particular, I want to suggest that there exist what we can call consumer lovemaps. This concept represents an adaptation of Money's (1984) lovemap theory. He defines a lovemap as (p. 165) as that which "carries the program of a person's erotic fantasies and their corresponding practices." Based on the lovemap concept, Money has developed a typology of paraphilias (perversions) each with their own lovemap (e.g. autonepiophilia - diaperism; hyphephilia - lover of fabrics). Each also follows certain strategies of sexual response - the two examples of autonepiophilia and hyphephilia, for instance, represent a fetishistic sexual strategy. In this context, we may define a consumer lovemap as including those aspects of the more general lovemap which involve consumption, i.e. the purchase and use of products in the process of attracting a mate, engaging in sexual activity, and developing and maintaining sexual-love relationships.

In sex research, there is nothing like a case to illustrate a point. The case I will quote in part here from Stekel (1952, p. 21) illustrates not only how a consumer lovemap works (as well as a fetishistic lovemap strategy) but also gives us an idea how sexuality and consumption are related. In the following passage, Stekel recounts the case of a rose fetishist:

He never had intercourse with women and even declared that he was a misogynist. One evening he saw a woman who was wearing a beautiful rose upon her breast and promptly fell in love - with the woman but primarily with the rose. Secretly he soon engaged himself to this woman, but his desire was

solely directed to her roses. He never rested
until the roses she wore became his property.
He would then take them home, smell them
over and over again and thereby sense the
deepest raptures. He finally collected quite a
museum of roses with a deal of industry.

This man never married the woman but
instead broke off the engagement. His passion was
for roses to which he had transferred the psychic
investment of his libido energy. However, while
such paraphilias might be of interest in their own
right to consumer researchers as representing
distorted lovemaps which involve various forms of
consumption, the paraphilia and lovemap concepts
might also be considered for what they say about
consumption in the 'normal range' of sexual
behavior. Here in using the term normal or
'normophilia', we follow Money who views
paraphiliacs as generally using unusual or
unacceptable stimuli to reach orgasm, i.e. the
normal sex act is not as arousing to them.
Nonetheless even those for whom the 'usual sex act'
is arousing and exciting may still exhibit all sorts
of peculiarities and specific tastes related to
partners, objects and settings as sexual stimuli, as
well as to interactions between these stimuli. In
considering these stimuli, based on the work of
Money and many others in the sex research field
(e.g. Singer 1985; Singer and Toates 1987), sexual
behavior may be viewed as being appetitive and
involving acquired (conditioned) motivation as
developed in various socialization theories -
although also possessing drive-like, unconditioned
qualities. It especially differs across cultures and
some individuals have reported that their whole
experience of sexuality changes when they try the
sexual practices of another culture (Gould 1990).

Consumer lovemaps represent this patterning
of acquired tastes and incorporate a broad range of
ordinary to extraordinary consumption behaviors.
Thus we can all describe to some degree what
composes our lovemap if asked, although we might
not know why. Some of us may know that we
particularly like to 'prime' our sexual behavior by
wearing certain clothes, watching certain videos,
eating certain foods, engaging in certain cleansing
and grooming rituals etc. Sex therapy often goes
back to the source of these tastes in one's lovemaps
and finds particular experiences in which the
investment of one's libido gets focused on particular
objects and rituals (cf. Money 1984).

IMPLICATIONS AND CONCLUSIONS

The consumer lovemap approach might help
us to sort out various questions of interest to
consumer researchers. For example, we might begin
to develop a framework for answering the most
famous question of all, "How much of consumption
is sexual?" Lovemap theory, along with other
approaches, suggests several things that might be
useful in this regard (cf. Money 1984):

(1) There are vast individual differences in
lovemaps so that what has sexual feeling
and/or connotation for one individual will
not for another.

(2) While lovemaps are largely psychogenic
in nature, individual differences in libido
may also play a role in their
determination.

(3) There are also likely to be gender, age and
other socio-demographic differences in
lovemaps.

(4) Specific life experiences, especially early
developmental ones, serve as the root of
various lifelong lovemap patternings.

(5) Some consumption experiences may be
seen to be more tied directly to actual
sexual experience while others may not.
This may account for our ambivalence
toward and difficulty with the study of
sexuality in consumer research, since it
may not be the consumption experience
per se that makes it sexual or not sexual
in feeling and association, but rather a
phenomenological question of experience
which may not be easy to trace. Thus, for
example, one individual may have at some
point had an acutely arousing experience
while eating an ice cream cone and
associate that with sexuality at some level
of consciousness, while another person
may have had no such experience.

(6) The relationship of sexual behavior and
consumption may be mapped. Moreover,
with regard to this mapping, we need not
rely solely on relatively abstract
psychotherapy, however useful and
suggestive for some research in this area
it might be - instead we can also explore
and identify specific networks of behavior
(conscious and unconscious) and see how
they are encoded in various schema and
scripts. In fact, I would argue that using a
lovemap approach provides a natural
bridge between so-called positivistic and
post-positivistic researchers as both
phenomenological-ethnographic and
cognitive social-psychological
methodologies should prove useful in
describing consumer lovemaps and also in
forming and testing predictive hypotheses
about them. Through the application of
the lovemap construct, we should begin to
understand in more specific terms how
libido comes to be cathected into
consumption objects.

It is hoped that this brief paper will inspire
researchers to look more closely at what may be the
most important and certainly one of the least

understood consumer behavior phenomena, i.e. sexually-related consumption. In this domain as well in others we have tended to undervalue things of the direct senses and to overvalue abstractions and constructs of the mind which are distal from felt experience (cf. Berman 1989). Yet if we want to go to the roots of consumer behavior and investigate the deeper linkages and networks of experiential phenomena at more fundamental levels of being, it is imperative that we have a sexual revolution of our own.

Thus, if we envision what consumer research might look like one hundred years from now, given that such a revolution has taken place, we almost certainly will see that many articles have been published on sexuality and consumption and that various aspects of their relationship will have been inscribed into our basic consumer research 'text' and discourse. Perhaps the idea of the consumer lovemap will be the guiding construct along with other ideas concerning libido and its psychic investment in objects. Moreover, we can almost certainly expect that sexuality, itself, as an object and aspect of consumption will have evolved so that the art and science of sexual stimulation and satisfaction will have moved into new spheres. It is likely, for instance, that new aphrodisiacal drugs; psychophysiological stimulating devices; consciousness altering mindbody psychotechnologies (cf. Roberts 1989), psychological interventions, and related sexual techniques and practices; and environments and objects surrounding and/or used in lovemaking will make the sex act even more an object of consumption than it already is, especially in our *perception of it as involving or even itself being an act of consumption*. Thus for us as consumer researchers it is most important that we discover and study male and female sexual consumers, i.e. *consumer eroticus* and *consumer erotica*, respectively.

REFERENCES

Berman, Morris (1989), *Coming to Our Senses*, New York: Simon and Schuster.

Douglas, Nik and Penny Slinger (1989), *Sexual Secrets: The Alchemy of Ecstasy*, Rochester, VT: Destiny Books.

Gould, Stephen J. (1990), "The Import of Asian Sexual Psychotechnologies into the United States: The 'New Woman' and the 'New Man' Go Tantric'," *Journal of Popular Culture* (in press).

Money, John (1984), "Paraphilias: Phenomenology and Classification," *American Journal of Psychotherapy*, 38 (April), 164-179.

New Woman (1990), "Sexually Speaking," 20 (May), 76.

Robert Lee Morris Jewelry and Accessories (undated catalog).

Roberts, Thomas R. (1989), "Multistate Education: Metacognitive Implications for the Mindbody Techonologies," *Journal of Transpersonal Psychology*, 21 (1), 83-102.

Singer, Barry (1985), "A Comparison of Evolutionary and Environmental Theories of Erotic Response Part I: Structural Features," *The Journal of Sex Research*, 21 (August), 229-257.

_____ and Frederick M. Toates (1987), "Sexual Motivation," *The Journal of Sex Research*, 23 (November), 481-501.

Stekel, Wilhelm (1952), *Sexual Aberrations: The Phenomena of Fetishism in Relation to Sex*, New York: Liveright.

Two Pornographies: A Feminist View of Sex in Advertising
Barbara B. Stern, Rutgers University

ABSTRACT

This paper presents the feminist concept of two pornographies, one for men, and one for women. It first distinguishes between them, and then presents the themes, characteristics, and underlying values of soft-core pornography known as the "women's romance." Next, it analyzes an advertisement to illustrate the romance elements. Last, it discusses the implications of different pornographies in three areas: alienation of target markets, feminist evaluations of romances, and the "pornographic society."

An "omnipresent sexuality" is said to permeate consumption, for advertising frequently relies on symbolic representations of sexuality (Gould 1990) for products not directly related to sexual activities. Some researchers say that the prevalence of this imagery reflects the importance of sexuality as an essential consumption element -- a bonding agent between consumer and product (Dichter 1990). The abundance and ubiquity of sexual imagery has been castigated at best as "Sex-cess in Advertising" (Pollay 1989), and at worst as commercial pornography (McLuhan 1951; Miller 1989; Prewitt 1990).

However, while all pornography (defined below) contains sexual imagery, not all sexual imagery is pornographic. Controversy surrounds the definition, nature, and function of pornography, and its differentiation from other kinds of sexual literature such as erotica and/or romances (Sontag 1967; Steinem 1978). Further, recent research indicates that the nature of pornography differs depending on whether its authors/audience are men or women. The concept of consumer "lovemaps" -- the "patterned acquired tastes that delineate an individual's erotic fantasies and corresponding practices" (Gould 1990) -- suggests the role gender differences play in what is experienced as sexually arousing. Thus two inter-related questions about sexuality, pornography, and consumption are of interest to researchers, one concerning text (the advertisement), and the second concerning reader response to text (the consumer). The first question is, what is the distinction between pornography and other sexual imagery? The second is, what is the distinction between what men and women consider sexually arousing stimuli?

The purpose of this paper is to address these questions. It presents the feminist concept of "two pornographies, one for men, one for women" (Snitow 1978, p. 257) and pays special attention to erotic romances as pornography for women. The paper will first distinguish between the two pornographies, and then present the themes, characteristics, and underlying values of soft-core pornography known as the "women's romance." Next, it will analyze an advertisement to illustrate the romance concepts. Last, it will discuss implications of the two pornographies for consumer research in three areas: unintentional alienation of target markets, feminist evaluations of romances, and societal effects of sexual advertising.

The rationale for this paper's reliance on feminist research is that it provides new insights into sexuality and consumption by viewing phenomena from the vantage point of the "other" -- that is, the female -- sex. Most of the sex-related research up to the 1970s was based on assumptions of male norms, implicitly held applicable to females as well. Feminist scholarship has questioned these assumptions. Its major contributions to cultural self-awareness have been the identification of a "masculinist" bias and the discovery of a female culture coexisting with the predominant male one in patriarchal societies. Since the most fundamental distinction between the two cultures is based on sex, feminist scholars often begin by hypothesizing differences between men and women in relation to words, images, and ideas related to sexuality.

Feminist scholarship is thus an additional but under-utilized resource available to consumer researchers bent on understanding the still-relevant question, "Why does sex sell?" (Russell 1990, p. 58). Since sexually-oriented appeals are unlikely to disappear, more accurate knowledge of what pornography is and is not as well as what sexual imagery appeals more to women than to men may encourage creation of advertisements that are more socially responsible *and* more effective.

Distinction Between Pornography Erotica

Both pornography and erotica are terms categorizing literary texts whose goal is sexual arousal (Sontag 1967). Yet the etymological roots of the terms reflect differences: pornography comes from the Greek *porne*, meaning "prostitute, harlot," and probably derived from *pernemi*, meaning "sell, as captives." Etymologically, the word's denotation of financial profit from the sale of female captives implies the connotation of an imbalance of power in a sex-for-sale marketplace. Erotica, in contrast, comes from the Greek *eros*, meaning passionate love (Steinem 1978). The denotative concept of sensual awakening connotes mutual rewards for equal partners in a love relationship.

Pornography is thus rooted in the concept of domination of women, and is often associated with sadomasochistic violence, in that the participants in the exchange are either male conquerors (sadists) or female victims (masochists). The literature sends messages of male aggression and superiority, for standard themes are misogyny, mistreatment of women as objects, and sex as a weapon. Nearly all pornography is written, sold, and bought by men (Morgan 1978), for, like rape, its aim is *power* through sexual humiliation rather than mutual erotic satisfaction (Brownmiller 1976). Some critics feel that the main subject of pornography is pain leading to death (Sontag 1967). Erotica, on the other hand, is the literature of pleasure (Steinem 1978): it depicts sensual images of shared sexual joy.

True pornography is said to "serve as aversion therapy for sex" for most women (Steinem 1978, p. 54), apparently repelled by the woman-hating themes and violence commonplace in X-rated literature. Feminists point out that what arouses women is different from what arouses men, a distinction that has led to the concept of "two pornographies" (Snitow 1978). One is "hard-core," more likely to arouse men sexually, and the other is "soft-core," more appealing to women. Erotica has been defined as synonymous with soft-core pornography since 1977, when the term first appeared in the journal *Lancet* (Oxford English Dictionary 1989, italics mine):

> A distinction could be drawn between *erotic art* (or *soft pornography*) and *hard pornography*, which by connecting sex with violence, hatred, pain, and humiliation, stimulated gratification of sexual desire in deviant ways.

Discussion of male-oriented hard-core pornography lies beyond the scope of this paper (see Prewitt 1990), and we now turn to closer examination of romances as pornography for women.

Pornography for Women: "Romance" Characteristics and Themes

The "romance" genre is considered a form of "soft-core pornography that women find socially acceptable and non-threatening" (Coles and Shamp 1984). The genre includes many species variously called gothics, historical romances, soap operas, and erotic romances (Ellis 1975). Its ancestry is traceable to Greek romances, and it bears remnants of medieval Arthurian tales and post-eighteenth century popular gothic novels. Unlike hard-core pornography, soft-core literature has traditionally been written by and for women. It describes sexual activities in veiled rather than overt terms: lovemaking is "bathed in romance, diffused, always implied rather than enacted" (Snitow 1978, p. 257). In a word, soft-core women's pornography presents foreplay, whereas male pornography describes penetration.

The reason that romances stop after foreplay is that they have but one major theme: courtship. Romances end with marriage -- "they lived happily ever after" -- a goal attainable only if the heroine retains her chastity. They are an unusual literary genre in that they are told from the woman's point of view, with a woman as the major protagonist (Cawelti 1975). The heroine occupies center stage in a love relationship, for in this literature, the male is the inscrutable "other" (De Beauvoir 1952; Stern 1991). Romances characteristically feature a lonely heroine, emotionally and often physically isolated, who tries to keep her virginity intact under pressure from a sporadically available but nonetheless powerful male. The gulf between the sexes is widened by this romanticized sexuality, for women's pleasure derives from the excitement of waiting to unravel the male mystery: "Not knowing may be more sexy than finding out" (Snitow 1978, p. 250). The Freudian question ("what do women want?") is reversed, and heroines puzzle over what *men* want.

But male-female communication is less a concern than sexual fantasizing. Because romances rarely depict sexual activities below the waist -- they are popularly called "bodice-rippers" -- they do not present mature sexual relationships. Since the only adventure open to women is the hunt for marriage, romances fantasize the early stages of love. Once the woman gets her man, this particular story is over. Romance literature, then, is the literature of courtship rather than of consummation, for "sex means marriage, and marriage, promised at the end, means, finally, there can be sex" (Snitow 1978, p. 248).

Romance themes (Coles and Shamp 1984) can be summarized as follows:

-- the glorification of courtship, that point in a woman's life cycle when she is the center of male attention and most optimistic about marriage

-- the ideal of virginity, for women's value in the marriage market depends on her purity (otherwise, she is "used goods")

-- the sign of success for women as marriage, postulated as the final truce in the sexual war ("living happily ever after")

-- the importance of domesticity, for women are judged by their goodness as wives and mothers

-- the emphasis on consumption, for women must fill time while waiting for their men by buying clothes, furniture, food, and so forth

These themes suggest values most recently enshrined in the 1950s, for romances can be read as pre-feminist stories about women whose lives center on men. Despite the societal changes in the past generation, traditionally feminine values seem to be coexisting with newer liberated ones. In this context, romances may function as repositories of fantasy as well as descriptions of reality, fulfilling the dual literary mission of defining sexuality while at the same time reflecting it. Advertising, like literature (Light 1986), plays a part in constructing sexual ideology and in defining the multiplicity of "femininities" that come to be lived, and its articulation of romance themes in 1950s terms indicates a pervasive media influence.

Analysis of A Romance Advertisement: Prell Shampoo

The romance advertisement selected for full analysis is a Prell shampoo ad from January, 1950, originally published in *The Woman's Home Companion*, and reproduced in *Advertising Age's* special section, *The House that Ivory Built: 150 Years of Procter & Gamble* (Freeman 1987, p. 46). It is used as an exemplar here for two reasons. First, it was selected by *Advertising Age's* editors as representative of one of Procter & Gamble's "memorable images," an indication that it tells society something important about itself. Second, it provides enough rich verbal and visual detail to enable close analysis of the romance themes that define the nature of this image.

The date of the ad suggests a link to popular romance themes, for 1950 was the start of the post-war decade most closely associated with "the feminine mystique" (Friedan 1963) and the full development of modern romanticized sexuality. This mystique is rooted in post-war optimism and prosperity (Light 1986). In the environment of abundance, women's "place" was once again the home (Welter 1966), for sexual and social fulfillment were circumscribed within the confines of marriage (Light 1986). "Normal" sexuality was what a woman experienced in her relationship with her husband, and femininity flowed from a guilt-free identity as wife and mother. A contemporary survey by Dichter points to the centrality of marriage in terms of the mystique (Friedan 1963, p. 210):

> The modern bride is deeply convinced of the unique value of married love, of the possibilities of finding real happiness in marriage and of fulfilling her personal destiny in it and through it....The modern bride seeks as a conscious goal that which in many cases her grandmother saw as a blind fate and her mother as slavery: to belong to a man, to have a home and children of her own, to choose among all possible careers the career of wife-mother-homemaker.

Glorification of Courtship: The Two Protagonists

The ad's romance themes cluster around four characters. Three are realistic -- the hero, the heroine (protagonists), and the doctor (see next section) -- and one is symbolic -- the Prell figure (see below). The first theme, the glorification of courtship, introduces the protagonists and the product message. The ad is about the heroine's entry into the marriage mart, and the product's benefit is to make her a winning player. The realistic level concerns the heroine's activity in the business of getting a man, step one on the road to domesticity. She is the center of male attention, winning admiration for her beautiful hair. Long shiny hair as a sexual lure links this text to folk-lore antecedents -- fairy-tales such as Rapunzel, Biblical tales such as Samson and Delilah, and modern variants such as the musical *Hair*.

The respective size and placement of the main characters (heroine and hero) illustrate their importance in the romance world: in the main picture, the woman is centered, and larger than the man. Interestingly, the heroine's hair (her bangs) obscures the hero partially. He is on a line with the conversation bubble below her fan, and seems to be emerging from the top of her head as a continuation of the unspoken thoughts signified by the bubble. The alignment of these thoughts, the heroine, and the hero on a diagonal suggests that his identity springs from her imagination. The heroine is thus the major character, with the hero off to one side, perhaps more imaginary than real.

Colors and clothing provide an important clue to the hero and heroine in romance, for this is a genre in which the characters are unidimensional and simplistic -- they are what they wear. The ad's hero is a generic "everyman," present only as an image of a future husband. He could be any available man, for he is a depersonalized character whose hair and dress -- brown-haired, clean-shaven, well-groomed, wearing a tuxedo -- describe anonymity. Brown is the commonest hair color in the United States, and a tuxedo resembles a uniform in that it masks distinctions among wearers. However, since tuxedos are commonly associated with wedding attire, the uniform also indicates that the hero matters less as an individual than as husband-fodder.

The Case for Chastity: The Virgin Heroine

Colors and clothing also provide insight into the more complex and ambiguous nature of the virgin heroine. She embodies the second theme -- the ideal of virginity. This ideal equates a woman's value in the marriage market with the cardinal virtue of chastity. Romances present women who are determined to preserve their virginity for their husbands, since non-virgins are considered, in marketplace terms, "used goods." Because marriage is the key to feminine identity, and because virginity once lost is irreplaceable, the chaste heroine symbolizes the pinnacle of desirability. However, her sexuality is ambivalent, since she must simultaneously project virtue at the same time as sufficient sexual availability to make her interesting to prospective mates.

The heroine's virgin/whore ambiguity is suggested by her blonde hair (a sign of virtue) versus her clothing, some of which is more vampish than virginal. Her black glove, most notably, is a sign of sexual experience, yet its color is what connects her visually with the hero's wedding attire -- his black tuxedo and tie. Her ambiguity is further complicated by the colors of her garments -- pink and blue -- hinting at baby innocence. Moreover, each garment has some white in its pattern, suggesting bridal innocence as well, for brides wear white in this culture as a symbol of purity. Thus the heroine reveals innocence as well as provocativeness, holding out the promise of an end to virginity, if it is preceded by matrimony.

The Doctor: A Character From Ritual to Romance

In the smaller picture, a secondary male character occupies a pivotal role: the doctor. His

FIGURE 1

presence is noteworthy, for he is the link between the third theme -- marriage as success -- and the underlying mythic level first identified by Weston as the foundation of modern romances (1919, repr. 1957). These mythic associations have been familiar since Eliot's *The Waste Land* popularized arcane folk matter for modern audiences. The doctor is a descendant of the "Medicine Man" in fertility rituals, a stock character whose function was to restore to life the wounded representative of a vegetation deity. By the time of the Arthurian romances, the Medicine Man had taken on elements of the Redeemer, for his original pagan task of healing the body had metamorphosed into the priestlike Christian mission of healing the soul.

The ad retains echoes of the doctor's dual function as both healer and priest. In the first role, he is a scientific authority schooled in medicinal remedies to cure physical ailments. As such, he provides the data that convinces the heroine of the shampoo's benefits -- "Doctors' examinations proved" Prell's ability to remove dandruff. But in his second and more important role, the doctor does more than simply describe or prescribe a remedy: he guides the curing ceremony, holding the shampoo while the heroine washes her hair. This is an allusion to the baptismal rite, where immersion in water becomes part of a purification ritual. The doctor's dual function is thus a remnant of fertility myths that has endured in quest-romances, paving the way for consideration of the sexual symbolism underlying the fourth character.

Prell as the Fourth Character: Sexual Symbolism

The Prell-figure's enactment of a sexual act harks back to familiar archetypal patterns that resurface in modern romances. The courtship theme, in Frye's words, is a reworking of an ancient one: "the search of the libido or desiring self for a fulfilment that will deliver it from the anxieties of reality but will still contain that reality" (1973, p. 193). The romance "reality" that subsumes fertility motifs is marriage, but the genre's conventions depend on resolution of the tension between the heroine's virgin/whore aspects. Tension exists because the heroine is in the difficult position of having to use virginity as a weapon in the war of sexual conquest without herself being conquered. In the romance literature, women have to "get" men by holding out sexual bait strong enough to attract a marriage proposal, but not so strong as to risk being judged an easy mark.

The ad communicates this tension between the virgin/whore sides of the heroine by means of her garments, and resolves it symbolically. The mythic theme -- "the victory of fertility over the waste land....the union of male and female" (Frye 1973, p. 193) -- is acted out by symbolic consumption of Prell. The Prell tube is a fourth character, an allegorical figure with a name ("Tallulah the Tube"), bearing all the hallmarks of medieval allegory (Stern 1988; 1990). Prell is a phallic symbol, a penis-substitute serving as a fictionalized character who acts out a consumer quest. Symbolic consummation is represented by the action of the tube: it is erect at the top of the ad and limp at the bottom, a mimetic representation of the tumescence-detumescence pattern of orgasm. The Prell character disguises the phallicism slightly with a female name, perhaps to render it more acceptable to women consumers.

Nonetheless, the character's penile nature is introduced as early as its name, the first clue to the symbolism: the name is "Tallulah *the Tube*" (italics mine), an unusual allegorical reference to the *package* rather than to the product (cf. Stern 1988). This directs attention to the qualities of the tube (rather than to its contents): upright, filled to the brim, and throbbing rhythmically. Further, the Prell-penis tells the audience what is wanted -- "all you've got to do is *get ahold of me*" (italics mine). The *double entendre* of the lyric introduces the heroine's ambiguous good girl/bad girl qualities, connected by subsequent word-play ("get"). If her hair is nice and shiny because she "gets ahold of Prell," she will also "get ahold of" the man. However, different meanings of "getting ahold of" depend on whether its object is the man/marriage, his penis/sexual satisfaction, or the tube/shiny hair.

These meanings underline a basic romance difference between men and women: to men, "getting hold of" means sex, while to women it means marriage. In the context of the ad, the unmarried heroine must remain virginal in fact if not in fantasy. The only long hard object she can "get ahold of" is a sex substitute. Her participation in the sex act is vicarious, as revealed in the bottom picture, which presents the climax of the real action and the symbolic sexual one. Here, the heroine holds an upright hairbrush in her right hand, and touches her hair with her left hand. She thus "gets" Prell, and "goes further than" any time before. Even more pertinent, she has also succeeded in getting hold of her man, for on the third finger of her left hand she is wearing a diamond ring, the traditional symbol of engagement. The ad, then, relies on symbolism and allegory to develop and structure the romance themes of courtship, virginity, and marriage.

Words and Sound Patterns

Those themes are reiterated by the words and sound patterns, further reinforcing the orgasmic sexual structure. This is presented in terms of a problem/solution format. At the outset, a problem is introduced: the needs of the erect penis, which must be relieved -- "removed," "fast." The sexual nature of the problem is stated in the following words -- "harder," "cream." The resolution in the next line hints at sexual satisfaction: a "curl" that is "easy to manage" and "do in any style." A solution is promised at once, for Prell "goes farther" than any other shampoo because it is "more concentrated" --that is, it is about to spurt out of the tube. The rhythm of the last line mimics this orgasmic spurt, for it is a three-word imperative ending a block of longer word groups (9 to 17 words). "Get Prell today" is the verbal analog to the sexual climax, bursting forth as a short, insistently trochaic command. The sound scheme thus reinforces the symbolic and thematic matter -- "getting" shiny hair (use Prell), getting a man, getting sexual release -- in a synergistic blend of form and content.

The language adds a richer dimension to feminized sexuality, for the ad relies on "women's language," the habitual tongue of romance literature (Lakoff 1976; Spender 1985; Stern 1991). First, the song ends with an exclamation point, an early indication of the hyperbole that characterizes women's colloquial speech. There are eight more exclamation points, totalling two-thirds of the ad's twelve sentences. Numerous italicized words and modifiers signifying excess ("beautifully, amazing, shiningly, gloriously") add to the stylistic overstatement.

The most frequently repeated word -- "radiant," used five times -- links stereotypically feminine overstated language with the heroine's success as a woman. It is a key word highlighting success in the romance quest, for the term refers not only to hair, but also to a popular diamond shape, the round or "radiant" cut. The gem symbolism is reinforced by a second key word -- "emerald" -- a rare instance of a word used by the heroine herself. "Emerald" is significant as a reference not only to the clear green shampoo, but also as the name of another popular diamond cut (rectangular). These key words hammer home the romance theme by associating Prell with the symbol of engagement: at the ad's end, the heroine's hair is shown in metonymic juxtaposition -- association by contiguity -- with the diamond on her ring finger. Thus, the ad is a rich source of romance themes, symbols, and language, all interwoven in a *gestalt* of form and content.

IMPLICATIONS

The Alienated Consumer

An understanding of romances as soft-core pornography appealing to women can assist the creation of advertising appeals that attract rather than alienate target markets. The creation of more accurately-targeted sexual appeals depends on sensitivity to differences between male and female sexual fantasies. Failure to recognize such differences can result in portrayals likely to alienate the very consumers they are designed to attract. This is a special danger when products are much more likely to be bought by one sex than the other, for if the target sex is turned off, who is left to buy the product?

One example of an alienating campaign seems to be the Maidenform ad series using Pierce Brosnan as a spokesman to sell women's lingerie. Since Maidenform products, like most basic undergarments, are bought primarily by women for their own use, the advertisement should logically appeal to women consumers. However, Brosnan seems more like a romance villain than a hero, and may appear threatening rather than enticing. The ads feature a large picture of Brosnan (no product is shown) delivering a solo recitation of a conversation about lingerie "with a woman friend." He appears as one of the people "listening" to the 150 ways Maidenform helps women "express themselves." Yet this campaign seems to appeal more to *male* fantasies of voyeurism, conversational sex, and undressing women in public than to female ones of virginal resistance culminating in marriage (Garfield 1990). Sexual imagery as the substance of an advertisement requires careful execution to insure that it does indeed appeal to the designated target market.

Male and Female Evaluations of Romances

Understanding some differences between male and female pornographies can also shed light on differences between male and female evaluations of sexual images in advertising. Here, feminist reader response theory (see Fetterley 1978; Flynn and Schweickart 1986) provides insight into the way men and women differ in reading a text's values. Male critics generally denigrate romances (and by implication, their readers) as masochistic, regressive, and passive. Questions have often been raised as to whether the polarizations of romance (hero vs. villain), its stereotypically bad characters (men) versus good ones (women), and its teasing depictions of incomplete sexual expression may be constricting. Romances have been called anxiety-enhancers, said to intensify women's conflicted sexuality (Modelski 1984) by presenting unrealistic values that distort the reality of male-female relationships.

But this view has not gone unchallenged by feminists, aware that "50 per cent of all women reading at any given moment are likely to be reading romance" (Radford 1986, p. 14). Not all feminist scholars are willing to label the sizable romance audience as neurotic. They are in opposition to the male critical model of reading as inadequate and reductive, pointing out that romances may contain positive values overlooked by the male literary establishment. A feminist point of view suggests that reading romances may have an integrative effect on women's lives (Radway 1983; 1985). In this view, romance narratives offer heroines (and readers) the love of a strong man, a satisfying mature sexual model of nurturance rather than the infantile one of seduction. Further, the hero's ability to care for the heroine is said to enhance her self-esteem by fostering her self-perception as the valued center of expert care and attention. Feminists also note that for the majority of American women, whose primary role in the family and workplace is a nurturing one, the romance convention of marriage to a strong and supportive man may represent their most utopian aspiration. Thus, romance literature -- including advertising based on its conventions -- may promote socially beneficial values by raising feminine self-esteem and presenting role models for adult sexuality.

The "Pornographic Society"

Differing evaluations of romance, however, exist in the context of a culture that seems to include a multiplicity of pornographies based not only on sex, but also on race, social class, gender orientation, and even age. The most important issue may not be how to use our understanding of what different segments view as pornography to encourage construction of better advertisements, but whether we should be doing this at all. More socially responsible advertisements that treat male *and* female sexuality with respect may best be achieved by decreasing the emphasis on sex rather than by getting it precisely right. Warmth, joy, love, and intimacy may be a more attractive set of appeals to all humans rather than violent hard-core or romantic soft-core depictions aimed at one sex or the other. The goal of humanization in advertising depends on a willingness to create messages that dignify the whole person rather than relying on those that reduce consumers of both sexes to no more than their sexual parts.

REFERENCES

Brownmiller, Susan (1976), *Against Our Will: Men, Women, and Rape*, New York: Bantam Books.

Cawelti, John G. (1976), *Adventure, Mystery, and Romance*, Chicago: University of Chicago Press.

Coles, Claire D. and N. Johanna Shamp (1984), "Some Sexual, Personality, and Demographic Characteristics of Women Readers of Erotic Romances," *Archives of Sexual Behavior*, 13 (No. 3), 187-209.

De Beauvoir, Simone (1952), *The Second Sex*, New York: Random House.

Dichter, Ernest (1990), "Examples of Sexual Signification in Consumption," in *Advances in Consumer Research*, Vol. 19, eds. Rebecca H. Holman and Michael R. Solomon, Provo: Association for Consumer Research, in press.

Ellis, Kate (1975), "Paradise Lost: The Limits of Domesticity in the Nineteenth-Century Novel," *Feminist Studies*, 2 (nos. 2/3), 55-63.

Fetterley, Judith (1978), *The Resisting Reader: A Feminist Approach to American Fiction*, Bloomington: Indiana University Press.

Flynn, Elizabeth A. and Patrocinio P. Schweickart (1986), "Introduction," in *Gender and Reading: Essays on Readers, Texts, and Contexts*, eds. Elizabeth A. Flynn and Patrocinio P. Schweickart, Baltimore: The Johns Hopkins University Press, ix-xxx.

Freeman, Laurie (1987), "Memorable Images," *Advertising Age: The House That Ivory Built -- The Story of Procter & Gamble*, Chicago: Crain Communications Inc., 46-48.

Friedan, Betty (1963), *The Feminine Mystique*, New York: Dell Publishing Co.

Frye, Northrop (1973), *Anatomy of Criticism: Four Essays*, Princeton, NJ: Princeton University Press.

Garfield, Bob (1990), "Brosnan works like a charm in latest Maidenform effort," *Advertising Age*, (February 19), 76.

Gould, Stephen J. (1990), "Toward a Theory of Sexuality and Consumption: Consumer Lovemaps," in *Advances in Consumer Research*, Vol. 19, eds. Rebecca H. Holman and Michael R. Solomon, Provo: Association for Consumer Research, in press.

Lakoff, Robin (1975), *Language and Woman's Place*, New York: Harper & Row.

Light, Alison (1986), "Writing Fictions: Femininity and the 1950s," in *The Progress of Romance: The Politics of Popular Fiction*, ed. Jean Radford, London: Routledge & Kegan Paul plc, 139-166.

McLuhan, Marshall (1951), *The Mechanical Bride*, Boston: Beacon Press.

Miller, Mark Crispin (1989), *Boxed In: The Culture of TV*, Evanston: Northwestern University Press.

Modelski, Tania (1984), *Loving With a Vengeance: Mass-Produced Fantasies for Women*, New York: Methuen, Inc.

Morgan, Robin (1978), "How to Run the Pornographers out of Town," *Ms. Magazine*, November, 55, 78

Pollay, Richard W. (1989), "Sex-cess in Advertising," in *Myth, Mysticism and the Meaning of Matrialism: Advertising as Myth Information*. 1989 Summer Seminar Series (July), Vancouver, B.C.: University of British Columbia, unpublished handout.

Prewitt, Terry J. (1990), "Dead Women and Other Pornographic Representations in Contemporary Advertising," in *Advances in Consumer Research*, Vol. 19, eds. Rebecca H. Holman and Michael R. Solomon, Provo: Association for Consumer Research, in press.

Radford, Jean (1986), "Introduction," *The Progress of Romance: The Politics of Popular Fiction*, London: Routledge & Kegan Paul plc, 1-22.

Radway, Janice A. (1985), *Reading the Romance: Women, Patriarchy, and Popular Literature*, Chapel Hill: University of North Carolina Press.

_____ (1983), "Women Read the Romance: The Interaction of Text and Context," *Feminist Studies*, 9 (Spring), 53-78.

Russell, Anne M. (1990), "Sex: It Still Sells, Boys and Girls, Part 1," *American Photo*, 1(July/August), 58-59.

Snitow, Ann Barr (1978), "Mass Market Romance: Pornography for Women is Different," *Radical History Review*, 29 (Spring/Summer) 245-263.

Sontag, Susan (1967), "The Pornographic Imagination," in *Styles of Radical Will*, New York: Farrar, Straus and Giroux, 35-73.

Spender, Dale (1985), *Man Made Language*, Second Edition, London: Routledge & Kegan Paul.

Steinem, Gloria (1978), "Erotica and Pornography: A Clear and Present Difference," *Ms. Magazine*, (November), 53-54, 75-76.

Stern, Barbara B. (1991), "Advertising to the "Other" Culture: Women's Use of Language and Language's Use of Women," in *Advertising and Consumer Psychology: Cross-Cultural Advertising*, eds. Basil G. Englis and D. Frederick Baker, Hillside, NJ: Lawrence-Erlbaum Publishers, in press.

_____ (1990), "Other-Speak: Classical Allegory and Contemporary Advertising," *Journal of Advertising*, 19 (no. 3), 14-26.

_____ (1988), "Medieval Allegory: Roots of Advertising Strategy for the Mass Market," *Journal of Marketing*, 52 (July), 84-94.

Welter, Barbara (1966), "The Cult of True Womanhood: 1820-1860," *American Quarterly*, 18 (Summer), 151-174.

Weston, Jessie L. (1919), *From Ritual to Romance*, Garden City, NY: Doubleday Anchor Books, repr. 1957.

Perceived Variability and Inferences about Brand Extensions
Frank R. Kardes, University of Cincinnati
Chris T. Allen, University of Cincinnati

ABSTRACT
Recent research on consumer reactions to brand extensions has focused on the judgmental effects of the match between the attributes, benefits, and uses of established versus new products sharing the same brand name. The present experiment extends this research by investigating the effects of two types of perceived variability on consumers' inferences about brand extensions: (a) the perceived variability of a firm's current offerings, and (b) the perceived variability of brands in an entry category. Inferences about the potential quality of the brand extension, and about the manufacturer's reasons for attempting to enter the new product category were measured. Repercussions of these inferences on judgments of the firm launching the brand extension were also examined. Implications of the results for product management are discussed.

A great deal of recent research has focused on the concept of *brand equity*, which refers to the value added to a product by a brand name (Farquhar 1989; Leuthesser 1988). A successful brand name is strongly associated with concepts designed to (a) enhance the perceived value of a product, and (b) differentiate a product from competitors' offerings. However, building a successful brand name requires the commitment of a large pool of resources for an extended period of time (Park, Jaworski, and MacInnes 1986).

Because organizations have limited resources, risks and costs must be managed in an efficient manner. One way to manage risks and costs is through brand leverage, which refers to the use of a successful, established brand name to facilitate entering new markets. This can be achieved by attaching the established brand name to a new offering in either the same (a line extension) or a new (a brand extension) product category. Extending a strong brand name should result in easier and wider acceptance, on the part of both consumers and distributors.

Recent research on consumer acceptance of brand extensions has focused primarily on the effects of the categorization process on judgment and choice (for reviews of the categorization literature, see Alba and Hutchinson 1987; Cohen and Basu 1987; Sujan and Bettman 1989). Several studies have shown that judgments of original brands are generalized to judgments of new brands only when there is a good match between the attributes, benefits, and uses of parent and new brands (Aaker and Keller 1990; Farquhar, Herr, and Fazio 1990; Leuthesser 1988; Tauber 1988). Hence, new products should benefit from established brand names if (a) concepts having favorable implications for the purchase decision are strongly linked to the brand name, and (b) generalization is likely due to a high degree of overlap between the attributes, benefits, and uses of parent and new brands.

Although the degree of similarity between new and parent brands is clearly an important mediator of consumer response to extensions, other factors are likely to be important as well. We suggest that some parent brands provide greater leverage than others, and that some new product entry categories are more receptive to extensions, even when one controls for similarity. Specifically, we focus on two new variables that should influence consumer response to extensions: the perceived variability of a parent brand's current offerings, and the perceived variability of existing brands in an entry category.

Perceived Variability and the Generalization Process
Why do people make sweeping generalizations on the basis of limited evidence, in some cases, whereas in others, they fail to generalize even when extensive evidence is available? In addressing this issue, it becomes immediately apparent that other factors besides perceived similarity are also likely to influence the generalization process. Theories of categorization must address not only the abstraction and use of distributional knowledge such as knowledge about the central tendency of category members on a given dimension (e.g., attributes, benefits, uses), but also knowledge about the perceived variability or dispersion of category members on focal dimensions (Flannagan, Fried, and Holyoak 1986; Fried and Holyoak 1984).

For example, social judgment research has shown that generalization is greater when perceived variability on a target dimension is low, as opposed to high (Linville, Fischer, and Salovey 1989; Nisbett, Krantz, Jepson, and Kunda 1983; Park and Hastie 1987; Quattrone and Jones 1980). That is, when perceived variability is low, the observed characteristics of one individual is attributed to all members of the individual's social category ("you've seen one, you've seen them all"). Because perceptions of variability are lower for unfamiliar categories (e.g., out-groups), and for abstraction-based (as opposed to instance-based) categories, greater generalization occurs for unfamiliar and for abstraction-based categories.

Perceived Variability of a Parent Brand's Current Offerings
Some firms attach a single brand name to a wide variety of products in several different categories. Other firms use one brand name for one current offering. Henceforth, these end-points of the breadth continuum will be referred to as umbrella vs. niche brands, respectively. Because there are advantages and disadvantages associated with each of

these alternatives, strategy selection calls for an analysis of costs and benefits.

One advantage of the umbrella strategy is that the manufacturer is likely to be perceived as having a wide variety of strengths and skills in several different product categories. Such a firm may be perceived to have the requisite knowledge and skills for entering new markets, and, consequently, brand extensions should seem legitimate. A firm adopting a niche strategy, on the other hand, may be perceived to possess highly specialized knowledge and skills that cannot be transferred readily to new markets.

Of course, an umbrella firm runs the risk of being perceived as a "jack-of-all-trades" (master of none); further extensions into new markets support and strengthen this perception. Moreover, images and values associated with a brand name become more ambiguous and more diffuse as extending increases (Ries and Trout 1981). In contrast, a niche firm can more readily build a strong brand name by linking it to unambiguous concepts that clearly differentiate the offering.

Perceived Variability of Existing Brands in the Entry Category

Some product categories may be more receptive to new brands than others. When perceived variability of an entry category is low, category members should be perceived as undifferentiated; new brands entering this category should be perceived as legitimate (e.g., if everyone else is doing it, you can, too), but not really new or exciting. Conversely, when perceived variability is high, there is "room" for extensions, but generalization is difficult and consumers may be unable to make predictions about the quality of new brands.

Research Propositions and the Experimental Design

Inferences about brand extensions should be affected by these two types of perceived variability: (a) the perceived variability of a firm's current offerings (i.e., umbrella vs. niche brands), and (b) the perceived variability of extant brands in an entry category. Perceptions of variability may be formed for several different dimensions of an existing category. We focused on one key dimension: perceived quality. Quality judgments of parent brands should generalize more readily to brand extensions when perceived variability is low in entry categories.

To investigate the role of perceived variability in consumer inference, an experiment was conducted in which brand name and new product concept information was manipulated. Subjects received either an umbrella brand name, a niche brand name, or no brand name, paired with concepts for six different packaged goods (i.e., the entry categories). On the basis of idiothetic ratings (Jaccard and Wood 1986), the entry categories were split into high and low perceived variability groups. Hence, a 3 (umbrella, niche, or no brand name [between-subjects]) X 2 (high or low perceived variability in the entry category [within-subjects]) factorial design was employed. This design has several advantages over previous correlational research on brand extensions: (a) subjects were randomly assigned to brand name conditions, (b) reactions to all possible combinations of brand name and concept information were examined, and (c) the no brand name control condition enables one to measure inferences about a new product concept while controlling for prior knowledge about a brand.

METHOD

Subjects

Sixty evening MBA students (40 males and 20 females) participated in the experiment. Thirty-five were married, and subjects reported that they personally shopped for groceries at least four times per month ($M = 4.29$, median = 4.00; only one subject reported shopping 0 times per month).

Procedure

Subjects received a booklet containing perceived variability measures, parent brand measures, and measures designed to tap inferences about new product concepts in six established packaged good categories. The instructions stated that we were "interested in your personal opinions about several new product ideas. Some of these ideas may lead to the introduction of a new product and some may be abandoned. We are not associated with the manufacturer in any way, so we are not concerned about whether your reactions are positive or negative."

First, subjects were asked to provide perceived quality distributions for several packaged goods categories (including the entry categories). Next, judgments of the parent brand were measured (pre-launch ratings). After these measures were taken, subjects were exposed to the new product concepts and inferences about these concepts were assessed. Finally, subjects were told to assume that the concepts would actually be launched and they were again asked to judge the parent brand (post-launch ratings).

Perceived Variability of Entry Categories

Subjects were asked to provide perceived quality distributions for 11 (6 target and 5 filler) packaged goods categories. They were asked to allocate 100 points to five levels of overall quality for each category. The variance of a distribution served as the perceived variability index (Linville et al. 1989). The instructions and the index are provided in the Appendix.

Pre-Launch Ratings

Subjects were asked to indicate their overall impressions of the parent brand (Nabisco or Sealtest) on a scale from 0 (Extremely unfavorable) to 10 (Extremely favorable). They also rated the quality of the parent brand's current offerings on a scale from 0 (Extremely low quality) to 10

TABLE 1
New Product Concepts

Garden Vegetable Flavored Potato Chips
Cajun Blackened Steak Frozen Dinner
Chunky Peach Cottage Cheese
Smoky Bacon Flavored Hot Dogs
Italian Spice Lunch Meat
Lemon Mint Soda

(Extremely high quality). The breadth of these offerings was measured by asking "when you hear the name Nabisco/Sealtest, does a wide variety of products or does only one product come to mind?" (a scale from 0 [one product] to 10 [An extremely wide variety of products] was provided).

New Product Concepts and Inference Measures

After the perceived variability and pre-launch measures, subjects received descriptions of new product concepts in six established packaged good categories. Care was taken to select entry categories that: (a) were new for both parent brands, and (b) were equally applicable to both parent brands. The new product concepts are presented in Table 1.

Each concept was paired with the umbrella brand name (Nabisco), the niche brand name (Sealtest), or no brand name. Each concept was printed in capital letters at the top of separate pages, and all measures pertaining to a brand extension were printed on the same page. Because we focused solely on responses to various pairings of brand names and concepts, detailed product descriptions were not provided.

Inferences about the perceived quality of a brand extension were measured on a scale from 0 (Extremely low quality) to 10 (Extremely high quality). Two attributional measures were included to assess inferences about why the manufacturer is attempting to extend into the entry category. Likelihood ratings on scales from 0 (Not at all likely) to 10 (Extremely likely) were assessed for the following questions: "How likely or unlikely is it that this product was developed because it capitalizes on the unique strengths and skills of the manufacturer?" and "How likely or unlikely is it that this product was developed because many manufacturers have jumped into this product category recently?"

Post-Launch Ratings

Finally, subjects were asked to rate the manufacturer of the parent brand, given that the manufacturer intends to launch each of the new product concepts. Overall impressions of the manufacturer, for each new product concept, were measured on scales from 0 (Extremely unfavorable) to 10 (Extremely favorable).

RESULTS

Manipulation Checks

Perceived variability of entry categories was operationalized by performing a median-split on the perceived variability indices for the six entry categories. The indices were averaged across the three high and across the three low perceived variability categories, separately, for each subject. A repeated measures analysis of variance performed on these indices showed that existing product offerings were perceived to be more dispersed in the high than in the low perceived variability entry categories ($Ms = .99$ vs. $.50$), $F(1, 59) = 170.97$, $p < .001$. Thus, our operationalization of the perceived variability of entry categories was effective.

It was predicted that the perceived variability of the parent brand's current offerings would be greater for the umbrella brand (Nabisco) than for the niche brand (Sealtest). As anticipated, the umbrella brand was perceived as having a much wider variety of current offerings than the niche brand ($Ms = 6.20$ vs. 3.00, for Nabisco vs. Sealtest, respectively), $F(1, 38) = 14.56$, $p < .001$. Thus, our operationalization of the perceived variability of the parent brand's current offerings was effective.

Inferences about the Quality of the Extensions Relative to Extant Offerings

To assess the inferential effects of the perceived variability of the parent brand's current offerings while controlling for judgments of the quality of these offerings (subjects had more favorable impressions towards the umbrella brand [$M = 7.35$] than towards the niche brand [$M = 5.85$], $p < .01$), a difference score was computed in which quality ratings of current offerings were subtracted from quality ratings of brand extensions. Positive scores on this index indicate that the brand extensions were rated as higher in quality, whereas negative scores indicate that the extensions were rated as lower in quality, relative to existing products associated with the parent brand name.

In the no brand name conditions, the scale midpoint was subtracted from quality ratings. Because no brand name information was provided, average ratings of current offerings were assumed. This provides a very conservative index because

TABLE 2
Quality Inferences

	Umbrella brand	Niche brand	No brand
High perceived variability	-1.82	-1.52	0.48
Low perceived variability	-1.78	-0.78	0.68

Note. $n = 20$ per cell. Higher scores indicate more favorable quality inferences.

consumers often infer below-average values for dimensions with unknown values in multiattribute evaluation (see Huber and McCann 1982; Meyer 1981). Scores on this index would be more extreme if below-average values were used.

Quality inference means as a function of brand name and perceived variability in entry categories are presented in Table 2. A 3 X 2 mixed analysis of variance performed on these scores yielded a main effect for Brand, $F(2, 57) = 14.55$, $p < .001$, and a marginal main effect for Perceived variability, $F(1, 57) = 3.11$, $p = .08$. The interaction was nonsignificant.

As Table 2 indicates, mean difference scores were higher in the no brand name than in the umbrella or niche brand conditions ($ps < .01$), and quality inferences did not differ between umbrella and niche brands. Moreover, mean difference scores were positive in no brand name conditions, suggesting that the new product concepts were evaluated favorably.

The new product concepts also tended to be rated as higher in quality in low ($M = -.63$) than in high ($M = -.95$) perceived variability conditions. This pattern suggests that a brand extension tends to be accepted more readily in low perceived variability entry categories.

Inferences about Manufacturers' Motives for Extending into Entry Categories

One reason for entering a new market is that the manufacturer's unique strengths and skills may be perceived to facilitate the development of a high quality brand extension (a unique skills attribution). Means for unique skills attributions as a function of brand and perceived variability are presented in the first two rows of Table 3. A 3 X 2 mixed analysis of variance performed on unique skills attributions yielded a significant main effect for Brand, $F(2, 57) = 3.73$, $p < .04$, and a significant Brand X Perceived variability interaction, $F(2, 57) = 5.31$, $p < .01$. Extending was attributed more to unique skills (as opposed to other factors) in no brand than in umbrella or niche brand conditions ($ps < .03$).

Moreover, perceived variability had a strong impact on unique skills attributions pertaining to the niche brand, $F(1, 19) = 9.10$, $p < .01$, but not to the remaining brands ($ps > .20$). In the niche brand condition, more extreme unique skills attributions were formed in low than in high perceived variability conditions.

Another reason for entering a new market is that many manufacturers may be entering this market (perhaps due to increased consumer demand), and the target firm may be perceived as following a reactive strategy (a copy cat attribution). Mean scores for copy cat attributions as a function of brand and perceived variability are presented in the bottom two rows of Table 3. More extreme copy cat attributions tended to be formed in the high perceived variability conditions, $F(1, 57) = 2.14$, $p < .15$. Copy cat attributions tended to be lowest in the niche brand - low perceived variability cell, but this effect was nonsignificant.

Pre- Versus Post-Launch Impressions of Parent Brands

To examine the degree to which judgments of a firm were adjusted, when subjects were asked to assume that the manufacturer would launch each extension, difference scores were computed on the basis of pre- and post-launch impressions (initial ratings of the parent brand were subtracted from "post-launch" ratings). In the no brand name condition, the scale midpoint was subtracted from post-launch ratings (because no brand name information was provided, average ratings were assumed; this provides a very conservative index because below-average values are common for dimensions with unknown values in multiattribute evaluation; see Huber and McCann 1982; Meyer 1981). Positive scores on this index indicate that overall impressions of firms became more favorable when subjects assume the extensions will be launched; negative scores indicate that launching would have a negative impact on judgments about the firms.

TABLE 3
Causal Inferences

	Umbrella brand	Niche brand	No brand
Unique skills attributions			
High perceived variability	4.78	4.00	6.50
Low perceived variability	4.82	5.22	6.10
Copy cat attributions			
High perceived variability	5.50	5.32	4.95
Low perceived variability	5.18	4.50	5.02

Note. $n = 20$ per cell. Higher scores indicate more extreme unique skills and copy cat attributions.

TABLE 4
Conditional Inferences

	Umbrella brand	Niche brand	No brand
High perceived variability	-1.93	-1.12	0.67
Low perceived variability	-2.00	-.042	0.65

Note. $n = 20$ per cell. Higher scores indicate more favorable conditional inferences.

Pre- versus post-launch difference scores as a function of brand and perceived variability are presented in Table 4. A 3 X 2 mixed analysis of variance performed on these scores revealed a main effect for Brand, $F(2, 57) = 19.55$, $p < .001$, a marginal main effect for Perceived variability, $F(1, 57) = 3.32$, $p < .08$, and a significant Brand X Perceived variability interaction, $F(2, 57) = 4.82$, $p < .02$.

As Table 4 indicates, when subjects assumed that the extensions would be launched, more favorable impressions were formed in no brand ($M = .66$) than in umbrella brand ($M = -1.97$), $F(1, 38) = 51.00$, $p < .001$, or in niche brand ($M = -.77$) conditions, $F(1, 38) = 10.89$, $p < .003$. Further, more favorable judgments were formed in niche brand than in umbrella brand conditions, $F(1, 38) = 6.91$, $p < .02$. Thus, the exact same product concepts that improve a brand's image when the brand name is unknown (i.e., the positive difference score in the control condition reflects an above average, post-launch impression), actually tarnish a brand's image when the brand name is known (i.e., the negative difference scores in the experimental conditions show unfavorable post-launch impressions). This effect is most robust for the umbrella brand.

Follow-up tests on the Brand X Perceived variability interaction revealed that, in the niche brand condition, more favorable brand image judgments were formed in low than in high perceived variability conditions, $F(1, 19) = 9.99$, $p < .01$.

However, perceived variability had no effect on judgments in the umbrella or in the no brand name conditions ($Fs < 1$).

DISCUSSION

Together, the quality inference, causal inference, and conditional inference data suggest that brand extensions can tarnish global evaluations of a parent brand. Even when favorably-evaluated parent brand names are paired with favorably-evaluated brand extensions, a less favorable overall impression of the parent brand can result. Furthermore, this negative reaction seems more pronounced for umbrella brands. Thus, an umbrella brand does not automatically provide more leverage than a niche brand. When a parent brand name is stretched too far, additional extensions can have negative repercussions on judgments about the parent brand.

The results also imply that the perceived variability of brands in an entry category is an important moderator of consumers' initial inferences about a new offering. When perceived variability is high, generalization is difficult and consumers tend to form conservative, moderate judgments. In contrast, when the perceived variability of a parent brand's current offerings is low (i.e., niche brands), and when the perceived variability of existing products in an entry category is low, there appears to be some opportunity for brand leverage.

Why is the brand extension strategy so difficult to manage? To address this complex issue, we should consider the multiple inferential implications of brand name information. When the brand name is unknown, consumers are unable to determine if a given new product extends an existing product line or if the new product is the firm's only offering. In contrast, when the brand name is known, less extreme unique skills and more extreme copy cat attributions tend to be formed. If a new product is not perceived to be a natural sequel to prior offerings, it may be perceived to be an inferior brand (because the manufacturer may lack the experience needed to develop a superior brand), or it may be perceived to be the result of a quickly implemented tactic designed to exploit a recently emerging opportunity (if it does not capitalize on unique strengths, why else would it be launched?). The former case suggests that line extensions may be effective, and the latter case suggests that both line and product extensions are likely to be ineffective.

Future research should attempt to replicate the findings from this project using a more generalizable set of umbrella and niche brands (we employed only two brands). Although we attempted to select entry categories that were equally applicable to both parent brands, more rigorous controls for similarity or fit between parent and extended brands are needed. Future research should also examine consumer response to line and brand extensions using different parent brand names and different entry categories. Finally, future research on brand equity should (a) include a no brand name control condition to establish the general appeal of a new product concept while controlling for prior knowledge about the parent brand, and (b) employ pre- and post-launch measures to assess the ramifications of extending for judgments of the original, parent brand.

REFERENCES

Aaker, David A. and Kevin Lane Keller (1990), "Consumer Evaluations of Brand Extensions," *Journal of Marketing*, 54 (January), 27-41.

Alba, Joseph W. and J. Wesley Hutchinson (1987), "Dimensions of Consumer Expertise," *Journal of Consumer Research*, 13 (March), 411-454.

Cohen, Joel B. and Kunal Basu (1987), "Alternative Models of Categorization: Toward a Contingent Processing Framework," *Journal of Consumer Research*, 13 (March), 455-472.

Farquhar, Peter H. (1989), "Managing Brand Equity," *Marketing Research*, 1 (September), 24-33.

_____, Paul M. Herr, and Russell H. Fazio (1990), "A Relational Model for Category Extensions of Brands," in *Advances in Consumer Research*, Vol. 17, eds. Marvin E. Goldberg, Gerald Gorn, and Richard W. Pollay, Provo, UT: Association for Consumer Research, 856-860.

Flannagan, M. J., L. S. Fried, and K. J. Holyoak (1986), "Distributional Expectations and the Induction of Category Structure," *Journal of Experimental Psychology: Learning, Memory, and Cognition*, 12, 241-256.

Fried, L. S., and K. J. Holyoak (1984), "Induction of Category Distributions: A Framework for Classification Learning," *Journal of Experimental Psychology: Learning, Memory, and Cognition*, 10, 234-257.

Huber, Joel and John McCann (1982), "The Impact of Inferential Beliefs on Product Evaluations," *Journal of Marketing Research*, 12 (August), 324-333.

Jaccard, James and Gregory Wood (1986), "An Idiothetic Analysis of Behavioral Decision Making," in *Perspectives on Methodology in Consumer Research*, eds. David Brinberg and Richard J. Lutz, New York: Springer-Verlag, 67-106.

Leuthesser, Lance, ed. (1988), "Defining, Measuring, and Managing Brand Equity: A Conference Summary," Report 88-104, Cambridge, MA: Marketing Science Institute.

Linville, Patricia W., Gregory W. Fischer, and Peter Salovey (1989), "Perceived Distributions of the Characteristics of In-Group and Out-Group Members: Empirical Evidence and a Computer Simulation," *Journal of Personality and Social Psychology*, 57 (August), 165-188.

Meyer, Robert J. (1981), "A Model of Multiattribute Judgments Under Attribute Uncertainty and Informational Constraint," *Journal of Marketing Research*, 18 (November), 428-441.

APPENDIX

For each of the product classes listed below, your task is to estimate the percentage of currently existing brands that fall into each of the five levels of overall quality. Assume that any given brand falls into one and only one level of quality. Please write your estimates above each level on the scales below, and be sure that the percentages you assign to the different levels add up to 100% for each product category.

CATEGORY

____	____	____	____	____
Very low quality	Low quality	Average quality	High quality	Very high quality

$$\text{Variance} = \sum p_i (X_i - M)^2,$$

where X_i is the scale value of the ith level of an interval scale dimension, and the number of levels of the dimension are discrete; M denotes the mean of the perceived distribution and is defined by:

$M = \sum p_i X_i$

Nisbett, Richard E., David H. Krantz, Christopher Jepson, and Ziva Kunda (1983), "The Use of Statistical Heuristics in Everyday Inductive Reasoning," *Psychological Review*, 90 (October), 339-363.

Park, Bernadette and Reid Hastie (1987), "Perception of Variability in Category Development: Instance- Versus Abstraction-Based Stereotypes," *Journal of Personality and Social Psychology*, 53 (October), 621-635.

Park, C. Whan, Bernard J. Jaworski, and Deborah J. MacInnes (1986), "Strategic Brand Concept-Image Management," *Journal of Marketing*, 50 (October), 135-145.

Quattrone, George A. and Edward E. Jones (1980), "The Perception of Variability within In-Groups and Out-Groups: Implications for the Law of Large Numbers," *Journal of Personality and Social Psychology*, 38 (January), 141-152.

Ries, Al and Jack Trout (1981), *Positioning: The Battle for Your Mind*. New York: McGraw-Hill.

Sujan, Mita and James R. Bettman (1989), "The Effects of Brand Positioning Strategies on Consumers' Brand and Category Perceptions: Some Insights From Schema Research," *Journal of Marketing Research*, 26 (November), 454-467.

Tauber, Edward M. (1988), "Brand Leverage: Strategy for Growth in a Cost-Control World," *Journal of Advertising Research*, 28 (August-September), 26-30.

The Effect of Negative Information on the Evaluations of Brand Extensions and the Family Brand

Jean B. Romeo, Boston College

ABSTRACT

While the number of brand extensions has proliferated, there is little theory or methodology to help managers understand how extensions may affect a family brand name. The purpose of this research is to explore the effect that negative information about extensions may have on evaluations of extensions and the family brand's image. The study manipulated an extension's product category and attribute similarity with the family brand. The results indicated that when extensions are in the same product category as the family brand, negative information is most detrimental to extension evaluations and evaluations of the family brand image. Thus, while introducing extensions that are closely related to the family brand does increase the probability of consumer acceptance, managers should realize that this strategy can be detrimental to the family brand if the new extension is the target of negative information.

INTRODUCTION

While the number of brand extensions in the marketplace has proliferated, managers have little insight into whether extensions affect consumers' perceptions of the family brand name. Yet, the potential influence that an extension may have on a brand name is most important because if it is negative, it could damage the family brand's image. For instance, if a known brand name gets attached to a product failure, the possibility exists for negative "ruboff" on the parent brand (Fannin 1987). The effect that brand extensions may have on the brand's image becomes even more critical when one considers that corporate licensing (one corporation linking up with another's successful brand or trademark to market new products that the trademark owning company does not produce) has become a $14 billion annual business (Norris 1987). Companies that license their brands in order to increase revenues should understand when this strategy could affect their brand. The purpose of this study is to provide some insight into how negative product information about a brand extension may affect evaluations of the extension as well as the family brand. The following questions are investigated:

- How does negative information about an extension affect the family brand's image?

- Will this effect depend on how closely associated the extension is to the family brand?

- What factors influence consumers' perceptions of how closely associated the extension is to the family brand?

BACKGROUND

Currently, there is little theory or methodology to guide managers in understanding the effect that an extension can have on the brand name (Jolley and Hawkins 1988). However, one can find opposing views in the literature on how extensions may affect a brand's image. One view is that line extensions are detrimental to a family brand's image since they blur the sharp focus of the brand in consumers' minds -- the more products positioned under a brand name, the less meaning the brand name has (Ries and Trout 1986). For instance, you cannot say Dial if you want soap (Dial makes deodorant, too) and Scott if you want paper towels (Scott also makes napkins and toilet tissue). Ries and Trout feel that a well-known name gets well known because it stands for something specific -- the more extensions under one brand name, the weaker that brand name becomes.

Some managers feel that many extensions surrounding a brand will enhance its image. The Sunkist brand is licensed to a variety of products because management believes that the diverse range of extensions (e.g., Sunkist Vitamin C, Sunkist Orange Soda) increases the frequency of the Sunkist message to the consumer and strengthens the desired association with good health and vitality (Kesler 1987). Park, Jaworski, and MacInnis (1986) present a framework for managing a brand's image over time which they call Brand Concept-Image Management (BCM). In this framework, the final stage (after introduction and elaboration) of brand image management is the fortification stage where the brand image is strengthened by linking it to products produced by the firm in different product classes. Their theory is that many products with similar images reinforce one another and strengthen the image of the brand. They provide the example of how the Vaseline brand was fortified by extending the brand to beauty care products (Vaseline Intensive Care Bath Beads) and baby products (Vaseline Wipe 'N Dipes, Vaseline Baby Powder).

While the long-term effect that an extension may have on a family brand remains unclear, it seems likely that negative information about an extension would be detrimental to the family brand. This is evident from the broad support throughout the behavioral and marketing literature for the potency of negative information. For instance, research has found that negative adjectives are more powerful than positive adjectives (Anderson 1965) and the weights given to negative adjectives have exceeded the weights given to positive adjectives when several must be combined into one overall evaluation (Feldman 1966, Richey, McClelland, and Shimkunas 1967). In a marketing context, unfavorable product ratings tended to have a greater impact on attitudes and purchase intentions than favorable ratings (Weinberger and Dillon 1980).

One explanation for the increased influence of negative information is that negative information stands out more than positive information because there are more positive cues in the environment. Thus, negative cues, which are more infrequent, attract more attention (Kanouse and Hanson 1971). Fiske (1980) hypothesized that cues which deviated from the moderate positive norm should be more informative. She found that subjects paid more attention and gave more preferential weighing to negative and extreme cues in forming likability ratings of people. Thus, cues that are more rare may be more informative because they discriminate among similar objects.

In order to provide insight into the effect that negative information about an extension may have on a family brand, recent brand extension research is summarized. The idea of a family brand schema is then introduced to provide a framework from which the hypotheses are derived.

Brand Extension Research

Brand extensions became the guiding strategies of product planners in the 1980's (Tauber 1988). One reason for the proliferation of brand extensions is that they promote marketing efficiencies. Promotion expenses and risk associated with a new product introduction are lowered because both consumer and retailer acceptance is greater for a new product with an existing brand name than with a new name. People may be more apt to buy a new product with an existing brand name because the known brand name provides the assurance that the new product is of the same quality as the other product(s) with the brand name. Thus, consumers can relate the new product to a product with which they are already familiar. Categorization research implies that "When a consumer has little experience with a product, being able to categorize it with products that are familiar may permit a set of important inferences to be made" (Cohen and Basu 1987, p. 470). This relates to brand extensions since, "New products may be perceived as members of an existing brand 'family' (category) simply by virtue of having the brand name" (University of Minnesota Consumer Behavior Seminar 1987, p. 228).

Recent brand extension research has focused on how consumers perceive and evaluate extensions. These studies have found that the greater the similarity between the extension and the family brand, the greater the transfer of positive attitudes from the brand to the extension. One study found the transfer of affect from the brand to the new extension depends on the similarity between the new extension and the original branded product (UMCBS 1987). In fact, these researchers found that a brand's reputation for excellence in one product category may have a negative effect on consumer ratings of new products in an unrelated product area. They concluded that a consumer may reason that a brand's specialization in one product area may prevent it from being associated with a good product in an unrelated product category.

Aaker and Keller (1990) investigated how consumer knowledge about a brand may affect perceptions about the extension's quality. They found that a positive quality image for the brand influenced perceptions of the extension only when there was a basis of fit between the two products. In this study, the "basis of fit" between a brand and an extension was measured using the following dimensions: 1) extent to which consumers viewed the two product classes as complementary, 2) extent to which consumers viewed the two product classes as substitutes, and 3) the perceived credibility of firms operating in the original product category to make a product in the extension's product category.

Family Brand Schema

The brand extension research described in the preceding section indicates that consumers may have a schema for a family brand. A schema is a cognitive structure that represents organized knowledge about a certain concept (Fiske and Taylor 1984, p. 140). A schema is developed through our experiences -- a collection of individual components becomes an integrated organization unit with strong associations among the once individuated components (Fiske and Dyer 1985). Once a schema is activated, it functions as an organized whole and serves as a perspective for attending to and interpreting events. Thus, when consumers become familiar with a brand name, they may form a type of schema representing the category of branded products. For instance, one could have a schema for "Ivory" branded products which might include features such as pure, wholesome, white, smooth, and gentle. Since schemata focus on how we assimilate new information with existing knowledge (Fiske and Taylor 1984), we would know what information is congruent to our schema (e.g., "new Ivory Shampoo is gentle enough for children") and incongruent (e.g., "new Ivory Detergent is tough on dirt").

A family brand schema may enable consumers to determine which extensions are similar to the brand and which are not. For instance, the brand Country Time Lemonade was so strongly associated with lemonade, that consumers couldn't accept Country Time Apple Cider. The set of associations consumers had for the Campbell's brand resulted in the belief that Campbell's Spaghetti Sauce would be orangy, runny, and not authentic Italian. This evaluation was based on consumers' schema for the Campbell's brand which was strongly associated with its tomato soup. (The company therefore introduced the sauce under a new brand, Prego).

HYPOTHESES

Positive brand beliefs will transfer to positive extension beliefs when the extension is perceived as similar to the family brand (Consumer Behavior Seminar 1988) and when there is a basis of fit between the brand and the extension (Aaker and Keller 1990). How will this transfer of positive brand attitudes be affected when the extension is clearly inferior to the family brand?

Research indicates that people are very attentive to information which is inconsistent with their schemas. For instance, people take longer to interpret and evaluate inconsistent information. In addition, inconsistency which is unambiguous, strong, or evaluative, is even more likely to capture attention and be remembered. The underlying principle is that people think about and remember the exceptions (Fiske and Taylor 1984, Chapter 5).

If the set of associations subjects have about a family brand name is positive, negative information about extensions that are perceived as similar to the brand is hypothesized to be distinctive since it is inconsistent with consumers' schema. Thus, subjects should pay attention to and remember this information which is strong, unambiguous, and evaluative. Negative information about products that are perceived as dissimilar to the family brand should be less distinctive since these products are not strongly associated with the family brand schema. Therefore, it is expected that negative information about an extension which is similar to the family brand will be more noticeable than negative information about an extension which is not similar to the family brand.

H1: Negative information should be more influential on evaluations of extensions that are closely related to the family brand (high perceived similarity) than on extensions that are not closely related (low perceived similarity).

Research has found that a positively evaluated brand will lead to positive extension evaluations when the extensions are similar to the original family brand. However, what influence will negative associations with extensions have on the brand's image? Since the transfer of affect from a brand to an extension (Family Brand --->Extension) is mediated by the "fit" between the brand and the extension, it is hypothesized that the transfer of affect from the extension to the brand (Extension --->Family Brand) is also be mediated by "fit."

H2: Negative information about extensions closely related to the family brand will have more of an effect on the family brand image than information about extensions that are not closely related to the family brand.

In this study, an extension that is considered to be closely related to the family brand (high perceived similarity) is in a similar product category and has similar attributes compared to the family brand. An extension that is not closely related (low perceived similarity) is in a dissimilar product category and has dissimilar attributes compared to the family brand.

EXPERIMENT

For this study, a decision had to be made whether to use a known brand or a hypothetical brand. Since subjects' prior experience and knowledge of the brand could affect evaluations, one brand extension study (UMCBS 1987) used a hypothetical brand in order to control for a priori information or impressions that are associated with a known brand name. However, using a hypothetical brand has a disadvantage in that it is unknown to consumers. When a company pursues a brand extension strategy, the brand is one which is familiar to consumers, thus consumers have most likely formed some sort of schema about that brand.

Following guidelines provided by Aaker and Keller (1990) in their study of consumer response to brand extensions, a known brand name should: 1) have a favorable overall quality image, 2) elicit relatively specific associations, and 3) not have already been broadly extended. For this study, a family brand name that was familiar to subjects and did not elicit a strong negative affective response was used. The extensions, however, were new products for the brand name. The family brand selected for this study was Tropicana. Tropicana was chosen since its association with orange juice would be equally relevant to men and women, and at the time of the study, it was not broadly extended. In order to check that Tropicana would elicit an overall positive affect, twenty six undergraduate business students (who did not participate in the main experiment) rated their attitude toward the brand on a series of semantic differential scales. The results indicated that subjects had a positive attitude towards the Tropicana brand. (Ratings on the 7-point evaluation scale where a rating of 1 was associated with a low evaluation and a rating of 7 was associated with a high evaluation were: Good=6.7, Pleasant=6.4, Superior=6.2, Interesting=4.8, Nice=5.9, Important=5.4).

The extensions' similarity to the brand name was manipulated in terms of their product category and attribute similarity to the family brand. Product category similarity was varied at two levels by selecting extensions in a similar product category (juice) to the family brand and in a different product category (sherbet). Attribute similarity was also varied at two levels by having extensions with many similar attributes (citrus-related) as the family brand and extensions with many different attributes (raspberry). Thus, four extensions under one family brand name were investigated (see Figure for extension manipulations). While similarity in terms of product category has been investigated in brand extension studies, similarity in terms of attributes has not. Research in categorization has found that if an object's attributes are consistent with the schema it evokes (e.g., category of branded products), category-based processing will result; if the object's attributes are perceived as inconsistent with the category, piecemeal processing will result (Fiske and Pavelchak 1986, Sujan 1985). For instance, the failure of Country Time Apple Cider, which is in a similar product

FIGURE
Tropicana Extension Manipulations

		PRODUCT CATEGORY	
		Similar	Dissimilar
ATTRIBUTES	Similar	Tropicana Citrus Guava Juice	Tropicana Citrus Guava Sherbet
	Dissimilar	Tropicana Raspberry Fruit Juice	Tropicana Raspberry Fruit Sherbet

category to the family brand (juice), yet has different attributes (apple cider instead of lemonade) indicates that attribute similarity as well as product category similarity may determine the basis of fit between an extension and a family brand. Thus, the purpose of manipulating the extensions' attributes as well as product category was to provide insight into the factors that may affect similarity perceptions.

A pre-test was conducted to check that the extension in a similar product category and with similar attributes was perceived as closely associated to the family brand compared to the extension with dissimilar product category and dissimilar attributes. This check was a modification of Rosch's (1975) rating tasks. Twenty subjects who did not participate in the main experiment were asked to rate how well each of ten products fit their image of a brand name. They were instructed that a 1 means that the product is a good example of their image of the brand name and a 7 means that the product fits poorly with their image of the brand name. The mean ratings indicated that the citrus juice extension was closely associated with the brand name (mean=1.65) and the raspberry sherbet was not closely associated with the brand (mean=5.75) As expected, the two remaining extensions were rated in between with citrus sherbet (similar attributes/dissimilar product category) receiving a rating of 4.30 and raspberry juice (dissimilar attributes/similar product category) receiving a rating of 4.80.

Experimental Procedure

Subjects were undergraduate business students recruited from a large northeastern university. The data was collected in two sessions. The first session was held during class time of four undergraduate marketing courses. The purpose of this session was to collect subjects' image of the Tropicana brand.

Brand image was assessed by having subjects respond to a series of seven-point semantic differential scales. The bipolar adjective pairs used to measure brand image were developed by integrating some of the bipolar adjective pairs used by Jacoby and Mazursky (1984) into the framework suggested by Osgood, Suci, and Tannenbaum (1957).

Three weeks later, students in the same marketing classes were told that they could receive extra credit points by participating in a research study. They were given the opportunity to sign-up for one of several sessions outside of class time. At the sessions, students read a case study that they were told was currently being developed for a textbook of case studies. Case study stimuli were used because they provided a realistic format to experimentally manipulate negative information about the brand extensions. The cases consisted of information about a new Tropicana product that had been introduced but where sales were disappointing. They were also shown an evaluation of the product similar to those in *Consumer Reports* magazine. Six product characteristics were listed in the first column, followed by five columns of evaluations ranging from excellent to poor. The product characteristics were determined from actual *Consumer Reports* evaluations of juice and sherbet products. The characteristics used were: *pleasantly sweet, agreeable aftertaste, flavor of fresh fruit, natural taste, freshness of flavor,* and *natural coloring.* Evaluations were all in the fair and poor categories. In addition, under the evaluation grid there was a comment section to reinforce the negative evaluation.

At each session, one of the case studies was distributed (case studies were randomly assigned to sessions). After reading the case, students answered questions about the case, evaluated the Tropicana extension on a series of seven-point scales and evaluated the Tropicana brand image (on the same set of scales used in the first study). Subjects also responded to three-item involvement scales to assess their involvement with orange juice and the extension's product category (either fruit juice or sherbet). The specific items used were product category interest, time spent thinking about the product category, and average importance of the product category (adapted from Bloch, Sherrel, and Ridgway 1986). In addition, subjects were asked if they ever had Tropicana Orange Juice or any other Tropicana products and whether they had seen any advertisements for Tropicana products.

RESULTS

A total of 80 subjects completed the initial survey and the follow-up survey three weeks later (treatment sizes ranged from 19 to 21). Almost all of the subjects (98%) indicated that they have had Tropicana Orange Juice (this confirms the pre-test

TABLE 1
Post-exposure Evaluations of Extensions

Extension Similarity (Product/Attribute)	All Subjects	Involvement with product class	
		Low	High
Similar/Similar	21.70 (20)	21 (11)	29.56 (9)
Similar/Dissimilar	21.89 (19)	17.86 (7)	28.67 (12)
Dissimilar/Similar	25.00 (21)	22.70 (11)	33.30 (10)
Dissimilar/Dissimilar	22.95 (20)	20.46 (11)	33.86 (9)

Involvement scale was split on median response to create high and low involvement groups
Cell entries are mean response to summated product rating scale (higher ratings = higher evaluations)
Cell sizes are in parentheses

which found students to be familiar with the Tropicana brand).

The family brand image measures taken at time 1 and time 2 were factor analyzed. As expected, the brand image measures loaded on three dimensions -- evaluation, potency, and activity. For the purpose of this study, only the evaluation dimension was of interest in order to investigate the effect of negative information on the evaluation of the family brand image. Family brand image was operationalized as the summed response across eight semantic differential scales that loaded on the evaluation factor: quality, taste, superior, fresh, natural, unique, high class (Chronbach's alpha = .9073 for time 1 and .8961 for time 2). Subjects who evaluated the Tropicana image as either neutral or negative were eliminated from the analysis (4% of respondents fell into this category).

In order to check that the four extensions were evaluatively equivalent, some subjects received case studies with positive information about the extension. A one-way ANOVA was performed across the four extensions using the overall extension evaluation as the dependent measure. The results indicated that there was not a significant difference in evaluations of the four extensions when subjects were not presented with negative information ($F(3,75) = .7999$, $p<.5$).

The first hypothesis concerns the expected effect that negative information may have on subjects' ratings of the extensions. It was expected that negative information about an extension closely associated with the brand would be most distinctive since it was inconsistent with the positive brand schema. Thus, the similar brand extension (similar product category and attributes) should be rated lower than the dissimilar extension (dissimilar product category and dissimilar attributes).

A 2 X 2 analysis of covariance was performed to investigate this hypothesis. The independent variables were product category (similar/dissimilar) and attribute (similar/dissimilar). The covariate was subjects' involvement with the product category (either juice or sherbet) and the independent variable was the summated product rating score (the rating scales were combined into an overall extension evaluation; Chronbach's alpha =.9171). The results indicated that the covariate was significant ($F(1,73) = 7.525$, $p<.01$).

Product category was the only significant main effect ($F(1,73) = 10.654$, $p<.003$). For both low and high involvement subjects, extensions that were similar to the brand in terms of product category (see Table 1) received lower evaluations than extensions that were dissimilar to the brand.

Subjects' schema for Tropicana was strongly associated with juice (similar product category), so that negative information about Tropicana juice products had more impact on evaluations than negative information about Tropicana sherbet products. Thus, subjects paid more attention to this information because it was distinctive, and lower extension evaluations resulted. There was no difference in extension evaluations across the attribute manipulations, thus it seems that product category was more important than attributes when evaluating the extension. Hypothesis 1 was supported when similarity is defined in terms of product category only.

The second hypothesis concerns the effect that negative information about extensions may have on the overall family brand image. It was expected that negative information about an extension closely associated with the brand (similar product category and similar attributes) would be more detrimental to evaluations of the family brand image than information about an extension not

TABLE 2
Family Brand Image Evaluations

Extension Similarity (Product/Attribute)	Time 1	Time 2	Change (T2-T1)
Similar/Similar	48.11	47.17	-.94
Similar/Dissimilar	47.44	47.28	-.16
Dissimilar/Similar	48.89	50.63	1.74
Dissimilar/Dissimilar	46.95	48.20	1.25

Cell entries are the summated evaluations of Tropicana image; higher values indicated more positive overall image.

closely associated (dissimilar product category and dissimilar attributes) with the brand schema.

A 2 X 2 analysis of variance was performed with the product category (similar/dissimilar) and attributes (similar/dissimilar) as the independent variables. The dependent measure was the change in brand image (difference in brand image before and after negative information about the extension was encountered). Involvement with the product category was not found to be a significant covariate, and thus dropped from the analysis.

The results indicated a marginally significant main effect for product category only ($F_{(1,71)} = 3.003$, $p<.08$). When the extension was in a similar product category to the brand (juice), the negative information led to an average decrease in family brand image of .56. However, when the extension was in a dissimilar product category (sherbet), the negative information led to an average increase in family brand image of 1.49. Table 2 shows the change in brand image that resulted after subjects encountered negative information about an extension.

Post hoc contrasts were performed to determine if the decrease in brand image is significant when the product category is similar to the family brand. The one-tailed tests were not significant for the two juice extensions, thus there is not adequate support for Hypothesis 2. Two additional post-hoc tests were conducted to determine if the change in image is significantly positive when the extension is in a dissimilar product category to the family brand. The results indicated that when the attributes are similar to the family brand, the change in brand image is positive ($p<.05$). The increase in brand image was not expected for subjects who encountered negative information about an extension in a dissimilar product category. One explanation is that people discounted sherbet as being a product associated with the family brand, and therefore its evaluation did not affect their overall schema for the brand. This explanation is developed further in the following section.

DISCUSSION

One purpose of this paper was to provide insight into the factors that influence consumers' perceptions of how closely associated the extension is to the family brand. While previous studies have manipulated extensions' product categories in order to vary similarity to the family brand, they have not manipulated extensions' attribute similarity. The results in this study indicated that the extension's product category was more important than its attributes when assessing similarity to the family brand.

The findings suggest the following relationship between negative information and the evaluation of brand extensions:

- negative information may lead to more negative extension evaluations when the extensions are in a similar product category than when they are in a dissimilar product category to the family brand.

This effect might be due to the fact that negative information about extensions closely associated with a family brand is incongruous with the brand schema. This inconsistency is distinctive and results in lower evaluations.

The findings were not conclusive as to the relationship between negative information about an extension and its effect on brand image. Future research is needed to investigate whether negative information may be more detrimental to the brand's image when it is targeted to extensions in a similar product category than when it is targeted to extensions in a dissimilar product category to the family brand.

Brand extension studies have found that the transfer of positive attitudes from a brand to an extension will be facilitated when there is a basis of fit between the brand and the extension. This study indicated that this basis of fit (in terms of product category) might also facilitate the transfer of affect from the extension to the family brand. Thus, while introducing a new brand in a similar product category has benefits, it could be a detrimental strategy for the family brand image if the extension is the target of negative information (i.e., does not perform well).

The increase in brand image when the extension was in the dissimilar product category was an unexpected result. Fiske and Taylor (1984) note that if behavior is inconsistent with a schema, it can be dismissed as due to temporary situational factors, and may not be remembered. In this case, subjects might resolve the inconsistency by attributing the negative extension to be the result of the brand's inability to produce an extension in a different product category. Thus, the negative evaluations were more reflective of the product and not the original brand image. In determining the fit of the extension to the family brand, Aaker and Keller (1990) investigated the perceived ability of the firm operating in the family brand product class to make the product in the second product class. They concluded that if consumers feel that the skills needed to make the original product would not transfer to the product extension, then the perceived quality of the brand or beliefs about the brand may not transfer to the extension. This study provides some insight into the fact that maybe these extensions will not affect a brand's image when the target of negative information.

CONCLUSION

Brand extensions have become attractive marketing strategies since they save companies millions of dollars promoting a new brand name to consumers. However, critics of extension strategies are concerned about the effect that unsuccessful extensions may have on a family brand's image. This study was designed to provide insight into the effect that unsuccessful extensions may have on a family brand's image. The results found here indicated that negative information about extensions that are closely related to the family brand may be more detrimental to the family brand image than information about extensions that are not closely related to the brand name.

This study's limitations include data collection in a laboratory setting and the use of student subjects. In addition, only one brand is investigated. Another limitation is the possibility that the two manipulations (product category similarity and attribute similarity) were not independent of each other. The pre-test results indicated that the perceived fit between the extension and the family brand was very high for the extension with the similar product category and similar attributes. The perceived fit for the remaining three extensions were all very similar. Thus, a "medium fit" may have not been achieved.

However, this study does provide some initial insight into how consumers use family brand schemas to assess negative information about extensions and the effect this information may have on the family brand image. Future studies might investigate the effect of negative information on a wider range of extensions for several family brands.

REFERENCES

Aaker, David A. and Kevin Lane Keller (1990), "Consumer Evaluations of Brand Extensions," *Journal of Marketing*, 54 (January), 27-41.

Anderson, Norman H. (1965), "Averaging Versus Adding as a Stimulus Combination Role in Impression Formation, *Journal of Personality and Social Psychology*, February, 1-9.

Bloch, Peter H., Daniel L. Sherrel, and Nancy M. Ridgway (1986), "Consumer Search: An Extended Framework," *Journal of Consumer Research*, 13 (June), 119-126.

Cohen, Joel and Kunal Basu (1987), "Alternative Models for Categorization: Toward a Contingent Processing Framework," *Journal of Consumer Research*, 13 (March), 455-472.

Fannin, Rebecca (1987), "Stretch," *Marketing and Media Decisions*, January, 22-28.

Feldman, Sheldon (1966), "Motivational Aspects of Attitudinal Elements and Their Place in Cognitive Interaction," *Cognitive Consistency*, S. Feldman, Ed., New York: Academic Press.

Fiske, Susan T. (1980), "Attention and Weight in Person Perception: The Impact of Negative and Extreme Behavior," *Journal of Personality and Social Psychology*, 38 (6), 889-906.

_____ and Linda M. Dyer (1985), "Structure and Development of Social Schemata: Evidence from Positive and Negative Transfer Effects," *Journal of Personality and Social Psychology*, 48 (4), 839-852.

_____ and Mark Pavelchak, "Category-Based versus Piecemeal-Based Affective Responses," in *Handbook of Motivation and Cognition*, R.M. Sorrentino and E.T. Higgins, Eds., New York: The Guilford Press, 167-203.

_____ and Shelley Taylor (1984), *Social Cognition*, Reading, MA: Addison-Wesley Publishing Company.

Jacoby, Jacob and David Mazursky (1984), "Linking Brand and Retailer Images: Do the Potential Risks Outweigh the Potential Benefits?" *Journal of Retailing*, 60 (2), 1-5-122.

Jolley, Bill and Dell Hawkins (1988), "Brand Extensions," in *Defining, Measuring, and Managing Brand Equity*, Lance Leuthesser, Ed., Report No. 88-104, Cambridge, MA: Marketing Science Institute.

Kanouse, David and Reid L. Hanson, Jr. (1972), "Negativity in Evaluations," in *Attribution: Perceiving the Causes of Behavior*, E.E. Jones et al. Eds., Morristown, NJ: General Learning Press.

Kesler, Lori (1987), "Extensions leave brand in new areas," *Advertising Age*, June 1, s1-s4.

Norris, Eileen (1986), "Companies bring logos and profits full circle," *Advertising Age*, June 9, s-1.

Osgood, C.E., G.J. Suci, and P.H. Tannenbaum (1957), *The Measurement of Meaning*, Urban: University of Illinois Press.

Park, Whan C., Bernard J. Jaworski, and Deborah J. MacInnis (1986), Strategic Brand Concept-Image Management," *Journal of Marketing*, 50 (October), 135-145.

Richey, M.H., L. McClelland, and A. Shimkunas (1967), "Relative Influence of Positive and Negative Information," *Journal of Social Psychology*, 97, 233-241.

Ries, Al and Jack Trout (1986), *Positioning: The Battle for Your Mind*, New York: McGraw-Hill Book Company.

Rosch, Eleanor (1973), "On the Internal Structure of Perceptual and Semantic Categories, in *Cognitive Developments and the Acquisition of Language*, T. E. Moore, Ed., New York: Academic Press.

Sujan, Mita (1985), "Consumer Knowledge: Effects on Evaluation Strategies Mediating Consumer Judgments," *Journal of Consumer Research*, 12 (June), 31-46.

Tauber, Edward (1988), "Brand Leverage: Strategy for Growth in a Cost-Control World," *Journal of Advertising Research*, 28 (August/September), 26-30.

University of Minnesota Consumer Behavior Seminar (1987), "Affect Generalizations to Similar and Dissimilar Brand Extensions," *Psychology and Marketing*, 4 (3), 225-237.

Weinberger, Marc G., Chris T. Allen, and William R. Dillon (1981), "Negative Information: Perspectives and Research Directions," in *Advances in Consumer Research*, Kent B. Monroe, Ed., 8, Ann Arbor: MI, 398-404.

―――― and William R. Dillon (1980), "The Effects of Unfavorable Product Information," in *Advances in Consumer Research*, J. Olson, Ed., 7, 528-532.

Role of Product Knowledge in Evaluation of Brand Extension

A. V. Muthukrishnan, University of Florida
Barton A. Weitz, University of Florida[1]

ABSTRACT

This paper examines the role of product knowledge in consumer evaluation of brand extensions. Specifically, we give a set of hypotheses on the moderating effect of the variables of product knowledge and type of similarity on similarity judgment between original and new product categories as well as on attitude extension. An experiment was conducted to test these hypotheses and the results of this experiment support some of our predictions.

INTRODUCTION

In recent years there has been an increased interest in research on brand extension. The thrust of this research has been on identifying a set of factors determining the success of brand extension (for example Aaker and Keller, 1990; Boush et al, 1987; Smith, 1990). The studies examining brand extension from a micro perspective concentrated on the product and brand characteristics that account for the judgement of similarity between the original and new product with the same brand name. However, one of the issues not addressed by these studies is the interaction of individual characteristics with brand or product characteristics in similarity judgment as well as in attitude extension. This paper examines the role of an important individual characteristic, product knowledge, in similarity judgment as well as in attitude extension.

Previous Research on Brand Extension

Though there is much evidence for the success of brand extensions (Tauber, 1981; 1988), there are many instances in which brand extensions resulted in diluting the value of original brand equity (Leuthesser, 1988). Recent research on branding has concluded that being a well known brand is not sufficient for extending the brand name to other product categories. As Tauber (1988) states, few consumers would want Jell-O shoe laces or Tide frozen entrees. The key to brand extension then is the logical fit or perceived similarity between the original and the new product bearing the same brand name.

The role of similarity in product evaluation has been examined by a few authors. The earliest studies in this area concluded that brand extension will be successful only when the consumers perceive a high degree of similarity between the original and extended product categories (for example, Boush et al 1987). The research that followed investigated the possible bases of similarity. Tauber (1988) after analyzing actual brand extensions involving 115 different brands in consumer durable and non durable categories suggests seven types of leverages a company should consider when seeking to extend its brands. These are 1) same products in different forms, 2) distinctive taste/ingredient/ component in the new item, 3) companion products, 4) same customer franchise 5) technical expertise 6) benefit/attribute/feature owned and 7) designer image/status. He terms the first two types of leverages as line extension opportunity and the rest as brand extension opportunity. The assumption behind the types of possible leverages listed above may be that a consumer sees some form of consistency between the original product and the new product. More recently some consumer researchers identified the types of perceived consistency or similarity used in product evaluation and their effect on the success of brand extension.

Although not specifically investigating the issue of brand extension, a study by MacInnis and Nakamoto (1989) identified the possible bases of similarity between pairs of products. While product attributes were the most recalled features, benefits and usage situations played the most important role in similarity judgment. The other factors in this study like manufacturing requirements and marketing factors did not have a significant role in the similarity judgment.

In a recently published article, Aaker and Keller (1990) present the results of two studies that explored the role of a set of moderator variables on attitude extension. In the first study the authors proposed that affect transfer to hypothetical brand extensions may depend on 1) the quality perceptions of the brand in the original product category, 2) the extent to which the new product is perceived as a "substitute" for or "complement" to the original product, 3) the extent to which the firm's manufacturing expertise could be transferred to the new product and 4) perceived difficulty of extension. The authors found that of the proposed set of factors only two,"transfer" and "difficulty of extension", had a significant effect on attitude toward the extended brands. In the second study, they manipulated positive quality cues about the brand (cue present or absent) and opportunity to elaborate (a neutral description of the extension attributes alone or in combination with positive quality cues). It was found that providing positive quality cues did not affect attitude extension while opportunity to elaborate did.

The studies discussed above have certainly improved our understanding of the factors accounting for the success of brand extension. However, there is a need to incorporate individual differences such as product knowledge as explanatory variables. As product evaluation may be a function of familiarity

---

[1] We thank John Lynch, Jr., and Rich Lutz for their suggestions at various stages of this project. We also thank Joe Alba, S. Ratneshwar, Barb Bickart and Susan Broniarczyk for their comments on the earlier versions of the manuscript.

with and expertise in a particular product category, these variables may play a significant role in attitude extension. More interestingly, these knowledge related variables may interact with product characteristics to affect one's similarity perceptions as well as attitude extension. The following section gives the theoretical rationale for including the variable of product knowledge in our study.

Product Knowledge and Attitude Extension

In recent years there has been a substantial amount of research on the role of product knowledge on various stages of consumer behavior (for example Bettman and Park, 1980; Brucks, 1985; Johnson and Russo, 1984; Rao and Monroe, 1987 and Sujan, 1985). These studies conclude that the decision processes and strategies of consumers who are high on product knowledge differ from those who are low. Based on an extensive conceptual analysis, Alba and Hutchinson (1987) suggest that familiarity (the number of product related experiences that have been accumulated by the consumer) and expertise (the ability to perform product related tasks successfully) are two separate components of product knowledge. Furthermore, these authors suggest that experts are superior to novices in terms of their cognitive structure, analytic capabilities, ability to make elaborate inferences and memory capabilities. On the basis of these conclusions, we suggest that the basis of similarity or fit judgment in an attitude extension may not be uniform across all segments of consumers; it may vary between experts and novices.

We extrapolate the following propositions of Alba and Hutchinson (1987) to the specific context of attitude extension. Because of their deep, richly intertwined category structure, experts may be able to comprehend similarity between two different classes of products although surface perceptual cues may not suggest any obvious similarity between those products. When novices process information selectively, they are more likely than experts to select peripheral surface cues for judging a brand extension processing (Alba and Hutchinson, 1987)

Furthermore, experts may more often use elaborate inferences to find fit between two product categories. For example, Gillette once test marketed a line of blank tape cassettes. Though, the Gillette name is not associated with sound reproduction, knowledge of the commonalities between the production of cassette tapes and shaving equipments made the association between the brand and the product seem less incongruent (Alba and Hutchinson, 1985).

Thus experts may find similarity between the original product and the new product with the same brand name on the basis of *deep cues*. We define deep cues as those factors that may account for the performance of the product in the original category and may also be related to the performance in the new category. At the attribute level, these may include similarity in terms of technology, design and fabrication and materials and components used in the manufacturing process. These may also include abstract benefits that require elaborate inference making.

Novices, on the other hand, may tend to relate the original and new products on the basis of *surface level cues*. These factors are not related to the performance of products. Rather these may include perceptual cues like package, shape, color, size, etc., perception of two products being either substitutes or complements, similar retail outlets and similar promotional techniques used. Also benefits that require no elaborate inference making may come under this category.

The findings of several streams of research in the areas of attitude formation and change support our propositions. Our proposition that similarity between two products may be judged on the basis of either surface level factors or deeper level factors is similar to the propositions of Petty and Cacioppo (1981) and Chaiken (1980). In both these models, ability is one of the factors that decide the type of processing a person engages in. In a framework on relationship among belief, attitude, intention and behavior, Feldman and Lynch (1988) propose that prior knowledge may be one of the factors that determine the "perceived diagnosticity" of an input.

As previous studies have shown, attitude extension is a function of perceived similarity between two products. Based on the logic given above we suggest that experts are more likely to transfer their attitude when the original and new product categories are similar in terms of deep properties. Conversely, novices are more likely to transfer their attitude when categories are similar only in terms of surface level factors. It has to be noted, however, that when two products are related at surface level, experts as well as novices may identify the similarity. Unlike novices, experts may not perceive such a similarity diagnostic and hence may not transfer their attitude from the original product to the new product bearing the same brand name.

The above discussion leads us to the following set of hypotheses:

H1(a): When similarity between the original product and the new product with the same brand name is based on surface factors, experts as well as novices are likely to identify the similarity.

H1(b): When similarity between the original product and the new product with the same brand name is based on deep factors, experts are more likely than novices to identify this similarity more accurately.

H2(a): When similarity between the original product and the new product with the same brand name is based on surface factors, novices are more likely than experts to transfer their positive or negative attitude toward the original product to the new product.

H2(b): When similarity between the original product and the new product with the same brand name is based on deep factors, experts are more likely than novices to transfer their positive or negative attitude toward the original product to the new product.

Although these hypotheses were proposed explicitly for the variable of expertise, we expected the same pattern of results for the variable of familiarity.

METHOD

Subjects

Subjects in this study were undergraduate students enrolled for Marketing Management and Marketing Research courses at a South-eastern university. There were 106 subjects (52% female and 48% male). The subjects participated in the study as a part of a course requirement.

Procedure

The subjects were told that the study was being conducted by the university for a sporting goods manufacturer. To increase the response involvement, subjects were told that their responses would be used as input for the product and promotional strategy of the company. Then they were asked to fill out a four section questionnaire. Each section of the questionnaire was distributed and collected separately. The sections of the questionnaire asked for information in the following order: a. attitude toward the brands in the original product category; b. attitude toward hypothetical brand extensions; c. judgment of similarity between original and new products; d. the level of familiarity with and expertise in the original as well as new categories. At the end of the session subjects were debriefed.

Design

There were three factors in this study - product knowledge at two levels (expert vs novice and high familiarity vs low familiarity), basis of similarity at two levels (deep vs surface), and attitude toward brands in the original category at two levels (positive vs negative). Product knowledge was a between subjects factor and the other two were with in subject factors. There were two brands nested in each combination of the two with in subjects factors and "brands" was treated as a fixed factor. Finally the set of subjects was treated as random factor nested in product knowledge.

Independent Variables

The study was conducted with tennis racquet as the proposed extension category using brand names of existing tennis shoes or golf clubs. Tennis racquets bear a surface similarity to tennis shoes. Probably the most obvious relationships between these products are that both of them are tennis products and thus may be viewed as complements and both are sold at the same retail outlets.

Tennis racquets were considered to be similar to golf clubs at a deeper level. It was learned through lengthy discussions with sporting goods sellers that same materials were used to manufacture components of these two products. Further the design and fabrication techniques for these products were quite similar.

The second factor in the study was the initial attitude toward the brand in the original category. The brands of golf clubs and tennis shoes considered by sellers of sporting goods to be high quality were used as "positive brands" and the ones they identified as low quality were used as "negative brands". Their classification highly correlated with the sales figures for these brands, suggesting that consumers may share their perceptions of quality.

The third factor was the level of subjects' knowledge in tennis and golf products. Both familiarity and expertise were measured, in order to ascertain whether differently moderated similarity judgments and attitude extension. Expertise was measured through two item self rating. In previous studies this measure of subjective knowledge was found to be correlated with objective knowledge (for example, Brucks, 1985). Familiarity was measured through a nine item scale. Some of the items were similar to those used by Sujan(1985) to measure familiarity in another product domain. Others were constructed on the lines of the components of familiarity identified by Alba and Hutchinson (1987). Appendix- A gives the items used to measure expertise and the contents of familiarity scale. Cronbach's alpha for subjective expertise was 0.969 for tennis shoes, 0.985 for golf club and 0.981 for tennis racquets. Median split was used to separate high and low knowledge groups in each of the product categories. Subjects falling in the upper half of all the three categories were classified as "high familiar group" and the others were classified as "low familiar group". A similar procedure was used to classify subjects as experts and novices.

Dependent Variables

Attitude toward brands in the original category, attitude toward the new product with the same brand names and judgment of similarity between the original and new product categories were used as dependent variables. Attitude toward brands in the original categories was included as a check for our manipulation of positive and negative brands. The manipulation check revealed that the ratings of the subjects did not agree with those of the sellers in the case of two brands each in tennis shoes and golf club categories. Hence although we collected data for six brands in each category, only data for four brands in each category were included in the final analysis.

Based on attitude scales used in a number of previous studies, attitudes toward brands in original as well as extended category was measured through a scale of four 7 point semantic differential items. The items in the scale were positive-negative, favorable-unfavorable, good-bad and like-dislike. Cronbach's alpha for scale items for attitude toward the original brand was 0.754 and it was 0.868 for scale items for attitude toward the extended brand. The overall attitude was the average of these four items.

The perceived similarity between the original category and new category was measured through two items (1= not at all similar to 7= highly similar and 1=not at all related to 7=extremely related). Cronbach's alpha for these items was 0.911 for the pair of tennis shoes-tennis racquet and 0.930 for the pair of golf club-tennis racquet. The subjects were also asked to give reasons for their similarity judgments which served as an indicator of the possible bases of similarity. Later these responses were coded by one of the researchers as deep and surface level factors.

Plan of Analysis

To test Hypotheses 1a. and 1b. two models were used. In the first model either expertise or familiarity and type of similarity (manipulated) were the independent variables and subjects' rating of similarity was the dependent variable. Expertise/familiarity was a between subjects variable and type of similarity was a two levels (surface and deep) repeated factor. A mixed factor analysis of variance was used to test these hypotheses. To support these hypotheses there should be a significant simple effect of product knowledge at deep level of similarity and there should be no such effect at surface level of similarity. In other words, there should be a significant expertise/familiarity * Type of similarity interaction.

In the second model, the reasons for similarity judgment for the pairs of tennis shoes-tennis racquet and golf club-tennis racquet, coded as accurate and inaccurate was used as the dependent variable and familiarity/expertise was the independent variable. This model was an additional test of hypothesis 1b. If our assertion that experts would identify the basis of similarity more accurately when two products are related at a deeper level is correct, then there should be a significant effect of expertise/familiarity. Categorical linear model (CATMOD) was used as the technique of analysis.

RESULTS AND DISCUSSION

Manipulation Checks

As mentioned earlier, data on some brands had to be excluded from analysis as the initial attitude expressed by a majority of subjects did not agree with the opinions of sellers. We conducted manipulation checks to ensure that the eight brands included in final analysis were perceived as positive or negative by subjects. We were interested in two effects. First, to show that our manipulations worked, there should be a significant main effect of the factor of initial attitude. Second, we tested whether the difference in liking between the positive and negative brands of tennis shoes was equal for experts and novices and whether the analogous difference in liking for positive and negative brands of golf clubs was equal for experts and novices. Such expert novice difference in attitudes toward the original brands could artificially produce differences in liking for the extended brands. This explanation could be ruled out by finding no significant three way interaction of product knowledge*initial attitude*type of similarity.

The results we obtained confirmed that the initial attitude manipulation was strong ($F (1,104)= 97.16, p < 0.0001$)[2]. The three way interaction was not significant ($F (1,104)= 2.35, p > 0.128$). This shows that there was no expert-novice differences in the liking for brands in the original product categories.

Similarity Judgments of Experts and Novices

The model using expertise as a between subjects variable, type of similarity as repeated factor and similarity judgment as dependent variable yielded partial support for our hypotheses 1(a) and 1(b). Table 1 gives the type of similarity x expertise mean scores.

The type of similarity x expertise interaction was highly significant ($F (1,104) =23.9, p < 0.0001$). The cell means for expertise x type of similarity were in the predicted direction. However, contrary to our prediction that the effect of expertise would be significant only at deeper level of similarity, we found that expertise had a significant simple effect at surface level ($F = 8.36\ p < 0.004$) as well as at deep level of similarity ($F = 16.9\ p < 0.0001$). These results suggest an interesting possibility that experts may perceive two product categories less similar when these categories are related only on the basis of surface factors.

Table 2 gives the results of categorical linear analysis done with bases of similarity rating (coded as relevant or irrelevant) given for the pairs of tennis shoes-tennis racquet ("surface" pair) and golf club - tennis racket ("deep" pair) as the dependent variable and expertise as independent variable. This is an additional test for Hypotheses 1(a) and 1(b).

We obtained strong support for our hypothesis 1 b(chi-square (1)=36.9, $p < 0.0001$). Experts gave deeper level reasons for similarity between the product categories of tennis racquets and golf clubs. Novices either judged the similarity to be low or gave surface level reasons for their judgment. We combined these two categories of

---

[2] In this section we are only discussing results for analyses using expertise as an independent variable. We did similar analyses using familiarity as an independent variable. The results supported Hypotheses 2(a) and 2(b) but not hypotheses 1(a) and 1(b). The results are given in the footnote.

TABLE 1
SIMILARITY JUDGMENT OF EXPERTS AND NOVICES

EXPERTISE	N	SURFACE CATEGORY	DEEP CATEGORY
Novice	87	5.149	3.196
Expert	19	3.947	4.948
N	106		

TABLE 2
FREQUENCIES OF REASONS FOR SIMILARITY X EXPERTISE FOR DEEP SIMILARITY PAIR

EXPERTISE	ACCURATE REASONS	INACCURATE REASONS
Novice	12 (13.8%)	75 (86.2%)
Expert	14 (73.7%)	5 (26.3%)

TABLE 3
FREQUENCIES OF REASONS FOR SIMILARITY X EXPERTISE FOR SURFACE SIMILARITY PAIR

EXPERTISE	ACCURATE REASONS	INACCURATE REASONS
Novice	81 (93.1%)	5 (6.9%)
Expert	18 (94.7%)	1 (5.3%)

responses and called it as inaccurate basis of similarity. Table 3 gives the frequencies for expertise by type of reasons for similarity for the pair of tennis shoes-tennis racquets. No one gave a reason that could be identified as deep. However, a few subjects perceived no similarity between these two product categories. Hence, the levels of the factor basis of similarity are appropriate (surface level) and inappropriate (no similarity between these two product categories).

As there are very few frequencies in the "inappropriate" cells, no further analysis is done on this data. An examination of frequencies in the cells appears to support hypothesis 1 (a).

Test of Hypotheses on Attitude extension

Table 4 gives the means of Expert x initial Attitude x Type of Similarity

The three way interaction was significant, ($F(1,104) = 9.58$, $p < 0.003$). Since the interaction is significant, we conducted a follow up test. In this test, we compared type of similarity x initial attitude interaction at each level of expertise. For the experts this interaction was moderately significant ($F(1, 18) = 3.68$, $p < 0.08$). For novices this interaction was highly significant ($F(1, 86) = 8.92$, $p < 0.004$. The directions were as predicted. Since the experts were smaller in number, power to detect this interaction effect may be low. This may explain the lower statistical significance for experts.

Limitations and Future Research Directions

Although we found evidence for most of our hypotheses, there are certain limitations in this study. First of all, we used only one product in each of the categories relevant to our research objectives. Secondly, the most important variable in this research, product knowledge, was measured rather than manipulated. However we recognize that manipulating product knowledge may be an extremely difficult task. A more important point is that when brands were treated as random factor nested in initial attitude and type of similarity, appropriate error terms changed, and the observed treatment effects sometimes failed to attain statistical significance. Hence the findings may not be generalizable to products or brands other than the

TABLE 4
ATTITUDE EXTENSION BY EXPERTS AND NOVICES

EXPERTISE	SURFACE		DEEP	
	Positive	Negative	Positive	Negative
Novices (n=87)	3.518	2.706	1.923	1.762
Experts (n=19)	2.670	2.210	3.343	1.917
N=106				

ones used in this study. It may be necessary to replicate this study using a number of products/brands. Finally, in the process of categorization, we suggested that our novice subjects' evaluation may be based on a similarity judgment. They may identify similarity between tennis shoes and tennis rackets as they are used in the same sport (complements). However it is also possible that they just went by the category label "Tennis" as this label was missing in the other pair.[3] Hence it is possible that novices' evaluation simply may be on the basis of the category label and not on the basis of perceptual fit of surface level factors. Future research could examine these competing explanations on the process of attitude extension.

GENERAL DISCUSSION AND CONCLUSION

In this research we suggested that experts and novices may differ in their reactions to brand extension on the basis of the type of relationship between the original product and the new product with the same brand name. Our results may have implications in the areas of branding and promotion. When a firm extends its brand name to another product category on the basis of commonality in technology, experts may appreciate such an extension while novices may not. Similarly, novices may find surface factors diagnostic while novices may not. In such a case, it will be advantageous for the firm to educate consumers on the technical/manufacturing commonalities and convince them that the extension is logical. The expert - novice differences may also be useful in positioning of the extended brand. However, when the global image of the firm is very high then there may not be any expert - novice difference in product evaluation. In such an instance experts as well as novices may have high attitude toward extended brand.

FOOTNOTE

The analyses with familiarity instead of expertise as an independent variable yielded results somewhat different from those reported in the results and discussion section. The type of similarity x familiarity was not significant at 0.05 level but was significant at 0.1 level (F (1,104) = 2.93, p < 0.1). For the pair of tennis racquet and golf club basis of judgment x familiarity interaction was significant (chi-square (1)= 12.67, p < .0005. The three way interaction among familiarity, initial attitude and type of similarity was significant (F (1,104)=4.38, p < 0.05). However, the mean in positive-surface condition (3.24) was higher than the mean in positive-deep condition (2.76) for High familiar group. This is contrary to our prediction. This shows that as Alba and Hutchinson (1987) argue, familiarity and expertise are different constructs and treating them as same may cause serious construct validity problems.

APPENDIX - A
The contents of Familiarity Scale

The items included in the familiarity scale sought information on (1) How long the subject been playing the sport? (2) How often does she play? (3) How often does she visit stores exclusively selling these products? (4) How many times has she bought tennis racquets, tennis shoes and golf clubs for herself or for others? (5) How often and how much is she consulted by her friends and relatives in the purchase of these products? (6) How much of attention does she pay to the ads for these products? (7) How many brands in each of these product categories could she recall? (8) What magazines pertaining to these product categories does she read? and (9) How much of time does she spend watching TV programs on these sports?

The subjective expertise scale had two items 1) I consider myself least knowledgeable = 1 to highly knowledgeable = 7 and 2) I consider myself novice = 1 to expert = 7. These were measured for each product category separately.

REFERENCES

Aaker, D and K. Keller (1990), "Consumer Evaluations of Brand Extensions", *Journal of Marketing*, 54, 27-41.

Alba, J. W and J. W. Hutchinson (1985), "A Framework for Understanding Consumer Knowledge II. Comparison and Inference Process", Working Paper, University of Florida, Center for Consumer Research.

---

[3] We thank Susan Broniarczyk for suggesting this possiblity

_____ (1987), "Dimensions of Consumer Expertise", *Journal of Consumer Research*, 13, 411-454.

Bettman, J. R and C. W. Park (1980), "Effects of Prior Knowledge and Experience and Phase of the Choice Process on Consumer Decision Processes: A Protocol Analysis", *Journal of Consumer Research*, 7, 234-248.

Boush, D et al.[University of Minnesota Seminar] (1987), "Affect Generalization to Similar and Dissimilar Brand Extensions", *Psychology and Marketing*, 4, 225-237.

Brucks, M (1985), "The Effects of Product Class Knowledge on Information Search Behavior", *Journal of Consumer Research*, 12, 1-16.

Chaiken, S (1980), "Heuristic versus Systematic Information Processing and the Use of Source versus Message Cues in Persuasion", *Journal of Personality and Social Psychology*, 39, 752-766.

Feldman, J. M and J. G. Lynch, Jr. (1988), "Self-Generated Validity and Other Effects of Measurement on Belief, Attitude, Intention and Behavior", *Journal of Applied Psychology*, 73, 421-435.

Johnson, E. J and E. Russo (1984), "Product Familiarity and Learning New Information", *Journal of Consumer Research*, 11, 253-263.

Leuthesser, L (1988), "Defining, Measuring, and Managing Brand Equity", MSI Report No. 88-104.

MacInnis, D and K. Nakamoto (1989), "Cognitive Associations and Product Category Comparisons": The Role of Knowledge Structures and Context", Working paper, University of Arizona.

Petty, R. E and J. T. Cacioppo (1981), "*Attitudes and Persuasion*: Classic and Contemporary Approaches", Dubuque, IA, William C. Brown.

Rao, A and K. B. Monroe (1988), "The Moderating Effect of Prior Knowledge in Cue Utilization in Product Evaluation", *Journal of Consumer Research*, 15, 253-263.

Smith, D (1990), "An Examination of Product and Market Conditions That Affect the Financial Outcome of Brand Extensions", Working paper, University of Wisconsin.

Sujan, M (1985), "Consumer Knowledge Effects on Evaluation Strategies Mediating Consumer Judgments", *Journal of Consumer Research*, 12, 31-46.

Tauber, E. M (1981), "Brand Franchise Extension: New Product Benefits from Existing Brand Names", *Business Horizons*, 24 (2), 36-41.

_____ (1988), "Brand Leverage: Strategy For Growth in a Cost-Control World", *Journal of Advertising Research*, 28, (August/September), 26-30.

The Effects of Advertising Context on Consumer Responses
Amna Kirmani, Duke University
Youjae Yi, The University of Michigan

ABSTRACT
This paper provides a summary of a special topic session organized to address how consumers' responses can vary as a function of advertising context. The papers presented in this session provide theoretical frameworks that can be useful for investigating the processes in which affective and cognitive ad context influence consumers' responses to advertisements. The theoretical and practical implications of advertising context effects are also discussed.

OVERVIEW
Many advertisements do not occur in a vacuum, but rather appear simultaneously with other materials such as programs on TV, articles in magazines, ads for other products, and station identifications. Such material within which ads are embedded are usually referred to as advertising context (Soldow and Principe 1981). Advertising context can vary to a great extent, and an important decision is selecting an appropriate context for advertisements. In this regard, a key question should be considered: What are the influences of advertising context on consumers' responses (e.g., brand recall, attitudes toward the ad or brand, purchase intentions). This question seems very important for an understanding of advertising effectiveness, given the wide variety of advertising context. In fact, several surveys show that the impact of advertising context is currently among the top research priorities for advertisers (Chook 1985; Schultz 1979).

A number of studies suggest that ad context can influence the audience's perception of the ad and thus its effectiveness, but studies have often yielded conflicting results. Furthermore, although many studies have examined the overall impact of advertising context, relatively little attention has been given to underlying mechanisms and specific effects (but see Goldberg and Gorn 1987). It seems useful to develop theoretical models that can systematically account for the effects of advertising context.

This session attempts to provide theoretical frameworks that can be useful for investigating the processes in which advertising context influences consumer responses to advertisements. It is proposed that advertising context may have at least two types of influence on the impact of advertisements: affective influence and cognitive influence. Affective influences of advertising context are examined in the first and second papers (e.g., how context-generated mood influences consumers' attitude toward the brand). The third and fourth papers investigate cognitive influences of ad context (e.g., how ad context influences consumers' processing of product information in ads).

The first paper by Douglas Stayman examines the impact of affective context (mood, program tone, other ads) on advertising effectiveness. This paper provides an overview of various streams of research on affective context (e.g., affect modeled either as a moderator or as a mediator). The second paper by Helen Anderson develops a conceptual model of change in emotional responses due to context by integrating a theory of adaptive response with a theory for the structure of emotions. It is proposed that perception of an ad stimulus will be a function of how close (or similar) that stimulus is to the current reference point. Specifically, close stimuli are assimilated, while distant stimuli are contrasted to the reference. To apply this theory to the affective domain, Anderson develops a measure of distance between emotion types based on a theory for the structure of emotions (Shaver et al. 1987).

The third paper by Kevin Keller and Amna Kirmani examines the effect of other ads in the environment on memory and evaluation of the target ad. Like Anderson, they derive predictions from assimilation-contrast theory, looking at how valence and nature of the surrounding ads affect the target ad. They use these predictions in an experiment using print advertisements. Finally, the last paper by Yi investigates a way in which advertising context can affect consumers' processing of ambiguous product information in advertisements (i.e., information that has multiple implications for the evaluation of the advertised product). Yi posits that prior exposure to contextual factors can prime certain product attributes and subsequently increase the likelihood that consumers interpret product information in terms of these activated attributes, thereby affecting consumers' evaluations of the advertised brand. More detailed abstracts of the papers provided by the authors are presented next.

ABSTRACTS

The Effect of Affective Context on the Effectiveness of Advertising
Douglas M. Stayman, Cornell University

This paper discusses the impact which the affect due to surrounding content can have on the effectiveness of advertising. The paper discusses two primary effects which have been identified. The first effect is the effect of context on the affective responses to advertising. Research suggests that the affective state which a viewer is in before a commercial starts can have predictable and substantial effects on the affective response of the viewer to the commercial. Research on the effect of editorial (for print) and programming (for television) content is first reviewed which suggests that the affective tone of programming can 'carry-over' to advertising (e.g., Goldberg and Gorn 1987). Second, work is reviewed that suggests that the advertising which precedes a commercial can have a contrast effect on the affective responses, inflating responses to commercials for which the affective appeal is different from those of preceding commercials (e.g., Aaker, Stayman and Hagerty 1986). Such effects of context on affective responses have been shown to influence such outcome measures as ad recall, ad attitudes, and brand attitude change.

The second effect discussed is the effect of affective context on the processing of the informational content in advertisements. Work in social cognition by Isen and others suggests that affective states can have significant impact on the processing of information in persuasive messages. For example, mood states have been shown to affect the amount and type of processing of print advertisements as well as the motivation to selectively process information about different types of products.

Finally, the paper concludes by combining these two areas in a discussion of affective context in differentially affecting informational versus emotional appeals. Implications for both additional theoretical work necessary as well as practitioner usefulness of the reviewed findings are made.

Contextual Effects on Responses to Advertising: The Role of Emotion Types
Helen M. Anderson, University of Arizona

This research examines the impact of contextual factors on affective responses to advertising. The contextual influence is operationalized as the emotional reaction to the television program in which the ad is embedded. Ad responses include affective reactions, involvement, and attitudes.

A conceptual model of change in emotional response due to context is developed by integrating a theory of adaptive response with a theory for the structure of emotions. In adaptation level theory (Helson 1964), perception of a stimulus is argued to be a function of the distance between a stimulus and the current reference point. Close stimuli are assimilated, or perceived to be more like the reference than objective measures of distance would indicate. Distant stimuli are contrasted, or perceived to be less like the reference.

Shaver, Schwartz, Kirson, and O'Connor (1987) posit a theory for the structure of emotions which incorporates a dimension of distance between emotion types. Thus, by integrating Shaver et al.'s work with that of Helson, predictions are generated for when the perception of emotions in the ad may be contrasted or assimilated based on emotion engendered by the television program. For example, predictions may be made as to when a given ad may be seen as more or less joyful.

Initial findings from a laboratory experiment indicate that reactions to the ad are affected by the programming context. These results are argued to have interesting managerial implications with regard to ad design and media placement. In addition, findings hold important implications for future research on assessing emotional reactions to advertising stimuli, especially in terms of research design and measurement.

Context Effects in Advertising: The Role of Other Ads in the Environment
Kevin Lane Keller, Stanford University
Amna Kirmani, Duke University

The basic proposition of this paper is that people seldom evaluate ads in a vacuum; they judge the merits of an ad relative to some standard or context. The context may be explicit, or externally imposed (e.g., from other ads in the environment); or it may be implicit, or internally generated from memory (e.g., from other product class ads stored in memory). The context that we examine is that of other ads in the environment.

We investigate context effects on both memory for and evaluations of a target ad. We propose that the target ad may be either assimilated or contrasted with competing ads. Several factors may moderate this process, leading to either assimilation or contrast: 1) adjacency (whether adjacent ads are from the same product class as the target ad); 2) valence of competing ads (whether the surrounding ads are judged as good or bad); and 3) position (whether the competing ads precede or follow the target ad). We hypothesize that people may use adjacent preceding ads as an anchor, and assimilate or contrast the target ad with their evaluation of the prior ad. We would expect interference effects to be stronger with adjacent ads in the same product class. We present evidence from an experiment which looks at these variables in the context of print advertising. We measure ad and brand recall, as well as ad and brand attitudes.

The Influence of Contextual Priming on Advertising Effects
Youjae Yi, The University of Michigan

Product information in an ad can often be perceived in different ways. For example, when an ad emphasizes that a piece of luggage is light, one might conclude either that the bag is easy to carry or that the bag is not durable. Then, what determines the particular interpretation given to such product information? An answer to this question may be found from the work on priming which demonstrates that an ambiguous stimulus is interpreted in terms of the concepts primed by contextual factors (e.g., Herr 1989; Meyers-Levy 1989).

This presentation investigates how contextual materials affect the processing of ambiguous product information in advertisements. It is proposed that contextual factors can prime certain product attributes and subsequently increase the likelihood that consumers interpret product information in terms of these activated attributes. These interpretations may result in the formation or change of beliefs about the advertised brand, thereby affecting consumers' evaluations of the brand.

This research should be of interest to researchers who study basic information processing, attitude change and consumer responses to advertising. The present research is also relevant to practitioners of advertising. By showing that an ad context is not merely a benign background but can influence the effectiveness of an ad, this study expands the scope of both strategic and tactical approaches to persuasion. The present study also helps advertisers to understand potentially dysfunctional effects of the ad context. If the ad context primes negative interpretations of the product, perceptions of the advertised product will be negatively affected.

ACKNOWLEDGEMENTS

The session co-chairs thank Christopher Puto of the University of Arizona for providing valuable comments as discussant.

REFERENCES

Aaker, David A., Douglas M Stayman, and Michael R. Hagerty (1986), "Warmth in Advertising: Measurement, Impact, and Sequence Effects," *Journal of Consumer Research*, 12 (March), 365-381.

Chook, Paul H. (1985), "A Continuing Study of Magazine Environment, Frequency, and Advertising Performance," *Journal of Advertising Research*, 25 (4), 23-33.

Goldberg, Marvin E. and Gerald J. Gorn (1987), "Happy and Sad TV Programs: How They Affect Reactions to Commercials," *Journal of Consumer Research*, 14 (December), 387-403.

Helson, H. (1964), *Adaptation Level Theory*, New York: Harper & Row.

Herr, Paul M. (1989), "Priming Price: Prior Knowledge and Context Effects," *Journal of Consumer Research*, 16 (June), 67-75.

Meyers-Levy, Joan (1989), "Priming Effects on Product Judgments: A Hemispheric Interpretation," *Journal of Consumer Research*, 16 (June), 76-86.

Schultz, D. E. (1979), "Media Research Users Want," *Journal of Advertising Research*, 19 (December), 13-17.

Shaver, P., J. Schwartz, D. Kirson, and C. O'Connor (1987), "Emotion Knowledge: Further Exploration of a Prototype Approach," *Journal of Personality and Social Psychology*, 52 (6), 1061-1086.

Soldow, Gary F. and Victor Principe (1981), "Response to Commercials as a Function of Program Context," *Journal of Advertising Research*, 21 (2), 59-65.

The Influence of Contextual Priming on Advertising Effects

Youjae Yi, University of Michigan

ABSTRACT

This study investigates a particular way in which contextual priming influences advertising effects. It is proposed that prior exposure to contextual factors can prime or activate certain product attributes in consumers' knowledge structure and subsequently increase the likelihood that they interpret ambiguous product information in terms of these activated attributes, thereby affecting the overall impact of the ad. Two experiments are conducted to test the main hypothesis and eliminate potentially confounding effects of experimental tasks. The results demonstrate that the specific attributes relevant to evaluating the advertised brand vary in their accessibility as a function of the ad context, and that these variations influence brand attitudes and purchase intentions. Step-down analyses show further that the effects of priming product attributes operate mainly through brand attitudes. Theoretical and practical implications of these findings are also discussed.

INTRODUCTION

Product information in advertisements can often have multiple implications for the evaluation of the advertised product. For example, when an ad emphasizes that a car is large, one might infer either that the car will be comfortable or that the car will yield low miles per gallon (MPG). In such a case, interpretations of the large size as high comfort would induce favorable brand evaluations, whereas interpretations as low gas mileage would yield unfavorable brand evaluations. A question then arises: What determines the particular interpretation given to the product information that has several possible meanings?

According to the research on priming, interpretations of ambiguous information can be very sensitive to the surrounding context (e.g., Herr 1989; Meyers-Levy 1989). Researchers have found that an ambiguous stimulus is often interpreted in terms of the concepts that are primed by contextual factors (Wyer and Srull 1981). These findings suggest that contextual factors might be an important determinant of how ambiguous information in the ad is perceived.

Thus, the present study proposes that contextual factors can affect consumers' processing of ambiguous product information in the ad by priming certain attributes. Specifically, contextual materials (e.g., a magazine article on oil prices) may activate particular product attributes (e.g., gas mileage) and guide consumers' interpretations of product information (e.g., car size). These interpretations may result in the formation or change of beliefs about the advertised brand, thereby affecting consumers' evaluations of the advertised brand.

CONTEXTUAL PRIMING EFFECTS

Researchers using the priming paradigm have shown that people's interpretation of information often depends on the particular knowledge structures (e.g., concepts and schemas) that are currently active (Higgins and King 1981; Wyer and Srull 1981). For example, the fact that someone gave a friend an answer during an exam could be interpreted as either "dishonest" or "kind." The type of interpretation given seems to depend on which of the related concepts (dishonest or kind) is easily accessible at the time when information is processed (Srull and Wyer 1980). Accessible concepts serve to direct attention to certain aspects of information and are likely to guide the interpretation of information (Yi 1990a). Priming effects have been demonstrated even when people are unaware of the activated concepts (Higgins, Bargh, and Lombardi 1985). These findings suggest that highly accessible attributes are likely to be used in interpreting an ambiguous description of a product.

Then, what makes certain attributes highly accessible? Many researchers in cognitive and social psychology have found that the accessibility (likelihood of retrieval from memory and subsequent use) of a certain concept is enhanced by prior exposure to the concept (Higgins and King 1981; Wyer and Srull 1986). A concept's temporary accessibility is directly related to its recency of activation; the more recently a concept is activated, the greater its accessibility (Higgins and King 1981). Although a variety of factors can provide exposure to product attributes, of particular interest to this study is the context for the ad.

Many advertisements occur with other materials such as articles in the magazine and other competing advertisements (Soldow and Principe 1981), and prominent aspects of the ad environment can activate certain sets of product attributes (Gardner 1983). When the ad context provides people with exposure to a certain attribute, such as occurs when they read a magazine article emphasizing the attribute, this attribute may become highly accessible. Subsequently, that attribute is likely to be used in processing the ad information and evaluating the advertised brand. That is, contextual factors may make certain attributes salient to ad recipients and guide their perceptions of product information in the ad (Shavitt and Fazio 1990).

The evaluation of the advertised brand would therefore depend upon which attribute is activated by the contextual factors preceding the ad. When the ad context primes an attribute (e.g., ease of handling) that has positive implications for evaluation of the target brand, overall product evaluations will be enhanced. In contrast, when the context primes an attribute (e.g., durability) whose evaluative implication is negative, overall product evaluations will be lowered. This suggests that the same ad can have different effects, depending upon the attribute activated by the context preceding the ad. Thus, it is hypothesized that how product information in an ad is perceived depends on what related attribute is primed previously by contextual factors.

One purpose of the present study is to investigate the priming effects of contextual factors for a print advertisement, especially when the ad contains ambiguous product information. The results should be informative of a way in which the ad context can influence ad perception. Another purpose of this research is to look deeply into the nature and process of contextual priming effects. In this regard, we analyze attribute level data elicited by subjects to assess the accessibility of primed attributes and examine the theoretical relation among dependent variables with step-down analyses. We have also employed the more powerful analysis of MANOVA designs via structural equation models (Bagozzi and Yi 1989). Finally, an attempt is made to replicate the results so that the findings can be generalized. By conducting a second experiment that overcomes certain methodological limitations of the first experiment, we attempt to eliminate alternative explanations and test the generalizability of the findings.

EXPERIMENT 1

The priming hypothesis was tested in an experiment in which subjects were exposed to an ad and asked to indicate their reactions to the advertised product. The contextual materials surrounding the target ad were manipulated to investigate the impact of the ad context. All the subjects saw the same target ad, except for the context.

Method

Subjects and Advertisement. Forty student subjects participated in the first experiment. Personal computers were selected as a focal product, because this product category should be highly relevant to the subjects. After a pretest was conducted with ten students, the availability of various features was chosen as the key message in the target ad. Accordingly, ease of use was chosen as the attribute to be primed in the negative interpretation condition, whereas versatility was chosen as the salient attribute in the positive interpretation condition (see also Yi 1990d).

The target ad focused on numerous features of a new personal computer (PC-3000). The ad featured a headline in bold face, "Get the PC-3000, satisfy your lust for power and performance." The ad contained three paragraphs of text emphasizing that the PC-3000 personal computer has numerous features. The ad also contained a picture of one person standing by the personal computer.

Procedure. After being seated in the research room, subjects were told that the study concerned consumers' evaluation of print advertisements for new personal computers in pre-production form. After the general instructions, they were given three booklets and told to complete the booklets in the order presented.

In the first booklet, subjects were asked for general background information such as their knowledge and familiarity with personal computers. The second booklet contained two advertisements: (1) an ad designed to prime certain product attributes and (2) an ad for the target brand (PC-3000). The first ad in this booklet represented the priming manipulation. The purpose of this ad was to prime a certain product attribute that could induce an either positive or negative interpretation of the advertised attribute in the target ad ("numerous features" of PC-3000). To do this, two different ads were created that emphasized one of the two attributes (versatility and ease of use). These ads will be called hereafter "prime ads." Each of the prime ads featured a personal computer (which is different from the target brand) that can activate one of the attributes relevant to evaluating the target brand. An ad was used as a prime, because it fit well with the cover story of the experiment (cf. Yi 1990b).

Half of the subjects saw a prime ad for the personal computer with a brand name in bold face, "Versa-Com." Centered at the top of the prime ad was the headline, "I didn't know it could do that," emphasizing the fact that the Versa-Com computer can perform many functions. This claim was bolstered by including a picture illustrating many different analyses and applications of the computer. The other half saw a prime ad emphasizing the ease of use for the computer with its brand name in bold face, "EZ-Com." This prime ad had the headline, "Our frills require no skills," at the top and contained a picture of a child working at the computer terminal. Each of the two prime ads had the same format: a headline, two paragraphs of copy text, and a picture. Both ads were approximately equal in length.

The objective of the priming manipulation was to enhance the likelihood that, later when reading the target ad mentioning that the PC-3000 computer had numerous features, subjects who had earlier seen the Versa-Com ad would encode the provided information in terms of versatility, whereas those who had earlier read the EZ-Com ad would perceive the product information in terms of ease of use. After completion of the priming manipulation, subjects saw the target ad for PC-3000. All subjects saw the same target ad, although they had previously read a different prime ad (either Versa-Com or EZ-Com).

In the third booklet, subjects were asked to generate salient attributes of a personal computer that would come to mind if they considered purchasing a personal computer. They listed the characteristics of a personal computer that they would consider in an open-ended format. Subjects were then asked to turn to the next page, where they were asked for brand evaluations such as brand attitude and purchase intentions. It was also checked whether there had been any demand artifacts. After completing the last questionnaire, subjects were asked to write down their thoughts concerning the purpose of the study. Results showed that no subjects guessed the true purpose of the study, indicating that few demand artifacts had operated.

Dependent Variables. Attitude toward the target brand (Ab) was assessed by three 7-point scales anchored by the phrases "good-bad," "like-dislike," and "favorable-unfavorable." Purchase intention toward the brand (PI), assuming a product category need, was also measured by asking a question, "What are your chances of buying PC-3000 the next time that you need to purchase a personal computer?" Given a single exposure to the ad, the conditional purchase intention, rather than the usual purchase intention, measure was considered appropriate. Subjects responded on three seven-point scales: "likely-unlikely," "possible-impossible," and "probable-improbable." The alpha coefficients for Ab and PI were .90 and .92, respectively, indicating a high degree of internal consistency.

Results

Contextual Priming Effects. A one-way multivariate analysis of variance (MANOVA) was run via SPSS^X on the set of two dependent variables (Ab and PI), each of which was operationalized by the sum of three items. The Box's M test indicated that the homogeneity assumption was valid: Box's M = 1.93, χ^2 (3) = 1.82, $p > .60$. MANOVA results showed that contextual priming had a significant effect on these measures of brand evaluations (F (2, 37) = 7.92, $p < .01$).

For an understanding of priming effects on individual variables, separate ANOVAs were subsequently run on each dependent variable. Results indicated that priming had significant effects on both Ab and PI (F (1, 38) = 12.59, $p < .01$; F (1, 38) = 10.74, $p < .01$, respectively). As expected, Ab was higher when the versatility attribute was primed, compared with the case when ease of use was primed (4.98 vs. 3.97). Also, BI was higher in the versatility condition (4.57) than in the ease-of-use condition (3.33).

We have thus far examined examined results of MANOVA and univariate ANOVAs for priming effects. There are, however, several limitations to this common use of MANOVA-ANOVA analyses (Bray and Maxwell 1985). First, the probability statements from separate ANOVAs are not meaningful, when the dependent variables are interrelated. Previous research shows that the dependent variables (Ab and BI) of this study are related to each other (e.g., Mackenzie, Lutz, and Belch 1986). Second, MANOVA or ANOVAs are not very useful for understanding the nature and process of the experimental effects on interrelated variables as in this study. Variation in a particular variable may be either due to a direct influence of the priming manipulation or due to the dependence of that particular variable on other variable.

A useful approach to such problems would be a step-down analysis (Roy 1958). The step-down analysis provides an examination of sequential relations among the set of dependent variables. By examining dependent variables in a predetermined way, one can assess the unique contribution of each variable to the between-group difference, as the variable is added to the dependent variable set. Unlike univariate ANOVA tests, the probability values associated with step-down analysis are independent. It can provide useful information by testing whether variation in a certain dependent variable is due to the direct effect of the experimental manipulation or due to the relationships of that dependent variable with other dependent variables.

Previous research suggests that the dependent variables are likely to be in a causal order of Ab to PI (e.g., Mackenzie, Lutz, and Belch 1986; Yi 1990b). Step-down analyses were thus conducted with a causal path from Ab to PI. Step-down analyses were conducted beginning with the last ordered variable (Ab), examining the step-down F values. The first step-down F value was the same as the univariate F value from ANOVA on Ab (F (1, 38) = 12.59, $p < .01$). But the next step tested the effect of contextual priming on PI, with the effect of Ab covaried out. The results showed that the effect of priming was statistically insignificant (F (1, 37) = 2.68, $p > .10$), whereas the effect of Ab as a covariate was significant (F (1, 37) = 19.08, $p < .01$).

Thus, when the causal relation between the dependent variables was taken into account by step-down analyses, one of the effects that had been significant in univariate ANOVAs became insignificant. Specifically, the priming effect on PI became insignificant in the step-down analyses. These results suggest that the variation in PI was due to the dependence of PI on Ab, rather than due to the direct influence of priming itself.

Attribute Accessibility. We have thus far examined the overall brand evaluations, and implicitly assumed that if priming effects on judgements were observed, the attribute must have been activated. However, since priming effects depend ultimately on the enhanced accessibility of a primed attribute, it is important to assess whether different attributes were indeed accessible to consumers across the two priming conditions. In this regard, the attribute data from the elicitation task were analyzed to gain better insights into the processes underlying the priming effects.

Two measures were constructed from the free elicitation data to operationalize the accessibility of attributes: (1) frequency of mention and (2) order of mention (Yi 1990b). The frequency of mention measures were based on the assumption that accessible attributes would be more frequently mentioned by subjects (Ryan and Holbrook 1982). The order of mention measure was used, because it is likely that a cognitively accessible concept comes first to mind (Jaccard, Brinberg, and Ackerman 1986; Wyer and Srull 1981). This measure is also consistent with the availability heuristic (Tversky and Kahneman 1973).

The frequency of mention measure was first examined. For the attribute of versatility, the priming manipulation had significant effects on the frequency of mention; 55% of the subjects mentioned versatility in the versatility condition, whereas 25% mentioned versatility in the ease-of-use condition ($p < .03$). On the other hand, ease of use was more frequently mentioned in the ease-of-use condition than in the versatility condition (55% vs. 30%; $p < .06$). The order of mention measure was also compared across groups. For the attribute of versatility, the mean order of mention was 6.2 in the versatility condition, compared with 7.1 for the ease of use (Mann-Whitney $U = 142.5$; $p < .05$). The ease of use was also elicited earlier in the ease-of-use condition than in the versatility condition (6.0 vs. 7.7; Mann-Whitney $U = 140.5$; $p < .05$). The results indicate that the priming manipulation indeed affected the relative accessibility of product attributes.

Overall, the results of Experiment 1 supported the main hypothesis. Evaluations of the target brand were influenced by the ad context priming different product attributes. Step-down analyses also showed that contextual priming affected Ab directly, but affected PI indirectly (through Ab). Further, attribute level data indicated that primed attributes were indeed highly accessible to consumers as expected.

Limitations. We can note several potential limitations of the first experiment. One problem concerns the requirement after reading the target ad that subjects generate salient attributes of a personal computer that would come to mind if they consider purchasing a personal computer. This task might have been intrusive and have biased the subjects' processing of the product information in such a way as to support the predictions of the priming hypothesis. That is, the task might have drawn the subjects' attention to these attributes, emphasizing them in a way unlike what would naturally occur. It is thus possible that the effects on Ab and PI might have been just the result of the attribute eliciting task, rather than the priming manipulation. To the extent that such a possibility exists, the interpretation of the results is ambiguous.

Second, the dependent variables (Ab and PI) in this study are inherently unobservable and they might have to be treated as latent constructs in analyses. In this regard, it seems instructive to test the hypothesis via more powerful analyses with structural equation models (Bagozzi and Yi 1989). However, the small sample size in this experiment does not permit us to do this analysis.

EXPERIMENT 2

Method

A second experiment was conducted to correct for the aforementioned limitations of the first experiment. The second experiment differed from the first experiment in two ways. First, the experiment eliminated the attribute elicitation task, which could be intrusive so as to distort the subjects' processing of ad information. Second, the sample size was large enough for structural equation analysis; the subjects were 120 students recruited from several business courses. The stimuli and procedures were identical to those of the first experiment in all other aspects.

Results

A one-way MANOVA was run first via SPSS^X on the set of two dependent variables (Ab and PI), each of which was operationalized by the sum of three items. The Box's M test indicated that the homogeneity assumption was valid: Box's $M = 4.34$, $\chi^2 (3) = 4.26$, $p > .23$. MANOVA results showed that attribute priming had a significant effect on these measures of advertising effectiveness ($F (2, 117) = 4.91$, $p < .01$). For an understanding of priming effects on individual variables, separate ANOVAs were also run on each dependent variable. Contextual priming had significant effects on both Ab and PI ($F (1, 118) = 7.93$, $p < .01$; $F (1, 118) = 4.26$, $p < .04$, respectively). An examination of the cell means reveals that the effects were in the expected direction. Both Ab and PI were higher when the versatility attribute was primed, compared with the case when the ease of use was primed (4.56 vs 3.98; 3.82 vs 3.32, respectively).

Note that F values and mean differences for the priming effects are lower in Experiment 2 than in Experiment 1 (e.g., MANOVA $F = 7.92$ vs 4.91). This is consistent with our prediction that the task of attribute elicitation might be intrusive so as to increase priming effects. However, the priming effects were still significant in Experiment 2 which did not involve this task. These results suggest that the attribute elicitation task cannot fully explain the mean differences between the two groups, and that contextual priming itself has significant effects on brand evaluations.

Step-down analysis was then conducted via structural equation models (Bagozzi and Yi 1989). This analysis enables one to employ latent constructs indicated by several items as the dependent variables. The augmented moment matrix, rather than the correlation or covariance matrix, was used as the input data for analyses with LISREL. Figure 1 illustrates the specifications of the structural equation models for the step-down analyses.

The initial stage was a MANOVA test performed on the dependent variables, which were operationalized as latent constructs underlying the observed variables (see Figure 1A). For example, Ab was used as a factor underlying the three measured variables (Ab1, Ab2, and Ab3). Notice that the two experimental groups were represented by a 0, 1 dummy variable, which was expressed as an exogenous latent variable (ξ_1). Note also that a pseudovariable (i.e., "one") was shown as another exogenous variable (ξ_2) to capture the means or locations of dependent variables. Because the dummy variable was 0 for one group and 1 for the other group, the paths from the dummy variable to dependent variables corresponded to the differences in the means across the two groups. Specifically, γ_1 and γ_2 were the mean differences between the two

TABLE 1
FINDINGS FOR STEP-DOWN ANALYSIS VIA STRUCTURAL EQUATION MODELS IN EXPERIMENT 2

First Stage

Full Model	Model with $\gamma_1^* = \gamma_2^* = 0$
$\chi^2 (16) = 32.49, p \approx .009$	$\chi^2 (18) = 41.63, p \approx .001$
$\gamma_1^* = .55 \ (2.78)^a$	Hence:
$\gamma_2^* = .46 \ (2.00)$	$\chi^2_d (2) = 9.14, p < .02$

Second Stage

Full Model	Model with $\gamma_2^* = 0$
$\chi^2 (16) = 32.49, p \approx .009$	$\chi^2 (17) = 33.98, p \approx .008$
$\gamma_1^* = .55 \ (2.78)$	Hence:
$\gamma_2^* = .29 \ (1.23)$	$\chi^2_d (1) = 1.49, p > .10$

Third Stage

Model with $\gamma_2^* = 0$	Model with $\gamma_1^* = \gamma_2^* = 0$
$\chi^2 (17) = 33.98, p \approx .008$	$\chi^2 (18) = 41.63, p \approx .001$
$\gamma_1^* = .56 \ (2.82)$	Hence:
	$\chi^2_d (1) = 7.65, p < .01$

[a] t-values in parentheses.

---

groups in Ab and PI, respectively. The global significance of the mean differences were tested with the chi-square difference tests of the zero restrictions for these parameters.

The top portion of Table 1 reports the findings for the initial stage of the step-down analysis: the omnibus test with all variables included but no causal relation implied between them. The full model specified in Figure 1A, which allows for the differences in means, gave the following results: $\chi^2 (16) = 32.49, p \approx .009$. The mean differences parameters (i.e., γ_1 and γ_2) were 0.55 ($t = 2.78$) and 0.46 ($t = 2.00$). The restricted model with the zero constraints for the mean difference parameters gave the following results: $\chi^2 (18) = 41.63, p \approx .001$. The chi-square difference was 9.14 with 2 degrees of freedom, which was significant at the .02 level. These findings suggested that the means of dependent variables were different across groups.

The next two steps consisted of testing the mean differences while controlling for the theoretical relation between dependent variables (see Figure 1B). In Step Two, the mean difference in PI was tested after considering the causal order between Ab and PI. In other words, γ_2 in Step Two could be interpreted as the mean difference in PI due to the priming manipulation when the effect of Ab had been controlled for. The chi-square difference test indicated that the mean difference in PI was not significant: $\chi^2_d (1) = 1.49, p > .10$. In the final step, the mean difference in Ab was tested for statistical significance. The chi-square difference regarding this mean difference was significant: $\chi^2_d (1) = 7.65, p < .01$.

When the causal relation among the dependent variables was taken into account, one of the effects that had been significant in univariate ANOVAs became insignificant. Specifically, the effect of attribute priming on PI became insignificant in the step-down analyses. These results suggest again that the variation in PI was due to the dependence of PI on Ab, rather than due to the direct influence of priming itself. In sum, these results replicate the findings of Experiment 1; the contextual priming of product attributes affected Ab directly, but influenced PI indirectly through Ab.

DISCUSSION

It is found that priming a particular attribute increases the likelihood that this attribute will be used to interpret product information in an ad, and thus influences the evaluation of the advertised brand. The activation of the attribute guided a person to select among possible interpretations of an ambiguous description (i.e., the number of features) of the target brand. When subjects were reading the prime ad on either of the two attributes (versatility or ease of use), this attribute should have been activated and become highly accessible. As a consequence, subjects should have had the "top of

FIGURE 1
STRUCTURAL EQUATION MODELS FOR STEP-DOWN ANALYSIS

A. Covariance between dependent variables unordered

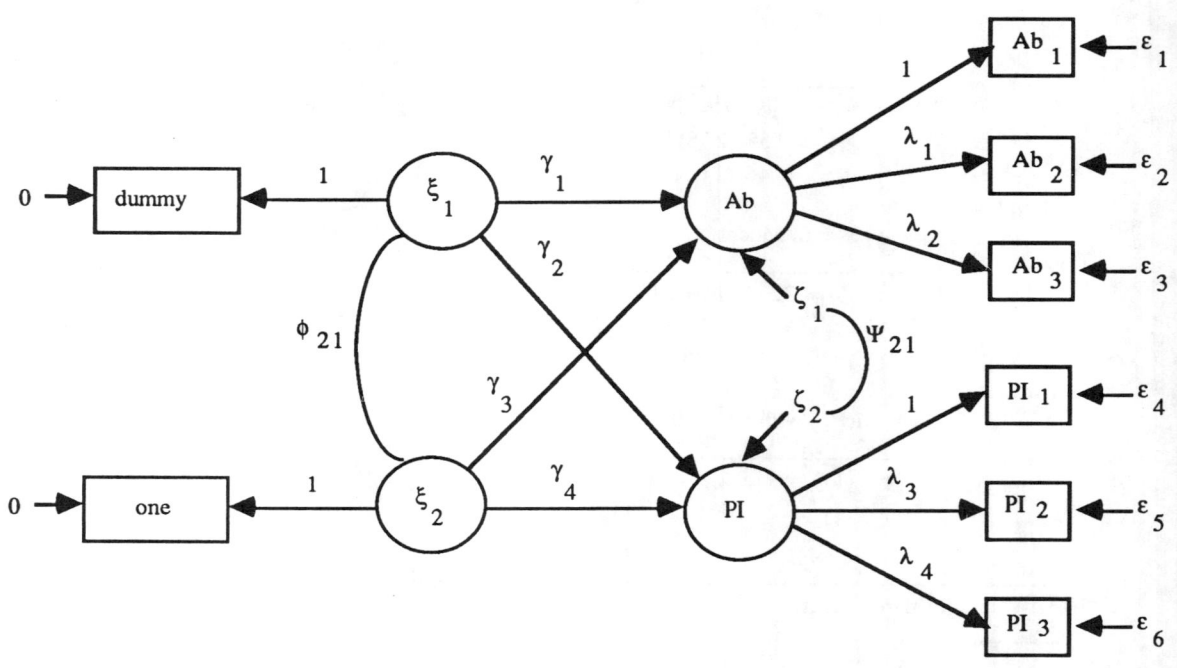

B. Covariance between dependent variables as a causal path

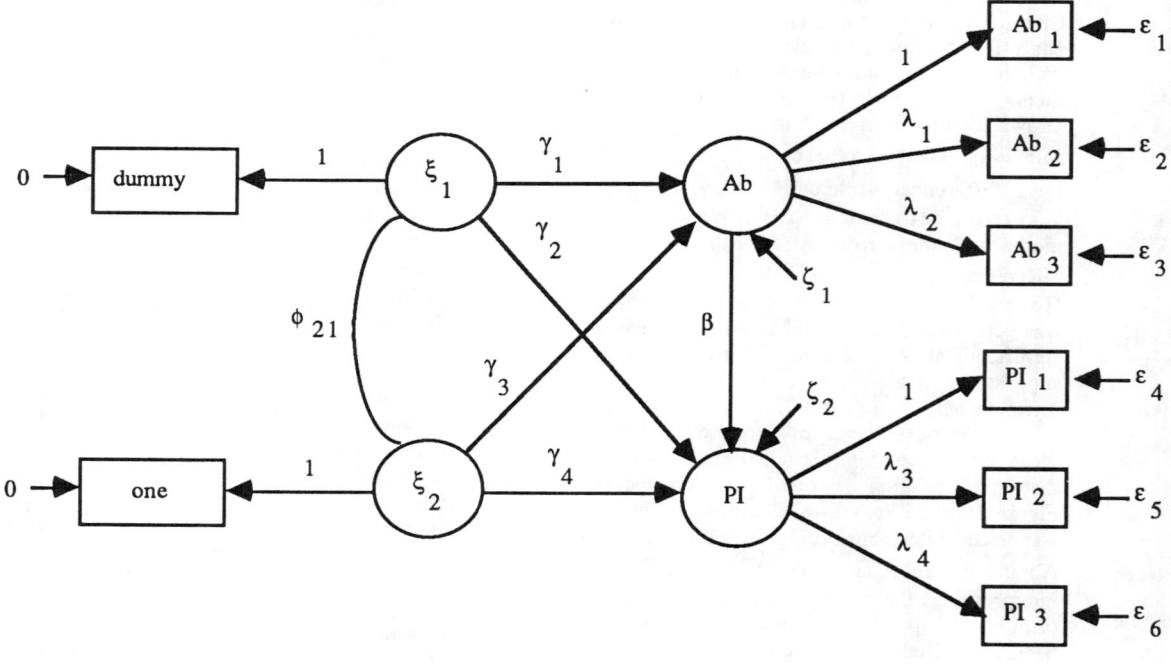

mind" awareness of the attribute when they subsequently read the target ad. That attribute was therefore highly likely to be used in processing product information in the ad. That is, the interpretation given depended on which attribute was most accessible when ambiguous information was received.

These results support research in social cognition showing that construct accessibility can increase temporarily from recent activation and affect people's judgment of an object (Wyer and Srull 1981). According to Wyer and Srull's "storage bin" model, a recently activated concept is placed on the top of a layered bin, and the construct at the top is most likely to be used in interpreting new incoming information. The elicitation data in Experiment 1 indicate that the attributes primed by the preceding context were indeed accessible for use in interpreting ad information. The results are also in line with the research on framing effects in consumer decision making (e.g., Bettman and Sujan 1987); priming different decision criteria (i.e., attributes) influences how a product is evaluated.

This research extends existing studies in several aspects. First, this study incorporates research on priming in investigating the effects of contextual materials preceding the ad (Herr 1989; Meyers-Levy 1989). This study has found that contextual factors may influence judgments of the advertised product by altering the way how information is perceived. The same product features in an ad can be evaluated in different ways, depending on the adjacent materials. This finding is consistent with the Gestalt psychology, decision making, and perception stressing that the context in which a stimulus appears affects the interpretation of that stimulus (e.g., Helson 1964; Payne 1982).

Second, this study links research on information accessibility and ad context effects within a single framework. On the one hand, researchers have found that information accessibility affects brand choice and attitudinal judgments (e.g., Biehal and Charkravarti 1983; Kisielius and Sternthal 1986). On the other hand, many studies have shown that ad contexts affect advertising effectiveness (e.g., Chook 1985; Soldow and Principe 1981). We found that consumers render evaluatively different judgments of the same product, depending on which attribute is activated by contextual factors. The present research suggests that the two streams of research can be integrated fruitfully.

This study also has an interesting implication for research on persuasion. The findings suggest an indirect persuasive attempt in which one provides seemingly neutral information (e.g., weight of a bag) and primes consumers to encode the information in terms of the target benefit (e.g., ease of handling). Such indirect approaches to persuasion are likely to offer several advantages over traditional techniques claiming the target benefit directly. For example, indirect persuasion has been found to generate less negative cognitive responses and to be more stable over time, compared with direct persuasion (Yi 1990a, 1990c).

Finally, this study provides useful insights into the process of priming effects by employing step-down analyses with structural equation models. Such analyses provide better understanding of priming effects by incorporating the relationships among dependent variables and correcting for measurement error (Bagozzi and Yi 1989). In contrast, existing research either used a single dependent variable or relied on MANOVA or separate ANOVAs of observed variables (e.g., Soldow and Principe 1981). For example, the univariate test for PI in the present study may have been interpreted as evidence for the direct link from priming to PI. However, step-down analyses ruled out this possibility by indicating that the priming effect on PI does not hold unless Ab is considered as a mediating variable.

The present research is also relevant to practitioners of advertising. First, an ad context can either inhibit or facilitate the effects of a particular ad on brand evaluations. The specific attributes (e.g., ease of use or versatility) relevant to evaluating an advertised product may vary in salience as a function of its context, and these variations may influence the favorability of brand evaluation. By showing that an ad context is not just a benign background but can influence the effectiveness of an ad, this study expands the scope of both strategic and tactical approaches to persuasion.

Also, the present study helps advertisers to understand the unintended effects of the ad context. If the ad context primes negative interpretations of the product, perceptions of the advertised product will be negatively affected. One should avoid placing the ad in such an environment. Alternatively, one should proactively create an advertising environment that can enhance the effect of the target ad. Finally, this study provides a new perspective into the effects of competitive advertising (cf. Burke and Srull 1988). The study suggests the possibility that ads for competing brands might be beneficial if competing brands can prime certain product attributes which are relevant to interpreting information about the target brand.

Several limitations of the present study are in order. First, this study used somewhat strong priming manipulations in a lab experiment, and one might argue that priming is unlikely to occur in the actual advertising context. However, advertisements for products that use product features or benefits as a basis for positioning (e.g., Budget Rent-A-Car) may prime certain attributes (e.g., economy) to consumers. Also, magazine articles (e.g., crime story) may make certain attributes (e.g., safety) salient to consumers. One should assess the extent to which the general ad context primes product attributes and examine whether the findings are generalizable.

It should also be noted that measurement procedures for attribute accessibility have been intrusive. A comparison of the results from Experiments 1 and 2 provides some evidence for the biasing effects of the attribute elicitation task on brand evaluations. One needs to develop subtler ways to assess attribute accessibility, which would not bias subjects' processing of ad information. This study focused on cognitive priming effects of the ad context, but it should be mentioned that the ad context can also have affective priming effects (Erdley and D'Agostino 1988). For example, a magazine article or a TV program may evoke certain affective/feeling states temporarily, such as when it contains pleasant or unpleasant stories. Indeed, Yi (1990b) shows that an ad context can prime affective reactions among ad recipients and influence their attitude toward the ad, which in turn affects brand evaluations.

We have examined competitive ads as a contextual priming cue that affects the accessibility of product attributes in brand evaluations. Future research can focus on other factors (e.g., point-of-purchase stimuli or program contexts) that may prime certain attributes to consumers in processing product information. Future research should also investigate variables that moderate the contextual priming effects such as involvement and knowledge.

REFERENCES

Bagozzi, Richard P. and Youjae Yi (1989), "On the Use of Structural Equation Models in Experimental Designs," *Journal of Marketing Research*, 26 (August), 271-284.

Bettman, James R. and Mita Sujan (1987), "Effects of Framing on Evaluation of Comparable and Noncomparable Alternatives by Expert and Novice Consumers," *Journal of Consumer Research*, 14 (September), 141-154.

Biehal, Gabriel and Dipankar Chakravarti (1983), "Information Accessibility as a Moderator of Consumer Choice," *Journal of Consumer Research*, 10 (June), 1-14.

Bray, James H. and Scott E. Maxwell (1982), *Multivariate Analysis of Variance*, Beverly Hills, CA: Sage.

Burke, Raymond R. and Thomas K. Srull (1988), "Competitive Interference and Consumer Memory for Advertising," *Journal of Consumer Research*, 15 (June), 55-68.

Chook, Paul H. (1985), "A Continuing Study of Magazine Environment, Frequency, and Advertising Performance," *Journal of Advertising Research*, 25 (4), 23-33.

Erdley, Cynthia A. and Paul D'Agostino (1988), "Cognitive and Affective Components of Automatic Priming Effects," *Journal of Personal and Social Psychology*, 54 (5), 741-747.

Gardner, Meryl Paula (1983), "Advertising Effects on Attributes Recalled and Criteria Used for Brand Evaluations," *Journal of Consumer Research*, 10 (December), 310-318.

Helson, Harry (1964), *Adaptation-Level Theory*, New York: Harper and Row.

Herr, Paul M. (1989), "Priming Price: Prior Knowledge and Context Effects," *Journal of Consumer Research*, 16 (June), 67-75.

Higgins, E. Tory, John A. Bargh, and Wendy Lombardi (1985), "Nature of Priming Effects on Categorization," *Journal of Experimental Psychology: Learning, Memory, and Cognition*, 11 (January), 59-69.

——— and Gillian King (1981), "Accessibility of Social Constructs: Information Processing Consequences of Individual and Contextual Variability," in *Personality, Cognition, and Social Interaction*, eds. Nancy Cantor and John Kihlstrom, Hillside, NJ: Erlbaum, 69-122.

Jaccard, James, David Brinberg, and Lee Ackerman (1986), "Assessing Attribute Importance: A Comparison of Six Methods." *Journal of Consumer Research*, 12 (March), 463-468.

Kisielius, Jolita and Brian Sternthal (1986), "Examining the Vividness Controversy: An Availability-Valence Interpretation," *Journal of Consumer Research*, 12 (March), 418-431.

MacKenzie, Scott B., Richard J. Lutz, and George E. Belch (1986), "The Role of Attitude Toward the Ad as a Mediator of Advertising Effectiveness: A Test of Competing Explanations," *Journal of Marketing Research*, 23 (May), 130-143.

Meyers-Levy, Joan (1989), "Priming Effects on Product Judgments: A Hemispheric Interpretation," *Journal of Consumer Research*, 16 (June), 76-86.

Payne, John W. (1982), "Contingent Decision Behavior," *Psychological Bulletin*, 92 (2), 382-402.

Roy, J. (1958), "Step Down Procedure in Multivariate Analysis," *Annals of Mathematical Statistics*, 29 (December), 1177-1187.

Ryan, Michael J. and Morris B. Holbrook (1982), "Importance, Elicitation Order, and Expectancy x Value," *Journal of Business Research*, 10 (September), 309-317.

Shavitt, Sharon and Russell H. Fazio (1990), "Effects of Attribute Salience on the Consistency of Product Evaluations and Purchase Predictions," in *Advances in Consumer Research*, Vol. 17, eds. Marvin E. Goldberg, Gerald Gorn, and Richard W. Pollay, Provo, UT: Association for Consumer Research, 91-97.

Soldow, Gary F. and Victor Principe (1981), "Response to Commercials as a Function of Program Context," *Journal of Advertising Research*, 21 (2), 59-65.

Srull, Thomas K. and Robert S. Wyer (1980), "Category Accessibility and Social Perception: Some Implications for the Study of Person Memory and Interpersonal Judgments," *Journal of Personality and Social Psychology*, 38 (June), 841-856.

Tversky, Amos and Daniel Kahneman (1973), "Availability: A Heuristic for Judging Frequency and Probability," *Cognitive Psychology*, 5 (September), 207-232.

Wyer, Robert S. and Thomas K. Srull (1981), "Category Accessibility: Some Theoretical and Empirical Issues Concerning the Processing of Social Stimulus Information," in *Social Cognition: The Ontario Symposium*, eds. E. Tory Higgins, C. P. Herman, and M. P. Zanna, Hillsdale, N.J.: Erlbaum, 161-197.

⎯⎯⎯ (1986), "Human Cognition in Its Social Context," *Psychological Review*, 93 (July), 322-359.

Yi, Youjae (1990a), "The Indirect Effects of Advertisements Designed to Change Product Attribute Beliefs," *Psychology and Marketing*, 7 (Spring), 47-63.

⎯⎯⎯ (1990b), "Cognitive and Affective Priming Effects of the Context for Print Advertisements," *Journal of Advertising*, 19 (2), 40-48.

⎯⎯⎯ (1990c), "Direct and Indirect Approaches to Advertising Persuasion: Which is More Effective?" *Journal of Business Research*, 20 (June), 279-291.

⎯⎯⎯ (1990d), "The Effects of Contextual Priming in Print Advertisements," *Journal of Consumer Research*, 17 (September), 215-222.

A Brief History of the Mall
Richard A. Feinberg, Purdue University
Jennifer Meoli, Indiana University of Pennsylvania

America has been "Malled." The "air-conditioned, sanitized, standardized" shopping malls "have become the new Main Streets of America" (Consumer Reports, 1986). Along with power mowers, "the pill," antibiotics, smoke detectors, transistors, and personal computers, the shopping mall was selected as one of the top 50 wonders that has revolutionized the lives of consumers (Consumer Reports, 1986). Because alternative retail settings may differ in important economic, social, and psychological characteristics, the shopping mall may exert a significant influence on individual and collective consumer behavior.

Why then has there been so little attention to the mall by the consumer research community, either as an important setting for consumer behavior or a social and consumer phenomenon in and of itself? While we can find Arnold Schwarzenegger and Chuck Norris defending malls against evil doers and Michael J. Fox taking off back to the future from the mall in recent movies, we would be hard pressed to find a scholarly treatment in our best journals.

History of Shopping Centers

Shopping malls didn't just happen. They are not the result of wise planners deciding that suburban people, having no social life and stimulation, needed a place to go (Bombeck, 1985). The mall was originally conceived of as a community center where people would converge for shopping, cultural activity, and social interaction (Gruen & Smith, 1960). It is safe to say that the mall has achieved and surpassed those early expectations. In today's consumer culture the mall is the center of the universe.

According to the history of shopping centers provided by Consumer Reports (1986, for other histories of the shopping center see Jacobs, 1985; Kowinski, 1985) shopping centers had their birth in the 1920's in California where supermarkets would anchor and serve as a magnet for a strip of smaller stores. According to Samuel Feinberg (1960) shopping centers got their start a bit earlier, in 1907, in a Baltimore neighborhood where a group of stores established off-street parking. In 1922 The Country Club Plaza in suburban Kansas City, a group of stores only accessible by car, was built. In 1931 the Highland Park Shopping Village in Dallas became the first group of stores that had its own parking lot with the stores facing away from the access road. The first enclosed mall was developed in a suburb of Minneapolis in 1956. Designed to get the shopper out of the harsh weather, it introduced the world to shopping complexes as worlds unto themselves--free from bad weather, life, crime, dirt and troubles. It is somehow fitting that the largest mall in the United States, called "The Mall of America," is now nearing completion outside Minneapolis.

Whatever and wherever its start, the phenomenal growth and development of shopping centers naturally followed the migration of population out from the cities and paralleled the growth of the use of the automobile. By 1960 there were 4500 malls accounting for 14% of retail sales. By 1975 there were 16,400 shopping centers accounting for 33% of retail sales. In 1987, there were 30,000 malls accounting for over 50% of all retail dollars spent (about 676 billion dollars, 8% of the labor force, and 13% of our gross national product--Keinfield, 1986; Turchiana, 1990).

Malls are now the retail, social and community centers of their communities. Indeed, shopping malls are the center pieces for rejuvenation of urban centers (e.g., City Center - Indianapolis, Faneuil Hall - Boston, South Street Seaport - New York City, Harbour Place - Baltimore). Some malls are so large that they are communities. Chicago's Water Tower place has hotels, restaurants, offices, stores, restaurants, and residential units. The West Edmonton Mall in Canada, The largest mall in the world, has over 800 stores, ice skating, 24 movie screens.

Despite unsupported forecasts that the country is over-malled (e.g., Turchiana, 1990) the increasing dominance of malls seems inevitable (Ballard, 1981; Burstiner, 1986). Many of these malls will be smaller strip centers ("Overbuilding: A real...," 1987), but there are plans for mega-malls modeled after the Edmonton Mall (Martin, 1987).

The competitive environment that a mall faces today is considerably different from that faced in their early days when their primary competition was a downtown business district. Many of the best "locations" are gone so that a mall's primary competition is now likely to be another mall. Shopping malls appear to be in a mature phase of the retail life cycle where market shares and sales may be leveling off (Sternlieb & Hughs, 1981). The challenges that face developers within this context will have to become more consumer oriented in the sense that more attention will need to be paid to the why, when, what, who, where, and how's of the consumer when it comes to all aspects of "the shopping mall" (for a complete review of published articles on shopping centers before 1982 see Dawson, 1982).

Research on Shopping Malls

Research on mall issues can be characterized as mainly centering on models of mall patronage/choice (e.g., Cox & Cooke, 1970; Howell & Rogers, 1981). These models have been guided by retail gravitational approaches. These approaches assume that a mall will be differentially attractive as a function of their utility. Research has identified a variety of factors that could define the utility of a mall: distance traveled - Bucklin, 1971;

travel time - Brunner & Mason, 1968; accessibility - Bucklin & Gautschi, 1983; size of mall -Bucklin, 1967; number of brands carried - Crask, 1979; number of stores - Weisbrod, Parcells, & Kern, 1984. The inability of these various studies to adequately account for mall patronage has led to studies focusing on more "subjective" types of variables such as social factors (Feinberg, Meoli, & Sheffler, 1989) and mall image and mall image variables (e.g., Gentry & Burns, 1977-1978; Nevin & Houston, 1980). Unfortunately these too have not led to overwhelming success and acceptance.

The enviable success and impact of the shopping mall may have something to do with the potential of shopping malls to enhance community life. There is no conflict between shopping malls, profits, and people. The basis for a shopping mall is to make it an "indispensable servant of the community" (Rouse, 1962). Right now consumer research seems to be on the sidelines of this phenomena. However, like the lead pack dog, since the mall is at its basics a consumer phenomenon, consumer researchers should be making the dust, not eating it.

REFERENCES

Ballard, C. (1981), "Trends in Retail Development: 1980's and Beyond," In George Sternlieb and James Hughes (Eds), *Shopping Centers: USA*, New Jersey: State University of New Jersey, Center For Urban Policy Research.

Bombeck, E (1985), "Lost Forever In A Shopping Mall," *The Daily News*, Sunday- December 22, p. 16.

Brunner, J., and Mason, J. (1968), "The Influence Of Driving Time Upon Shopping Center Performance," *Journal of Marketing, 32*, 57-61.

Bucklin, L. (1967), "The Concept In Mass In Intraurban Shopping," *Journal of Marketing, 32*, 32-36.

Bucklin, L. (1971), "Retail Gravity Models and Consumer Choice: A Theoretical and Empirical Critique," *Economic Geography , 47*, 489-497.

Bucklin, L. and Gautschi, D. (1983), "The Importance Of Travel Mode Factors in the Patronage of Retail Centers," In William Darden and Robert Lusch (Eds), *Patronage and Retail Management*, New York: Elsevier Science Publishing Company.

Burstiner, I. (1986), "Retailing For the Next Twenty Years: Looking Forward In Time," *Basic Retailing* , Il: Irwin Publishing, 648-671.

Consumer Reports (1986), *I'll Buy that: 50 small wonders and big deals that revolutionized the lives of consumers*, New York: Consumers Union of the United States

Cox, W., and Cooke,E. (1970), "Other Dimensions Involved In Shopping Centyer Preference," *Journal of Marketing, 34*, 12-17.

Crask, M. (1979), "A Simulation Model of Patronage Behavior Within Shopping Centers," *Decision Sciences, 10*, 1-15.

Dawson, J. (1982), *Shopping Centers: A Bilbliography* , Il: Council of Planning Librarians.

Feinberg, R., Meoli, J., & Sheffler, B (1989), "There's Something Social Happening At The Mall," *Journal of Business and Psychology, 4* , 44-63.

Feinberg, S (1960), *What Makes Shopping Malls Tick* , New York: Fairchild Publications.

Gentry, J., and Burns, A. (1977-1978), "How Important Are Evaluative Criteria In Shopping Center Patronage," *Journal of Retailing, 53*, 73-86.

Gruen, V., and Smith, L. (1960), *Shopping Towns, U.S.A.: The Planning of Shopping Centers.* New York: Van Nostrand Reinhold.

Howell, R., and Rogers, J. (1981), "Research Into Shopping Mall Choice Behavior,", In K. Monroe (Ed.), *Advances In Consumer Research, 8*, MI: Association for Consumer Research, 671-676.

Jacobs, J. (1986), *The Mall: An Attempted Escape From Everyday Life*, IL: Waveland Press.

Keinfeld, N. (1986), "Why Everyone Goes To The Mall," *The New York Times*, December 21, Sec 3, F1, F33.

Kowinski, W (1985), *The Malling Of America: An Inside Look At The Great Consumer Paradise*, New York: W. Morrow.

Martin, D. (1987), "Behemoth On The Prairie: In Edmonton The World's Largest Mall Mixes Shopping And Show Business," *The New York Times*, January 4, 19-20, 29.

Nevin, J., and Houston, M. (1980), "Image As A Component Of Attraction to Intrurban Shopping Areas," *Journal of Retailing, 56*, 77-93.

"Overbuilding: A Real or Imagined Issue" (1987), *Chain Store Age Executive, 63*, 48-50.

Rouse, J. (1962), "Must Shopping Centers Be Inhuman," *Architectural Forum, 116*, 105-119.

Sternlieb, G., and Hughs, J. (1981), *Shopping Centers: USA*, New Jersey: State University of New Jersey, Center For Urban Policy Research.

Turchiana, F. (1990), "The Unmalling of America," *American Demographics*, April, 36-39.

Weisbrod, G., Parcells, R., and Kern, C. (1984), "A Disaggregate Model For Predicting Shopping Area Market Attraction," *Journal of Retailing, 60*, 65-83.

Retail Shopping Mall Semiotics and Hedonic Consumption
Frederick W. Langrehr, Valparaiso University

The purchase of goods may be incidental to the experience of shopping. People buy so they can shop, NOT shop so they can buy. Thus consumers shop not only for goods and services or specific information but for experiential and emotional reasons (Hirschman and Holbrook 1982).

Hirschman and Holbrook (1982:92) state, "Hedonic consumption designates those facets of consumer behavior that relate to the multi-sensory, fantasy and emotive aspects of one's experience with products." The activity of shopping is part of the experience of the product. But "retail mall" could replace "product" and hedonic consumption can be directly linked with the mall shopping experience in and of itself.

Mall environments are part of a shopper's hedonic consumption activity. Retailers appeal to the multiple senses of sight, sound, scent, tactile and in the case of food, taste. Fantasies can be played out in a mall as a shopper walks in the mall, sits in a mall atrium or is "waited on" by a responsive retail sales associate (Campbell 1987).

Some writers have made conceptual links between shopping malls, semiotic messages and consumer emotions, fantasy and acting (Kowinski 1985, Zepp 1986). Because the mall is enclosed it is protected from the outside world and controlled inside. The mall is thus a theatre where consumers can create their own world and fantasize their parts in a play. Retailers provide the staging, props, lighting, and mannequins (Kowinski 1985).

Mall semiotics have also been conceptualized as creating sacred space again because the mall is separated from the outside world. A mall is safe, habitable, and serves as a substitute from the medieval church. Zepp (1986) continues this analogy when he suggests that the church floor plan in the shape of a cross is reflected in the mall's cross layout. The atmospherics of space, height, and light also play a role in continuing this comparison.

Surprisingly little research has been done on consumer reactions to retail environmental variables. There has been a little research on store atmospheres but no reported research in mall settings. The above mentioned observations of mall interiors are suppositions not supported by consumer research.

The purpose of this review is to answer four questions. First, are visual presentations of retail interiors important in forming retail image? Next, how do retail environments work to influence consumer affective evaluations and buying decisions? Then, how do specific environmental variables such as crowding, color, sounds, influence shopper images and behavior? Finally, because of the relative paucity of retail semiotic analysis, what research is needed in the fields of retail environment, semiotics and consumer response?

IMPORTANCE OF VISUAL IMAGES

It appears that depictions of a retail interior have a greater impact on consumer perception than does written description. When respondents were shown combinations of favorable/unfavorable pictures (slides of restaurant interiors) along with favorable/unfavorable written descriptions, visuals had a more lasting impact. The favorable pictures/unfavorable written combination led to an improving retail image after the passage of time. By contrast, the image of the unfavorable pictures/favorable written description deteriorated over time (Gardner and Houston 1986).

The impact of visual description was also shown in a pricing study conducted by Buyukkurt (1986). Respondents were given two grocery store descriptions. One store, family owned, had service departments such as a deli and in-store bakery. It had few weekly specials, but customers rarely waited in line, and the store bagged and carried out the shoppers' purchases. The other supermarket was part of a large chain operation, had no service departments, and advertised weekly specials. Shoppers had to wait in line and bag their own groceries. The interior of the first store was described as elegant, the second as spartan. These two descriptions were part of a pricing experiment, and even when the researchers set the prices in the two stores equal, the respondents thought the first store still had the higher prices. The researcher concluded that the services offered and the store interiors made a price statement; and even if the store's actual prices were the same, shoppers would still believe the store that portrayed a service image would have the higher prices.

But we must be careful in overplaying the impact of retail atmospherics. In a study conducted in England, Downs (1970) found store service features were more important that shopping center design factors in explaining the respondent's image of a shopping center. Specifically, he explained 38 percent of the variance in retail image was due to store factors such as service quality, price, shopping hours, selection, and quality. On the other hand, only 16 percent of the variance in the image of the shopping center was explained by its structural features such as design, internal pedestrian movement, visual appearance, and traffic conditions. However, Downs' main thrust was a measurement of shoppers' cognitive, not their affective or behavioral, responses.

Thus we know that depictions may influence retail image, but do the environments work to influence behavior?

THEORY OF ENVIRONMENTAL IMPACTS

The link between the semiotic variables and behavior may be the shopper's emotional reaction to retail environments. This emotional reaction may be influenced by the individual's personality, the amount of stimulus screening, and both shopper's mood and mood inducing capabilities of the shopping experience.

Belk (1975) suggested that situational variables were as important as individual consumer characteristics in explaining consumer behavior. He suggested that physical and social surroundings such as location, decor, noise, aromas, lighting intensity, physical layout, and other persons present may affect a consumer's purchasing behavior.

Kotler (1973), author of one of the first articles appearing in the retail literature on environmental impacts of store interiors, suggests that a store's atmosphere creates a retail image in the shopper's mind. If the image is positive, it will incline the consumer to shop in the store. He gave a number of anecdotal examples of the type of atmospheres specific types of retailers had created. A few years later, Markin et al. (1976) suggested in a general way how retail environments could influence shopper behaviors. Neither of these reports, however, related how various physical features could serve as effective stimuli for a shopper.

Russell and Mehrabian (1976) believe that emotional states resulting from exposure to retail atmospherics should be analyzed. Instead of only describing environmental factors, researchers should focus on the following emotional states of retail shoppers: pleasure-displeasure, degree of arousal (feelings of alertness and excitement), and dominance-submission. Specifically, environments that created heightened arousal and pleasure and stimulated mild feelings of dominance would lead to maximum buying (Mehrabian 1976).

When this theory was tested in a quasi-field setting, two of the three dimensions did have a positive effect on predispositions to buy. Store environments that induced pleasure or good feelings did lead to potentially greater impulsive shopping behavior. Also, increased levels of arousal, feelings of alertness and excitement, led to a greater desire to linger in a store and interact with store personnel. The dominance dimension did not have an impact on interest in the store or buying from that store (Donovan and Rossiter 1982). Other researchers found that actual shopping behavior was affected by mood. When using the PAD scale to measure mood Sherman and Smith (1986) found in a survey of shoppers that a more positive mood resulted in purchasing more items and spending more money in a store. However, the foregoing researchers did not enumerate the store characteristics that led to these positive emotional feelings. The possible negative behaviors that arise from this arousal also need to be considered. High arousal may lead to impulsive and excessive consumption (O'Guinn and Faber 1986, Rook 1987).

Personality, however, may be an intervening variable in the emotional response. High stimulus need, high sensation seekers are more environmentally sensitive than low sensation seekers. Shopping behavior, number of stores shopped, duration of shopping trip, and frequency of shopping trips are also related to these personality variables (Grossbart et al. 1975). The researchers point out that these findings were based on macro-environments--shopping centers; however, they believed they may also be relevant for micro-environments--stores as well.

Another personality variable may be the level of stimulus screening. The more people screen out the environment, the lower their environmental load and arousal level. People who do little screening out of stimuli will have longer lasting arousal reactions to unusual or different environments. People who are more active screeners will have lower arousal levels and shorter arousal periods. Because nonscreeners have such strong reactions to their environment, they are much more likely to seek pleasing high arousal environments and avoid displeasing surroundings. Screeners will be more ambivalent, since the stimuli have a lesser impact, and they can more easily screen out unpleasant stimuli (Mehrabian 1976).

Moods and emotional states also govern how consumers react to store environments. Gardner (1985) suggests that store atmospherics and salespeople may affect consumers' moods, and the mood states may then influence purchase behavior. However, she also believes that the interaction is two-way. Consumers' moods could also influence how they perceived a given environment. Thus the impact was not only environment --> mood, but also mood --> environment. Gardner (1985) further posits that shoppers probably select stores that induce positive moods and avoid those that create negative ones. She does not indicate the types of environments or the specific environmental features that lead to positive moods.

Thus we know that numerous authors believe that retail semiotics do lead to a response on the part of shoppers. Some focused on situational or physical variables, while others looked at the emotions stimulated by the physical setting. Personality and stimulus need will influence the type and intensity of emotional response. Finally, the environment induces an emotion or mood but a consumer's mood at the time of exposure to retail atmosphere will also influence how these messages are interpreted and what the resulting responses are. Therefore, shoppers' affective and connotative responses may vary in the same retail environment, depending on the consumer's mood upon entering the store.

We now need to look at how specific environmental features will influence shoppers' affective and behavioral responses.

INTERIOR PHYSICAL FEATURES' INFLUENCE ON CONSUMERS

How do specific interior features relate to consumer affective and behavioral responses? Unfortunately, little research has been conducted in retail settings on this question. Thus this section contains the findings of studies undertaken in both retail and nonretail settings. The physical features discussed are crowding, color, music and noise, temperature and miscellaneous factors.

BEHAVIORAL IMPACTS OF STORE INTERIORS

Crowding - Retail Settings

A crowded, cluttered environment fosters a low price image. But crowding does have negative connotations. In crowded stores, respondents said they
- spent less time shopping in the store,
- did less impulsive shopping,
- purchased fewer items per trip (lower priority needs are deleted),
- were less likely to socialize or seek contact with store personnel,
- were less receptive to new store layouts (too hard to find things in the crowd or clutter),
- were more nervous, tense and confused and thus less confident about their purchases.

These findings were especially true for time-constrained shoppers (Harrell and Hunt 1976). Task-oriented shoppers, ones who make fewer unplanned purchases and spend less time per shopping trip, may also be more sensitive to crowded conditions (Eroglu and Harrell 1986).

Crowding - Other Environments

The impact of crowding on individuals was the most popular by far of all interior environmental topics. Indeed, an entire issue of *Environment Behavior* (1975) was devoted to this topic. Crowding had universally negative impacts on individuals. In crowded conditions, people performed complex tasks more poorly and became more frustrated (Evans 1979). Crowded subjects experienced higher levels of hostility and increased anxiety (Zeedyk and Smith 1983). Finally, other researchers found greater levels of arousal (a negative reaction in this study) and greater levels of tension. Also, people did not become accustomed to crowded conditions (Epstein et al. 1981). But reactions to crowding are not the same for all people. They are partially influenced by national origin. Gillis et al. (1986) found that Asians were more tolerant of crowding than Southern Europeans and that the British were the least tolerant of all three groups.

Color - Retail Setting

Warm colors, red and yellow, will attract people to a store, while cool colors (blue and green) encourage more contemplation and less avoidance of the environment. Interestingly, the two types of colors were not related to price or quality perceptions of the store (Bellizzi et al. 1983).

Music - Retail Settings

People will spend more time and more money in a store if slow-tempo versus fast-tempo music is played in the store. Respondents did not notice a difference in the tempo of the music. In a similar study in a restaurant, the slow tempo manipulation also yielded higher total expenditures (Milliman 1986, 1982).

Noise - Other Settings

Noise, like crowding, is also detrimental to human performance. People who lived in a high aircraft noise environment reported more errors in daily tasks than those who did not live in these noisy conditions (Smith and Stansfeld 1986). Bronzaft and McCarthy (1975) also found that students in a room near elevated train tracks had a lower level of reading performance than students in rooms on the quiet side of the same building. Noise also had a negative impact on helping behavior, people being less helpful in noisy environments (Page 1977). For retail settings, the implication is that shoppers will avoid or quickly leave a noisy environment.

Temperature - Other Settings

Schneider and his colleagues (1980) did not find any decrease in helping behavior as the temperature changed. Subjects in hot or cold environments were as likely to give assistance as subjects in a comfortable room. However, in an earlier study Griffith (1970) found that subjects who were hot reacted less positively to other people than subjects who were comfortable. The implication seems to be consumers would avoid shopping environments that had temperature outside of their comfort range. Of course this range might vary according to person, season, setting, and shopping purpose.

Signing - Retail Settings

The presence and type of sign may or may not influence the level of sales. Namely, a benefit sign (a sign that gave some information about the product) would lead to higher sales for both regularly and sale priced merchandise (McKinnon et al. 1981). The impact on the consumers' overall perception of the store was not measured. Perhaps as signs are added to the store environment, the store may look more cluttered and communicate a more "down" market image.

Other research on the use of signs found that nutritional signing in the produce department had little, if any, effect on produce sales. The researchers thought that their findings may have been an artifact of the size (too small) and placement (out of line of sight of the produce) of the signs (Achabal et al. 1987). But other research on nutritional signing is equivocal (Russo et al. 1986). Signs that presented positive benefits of certain nutrients did not have an effect on sales of more nutritional products. But in another experiment where negative nutritional information was emphasized (sugar content of cereals) there was a dramatic change in sales to lower sugar content cereals. But this change in sales was within the product category and did not lead to higher overall sales for the store. An important finding of both studies was that even if consumers did not change their purchasing patterns the signs still increased customer good will towards the supermarket (Achabal et al. 1987, Russo et al. 1986).

The format information presented in a store has an impact on sales (Russo 1977). Shoppers were much more likely to shift to cheaper store brands when unit prices in a product class were presented in a list versus only displayed on individual shelf tags. This could potentially result in a lower sales volume, albeit higher profit margin since store brands are cheaper to the consumer but have a higher profit margin for the retailer. But Russo thought that, over all, the retailer would lose money if the shopper switched to lower unit priced merchandise. He believed, however, that shoppers would have an improved image of the supermarket that provided the easiest to use unit price information. This possible change in image was not measured in his study.

In summary, even if signs do not change purchase behavior, if the signs provide information consumers think is beneficial, shoppers will have an improved image of the store.

Other Factors

Smells may convey a certain image. Thus perfume or odors of prepared food may have an impact on shoppers. Tactile sensation of handling merchandise may also create an emotional response. Unfortunately, these two factors were only hypothesized on the basis of unstructured interviews; no testing of their relationships was undertaken (Tauber 1972).

The number of shelf facings may or may not influence the level of sales of a brand item; the results of two studies were mixed. One study found that in increasing the shelf facings of four products, only one product had an increase in sales (Cox 1964). Another study found a sales increase for three of four products (Kotzan and Evanson 1969). These authors did point out that this did not mean total store sales increased. Rather, sales may have simply shifted between brands in a category.

FUTURE RESEARCH

Little research has been done on retail semiotics. Retail management textbooks always discuss store interiors and atmospheres, but, except for the studies cited, the impact of various environmental features is based largely on anecdotal evidence (Berman and Evans, 1986, Mason and Mayer 1987). Trade literature is frequently cited as a source for information on store interiors. Unfortunately, this "research" is ofttimes based on observations outside a controlled experiment, where the effect of extraneous variables was not controlled.

A research program investigating the major components of mall and store design and their impact on shopper emotions, evaluations and behavior is required. (The conceptualization of this research design was partially based on Belk 1975a, 1975b, 1976; Eroglu and Harrell 1986, Frederiksen 1972.) However, this is more than simply a case of developing a taxonomy of retail symbols and investigating each element of retail semiotics. Rather one course of action is to develop a typology of retail environments. Then researchers need to focus on the total environment, the gestalt, of the retail mall or store. Next, how the individual elements of retail design work to form this total image should be studied. Finally, these studies need to focus on shopper segments.

We need to determine if there is a typology of retail environmental messages. Historically we have focused on developing a taxonomy of shoppers (Anderson 1971, Bellenger and Korgaonkar 1980, Darden and Ashton 1974-75, Darden and Reynolds 1971, Monroe and Guiltian 1975. Moschis 1975, Stephenson and Willet 1969, Stone 1954, Williams et al. 1978). But a typology of environments is also necessary.

Since shoppers differ (Gutman and Mills 1982), all people will not react the same way to an environment. It is important to test the reaction of different groups of customers or a specific retailer's target group to store atmospherics. Thus the research program needs to be market-segment and store-type specific (King and Ring 1980). The segmentation variables may include shopper demographics, psychographics, moods, and shopping involvement (Salma and Tashikian 1985). But other classification variables may be types of store (department store, supermarket, etc.), types of goods (convenience, shopping, specialty), and purpose of trip (entertainment, fact finding, purchase).

Two recent developments encourage experimentation. Larger chain organizations with increasing numbers of stores facilitate on-side versus laboratory experiments. Because these large chains have more locations in which to use the information, they can use three or four stores out of 1,000 or 2,000 units to serve as experimental sites to test color, sound, aisle width and configuration, or light intensity and type. Because of the large number of stores in the chain, researchers likely could find stores to serve as controls for the experimental stores. The second facilitation mechanism is point-of-sale systems than can capture unit sales volume. The best example of the systems is universal product code scanners in the supermarket and discount store industry. These point-of-sale systems will allow an accurate and timely recording of unit-sales volume as various aspects of a store's interiors are tested.

REFERENCES

Achabal, Dale D., Shelby H. McIntyre, Cherryl H. Bell and Nancy Tucker, (1987), "The Effect of Nutrition P-O-P Signs on Consumer Attitudes and Behavior," *Journal of Retailing*, 63 (Spring) 9-24.

Anderson, W. Thomas Jr., (1971), "Identifying the Convenience-Oriented Consumer," *Journal of Marketing Research*, 8 (May) 179-183.

Belk, Russell W., (1975), "Situational Variables and Consumer Behavior," *Journal of Consumer Research*, 2 (December) 157-164.

_____, (1975b), "The Objective Situation as a Determinant of Consumer Behavior," in Mary Jane Schlinger (ed.), *Advances in Consumer Research*, Vol. 2, Chicago: Association for Consumer Research, 427-437.

_____, (1976), "Situation Mediation and Consumer Behavior: A Reply to Russell and Mehrabian,"*Journal of Consumer Research*, 3 (December) 175-177.

Bellenger, Danny N. and Pradeep K. Korgaonkar, (1980), "Profiling the Recreational Shopper," *Journal of Retailing*, 56 (Fall) 77-92.

Bellizzi, Joseph A., Ayn E. Crowley, and Ronald W. Hasty, (1983), "The Effects of Color in Store Design," *Journal of Retailing*, 59 (Spring) 21-45.

Berman, Barry and Joel R. Evans, (1986), *Retail Management*, Third Edition, New York: Macmillan Publishing Co.

Bronzaft, Arline L. and Dennis P. McCarthy, (1975), "The Effect of Elevated Train Noise on Reading Ability," *Environment and Behavior*, 7 (December) 517-527.

Buyukkurt, B. Kemal, (1986), "Integration of Serially Sampled Price Information: Modeling Some Findings," *Journal of Consumer Research*, 13 (December) 357-373.

Campbell, Colin, (1987), *The Romantic Ethic and the Spirit of Modern Consumerism*, NY: Basil Blackwell.

Cox, Keith, (1964), "The Responsiveness of Food Sales to Shelf Space Changes in Supermarkets," *Journal of Marketing Research*, 1 (May) 63:67.

Darden, William R. and Dub Ashton, (1974-75), "Psychographic Profiles of Patronage Preference Groups," *Journal of Retailing* 50 (Winter) 99-112.

_____ and Fred P. Reynolds, (1971), "Shopping Orientations and Product Usage Rates," *Journal of Marketing Research* 8 (November) 505-508.

Donovan, Robert J. and John R. Rossiter, (1982), "Store Atmosphere: An Environmental Psychology Approach," *Journal of Retailing*, 58 (Spring) 34-57.

Downs, Roger M., (1970), "The Cognitive Structure of an Urban Shopping Center," *Environment and Behavior*, 2 (June) 13-39.

Epstein, Yakov M., Robert L. Woodfolk and Paul H. Lehrer, (1981), "Physiological, Cognitive, and Nonverbal Responses to Repeated Exposures to Crowding," *Journal of Applied Social Psychology*, 11 (January-February) 1-13.

Eroglu, Sevgin and Gilbert D. Harrell, (1986), "Retail Crowding: Theoretical and Strategic Implications," *Journal of Retailing*, 4, 346-363.

Evans, Gary W., (1979), "Behavioral and Physiological Consequences of Crowding in Humans," *Journal of Applied Social Psychology*, 9 (January-February) 27-46.

Frederiksen, Norman, (1972), "Toward a Taxonomy of Situations," *American Psychologist*, 27 (February) 114-123.

Gardner, Meryl P. and Michael J. Houston, (1986), "The Effects of Verbal and Visual Components of Retail Communications," *Journal of Retailing*, 62 (Spring) 64-78.

_____, (1985), "Mood States and Consumer Behavior: A Critical Review," *Journal of Consumer Research*, 12 (December) 281-300.

Gillis, A.R., Madeline A. Richard, and John Hagan, (1986), Ethnic Susceptibility to Crowding An Empirical Analysis,"," *Environment and Behavior*, 18 (November) 683-706.

Griffith, William, (1970), "Environmental Effects on Interpersonal Affective Behavior: Ambient Effective Temperature and Attraction," *Journal of Personality and Social Psychology*, 15 (July) 240-244.

Grossbart, Stanford L., Robert A. Mittelstaedt, William W. Curtis and Robert D. Rogers, (1975), "Environmental Sensitivity and Shopping Behavior," *Journal of Business Research*, 3 (October) 281-294.

Gutman, Jonathan and Michael K. Mills, (1982), "Fashion Lifestyle, Self-Concept, Shopping Orientation, and Store Patronage: An Integrative Analysis," *Journal of Retailing*, 58 (Summer) 64-86.

Harrell, Gilbert D. and Michael D. Hutt, (1976), "Crowding in Retail Stores," *MSU Business Topics*, (Winter) 33-39.

Holbrook, Morris B. and Elizabeth C. Hirschman, (1982), "The Experiential Aspects of Consumption: Consumer Fantasies, Feelings, and Fun." *Journal of Consumer Research* 9 (September):132-240.

King, Charles W. and Lawrence J. Ring, (1980), "Market Positioning Across Retail Fashion Institutions: A Comparative Analysis of Store Types," *Journal of Retailing*, 56 (Spring) 37-55.

Kotler, Phillip, (1973-74), "Atmospherics as a Marketing Tool," *Journal of Retailing*, 49 (Winter) 48-64.

Kotzan, Jeffery A. and Robert V. Evanson, (1969), "Responsiveness of Drug Store Sales to Shelf Space Allocations," *Journal of Marketing Research*, 6 (November) 465-469.

Kowinski, William S., (1985), *The Malling of America*, NY: William Morrow and Co.

Markin, Rom J., Charles M. Lillis, and Chem L. Narayana, (1976), "Social-Psychological Significance of Store Space," *Journal of Retailing*, 52 (Spring) 43-54.

Mason, J. Barry and Morris L. Mayer, (1987), *Modern Retailing*, Fourth Edition, Plano, Texas: Business Publications Inc.

McKinnon, Gary F., J. Patrick Kelly and E. Doyle Robison, (1981), "Sales Effects of Point of Purchase In-Store Signing," *Journal of Retailing*, 49-63.

Mehrabian, Albert, (1976), *Public Places and Private Spaces*, New York: Basic Books.

Mick, David Glen, (1986), "Consumer Research and Semiotics: Exploring The Morphology of Signs, Symbols, and Significance," *Journal of Consumer Research*, 13 (September) 196-213.

Milliman, Ronald E., (1986), "The Influence of Background Music on the Behavior of Restaurant Patrons," *Journal of Consumer Research*, 13 (September) 286-289.

———, (1982), "Using Background Music to Affect the Behavior of Supermarket Shoppers," *Journal of Marketing*, 46 (Summer) 86-91.

Monroe, Kent B. and Joseph P. Guiltinan, (1975), "A Path-Analytic Exploration of Retail Patronage Influences," *Journal of Consumer Research*, 2 (June) 19-28.

Moschis, George P., (1976), "Shopping Orientations and Consumer Uses of Information," *Journal of Retailing* 52 (Summer) 61-70.

O'Guinn, Thomas and Ronald J. Faber, (1986), "Mass Mediated Consumer Socialization: Non-Utilization and Dysfunctional Outcomes," in Melanie Wallendorf and Paul Anderson (eds.) Vol. 14, *Advances in Consumer Research*, Provo, UT, Association for Consumer Research, 473-477.

Page, Richard A., (1977), "Noise and Helping Behavior," *Environment and Behavior*, 9 (September) 311-334.

Rook, Dennis W., (1987), "The Buying Impulse," *Journal of Consumer Research*, 14 (September) 189-199.

Russell, James A. and Albert Mehrabian, (1976), "Environmental Variables in Consumer Research," *Journal of Consumer Research*, 3 (June) 62-63.

Russo, J. Edward, (1977), "The Value of Unit Price Information," *Journal of Marketing Research*, 14 (May) 193-201.

———, Richard Staelin, Catherine A. Nolan, Gary J. Russell, Barbara L. Metcalf, (1986), "Nutrition Information in the Supermarket," *Journal of Consumer Research* 13 (June) 48-70.

Salma, Mark E. and Armen Tashckian, (1985), "Selected Socioeconomic and Demographic Characteristics Associated with Purchasing Involvement," *Journal of Marketing*, 49 (Winter) 72-82.

Schneider, Frank W., Wayne A. Lesko and William A. Garrett, (1980), "Helping Behavior in Hot Comfortable and Cold Temperatures: A Field Study," *Environment Behavior*, 12 (June) 231-240.

Sherman, Elaine and Ruth Belk Smith, (1986), "Mood States of Shoppers and Store Image: Promising Interactions and Possible Behavioral Effects," in Melanie Wallendorf and Paul Anderson (eds.) Vol. 14, *Advances in Consumer Research*, Provo, UT: Association for Consumer Research, 251-254.

Smith, Andrew and Stephen Stansfeld, (1986), "Aircraft Noise Exposure, Noise Sensitivity and Everyday Errors," *Environment and Behavior*, 18 (March) 214-226.

Stephenson, P. Ronald and Ronald P. Willet, (1969), "Analysis of Consumers' Retail Patronage Strategies," in P. R. McDonald (ed.) *Marketing Involvement in Society and the Economy*, Chicago: American Marketing Association, 316-322.

Stone, Gregory P., (1954), "City Shoppers and Urban Identification: Observations on the Social Psychology of City Life," *American Journal of Sociology* 60 (July) 36-45.

Tauber, Edward M., (1972), "Why Do People Shop," *Journal of Marketing*, 36 (October) 46-59.

Williams, Robert H., John J. Painter and Herbert R. Nicholas, (1978), "A Policy-Oriented Typology of Grocery Shoppers," *Journal of Retailing*, 54 (Spring) 27-42.

Zeedyk-Ryan, Janice and Gene F. Smith, (1983), "The Effects of Crowding on Hostility, Anxiety and Drive for Social Interaction," *Journal of Social Psychology*, 120 (August) 245-252.

Zepp, Ira G. Jr., (1986), *The New Religious Image of Urban America: The Shopping Mall as Ceremonial Center*, Westminster, Maryland: Christian Classic Inc.

Shopping Choices: The Case of Mall Choice

Jeffrey J. Stoltman, Wayne State University
James W. Gentry, University of Nebraska-Lincoln
Kenneth A. Anglin, Central Michigan University

The focus of this paper is on a specific retail patronage phenomenon: mall shopping. Though this form of retailing may have a less promising future than once thought (Turchiano 1990), mall shopping clearly constitutes a significant aspect of retail patronage. The retail sales volume estimates and the affinity of certain consumer segments for this retail venue underscores this point (see Feinberg 1991). While malls have been a formidable aspect of the retailing environment for decades, and a variety of mall-types dot the landscape (e.g., off-price malls and festival malls), surprisingly little research has focused on this general phenomenon. A better understanding of this important form of consumer behavior will result as efforts are made to delineate and empirically estimate the nature of and underlying reasons for this behavior.

Rather than to categorize consumers as patrons or non-patrons with respect to malls, it makes more sense to explore the form and strength of their patronage. This is important because other retail outlets (e.g., shopping plazas, retail centers, etc.) can offer several of the benefits of malls (e.g., broad product assortments in close proximity to one's residence). Although the terms shopping-"area," "center" and "mall" have been used interchangeably in the past, there are important conceptual distinctions to be drawn. Just as a downtown shopping center or area may or may not be mall-like, a shopping center can be a plaza or a mall. So-called "festival areas" have been developed to help revitalize some downtown districts (cf. Maronick and Stiff 1985), plazas now include both covered and "power" formats (where a national discount department store operates like anchor stores in conventional mall development), and malls now come in the "standard", mixed-use format, as well as in mini, mega, regional, high-fashion/specialty, and off-price/outlet formats. The emergence of the hypermarket/ superstore concept in this country promises to complicate things even further. Whether consumers do, in fact, vary in their propensity and affinities with respect to these many options is undetermined. Researchers have not even scratched the surface with respect to these many variants and the choice alternatives they present to shoppers.

That such developments have not been noted and examined previously underscores the fact that in addition to being limited in quantity, the extant literature is dated. Moreover, findings reported when central business districts were in decline and malls were in a relative growth stage may no longer hold. It was during this period that a gravitational theory of center/area patronage gained strength. These studies demonstrated that the size of a trading area and driving time/distance to that area offered a suitable prediction of patronage. However, it has been shown that this explanation is incomplete because it fails to recognize important qualitative distinctions between shopping choices (cf. Gautschi 1981). The importance of these qualitative factors needs to be considered in light of the many ways in which shopping areas have been developed and promoted. Furthermore, as retail choices have proliferated, shoppers have undergone many important changes in their lifestyles, spending habits, and shopping tendencies and strategies. For example, May (1989) discusses the increasing demands on time and changing requirements regarding variety and value. Collectively, these observations send a clear signal to the research community: There is a need to review and redirect research exploring retail patronage phenomena in general, and mall choice in particular.

The primary purpose of this paper is to provide additional perspective and exploratory evidence regarding the consumer shopping tendencies and motives underlying mall shopping. Individually, most of the points raised are neither new nor particularly difficult to accept. However, in addition to being dated and limited in quantity, an integration of the several explanations implied in past research has not been provided to date. Accordingly, a synthetic view of the general retail patronage literature is provided. In addition, given the *zeitgeist* in consumer research, consideration must be given to affective dimensions of this form of behavior.

In the following discussion mall shopping is viewed as a relative choice phenomenon, i.e., a consumer chooses to shop at malls over other outlets and chooses some malls over other malls where this choice is given-- patronage is contingent upon the choice alternatives. Furthermore, mall patronage doesn't occur in the abstract, it is a context-driven choice. A consumer may (prefer/ expect to) shop malls for clothes, but not for home electronics; they may shop malls when many purchasing needs exist but few solutions have been identified (e.g., holiday gift shopping); or, they may shop malls when pressed for time. In addition, those who have certain shopping orientations may prefer to shop at malls, as in the case of the browser. Mall shopping can also reflect more economic, or functional, shopping orientations because they provide a convenient/efficient way to comparison shop across a variety of goods, and/or a way to complete several purchase tasks in one trip. As implied in these examples, shopping tendencies and motives can provide several promising bases for the exploration of mall choice.

OVERVIEW OF RELEVANT RETAIL PATRONAGE LITERATURE

Previous research on the topic of mall/center choice and patronage can be classified as falling into three categories: gravitational attraction of shopping centers (cf. Gautschi 1981; Nevin and Houston 1980); the dimensions and predictive power of shopping area image (cf. Gentry and Burns 1977-78; Howell and Rogers 1980; Wee 1985); and the motivational and experiential aspects of mall shopping (cf. Bellenger, Robertson, and Greenberg 1977; Bloch, Ridgway, and Sherrel 1989). Despite their dissimilar methodologies and focal points, the results of these studies can be integrated.

An important starting point in the process of investigating mall patronage phenomena is to recognize that, while most consumers shop at malls, some shoppers are clearly more frequent and more likely shoppers. This general premise has been explored by examining the influence of driving time/distance and center size (mass) on area/center/mall patronage (cf. Brunner and Mason 1968; Bucklin 1967; Cooke and Cox 1970). This gravitational explanation for mall/area attraction is highly touted because of the predictive capability that has been observed. Yet, findings have been sufficiently different from study to study to give pause. One concern is that the gravitational "pull" varies across the population centers chosen for study (see Cooke and Cox 1970). Clearly, the infrastructures and population patterns have a bearing on this relationship, as does the commercial development communities' adherence to and/or (self-fulfilling) instigation of these patterns.

Given the effects that have been observed and the variance in the transportation infrastructures and the population patterns of cities the gravitational view must continue to be tested. However, it is important to remind ourselves that shoppers are not inexorably drawn to a trading area. They make choices given the alternatives and the facilitating and inhibiting conditions that prevail in a given market (or from some point in the market to some other point). While driving time/distance may be related to mall choice, given the increased demands on time resources, this applies to all retail choices. Thus, the concept offers little in the way of explaining the relative choice of shopping at a mall over other alternatives. This finding does not explain the success of downtown redevelopment efforts (cf. Maronick and Stiff 1985), nor does it explain the (implied) success of mall developer/retailers who present the right "mix" of stores to the market (cf. Carlson 1990). In attempting to attract shoppers, mall operators promote a specific identity for their facility and devise programs designed to woo the shopper. Additionally, the choices that exist often vary in quality of location, clientele attracted, safety, ease of parking, etc.. Clearly, something more than mass/ distance is at work here and we need to look elsewhere for an explanation of mall/area patronage. There are two ways to go about this task.

Several authors have noted that the gravitational explanation rests on the assumption that shopper perceptions of retail alternatives are equivalent or irrelevant (cf. Gautschi 1981; Gentry and Burns 1977-78; Nevin and Houston 1980; Wee and Pearce 1985). One approach is to add these factors to a gravitational model. When these factors are incorporated a significant improvement in explanatory power has been found. However, this approach is not without its problems. While store images have been the subject of considerable study (cf. Lindquist 1974-75; Peterson and Kerin 1983), shopper images of the range of mall, area and center types note above have not. Measurement has basically involved various "adaptations" of the instruments developed for stores/store-types. While attempts have been made to address this problem, dissimilar measures have been used and, as a result, there has been no consensus reached. Nevin and Houston (1980) provide the most systematic approach, while others have sampled a greater range of attributes (Howell and Rogers 1980; Wee 1985). A related matter is the comparability of these measures and their basic structure. For example, while Howell and Rogers (1980) felt their measure compared favorably to the findings reported by Nevin and Houston, their solution produced 5 underlying dimensions versus the 3 reported by Nevin and Houston (see also Houston and Nevin 1980). Wee (1985) used 31 attributes and derived 4 factors. Each of these studies used non-comparable items and applied the measures of image to a mix of "shopping area," including downtown centers, malls, and unspecified "areas." A related issue that persists is whether the basic structure of mall/area image is consistent across venues/types. Though Nevin and Houston found considerable stability, there were important differences between the image components of downtown and "outlying" shopping areas. This indicates that shoppers do not judge these entities on the same dimensions. Each of these issues will need to be resolved before image or image-enhanced gravitational explanations of patronage can be accepted.

There is a more fundamental issue that also requires attention. In the studies noted, the importance of the attribute dimensions is inferred from the structural findings (which are, as we have noted, inconsistent across studies). This is crucial because of the explanation that typically accompanies the findings of gravitational pull: Consumers who frequent malls/areas/centers in a manner consistent with the gravitational model are said to be doing so because *they wish to be* economical with respect to time and other resources. Shoppers seek to minimize resource expenditures and maximize search or other benefits derived from patronage. The assortments provided in a shopping area provide utility, as can proximal location. Upon close examination, there are, in fact, several possible motivations and behavioral dispositions implicated in such an explanation. Based upon the analysis provided below it is predicted that some shoppers will be attracted to malls/centers for economic motives (e.g., for matters of convenience, search efficiency, etc.), while others may be attracted for affective reasons.

One study did investigate the importance of area attributes and produced an interesting finding. Gentry and Burns (1977-78) reported that, while shoppers felt a variety of center/area attributes were important, driving time (a factor associated with the gravitational view) was the best predictor of past patronage activity. In focusing only on past behavior, the Gentry and Burns study leaves open the question as to whether the same finding holds with respect to shopping intentions or future behavior. It is clear that additional empirical evidence is needed regarding the impact, or lack of impact of the influence implied in the "importance" measure. However, the importance explanation provides a bridge to the second basic explanation for mall choice.

From a broader perspective, the importance of mall/area attributes will be a function of shopper motives and behavioral tendencies of the shopper (see Westbrook and Black 1985). Given this view, it is apparent that other means of incorporating the influence reflected in importance measures are available. The conjecture that accompanies gravitational research and research focused on the nature and influence of image factors has touched upon several motivational dimensions of shopping. Given the assortment of goods presented, a mall should be attractive to functional browsers (e.g., those who search on a continuing basis to solve future problems), as well as recreational browsers (see Bloch, Ridgway and Sherrel 1989). To the degree shopping task requirements have even been partially defined, mall settings offer the opportunity for greater search efficiency due to the close proximity of a greater number of choice alternatives. Malls also provide an efficient means of "getting ideas" when the purchase has been only loosely-specified (see Jarobe and McDaniel 1987). Browsing behavior also creates an opportunity for impulse purchasing, i.e., "If I see something I like, I buy it." While the "looking" behavior constitutes a form/facet of browsing, the basic orientation of the impulsive shopper may be directly satisfied by the number of opportunities (or temptations) the mall environment provides.

Multi-purpose shopping tendencies/motives are also compatible with the mall environment. This relationship may be particularly important because of the demands on time already noted; it may also reflect the reluctance or apathy of some shoppers (Tauber 1972). As noted by Stoltman, Anglin and Gentry (1989), multi-purpose shopping can take many forms. For example, it can be defined as a general tendency to combine shopping trips/needs, or it may be contextually-defined, e.g., one may tend to shop in this way for clothing or groceries, but not for appliances. Though the importance of the concept seems obvious, it has received little attention. In offering a different twist on gravitational models of center patronage, Ghosh (1986) briefly commented upon the importance of multi-purpose shopping to both the shopper and the retailer. The possibility should be explored further. Malls would afford those pursuing a multi-purpose agenda the opportunity to do so more effectively and in a pleasant environment.

The motives and shopping orientations noted here represent distinct, though related, reasons why (some) individuals would prefer to shop at malls. As suggested by May (1989; see also Jarobe and McDaniel 1987), it is unreasonable to categorize mall shoppers as either recreational or economic, or to expect that a single motive underlies this form of shopping (see also Westbrook and Black 1985). Consequently, we conducted an exploratory analysis of the full complement of motives and orientations noted above. In addition, given the findings from gravitational studies, the role of driving time was examined. Rather than explore image per se, we also tested the explanatory power of mall/center attribute importance. While formal hypotheses were not tested, the preceding discussion indicates the relationships expected: Mall shoppers would exhibit a tendency to be economically motivated, to engage in multi-purpose shopping, and to be browsers. These orientations/motives were measured in several ways to gain further insights.

METHOD

The data analyzed here are drawn from a data base created using a 15-page survey that examined a range of shopping behaviors and influences. One thousand surveys were distributed in a midwestern city (combined population approximately 200,000) across the 42 census tracks, in proportion to the size of the census track, and randomly within tracks. The procedure used (i.e., drop-off/mail-back), the questionnaire length, and the absence of response incentives yielded 289 usable questionnaires. This rate compares favorably to several previous studies, but is low enough to be of concern. Analysis of the sample characteristics and the market demographics indicated a high-level of comparability existed. However, seven low-income tracts had lower response rates.

Three shopping choice alternatives were examined: a mall, the downtown area (a four-square block mixed-use development), and the largest shopping plaza in the market. At the time of the study, the downtown area was being considered for a major redevelopment effort. An enclosed two-story "mall" was part of the downtown center, but, as in many downtown areas, the shopping center was spread in a loose fashion over a several block area. Furthermore, in the previous decade, two major local department stores had vacated the area. The area could aptly be described as transitional. The mall was formerly a shopping plaza which had been enclosed and which had received several "grafts" (including the addition of three additional department store anchors). The plaza was located on property adjacent to the mall development and it is more properly labeled a mini-mall. Because of the arbitrary nature of a square-footage measure (exacerbated in this case because of the manner these three properties were developed), driving time served as the measure of gravitational pull. Each of these locations offered approximately the same number of clothing stores/clothing outlets.

Specific measures of patronage were obtained within the context of shopping for clothes for reasons suggested by Peterson and Kerin (1983): shoppers make evaluations and decisions within a context, not in the abstract (see also Howell and Rogers 1980). Patronage was measured in several ways. The recency and frequency of purchasing clothing with respect to each of the retail options was measured using 6-point scales with categories ranging from "Never" (1) to "Last 2 days" (6), or to "Weekly" (6), respectively. Purchase intentions for the following 30-day period were measured using 4-point scale with categories ranging from "Very Unlikely" (1) to "Very Likely" (4). Respondents were also asked to provide an estimate of the driving time from their residence to each of the three locations. These are the same measures used by Nevin and Houston (1980), except they did not examine recent patronage. For the purposes of analysis all measures were standardized.

Two sets of attribute importance measures were also obtained; each required the respondent to consider mall/center features in the context of clothing purchases. The Nevin and Houston (1980) 16-item attribute list was adapted by for this purpose and importance was measured on a 7-point scale (1= "Very Unimportant", 7= "Very Important"). Four dimensions were identified via factor analysis. Previous research has been criticized for under-sampling the attribute domain. Thus a separate and alternatively worded list of 33 attributes was created based upon the work of Howell and Rogers (1980) as well as observations made during a series of in-depth and focus group interviews conducted prior to the development of the survey instrument. Respondents were asked to rate the desirability of the attributes using a 5-point scale (1 = "Very Undesirable" and 5 = "Very Desirable"). Six dimensions were identified based on a factor and reliability analysis. The identities, composition and reliability estimates for two sets of importance measures are reported in Table 1. While conceptually these dimensions seem related, the highest correlation across these two sets of measures was .36. The assortment measure obtained using the Nevin and Houston list was more strongly correlated with the second set of measures, and the four Nevin and Houston-based measures were most strongly correlated with the facilities dimension of the alternative measure. The additional shopping motive/orientation measures reported in Table 1 were obtained using 4-point frequency (1 = "Never" to 4 = "Very Frequently") and 5-point agreement (1 = "Strongly Disagree" to 5 = "Strongly Agree") response scales.

RESULTS

As was the procedure in several prior studies (Gentry and Burns 1977-78; Nevin and Houston 1980; Wee 1986), a step-wise regression was performed on the three criterion measures. The results are summarized in Table 1. While significant, the amount of variance accounted for is exceptionally low (prior studies often report R^2 in the .20-.30 range). There are still several insights provided in these findings. Differences arise both as a function of the criterion and as a function of the mall/center examined. In particular, driving time is significantly related to past behavior (i.e., recency and frequency of mall/area patronage) for both the mall and downtown choice alternatives. This variable is the first to enter the regression equation in three of the four models. The relationship also appears stronger in the case of past mall patronage as defined by the amount of variance range accounted for in the models of recency and frequency. Also note that small, though significant gains are made in prediction through the addition of the other factors. As expected, the mall choice was significantly related to several of the shopping orientations and motives measures. In particular, impulse shopping is related to past behavior in the case of the mall and the plaza, yet related to shopping intention in the case of the downtown option. Browsing shows up in several of these models, and it too is more strongly related to past patronage. One orientation that consistently shows up is shopping frequency. Though one-interpretation is that this is, essentially, a manipulation check, the finding can also mean that heavy shoppers are more likely to shop *each* of these areas. While the multi-purpose shopping orientation contributes in only two cases, both instances involve the mall choice. Frequency of shopping malls and future intentions are both related to this orientation. Finally, the sporadic contributions of the dimensions derived from the two sets of attribute importance measures should be noted. Overall, these measures do not contribute much, but the measures derived from Nevin and Houston seem better suited to a downtown center, while the alternative measures contributed in the models of mall patronage.

DISCUSSION

Since considerable variance is left unaccounted for (both here and in prior studies), attention should clearly be focused on measurement issues. Those used here may be inadequate in many respects, and undoubtedly there are better ways to operationalize and explore the logic presented in the introduction to this paper. It is also a certainty that important factors relating to mall choice have been omitted. Coupled with past findings (e.g., Gentry and Burns 1977-78; Nevin and Houston 1980), these findings point to the fact that different definitions of mall patronage (e.g., past as opposed to intended behaviors) must be examined. While economic factors captured in gravitational models (e.g., driving time) are predictive of past behavior, intentions are less influenced by this factor.

Differences also arose here across retail choice alternatives. In general, there is a need to begin exploring retail patronage in a manner which incorporates the range of intra-urban choices

TABLE 1
Results of Stepwise Regression

Area	Criterion Variables		
	Recency	Frequency	Intention
Mall	$[R^2 = 10 \to 19]_a$	$[R^2 = 07 \to 18]$	$[R^2 = 5 \to 12]$
	*1. Drive-time	1. Drive-time	1. Frequently
	2. Frequent	2. Impulse	2. Saves Time
	3. Impulse	3. Multi-C	3. Search
	4. Socialize	4. Socialize	4. Sales
	5. Browsing	5. Assortment-II	5. Drive-time
	$[F=9.4\ (5,278)]_b$	$[F=14.02\ (4,279)]$	$[F=6.54\ (5,278)]$
Downtown	$[R^2 = 03 \to 05]$	$[R^2 = 04]$	$[R^2 = 03 \to 11]$
	1. Time	1. Impulse	1. Impulse
	2. Browsing		2. Assortment
			3. Economics
	$[F=5.32\ (1,281)]$	$[F=8.9\ (1,282)]$	$[F=6.54\ (3,278)]$
Plaza	$[R^2 = 05 \to 11]$	$[R^2 = 04 \to 08]$	$[R^2 = 05 \to 10]$
	1. Impulse	1. Frequent	1. Frequent
	2. Frequent	2. Atmosphere-II	2. Search
	3. Search		
	$[F=9.89\ (3,280)]$	$[F=9.15\ (2,281)]$	$[F=10.59\ (2,281)]$

Description of Predictors Tested:

Importance
Dimensions	#Items:Sample Items (Coefficient alpha)
Assortment:	4: Quality of Stores, Variety of Merchandise (.87)
Amenities:	3: Layout of Shopping Area, Special Exhibits (.74)
Atmosphere:	4: Atmosphere, Personnel, Saftey (.80)
Economics:	4: General Price Levels, Special Sales (.78)

Desirability	#Items:Sample Item (Coefficient alpha)
Atmosphere-II	5: Clean Area, Visually Exciting, Attractive (.85)
Assortment-II	4: Variety of Clothing Stores, Latest Fashions (.89)
Sales	4: Frequent Sales, Special Sales, Special Events (.84)
Facilities	6: Refreshments, Eating Establishments, Restrooms (.81)
Conveniences	3: Easy to Walk Around, Open Weekends, Open Evenings (.79)
Socialize	3: Friends Shop There, Friends Recommend (.88)

Shopping Orientations/Tendencies
Frequent	-- "How often do you shop for clothes?"
Impulse	-- "I find it hard to resist buying a product on sale."
Browsing	-- "I like to browse with no specific item in mind."
Compare	-- "I like to shop at several stores before I buy."
Search	-- "How often..shop strictly for information gathering?"
Multi-C	-- "How often do you shop for several clothes items?"
Multi-G	-- "How often do you shop for several different items?
Saves Time	-- "I always shop where it saves me time."

a: R^2 for first through last model.
b: F-ratio for final (full) model.
*: Order of entry into regression model.

shoppers face. This may be particularly true when malls are compared to downtown areas because of the problems the latter have experienced. Additionally, many shopping "centers" do not compare favorably to most mall operations: malls tend to have more clearly defined images due to their relative newness, their amenities, the promotional programs (including both sales and image development strategies) and because they occupy a definable physical space. In most markets, alternatives exist such that both inter-type and intra-type choices must be made. That is, consumers would need to pick malls over options such as the central business district, strip plazas, direct marketing options (e.g., catalogs), etc. Beyond this, if several malls are accessible, the consumer must choose which malls to shop. Clearly, such choices will be guided by the presence/absence of certain stores (anchors), the relative accessibility of the mall (drive time, routing convenience, conditions of crowding), etc.. These possibilities must be explored.

Furthermore, given the choice alternatives, a consumer will tend to patronize malls to the extent the orientations and motives noted here are present and appropriate to the shopping task. Differences as a function of task may be important, indeed should be expected according to Peterson and Kerin (1983). At a minimum, this should be taken into account and a task-based frame of reference should be provided when asking patronage, choice, attitude, attribute importance, and image questions. The fact that the relationships reported here may be specific to clothes shopping needs to be explored. Mall shopping can either be defined as a general preference or pattern of shopping, or it may be defined within a given range of purchasing/shopping contexts, e.g., clothes or gift shopping. That is, malls may be viewed as more attractive choices under certain conditions and not others. In this study, mall patronage was explored on a relative basis (i.e., the explanatory framework was applied across several retail centers, including a mall), across several different manifestations of patronage, and within a specific context. The fact that different patterns emerged across retail choices needs to be explored further.

These findings need to be replicated and extended, with particular emphasis placed on the role of task influences. These influences can include, but are not limited to the following: need specificity (degree to which a product- level acquisition has been developed), urgency, solution familiarity (degree to which analogous situations have been previously encountered and successfully resolved -- particularly at certain venues), etc.. Having focused primarily on clothes shopping, the generalizability of these findings across other categories is an open question. In addition, since the selection of any given retail alternative is also based on one's assessment of the mall's "performance" along dimensions of importance, the theory that underlies the image study approach to this question must be reviewed.

Finally, one issue stands above all others as deserving further development: A clearer understanding of the nature and influence of consumer motives is needed. The study of this issue promises to offer important insights across a number of research domains; however such clarity will not be achieved until additional conceptual and empirical efforts are made. The extant literature is limited in quantity and is equivocal on a number of issues. These empirical findings certainly offer little relief with respect to the last point, but several research directions clearly emerge from the approach discussed here. Given the amount of mall shopping that occurs, the possibility that mall shopping will be undergoing important changes in the next decade (see Turchiano 1990), and the number of directions that can be followed, there is clearly enough to occupy those consumer researchers who are attracted to this area. Significant resources are marshalled by practitioners in an attempt to stimulate, direct, and sustain patterns of patronage. However, we have basically neglected retail patronage phenomena. This circumstance has profound implications for the direction and status of this discipline. It is hoped that this session will promote the effort needed to begin filling the void that persists.

REFERENCES

Bearden, William O. (1977), "Determinant Attributes of Store Patronage: Downtown Versus Outlying Shopping Centers," *Journal of Retailing*, 53 (Summer), 15-22, 92.

Bellenger, Danny N., Dan H. Robertson and Barnett A. Greenberg (1977), "Shopping Center Patronage Motives," *Journal of Retailing*, 53 (Summer), 29- 38.

Bloch, Peter H., Nancy M. Ridgway and Daniel L. Sherrel (1989), "Extending the Concept of Shopping: An Investigation of Browsing Activity," *Journal of the Academy of Marketing Science*, 17 (Winter), 13-21.

Brunner, James A. and John Mason (1968), "The Influence of Driving Upon Shopping Center Preference," *Journal of Marketing*, 32 (April), 57-61.

Bucklin, Louis P. (1967), "The Concept of Mass in Intra-Urban Shopping," *Journal of Marketing*, 31 (October), 37-42.

Carlson, Eugene (1990), "New Retailers Face Struggle Getting in Malls," *Wall Stree Journal*, (July 24), B1-B2.

Cox, William E. and Ernest F. Cooke (1970), "Other Dimensions Involved in Shopping Center Preference," *Journal of Marketing*, 34 (October), 12-17.

Darden, William R. and Fred D. Reynolds (1971), "Shopping Orientations and Product Usage Rates," *Journal of Marketing Research* 8 (November), 505-508.

Feinberg, Richard (1991), "A Brief History of the Mall," *Advances in Consumer Research*, Volume 18, forthcoming.

Gautschi, David A. (1981), "Specification of Patronage Models for Retail Center Choice," *Journal of Marketing Research*, 18 (May), 162-174.

Gentry, James W. and Alvin C. Burns (1977-78), "How 'Important' are Evaluative Criteria in Shopping Center Patronage?" *Journal of Retailing*, 53 (Winter), 73-86, 94-5.

Ghosh, Avijit (1986), "The Value of a Mall and Other Insights From a Revised Central Place Model," *Journal of Retailing*, 62 (Spring), 79-97.

Houston, Michael J. and John R. Nevin (1980), "Retail Shopping Area Image: Structure and Congruency Between Downtown Areas and Shopping centers," *Advances in Consumer Research*, Volume 8, 677-681.

Howell, Roy D. and Jerry D. Rogers (1980), "Research Into Shopping Mall Choice Behavior," *Advances in Consumer Research*, Volume 8, 671-676.

Jarobe, Glen R. and Carl McDaniel (1987), "A Profile of Browsers in Regional Shopping Malls," *Journal of the Academy of Marketing Science*, 15 (Spring), 46-53.

Lindquist, Jay (1974-75), "Meaning of Image: A Survey of Empirical and Hypothetical Evidence," *Journal of Retailing*, 50 (Winter), 29-38, 116.

Maronick. Thomas and Ronald M. Stiff (1985), "The Impact of a Specialty Retail Center on Downtown Shopping Behavior," *Journal of the Academy of Marketing Science*, 13 (Summer), 292-306.

May, Elanor (1989), "A Retail Odyssey," *Journal of Retailing*, 65 (Fall), 356-367.

Nevin, John R. and Michael J. Houston (1980), "Image as a Component of Attraction to Intraurban Shopping Areas," *Journal of Retailing*, 56 (Spring), 77-93.

Peterson, Robert and Roger Kerin (1983), "Store Image Measurement in Patronage Research: Fact and Artifact," in *Patronage Behavior and Retail Management* W.R. Darden and R.F. Lusch (eds.), New York, Elsevier-North Holland, 293-306.

Stoltman, Jeffrey J., Kenneth A. Anglin and James W. Gentry (1989), "The Impact of 'Shopping Trip Orientation' on Retail Perceptions," in *Proceedings of the Symposium on Patronage Behavior and Retail Strategy: The Cutting Edge*, W.R. Darden (ed.), Louisiana State University, 69-81.

Tauber, Edward M. (1972), "Why Do People Shop?", *Journal of Marketing*, 36 (October), 46-59.

Turchiano, Francesca (1990), "The Unmalling of America," *American Demographics*, April, 37-39.

Wee, Chow Hou (1986), "Shopping Area Image: Its Factor Analytic Structure and Relationships with Shopping Trips and Expenditure Behavior, *Advances in Consumer Research*, Volume 13, 48-52.

──── and Michael R. Pearce (1985), "Patronage Behaviour iToward Shopping Areas: A Proposed Model Based on Huff's Model of Retail Gravitation," *Advances in Consumer Research*, Volume 12, 592-597.

Westbrook, Robert A. and William C. Black (1985), "A Motivation- Based Shopper Typology," *Journal of Retailing*, 61 (Spring), 78-103.

A Reinforcement-Affect Model of Mall Patronage

Jennifer Meoli, Indiana University of Pennsylvania
Richard A. Feinberg, Purdue University
Lori Westgate, Purdue University

ABSTRACT

Learning theory provides a basis for understanding and predicting consumer attraction to a mall. The stimulus response relationship between stores in a mall and attraction to a mall can be theoretically modeled as a mathematical function. Quantifying consumer attraction to a mall as a function of the reinforcement potential of the array of stores, provides a way to reconcile the absence of consumer based variables in applied patronage models. Market variables dominate patronage prediction equations despite researchers efforts to blend image measures into the retail gravity model. The reinforcement-affect model is proposed as a guide to understanding the relationship between consumer preferences and patronage in the context of marketplace variables.

INTRODUCTION

The purpose of this paper is to introduce an alternative approach to incorporating consumers' feelings of attraction into the process of understanding and predicting retail mall patronage. Sheth (1983) and Darden's (1979, also Darden and Dorsch 1989) comprehensive theoretical models of patronage provide insight and direction for untangling the complex organization of factors influencing consumers' shopping motivation and behavior. In contrast, Huff's (1964 and Huff and Rust 1984) retail gravity model, provides a formula for predicting mall patronage based on the principle of cost (accessibility) verses utility (size). The strength of retail gravity model is that, by using essentially two variables to predict patronage behavior, it is an elegantly simple tool for managerial decision making. Infusing a measure of consumers' feelings of attraction into the retail gravity model would be expected to contribute to the power of the prediction equation, as well as to the understanding of how patronage patterns are influenced by accessibility, size and consumers' differential preferences.

Including a quantified measure of consumers' feelings of attraction to a mall, based on the combined pull of specific retailers, may become a necessary component of retail patronage models. The challenge of accurately predicting mall patronage has been heightened by the anticipated increasingly intense competition between various types of malls within market boundaries (e.g., Milford 1989, "Shopping Centers Suffer" 1986, "Overbuilding" 1987). Industry growth and innovation have stimulated spiraling increases in the density of shopping center alternatives in many geographic regions. These changes in the marketplace diminish the predictive power of retail gravity models by accentuating the limitations of relying on size and location to predict patronage share between relatively equally accessible alternatives of comparable size (Bucklin, 1971). Size, as measured by square feet of selling space, provides a convenient operational definition of attraction for retail managers (Mason and Mayer, 1990). In an overmalled market, when consumers have choices for variety and several shopping center options for multiple purpose trips, the need arises for a measure of attraction which grasps the essence of consumers' liking, and can also be practically applied.

THE RELATIONSHIP BETWEEN STORES AND PATRONAGE MODELING

Implicit in the retail gravity model is the assumption that a larger mall, with a greater number of stores, is more attractive to consumers. As increased alternative shopping centers with location accessibility reduce the cost aspect of patronage, malls within a market area turn to manipulating the utility function by increasing the number of stores. Consistent with the assumption that size defines attraction for consumers, developers' objective in altering the tenant mix has been to design larger malls that have a greater number of stores, and to reduce the size of each store (Peterson 1989). Older malls have manipulated size by reducing the square foot of each store by 30-40 percent, slivering into a plethora of downscaled stores. Revising the definition of utility to reflect preferences for particular retailers may necessarily yield strategic implications which contradict the recommendation that a mall should maximize tenant occupancy.

There is a basis for assuming that consumers may be attracted to a mall by feelings evoked by qualitative aspects of a particular amalgam of stores, rather than by the illusion of variety a large quantity of stores, with limited width and depth of merchandise, may present. Considering the generally homogeneous national chain stores common to most large malls, size and variety, as defined by the number of stores may not be a sustainable advantage. Mall choice may be a function of attraction to particular stores which consumers have identified as rewarding enclaves in an overwhelming stimulus environment. The idea that mall choice may be a function of attraction to particular stores or types of stores has been asserted by several researchers (Nevin and Houston 1980, Stanley and Sewall 1976, Sheth 1983, Weisbrod, Parcells and Kern 1984). While the need to incorporate consumers' subjective preferences for certain stores has been identified as a way to better understand and predict individual and aggregate mall patronage, a theoretical underpinning to guide the application of this idea has not been established.

In efforts to account for consumers' subjective attraction, measures of the unified image of a mall have been included as a component of retail patronage models. Image, as a concept representing the qualitative attractiveness of a retail unit, although useful in predicting attraction to a store, has not been successfully applied to the problem of predicting attraction to a mall (e.g. Gentry and Burns 1977-1978, Nevin and Houston 1980, Peterson and Kerin, 1983). Quantifying the overall image of a mall presents methodological and practical problems because the concept of store image does not translate smoothly into mall image. Image is measured by mostly store specific attributes, such as prices and salespeople (Lindquist 1974-1975). Asking consumers to describing the image of a mall, which has an array of stores all with their own varied images, may be forcing a definition of the qualitative attractiveness which is not a realistic reflection of how consumers formulate their feelings of attraction. (Howell and Rogers 1981). Image research leads to the implication that stores should be treated as units with identity and meaning that consumers' readily discern (Meoli 1989).

THE REINFORCEMENT-AFFECT MODEL

The theoretical basis for a reinforcement-affect model of mall patronage is Byrne's (1971) landmark reinforcement-affect model of interpersonal attraction. Byrne used behavioral learning theory as a guide to understanding and predicting interpersonal attraction. Byrne demonstrated that attraction was a function of the proportion of reinforcing stimuli present in another person. The stimuli Byrne used in controlled experiments was attitudes. Similar attitudes in a stranger are reinforcing stimuli which can be modeling in a mathematical function to predict attraction. To make the analogous comparison, attraction to a mall would be a function of the proportion of reinforcing stimuli in a mall. The stores which compose a mall are the relevant basis for stimulus reinforcement, both from a theoretical and practical point of view. Stores which a consumer likes or prefers shopping in represent reinforcing stimuli contributing to the attraction response toward the mall. If it can be established that the same structural relationship between stimulus cues and attraction that has been successfully used to illuminate interpersonal attraction, can be applied to retail malls, then Byrne's work can serve as a guide for retail patronage research.

The initial exploration of the congruence between interpersonal attraction and attraction to a retail mall followed the progress of Byrne's work (Meoli and Feinberg 1989). This series of experiments, the latter two using hypothetical malls, accomplished three objectives;

1. A measure of attraction to a retail mall adapted from the measure of interpersonal attraction was developed and validated. The mall judgement scale (MJS) is a two item assessment of feelings of attraction, and feelings about spending time in a mall. Comparing two malls which consumers reported regularly shopping at, malls with a greater share of reported patronage had significantly higher MJS scores.

2. The hypothesis that attraction to a retail mall is a linear function of the number of liked stores in the mall was confirmed. Holding the number of stores constant, a mall with a greater number of liked stores is more attractive than a mall which has an equal number of stores, but those stores are not preferred.

3. The hypothesis that attraction to a mall could be modeled as a function of the proportion of reinforcing stimuli present in a mall was tested. Attraction was a function of both proportion and the absolute number of liked stores. Attraction to a mall is a function of the relative number of liked stores among the total stimulus array. Larger malls, with a greater number of stores, were not necessarily more attractive than malls with fewer stores. The reinforcement potential of the composite stores influenced the attraction response.

This preliminary set of studies were controlled experiments in which the array of combined stores was manipulated using hypothetical malls. Experimental design was the optimal way to test the theoretical relationship between liked stores and attraction that was predicted by the reinforcement-affect model. If this relationship was not observed in this context, the reinforcement-affect model would not be expected to be observed in the actual marketplace context of mall patronage. There were differences between interpersonal attraction and attraction to a mall in the slope of the response function and the significance of the number, as well as the proportion of reinforcing stimuli influencing the attraction response. However, both relationships can be understood by behavioral learning theory, and by considering the nature of the difference between attraction to a person and attraction to a place.

THE REINFORCEMENT-AFFECT MODEL AND PATRONAGE MODELS

The relationship between liked stores and mall attraction is consistent with concepts proposed in theoretical patronage modeling. In Sheth's (1983) theory, personal value determinants of patronage lead into shopping motives, and then marketplace determinants. Darden and Dorsch (1989) describe a hierarchical "bundle of benefits" which shifts according to patronage intentions. Defining personal determinants of patronage by

FIGURE 1
Revising The Retail Gravity Model

$$P(C_{ij}) = S_j T_{ij} R_{ij} / \sum_{j=1}^{n} S_j T_{ij} R_{ij}$$

Where

$P(C_{ij})$ = The probability of a consumer in area i shopping at mall j.

S_j = A measure of the size of the mall. Either square feet of selling space or number or the absolute number of stores.

T_{ij} = Time for a consumer to travel from area i to mall j.

R_{ij} = The number and the proportion of stores at mall j that are reinforcing stimuli to consumers in area i.

n = The number of malls (j) in the consumers choice set.

---

preference for stores is a strategy to integrate the recognized role of personal values and benefits sought and the influence of store image. The image of the mall is embedded in the feelings toward the stores. We can expect that a consumers will have preferences for stores which are compatible with personal value systems and have meaningful benefits.

The results of this study have major implications for mall development strategy if the theoretical relationship between the number and the proportion of liked stores and attraction can be demonstrated in an applied patronage model. In order to test the effectiveness of the reinforcement-affect model of mall patronage, a measure of the number and the proportion of liked stores must be input into the retail gravity model. The predictive ability of mall image inputs was tested in the context of accessibility and size variables (e.g. Gautschi 1981, Howell and Rogers 1981, Nevin and Houston, 1980). The revised model, including the reinforcement inputs is presented in Figure 1.

DIRECTIONS FOR FUTURE RESEARCH

The next stage in theoretical modeling would be to explore how the liking for certain stores or types of stores may be weighted. Byrne (1971) showed that while attraction was a function of the proportion of similar attitudes in a stranger, similar attitudes on issues of importance to the individual, were a more salient positive reinforcement, and therefore had a greater impact on the attraction response than similar attitudes toward trivial matters. In the corresponding stimulus response relationship between an individual and a mall, certain stores or types of stores, perhaps tied to purchase intentions, may have greater reinforcement potential and impact on patronage.

The reinforcement-affect model poses the possibility that stores in a mall can be negative reinforcement, as well as positive. A store that is not liked, or not compatible with the values or the benefits sought by the target served by the mall, may inhibit attraction to a mall. While it is understood that consumers limit the focus of the stores they visit when shopping at a mall (Rothenberg 1986), the idea that stores which are not liked in a mall could have an inverse impact on attraction has not be considered.

Drawing a plan to operationalize conceptual research so that it may be translated into a guide for managerial decisions is an exceptionally difficult challenge. Marketplace determinants muddy the clarity of understanding consumer choice patterns. The reinforcement-affect model is presented as a reworking of the same underlying concept of personal preference for qualitative differences, which image embodied. The advantage of the reinforcement-affect model is that it is developed from a history of behavioral learning theory applications. The reinforcement-affect model of mall patronage can follow the application of learning theory to interpersonal attraction. However, this model can only serve as a guide to understanding the relationship between stimulus cues in the mall and patronage if empirical support for the revised retail gravity model demonstrate that the stimulus response relationship between the stores in the mall and attraction is maintained in the environment of competing marketplace variables.

REFERENCES

Bucklin, Louis P. (1971) "Retail Gravity Models and Consumer Choice: A Theoretical and Empirical Critique," *Economic Geography*, 47 (4), 489-497.

Byrne, Donn (1971) *The Attraction Paradigm*, New York: Academic Press.

Gautschi, David A. (1981) "Specification of Patronage Models for Retail Center Choice" *Journal of Marketing Research*, 18 (2), 165-183.

Gentry, James W. and Alvin C. Burns (1977-1978) "How Important are Evaluative Criteria in Shopping Center Patronage?," *Journal of Retailing*, 53 (4), 73-86, 94.

Darden, William R. (1979) "A Patronage Model of Consumer Behavior," in *Competitive Structure in Retail Markets: The Department Store Perspective*, eds. Ronald W. Stampfl and Elizabeth Hirschman, Chicago: American Marketing Association, 43-52.

Darden, William R. and Michael J. Dorsch (1989) "Upgrading a Patronage Model of Consumer Behavior," in *The Proceedings of The Symposium on Patronage Behavior and Retail Strategy: The Cutting Edge*, ed. William R. Darden, 193-202.

Howell Roy D. and Jerry D. Rogers (1981) "Research into Shopping Mall Choice Behavior," in *Advances in Consumer Research*, Vol. 8, ed. Kent B. Monroe, Ann Arbor, MI: Association for Consumer Research, 671-676.

Huff, David L. (1964) "Defining and Estimating a Trade Area," *Journal of Marketing*, 32 (4), 34-38.

Huff, David L. and Rowland T. Rust (1984) "Measuring the Congruence of a Trading Area," *Journal of Marketing*, 48 (4), 68-74.

Mason, Joseph B. and Morris L. Mayer (1990) *Modern Retailing: Theory and Practice*, Richard D. Irwin, Inc., 660-692.

Meoli, Jennifer (1989) "Predicting Retail Patronage: Should Attraction to Individual Stores be Considered?," *Proceedings of the International Academy of Management and Marketing* 1 (1), 185-190.

Meoli Jennifer (1989) "Stores as Reinforcing Stimuli: A Learning Theory Approach to Retail Mall Assortment," in *The Proceedings of The Symposium on Patronage Behavior and Retail Strategy: The Cutting Edge*, ed. William R. Darden, 149-159.

Milford, Maureen (1989) "Expansion Casts Pall on Malls," *The New York Times*, June 4, Section 10, 21.

Nevin, John R. and Michael J. Houston (1980) "Image as a Component of Attraction to Intraurban Shopping Areas," *Journal of Retailing*, 56 (1), 77-93.

"Overbuilding: a Real or Imagined Issue?," (1987) *Chain Store Executive*, 63 (5), 48-50.

Peterson, Eric C. (1989) "Economic of Space," *Stores*, 71 (5), 67-68.

Peterson Robert A. and Roger A. Kerin (1983) "Store Image Measurement in Patronage Research: Fact and Artifact," in *Patronage Behavior and Retail Management*, ed. William R. Darden and Robert F. Lusch, New York: Elsevier Science Publishing Co., 293-306.

Rothenburg, Marvin J. (1986) "Mall Marketing Principles That Affect Merchandising," *Retail Control*, 8, 3-36.

Sheth, Jagdish N. (1983) "An Integrative Theory of Patronage Preference and Behavior," in *Patronage Behavior and Retail Management*, ed. William R. Darden and Robert F. Lusch, New York: Elsevier Science Publishing Co., 9-27.

"Shopping Centers Suffer From Overbuilding in Many Areas," *Wall Street Journal*, July 31, 1986, 1.

Stanley, Thomas J. and Murphy A. Sewall (1976), "Image Inputs to a Probabilistic Model," *Journal of Marketing*, 40 (3), 48-53.

Weisbrod, Glen E. and Robert J. Parcells and Clifford Kern (1984) "A Disaggregate Model for Predicting Shopping Area Market Attraction," *Journal of Retailing*, 60 (1), 65-83.

Leisure and the Shopping Mall

Peter H. Bloch, University of Massachusetts
Nancy M. Ridgway, University of Colorado
James E. Nelson, University of Colorado

Shopping is my hobby. Every day I come to the mall to see something new (Graham 1988, p. 6)

In truth, I don't go to the malls to shop. Sure I might buy something, but it's not opportunity or need that brings me to a mall--it's the glitter and glitz, the chance to mingle...A good mall is like a good man: it offers entertainment, excitement and enlightenment. (Gershman 1988, p. 43)

INTRODUCTION

In the past few years, hedonic or recreational aspects of consumption have become increasingly salient to consumer researchers (see Holbrook and Hirschman 1982; Hirschman and Holbrook 1982; Hirschman 1984; Bloch and Bruce 1984; Belk 1982). Consumers are no longer viewed only as problem solvers, but as individuals who frequently enjoy aspects of the consumption process apart from its tangible outcomes. Holbrook et al. (1984) defined experiential or playful consumption as:

> intrinsically motivated consumer behavior that includes leisure activity, hobbies, creativity, games, sports, and aesthetic appreciation. All such intrinsically motivated phenomena involve the expenditure of time on activities that produce experiences enjoyed for their own sake (pp. 728-9)

Under this orientation, the attention shifts from the goods obtained via consumption to the fun, emotions, sensory stimulation, fantasy, and amusement elements that may accrue along with the goods or alone.

Arguably, the most common site for recreational or hedonic consumption is the large, enclosed shopping mall. Kowinski (1985) describes the shopping mall as one of the central elements in modern society. Today there are more malls than movie theaters and time budget analysis shows that we spend more time in malls than anywhere else outside of home and work. Americans make 7 billion trips per year to and from malls and one study reports that the most commonly mentioned reason for these visits is entertainment (Stoffel 1988). Today, mall development and remodeling increasingly emphasize entertainment and recreational elements. Thus, in order to add a place dimension to research on hedonic consumption, shopping malls as leisure venues will form the primary focus of this paper. It is the purpose of this paper to explore recreational use of shopping malls and to present the results of a preliminary study exploring this phenomenon.

SHOPPING AS RECREATION

There appear to be two broad categories of leisure activity that may occur while in a shopping mall--recreational shopping and traditional recreation. Nearly thirty years ago, Downs (1961) noted that consumers receive pleasure in addition to merchandise as outcomes of a shopping trip. In the ensuing years, relatively few studies have examined recreational shopping see (Bellenger and Korgoankar 1980; Jansen-Verbeke 1987; Bloch, Ridgway, and Sherrell 1989; Tauber 1972). The limited empirical attention is due to consumer researchers' narrow emphasis on task-oriented shopping and the focus of leisure scholars on outdoor rather than on commercial settings. Regardless of the level of empirical attention, even casual observers encountering "born to shop" bumper stickers must agree that shopping is a pervasive recreational activity in modern society.

Recreational shopping appears to vary in its character. For some individuals, recreational shopping takes on the characteristics of a hunt with the emphasis on the pursuit and discovery of bargains (Thaler 1985). These individuals spend weekends haunting garage sales and flea markets in pursuit of discounted treasures (Belk, Sherry and Wallendorf 1988). Considerable portions of discretionary time also may be devoted to frequenting discounters and stores offering special sales. These individuals may receive many of the same leisure satisfactions that accrue to hunters in the outdoors: affiliation, a sense of accomplishment, and esteem in the eyes of their like-minded peers (Vaske, Fedler and Grafe 1986). These consumers have also become a significant force as shopper/tourists given the rise of the factory outlet. Many small towns have become vacation destinations due to their heavy concentration of factory outlets (Patton 1986).

Recreational shopping may be more commonly exemplified by those who enjoy the recreational aspects of store browsing whether or not a purchase occurs (Bloch and Richins 1983; Bloch, Ridgway and Sherrell 1989; Jarboe and McDaniel 1987). Recreational store visits provide many of the same benefits available through alternative forms of recreation (Harper 1986; Tinsley and Kass 1979; Ragheb and Beard 1980). For example, Tauber and others (Tauber 1972; Westbrook and Black 1985) have suggested that shopping pleasures include the opportunity for social interactions with friends, family or even strangers that one encounters on site. In addition, shoppers may welcome the sensory stimulation, break from routine, and new information that come from a visit to a retail setting. Hirschman (1980) discusses vicarious innovation, the examination of appealing new goods and imagining ownership as substitutes for actual purchase. Although this behavior was not presented in the context of shopping related satisfactions, it appears to be another recreational or hedonic benefit obtainable in the mall. Large enclosed malls with 100, 200, or 300-plus stores provides ample opportunity for browsing and the experience of such satisfactions.

TRADITIONAL RECREATION OPPORTUNITIES AT THE MALL

Although recreational shopping draws consumers to malls, other more traditional entertainments are increasingly available within the air-conditioned space. Kowinski (1985) notes that malls have become community centers, offering visitors such long standing recreational attractions as music, movies, games, and dining out. A mall visitor can meet with friends, play a round of miniature golf, and then see a hit movie at a resident cineplex. Patronizing stores may be completely irrelevant during such visits. In such instances, the mall itself independent of its constituent stores provides the draw.

LEISURE ATTRACTIONS OF THE MALL

There are many elements that draw consumers to malls for recreational purposes. One obvious asset of malls is their *size* and assortment of stores. A recent study reported that looking around and browsing is a more common reason (42% mentioning) for mall patronage than is accomplishing a specific purchase objective (27%) (Monitor 1988). Consumers differ in the types of stores they find pleasurable for browsing because of variable involvement in the merchandise presented for sale (Bloch, Ridgway, and Sherrell 1989). For example, a man who takes considerable pleasure in looking around hardware or electronics stores may derive no recreational benefit from visits to fashion boutiques or jewelry showrooms. Thus, the more stores in one location, the greater the percentage of a population that will find some outlet worth their leisure time.

Several additional elements appear to enhance the attractiveness of shopping malls as leisure destinations. It is obvious that enclosed shopping malls provide a weatherproof environment in which to spend free time. Thus, they represent *comfortable* places to be regardless of time of day or season. In rigorous climates where outdoor recreation often seems untenable, the mall allows consumers to get out of the house to a large space while avoiding extremes of heat or cold. Malls share some of the environmental characteristics of Las Vegas casinos in that it is difficult while inside a mall to determine the correct time or weather.

Regardless of actual statistics, people also believe shopping malls are *safe* places. One study reported that over 90% of respondents feel that a mall is safe or very safe (Monitor 1988). Thus, parents are willing to drop their children off at malls and women feel comfortable going there alone. Mall crime seems to be concentrated in the parking lots, leading visitors to hustle in from the always threatening outside world into the safe confines of the temperate interior. Perhaps because the parking lots are not viewed as any less safe than other alternatives, however, malls remain attractive.

Another draw of the shopping mall is the *low cost* of entry. Essentially it costs nothing to go into a shopping mall. Although impulse buying is common and certainly encouraged in the mall, window shopping and vicarious purchasing are free of charge and provide an inexpensive way to while away a rainy Saturday. Given the increasing cost of alternative entertainment forms, this mall advantage should continue to be significant.

Malls are also attractive leisure sites because of the large variety of *stimuli* available to visitors. A number of leisure scholars have suggested that a significant benefit of leisure pursuits is their ability to provide novelty and stimulation (Beard and Ragheb 1983; Tinsley and Tinsley 1986). Westbrook and Black (1985) also portray stimulation as a notable non-purchase satisfaction available through shopping. Constantly changing displays and merchandise arrayed among over dozens of outlets provides the mall with high levels of sensory stimulation and excitement.

Social variables also make malls attractive leisure sites. A commonly noted recreational and shopping benefit is *affiliation* with others (Feinberg 1989). Interestingly, malls appear to be particularly versatile in terms of social dimensions of leisure. Kelley (1983) discusses mass, group, solitary leisure--all of which are available in the mall. During Saturday afternoons and all during the Christmas season, the large numbers of mall visitors allows the experience of leisure in a mass production setting. The mall resembles a PGA tournament with large galleries striding from location to location to follow the action.

More commonly, malls act as group-level gathering sites allowing people to meet and recreate with friends, as is common among teens. The low cost of entry also makes malls economical entertainment venues for families. Unlike many recreational outlets, shopping malls are also hospitable to people who are alone. While there are stigmas attached to attending movies or dining out alone, visiting a mall alone is common and free of negative associations (Kowinski 1985).

MANAGEMENT OF THE MALL AND PROMOTION OF LEISURE ELEMENTS

Malls compete with other retail establishments and with other leisure activities for individuals' free time. In addition, the growth in mall development has meant that consumers frequently have a choice among several alternative malls (Christman 1988). This competition has led mall developers to provide more varied stimulating environments and greater potential for leisure satisfaction. It also appears that traditional leisure activities are being emphasized in trying to attract people to the mall.

Malls are being designed and remodeled to increase their recreational content in a number of ways. First, planners are devoting increasing resources to environmental and architectural aspects of the mall. Consumers can visit high fashion centers with lavish interiors such as Dallas' Galleria or Boston's Copley Place (Gregorson 1988). Even the more common regional centers are being enhanced with features such as high ceilings, interior landscaping and natural lighting to emulate open space while retaining all the benefits of a controlled environment. These architectural elements are being employed to increase the drama of the mall interior and satisfy those seeking sensory stimulation (Stockil 1972; Donovan and Rossiter 1982). In some malls, patrons seeking a more relaxing experience during their mall-oriented leisure are offered quieter, less intense spaces to counter the generally demanding mall context.

Social satisfactions noted above have been also been recognized by mall managers. In addition to planned group events, such as mall walking clubs for seniors, the expansion of restaurant and entertainment options also serve to bring people together. Recently, however, the social aspects of the mall may have gone too far in the case of teenage visitors. Some malls are now limiting the hours that teens may visit in order to prevent the intrusion of large gatherings of youths which keep older patrons away (Graham 1988).

Mall managers are specifically enhancing the traditional recreation available inside the mall (Christman 1988; Henry 1986; Kowinski 1986; Stoffel 1988). Day care centers, for example, allow parents to browse leisurely in shops not suitable for small children. Food courts, movies, arcades, home improvement expos, art exhibits, auto shows and live entertainment are all being developed and emphasized which increase the recreational benefits available during a mall visit.

Where real estate and financial projections allow, some developers are giving the ultimate expression of the recreational aspects of malls. In Edmonton, Alberta, the West Edmonton Mall has a 400,000 square foot theme park within the mall offering water slides and submarine rides (Kowinski 1986; Henry 1986). This leisure center is surrounded by 800 stores and scores of restaurants, movies and hotel rooms. Transcending the mall context, West Edmonton has become Canada's premier tourist stop. A similar project encompassing a Knott's Berry Farm park is under way in Bloomington Minnesota and is appropriately named The Mall of America (Christman 1988). The distinction between shopping environment and recreational environment is impossible to see in such centers.

Christman (1988) points to several reasons for the increasing leisure content of malls. He argues that leisure and entertainment facilities and architectural features allow a mall to distinguish itself from competing centers. The sameness of malls nationwide has begun to bore consumers. In addition, the declining importance of anchor stores is being met by a growth in recreational anchors as mall magnets.

EXPLORATORY STUDY

As part of a larger research effort examining mall behavior, several preliminary findings regarding recreational shopping in the mall are presented below.

Method and Sample

Exit interviews were conducted with 200 mall patrons at each of six malls located throughout the United States for a total sample of 1200. Two separate questionnaires were used in the study. Study participants at three malls (representing 600 patrons) received one questionnaire while the other 600 participants received an entirely different questionnaire. Data reported in this paper come from both questionnaires. Individual malls were chosen to represent a variety of geographic locations and city sizes. Consumers were chosen by a judgmental sampling procedure designed to obtain widespread demographic representation (particularly on the variables of sex and age). Contacts with patrons were made by professional interviewers who were employed by survey research firms based in each of the six malls. Mall patrons were approached, offered a small financial incentive for participation in the study and those agreeing were given a self-administered survey to fill out. When completed, the surveys were collected by the interviewers and the patrons were given their financial reward.

Measures

Two pretests of the measures used in the questionnaires were conducted prior to data collection. Attitudinal measures were refined by a pretest using college students at three universities. All measures were then pretested in a mall setting to refine question understandability and ease of questionnaire completion. Specifics about the measures used in the data analysis are detailed in the next section.

Analysis and Results

Data from Sample 1 were used to explore the structure of respondents' consumption activities at the three shopping malls, with emphasis on isolating browsing behavior. Specifically, respondents' yes/no reports of engaging in 14 specific activities (shown in Table 1) were factor analyzed using principal axes factoring and oblique rotation. It should be noted that this procedure was used not to generate a theoretical model but simply as a heuristic (Kim and Mueller 1978) to inspect consumption activities for possible structure. In addition, any evidence of structure uncovered in the analysis will be attenuated because of the inevitable restriction in range for correlations among the activities due to the dichotomous measurements (Rummel 1970, pp. 216-19). A summary of the yes/no reports of activities appears in Table 1.

TABLE 1
Summary of Respondents' Mall Activities Engaged in Today

	Activity	Number Responding Yes	No
1.	Shopped to buy something today	435	165
2.	Shopped to buy something in the future	336	261
3.	Browsed in a store without a plan to buy something	366	232
4.	Looked at special mall exhibits or shows	218	380
5.	Socialized with friends or others	250	350
6.	Walked for exercise	139	460
7.	Had a conversation with sales clerks	348	252
8.	Eaten a snack/treat/ or had a soft drink	281	318
9.	Eaten a lunch or dinner	179	419
10.	Visited a medical/dental/vision-care office	41	550
11.	Had a conversation with other shoppers I just met today	136	463
12.	Had a haircut/hairstyling	48	551
13.	Played video games	43	555
14.	Gone to a movie	28	570

Results of the factor analysis appear in Table 2, showing a six factor solution. The solution represents an "overfactoring" result in reference to an eigenvalue greater than 1 criterion. However, many researchers recommend overfactoring compared to the alternative as a way to improve interpretation of the final solution (Stewart 1981). Results in Table 2 indicate the existence of a unique factor for "Browsing," (i.e., looking around the mall with no intent to buy)--Factor VI. Inspection of the other factor loadings permits identification of Factor I as "Eating," II as "Video/Movie," III as "Walking for Exercise," IV as "Shopping to Buy," and V as "Socializing." Factor correlations indicate that browsing behavior tends to be positively associated with "Eating" and negatively with "Socializing" and "Walking;" browsing behavior appears to be uncorrelated with "Shopping to Buy" and "Video/Movie."

Similar analyses were also completed for a four, five, and seven factor solution, with the latter failing to converge (25 iterations). Consistent with preceding results, the four and five factor solutions forced the browsing item (Activity 3) to load on the "Eating" factor.

Data from Sample 2 were used to examine relationships between browsing activity, demographic characteristics, and types of stores in which respondents enjoyed browsing. Analysis here began by constructing a browsing index as the sum of three items:

1. Approximately how many times have you browsed in a mall or shopping center during the past 30 days?
2. How would you rate the importance of browsing as a recreational activity for you?
3. During your trip to the Mall today, approximately what percentage of your time has been spent browsing?

In developing the index, responses to each item were first divided into five categories and values from 1 to 5 assigned to represent increasing degrees of browsing intensity. Assigned values were then summed to create the index. As summary, the index ranged from a minimum of 3 to a maximum of 15; the mean was 9.1, median 9.0, and standard deviation 2.7. A demographic profile of respondents in the bottom and top quartiles of index scores appears in Table 3. Briefly, respondents in the top quartile are younger, with less income, and tend not to possess a major credit card than respondents in the bottom quartile.

The index was used as an dependent variable in a series of one-way ANOVAs using demographic variables and type of store as independent variables. Summary results appear in Table 4, showing significant differences in the browsing index for age, income, and type of store. Table 5 shows mean values for each group for each independent variable. The index indicates a U-shaped relationship with income and age, although the latter result is quite tentative given the small number of respondents age 65 and older (n=9). Most enjoyable stores for browsing appear to be art galleries, record and tape stores, clothing stores, and department stores. Least enjoyable include book, hardware, and kitchen stores.

Briefly, results of this exploratory study indicate that there exist consumers who come to the mall specifically to browse. In addition, browsers are more likely to be social while at the mall (i.e., have conversations with other shoppers or friends) than others. In addition, consumers who score high on a browsing index appear to be younger, with

TABLE 2
Factor Analysis Results for Mall Activities*

Initial Statistics

Activity	Communality	Factor	Eigenvalue	% of Var.	Cum. %
1	.07442	1	2.23199	15.9	15.9
2	.05124	2	1.42408	10.2	26.1
3	.07129	3	1.18736	8.5	34.6
4	.09599	4	1.14374	8.2	42.8
5	.12286	5	.97056	6.9	49.7
6	.10802	6	.95703	6.8	56.5
7	.10641	7	.91795	6.6	63.1
8	.15437	8	.90097	6.4	69.5
9	.14751	9	.84356	6.0	75.6
10	.04290	10	.77370	5.5	81.1
11	.13717	11	.73405	5.2	86.3
12	.04566	12	.68872	4.9	91.2
13	.15239	13	.61802	4.4	95.7
14	.17421	14	.60828	4.3	100.0

Oblique Rotation Solution
*Pattern Matrix***

Activity	Factor I	Factor II	Factor III	Factor IV	Factor V	Factor VI
1				0.52		
2						
3						0.53
4						
5					-0.60	
6			-0.64			
7				0.39		
8	0.56					
9	0.53					
10						
11					-0.32	
12						
13		-0.44				
14		-0.70				

Factor Correlation Matrix

	Factor I	Factor II	Factor III	Factor IV	Factor V	Factor VI
Factor II	-0.24					
Factor III	-0.22	0.16				
Factor IV	0.12	0.08	-0.14			
Factor V	-0.34	0.23	0.37	-0.38		
Factor VI	0.46	-0.01	-0.15	0.04	-0.28	

* Activities are identified in Table 2.
**Only factor loadings > .30 are shown for the sake of clarity.

---

lower income. Finally, certain types of stores hold more appeal to browsers than others.

LEISURE AND THE MALL: RESEARCH OPPORTUNITIES

There are a number of promising issues for future research on recreational aspects of malls. One possible area of inquiry is the role of recreational elements in the multi-purpose mall trip. It is likely that the typical mall visit includes both required shopping tasks and recreational elements. It might prove interesting to identify whether recreational or purchase needs drive a visit to the mall. For example, a purchase need may drive the trip and while at the mall the consumer indulges in some browsing or other recreational activity. On the other hand, a consumer may feel bored and go to the mall just to get out of the house and have some fun

TABLE 3
Respondent Characteristics by Bottom (N=145) and Top (N=166) Quartiles of the Browsing Index

Characteristic	Bottom Quartile	Top Quartile	Significance
Male	48.3%	46.4%	ns
Female	51.7%	53.6%	
Married	55.9%	64.5%	ns
Not Married	44.1%	35.5%	
Household Size	2.7	2.9	ns
Possess Credit Card	34.5%	48.2%	$p < .02$
Age (years)	32.2	28.7	$p < .02$
Income ($000)	35.6	29.0	$p < .001$

TABLE 4
ANOVA Results for the Browsing Index

Independent Variable	F (df.)	Signif.	Eta^2
Age	2.34 (6, 537)	0.031	0.026
Sex	0.21 (1, 542)	0.644	0.000
Income	3.33 (5, 534)	0.006	0.030
Type of Store	2.72 (12, 468)	0.001	0.065

looking around. While on the mall premises, this browsing may trigger recall of certain product needs and thus stimulate more purposeful shopping behavior. Based on the increasing leisure content of malls, one must assume that managers view recreation potential as a draw that later culminates in purchase.

The significance of novelty in mall attractiveness also warrants further study. In particular, does the recreational attractiveness of a mall wane as it ages. In other words, does familiarity with mall offerings and layout decrease its attractiveness as a recreation destination? Furthermore, what is the relative importance of novelty and change in the mall itself versus change in the merchandise sold. Are new stores more desirable than new goods offered in existing retail outlets for those with hedonic motives?

Conversely the potential for sensory overload in mall environments could also be investigated. Researchers typically agree that people seek some optimal level of stimulation (Raju 1980). It is possible that infrequent mall visitors may be those who find the mall environment is over or under-stimulating.

Finally, some may wish to discover more about the impact of the mall on the culture. Leisure scholars have shown concern with the commodification of leisure which is exemplified by substituting mall visits for park visits. One may even speculate about mall visits increasing tendencies toward materialism. As recreational shoppers and browsers come into contact with so many products, they may become dissatisfied with their inability to buy them, decreasing overall satisfaction levels. Certainly these issues deserve additional attention. The profit seeking orientation of mall managers should encourage them to build and remodel shopping centers to make them increasingly appealing places to spend discretionary time. Therefore, the popularity of the mall as for recreation is unlikely to diminish.

TABLE 5
Descriptive Statistics for the Browsing Index by Groups

	Mean	Std. Dev.	N
Demographic variables			
Males	9.08	2.77	255
Females	9.18	2.73	289
15-17 years	9.91	2.77	33
18-24 years	9.95	2.38	216
25-34 years	8.85	2.78	159
35-44 years	8.82	3.30	67
45-54 years	8.53	2.88	34
55-64 years	8.26	3.15	27
65 years and older	9.75	2.92	9
Under $15,000 income	9.96	2.52	101
$15,000 to $24,999	9.43	2.56	112
$25,000 to $34,999	8.72	2.76	115
$35,000 to $49,999	8.83	2.67	96
$50,000 to $74,999	8.70	2.93	73
$75,000 and over	9.16	2.84	43
Favorite Browsing locale			
Book Stores	7.79	3.09	72
Kitchen Stores	8.00	2.94	4
Sporting Goods Stores	8.44	2.97	50
Record/Tape Stores	9.78	2.35	45
Hardware Stores	7.71	2.36	7
Antique Stores	8.21	2.19	14
Shoe Stores	8.86	2.68	14
Art Galleries	10.21	2.63	14
Home Ent./Electronic Stores	9.55	2.39	20
Jewelry Stores	9.33	3.35	15
Home Furnishings Stores	8.76	2.17	13
Department Stores	9.18	2.58	73
Clothing Stores	9.51	2.67	140

REFERENCES

Beard, Jacob G and Mounir G. Ragheb (1983), "Measuring Leisure Motivation," *Journal of Leisure Research*, 15 (3), 219-228.

Belk, Russell W. (1982), "Acquiring, Possessing and Collecting: Fundamental Processes in Consumer Behavior," in *Marketing Theory: Philosophy of Science Perspectives*, ed. R. Bush and S. Hunt, Chicago: American Marketing Association,

Belk, Russell W., John F. Sherry and Melanie Wallendorf (1988), "A Naturalistic Inquiry into Buyer and Seller Behavior at a Swap Meet," *Journal of Consumer Research*, 14 (March), 449-470.

Bellenger, Danny N. and Pradeep Korgoankar (1980), "Profiling the Recreational Shopper," *Journal of Retailing*, 58 (Spring), 58-81.

Bloch, Peter H. and Bruce Grady D (1984), "Product Involvement as Leisure Behavior," in *Advances in Consumer Research, Vol. 11*, ed. Thomas Kinnear, Ann Arbor, MI: Association for Consumer Research, 197-202.

_____ and Marsha L. Richins (1983), "Shopping Without Purchase: An Investigation of Consumer Browsing Behavior," in *Advances in Consumer Research, Vol. 10*, ed. R. Bagozzi and A. Tybout, Ann Arbor, MI: Association for Consumer Research, 389-393.

_____ , Nancy M. Ridgway and Daniel L. Sherrell (1989), "Extending the Concept of Shopping: AN Investigation of Browsing Activity," *Journal of the Academy of Marketing Science*, 17 (Winter), 13-21.

Christman, Edward (1988), *Mixing Entertainment, Retail*. Shopping Centers Today. 1, 4-5.

Donovan, Robert J. and John R. Rossiter (1982), "Store Atmosphere: An Environmental Psychology Approach," *Journal of Retailing*, 58 (Spring), 34-57.

Downs, Anthony (1961), "A Theory of Consumer Efficiency," *Journal of Retailing*, 37 (Spring), 50.

Feinberg, Richard A. et al (1989), "There's Something Social Happening at the Mall," *Journal of Business and Psychology*, 4 (Fall), 49-63.

Gershman, Suzy (1988), *Mad About the Mall*. Travel & Leisure. 43-48.

Graham, Ellen (1988), *The Call of the Mall*. Wall Street Journal. 7R.

Gregorson, John (1988), "Tailoring a fashion Mall to its Urban setting," *Building Design and Construction*, 29 (March), 74.

Harper, William (1986), "Freedom in the Experience of Leisure," *Leisure Sciences*, 8 (2), 115-130.

Henry, Gordon M. (1986), *Welcome to the Pleasure Dome*. Time. 128: 75.

Hirschman, Elizabeth C. (1980), "Innovativeness, Novelty Seeking, and Consumer Creativity," *Journal of Consumer Research*, 7 (December), 283-295.

_____ (1984), "Experience Seeking: A Subjectivist Perspective of Consumption," *Journal of Business Research*, 12 115-136.

_____ and Morris B. Holbrook (1982), "Hedonic Consumption: Emerging Concepts, Methods, and Propositions," *Journal of Marketing*, 46 (Summer), 92-101.

Holbrook, Morris B. and et al (1984), "Play as a Consumption Experience: The Role of Emotions, Performance and Personality in the Enjoyment of Games," *Journal of Consumer Research*, 11 (September), 728-739.

_____ and Elizabeth C. Hirschman (1982), "The Experiential Aspects of Consumption: Consumer Fantasies, Feelings and Fun," *Journal of Consumer Research*, 9 (September), 132-140.

Jansen-Verbeke, Myriam (1987), "Women Shopping and Leisure," *Leisure Studies*, 6, 71-86.

Jarboe, Glen R and Carl D. McDaniel (1987), "A Profile of Browsers in Regional Shopping Mall," *Journal of the Academy of Marketing Science*, 15 (Spring), 45-52.

Kelley, John R. (1983), *Leisure Identities and Interactions*, London: George Allen.

Kim, Jae-On and Charles W. Mueller (1978), *Factor Analysis: Statistical Methods and Practical Issues*, Sage University Paper Series on Quantitative Applications in the Social Sciences, Series No. 07-014, Beverly Hills and London, Sage Publications.

Kowinski, William S. (1985), *The Malling of America*, New York: William Morrow and Co.

_____ (1986), "Endless Summer at the World's Biggest Shopping Wonderland," *Smithsonian*, 17 (9), 34-43.

Monitor (1988), *Consumer Behavior in the Shopping Center*. Monitor. 18: 19-40.

Patton, Spiro G. (1986), "Factory Outlets and Travel Industry Development," *Journal of Travel Research*, (Summer),

Ragheb, Mounir G. and Jacob G. Beard (1980), "Leisure Satisfaction: Concept, Theory, and Measurement," in *Social Psychological Perspectives on Leisure and Recreation*, ed. Seppo E. Iso-Ahola, Springfield, IL: Charles C. Thomas, 329-353.

Raju, P. S. (1980), "Optimum Stimulation Level: Its Relationship to Personality, Demographics, and Exploratory Behavior," *Journal of Consumer Research*, 7 (December), 272-282.

Rummel, R. J. (1970), *Applied Factor Analysis*, Evanston, Ill.: Northwestern University Press.

Stewart, David W. (1981), "The Application and Misapplication of Factor Analysis in Marketing Research," *Journal of Marketing Research*, Vol. 18 (February), 51-62.

Stockil, Peter (1972), "The Mall," in *Enclosed Shopping Centres*, ed. Clive Darlow, London: Architectural Press, 52-62.

Stoffel, Jennifer (1988), *Where America Goes for Entertainment*. New York Times. 11F.

Tauber, Edward M. (1972), "Why Do People Shop?," *Journal of Marketing*, 36 (October), 46-59.

Thaler, Richard (1985), "Mental Accounting and Consumer Choice," *Marketing Science*, 4 (Summer), 199-214.

Tinsley, Howard E. and Richard A. Kass (1979), "The Ltent Structure of the Need satisfying Properties of Leisure Activities," *Journal of Leisure Research*, 11 (4), 278-291.

_____ and Diane J. Tinsley (1986), "A Theory of the Attributes, Benefits and Causes of Leisure Experience," *Leisure Sciences*, 8 (1), 1-43.

Vaske, Jerry J., Anthony J. Fedler, and Alan R. Grafe (1986), "Multiple Determinants of Satisfaction from a Specific Waterfowl Hunting Trip," *Leisure Sciences*, 8 (2), 149-166.

Westbrook, Robert A. and William C. Black (1985), "A Motivation-Based Shopper Typology," *Journal of Retailing*, 61 (Spring), 78-103.

Consumer Research and its Role in Shopping Center Development
Peter A. Doherty, Impact Resources, Inc.

Shopping center development in the 1990s will require increased reliance upon well-selected consumer information. Markets are becoming saturated with gross leasable area and market shifts are placing pressure upon the redevelopment and repositioning of existing centers.

Local market syndicated consumer information can provide important input to guide the development and redevelopment of America's shopping center industry. This paper explores the application of a syndicated local market consumer survey which can dramatically decrease the amount of expensive, customized research required. This survey is called MA•RT, which is an acronym for Market Audience • Readership Traffic. MA•RT, with its retail focus, can be used in all levels of shopping center development, including:

- Understanding the target consumer
- Developing the product/service mix
- Developing center image/design/signage
- Lease planning

MA•RT SYNDICATED CONSUMER RESEARCH

MA•RT measures local markets, collecting at either the Consolidated Metropolitan Statistical Area (CMSA) or the Metropolitan Statistical Area (MSA) levels. MA•RT currently measures 49 local markets annually that account for over 80 MSAs and 50 percent of the United States population. Within each of the MA•RT-measured markets, 5,000 to 18,000 surveys are collected, the exact number varies by the size and complexity of the market.

The destination-oriented collection scheme is designed to sample in areas of general retail consumer traffic flow. There are typically between 20 and 100 collection sites per market, including:

- Super-regional and regional malls
- Community and neighborhood shopping centers
- Other areas of high retail traffic (e.g. downtown shopping districts and grocery and other destination stores).

ACCURATE REPRESENTATION OF THE CONSUMER MARKETPLACE

Tight controls are set during the collection process to assure an accurate representation of the consumer marketplace. Controls consist of census-based information relating to:

- Age
- Sex
- Income
- Ethnicity
- Geography

These characteristics have been found to exhibit a close correlation with a wide cross-section of consumer behaviors and therefore function as important drivers or independent controls for these behaviors. The network of collection sites are set up across the market and a target number of surveys assigned per site with these controls in mind.

ACTIONABLE INFORMATION FOR SHOPPING CENTER DEVELOPMENT

The MA•RT consumer survey collects over 450 actionable pieces of consumer information, most of which can be useful in the development or redevelopment of shopping centers.

Demographic Information

MA•RT collects over twenty pieces of basic demographic information from each consumer respondent. These accumulated characteristics give an overall profile of a market's consumer population or of specific consumer groups (e.g. cellular telephone owners or Saks Fifth Avenue shoppers).

Lifestyle Characteristics

Consumers lifestyle characteristics, especially leisure time activities, can be helpful in store design, signage, advertising and merchandising. Is the target consumer interested in sports, fitness, outdoor activities, or theatre?

Retail Behavior

MA•RT collects consumers store preferences and reasons for shopping the store for sixteen merchandise categories. Consumers store preferences are useful not only for developing specific store shopper profiles, but also in developing leasing plans. MA•RT has information on over 1,500 retailers nationwide. Over 450 data points are available for every retailer in the MA•RT database, so a thorough understanding of each retailer's customer is at hand.

Consumers shopping motivations and fashion orientation are useful in developing a focus or image for a shopping center. Should the center focus around low price, or do the consumers mandate a quality/service/fashion-oriented center?

Purchase Intentions

MA•RT's major purchase intentions shed light on current opportunities. The MA•RT survey asks definite, probable, and undecided intentions to purchase each of twelve categories within the year.

Cross Media Measurement

The relative importance of different forms of media for each specific consumer group can be seen through MA•RT, taking the guesswork out of developing a media strategy. What times of the day do my shoppers tune in to which radio stations? Do my shoppers really read the lifestyle section of the paper? How much time does my target customer spend watching TV? Are my newspaper ad inserts effective?

MAJOR ISSUES FACING SHOPPING CENTER DEVELOPMENT

To state the obvious, shopping center development or redevelopment is a task of great complexity. However, there are a number of critical elements that can be identified for which MA•RT consumer information can provide vital decision-making insights. These include:

- Local market differences
- Micromarketing demands
- Tenant mix criteria
- Research needs for the 1990s

Major Issue No. 1: Local Market Differences

Consumers are not the same across all markets. A shopping center concept developed for New York may not work in Kansas City. MA•RT's database of local market information allows one to quickly understand a city's unique qualities, understand its strengths and weaknesses, and understand its competitors, other markets, strengths and weaknesses. In other words, MA•RT can help us profile a market and establish its competitive position.

Many cities have a well-established image, such as New York, for being sophisticated and fashion forward. New York City, Boston and Los Angeles are the top ranked cities for fine dining. (Figure 1). Detroit is not far behind. When looking at the percentage of consumers that attend live theatre, Washington D.C., Los Angeles and Detroit are the top ranked. New York follows directly behind. And if our focus was on people who like to go to sporting events, then Minneapolis is the clear winner. But Cincinnati and Kansas City are up there too.

Concentrations of specific target customer groups vary radically by market (e.g. Hispanics, Blacks, Asians, or seniors). A large sample syndicated survey can provide detailed information on once undervalued segments. (Figure 2). If it is large enough, it can also go beyond just size and examine details. Is there a market for fashion forward women aged 65 and older? West Palm Beach and Miami have strong presence of fashion forward seniors, in stark contrast to Phoenix and Tampa.

For those developments or retailers that focus on service as an important differential advantage, knowing service-oriented markets is a major leg up. These markets have the customers who demand service and the retailers who have cultivated this market demand. In other words, the markets are prepared.

The top five markets for service as a reason for department store choice are shown in Figure 3. The impact of Nordstrom is evident, being present in all these markets.

Looked at by merchandise line, the top five markets vary. When considering service as a reason for selecting a men's casual clothing store, the influence of Nordstrom is again apparent. Nordstrom is presently in three of the top five ranked markets - Seattle, San Diego and Salt Lake City.

If you are developing a price-first center concept, markets where consumers focus on price should be high on your list. Cincinnati, San Antonio and Phoenix top the list of MA•RT-measured markets for concentration on price as a reason for selecting a women's casual clothing store. For TV/VCR, Cincinnati, Sacramento and Minneapolis are the top three price-oriented markets.

Major Issue No. 2: Micromarketing Demands

Shopping centers in the 1990s face the same problems that faced the traditional department store in the 1970s and 1980s. They can no longer be all things to all people. Increased competition in saturated markets, together with a more individualistic and demanding consumer, have led to an age of target marketing, niche marketing and micromarketing.

The traditional department store has had to compete with discount stores, specialty stores, mass merchandise stores, hypermarkets, off-price stores, membership warehouse clubs, and direct mail/catalog retailers. In a similar manner the (now) traditional regional mall competes with fashion malls, power centers, home center malls, off-price malls, factory outlet centers, and many more. Each center is attempting to develop a niche based upon a specific segment of the consumer population. Successful centers are able to identify a clear target consumer group, put in place a mixture of stores with the right product at the right price, quality and service level to meet their demands and do so by creating an ego pleasing shopping environment.

Micromarketing, niche marketing and target marketing are the buzz-words of retailing today. One example of a consumer niche is fashion orientation. The MA•RT survey asks respondents to identify with one of three fashion focuses: newest trends and styles, conservative or traditional fashion, or value and comfort instead of fashion. (Figure 4).

The typical target for a department store, the 25-54 year old, is well-represented in all components. If you go after one fashion component you miss over half the group, but you can't be all things to all people. Highly targeted specialty stores have responded to this:

- Fashion forward -- The Limited
- Conservative -- Talbots
- Value and comfort -- Eddie Bauer

In contrast to those shopping centers serving relatively homogeneous populations, downtown

FIGURE 1
Fine Dining Is On the Menu Across America's Largest Cities

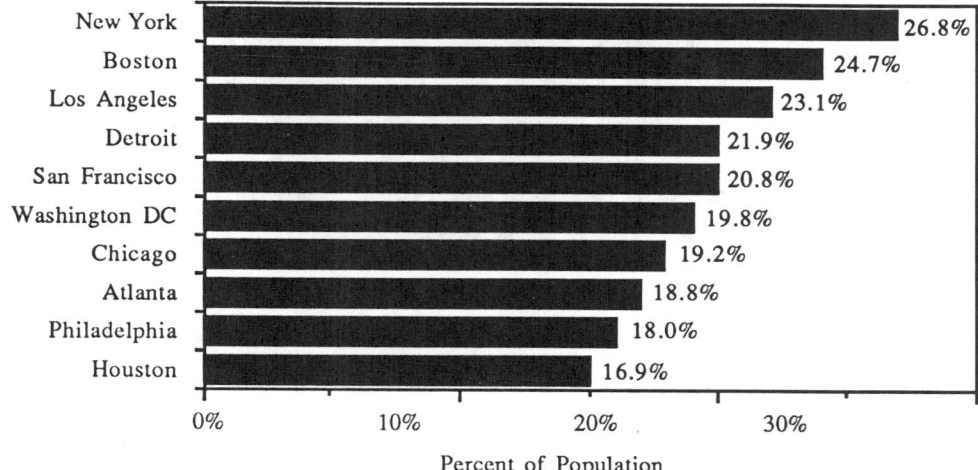

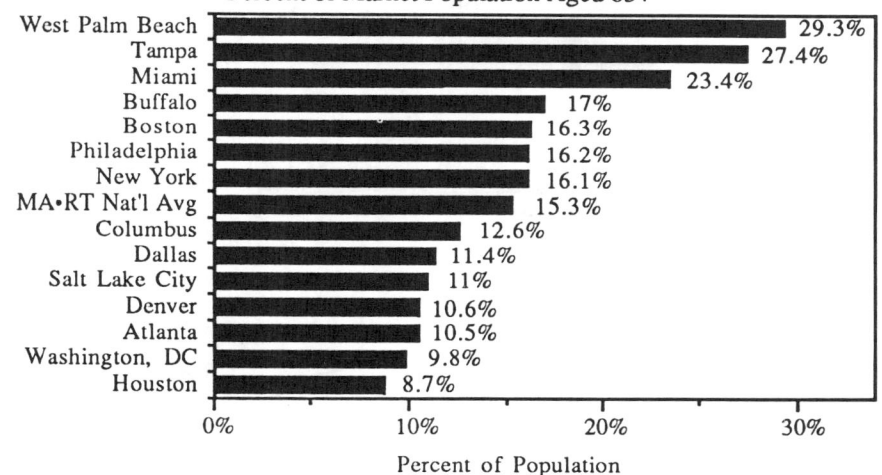

FIGURE 2
Percent of Market Population Aged 65+

retail often must cater to several different constituent groups, including downtown workers, residents, shoppers, and visitors. Downtown mall developers must recognize these consumer differences. Who will be the core customer? The fringe customer?

In Cleveland, important constituents are the downtown workers and downtown residents. (Figure 5). As the shopping is improved the affluent will become part of the core shopper group. As we can see there are clearly different segments with different needs and capabilities. The proportion aged 25-54 is relatively similar, but there are dramatic differences in income and education.

With a major focus of retailing on service, service quality may well be the competitive position of a mall and its tenants. What does a service-oriented consumer look like? Other centers may focus on price-oriented consumers. What does a price-oriented customer look like?

Using Los Angles consumers as an example, we examine service-oriented consumers, and to make their attributes pop out, we have contrasted them with price-oriented consumers. (Figure 6).

Compared to price-oriented consumers, service-oriented consumers are more likely to be married, highly educated, hold white collar jobs, and be slightly more concentrated in the 25-44 year old age group. When it comes to income, service-oriented consumers are strongly concentrated in the upper income groups, over half have household

FIGURE 3
Service as a Reason for Department Store Choice

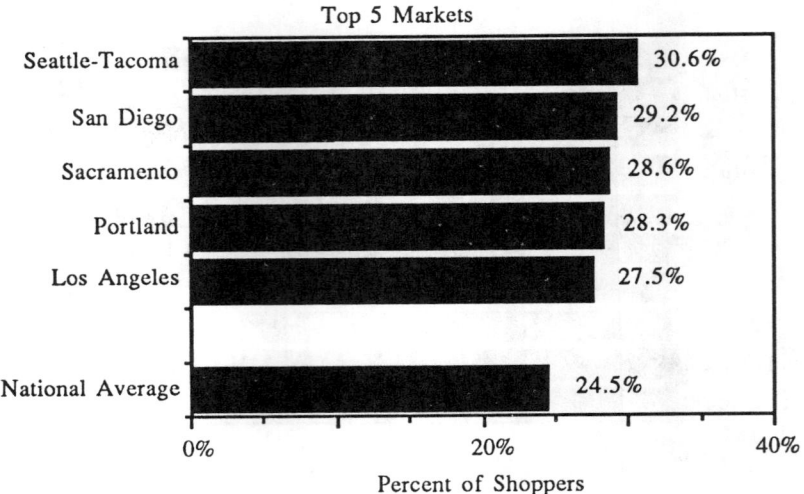

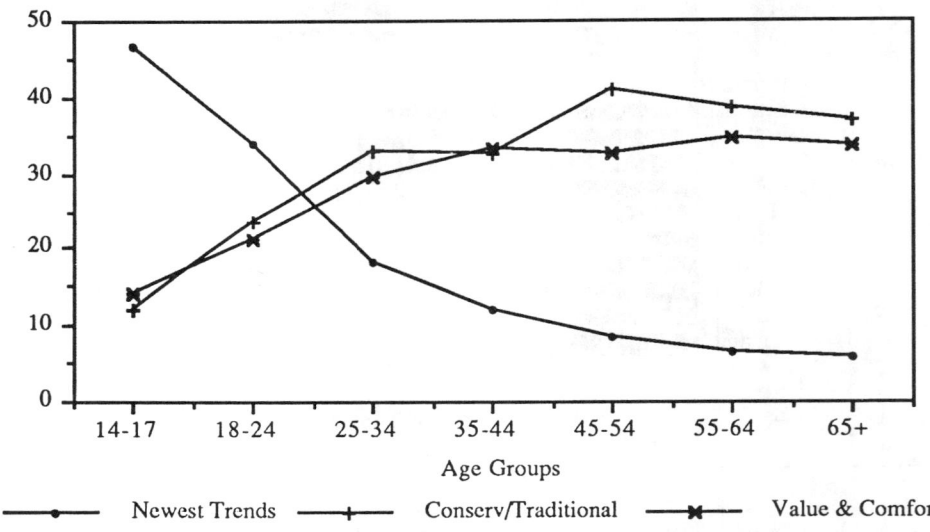

FIGURE 4
Fashion Consciousness Among Age Groups

incomes of $50,000 or above. Service-oriented consumers have a somewhat lower proportion of dual income households than their price-oriented counterparts.

Service-oriented Los Angeles consumers are very fashion forward, over twice as likely to favor the newest trends and styles than their price-oriented neighbors. A slightly smaller percentage allies with conservative and traditional fashions, while only a very small percentage are not fashion conscious. It therefore comes as no surprise that service-oriented consumers are four times as likely to prefer specialty department stores as price-oriented consumers. And price-oriented consumers are eight times as likely to prefer discount stores.

Major Issue No. 3: Tenant Mix Criteria
The development of a shopping center tenant mix has many determinants, including:

- The image of the center and the city
- The competitive position
- The target constituencies
- The merchandise mix

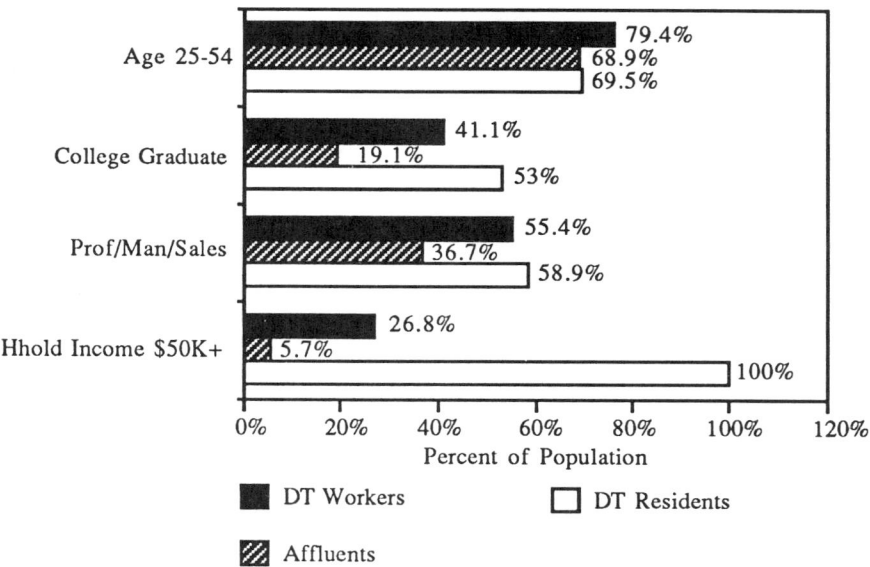

FIGURE 5
Downtown Workers/Downtown Residents/Affluents
Select Demographics
Cleveland

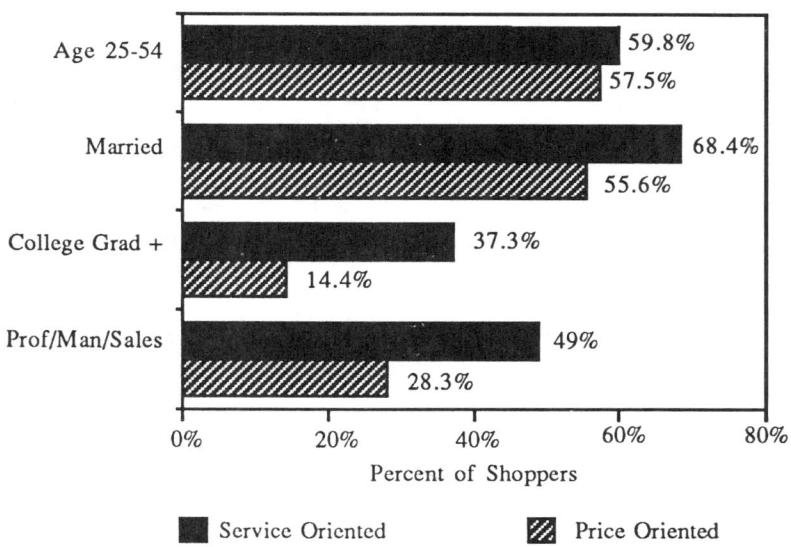

FIGURE 6
Service vs. Price Oriented Consumers
Select Demographics
Los Angeles

FIGURE 7

Women's Specialty Apparel — Regional Selection Leaders

Target Shoppers: Women Only

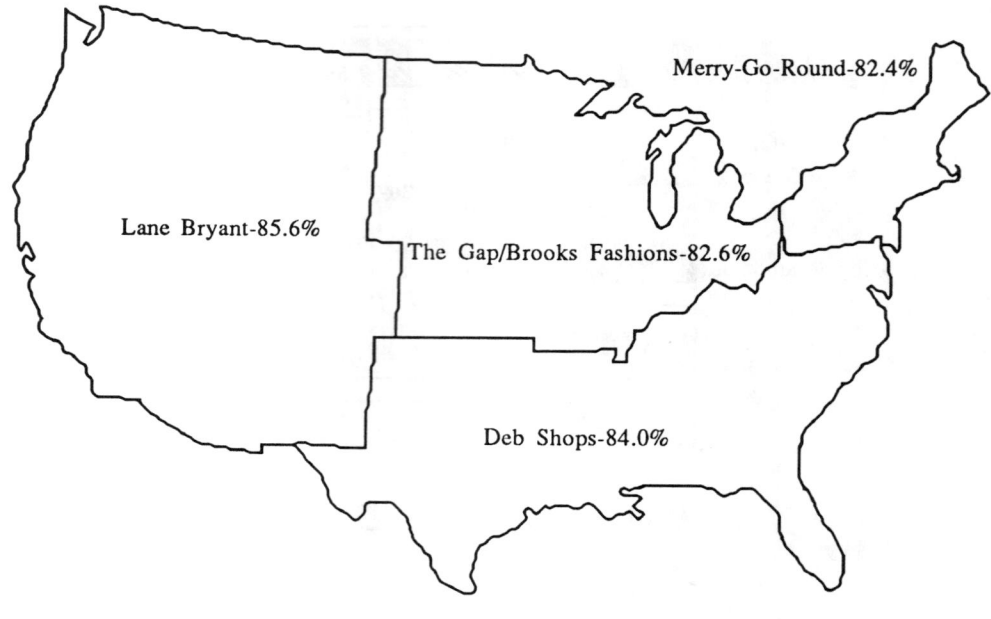

The MA•RT database, rich in retail information and with profiles of over 1,500 retailers, can be an invaluable tool for developing a tenant mix. Impact Resources has analyzed consumers retail preferences and their motivations for shopping specific stores. In our version of the People's Choice Awards, retail leaders in each merchandise line for every shopping motivation are identified by census region. Retail winners are those retailers whose regular customers identified a given motivation more often than regular customers at other stores in the same merchandise line. These retail winners are published annually in the *Consumer Viewpoint Study*, a joint publication with the Retail Advertising and Marketing Association.

Women's specialty apparel selection leaders are identified (Figure 7).

- Merry-Go-Round leads in the Northeast (82.4% of women in the Northeast who shop at Merry-Go-Round for women's clothing choose this store because of selection).
- The Gap and Brooks Fashions tie as leaders in the Midwest
- Deb Shops in the South
- Lane Bryant in the West

Casual Corner has succeeded in impressing its customers with quality merchandise across the country, with the exception of the Midwest where The Gap wins out. The Limited receives second place in all four regions. Casual Corner and the Limited have low ratings on price and high ratings on quality. The Gap has developed strengths in both quality and selection.

Casual Corner also succeeds in offering high service levels consistently across the country. The advertising message, "Build Your Wardrobe at Casual Corner," and a complete line of merchandise offered in addition to Casual Corner's "investment dressing" and "private consultation" programs have helped this service image.

Yet Casual Corner's direct competition, The Limited, wins the market share game hands down. How does the Casual Corner shopper differ from The Limited? While they both target the younger female and student shopper, The Limited niches much more strongly. (Figure 8). The same is true for fashion. Both stores appeal to the fashion-forward shopper, but The Limited is much more dramatic. Casual Corner also appeals strongly to the more conservative traditional shopper and has made strong inroads into the black consumer marketplace.

If you are looking for a service-oriented anchor, department store service winners may be of interest. (Figure 9). As you would expect, Nordstrom's legendary service makes it a dominant force in every market in which it competes. As this company expands into the Northeast, its reputation precedes it. Look out B. Forman and then look out Jacobsons!

We cannot tenant a mall without important inputs on the market, target customer, competitive

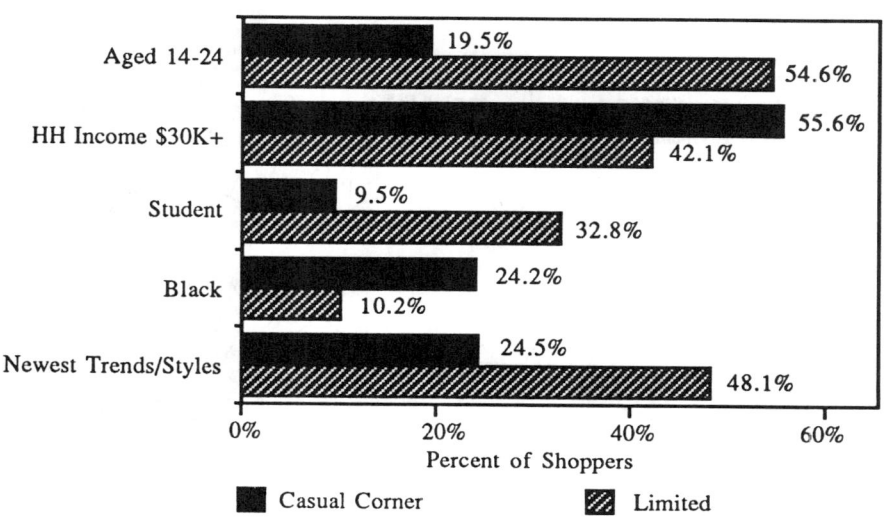

FIGURE 8
Casual Corner vs. Limited Shprs
Midwest Profile

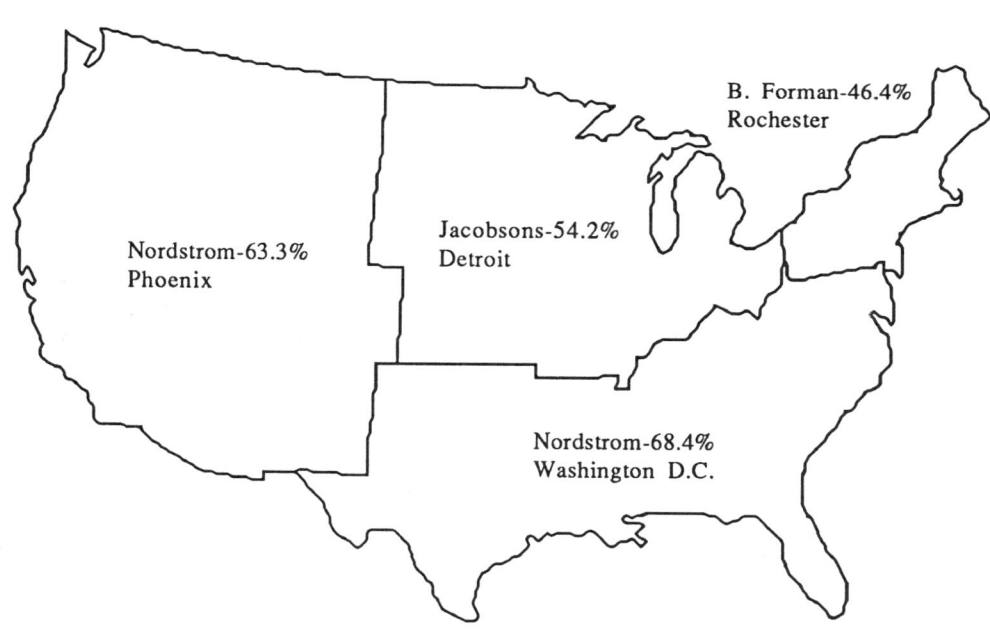

FIGURE 9

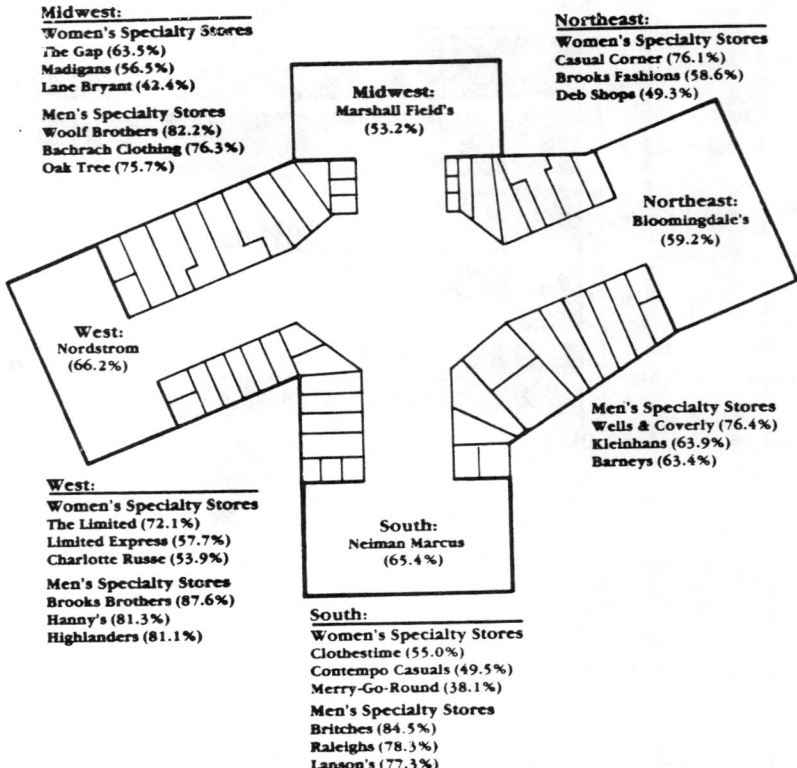

FIGURE 10
Fashion Mall of America

position, and center image. However, as an illustration of the use of a large local market syndicated survey, we can construct certain ideal mixes for, say the "Off-Price Mall of America," or the "Power Center of America," or the "Fashion Mall of America." For example, if you were developing a fashion center that incorporates quality leaders across the country, the retailers that you would want to include appear in figure 10. Bloomingdale's, Neiman-Marcus, Nordstrom and Marshall Field's anchor the "Fashion Mall of America."

Major Issue No. 4: Research Needs for the 1990s

The 1990s will be an era of increasing fragmentation in retail and media. Gone are the days of mass marketing. Shopping center developers will need to find the niche that gives their centers quality growth opportunities. Research will be required that is appropriate for this decade.

Information users deserve data that is accurate and actionable for the needs of market analysis of shopping center development. The critical criteria for choosing an information source include:

- Local market information
- Large sample sizes
- True single source
- Cross media measurement

Is the sample size large enough for micromarketing? All consumers are not the same. If we divide our sample, is it large enough to efficiently measure that segment?

Benefits Of A Large Sample Size

	Large Sample	Average Sample
Total Sample	5,882	1,000
Affluents (20.4%)	1,200	204
And Intend to Purchase Jewelry (11.1%)	133	22

For example, MA•RT measures 5,000 to 18,000 respondents. How many other sources go much beyond 1,000? Look at the significance of sample size. If you were targeting affluents and then broke the group further, would you make million dollar decisions on a sample under thirty?

Is the information from a true single source, or is it merged data? If you want to know about *my* retail behavior or my media usage...ask me, not someone who looks like me. Not someone who lives in my zip code.

Media habits may not be something you think of, but any master plan must include procedures for reaching and communicating with targeted groups. Developers need this. Retailers need this. What is the best mix of media? You need cross-media measurement, not just TV or radio ratings or newspaper circulation.

As you search for tools appropriate for the 1990s, look at syndicated consumer surveys developed for the complexities of this decade. Look for one that will allow you to answer many critical questions you ask of research, and enable you do so from the comfort of your office. One that provides a detailed local market database, with comparable information across the nation. Isn't this what you have been looking for?

The Negative Attraction Effect?
A Study of the Attraction Effect Under Judgment and Choice
Jennifer Aaker, University of California at Berkeley[1]

ABSTRACT

This study focuses on the interaction between judgment vs. choice and the impact of justification on the attraction effect, which refers to the increase in the choice probability of the alternative most similar to a newly added inferior alternative brand in a choice set. One unexpected result, a strong negative attraction effect that appeared in the choice/low justification cell, could be caused by the appeal of a "black sheep" alternative. A second unexpected finding, the appearance of the attraction effect in the judgment/high justification cell, may be due to the force of the justification manipulation which alters the judgment task to one of choice.

Choice modeling has stimulated considerable research in the fields of consumer behavior and psychology (Luce, 1959; Tversky, 1972; Payne, 1982). One issue in marketing focuses on how the addition of an inferior brand into a two brand set affects choice. The conflicting predictions that can be hypothesized are based upon: the principle of regularity (Luce, 1959), the attraction effect (Huber et al., 1982), and a "negative attraction effect".

The principle of regularity, assumed by most choice models (Luce, 1977), indicates that the addition of a new object into a two object choice set cannot change the relative attractiveness of the two original objects (1959). It is based upon the Luce axiom that the choices are made by adding up the utility of the attributes.

A context effect violating regularity, the attraction effect, demonstrates that Luce's axiom does not apply in certain instances (Payne, 1982). The attraction effect refers to the increase in choice probability of the alternative most similar to a newly added *inferior* alternative brand in the original choice set (Huber, Payne and Puto, 1982; Huber and Puto, 1983; Ratneshwar, Shocker and Stewart, 1987). Consider a set of two equally-valued brands; Brand A is superior or "dominant" in one dimension (i.e. cost), while Brand B is superior or "dominant" in a second dimension (i.e. quality). By adding a third "asymmetrically inferior" alternative C (closest to alternative B) to the choice set, the choice probability of B increases (Huber et al., 1982). (An alternative is "asymmetrically inferior" if it is dominated by one alternative in the set, but not by the second alternative).

The choice literature has explored regularity vs. the attraction effect. However, *the negative attraction effect*, where an asymmetrically inferior alternative actually decreases the attractiveness of those with which it is most similar, has been left out of the literature--possibly because the attractiveness of the dissimilar or "black sheep" alternative always decreases or because no choice situations have been tested in which the negative attraction effect occurs. In the study to be described a negative attraction effect was found in one of the cells. We will suggest reasons why it emerged.

PURPOSE OF THIS RESEARCH

One purpose is to focus on the two decision making tasks, *judgment* and *choice*, to determine if the attraction effect (or negative attraction effect) occurs in judgment as it does in choice. The second purpose is to explore the concept of the justification effect in another context from that which was used in Simonson's study (1989).

The Justification Explanation of the Attraction Effect

One partial explanation for the attraction effect is that people select the alternative that is easiest to justify to themselves and others (Simonson, 1989). When an asymmetrically inferior alternative is added to a choice set, the asymmetrically dominating alternative becomes easier to justify--hence the attraction effect.

Simonson (1989) supports the justification hypothesis by showing that when subjects are asked to justify their decision to an authority or reference group (a condition of high justification), the attraction effect is large. In contrast, in low justification conditions, the attraction effect is much smaller if it exists at all (Ratneshwar, Shocker et al., 1987; Huber, Payne and Puto, 1982). In the present paper, the levels of justification (low and high) will both be studied in order to examine the effect of justification on the decision making process in another context.

Judgment vs. Choice

Past research in decision making in general and the attraction effect in particular has focused upon choice (i.e. one alternative is selected from the choice set) rather than judgment (i.e. all alternatives are evaluated using a seven point scale.) In fact, the question of what happens under judgment has not really been considered. Many researchers have used the terms, judgment and choice interchangeably (Slovic and Lichtenstein 1971). Only recently have the two response modes been distinguished (e.g., Bettman, 1982; Einhorn & Hogarth, 1981; Payne, 1982).

Different decision-making strategies, *non-compensatory* and *compensatory*, have been associated with the two response tasks (Einhorn & Hogarth, 1981). Under choice, a non-compensatory decision making strategy is more likely to be used (Johnson & Russo, 1984), where less information is utilized (Billings and Sherer 1988). For example,

---

[1] The author wishes to acknowledge the helpful comments and assistance from Professor Philip Tetlock and Itamar Simonson.

given a choice the respondent may simply eliminate an alternative based on one attribute. Therefore, if one alternative appears to stand out or be in an attractive position based on an attribute, the choice will be easily made.

Under judgment, a more compensatory process is more likely be used which involves more deliberative thinking, time and effort (Einhorn et al. 1979). Therefore, when asked to *rate* (a judgment task) the alternatives, the respondent may make the initial assessment of the alternatives (with respect to one attribute and perhaps their relationship to each other), but then s/he may continue to consider each alternative individually, weighing each of the alternatives respective attributes against each other. The compensatory process involves more effort to evaluate all the available information and rank order the alternatives. Therefore, the attraction effect bias (which emerges using a non-compensatory strategy--elicited under choice) should be lessened using a compensatory strategy--elicited under judgment. Thus, the attraction effect should differ under judgment and choice, especially in the high justification cells where DMs (decision makers) feel more accountable for their decisions. In low justification, Simonson has shown that little, if any, attraction effect occurs even under choice (1989). Therefore, logically there should be no real attraction effect under judgment in low justification.

The hypotheses follow:

1a. Under a choice task, the attraction effect will emerge in a high justification condition.

1b. Under a choice task, a small attraction effect will appear in a low justification condition.

2a. Under a judgment task, the attraction effect will not emerge in a high justification condition.

2b. Under a judgment task, the attraction effect will not appear in a low justification condition.

METHOD

Subjects and Design.

Undergraduate psychology students (N=450) at the University of California at Berkeley were asked to participate in the experiment for class credit. The response tasks, judgment vs. choice, were within-subject, whereas the two other variables, justification level and number of people in the choice set, were between-subject. Approximately an equal number of males and females were in four cells; the two conditions of justification (low vs. high) and two vs. three people in the choice set (Person A, Person B, with or without Person C). The two person choice set was included as a control set which will be the basis for comparisons of the three person choice set.

Procedure.

The context of people evaluation to test the attraction effect was selected for three reasons. First, Ratneshwar, Shocker and Stewart (1987) suggest that the subject may perceive the "microworld" of products used in attraction effect studies differently from the realistic world of brands that they confront everyday in the market place. Most products have brand names which carry associations and attitudes. Therefore, it is suggested that the decision making process using products without brands is relatively unrealistic. In an evaluation context where brands are not involved, this problem does not arise.

Second, a validated scale was found in which adjectives describing people were known to be equal in value (Anderson, 1965). Equally-valued adjectives provide a more sensitive experiment because the choice task is more likely to result in 50/50 splits. In brand choice contexts, it is not necessarily true that commonly used traits such as quality and price are equally-valued in all product classes.

Third, the stimuli are described by common characteristics which are easy to conceptualize. Whereas, it is difficult to understand the value of a TV set with a quality rating of 70 (vs. 50) and a distortion level of 2.5% (vs. 1.5%), the idea that a person is "very humorous" (an 8 on a 1-10 scale), but "not at all open-minded" (a 2 on a 1-10 scale) is more understandable.

In the questionnaires, subjects were asked to choose to befriend one of two or three people and evaluate (rate) each of them. There were three choice tasks. In the first, people were described by their level of "*imaginativeness*" and "*intelligence*", in the second "*open-mindedness*" and "*humor*" were used and in the third "*friendliness*" and "*thoughtfulness*" provided the dimensions. Person C was inferior to Person A in one trait, thoughtfulness but not on friendliness, so dominance here does not necessarily exist. (see Figure 1a). In addition, the third added Person C was clearly inferior to Person B on both traits, thoughtfulness and friendliness; thereby making Person B asymmetrically dominating.

After the evaluation, subjects were asked to write a short paragraph justifying each of their choices. The length of the paragraphs provides one manipulation check for the level of justification felt. The theory behind such a check is that people may tend to write more if they feel highly accountable. In addition, the Crown-Marlowe Social Desirability Test (1967) was included to test for individual differences in social desirability and to provide covariates. Lastly, as another manipulation check on the justification manipulation, three questions were added which assessed how accountable the individual subjects felt. (e.g. "How accountable do you feel to provide justifications for your decisions?")

Fifty undergraduate subjects at the University of California, Berkeley participated in a pretest to find pairs of personality characteristics which were 1) equally valued and 2) unique in meaning.

FIGURE 1

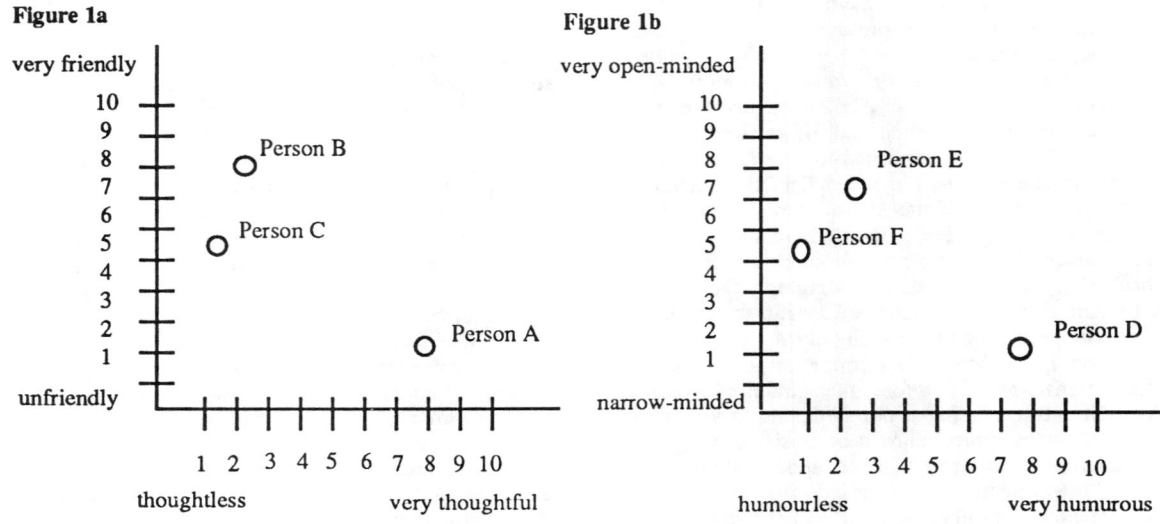

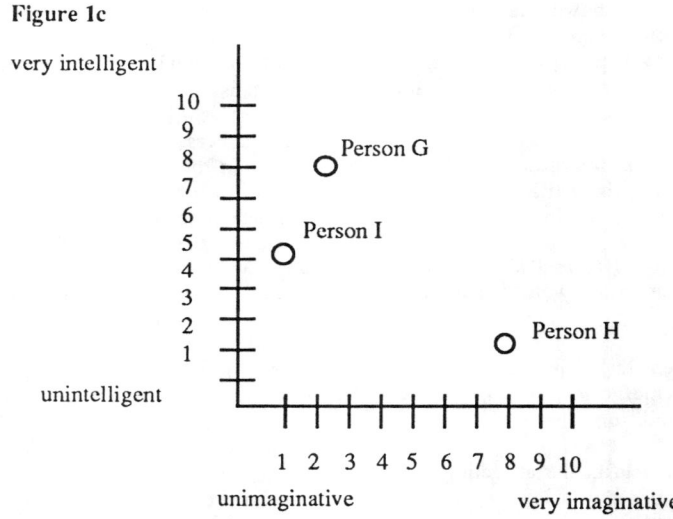

(Although the adjectives picked were rated equal in value in Anderson's list of 555 personality-trait words (1965), certain adjectives were too similar in meaning or not as equally-valued).

Manipulation.

Justification. Subjects in the low justification condition were told that their responses would remain totally confidential and would be used for statistical purposes only. They were instructed to not write their names on the questionnaire. In the high justification condition subjects were informed that their responses would be evaluated by a team of psychological researchers and they would be asked to justify their decisions in the questionnaire and possibly in an interview. Subjects were required to include their name and telephone number before starting and their initials on each page of the questionnaire.

Number of People. There were either two or three people in each choice set. In the first choice set, used for a control, only two people were described using two attributes (e.g. friendliness and thoughtfulness). For each attributes, a specific value (ranging from one to ten) was given.

In the second choice set, as shown in Figure 1a-c, a third asymmetrically inferior Person C was added. Person C was described as the worst "1" on thoughtfulness and a mediocre "5" on friendliness, whereas Person B was a "2" on thoughtfulness and a high "8" on friendliness. The third person, Person

C, was clearly inferior to one of the two alternatives, Person B.

Dependent Measures.

Subjects were asked to select the person they would choose to befriend, a measure of choice. In addition, subjects were asked, "How much do you think you would like this person?", a measure of judgment. They responded using a seven-point scale ranging from 1 ("dislike very much") to 7 ("like very much"). The order of the choice and judgment tasks was counterbalanced to test the existence of an affect of one dependent measure on the other.

RESULTS

Manipulation Checks

A significant difference in the justification paragraph length suggested that the manipulation worked--average of words: 35.3 vs. 47.7, p<0.01. A second manipulation check involved three 7-point scales assessing accountability felt during the experiment. The high justification subjects felt more sensitive to what others would think of their selection (5.12 vs. 4.89; p<0.1), and felt accountable to others in case they had to justify their decision (5.04 vs. 4.89; p<0.05). The third scale (whether others would understand the subject's decisions) did not result in significant differences but was less on target. No effect due to response task order existed. The Crown-Marlowe scale did not detect individual differences.

Lastly, in order to prove that the asymmetrically dominated alternative (Person B) was indeed asymmetrically dominating, the choices and ratings of Person C were compared to those of B. The percentage preference ratio of B over C was more than 50 to 1 in all three choice sets, thereby demonstrating that B was the asymmetrically dominating.

Hypothesis 1

The choice results, which were based on the percent of respondents who rated person B on a 1-7 likeability scale, are shown in Figure 2. Hypothesis 1a is clearly supported. There was a significant attraction effect in the aggregate (t=4.83, p>0.01) and in each of the individual cases for the high justification condition (t-5.46, p<0.01; t=4.80, p<0.05; t=4.75, p<0.05). However, hypothesis 1b was not supported--there was no attraction effect in the low justification condition. In fact, there was actually a strong negative attraction effect (t=5.03, p<0.01). Note the sharp negative slope in the aggregate and in the individual cases (all significant at the 0.01 level).

Hypothesis 2

Hypothesis 2b was supported in that there was no attraction effect under low justification in the judgment results, which were based on the percent of respondents who rated person B on a 1-7 likeability scale (see Figure 3). In fact, again there was a negative attraction effect. However, it was not significant in the aggregate and only appeared in one of the three cases.

A second unexpected finding was that hypothesis 2a was not supported. In fact, there was a strong attraction effect under high justification under the judgment task.

DISCUSSION

In this discussion we will focus upon the two unexpected findings--the negative attraction effect that appeared especially in the choice/low justification cell and the attraction effect that appeared in the judgment /high justification cell.

The Negative Attraction Effect Under Choice and Low Justification

Clearly the attraction effect applies in the high justification condition. However, in the low justification condition other forces are at work.

One possible explanation is Tversky's low of similarity (1972), where the choice probability of Person A (the "dissimilar alternative) increased because Person C took a disproportionate share from Person B. Based on the elimination-by-aspects model, the law of similarity refers to the idea that similar items divide the DM's loyalty. However, in the present study the increase in choice of Person C was not significant, so the negative effect of similarity does not apply.

Another possibility is that the dissimilar alternative A simply looks more interesting because it is different than the others. DMs may prefer the "black sheep" alternative because it stands apart. The DM may feel that the B and C types are more common. A preference for the unusual of different is consistent with the variety-seeking literature in consumer behavior.

In what conditions would the DM "go for" the black sheep alternative? One condition may be low justification in which the DM is not held accountable to anyone and the DM's responses are kept completely confidential. The state of an individual, who is not seen or treated like an individual, is termed "de-individuation" by Festinger, Pepitone and Newcomb. (1952). When a subject is assured of total confidentiality and told that their responses will be combined for statistical measures only, subjects feel free from restraints, less inhibited and able to indulge in forms of behavior in which, under high justification, they would not indulge (Festinger et al., 1951). Without self-monitoring or self-attention, subjects may become "more reactive to stimuli and emotions and are unresponsive to norms and long-term consequences of their behavior". (Festinger et al., 1951, p. 210) The "norms" and "long-term consequences" in this case may be the justifications needed for a decision. Without a need to justify the decision to others, DMs will "go for" the dissimilar "black sheep".

Research in social perception consistent with the "black sheep"/ de-individuation hypothesis exists. Under certain conditions (i.e. low justification or confidentiality), individuals prefer friends who are perceived unusual and who stand

FIGURE 2
CHOICE CHARTS

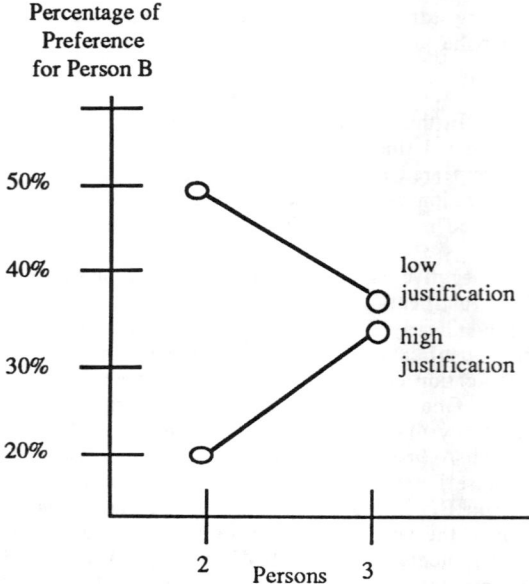

Figure 2a (friendly vs. thoughtful)

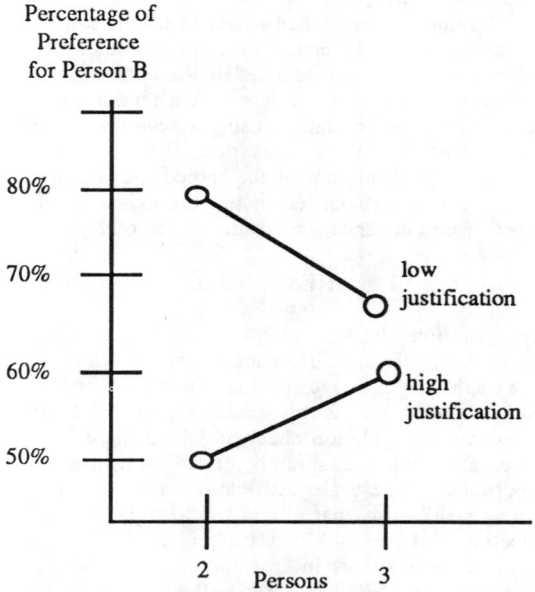

Figure 2b (open-minded vs. humurous)

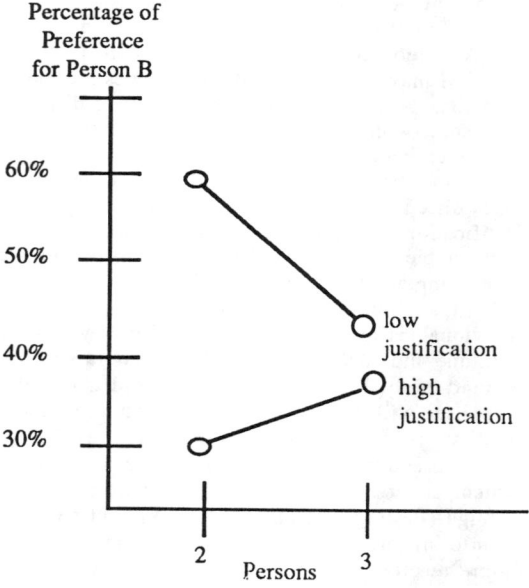

Figure 2c (intelligent vs. imaginative)

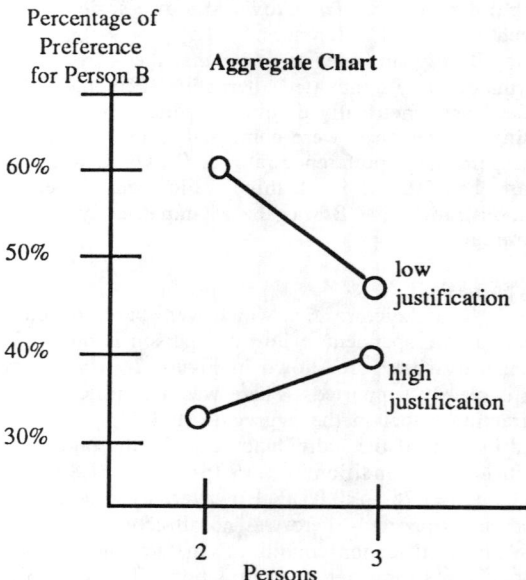

Figure 2d

FIGURE 3
RATING CHARTS

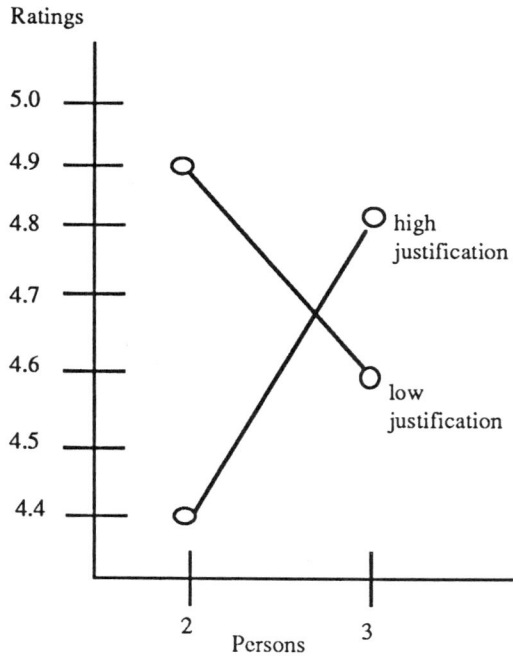

Figure 3a (friendly vs. thoughtful)

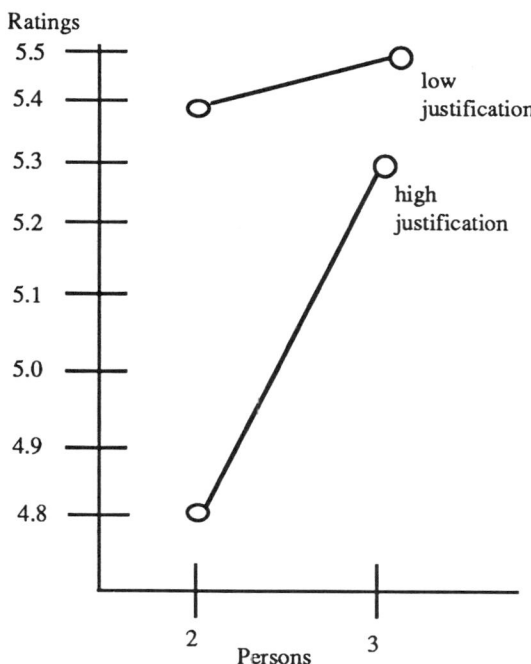

Figure 3b (open-minded vs. humurous)

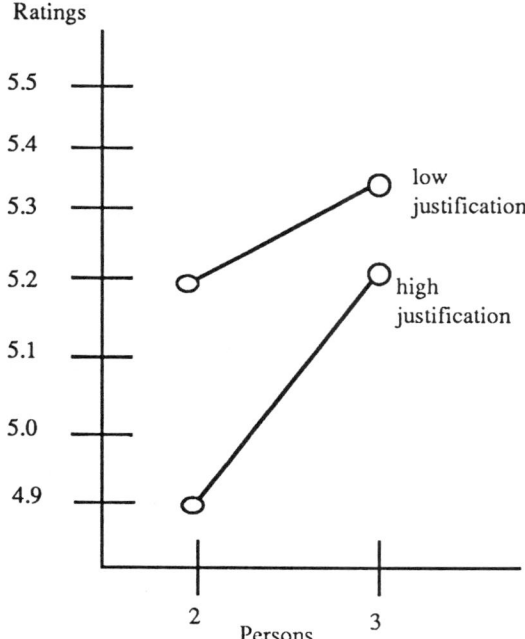

Figure 3c (intelligent vs. imaginative)

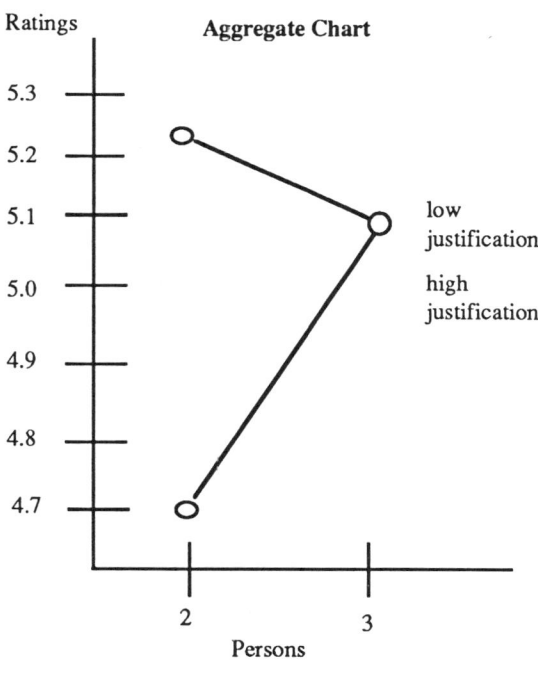

Figure 3d

away from the crowd (Heider, 1958; Newcomb, 1953). Individuals may prefer the "dissimilar" alternative because s/he is more interesting. However, such reasoning is not easily justified to others.

Why is the negative attraction effect under low justification stronger in choice than in judgment? Perhaps it is due to the different decision making strategies which are associated with the two response tasks (Johnson & Russo 1984). In choice, given a difficult trade-off decision, a non-compensatory strategy is more likely where alternatives are simply eliminated. In judgment, a compensatory strategy is more likely where alternatives are weighed and DMs may rate the alternatives equally (Einhorn and Hogarth 1981). Therefore, the preference for the black sheep alternative will be more likely in choice.

The different levels of negative attraction effect in the two response tasks is particularly interesting. It could be related to the general problem in the decision making literature where preferences are not necessarily accurate predictors of choice.

The Positive Attraction Effect under Judgment and High Justification

One influence of the asymmetrically inferior alternative is to make the asymmetrically dominating alternative (which dominates on one or two attributes) easier to justify to oneself and others. However, why would the strong positive attraction effect occur under judgment, where DMs may evaluate the alternatives separately and can rate the alternatives equally? There is no *choice* to justify.

One possible explanation is that the forces underlying the attraction effect under high justification are so strong that they apply even under an judgment task. In fact, in a strong justification manipulation, judgment tasks may resemble choice tasks. By making subjects highly accountable for their *decisions*, the experimenter implicitly implies a sort of decision (or choice) must be made. In such a situation, the decision making strategies used under choice may be elicited even though the response task is judgment.

LIMITATIONS/FUTURE RESEARCH

First, the present research is based on the premise that "more is better"--with respect to the attributes describing the people in each choice set. Specifically, it is assumed that a person who is very friendly (an "8" on a 1-10 scale) would be more attractive than another who is unfriendly or moderately friendly (a "2" or a "5"). The optimal level of an attribute was not tested in the present paper. As in product examples, the premise that "more is better" is not always true.

Moreover, the *meaning* of each attribute may change when paired to another specific attribute. For example, friendliness may be a positive attribute when paired with thoughtfulness but a negative one when paired with humor (both of which were equally-valued according to Anderson's list). Future research could focus on the effect of one attribute on the other as well as the optimal level of each attribute.

Second, further study may be done on the negative attraction effect and conditions under which it occurs. In addition, research may focus on why the negative attraction effect occurs by taking process measures. In particular, it would be useful to show if, indeed, a focus on choice occurs in a judgment task under high justification.

Third, no steps were taken to show that the different response modes, judgment and choice, actually elicited different decision making strategies. The presence of these decision processes may be tested as Tversky, Slovic and Sattath did in Contingent Weighting in Judgment and Choice (1988). For example, a coding scheme, such as Integrative Complexity Coding, may be used to code the level of complexity in the DM's reasoning and investigate changes in cognitive processing or decision-making strategies.

Fourth, future research would be productive in the realm of cross-cultural literature concerning the attraction effect. Specifically, does the attraction effect occur in other cultures? If so, do the same explanations of the phenomenon apply (e.g. justification)?

The present study was replicated in Paris with 40 subjects. Results showed similar findings as the present experiment, thus indicating that the attraction effect is cognitive process, not a cultural norm. However, such an interpretation is tentative. The evidence is weak because of small sample size, different age and profession in subject pool and translation differences. Much room remains in the social perception and consumer behavior literature for such cross cultural research.

Lastly, "real world" marketing implications of the present research can be seen in the realm of new product introduction or development. Given a situation where two (or more) equally-valued brands are on the market, an existing competing manufacturer may consider the possibility of introducing an asymmetrically inferior new brand in order to increase the market share of their existing (asymmetrically dominating) brand and decrease the market share of the competitor(s).

More interestingly, a manufacturer could explore the realm of justification to change market share in a specific market. By increasing the level of accountability through advertising or direct marketing, a manufacturer may increase market share for their brand. For example, given a brand situation with three alternatives positioned as in Figure 1, under low justification (a "normal" choice situation, where the consumer does not have to justify his/her choice to anyone), the consumer may be choosing brand A---the dissimilar alternative (i.e. the negative attraction effect occurs). By holding the consumer accountable for their decision by first asking them *why* they choose their choice and then listing some of the reasons why the DM *should* choose their brand, the choice probability of the manufacturer's brand B may increase.

REFERENCES

Abelson, Robert (1964), "The Choice Theories," in S. Moscow and A. Brayfield (Eds.) *Decision and Choice*, NY: McGraw Hill.

Anderson, Norman H. (1981), "Likableness Ratings of 555 Personality-Trait Words," *Journal of Personality and Social Psychology*, 9, 272-279.

Assar, Amardeep and Dipankar Chakravarti (1984), "Attribute Range Knowledge: Effects on Consumers' Evaluation of Brand-Attribute Information and Search Patterns in Choice," in *EMA Educators' Proceedings*, eds. Russell W. Belk et al., Chicago: American Marketing Association, 62-67.

Bettman, J.R. (1982), "A Functional Analysis of the Role of Overall Evaluation of Alternatives in Choice Processes", *Advances in Consumer Research*, 9, 87-93.

Billings, Robert S. and Lisa L. Scherer (1988), "The Effects of Response Mode and Importance on Decision-Making Strategies: Judgment versus Choice", *Organizational Behavior and Human Decision Processes*, 41, 1-19.

Chaiken, Shelly (1980), "Heuristic Versus Systematic Information Processing and the Use of Source Versus Message Cues in Persuasion," *Journal of Personality and Social Psychology*, 45 (March), 560-570.

Curley, Shawn P., J. Frank Yates, and Richard A. Abrams (1986), "Psychological Sources of Ambiguity," *Organizational Behavior and Human Decision Processes*, 38 (2), 230-256.

Dipboye, Robert L. (1977), "Alternative Approaches to Deindividuation", *Psychological Bulletin*, 84 (6), 1057-1075.

Einhorn, H.J., and Hogarth, R.M. (1981), "Behavioral Decision Theory: Processes of Judgment and Choice", *Annual Review of Psychology*, 32, 52-88.

Festinger, Leon, "A Theory of Cognitive Dissonance," Evanston, Illinois: Row, Peterson, 1957.

Festinger, L., Pepitone, A., Newcomb, T. (1952), "Some Consequences of Deindividuation in a Group", *Journal of Abnormal and Social Psychology*, 47, 382-389.

Hagafors, R. and B. Brehmer (1983), "Does Having to Justify One's Judgments Change the Nature of the Judgment Process?" *Organizational Behavior and Human Performance*, 31, 223-243.

Heider, Fritz, "The Psychology of Interpersonal Relations," New York, Wiley, 1958.

Huber, Joel, John W. Payne, and Christopher Puto (1982), "Adding Asymmetrically Dominated Alternatives: Violations of Regularity and the Similarity Hypothesis," *Journal of Consumer Research*, 9, 90-98.

Huber, Joel and Christopher Puto (1983), "Market Boundaries and Product Choice: Illustrating Attraction and Substitution Effects," *Journal of Consumer Research*, 10, 31-44.

Johnson, E.J., and Russo. (1984), "Product Familiarity and Learning New Information", *Journal of Consumer Research*, 11 542-550.

Kahneman, D., and Tversky, A. (1984), "Choices, Values, and Frames", *American Psychologist*, 39, 341-350.

Lerner, Melvin J. and Selwyn Becker (1965), "Interpersonal Choice as a Function of Ascribed Similarity and Definition of the Situation."

Luce, R. Duncan (1959), *Individual Choice Behavior*, New York: Wiley.

Luce, R. Duncan (1977), "The Choice Axiom After Twenty Years," *Journal of Mathematical Psychology*, 15, 215-233.

McAllister, D.W., Mitchell, T.R., & Beach, L.R., (1979), "The Contingency Model for the Selection of Decision Strategies: An Empirical Test of the Effects of Significance, Accountability, and Reversibility", *Organizational Behavior and Human Performance*, 24, 228-244.

Newcomb, Theodore, M., (1953), "Social Psychology and Group Processes," *Annual Review of Psychology*, (4), 183-214.

Payne, John W. (1982), "Contingent Decision Behavior," *Psychological Bulletin*, 92 (Sept.), 382-402.

Ratneshwar, Srinivasan, Allen D. Schocker, and David W. Stewart (1987), "Toward Understanding the Attraction Effect: The Implications of Product Stimulus Meaningfulness and Familiarity," *Journal of Consumer Research*, 13, 520-533.

Simonson, Itamar (1989), "Choice Based on Reasons: The Case of Attraction and Compromise Effects", *Journal of Consumer Research*, 16, 158-173.

Slovic, Paul (1975), "Choice Between Equally-Valued Alternatives," *Journal of Experimental Psychology: Human Perception and Performance*, 1, 280-287.

Slovic, Paul, Baruch Fischhoff, and Sara Lictenstein (1982), "Response Mode, Framing and Information Processing Effects in Risk Assessment," *New Directions in Methodology of Social and Behavioral Science: The Framing of Questions and the Consistency of Response*, San Francisco, Calif.: Josey Bass.

Tetlock, Philip E. (1985), "Accountability: The Neglected Social Context of Judgment and Choice," *Research in Organizational Behavior*, 7, 297-332.

Tetlock, Philip E. (1985), "Accountability: A Social Check on the Fundamental Attribution Error," *Social Psychology Quarterly*, Vol. 48, 3, 227-236.

Tversky, Amos, Paul Slovic, Samuel Sattath (1988), "Contingent Weighting in Judgment and Choice", *Psychological Review*, 95, (3), 271-384.

Tversky, Amos (1977), "Features of Similarity", *Psychology Review*, 84, 327-352.

Causes of Delay in Consumer Decision Making: An Exploratory Study

Eric Greenleaf, New York University
Donald Lehmann, Columbia University

ABSTRACT

This paper conducts an exploratory study of reasons why consumers delay making decisions. A survey on purchases costing more than $100 reveals five causes of delay. Three of these - task avoidance and unpleasantness, time pressure, and uncertainty - have been identified in other decision contexts, while causes related to the difficulty of selecting the best brand and perceived risk of product performance are more specific to consumer decision making. We find that difficulty of selection and time pressure are the most important causes of consumer delay and task avoidance the least important. Correlations between delay causes and time spent in each stage of the consumer decision making process provide tentative evidence that the different delay causes tend to prolong decision time in particular stages.

INTRODUCTION

Rare is the individual who never delays making decisions and taking actions. Delay and procrastination can improve decision making (Janis and Mann, 1977) and be an adaptive reaction to a decision (Taylor, 1979), but excessive delay can become maladaptive, prolonging a decision so long that it is finally made at the last minute in a slipshod fashion (Lay, 1986, 1988; Solomon and Rothblum, 1984), perhaps so late that the situation requiring the decision becomes moot (Simmons, Klein, and Thornton, 1974). The causes and effects of decision delay should be of interest whenever decision making and actions are studied. To quote Hogarth, Michaud, and Mery (1980): "whereas understanding how people make decisions is important, it is also necessary to understand why people *delay* making decisions . . . " (pg. 112).

Decision and task delay have been investigated in a number of contexts, including seeking help for a distressing personal problem (Amato and Bradshaw, 1985), donating a kidney (Simmons, Klein, and Thornton, 1973), urban development and business relocation (Hogarth, Michaud, and Mery, 1980), writing undergraduate term papers (Lay, 1988; Solomon and Rothblum, 1984), and completing personal projects (Lay, 1986) or small, everyday tasks (Milgram, Sroloff, and Rosenbaum, 1988). More general typologies of "nondecisions" have also been proposed (Corbin, 1980), including refusal, inattention, and delay.

However, little attention has been given to delay in consumer decision making. Decision and reaction time have been studied in experimental contexts, but a general study of reasons why consumers delay decisions has not been attempted.

The purpose of this paper is to investigate, in an exploratory fashion, the causes of consumer decision delay. Past research on delay has revealed that causes which may generalize to other contexts often exist alongside context-specific causes. We propose that this may apply to consumer decision making. This paper next discusses causes of delay which have been identified in other contexts and propose aspects of consumer decision making which may create context-specific causes. We then describe a study designed to identify the structure of these causes, examine their different importance in causing delay in consumer decision making, and investigate their relationship to elapsed decision times in different stages of the consumer decision making process.

CAUSES OF DECISION DELAY AND PROCRASTINATION.

Causes from other contexts.

Several investigators have found that delay and procrastination can be caused by a person's tendency to avoid an unpleasant task or decision. Milgram, Sroloff, and Rosenbaum (1988) find high correlations between procrastination in everyday tasks and dysphoric affect ("the negative emotional response associated with doing a particular task"), as well as covert negativism ("an avoidant reaction" towards "demands imposed on us by resented authority figures"). Amato and Bradshaw (1985) identify "fear and stigma" and "problem avoidance and denial" as two reasons for procrastination in seeking help for a personal problem (derived with clustering procedures, these causes may not be orthogonal). Hogarth, Michaud, and Mery (1980) find that decision makers may delay when psychological regret (the anticipation of adverse consequences from future decisions) causes them to fear "possible accusations of irresponsibility, from others or even themselves." Solomon and Rothblum (1984) find that procrastination in writing term papers can be caused by two general factors relating to negative reactions to the task: (a) fear of failure, involving both one's own and other people's standards, as well as lack of self-confidence, and (b) aversion to the task and laziness. Lay (1988), also in the term paper context, finds that pessimistic procrastinators are likely to develop negative reactions by anticipating problems completing this task, such as suffering from writer's block, or misplacing notes, and may also develop these reactions from overestimating the amount of time necessary to complete the task. Janis and Mann (1977) discuss how defensive procrastination is one form of defensive avoidance, used by the decision maker as "a means of coping with the painful stresses of decison making . . ."(pg. 6). They contrast this strategy with "vigilant information processing" which satisfies "ideal procedural criteria" for decision making (pgs. 11-12). Given the ubiquity of this cause across many different tasks, we would also expect it to emerge as a cause of delay in a consumer context.

Hogarth, Michaud, and Mery (1980) find that decision delay also can be caused by three types of uncertainty: "(a) lack of knowledge about events that could affect outcomes, (b) ambiguity concerning the consequences of actions, . . . and (c) procedural uncertainty, concerning means to handle and process the decision, e.g. specifying relevant uncertainties, what information to seek and where, how to invent alternatives and assess consequences, etc." (pg. 110). This source of delay may also affect consumer decision making, since consumers must determine products' attributes as well as which attributes are important to them, and other people may need to approve the decision.

Amato and Bradshaw (1985) find that "negative helper evaluation" may prompt decision delay when seeking help for a distressing personal problem. This cause may be quite relevant to a consumer context, since consumers seeking help in decision making often turn to friends or salespeople. Amato and Bradshaw (1985) find that lack of available time can cause decision delay, while Lay (1988) finds that perceptions of how much time a task will take can also lead to delay, and that procrastinators perceive that they spend less than adequate time on projects (Lay, 1986). Time pressure and availability should also cause delay in consumer decision making, since other tasks and decisions compete for time.

Delay causes peculiar to consumer decision making.

Some aspects of consumer decision making may create delay reasons not usually found in other contexts. One reason which may arise in consumer contexts is the difficulty of deciding which alternative to choose from among a set of brands or models. Unlike many other types of decisions or tasks, which require either a yes/no decision or simply getting on with the matter (such as writing a term paper), consumer decisions require comparing a set of alternatives which may be quite similar. This comparison involves assembling the set of considered alternatives, identifying the relevant attributes, comparing the alternatives on these attributes, and determining which is most preferred; these tasks comprise the information search and evaluation stages of the consumer decision making process. Accordingly, we conjecture that difficulty in deciding which alternative to choose may be a delay cause peculiar to the consumer decision making context. Many aids in consumer decision making, such as consumer magazines and personal computer software which allows consumers to readily compare data on different alternatives in a product category, seem to be directed at aiding consumers in this stage of decision making.

Delay and stages of the consumer decision making process.

Four of the stages in the consumer decision making process are relevant to the study of delay in these decisions: 1) identify the consumer need, 2) search for information, 3) evaluate alternatives, and 4) purchase. One purpose of the present study is to investigate how each reason for delay is related to the amount of time a consumer takes to complete each stage in the decision making process. Due to the exploratory nature of this research, we do not hypothesize specific relationships between causes of delay and decision time spent in each phase; significant relationships found in the present work will provide areas for future investigation.

STUDY DESIGN

To examine the causes of consumer decision delay, the authors designed a survey asking consumers why they delayed making a major purchase (a product costing at least $100) and how much time they took to complete various stages of the decision making process. Fifty-nine students, drawn from classes in two graduate schools of business in New York City, completed the survey. This sample is not intended to be representative of all consumers, but does provide insights into consumer delay for a well-educated segment that makes a considerable number of high involvement purchases, as suggested by the variety of product caegories mentioned in the surveys.

Subjects were asked to describe purchases which they were aware of delaying. Although this limits the scope of the study to conscious reasons for delay, it might be difficult to ask consumers to give delay reasons and delay times for purchases which they felt had been made promptly. Delay reasons for such purchases may show a different structure than for the purchases reported here.

Forty items, reproduced in Table 1, were composed to probe causes of consumer delay. Each item was designed to probe either an already identified source of delay which might also influence consumer decisions (task avoidance and unpleasantness, uncertainty, helper evaluation, and time pressure), or a cause related to the consumer-specific source of choosing which alternative to purchase. Reasons which had already been identified were selected from a review of the literature. Additional reasons were selected using a small pilot study, where six consumers were asked in a written survey to report reasons why they delay purchases. Table 1 also indicates each item's source.

Respondents were asked to indicate "how important each reason was in causing you to defer the [purchase] decision" by marking a Likert scale with the response intervals (1) no influence, (2) a minor influence, (3) a moderate influence, (4) an important influence, (5) a very important influence, and (6) an extremely important influence.

Respondents also indicated how much total time (not just time spent on the decision) elapsed (1) after they recognized the consumer need but before they began information search, (2) during information search and evaluation, and (3) after choosing which brand to purchase but before actual purchase (description of each phase on the survey is more extensive than the terms used here). Elapsed time between need identification and the onset of

TABLE 1
Means, factor loadings, and sources of items measuring reason for consumer delay

Source	TAVOID I	SELECT II	UNCERT III	TPRESS IV	PPRISK V	MEAN
1) P Other things had higher priority.	*	*	*	.43	.30	4.12
2) U I couldn't use the product until the future.	.34	*	*	*	*	2.47
3) T The problem/situation for which the product was intended was unpleasant to think about.	<u>.71</u>	*	−.31	*	*	1.38
4) T I hoped the situation for which the product was needed would go away.	.61	.31	.32	*	*	1.30
5) U I needed to know more about what I could use the product for.	*	*	<u>.67</u>	*	*	2.03
6) C I wanted to know more about different brands or models.	*	<u>.57</u>	*	*	*	4.11
7) U I thought a better product might be introduced soon.	.32	.47	.36	*	*	2.11
8) C I expected the price to decrease soon.	*	.31	*	*	−.48	2.72
9) C I didn't want the shopping process to end.	.40	*	*	−.52	*	1.44
10) C There was no urgency to make the decision.	*	*	*	.35	*	3.76
11) C I couldn't afford to make the purchase at that time.	*	*	*	*	−.69	3.16
12) P Shopping for the product was difficult/inconvenient.	*	*	*	<u>.71</u>	*	3.61
13) T Shopping for the product was unpleasant.	<u>.70</u>	*	*	.35	*	2.00
14) U I was unsure I would use the product enough to justify buying it.	*	*	<u>.62</u>	*	*	2.45
15) U I needed to get other people to agree on the choice.	*	*	<u>.60</u>	*	.32	2.35
16) H I didn't like the salespeople I had to deal with.	.43	*	*	*	.35	1.79
17) U The decision depended on another decision which was not yet made.	.34	*	.60	*	*	1.76
18) T The product was difficult to evaluate objectively.	.43	.50	*	*	*	2.32
19) C It was difficult to find a place where I could examine or buy the product.	.64	*	*	*	*	1.77
20) C There were many alternative brands or models to consider.	*	<u>.83</u>	*	*	*	3.88
21) C There were many different product characteristics/features to consider.	*	<u>.84</u>	*	*	*	3.79
22) C The alternatives were so similar that it was hard to select the best one.	*	<u>.75</u>	*	*	*	3.32
23) C The alternatives were so different that it was hard to compare them.	.55	*	.42	*	*	1.50

TABLE 2
Correlations between measures of reasons for delay

	SELECT	UNCERT	TPRESS	PPRISK
TAVOID	1.11	.39	.26	.44
SELECT		.21	-.09	.37
UNCERT			.12	.44
PPRISK				-.01

information search was requested since this period, when the consumer wants the product but is distracted by other activities and has not yet acted to gather information, may form an important area of decision delay. Elapsed time for the information gathering and alternative evaluation phases were combined into a single question since the consumer-specific delay cause, if found, was expected to affect elapsed time for both of these stages. Time between selecting an alternative and actual purchase again represents a period where the consumer is not active in decision making.

Respondents had the choice of providing elapsed time information in either years, months, weeks, days, hours, or minutes, and were asked to indicate how many units of the most appropriate time had elapsed in each stage. This information was subsequently reexpressed in weeks and used to create time variables for need recognition (abbreviated as NEED), search and evaluation (abbreviated as SEARCHEVAL), and purchase (abbreviated as PURCH). Since these elapsed times are based on retrospective reporting, they are subject to errors of memory that can affect such data.

RESULTS.

Respondents reported purchases involving a wide range of goods, including clothing (19 respondents), computers (14), television and stereo equipment (7), watches (4), furniture (4), jewelry(2), and other purchases (7). Purchase prices ranged from $120 to $6500. This variety of products and prices suggests that the study describes decision delay for a broad cross section of consumer decisions.

Respondents spent, on average, 12.1 weeks after they recognized the need for the product but before they began searching for information, 8.9 weeks searching for information and evaluating alternatives, and 7.7 weeks between choosing an alternative and actual purchase. It is interesting to note that the first stage, which in some sense represents "pure" procrastination, is the longest, whereas the final choice stage, which is the focus of much consumer research, is the shortest.

Interpreting causes of consumer procrastination.

To identify the underlying structure of reasons for delay, the 40 items were subject to factor analysis using varimax rotation. A five-factor solution, explaining 56.2% of total variance, was chosen based on the scree plot and the interpretability of the factors. To check for stability in the solution, ten observations were withheld and the analysis repeated; the factor loadings remained stable and their interpretation did not change.

Loadings for these five factors are reported in Table 1. Interpretation of these factors and construct multiple-item measures of each delay cause proceeded as follows:

Factor I: Six items (3, 13, 25, 27, 28, and 37) loaded at $\geq$ .7 on this factor. Four were intended to probe task avoidance and unpleasantness, while two others were designed to probe the consumer-specific delay cause. This factor appears to represent the cause related to task avoidance and unpleasantness found in prior investigations. These items are not concerned with the product itself, but the respondent's reaction to the prospect of having to make this decision (items 3, 13, 27, and 37), to initiate the decision process (item 1), and to future consequences of this decision, unrelated to product satisfaction (item 25). Each respondent's scores on these six items were summed to create the task avoidance scale TAVOID (coefficient alpha = .88).

Factor II: Five items (6, 20, 21, 22, and 34) loaded at $\geq$ .57 on this factor and at low levels on other factors. Four of these items had consumer-specific sources, while the fifth concerned uncertainty. This factor appears to represent the hypothesized delay cause arising from consumers' difficulty choosing the most preferred brand or model from a set of alternatives. The items refer to either describing and comparing alternatives on relevant product attributes (items 6, 20, 21, 22) or choosing an alternative that subsequently turns out to be inferior to others (item 34). These five items were summed to create the alternative selection scale SELECT (alpha = .84).

Factor III: Five items (5, 14, 15, 26, and 40) loaded at $\geq$ .60 on this factor and possessed low loadings on other factors (the latter criterion eliminated items 17 and 24). All these items were esigned to probe delay caused by uncertainty. This uncertainty can have different sources, related to consumer's use of the product (items 5 and 14),

TABLE 3
Correlations between delay reasons and elapsed time in decision stages

Delay Measure	Decision Stage		
	NEED	SEARCHEV	PURCH
TAVOID	.00	.05	-.02
SELECT	.04	-.18	-.10
UNCERT	.23*	.04	-.02
TPRESS	.26**	.29**	.03
PPRISK	-.15	-.07	-.11

* p < .10   ** p < .05

---

dalternative uses for the money (item 26) and other people's approval (items 15 and 40). None of these reasons concern the comparison and selection task, the realm of items in the SELECT factor. These five items were summed to create the uncertainty scale UNCERT (alpha = .75).

Factor IV: Two items (12 and 38) loaded at ≥ .7 on this factor. Both concern time pressure, caused either by the respondent's busy schedule (item 38) or the inconvenience of travelling to and shopping at outlets offering the product (item 12). These two items were summed to create the time pressure scale TPRESS (alpha = .80).

Factor V: Four items (8, 11, 30, and 33) had loadings with absolute values ≥ .48 on this factor (the next highest loading was .35). Two were designed to probe consumer-specific reasons, one helper-specific, and one uncertainty. Items 8 and 11, which had negative loadings, were concerned with financial factors, while items 30 and 33 appeared to probe perceived risk of poor product performance, due either to inaccurate salesperson information or faults of the product itself. The fact that the first pair of items posessed low correlations with the second recommended against including all four items in a single measure, regardless of the factor structure. Since items 30 and 33 were highly correlated (rho = .68) while items 8 and 11 were not (rho = .26), only the former two items were combined to create a measure of reason for consumer delay. Scores from items 30 and 33 were summed to create the scale for perceived performance risk, PPRISK (alpha = .81).

Correlations between the five scales, reported in Table 2, reveal moderate levels of intercorrelation between some of the scales. The highest correlations concerned the scale PRISK. The alternative method of computing factor scores avoids this problem, but creates problems of interpretability when applied to 40 items. These correlations among scales suggest that causes of delay may be related rather than independent, especially delay due to perceived risk.

Importance of delay reasons.

Table 1 also reports mean importance ratings for each of the 40 items. The three reasons rated highest in importance (items 1, 6, and 34) related to selecting alternatives or to time pressure, while the four rated lowest in importance (items 4, 25, 27, and 36) concerned task avoidance or uncertainty.

Mean item importance ratings for each of the five delay measures were also calculated, yielding: TAVOID (1.49), SELECT (3.82), UNCERT (2.26), TPRESS (3.66), and PPRISK (1.89). Taken together, the results for item and scale importances suggest that selecting an alternative and time pressure are the most important reasons for delay, whereas task avoidance and perceived risk are the least importance. Apparently respondents found the consumer-specific reason (SELECT) to be very important, but did not consider the decision making process as an unpleasant task to be avoided.

Correlations between delay reasons and decision times.

Another purpose of this study is to examine whether each delay reason is related to delay in a particular stage of the consumer decision making process. Table 3 reports correlations between each of the five delay measures and the decision time measures NEED, SEARCHEV, and PURCH. Significant correlations (p < .10) occured between TPRESS and NEED, between TPRESS and SEARCHEV, and between UNCERT and NEED. Time pressure clearly lengthened the time between need recognition and search as well as the search process itself, as expected. Also, greater uncertainty led to a longer time between need recognition and beginning search. Although these results are tentative, it appears that there may be some relationships between reasons for delay and the length of the decision process, and some decision stages may be more sensitive to delay than others.

DISCUSSION.

This exploratory investigation of reasons for delay in consumer decision making has provided several interesting, if preliminary, results. Consumers appear to delay major purchases for several reasons. Some of these, such as task avoidance and unpleasantness, uncertainty, and time pressure, occur also in other decision making contexts, while other reasons, such as selecting the most preferred alternative, are more specific to consumer decision making. The latter category may also include delay due to perceived performance risk, although the equivocal evidence for this cause makes this conclusion tentative until further work is done.

Some causes identified in other contexts may not translate directly to consumer decision making. The items intended to probe helper evaluation, which emerged in Amato and Bradshaw's (1985) study of delay in seeking help for a distressing personal problem, did not form a coherent reason for delay but instead were dispersed among other reasons. This further suggests that the structure of delay reasons may be partially context dependent.

The importance of these causes in delaying consumer decisions for products costing more than $100 varied considerably. Interestingly, but not surprisingly, task avoidance is not a major reason for delay in consumer decision making. Rather, the competing demands of other higher priority activities (which delays the start of the search process) and the complexity of the set of alternatives explain the long delay between need recognition and final choice. Time pressure appears to be related to elapsed time spent between need recognition and the beginning of information search, as well as to length of search and evaluation, while uncertainty is related to the former stage.

Future research may focus on what can be done to shorten (or lengthen) the period of delay. In naturally occurring environments, it may be interesting to focus on the length of time the consumer spends in the two information processing stages and how this is related to the nature of processing (ie., by brand or by attribute).

The rank order of importance found here is considerably different from that found in some other contexts; for example, Amato and Bradshaw (1985) found that reasons relating to problem avoidance were rated as considerably *more* important than time pressure.

The present study suggest several fruitful areas for future research. There is a need to validate further the delay causes found in the present study, resolve areas of ambiguity such as occured with perceived risk factor, and search for additional reasons for delay. Once convergent validity is established for the existence of these reasons across several studies, reliable and valid scales must be developed to measure the importance of these causes. Such research should also seek to resolve whether delay reasons are related or independent.

Further work is also needed to determine whether the structure of delay causes is stable across different types of consumer decisions or varies across decision types. We have studied purchases which cost at least $100, and probably elicited high involvement and complex decision making from most consumers, but purchases of low-involvement goods may exhibit different structures of reasons for delay. The relative importance of delay reasons may also depend on the decision context, as well as on consumer characteristics such as expertise, age, education, lifestyle, and household size and composition.

Further investigations of elapsed time in each stage of the decision making process and particular reasons for delay are also needed. This work should extend beyond the preliminary, correlational analyses presented here and search for causality between delay reason and decision time.

REFERENCES

Amato, Paul R. and Ruth Bradshaw (1985), " An Exploratory Study of People's Reasons for Delaying or Avoiding Helpseeking," *Australian Psychologist*, 20 (March), 21-31.

Corbin, Ruth M. "Decisions that Might Not Get Made," pgs. 47-67 in *Cognitive Processes in Decision Making*, Thomas Wallsten, ed., Lawrence Erlbaum.

Hogarth, Robin M., Claude Michaud, and Jean-Louis Mery (1980), "Decision Behavior in Urban Development: A Methodological Approach and Substantive Considerations," *Acta Psychologica*, 45, 95-117.

Janis, Irving L., and Leon Mann (1977), *Decision Making*, New York: The Free Press.

Lay, Clarry H. (1986), "At Last, My Research Article on Procrastination," *Journal of Research in Personality*, 20, 474-95.

Lay, Clarry H. (1988), "The Relationship of Procrastination and Optimism to Judgements of Time to Complete and Essay and Anticipation of Setbacks," *Journal of Social Behavior and Personality*, 3, 201-14.

Milgram, Norman A., Barry Sroloff, and Michael Rosenbaum (1988), "The Procrastination of Everyday Life," *Journal of Research in Personality*, 22, 197-212.

Simmons, Roberta G., Susan D. Klein, and Kenneth Thornton (1973), "The Family Member's Decision to be a Kidney Transplant Donor," *Journal of Comparative Family Studies*, 4 (Spring), 88-115.

Solomon, Laura J., and Esther Rothblum (1984), "Academic Procrastination: Frequency and Cognitive-Behavioral Correlates," *Journal of Counseling Psychology*, 31, 503-9.

Taylor, William L. (1979), "A Psychology of Decision Delay and Decision Avoidance," *Psychology*, 16 (Winter), 41-6.

Importance Weight Effects On Self-explicated Preference Models: Some Empirical Findings

Paul E. Green, University of Pennsylvania
Catherine M. Schaffer, University of Denver[1]

The self-explicated preference model (in which preference is assumed to be a simple additive function of attribute importances times attribute level desirabilities) has received renewed attention in recent developments of hybrid conjoint and computer-based (adaptive) conjoint models. This paper explores the effect of varying attribute importance weights on the self-explicated model's predictive validity across conjoint-based full profile evaluations.

Counter to conventional wisdom, we find that modifying importance weights, so that the less important attributes are reduced even further in relative importance, *reduces* predictive validity. That is, individuals' originally stated importances are the best predictors of their subsequent full-profile evaluations.

INTRODUCTION

The venerable self-explicated preference model, in which preference is assumed to be a simple additive function of attribute importance weights times attribute-level desirabilities, has recently undergone a resurgence of interest. At the academic research level, new classes of models, such as hybrid conjoint (Green, Goldberg, and Montemayor 1981; Cattin, Hermet, and Pioche 1982; Akaah and Korgaonkar 1983), have utilized self-explicated data as a first stage in the development of a compositional/conjoint model.

At the industry application level, Sawtooth Software's Adaptive Conjoint Analysis (Johnson 1987) incorporates self-explicated data as a first step prior to "Bayesian" updating, based on individuals' evaluations of paired comparisons stimuli. M/A/R/C, a national marketing research firm, has developed CASEMAP (Srinivasan 1988), a telephone interviewing method that collects only self-explicated data for preference modeling (i.e., there is no conjoint data collection stage).

Self-explicated preference models frequently predict conjoint-based profile responses reasonably well (Leigh, MacKay, and Summers 1984; Srinivasan 1988; Green and Helsen 1989). Of course, one could describe sets of conditions (e.g., preference evaluations of "holistic" stimuli such as food/beverage formulations, package designs, and physical stimuli in general) where the collection of self-explicated data would not make much sense.

Still, these are applied contexts in which the self-explicated model may be appropriate.

Since the inception of linear additive models in marketing (see Wilkie and Pessemier 1973), questions have been raised about whether importance weights are really necessary in self-explicated judgments and, if so, how they should be applied (Dawes and Corrigan 1974; McClelland 1978). Green and Krieger (1986) have examined this question in the context of marketing as have Curry and Faulds (1986).

The question addressed in the present paper, however, appears to be almost as old as the self-explicated model itself. In the early 1960s Shepard (1964), citing research on self-explicated models by Hoffman (1960) and Pollack (1962), stated (p. 266) that:

> In both cases subjects were asked not only to make an overall evaluation of each stimulus but also to judge the extent to which each attribute of the stimuli was subjectively weighted, on the average, in making these evaluations. The degree of "insight" of a subject could then be assessed by comparing his announced subjective weights with the weights that were in reality controlling his overall evaluations (as determined by multiple regression procedures, for example). The results suggest that although the weights controlling the subjects' responses are usually concentrated on only one or two attributes, the subjective weights reported by the subjects tended to be more evenly distributed over the whole set of attributes. Indeed, there is some indication in Pollack's findings that the announced subjective weights tended to err in the opposite direction of ascribing too much importance to the less important variables.

Shepard's comments seem plausible and in accord with one's own intuitions. They have remained a part of the conventional wisdom to this day.

The purpose of the study reported here is to examine the issue of whether appropriate transformations of individuals' self-explicated importances can actually *improve* cross-validities in sets of holdout stimuli where respondents evaluate conjoint profiles holistically from a preference standpoint. We first briefly review the main characteristics of the self-explicated model. We then describe the empirical study and report cross-validation findings. We conclude the paper with a further discussion of the problem and areas for future research.

---

[1] The authors would like to acknowledge support of the Citibank Fellowship from the Sol C. Snider Entrepreneurial Center and the SEI Center for Advanced Studies in Management at the Wharton School.

THE SELF-EXPLICATED PREFERENCE MODEL

The self-explicated preference model has been described by Green (1984). Following his notation, we let

$$\underline{i} = (i_1, i_2, \ldots, i_j, \ldots, i_J)$$

denote a multiattribute profile in which the vector component i_j denotes level i_j ($i_j = 1, I_j$) of attribute j ($j = 1, J$). Next, we let

u_{ijk} = respondent k's (k = 1, K) self-explicated desirability (or acceptibility) score for level i of attribute j,

w_{jk} = respondent k's self-explicated importance weight for attribute j; $w_{jk} \geq 0$;

$$\sum_{j=1}^{J} w_{jk} = 1.0$$

Then,

$$U_{i_1, i_2, \ldots, i_J, k} = \sum_{j=1}^{J} w_{jk} u_{ijk}$$

denotes respondent k's overall preference score, or utility U, for profile $\underline{i}$ as a weighted sum of the desirability scores u_{ijk}.

The u's are usually obtained as rating scale values on (say) a 0 to 10 scale. Depending upon the number of attributes, the w's may be obtained from constant sum tasks or from rating scales (where the non-negative importance ratings are later normalized to sum to unity). However, Johnson (1987) obtains desirability scores as integer rank numbers across the levels of each attribute and importance weights as ratings on a 4-point scale.

Data collection techniques also differ on how the u's are normalized. Here we shall first assume that, within attribute, the original ratings are simply transformed by a multiplicative constant to vary between 0 and 1.0. In some cases, however, the researcher may translate and stretch the original scale so that, within attribute, the lowest desirability scale value is coded 0 and the highest is coded 1, with interpolated intermediate values. (We comment later on the advisability of this transformation.)

EXPERIMENTAL DESIGN

The stimuli of this experiment consisted of privately offered, unfurnished apartment descriptions, a rather popular area for academic research in conjoint analysis (Johnson and Meyer 1984; Green, Helsen, and Shandler 1988). Subjects for the experiment were business students, most of whom were already living in a student apartment or were considering renting one during the next school year. Complete data were obtained from 177 respondents; all data were collected during March-April 1989.

Table 1 shows the attributes and levels used in the study. Data collection entailed four phases. Phase I consisted of the self-explicated task. For each attribute level of Table 1 the respondent was asked to rate its acceptability on a 0-10, equal-interval rating scale, ranging from completely unacceptable to completely acceptable. Following this, each respondent was asked to allocate 100 points across the six attributes, so as to reflect their relative importance in selecting an apartment for rent.

In phase II, each respondent received (in randomized order) 18 full-profile cards developed from an orthogonal main effects plan (see Table 2). In each case the respondent was asked to indicate the likelihood (on a 0-100 scale) of renting an apartment of that description, assuming he or she were in need of an apartment within walking distance of the university.

In phase III each respondent received 16 profiles, based on an orthogonal design, utilizing levels 1 and 3 of the attributes shown in Table 1. The same 0-100 likelihood of renting scale was used again. The data of phases I-III were all collected in one sitting. (Respondents received class credit for their participation.)

Two weeks later, each respondent participated in phase IV. A different experimental design (one that was constructed to make the profiles easier to judge) was used to construct 16 apartment profiles, again drawn from levels 1 and 3 of Table 1. Respondents rated these 16 "easier" profiles on the same 0-100 likelihood of renting scale used earlier. Hence for each of 177 respondents, data were available for constructing an individual-based self-explicated model and then validating that model on three separate holdout samples of 18, 16, and 16 profiles, respectively.

Analysis of the Individual Self-Explicated Models

All analyses were made at the individual subject level and then summarized. The principal experimental variable under study was the vector of self-explicated importances, i.e., the w's described earlier.

In keeping with the spirit of Shepard's comments, we operationalized the idea of giving differential weight to the most important attributes by means of a power function ß, where the following transformation of the original w_{jk}'s was made:

$$w_{jk}^* = w_{jk}^\beta$$

for ß = 1, 2, 4, 8, 16, respectively. For example, suppose a subject's original importance weights (from the constant sum task) were 0.15, 0.03, 0.42, 0.10, 0.08, and 0.22 for walking time, noise level, safety, condition, size, and rent, respectively. If

TABLE 1
Attributes and Levels Used in Conjoint Study

A. Walking Time to Classes
1. 10 minutes
2. 20 minutes
3. 30 minutes

B. Noise Level of Apartment House
1. Very quiet
2. Average noise level
3. Extremely noisy

C. Safety of Apartment Location
1. Very safe location
2. Average safety
3. Very unsafe location

D. Condition of Apartment
1. Newly renovated throughout
2. Renovated kitchen only
3. Poor condition

E. Size of Living/Dining Area
1. 24 by 30 feet
2. 15 by 20 feet
3. 9 by 12 feet

F. Monthly Rent (Utilities Incl.)
1. $540
2. $360
3. $225

TABLE 2
Profile Descriptions Used in Phase II

Profile	A	B	C	D	E	F
1	1	1	1	1	1	1
2	2	2	3	2	2	2
3	3	3	2	3	3	3
4	1	2	2	2	3	1
5	2	3	1	3	1	2
6	3	1	3	1	2	3
7	1	3	3	2	1	3
8	2	1	2	3	2	1
9	3	2	1	1	3	2
10	1	3	2	1	2	2
11	2	1	1	2	3	3
12	3	2	3	3	1	1
13	1	1	3	3	3	2
14	2	2	2	1	1	3
15	3	3	1	2	2	1
16	1	2	1	3	2	3
17	2	3	3	1	3	1
18	3	1	2	2	1	2

FIGURE 1
Average Desirability Scale Values (original units) from Self-Explicated Task

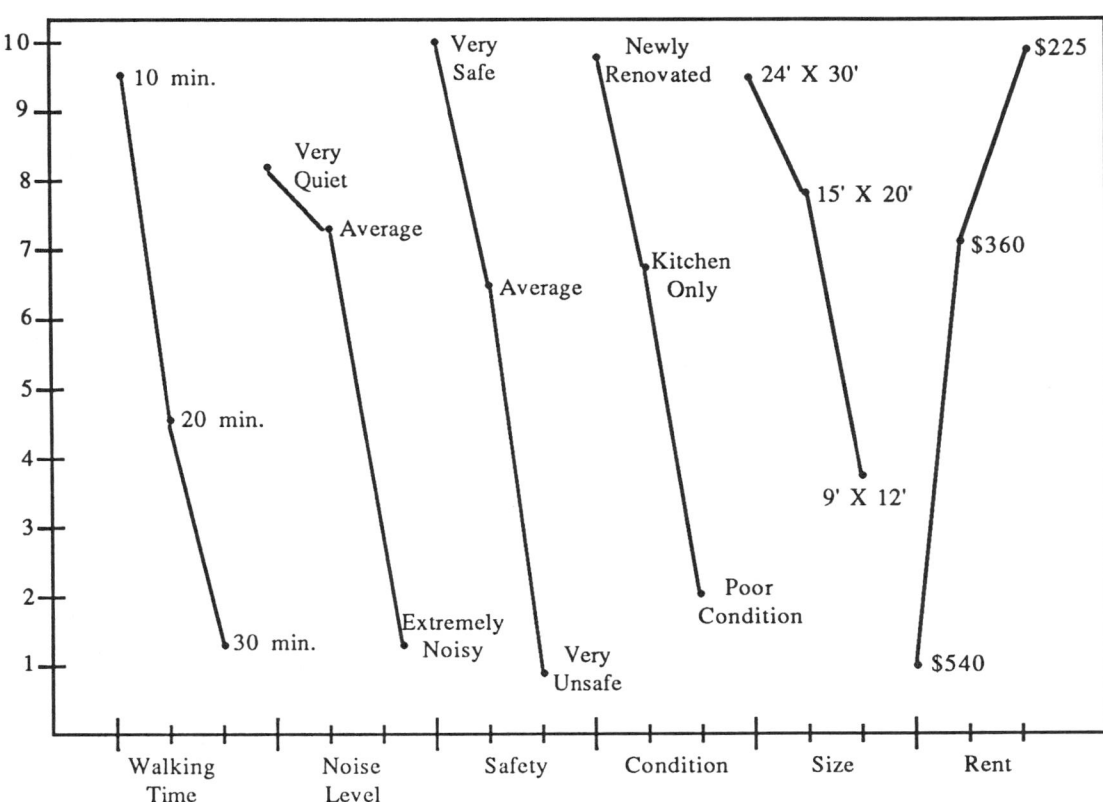

$\beta = 2$, the respective weights (after normalization) would be 0.085, 0.003, 0.667, 0.038, 0.024, and 0.183, respectively. As noted, the most important attribute (safety) receives differentially high importance after the power transformation.

In addition, we set up an experimental condition were $\beta = 0$, thereby constructing a set of unit (equal) weights in accord with the research of Dawes and Corrigan (1974). In this case, an effect that is *opposite* to Shepard's remarks would occur in which respondents' transformed weights are made more equal (i.e., precisely equal) than their original, self-stated weights.

Response Measures

Two kinds of tests on the effect of importance weight modifications were run. First, the control condition ($\beta = 1$) and the five test conditions ($\beta = 0, 2, 4, 8, 16$) along with the acceptability ratings, were used to obtain self-explicated part worths. Each of the six self-explicated models was then used to predict responses to the Phase II, III, and IV full-profile evaluations. As measures of cross-validity we employed Pearson's product moment correlation between actual and predicted likelihoods of renting and the incidence of predicted first-choice hits.

CROSS-VALIDATION RESULTS--HOLDOUT DATA

We first report results involving the cross-validation of each importance-weight power transformation with the three holdout samples obtained from phases II, III, and IV. However, by way of background, Figure 1 shows the average acceptability scores for the sample of 177 respondents (in their original, 0-10 rating scale units). As might be surmised, all attribute level ratings, on average, maintained monotonicity.

We now turn to the cross-validation results (Table 3) in which, for each individual, the appropriate self-explicated model was used to predict the actual evaluations of the holdout profiles of phases II, III, and IV.

Product Moment Correlations

As Table 3 shows, the effect of the power transformation (for $\beta = 2, 4, 8,$ and 16) is to *reduce* the self-explicated model's validity as β increases beyond $\beta = 1$. This pattern holds true across all three sets of holdout profile evaluations. We note that the use of equal weights (i.e., $\beta = 0$) also fails to improve on the original, self-stated attribute importances. (This result is less surprising since

TABLE 3
Cross-Validation Results by Power Transformation and Holdout Profile Sets (Phase II, III, or IV) Correlations and First-Choice Hits*

Power Function	Correlations			Incidence of First-Choice Hits		
	II	III	IV	II	III	IV
0	.676	.647	.701	.371	.277	.774
1 (Control)	.712	.721	.761	.379	.453	.798
2	.681	.699	.731	.339	.413	.783
4	.629	.650	.675	.323	.412	.742
8	.580	.600	.623	.298	.344	.570
16	.553	.573	.594	.239	.289	.369

* Correlations and first-choice hit incidences are averages of individual respondent results for N = 177.

the gist of Dawes and Corrigan's remarks relates to errors in regression-estimated weights rather than self-stated weight transformations.) The more important point is that cross-validation performance is diminished as one departs on "either side" of the self-stated weights, via a specified monotonic function of the original weights.

With the exception of the ß = 0 condition, we note that the correlations are always in the rank order of phase IV (best), followed by phase III, and finally by phase II. To a large extent this ordering is due to the fact that the stimuli in phase IV (which were not constructed by an orthogonal design) were easier to judge. In phase IV there were two highly desirable profiles (where five out of six attributes were all at their high levels) and two extremely poor profiles (only one of the six attributes was at its high desirability level). The remaining 12 profiles were all "intermediate," with exactly three high-level and three low-level attributes each.

The orthogonally-designed stimuli of phase III had only one extremely good profile (five out of six attributes at their high levels) and one extremely poor profile (one out of six at its high level). Of the 14 remaining stimuli, five profiles had two attributes at their high levels, six profiles had three attributes at their high levels, and three profiles had four attributes at their high levels.

Phase IV and phase III stimuli were expressly constructed to examine the differential impact that more easily evaluated profiles might have on various validation measures. (In this regard the phase II orthogonally-designed profiles were even more difficult to judge, given the fact that three levels of each attribute were independently varying.)

First-Choice Hits

Table 3 also shows the counterpart results for the first-choice hit measure, by phase. As noted, for the control case there is a 0.371 chance that the respondent's actual first choice among the 18 profiles of phase II is predicted by his/her self-explicated model. Because of the presence of ties in either the actual ratings and/or the self-explicated predictions, all first-choice incidences have been adjusted to allow for multiple first-choice hits. For example, if in phase III the subject's highest rated profile is #14 and the highest self-explicated predictions show ties among profiles #1, #11, and #14, the first-hit incidence is recorded as 0.33, instead of 1.0. (This procedure adjusts for the fact that as the power of ß increases, there is a greater incidence of tied self-explicated predictions.)

We note from Table 3 that the incidence of first-choice hits also decreases as ß departs on either side of its control value of 1.0. Similar to the correlations pattern, we note that the predictive accuracies of phase IV dominate their counterparts in phases II and III. With one exception (ß = 0), phase III accuracies are higher than their phase II counterparts. In short, both validation measures (correlations and first-choice hits) result in similar conclusions.

Significance Tests

The three-way matrix (of order 177 X 6 X 3) of correlations was analyzed by repeated measures ANOVA. Both main effects (levels of ß and the three sets of holdout profiles) were significant beyond the 0.01 level.

TABLE 4
Cross-Validation Results by Zeroing-Out Rule and Holdout Profile Sets (Phase II, III, or IV)

Number Zeroed Out	Correlations II	III	IV
1	.705	.714	.753
2	.691	.702	.736
3	.662	.674	.707
4	.614	.635	.658
5	.545	.564	.586
Control Case	.712	.721	.761

The incidence of first-choice hits (Table 3) was also analyzed. Significant results were also found for the effect of ß and the effect of holdout sample (phases II, III, and IV).

Data Rescaling

The preceding analyses were then repeated for the original acceptabilities data that were rescaled so that, within subject, each acceptability score was "stretched" to range from 0 (least acceptable) to 1.0 (most acceptable); the original intermediate scale values were linearly interpolated on the new scales. We found that the resulting correlations and first-choice hits were dominated by their counterpart values of Table 3, based on the *original* acceptabilities scaling. Given this poor performance, no additional analyses were carried out with the alternative scaling. For this data set, at least, the alternative scaling (of stretching each acceptability range to be anchored at zero and one) resulted in significant information loss.

DISCUSSION

To the best of our knowledge this is the first empirical study that has examined the empirical consequences of Shepard's 1962 comments. We have found that transformations which make the attribute importances more disparate (e.g., higher values of ß) lead to poorer cross-validations. Assigning equal importance weights also leads to lower cross-validations.

Moreover, although not shown here, part worth model misspecification also shows effects at the market share level, particularly if choice rules approximating the maximum utility rules are applied. Finally, transformations that alter the original acceptabilities ratings so that all acceptabilities exhibit the same range (i.e., 0 to 1) significantly *lower* the cross-validations, at least for this data set.

Clearly, the findings of this study are limited. First, we have considered only six attributes. It is possible that Shepard's comments could be appropriate for larger numbers of attributes and levels within attributes. More complex attribute combinations, including non-monotonic functions (e.g., ideal points) could also prompt the greater use of simplifying strategies that focus on a reduced number of attributes and attribute-level variations.

What about other transformations of the original importances that also have the effect of making the less important attributes even less influential? To this end, we examined another transformation rule, referred to as a "zeroing-out" rule. Under this procedure one takes the attribute that is *least* important (from the self-explication task) and sets its importance weight to zero. The remaining attribute importances are renormalized to sum to unity. The procedure is repeated for the two least important attributes, and so on.

This rule is somewhat gentler than the ß procedure, described earlier, inasmuch as the ß rule effectively lowers all attribute importances except the attribute carrying the highest importance. The zeroing-out rule was followed for all possible cases, leaving out 1, 2, 3, 4, or 5 of the less important attributes. We then ran validation correlations similar to those shown earlier in Table 3.

Table 4 shows the results of the zeroing-out rule. Again we note the same pattern of decrease in predictive accuracy as predictions are made on fewer and fewer attributes. We also note the same pattern in which phase IV correlations exceed those of phase III which, in turn, are higher than those of phase II. In sum, the "gentler," zeroing-out rule produced similar results, i.e., lower validities compared to the control case in which all attribute importances were retained.

While we have examined (in Table 3) cross-validation behavior for both correlations and the incidence of first choice hits, we have a predilection for the former measure. Correlations consider the whole set of predictions, not just the top choice (under a maximum utility rule). Correlations are also more sensitive to the types of transformations considered here. With the increasing application of logit-type models (Johnson 1987) and other varieties of share-of-utility rules, we feel that sole reliance on first-choice prediction could present, for some data sets and contexts, an incomplete description of cross-validation performance.

REFERENCES

Akaah, Ishmael P., and Pradeep K. Korgaonkar (1983), "An Empirical Comparison of Predictive Validity for the Self-Explicated, Huber-hybrid, Traditional Conjoint and Hybrid Conjoint Models," *Journal of Marketing Research*, 20 (May), 187-97.

Cattin, Philippe, Gerard Hermet, and Alan Pioche (1982), "Alternative Hybrid Models for Conjoint Analysis: Some Empirical Results," in Raj Srivastava and Allan D. Shocker (eds.), *Analytical Approaches to Product and Market Planning: The Second Conference*. Cambridge, MA: Marketing Science Institute (October), 142-52.

Curry, David J. and David J. Faulds (1986), "Indexing Product Quality: Issues, Theory and Results," *Journal of Consumer Research*, 13 (June), 134-45.

Dawes, Robyn M. and Bernard Corrigan (1974), "Linear Models in Decision Making," *Psychological Bulletin*, 81, 95-106.

Green, Paul E. (1984), "Hybrid Models for Conjoint Analysis: An Expository Review," *Journal of Marketing Research*, 21 (May), 155-9.

―――, Stephen M. Goldberg, and Mila Montemayor (1981), "A Hybrid Utility Estimation Model for Conjoint Analysis," *Journal of Marketing*, 45 (Winter), 33-41.

――― and Kristiaan Helsen (1989), "Cross-Validation Assesment of Alternatives to Individual-Level Conjoint Analysis," *Journal of Marketing Research*, 26 (August), 346-350.

―――, Kristiaan Helsen, and Bruce Shandler (1988), "Conjoint Internal Validity Under Alternative Profile Presentations," *Journal of Consumer Research*, 15 (December), 392-7.

――― and Abba M. Krieger (1986), "The Minimal Rank Correlation, Subject to Order Restrictions, with Application to the Weighted Linear Model," *Journal of Classification*, 3, 67-96.

Hoffman, Paul J. (1960), "The Paramorphic Representation of Human Judgement," *Psychological Bulletin*, 57, 116-31.

Johnson, Eric J. and Robert J. Meyer (1984), "Compensatory Choice Models of Noncompensatory Processes: The Effect of Varying Context," *Journal of Consumer Research*, 11 (June), 528-41.

Johnson, Richard M. (1987), "Adaptive Conjoint Analysis," *Sawtooth Software Conference on Perceptual Mapping, Conjoint Analysis, and Computer Interviewing*. Ketchum, ID: Sawtooth Software.

Leigh, T. W., David B. MacKay, and John O. Summers (1984), "Reliability and Validity of Conjoint Analysis and Self-Explicated Weights: A Comparison," *Journal of Marketing Research*, 21 (November), 456-62.

McClelland, Gary H. (1978), "Equal Versus Differential Weighting for Multiattribute Decisions: There Are No Free Lunches," Center Report No. 207, Boulder, CO: Institute of Behavioral Science, University of Colorado.

Pollack, I. (1962), "Action Selection and the Yntema-Torgenson 'Worth' Function," paper presented at the 1962 Meeting of the Eastern Psychological Association, April.

Shepard, Roger N. (1964), "On Subjectively Optimum Selections Among Multiattribute Alternatives," in M. W. Shelley, II and G. L. Bryan (eds.), *Human Judgments and Optimality*. New York: John Wiley, 257-81.

Srinivasan, V. (1988), "A Conjunctive-Compensatory Approach to the Self-Explication of Multiattributed Preferences," *Decision Sciences*, 19 (Spring), 295-305.

Wilkie, William L. and Edgar A. Pessemier (1973), "Issues in Marketing's Use of Multiattribute Attitude Models," *Journal of Marketing Research*, 10 (November), 428-41.

An Evaluation of the SERVQUAL Scales in a Retailing Setting
David W. Finn, Texas Christian University
Charles W. Lamb, Jr., Texas Christian University

ABSTRACT

A series of articles by Parasuraman, Zeithaml, and Berry has traced the development of a theory that attempts to explain how consumers acquire perceptions of the quality of service firms. Parallel with their theory development, Parasuraman, et al. have experimented with various ways of *measuring* the hypothetical dimensions of service quality. Their latest effort resulted in a set of scales they have named SERVQUAL.

The research reported here examined the usefulness of SERVQUAL in a retail setting. Results do not support the proposition that the instrument can be used to assess perceived service quality in retailing.

INTRODUCTION

One of the most critical challenges that U.S. firms faced in the 1980s was to provide consistently high quality goods and services (Leonard and Sasser 1982; Zeithaml, Berry, and Parasuraman 1986;). There is a growing body of evidence indicating that providing high quality goods and services enhances profitability, improves productivity, increases market share and return on investment, and reduces costs (Thompson, DeSouza, and Gale 1985; Rudie and Wansley 1985; Phillips, Chang, and Buzzell 1983; Garvin 1983; Deming 1982; Gale and Klavans 1985; Ishikawa 1985). It seems likely that the current emphasis on improving and maintaining high quality will have a substantial influence on management practice throughout the 1990s. As John Young, president of Hewlett-Packard has noted, "A corporate strategy that focuses on quality as a key element is the best way companies can respond to the [competitive] pressure they face" (Young 1985).

Quality, however, "is an elusive and indistinct construct" (Parasuraman, Zeithaml, and Berry 1985). Defining and measuring quality are complicated because the concept can be viewed from several different perspectives. Garvin (1983), for example, identified five completely different approaches to defining quality. Lewis and Booms (1983) and Gronroos (1982) have also discussed problems associated with defining and measuring quality. It is even more complicated when the quality is associated with the intangible aspects of *services* as compared to the tangible characteristics of *physical products*.

BACKGROUND

In a 1986 Marketing Science Institute Working Paper (MSI), Parasuraman, Zeithaml, and Berry (1986) offered a theory that consumers' perception of the quality of a service offering is a function of five separate quality perceptions. Figure 1 illustrates their theory that: (1) perceived quality of tangibles (physical facilities, equipment, and appearance of personnel), (2) perceived quality of reliability (ability to perform the promised service dependably and accurately), (3) perceived quality of responsiveness (willingness to help customers and provide prompt service), (4) perceived quality of assurance (knowledge and courtesy of employees and their ability to convey trust and confidence), and (5) perceived quality of empathy (caring and individualized attention the firm provides its customers) all influence consumers' perception of the overall service quality of a service firm.

In the original MSI piece and in related articles (1985, 1988), Parasuraman et al. hypothesized that the five dimensions of service quality are, themselves, related to the discrepancy between consumers' *expectations* and *perceptions*. Specifically, they proposed that "service quality, as perceived by consumers, stems from a comparison of what they (consumers) feel service firms should offer (i.e., from their expectations) with their perceptions of the performance of firms providing the services"(p. 16). As Figure 1 illustrates, their theory holds that perceived service quality is a function of the magnitude and direction of five specific perceptual discrepancies.

To test the adequacy of this theory, *measures* of the constructs were needed. In a 1988 *Journal of Retailing* article, Parasuraman, et al. described a series of iterations that led to the identification of 22 items that appear to measure the five dimensions. They labeled their scales SERVQUAL. SERVQUAL is comprised of 22 pairs of questions: one question from each pair asks consumers to describe their expectations, the other question asks for their perceptions. The instructions for using SERVQUAL are to subtract the expectations score from the perceptions score and to use the result as one of 22 measurement items. Table 1 lists the components of the SERVQUAL scales. Four items purport to measure consumers' perceptions of TANGIBLES quality, five items measure RELIABILITY quality, four items measure RESPONSIVENESS quality, four items measure ASSURANCE quality, and five items measure EMPATHY quality.

PURPOSE

The SERVQUAL scales that have been offered to consumer researchers are the result of ONE data collection. Parasuraman, et al.'s exploratory factor analysis of that data set led them to propose the 22 items as measures of the 5 dimensions. Before they are accepted as "off the shelf" measures of the dimensions of perceived service quality, they must be subjected to further testing. To date, very few studies have appeared that test the accuracy of either the theory or the measurement scales. One study by Babakus and Mangold (1989) concluded that SERVQUAL is not 5-dimensional in a health care

FIGURE 1
THE PARSURAMAN, ZEITHAML, AND BERRY (1988) THEORY OF THE DETERMINANTS OF PERCEIVED QUALITY

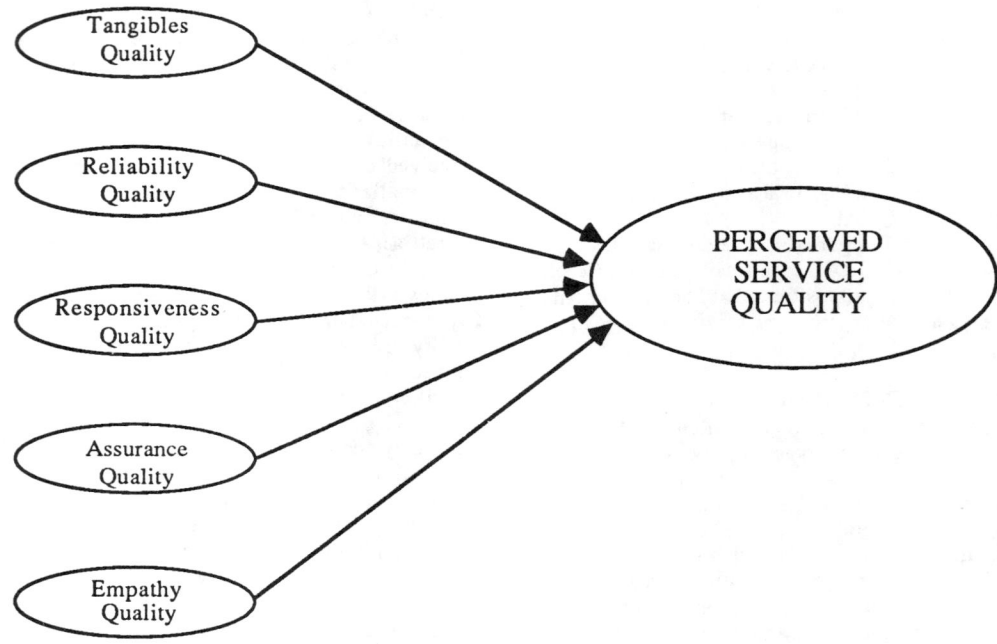

The 5 dimensions represent the differences between consumers' expectations and perceptions of a firm's performance along each quality dimension. Perceived service quality is a function of the magnitude and direction of the 5 perceptual dimensions.

---

setting. This paper tests whether SERVQUAL can be used in a retail setting.

THE MEASUREMENT MODEL

The five dimensions identified in Figure 1 and Table 1 are not directly observable; they are theoretical constructs. To say that items 1 through 4 form a *measure* of the construct named tangibles quality is to say that the answers an individual gives to those pairs of questions depend upon how much tangibles quality s/he perceives. Similarly, unobserved reliability quality causes the answers to question pairs 5 through 9; responsiveness quality causes the answers to question pairs 10 through 13, and so on. Figure 2 illustrates these relationships.

Figure 2 can be thought of as a representation of a factor analysis model where the λ_{ij}'s are factor loadings linking the theoretical factors to the measures. The δ_i's symbolize the presence of measurement error. The curved lines linking the factors represent possible correlations among the factors, and the magnitudes of the correlations are represented by Φ_{ij}'s. As Figure 2 shows, each measured item is linked to only one theoretical dimension. This illustrates the requirement that each measure is a manifestation of only one construct, and therefore measures only that construct (in practice, the items that represent one factor are combined into a composite score (often the mean of the item scores) to provide a measure of the factor. The composite score is meaningful only if each of the measures is unidimensional (Gerbring and Anderson 1988)).

If the SERVQUAL scales possess construct validity in a retail setting (i.e., if the twenty-two items included in the instrument measure the five distinct dimensions identified by Parasuraman, et al.(1988)), then a survey of retail store customers should produce results that conform to the model as specified in Figure 2.

METHODOLOGY

The Sample

To insure that a variety of retail firms was included, a quota of 60 - 70 shoppers from each of four different retail store types was set. The four different types of stores were: (1) stores like K-Mart, Wal-Mart, etc., (2) stores like J.C. Penney, Sears, etc., (3) stores like Dillards, Foley's, etc., and (4) stores like Saks, Neiman Marcus, etc.

Eleven hundred random telephone numbers were purchased from a commercial sampling house.

TABLE 1
DESCRIPTION OF SERVQUAL[a,b]

TANGIBLES QUALITY
1. should have up-to-date equipment
2. physical facilities should be visually appealing
3. employees should be well dressed and appear neat
4. appearance of physical facilities should be in keeping with the type of services provided

RELIABILITY QUALITY
5. should do things by the time they promise
6. when customers have problems, they should be sympathetic and reassuring
7. should be dependable
8. should provide their services at the time they promise
9. should keep accurate records

RESPONSIVENESS QUALITY
10. should not be expected to tell customers exactly when services will be performed (reverse coded)
11. not realistic for customers to expect prompt service (reverse coded)
12. employees do not always have to be willing to help customers (reverse coded)
13. is OK if they are too busy to respond to requests promptly (reverse coded)

ASSURANCE QUALITY
14. customers should be able to trust employees
15. customers should feel safe in their transactions with these stores' employees
16. the employees should be polite
17. employees should get adequate support to do their jobs well

EMPATHY QUALITY
18. company should not be expected to give customers individual attention (reverse coded)
19. employees cannot be expected to give customers personal attention (reverse coded)
20. unrealistic to expect employees to know what the needs of their customers are (reverse coded)
21. unrealistic for them to have customers' best interests at heart (reverse coded)
22. should not be expected to have operating hours convenient to all customers (reverse coded)

NOTE: This is not the EXACT wording of the SERVQUAL questions. Some sentences have been shortened to fit in the table. The questions in this Table represent the EXPECTATIONS questions. The parallel questions that asked for people's PERCEPTIONS asked if "XYZ company" *does* that thing.

[a] A 5-point scale ranging from "strongly agree" (=5) to "strongly disagree" (=1) is used to gather consumers' perceptions.

[b] To compute scores on each dimension, average the difference scores (PERCEPTIONS minus EXPECTATIONS) on the items making up that dimension. If the theory in Figure 1 is correct, "SERVQUAL can also provide an overall measure of quality in the form of an average score across all five dimensions" (Parasuraman, Zeithaml, and Berry 1986, pg. 29).

Each telephone interviewer sought female shoppers from one of the four store types. The interviewer asked a filter question to see if any female in the household had shopped at that type of store before continuing into the questionnaire.

The Questionnaire

The questionnaire was the same as the Parasuraman, Zeithaml and Berry (1988) instrument except that a 5-point, rather than a 7-point, scale was used (this change was suggested by the developers of the scale. Also, a five point scale is easier to use in telephone interviewing). Table 1 explains how the answers were coded.

Data Collection

The interviewers dialed 1,100 telephone numbers to get the target samples of users of the different types of retailers. The response rate was 31.9 percent. The final sample had 65 users of stores like K-Mart, 66 users of stores like Sears, 58 users of stores like Dillards, and 69 users of stores like Neiman Marcus.

FIGURE 2
THE SERVQUAL MEASUREMENT MODEL[a]

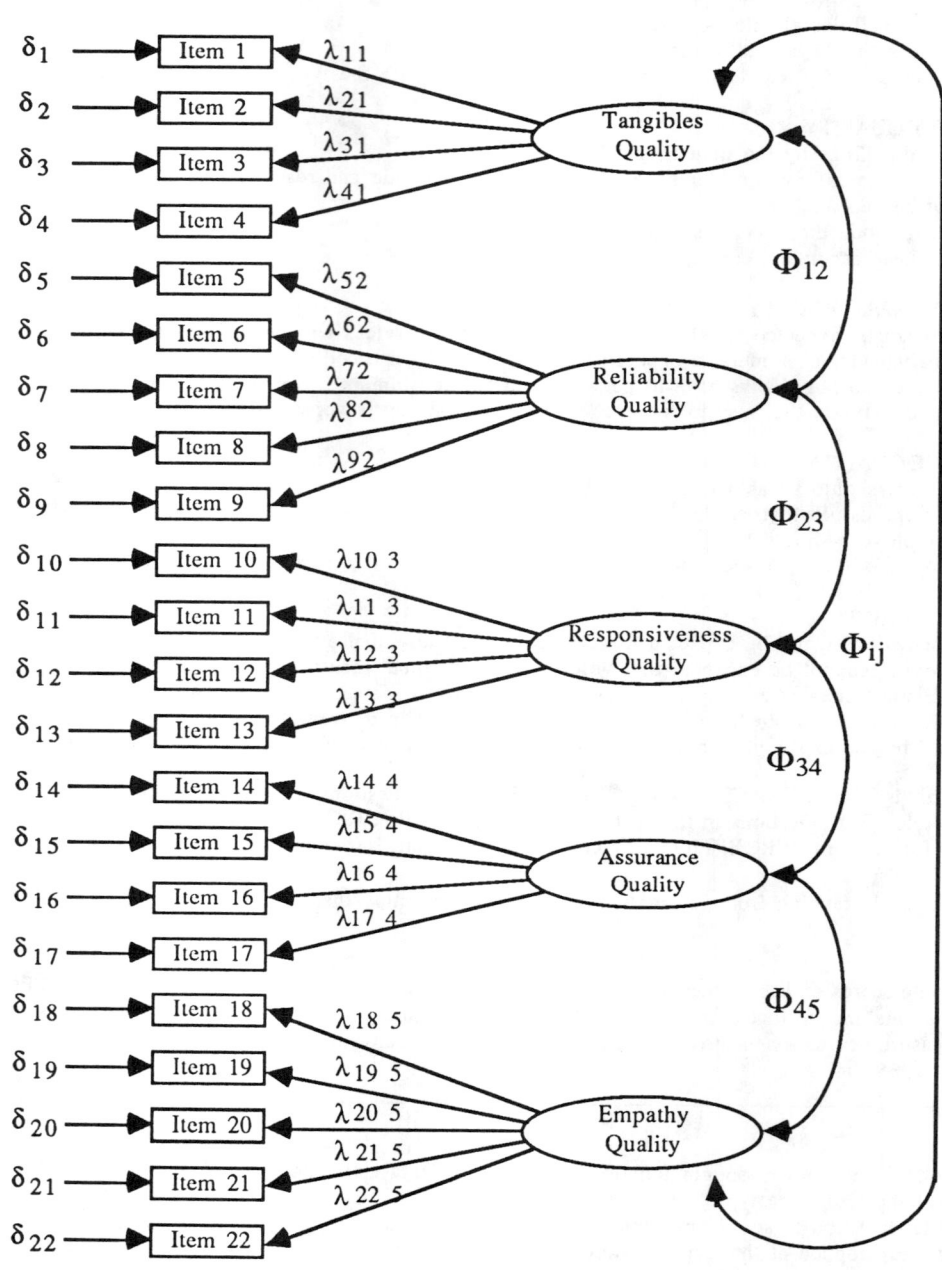

[a] In keeping with the conventions of structural equations analysis, latent variables are circled, and measures (or operationalizations) of those latent variables are within rectangles.

[b] Item numbers correspond to the statement numbers in Table 1

RESULTS

Analysis

Confirmatory factor analysis using LISREL V (Jöreskog and Sörbom 1981) was used to assess the fit of the data to the model. Confirmatory factor analysis is based on the matrix of variances and covariances (or a correlation matrix when the data are standardized) of the observed variables (the 22 items). The fit of this actual data to the theoretical model is computed by constructing a covariance matrix that *should* occur if the model is correct (Figure 2), and then comparing the observed covariance matrix to that theoretical covariance matrix.

If the data fit the model, confirmatory factor analysis can supply estimates of the λ_{ij}'s, the correlations among the factors, and the variances of the δ_i's. Equally important, the LISREL program can supply various indicators of how well the observed data fit the hypothesized model as well as diagnostic tools for identifying problems with the model.

One measure of fit is the Chi-Square goodness-of-fit statistic. This statistic is computed under the null hypothesis that the observed covariances among the answers came from a population that fits the model. A statistically significant value in the goodness-of-fit test would suggest that the data do not fit the proposed model, i.e., that the observed covariance matrix is statistically different than the hypothesized matrix. Strictly speaking, it is rare to have empirical data that meet all the assumptions required to use the Chi-square test. Jöreskog and Sörbom (1986, pp. I.38 - I.39) state:

> the statistical problem is not one of testing a given hypothesis . . . but one of fitting the model to the data and to decide whether the fit is adequate or not. . . . Instead of regarding χ^2 as a test statistic one should regard it as a goodness (or badness) of fit measure in the sense that large χ^2 values correspond to bad fit and small χ^2 values correspond to good fit.

When the overall fit is bad, Jöreskog and Sörbom suggest comparing every observed covariance with every theorized covariance and computing the normalized residuals. A residual greater than two in magnitude provides a hint at where the model is incorrect.

Assessment of the Overall Fit of the Model

Bagozzi and Yi (1988, p.76) have pointed out that "one of the first things that should be done before examination of the global criteria...is to see if any anomalies exist in the output." Examples of anomalies in the output are (1) negative estimates for the variances, (2) correlation estimates greater than 1, and (3) extremely large estimates for the parameters. None of these anomalies were present in the output reported here.

Table 2 shows the evaluation of the fit of the retail store data to the SERVQUAL measurement model. The large chi-square value of 377.64 implies that it is extremely unlikely that the data represent random variation from the model. Therefore, it is appropriate to look at other indicators. All the other indicators of fit demonstrate a decided lack of fit. Notice particularly the normalized residuals. The twelve normalized residuals that are greater than two involve fifteen of the twenty-two variables included in the model. Measured items 19 and 21 (Table 1) accounted for six of these large residuals in their pairings with other items.

One of the diagnostic tools available in LISREL is a table of modification indices, which helps to identify specific problems with models. An analysis of the output used to construct Table 2 suggested that items 19 and 21 are not unidimensional measures of the "empathy" construct. Accordingly, an alternative measurement model was tested. The SERVQUAL measure of Empathy Quality was reduced from a five item scale to a three item scale (composed of items 18, 20, and 22 in Table 1). Indicators of the fit of that model are shown in Table 3.

The large Chi-Square value again suggests that the model is not properly specified. A further hint at bad fit is the root mean square residual, which is almost 25 percent of the size of the correlation estimates. These results indicate that *the SERVQUAL measurement model is not appropriate in a retail store setting.*

Interestingly, the five multi-item scales proposed by Parasuraman, et al. meet acceptable standards of reliability for exploratory research, ranging from .59 for Tangibles Quality to .83 for Reliability Quality. This quirk underscores the well known dictum that *correlated sets of items do not necessarily measure anything.*

DISCUSSION

The results of this study challenge the validity of the SERVQUAL scales as measures of the determinants of perceived quality in retailing. Four possible explanations for this conclusion are as follows: (1) the study reported here produced results that are atypical; (2) the SERVQUAL scales do not capture the essence of the service quality construct in retailing; (3) perceived service quality in retailing is not a function of the 5 constructs identified by Parasuraman, Zeithaml, and Berry (1988); or (4) the differences in data gathering methodologies used (telephone versus self-administered questionnaires) accounted for the differences between the results the two studies.

TABLE 2
The Fit of the Data to the Model

Chi-square value	377.64
df	199
p value	<.001
Adjusted goodness of fit index	.802
Root mean-square residual	.064
Number of normalized residuals >2	12 [a]

[a] NOTE: 6 of these involved 2 measurement items (item 19 and item 21 in Table 1).

TABLE 3
The Fit of the Data to the Adjusted Model

Chi-square value	266.15
df	160
p value	<.001
Adjusted goodness of fit index	.849
Root mean-square residual	.057
Number of normalized residuals >2	5

Atypical Results

Although it is possible that the sample population is atypical, this is not likely. The sample was randomly drawn from a medium size (about 1 million people) SMSA by a commercial sampling firm. Respondent selection procedures were standard for a telephone survey. There is no apparent reason to believe that the study produced atypical results.

Service Quality in Retailing

Parasuraman, et al.(1988) followed rigorous procedures to develop general scales for measuring the dimensions of perceived service quality in a wide range of service categories, but these scales have never been tested beyond the ONE data set that resulted in the scale. That data set was collected from banking, credit card, repair and maintenance, and long distance telephone firms.

Babakus and Mangold (1989) reported problems with the SERVQUAL scales for measuring perceived quality of hospital service. Retailing may be another example of a service industry in which the SERVQUAL scales are inappropriate for measuring the five constructs identified and described by Parasuraman et al. (Tangibility Quality, Reliability Quality, etc.).

Different Constructs in Retailing

It is also possible that perceived service quality in retailing is not a function of the 5 dimensions identified by Parasuraman, et al. (1988). As Zeithaml, Parasuraman, and Berry (1985, p.43) themselves have noted,

While it is useful to generalize about the characteristics of services and service businesses, it appears to be equally important to recognize that differences exist *among* various services and among the firms that market them.

The service categories that were used in the development of SERVQUAL (appliance repair and maintenance, retail banking, long distance telephone, and credit cards) are very different than goods retailing, and clearly fall closer to the pure service end of the pure service - pure goods continuum than store retailing. It may well be that consumers use different criteria to evaluate competing goods retailers than they use to evaluate retailers that are primarily or exclusively service firms.

Different Methods

Parasuraman et al. (1988) used self administered questionnaires to gather their data. The results reported here are based upon data gathered using a telephone survey instrument. Although it is possible that differences in data gathering methodology accounted for some differences in results, it is unlikely that the differences would be of sufficient magnitude to reject the model.

SUMMARY

A major challenge facing many retailers is finding ways to differentiate themselves from competitors. One alternative available to some retailers is to provide superior customer service. Unfortunately, the quality of an organization's services cannot be measured objectively and precisely, making it difficult to gauge success in reaching that goal.

The purpose of the study reported here was to assess the validity of an instrument designed to measure perceived service quality in a variety of business settings including retailing. If valid, the instrument could be used for a variety of purposes such as tracking customers' perceptions of the quality of service provided by a retailer or measuring consumers' perceptions of the differences in service quality among competing outlets and organizations. This information would be useful for designing marketing strategies.

The results of this study do not support Parasuraman, Zeithaml, and Berry's (1988) conclusion that SERVQUAL can be used to assess the quality of firms in a wide range of service categories. Specifically, data gathered regarding different types of retail stores did not fit the SERVQUAL measurement model.

The immediate implication is that retailers and consumer researchers should not treat SERVQUAL as an "off the shelf" measure of perceived service quality. Much refinement is needed for specific companies and industries.

In the longer term, further research in retailing and other service categories is needed to examine the construct validity of SERVQUAL. Unresolved questions include the following: (1) Are the dimensions of service quality the same regardless of service category? (2) Are the five dimensions of service quality identified by Parasuraman, Berry, and Zeithaml (1988) generic? And (3), does the SERVQUAL instrument measure the determinants of perceived service quality in all service industries? The results reported here suggest that the construct validity of SERVQUAL should be examined on an industry by industry basis before it is used to gather consumers' perceptions of service quality.

REFERENCES

Babakus, Emin, and W. Glynn Mangold. 1989. "Adapting the 'SERVQUAL' Scale to Health Care Environment: An Empirical Assessment." In *Enhancing Knowledge Development in Marketing*. Eds. P. Bloom, R. Winer, H. Kassarjian, D. Scammon, B. Weitz, R. Speckman, V. Mahajan, and M. Levy. Chicago: American Marketing Association: 195.

Bagozzi, Richard P. and Youjai Yi. 1988. "On the Evaluation of Structural Equations Models." *Journal of the Academy of Marketing Science* 16 (Spring): 74-94.

Deming, W. Edwards. 1982. *Quality, Productivity, and Competitive Position*. Cambridge, Massachusetts: Massachusetts Institute of Technology.

Gale, Bradley T. and Richard Klavans. 1985. "Formulating a Quality Improvement Strategy." *The Journal of Business Strategy* (Winter): 21-33.

Garvin, David A. 1983. "Quality on the Line." *Harvard Business Review* (September-October): 64-75.

Gerbring and Anderson. 1988. "An Updated Paradigm for Scale Development Incorporating Unidimensionality and Its Assessment." *Journal of Marketing Research* 25 (May): 186-192.

Gronroos, Christian. 1982. *Strategic Management and Marketing in the Service Sector*. Cambridge, Massachusetts: Marketing Science Institute.

Ishikawa, Kaori. 1985. *What is Total Quality Control?* Englewood Cliffs, New Jersey: Prentice-Hall, Inc.

Jöreskog, Karl G. and Dag Sörbom. 1981. *LISREL V*. Chicago: National Education Resources.

_____ and _____. 1986. *LISREL VI*. 4th Ed. Mooresville, Indiana: Scientific Software, Inc.

Leonard, Frank S. and W. Earl Sasser. 1982. "The Incline of Quality." *Harvard Business Review* (September-October): 163-171.

Lewis, Robert C. and Bernard H. Booms. 1983. "The Marketing Aspects of Service Quality." In *Emerging Perspectives on Services Marketing*. Eds. L. Berry, L. Shostack, and G. Upah. Chicago: American Marketing Association: 99-107.

Parasuraman, A., Valarie A. Zeithaml, and Leonard L. Berry. 1985. "A Conceptual Model of Service Quality and Its Implications for Future Research." *Journal of Marketing* 49 (Fall): 41-50.

_____ , _____ , and _____. 1986. "SERVQUAL: A Multiple-Item Scale for Measuring Consumer Perceptions of Service Quality." Cambridge, Massachusetts: Marketing Science Institute.

_____ , _____ , and _____. 1988. "SERVQUAL: A Multiple-Item Scale for Measuring Consumer Perceptions of Service Quality." *Journal of Retailing* 64 (Spring): 12-40.

Phillips, Lynn W., Dae R. Chang, and Robert D. Buzzell. 1983. "Product Quality, Cost Position and Business Performance: A Test of Some Key Hypotheses." *Journal of Marketing* 47 (Spring): 26-43.

Rudie, Mary J. and H. Brant Wansley. 1985. "The Merrill Lynch Quality Program." In *Services Marketing in a Changing Environment*. Eds. T.M. Bloch, G.D. Upah, and V.A. Zeithaml. Chicago: American Marketing Association.

Thompson, Phillip, Glenn DeSouza, and Bradley T. Gale. 1985. *The Strategic Management of Services Quality*. Cambridge, Massachusetts: Strategic Planning Institute.

Young, John A. 1985. "The Quality Focus at Hewlett-Packard." *The Journal of Business Strategy* (Winter): 6-9.

Zeithaml, Valarie A., Leonard L. Berry, and A. Parasuraman. 1985. "Problems and Strategies in Services Marketing." *Journal of Marketing* 49 (Spring): 33-46.

_____ , _____ , and _____. 1986. "Communication and Control Processes in the Delivery of Service Quality." *Journal of Marketing* 52 (April): 35-48.

An S-O-R Model of The Purchase of an Item in a Store

Patrick G. Buckley, Queen's University

ABSTRACT

An S-O-R model is developed for consumers' purchases of items in stores. Part of the model is tested with the BehaviorScan panel data of Information Resources Incorporated. The results show significant influences on consumers' item purchases and store patronage. There are important influences of store attributes, item characteristics, and consumer characteristics. The selection of a store is not found to be significantly related to which item is purchased by a consumer. The results imply that brands' marketing strategies should include stores' attributes as well as item and consumer characteristics.

AN S-O-R MODEL OF THE PURCHASE OF AN ITEM IN A STORE

In this paper, a model is developed for consumers' purchases of items in stores. The acquired item may be a branded good or a generic, may be large or small, and may have a particular flavor. For example, you need some jam. Do you want raspberry or strawberry or blueberry? Which brand? What size? Where will you get it? At which store?

There are many models of the purchases of consumers (e.g., Lilien and Kotler 1983). The present concern is with purchases made in particular contexts in stores. In a later section of the paper, part of the proposed model is tested with data from a consumer panel.

Models have been developed for a consumer's purchase of an item in a store (Lusch 1982; Monroe and Guiltinan 1975). These models are only used to guide the present research because many of their parts have only been hypothesized, not proven. The relationships of two previous models to the variables of the present research are outlined in Table 1.

The basic model of the present study has origins in previous research. The model includes variables for consumers, items, and store attributes. There are variables for the consumers' characteristics since many previous research results show that a person's characteristics have some influence on his or her actions (e.g., Blattberg, Buesing, Peacock and Sen 1978). There are variables for the items for sale since past research results indicate that such variables have some influence on consumers' behaviors (e.g., Monroe and Della Bitta 1978). There are variables for the store attributes because of research results in environmental psychology. These imply that human actions are influenced by the surrounding environment (Fisher, Bell and Baum 1984; Donovan and Rossiter 1982). A store's attributes are part of the environment surrounding a consumer's purchase.

Many of the above variables can be included in a Stimulus-Organism-Response (S-O-R) model of consumer behavior. An S-O-R a model was developed for involvement by Arora (1982) and Slama and Tashchian (1987). Here, an S-O-R model is proposed for a consumer's purchase of an item in a store. The model is outlined in Figure 1. In this model the stimuli are variables which can be controlled by marketing managers. The organism and response sectors of the S-O-R model are more directly controlled by consumers.

The proposed model (Figure 1) has some origins in environmental psychologists' discussions of Brunswick's Lens Model (Brunswick 1943, 1953; Craik 1983; Fisher, Bell and Baum 1984; Holahan 1982). Parts of the S-O-R model are similar to the Lens Model's concepts of ecological validity and cue utilization. The interpretation of physical-store-attributes as perceived-store-attributes is a process of ecological validity. The influence of the perceived-store-attributes on purchasing behavior is a process of cue utilization. Ecological validity is the accuracy with which environmental stimuli are perceived as environmental cues. Cue utilization shows the degree to which the environmental cues influence attitudes and actions. The environmental cues filter the influences of the environmental stimuli on consumers' actions. A probabilistic relationship exists between the physical-store-attributes and the perceived-store-attributes because of ecological validity. A probabilistic relationship exists between the perceived-store-attributes and consumer behavior because of cue utilization.

Variables in the Proposed Model

The characteristics of the items for sale in the proposed model include price, quality, branding, and promotions. There is evidence that these characteristics have differential impacts on consumers' purchases. Both price and quality have some influence on choice (e.g., Monroe and Della Bitta 1978; Rao 1984). The drop in price of an autonomous brand (i.e., a "branded" good) is perceived as good value for the money since autonomous brands are perceived by consumers for their quality; whereas, the drop in price of a price brand (i.e., a "generic" good) is perceived as a resetting of the fair price, not as an offering of quality at a lower price (Bemmaor 1984; Bliemel 1984; Laroche, Rosenblatt, Wahler and Bliemel 1986). The promotions which influence consumers' behaviors include: special price-reductions, coupons, in-store displays, and advertisements. More consumers respond when the price reduction of a promotion is larger (Blattberg and Sen 1976; Blattberg, Eppen and Lieberman 1981; Chevalier 1975; Eskin and Baron 1977; Guadagni and Little 1983; McKinnon, Kelly and Robison 1981; Moriarty 1983; Strang 1976; Wilkinson, Mason and Paksoy 1982; Wilkinson, Paksoy and Mason 1981; Woodside and Waddle 1975).

TABLE 1
Models of Retailing

Variables	Monroe and Guiltinan (1975)	Lusch (1982)
Item characteristics	(In-store information processing)	Store visit
Consumer characteristics	Household or buyer characteristics	Situational factors
	General opinions and activities concerning shopping/search	
Physical store attributes		Shopping alternatives
Perceived store attributes	Importance of store attributes	Filtering
	Perceptions of store attributes	
	Attitude toward store	
Purchase of an item	Product and brand choice	Outcome
Store patronage	Store choice	Store choice

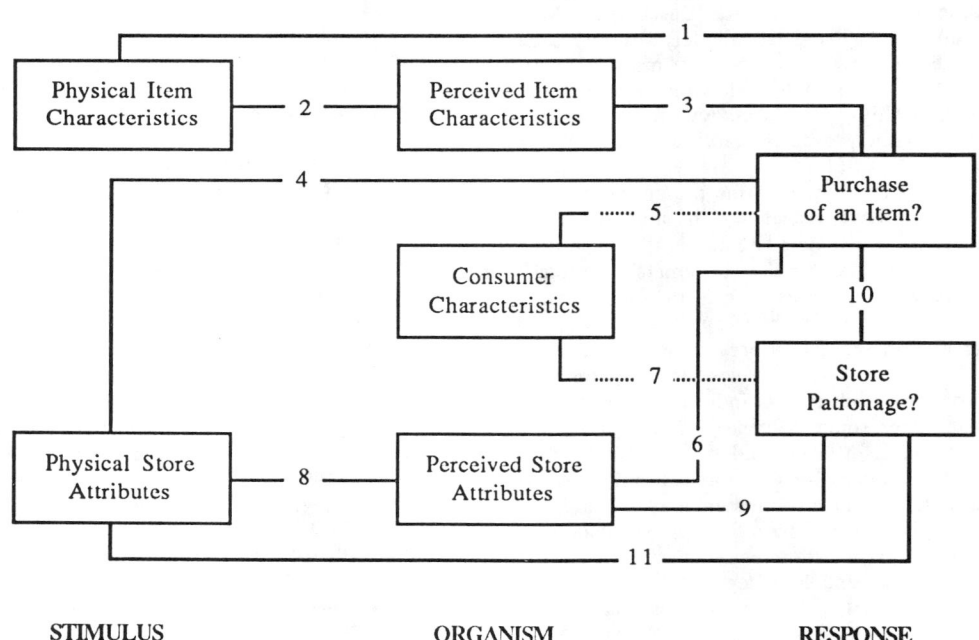

FIGURE 1
S-O-R Model of the Purchase of an Item in a Store

Our research assumes a one-to-one relationship between the item's perceived and physical characteristics. Such an assumption is like much other research (Blattberg et al 1978; Blattberg, Eppen and Lieberman 1981; Blattberg and Sen 1974 1976; Guadagni and Little 1983; Cotton and Babb 1978; Hackleman and Duker 1980; Winer 1986), and is true when the consumers perceive stimuli accurately.

The perceived store attributes which are included in the proposed model are those which have been found to have a differential impact on consumers' patronage. These attributes are: convenient locations, price levels, merchandise quality, merchandise assortment, atmosphere, service, salespeople, and amount of advertising. These attributes are found in reports of much previous research on store image, store location, and store patronage (e.g., Arnold, Oum and Tigert 1983; Black, Ostlund and Westbrook 1985; Lindquist 1974/5; Martineau 1958; Schuler 1981).

Some of the above perceived store attributes appear related to certain physical store attributes. Such relationships exist if consumers' perceptions of stores are based on the stores' physical attributes. For example, the store's price level appears to be related to the average price per ounce of the items sold in the store; the store's level of merchandise quality appears related to the average quality of the items sold in the store; the store's merchandise assortment appears related to the number of items for sale in the store; the level of advertising of a store appears related to the store's number of newspaper or store flyer advertisements each week.

Characteristics of consumers which are included in the proposed model are those which have been shown to influence consumers' behaviors. These characteristics include: demographics, psychographics, brand loyalty, store loyalty, and the shopping trip's purpose (Bellenger, Robertson and Greenberg 1977; Blattberg, Buesing, Peacock and Sen 1978; Cotton and Babb 1978; Gupta 1988; Lloyd and Jennings 1978; Teel Williams and Bearden 1980; Webster 1965). For example, consumers who do not display as much brand and store loyalty respond more favorably to special price reductions and other promotions. They tend to stock up when a special occurs (Aaker 1973; Blattberg and Sen 1976; Hackleman and Duker 1980; Kuehn and Rohloff 1967; Massy and Frank 1965; Shoemaker and Shoaf 1977; Webster 1965).

The research is concerned with the interactive effects of many variables in the proposed model as well as the simple effects of these variables. For example, results may have significant interactions between the stores' attributes and items' characteristics. Such findings would indicate that different kinds of items are preferred in stores with different kinds of environments. Many environmental psychologists have mentioned the important influence on behavior of interactive effects (Belk 1974 1975 1976; Hansen 1976; Lewin 1936; Punj and Stewart 1983).

TESTING THE MODEL

As noted in the preceding discussion, some parts of the proposed model have been researched extensively. Much research has examined the influence of item characteristics on the purchase of items (paths 1, 2, and 3 in Figure 1) (Bemmaor 1984; Bliemel 1984; Blattberg and Sen 1976; Blattberg, Eppen and Lieberman 1981; Chevalier 1975; Eskin and Baron 1977; Laroche, Rosenblatt, Wahler and Bliemel 1986; McKinnon, Kelly and Robison 1981; Monroe and Della Bitta 1978; Moriarty 1983; Rao 1984; Strang 1976; Wilkinson, Mason and Paksoy 1982; Wilkinson, Paksoy and Mason 1981; Woodside and Waddle 1975).

Some research has examined the influences of consumers' characteristics on the purchasing of items and the patronizing of stores (paths 5 and 7 in Figure 1) (Aaker 1973; Bellenger, Robertson and Greenberg 1977; Blattberg, Buesing, Peacock and Sen 1978; Blattberg and Sen 1976; Cotton and Babb 1978; Gupta 1988; Hackleman and Duker 1980; Kuehn and Rohloff 1967; Lloyd and Jennings 1978; Massy and Frank 1965; Shoemaker and Shoaf 1977; Teel Williams and Bearden 1980; Webster 1965).

Much research has also shown the influence of perceived store attributes on store patronage (path 9 in Figure 1) (Arnold, Oum and Tigert 1983; Black, Ostlund and Westbrook 1985; Lindquist 1974/5; Martineau 1958; Schuler 1981).

A question asked by the present study is: Do physical store attributes influence both consumers' purchases and store patronage? (Paths 4 and 11 in Figure 1). The multivariate influences of the physical store attributes are studied along with those of the items and the consumers. The influences of the physical store attributes are tested for after accounting for the influences of the other variables.

Also examined is the influence of store patronage on the purchase of an item (path 10 in Figure 1). In other words, does which store is patronized influence which item is purchased?

Data

The proposed model is tested with data from a consumer panel. The data is from the BehaviorScan panel of Information Resources Incorporated (IRI). The purchases of panel members were recorded with electronic scans of the UPC codes when the purchases occurred. The purchases are linked to panel members' demographic characteristics and each store's attributes. For the present study, a random sample of 1000 purchases is drawn from the 11,319 purchases of ground coffee made by 1000 panel members at six stores in Pittsfield, MA between 24 March 1980 and 5 April 1981. The average panel member who visits more than one store makes a purchase at 3.1 of the 6 stores.

At each purchase occasion there is only a limited number of brands, sizes, types, and stores for the consumers to choose among. In our model, the choice set of a purchase-occasion is like an evoked set (Brisoux and Laroche 1981). Each

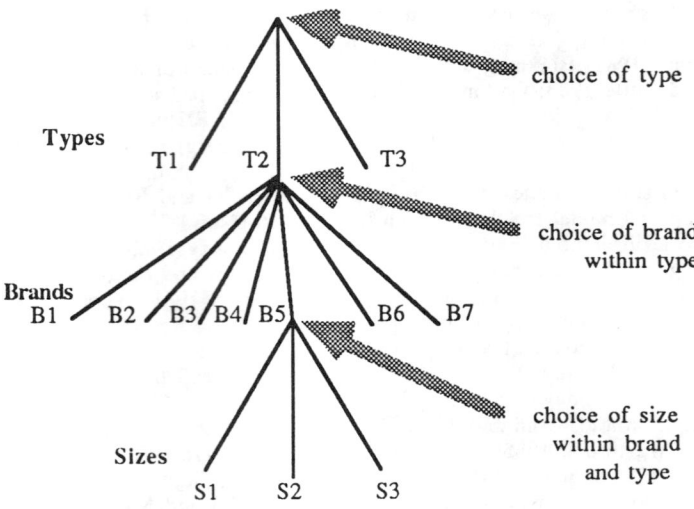

FIGURE 2
Hierarchical Choice of a Grocery Product

purchase-occasion's choice set contains those brands, sizes, and types which the consumer purchased over a two year period and those stores which the consumer patronized at least once over the same period.

The data are quite reliable. A quality control program was constantly run when collecting data. Panelists were encouraged to identify themselves at check-out counters. Check-out clerks were encouraged to scan all items. The in-store information was collected manually. It is estimated to have an error rate of about 0.1 percent.

Ratings of the quality of brands of drip coffee were obtained from *Consumer Reports* (1983). These ratings of relative quality are assumed to apply to all types of coffee and were added to the data set with a four-point scale which corresponds to the major breaks in the quality ratings of *Consumer Reports*.

The variable for advertising indicates that an item is featured in a store flyer or advertisement during the week when the purchase occurs.

An item is considered to be at a special price reduction when the item initially has a price-reduction of at least five cents and the item has a price increase of at least five cents in one of the four weeks following its price reduction. The item must have a price reduction and a succeeding price-rise to be considered on special. Items with just price reductions are not on special, since their prices fall because of a general decline in market prices.

RESULTS

Purchase of an Item

The purchase of an item of ground coffee involves at least the three choices of brand, size, and type of coffee. A hierarchical choice model of this purchase was developed with nested multinomial logit analysis (Ben-Akiva and Lerman 1985; Berkman, Brownstone and Associates 1979).

The nested multinomial logit solution was calculated with a sequential estimation procedure. The results of this procedure are separate multinomial logit equations for each of the choices of brand, type, and size of coffee container. Inclusive values link these equations. A hierarchical structure is implied if the inclusive values are statistically significant. The inclusive values in the equations for type and brand are significant. This implies that the choice model is hierarchical.

In summary, the model for the choice of an item of coffee has 3 equations: one for size, one for brand, and one for type of coffee (Tables 2, 3, and 4). These three equations are linked in the hierarchical structure shown in Figure 2. Each equation defines one level in this hierarchical choice model. Note that the structure shown in Figure 2 which results from the nested multinomial logit analysis is not the only structure that was examined. Alternative hierarchical structures were examined. The one presented here (in Tables 2, 3 and 4 and Figure 2) is that which fits the data best. Alternative hierarchies are discussed in Buckley (1988, 1989).

The equations for type and size contain alternative specific variables (ASV's). An ASV is like a covariate of an alternative in a regression equation. ASV's are formed since the variables in multinomial logit cannot have the same value for all alternatives. An ASV only varies on the alternative to which it is attached since it has its original value for this alternative. An ASV does not vary on the other alternatives since it is coded zero for all of these. The number of ASV's that can be created for each original variable is the number of alternatives minus one. For example, if there are 3 alternatives

TABLE 2
Choice of Type

	Logit Coefficient	T-Value	Elasticity
Regular Coffee			
ASC[1]	18***	4.16	
Average price per ounce for regular[2]	-6.4	-2.88	-.24
At least one in store display for regular[2]	.52**	2.29	.043
At least one advertisement for regular[2]	-.40*	-1.84	-.044
Brand switching behavior[2]	1.3***	6.00	.30
Perk Coffee			
At least one special price reduction for perk[3]	.59***	2.71	.022
Average quality[3,5]	6.8***	4.70	12
Drip Coffee			
ASC[1]	20***	4.45	
Average price per ounce for drip[4]	-11**	-1.99	-.35
At least one in store display for drip[4]	.68***	3.69	.043
Brand switching behavior[4]	1.4***	6.19	.30
Social class of residence[4]	.049**	2.41	.099
Average number of items for sale[4,5]	.069***	3.24	.30
Inclusive Values for Brand			
Regular coffee	.17***	3.14	1.9
Drip coffee	.018	.32	.25
Per cent correct	57.		
Log likelihood	-765.		
Likelihood ratio index	.18		

* $p<.10$; ** $p<.05$; *** $p<.01$.
1. ASC's: alternative specific constants.
2. Regular coffee alternative specific variable (ASV).
3. Perk coffee ASV.
4. Drip coffee ASV.
5. Store environment variable.
6. N is 907. This is the number of purchase occasions that have more than one type in the choice set.

(e.g., in the equation for choice of type), only 2 ASV's can be formed for each original variable. For example, the size equation has two ASV's for the Average-Price-Per-Ounce-Paid-by-Consumer (Table 4). The first ASV is for the 16 ounce size. The second is for the 32 ounce size. The ASV for the 16 ounce size has the original value of Average-Price-per-Ounce-Paid-by-Consumer for the 16 ounce size, and values of zero for the other sizes.

Besides ASV's, multinomial logit equations contain generic variables. An example of a generic variable is "Advertisement" in the equation for choice of brand (Table 3). Generic variables have different raw data values for each alternative on each purchase-occasion.

Elasticities are shown for all of the coefficients of the multinomial logit equations. These elasticities are aggregates of direct point elasticities (Ben-Akiva and Lerman 1985; Hensher and Johnson 1983). The direct point elasticities are computed for each alternative for each individual. A coefficient's elasticity is the change in choice probability which occurs when an independent variable changes one percent. Thus, the elasticities indicate the relative impacts of the variables on the choice probabilities.

In more detail, the elasticities for alternative specific variables (ASV's) are aggregates of direct point elasticities which are weighted by the estimated probability of each individual choosing each alternative. The elasticities for variables which span all alternatives (i.e. generic variables) are aggregates of direct point elasticities across individuals and alternatives -- the sum across individuals is weighted by the estimated probability of each individual choosing each alternative; the sum across alternatives is weighted by the frequency that the alternative is chosen (see p. 59 of Hensher and Johnson (1981) or p. 113 of Ben-Akiva and Lerman (1985) for more details).

TABLE 3
Choice of Brand

	Logit Coefficient	T-Value	Elasticity
Purchase brand last time	.79***	6.05	.063
Purchase brand second last time	.88***	6.35	.063
Purchase brand third last time	.63***	3.93	.037
Purchase brand fourth last time	.029	.18	.0016
Purchase brand fifth last time	.68***	4.16	.035
Advertisement	2.1***	6.35	.079
Store coupon	1.7***	4.66	.033
Price per ounce of autonomous brand	-48***	-3.97	-2.0
Square of price per ounce of autonomous brand	48***	4.27	.38
Quality of autonomous brand	16**	2.12	12
Square of quality of autonomous brand	-4.1***	-3.65	-9.6
Price per ounce of generic or store brand	-3.1	-.26	-.020
Special Price Reduction	-6.0***	-3.72	-.20
Percent off	11***	3.90	.070
% Purchase of favorite brand	-3.6***	-3.09	-.053
# Other stores with specials in previous week	.61***	3.56	.042
Store Environment			
Average quality BY quality	2.0**	2.16	4.6
Average number of items for sale BY special price reduction	.17***	3.26	.13
Number of special price reductions this week BY price	-.051*	-1.93	-.038
Number of advertisements this week BY special price reduction	.43***	2.73	.030
Inclusive Values for Size			
Maxwell House	.013	.17	.0027
Chock Full O'Nuts	.47***	4.72	.15
Generic/store brand	.69***	6.36	.26
Constants			
Martinson brand	-.42		
Hills Brothers Brand	-.49		
Folgers brand	3.5***		
Savarin brand	2.7*		
Chase and Sanborn	-.65		
Sanka	3.0		
Brim	3.9*		
Maxwell House	-1.7***		
Mellow Roast	1.3		
Chock Full O'Nuts	-1.3**		
Master Blend	xxx		
Generic/Store brand	23**		
Per cent correct	77		
Log likelihood	-514		
Likelihood ratio index	.71		

* p<.10; ** p<.05; *** p<.01.
1. N is 923. This is the number of purchase occasions that have more than one brand in the choice set.

TABLE 4
Choice of Size

	Logit Coefficient	T-Value	Elasticity
Purchase item last time	.66**	2.40	.037
Purchase item second last time	.74**	2.25	.025
Purchase item third last time	.97***	2.83	.041
Purchase item fourth last time	1.5***	3.62	.046
Advertisement	1.6***	3.29	.14
In store display	.94*	1.69	.048
13 Ounce Size			
number of stores patronized by consumer[2]	-.37*	-1.77	-.39
16 Ounce Size			
ASC[1]	-3.2	-.59	
Price[3]	-1.6***	-2.69	-.21
Quality[3]	-.36**	-2.10	-.045
Average price per ounce paid by consumer[3]	-14***	-2.64	-.14
Average quality[3,5]	3.8**	2.02	.56
32 Ounce Size			
ASC[1]	9.3***	2.91	
Price[4]	-1.5***	-2.92	-4.6
Average price per ounce paid by consumers[4]	-11*	-1.75	-1.1

Per cent correct	86
Log likelihood	-149
Likelihood ratio index .48	

* $p<.10$; ** $p<.05$; *** $p<.01$.
1. ASC: alternative specific constant.
2. 13 ounce size alternative specific variable (ASV).
3. 16 ounce size ASV.
4. 32 ounce size ASV.
5. Store environment variable.
6. N is 413. This is the number of purchase occasions that have more than one size in the choice set.

At each level in the choice model the first variables entered in the equation are product characteristics, promotions, and purchase loyalty. The product characteristics include price and quality. The promotions include special price reductions, advertisements, and in-store displays. The variables for purchase loyalty are the lags of the last five purchases. The results show: price and promotion variables are in all equations, and variables for quality and purchase loyalty are in the equations for choice of brand and size.

Next, the influences on item choice of the store attributes are tested. The store attributes indicate the store environment when coffee is sold. The store attributes include the average price and quality of coffee and the numbers of price reductions and advertisements of coffee. The results show: one variable for the store environment in the size equation, two in the type equation, and four in the brand equation.

There is a variable for average-quality in each of the three equations. This suggests that the level of merchandise quality in a store influences which types, brands, and sizes of products are purchased.

There is a variable for the average-number-of-items-for-sale in both the type and brand equations. This suggests that the level of merchandise assortment in a store influences which brands and types of products are purchased.

The other store attributes in the brand equation are for the number-of-special-price-reductions and the number-of-advertisements. This suggests that which brand of a product is purchased is influenced by the overall level of advertising and promotion carried out by a store.

Store Patronage

A model for store patronage is developed with a multinomial logit equation (Table 5). This equation contains generic variables for some physical store attributes. The variables' relative influences are indicated by the absolute values of the elasticities. The largest influences are for Average-Price-per-ounce and Average-Quality-in-Store. Thus, which

TABLE 5
Choice of Store

	Logit Coefficient	T-Value	Elasticity
Average price per ounce this week	-8.0***	-2.59	-.67
Average quality this week	.35***	2.61	.57
Number of items this week	.011	.80	.13
Number of special price reductions this week	-.058*	-1.84	-.049
Number of displays this week	.081*	1.79	.044
Number of advertisements this week	.13***	3.33	.10
Per cent correct	44		
Log likelihood	-881		
Likelihood ratio index	.38		

* $p<.10$; ** $p<.05$; *** $p<.01$.
1. Alternative Specific Constants were calculated for 5 of the 6 stores. These are not shown due to reasons of confidentiality.
2. N is 827. This is the number of stores that have more than one store in the choice set.

store is patronized is influenced by its relative price level and its merchandise quality.

There are significant, secondary influences on store choice of number-of-price-reductions, number-of-displays, and number-of-advertisements. This suggests that store patronage is also influenced by a store's overall levels of advertising, promotions, and displays.

The influence of the store patronized on which item is purchased (path 10 in Figure 1) is tested with a nested multinomial logit model which contains four equations: one for each of the choices of store, type of coffee, brand of coffee, and size of coffee container. The inclusive value linking the choice of store and the sub-hierarchy for the choices of type, brand, and size of coffee is not statistically significant. Thus, the choice of store is not related to the choices of an item of ground coffee.

DISCUSSION

The results confirm much of the proposed model for consumers' purchases in stores (Figure 1). Multivariate influences on these purchases are found for item, consumer, and store attributes. The stores' attributes also influence store patronage.

Store patronage is not found to have a significant influence on which item is purchased. This is not surprising since there are undoubtedly several reasons for choosing a specific grocery store besides the container of coffee that one wishes to purchase. Such a finding agrees with those of Wrigley and Dunn (1984), but is contrary to the models of retailing of Monroe and Guiltinan (1975) and Lusch (1982).

The results imply that brands' strategies should include stores' attributes as well as item and consumer characteristics. The larger elasticities (Tables 2, 3, 4, and 5) indicate the attributes which are the most important influences. These are the stores' price levels, merchandise quality, and merchandise assortment. For example, the influence on brand choice of the variable "Average number of items for sale BY special price reduction" indicates that it is more important to have price reductions in stores which have a higher level of merchandise assortment.

Support for the proposed model can be expanded with further research. The present study just examines consumers' purchase of one product, ground coffee, in one city's major grocery stores. Would similar results be found with other products? Would the results vary in some systematic fashion for different kinds of products? Can better results be found, for the influences of store attributes, with a larger sample of stores? Perhaps one including both large and medium sized grocery stores and corner stores?

REFERENCES

Aaker, David A. (1973), "Toward a Normative Model of Promotional Decision Making," *Management Science*, 19 (6), 593-603.

Arnold, Stephen J., Tae H. Oum and Douglas J. Tigert (1983), "Determinant Attributes of Retail Patronage: Seasonal, Temporal, Regional, and International Comparisons," *Journal of Marketing Research*, 20 (May), 149-157.

Arora, Raj (1982), "Validation of an S-O-R Model for Situation, Enduring, and Response Components of Involvement," *Journal of Marketing Research*, 19 (Nov), 505-516.

Belk, Russell W. (1974), "An Exploratory Assessment of Situational Effects in Buyer Behavior," *Journal of Marketing Research*, 11 (May), 156-163.

Belk, Russell W. (1975), "Situational Variables and Consumer Behavior," *Journal of Consumer Research*, 2 (Dec), 157-164.

Belk, Russell W. (1976), "Situational Mediation and Consumer Behavior: A Reply to Russell and Mehrabian," *Journal of Consumer Research*, 3 (Dec), 175-177.

Bellenger, Danny N., Dan H. Robertson, and Barnett A. Greenberg (1977), "Shopping Center Patronage Motives," *Journal of Retailing*, 53 (2), 29-38.

Bemmaor, Albert C. (1984), "Testing Alternative Econometric Models on the Existence of Advertising Threshold Effect," *Journal of Marketing*, 21 (Aug), 298-308.

Ben-Akiva, Moshe and Steven R. Lerman (1985), *Discrete Choice Analysis*, Cambridge, MA: MIT Press.

Berkman, Jerry, David Brownstone and Associates (1979), *QUAIL 4.0 User's Manual*, Berkley, CA: Department of Economics, University of California Berkeley (Feb).

Black, William C., Lyman E. Ostlund and Robert A. Westbrook (1985), "Spatial Demand Models in an Intra-brand Context," *Journal of Marketing*, 49 (Summer), 106-113.

Blattberg, Robert and Subrata Sen (1974), "Market Segmentation Using Models of Multidimensional Purchasing Behavior," *Journal of Marketing*, 38 (Oct), 17-28.

Blattberg, Robert C. and Subrata K. Sen (1976), "Market Segments and Stochastic Brand Choice Models," *Journal of Marketing Research*, 13 (Feb), 34-45.

Blattberg, Robert, Thomas Buesing, Peter Peacock and Subrata Sen (1978), "Identifying the Deal Prone Segment," *Journal of Marketing Research*, 15 (Aug), 369-77.

Blattberg, Robert C., Gary D. Eppen and Joshua Lieberman (1981), "A Theoretical and Empirical Evaluation of Price Deals for Consumer Durables," *Journal of Marketing*, 45 (Winter), 116-29.

Bliemel, F.W.A. (1984), "Brand Choice Under Price-Quality Considerations: An Integrative Theory," Working Paper, School of Business, Queen's University, Kingston, Ontario, Canada.

Brisoux, Jacques E. and Michel Laroche (1981), "Evoked Set Formation and Composition: An Empirical Investigation under a Routinized Response Behavior Situation," in *Advances in Consumer Research, Volume VIII.*, Kent B. Monroe, ed., Ann Arbor, MI: Association for Consumer Research, 357-361.

Brunswick, E. (1943), "Organismic Achievement and Environmental Probability," *Psychological Review*, 50, 255-272.

Brunswick, E. (1955), "Representative Design and Probabilistic Theory in a Functional Psychology," *Psychological Review*, 62, 193-217.

Buckley, Patrick G. (1988), "Nested Multinomial Logit Analysis of Scanner Data for a Hierarchical Choice Model," *Journal of Business Research*, 17, 133-154.

Buckley, Patrick G. (1989), *The Purchase of an Item in a Self Service Store: a Model With Tests of a Grocery Product Using a UPC Scanner Panel*, Ph.D. Thesis, School of Business, Queen's University, Kingston, Ontario, Canada.

Chevalier, Michel (1975), "Increase in Sales Due to In-Store Display," *Journal of Marketing Research*, 12 (Nov), 426-431.

Consumer Reports (1983), "Looking for a good cup of coffee?" 48 (March), 110-114.

Cotton, B. C. and Emerson M. Babb (1978), "Consumer Response to Promotional Deals," *Journal of Marketing*, 42 (July), 109-113.

Craik, Kenneth H. (1983), "The Psychology of the Large Scale Environment," in Nickolaus R. Fermer and E. Scott Geller, eds., *Environmental Psychology: Directions and Perspectives*, New York: Praeger, p. 67-105.

Donovan, Robert J. and John R. Rossiter (1982), "Store Atmosphere: An Environmental Psychology Approach," *Journal of Retailing*, 58 (1), 34-57.

Eskin, Gerald J. and Penny H. Baron (1977), "Effects of Price and Advertising in Test-Market Experiments," *Journal of Marketing Research*, 14 (Nov), 499-508.

Fisher, Jeffrey D., Paul A. Bell and Andrew Baum (1984), *Environmental Psychology*, 2nd edition, Holt, Rinehart and Winston, New York.

Guadagni, Peter M. and John D. C. Little (1983), "A Logit Model of Brand Choice Calibrated on Scanner Data," *Marketing Science*, 2 (Summer), 203-38.

Gupta, Sunil (1988), "Impact of Sales Promotions on When, What, and How Much to Buy," *Journal of Marketing Research*, 25 (November), 342-355.

Hackleman, Edwin C. and Jacob M. Duker (1980), "Deal Proneness and Heavy Usage: Merging Two Market Segmentation Criteria," *Journal of the Academy of Marketing Science*, 8, 332-44.

Hansen, Flemming (1976), "Psychological Theories of Consumer Choice," *Journal of Consumer Research*, 3, 117-142.

Hensher, David A. and Lester W. Johnson (1981), *Applied Discrete Choice Modelling*. London: Croom Helm.

Holahan, Charles J. (1982), *Environmental Psychology*, New York, Random House.

Kuehn, Alfred Albert and A.C. Rohloff (1967), "Consumer Response to Promotions," in *Promotional Decisions Using Mathematical Models*, P.J. Robinson, ed., Boston: Allyn & Bacon, 45-145.

Laroche, Michel, Jerry Rosenblatt, Leon Wahler, and Friedhelm Bliemel (1986), "Economic Considerations for Dispensing Pharmacists: The Impact of Price-Quality Evaluations on Brand Categorization," *Journal of Pharmaceutical Marketing and Management*, 1 (Fall), 41-60.

Lewin, Kurt (1936), *Principles of Topological Psychology*. New York: McGraw-Hill.

Lilien, Gary L. and Philip Kotler (1983), *Marketing Decision Making: A Model Building Approach*, New York: Harper and Row.

Lindquist, Jay D. (1974/5), "Meaning of Image: A Survey of Empirical and Hypothetical Evidence," *Journal of Retailing*, 50 (4), 29-38, 116.

Lloyd, Robert and Diana Jennings (1978), "Shopping Behavior and Income: Comparisons in an Urban Environment," *Economic Geography*, 54, 157-167.

Lusch, Robert F. (1982), *Management of Retail Enterprises*, Boston, MA: Kent Publishing.

Martineau, Pierre (1958), "The Personality of the Retail Store," *Harvard Business Review*, 36 (Jan-Feb), 47-55.

Massy, William F. and Ronald E. Frank (1965), "Short Term Price and Dealing Effects in Selected Market Segments," *Journal of Marketing Research*, 2 (May), 171-85.

McKinnon, Gary F., J. Patrick Kelly and E. Doyle Robison (1981), "Sales Effects of Point-of-Purchase In-Store Signing," *Journal of Retailing*, 57 (2), 49-63.

Monroe, Kent B. and Albert J. Della Bitta (1978), "Models of Pricing Decisions," *Journal of Marketing Research*, 15 (Aug), 413-428.

Monroe, Kent B. and Joseph P. Guiltinan (1975) "A Path-Analytic Exploration of Retail Patronage Influences," *Journal of Consumer Research*, 2 (June), 19-28.

Moriarty, Mark (1983), "Feature Advertising-price Interaction Effects in the Retail Environment," *Journal of Retailing*, 59 (Summer), 80-98.

Punj, Girish N. and David W. Stewart (1983), "An Interaction Framework of Consumer Decision Making," *Journal of Consumer Research*, 10 (Sept), 181-196.

Rao, Vithala R. (1984), "Pricing Research in Marketing: The State of the Art," *Journal of Business*, 57 (1), S39-S61.

Schuler, Harry J. (1981), "Individual Preferences Based on Store Attractiveness and Distance," *Environment and Behavior*, 13 (3), 331-347.

Shoemaker, Robert W. and F. Robert Shoaf (1977), "Repeat Rates of Deal Purchases," *Journal of Advertising Research*, 17 (April), 47-53.

Slama, Mark E. and Armen Tashchian (1987), "Validating the S-O-R Paradigm for Consumer Involvement with a Convenience Good," *Journal of the Academy of Marketing Science*, 15 (Spring), 36-45.

Strang, Roger A. (1976), "Sales Promotion--Fast Growth, Faulty Management," *Harvard Business Review*, 54 (July), 115-24.

Teel, Jesse E., Robert H. Williams and William O. Bearden (1980), "Correlates of Consumer Susceptibility to Coupons in New Grocery Product Introductions," *Journal of Advertising*, 9, 31-35, 46.

Webster, Frederick E. (1965), "The "Deal-Prone" Consumer," *Journal of Marketing Research*, 2 (May), 186-189.

Wilkinson, J.B., J. Barry Mason and Christie H. Paksoy (1982), "Assessing the Impact of Short-Term Supermarket Strategy Variables," *Journal of Marketing Research*, 19 (Feb), 72-86.

Wilkinson, J.B., Christie H. Paksoy and J. Barry Mason (1981), "A Demand Analysis of Newspaper Advertising and Changes in Space Allocation," *Journal of Retailing*, 57 (Summer), 30-48.

Winer, Russell S. (1986), "A Reference Price Model of Brand Choice for Frequently Purchased Products," *Journal of Consumer Research*, 13 (Sept), 250-256.

Woodside, Arch G. and Gerald L. Waddle (1975), "Sales Effects of In-Store Advertising," *Journal of Advertising Research*, 15 (3), 1975.

Wrigley, N. and R. Dunn (1984), "Stochastic Panel-Data Models of Urban Shopping Behavior: 3. The Interaction of Store Choice and Brand Choice," *Environment and Planning A*, 16, 1221-1236.

Using a Theoretical Perspective to Examine the Psychological Construct of Coupon Proneness

Donald R. Lichtenstein, University of Colorado
Richard G. Netemeyer, Louisiana State University
Scot Burton, Louisiana State University

ABSTRACT

Transaction utility theory (Thaler 1985) has recently been used as a theoretical basis for delineating coupon proneness from the correlated, but distinct, construct of value consciousness. This study further examines the relationship between these two constructs by hypothesizing differential relationships between coupon proneness, value consciousness, and several price and deal-related constructs. Results indicate that value consciousness is more strongly related to the use of internal reference prices than is coupon proneness, and this difference is more pronounced when the internal reference price is market price-based as opposed to product utility-based. Differential correlations with other constructs provide further support for the theoretical distinction drawn between coupon proneness and value consciousness based on utility theory.

Most previous research on "deal proneness" or "coupon proneness" has measured these constructs strictly in behavioral terms and attempted to identify variables that are related to a behavioral response to promotional offers. Such dealing research has been criticized due to its lack of a theoretical framework, its lack of conceptual definitions of the key constructs, as well as its focus on descriptive variables (Raju and Hastek 1980). Such problems have led to limited research on the psychological processes that underlie consumer responses to coupon offers (Shimp and Kavas 1984).

A different approach to the study of coupon proneness has been provided recently by Lichtenstein, Netemeyer, and Burton (1990). These authors argue that coupon proneness is but one of potentially many psychological constructs that may have an impact on an individual's response to a coupon offer. They further argue that coupon (and deal) proneness should be conceptualized and measured at the psychological level and viewed as an antecedent of the behavioral response to a coupon. Support for their position was provided by demonstrating that the correlated but distinct construct of value consciousness had a significant effect on coupon-responsive behavior beyond that explained by coupon proneness.

The purpose of this paper is to extend recent research on the coupon proneness construct in three primary ways. First, utility theory (Thaler 1985) implies that consumers high in coupon proneness may establish internal reference prices (i.e., the mentally-stored price against which other prices are judged (Rosch 1975)) in different ways than other consumers. This paper offers explicit hypotheses drawn from utility theory and provides initial tests of some relationships pertaining to coupon proneness, value consciousness, and the basis of the IRP. Second, hypotheses pertaining to the differential relationships between coupon proneness, value consciousness, and some deal-related theoretical constructs are proposed and tested. Lastly, given the previous interest in the association of demographics and *behavioral* response to coupons, relationships between demographics and the measure of coupon proneness are assessed.

CONCEPTUAL BACKGROUND AND HYPOTHESES

Coupon proneness has been defined as "an increased propensity to respond to a purchase offer because the *coupon form* of the purchase offer positively affects purchase evaluations," while value consciousness has been defined as "a concern for paying low prices, subject to some quality constraint" (Lichtenstein et al. 1990). Combining these definitions with the conceptualization of utility proposed by Thaler (1985) allows a conceptual distinction to be drawn between coupon proneness (CP) and value consciousness (VC). Thaler states that total utility is comprised of (1) acquisition utility (i.e., the economic gain or loss from a purchase transaction) and (2) transaction utility (i.e., the pleasure (or displeasure) associated with the financial terms of the deal, per se). Based on these conceptualizations, Thaler equates acquisition utility to the difference between the estimate of the utility derived from the purchased good and the price paid for the good, and transaction utility as the difference between the internal reference price (IRP) and the purchase price.

If IRPs are largely a function of product utility-related experience (e.g., a fair price based on the need satisfying ability of the product), transaction utility appears to be a function of acquisition utility (i.e., acquisition utility affects transaction utility via the IRP). If, on the other hand, the IRP is based more exclusively on external price information (e.g., price of similar products, price most frequently charged), transaction utility is less dependent upon acquisition utility (Lichtenstein et al. 1990).

Thus, the conceptual equations for acquisition and transaction utility suggest that the use of coupons can increase both types of utility via a lower purchase price. However, Lichtenstein et al. (1990) proposed that beyond affecting both types of utility via a lower purchase price, a coupon will have greater impact on transaction utility than acquisition utility because it also affects the IRP (the component unique to transaction utility), but not the inherent need satisfying ability of the product (the component unique to acquisition utility). The coupon suggests that the IRP should be the non-coupon price. While assimilation-contrast theory indicates that assimilation of the non-coupon price may not increase the IRP to the non-coupon price level, it should increase the IRP *toward* the non-coupon price (Monroe and Petroshius 1981; Urbany, Bearden, and Weilbaker 1988). Also, by considering Thaler's equations in conjunction with the conceptual definitions of VC and CP, Lichtenstein et al. (1990) argued that because VC is concerned with the relationship between quality received for price paid, VC is more highly related to acquisition utility (inherent need satisfying ability of the product in relation to price paid) than is CP. Alternatively, because CP is more strongly related to the specific financial terms of the deal, it is more strongly related to transaction utility (the IRP in relation to price paid) than is VC.

Hypotheses between VC, CP and several theoretically-related constructs (e.g., price-based dissonance, shopping enjoyment) which have not been assessed in the literature are proposed and tested here based on this rationale. The hypotheses are segmented into three categories. The first two hypotheses address the rationale offered by Lichtenstein et al. (1990) pertaining to CP, VC and two possible bases for the IRP. Hypotheses 3 through 6 concern differential relationships between CP, VC, and several deal/shopping-related theoretical constructs. H7 and H8 concern the relationship between CP and selected demographics. Except for the final two hypotheses, all hypotheses are two-part. The first part hypothesizes a direction between VC, CP and the respective construct, while the second part hypothesizes if the theoretically-related construct referred to in the hypothesis is more strongly related to VC or CP.

VC, CP and the IRP

Because both acquisition and transaction utility encompass a focus on paying lower prices, both VC and CP consumers can be characterized as somewhat more price vigilant than other consumers. Hence, both VC and CP are expected to be positively correlated to the level of use of external market price-based IRPs and product utility-based IRPs. However, the theoretical framework discussed above suggests some differences in the bases of the IRP for the CP and VC consumers. Because of their greater focus on transaction utility (and, hence, greater exclusive focus on price information), it was proposed that CP consumers' IRPs are based more on external market-based prices than are VC consumers. Conversely, because of their greater focus on acquisition utility (and, hence, greater focus on the utility of the product), it was proposed that VC consumers' IRPs are based more on product utility-related factors than are CP consumers. While these conceptual arguments involving the basis of the IRP and its relationship to VC and CP were offered by Lichtenstein et al. (1990), they were not empirically assessed. Consequently, based on the rationale above, we offer the following two hypotheses regarding the differential relationships of VC and CP with market price and product utility-based IRPs.

H1a: The correlations between CP and external, market price information-based IRPs and VC and external, market price-based IRPs are both positive.

H1b: The correlation between CP and external, market price information-based IRPs is greater than the correlation between VC and external, market price information-based IRPs.

H2a: The correlations between VC and product utility-based IRPs and CP and product utility-based IRPs are both positive.

H2b: The correlation between VC and product utility-based IRPs is greater (more positive) than the correlation between CP and product utility-based IRPs.

VC, CP and Deal/Shopping-Related Constructs

Given that purchase price is a component of both acquisition and transaction utility, it seems probable that learning about a lower price after the purchase will create dissonance for both VC and CP customers. Given the importance of purchase price for both VC and CP consumers, price-related dissonance should be positively correlated to both CP and VC. In addition, Thaler's utility theory suggests that CP individuals should perceive more dissonance from learning that the market-based IRP which was used in judging the value of the deal was not valid. That is, learning that other consumers were not actually paying more and/or that other merchants were not actually charging more should cause greater dissonance for the CP consumer than for the VC consumer. The VC individual will be less affected by such information because the product still is capable of delivering the need fulfilling benefits for which it was purchased.

H3a: The correlations between VC and price-based dissonance and CP and price-based dissonance are both positive.

H3b: The correlation between CP and price-based dissonance is greater than the correlation between VC and price-based dissonance.

One method by which dissonance is reduced is rationalization. Given the importance of purchase price and the dissonance hypothesized above, upon learning that the price paid was not as favorable as initially perceived, positive correlations between VC, CP, and price-related rationalizations may be anticipated. However, Thaler's (1985) utility theory suggests that CP consumers may be more likely to make such price-related rationalizations (e.g., "The price I paid was still cheaper than that paid by many others") because of the relative importance of purchase price and lesser importance of product utility, compared to VC consumers.

> H4a: Given the knowledge that an acted-upon deal price was not as favorable as originally perceived, the correlations between CP and price-related rationalizations and VC and price-related rationalizations are both positive.
>
> H4b: The correlation between CP and price-related rationalizations is greater than the correlation between VC and price-related rationalizations.

Because of their emphasis on low prices and obtaining "good" deals and the positive correlation found between situational shopping involvement and both CP and VC (Lichtenstein et al. 1990), it may be hypothesized that both VC and CP consumers will derive enjoyment from the shopping process. Further, Lichtenstein et al. found a stronger correlation between CP and situational shopping involvement than VC and situational shopping involvement. Given that CP consumers appear more involved with the shopping process itself (i.e., situational shopping involvement), it may be hypothesized that the correlation between CP and shopping enjoyment is more positive than the correlation between VC and enjoyment.

> H5a: The correlations between VC and shopping enjoyment and CP and shopping enjoyment are both positive.
>
> H5b: The correlation between CP and shopping enjoyment is greater than the correlation between VC and shopping enjoyment.

The purchase price of a good generally is only one of the costs involved in obtaining the product. There also may be nonmonetary costs that include time costs, travel costs, etc. (Zeithaml 1988). It seems logical to postulate that because of the importance of low monetary price to both VC and CP consumers, the perception of nonmonetary costs as adversely affecting the value of a deal should be negatively related to both (i.e., both types of consumers should feel that getting low prices is so important that nonmonetary costs play a lesser role). However, because CP consumers are hypothesized to be very concerned with the difference between the market-based IRP and the purchase price, as well as more involved in the shopping experience, these other costs may not be given too much consideration. Relative to CP consumers, VC consumers have been shown to be less influenced by situational involvement regarding "getting a good deal" (Lichtenstein et al. 1990), and thus may be more likely to consider a broader range of acquisition-related costs. Based on this rationale, it is postulated that VC consumers will be less willing to accept nonmonetary costs (i.e., to drive further distances, wait in longer lines, spend time clipping coupons) in order to take advantage of a coupon deal.

> H6a: The correlations between CP and the perception that nonmonetary costs adversely affect the value of a promoted deal and VC and the adverse effect of nonmonetary costs are both negative.
>
> H6b: The correlation between VC and the perception that nonmonetary costs adversely affect the value of a promoted deal is less negative than the correlation between CP and the perception that nonmonetary costs adversely affect the value of a promoted deal.

CP and Selected Demographics

While relationships between demographics and deal proneness (operationalized as a behavioral response to a coupon promotion) often has been examined in previous research (e.g., Blattberg et al. 1978; Levedahl 1988; Webster 1965), when CP is assessed at a *psychological level* it is not clear that results concerning demographics and *coupon usage* will extend to the relationship between demographics and CP. Economic factors may play some role in the development of CP because of the need/desire to lower purchase costs. However, while these economic factors may affect the psychological state of CP, it should be noted that such a relationship may not extend to redemption rates due to lower income consumers' lesser ability to locate and organize coupons and the lack of mobility necessary to redeem the coupons (Blattberg et al. 1978; Levedahl 1988). Possible differences in shopping orientations across sex may translate into a relationship between CP and gender. However, at this point, hypothesizing any direction appears premature. Thus, the following hypotheses between these demographic variables and CP are offered in an exploratory manner.

> H7: Family income is negatively related to CP.
>
> H8: CP is related to gender.

METHOD

Except for demographic variables, all measures of constructs of interest in the hypotheses were assessed with seven point scales with endpoints ranging from strongly agree to strongly disagree. Measures of CP and VC consisted of eight and seven items, respectively, and were drawn directly from those developed by Lichtenstein et al. (1990). The coefficient alpha reliability estimates were .88 for the CP measure and .80 for the VC measure. The Pearson correlation between the CP and VC constructs was .17 ($p < .01$). The scale items, along with complete scale develop procedures for the CP and VC constructs, are described in Lichtenstein et al. (1990).

Other constructs of interest in the study were measured with multi-item scales consisting of two to four items. The measure of a price basis for the IRP was a three-item scale that had an alpha of .71. Items used to assess this construct were "In judging if an advertised price represents a good deal I consider the prices other merchants are charging"; "In judging if an advertised price represents a good deal I consider the price of similar or competing brands"; and "In judging if an advertised price represents a good deal I consider the price the product normally sells for." The product utility-related basis for the IRP was assessed with two items (i.e., "In judging if an advertised price represents a good deal I consider the amount of use I will get for the product or brand" and "In judging if an advertised price represents a good deal I consider the quality of the product"). The correlation between these two items was .66.

Shopping enjoyment and non-monetary costs were both assessed with four items and reliabilities for these two scales were .82 and .72, respectively. The shopping enjoyment items were drawn from those proposed by Tauber (1972). A sample item used for the non-monetary cost measure was "The time it takes to find a bargain is usually not worth the effort."

Price dissonance and price dissonance reduction constructs were measured with two items each. The price dissonance items were "I get upset when I purchase an item on sale only to find that I could have bought it cheaper some place else" and "It does not really bother me to pay a certain price for a product and find out later I could have bought it for a lower price elsewhere" (reverse coded). The dissonance reduction items were "When I discover that I could have gotten a better deal on a product, it makes me feel better to know that I still got it cheaper than most everyone else" and "When I find that I did not pay the lowest price possible for a product I will try to convince myself that I got it cheaper than most others did." Correlations between the two items for both measures were .49. All demographics were assessed with single-item measures.

Data were gathered from a convenience sample of 350 respondents residing in a southeastern SMSA. Students were trained on how to administer and answer questions pertaining to the survey. Surveys were administered to non-student respondents who were the primary grocery shoppers for their household. The median age of the respondents was 40.3 years, and the median family income was $34,666. The median education level was 1 year of college and 57% were female. These median age, income, and education levels were similar to those of the SMSA population.

RESULTS

H1 and H2 pertained to the relationship between the basis for the IRP and CP. Following from rationale drawn from Thaler's utility theory, it was predicted that because both acquisition and transaction utility are enhanced by low prices, and based on the hypothesized association of VC with the former and CP with the latter, both VC and CP should be positively correlated with a concern for price, and, hence, more likely to use both external price-based (H1a) and product utility-based (H2a) IRP's. It was further hypothesized that while VC and CP should both be positively related to both IRP bases, CP should be more strongly related to the external price-based IRP (H1b), while VC should be more strongly related to the product utility-based IRP (H2b). Results relevant to the first six hypotheses are shown in Table 1.

With the exception of the nonsignificant (but directionally consistent) correlation between CP and the product utility-based IRP, the correlations between CP, VC and the two IRP bases were positive and significant. Consequently, H1a is supported, while only partial support is offered for H2a. Contrary to H1b, CP was not more strongly correlated than VC to the external price-based IRP, however, consistent with H2b, VC was more strongly related than CP to the product utility-based IRP (.43 vs. .07, $t = 5.76$, $p < .01$).

H3a and H3b concerned the relationship between CP, VC, and price dissonance. Because both VC and CP constructs are associated with a concern for paying low prices, it was postulated in H3a that higher levels of both VC and CP would be associated with higher levels of perceived price dissonance. Correlations between VC and price dissonance and CP and price dissonance were .36 ($p < .01$) and .25 ($p < .01$), respectively, thus offering support for H3a. However, H3b predicted that the greater correlation would be between CP and price dissonance. The above correlations are in the opposite direction of the one hypothesized indicating that these data do not support H3b.

H4a and 4b concerned price-related rationalizations used by consumers to reduce price-related dissonance. Given an overall concern about price and significant perceived price dissonance, it was hypothesized that both VC and CP would be related to the use of price related rationalizations to reduce dissonance (H4a), but that the correlation would be greater for CP than for VC (H4b). The correlation between price-related rationalizations and CP ($r = .29$, $p < .01$) was greater than the correlation between VC and price-related rationalizations ($r = .05$, n.s.) providing support for H4b ($t = 3.92$, $p < .01$). However, the data do not offer support for H4a, given the nonsignificance of the latter correlation.

H5a predicted a positive relationship between VC, CP and shopping enjoyment. As hypothesized the correlations between CP and enjoyment and VC and enjoyment were both significant ($r = .31$ and .23, respectively, $p < .01$ for both correlations, H5a supported). The difference between the two

TABLE 1
Summary of Results of Hypotheses 1 through 6

Hypothesis/Constructs	Hypothesized Direction of CP and VC Correlations	Hypothesized Difference in Correlation	Correlational Results CP	VC	Support for Hypothesized Direction	Support for Hypothesized Difference[b]
H1: External price-based IRP	positive	CP > VC	.28[a]	.49[a]	H1a supported	H1b not supported
H2: Product utility-based IRP	positive	VC > CP	.07	.43[a]	H2a partially supported	H2b supported
H3: Price-based dissonance	positive	CP > VC	.25[a]	.36[a]	H3a supported	H3b not supported
H4: Dissonance reduction	positive	CP > VC	.29[a]	.05	H4a not supported	H4b supported
H5: Shopping enjoyment	positive	CP > VC	.31[a]	.23[a]	H5a supported	H5b supported
H6: Nonmonetary costs	negative	VC < CP	-.39[a]	-.34[a]	H6a supported	H6b not supported

[a] For all correlations, $p < .01$; all other correlations are not significant.

[b] Hypothesized differences were tested using t-tests for the difference in correlations within the same sample (Cohen and Cohen 1975). Hypothesized differences in H2 and H4 are significant at $p < .01$; weak support was found for H5b where $p < .10$.

correlations was in the hypothesized direction, but was only marginally significant ($t = 1.33$, $p < .10$). These data thus offer weak support for H5b.

H6a predicted that the relationship between VC, CP, and perceptions about the adverse effect of nonmonetary costs on the value of a coupon deal would be negative for both VC and CP constructs. Strong support was found for this hypothesis, as evidenced by the respective correlations of -.34 and -.39 ($p < .01$ for both). However, only directional support was found for the prediction that the correlation between CP and the perception that nonmonetary costs adversely affect the value of a promoted deal would be more negative than the correlation between VC and perceptions about nonmonetary costs (H6b not supported).

A profile of the relationships between demographic variables and the CP measure is shown in Table 2. Offered from a exploratory perspective, H7 predicted a negative relationship between CP and family income, while H8 postulated a relationship between CP and gender. Consistent with H7, CP was significantly related to income ($F = 4.55$, $df = (4,338)$, $p < .01$). However, the mean scores in Table 2 show little difference for the middle income categories, with larger CP scores for the low income group (i.e., less than $20,000) and much lower CP scores for the high income respondents (i.e., greater than $60,000). Consistent with H8, CP scores were significantly higher for females ($t = 5.30$, $p < .01$), as shown in Table 2.

Although no explicit hypotheses were offered concerning the relationships between age and education and CP, results are shown in Table 2. Neither of the overall relationships are statistically significant; however, for education there appears to be a relatively sharp decline in CP for respondents with graduate degrees. Previous research on the relationship between age and coupon redemption behavior has offered inconsistent results; for example one study has shown that coupon users are younger than non-users, another has indicated that

TABLE 2
Relationships Between Demographics and CP

Demographic Variable	n	Coupon Proneness	F/t Value[a]	P Value
Sex				
Male	148	34.7		
Female	201	43.5	5.30	<.01
Family Income				
Less than $20,000	85	43.6[a]		
$20,000 - $29,999	59	40.7		
$30,000 - $39,999	66	39.8	4.55	<.01
$40,000 - $59,999	71	40.7		
$60,000 or higher	62	32.9		
Education				
High school or less	93	40.7		
Some college	118	40.0		
College graduate	93	40.5	1.81	<.15
Post graduate degree	49	34.8		
Age				
Under 35	132	41.8		
35 - 54	164	38.9	1.95	<.15
55 or over	53	37.5		

[a] A t-value is reported for the effect of sex; all other statistics are F values.

users are more likely to be middle-aged, and a third study reported that coupon users are either young or old but not middle-aged (Levedahl 1988). For the measure of CP used here, although nonsignificant, there was a monotonic negative relationship between age and CP for this particular group of respondents. All interactions between the demographic variables were not statistically significant.

DISCUSSION

Eight hypotheses were proposed and tested. The first two hypotheses postulated relationships between CP, VC, and two possible bases for the IRP. H3 through H6 offered predictions about differential relationships between CP, VC and several shopping and deal-related constructs. Results displayed mixed support for the six hypotheses. The last two hypotheses were exploratory and looked at the relationship between CP and demographic variables.

Because of the explicit role of the IRP in Thaler's utility theory, H1 and H2 are seen as critical in assessing the applicability of Thaler's theory to the domain of CP. The joint prediction of H1a and H1b was that CP and VC would both be positively related to the use of an external price-based IRP, but that CP would be more strongly related. The joint prediction of H2a and H2b was that CP and VC would both be positively related to the use of a product utility-based IRP, but that VC would be more strongly related. Taking H1 and H2 in conjunction, only mixed support was found. However, considering both H1 and H2 jointly also suggests that the rationale on which they are based may have been stated too strongly, but appears reasonably valid.

That is, results relevant to H1 and H2 suggest that VC is more strongly correlated to the use of IRPs, in general, than is CP. Although the correlations between VC and the two IRP measures were higher than the respective correlations involving CP, the magnitude of the difference was much greater for the product utility-based IRP measure (i.e., difference in correlations = .21 and .36 for H1b and H2b, respectively). Hence, when viewed relative to H2, the correlations involving H1 do appear to make some sense. It may be that VC individuals, in general, have (or make use of) IRPs to a greater degree than CP individuals, but more so for product utility-based IRPs than for external price-based IRPs.

In retrospect, the results regarding the stronger correlation between VC and the use of IRPs in general appears consistent with the suggestions of other researchers. For example, Henderson (1988) suggests that consumers with a "coupon primacy" have a strong "commitment to a coupon" that prevents attention to other factors such as net lowest price (requiring external price information) or best value for the money (requiring price and product utility information (cf. Monroe and Petroshius 1981)). Similarly, Zeithaml (1988) found that some consumers use coupons as extrinsic signals of good deals without actually comparing the reduced price of the couponed brand with the prices of other brands. CP consumers may follow well-defined "scripts" that result in very minimal attention and processing of information that is highly relevant to other consumers (Gardner and Strang 1984, p.421). Consequently, consistent with these perspectives and our findings, there may be a "coupon commitment" among a certain consumer segment that leads the consumer to focus directly on coupon possession, while diminishing consideration of non-coupon decision-related factors, perhaps including the use of a memory-based IRP. That is, compared to VC consumers, CP consumers may be less likely to incorporate previous marketplace information into IRP points that they use in evaluating a market price, and instead rely more upon the (heuristic) information offered directly from the coupon.

Results pertaining to H3 though H6 demonstrated that VC and CP have significant but differential relationships with other shopping and deal-related constructs. These results support the discriminant validity of the constructs.

Researchers that have examined the relationship between demographics and coupon redemption behavior may be interested in these demographic results for the psychological measure of CP examined here. Results differ from some previous findings that have shown a positive relationship between coupon redemption behavior and family income. In this study there was a large dropoff in CP for respondents with family incomes in excess of $60,000 and post-graduate degrees. Also, males were lower in CP than females, and although not significant, there was a negative monotonic relationship between CP and age.

Implications For Future Research

When compared to the correlations between VC and the bases of the IRP, the relatively weak correlations between CP and the IRP bases suggest some intriguing research questions. For example, given the lack of a strong basis for the IRP, in the absence of a coupon, these results may suggest that CP consumers may be more vulnerable to other promotional techniques (e.g., reference price advertisements) designed to impact the IRP. Similarly, given the much stronger correlations between VC and the bases for the IRP, it may be postulated that promotions designed to affect the IRP may be relatively less successful for VC consumers. While there is a great deal of interest in the effects of advertising a reference price (cf. Urbany et al. 1988) and whether such ads are used to illegally deceive consumers (Colorado vs. May Department Stores 1989; Maryland vs. Hecht Company 1989), research has rarely focused on whether certain segments of the population are more likely to be deceived by such ads.

In general, results of this study suggest the need for the specification and testing of more complex theoretical models of deal-related processes that include both CP and VC, as well as other psychological antecedents. Future research also may explore the underlying cause of the significant relationships between CP and demographics.

Limitations

There are several limitations concerning some of the measures employed in this study. Measures of two possible bases of the IRP were used, but it may be argued that there are other possible bases for the IRP that have been ignored (Klein and Oglethorpe 1987). Because of the variety of possible IRPs and the uncertainty about the cognitive process used by any individual to formulate any specific IRP, any measure may be considered exploratory and its degree of validity questioned.

The correlations between the individual items used to measure some of the other constructs in the study were lower than desired. Specifically, for price dissonance and price dissonance reduction, only two items were used to measure each construct, and in both cases the correlations between the items were only .49. Mixed results were obtained for hypotheses concerning these constructs; stronger results possibly may have been found with better measures.

A convenience sample was used in the study and thus results may not be generalized to any specific population. While this sample does not seem inappropriate given the primarily theoretical nature of the study, practitioners interested in the effects of CP, VC, and other psychological variables on coupon usage behavior will have an interest in future research that uses probability samples that may be generalized to a specific population.

Despite these limitations, this study offers several findings that researchers concerned with price perceptions may view as interesting. In particular, we feel that results concerning the relationships between CP, VC, and the basis of the IRP are of theoretical importance and suggest several directions for some intriguing future research.

REFERENCES

Blattberg, Robert, Thomas Buesing, Peter Peacock, and Subrata Sen (1978), "Identifying the Deal Prone Segment," *Journal of Marketing Research*, 15 (August), 369-377.

Cohen, Jacob and Patricia Cohen (1975), *Applied Multiple Regression/Correlation Analysis for the Behavioral Sciences*, Hillsdale, NJ: Lawrence Erlbaum Associates.

Colorado vs. The May Company (1989).

Gardner, Meryl P. and Roger A. Strang (1984), "Consumer Response to Promotions," in *Advances in Consumer Research*, Vol. 11, Thomas C. Kinnear, ed., Provo, UT: Association for Consumer Research, 420-425.

Henderson, Caroline M. (1988), "The Interaction of Coupons With Price and Store Promotions," in *Advances in Consumer Research*, Vol. 15, Michael J. Houston, ed., Provo, UT: Association for Consumer Research, 364-371.

Klein, Noreen M. and Janet E. Oglethorpe (1987), "Cognitive Reference Points in Consumer Decision-Making," in *Advances in Consumer Research*, Vol. 14, Melanie Wallendorf and Paul Anderson, eds., Provo, UT: Association for Consumer Research, 183-187.

Levedahl, J. William (1988), "Coupon Redeemers: Are They Better Shoppers?" *The Journal of Consumer Affairs*, 22 (Winter), 264-283.

Lichtenstein, Donald R., Richard G. Netemeyer, and Scot Burton (forthcoming), "Distinguishing Coupon Proneness from Value Consciousness: An Acquisition-Transaction Utility Perspective," *Journal of Marketing*.

Maryland vs. Hecht Company (1989).

Monroe, Kent B., and Susan M. Petroshius (1981), "Buyers' Perceptions of Price: An Update of the Evidence," in *Perspectives in Consumer Behavior*, H. Kassarjian and T.S. Roberston, eds., 43-55.

Raju, P.S. and Manoj Hastek (1980), "Consumer Response to Deals: A Discussion of Theoretical Perspectives," in *Advances in Consumer Research*, Vol. 10, Jerry C. Olson, ed., Ann Arbor, MI: Association for Consumer Research, 296-301.

Rosch, Eleanor (1975), "Cognitive Reference Points," *Cognitive Psychology*, 7, 532-547.

Shimp, Terence A. and Alican Kavas (1984), "The Theory of Reasoned Action Applied to Coupon Usage," *Journal of Consumer Research*, 11 (Dec), 795-809.

Tauber, Edward M. (1972), "Why Do People Shop?," *Journal of Marketing*, 36 (October), 46-49.

Thaler, Richard (1985), "Mental Accounting and Consumer Choice," *Marketing Science*, 4 (Summer), 199-214.

Urbany, Joel E., William O. Bearden, and Dan C. Weilbaker (1988), "The Effect of Plausible and Exaggerated Reference Prices On Consumer Perceptions and Price Search," *Journal of Consumer Research*, 15 (June), 95-110.

Webster, Frederick E. Jr. (1965), "The 'Deal Prone' Consumer," *Journal of Marketing Research*, Vol. 2 (May), 186-189.

Zeithaml, Valarie A. (1988), "Consumer Perceptions of Price, Quality, and Value: A Means-End Model and Synthesis of Evidence," *Journal of Marketing*, 52 (July), 2-22.

Defining Impulse Purchasing
Francis Piron, University of Texas at San Antonio

Impulse purchasing is an important phenomenon for researchers in consumer behavior and retailing. A multitude of empirical evidence has been collected in an effort to measure the prevalence of purchases made on impulse. Unfortunately, existing definitions come short of fully capturing the phenomenon, and in turn yield measurements that do not accurately reflect the pervasiveness of impulse purchasing. The definition offered in this paper will help measure the pervasiveness of impulse purchasing more faithfully. The proposed definition is constructed on elements from existing definitions, and introduces and defines a new dimension: "on-the-spot."

Impulse purchasing is a phenomenon that started to trigger consumer researchers' interest forty years ago (Clover 1950; DuPont Studies 1945, 1949, 1959, 1965; West 1951). In response to this interest, considerable efforts have been invested toward defining impulse purchasing, and have resulted in a proliferation of definitions. Typically, as researchers strived to frame a "better" definition of impulse purchasing, their attempt was combined with an investigation on the pervasiveness of impulse purchasing. One of the results of this "growth" process is that consumer researchers are left with a wealth of ambiguous information. One cannot compare impulse purchasing defined by Kollat and Willett (1967) simply as unplanned purchasing with the "relatively extraordinary and exciting" phenomenon that Rook (1987, p.191) defines as impulse purchasing. The purpose of this paper is 1) to offer a review of existing definitions of impulse purchasing, 2) propose a new definition of impulse purchasing, and 3) demonstrate how the new definition improves over the previous ones.

REVIEW OF EXISTING DEFINITIONS

Impulse Purchasing = Unplanned Purchasing

As illustrated in Table 1 (for a full discussion on and comparison between the definitions, see Piron 1989), the early studies viewed impulse purchasing to be strictly similar to unplanned purchasing (Clover 1950; DuPont Studies 1945, 1949, 1954, 1959, 1965; West 1951), and were conducted with managerial interests in mind (i.e., for the retailers' benefit). The purchase, *not* the consumer, was investigated. Researchers were solely interested in the pervasiveness of impulse purchasing and recorded it as the difference between shoppers' intended and actual purchases.

Impulse Purchasing = Unplanned Purchasing + Exposure to a Stimulus

While Applebaum (1951) was the first to suggest that impulse purchasing may stem from the consumer's exposure to a stimulus while in the store, Nesbitt (1959) viewed it as intelligent shopping. In other words, smart shoppers do not plan their purchases, but search for and take advantage of in-store promotions, thus maximizing their buying power.

The understanding of impulse purchasing was greatly improved through Stern's (1962) identification of four distinct types of impulse purchasing: planned, pure, reminder and suggestion impulse purchasing. Planned impulse purchasing is equivalent to Nesbitt's (1959) understanding of the phenomenon, as described above. Pure impulse purchasing occurs when consumers experience "truly impulsive buying, the novelty or escape purchase which breaks a normal buying pattern" (Stern 1962, p.59). Reminder impulse purchasing occurs when the consumer is reminded of the need to buy an item upon seeing it. Finally, suggestion impulse buying

> occurs when a shopper sees a product for the first time and visualizes a need for it ... [s]uggestion buying is distinguished from reminder buying in that the shopper has no prior knowledge of the product to assist her in the purchase (p.59-60).

Stern's conceptualization of impulse purchasing is based on the premise that the making of an impulse purchase, be it planned, pure, reminder or suggestion, is linked to the consumer's exposure to a stimulus (e.g., "a shopper sees a product" above).

"Traditional" marketer-controlled stimuli such as the product itself, the product's position on the shelf, atmospherics (Kotler 1972), salesmanship, tie-ins have been identified by consumer researchers as prompts for unplanned or impulse purchases. Departing from the more conventional view of stimuli described above, Hirschman (1985) proposed that autistic (i.e., self-generated) stimuli are also accountable for unplanned and impulse purchases. Hirschman's suggestion implies that the consumer's own train of thoughts may trigger the desire to make an unanticipated purchase. For example, as she is grocery shopping, a housewife may start thinking about the coming week-end, and decide to surprise her family with a picnic for which she will now have to purchase unplanned items.

Impulse Purchasing = a "Hedonically Complex" Experience

Rook and Hoch's (1985) article has focused attention on the cognitive and emotional responses which consumers may experience during an impulse purchase. In their eyes, these responses define the essence of an impulse purchase. Rook and Hoch (1985) and Rook (1987) constructed a definition of the phenomenon resting on consumers' descriptions of thoughts and emotions experienced during impulse purchasing situations. An analysis of the descriptions yielded the following five "crucial

TABLE 1
DIMENSIONS OF THE IMPULSE PURCHASE DEFINITION

DEFINITIONAL ELEMENTS

STUDIES	1	2	3	4	5	6	7	8	9	10	11	12	13
DU PONT STUDIES (1945 TO 1965)	X												
CLOVER (1950)	X												
APPLEBAUM (1951)	X	X											
WEST (1951)	X												
NESBITT (1959)			X										
STERN (1962)													
1) Reminder Impulse	X	X											
2) Suggestive Impulse	X	X											
3) Planned Impulse		X	X										
4) Pure Impulse	X	X		X									
DAVIDSON (1966)	X				X								
DAY (1970)			X										
MC NEAL (1973)	X						X						
RUNYON (1977)	X												
ENGEL & BLACKWELL (1982)	X							X	X				
WEINBERG & GOTTWALD (1982)	X											X	
LOUDON & DELLA BITTA (1984)			X										
ROOK & HOCH (1985)									X	X	X	X	X
COBB & HOYER (1986)							X	X					
ROOK (1987)									X		X		X

elements that distinguish impulsive from nonimpulsive consumer behavior" (p.23): 1) feeling a "sudden and spontaneous desire to act," 2) being in a "state of psychological disequilibrium," 3) experiencing a "psychological conflict and struggle," 4) reducing "cognitive evaluation," and 5) consuming "without regard for the consequences."

The first dimension is viewed as a "rapid change in psychological states," capturing the quickness and unexpectedness of the stimulation that is transformed into a desire to purchase. The second dimension ("state of psychological disequilibrium") is seen as a temporary loss of self-control caused by a "sudden and spontaneous desire to act." The "psychological conflict and struggle" arises as the consumer strives to regain some of the temporarily lost self-control, evaluating the immediate positive or pleasant aspects of the purchase against the delayed negative or unpleasant aspects of the purchase. As s/he experiences a reduction in "cognitive evaluation," the consumer becomes "the antithesis of classical models of 'economic man' as a rational expected utility maximizer" (p.24). In other words, the unexpected confrontation with the stimulus impairs the consumer's rationality. The fifth dimension ("disregard for future consequences") defines the consumer who chooses a small but immediate reward over a larger but delayed

TABLE 1 (CONTINUED)
DIMENSIONS OF THE IMPULSE PURCHASE DEFINITION

DEFINITIONAL ELEMENTS	EXPLANATION
1	UNPLANNED PURCHASE
2	RESPONSE TO STIMULUS
3	DELIBERATELY PLANNED TO BENEFIT FROM SPECIAL OFFERS
4	THRILL SEEKING
5	DECISION MADE ON THE SPUR OF THE MOMENT
6	RESULT OF A DELIBERATION PROCESS
7	NOT IN RESPONSE TO A PREVIOUSLY RECOGNIZED PROBLEM
8	NO BUYING INTENTIONS FORMED PRIOR TO ENTERING THE STORE
9	SUDDEN AND SPONTANEOUS DESIRE TO ACT
10	STATE OF PSYCHOLOGICAL DISEQUILIBRIUM
11	PSYCHOLOGICAL CONFLICT AND STRUGGLE
12	REDUCTION OF COGNITIVE EVALUATION
13	NO EVALUATION OF CONSEQUENCES

remuneration. Rook and Hoch refer to this dimension as the "pathological aspects of impulsive consumption" that may "deteriorate into a destructive character disorder."

Finally, summarizing the five dimensions identified earlier, Rook (1987) identifies impulse purchasing to be:

> when a consumer experiences a sudden, often powerful and persistent urge to buy something immediately. The impulse to buy is hedonically complex and may stimulate emotional conflict. Also impulse buying is prone to occur with diminished regard for its consequences (p.191).

He then describes the phenomenon as "extraordinary," "a fast experience," "more emotional than rational," and concludes that "this interpretation is close in spirit to the 'pure impulse' behavior that Stern (1962) identified" (p.191).

In summary, a distinct shift can be observed with respect to the elements comprising the definitions of impulse purchasing formulated over the past forty years (see Table 1). Beginning with the simple equation where unplanned purchasing equals impulse purchasing, components such as "response to a stimulus," "thrill seeking," to name but a few, were incorporated in the definitions, eventually portraying a more "hedonically complex" phenomenon.

CRITIQUE OF PREVIOUS DEFINITIONS

The second objective of this paper, to offer a definition of impulse purchasing that more accurately captures the phenomenon, rests on the premise that existing definitions do not adequately depict impulse purchasing. Specifically, equating impulse to unplanned purchasing fails to consider the many instances where unplanned purchases are not made impulsively. For example, consider an unplanned purchase where the consumer decides on buying a particular product after examining and comparing brands, contents and price, the purchase would be hard pressed to qualify as an impulse purchase.

Further, when, without regard for the consumer's reactions, impulse purchasing is simply defined as an unplanned purchase prompted by an exposure to a stimulus, the understanding of the phenomenon is seriously limited by its exclusion of the purchasing decision maker. However, when the definition implies that emotional and cognitive reactions *must* accompany the purchase (i.e., Rook 1987; Rook and Hoch 1985), the phenomenon may then be too narrowly defined. For instance, the shopper who, upon seeing canned vegetables,

TABLE 2
Analysis of Respondents' Answers

Dimension Mentioned	Frequency	Percentage
Unplanned	120	47.4%
Exposure to stimulus	78	30.8%
On-the-spot	7	2.8%
Emotional reactions	13	5.1%
Psychological reactions	9	3.6%

(Note: totals do not add up to 253 (i.e., number of respondents). Some respondents used two or more of the dimensions in their definitions).

decides to purchase a can of the product may have made a suggestion or reminder impulse purchase (Stern 1962); yet s/he is not expected to experience emotional or cognitive reactions such as those identified by Rook and Hoch.

In sum, existing definitions fail to adequately capture impulse purchasing by focusing on one element of the phenomenon (i.e., the purchase itself) to the expense of another (i.e., the consumer). Yet, when the consumer is considered, it is only with respect to his/her unusual behavior.

A COMPREHENSIVE DEFINITION OF IMPULSE PURCHASING

The above review indicates that none of the available definitions fully describes impulse purchasing (previous definitional shortcomings will be further discussed in a subsequent section). This state of affairs is not new and was noticed by previous researchers (Kollat and Willett 1969; Rook 1987; Rook and Hoch 1985). In this section, a simple statement defining impulse purchasing is offered, while the definitional elements are specified and illustrated in a following section. While the definition proposed in this paper integrates previously outlined dimensions into one definition, it also considers the responses given by 253 undergraduate students from two major universities (see Table 2) who were asked "to define impulse purchasing in [their] own words."

Impulse purchasing is formally defined as a purchase that is 1) unplanned, 2) the result of an exposure to a stimulus, 3) decided "on-the-spot." Impulse purchases can be further classified depending on the consumer's experiencing emotional and/or cognitive reactions, as defined later: An "Experiential Impulse Purchase" differs from a "Non-Experiential Impulse Purchase" as only the former is accompanied by emotional and/or cognitive reactions. As a brief illustration, the consumer who purchases an expensive designer leather jacket on impulse may experience a mixture of guilt and excitement (Experiential Impulse Purchase), but may not experience such reactions when purchasing a can of vegetables on impulse (Non-Experiential Impulse Purchase). The next section focuses on outlining and illustrating the elements making up the definition proposed in this paper, and is followed by a discussion describing how the proposed definition improves upon the previous ones.

Unplanned Purchasing

The definition of unplanned purchasing used here follows from Engel, Kollat and Blackwell (1968). An unplanned purchase is:

> a buying action undertaken without a problem having been previously recognized or a buying intention formed prior to entering the store (p.483).

The concept that an impulse purchase is unplanned is central to all definitions of impulse purchasing. Also, almost 50% (see Table 2) of the students who were asked to define impulse purchasing did so using terms implying a lack of planning (e.g., "unexpected purchase," "I was not looking for the [product]") in the purchasing decision.

Exposure to a Stimulus

Only two of the previously conceived definitions of impulse purchasing (Applebaum 1951; Stern 1962) specifically include "exposure to a stimulus" in their formulation of an impulse purchase (see Table 1). However, almost 31% (see Table 2) of the students who were asked to define impulse purchasing incorporated the concept in making statements such as "[w]hen you see something you had not planned to buy ...," or as "[b]uying a product without planning because it is on sale."

A review of the consumer research literature indicates that the stimuli associated to impulse purchasing can be categorized along four broad dimensions. First, impulse purchases can be made in response to marketers' suggestions and/or reminders (Stern 1962). Second, impulse purchasing may occur as a result of marketers' environmental manipulations through atmospherics (Kotler 1974), point-of-purchase and end-aisle displays (see Shimp and DeLozier 1986 for a comprehensive review), shelf and product positioning (Bergman and Gilson 1986, Cox 1964, Engel et al. 1968), tie-ins ("relating different items in displays on the basis of how the products will be used" Berkman and Gilson 1986, p.505). Third, non-satisfactory or unavailable planned purchases (e.g., Iyer and Ahlawat's (1987) "shortfalls") may translate into impulse purchases. Finally, Hirschman (1985) identified autistic stimulation as a potential origin of impulse purchasing: Autistic stimulation refers to consumer-generated, non-environmentally induced arousal.

"On-The-Spot"

The third characteristic of an impulse purchase, as defined here, involves the time and location of the purchase. While earlier research identified the location element in the definition of impulse purchasing (cf. Engel et al. (1968) above), only very recently did researchers propose that both location and time elements of the purchase decision making are instrumental in differentiating impulse from non-impulse purchasing. Specifically, Settle and Alreck (1986) contend that:

> the whole purchase decision process for impulse goods takes place at the point of sale and may take only a few seconds time (p.335).

Within the context of the definition of impulse purchasing proposed here, "on-the-spot" is defined as the immediate time and place where the purchase decision is processed and made. In other words, considering the first two definitional elements (i.e., the purchase is unplanned, and the desire to purchase is stirred by an unexpected encounter with a stimulus), impulse purchasing occurs when the decision to purchase is made immediately upon seeing the product or the stimulus representing the product.

While only 3% (see Table 2) of the students surveyed specifically mentioned "on-the-spot," another 18% of the sample defined the decision to make an impulse purchase using terms such as "on the spur of the moment," "spontaneously," "on a whim," "suddenly," and "spontaneously." While such terms unequivocally incorporate the "time" element of "on-the-spot", they do not specifically refer to the "location" element inbedded in our definition of "on-the-spot."

The location element of the definition is nevertheless primordial since a purchase decision made immediately upon exposure to a stimulus, but away from the point-of-purchase, can translate either into a planned purchase or into a rescinded purchase decision. For example, a consumer who views a commercial and immediately decides s/he wants the product would still have to transport him/herself to the point-of-sale to acquire the product. In other words, the purchase would then be planned.

Emotional and/or Cognitive Reactions

The final element of the proposed definition relates to the consumer him/herself. Surely, and as illustrated earlier, not all unplanned purchases bought on the spot as a result of an exposure to a stimulus are accompanied by excitement, pleasure, or forgetfulness of reality, yet experiential impulse purchasing does occur. It is argued here that, contrary to assertions made in the most recent research (Rook 1987; Rook and Hoch 1985), experiencing emotional and/or cognitive reactions (i.e., feeling a "sudden and spontaneous desire to act," being in a "state of psychological disequilibrium," experiencing a "psychological conflict and struggle," reducing "cognitive evaluation," and consuming "without regard for the consequences.") are not the determinant characteristic of an impulse purchase. In fact, both planned and unplanned purchases can be accompanied by emotions and cognitive reactions such as guilt, disregard for future consequences, to name but a few. In sum, as was proposed earlier, and since not all impulse purchases are accompanied with emotional and/or cognitive reactions, impulse purchasing can be experiential or non-experiential.

Previous study of the emotional and cognitive aspects of impulse purchasing is limited (for two exceptions, see Rook 1987; Rook and Hoch 1985). The emotion and cognitive reactions incorporated in the proposed definition are those identified by previous research, and defined in an earlier section. Specifically, Rook (1987) identified the "excitement and stimulation," "hedonic elements: feeling good, bad, guilty," "purchasing in response to moods," and a "sudden and imperative desire to purchase" as emotion reactions that may accompany an impulse purchase.

Rook (1987) and Rook and Hoch (1985) also identified the following cognitive reactions: (1) being in a state of psychological disequilibrium, which may result in experiencing a feeling of helplessness, (2) experiencing a psychological conflict and struggle, (3) experiencing a reduction of choice evaluation.

Another interesting "cognitive reaction" dimension is the one Navarick (1987) uses to define impulsivity and which can be labeled "reduced evaluation of consequences." That is, impulsive behaviors result from choosing an immediately available option over a future option as a result of a mental accounting where the present value of the future outcome compares unfavorably with the value of an immediate outcome.

Finally, a cognitive trait labeled: "discounting of own responsibility" is introduced. This trait became salient when analyzing the answers given by the sample of students mentioned above: A small percentage of students described the episode as an experience that could well fit in "the-devil-made-me-do-it" category.

SUMMARY

A complete definition of impulse purchasing must recognize that emotional and cognitive reactions may accompany, but are not a sine qua non condition to an impulse purchase. Further, a consumer does not have to experience all the reactions mentioned in the definition to make an experiential impulse purchase. Further, due to the lack of available evidence, it is acknowledged that this discussion is somewhat speculative and that the field of consumer research needs to spend renewed efforts, focused on the discovery and comprehension of such reactions, as well as on the acquisition of an understanding of the personal and environmental factors that may influence such experiences.

Finally, the definition proposed in this paper improves upon the previous definition as it offers both discernment and flexibility. First, discernment is found as unplanned purchasing is unequivocally differentiated from impulse purchasing because of the "on-the-spot" definitional requirement: Unplanned purchases not decided immediately upon the first encounter with the stimulus cannot qualify as an impulse purchase. Second, flexibility is offered as impulse purchases can be categorized according to the experiencing or non-experiencing of emotion and cognitive reactions.

BIBLIOGRAPHY

Applebaum, William (1951), "Studying Consumer Behavior in Retail Stores," *Journal of Marketing*, 16 (October), 172-178.

Berkman, Harold W. and Christopher C. Gilson (1986), *Consumer Behavior: Concepts and Strategies*, Kent Publishing Co., Wadsworth, Inc., Boston, massachussetts.

Clover, Vernon T. (1950), "Relative Importance of Impulse Buying in Retail Stores," *Journal of Marketing*, 25 (July), 66-70.

Cobb, Cathy J. and Wayne D. Hoyer (1986), "Planned versus Impulse Purchase Behavior," *Journal of Retailing*, 62 (Winter), 67-81.

Consumer Buying Habits Studies, E.I. DuPont de Nemours and Co., 1945, 1949, 1959, 1965.

Cox, Keith (1964), "The Responsiveness of Food Sales to Shelf Space Changes in Supermarkets," *Journal of Marketing Research*, 1 (May), 63-67.

Davidson, William R. (1966), *Retailing Management*, The Ronald Press Co., New York, NY.

Day, George S. (1970), *Buyer Attitudes and Brand Choice Behavior*, The Free press, New York, NY.

Engel, James F. and Roger D. Blackwell (1982), *"Consumer Behavior,"* Hinsdale, IL: Dryden Press.

Hirschman, Elizabeth C. (1985), "Cognitive Processes in Experiential Consumer Behavior," in *Research in Consumer Behavior*, ed. Jagdish N. Sheth, Vol. 1, Jai Press, Inc.

Iyer Easwar S. and Sucheta S. Ahlawat (1987), "Deviations from a Shopping Plan: When and Why Do Consumers Not Buy as Planned," in *Advances in Consumer Research*, Vol. 14, eds. Melanie Wallendorf and Paul Anderson, Provo, UT.: Association for Consumer Research, 246-249.

Kollat, David T. and R.P. Willett (1967), "Consumer Impulse Purchasing Behavior," *Journal of Marketing Research*, 4 (February), 21-31.

Kollat, David T. and R.P. Willett (1969), "Is Impulse Purchasing Really a Useful Concept in Marketing Decisions?," *Journal of Marketing*, 33 (January), 79-83.

Kotler, Philip (1974), "Atmospherics as a Marketing Tool," *Journal of Retailing*, Vol. 49, 4, (Winter), 48-64.

Loudon, David L. and Albert J. Della Bitta (1984), *Consumer Beha-vior: Concepts and Applications*, 2d Edition, Mcgraw-Hill Book Co.

McNeal, James U. (1973), *An Introduction to Consumer Behavior*, John Wiley & Sons, Inc., New York, NY.

Navarick, Douglas J. (1987), "Reinforcement Probability and Delay as Determinants of Human Impulsiveness," *The Psychological Record*, 37, 219-226.

Nesbitt, Saul (1959), "Today's Housewives Plan Menus as They Shop," *Nesbitt Associates Release*, 2-3.

Piron, Francis (1989), "A Definition and Empirical Investigation of Impulse Purchasing," Unpublished Dissertation, The University of South Carolina.

Rook, Dennis W. (1987), "The Buying Impulse," *Journal of Consumer Research*, 14 (September), 189-199.

Rook, Dennis W. and Stephen J. Hoch (1985), "Consuming Impulses," in *Advances in Consumer Research*, Vol. 12, eds. Morris B. Holbrook and Elizabeth C. Hirschman, Provo, UT: Association for Consumer Research, 23-27.

Runyon, Kenneth E. (1977), *Consumer Behavior and the practice of Marketing*, Charles E. Merril Publishing Co., Columbus, OH.

Settle, Robert B. and Pamela L. Alreck (1986), *Why They Buy: American Consumers Inside and Out*, John Wiley & Sons, New York.

Stern, Hawkins (1962), "The Significance of Impulse Buying Today," *Journal of Marketing*, 26 (April), 59-62.

West, John C. (1951),"Results of Two Years of Study into Impulse Buying," *Journal of Marketing*, 15 (January), 362-363.

Perspectives From Industry and Academic Research on Elderly Adults' Responses To Advertising
Summary Of A Special Session
Catherine A. Cole, University of Iowa

INTRODUCTION

Demographic trends all point to the increasing size of the elderly market. For example, the over-65 group is growing twice as fast as the general population. By the year 2010, 25% of the total U.S. population will be at least 55 years old; by 2050 this segment will comprise about 33% of the population. Although this segment is an attractive one, marketing professionals cannot always expect to use the same types of communications strategies with this group as with younger consumers.

SUMMARY

This session brought together researchers from academic settings and industry to discuss developments in advertising to the elderly market. The four papers focused on ways in which elderly adults' cognitive, affective and behavioral responses toward advertising differ from and resemble those of younger adults. We also discussed what these differences and similarities imply for theory and practice.

To develop focus questions, we used the literature from life-span psychology which identifies three types of influences on humans in later life: normative age graded, normative history graded and non-normative life events. Normative age graded changes are biological and environmental influences that are closely related to chronological age in terms of when they start and how long they last. They are normative because they happen to everyone. For example, some of us will have some degree of hearing loss in the third decade of life, but by the 70's all of us lose some hearing. This literature suggested that we use the following question as a focus question: *How do elderly adults' responses to advertising differ from those of younger adults? Why do they differ?*

PRESENTATION #1
Age Differences in Response to Advertising
Harlan Spotts, Northeastern University

This talk reported on an experiment assessing age differences in cognitive responses to two versions of a print ad for a fictitious cereal product. In this experiment the target print ad, which was either concrete or abstract in content, was embedded in a magazine. Respondents read the magazine at their own pace, were shown a reminder headline and then completed questions designed to obtain cognitive response, recall and recognition data. Elderly generated fewer total thoughts and fewer product oriented and neutral thoughts than younger adults. While not statistically significant, the directional trend for the elderly was to generate fewer negative and more positive thoughts than young adults. In the analysis, education was a significant covariate having a positive influence on cognitive response generation. Age effects, however, were still significant in light of education effects. Advertisement involvement, while having a significant main effect, had no interactive effect with age on cognitive response. In addition, elderly recalled and recognized less material from the ad than younger adults.

From a theoretical perspective, the study suggests that at very low exposure levels, regardless of the type of ad, elderly fail to elaborate spontaneously on print advertising messages. This failure may result from a general slowing of processing speed, a normative age graded change which is highly correlated with aging. Future research might explore ways of redesigning ads to increase the amount elderly elaborate on messages. From a practical perspective, this study suggests that to generate high levels of learning among the elderly it may be necessary to increase repetition levels of messages in advertising campaigns.

PRESENTATION #2
Developing Advertising Campaigns for the 65+ Market
Joyce Wackenhut, D'Arcy, Masius, Benton & Bowles, Inc.

This talk began with slides summarizing demographic and psychographic trends in the elderly market. These data emphasized that the 65+ plus market should not be characterized as impoverished, inactive or sickly. Instead, the market can be described as diverse and active. The speaker argued that advertising targeted to this market should communicate meaningful benefits about the good or service. In fact, the procedure for developing good creative concepts should be the same as that followed for developing creative concepts for the younger market.

SUMMARY (CONTINUED)

Several currently running commercials were shown. The successful spots avoided stereotypes of elderly and showed clear benefits from brand usage. The unsuccessful spots negatively portrayed elderly and used a overly general life style appeal.

The second set of influences on development, normative history graded, are biological and environmental forces that are associated with an historical time and are related to cohort. These influences are considered normative because they tend to occur in a highly similar way for all individuals in a given culture or subculture at a given period of time. Thus, for example, people who were teenagers during the depression may have different attitudes toward risk than people who were born at the start of the depression even though both groups are now over 60.

The third influences, non-normative life events, are biological and environmental and do not occur in any normative or universal way. There is a lack of consistency across time and individuals about these events. Illness, accidents, loss of a significant other, and retirement are all examples. Both these last two influences suggest a second focus question: *Is there heterogeneity among elderly adults in their responses to advertising? What causes this heterogeneity?*

PRESENTATION #4
Cognitive Age and Memory Performance of Elderly Consumers in Information Processing: Individual Differences Approach
Bonnee Wettlaufer, Peter D. Bennett, Sung-Soon Lee Pennsylvania State

This paper assessed age differences in cognitive responses to a print advertisement for a newly developed product designed to help people remain in their homes as long as possible. In a result contrary to the Spotts' study, elderly generated more cognitive responses than younger adults, suggesting that for highly involving products elderly may elaborate more extensively than younger adults do for relatively uninvolving products. However, the content of the thoughts indicated that the younger adults were processing the information more deeply than older adults, supporting previous work on encoding deficits among the elderly.

A unique contribution was the discussion of the cognitive age variable, used to asses "felt" age, which may be the result of non-normative influences on development. The authors classified elderly adults into three groups based on the size of the difference between their chronological age and their felt age. They found that subjects who felt the youngest generated thoughts at a deeper level of encoding than those whose felt age was close to their chronological age, but there was no effect of felt age on the number of thoughts generated. Thus the encoding deficit varies among the different segments of the elderly market.

PRESENTATION #5
A Cohort Study of the Elderly For The Insurance Industry
Seth Ginsberg, J. Walter Thompson

The presenter discussed the unique perspective provided by cohort studies in targeting marking strategies to members of the mature market. He described a specific study and explored the relevance of the findings to the financial services category.

In the presentation, he reviewed the philosophy guiding cohort analyses. Cohort membership is a function of shared social history, not age per se. Assumptions about the world shared by cohort members form the basis for their future expectations. He also reviewed a cohort based model of the mature market. By seeing the mature market in terms of three cohorts, and understanding their experiences (or lack thereof) with the world before the Depression, the Depression and the post-war American ascendence, one can predict may of their attitudes--particularly those concerning financial matters. He also reviewed a study of financial attitudes among members of these three cohorts. He demonstrated how the cohort centered approach revealed patterns in mature citizens' attitudes about saving and investing money--helping the agency to more effectively target an advertising campaign.

CONCLUSION

The final focus question was: What are the implications of these differences for theory and practice. At least three generalizations about elderly adults' responses to advertising can be made. First, like younger adults, elderly adults respond well to message appeals that promise clear unique benefits from brand usage. Second, elderly adults appear to think less about advertising (i.e. elaborate less) than younger adults. Even though in high involvement situations they may elaborate more on messages than younger adults, the content of their thoughts suggests that they are not encoding material deeply. Finally, the elderly market is a diverse market. Possible segmenting variables include actual age, which will capture birth cohort, and felt age, which may rapture cognitive functioning.

Moschis concluded by arguing that (1) there is a need for continued research on the elderly market from both industry and academics and (2) there is a need for researchers to continue drawing on aging models from psychology, sociology and communications.

Approaches to the Study of Consumer Behavior in Late Life

George P. Moschis, Georgia State University

The increasing focus on the aging population has generated interest in understanding the consumer behavior of older adults. As a result, the need for using effective approaches to study this segment becomes apparent. This paper presents several approaches developed in social sciences; it attempts to make those interested in the area aware of these approaches and their potential for contribution to the field of consumer behavior.

BACKGROUND

Approaches to the study of human behavior in late life can be classified into two categories. Those which can be considered as traditional theories and those which fall into humanistic science.

"Traditional" Theories of Aging

"Traditional" theories correspond to the unreflective elaboration of the empirical-analytic sciences, all sharing common logical rules and ideal principles of explanation aimed at prediction and control of phenomena (cf. Moody 1988). Traditional theories can be classified in three categories, reflecting three different approaches to studying aging and age-related behaviors in late life. First, aging can be viewed as a *biological phenomenon* involving maturation and decline in various functions of the body. This model is primarily useful for guiding the work of physiologists and biologists who are interested in examining changes in various bodily functions over the life span.

Aging can also be viewed as a *psychological development* (process). Psychological aging has been studied either as a process of change in mental factors, or as a continuous process of evolution in the mind, commonly referred to as "human development." Unfortunately, one cannot predict patterns of aging effects on mental capacities and performance due to the dependence of these functions upon the body and its level of functioning which, in turn, shows wide variability. Human development, on the other hand, can be viewed either as a process moving through several discrete stages or as a continuous process of interaction with, or adjustment to, one's environment (Atchley 1987).

Finally, *social aging* involves the assignment of people to positions and roles by society based on ideas about what people at various ages or life stages are capable of and about what is appropriate for them. Age norms are conveyed to them through socialization, although people often anticipate and learn age-related changes before they encounter them (i.e., anticipatory socialization). The actual learning of these age norms is achieved through acculturation, while adaptation and negotiation allow people to fit themselves to new roles and vice versa (Atchley 1987).

Humanistic Theories of Aging

The contribution of humanities to theories of aging is reflected in three different approaches: dialectical gerontology, hermeneutic gerontology, and critical gerontology (Moody 1988). *Dialectical gerontology* is an approach which acknowledges the contradictory features of old age, trying to locate the contradictions within a historical and developmental framework. This approach would highlight contradictions rather than seeking theories of aging that would eliminate them. *Germeneutic gerontology* focuses on interpretations of facts or events, both in relationships between theory and fact and the relationship between theory and fact and the social behavior. *Critical gerontology* focuses on progressive and unfolding capacities of the human state, and refers to human development that recognizes aging as a movement toward freedom beyond domination (wisdom, autonomy, transcendence).

RELEVANCE TO THE STUDY OF OLDER CONSUMERS

Traditional theories of aging include three types of theories: biological, psychological and social theories. These can be classified on the basis of the assumption about the location of causal factors: individual, environment, or both (Table 1).

Biological Theories. These theories assume that aging is affected by either genetic factors or environmental causes. Examples of the first category include theories such as wear-and-tear, cross-linkage, metabolic, programmed senescence, neuroendocrine, and immunological theory. Examples of environmental theories include free radical, somatic mutation, and error theory. All these theories attempt to explain aging of the body and its parts.

The biophysical approach suggests a wide variation among the older population with respect to aging. While explanations for aging and age-related behaviors are far from being adequate, the available data in this field suggest two important implications. First, physiological and biological changes may not occur at the same rate for all segments of the older market, and chronological age is not the appropriate variable to capture these changes. Thus, when we make inferences about the corresponding consumer behavior as a result of declining ability in certain areas (e.g., Schewe 1988 and 1989), we must keep in mind the wide variation in responses. The tendency to assume homogeneous responses from the aged market is a concern that has captured the attention of theorists and practitioners. For example, Hendricks and Hendricks (1977) note that: "In constructing their explanations social scientists are forced to treat all members of a category as though they were identical." Second, the use of variables that measure a person's functional or physiological capacity may more

TABLE 1
TRADITIONAL THEORIES OF AGING

		Biological	Psychological		Social
			Cognitive	Personality	
Focus of Theory	Individual	Wear-and-Tear Cross-Linkage Metabolic Immunological Neuroendocrine Programmed Senescence	Organismic	Stage Theories Continuity Theory Self-congruity	
	Environment	Free-Radical Somatic Mutation Error Theory	Mechanistic		Activity Disengagement Exchange Labeling Subculture Modernization Political Economy
	Both		Contextual	Cognitive Personality	

appropriately capture aging than chronological age per se.

Psychological Theories. Psychological theories address the development and change of cognition (human development), and personality and self in late life. These theories explore adult cognitive development as it may be affected by biophysical factors (organismic), environmental influences (mechanistic), or both (contextual); they also focus on personality and self, attempting to explain changes over the life span either as an abrupt process (stage theories) or as a smooth transition (continuity theory and cognitive personality theory). Since the focus of these theories has been on explaining changes in personality and self-concept over the lifespan, their usefulness in explaining consumer behavior in late life is not apparent. Theories of self appear to hold promise but researchers must resolve the issue of appropriate research design to be used (e.g., Sirgy 1982).

Theories of Social Aging. Theories of social aging focus on adaptation to old age or socialization to appropriate roles in late life. Among the most popular theories are activity, disengagement, and exchange theory. These are either of little usefulness to researchers of consumer behavior or have not been adequately supported (Passuth and Bengtson 1988). However, even though these theories may not prove useful in explaining a wide variety of consumer behaviors they may play important role in explaining linkages in broader conceptual or theoretical models. For example, these theories might help us explain patterns of social interaction in the broader model of age stratification.

The subcultural theory, on the other hand, is more pervasive in terms of its potential for application to the consumer field. Although the theory has not been rigorously tested it holds promise for its potential to explain homogeneity of consumer behavior in the aged subculture as well as specific subsegments (Moschis 1990).

The social breakdown theory is perhaps the model that most accurately depicts relationships between the individual and his/her environment. It offers sociological and psychological explanations of the development of a psychological construct (self-concept). Yet, the model appears to be untestable. Even testing parts of the model based on labeling theory would be of questionable desirability, since previous testing failed to provide adequate support amidst controversies about its value and appropriateness (Moschis 1990). Modernization theory and political economy theory are macro-theories aimed at explaining consumer behavior of the elderly using countries or subcultures as unit of analysis.

The age stratification model is considered to be a vast improvement over other models of social aging (Hendricks and Hendricks 1977). Although it could be applied to several aspects of consumer behavior, its value is expected to be in explaining those for which society holds norms and expectations for older consumers in late life. One appeal of this model is its capability to accommodate several theoretical perspectives into a broader, more cohesive framework. Although cross-sectional data may be adequate for initial stages of

TABLE 2
RATING OF APPROACHES[1]

"Good"	"Fair"	"Poor"	"Questionable"
Age Stratification	Cognitive Personality	Activity	Critical
Interpretive Science	Exchange	Continuity	Dialectic
Life-Course Perspective	Modernization	Disengagement	Labeling
Political Economy	Personality Theories	Error Theories	Self-congruity
Processing-Resource Perspective	Stage Theories	Programming Theories	Social Breakdown
Socialization Perspective	Subculture		
Three-Tier Model of Cognition			

[1] Ratings ("Good," "Fair," "Poor") are based on relative acceptance of frameworks in disciplines and potential application to the field of consumer behavior. "Questionable" frameworks are those which pose issues of clarity of the appropriate research tradition required (positivistic, humanistic) and/or of overcoming methodological and conceptual issues before they can be applied to the consumer field.

research, longitudinal data are more appropriate for testing relationships between processes and their outcomes. Investigators working in this area should be aware of the plethora of issues surrounding the conceptualization and measurement of socialization processes and outcomes (Moschis 1987).

In testing the various theories researchers should focus on cognitive and overt *processes* and their influence on consumer behavior, rather than inferring the presence of such processes from differences in the observed behaviors. This is because observations of behaviors based on cross-sectional data could potentially provide explanation or support for more than one theory or perspective. For example, decline in consumer behavior measured as "age-differences," could be the effect of decline in biophysical abilities, psychological changes or social aging (e.g., disengagement); sustenance of self-concept could be explained by both activity and personality theories, and so on. Similarly, the measurement of processes using situations (e.g., the presence or absence of social visibility) should be validated, since they are based only on the researcher's judgment rather on the older person's perceptions and interpretation of the situation.

Multitheoretical Perspectives. It is widely accepted that there is no single approach to the study of human behavior and age-related changes in late life. This is because aging is multi-dimensional -- that is, people age as biological beings, social beings, psychological beings and even as spiritual beings (Moody 1988). Thus, the study of human behavior in late life must take into account the variety of aging perspectives.

The multidimensional nature of aging has given impetus to the development of conceptual frameworks developed to incorporate several, and often diverse, theoretical perspectives. The *processing-resource framework* and the *three-tier model* of cognition are recent developments in the field of cognitive psychology of aging (cf. Moschis 1990). The *psychometric approach* is an atheoretical quantitative method designed to uncover traits and various aspects of cognition over the life span. The *socialization perspective* has been the topic of considerable attention in the areas of sociology, psychology, anthropology, mass communications, and more recently in consumer behavior (Moschis 1987). However, it is closest related to the field of sociology and is considered to be a more elaborate model than age stratification theory. The latter theory has also been a major influence on the development of another multitheoretical framework, the *life-course* perspective (Passuth and Bengtson 1988).

Humanistic Science. Finally, the use of the interpretive perspective is suggested to study concepts that can not be easily explicated, described, measured, and defy explanation via traditional scientific approach. This perspective has been receiving increasing attention by social scientists and should not be ignored by consumer researchers who often claim to rely heavily on other disciplines.

SUMMARY

Table 2 summarizes the usefulness of various approaches to the study of consumer behavior in late life. The ratings reflect potential for contribution to the field of consumer behavior based on criteria such as acceptance of the approach in other disciplines, potential for overcoming methodological and conceptual issues and for its potential to explain consumer behavior. These considerations, criteria and other basis for evaluating these approaches are discussed in detail elsewhere (Moschis 1990). The present classification is offered only as a rough guideline for future research, since there is some subjectivity involved in rating the various approaches.

In summary, the approaches available in other disciplines that could be used to study the older consumer are not full-fledged theories. Some are still in the initial stages of developing propositions, while others have progressed at a more advanced stage of gathering data (Barrow and Smith 1983). The researcher should be constantly alert of developments in other disciplines that might provide insights into the value of an approach in understanding the older consumer.

REFERENCES

Atchley, Robert C. (1987), *Aging: Continuity and Change*. (2nd Edition). Belmont, CA: Wadsworth Publishing Company.

Barrow, George M. and Patricia A. Smith (1983), *Aging, the Individual, and Society*. St. Paul, Minnesota: West Publishing Company, 51-69.

Hendricks, J. and C. Hendricks (1977), *Aging in Mass Society: Myths and Realities*, Cambridge, MA: Winthrop.

Moody, Harry R. (1988), "Toward a Critical Gerontology: The Contribution of the Humanities to Theories of Aging," in *Emergent Theories of Aging*, James E. Birren and Vern L. Bengtson (eds.). New York: Springer Publishers.

Moschis, George P. (1987), *Consumer Socialization: A Life-Cycle Perspective*. Boston: Lexington Books.

⎯⎯⎯⎯ (1990), "Frameworks for Studying Older Consumers: Present Status and Methodological Issues," Georgia State University, Center for Mature Consumer Studies (Working Paper No. 06-90).

Passuth, Patricia M. and Vern L. Bengtson (1988), "Sociological Theories of Aging: Current Perspectives and Future Directions," in *Emergent Theories of Aging*, James E. Birren and Vern L. Bengtson (eds.). New York: Springer Publishers.

Schewe, Charles D. (1988), "Marketing to Our Aging Population: Responding to Physiological Changes," *Journal of Consumer Marketing*, Vol. 15 (3) (Summer), 61-73.

⎯⎯⎯⎯ (1989), "Effective Communication with Our Aging Population," *Business Horizons* 32, no. 1 (January/February): 19-25.

Sirgy, Joseph M. (1982), "Self-Concept in Consumer Behavior: A Critical Review," *Journal of Consumer Research*, 9(December), 287-300.

Can't Buy Me Love: Dating, Money, and Gifts
Russell W. Belk, University of Utah
Gregory S. Coon, University of Utah

I had an overwhelming desire to shower the girl with gifts. I bought her all kinds of things such as stuffed animals, clothing, and jewelry. Unlike before when I viewed dates and gift giving an investment, I was now making decisions about buying from my heart instead of my head. I spent so much money on the girl that I had to quit school for a quarter and work full time. I guess that's what true love is [M 25].

In America, money seems to have taken a big role in dating. I don't think that it should. Like the Beatles song, I believe strongly that "money can't buy me love". True love is developed through true friendship and trust, and generosity is only one of those features....I don't think that money should be a big issue in dating, and I wanted to find someone who didn't care too much for money [M 24].

Money is a part of everything, even dating. It is impossible to date without money. I guess I find it difficult to separate love from money. Not that money can buy love, but rather money is an essential part of the dating process. I don't know if you can possibly have one without the other [F 24].

It seems sick to me. Like they try to buy each other or show how much they love each other in how much money they spend on the gift to the other person [F26].

American dating, mating, and courtship activities employ money and tangible gifts as key ritual elements and as focal symbolic vehicles. Gifts and dating expenditures "say" what cannot be said in words. However, perhaps due to the crass associations of exchanging money and gifts for the attentions and sexual favors of prostitutes, mistresses, gigolos, and gold-diggers, research on Western dating has largely ignored the monetary and material aspects of these relationships. A related explanation for this lack of attention is the inappropriate intrusion of the profane into the supposed realm of the sacred when cash and gifts become too prominent in our view of dating (Belk, Wallendorf, and Sherry 1989, Belk and Wallendorf 1990). Treating dating as an exchange relationship may threaten to commoditize and destroy the illusions provided by the romantic model of love. The present study presents a brief historical perspective and qualitative data that illuminate the tabooed and neglected intersection of the material, the sexual, and the romantic in the dating practices of U.S. college students.

HISTORIC VARIATIONS IN THE U.S. DATING AND COURTSHIP

The role of material possessions in early middle class American courtship practices was not so much in impressive gift-giving as in displaying command of the resources for providing comfort and earning a living. Rothman (1984, p. 24) explains:

> Before a man could marry, he had to possess the means to support a wife and children....His marriage "portion"--the land he would farm, the house in which he and his bride would live--came from a share of his father's property.

Furthermore, these standards escalated with time and economic progress:

> Where the eighteenth-century man had looked to provide a simply furnished house for his family, men who married in the increasingly industrialized middle years of the nineteenth century set higher standards for themselves. They aspired to equip their households with cook stoves, pianos, Irish servant girls, indoor plumbing, or whatever they and their families needed to enjoy and demonstrate middle-class status (Rothman 1984, p. 151).

At the same time, it was the responsibility of the bride and her family to provide a trousseau of clothes, linens, and "fancy things" to set up the household. In addition, a woman's home and schooling might limit her exposure to certain men. Lystra (1989, p. 163) reports a 19th century woman's derision of a neighbor's daughter whose marriage to an Army officer "was because her mother and brother never took the trouble to have a suitable home for her, and bring into it, the class of young men, whom after all they would have liked her to marry." The home of a woman's family was both the meeting and screening ground for her future marriage prospects. Upper middle class families also tried to provide their daughters with an education at a "proper" school where they could meet "appropriate" members of the other sex.

Middle class calling rituals, calling cards, flowers, and other small courtship gifts became increasingly elaborated, common, and expensive during the Victorian era (Ames 1978). The cost of courtship also increased due to more commercial entertainments such as "Taking a train or streetcar to a nearby town to see a show, ride a carousel, or dance in a cabaret" (Rothman 1984, p. 205). If men felt an increased economic burden in these rituals, women felt increasingly uneasy about the economic dependency that such gift-giving fostered (Lystra 1989, p. 9).

However, it was not until the emergence of dating during the 1920s that the cost and scale of interactions among unmarried men and women, especially those in college, made a quantum leap. Whereas courtship involves socializing with the intention of marriage (Rothman 1984, p. 23), dating is recreational and involves no commitment beyond the occasion of the date (Winch 1968). Factors affecting the development of dating include growing affluence, more recreational venues, longer periods of primarily coeducational schooling, employment of parents at increasing distances from the home (making it difficult for them to supervise activities of adolescent children), widespread adoption of the automobile, and increasing emphasis on consumption (Whyte 1990). Others cite the declining influence of religion, increased emancipation of women, the transition from a rural to an urban population, broadened mass media, declining emphasis on home, family, and marriage, and increased individualism and anonymity as causes of the development of recreational dating (Burgess and Wallin 1953). Bailey (1988) summarizes the effect of these changes succinctly: "Money -- Men's money -- became the basis of the dating system" (p. 13). With increased expenditures on dating by men, they began to regard dating as an investment in sexual pleasure: "...boys planned and paid for `a good time' and asked of their girls a bit of physical intimacy" (Modell 1983).

Another trend that started in the 1920s was detected by Waller (1937) a decade later and dubbed "the rating and dating complex." This involved a woman dating many desirable men for the prestige value of appearing popular:

> In order to have Class A rating they must belong to one of the better fraternities, be prominent in activities, have a copious supply of spending money, be well-dressed, 'smooth' in manners and appearance, have a 'good line,' dance well, and have access to an automobile (Waller 1937, p. 730).

Coeds were seen to lose prestige if they dated less desirable men, dated too few men, or accepted last minute dates. For their part, women also needed to dress, dance, and talk well, plus be physically attractive. Dress became such a restrictive social barrier that women even quit going to school because of insufficiently fashionable wardrobes (Modell 1983). While Waller's analysis has been criticized (Lasch 1977, Gordon 1981), it is generally accepted as describing a dating system that persisted in colleges from the 1920s into the 1940s. Within this system Waller (1938/1970) saw a danger of exploitation by both parties. Men were potentially able to use money and presents to obtain sexual "favors" from women, while women were potentially able to use their sexuality to "gold-dig" money and gifts from men. According to his "principle of least interest," the party least interested in perpetuating the relationship was best able to exploit the other. The result, according to Waller's analysis was for both men and women to feign true love while attempting to secretly remain indifferent.

After the World War II disruption of domestic dating, the marriage boom helped precipitate the baby boom which lasted into the 1960s in the U.S.. Bailey (1988) notes that by 1950, going steady had completely replaced the rating and dating complex. Nevertheless, Bailey (1968) finds that spending money on dates continued to escalate and advice books advocated judging a man's seriousness by the amount of money he was willing to spend on a date. Material generosity by males and sexual generosity by females continued to be taken as signs of love (Katz 1976). Scott (1965) insightfully detected the role of college sororities in screening to assure matches that were endogamous (in this case within ethnic group) and hypergamous (with a man of a higher social class). Sorority women who attempted to date someone "beneath them" were quickly brought into line through the social sanctions of their sorority sisters.

Sexual practices on dates during the 1940s continued to be conservative in comparison to the sexual revolution of the late 1960s and 1970s (Whyte 1990). Dating advice manuals continued to warn against excessive generosity in women's sexual giving:

> Offering your body to him in a bout of excessive necking will also cause his love for you to cool eventually, if not immediately. This kind favor which, like the others, is too personal and too expensive will make him feel so obligated that soon he will start squirming to free himself from the obligation you have imposed (Jackson 1955, p. 69).

Even after the most recent sexual revolution, "Miss Manners" continues to advise: "Another thing that has not changed is what a lady who accepts an expensive present from a gentleman is expected to do in return" (Martin 1982, p. 526). Paradoxically, increased pre-AIDS sexual freedom may have encouraged men to be more demanding about sexual favors, resulting in what is now recognized as date-rape (Bailey 1988).

It will be noted that traditional dating guidelines, including the man's obligation to pay for the date and the woman's obligation to withhold sex and "bestow" it only as a special "favor" to the man she loves, were born in an era when women were less likely to work and were economically disadvantaged compared to men (Harayda 1989). But while women are increasingly sharing the expenses of dating (Korman 1983), feminism does not appear to have been successful thus far in reducing sexual aggression by men (Korman and Leslie 1982). Nor, on the other hand, do contemporary ideological changes seem to have reduced the tendency for some women to be mercenary in extracting money and expensive gifts in exchange for sexual favors (Bushnell 1989, McRay 1990). The less extreme forms of contemporary giving of sex, money, and gifts in the context of dating have not been studied however. The present research is an effort to begin to understand such giving.

METHODS

Following preliminary depth interviews with five young adults, conducted by the second author and two other graduate students, 30 University of Utah undergraduates and 25 graduate students wrote essays on their dating histories and the role of gifts and money in their dating experiences. Fewer than 10 percent of those sampled had dated members of the same sex. Approximately one-third were married. Each student was assigned a random identification number in order to provide confidentiality. Students were given the option, after final grades were given, of having their data removed from the data base; none chose to this option. After these self-report journals were completed, the data were reviewed and a brief topical outline (like one given to guide the journals) was prepared. Based on this outline, the graduate students then conducted fifty in-depth interviews, which were recorded and transcribed along with the interviewer's reflective journals for each interview. Data from the 110 informants (58 M, 52 F) produced over 700 pages of text.

While the age distribution (18-38) of informants is wider than most college based samples, ethnicity is predominantly white with few blacks and Hispanics. Ten informants who were not raised in the United States were eliminated from the present analysis. The remaining informants roughly parallel the Salt Lake City community, which has only a 3% minority population and is nominally 48% Mormon. Notably, the Mormon (Latter Day Saints) religion encourages early dating and early marriage (Smith 1988). Such factors may limit the generalizability of these results since ethnic differences in dating practices seem evident (Porter 1979).

RESULTS

The Role of Money in Dating

As the opening quotations in this paper suggest, money is often a problematic issue in dating. While the current set of informants sense some change in who pays for a date and often make it a point to both pay some dating costs, the majority of dating expenses are still paid for by the man, and some women never pay. These findings parallel those of Rose and Frieze (1989). A common rule is that the one who asks for the date pays, but this was overwhelmingly the man. For others, all of whom are relatively impoverished women, there is some justification that the one with the most income should pay. There is also awareness of changes over the course of a dating relationship. For most, the man paid for earlier and more expensive dates, with later dates involving more sharing of expenses and less expensive activities (e.g., preparing a meal rather than dining out). A smaller group, composed entirely of men, believed in keeping dating expenses at a minimum until it could be determined whether the relationship seemed promising.

A number of women saw the issue of who pays in dating in terms of power and control.

> That's how I felt with Jed and I liked it. I liked having the control. You know when he's paying and asks where I want to go to eat I have to choose a place with the price in mind. But when I was the one paying it was great because I could go where I wanted and order anything I wanted. That's what I did with Jed. It was like I was leading him around by his nose [F 18].
>
> I felt like I was being bought but I also felt mean because he really wanted to show how he cared by buying me things. He was well settled in a career and doing well financially and I was a broke student. I somehow perceive money and control as one in the same [F 25].

Other women said that they had known men who felt threatened if they paid.

> Umm, when I got out of school I went straight to work as an office manager for an apartment complex and I was making pretty good money and he was going to school. So, I ended up paying for our dates and driving him around because he didn't have a car and I think he had a problem with that -- an ego problem. So, umm, we just kind of grew apart [F 29].

Men were not alone in feeling tension from the issue of who pays. Women often expressed feeling guilty or indebted from having money spent on them.

> I was never into expensive dates because I felt guilty because the guy would be paying and I also enjoyed going out to places where I could be more relaxed [F 32].

Others felt that having large amounts of money spent on them was tantamount to being purchased, although this was not always an unwelcome feeling.

> Traveling with someone I enjoy, who is romantic and obliging, and who is paying for all the fun, is a lethal combination for me. I definitely am not trying to say I can be bought -- but I am definitely saying one can score big points with me with the lure of travel [F 36].

A few women used the traditional man-pays dating system to their advantage.

> My friend...put it this way, 'If you're going to go out, you might as well have someone else pay for it" [F 35].

Other problems created by money in dating occur when that one partner is relatively free-spending while the other is parsimonious or when the two have very different ideas about appropriate spending. One function of dating appears to be to screen out such mismatches and bring together pairs who have similar values regarding money.

> ...money does "talk" in a dating situation. At least it communicates whether a person is willing to share or put some monetary investment into the relationship. It also shows what kind of value the person puts on people and relationships as opposed to him or herself and/or material things [F31].

Some men saw money as a key element in their ability to compete for dates.

> For those who can afford it, they may have an edge on those who can't in the case that a woman needs a man to support her. I think if you give gifts on regular first or second dates then you make it conspicuous that you have excess money to spend on her [M 25].

More males than females also believed that some women exploited men for their money.

> ...gift giving on a first date implies that the giver will spend money. This is not ideal for someone that doesn't want to be hurt later when he or she learns that the other was using him/her for money [M 25].

The source of many of the problems discussed is the polyvocal nature of money (Belk and Wallendorf 1990). The more cynical interpretations of being bought, investing in a date, and being used by a date are a subtext and involve the profane or utilitarian meanings of money. On the other hand the more sacred meanings of money allow a surface text that, genuinely or not, maintains that money expenditures are an index of caring in contemporary American dating.

> I felt unloved when my ex-fiance said he would not spend over $1500 for my wedding set. I felt he had put a low budget limit on his love for me. On the other hand, he bought me a car when I needed one, and that made me feel very important and loved [F 35].

Others recognize but reject the model that money equals caring.

> Money, money, money, what effect does money have on dating? In the ideal sense it shouldn't have much effect at all, but in reality it seems to have an effect. I think there are some people who think that how much is spent is a direct reflection of how much is felt [M 25].

The Role of Gifts in Dating

Gifts given to dates by this group of informants are quite varied, but traditional gifts are common, including flowers, candy, clothes (especially sweaters), clothing accessories, stuffed animals, and jewelry. Occasionally, recreational drugs, trips, dinners, and dating entertainments were considered to be gifts. There was general agreement among informants that the nature of gift-giving changed over the course of a relationship. As with dating expenses, a few men tried to minimize (or eliminate) gift-giving during the early part of a dating relationship.

> I never spent very much money on a girl in the early stages of dating. I didn't want to drain my savings account on a girl and have her dump me the next day. That happened to a friend of mine. He bought his girlfriend a television set. When he gave it to her she said, "I don't want to see you anymore, by the way thanks for the T.V."....Men have to be careful about spending money on women, you may spend hundreds of dollars on a girl in a couple of weeks and then BAM she decides she doesn't like you anymore. I view money and dating as an investment. You want to get marginal return on the dollar [M 25].

For most people, however, early gifts were intended to impress dates, to say "thank you" for going out with me, and to suggest the sincerity of the gift-giver's interests. It is men who are most apt to give a gift during a first date, but several women reported giving gifts soon after a first date -- both to reciprocate and to initiate gift-giving. As a relationship progresses, informants report that giving becomes more costly and gifts become more intimate. Eventually, in continuing relationships, the extravagance of material gift-giving tends to decline at the same time that non-material gifts of time, compliments, attention, and talents become more common. One woman [F 24] explained these changes as occurring in three stages:

> ...as a couple begins to date...mainly money is exchanged. Not that actual cash exchanges hands, but the gifts are basically little more than gifts of cash. For example, if a gift of flowers is given it is usually done at this stage in the dating in the context of I need to give you something. (Usually very little thought is put into the content of the gift). As the dating relationship develops I have noticed that the exchange resembles more of what I consider gift giving. By this I mean the gift giver puts more thought into the gift, the gifts are more personal, have more meaning etc.. The third stage of gift giving (over the course of dating) develops as the couple gets to know one another better. This is when the gifts are non-material in nature. These gifts include helping the other person

when one is stressed for time, lending a good
ear, etc.. I also believe that as the length of
time a couple is married increases this pattern
is further magnified. For example, I have
noticed that my parents and in-laws rarely
give each other Christmas or birthday
presents. My husband and I are at the stage
when we rarely give each other gifts that are
total surprises. The gifts are usually needed
or well expressed items [F30].

The timing of the early escalation in gift-giving is often seen as critical. A gift can be too expensive for the degree of commitment desired by the gift-recipient or too personal for the recipient's desired level of intimacy. As one informant put it, "He's got to understand where you are coming from. He can't be giving you rings when you are only interested in popcorn" [F 21]. Unless the escalation implied by an expensive gift is desired, it can lead to rejection:

If someone gave me a gift on the first,
second or third date I would not feel obligated
to continue dating. It would make me
consider this guy more closely. I would
examine his potential and attributes more
closely because he had impressed me and I
would be more interested in him because of
his concern with making a good impression.
Although, if I was already nervous about a
guy and didn't think that I liked him, a gift
would make me even more nervous and make
me really back off. I think I would give him
the cold shoulder [F 22].

It is clear that gifts are a form of communication (Belk 1979), and the messages they convey are multiple. As one woman [F 24] noted, "Gifts are used as an expression for they carry meaning. It is easier for me to express love through gifts than it is to do it verbally." One message conveyed by dating gifts is that the giver has confidence in the relationship and is committed to the partner receiving the gift. Gifts are sometimes seen as tests of the giver's sincerity:

I pointed out a necklace and said something
like, "This is the kind of thing I would like
to have someone give me." I was testing
him....it was almost as if I felt I had to
identify something as a test of his
commitment and ability to provide [F 38].
We went up to Snowbird Ski Lodge and he
presented me with the first piece of jewelry
he ever bought me: a gold bracelet. That
bracelet meant the world to me for two
reasons: 1-) It showed that he was just as
serious about me as I was about him and 2-)
It was a personal triumph over the loser he
dated before me because he told me he had
never given another girl jewelry in his life
(so maybe I was a little insecure about the
little tramp) [F 25].

One 34-year-old woman broke off a relationship with a "workaholic" who gave her expensive gifts (e.g., $600 in cash, matching snowmobiles, matching jetskis), but was unwilling to give her his time. He had his secretary buy gifts for her and didn't take time to use the motorized toys he bought for them. In this case, buying expensive gifts was not enough without a commitment of time as well.

Sometimes gifts act as a thank-you or an apology:

I remember getting roses from a friend of my
big brother's that I had was madly in love
with as a 14 year old. He had been trying to
get in my pants for years (I was now about
21). I finally succumbed and then flowers
were arriving left and right when I got back
to college [F 25].
A couple weeks before Valentine's Day we got
in a really bad fight. He hit me several times
on my shoulder. I wouldn't have anything to
do with him and I was very confused. I was
on the verge of ending the whole damn thing
when he cooked this dinner. He wasn't dumb,
he knew he was loosing me. So he cooked
this wonderful dinner and I was so amazed
that I figured he must care a lot [F 25].

Another woman [F 35] noted that she has received the most flowers after arguments and when she has tried to end a relationship.

Many informants mentioned that they looked at gifts as giving part of self. Because gifts are seen as a part of the giver's extended self (Belk 1988), they are found by some informants to involve high vulnerability and risk in self presentation:

It has sometimes been difficult to give gifts
because I see it as giving something of me to
the other person. If I don't know the person
well, or am not yet comfortable with them,
then I have a particularly difficult time giving
a gift....I am just a little insecure in myself
and it shows in my relationships [F 24].
...buying a gift and then having to give it to
someone is scary. Giving something as
serious as a sweater shows that you are ready
to make a commitment [F 24].

One man explained how this fear of failure in self presentation, coupled with the mnemonic functions of gifts affect his gift-giving strategies:

I'm not a big gift giver because giving gifts
is too dangerous.....I don't like giving
serious gifts. The last thing that you want to
do is to give a gift that ties you up. There
are two things to keep in mind before you
give a gift -- what happens when you break
up? You don't want to give a present that
your old girlfriend is going to want to throw
away because it reminds her of you. And you
definitely don't want to give her something

that you are going to want back if things don't work out. Food is the best gift that you can give or get. After all how threatening can a cake be? [M 22].

But besides giving "neutral" gifts that don't act as part of extended self, many people try to do just the opposite. To many people, non-material gifts best demonstrate that a part of self is being given:

> Non-material gifts are much more powerful as true expressions of love than that of material gifts. Non-material gifts are a part of you and not just a part of a department store [F 24].

Because gifts are seen as expressing the giver's personality, gifts that the recipient judges as showing poor taste may signal incompatibility:

> I remember a man giving me a blouse as a gift. He was an appropriate person for me to be dating, in fact he was really a very good catch, but I suspected I would likely not fall in love with him. The blouse, as he saw it, was very much "my style." It was the right color (red), but the fabric was polyester, which was a big "no no." I wore it on a date with him, received compliments on it from others, but felt uncomfortable all night. I kept it for a few months, maybe even a year, but never really liked it. Actually, because the gift was not really "right," it helped confirm my notion that this was not a guy for me [F 38].

Another woman [F 28] received an electric frying pan for Christmas from a man she was dating. "I got the feeling he had visions of me barefoot and pregnant." She quit dating him shortly after this gift.

Gifts also produce feelings of obligation that are sometimes unwelcome.

> I had been dating a man for a couple of months, and for Valentines Day he had a messenger deliver a black negligee from Victoria's Secret. I could see why he didn't have the nerve to bring it over himself! I knew it had cost a lot of money, and I had been planning to break off with him, so I felt like I had to wait a couple of weeks to do that after having received that gift [F35].
> There was a girl who I had met once on a blind date; a couple days after the date she brought me cookies, balloons, and a stuffed animal. I thought that it was a kind gesture, but I hardly knew the girl and felt very uncomfortable accepting the gift. I felt obligated to reciprocate the deed [M25].
> In the past, I have accepted gifts which I wish I had not. I always feel as though I owe that person at least another date or a few more weeks of my time. Gifts can put you in that awkward position of "now I owe you something in return" [F 28]

Besides feelings of obligation, there are also feelings of guilt sometimes stimulated by gifts.

> I remember feeling so guilty from receiving those roses from that guy after I broke up with him. I didn't want our relationship to have meaning, and I certainly didn't want to return the favor. Those next few days, while the flowers were alive, they were a constant reminder of the times we spent together, and I actually resented those flowers because of it [F 25].

For similar reasons, many gift recipients were reluctant to keep gifts from relationships that had ended. However, in other cases people, particularly women, kept gifts from prior suitors in order to remember them.

> I still have the all the gifts that I have received and the cards that go with them, including the corsages, which my mother made me save. I am a sentimental person and save everything that has meant something to me [F 24].

Belk (forthcoming) notes that keeping gifts from prior romances is a way of providing a sense of past. Such gifts remind us that people have professed to love us.

CONCLUSIONS

On the basis of this preliminary analysis of our data on college student dating in Salt Lake City, both expenditures of money and gift-giving appear to be key symbolic communication media. In pre-courtship and non-courtship dating, there is a careful attempt to invoke gifts and expenditures to express interest, gratitude, and sincerity, to exercise or attempt to exercise power, to apologize, and to please a date. Gift recipients react with discounting, resentment, guilt, disappointment, joy, and feelings of self-affirmation, depending upon the giver and the nature of the gift. Men and women often hold different opinions and reservations in these exchanges. The process of gift-giving and paying for dates is generally seen to become easier and less expensive as a relationship becomes more long-standing.

Dating is a key context for further research on gift-giving and consumption expenditures. Emotions and stakes in dating, mating, and courtship are high. Those involved in dating attempt to assess their own feelings as well as those of dating partners through a material system of ritual gifts. All of this is played out against the backdrop of cultural models of dating, love, sex, and images -- albeit sometimes conflicting -- of the role of gifts and money in these intense personal interactions. Even more than gift-giving in general, dating gift-giving seems a highly emotionally charged as well as significant area for further consumer research.

REFERENCES

Ames, Kenneth (1978), "Meaning in Artifacts: Hall Furnishings in Victorian America," *Journal of Interdisciplinary History*, 9 (Summer), 19-46.

Bailey, Beth L. (1988), *From Front Porch to Back Seat: Courtship in Twentieth Century America*, Baltimore: Johns Hopkins University Press.

Belk, Russell W. (1979), "Gift-Giving Behavior," *Research in Marketing*, Vol. 2, Jagdish N. Sheth, ed., Greenwich, CT: JAI Press, 95-126.

Belk, Russell W. (1988), "Possessions and the Extended Self," *Journal of Consumer Research*, 15 (September), 139-168.

Belk, Russell W. (forthcoming), "Possessions and the Sense of Past," *Highways and Buyways: Naturalistic Research from the Consumer Behavior Odyssey*, Russell W. Belk, ed., Provo, UT: Association for Consumer Research.

Belk, Russell W. and Melanie Wallendorf (1990), "The Sacred Meanings of Money," *Journal of Economic Psychology*, 11 (March) 35-67.

Belk, Russell W., Melanie Wallendorf, and John F. Sherry, Jr. (1989), "The Sacred and the Profane in Consumer Behavior: Theodicy on the Odyssey," *Journal of Consumer Research*, 16 (June), 1-38.

Burgess, Ernest W. and Paul Wallin (1953), *Engagement and Marriage*, Chicago: J. B. Lippincott.

Bushnell, Candace (1989), "Gold Diggers of 1989," *Mademoiselle*, (November), 176-177, 246-249.

Gordon, Michael (1981), "Was Waller Ever Right? The Rating and Dating Complex Reconsidered," *Journal of Marriage and the Family*, 43 (February), 67-76.

Harayda, Janice (1989), "The New Dating Game," *New Woman*, 19 (November), 55-57.

Jackson, Joyce (1955), *Guide to Dating*, New York: Prentice-Hall.

Katz, Judith M. (1976), "How Do You Love Me? Let Me Count the Ways (The Phenomenology of Being Loved)," *Sociological Inquiry*, 46 (1), 17-22.

Korman, Sheila K. (1983), "Nontraditional Dating Behavior: Date-Initiation and Date Expense-Sharing Among Feminists and Nonfeminists," *Family Relations*, 32 (October), 575-581.

Korman, Sheila K. and Gerald R. Leslie (1982), "The Relationship of Feminist Ideology and Date Expense Sharing to Perceptions of Sexual Aggression in Dating," *Journal of Sex Research*, 18 (May), 114-129.

Lasch, Christopher (1977), *Haven in a Heartless World: The Family Besieged*, New York: Basic Books.

Lystra, Karen (1989), *Searching the Heart: Women, Men, and Romantic Love in Nineteenth-Century America*, New York: Oxford University Press.

McRay, Leslie (1990), *Kept Women: Confessions From a Life of Luxury*, New York: William Morrow.

Martin, Judith (1982), *Miss Manners' Guide to Excruciatingly Correct Behavior*, New York: Atheneum.

Modell, John (1983), "Dating Becomes the Way of American Youth," *Essays on the Family and Historical Change*, David Levine, Page Moch, Louise A. Tilly, John Modell, and Elizabeth Peck, eds., College Station, TX: Texas A & M University Press, 91-126.

Porter, John R. (1979), *Dating Habits of Young Black Americans*, Dubuque, IA: Kendall/Hunt.

Rose, Suzanna and Irene H. Frieze (1989), "Young Singles' Scripts for a First Date," *Gender and Society*, 3 (June), 358-368.

Rothman, Ellen K. (1984), *Hands and Hearts: ; A History of Courtship in America*, Cambridge, MA: Harvard University Press.

Scott, John F. (1965), "Sororities and the Husband Game," *Trans-action*, 2 (September/October), 10-14.

Smith, James E. (1985), "A Familistic Religion in a Modern Society," *Contemporary Marriage: Comparative Perspectives on a Changing Institution*, Kingsley Davis, ed., New York: Russell Sage Foundation, 273-298.

Waller, Willard W. (1937), "The Rating and Dating Complex," *American Sociological Review*, 2 (October), 727-734.

Waller, Willard W. (1938/1970), "Bargaining and Exploitative Attitudes," *Willard W. Waller, On the Family, Education, and War: Selected Writings*, Willard Goode, Frank Furstenberg, and L. Mitchell, eds., Chicago: University of Chicago Press, 181-192.

Winch, Robert F. (1968), "The Functions of Dating in Middle-Class America," *Selected Studies in Marriage and the Family*, 3rd edition, Robert F. Winch and Louis W. Goodman, eds., New York: Holt, Rinehart and Winston, 505-507.

Whyte, Margaret K. (1990), *Dating, Mating, and Marriage*, New York: Aldine de Gruyter.

When the Thought Counts: Friendship, Love, Gift Exchanges and Gift Returns

Margaret Rucker, University of California, Davis
L. Leckliter, University of California, Davis
S. Kivel, University of California, Davis
M. Dinkel, University of California, Davis
T. Freitas, University of California, Davis
M. Wynes, University of California, Davis
H. Prato, University of California, Davis

ABSTRACT

The present study investigated gift exchange behavior of opposite-sex and same-sex pairs. Findings indicated that in only the condition of males estimating female economic contributions did underestimation occur. In all other conditions, contributions of partners were overestimated. Furthermore, males were more likely to use price as a basis for judging equity of the exchange whereas females were more prone to consider whether both partners liked the gifts. A relatively high rate of return for clothing gifts was noted and economic and social reasons for this phenomenon were proposed.

INTRODUCTION

As a universal behavior with important economic and social functions, the gift giving process has been examined by scholars from a variety of perspectives. The significance of gift exchanges in romantic relationships has been suggested by Baxter (1987) in a study of the symbols of relationship identity. In comparing romantic and friendship relationships, it was found that physical object symbols were especially important for the former while behavioral action and event/time symbols were more prominent in the latter. Frequently, the physical objects were gifts that one partner had given to the other.

Although the folk definition of gift implies a voluntary contribution with no expectation of compensation, scholars from Mauss (1925/1967) on have acknowledged the reciprocal nature of gift exchanges. Pin and Turndorf (1985) talked about the "dynamism of reciprocity" being true of all gifts. To distinguish between economic exchange and gift exchange, they contended that economic exchange generally does not forge a personal link between the two parties and consists of exchanging two objects of equivalent value. On the other hand, gift exchanges affect social relations and the recipient can decide how to repay. However, to maintain a friendly social relationship, repayment must be commensurate with the gift.

Belk (1979) observed that while it is normally important to have a balanced exchange, what is seen as "adequate" repayment may vary with the recipient's resources. Moschetti (1979) analyzed situations in which classes of people receive more than they give and concluded that receiving more than is given is associated with social dependency. The asymmetric exchange is a symbolic reminder of the agentive power difference. Cheal (1986, p. 434) specifically points to gender positions as one of the social statuses that affect symmetry of the exchange. He found that even when economic factors were controlled, sex was still related to exchange values. He described the unequal exchanges as "ritual enactments of the support/dependence relationships that are conventionally assumed to exist between men and women in general...." In an expansion of that theme, Bailey (1988) noted the importance of public gifts in symbolizing what the man could afford and what the woman was worth.

A major thesis in an article by Schieffelin (1980) is that reciprocity itself is a process for making social distinctions and defining identities. He suggests that understanding of different types of exchanges could benefit from determining how the norm of reciprocity is related to other patterns of cultural thought. Prior to that, however, one must determine what attributes of the exchange are considered important in judging reciprocity and how partners might vary in their perceptions of these attributes. Attributes that have been suggested in the literature include cost, value, number and variety of items (Belk, 1979; Caplow, 1984; Moschetti, 1979).

The present study was designed to extend previous work (Rucker et al., 1989) on perceptions of cost and equity in exchange situations by collecting data on same-sex pairs as well as opposite-sex pairs. It was also designed to investigate attributes other than price that could affect perception of equity, as well as factors affecting gift return decisions.

METHOD

Subjects were obtained by placing advertisements in a university newspaper and on a campus bulletin board. Volunteers had to have exchanged gifts with each other within the previous six months and both partners had to agree to be interviewed separately. A small reward was offered for participation. A total of sixty couples completed the interview.

Items in the interview included questions about overall evaluation of equity in the exchange, cost and estimated price of the gifts, and gift return attitudes and practices. The interviews were taped and transcribed for later analysis.

RESULTS

Data from the male/female couples on costs and estimated prices of their gifts were similar to

TABLE 1
MALE/FEMALE COUPLES' ESTIMATES OF COSTS OF GIFTS RELATIVE TO GIVERS' REPORTS

	Sex of Respondent	
	Female	Male
Estimate		
Over/Equal	25 (64%)	15 (41%)
Under	14 (36%)	22 (59%)

$X^2 = 4.23$, df = 1, $p < .05$

TABLE 2
ALL COUPLES' ESTIMATES OF COSTS OF GIFTS RELATIVE TO GIVERS' REPORTS

	Sex of Respondent and Pair			
	Female/Same	Male/Same	Female/Opposite	Male/Opposite
Estimate				
Over/Equal	40 (64%)	10 (63%)	25 (64%)	15 (41%)
Under	22 (35%)	6 (38%)	14 (36%)	22 (59%)

findings of the 1989 Rucker et al. study and so were pooled for the first analysis. As shown in Table 1, females were more prone to overestimate the monetary contributions of their partners whereas males tended to underestimate. A comparison of same-sex couples with opposite-sex couples (Table 2) indicated that underestimation characterized only males' evaluations of gifts from females. The combination of results failed to support the proposition that males were underestimating female contributions because they were infrequent shoppers and so would underestimate prices of products in general. Rather it seems to suggest that perceptions of contributions are being adjusted to fit sex status stereotypes.

Work by Burns and Hopper (1986) has shown that estimates of influence can be affected by the resources contributed to a dyad. Specifically, they found that husbands underestimated influence of wives when resource contributions such as income were low. To see if a similar effect could be depressing males' estimates of females' gift-giving contributions, average price paid was computed for males and females in same-sex and opposite-sex dyads. The results are presented in Table 3. These results suggest that lower overall contribution of females is not a factor in influencing underestimation by males; females actually paid somewhat more on the average than their male counterparts. Males' contributions were also lower when same-sex pairs were compared. In addition, when opposite-sex pairs in which the male paid more were compared with opposite-sex pairs in which the male paid less, it was found that males were slightly more likely to underestimate when the female paid *more* for the gift than they did.

The next question concerned attributes used by partners in assessing the equity of an exchange. These data are shown in Table 4. Content analysis of all answers to the equity question indicated that price was most often considered, closely followed by whether the partners liked their respective gifts. In reviewing the less frequently reported attributes, it should be noted for "surprise" that the comments were generally positive and reflected a sense of not expecting anything and therefore being pleasantly surprised. On the other hand, it was also used to explain the inequity that resulted when one person was so caught by surprise that he/she had little or nothing to offer in return. With respect to "permanence," durable goods seemed to be valued more highly than nondurables for two reasons. As noted by Camerer (1988), gifts can serve as signals of intentions of future investment in the relationship. Nondurables were viewed as a lack of commitment, and therefore as a negative cue by some respondents. Also when one partner received a durable gift and the other a nondurable, there was some resentment over continued enjoyment by only one person.

When only the first response concerning attributes used to judge equity was compared for

TABLE 3
AVERAGE AMOUNT SPENT ON THE EXCHANGE

Male/Male	Female/Female	Male/Female	Female/Male
$10.17	$24.82	$81.76	$85.02

TABLE 4
ATTRIBUTES USED TO EVALUATE EQUITY OF THE GIFT EXCHANGE - ALL RESPONSES

Attributes	N
Price	50
Liking	45
Thought/Effort	19
Utility	8
Surprise	8
Number/Type	6
Appropriateness	5
Permanence	2

TABLE 5
USE OF PRICE AND LIKING IN EVALUATING EQUITY BY SEX-FIRST RESPONSE

	Sex of Respondent				
	Male		Female		
Attributes	N	% of Total	N	% of Total	Z
Price	11	31%	14	17%	1.70
Liking	7	19%	30	36%	1.84

males and females, it appeared that males placed more emphasis on price whereas females were more concerned with how much both partners liked their gifts (Table 5). The test for difference between two proportions resulted in Z scores that only approached significance, but the findings are consistent with communications research that indicates women talk more about relationship problems whereas men talk more about money (Haas and Sherman, 1982). They are also consistent with the vast body of related work on sex-role standards and gender-related traits which identifies nurturent activities as feminine and business skills as masculine (e.g., Broverman et al., 1972; Spence, 1984).

A comparison of couples' opinions about the equity of their exchanges is presented in Table 6. As might be expected from the previous findings on prices actually paid and price estimates, opposite-sex couples were least likely to have both partners report that the exchange was equitable.

In response to questioning about gift returns, only five (4%) of the respondents reported that they had returned the gifts they were describing in the interview whereas 91 (76%) stated that they had returned other gifts on at least one other occasion. The 91 respondents who had engaged in gift return behavior were then asked to describe their most recent return experience.

For both sets of data on gift returns, clothing was the type of item mentioned most often. Finding clothing to be the type of product most often returned was not surprising in light of previous work listing clothing as one of the most frequently given gifts, at 25% to 35% of total gifts (Belk, 1979; Caplow, 1982). However the values for clothing as a percentage of returns far exceeded the values for clothing as a percentage of gifts. For the interview gift, clothing accounted for 3 of the 5 returns (60%) and, for other gifts, 77 of the 91 returns (85%). Respondents' explanations of return actions suggested that economic and social factors prompted more willingness to return clothing than other

TABLE 6
COUPLES' OPINIONS ABOUT EQUITY OF THEIR EXCHANGE

	Female/Female	Male/Male	Male/Female
Yes/Yes	25 (83%)	6 (75%)	10 (53%)
No/No	1 (3%)	2 (25%)	5 (26%)
Yes/No	4 (13%)	--	4 (21%)

products. A bad fit and the wrong color were viewed as socially acceptable reasons for a clothing return. Indicating that one just did not like a gift, as would be necessary for many other types of products, was often noted as overly rude or hurtful. In economic terms, clothing was cited as generally being of sufficient value to make the gain from a return worth the effort expended in making that transaction.

CONCLUSIONS

This study has implications for equity and gender theory by showing evidence of both the affective or romantic and marketing model of value and equity in the gift exchange process. The existence of two competing perspectives becomes problematic when models clash in male/female relationships, since males are more prone to take the marketplace view and underestimate the economic contributions of their female partners. The study also has implications for the gift market itself by suggesting the range and order of attributes that can affect consumers' gift selection decisions. In addition, the information on product returns can be useful in anticipating changes in inventory following holiday seasons.

REFERENCES

Bailey, B. L. (1988), *From Front Porch to Back Seat*, Baltimore, MD: Johns Hopkins.

Baxter, L. A. (1987), "Symbols of Relationship Identity in Relationship Cultures," *Journal of Social and Personal Relationships*, 4, 261-280.

Belk, R. W. (1979), "Gift-giving Behavior," *Research in Marketing*, 2, 95-126.

Broverman, I. K., S. R. Vogel, D. M. Broverman, F. E. Clarkson and P. S. Rosenkrantz. (1974), "Sex-Role Stereotypes: A Current Appraisal," *Journal of Social Issues*, 28(2), 59-78.

Burns, A. C. and J. A. Hopper. (1986), "An Analysis of the Presence, Stability, and Antecedents of Husband and Wife Purchase Decision Making Influence Assessment Agreement and Disagreement," in R. L. Lutz, ed., *Advances in Consumer Research*, Vol. XIII, Provo, UT: Association for Consumer Research, 175-180.

Camerer, C. (1988), "Gifts as Economic Signals and Social Symbols," *American Journal of Sociology*, 94, 180-214.

Caplow, T. (1982), "Christmas Gifts and Kin Networks," *American Sociological Review*, 47, 383-392.

Caplow, T. (1984), "Rule Enforcement without Visible Means: Christmas Gift Giving in Middletown," *American Journal of Sociology*, 89, 1306-1323.

Cheal, D. J. (1986), "The Social Dimensions of Gift Behaviour," *Journal of Social and Personal Relationships*, 3, 423-439.

Haas, A. and M. A. Sherman. (1982). Reported Topics of Conversation Among Same-Sex Adults. *Communication Quarterly*, 30(4), 332-342.

Mauss, M. (1967). *The Gift: Forms and Functions of Exchange in Archaic Societies* (I. Cunnison, Trans.), New York: W. W. Norton. (Original work published 1925).

Moschetti, G. J. (1979). The Christmas potlatch: A refinement on the sociological interpretation of gift exchange. *Sociological Focus*, 12, 1-7.

Pin, E. J. and J. Turndorf (1985). *The Pleasure of Your Company: A Socio-Psychological Analysis of Modern Sociability*, New York: Praeger.

Rucker, M., T. Freitas, J. Herron, H. Prato, L. Boynton and B. Hackett. (1989), Measuring Equity in Exchange Situations, in C. N. Nelson, ed., *ACPTC Proceedings*, Monument, CO: Association of College Professors of Textiles and Clothing, Inc., 74.

Schieffelin, E. L. (1980), "Reciprocity and the Construction of Reality," *Man*, 15, 502-517.

Spence, J. T. (1984), "Masculinity, Femininity and Gender-Related Traits: A Conceptual Analysis and Critique of Current Research," *Progress in Experimental Personality Research*, 13, 1-97.

Two Views of Consumption in Mating and Dating

Aaron Bernard, Northwestern University
Mara B. Adelman, Northwestern University
Jonathan E. Schroeder, University of Rhode Island

Endless types of markets are available for analysis, yet few are as consequential as those that facilitate finding a lifelong partner. The process by which single men and women meet and agree to marry can readily be seen as a market phenomenon in which both material and psychological benefits are exchanged in the process of forming and formalizing ongoing relationships. This social process is frequently referred to as the "marriage market."

Due to the important role that exchange plays in the courtship process, many academics from disciplines traditionally concerned with the world of commerce have turned their attention to dating and mate selection. For example, Becker (1973, 1974, 1976, 1981), Freidan (1974), and Parsons (1980) have applied economic models to these social relationships. As the disciplines of marketing and consumer behavior have come to be understood as the study of exchange (Bagozzi, 1975) rather than the study of a particular business function, Kotler and Levy (1969) coined the term *personal marketing* and Levy and Zaltman (1975, p. xix) used the phrase *intimate marketing* to refer to certain aspects of romantic relationships. More recently, Hirschman (1987) and Bernard and Adelman (1990) have looked at formal mate-selection networks (i.e., dating services, singles ads, etc.) to show how courtship can be studied as a special case of marketing and/or consumer behavior. Indeed, because consumer researchers combine a theoretical interest in exchange per se with a solid understanding of the commercial marketplace, they are particularly well suited to perform studies involving formal mate-selection services.

As the number of singles reached record proportions (Bennet 1989, Cutler 1989, Fuchs 1988, and Masnick and Bane 1980), the development of products and services targeting this group became a major strategy for the business community as well as nonprofit service providers. A somewhat surprising outgrowth of this larger trend was the rapid increase in the number of formal methods for singles to meet each other. For example Adelman and Bernard (1990) found that

> in the ten years between 1978 and 1988, the number of social introduction services listed in the Chicago area yellow pages increased from 5 to 23. Over the same period, singles ads, once the exclusive domain of off-beat publications, have become an established feature in most major newspapers and many magazines such an the *New York Review of Books*. Movies, like *Crossing Delancy* and *Sea of love*, along with television shows like *Thirty Something*, all incorporate these new introduction techniques into their story lines. Talk shows such as *Oprah Winfrey* and *Phil Danahue*, as well as news shows like *20/20* (Pfifferling 1989), seem to have an endless fascination with these services. Even the *Wall Street Journal* (Freedman 1989) devoted front page coverage to a renowned matchmaker. The singles business is booming (Andrews 1988, Bennet 1989, Blodgett 1986, Brand 1988, and Mullan 1984) and represents a significant change in the way many Americans go about finding a mate. (p.1)

These events have not been overlooked by academic researchers (see Adelman and Bernard 1990, for review). In some cases, researchers have used these services as a convenient vehicle to investigate basic questions about mate selection (Curran 1972, 1973a, 1973b, Curran and Lippold 1975, Woll and Cozby 1987, and Woll and Young 1989), whereas other researchers have sought a better understanding of this phenomenon in its own right (Adelman 1987, Bolig, Stein, and McKenry 1984, Cameron, Oskamp and Williams 1977, Godwin 1973, Jedlicka 1981, and Woll 1986).

This paper presents two examples of research involving formal social intermediaries, one from each of these two categories. Schroeder's work extends basic questions about mate selection, as he uses singles ads to investigate the ability of evolutionary theory to explain the role of consumption in human courtship. A summary of Schroeder's research is presented immediately below in the section labeled "Consumer Activities in Romantic Self-Presentation". Bernard and Adelman's work falls into the second category and furthers understanding of these services themselves. Although this research deals specifically with the clients of a matchmaking service, the findings have wider implications for general theories regarding the role of self-image in product or service utilization. This research is presented in the second major section entitled, "An Empirical Test of Client Utilization Models for Social Introduction Services".

CONSUMER ACTIVITIES IN ROMANTIC SELF-PRESENTATION

The quest for a romantic partner can require an enormous investment in time and goods. The market for products designed to enhance one's attractiveness, such as personal care items, is substantial. And, of course, advertising utilizes sexual attractiveness to promote products. The use of products and consumer activities can play an important role in how people define, present, and symbolize themselves to others, which is a critical step in the dating and mating process. One dating arena where the link between consumer activities and romantic self-presentation is explicit is personal advertisements, designed to attract responses from readers. This study surveyed a sample of personal ad writers to examine the role that consumer activities play in presenting the self and attracting a potential mate.

Research on mate selection involves a myriad of theoretical approaches, ranging from genetic theories to Jungian psychology. This study draws on three diverse, yet complementary research areas: self-presentation; possessions as symbols; and an evolutionary approach to mate selection and parental investment. The evolutionary framework offers the chance to understand consumer behavior as an extension of behavior patterns established long before the age of consumer goods.

Mate selection is central to the evolutionary drive to maximize one's genetic representation in the gene pool. Thus, the selection of a mate ought to be governed, at one level, by evolutionary mechanisms. This does not imply, however, that individuals are *consciously* attempting to maximize their ability to produce viable offspring. Furthermore, culture has reinforced male and female evolutionary preferences through institutions such as marriage and more recently the media. Therefore an evolutionary approach does not tell the whole story. Rather it offers one level of analysis. Barkow (1980) suggests that social (and presumably consumer) behavior can be explained by at least four different levels of analysis: physiological, individual differences, culture, and evolution (see also Tooby and Cosmides, 1989). These levels should be complementary, but they are not necessarily derivable from each other. Certainly when dealing with a complex behavior, such as mating, multiple approaches are called for.

Trivers (1972) introduced a theory of parental investment to account for sex differences in mating behavior. Briefly, the theory states that females, who invest greater time, energy, and resources in any given pregnancy than their male partner, will therefore be highly discriminating when selecting a mate. This is because once a female has made a choice of a male partner and becomes pregnant, she is locked into that choice for an extended period of time. If shortly after becoming pregnant, a more desirable male becomes available to her, it's too late for her to change her mind. Therefore, females have an intrinsic motivation to be highly selective in the choice of a partner.

Males, on the other hand, must display the potential to be a good partner, in order to convince females to take the risks involved in making these investments. While females will be concerned with the biological fitness of their mate, this concern will focus on the males' genetic fitness and will only consider males' phenotypic fitness to the degree that it influences the males' ability to contribute resources to the relationship throughout the child-rearing period. Males, on the other hand, will focus more on the phenotypic health of their partner due to the physical demands of pregnancy and childbirth. They will also display a strong preference for youth so as to maximize the fecundity of the relationship. In this way, the current sex differences in mate selection can be understood by the increased reproductive success that they gave to past generations.

In the modern world of mate selection, consumer goods and activities provide clues to potential mates' desirability. Thus, consumption may serve as a signal that the consumer possesses evolutionarily adaptive characteristics. Personal ads provide an excellent data source to test evolutionary theories as applied to consumer behavior, because these ads frequently mention consumer goods and activities in connection with describing the self or the desired other.

This study extends earlier work on singles ads (Baize and Schroeder 1989, Deaux and Hanna 1984, Harrison and Saeed 1977, Hirschman 1987, Koestner and Wheeler 1988) by interpreting results in terms of evolutionary significance. As reasoned above, evolutionary theory predicts that males will be more successful in attracting potential mates when displaying symbols of economic fitness, and females will be more successful when mentioning or displaying symbols of physical fitness. Thus, a given strategy will have a different level of success depending on the sex of the ad writer.

Methodology

To investigate this hypothesis, 240 heterosexual romantic ads were randomly selected from two geographically distinct publications that carry a substantial number of personal ads for the purposes of arranging and attempting romantic relationships. Ads were eliminated from this study if they mentioned relationships other than exclusively heterosexual. To standardize the length of exposure to the ad audience, only ads that appeared for the first time were used. One hundred and sixty-one ads written by men and 142 ads written by women met the criteria; 120 of each sex were then randomly selected for inclusion in the sample. A questionnaire on university letterhead was then mailed to all potential subjects, using their anonymous post office box supplied in the ad.

Responses from 92 heterosexual romantic advertisers to several individual difference measures and the number and quality of answers received were analyzed to assess the relationship between individual characteristics and the success of the personal ads. Three domains were utilized: demographic information gained from the ad writer; scores on individual difference measures; and extensive codings of the content of the ad itself. The entire sample of ads was content analyzed in two phases. First, the content categories of prior research on personal ads was replicated. The second phase focused on the terms the ad writer used to describe him or herself and the terms used to describe the person sought. The terms used in each ad were rated for their inclusion into a coding framework that encompassed attractiveness, personality items, and categories of what the ad writer desired and offered. Two independent

TABLE 1
Means

	Women	Men	t
Demographics			
Income	$24 K	$35 K	-3.480***
Education (years)	17.49	17.79	-0.053
Age	37.25	36.54	0.037
Ad production/response			
Responses	17.58	11.68	2.14*
Desirable responses	5.72	3.73	2.23*
Prior ads	1.06	2.59	-2.19*
Writing assistance	0.43	0.20	2.45*
Number of words	48.70	41.00	1.33

n = 92   *p < .05, ***p < .001

undergraduate research assistants, blind to the study's hypothesis, were trained in the coding procedure using other ads not in the study. They then each coded a portion of all 240 ads that were sent materials. For the 36 ads that both assistants coded, inter-coder agreement averaged 85 percent; discrepancies were resolved by the authors. The number of responses subjects received serves as a criterion variable for success in attracting potential mates.

Results

Results show a significant negative relationship between age of women and number of responses; older men received more responses, as did more educated and higher income males (see table 1). This supports the general hypothesis derived from evolutionary theory that men and women will have differing emphases in evaluating potential mates. The content codes provide insight into the role that consumption activities play in mate selection (see table 2). Ads that mentioned an expensive cultural activity, such as European vacations, were significantly correlated with number of responses for men, but not for women. This is interpreted as a symbol of financial security. Ads that mentioned active sports, such as skiing, were positively correlated with response rate for women, but not for men, underscoring male preference for physically active and attractive mates.

Discussion

These cultural activities may be understood through their relationship to the evolutionary framework suggested by Trivers (1972) and Buss (1987), in which the sexes are expected to differ in their strategies for attracting mates. Kenrick and Trost (1989) suggested that the mate-selection process that underlies writing a personal ad can be understood in its evolutionary context for fitness and reproductive potential. According to this approach, males are expected to value physical qualities that serve as cues to reproductive capacity in women. Women, on the other hand, attempt to attract a stable, providing mate. Women show a distinct preference for men who are older, more educated, interested in expensive cultural activities, and who are more masculine. All of the characteristics are related to status and access to material resources. Conversely, men preferred younger, active women, qualities that can be considered examples of physical resources.

The evolutionary approach can be considered one level of analysis of a complex activity. Clearly, personal advertising is a social phenomenon that involves marketing oneself and responding (consuming) to the advertisements. Personal ads provide an excellent forum to study the marketing or presentation of the self in a meaningful, unobtrusive context. By applying evolutionary theory to these investigations, it is possible to integrate some aspects of consumer behavior into widely held biological theories of mate selection.

AN EMPIRICAL TEST OF CLIENT UTILIZATION MODELS FOR SOCIAL INTRODUCTION SERVICES

"Lonely and desperate"
(description of people who use dating services, *Wall Street Journal*, 1989)

Despite the stigma associated with using introductory services, the past decade has seen a meteoritic rise in the number of introductory services for mate-seeking (Adelman and Bernard 1990). The emergence and viability of these innovative channels as conduits for romance calls for an investigation of these intermediaries and a questioning of negative stereotypes (i.e., lonely and desperate) associated with client utilization.

Research

In this research users of one of these matchmaking services are contrasted (N=98) with a closely matched comparison group (N=57). This data was used to test two models of client utilization for these services to understand the role the services

TABLE 2
Correlations of ad content ratings with number of responses to ad

	Total	Women	Men
Offered by ad writer			
Attractive-general	.15	.35*	.24*
Attractive-sexual	.28*	-.16	.07
Marriage	.05	.20	.10
Culture - expensive	-.15	.44**	.10
Culture - inexpensive	-.07	-.08	.04
Sports - expensive	.31*	.18	-.06
Sports - inexpensive	.23	.26+	.18+
Sought by ad writer			
Attractive - general	.24+	.53***	.34***
Attractive - sexual	-.03	-.23	-.12

male n = 41, female n = 51
+p < .10, *p < .05, **p < .01, ***p < .001

play in changing social norms. The two models were,

A. The Social Skills Deficiency Model.

The deficiency model is based on the popular stigma associated with clients of these services. It holds that people join dating services because they have social, psychological, and behavioral deficiencies that prevent them from establishing romantic relationships through conventional channels.

B. The High Selectivity Model.

The selectivity model is the rival to the deficiency hypothesis and is based on the data gathered in exploratory interviews. These interviews revealed that the deficiency stereotype did not accurately reflect the interview responses. Rather, a common thread in comments by members of the matchmaking service was that they were socially active and people of worth, but for various reasons they were simply unable to meet the person they were looking for and sought a service that would provide a selective and efficient mode for meeting prospective mates. A result is the hypothesis that they may have high standards in a potential mate and this partly accounted for their inability to meet an acceptable partner and thus their involvement in an introductory service. This notion is formally presented by the hypotheses that users of introductory services are more likely to be "selective" in regards to their criteria for a mate, (i.e., economic, physical, and personhood attributes) than non-users of these services.

Methodology

All respondents in this study were associated with a large Jewish agency that sponsored a wide variety of programming and activities for singles. The agency is located in an upscale neighborhood community center in a major metropolitan area. The targeted audience for this service is professional, well-educated Jewish singles ranging from their mid-twenties to mid-forties who are looking for lifelong partners.

The target group (henceforth referred to as "members") was drawn from the current and former clients of a non-profit, matchmaking service sponsored by this agency. A comparable group of non-users (herein referred to as "comparison group") was drawn from the single members of the larger Jewish community organization that sponsors the introductory service. Both groups of respondents were sent extensive questionnaires covering the experience of single life and including psychological scales measuring loneliness, ability to elicit self-disclosure from others, shyness, satisfaction with the friendship network, and self-esteem. The questionnaires also included items pertaining to how selective the respondent was in his or her choice of a spouse.

Results

The deficiency model represents the popular stereotype of matchmaking clients as more "deficient" in social and psychological characteristics than non-users of these services. This stereotype was strongly disconfirmed by the data. In fact, members were found to be less shy than the comparison group (p< .10), and they were found to have higher self-esteem than the comparison group (p< .01).

The investigation of possible gender differences revealed that the differences (or lack of differences) between the members and the comparison group were not dependent on the gender of respondents. No significant interaction effects between gender and group membership were found.

The rival hypothesis points to the greater selectivity of members in regards to their criteria for a mate (i.e., economic, physical, and personhood attributes) than non-users of these services. This hypothesis was supported by findings that members were more selective regarding physical attractiveness (p<.10) and more selective regarding several desirable personality characteristics (p<.01). Once again, the investigation of possible gender differences revealed that these findings were not dependent on the gender of respondents. No significant interaction effects between gender and group membership were found.

Discussion

Because the social conditions that gave rise to these services show no signs of abating, it is possible that utilization of these social channels could expand over the coming years. If this is the case, these conduits to romance represent a major change in the social ethos that has governed dating and courtship since the 1920s. To better grasp this trend and the way service intermediaries are permeating social relations and culture, requires a better understanding of the people who are experimenting with these innovative social channels. Furthermore, the stigma associated with these channels may in itself be detrimental to the development of romantic relationships on the part of their members. Apart from these services being perceived as anti-romantic, clients may make unfounded negative attributions toward the other clients they meet through these services because they may see themselves as the rare exception to the loser stereotype. In stripping away the stigma, one sees that introductory services are not the last resort of social rejects, but rather a professional service for a self assured and *very demanding* clientele.

Conclusion

In the introduction this paper discussed the two basic approaches that research involving formal mate-selection networks have taken. The first used these networks to investigate general theoretical concerns, and the second sought to illuminate the nature of the networks themselves. While this distinction is useful, it is clear from the examples summarized here that there is broad overlap between these two categories. Schroeder's work, while ostensibly only using singles ads as a means to test evolutionary theory, can still provide insight into the functioning of singles ads themselves. Likewise, the work of Bernard and Adelman goes beyond a descriptive study of a matchmaker's clientele and offers new data on the role of self-image in product and service utilization. Future work along these lines is needed, both to increase understanding of human mate selection in general and in explaining emerging social and cultural institutions.

REFERENCES

Adelman, M. (1987), "Love's Urban Agent: Social Support and the Matchmaker," paper to Iowa Conference on Personal Relationships, University of Iowa, May-June.

Adelman, M. and A. Bernard (1990), *Marriage Market Intermediaries: A Critical Appraisal*, working paper, Department of Communications, Northwestern University, Evanston, IL.

Andrews, E. L. (1988), "The King Kong of Video Dating," *Venture*, 10(2), 24-25.

Bagozzi, R. P. (1975), "Marketing as Exchange," *Journal of Marketing*, 39, 32-39.

Bailey, R. C. and D. G. Garrou (1983), "Dating Availability and Religious Involvement as Influences on Interpersonal Attraction," *The Journal of Psychology*, 113, 95-100.

Baize, H. R., & J. E., Schroeder (1989). "Prototypes in personal ads: An application of the big five personality dimensions," Paper presented at the annual meeting of the American Psychological Association, New Orleans, LA, August.

Barkow, Jerome H. (1980), "Sociobiology: Is this the new theory of human nature?" In Ashley Montagu (Ed.) *Sociobiology Examined* (pp. 171-197). Oxford: Oxford University Press.

Becker, G. S. (1973), "A Theory of Marriage: Part I," *Journal of Political Economy*, 82, 813-846.

Becker, G. S. (1974), "A Theory of Marriage: Part II," *Journal of Political Economy*, 82, 11-27.

Becker, G. S. (1976), *The Economic Approach to Human Behavior*, Chicago IL: The University of Chicago Press.

Becker, G. S. (1981), *A Treatise on the Family*, Cambridge: Harvard University Press.

Bennet, J. (1989), "The Data Game," *The New Republic*, Feb. 13, 20-22.

Bernard, A. and M. Adelman (1990), "Market Metaphors for Meeting Mates," in *Advances in Consumer Research*, 17, 78.

Blodgett, N. (1986), "The Dating Game: Regulating the Video Matchmakers," *ABA Journal*, September 1, 25.

Bolig R., P. J. Stein, and P. McKenry (1984), "The Self-Advertisement Approach to Dating: Male-Female Differences," *Family Relations*, 33, 587-592.

Brand, D. (1988), "Make Me a Perfect Match," *Time*, Nov. 28,14-15.

Buss, David M. (1987), "Sex Differences in Human Mate Selection Criteria: An Evolutionary Perspective." In C. Crawford, M. Smith, and D. Krebs (eds.), *Sociobiology and Psychology: Ideas, Issues, and Applications*. (p. 335-351). Hillsdale, NJ: Erlbaum.

Cameron, Catherine, Oskamp, Stuart, & Sparks, William (1977), "Courtship American Style: Newspaper ads." *The Family Coordinator*, 26, 27-30.

Curran, J. P. (1972), "Differential Effects of Stated Preferences and Questionnaire Role Performance on Interpersonal Attraction In the Dating Situation," *The Journal of Psychology*, 82, 313-327.

Curran, J. P. (1973a), "Correlates of Physical Attractiveness and Interpersonal Attraction in the Dating Situation," *Social Behavior and Personality*, 1(2), 153-157.

Curran, J. P. (1973b), "Examination of Various Interpersonal Attraction Principles in the Dating Dyad," *Journal of Experimental Research in Personality*, 6, 347-356.

Curran, J. P., and S. Lippold (1975), "The Effects of Physical Attraction and Attitude Similarity on Attraction in Dating Dyads," *Journal of Personality*, 43(3), 529-539.

Cutler, B. (1989), "Bachelor Party," *American Demographics*, 11 (2), 22-26.

Deaux, K., & R. Hanna (1984) "Courtship in the Personals Column: The Influence of Gender and Sexual Orientation," *Sex Roles*, 11, 363-375.

Freedman, A. M. (1989), "Beautiful Women Don't Go to Bars, But Helena Does," *Wall Street Journal*, September 22, 1.

Freidan, A. (1974), "The United States Marriage Market," *Journal of Political Economy*, 82, 11-27.

Fuchs, V. R. (1988), *Women's Quest for Economic Equality*, Cambridge, MA: Harvard University Press.

Godwin J. (1973), *The Mating Trade*, Garden City, NY: Doubleday.

Harrison, A. A., and L. Saeed (1977) "Let's Make a Deal: An Analysis of Revelations and Stipulations in Lonely Hearts Advertisements," *Journal of Personality and Social Psychology*, 33, 257-264.

Hirschman, E. C. (1987), "People as Products: Analysis of a Complex Marketing Exchange," *Journal of Marketing*, 51, 98-108.

Jedlicka, D. (1981), "Automated Go-Betweens: Mate Selection of Tomorrow?" *Family Relations*, 30, 373-376.

Jones, E.F., A. Farina, A. H. Hastorf, H. Markus, D. T. Miller, R. A., Scott (1984), *Social Stigma: The Psychology of Marked Relationships*. New York: W.H. Freeman and Company.

Kenrick, D. T., and M. R. Trost (1989), "Reproductive Exchange Model of Heterosexual Relationships: Putting Proximate Economics in Ultimate Perspective," In C. Hendrick (ed.), *Review of Personality and Social Psychology* (Vol. 10, pp. 53-67). Newbury Park, CA: Sage.

Koestner, R., and L. Wheeler (1988), "Self-Presentation in Personal Advertisements: The Influence of Implicit Notions of Attraction and Role Expectations," *Journal of Social and Personal Relationships*, 5, 149-160.

Kotler, P., and S. J. Levy (1969), "Broadening the Concept of Marketing," *Journal of Marketing*, 33, 10-15.

Levy, S. and G. Zaltman (1975), *Marketing, Society, and Conflict*, Englewood Cliffs, NJ: Prentice-Hall.

Masnick, G. and M. J. Banc (1980), *The Nation's Families: 1960-1990*, Cambridge, MA: Joint Center for Urban Studies.

Mullan, B. (1984), *The Mating Trade*, Boston: Routledge and Kegan Paul inc.

Parsons, D. O. (1980), "The Marriage Market and Female Economic Well-Being," *Journal of Mathematical Sociology*, 7, 113-138.

Pfifferling, J. (1989), "Matchmakers," ABC News, *20/20* segment, February 17. Television interview with Abbey Hirsh.

Sirgy, M. J. (1982), "Self-Concept in Consumer Behavior: A Critical Review," *Journal of Consumer Research*, (9) 287-300.

Tooby, John, & Cosmides, Leda (1989). "Evolutionary psychology and the generation of culture, Part I." *Ethology and Sociobiology*, 10, 29-49.

Trivers, R. L. (1972), "Parental investment and sexual selection," in B. Campbell (Ed.), *Sexual selection and the descent of man: 1871-1971*, Chicago, IL: Aldine.

Woll, S. B. (1986), "So Many to Choose From: Decision Strategies in Videodating," *Journal of Social and Personal Relationships*, 3, 43-52.

Woll, S. B. and C. P. Cozby (1987), "Videodating and Other Alternatives to Traditional Methods of Relationship Initiation," in *Advances in Personal Relationships*, (1), 69-108.

Woll, S. B. and P. Young (1989), "Looking for Mr. or Ms. Right: Self-presentation in Videodating," *Journal of Marriage and the Family*, 51, 483-488.

Moment By Moment Analyses of TV Commercials: Their Theoretical and Applied Roles
Summary of the Panel
Esther Thorson, University of Wisconsin-Madison

Marshall McLuhan (1964) called advertising professionals "frogmen of the mind," diving into and scrutinizing moment-by-moment human responses to their messages. Despite his perjorative intention, the phrase nicely characterizes the research area represented here. While much of advertising research has been concerned with the performance of entire commercials, all of the approaches developed here are concerned with momentary events occurring within commercials.

In the October 1989 issue of the newsletter of the Society for Consumer Psychology, one of the panel's chairs, Bill Wells, was asked what he thought the next important topics would be in advertising research and practice. Bill's first choice of important topics was what he termed "scene-by-scene analysis." He noted that much of the industry's present measurements tend to give each ad one overall score for how memorable the ad was or how much attitudes changed as result of exposure. But, he said, a commercial is in fact a complex set of events that proceeds through time. In the same way that one can analyze a play scene-by-scene, one can analyze a commercial scene-by-scene, and get new insight about how the commercial is processed and how it affects the viewer.

As we thought through this idea and talked to our colleagues in business and academe, it seemed to us that indeed there was considerable interest in individual moments in ads. And, in fact, there existed many different ways to theorize and to measure occurrences in those moments. So we decided to try to bring together a diverse sample of research programs that were focusing on ad moments and ask of each paper that the authors consider both theoretical foundations or implications of their work *and* to discuss how their theorizing and findings could be applied to advertising in the 90's. We found that all of our chosen participants were way ahead of us and quite prepared to take this approach. As will be seen, the two practitioner papers on the panel have major theoretical concerns about these moment-by-moment events, and the academic paper has major practical interests.

Of course, moment-by-moment analysis is not new to either ACR or to communication research, although we could find no precedent for a panel devoted to the topic. In the communication literature, one of the earliest moment-by-moment studies was carried out by Dysinger and Ruckmick (1933) who recorded galvanic skin responses and changes in breathing patterns in children who were watching various film genres. In the next decade, Lazarsfeld, the eminent sociologist, and Stanton, the future president of CBS, patented the program analyzer. This piece of equipment allowed people to push buttons to indicate their like or dislike while they listened to radio music. Initially there was great interest in what this technology could tell us about momentary cognitive processes in response to messages (e.g., Perterman, 1940). Unfortunately, the interest in basic psychological questions died and the method faded into the oblivion of minor use as a predictor of commercial success of radio and eventually television programs and commercials. Further developments in fine-grained analyses started to bloom again in the 1980's when microcomputerization put moment-by-moment technology into more general availability (Biocca and David, in press).

Some of the most important contributions to theory and methodology in this area have come from ACR members. German consumer researcher Kroeber-Riel (1979) has been concerned with how overtime patterns in psychophysiological measures inform us about ads. His colleague, Neibecker (1987) has been developing a program analyzer much like Lazarsfeld and Stanton's, and using it to look at over-time responses to music. Friestad and Thorson (1986) have been developing a dial-turning method to look at emotional response to ads, and Aaker, Stayman, and Hagerty (1986) have explored the "warmth monitor." And our discussant, Linda Alwitt introduced the Leo Burnett Moment-By-Moment system^{TM} (1985).

With all this activity and some belief that this area is coming into it own in the ad industry, the time seems ripe to take a close look at some newer fine-grained methods, as well as the theories that guide their application. We therefore reached into Michigan Avenue and the ivory tower for interesting examples of programs of moment-by-moment ad research. The three papers presented in the panel differed in interesting ways in terms of how they conceptualize their chosen moments.

The first paper was authored by Mark Polsfuss of Viewfacts. This Chicago company specializes in the Program and Evaluation and Analysis Computer (PEAC) system. PEAC collects momentary liking responses to commercials from either individuals or groups, and then uses the over-time patterns generated during an initial viewing to guide a group interview about what in the commercial was liked, what was disliked, and the reasons for those patterns of liking. This diagnostic procedure allows clients to determine exactly what works in their ads and what doesn't. This knowledge can be used to decide among their own competing executions, to see how they stack up against the advertising of competitors, and to determine what sections of their messages might bear replacement with more effective material. In addition to the practical application, however, the researchers at Viewfacts are developing ways to quantify the liking patterns. Doing so has allowed exploration of generalizations about what various over-time patterns tell us about processes of comprehension and attitude management. In his paper, Mr. Polsfuss overviews the details of the method and its utility, and then summarizes some theoretical efforts.

The second paper was presented by Charles E. Young of the Chicago ad agency, Tatham-Laird and Kudner. The previous work of Mr. Young and his colleague Mike Robinson is probably already familiar to readers of *Journal of Advertising Research*. (Young & Robinson, 1987; 1989). Young and Robinson use a technique in which people watch a commercial and then are shown a series of pictures which they must identify as having appeared in the ad or not. Ordinarily 50 to 100 respondents are tested for each ad. From these data, they generate a graph of the percent of correct recognitions for each ad location represented by a picture. This measure of over-time recognition accuracy has been shown to be sensitive to such ad variations as the amount of redundancy in script and visuals, emotional impact of particular pictures, and the amount of complexity occurring at particular moments in the ads. Young and Robinson are developing a theory of video rhythms (Young & Robinson, 1989) to account for their results and predict to new ones. In the paper presented at the panel they compare the video rhythm differences they are observing for established and new brands.

The third paper on the panel was authored by Marian Friestad and Peter Wright. These academic consumer researchers are interested in momentary events that consumers perceive to be specifically designed to add impetus to the persuasive impact of the message. In other words, they are trying to understand which moments of commercials are perceived by consumers as manipulative. In the moment-by-moment technique the authors developed, consumers watched ads and respond on a key pad to the occurrence of "key moments" that the viewers believed were there as a tactical move by the advertiser. In the initial study, the authors sampled eight commercials from each of four product categories and presented them to viewers. The results indicated that consumers did identify consistent moments in the ads as being there for reasons of persuasion. The next stage of the research is to attempt to determine how the patterns of the identified key moments relate to either specific attitudes (i.e., to the brand) or to more generalized attitudes, (i.e, to the integrity and motivations of the advertiser and beliefs about the quality of the products).

The panel discussant, Linda Alwitt, was uniquely qualified to deal with the issue of moment-by-moment processes. Not only has her own psychophysiological (Alwitt, 1985) and event-monitoring work (Alwitt, 1985) contributed to the literature, Alwitt spent nine years as a research manager at Leo Burnett. Professor Alwitt is now on the business school faculty at DePaul University. This combination of interest in the area and both practical and academic experience makes Alwitt's comments particularly interesting and relevant.

REFERENCES

Aaker, D.A., Stayman, D.M., & Hagerty, M.R. (1986). Warmth in advertising: Measurement, impact and sequence effects. *Journal of Consumer Research* 12, March, 365-381.

Alwitt, Linda (1985). Monitoring the emotional flow of commercials. Paper presented at the Advertising Research Foundation, Chicago, Sept 4-6.

Alwitt, Linda (1985). EEG activity reflects the content of commercials. In Linda Alwitt and Andrew Mitchell (Eds.), *Psychology Processes and Advertising Effects*. Hillsdale, NJ: Erlbaum.

Biocca, Frank, & Prabu, David (in press). Continuous on-line audience response measures. In Joan Schleuder (Ed.), *Measuring Cognitive Responses to Media Messages*. Hillsdale, NJ: Erlbaum.

Dysinger, W.S., and Ruckmick, Christian A. (1933). *The Emotional Responses of Children to the Motion Picture Situation*. New York: Macmillan.

Friestad, Marian, & Thorson, Esther (1986). Emotion-eliciting advertising: Effects on long term memory and judgment. *Advances in Consumer Research, Vol. 13*. R. Lutz (Ed.), Provo UT: Association for Consumer Research.

Kroeber-Riel, W. (1979). Activation research: Psychobiological approaches in consumer research. *Journal of Consumer Research*, 5, 240-250.

McLuhan, Marshall (1964). *Understanding Media: The extensions of man*. New York: McGraw-Hill.

Neibecker, Bruno (1987). The dynamic component in attitudes toward the stimulus. In Melanie Wallendorf and Paul Anderson (Eds.), *Advances in Consumer Research, Vol 14*, 482-486.

Perterman, J. (1940). The "program analyzer": A new technique in studying liked and disliked items in radio programs. *Journal of Applied Psychology*, 718-741.

Rothschild, Michael L., & Hyun, Yong J. (1990). Predicting memory for components of TV commercials from EEG. *Journal of Consumer Research*, 16(4), 472-478.

Young, Charles, and Robinson, Michael (1987). Guideline: Tracking the commercial viewer's wandering attention. *Journal of Advertising Research*, 27(3), 15-22.

Young, Charles, and Robinson, Michael (1989). Video rhythms and recall. *Journal of Advertising Research*, June/July, 22-25.

"Liking" Through Moment-To-Moment Evaluation; Identifying Key Selling Segments In Advertising

Mark Polsfuss, Viewfacts, Inc.
Mike Hess, Viewfacts, Inc.

Historically the advertising industry has used two primary approaches to judge television advertising. These have been termed "evaluative" and "diagnostic." The evaluative techniques of recall and persuasion normally employ some sort of established category norm. Depending on the technique, commercials that obtain a recall or persuasion score exceeding the norm usually go to air, while those that fall short are either reworked or abandoned. Over the past several years the industry has largely relied on these two measures as their ultimate decision criteria. For this reason "evaluative" measures have also sometimes been referred to as "criterion" measures.

In contrast the "diagnostic" approaches have tried to understand how advertising works. Primarily this has been done through one-on-one interviews or focus groups. The diagnostics go beyond recall and persuasion to examine issues such as the main message of the commercial, what people liked or disliked, whether there was confusion about anything, etc.

In this paper we will discuss how "liking," in the past generally used as a diagnostic variable, is currently in the process of becoming a criterion variable as a result of research reported in recent papers. In addition, we will examine how a comprehensive understanding of liking through moment-to-moment analysis allows us to pinpoint key selling seconds in the commercial that lead to more effective advertising.

Let's first examine what Viewfacts means by moment-to-moment analysis and how to measure it.

During the late '70's, technological applications to the entire market/media research industry began to appear with increasing frequency. One such application was a small hand-held microcomputer developed by PEAC Media Research, Inc. (PMRI) in Toronto, Canada. The unit was designed to track a respondent's moment-to-moment (M-T-M) response to any audio/visual material.

The original motivation for developing the technique was to facilitate understanding of childrens' reactions to programming. In conjunction with the Children's Television Workshop and TV Ontario, PMRI began using their "PEAC System" (Program Evaluation and Analysis Computer) with children. The basic idea was to use the data to enhance a qualitative exploration. This approach worked so well with children that it also was easily adapted for use with adults. Over the years a variety of improvements have been made to the technique, which is now in use worldwide. Here is how it works today.

Respondents continuously enter their reactions on the wireless hand-units by pressing keys (A-E) which correspond to a 5-point scale from very positive to very negative. While they are giving us their anonymous, spontaneous reactions, their responses are instantly aggregated and displayed for both the moderator as well as for the clients in the viewing room. We have the option of displaying the data by total sample, by sub-groups i.e. age, sex, etc., by the number of negative key pressers, or deviations from the group average and so on. The group moderator subsequently utilizes the movement in the line as a discussion tool, probing for the reasoning behind those reactions. What we get as a result, then, is diagnostic information explaining what's working, what's not working, and most importantly - why. Clients have considered this approach a significant improvement over standard focus groups because it gives the moderator structured feedback from the audience itself to use in the ensuing group discussion.

As mentioned, this data was used in a structured way to elicit qualitative responses. The M-T-M line has proven itself to be an excellent tool for examining a commercial's ability to involve viewers, to determine its level of appeal and to find out what the commercial was communicating. Since we frequently have used a positive to negative scale, we at Viewfacts often felt we were getting a good read on what was "likeable" about the commercial as well. How useful this knowledge was in terms of creating "successful or persuasive advertising" has always been somewhat controversial, because likability, while considered an excellent "diagnostic" variable, has not generally been considered a "decision criterion" variable, in contrast to recall and persuasion.

Alexander Biel, Executive Director of the Center for Research and Development and an authority in the area of "commercial liking," was a pioneer in tackling the likability issue by conducting a large-scale study in 1985 which investigated whether liking a commercial had anything to do with persuading consumers to buy the advertised brand. In a recent discussion of that research he and his co-author Carol Bridgwater (1990), found that "people who liked a commercial a lot were twice as likely to be persuaded by it than people who simply felt neutral towards the advertising." The study went on to define what likeable advertising was and was not. Without getting into that issue in depth, its overall conclusions were that "commercial liking went far beyond mere entertainment. Viewer involvement and perceived relevance are factors that link commercial liking to persuasion in the first place. People like commercials which they feel are relevant and worth remembering." The study also found that "liking was a function of product category..." That is, the way in which liking works in one category, is different than how it works in another, in terms of being persuasive.

FIGURE 1

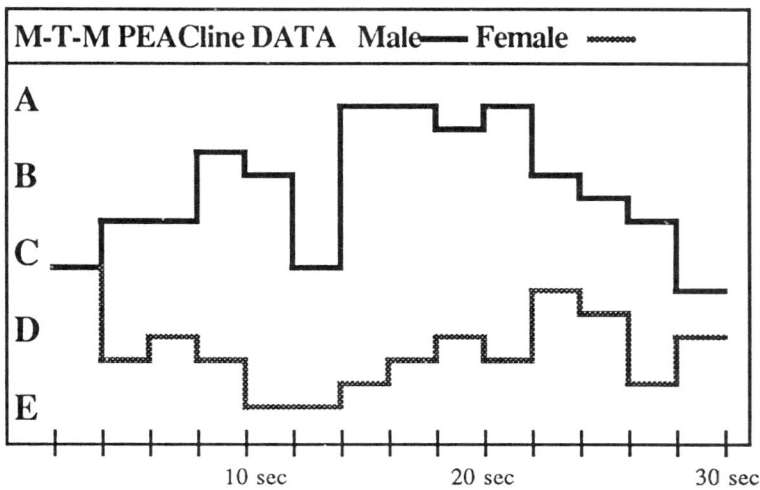

Vertical axis represents Positive to Negative 5 point rating scale
Horizontal axis represents passage of time
M-T-M- PEAClines are cumulative affective reaction of subgroups over time
M-T-M data provides evaluative and diagnostic insight into commercial performance

FIGURE 2
1989 Viewfacts Validity Study

o Multi-variate model selected "winner" 100% of the time
   - Overall liking
   - Other attributes
   - Several M-T-M variables
o Attribute-only model 70% accurate
o M-T-M only model 90% accurate

In our own continuing effort at Viewfacts to understand the moment-to-moment response data and its relationship to such measures as likability and persuasion, we had always believed that there was more to the measure in terms of its quantifiable aspects. Some of our clients had also felt this way. Intuitively recognizing a relationship between persuasion and the moment-to-moment data, our regular clients have, over the years, built their own norms for acceptable performance of their own advertising. During the last two years Viewfacts has learned how to statistically transform the M-T-M data into measures that are directly correlated to internal measures of persuasion, and even to actual product purchase (Polsfuss and Hess, 1989; Spaeth, Hess and Tang, 1990). We would now like to discuss how this has come about.

In 1989, Viewfacts, along with our client Time, Inc., undertook the challenge to determine if the moment-to-moment data could be mathematically related to commercial success or failure. By obtaining M-T-M data for ten direct response television commercials (Call 1-800...) and a measure of actual marketplace performance for each commercial (based on cost-per order) Time, Inc. and Viewfacts divided the ten cases into two groups: 5 successful and 5 unsuccessful commercials.

With the M-T-M data on each commercial, an overall liking score and additional standard scalar attribute data, we set out to develop a multivariate model that would hopefully reveal relationships between these variables and commercial success.

One conclusion was that there was a strong inverse correlation between overall liking and cost per order. That is, the more the commercial was liked, the lower the cost per order, in general, and of course, the more likely that the commercial was a success. In the end, the resulting discriminant model was able to predict which of the commercials in each pair would be the superior sales producer 100 percent of the time. As mentioned, this model employed overall liking as one variable, several additional closed-end attribute variables, as well as several very specific moment-to-moment variables.

FIGURE 3
ARF Copy Research Validity Study (Haley, 1990)

Commercial Reaction

(5) I liked it very much
(4) I liked it
(3) I neither liked it nor disliked it
(2) I disliked it
(1) I disliked it very much

FIGURE 4
What Worked?

o   M-T-M response to the Product Attributes
o   Other M-T-M variables
o   1-2 other summary measures of viewer interest

Time, Inc. has agreed that we may share these basic modeling outcomes. We are not at liberty to reveal the exact identity of the variables themselves for proprietary reasons.

As indicated in the above summary chart, it is important to note that when simpler models were tried, the results were good, but did not explain 100% of the commercial winners and losers correctly. For example, a model consisting only of closed-end attributes was able to classify 7 of the 10 commercials correctly, while a model that employed just M-T-M variables got 9 of 10 right.

The primary conclusion of this project, which was reported at the 1989 ARF Copytesting with our client's permission (Polsfuss and Hess, 1989), was that models using both overall and moment-to-moment viewer reactions can be used successfully to predict a commercial's in-market sales performance. *Both* types of variables were important to the success of the modeling effort. An interesting notion which flowed from these findings was the idea that the moment-to-moment variables enabled us to dissect the *overall* liking of a commercial into the *specific* liking for each commercial element. In fact we found that the overall liking measure correlated with the mean moment-to-moment score with a .96 coefficient. Clearly the moment-to-moment measure of liking and the overall measure of liking, were measuring essentially the same thing. The difference is that the moment-to-moment measure can be broken down into its constituent elements, whereas the overall measure is a simple pass/fail grade in the form of just one number.

This past summer at the annual ARF Copytesting Workshop, Russ Haley, Professor Emeritus of Marketing, University of New Hampshire delivered the results of the ARF Copy Research Validity Study (Haley, 1990). This study, some eight years in the making, was based on comparing 5 pairs of packaged goods television commercials that were run in BehaviorScan split cable tests. The only variable that differentiated each member of a commercial pair from the other was a difference in advertising copy. All other variables, ad weight, in-store promotion, etc. were held constant.

The primary conclusion that one can draw from the findings, is that copy tests do work. They can be predictive of a commercial's in-market sales effectiveness. We've had pre-test measures of copy for a long time, but the industry has rarely had such a solid demonstration of the relationship between those copy pre-test measures and the eventual sales effectiveness of the advertising. A second conclusion is that with few exceptions, all of the various types of copy testing measures tried, worked in one form or another. This means that recall, persuasion, commercial reaction, etc. all were effective measures at differentiating winning from losing commercials.

The new ground here is that of all the measures tested, the one that ranked first in terms of predicting sales effectiveness was "commercial reaction," consumer reaction to the commercials. But what exactly was this reaction measurement? It was a simple five point liking scale as configured below.

The simplicity of this measure is its great power. We're all familiar with the difficulty of getting a reasonably valid measure of recall, and the even greater difficulty of getting a useful and valid measurement of persuasion. Measuring liking, however, is more direct.

Based on this "commercial reaction" finding, Haley concluded, "Commercials that are liked, sell better than those that are not liked." Couple this with Biel's conclusion that "people who liked a commercial 'a lot' were twice as likely to be persuaded by it..." and we have some solid motivation for now proceeding to determine what

FIGURE 5
% Variance Explained in Liking
Complete M-T-M Model vs. Product Attributes

Seven-Up

Commercial	Complete M-T-M Model	Product Attribute Only M-T-M Model
#1	.86	.75
#2	.89	.83
#3	.95	.78

Volkswagen

Commercial	Complete M-T-M Model	Product Attribute Only M-T-M Model
#1	.93	.87
#2	.96	.91
#3	.90	.82

FIGURE 6
Modeling Summary

o Consumer's overall liking depends on their reaction to a few key seconds of the commercial.
o M-T-M measurement can isolate those key seconds

M-T-M Response To → Overall → Believe Brand →
Brand Attributes   Liking   Attributes   Sales

---

elements contribute to making a commercial likeable. Is it the overall impact, or are there segments that may be doing most of the work?

We at Viewfacts were motivated to address this critical issue for three reasons, as shown below.

o Viewfacts' own 1989 research for Time, Inc. linking "liking" to the M-T-M line and the M-T-M line, in turn, to sales.

o The recent studies reported by Haley and by Biel and Bridgwater clearly indicated liking was predictive of commercial effectiveness.

o The development of the Viewfacts M-T-M database, which would allow us to dissect the time periods in a commercial for over 1,000 commercials.

In an extensive analysis of that database during the current year, we looked at a broad range of product categories, as shown below.

o Tourism
o Computers
o Soft Drinks
o Automobiles

In each of these categories we found, as we had previously learned in the Time, Inc. study, a high correlation between the M-T-M data and a separate measure of liking, or commercial reaction. In the computer category, for example we found that 86% of the variance in commercial reaction for 9 IBM commercials could be explained by a model consisting primarily of variables created from the M-T-M line. What variables were these?

The most important variables were those segments of the M-T-M line that were generated during the specific few seconds of the commercial in which the "key selling points" were presented. In fact, the specific correlation with overall liking of this M-T-M response to *just a few seconds* of the commercial, when the product attributes were presented, ranged from .73 to .89 across the 9 commercials tested.

When we turned our attention to the soft drink and automobile categories, we found a similar pattern, as shown in the chart below. For both 7-Up and Volkswagen, a model consisting only of M-T-M responses when product attributes were shown, was almost as good at predicting liking than a more complete M-T-M model containing additional time periods.

By now, you may be wondering exactly what the contents of those key selling segments are and also, why they are so effective at predicting liking. Well, for proprietary reasons I can't answer the first question because to answer it would be to tell you what that firm's key selling variables are.

The second question, I'll try to answer with the help of another diagram.

The diagram indicates a conceptual scheme that might be helpful at understanding the relationships that may be at work here. It has been compiled by synthesizing the findings from the Biel, Haley and Viewfacts research studies referred to throughout the course of this paper.

The analysis goes like this:

- Commercials that are *liked*, lead viewers to believe the brand attributes that are presented in the commercial.
- When these same attributes are compelling and persuasive, they provide good reasons to buy the product.
- If we also assume that marketing management and the ad agency have done their jobs prior to development of the commercial, then the proper product attributes for the category and brand have already been identified.
- Therefore, if the commercial is presented in an essentially believable fashion and it "penetrates your consciousness," then those same attributes will help sell the product.
- The role of the commercial, in this sense, is to credibly and pleasantly present persuasive brand attributes.
- In turn the viewer response to that portion of the commercial is critical to subsequent sales effectiveness.

Put another way, if a commercial has done its job well, pleasantly and effectively, then it is liked. After that, it is up to those few key seconds during which the commercial delivers its message, to "make the sale."

So much for theory and analysis; where is Viewfacts now with respect to practical application of these findings?

We are currently giving our clients the following summary of our thinking on this topic.

1. The ARF and Viewfacts have now both reported findings that indicate commercial liking is linked to sales.
2. Viewfacts has found that its M-T-M PEACline and liking are highly correlated. Therefore, the M-T-M line can be linked to sales as well.
3. Although an understanding of the *entire* M-T-M line taken as a whole is necessary to adequately model liking mathematically...
4. Within the M-T-M line there exist certain "key selling segments" that appear to be more predictive of commercial liking than are other segments of the line.
5. These "hot spots" of selling power tend to be both brand-benefit oriented and positional (beginning/end of commercial).
6. Key selling segments, as well as the meaning of likability appear to vary from category to category. Therefore, it will be necessary to create separate models for each advertised category.
7. These models will be similar to each other in that each will depend on the shape of the M-T-M line; critical positional effects; creative elements; and brand benefits. But they will differ from each other with respect to the exact *location* of positional effects and to the *nature* of relevant brand benefits.

Overall liking of commercials, we have found, is driven by consumer's moment-to-moment response to key commercial segments. We are continuing our efforts to build an expert system that identifies those key positive selling segments for our clients.

The marketplace is dynamic, and what is "hot or not" is always changing. By understanding advertising on a moment-to-moment basis as we have outlined in this paper, one can optimize the selling power of a commercial. The blending of this scientific approach to understanding the art of advertising is useful when trying to stay with or ahead of an ever-changing world.

REFERENCES

Biel, Alexander L., and Bridgwater, Carol A. (1990). *Attributes of Likable Television Commercials*. Journal of Advertising Research, June/July, 38-44.

Haley, Russell I. (1990). *The ARF Copy Research Validity Project*. Transcript Proceedings, Seventh Annual ARF Copy Research Workshop, New York, July 11-12.

Polsfuss, Mark and Hess, Michael (1989). *The Relationship Between Second-To-Second Response and Direct Response: What Is The Link? Transcript Proceedings, Sixth Annual ARF Copy Research Workshop*, New York, May 22-23.

Spaeth, Jim; Hess, Michael and Tang, Sidney (1990). *The Anatomy of Liking. Transcript Proceedings, Seventh Annual ARF Copy Research Workshop*, New York, July 11-12.

The Visual Experience of New and Established Product Commercials

Charles E. Young, TLK Advertising
Michael Robinson, TLK Advertising

ABSTRACT

This study uses a moment-by-moment copytesting technique to examine the differences between new product and established brand tv commercials from an information theory perspective. Based on a theoretical dichotomy suggested by earlier researchers, two types of visual information were identified in pictures taken from a sample of 41 commercials. P-type information was explicit, product-related content and E-type information was the esthetic, execution-related content. Using the TLK Picture Sort recognition technique, it was found that viewers process more of the E-type information present in established brand ads, while more P-type information was processed by viewers of new product ads.

INTRODUCTION

From a theoretical standpoint, advertising for new products clearly differs in a number of fundamental ways from advertising for established brands. Coming in the critical first stage of the product life cycle, a new product commercial has the job of generating awareness of the new product starting from a zero base. It must, therefore, communicate a large amount of new information. It must communicate the brand name; it must communicate the category in which the product competes; it must communicate the attributes of the product and how those attributes are different from other products in the category and what the benefits of those differences are. By contrast, advertising for established brands has the benefit of prior advertising or marketing history. Usually its job is to remind consumers of the brand and to reinforce existing attitudes and loyalties toward the brand. Typically, established brand advertising has much less factual information to convey than advertising for new products.

It is reasonable to assume, therefore, that consumers would in general respond differently to new product than to established brand advertising and this assumption has been confirmed empirically by a number of researchers in recent years. Interestingly, the differences that have been found confirm not only that the information content of the two kinds of advertising is different but suggest that how consumers process the information content of new product ads is different from how they process the information in established brand ads. This difference in information processing is not fully understood.

This paper uses a moment-by-moment copytesting technique, the TLK Picture Sort, to provide a new perspective on this subject. In particular, we will attempt to bring a new precision to the measurement of the information content of an ad by defining two types of visual information that might be present in a tv commercial. Then we will report empirical results that demonstrate significant differences in how viewers process the information content of new product versus established brand tv commercials.

LITERATURE REVIEW

Olson, Schlinger and Young (1982) analyzed a large sample of tv commercials for new and established packaged goods using the Viewer Response Profile, a multidimensional rating system. They found significant differences in viewer response to the two types of advertising on a number of dimensions, with new product ads rated higher on the dimension of relevant news but lower on the dimensions of familiarity and stimulation. Notably, their interpretation of the lower stimulation scores for new product commercials was that it was due to the information overload of product news that would typically be carried by introductory advertising. They concluded that in terms of viewer response "new product advertising forms a distinctive and important genre or category of advertising."

Stewart and Furse (1986), in their analysis of the recall and persuasiveness scores of a large sample of tv commercials, suggested that the "communication and persuasion process may not be the same for new product commercials as for established product commercials." For new product commercials they found recall and persuasion scores to be highly correlated, whereas for established brand commercials the two measures were uncorrelated.

Jones (1986) pointed out in his review of the hierarchy of effects models first described by Ramond (1976) and based on the low involvement theory propounded by Krugman (1965) that the "Learn-Do-Feel" hierarchy is "relevant to the vast majority of packaged goods in their introductory phase" while the "Do-Feel-Do" hierarchy, or reinforcement model, is relevant in the majority of cases of established brand advertising. Implicit in these two models of advertising are two types of information content that might be found in commercials. "Learning" in this context pertains to the the factual content of the ad, such as the product name, product attributes and benefits, etc. which produces a cognitive response from the viewer. "Feeling" pertains to the other executional content of an ad that produces affective or emotional response.

Young (1972) drew a similar distinction between two types of advertising copy. The first type she described as "explicit" copy, which "communicates concrete, product-related benefits." The second type is "implicit" copy, which "communicates less tangible or more psychological benefits." The implication that new product ads tend to be more explicit while established product ads tend to be more implicit is clear. Jones, in the same review, commented that "It is obvious that in most circumstances, with increases in a brand's store of added values, implicit copy will become relatively more important as it takes on some of the prominence that was held by explicit copy during a brand's introduction."

Shannon's invention of information theory (1947) has spawned many information processing models of communication but perhaps the most interesting in the light of the preceding discussion is the work done by Moles (1966) on information theory and esthetic perception. Moles proposes the existence of two types of information in messages in general. The first type of information he calls "semantic". Semantic information refers to logical, translatable, utilitarian information about the state of the external world and pertains to decisions about present or future actions. It would seem to correspond to the type of copy Young labeled explicit and which produces a learning response in the hierarchy of effects models. Esthetic information, on the other hand, relates to internal states. Instead of to a universal or logical repertoire, esthetic information refers to a repertoire of knowledge common to a particular transmitter and to a particular receiver and as such it is like "personal" information. In general, esthetic information is untranslatable from one channel of transmission to another. For example, the esthetic information content of a picture cannot readily be translated into words. Esthetic information would seem to correspond to the type of copy Young labeled implicit and which produces a feeling response in the hierarchy of effects models.

Young and Robinson (1989) used a moment-by-moment picture recognition technique to show that the type of information contained in the peaks of their video attention curve is related to the recall score generated by an ad. Specifically, peak experiences of explicit product information appears to drive recall. They have also shown (1990) that the number of peak experiences produced by an ad is related to its persuasiveness, at least as persuasiveness is measured by the RSC copytesting system. The relationship between persuasiveness and the type of information attended to has not yet been explored, but anecdotal results obtained to date suggest that it need not be explicitly product-related.

Building on this research, this study uses the moment-by-moment picture recognition technique to explore in further detail the differences between new product and established brand commercials. Specifically, we will examine differences in the information content of new and established brand commercials and how that information is processed by viewers.

METHODOLOGY

The sample consisted of 41 finished 30-second commercials. This included 23 commercials for established national brands of consumer packaged goods and 18 commercials for both successful and unsuccessful new products. All of the commercials had been tested prior to airing within the last five years.

The tests were conducted in one-on-one consumer interviews during which respondents individually viewed the test commercial one time and then answered a series of open-ended and closed-ended questions describing their reactions to the advertising. Sample sizes typically consisted of from 50 to 100 respondents recruited by mall intercept on the basis of category usage.

Part way through the interview respondents were taken through the TLK Picture Sort (See Young and Robinson, 1987). The procedure uses a deck of still photographs taken of the commercial directly from a television screen. This deck represents a visual "sample" of the commercial's images and typically consists of from 15 to 20 photographs for a 30-second ad. Respondents were given a randomized deck of photographs to look through and asked to sort them into two piles--the pictures they recognized from the commercial and the ones they did not recognize. The resulting recognition scores were then plotted as a time series representing the viewer "attention curve" for the ad.

The information content of the individual frames or pictures used in the test was subsequently coded using a two-way classification scheme. Pictures were classified as either P-type or E-type. P-type pictures were pictures containing explicit product-related content, such as the name, the package, visualizations of product attributes or benefits, or pictures of the product in use. E-type pictures were basically all other visuals in the execution. The images in E-type pictures could be said to represent much of the esthetic content of the video portion of the commercial.

Examples of the patterns produced by this coding are shown in Exhibit 1. Three commercials are shown. Each series of P's and E's represents the sequence of pictures taken from one commercial, in the order shown, and coded according to our categories. As can be seen, the proportion of P-type to E-type pictures present in a commercial and the order in which each type of picture occurs in the flow of commercial images varies considerably from ad to ad.

The data for the new product commercials were then aggregated and compared to the data for established brand commercials.

DISCUSSION OF FINDINGS

A summary of the basic recognition measures for the two samples of commercials is shown in Exhibit 2.

In a sense, the *total* information content of the video portion of a commercial is a function of the visual complexity of the ad. A measure of that complexity is the number of pictures needed to describe a commercial with a picture sort deck. Looking at that measure as a starting point, we see that the total information content of the visual component of new product ads is comparable to that for established brand commercials. The average number of pictures used to describe new product

EXHIBIT 1
Information Type Frame By Frame

Ad 1: E P E E E E E E P P P P E E E E P

Ad 2: P P P E P P P E P E P P P

Ad 3: E E E E E E E P E E P

EXHIBIT 2
Average Picture Recognition

	New Products	Established Brands
N =	18 Commercials	23 Commercials
Average Number of Pictures Per Ad	16.3 Per Ad	14.6 Per Ad
Pictures Recognized	60%	66%
Pictures Recognized By ≥ 75% of Respondents (Peak Experience)	24%	37%

commercials, 16.3 pictures, is only directionally higher than the number needed to describe established brand commercials, 14.6 pictures.

The amount of visual information actually *processed* by the viewer, as measured by the percentage of pictures recognized, is higher for established brand commercials, 66% versus 60% which is signficant at p<.05. Importantly, this difference in the amount of information processed is due to the higher rate of "peak visual experiences" viewers had of established brand commercials. (Signficant at p<.001.) We define a "peak experience" as a picture recognized by 75% or more of viewers. Here we find that while one-fourth of the pictures in new product ads were peak experiences, over one-third of the visuals in established brand commercials were experienced at peak levels.

A lower rate of information processing was expected for new product ads given the finding of Olson, Schlinger and Young that new product ads are perceived to be less familiar and more newsworthy. Since the information content of new product ads is in general more original, it should be more difficult to process. However, the higher rate of *peak* experiences for established brand commercials was not expected, but this is possibly related to the finding that established brand advertising is generally perceived to be more stimulating or entertaining.

The difference in the amount of pictorial information processed, while significant, is smaller than what we might expect given the greater load of information that new product commercials are generally expected to carry. To reconcile our intuition with empirical results we must first be clear about the type of information to which we are referring. Exhibit 3 shows the results of our analysis for our two categories of information, P-type and E-type visuals.

New product commercials were found to contain substantially more P-type information than established brand commercials. Less than half, or 47%, of the visuals in established brand commercials were of the P-type while 69% of the visuals in new product ads were, a level nearly one-and-a-half times higher. This is consistent with the commonly held perception that new product ads tend to be loaded down with "information".

Now if we look at the type of information that is actually processed by the viewer we see a much larger difference than before, with 41% of the P-type visuals being recognized in the new product ads and only 29% of the P-type visuals recognized in the established brand ads. This is potentially misleading, however, because these differences simply reflect the proportions of P-type to E-type visuals in the two categories of advertising.

The results for peak experiences, however, are more interesting. Here we see the same number of P-type visuals in the viewer's peak experience of

EXHIBIT 3
Type of Information Processed by Viewers

	New Products	Established Brands
(Base: Total Pictures)	(293)	(337)
	%	%
Information Content		
P-type pictures	69	47
E-type pictures	31	53
Information Processed		
P-type recognized	41	29
E-type recognized	19	37
Peak Experiences		
P-type recognized by ≥ 75% respondents	17	16
E-type recognized by ≥ 75% respondents	7	21

both categories of advertising, 17% for new products and 16% for established brands, despite the beginning imbalance of P-type information in favor of new products ads. Moreover, E-type information occurs in peak experiences at a rate three times higher for established brand commercials than for new product commercials.

This finding helps to explain a number of previous research results.

For example, the finding that the same amount of P-type information is processed into the peak experiences of both new and established product commercials explains why the recall norms for most major copytesting systems for new and established product commercials are so similar. Young and Robinson have shown that it is the P-type content of peak experiences that drives recall.

Also, to the extent that the P-type content is motivating to consumers, this would explain the correlation between persuasiveness and recall scores found by Stewart and Furse for new product ads. P-type information, that is, explict product-related information, is the dominant type of information processed at peak levels by viewers of new product ads.

It is likely, however, that E-type content can be just as motivating to consumers as P-type information. Given our previous research which found no relationship between E-type information in attention curve peaks and recall, we also have an explanation for the lack of correlation between recall and persuasion for established brand commercials. E-type information is the dominant type of information processed at peak levels by viewers of established brand ads.

From a theoretical standpoint, P-type information is the type of information we would expect to produce the cognitive or learning response predicted by the first hierarchy of effects model, learn-do-feel. This is exactly what happens with viewer processing of new product ads. E-type information, that is, esthetic or emotion-generating information, is the type of information most freqeuently processed at peak levels by viewers of established brand commercials. In terms of the hierarchy of effects, this is the do-feel-do model. And this, importantly, is consistent with the assumption made by many advertising practitioners that established brand advertising often works by an emotional rather than a rational mechanism.

Finally, we should point out that we do not yet understand how peak experiences are created in an ad--that is still one of the mysteries of the creative process. Given the relationship between peak experiences and recall and persuasion, however, this is clearly an important subject. An intriguing line of inquiry for further work on this subject is suggested by the recent studies of Csikszentmihalyi (1990) who has developed an analogous concept in the larger arena of the psychology of optimal human experience. Writing about his concept of "flow", or peak human experience, he says,

"Because attention determines what will or will not appear in consciousness, and because it is also required to make any other mental events--such as remembering, thinking, feeling, and making decisions--happen there, it is useful to think of it as psychic energy. Attention is like energy in that without it no work can be done, and in doing work it is dissipated. We create ourselves by how we invest this energy....When a person is able to organize his or her consciousness so as to experience *flow* as often as possible, the quality of life is inevitably going to improve....In flow we are in control of our psychic energy and everything we do adds order to consciousness."

Understanding the "micro-flow" of images in a tv commercial, whether it be for a new product or an established brand, would appear to be an important step towards understanding advertising effectiveness.

REFERENCES

Csikszentmihalyi, Mihaly (1990), *Flow: The Psychology of Optimal Experience*, New York: Harper and Row

Jones, John Philip (1986) *What's In a Name? Advertising and the Concept of Brands*, Lexington: D C Heath and Co. pp 132-49

Krugman, Herbert E. (1965), "The Impact of Television Advertising: Learning without Involvement," *Public Opinion Quarterly* 29: 350-56

Moles, Abraham (1966, trans. by Joel E. Cohen), *Information Theory and Esthetic Perception*, Urbana: University of Illinois Press

Olson, David, Mary Jane Schlinger and Charles E. Young (1982) "How Consumers React to New-Product Ads," *Journal of Advertising Research* 22 (June/July) 24-30

Shannon, C. E. and Weaver, W. (1949) *The Mathematical Theory of Communication*. Urbana: University of Illinois Press

Stewart, David W. and David H. Furse, (1986) *Effective Television Advertising: A Study of 1000 Commercials*, Lexington: D C Heath and Co. pp 23-24

Young, Shirley (1972), "Copy Testing without Magic Numbers," *Journal of Advertising Research* (February), 3-12

Young, Charles E., and Michael Robinson, (1987), "Guideline: Tracking the Commercial Viewer's Wandering Attention," *Journal of Advertising Research* 27 (June/July), 15-22

_____ (1989), "Video Rythms and Recall", *Journal of Advertising Research* 29 (June/July), 22-25

_____ "Video Connectedness and Persuasion," pending publication in the *Journal of Advertising Research*

Analysis Approaches to Moment by Moment Reactions to Commercials: Discussion for Special Session on Moment by Moment Analyses of TV Commercials

Linda F. Alwitt, DePaul University

Most evaluations of advertising are overall reactions collected after exposure of the advertisement. These evaluations are either short-term, like recall or persuasion, or long-term like ad or sales tracking. Post-exposure copytesting assumes that reactions to advertising depend on the effect of the total commercial, and that they transcend the sum of reactions to each part of an ad. The latter assumption makes sense because parts of an ad interact with each other to produce an overall effect, and because the past experiences and current mood states of individuals interact with the content of a commercial to produce an overall reaction. However, when post-exposure reactions to advertising are analyzed, one must *infer* what caused consumers to reach their evaluations. That is, one must infer what a marketer must do to persuade a consumer to take action such as buying the advertised brand.

Moment by moment approaches to evaluating reactions to television commercials offer an opportunity to learn how consumers form their evaluations. These approaches allow us to dissect overall reactions and extract the aspects of a commercial that can be controlled by marketers. This is potentially the most valuable contribution of moment to moment analyses of television commercials.

Four types of variables can be used to dissect overall reactions to advertising using moment by moment approaches: person; product; medium; content.

Person variables include traits such as the speed of reaction to events within a commercial, the time delay between comprehending the content of a commercial and crystallizing an evaluation, the influence of mood due to the program context, and persistence. Persistence refers to the tendency of a viewer to respond at time t in the same way he responded at time t - 1. Examples of product variables are levels of involvement with the category and the brand, awareness of the brand's current and past positioning, and the brand's advertising history. Variables related to the medium of television involve how people react to on-going events. One example is the phenomenon of attentional inertia (Anderson 1985). Another is how people chunk on-going events into meaningful units (e.g., Newtson 1973). Content variables include the relevance of the message, the creative approach such as the distinction between lecture and drama commercials (Wells 1989) and the structure of the ad. An example of ad structure is a 'poignant' emotional problem-solving ad (Thorsen 1989). Research on moment by moment reactions to advertising has just started to examine these types of variables.

Moment by moment researchers have developed rather sophisticated ways of gathering and describing their results (e.g., Polsfuss and Hess this volume; Young & Robinson this volume), but have just started to explore ways to analyze the data in order to address some of the issues involved in dissecting overall evaluations of a brand based on its advertising. Two methodological questions are important:(1) what should be the units of analysis? (2) what analytic techniques should be used?

The unit of analysis depends on the issue being addressed. The total pattern of response for an entire commercial, for example, might be an appropriate unit of analysis for evaluating persistence, positioning, chunking of events into meaningful units, or creative strategy. Reactions to specific events within a commercial might be the appropriate unit for studying the speed of reaction to events, positioning, context effects within a commercial or ad structure. Individual viewers might be the appropriate unit of analysis for evaluating response styles, involvement, familiarity with the brand's advertising history, or message relevance.

A great strength of the moment by moment approach is that it tells us how a viewer changes over the course of a commercial. This calls for analytic techniques that take into account that:

a. events in a commercial are ordered in a sequence;
b. an event at time t is related to events at time t-n and t+n;
c. the response at time t is likely to be related to the response at time t - n as well as events at time t - n.

That is, analysis of moment by moment data calls for time-series analysis. Since time-series analysis has not been commonly used for evaluating reactions to advertising, we must learn how to apply and interpret these methods. Different time-series approaches suit different issues. For example, to analyze the pattern of reactions to an entire commercial, one might use Fourier analysis (Kaplan 1983), ARIMA and econometric regression approaches (Makridakis, Wheelwright & McGee 1983), or profile analysis (Greenhouse & Geisser 1959; Cole & Grizzle 1966). To analyze the effects of specific events within a commercial, Markov analysis or lag sequential analysis (e.g., Gottman & Roy 1990) should be useful.

Analysis of moment by moment reactions to television commercials is in its infancy. It offers opportunities to address issues which can only be inferred from post-viewing reactions to commercials, issues about how persuasion works. To take advantage of these opportunities, we will have to apply new techniques such as the various time-series analytic approaches.

REFERENCES

Anderson, Daniel R. (1985) Online cognitive processing of television. In L.F. Alwitt & A.A. Mitchell (Eds), *Psychological Processes and Advertising Effects*, Hillsdale,N.J.: Erlbaum.

Cole, J.W.L. & James E. Grizzle (1966) Applications of multivariate analysis of variance to repeated measures experiments. *Biometrics*, 22, 810-828.

Gottman, John M. & Anup K. Roy (1990) *Sequential Analysis*. Cambridge: Cambridge University Press.

Greenhouse, Samuel W. & Seymour Geisser (1959) On methods in the analysis of profile data. *Psychometrika*, 24(2), 95-112.

Kaplan, Howard L. (1983) Correlations, contrasts, and components: Fourier analysis in a more familiar terminology. *Behavioral Research Methods and Instrumentation*, 15(2), 228-241.

Newtson, Darren. (1976) Attribution and the unit of perception of ongoing behavior. *Journal of Personality and Social Psychology*, 28, 28-38.

Makridakis, Spyros, Steven C. Wheelwright & Victor E. McGee (1983), *Forecasting:Methods and Applications*, 2nd ed., New York: Wiley.

Polsfuss, Mark & Mike Hess (1990), 'Liking' through moment-to-moment evaluation: identifying key selling segments in advertising, *Advances in Consumer Research*, this volume.

Thorsen, Esther & Marion Friestad (1989) The effects of emotion on episodic memory for television commercials. In P. Cafferata & A. Tybout (Eds.) *Cognitive and Affective Responses to Advertising*. Lexington, MA: Lexington Books.

Wells, William D.(1989) Lectures and Dramas, In P. Cafferata & A. Tybout (Eds.) *Cognitive and Affective Responses to Advertising*. Lexington, MA: Lexington Books.

Young, Charles & Michael Robinson (1990) The visual experience of new and established product commercials, *Advances in Consumer Research*, this volume.

Clarifying the Simple Assumption of the Secondary Task Technique

Robert S. Owen, Ohio State University

ABSTRACT

The secondary task technique has been used in the detection and measure of constructs described variously as attention, effort, elaboration, cognitive capacity, processing intensity, and such, which in turn may provide an indication of learning and automatism. The assumption that the secondary task provides evidence for the detection of such a variety of constructs may not always be valid. This paper attempts to clarify our current understanding of how the secondary task technique works.

INTRODUCTION

Our inability to perform some combination of tasks without a decrement in performance of one or all tasks is the basis of the secondary task technique. Until the skill to concurrently perform two tasks has been acquired, focusing one's attention on the performance of one task can often cause a measurable degradation in the performance of the other. The observation of performance changes in one task can often be taken as a measure of changes in processing resources being devoted to the performance of a concurrent task, presumably providing an operational indication of attention, of the expenditure of effort, or of various other constructs or processes, which in turn can provide evidence of learning and skill acquisition.

The secondary task technique has been used in a number of contexts that are of interest to both marketing academicians and practitioners. For example, the secondary task technique has been used by Thorson, Reeves, and Schleuder (1985, 1987) to investigate the amount of viewer "attention" allocated to the processing of television messages; by Lord and his colleagues (Lord and Burnkrant 1988; Lord, Burnkrant, and Owen 1989) to measure changes in television viewer "involvement" and "elaboration"; and by Moore, Hausknecht, and Thamodaran (1986) in the investigation of the amount of "attentional capacity" allocated to the processing of audio commercials. The secondary task technique has also been used by several researchers in psychology as a measure of the amount of "cognitive capacity" dedicated to the reading of text (e.g., Inhoff and Fleming 1989; Britton and Tesser 1982). Secondary task performance has even been associated with personality (Huddleston and Wilson 1974) and demographic variables (Stapleford 1973).

Although the secondary task technique, particularly the "RT-probe", does appear to be useful in the detection and measure of a variety of constructs and processes in a variety of situations, several questions can be raised regarding such uses. How is it that the same technique can be used in different studies to measure "attention", "effort", "elaboration", and so on? Do identical operationalizations in the detection and measure of these imply that these are identical constructs or processes? What are the implications when a secondary task probe fails to detect these constructs or processes? Does this failure necessarily imply that the construct or process was non-existent at the time of the measure?

The focus of this paper is on clarifying our current understanding of what it is that the secondary task technique, particularly the "RT-probe", actually measures. The generally accepted assumption, that the existence of some limited pool of resources is a phenomenal given and that the secondary task probe is the dipstick by which this pool is measured, may not always be valid justification for claims that may be made as a result of the use of the secondary task technique. A theoretical problem with this assumption as the basis for using the secondary task probe as a measurement instrument is its circularity as a theoretical claim (cf., Navon 1984, 1985). An operational problem with this assumption in its simple form is that it does not account for evidence of apparently "resource free" processing, including apparent parallel processing and automatism. What we *do* know is that changes in secondary task performance do seem to provide evidence of changes in the use of processing resources, whatever these "resources" really are, and that these changes may in turn provide evidence for the detection of *one (and only one) dimension* of a variety of constructs and processes.

THE RT-PROBE SECONDARY TASK

Although most recent users of the secondary task technique have used the RT-probe, a variety of secondary tasks could be used (Ogden, Levine, and Eisner 1979), including the maintenance of hand pressure (Welch 1898) and finger tapping tasks (Friedman, Polson, and Dafoe 1988; Jastrow 1892). Of greatest interest to most current users of the secondary task technique is the measurement of response times to visual or auditory stimuli while performing a concurrent primary task. A brief audible beep, to which the subject must respond by pressing a button switch, can presumably function as a probe into the processing of a concurrent *primary* task. Changes in response times to the *secondary* or *probe* task are taken as an indicator of changes in the use of processing resources devoted to the performance of the primary task. There are variations on the secondary stimuli and response tasks that can be used, such as the use of a flash of light and a verbal response, but all are based on the same basic underlying assumption: that there appear to be limits in our abilities to utilize processing resources and that greater expenditure of resources toward the performance of the primary task can measurably degrade the performance of the concurrent secondary task. There is yet, however, some amount of controversy regarding just what these "resources" might be and how they function.

ATTENTION, EFFORT, ELABORATION, ETC.: WHAT'S THE DIFFERENCE?

Although the secondary task technique is most certainly a valuable research tool, it really cannot detect anything other than apparent interference between concurrently performed tasks. Under the assumption that concurrently performed tasks will interfere with each other, the secondary task technique has been used to measure constructs and processes described variously as attention, effort, elaboration, processing intensity, and such. Is it really possible that the response time to an audible beep can become a common operational definition of these various constructs which may not have common theoretical meanings? If these constructs are theoretically different, how is it that they can all be measured in exactly the same manner? That is, if all are defined in the amount of secondary task interference that they cause, how can they be any different? A yardstick only provides a measure of length and nothing more: can the secondary task probe provide a direct measure of attention *and* of effort *and* of elaboration?

Although such constructs may be related, they are theoretically somewhat different. What we need is to know what *specific dimensional aspect* the secondary task describes about the construct under investigation. The RT-probe secondary task generally does not provide a *direct* measure of attention or of elaboration or of most other constructs we would usually want to investigate, but provides a measure of only a single dimensional quantity which is *common* to these constructs. Evidence that the secondary task measured *something* is not alone sufficient evidence of whatever construct the investigator might claim to measure. There must be some *a priori* theoretical reason for considering that the secondary task probe provides evidence of some dimension of a construct.

Consider, for example, two tasks with which we might use the RT-probe secondary task. The first primary task involves mental arithmetic and the second primary task involves reading an interesting story. Both primary tasks can be expected to produce measurable decreases in RT-probe secondary task performance. It might be reasonable to assert that we have measured "effort" in the arithmetic task and "elaboration" in the interesting reading task, even though we might not think that "elaboration" was involved in the mental arithmetic task or that subjects would regard reading an interesting story as especially effortful. This is because we do have some feel for other dimensions such as how and when processing resources might be utilized in performing these tasks and for the outcome of the performance of these tasks. In this example, we might consider *recall* as another dimension associated with the elaboration construct but not with the effort construct. We might consider certain *skill improvements* to be associated with the effort construct, but not with the elaboration construct.

As long as the theoretical context of the construct was considered and more than a single dimension of the construct under test was investigated, we might have reasonable strength in our claim of evidence for the construct under investigation. The cautionary note, then, is that there must first be some *theoretical* justification for using this methodology and that it should not be the *sole* measurement instrument of a multidimensional construct. One possible multidimensional framework, which attempts to integrate measures of attention with measures of attitude, has been suggested by Owen (1990).

So what exactly is this single common dimension that is detected or measured by the secondary task probe? Why and how do concurrently performed tasks interfere with each other? The basic assumption in using the secondary task probe is that it provides an index of primary task consumption of "processing resources". Precisely what are these "resources" upon which the use of the secondary task technique is grounded? If a change in the use of these resources as indicated by the secondary task probe has some sort of meaning, what is the meaning of a failure of the secondary task probe to detect resource usage?

WHAT IS A "LIMITED RESOURCE"?

The theoretical basis for using the secondary task probe in the measure or detection of a particular construct is a little more problematic than one might initially assume; it is still not clear just what it is that the secondary task probe measures and does not measure beyond concurrent task interference. The theoretical justification for the secondary task technique is based on the assumption that the construct or process under investigation consumes from some asymptotically limited pool of processing resources; changes in secondary task performance are presumed to provide a measure of changes in the use of those resources, providing evidence as to the investigator's claims regarding the construct under investigation. Acceptance of this assumption requires that one adopt a circular form of reasoning. Although the relationship between secondary task performance and "attention", "effort", "capacity", or "processing resources" seems obvious enough to some researchers, others have found the conceptual, theoretical, and operational definition of these constructs and processes to be more elusive (cf., Hirst and Kalmar 1987; Kinchla 1980; Navon 1984; Stelmach and Hughes 1983; Wickens 1984). Secondary task performance can be explained in terms of structural limitations, processing channel limitations, central processor limitations, resource sharing, and so on, and none of these explanations seems to have completely obsolesced the others.

Earlier studies of the mechanism of information processing viewed the processing system as something like a single channel transmission line (see Welford 1967 for review). Miller (1956), for instance, viewed the human as "a kind of communication system" with a finite limit in its *channel capacity*. Many of the earlier studies of attention and the mechanism of the information processing system were attempts to locate where this capacity limitation, or "bottleneck", occurred. Broadbent (1954) concluded that there seemed to be a many-to-one selection switch in this channel and that there was a limit as to how fast this switch could operate in selecting parallel input signals for sequential passage through a single channel processing system. The idea that this processing bottleneck occurred near the input of the processing channel was to result in Broadbent's "Filter Theory" (Broadbent 1957, 1958).

Although Broadbent's theory is one of the most well known of the earlier theories of attention, it very quickly came under attack regarding the location of the channel bottleneck and the mechanism of this bottleneck. Two well known attempts to refine the Filter Theory in these regards were those of Deutsch and Deutsch (1963) and Treisman (1966). It became evident, however, that there could be situations in which the processing system did not behave as if it was a single channel transmission line.

If the processing system operates in a serial manner as proposed by the single channel hypotheses, i.e., being able to sequentially process only one task at a time, then the time taken to perform two tasks concurrently should be linearly additive. That is, if the system must function by completing one task and then "switching" to the other, then the amount of time taken to complete both tasks should be predicted by adding the times to complete each task individually. Empirical evidence has shown otherwise; the time taken to perform the tasks concurrently is sometimes much less than the sum of the times taken to perform the tasks individually (Keele 1967). This seems to provide evidence against a single-channel serial system.

Further evidence against the single channel hypothesis was provided by experiments that allowed for compatible input and output tasks. In a manner similar to Broadbent's (1954) dichotic listening task, Moray and Jordan (1966) presented subjects with different but simultaneous messages in each ear. Subjects were asked to type these messages, the numbers zero through nine, on keyboards with ten keys labeled zero through nine; the subject was to type the left ear messages on left hand switches, and right ear messages on right hand switches. This was assumed to provide subjects with a means of parallel output matched to parallel input. The results seemed to indicate that something more than single channel transmission was possible.

This led Moray (1967) to propose that apparent limits in the ability to process information may be better conceptualized in terms of a limited capacity *central processor* rather than a limited capacity *communication channel*. Under this central processor conceptualization, the overall size of the processor is limited but the processor is very flexible. This limited capacity central processor conceptualization was expanded and refined by Kahneman (1973). Kahneman did not view this model as a replacement for the earlier models. The earlier models were viewed as explanations of *structural limitations* in processing (e.g., eyes cannot be focused on two objects simultaneously, regardless of the processing abilities of the rest of the system) and the limited capacity processor model as an explanation of how some processing activities can be carried out together; neither view was considered as adequate alone. The model that was proposed by Moray and Kahneman has been labeled the *undifferentiated capacity hypothesis* by Kerr (1973).

Kahneman seemed deliberately vague in labeling this limited processing resource, noting that it "may be variously labeled 'effort', 'capacity', or 'attention'" (p. 9). Kahneman's conceptualization viewed the processing system as possessing a very *general* pool of "capacity" or "effort" or "attention" which may be allocated to the performance of various tasks.

A problem with this undifferentiated resource capacity model is that the processing of some tasks *does* appear to be differentiated. For example, it is easier to attend to auditory and visual messages concurrently than to two auditory messages (Rollins and Hendricks 1980; Treisman and Davies 1973). This could be due to structural limitations or it could be possible that there are separate processing channels for auditory and visual information prior to input to the central processing mechanism. According to the *multiple resource theory*, it could also be possible that there are different kinds of resource pools, and that dual task performance interference occurs when two processes attempt to use the same pool (Navon and Gopher 1979; Wickins 1980, 1984). Friedman, Polson, and Dafoe (1988), for instance, found differences between each cerebral hemisphere and task interference. This explanation implies that not all primary tasks will interfere in the same way with secondary task performance; *the detection of differences in secondary task performance between two tasks may be not necessarily be due to differences in "attention" or in the expenditure of "effort"*.

Yet another explanation is the *dual process theory*, which recognizes a continuum of information processing, anchored by slow, effortful, serial controlled processing at one extreme and by fast, resource-free, parallel automatic processing at the other (e.g., Schneider and Shiffrin 1977; Shiffrin and Schneider 1977). Related to this latter notion is the "processing is a skill" explanation (Hirst 1986; Hirst, Spelke, Reaves, Caharack, and Neisser 1980; Spelke, Hirst, and Neisser 1976). These explanations attempt to explain how processing can sometimes appear to be resource free; *processing can take place yet remain undetected by a secondary task probe*.

A more recent explanation is that concurrent task interference may not be due to limitations in "capacity" in the sense of some entity being *divided* in the processing of concurrent tasks, but is due instead to attention *sharing*. David Navon, who was once an advocate of the capacity explanations of concurrent task interference, has become somewhat more hesitant toward the capacity assumption in recent years. A possible explanation for differences in the interference of various dual tasks is in the way they share a relatively limitless resource; there may be no limitations in a capacity sense, but interference may be a result of some sort of confusion due to what Navon calls *outcome conflict* (Navon 1985; Navon and Miller 1987). One possible source of outcome conflict discussed by Navon is "cross talk" among parallel, independent processes similar to electrical cross talk in parallel wires.

Given that there can be so many viable explanations for dual task interference, it might seem that the secondary task technique is not a useful technique beyond the investigation of its own theoretical basis. Navon (1984) questions the validity of tests which rely on a resource explanation and suggests that an uncritical acceptance of such resource assumptions can result in experimental results that might only be methodological artifacts (Navon 1985). On the other hand, the secondary task technique does appear to detect and measure *something* related to the interference between concurrently performed tasks. As long as this observation allows us to make inferences regarding constructs and processes such as attention, effort, or elaboration, then the secondary task technique would appear to be useful and valid regardless of our inability to completely understand why or how it works (cf., Navon 1984).

A cautionary note is again, then, that there should be some theoretical justification behind using this methodology. One report in the marketing literature, for instance, justifies the use of the secondary task technique on the grounds that "psychologists have used this method for many years" and by discussing what sorts of findings are "typical" of such studies. It is important to be explicit about assumptions regarding the resource requirements of specific pairs of tasks (cf., Friedman, Polson, and Dafoe 1988); careful consideration needs to be given as to why a particular pair of tasks may or may not be expected to interfere in a predictable, detectable, and measurable way.

CONCLUDING REMARKS

The secondary task technique does appear to be a very useful tool, but our current understanding of its underlying assumptions with regard to a variety of constructs is not so strong as one might initially believe. What has been emphasized in this paper is that there must be a stronger theoretical basis when using the secondary task technique than a casual, vague reference to "limited processing resources". Not all pairs of tasks will always cause detectable interference, yet some form of processing can still take place. Most importantly, the construct that is detected is generally not the construct of interest, but only a single dimension of that construct, evidenced only by concurrent task performance interference.

One must fully consider, then, what dimensional aspect of a construct or process the secondary task probe is expected to measure. One must be cautious in claims that a change (or no change) in secondary task performance alone provides conclusive evidence regarding the construct under investigation. The studies of Britton suggest, for instance, that the reading of difficult text can at times consume more "processing resources" than simple text (Britton and Tesser 1982), but also suggest that simple text can at times consume more "processing resources" than difficult text (Britton et al. 1978, 1979, 1980). We cannot really say what is "typical" of such studies, nor can we expect in both cases that the construct that was detected was, say, "elaboration" or "effort". The detection of decreased secondary task performance during, say, the processing of a marketing communication is also not universally an indication of any particular construct or process.

The secondary task probe merely detects apparent changes in the use of "processing resources". Whether this indicates a change in the quantity of usage of a particular resource, a change in the way a resource is shared, or a change to a different resource is currently unclear. Although it would seem reasonable to assume that changes in secondary task performance are an indication of *something*, regardless of our current ability to fully understand whatever that "something" really is, it is currently not clear how such changes relate to a variety of constructs such as attention, effort, elaboration, and so on. Perhaps we need to better define the various dimensions which might be used to conceptually, theoretically, and operationally describe these constructs and processes.

It seems appropriate to conclude with two quotes that are so often used to introduce papers on the subject of attention:

"Everyone knows what attention is."
(William James 1890, p. 403)

"The discovery of attention didn't result in any immediate triumph of experimental method. It was something like a hornet's nest: The first touch brought out a whole swarm of instant problems. . . The discovery of a reliable measure of attention would appear to be one of the most important problems that await solution by experimental psychology in the future." (Edward Titchener 1908, ch. 5)

REFERENCES

Britton, Bruce K., Timothy S. Holdredge, Cheryl Curry, and Robert D. Westbrook (1979), "Use of Cognitive Capacity in Reading Identical Texts with Different Amounts of Discourse Level Meaning," *Journal of Experimental Psychology: Human Learning and Memory*, 5, 262-270.

_____ and Abraham Tesser (1982), "Effects of Prior Knowledge on Use of Cognitive Capacity in Three Complex Cognitive Tasks," *Journal of Verbal Learning and Verbal Behavior*, 21, 421-436.

_____, Robert D. Westbrook, and Timothy S. Holdredge (1978), "Reading and Cognitve Capacity Usage: Effects of Text Difficulty," *Journal of Experimental Psychology: Human Learning and Memory*, 4, 582-591.

_____, Robbie Zeigler, and Robert D. Westbrook (1980), "Use of Cognitive Capacity in Reading Easy and Difficult Text: Two Tests of an Allocation of Attention Hypothesis," *Journal of Reading Behavior*, 12, 23-30.

Broadbent, D.E. (1954), "The Role of Localization in Attention and Memory Span," *Journal of Experimental Psychology*, 47, 191-196.

_____ (1957), "A Mechanical Model for Human Attention and Immediate Memory," *Psychological Review*, 64, 205-215.

_____ (1958), *Perception and Communication*. London: Pergamon Press Ltd.

Deutsch, J. and D. Deutsch (1963), "Attention: Some Theoretical Considerations," *Psychological Review*, 70, 80-90.

Friedman, Alinda, Martha Campbell Polson, and Cameron G. Dafoe (1988), "Dividing Attention Between the Hands and the Head: Performance Trade-offs Between Rapid Finger Tapping and Verbal Memory," *Journal of Experimental Psychology: Human Perception and Performance*, 14, 60-68.

Hirst, William (1986), "The Psychology of Attention," in *Mind and Brain*, eds. Joseph E. LeDoux and William Hurst, New York: Cambridge University Press. 105-141.

_____ and David Kalmar (1987), "Characterizing Attentional Resources," *Journal of Experimental Psychology: General*, 116, 68-81.

_____, Elizabeth E. Spelke, Celia Reaves, George Caharack, and Ulric Neisser (1980), "Dividing Attention Without Alternation or Automaticity," *Journal of Experimental Psychology: General*, 109, 98-117.

Huddleston, E. F., and R. V. Wilson (1971), "An Evaluation of the Usefulness of Four Secondary Tasks in Assessing the Effort of a Lag in Simulated Aircraft Dynamics," *Ergonomics*, 14, 371-380.

Inhoff, Albrecht Werner, and Kevin Fleming (1989), "Probe-Detection Times During the Reading of Easy and Difficult Text," *Journal of Experimental Psychology: Learning, Memory, and Cognition*, 15(2), 339-351.

James, William (1890), *The Principles of Psychology*. New York: Holt.

Jastrow, J. (1892), "The Interference of Mental Processes," *American Journal of Psychology*, 4, 219-223.

Kahneman, Daniel (1973), *Attention and Effort*, Englewood Cliffs: Prentice Hall, Inc.

Keele, S.W. (1967), "Compatibility and Time-Sharing in Serial Reaction Time," *Journal of Experimental Psychology*, 75, 529-539.

Kerr, Beth (1973), "Processing Demands During Mental Operations," *Memory and Cognition*, 1, 401-412.

Kinchla, R.A. (1980), "The Measurement of Attention," in *Attention and Performance VIII*, ed. Rayond S. Nickerson, Hillsdale: Lawrence Erlbaum Associates, Publishers. 213-238.

Lord, Kenneth R. and Robert E. Burnkrant (1988), "Television Program Elaboration Effects on Commercial Processing," in *Advances in Consumer Research*, vol. 15, ed. Michael J. Houston, 213-218.

_____ _____, and Robert S. Owen (1989), "An Experimental Comparison of Self-Report and Response Time Measures of Consumer Information Processing," in *Proceedings of the American Marketing Association 1989 Summer Educator's Conference*.

Miller, George A. (1956), "The Magical Number Seven, Plus or Minus Two: Some Limits on our Capacity for Processing Information," *Psychological Review*, 63(2), 81-97.

Moore, Danny L., Douglas Hausknecht, and Kanchana Thamodaran (1986), "Time Compression Response Opportunity in Persuasion," *Journal of Consumer Research*, 13(June), 85-99.

Moray, N. (1967), "Where is Capacity Limited? A Survey and a Model," in *Attention and Performance*, ed. A.F. Sanders, Amsterdam: North-Holland Publishing Co., 84-92.

_____ and A. Jordan (1966), "Practice and Compatibility in Two-Channel Short-term Memory," *Psychonomic Science*, 4, 427.

Navon, David (1984), "Resources - A Theoretical Soupstone?" *Psychological Review*, 91, 216-234.

_____ (1985), "Attention Division or Attention Sharing?" in *Attention and Performance XI*, eds. Michael I. Posner and Oscar S.M. Marin. Hillsdale: Lawrence Erlbaum Associates, Publishers, 133-146.

_____ and Jeff Miller (1987), "Role of Outcome Conflict in Dual-Task Interference," *Journal of Experimental Psychology: Human Perception and Performance*, 13(3), 435-448.

_____ and D. Gopher (1979), "On the Economy of the Human Processing System," *Psychological Review*, 86, 214-255.

Ogden, George D., Jerrold M. Levine, and Ellen J. Eisner (1979), "Measurement of Workload by Secondary Tasks," *Human Factors*, 21(5), 529-548.

Owen, Robert S. (1990), "Integrating Attitude and Attention Theories," in *Developments in Marketing Science*, Vol. 13, ed. B. J. Dunlap, The Academy of Marketing Science, 52-55.

Rollins, H.A. and R. Hendricks (1980), "Processing of Words Presented Simultaneously to Eye and Ear," *Journal of Experimental Psychology: Human Pereption and Performance*, 6, 99-109.

Schneider, Walter and Richard M. Shiffrin (1977), "Controlled and Automatic Human Information Processing: I. Detection, Search, and Attention," *Psychological Review*, 84, 1-66.

Shiffrin, Richard M. and Walter Schneider (1977), "Controlled and Automatic Human Information Processing: II. Perceptual Learning, Automatic Attending, and a General Theory," *Psychological Review*, 84, 127-190.

Spelke, Elizabeth, William Hirst, and Ulric Neisser (1976), "Skills of Divided Attention," *Cognition*, 4, 215-230.

Stapleford, R. L. (1973), "Comparisons of Population Subgroups' Performance on a Keyword Psychomotor Task, " *Proceedings of the Ninth Annual Conference on Manual Control*, Massachussetts Institute of Technology, Cambridge, Massachussetts.

Stelmach, George E. and Barry Hughes (1983), "Does Motor Skill Require a Theory of Attention?" in *Memory and Control of Action*, ed. Richard A. Magill, New York: North-Holland Publishing Company, 67-92.

Thorson, Esther, Byron Reeves, and Joan Schleuder (1985), "Message Complexity and Attention to Television," *Communication Research*, 12(4), 427-454.

_____ (1987), "Attention to Local and Global Complexity in Television Messages," in *Communication Yearbook 10*, ed. Margaret McLaughlin, Newbury Park, CA: Sage Publications, 366-383.

Titchener, Edward B. (1908), *Lectures on the Elementary Psychology of Feeling and Attention*, New York: McMillan.

Treisman, Anne M. (1966), "Our Limited Attentention," *Advances in Science*, 22, 600-611.

_____ and Alison A. Davies (1973), "Divided Attention to Ear and Eye," in *Attention and Performance IV*, ed. Sylvan Kornblum, New York: Academic Press, 101-125.

Welch, Jeannette C. (1989), "On the Measurement of Mental Activity through Muscular Activity and the Determination of a Constant Attention," *American Journal of Physiology*, 1, 283-306.

Welford, A.T. (1967), "Single-Channel Operation in the Brain," in *Attention and Performance*, ed. A.F. Sanders, Amsterdam: North-Holland Publishing Co., 5-22.

Wickens, Christopher D. (1980), "The Structure of Attentional Resources," in *Attention and Performance VIII*, ed. Raymond S. Nickerson, Hillsdale: Lawrence Erlbaum Associates, Publishers, 239-257.

_____ (1984), "Processing Resources and Attention," in *Varieties of Attention*, eds. Raja Parasuraman and D.R. Davies, Orlando: Academic Press, Inc., 63-102.

An Exploratory Investigation Of Questionnaire Pretesting With Verbal Protocol Analysis

Ruth N. Bolton, GTE Laboratories Incorporated

ABSTRACT

This paper explores how cognitive research methods can be used to identify defective questions in survey questionnaires. Concurrent verbal protocols are elicited during face-to-face interviews to investigate respondents' cognitive processes as they respond to survey questions. The protocols are segmented and then coded using categories that represent comprehension, retrieval and judgment problems. This procedure is used to pretest two versions of a telecommunications survey. The results indicate that this procedure is useful for evaluating draft questionnaires, and for identifying questions that are associated with information processing problems.

INTRODUCTION

Questionnaire pretesting is a relatively straightforward, low-cost method for detecting problems with a questionnaire. It entails a small pilot study to determine how a questionnaire can be improved to minimize response errors, such as a respondent misinterpreting a question (Converse and Presser 1986). Individual items (i.e., questions) can be pretested for an acceptable level of response variation, meaning, task difficulty, and respondent interest/attention. Or, the overall questionnaire can be pretested for appropriate vocabulary, the order of questions, skip patterns, timing, and overall respondent interest, attention and respondent well-being. These tests enable a researcher to identify and change questionnaire design features to minimize response errors.

Since nonsampling error (i.e., response and nonresponse error) is the major contributor to total survey error (Assael and Keon 1982), questionnaire pretests should be central to the survey design process. However, as several authors have noted (e.g., Lehmann 1979), researchers frequently neglect to pretest survey questionnaires. Furthermore, academic researchers have failed to examine methodological issues in questionnaire pretesting. In a notable exception, Hunt, Sparkman and Wilcox (1982) found that traditional methods of pretesting (i.e., a face-to-face or telephone interview followed by a debriefing) were effective in identifying some, but not all, types of problem questions.

This paper explores how cognitive research methods can be used to pretest questionnaires. It describes a new method of identifying defective questions and illustrates the method by pretesting two versions of a survey. Concurrent verbal protocols are elicited during face-to-face interviews to investigate respondents' cognitive processes as they respond to survey questions. In contrast with prior questionnaire pretests, the unit of analysis is a speech burst, rather than the complete response to a survey question. Segmenting protocols into speech bursts enables the use of a coding scheme that identifies the macroprocesses associated with answering a survey question. Protocols are coded using categories that represent comprehension, retrieval and judgment problems. This procedure is useful for evaluating draft questionnaires and diagnosing problems.

LITERATURE REVIEW

The survey research literature provides guidance about *developing* questionnaires and multi-item measures of constructs for questionnaires (Sudman and Bradburn 1982; Churchill 1979), but there is very little guidance about *pretesting* questionnaires. Most researchers agree that the first pretest should be administered by personal interview to elicit concurrent or retrospective protocols, even if the questionnaire will ultimately be administered by mail or telephone. However, they are almost completely silent about how the pretest data should be collected and analyzed. Fortunately, recent interdisciplinary research in cognitive psychology and survey research provides some direction (Jadine, Straf, Tanur and Tourangeau 1984; Hippler, Schwarz and Sudman 1987).

Pretest Data Collection

Researchers have used a variety of methods of pretest data collection. For example, the National Center for Health Statistics (NCHS) has used concurrent protocols, paraphrasing, retrospective protocols, confidence ratings, and response latency measurements (Royston, Bercini, Sirken and Mingay 1986; Royston 1987). Although there is little information available about their methods, they seem to have primarily relied on retrospective protocols. In a study of the processes respondents use in answering behavioral frequency questions, Blair and Burton (1987) also elicited retrospective protocols by asking "How did you come up with that answer?" They argued that a retrospective protocol was an appropriate measure of process because: (a) a concurrent protocol would have altered "natural survey conditions," (b) previous authors have recommended retrospective protocols when they can be taken immediately and the processing episode is brief, and (c) demand effects that would lead respondents to distort the process did not seem likely.

Retrospective reports may be accurate in some contexts (Wright and Rip 1981), but there are potential problems (Ericsson and Simon 1984; Nisbettt and Wilson 1977). Respondents may fail to retrieve and accurately verbalize the processes used, and they may report processes they feel they should have used rather than those they actually used. In contrast, concurrent verbalization is closely related to the actual survey task -- responding to the interview questions -- so that the request to verbalize should not interfere/change the respondents' thought processes. For this reason, the elicitation of concurrent protocols seems particularly appropriate for identifying defective questions. However, Hunt, Sparkman and Wilcox (1982) did not find any difference between the effectiveness of concurrent and retrospective protocols. Surprisingly, they did find that verbal protocols collected during telephone interviews were more effective in detecting defective questions than verbal protocols collected during in-store (i.e., face-to-face) interviews.

Pretest Data Analysis

Recent research on the cognitive processes underlying a respondent's answer to a survey question provides a theoretical context for a new method of analyzing pretest data. Building on work concerning the structure of attitudes, Tourangeau (1987; Tourangeau and Rasinski 1988) proposed that the respondent's answer to an attitude question is the product of four stages or macroprocesses: comprehension of the question, the retrieval of relevant beliefs and feelings from memory, the weighing of information to form a judgment, and the selection of an appropriate response alternative. If the content characteristics of a respondent's verbal protocols arise from these four macroprocesses, an analysis of pretest data should be able to identify defective survey questions by coding respondents' processing difficulties.

Although content analysis has been used to code and analyze open-ended questions, it has not been applied to questionnaire pretest data (Weber 1985). In prior research that has coded verbal protocols from surveys, the unit of analysis has been the complete response to a question. Hunt, Sparkman and Wilcox (1982) coded five types of faulty questions: loaded questions, double questions, ambiguous questions, inappropriate vocabulary, and missing alternatives. An error identification was scored if the respondent made comments "which could help in recognizing the error" (p. 272). However, Tourangeau's model suggests that a pretest should trace the thought processes that occur as a respondent forms an answer to a question. Hence, in order to identify difficulties in the response process, the unit of analysis for verbal protocols elicited during questionnaire pretests should be a speech burst or segment.

A PROPOSED PRETEST METHODOLOGY

This section describes a pretest methodology that uses cognitive research methods to identify defective questions. This methodology entails the elicitation of concurrent verbal protocols -- a process tracing technique that requires the respondent to think aloud while making a decision (Ericsson and Simon 1984). The verbal protocols are segmented into speech bursts and coded to identify respondents' difficulties in forming answers to the survey questions.

The core of this pretest methodology is the coding scheme. Coding schemes in consumer research have typically identified information processing strategies, such as attribute comparison versus within brand processes (e.g., Bettman and Park 1980). In contrast, this coding scheme identifies respondents' comprehension, retrieval, judgment and response difficulties. The conceptual framework for this coding scheme is described in the following paragraphs.

Comprehension.

A respondent's ability to comprehend a survey question should be facilitated when the survey provides contextual information, such as bridging statements, a logical sequence of questions, groups of related questions and explicit (perhaps lengthy) questions (Tourangeau 1984). If a survey question is defective, respondents frequently indicate comprehension difficulties by asking a question. Hence, a coding category was created to count questions *asked by the respondent*. In the context of many inter-related survey questions, respondents frequently indicate comprehension difficulties by statements about the similarity of the questions. These statements can be identified by a category of verbal cues such as "I've already answered that question."

Retrieval

Surveys typically elicit memory-based rather than stimulus-based judgments, necessitating the retrieval of information or earlier judgments. In a typical survey context, the respondent retrieves information -- rather than earlier judgments -- because he/she acquired information without knowing that a judgment would be required. Consequently, a respondent's ability to retrieve information in response to a survey question depends on whether the cues provided match the cues available during encoding. The respondent's failure to retrieve information -- that is, forgetting -- can occur when the relevant information was not stored in long-term memory, it cannot be retrieved from available cues, or it is difficult to distinguish from related information (Tourangeau 1984). The respondent's difficulty in retrieving information from memory can be identified from the respondent's verbal protocols concerning the retrieval process: either information was not stored in long-term memory (e.g., "no experience") or information cannot be retrieved (e.g., "don't remember").

Judgment

There are numerous studies that document the existence of judgment heuristics and response biases in decision-making contexts. In a survey context, response biases may be associated with questions for which respondents experience difficulty forming judgments. Respondents' verbal protocols may provide verbal cues that indicate they are experiencing difficulty forming a judgment (e.g., "difficult to say") or that they lack confidence in their answer to the question (e.g., "maybe"). These two categories of verbalizations should identify defective questions, but they are not completely diagnostic. The respondent may not distinguish between difficulty retrieving information versus difficulty evaluating information.

EXHIBIT ONE
Alternative Versions of Questionnaire

CURRENT VERSION

Now I would like to ask your opinions about the quality of different services you think you would get from GTE if you should need them. You may base your responses either on your own experience, what you have heard from others, or the level of service quality you believe GTE would provide.

1. If you were to need repair service, how would you evaluate the quality of repair service that you think you would get from GTE?
2. If you wanted a change in your current telephone service, such as ordering new service features, extensions or for transferring your service to a new residence; how would you evaluate the quality of service you think you would receive from the GTE representative who would handle your request?
3. Now thinking about the new service or service change that you might request, how would you evaluate the quality of how GTE would handle this change?
4. There are times when directory assistance is needed to find a local telephone number. If you should need such assistance, what kind of service quality do you think you might receive from GTE?

REVISED VERSION

In the next few questions, I will be asking you to rate various aspects of GTE's service. We are interested in your opinion even if you have had no direct experience with a particular aspect of service. If you have not had experience with a particular item, please base your opinion on what you think to be true of GTE's service.

1a. How would you rate GTE on the overall quality of repair service?
1b. How would you rate GTE on fixing problems with telephone service the first time?
1c. How would you rate GTE on the length of time to fix telephone service problems?
2. How would you rate the handling of your request for ordering new service features by GTE representatives?
3. How would you rate the handling of the actual new service installation or service change itself?
4. How would you rate GTE on handling directory assistance requests for telephone numbers?

Response

This study does not examine response difficulties because they are related to measurement and scaling issues. However, it is conceptually straightforward to code respondents' use of scale items or use of fixed response alternatives. The coding scheme does code pauses because they indicate unidentified, nonverbalized processing. For example, if many respondents pause when answering a specific question, the question may require extensive information processing so that it is inappropriate for a brief telephone interview.

THE DATA BASE

The previous section described a questionnaire pretest methodology. This section describes how the methodology was applied in a split ballot experiment that pretested a customer satisfaction survey used by GTE Telephone Operations. GTE, like most franchised suppliers of local telephone service, regularly surveys its customers to identify potential service enhancements, to evaluate the effect of enhancements, and to meet public utilities commission requirements. In 1989, GTE conducted an experiment to compare the current version of its residential customer survey with a revised version (that was intended to replace it in 1991). The entire survey instrument was pretested, but (due to space limitations) this study only examines the pretest data from one section of the instrument in which the current version (CV) measured service quality dimensions with a sequence of "hypothetical" questions while the revised version (RV) measured the same dimensions with conventional perceptual ratings questions. The two versions of this section of the questionnaire are shown in Exhibit 1.

Residential customers were recruited by telephone to participate in face-to-face interviews lasting approximately forty-five minutes to an hour. Prior to the interview, respondents were informed of the purpose of the study and were informed that their responses would be audiotaped. As with virtually all pretests, this pretest employed a small convenience sample. Six customers were administered the revised version and fifteen customers were administered the current version (because GTE management was particularly interested in the latter's performance).

Task Instructions

The task instructions for the elicitation of concurrent protocols during the questionnaire pretest differ somewhat from the instructions used in problem-solving situations. They asked the respondent to "constantly THINK OUT LOUD while you are deciding about your answers." The interviewers were trained to strictly follow the questionnaire, but they were permitted to backchannel. (Backchanneling is the occurrence of a speaking turn of one word (e.g., "uh-uh") that does not follow a question. This activity is the equivalent of a nod or other indication that the interviewer "hears" the respondent.) The interviewer administered two practice questions similar in format to the actual survey questions. Afterward, the introductory sentences of the survey provided the transition to the actual survey questions. The interviewer used the phrases "Remember, I'm interested in what you are thinking," and "You're doing a good job of thinking aloud" to reinforce the respondents' behavior.

Segmentation, Precoding and Coding

The audiotapes of the interviews were transcribed into electronic form and the transcripts were segmented for analysis. The respondents' speech was segmented into speech bursts or utterances using short pauses, intonation, and syntactical markers (for complete phrases, clauses or sentences) as cues. The transcripts were pre-coded by marking the text to indicate pauses (of three seconds or more) and questions (identified by an interrogative voice inflection).

Each coding category is a list of key words or word strings that have similar meanings or a nonverbal cue (such as a pause). The initial lists were developed from a pretest of a cafeteria survey. Respondents' protocols were examined to (1) identify key words (e.g., evaluate), and (2) generate synonyms (e.g., judge, rate), including colloquialisms. The coded transcripts were reviewed to ensure that the key words were associated with appropriate segments, and the coding categories were revised several times. Revisions usually resulted in more restrictive word strings or new word strings. These steps were repeated using transcripts from the pretest of the telecommunications survey. Exhibit 2 shows the lists of key words for each category.

Analysis

After the interviews were transcribed, segmented and precoded, the transcripts were coded with Miller and Chapman's (1982) computer program, *Systematic Analysis of Language Transcripts* (SALT). This program was not designed for the analysis of pretest data, but it can be adapted to this purpose. There are several advantages to automatic encoding (Ericsson and Simon 1984). It requires all of the underlying vocabulary and inference rules to be defined and applied consistently; its reliability is perfect; and its robustness to changes in vocabulary and rules can be tested. Since the coding scheme was not intended to completely describe the processing strategy of each respondent, a code was not assigned to every segment. Multiple codes were sometimes assigned to a single segment when it contained verbal cues for more than one category.

RESULTS

The SALT program was used to count the number of occurrences of each category for each question answered by each respondent. These "counts" were converted into percentages by dividing by the total number of segments uttered by the respondent (to adjust for the fact that some respondents are more verbose than others). Then, an exploratory factor analysis was conducted to investigate the interdependence among the coding categories. Afterward, the percentage of segments in each category of information processing difficulty were tabulated to provide diagnostic information about potential defects in the current and revised questionnaires.

Factor Analysis

Since the development of the coding categories relied heavily on the face validity of the lists of verbal cues, our analysis began by examining the convergent and discriminant validity of the seven coding categories. The proportions of segments in each coding category for each question were subjected to a principal components analysis with a varimax rotation. The results are displayed in Table 1. Three factors with eigenvalues greater than one explain 55% of the variance in the original seven categories. Appropriate labels for these three factors seem to be COMPREHENSION, RETRIEVAL and JUDGMENT. The comprehension factor has heavy loadings on the categories for questions and "similar" statements; the judgment factor has heavy loadings on the categories measuring uncertainty and "can't judge," and the retrieval factor has a heavy loading on the category that measures "don't remember." Pauses and segments about "no experience" tend to load on more than one factor, indicating that they reflect multiple information processing problems. This factor analytic structure supports the notion that respondents' verbal protocols reflect three *independent* underlying information processes.

Tabulation of Coding Categories

The percentage of segments in each category of information processing difficulty are shown in Table 2. These percentages are intrinsically interesting because they are measures of the extent of information processing problems. For example, the average respondent uttered 11 segments in response to the CV of question two. 7.9% percent of these segments were pauses, so that the average customer must have paused once (i.e., 11.4 segments x 7.9% = 0.90 segments) during his response. This statistic demonstrates that most customers engaged in nonverbalized processing while responding about the service representative -- implying that the question did *not* elicit a "top of mind" response. The following paragraphs examine the pattern of the results in Table 2 to determine whether the coding categories are providing diagnostic information about defective questions. Although statistical tests of differences in proportions between the two versions of each question are reported, the results of these tests should be viewed with caution due to the small sample size.

EXHIBIT TWO
Coding Categories

1) <u>Comprehension - Similar</u>
identical&question
same&question
similar&question
identical&answer
same&answer
similar&answer
answer&again
sound&alike
question&close
sound&identical
I&answered&that&question
like:I:said
like:I:siad&before
experience:again
opinion:again
there:again
is:that:what:you're:asking
repetitious

2) <u>Retrieval - No Experience</u>
no:experience
never:experienced
not:experienced
any:experience
never:experience
not:experience
haven't:experienced
not:familiar:with
no:need:for&service
no:need:for&option
never:use
never:done
never:used
don't use
haven't:used

3) <u>Retrieval - Don't Remember</u>
dont:remember
forget
can't:think
I'm:trying:to:think
or:something

4) <u>Judgment - Can't Judge</u>
I:can't:say
I:can't:tell
I:can't:rate
I:can't:evaluate
I:can't:judge
tough&rate
not:easy&rate
difficult&rate
hard&rate
tough&evaluate
not:easy&evaluate
difficult&evaluate
hard&evaluate
tough:to:say
not:easy&to:say
difficult:to:say
hard:to:say
tough&judge
not:easy&judge
difficult&judge
hard&judge
tough&to:tell
not:easy&to:tell
difficult&to:tell
hard&to:tell

5) <u>Judgment - Uncertain</u>
approximately
perhaps
kind:of
unless
somewhere:in:there
I:reckon
not:certain
I&imagine
depends
mostly
sort:of
not:sure
whatever

---

* The string "word1:word2" is interpreted "word1 immediately followed by word2 in a given segment."
The string "word1&word2" is interpreted "word1 and word2 occurring in a given segment," where word 1 and word2 can appear in any order, with or without intervening words.

Question One - Repair. The RV asks three separate questions about repair, whereas the CV asks a single question. Respondents generate substantially more thoughts and they make significantly ($p < 0.15$) more statements about question similarity in response to the RV questions. Thus, respondents are supplying more information, but they perceive redundancy among the three repair questions in the RV. Furthermore, respondents are slightly less likely to verbalize retrieval difficulties ("no experience") and slightly more likely to verbalize judgment difficulties ("uncertain") in the RV.

Question Two - Service Representative. The second question asks customers to rate the service representative's handling of their requests. The CV provides examples of situations in which the customer might have contacted a service representative about a service order whereas the RV does not. (From the telephone company's

TABLE 1
Factor Analysis of Category Proportions*

	Factor 1 (Comprehension)	Factor 2 (Judgment)	Factor 3 (Retrieval)
Questions	<u>0.62175</u>	0.35259	-0.04825
Similar	<u>0.79730</u>	-0.10436	0.00485
Uncertain	0.02546	<u>0.78603</u>	0.35657
Pause	0.32621	0.16105	0.52887
Can't Judge	-0.12370	<u>0.63009</u>	-0.22994
Don't Remember	-0.20832	-0.12098	<u>0.77454</u>
No Experience	0.59431	-0.28376	0.04654
Eigenvalue	1.55	1.31	1.02
% Variance Explained	22.1	18.7	14.6

* Varimax rotation. Factors with eignenvalues greater than one were retained.

TABLE 2
Processing Difficulties**

		Repair	Service Rep	Service Change	Directory Assistance	All Questions
Comprehension						
Questions	- CV	3.1	4.0	9.1	4.3	5.2
	- RV	4.1	1.5	5.0	0.8	3.0
Similar	- CV	0.3	0.3	0.7	0.0	0.3
	- RV	1.9*	0.0	4.1	0.0	1.6*
Retrieval						
No Experience	- CV	2.9	0.7	0.0	4.8	2.1
	- RV	0.0	0.0	4.2*	3.3	1.8
Don't Remember	- CV	0.0	0.0	0.0	0.0	0.0
	- RV	0.0	1.0*	0.0	0.0	0.3*
Evaluation						
Uncertain	- CV	4.0	3.0	9.3	5.3	5.4
	- RV	5.5	8.7	3.3	5.1	5.6
Can't Judge	- CV	0.0	0.0	0.0	0.0	0.0
	- RV	0.0	1.3*	0.0	0.8*	0.5*
Pauses						
	CV	13.5	7.9	10.3	2.5	8.5
	RV	5.4	3.3	5.9	7.4	5.4
Average Number of Segments						
	CV	13.5	11.4	12.2	8.3	11.3
	RV	27.8	11.2	9.5	13.2	15.5

* Difference between proportions in versions one and two is statistically significant at p < 0.15. Recall that the sample size is larger for the current version of the questionnaire.

** The numbers in this table represent the number of segments in each category, expressed as a percentage of total segments.

viewpoint, service orders include requests for additional directory listing(s), requests for new services such as call waiting, and the installation of additional lines or equipment, as well as changes in service (e.g., flat rate versus measured unit service). Customers typically place these orders by telephoning a company service center and speaking to a representative.) Respondents' verbal protocols indicate proportionally more retrieval problems ("don't remember," p < 0.15) and judgment problems ("can't say," p < 0.15) in response to the RV. This result suggests that customers have difficulty evaluating the service representative's handling of their request because the RV does not supply appropriate cues for customers to retrieve this information from memory.

Question Three - Service Change. The RV's failure to provide cues that match customers' encoding of information about service order requests is compounded in question three, in which the customer is asked to rate how service changes are handled. Respondents' verbalizations indicate their inability to retrieve information ("no experience," p < 0.15) in response to the RV. Apparently, customers' recollections of service order contacts are less vivid than their recollections of repair contacts.

Question Four - Directory Assistance. The RV provides a less detailed description of directory assistance service than the CV. Respondents do not seem to experience more comprehension or retrieval difficulties with the RV, but they generate proportionally more segments about their inability to judge (p < 0.15). One explanation for this result is that respondents confuse toll operators (that handle requests for *connections to long distance numbers*) with directory assistance operators (that handle requests for *information about local numbers*). They are probably unable to retrieve information to form a judgment because their contacts with operators are rare, brief, low-involvement experiences.

All Questions. Excepting question one, respondents ask fewer questions and make fewer comments about similarity of questions in response to the RV of the questionnaire. This finding suggests that they typically experience fewer *comprehension difficulties* with the RV. Respondents produce significantly more (p < 0.15) segments indicating that they "don't remember" across all four RV questions. This result is due to fewer *retrieval difficulties* with questions one and four and more retrieval difficulties with questions two and three. Respondents make more statements about *judgment difficulties* ("can't judge," p < 0.15) with the RV. Their difficulties arise in questions two and four, in which respondents are provided with few retrieval cues and asked to judge brief contacts with telephone company personnel.

DISCUSSION

The diagnostic information provided by our content analysis of verbal protocols cannot be obtained from conventional pretest methodologies. Only a coding scheme that focuses on respondents' cognitive processes as they respond to a survey question can determine whether the question poses a processing difficulty. For example, Table 2 shows that customers' responses to both versions of the directory assistance question include relatively frequent (4.8% and 3.3%) mentions of "no experience." This statistic is based on a detailed count of the number of times the relevant key words/strings listed in Table 1 occur in customers' speech bursts. The verbal cues are quite subtle. For example, one customer responded to the CV of this question by saying, "I *haven't used* it in a long time / but I would say good." Coding schemes that focus on the entire response (e.g., Hunt, Sparkman and Wilcox 1982) are very useful for some types of problem questions, but they do not provide this type of information.

Inspection of respondents' protocols suggests that additional coding categories could be helpful in revising defective questions. For example, the CV seems to create comprehension difficulties for respondents because the questions are framed in a "hypothetical" way and the phrasing "how would you evaluate" is less comprehensible than the more colloquial phrase "how would you rate." For example, one customer responded to the CV of question two by saying, "In other words, *you're asking* me to do a pre-evaluation of what I might do in the future." Another coding category could be created that counts occurrences of such interpretive comments, perhaps including the word string "you're asking."

The information from these analyses can be used (and was used) to create a new version of the questionnaire that improves upon both pretested versions. For example, the pretest results suggest that the RV of the service representative question is defective because it does not provide appropriate cues for service order requests. An introductory statement could be added to provide this information.

CONCLUDING REMARKS

This study described a new questionnaire pretesting methodology. The content characteristics of verbal protocols elicited in a pretest were found to reflect comprehension, retrieval and judgment processes. Coding categories representing these macroprocesses provided diagnostic information about defective questions in a split ballot pretest of a telecommunications questionnaire. The methodology yielded useful recommendations for further questionnaire revisions.

In this study, respondents experienced comprehension difficulties due to the phrase "How would you evaluate" and retrieval difficulties due to inappropriate cues/phrases in questions about telephone service changes and directory assistance. Hence, the questionnaire pretesting methodology seems better suited to identifying question-phrasing problems than question-sequencing problems. Repeated usage of this methodology may yield some rules for "good" question phrasing. Eventually, standards may evolve that indicate "acceptable" levels of response difficulties.

This methodology complements, rather than replaces, existing methods because it cannot identify all types of defective questions. Content analysis depends heavily on the specification and measurement of theoretically-justified content characteristics. Further research is necessary to improve our understanding of the cognitive processes underlying a respondent's answer to a survey question increases and to generalize the measurement/coding scheme to other survey contexts.

This approach is time consuming and labor intensive. In some instances, sufficient information for questionnaire revisions can be obtained from coding schemes that are used in observational monitoring (Bercini 1989) or coding schemes that focus on questionnaire design errors (Hunt, Sparkman and Wilcox 1982). However, a content analysis of verbal protocols is warranted in pretests of large-scale government and industry surveys that generate data for policy decisions. For example, GTE's survey programs provide vital -- and expensive -- inputs to corporate decisions. Consequently, the benefits of pretesting GTE's surveys outweighed the associated costs -- which constituted less than 5% of total survey program costs.

REFERENCES

Assael, Henry and John Keon (1982), "Nonsampling vs. Sampling Errors in Survey Research," *Journal of Marketing*, 45 (Spring), 114-123.

Bercini, Deborah (1989), "Observation and monitoring of interviews," *Quirk's Marketing Research Review* (May).

Bettman, James R. and C. W. Park (1980), "Implication of a Constructive View of Choice for Coding Protocol Data: A Coding Scheme for Elements of Choice Processes," in *Advances in Consumer Research*, 7, San Francisco: Association for Consumer Research: 148-153.

Blair, Edward and Scot Burton (1987), "Cognitive Processes Used by Survey Respondents to Answer Behavioral Frequency Questions," *Journal of Consumer Research*, 14 (September), 280-288.

Churchill, Jr., Gilbert A. (1979), "A Paradigm for Developing Better Measures of Marketing Constructs," *Journal of Marketing Research*, 16 (February), 64-73.

Converse, Jean M. and Stanley Presser (1986), "Survey Questions: Handcrafting the Standardized Questionnaire," Sage University Paper series on Quantitative Applications in the Social Sciences, 07-063, Beverly Hills: Sage Publications.

Ericsson, K. Anders and Herbert A. Simon (1984), *Protocol Analysis: Verbal Reports as Data*, Cambridge, MA: MIT Press.

Hippler, Hans-J., Norbert Schwarz and Seymour Sudman (1987), *Social Information Processing and Survey Methodology*, New York: Springer-Verlag.

Hunt, Shelby D., Richard D. Sparkman, Jr., and James B. Wilcox (1982), "The Pretest in Survey Research: Issues and Preliminary Findings," *Journal of Marketing Research*, 19 (May), 269-73.

Jadine, Thomas B., Miron L. Straf, Judith M. Tanur, Roger Tourangeau (1984), *Cognitive Aspects of Survey Methodology*, Washington: National Academy Press.

Lehmann, Donald R. (1979), *Market Research and Analysis*, Homewood, IL: Richard D. Irwin, Inc.

Miller, J. and Chapman, R. (1982), "Systematic Analysis of Language Transcripts (SALT)," Unpublished manuscript, University of Wisconsin.

Nisbett, Richard and Timothy Wilson (1977), "Telling More Than We Know: Verbal Reports on Mental Processes," *Psychological Review*, 84 (May), 231-59.

Royston, Patricia (1987), "Application of Cognitive Research Methods to Questionnaire Design, Paper Presented at the Society for Epidemiological Research Twentieth Annual Meeting.

Royston, Patricia, Deborah Bercini, Monroe Sirken and David Mingay (1986), "Questionnaire Design Research Laboratory," Paper Presented at the Meetings of the American Statistical Association.

Sudman, S. and N. Bradburn (1982), *Asking Questions: A Practical Guide to Questionnaire Design*, San Francisco: Jossey-Bass.

Tourangeau, Roger (1987), "Attitude Measurement: A Cognitive Perspective," in H. Hippler, N. Schwarz, and S. Sudman (Eds.), *Social Information Processing and Survey Methodology*, New York: Springer-Verlag, 149-162.

_____ and Kenneth A. Rasinski (1988), "Cognitive Processes Underlying Context Effects in Attitude Measurement," *Psychological Bulletin*, 103 (3), 299-314.

Weber, Robert Philip (1985), *Basic Content Analysis*, Sage University Series on Quantitative Applications in the Social Sciences, 07-049, Beverly Hills and London: Sage Publications.

Wright, Peter and Peter D. Rip (1981), "Retrospective Reports on the Causes of Decisions," *Journal of Personality and Social Psychology*, 40 (4), 601-14.

Respondents' Moods as a Biasing Factor in Surveys: An Experimental Study
Morten Heide, Rogaland Research
Kjell Grønhaug, Norwegian School of Economics and Business Administration

ABSTRACT
This paper reports an experiment conducted to estimate the impact of subjects' mood states on their evaluations. Four experimental groups were induced by either a very negative, mildly negative, neutral or positive mood-inducing film. As hypothesized, systematic differences were found between the groups in their evaluations. Factual knowledge about the evaluation object was, contrary to expected, not found to modify mood effects. This negative finding could, however, be explained by a strong stereotypical impression of the product (a distant travel destination) held by the respondents.

INTRODUCTION
Response effects are factors that make the reported response differ from the actual or true value of the variables being investigated (Bradburn and Sudman 1974). Survey researchers have long been aware of the potentially disturbing impact response effects may have on self-report data. The sources of response effects have traditionally been viewed as *uncontrollable* environmental influences external to the individuals from which data are being collected. In recent years, however, researchers have started to look at internal, and especially psychological characteristics that may be sources of response effects (Peterson and Sauber 1983). Cognitive psychologists have found that an individual's temporary mood state, that is the transient feeling state perceived by the individual, may influence the evaluations s/he makes.

Several studies have investigated mood effects on evaluations, and the results indicate *asymmetric* effects of positive and negative moods. This implies that while a positive mood tends to give more favorable evaluations, the opposite will not always be true for negative moods (Isen 1984). It has been suggested that a negative mood will lead to a more pessimistic view of the world which in turn will result in less favorable evaluations, and some studies do indeed confirm this characterization. For example, Isen and Shalker (1982) found that subjects rated ambiguous slides as less pleasant when they were in a negative mood. Other studies (Griffitt 1970, Veitch and Griffitt 1976) indicate that being in a negative mood state may result in less favorable conceptions of others, and higher estimates of the likelihood of various types of disasters and unpleasant events occuring (Johnson and Tversky 1983). On the other hand, some studies do not report symmetric effects of positive and negative moods. Masters and Furman (1976) found that a positive mood was associated with higher expectations among children, but not more pessimistic expectations among children in the negative mood condition. Schwarz and Clore (1983) in their study of judgements of well-being, discovered that the negative impact of bad moods was eliminated when subjects were induced to attribute their present feelings to transient external sources irrelevant to the evaluation of their lives. Subjects who were in a good mood, on the other hand, were not affected by misattribution manipulations. Studies of person-perception judgements (Forgas et. al. 1984, Forgas and Bower 1987) clearly indicate that negative mood effects appear to be less pronounced and may depend on a variety of contextual factors. Thus, based on previous research we can conclude that while the effects of positive mood on evaluations seem to be consistently in a mood-congruent direction, the effects of negative moods are found to be more diffuse.

Srull (1984) raises the important issue of *familiarity* with regard to mood effects on evaluations. For instance when asked for their opinion about a low familiarity object, most people will act in accordance with a *computational model*. This means that they will use some form of a reference frame and "compute" their answer in accordance with this. For example, imagine that you are asked the following question: "Is Buick Regal a luxury automobile?". A computational model implies that you will compare Buick Regal with your references for "luxury automobile", and figure out an answer. For high familiarity objects it will be different, as the answer to the question has already been determined and stored in memory. The subject will use a *retrieval model*, which implies that s/he just has to retrieve the answer from the memory. Srull (1984) argues that mood states will be of greatest importance when dealing with *low* familiarity objects. For such objects the person has to "compute" an evaluation, and, as discussed above, such an evaluation may very well be biased by the present mood state. In contrast, when asked about an object with which s/he is already highly familiar, the person will often already have made an evaluation, and thus be more or less immune to the effects of temporary mood states. The importance of familiarity has been tested empirically, and the findings clearly support Srull's hypothesis (Srull 1983). For low familiarity subjects, the evaluations were biased in a mood-congruent direction, in other words, the subjects who were in a negative mood rated the products lower than the control group and vice versa for subjects in a good mood. The high familiarity subjects, on the other hand, were not affected by their temporary mood states.

The *complexity* of the evaluation task is another important issue. Previous research has shown that faced with a complex evaluation task, people will often employ some form of a *simplifying* strategy (Isen et. al. 1982). One such strategy may be to rely on an availability heuristic (Tversky and Kahneman 1973). Research has shown that mood can serve as a *retrieval cue*, which implies that mood-congruent material will have a memory advantage. If an availability heuristic is employed, this memory advantage may cause a mood-biased evaluation. Another strategy may be to simplify the evaluation task by using the *informative function* of mood states (Schwarz and Clore 1983). This function implies that the individuals use their perceived *affective* reactions as a basis for their evaluations, rather than computing a judgement on the basis of recalled features of the target object (Schwarz and Clore 1988). Whatever strategy is used, chances are that the severity of the mood-biases will increase in accordance with the complexity of the evaluation task.

An intuitive implication from the above literature review is that since mood states may influence people's evaluations, mood may influence people's responses and thus be a source of response effects.

Below are reported our hypotheses, target object, and research method.

HYPOTHESES

The preceding discussion suggests the following study hypotheses:

H1: When subjects are in a positive mood, we expect the evaluations to be systematically higher then when in a neutral mood, while no certain direction is hypothesized for the mood-biases among respondents holding negative moods.

The rationale for hypotheses H1 lies in the asymmetry between the effects of positive and negative moods. As discussed above, studies of mood effects on evaluations generally report mood-congruent findings for positive moods, while more diverse effects have been obtained for negative moods.

H2: We expect to find a negative correlation between mood effects and level of knowledge about the target object.

The subjects' level of knowledge about the object to be evaluated is predicted to be an important determinant of the severity of mood-biases. High level of knowledge indicates that the subject is familiar with the target object and is therefore expected to be a safeguard against mood effects, while subjects low in knowledge are anticipated to be more biased by their temporary mood states in the evaluations they make about the target object. A negative correlation between mood effects and level of knowledge is thus hypothesized.

TARGET OBJECT

Most studies of mood effects on product evaluations have focused on *high* familiarity products. Isen et. al. (1978) for instance, asked their subjects to evaluate products they owned. Here a low familiarity object,"Norway as a travel destination",was selected as the target object. This particular travel destination was expected to be a *low* familiarity "product" as previous information indicates that the familiarity with Norway, both in general and as a travel destination is fairly limited among distant foreigners. By focusing on a low familiarity product, instead of a high familiarity product, our study represents a fairly new approach.

Another reason for the choice of target object, lies in its *complexity*. The tourist product constitutes a rather complex combination of goods and services. In the evaluation of a travel destination, a thorough evaluator has to compare and weigh a great number of product dimensions against each other, before s/he can reach an overall judgement. As the majority of studies of mood effects on evaluations (see Gardner 1985 for a review) have focused on rather trivial objects, the present choice of product also in this respect, represents a rather new approach for research on mood effects.

METHOD

An experimental approach was preferred to examine the research problem.

Experimental Stimuli

Four mood states were induced, i.e. a very negative, a mildly negative, a neutral, or a positive mood. As discussed above, the effects of negative moods are found to be more diverse than for positive moods, which is the reason why two negative mood groups were included. The mood states were induced by exposing subjects to approx. 15 minutes of videotaped films.

(1) For the very negative mood induction, the film *Night and Fog* was used. This is a documentary film depicting Nazi concentration camps. With its authentic scenes of torture and genocide, the film was expected to have a very strong negative mood inducing effect.

(2) The second film, *But Jack was a Good Driver* was used for the mildly negative mood induction The theme here is teen-suicide. Although the film was intended to induce a negative mood, the mood inducing properties were not anticipated to be as powerful as those of *Night and Fog*.

(3) Neutral mood was induced by *Forces and Moments*, an instructional film which illustrates the way the effects of forces are used in engineering.

(4) Positive mood was induced by a 15-minutes segment of *The Best of Candid Camera*. This film shows people who are tricked into different awkward situations, without knowing that they are being filmed. As this is a recognized humorous film, it was

expected to have a strong positive mood inducing effect.

Groups and Subjects

Four groups were used in the actual experiment. Each group was exposed to one of the films noted above. Subjects were 34 male and 31 female students at a major U.S. university. All subjects were in their junior- or senior-year and received course-credit for their participation. Male-female composition varied somewhat in the different groups with between 41% and 69% men in each group.

Procedure

Subjects were randomly assigned to one of the four conditions, all with roughly 16 participants. All sessions were conducted using the same classroom setting. After the subjects had been seated they were informed that they would be asked to complete a questionnaire, where most of the questions concerned Norway as a travel destination. However, first the subjects were asked to watch a film. They were told that the film should be used in another study, next term, but before it was decided whether or not to use the film it was important to learn people's general reaction to the film. The subjects were instructed not to memorize anything from the film, but just to watch it. The purpose of this procedure was to legitimize the mood induction procedure, and to prevent the subjects from suspecting any connection between the film and the evaluation task. The procedure has previously been used with success by Isen et. al. (1987). When talking with the subjects after they had completed the questionnaire, it was learned that they had no suspicion that the film had anything to do with the evaluation task.

Measurements

Nowlis' (1965) Mood Adjective Check List was used in the present study. This list is perhaps the most widely used mood measure (Peterson and Sauber 1983), and it has been employed in numerous studies in the last couple of decades (see e.g. Samuel 1980, Stone and Neal 1984, Hedges et. al. 1985). The list consists of 35 adjectives, where the respondent is asked to indicate to what extent each of them describes his/her current mood. A varimax-rotated factor analysis of the subjects' answers revealed two major factors, explaining 38% of the total variance. The factors could easily be interpreted as Negative affect and Positive affect, and for each subject a mood score was computed as follows:

Mood score = Factor score on the Positive affect factor - Factor score on the Negative affect factor

The subjects also completed an evaluation of 26 different aspects of the target object. For all evaluations, the following response-scale was used:

```
very                                   very
poor                                   good
 -3    -2    -1    0    1    2    3
```

The majority of the evaluation-aspects were sampled from a *previous tourist survey*[1] conducted in Norway, which was done because of two reasons. First, since these variables had already been used in the survey, a comprehensive pretesting of the variables was superfluous. Second, using the same variables gave us an opportunity to *compare* the evaluations made by the subjects with those made by tourists that had actually been to Norway. As we shall see later, this type of comparison proved to be very useful. The evaluation-aspects were related to four different domains; 1) nature, peace and quiet-aspects, 2)vacation activities, 3)general aspects, 4)overall evaluation of Norway as a travel destination. The various aspects are listed in the appendix.

Following the evaluation task, several questions were included to measure the subject's level of knowledge about the target object by using indicators such as an estimate of the population in Norway, name of the capital of Norway, three Norwegian cities, and countries bordering Norway. Furthermore, the subjects were asked to name the three most important industries, i.e. the industries with highest annual sales and pick out the Norwegians from a list of ten famous persons. The answers to the questions were used to compute a knowledge score as a measure of how familiar the subjects were with the target object. The last section of the questionnaire was comprised of questions about the film (the answers to these questions proved to be very useful in a later study where the same films were employed). Also information about gender was gathered.

ANALYSIS AND RESULTS

Manipulation Check

Table 1 presents the mean mood scores in the four groups. As we can see from the table, the observations correspond with the expected effects. The film, *Night and Fog* appears to have had a powerful negative effect on the subjects' mood, while the negative effect of *But Jack was a Good Driver* seems to be more moderate. In accordance with our expectations *Forces and Moments* does not seem to have any mood inducing properties, while a

---

[1] The tourist survey was sponsored by the Tourist Department of the Royal Norwegian Ministry of Transportation, and was carried out in the summer of 1987. Approximately 1800 questionnaires were returned from foreign tourists on vacation in different parts of Norway.

TABLE 1
Mood Scores in the Four Experimental Groups

Mood-condition	Film	mood score	Mean mood score	St. dev. n
Very negative	Night and Fog	-1.78	.74	17
Mildly negative	But Jack was a Good Driver	.07	1.06	16
Neutral	Forces and Moments	.49	.66	16
Positive	The Best of Candid Camera	1.37	.63	16

positive mood is induced by *The Best of Candid Camera*.

An analysis of variance (ANOVA) was performed on the data. The analysis contrasting the four different film conditions indicated a significant effect of the mood manipulations, $F(3,60) = 46.54$, $p < .001$. Subsequent one-tailed t-tests revealed that the subjects in the Candid Camera group after they had watched the film, were in a significantly more positive mood than was the case for the neutral control group, $t(29) = 3.77$, $p < .001$. Subjects in the Night and Fog group had a significantly more negative mood, $t(30) = 9.14$, $p < .001$. As for the effect of the film "But Jack was a Good Driver", the effect on mood although not significant ($t(29) = 1.32$, $p = .097$) was in the predicted direction. Thus, the manipulation check data confirm the expected mood induction properties of the four films.

Mood Effects on Evaluations

It was hypothesized that the evaluations would differ in the various groups. For positive mood, a mood-congruent bias in evaluations was hypothesized, which implies that more positive evaluations in the positive mood group than in the neutral control group were expected. Because of the inconsistent effects of negative moods, reported in past research, no specific direction for the mood-biases was hypothesized for the two groups exposed to negative mood induction.

In our first analysis we computed the grand-mean of all evaluations for each subject. By looking at the grand-mean random fluctuations in the individual variables should be eliminated, and any true differences between the groups should thus be easier to detect. An analysis of variance (ANOVA) contrasting the four groups revealed a significant difference between groups with regard to grand-mean evaluations, $F(3,61) = 2.998$, $p < .05$. To investigate the directions of the mood-biases, the evaluations in the positive and the two negative mood groups were compared with those in the neutral control group. A graphical illustration of the first comparison is presented in figure 1.

On the X-axis we find the various aspects of Norway which the subjects were asked to evaluate. On the Y-axis the group-mean ratings in the positive and the neutral groups are shown. A visual inspection of figure 1 indicates that the evaluations seem to be generally higher in the *positive mood group*. Of the 26 evaluations, 20 are highest in the positive group, while only four are higher in the neutral group. For the remaining two evaluations, the group-means are identical in the two groups. Because of the relatively low number of participants (16 in each group), only one of the evaluations (#1) shows a significant difference ($p < .05$) between the two groups. Computing the grand-mean of all evaluations, we found this figure to be 1.28 in the positive mood group as opposed to .95 in the neutral control group. A one-tailed t-test established that the difference between the two groups was significant, $t(30) = 2.25$, $p < .05$. The results support hypothesis H1 concerning a mood-congruent evaluation-bias in the positive mood group.

Another way of testing the hypothesis, is to look at the evaluations as an approximate binomial series. The results from running a non-parametric sign test show that the probability that at least 20 out of 24 evaluations (i.e. the 24 evaluations where the group-means differ) are highest in the positive mood groups is less than .001 (one-tailed) if the two groups were drawn from the same population. In other words, it is not very likely that the group-differences were obtained by chance. In a binomial series, there is a requirement that the variables should be independent of one another. In the experiment, some of the evaluation-variables are correlated, and this violates the independence-assumption. To what extent this will influence the binomial probabilities reported above, is difficult to say, but it is likely that it will increase the probability somewhat.

Because of the widely reported asymmetry between the effects of positive and negative moods, we did not predict any mood-congruent mood-biases for negative moods. Still it will be interesting to compare the evaluations in the two negative mood groups with those in the neutral control group. A comparison between the *mildly negative group* and the neutral group showed that as many as 23 of the 26 were highest in the mildly negative mood group. The probability of this occuring at random is .0002 (two-tailed). The grand-mean of all evaluations was significantly higher in the mildly negative group, $t(30) = 3.50$, $p < .01$ (two-tailed).

FIGURE 1
Group-Mean Evaluations for Each Aspect in the Positive Mood Group vs. the Neutral Control Group

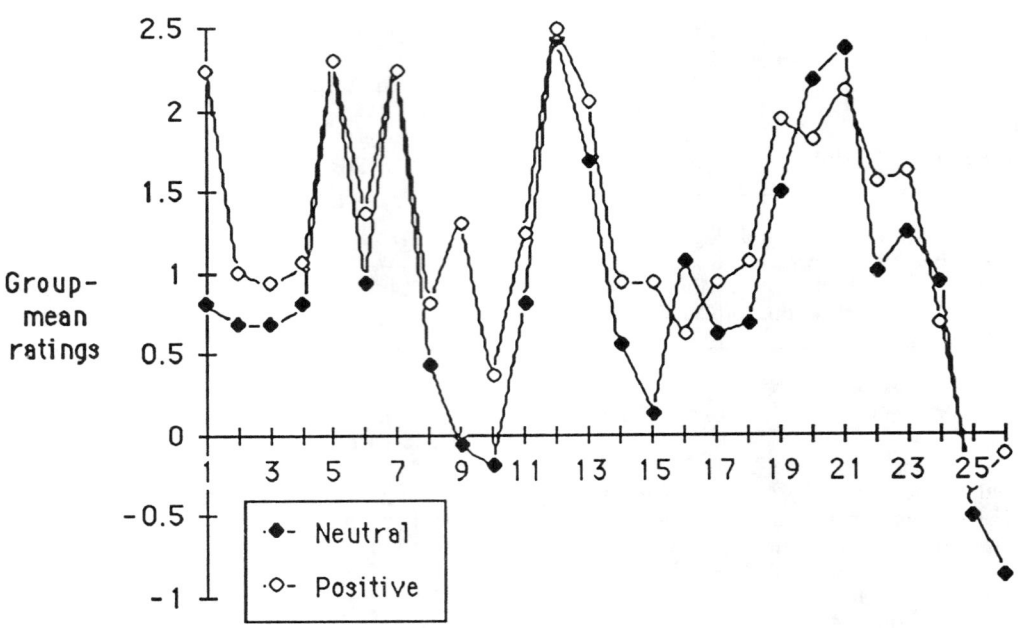

TABLE 2
Intercorrelations between the Group-Mean Evaluations in the Different Groups

	Neutral	Positive	Very negative	Mildly negative
Positive	.8638			
Very negative	.9065	.7989		
Mildly negative	.8923	.8223	.8096	-

all correlation coefficients significant at $p < .001$, (n=26)

By comparing the *very negative mood group* with the neutral control group, we found that 19 of the 26 aspects were rated highest in the very negative group, while the remaining 7 were highest in the control group. The two-tailed binomial probability is .03. A comparison of grand-mean evaluations showed a higher grand-mean in the very negative mood group, but the difference was not significant, $t(31) = 1.13$, $p > .25$ (two-tailed). The findings indicate mood-incongruent evaluation-biases for both of the negative mood groups.

Response Pattern

In Figure 2 we have reported the group-means for each aspect to be evaluated. It is evident that the overall response pattern is very similar in all groups, although mood-biases have been traced.

An inspection of figure 2 reveals that all groups seem to follow the same pattern. By inspecting the intercorrelations between the different group-means the following is observed:

From table 2 it can be seen that the means in the various groups are highly intercorrelated. This confirms that the response pattern is generally the same in all groups. By treating each group as a case and each group-mean evaluation as an observation, the Kendall's coefficient of concordance was computed to get an estimate of the similarity of the ratings between the four groups. The computed coefficient of concordance (W) was .8658 ($p<.0001$), which means that the four groups are fairly similar in their ratings of the different aspects of the target object.

TABLE 3
Variations in Evaluations by Group-Differences and Knowledge

SOURCE OF VARIATION	MEAN OF ALL EVALUATIONS				
	SS	DF	MS	F	p
Within cells	12.91	60	.22		
Regression	.03	1	.03	.15	.703
Between groups	1.94	3	.65	3.00	.037

TABLE 4
Variations in Evaluations by Group-Differences and Interaction with Knowledge

SOURCE OF VARIATION	MEAN OF ALL EVALUATIONS				
	SS	DF	MS	F	p
Within + residual	12.66	58	.22		
Group	1.05	3	.35	1.60	.198
Group by knowledge score	.28	3	.09	.43	.735

The Impact of Knowledge

A negative correlation between knowledge about the target object and mood effects on evaluations was hypothesized (H2), which implies that subjects with a high level of knowledge about Norway, were expected to be less influenced by their current mood in their evaluations about Norway. To test the hypothesis an analysis of covariance was performed, using the knowledge score as a covariate to determine how much of the variance in the grand-mean evaluation could be explained by differences in knowledge about Norway.

From table 3, it is obvious that the knowledge score does *not* have any significant explanatory power as a covariate (F= .15, p = .703). An analysis of variance was included to determine if the interaction between group and knowledge score was able to explain a significant part of the variance in the mean of all evaluations. The output from this analysis is presented below.

The interaction term between group and knowledge score is reported on the last line. As we can see the F-value for the interaction term is only .43 and definitely not significant (p= .735). The analyses show that the knowledge score is *not* able to explain any significant part of the variation in the mean of all evaluations, either as a covariate or in interaction with group. Thus, our prediction that subjects high in knowledge about the target object would be less likely to be influenced by their current mood states in their evaluations, did not come true.

DISCUSSION

In the experiment, we compared one positive mood group and two negative mood groups with a neutral control group to see how the subjects' evaluations were influenced by their mood states. Subtle but consistent mood biases for both positive and negative moods were detected. The biases were in a mood-congruent direction for the positive mood group, as hypothesized. For negative mood, no direction was hypothesized, but the results indicate mood incongruent mood effects for both negative mood groups. Even though there were differences between the various groups, the overall response pattern seemed to be the same in all groups. It was also hypothesized that subjects familiar with the object, i.e. respondents high in knowledge about Norway would be less likely to be influenced by their current mood states in their evaluations. In the experiment, however, no support for this hypothesis was found. Can this negative finding be explained?

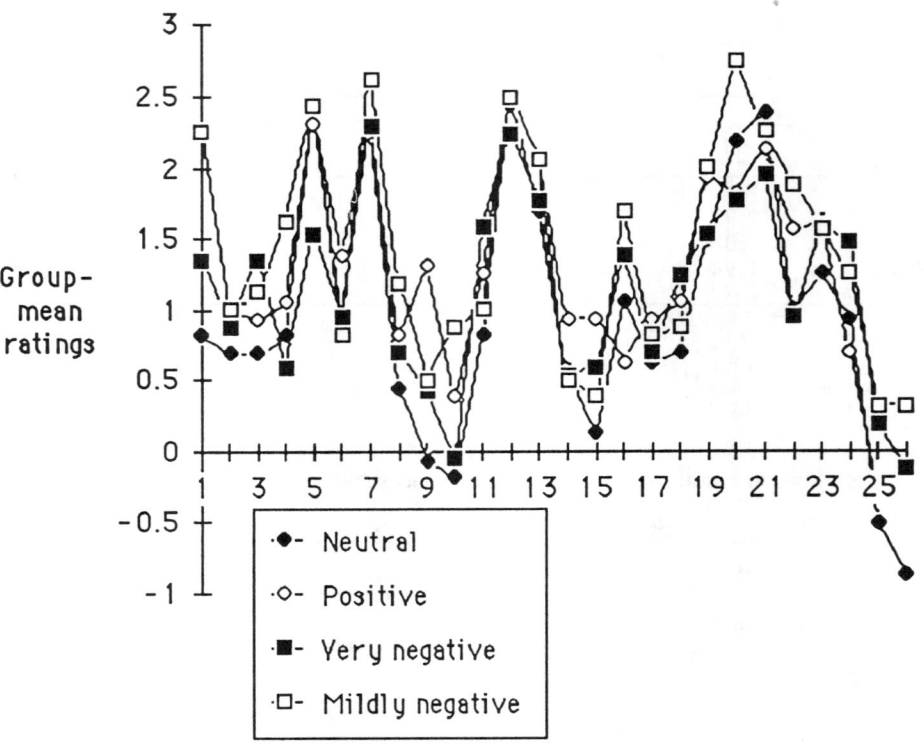

FIGURE 2
Group-Mean Evaluations for Each Aspect

In their answers to the knowledge questions, the subjects revealed *very limited* knowledge about the target object. The findings show that most subjects were unable to name any cities or major industries in the country. Nor had they any knowledge about the population size of Norway, its neighboring countries, neither were they able to identify famous people from the country. Consequently, out of a possible score of 17, the mean knowledge score was only 3.7 (with st. dev. = 2.3). Based on the subjects' modest knowledge-level it is tempting to classify "Norway as a travel destination" as a low familiarity product. As mood effects, according to Srull (1984), will be greatest when subjects evaluate low familiarity products, it is very surprising that knowledge was not found to be an important determinant in how sensitive the subjects were to mood effects. It was also expected that the mood-biases that were detected in the evaluations should be more severe.

There are, however, reasons to believe that we just cannot equate knowledge-level with familiarity. When looking at the evaluations made by the subjects, it is found that aspects like weather and the possibilities of having a reasonably priced vacation in Norway are rated extremely low, while possibilities for hiking and possibilities of experiencing clean and undisturbed nature are highly rated aspects. These ratings are very much in line with the general strengths and weaknesses of the Norwegian tourist product. This indicates that the subjects, even though they know little about Norway in general, nonetheless *are familiar* with Norway as a travel destination.

As mentioned earlier, some of the aspects that were evaluated by the subjects were sampled from a survey conducted among actual tourists in Norway (see footnote 1). To investigate further how familiar the subjects in the experiment were with Norway, a comparison with the actual tourists' evaluations was made. A graphical presentation of the comparison is found below.

Figure 3 compares the mean scores of all subjects in the experiment with the mean scores of approximately 1800 foreign tourists visiting Norway for various aspects of the travel product. It is evident that the response-patterns are very similar. The correlation between the means in the two groups is $r = .704$, $p < .01$. An intuitive interpretation of this finding is that the subjects in the experiment hold a strong *stereotype* about Norway as a travel destination, and that this stereotype is very much in line with the attitude of tourists that have actually visited Norway. It is not surprising that the mood effects were found to be as modest as was the case in the experiment, as the subjects could use the stereotype as basis for their evaluations, and thus were less influenced by their

FIGURE 3
Comparison between Subjects in the Experiment and Actual Tourists

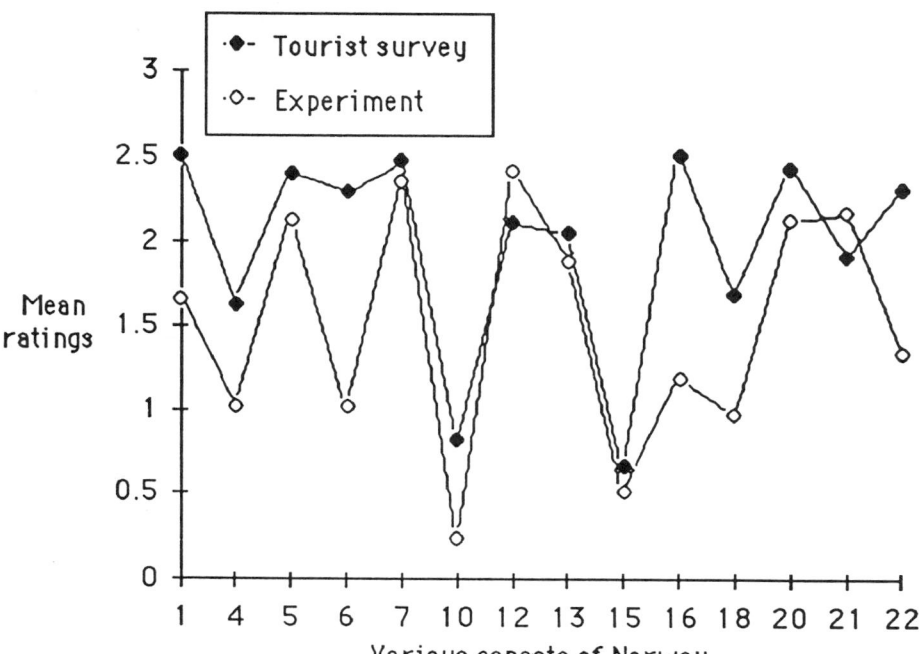

temporary mood states. In other words, even though the subjects' level of factual knowledge about the target object was low, they could act in accordance with a retrieval model (Srull 1984) by simply retrieving the evaluations from memory.

IMPLICATIONS

Our study raises several important implications. In the experiment we found consistent mood biases on evaluations. This indicates that mood may be considered as a *biasing* factor in surveys, and thus constitute a source of *response effects*. However, although the mood biases were present, the overall response pattern was very similar in all groups. We recall that the coefficient of concordance was higher than .86, and taking the small sample sizes into account (roughly 16 subjects in each group), any higher concordance would be difficult to obtain even if the groups were drawn from the same population, simply because of sampling variance. Our conclusion is therefore that even if the subjects' evaluations seem to be influenced by their mood, the damaging impact of the mood effects seems to be rather minimal.

The second implication is that our results seem to bolster the already well-documented findings about *asymmetric* effects between positive and negative mood states. As hypothesized we found mood-congruent effects for the positive mood group, i.e. the evaluations were biased in an upward direction. For the two negative mood groups, the results indicated mood-incongruent effects. The evaluations in the suicide-film group were significantly higher than those in the neutral control group. For the Night and Fog group too, the evaluations, although the differences were not very significant, appeared to be more favorable than was the case for the control group. By including two instead of only one negative mood group, we have reduced the probability that the incongruent results occurred by chance only. What are the mechanisms by which these effects occurred? According to Isen (1985) there may be both a *motivational* and a *cognitive* interpretation of the asymmetric effects of positive and negative moods. The motivational interpretation is that of positive-affect maintenance and negative-affect repair. Seen in relation to our study, this explanation suggests that subjects who have been exposed to the positive mood inducing film will try to retain their good feelings, while subjects in the negative film groups will try to chase "the blues" away. According to the cognitive interpretation the explanation may be that cognitive material associated with negative affect may be structured differently from that associated with positive affect. For example, depressing material may come to be less well elaborated and interconnected in the cognitive system than positive (Isen 1985). The idea of focusing on arousal instead of valence may also help to explain our findings. Our results indicate that all three affect groups yield higher evaluations than the neutral control group. It may then be that arousal and not hedonic tone is the key issue for explaining the observed asymmetry.

The third implication our study raises is the issue of *familiarity*. In the experiment, the subjects' factual knowledge about the target object was found to be rather marginal. We had predicted that subjects with a high level of knowledge would be less likely to be influenced by their current mood states in their evaluations, but no support was found for this hypothesis. This could have led us to conclude that product-familiarity was of little importance. However, by comparing the subjects' evaluations with those made by actual tourists in Norway, we were able to determine that the subjects had a clear and reasonably stereotypical impression of the target object (Norway as a travel destination). In other words, even though the subjects had little factual knowledge about Norway, their familiarity with the travel product was fairly high. This finding has the important implication that we just *cannot* always *equate* familiarity with level of knowledge, as it may occur that the stereotype and not the mood states provided most of the basis for respondents' evaluations. It may be argued that the lack of impact of knowledge resulted from a floor effect exhibited by knowledge itself. However, because of the clear stereotype we do not consider this alternative explanation to be very probable.

In this study we have found that mood states may bias evaluations and thus constitute a source of response effects in surveys. However, if the respondents are familiar with the object they are asked to evaluate, or if they have a clear stereotype of the object, chances are that the mood biases will be rather marginal, and thus not represent a serious threat to the validity of the survey measurements. In the current study only films have been used as mood induction stimuli. It may be argued that films trigger a number of different processes and that it is therefore difficult to be sure that it is mood change per se that causes the evaluation changes. To eliminate the possibility of a mono-method bias the study should thus be replicated using other types of mood induction procedures, preferably procedures that are fairly clean, i.e. they only manipulate mood. Basing our conclusions on only one target object (Norway as a travel destination) is problematic, because much of what we have found may result from the clear stereotypes and the low knowledge levels described above. The study should therefore be replicated using different target objects, different involvement levels, different prior knowledge levels, and so on. Furthermore, due to the asymmetry between positive- and negative moods the relationship between mood states and mood effects on evaluations appears to be a non-linear one. In other to estimate the true relationship future studies should employ a large number of stimuli to induce moods of different intensities, and measure their effects on evaluations. Finally, to increase external validity the current study should be replicated in field-settings using random samples of the general population.

REFERENCES

Bradburn, Norman M. and Seymour Sudman (1974), *Response Effects in Surveys: A Review and Synthesis*, Chicago: Aldine.

Forgas, Joseph P., Gordon H. Bower, and S. Krantz (1984), "The Influence of Mood on Perceptions of Social Interactions," *Journal of Experimental Social Psychology*, 20, 497-513.

Forgas, Joseph P. and Gordon H. Bower (1987), "Mood Effects on Person-Perception Judgements," *Journal of Personality and Social Psychology*, 53 (1), 53-60.

Gardner, Meryl P. (1985), "Mood States and Consumer Behavior: A Critical Review," *Journal of Consumer Research*, 12 (December), 281-300.

Griffitt, William (1970),"Environmental Effects on Interpersonal Affective Behavior: Ambient Temperature and Attraction," *Journal of Personality and Social Psychology*, 15 (3), 240-244.

Hedges, Susan M., Lina Jandorf, and Arthur A. Stone (1985),"Meaning of Daily Mood Assessments," *Journal of Personality and Social Psychology*, 48(2), 428-434.

Isen, Alice M. (1984),"Toward Understanding the Role of Affect in Cognition," in *Handbook of Social Cognition*, eds. Robert Wyer and Thomas Srull, Hillsdale, N. J.: Erlbaum, 179-236.

Isen, Alice M. (1985),"Asymmetry of Happiness and Sadness in Effects on Memory in Normal College Students: Comment on Hasher, Rose, Zacks, Sanft, and Doren," *Journal of Experimental Psychology: General*, 114(3), 388-391.

_____, Thomas Shalker, Margaret Clark, and Lynn Karp (1978),"Positive Affect, Accessibility of Material in Memory and Behavior: A Cognitive Loop?," *Journal of Personality and Social Psychology*, 36, 1-12.

_____ and Thomas Shalker (1982),"The Influence of Mood State on Evaluation of Positive, Neutral, and Negative Stimuli: When You 'Accentuate the Positive,' Do You 'Eliminate the Negative'?," *Social Psychology Quarterly*, 45, 58-63.

_____, Barbara Means, Robert Patrick, and Gary Nowicki (1982),"Some Factors Influencing Decision-Making Strategy and Risk Taking," in *Affect and Cognition*, eds. Margaret Clark and Susan Fiske, Hillsdale, N. J.: Erlbaum, 243-261.

_____, Kimberly Daubman, and Gary Nowicki (1987),"Positive Affect Facilitates Creative Problem Solving," *Journal of Personality and Social Psychology*, 52 (6), 1122-1131.

Johnson, Eric J. and Amos Tversky (1983),"Affect, Generalization, and the Perception of Risk," *Journal of Personality and Social Psychology*, 45 (1), 20-31.

Masters, John and Wyndol Furman (1976),"Effects of Affective States on Noncontingent Outcome Expectancies and Beliefs in Internal or External Control," *Developmental Psychology*, 5, 481-482.

APPENDIX

In the experiment the subjects were asked to evaluate the following aspects:

1. The possibility to see and experience nature in Norway is..... *
2. The health-care system in Norway is.....
3. The educational system in Norway is.....
4. The swimming possibilities in Norway are..... *
5. The possibilities for hiking in Norway are..... *
6. The possibilities for nightlife and entertainment in Norway are..... *
7. The possibilities for a calm and peaceful stay in Norway are..... *
8. Democracy and civil-rights in Norway are.....
9. The suicide-rate in Norway is.....
10. The weather in Norway is..... *
11. The standard of living in Norway is.....
12. The possibilities to experience something new during a vacation in Norway are..... *
13. The possibilities to eat well during a vacation in Norway are..... *
14. The unemployment-rate in Norway is.....
15. The possibilities to have a reasonably priced vacation in Norway are..... *
16. The possibilities to become physically fit during a vacation in Norway are..... *
17. Communications and transportations in Norway are.....
18. The shopping possibilities in Norway are..... *
19. The safety as a tourist in Norway is.....
20. The possibility to experience clean and undisturbed nature in Norway is..... *
21. The possibilities for cultural experiences during a vacation in Norway are..... *
22. Service and helpfulness in Norway is..... *
23. Overall, I would rate Norway as a travel destination as.....
24. In comparison with other *Scandinavian* countries, Norway as a travel destination is.....
25. In comparison with other *European* countries, Norway as a travel destination is.....
26. In comparison with travel-destinations *in general*, Norway as a travel destination is.....

* indicates that the evaluation-aspect is sampled from the tourist survey.

Nowlis, Vincent (1965),"Research With the Mood Adjective Checklist," in *Affect, Cognition, and Personality,* eds. S. S. Tomkins and C. E. Izard, New York: Springer, 352-389.

Peterson, Robert and Matthew Sauber (1983),"A Mood Scale for Survey Research," In *1983 AMA Educator' Proceedings,* eds. Patrick Murphy et. al., Chicago: American Marketing Association, 409-414.

Samuel, William (1980),"Mood and Personality Correlates of IQ by Race and Sex of Subject," *Journal of Personality and Social Psychology,* 38(6), 993-1004.

Schwarz, Norbert and Gerald Clore (1983), "Mood, Misattribution, and Judgements of Well-Being: Informative and Directive Functions of Affective States," *Journal of Personality and Social Psychology,* 45 (3), 513-523.

Schwarz, Norbert and Gerald Clore (1988), "How do I Feel About it? The Informative Function of Affective States," in *Affect, Cognition and Social Behavior,* eds. Klaus Fiedler and Joseph Forgas,. Lewiston, N. Y.: C. J. Hogrefe, 44-62.

Srull, Thomas (1983),"The Role of Prior Knowledge in the Acquisition, Retention, and Use of New Information," in *Advances in Consumer Behavior,* Vol. 10, eds. Richard Bagozzi and Alice Tybout, Ann Arbor, MI: Association for Consumer Research, 572-576.

Srull, Thomas (1984)," The Effects of Subjective Affective States on Memory and Judgment," in *Advances in Consumer Behavior,* Vol. 11, ed. Thomas Kinnear, Provo, UT: Association for Consumer Research, 530-533.

Stone, Arthur A. and John M. Neale (1984),"Effects of Severe Daily Events on Mood," *Journal of Personality and Social Psychology,* 46(1), 137-144.

Tversky, Amos and Daniel Kahneman (1973),"Availability: A Heuristic for Judging Frequency and Probability," *Cognitive Psychology,* 5, 207-232.

Veitch, R. and Griffitt, W. (1976),"Good News-Bad News: Affective and Interpersonal Effects," *Journal of Applied Social Psychology,* 6 (1), 69-75.

Sampled Survey Data: Quota Samples Versus Probability Samples

E. L. Melnick, New York University
R. Colombo, New York University
R. Tashjian, New York University
K. R. Melnick, D'Arcy, Masius, Benton & Bowles

ABSTRACT

Marketing decisions are often based upon measurements of the market place, which are usually constructed from sampled data. These data are obtained from mail surveys, telephone surveys, door-to-door interviews and from interviews at shopping centers and central location facilities. The recommended procedure is to capture data from a probability sampling scheme based on the assumption that the observations will be well balanced against all variables, independent of experimenter bias and necessary for accurate inferences about the unknown population. The discussion in this paper compares the relevance of probability sample inference to model based inference. We argue that inferences based upon models are more useful than probability sampling inferences and that quota samples are most informative for providing data for the estimation of the models. This is especially true in the presence of nonresponses.

INTRODUCTION

Most market research textbooks extol the virtues of probability sampling and suggest that non-probability sampling in general, and quota sampling in particular, is scientifically suspect. For example, Aaker and Day (Marketing Research, 1989, p. 349) state that "Probability sampling has several advantages over non-probability sampling. First, it permits the researcher to demonstrate the representativeness of the sample. Second, it allows an explicit statement as to how much variation is introduced because a sample is used instead of a census of the population. Finally, it makes possible the more explicit identification of possible biases". Churchill (Marketing Research, 1986, p. 433) in considering whether quota samples can be considered representative even though they accurately reflect the population with respect to the control characteristics makes three points. "First, the [quota] sample could be very far off with respect to some other important characteristic likely to influence the result...Second, it is difficult to verify whether a quota sample is indeed representative... Third, interviewers left to their own devices are prone to follow certain practices. They tend to interview their friends in excessive proportions..."

In spite of such positions many, or perhaps most, market research studies use some form of explicit non-probability sampling such as mall intercepts or quota sampling. Jacoby and Handlin (*Trademark Reporter*, 1991) report a study by the Council of American Survey Research Organizations, conducted in 1985, that showed that the overwhelming proportion (95% or more) of in-person interviews did not involve probability selection. They further report, on the basis of a sampling of the academic literature, that a similar proportion of (94-97%) of academic studies do not employ probability sampling designs.

In the light of such a discrepancy between the prescription of the textbooks and the custom of practitioners we pose two questions. First, why does such a discrepancy between theory and practice exist? And second, who is right - the textbooks or the practitioners?

One possible answer to the first question is not hard to find. Much of the theory of survey sampling has been developed and expounded by statisticians working for government agencies (Deming; Hansen, Madow and Tepping; Hansen and Hurwitz) or for large survey organizations (Kish; Cochran). Surveys conducted by these organizations tend to differ from those conducted by marketers. Typically, government surveys or those conducted by large social research organizations have the following characteristics:

- they are carried out to provide simple descriptive statistics of the survey population;

- the survey findings are required to be as objective as possible;

- they are multi-purpose - many variables are collected;

- the surveys often end up in the public domain (since they are often financed from public funds) where they are analyzed by different researchers for different purposes;

- sample sizes are typically quite large (often 2000 or more);

- time from commissioning a survey to reporting is often quite long (a year or more).

In contrast, cross-sectional studies carried out by market research companies and advertising agencies typically have the following characteristics[1]:

---

[1] Diary panel and scanner panels have characteristics more similar to governmental-type studies. Their longitudinal nature makes them especially suitable for measuring change (e.g. change in sales due to a promotion or advertising campaign) and assessing causal relationships. Academic studies have more or less the same characteristics as

- they are designed for a specific purpose - to help managers make a decision;

- they are often a part of a whole program of research (e.g. as part of the research carried out for a new product introduction);

- the sample sizes are quite small (often 200-300);

- time from commissioning the survey to reporting the findings is often quite short (a few weeks);

- non-response is relatively high (35-40%) or more.

These differences are important. We will argue that the relatively small sample sizes, high non-response, single-purpose nature of market research studies conspire to make non-probability sampling *theoretically and practically* more attractive than probability sampling. Thus our answer to the second question, "who is right the textbooks or the practitioners?" is, "it depends on the type of survey and the resources available." For large scale multi-purpose surveys, well designed probability samples and inferences that do not rely on a model for the population may be advantageous. For small scale surveys and especially where the non-response may be quite large, non-probability sampling and inference based on models for the population have the advantage.

We will support this view in the following way. First we will briefly compare the classical finite population approach to survey sample design and analysis as exemplified in the textbooks with the newer model based approach. Then, by means of a simple example and by simulations we show that model-based sampling inference outperforms design-based sampling inference. Finally we conclude with some general advice for market researchers on how to design and analyze survey studies.

PROBABILITY SAMPLING

Classical finite population sampling theory eschews making any assumptions about the distribution of a variable in the population. The main reason for this seems to be the acceptance that human and animal populations are not "perfectly mixed" so that the values of variables describing the population will be clustered or clumped. Since the population does not come "pre-randomized", the survey sampler cannot, it is argued, rely on a set of random variables representing observations from the population to be independently and identically distributed. Thus, in the absence of a probability distribution for the population the survey sampler, if he is to use statistical theory, has to induce a probability distribution by means of a selection

mechanism. More formally, the classical finite population approach assumes that a finite population is a set of values Y_i, $i = 1,...,N$ (for example, Y_i is the income for the ith person in the United States where there are N individuals). The values are assumed to be constants (there is an exact income number associated with each individual) and for each label i there exists a value Y_i. A population parameter, say the population mean, $\overline{Y}$ is defined by the set of all Y's,

$$\overline{Y} = \frac{1}{N} \sum_{i=1}^{N} Y_i$$

so that no probability function is invoked to generate the data. A sample, s, is a subset of n units of the population denoted $i_1, i_2,...,i_n$. A sample design assigns a probability p(s) to each s where the sum of the probabilities defined over all samples occurring is one. The only probabilities in this scheme are those induced by the sample design and different sampling designs will induce different probabilities. The sample design is therefore a vital part of the analysis of the sample data.

A serious problem with this approach is that no direct mechanism is specified by which we can know the values of elements not in the sample and therefore no mechanism by which we can deduce population characteristics. Finite population theory gets around this difficulty by invoking the Central Limit Theorem. If the sample size is sufficiently large and the sample was drawn at random, then the sample mean, being a linear combination of random variables, should be approximately normally distributed with mean $\overline{Y}$ and variance

$$s^2 = \left(1 - \frac{n}{N}\right) \frac{\Sigma (y_i - \overline{y})}{n-1}$$

The classical infinite population approach to inference proceeds in a different way. A model is postulated for the data, for example that the Y_is are a sample from a normal distribution with mean μ and variance σ^2. The data from the observed sample are used to estimate the parameters μ and σ^2. The model provides the link from sample to population and the sample design plays no role in the inference - the probability model and the data are sufficient to estimate the population parameters. (See Example).

NONRESPONSE IN SAMPLE SURVEYS

The inference problem under probability sampling is the estimation of a population quantity based upon a known sampling distribution and a sample of size n. In the presence of nonresponse, modelling is necessary to relate these measurements to those obtained from the respondents since the nonrespondents are not under control of the sampler. Based upon an assumed model, the EM algorithm was demonstrated under general conditions by Dempster, Laird and Rubin (JRSS series B, 1977) to produce an estimator that converges to the maximum likelihood estimator of the population quantity, even in the presence of non-response. In the absence of a model, inference can be made on the observed data if the inference can be assumed to be

---

market research studies but with the difference that interest is more analytical than descriptive in character.

EXAMPLE

POPULATION IN 1990 Y_i: 5, 7, 1200

POPULATION IN 1989 X_i: 3, 10, 1280

PROBLEM: ESTIMATE THE MEAN IN 1990 BASED ON A SAMPLE OF 2 OBSERVATIONS.

UNKNOWN: POPULATION MEAN IN 404

PROBABILITY SAMPLES

SAMPLE 1:	5, 7	MEAN IS 6
SAMPLE 2:	5, 1200	MEAN IS 602.5
SAMPLE 3:	7, 1200	MEAN IS 603.5

SUMMARY: AVERAGE OF SAMPLE MEANS IS 404 (UNBIASED)
STANDARD ERROR OF SAMPLE MEANS IS 345

MODEL: RATIO ESTIMATOR $R_i = \dfrac{\sum_{j}^{2} y_j}{\sum_{j}^{2} x_j} \; \bar{x}$

SAMPLE 1:	5, 7	$R_i = 398$
SAMPLE 2:	5, 1200	$R_i = 405$
SAMPLE 3:	7, 1200	$R_i = 403$

SUMMARY: AVERAGE OF ESTIMATORS IS 402 (BIASED BY 2 UNITS)
STANDARD ERROR OF ESTIMATOR IS 3.6

---

equivalent to an inference based on the full distribution (this type of sample design is called ignorable by Rubin (Biometrika, 1976) and Little (JASA, 1982)). If the nonresponses are a function of the sample design, the estimator and its variance might have a large bias thus invalidating the inference. This situation is very common in probability samples based upon human populations. However, data collected from individuals sampled from a panel are more likely to be based upon ignorable designs. An individual refuses to become part of the sample because he/she does not want to participate in a sample survey, *not* because of the specific components of a particular sample design. In a probability sample there is no way of knowing whether the nonresponse is due to an unwillingness to participate in any survey and/or an unwillingness to participate in a particular survey. The latter situation is more likely to create a nonignorable design.

Probability sampling serves two main objectives: (1) Generate a representative sample from the population free of any selection bias and (2) Provide a good balance on uncontrolled ancillary variables. These objectives are laudable and on average achievable for large samples when all sampled units participate in the survey. Once the sample is selected inferences based on the observations are made to the unobserved individuals' characteristics. These inferences can be quite inaccurate if the sample is not balanced and the situation is not improved by knowing that this would not happen if many samples had been taken and the inferences had been based upon the average of those computed from all hypothetical samples not selected.

All advantages of randomization disappear in the presence of non-response. First, there is no way of knowing the reason for the non-response and therefore one must suspect that the design is nonignorable. Second, the non-respondents might have different characteristics from those responding to the survey resulting in an un-representative sample. Thirdly, poor representation of certain subsets of the population produce unbalanced samples. Finally, a truly balanced sample requires balance on many characteristics. This cannot be guaranteed for any probability sample, even stratified sampling designs, because of the requirement of impractically large samples. None of these problems exist with samples drawn from a well constructed panel, that is, if we assume that the panel is the population to which we wish to make inferences, or is representative of that population.

ILLUSTRATIONS COMPARING INFERENCES FROM PROBABILITY SAMPLES AND QUOTA SAMPLES IN THE PRESENCE OF NONRESPONSE

Two data sets were used as populations for this study. Each data set was balanced against the United States population on 6 demographic characteristics. The parameter of interest in the first study is the total number of households having personal computers. This parameter, T, is computed as

$$T = \sum_{1}^{N} Y_i$$

where

$$Y_i = \begin{cases} 1 \text{ if the } i^{th} \text{ household has a PC} \\ 0 \text{ otherwise.} \end{cases}$$

The covariate X_i is the combined salary for household i. The dependent variate, Y_i, in the second study is

$$Y_i = \begin{cases} 1 \text{ if the } i^{th} \text{ household has cable TV} \\ 0 \text{ otherwise.} \end{cases}$$

In the first study the population size, N was 12,609 and in the second study, the population size was 12,651. Simulations were run in each study to represent both probability and quota samples. Probability samples were selected by taking 1000 samples of 600 observations; the individuals in each sample were selected using a random number generator. Sampled information was compared based upon data selected by both replacement and also without replacement designs. Negligible differences were detected so that with replacement designs were used for the comparisons since they were obtained more economically. Quota samples were simulated by selecting the first 2400 individuals that satisfied a design that was balanced on income and geographic dimensions. These individualss were selected from a list in the order that they joined the quota sample. This selection process attempted to capture an unknown correlation structure, induced by the selection mechanism, which is often suspected to exist in quota samples. The larger quota sample was arbitrarily set at 4 times the size of a random sample and was intended to reflect the lower cost for conducting the survey. The 1000 probability samples selected were used to show that although any one sample could provide poor estimates of population parameters, averaging over many samples would result in accurate estimators. This illustrates the statistical concepts of unbiased, consistent estimators but is of no practical importance since only one sample is ever drawn.

The results of the simulations comparing 1000 combined random samples of size 600 to one quota sample of size 2400 are presented in Figures 1, 2 and 3. The average of the probability based estimators has small error but the range of individual estimates reflects a greater variability than quota sample based estimates. Sampling theory states that if the CDF of the covariates of a sample is similar to the population CDF of the covariates, then the sample is a good representation of the population. The average covariates associated with the extreme estimates in Figure 2 show that similar averages is not a sufficient condition for similar CDF's. The only way to guarantee this property is by purposive sampling and this can best be achieved with quota panel data.

In the second simulation study, the population was partitioned into sixty cells classified by ten income levels and six geographic locations. The six geographical regions were: 1) New England and Middle Atlantic, 2) North Central, 3) South Atlantic, 4) East South Central, 5) West South Central and 6) Mountain and Pacific. Under the assumption that the response rate is poor for low and high income families, a nonresponse pattern in the study omitted all households with incomes less than $8000 dollars or more than $70,000 dollars. Further, in regions 1, 3, and 4, nonresponse was set at under 12,000 dollars and in regions 1 and 6 nonresponse was set at above $50,000 dollars.

The results from the two studies are presented in Figure 3. Comparing these results to the population characteristics (Figure 1) shows the larger bias with the probability based estimators. For example, in Study 1, the population total number of positive responses is 5941 whereas the quota sample based estimate is 6004 and the average probability sample based estimators is 6184. Further, the probability sample estimates range from 5376 to 7004.

Probability sample estimates may be extremely biased especially when the sample has a large proportion of nonrespondents. Suggested strategies for determining the effect of missing data are follow-up studies and applications of models relating responses from respondents to those of nonrespondents. The first strategy is rarely useful. It is expensive, thus limiting the size of the follow-up study. Also, based upon documented evidence, it seldom supplies the required information. Introduction of models *after* obtaining missing data is questionable since the formulation is confounded with the sampler's bias. If modelling is to be performed, it should be done *before* the data is collected, consistent with the scientific method.

In practice, the presence of missing data renders a probability sample as suspect. This problem does not exist for model based samples, especially those constructed from quota data. Firstly, the model is constructed before obtaining

FIGURE 1
Population Characteristics

STUDY	TOTAL POPULATION SIZE	NUMBER OF POSITIVE RESPONSES	AVERAGE INCOME
1. Subscribers to Cable Television	12651	5941	23,400
2. Ownership of Personal Computers	12609	1706	23,400

FIGURE 2
Sample Estimates of Positive Responses

STUDY	QUOTA SAMPLE		PROBABILITY SAMPLES		
	ESTIMATED POSITIVE RESPONSES	AVERAGE INCOME	AVERAGE ESTIMATED POSITIVE 1000 SAMPLES	AVERAGE INCOME 1000 SAMPLES	RANGE OF ESTIMATES (ASSOCIATED AVERAGE INCOME)
1. Subscribers to Cable Television	5703	23,400	5935	23,420	5105 (23,600), 6699 (23,950)
2. Ownership of Personal Computers	1555	23,280	1705	23,380	1163 (21,890), 2322 (22,520)

the data so that the responses from the nonrespondents can be imputed from the model. Secondly, quota samples are formed so that the individuals selected have covariates balanced against the population's characteristics. Therefore, the characteristics of the nonrespondents are known and this information can be exploited when imputing the missing data. In the two data sets considered in this section, the quota samples were drawn balanced on the income and geographic variables. Assume that the purchase rate of a product as a function of income is independent of geographical region, but that the number of products purchased is a function of the geographical region. These assumptions can be modelled by considering partitioning of the population into the cells $A(i,j)$ $i=1,...,10$ and $j=1,...,6$ representing the income and geographic categories. A logistic model is used to estimate the nonresponse rate since the basic input variable is binary, either the household purchased or did not purchase the product. Let P_{ij} be the proportion of positive responses in the $(i,j)^{th}$ cell and the log of the odds ratio be $Z_{ij} = \log(P_{ij}/1 - P_{ij})$. Based upon the assumption that the relationship between Z_{ij} and income is independent of geographical region, the nonresponse model is $Z_{ij} = \alpha_j + \beta$ (Income) $+ \varepsilon_{ij}$. The seven parameters β and α_j $j=1,...,6$ were estimated by least squares. The estimated model was used to estimate the nonresponding cells and smooth the data within the cells. The adjusted data were then used to produce an accurate estimate of the number of positive responses from the population. This methodology is not available within the probability sampling framework since there is no available information on the characteristics of the nonrespondents. Further, the randomization principle which states that the probability sampling plan creates the only probability distribution for reliable statistical inference must be discarded in the presence of nonrespondents unless the nonrespondents have the same characteristics as the respondents, which is very unlikely. The nonresponse problem is not serious for samples drawn from panels, if the panel is assumed to be representative of the population.. The nonrespondents are easily determined and their characteristics are known. Models can be constructed for estimation of the responses from the nonresponding units.

CONCLUSION

Most surveys are multipurpose so that globally optimal designs rarely exist and optimal designs for different purposes are usually in conflict. It is even difficult to design optimal sampling plans for single purpose studies in market research where

FIGURE 3
Sample Estimates of Positive Responses Based on Samples with Nonresponses

	QUOTA SAMPLE			PROBABILITY SAMPLES			
STUDY	ESTIMATED POSITIVE RESPONSES	AVERAGE INCOME	RESPONSE RATE	AVERAGE ESTIMATED POSITIVE RESPONSES	AVERAGE INCOME	RESPONSE RATE	RANGE OF ESTIMATES (ASSOCIATED AVERAGE INCOME)
1. Subscribers to Cable Television	6004	26,070	0.77	6184	26,260	0.75	5376 (26,080), 7004 (26,510)
2. Ownership of Personal Computers	1787	26,080	0.75	1913	26,220	0.75	1403 (24,620), 2436 (26,130)

well defined sampling frames rarely exist. Probability sampling plans do not attempt to describe the process generating the data, and in fact, probabilities are induced by the selection of the sampling plan. In this setting there are no unknown parameters, no discussion of goodness of fit and the design is primarily based on cost efficiency considerations. Of major concern is the sampling variance, which is usually the smallest source of error in a survey. The distinction between probability samples and model based inference is described by Little (JASA, 1982). "In the randomization approach the population values are treated as fixed, and inferences are based on the probability distribution used to select the sample. In the modeling approach, the population values are treated as realizations of random variables that are distributed according to some model. The model distribution forms the basis of inferences, and the sample selection procedure has an ancillary role, namely to avoid selection bias." Quota sample based surveys are constructed within the restrictions of multistage designs where members of the panel are selected from a well defined sampling frame (for example, households in the United States). Data selected from these panels are randomly chosen from the strata having the same socio-demographic characteristics present in the population to which the product attitude inferences are to be made. The hypothesized models are constructed and then perhaps checked against independently obtained data for model consistency. This methodology is consistent with usual scientific inquiry. That is: (1) a model is proposed to describe the random phenomena generating the data, (2) data are obtained, (3) parameters are estimated, (4) the model fit is tested, (5) modified and (6) used for making inferences to the population. In this process randomization is used to guard against selection bias, but once a sample is selected it is unique and the selection process is unimportant. Inferences are based upon the constructed model, which can be used to estimate unobserved data and error sources. The model smooths the data and does not require the assumption of large sample normality. Thus high quality quota data has advantages over probability sampled data since it is plentiful, inexpensive and useful input for the formulation of mathematical models. Once the models have been verified they can be used to explain the process generating the data and to predict characteristics of the sampling frame. In the presence of non-response, randomization loses its important properties. The design might be nonignorable, the respondents might not be representative and the balance on ancillary variables might be lost. None of these problems occur with quota samples. Even in the presence of non-response, the non-respondents and their characteristics are known so that models can be developed. Further, since the quota sample was developed to guarantee balance this data is useful for the development of models describing the characteristics of and projecting the responses to the non-respondents in order to generate accurate parameter estimators and their mean square errors.

REFERENCES

Aaker, D. A. & George S. Day, "Marketing Research", Wiley, New York, 1989.

Churchill, G. A., "Marketing Research", Dryden, Chicago, 1986.

Deming, W. E. (1953), "On a probability Mechanism to Attain an Economic Balance Between the Resultant Error of Response and Bias of Nonresponse," *Journal of the American Statistical Association* 58 (December), 766-783.

Dempster, A. P., N. M. Laird and D. B. Rubin (1977), "Maximum Likelihood from Incomplete Data Via the EM Algorithm (with Discussion)," *Journal of the Royal Statistical Society* Series B, 39, (1), 1-38.

Godambe, V. P. (1955), "A Unified Theory of Sampling from Finite Populations," *Journal of the Royal Statistical Society* Series B, 17 (2), 269-278.

Hansen, M. H., W. G. Madow and B. J. Tepping (1983), "An Evaluation of Model-Dependent and Probability-Sampling Inferences in Sample Survey," *Journal of the American Statistical Association* 78 (December), 776-807.

Horvitz, D. G. and D. J. Thompson (1952), "A Generalization of Sampling without Replacement from a Finite Universe," *Journal of the American Statistical Association* 47 (September), 663-685.

Jacoby, J. and Hanlin, A. (1991), "Non-probability Sampling Designs for Litigation Surveys", *Trademark Reporter*, In press.

Lipstein, B. (1975), "In Defense of Small Samples," *Journal of Advertising Research* 15 (February), 33-40.

Little, R. J. A. (1982), "Models for Nonresponse in Sample Surveys," *Journal of the American Statistical Association* 77 (June), 237-250.

Royall, R. (1970), "On Finite Regression Models," *Biometrika* 57 (August), 377-387.

Royall, R. and W. G. Cumberland (1978), "Variance Estimation in Finite Population Sampling," *Journal of the American Statistical Association*, 73 (June), 351-358.

Royall, R. and W. G. Cumberland (1981), "An Empirical Study of the Ratio Estimator and Estimators of the Variance," *Journal of the American Statistical Association* 76 (March), 66-88.

Rubin, D. R. (1976), "Inference and Missing Data, *Biometrika* 63 (December), 581-592.

Smith, T. M. F. (1976), "The Foundations of Survey Sampling: A Review (with Discussion)," *Journal of the Royal Statistical Society* Series A, 139(2), 183-204.

Sudman, S. (1964), "On the Accuracy of Recording of Consumer Panels," *Journal of Market Research* 1 (May), 14-20.

Wind, Y. and D. Lerner (1979), "On the Measurement of Purchase Data: Surveys Versus Purchase Diaries," *Journal of Market Research* 16 (February), 39-47.

Wiseman, F. and P. McDonald (1979), "Noncontact and Refusal Rates in Consumer Telephone Surveys," *Journal of Market Research* 16 (November), 478-484.

Your Opinion Counts (1986), "Refusal Rate Study," Chicago, Illinois: Marketing Research Association.

Some Methodological Issues in Consumer Research
Naresh K. Malhotra, Georgia Institute of Technology

ABSTRACT

This paper offers comments on the four papers presented in the session on Methodological Issues. The four papers are considered in the order in which they were presented. Comments are made on the use of secondary task technique, questionnaire pretesting with verbal protocol analysis, respondents' moods as a biasing factor in surveys, and quota samples versus probability samples.

THE SECONDARY TASK TECHNIQUE

The secondary task technique has been applied in a variety of contexts in the behavioral sciences (e.g., Inhoff and Fleming 1989). Applications in marketing have also surfaced recently (e.g., Lord and Burnkrant 1988; Lord, Burnkrant, and Owen 1989). Marketing history abounds with cases where techniques used in other disciplines were borrowed hastily and applied in marketing settings without an adequate examination of the underlying assumptions and without critically evaluating the applicability of those techniques. Hence, the paper by Owen (1990) addressing the assumptions of the secondary task technique is certainly in order. Beyond the assumptions identified by Owen, the following limitations of the secondary task technique are emphasized to caution readers against ill-considered applications of this technique.

The theoretical relationship between the performance on the secondary task and constructs such as attention, elaboration, and effort devoted to the primary task is not well understood. Note, understanding the theoretical relationship of a measure with other constructs it is supposed to measure, or is related to, is an essential requirement for construct validity. This means that given the lack of theoretical understanding, it would be very difficult to even begin to establish the construct validity of the secondary task techniques, such as the RT-probe, as measures of constructs such as attention, elaboration, and effort.

The use of the secondary task technique becomes all the more problematic in a study where attention, elaboration, and effort are all being measured. In such a case, it is not clear which one of these constructs the secondary task technique is measuring. The secondary task technique is incapable of detecting anything other than apparent interference between concurrently performed tasks. Furthermore, it should be realized that attention, elaboration, and effort are multidimensional constructs. The secondary task technique measures only one dimension of these constructs, perhaps a dimension which is common to all. Hence, exclusive reliance on the secondary task technique to provide a sole measure of these constructs is not appropriate.

The secondary task technique provides an indirect measure of attention, elaboration, and effort. Given the limitations associated with this technique, it should be used with extreme caution. Perhaps, its use to carry out manipulation checks is more defensible than its use to measure attention, elaboration, and effort.

QUESTIONNAIRE PRETESTING WITH VERBAL PROTOCOL ANALYSIS

Designing a questionnaire has many facets. The objectives and steps involved in questionnaire design may be described by the acronym QUESTIONNAIRE (Malhotra 1991, 1992):

Objectives
- Q uestions that respondents can answer
- U plift the respondent
- E rror elimination

Steps
- S pecify the information needed
- T ype of interviewing method
- I ndividual question content
- O vercoming inability and unwillingness to answer
- N onstructured versus structured questions
- N onbiasing question wording
- A rrange the questions in proper order
- I dentify form and layout
- R eproduction of the questionnaire
- E liminate bugs by pretesting

Verbal protocol analysis, as advocated by Bolton (1990) tests only one aspect of questionnaire design, namely question wording. Furthermore, there are many issues involved in determining the exact wording for each question. These may be summarized by the acronym WORDING (Malhotra 1991, 1992).

- W ho, where, what, when, why, and how
- O rdinary words
- R egularly, normally, usually etc. should be avoided
- D ual statements (positive and negative)
- I mplicit alternatives and assumptions should be avoided
- N on leading and nonbiasing questions
- G eneralizations and estimates should be avoided

The approach by Bolton examines only limited aspects of question wording. Nevertheless, the use of protocols to test the comprehension, retrieval, judgment and response difficulties associated with questions is interesting. It is important that this framework be applied taking the context of the survey appropriately into account. For example, in encoding retrieval, Bolton (1990) assumes that "surveys typically elicit memory-based rather than stimulus-based judgments". This assumption is obviously grossly violated in conjoint analysis and other information processing surveys, where the respondents are asked to evaluate a given set of stimuli described in terms of the information provided. At the heart of this pretest methodology lies the coding scheme. Hence, it is important that the codes developed be consistent, complete, and applied uniformly to the protocols. Given the limited aspects of the questionnaire which are examined in this methodology, it should not be used as the sole method of pretesting. However, it could be useful when used in conjunction with other pretest procedures.

RESPONDENTS' MOODS AS A BIASING FACTOR IN SURVEYS

There is evidence to suggest that mood states have a direct and indirect effect on consumer behavior (Gardner 1985). In the context of judgment and affective reactions a direct link may involve associations in memory between mood states and affective responses. An indirect effect may involve the effect of mood being mediated by cognitive activity such as information retrieval. In an indirect way mood states may affect evaluations by making mood congruent items more accessible in memory and thus influencing affective responses (Isen et al. 1978). In examining the impact of moods on Norway as a travel destination, Heide and Gronhaug (1990) do not distinguish between the direct and indirect effects.

Based on the available literature, Heide and Gronhaug (1990) hypothesized that positive mood would result in higher evaluations than neutral mood. However, they did not hypothesize any directional effect of negative mood. Literature does indicate that the effect of negative mood states seems to be more heterogenous than the effects of positive mood states (Isen 1984). The heterogeneity in the effects of negative moods may be attributed to at least two factors. Negative mood states may be themselves more heterogeneous than positive mood states. Secondly, processes that terminate negative moods may compete with automatic tendencies to engage in mood-congruent behavior (Clark and Isen 1982; Gardner 1985; Isen 1984). In their study, Heide and Gronhaug (1990) found biases in mood-congruent direction for both positive and negative moods.

Heide and Gronhaug (1990) also hypothesized a negative correlation between mood effects and level of knowledge about Norway. However, they did not find support for this hypothesis. The reason may well be that almost all the respondents (students in the USA) lacked knowledge about Norway. Hence, there was not enough variation on this variable in the sample. To examine the impact of knowledge, this variable should have been experimentally manipulated, just as mood states were. For example, some subjects could have been provided with information about Norway to induce a high knowledge state. Another, reason for the weak/inconclusive results might be that the sample size was small. There were a total of only 65 respondents with about 16 being assigned to each treatment condition.

It appears that the mood states are more likely to have an impact on consumer evaluations when the stimuli are ambiguous, the perceived benefits of being precise are low, and induction and action are contiguous (Gardner 1985). However, more research investigating the effects of specific positive and negative moods on consumer behavior is certainly needed.

QUOTA SAMPLES VERSUS PROBABILITY SAMPLES

The contention of Melnick et al. (1990) that under certain conditions, quota samples may be preferred to simple random samples is a reasonable one. Few would argue with it. However, reservations may be expressed about some of the comments and the two studies conducted by Melnick et al. (1990). First, it should be noted that telephone interviews, and not personal interviews, are the dominant mode of data collection in marketing research conducted in the USA (Malhotra 1990). Probability sampling is often employed in telephone surveys. Variants of random digit dialing, particularly directory based designs, are often used to generate telephone samples. Melnick et al. (1990) are also not quite correct in assuming that the sample size in marketing research is small (200-300). In most commercial applications in marketing research, the sample size is much larger. Syndicate services using omnibus panels, often use large samples of 2000 or more. In their discussions, the authors imply that panels always use quota samples. This is not true. Probability sampling schemes can be and have been applied to select samples from panels.

The empirical comparison reported by the authors raises several questions. They have compared quota sampling with simple random sampling. However, stratified random sampling is more similar to quota sampling and should have been the probability sampling technique selected for comparison. The population should have been stratified on the same variables and levels used to select quotas. A second factor which makes the comparison uneven is sample size. The sample size for quota sampling is 2400 whereas for simple random sampling it is only 600. Since the sample size for quota sampling is four times the sample size for simple random sampling, is it surprising that quota sampling does better? A further factor biasing the results against simple random sampling is that the pattern of nonresponse was deterministic. In practice, nonresponse may not be truly random but is also not truly deterministic. A biasing factor in favor of simple random sampling is that 1000 samples were drawn, when in practice only a single sample is drawn.

The authors' conclusion though may still be reasonable, but for reasons other than those emphasized in their paper. In certain situations, quota sampling may be preferred because the cost of probability sampling is high, sampling errors are small in comparison to nonsampling errors, nonresponse rate may be high and nonrandom, and the sample size is small. Yet, in other instances, where the conditions are just the opposite, probability sampling might well be preferred.

CONCLUSIONS

It is indeed appropriate to have one or more sessions on methodological issues in ACR conferences. The four papers discussed here emphasize the need to examine and validate our measures, pretest the questionnaires and other research instruments, take into account the effect of relevant variables which may have a direct or mediating influence on the phenomenon of interest, and adopt a suitable sampling plan. These, and other methodological issues are central to the quality of consumer research. If the goal is to accumulate unequivocal findings in consumer behavior, it is imperative that the research conducted be methodologically sound.

REFERENCES

Bolton, Ruth N. (1990), "An Exploratory Investigation of Questionnaire Pretesting With Verbal Protocol Analysis", in *Advances in Consumer Research*, Vol. 18, eds. Rebecca H. Holman and Michael R. Solomon.

Clark, Margaret and Alice Isen (1982), "Toward Understanding the Relationship Between Feeling States and Social Behavior, in *Cognitive Social Psychology*, eds. Albert Hastorf and Alice Isen, New York: Elsevier/North Holland, 73-108.

Gardner, Meryl P. (1985), "Mood States and Consumer Behavior: A Critical Review," *Journal of Consumer Research*, 12 (December), 281-300.

Heide, Morten and Kjell Gronhaug (1990), "Respondents' Moods as a Biasing Factor in Surveys: An Experimental Study", in *Advances in Consumer Research*, Vol. 18, eds. Rebecca H. Holman and Michael R. Solomon.

Inhoff, Albrecht W. and Kevin Fleming (1989), "Probe-Detection Times During the Reading of Easy and Difficult Text", *Journal of Experimental Psychology: Learning, Memory, and Cognition*, 15(2), 339-351.

Isen, Alice (1984), "Toward Understanding the Role of Affect in Cognition", in *Handbook of Social Cognition*, eds. Robert Wyer, Jr. and Thomas Srull, Hillsdale, NJ: Lawrence Erlbaum, 179-236.

Isen, Alice, Thomas Shalker, Margaret Clark, and Lynn Karp (1978), "Affect, Accessibility of Material in Memory, and Behavior: A Cognitive Loop?," *Journal of Personality and Social Psychology*, 36 (January), 1-12.

Lord, Kenneth R. and Robert E. Burnkrant (1988), "Television Program Elaboration Effects on Commercial Processing", in *Advances in Consumer Research*, Vol. 15, ed., Michael J. Houston, 213-218.

Lord, Kenneth R., Robert E. Burnkrant and Robert S. Owen (1989), "An Experimental Comparison of Self-Report and Response Time Measures of Consumer Information Processing", in *Proceedings of the American Marketing Association 1989 Summer Educators' Conference*.

Malhotra, Naresh K. (1990), "Administration of Questionnaires for Collecting Quantitative Data in International Marketing Research," *Journal of Global Marketing*, Vol. 4, No. 2, forthcoming.

Malhotra, Naresh K. (1991), "Mnemonics in Marketing: A Pedagogical Tool", *Journal of the Academy of Marketing Science*, forthcoming.

Malhotra, Naresh K. (1992), *Marketing Research: An Applied Orientation*, New York: Harper-Collins, forthcoming.

Melnick, E. L., R. Colombo, R. Tashjian, and K. R. Melnick (1990), "Sampled Survey Data: Quota Samples Versus Probability Samples", in *Advances in Consumer Research*, Vol. 18, eds. Rebecca H. Holman and Michael R. Solomon.

Owen, Robert S. (1990), "Clarifying the Simple Assumption of the Secondary Task Technique", in *Advances in Consumer Research*, Vol. 18, eds. Rebecca H. Holman and Michael R. Solomon.

Door-In-The-Face, That's-Not-All, and Legitimizing A Paltry Contribution: Reciprocity, Contrast Effect and Social Judgment Theory Explanations

Ian Brennan, University of Texas at Arlington
Kenneth D. Bahn, University of Texas at Arlington

ABSTRACT

Research has shown how a small family of techniques (Door-in-the-face, That's-not-all and Legitimizing a paltry contribution) have proven successful in increasing the proportion of compliant responses without reducing average response magnitudes. The concept of reciprocity has been proposed to explain the success of the Door-in-the-face and the That's-not-all techniques. The present study attempts to build a theoretical framework to explain the success of the That's-not-all technique via the contrast effect and the Legitimizing a paltry contribution technique via social judgment theory.

INTRODUCTION

A number of studies have focused on the question of which factors influence a person's compliance with a request. In particular, a small family of techniques ("Door-in-the-face," "Legitimizing a paltry contribution," and "That's-not-all") have proven successful in increasing the proportion of compliant responses without reducing the average response size (Cann, Sherman and Elkes 1975; Cialdini and Schroeder 1976; Berger 1986).

Door-in-the-face (DTF), Legitimizing a paltry contribution (LPC) and That's-not-all (TNA) may be thought of as a related group of techniques in the sense that each relies on the requestor retreating from a larger request to a smaller one in an attempt to gain compliance.[1] In the DTF approach, an extreme first request is made. If it is rejected, a second more moderate request is made (Cialdini, Vincent, Lewis, Catalan, Wheeler and Darby 1975). In the case of the LPC technique, a standard request for an unspecified donation is followed by the phrase "even a penny would help" (Cialdini and Schroeder 1976). Finally, the TNA technique consists of offering a product at a high price and then offering to sell the product at a lower price before the customer has a chance to respond (Burger 1986).

The concept of reciprocation has been proposed to explain both the TNA technique (Burger 1986) and the DTF technique (Cialdini et al. 1975; Mowen and Cialdini 1980; Tybout 1978). Gouldner (1960) explains the norm of reciprocity as: "You should give benefits to those who give you benefits." In a similar manner, Cialdini et al. (1975) postulate a reciprocal concessions corollary to the general norm of reciprocity: "You should make concessions to those who make concessions to you." The fact that the requestor makes a concession by dropping from a large to a small request is the foundation of the reciprocity explanation of both the DTF and TNA techniques.

An alternative explanation for the success of both the TNA and DTF techniques may be found in assimilation and contrast theory, as introduced by Sherif, Taub and Hovland (1958). A contrast refers to a shift in judgment away from an anchor or reference point. Assimilation, on the other hand, refers to a shift in judgment toward the anchor. A contrast effect has been demonstrated to occur with both physical and social stimuli. Kenrick and Gutierres (1980) found that when college men were asked to judge the physical attractiveness of a potential date, the date was rated as significantly less attractive if the men had just finished watching a television program starring three very attractive women ("Charlie's Angels") than if they had watched a control program.

In the case of social stimuli, Pepitone and DiNubile (1976) showed support for the existence of a contrast effect in the area of judicial sentencing. The order in which cases were heard affected the prison sentences handed out. Thus, a homicide case judged after another homicide case drew an average of twenty-two years of punishment, but a homicide case judged after an assault drew thirty-three. Similarly, an assault case judged after another assault case drew eight years, whereas an assault case judged after a homicide drew only five. Clearly, in the case of both the DTF and TNA techniques, the initial request may serve as a large anchor point which makes the second (smaller) request appear less of a burden than it would in the absence of the anchorpoint. As Burger (1986) notes, "If the salesperson first introduces an anchorpoint of $1 and allows for this to operate as a basis of the customer's deliberations, then a price of 75 cents for the same product would appear more reasonable than if an anchorpoint of 75 cents was introduced initially."

Both Burger (1986) and Cialdini et al. (1975) designed experiments to test the aforementioned alternative explanations for the success of the TNA and DTF techniques. The empirical results of both researchers support the reciprocity explanation and reject the contrast explanation.

In an attempt to build a theoretical framework to explain the DTF, TNA, and LPC techniques, the current paper questions Burger's rejection of the contrast explanation for the success of the TNA technique and also purports to explain the success of the LPC technique through social judgment theory. The hypothesized social judgment explanation for the success of the LPC technique and the hypothesized contrast effect explanation for the

---

[1] The authors wish to consider techniques that involve the requestor retreating from a large (explicit or implicit) request to a smaller one. Thus, the Foot-in-the-Door technique was not considered since it reverses the order of request magnitudes.

FIGURE 1
Conceptual Model of DTF, TNA and LPC Techniques*

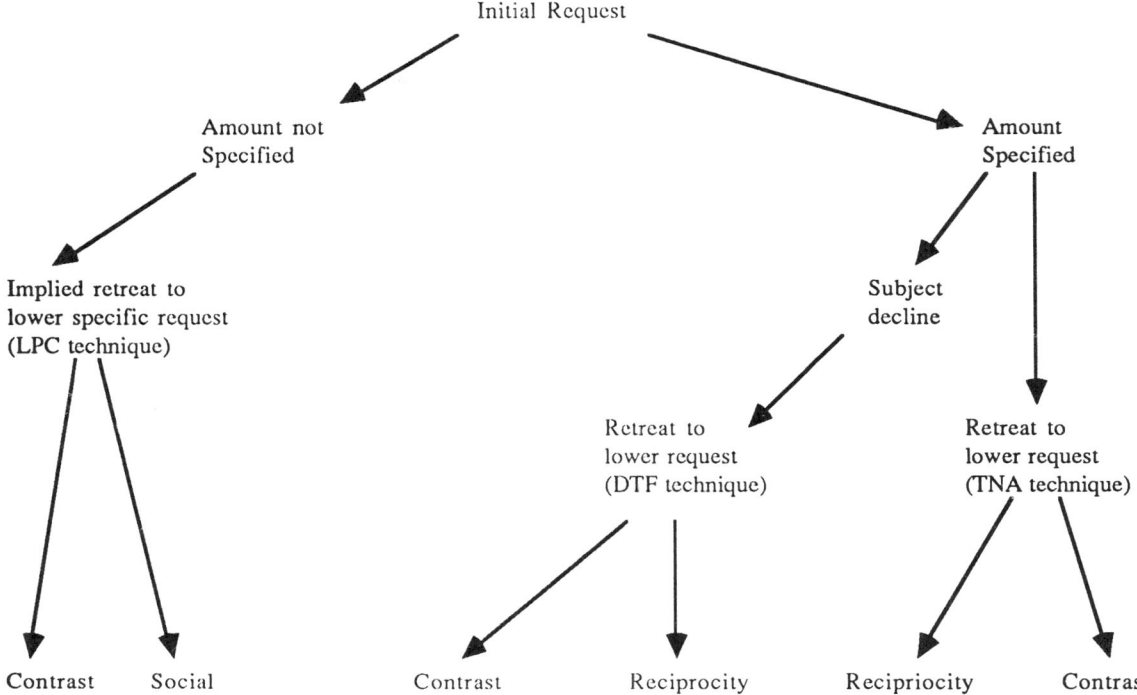

* The authors advocate Social Judgement Theory, Reciprocity Theory and the Contrast Effect as explainers of the LPC, DTF and TNA techniques, respectively.

success of the TNA technique opens the door to innovative combinatory techniques that employ more than one theory. Such innovations are addressed in the final section of this paper.

THEORETICAL FRAMEWORK

A conceptual model of the DTF, TNA and LPC techniques appears in Figure 1. The theoretical explanations for all techniques are discussed individually in the sections below.

The Door-in-the-Face Technique

In the case of the DTF technique, Cialdini et al. (1975) argue that success depends upon invoking the norm of reciprocity. The norm of reciprocity depends upon two conditions. First, the same individual must deliver both requests. Second, the initial request must be rejected by the respondent before the second request is delivered.

If different people make the requests, then Cialdini et al. (1975) maintain that the first (large) request serves only as a large anchorpoint (which is the only requirement of the contrast effect explanation); thus, the second request can no longer be seen as representing a concession violating one of the conditions of reciprocity. Both Cialdini et al. (1975) and Fern, Monroe and Avila (1986) found higher compliance rates when the same person delivered both requests than when the two requests were delivered by different individuals.

Cialdini et al. (1975) also argue that if a requestor delivers two requests (one large and one small) and asks the subject to perform either of them, then the contrast effect of a large and a small anchorpoint is present (contrast effect) but reciprocity is absent, since the reciprocal concessions explanation requires the subject's refusal of the large request rather than mere exposure to it. Again, the rate of compliance with the second request was higher when the subject rejected the first request (reciprocity explanation) than when he was merely exposed to it (contrast effect). Thus, empirical tests support the reciprocity explanation of the DTF technique.

The That's-Not-All Technique

The evidence supporting a particular theoretical explanation for the TNA technique is less conclusive. Burger (1986) argues that reciprocity accounts for the success of the TNA technique. In an experiment in which two experimenters sell cupcakes at a bake sale, three experimental conditions are manipulated:

> "In the reciprocity condition, subjects were told that the price of a cupcake was $1.25. At this point the second experimenter interrupted. The customer's response was delayed, with a raised hand and a wait a second by the first experimenter. After two to three seconds, the first experimenter turned to the customer and said that because they were planning to close down pretty soon, he or she would be willing to sell the cupcake for only $1.00." Subjects in the contrast effect condition were told, "These are only a dollar now. We were selling them for $1.25 earlier." Subjects in the control condition were told that the price of a cupcake was $1.00 (Burger 1986).

The purchase rate in the reciprocity condition was higher than in the contrast effect condition. Burger's conclusion is that the success of the TNA technique is based on reciprocity. This conclusion, however, may be questioned in view of the absence of the first condition for reciprocity, namely the rejection of the large request. Moreover, it may be argued that the reduction in price is motivated by the self interest of the experimenters (i.e., the desire to close the stall) rather than as a concession towards the customer. Thus it may be argued that the contrast effect provides an alternative explanation for Burger's results, since in the reciprocity condition, the $1.25 acts as an anchorpoint against which the $1.00 price appears reasonable. In the contrast effect condition, however, the $1.25 is a weaker/nonexistent anchorpoint, since it is introduced *after* the current price of $1.00.

Legitimizing a Paltry Contribution Technique

In the case of the LPC technique, researchers have, for the most part, focused on demonstrating the success of the technique (Frazer, Hite and Sauer 1988; Brockner, Guzzi, Kane, Levine and Shaplan 1984; Cialdini and Schroeder 1976; Reeves, Macolini and Martin 1987; Reingen 1978) rather than providing a theoretical framework to explain success.

The LPC technique has been tested most frequently in a charitable gift-giving context. It would appear that the decision to give to charity is based on social norms and/or to bolster self image. Brockner et al. (1984) observe that individuals may make charitable contributions to "look good in their own and/or other eyes." Clearly, one obstacle that may inhibit an individual from making a charitable contribution is that the individual may feel that the amount of the donation he can afford would be socially unacceptable. On the other hand, as Mowen and Cialdini (1980) observe, "the individual may perceive that they will be disliked if they break an operative norm," which in the gift-giving situation would be to act perniciously. It is contended in this paper that the LPC technique, which relies on the above mentioned concepts for its conceptual development, may be explained by cognitive dissonance (Festinger 1957), which is acted upon and resolved through the concepts forwarded in Social Judgment Theory (see Figure 1).

Festinger (1957) notes that two objects are dissonant when knowledge of one suggests the opposite of the other. Moreover, dissonance will give rise to activity designed to reduce the unpleasant feeling of dissonance. One method of reducing dissonance is to change one of the elements. Thus, under the cognitive dissonance conceptualization of the LPC technique, a subject experiences dissonance when he would like to comply with a charitable request but feels the financial magnitude of his donation would be smaller than that which he perceives to be socially acceptable. It should be evident that the tension felt by the subject is reduced if such a donation is legitimized as socially acceptable.

The process of changing the social acceptability of a donation while holding the donation size constant may be explained by Social Judgment Theory (Sherif and Sherif 1967). Social Judgment Theory maintains that attitudinal judgments such as agreeing or not agreeing with a statement, need to be considered within the particular frame of reference of an individual making the judgment. According to Social Judgment Theory, an attitudinal dimension is comprised of three categories or latitudes (Petty and Cacioppo 1981). The latitude of acceptance includes a person's most preferred position, but also includes the range of other opinions on an issue that the person finds acceptable. The latitude of rejection comprises the range of opinions that the person finds objectionable. Finally, the latitude of noncommitment comprises those positions that the person finds neither acceptable nor objectionable. In the charitable gift-giving situation, the attitudinal dimension appears dichotomous (i.e., an individual may consider donation size either socially acceptable or socially unacceptable). Clearly, for those individuals who feel that their economically affordable donation is socially unacceptable (i.e., in the latitude of rejection), the phrase "even a penny would help" is a discrepant communication which is designed to extend the latitude of acceptance (i.e., the range of donation sizes that are considered socially acceptable), and reduce the latitude of rejection (the range of donations that are considered socially unacceptable).

Although Cialdini et al. (1975) in the case of the DTF technique, and Burger (1986) more questionably in the case of the TNA technique, have built support for reciprocity, that explanation seems inappropriate in the case of the LPC technique. This notion is predicated on the positions forwarded by Cialdini et al. (1975) and Mowen and Cialdini (1980). They observed that for reciprocity to be invoked, the requestor must be perceived as making a legitimate request and a concession must be perceived in the movement from the large to the small request. Previous field tests of the LPC (e.g., Cialdini and Schroeder 1976; Brockner et al. 1984) have not specified the size of the donation in the initial request.[2] Therefore, since the addition of the phrase "even a penny will help" has not been preceded by a large request, it cannot be viewed as a concession by the requestor. If we accept the conditions of reciprocity to be true, then reciprocity as an explanation for the LPC technique appears to be invalid.

Finally, a contrast effect explanation of the LPC technique must be considered. It would appear that for the contrast effect to be effective, the subject must first anchor on the relatively unfavorable (high price) request for the second (lower price) to be perceived more favorably. Reversing the order of request presentation appears to weaken the power of the technique (see the results of Burger's (1986) operationalization of a contrast-effect quoted above). A contrast effect explanation of the LPC technique implies that the respondent's first perception of a socially acceptable donation is financially unacceptable so that the legitimizing of a paltry contribution allows the respondent to perceive a smaller donation size as socially acceptable. The contrast effect explanation of the LPC technique is, however, inconsistent with empirical tests of the LPC which have demonstrated that when compliance rates increase, average donation sizes are not significantly affected (Brockner et al. 1984; Reeves et al. 1987; Reingen 1978).

Directions for Future Research

Clearly, the conceptualization that the contrast effect and Social Judgment Theory explain the TNA technique and the LPC technique, respectively, requires empirical testing. It is possible that results of both techniques might be improved if an attempt is made to augment them with reciprocity.

Tybout (1978) has observed that the trustworthiness of the requestor appears to be an important factor in the success of techniques that attempt to invoke the norm of reciprocity in the subject. Thus, future research might combine the LPC or TNA with methods to build trust and reciprocity in the requestor. For example, in the case of the LPC technique, the requestor could explain to the subject that he (the requestor) was giving up his leisure time without compensation on behalf of the charity in question. Such a statement might reassure the subject as to the ultimate destination of the donation (build trust in the requestor) as well as invoking the norm of reciprocity through the concession of free time by the requestor to the cause of the charity.

REFERENCES

Brockner, Joel, Beth Guzzi, Julie Kane, Ellen Levine, and Kate Shaplan (1984), "Organizational Fundraising: Further Evidence on the Effect of Legitimizing Small Donations," *Journal of Consumer Research*, 11, 611-614.

Burger, Jerry M. (1986), "Increasing Compliance by Improving the Deal: The That's-Not-All Technique," *Journal of Personality and Social Psychology*, 51, 277-283.

Cann, A., S. J. Sherman and R. Elkes (1975), "Effects of Initial Request Size and Timing of a Second Request: The Foot-in-the-Door and the Door-in-the-Face," *Journal of Personality and Social Psychology*, 32, 774-782.

Cialdini, Robert B. and David A. Schroeder (1976), "Increasing Compliance by Legitimizing Paltry Contributions: When Even a Penny Helps," *Journal of Personality and Social Psychology*, 51, 599-605.

_____, Joyce E. Vincent, Stephen K. Lewis, Jose Catalan, Diane Wheeler, and Betty Lee Darby (1975), "Reciprocal Concessions Procedure for Inducing Compliance: The Door-in-the-Face Technique," *Journal of Personality and Social Psychology*, 31, 206-215.

Fern, Edward F., Kent B. Monroe and Ramon A. Avila, "Effectiveness of Multiple Request Strategies: A Synthesis of Research Results," *Journal of Marketing Research*, 23, 144-152.

Frazer, Cynthia, Robert E. Hite, and Paul L. Sauer (1988), "Increasing Contributions in Solicitation Campaigns: The Use of Large and Small Anchor Points," *Journal of Consumer Research*, 15, 284-287.

Gouldner, Alvin W. (1960), "The Norm of Reciprocity: A Preliminary Statement," *American Sociological Review*, 25, 161-178.

Helson, Harry (1964), *Adoption-Level Theory: An Experimental and Systematic Approach to Behavior*, New York: Harper and Row.

Kenrick, Douglas T. and Sarat E. Gutierres (1980), "Contrast Effects and Judgments of Physical Attractiveness: When Beauty Becomes a Social Problem," *Journal of Personality and Social Psychology*, 38, 131-140.

Mowen, John C. and Robert B. Cialdini (1980), "On Implementing the Door-in-the-Face Compliance Technique in a Business Context," *Journal of Marketing Research*, 27, 253-258.

Pepitone, Albert and Mark Dinubile, "Contrast Effects in Judgments of Crime Severity and the Punishment of Criminal Violators," *Journal of Personality and Social Psychology*, 33, 448-459.

Petty, Richard and John Cacioppo, 1981, *Attitudes and Persuasion: Classic and Contemporary Approaches*, Iowa: W. C. Brown.

---

[2] The one exception: Frazer, Hite and Sauer (1988) combined a large anchorpoint ($20) with the LPC but found the distant anchorpoints cancelled each other's effectiveness. As Frazer et al. (1988) observe, "He says a penny would help, but he wants $30. I can't afford $30 and he can't be serious about accepting a penny."

Reeves, Robert A., Ruthann M. Macolini, and Roy C. Martin (1987), "Legitimizing Paltry Contributions On the Spot vs. Mail-In Service," *Journal of Applied Social Psychology*, 17, 731-738.

Reingen, Peter (1978), "On Inducing Compliance with Request," *Journal of Consumer Research*, 5, 96-102.

Sherif, Muzafer and Carolyn W. Sherif, eds. (1967), *Attitude as the Individuals Own Categories: The Social Judgment-Involvement Approach to Attitude and Attitude Change, in Attitude, Ego-Involvement and Change*, Westport, CT: Greenwook, 105-139.

_____, Daniel Taub and Carl I. Hovland (1958), "Assimilation and Contrast Effects of Anchoring Stimuli on Judgments," *Journal of Experimental and Social Psychology*, 55, 150-155.

Tybout, Alice M. (1978), "Relative Effectiveness of Three Behavioral Influence Strategies as Supplements to Persuasion in a Marketing Context," *Journal of Marketing Research*, 15, 229-242.

Deal Search: An Approach for Computer-Controlled Information Processing Experiments Involving Bargainable Attributes

Paul H. Schurr, State University of New York - Albany

Merrie Brucks, University of Arizona[1]

ABSTRACT

Deal Search is a microcomputer program that can facilitate the study of information processing issues concerning bargainable and non-bargainable attributes. This article (1) discusses an information processing approach to bargaining, (2) provides details on how Deal Search may be used in computer-controlled experiments in this area, and (3) proposes some starting points for future research.

INTRODUCTION

In a recent article by Brucks and Schurr (1990) the bargaining purchase process was examined as a multiattribute, multialternative choice task in which the attribute values are subject to change. Knowledge of attribute value ranges was manipulated to examine its effects on bargaining and non-bargaining purchase tasks. They found that buyers reduce information search when they have the option of bargaining. Also, knowledge of attribute value ranges appears to increase the degree to which buyers replace information search with bargaining. This study demonstrates the use of a computer-controlled experiment to gain understanding about how consumers search for information and make choices when product attributes are bargainable.

Their work utilized Deal Search, a menu-driven user interface that combined a number of novel features: (1) comparability between purchase tasks that do and do not include a bargaining component, (2) multiple brands or dealers, representing alternative bargaining partners, and (3) an offer-sensitive algorithm for generating responses to subjects who elected to bargain.

The Brucks and Schurr (1990) article provides sufficient description of their methods for the purpose of reporting their experiment. However, their article did not attempt to discuss Deal Search in such a way that would allow other researchers to easily envision how this same approach might be used to address other research issues in bargaining and information processing. Similar to Brucks' (1988) article on Search Monitor, the purpose of this paper is to suggest research problems for which Deal Search is appropriate and to briefly describe its features and options.

This paper is divided into four sections. First background is provided on an information processing approach to bargaining. The next two sections give the essential characteristics of Deal Search and summarize how the program operates. The fourth section discusses research issues that might be addressed using Deal Search or similar software.

BACKGROUND

An Information Approach to Bargaining

When attributes are bargainable, additional tasks confront the consumer: the consumer must interact with the seller and mutually define the attribute values for the product. This means buyers in a bargaining situation evaluate the implications of sellers' offers relative to potential final agreement levels. And they must also formulate messages and counter-offers that will induce the sellers to make favorable concessions.

The increased cognitive load associated with bargaining changes information search and decision-making processes in purchase situations. For example, when bargaining is required, a buyer may curtail information search in order to devote more cognitive effort to the bargaining task. The Brucks and Schurr (1990) article proposes that such changes in information search and decision-making processes have not been examined in the bargaining literature. Even in marketing, this important aspect of buying behavior -- relevant to house and car buying, for example -- has received little attention. One reason for this lack of attention, we believe, is that until recently adequate methods were not available to study bargaining from an information processing approach.

Adding Bargaining to the Information Search Paradigm

When product attributes are not bargainable, decision making requires finding out the value of attributes for the various alternatives. It also requires evaluating those values relative to some absolute criteria or the other decision alternatives. Thus, the consumer information processing literature (cf. Bettman 1979) studies the multiattribute brand choice problem as follows. Subjects are presented with a choice of several brands, each characterized by values on several attributes. Data are collected on the information search and/or evaluation process by monitoring subjects' acquisition of attribute information and/or thoughts produced during choice.

Deal Search overlays the possibility of bargaining on this basic paradigm. For example, as in the purchase of a house or a computer for a small business, a subject might begin by gathering attribute information about different alternatives. At some point, however, the subject may choose to bargain with the seller to obtain desired values for particular attributes. In Deal Search, information search when attributes are bargainable is analogous to information search in non-bargaining tasks, except that the attribute values that are acquired are

---

[1] The software discussed in this paper is available from either author. The copyright to Deal Search ((C) 1986) is owned by Paul H. Schurr and Merrie Brucks.

subject to change through an exchange of offers and counter-offers regarding specific attributes.

DEAL SEARCH'S CHARACTERISTICS

Deal Search itself has roots in a prior information search study (Brucks 1985) and a multiple-opponent bargaining study (Schurr and Ozanne 1985). These prior studies provide the rationale for using a computer-controlled task in consumer behavior studies (see also Brucks 1990). The following discussion focuses on the specific characteristics of Deal Search.

Degree of Customization

Deal Search can be modified to adapt a number of design characteristics to the needs of the research: the number and type of alternatives (i.e., dealers, stores, or brands), the number and type of attributes, the bargainability of the attributes (bargainable or non-bargainable), the values of attributes, and the pattern of counter-offers in the bargaining mode. (In addition, the researcher can design both pre-test and post-test questionnaires that are administered by the computer.) This adaptability applies to both the warm-up familiarization task and the main experimental task. As operationalized in the Brucks and Schurr (1990) article, subjects purchased a business computer from one of 6 dealers. Twelve product attributes described the computers. The following discussion refers to this version of Deal Search.

Sequential Decisions

There are two fundamental decisions relating to alternatives and attributes. Essentially, a subject first must choose which store to visit. Then the subject must decide which product attribute(s) to ask (or bargain) about while at the store. The stores are the alternatives, and could be relabeled as brands if the researcher so desired. The following menus indicate the options that are related to the basic store-choice and attribute-choice decisions.

The menu for choosing a store to visit. The focal buying task requires a series of sequential decisions, and these decisions vary according to where the subject is in the search process. First, the subject chooses which store to visit. Then the computer provides a waiting-time graphic to denote travel time to the store.

The menu for making an initial inquiry at a store. On the first visit to a store the choices include: asking about attributes, purchasing the product without further ado, or backtracking so that a different store can be visited. This latter option is necessary to allow for times when a subject goes to a store and then discovers that s/he intended to visit a different store.

Choosing an attribute to inquire about. If the subject opts for asking about attributes, the subject must type in the name of the attribute. In the Brucks and Schurr (1990) study the subjects knew about the attribute names by reading about them in a pre-task instruction set.

The menu accompanying attribute value information. Upon receiving attribute information, the choices become: ask about a different attribute, go to a different store, or purchase the product. The latter option recognizes that a consumer may elect to make a purchase at any point in the search process.

In the bargaining mode this menu also includes the option to bargain about the attribute. The option to bargain also appears in the preceding menu, but only if a subject has already asked about the store's offering (i.e., attribute values). (Generally speaking it would be unnatural for a person to walk into a store and launch into bargaining without first asking some questions aimed at revealing a seller's initial offer. However, in non-retail settings the seller may or may not make the first offer; Deal Search would require modification in this case.)

The bargaining option. If the subject elects to bargain, the following screen requests the subject's counter-offer in a fill-in-the-blank format. Accompanying the seller's response are the same options as in the preceding menu plus the option to continue bargaining about the same attribute.

As the preceding details indicate, the menu options are tailored to a particular step in the subjects' information search task and to whether the attributes are bargainable or not. Because of this sequential structure, of course, the key-stroke-and-time sequential trace of a subject's decisions provides appropriate data for information search analyses.

Methods for Requesting Information and Making Counter-Proposals

Requesting attribute information. In Deal Search subjects make inquiries about a particular attribute by typing in the name of that attribute. This approach has both advantages and disadvantages (also see Brucks 1988). One advantage of this approach is that people normally have to bring to mind which attributes they want to ask about and then communicate their choices. Another advantage of this approach is that it offers the researcher flexibility in the way attribute information is presented to subjects. For example, in Brucks and Schurr (1990) the knowledge manipulation was incorporated in the hard-copy attribute descriptions. Another consideration is that the format of hard-copy attribute information can be varied, recognizing the possibility that information presentation may affect consumer search. To avoid order effects in attribute listings, order may be varied in the different versions of the instruction sets.

The primary disadvantage of forcing a subject to type in an attribute name is that it imposes a cost of search that may vary according to the typing skills of the subject. This problem is minimized by keeping keywords short. While Deal Search can handle some variations of the attribute keywords, typing errors evoke a message indicating that the input is not recognized.

Making counter-proposals. Subjects make counter-proposals to a seller's offers by stating an attribute value for the attribute selected. Counter-proposals can be made for only one attribute at a time. On one hand, this one-at-a-time feature preserves the sequential nature of a subject's decisions; this facilitates the monitoring of information search (e.g., Brucks and Schurr 1990). On the other hand, it does remove the possibility of log-rolling through the simultaneous presentation of counter-proposals on, say, three attributes at one time. Log-rolling refers to giving concessions on one attribute so that gains can be obtained on an alternative attribute (Pruitt 1981; for a paradigm that incorporates computer-controlled log-rolling see Schurr and Ozanne 1985).

Allowing subjects to enter any attribute value they choose for their counter-proposals creates some challenges for the algorithm that determines the computerized responses. However, this characteristic is in some respects a significant advance over the widely used Kelly (1966) paradigm (e.g., Graham et al. 1988; Schurr 1987) because the Kelly paradigm reveals the feasible range of attribute value offers; Deal Search does not require that subjects know the researcher's pre-conceived range of bargainable attribute values. Thus, a primary advantage of this approach is that the range of possible responses is not communicated to subjects unless the researcher so chooses. This means researchers can study the effect that a subject's attribute-value knowledge has on counter-proposals that are made. Another possible advantage not exploited in the Brucks and Schurr (1990) study is that more latitude is provided for the study of how consumers formulate a series of counter-proposals in a bargaining situation.

Search Costs

As discussed in Brucks (1988), the major advantage of building waiting time into a computer-controlled experiment is that it parallels the cost of search in actual purchase situations. In Deal Search, waiting time can be adjusted for any of the menus or computerized responses. One of the more important search cost variables is the time it takes to go from store to store. When the cost of traveling to alternative stores increases, one might expect consumers to increasingly focus on bargaining rather than search since bargaining may achieve more favorable outcomes without traveling to another store.

Bargaining Interaction

An important characteristic that distinguishes Deal Search from other computer-controlled approaches to the study of bargainable attributes (e.g., Clopton 1984; Schurr and Ozanne 1985) is the strategy employed for developing computerized responses to a subject's counter-proposals. Each rule governing the bargaining process was designed to be consistent with certain assumptions about a realistic bargaining process. The following discussion presents these rules and explains the underlying assumptions and rationale for the rules.

1. In non-bargaining and bargaining conditions dealers make the initial offers that are predetermined by the researcher. In the bargaining condition, concessions are then determined in response to a subject's counter-offer.

This rule fits selling situations, particularly retail situations, where the product has an "asking" price. An advantage of this rule is that it keeps non-bargaining and bargaining tasks identical until the subject in the bargainable attribute condition chooses to bargain. However, in bargaining situations opening offers commonly are different from agreement points. Yet Deal Search equates a seller's opening offer in a bargaining situation with a seller's best and only offer in a non-bargaining situation. This may mean that an attribute value that a subject perceives as a reasonable opening offer in a bargaining situation (say, a list price of a house in a buyer's market) will be perceived as less than reasonable in a a non-bargaining situation (see Brucks and Schurr 1990 for a discussion of this point).

2. If a subject's counter-offer is poorer than (less attractive to the seller) or the same as that subject's most recent offer, then the dealer will not make a concession. A dealer will never retract an offer once it is made.

This rule assumes that in general bargainers do not backtrack on their previous offers, and a seller will not reward such backtracking with a concession. Exceptions to this norm are possible in real life, of course.

3. However, if a subject persists in making offers that do not represent a concession, the dealer will occasionally respond with a small concession.

Osgood (1959) introduced a widely discussed notion of initiating reciprocity by making a small concession in a stand-off situation. Deal Search casts the seller in the position of trying to stimulate a give-and-take exchange. However, in a laboratory setting subjects will try to "game" the task if they discover that the simple rule "be persistent" yields consistent rewards in bargaining. Therefore, Deal Search is designed such that persistence by itself is an inefficient strategy for reaching favorable agreements. In fact, the researcher can control when and how the programmed seller responds to a subject's persistence -- even retracting a previous concession, if this makes sense in the research context.

4. If a subject's current offer represents a concession when compared to the

subject's most recent offer, then the dealer will make a concession. The computer determines an appropriate concession by first matching the subject's offer to one of a number of predetermined offer ranks for a particular dealer. An offer rank is a subset of attribute values defined by an upper and lower bound between which a buyer's offer to a seller may fall. Each offer rank is associated with a specific concession size for the dealer.

For example, suppose a subject asks a dealer about the attribute "free software," and the dealer replies by offering free software valued at $100. Then suppose the subject counters with a higher figure: free software valued at $1200. The Deal Search algorithm first examines the attribute's offer ranks in order to classify the subject's proposal for the value of free software:

Offer Rank	Value Range for Subject's Offer	Dealer's Concession
7	Over $1300	$200
6	$1150 - $1299	$200
5	$1000 - $1149	$150
4	$850 - $999	$150
3	$700 - $849	$100
2	$550 - $699	$100
1	$400 - $549	$50

Deal Search determines that the subject's $1200 proposal falls within Offer Rank 6 (bounded by $1150 and $1299) and determines that a concession of $200 is called for. Consequently the dealer would add $200 worth of free software to the initial offer of $100, resulting in a counter-proposal of free software valued at $300.

Rule 4 utilizes Osgood's 1959 notion of graduated reciprocity, which says that an opponent's concessions should be reciprocated in order to facilitate agreement. To implement this reciprocity, the Deal Search algorithm requires that the researcher predetermine dealer responses by creating offer rank ranges and corresponding dealer concessions. Each dealer can have different initial offers (e.g., see Table 1 in Brucks and Schurr 1990). Because a dealer's concessions are added to a dealer's initial offer, each dealer's attribute value offers varies accordingly.

5. Concessions for some attributes (i.e., where feasible) are smaller as a dealer approaches the preset settlement point for that dealer.

This rule assumes Siegal and Fouraker's (1960) notion that bargainers signal that their settlement point is approaching by making smaller concessions. By incorporating this rule into Deal Search we approach the goal of making a dealer's pattern of offers informative to the alert subject. The implementation of this rule can be observed by inspecting the Dealer's Concession column in the preceding example. Note that as a subject's offers fall into progressively lower offer ranks, the dealer's concessions decrease.

Also, if a subject makes a second offer that falls within the same offer rank, the dealer responds with the smallest concession the subject could make -- $50 in the case of free software. Subsequent concessions are treated in the same way as repetitive offers (Rule 3). Note that a subject whose initial counter-proposal corresponds to a lower offer rank may actually obtain a less favorable final settlement point with a dealer than will a subject whose initial offer falls into a higher offer rank. This aspect of Deal Search bargaining agrees with observed patterns of bargaining outcomes (Siegal and Fouraker 1960).

6. Agreement is reached when a subject agrees to a dealer's standing offer (either the initial offer or an offer that has resulted from one or more concessions) or when a dealer makes a concession that results in agreement with a subject's most recent offer.

This rule assures that the dealer will stop making concessions when a point of agreement has been reached.

7. A dealer never agrees to a final settlement less favorable to the dealer than a preset best offer.

This rule prevents persistent subjects from obtaining unrealistically favorable deals. Also, note that by manipulating the best offer that is made by a dealer, the researcher can create a task in which some alternatives (i.e., dealers) dominate other alternatives. By observing the efficiency and effectiveness that subjects exhibit in terms of identifying the dominant alternatives, a researcher can draw some conclusions about the effectiveness of alternative patterns of bargaining or information search.

RUNNING THE PROGRAM

From the subject's standpoint, Deal Search is easy to use. Deal search tells subjects when to read instructions contained on separate pages, solicits responses to pretest and post-test questionnaires, and manages the menu-driven search task as well as keyword and attribute value input. Creation of the keystroke trace, which is the researcher's raw data, is invisible to subjects.

From the researcher's standpoint, Deal Search is not especially user friendly. While Deal Search incorporates debugging features, structured data entry for many parameters, and special operator-only screens, understanding of the source program is necessary in order to use Deal Search. Adapting Deal Search to the research project at hand and transforming data traces to data bases suitable for statistical analysis requires knowledge of BASIC and competent programming skills.

Input Required

Deal Search requires information for a variety of parameters, including: store names, attribute keywords, units that describe how the attribute values are measured, the number of offer ranks for each attribute, concession range information for each rank, concessions for each offer rank, and additional parameters that control certain aspects of bargaining. A variety of waiting time parameters can also be adjusted.

Program Requirements and Documentation

Deal Search currently utilizes Zenith's Microsoft GW-BASIC (Version 2). Currently it operates on computers with 512K of memory and one disk drive. Deal Search contains documentation in the programming statements. Some additional documentation is available from the authors.

RESEARCH ISSUES

We believe that there is considerable merit in approaching bargaining as an information search and evaluation task. Such an approach reveals new issues for study that have received very little attention. Because this approach to bargaining is so new, the value of Deal Search probably lies more with the issues a researcher might address, rather than with the program itself. Three general research streams appear appropriate: (1) comparing bargainable to non-bargainable purchases, (2) examining the factors that affect the trade-off between bargaining and information search, and (3) examining the factors that produce various bargaining strategies. In this concluding section we enumerate a few starting points for such research.

1. Bargaining and Decision Frames

Starting with the notion that a major task of bargainers is to process the great variety of information pertaining to a negotiation, it is interesting to consider the effects of different frames of reference that might influence how a bargainer interprets information. For example, it was found in one negotiation study concerned with risky decisions (Schurr 1987) that the very same pay-offs stated in terms of "the chances of obtaining net profits" (i.e., potential gains, a positive frame) instead of "the chances of incurring expenses" (i.e., potential reduced losses, a negative frame) caused negotiators to make less risky bargaining agreements. Besides affecting outcomes, risk aversion may also affect (1) the trade-off between bargaining and information search and (2) bargaining strategy.

2. The Perceived Cost of Information Search and Bargaining

Search costs have received almost no attention in the bargaining literature. More research is needed on how time pressure and time-costs of information affect consumer behavior in connection with both bargainable and non-bargainable attributes. It has become conventional wisdom that when one bargainer is subject to time pressure and his or her opponent is not, the opponent has an advantage. Yet we know little about patterns of information search and bargaining or about the effectiveness of these efforts in connection with time costs.

3. Perceived Benefits of Information Search and Bargaining

In the study reported in Brucks and Schurr (1990) subjects varied considerably in the degree to which they engaged in bargaining to achieve a favorable outcome. While much research has been carried out regarding individual differences in amount of information search (see Moore and Lehmann 1980), little has been published in the consumer literature on individual differences in the amount of bargaining. Motivational factors, such as involvement and past enjoyment, should be examined.

4. Attribute Level Knowledge

Attribute level knowledge emerged as an important factor in the Brucks and Schurr (1990) study, which suggested that bargainers tended to discount the value of initial offer information and utilize bargaining influence to improve their outcomes. Future research can explore the effects of knowledge that gives greater meaning to initial offers. For example, industry norms or other sources of expectations would influence the ability of a consumer to utilize initial offers to screen dealers by means of initial offers. Alternatively, bargainers may be most interested in knowing the feasible zone of agreement and indifference points to use in their bargaining efforts.

5. Reputational Knowledge

Reputational knowledge is another factor that affects a consumer's ability to form evaluations about dealers. For example, dealers in the Brucks and Schurr (1990) study had no established reputation, which may be realistic in some, but not all, settings. Reputations take different forms. Reputations for quality or service reliability would affect expectations for product attributes levels. In contrast, reputation for fairness and honesty is more likely to influence the process of bargaining, rather than information search (cf., Schurr and Ozanne 1985).

In addition to the effects of reputational knowledge, interactions between reputation and product attribute information deserves consideration. For example, an interesting research issue concerns the affects of disconfirming information on search patterns and choice behavior. Disconfirming information may cause consumers to discount reputational knowledge, leading to increased information search.

6. Bargaining Strategies

Bargaining processes reflect a bargaining strategy or an absence of one. While in the Brucks and Schurr (1990) study a bargaining strategy was suggested to subjects in order to reduce variance from different strategies, bargaining strategy itself warrants attention as a research variable. One might examine the buyer's bargaining strategy as a function of the different bargaining strategies of the different sellers.

CONCLUSION

Our purpose in this paper has been to (1) suggest an information processing approach to bargaining, (2) provide details on how Deal Search could be used to conduct a computer-controlled experiment in this area, and (3) propose some starting points for future research. The Deal Search software is available from either author.

REFERENCES

Bettman, James R. (1979), *An Information Processing Theory of Consumer Choice*, Reading, MA: Addison-Wesley.

Brucks, Merrie (1985), "The Effects of Product Class Knowledge on Information Search Behavior," *Journal of Consumer Research*, 12 (June), 1-16.

_____ (1988), "Search Monitor: An Approach for Computer-Controlled Experiments Involving Consumer Information Search, *Journal of Consumer Research*, 15 (June), 117-121.

_____ (1990), "Computer-Controlled Experimentation in Consumer Decision Making and Judgment," in Marvin E. Goldberg, Gerald J. Gorn, and Richard Pollay, eds. *Advances in Consumer Research*, Vol. 17, in press.

_____ and Paul H. Schurr (1990), "The Effects of Bargainable Attributes and Attribute Range Knowledge on Consumer Choice Processes," *Journal of Consumer Research*, 16 (March), 409-419.

Clopton, Stephen W. (1984), "Seller and Buying Firm Factors Affecting Industrial buyers' Negotiation behavior and Outcomes," *Journal of Marketing Research*, 21 (February), 39-53.

Graham, John L., Dong Ki Kim, Chi-Yuan Lin, and Michael Robinson (1988), "Buyer-Seller Negotiations Around the Pacific Rim: Differences in Fundamental Exchange Processes," *Journal of Consumer Research*, 15 (June), 48-54.

Kelley, Harold H. (1966), "A Classroom Study of the Dilemmas in Interpersonal Negotiations," in *Strategic Interaction and Conflict*, ed. Kathleen Archibald, Berkeley, CA: Institute of International Studies, University of California, 49-73.

Moore, William L. and Donald R. Lehmann (1980), "Individual Differences in Search Behavior for a Nondurable," *Journal of Consumer Research*, 7 (December), 296-307.

Osgood, Charles E. (1959), "Suggestions for Winning the Real War with Communism," *Journal of Conflict Resolution*, 3 (4), 295-325.

Pruitt, Dean G. (1981), *Negotiation Behavior*, New York: Academic Press.

Schurr, Paul H. (1987), "The Effects of Gain and Loss Decision Frames on Risky Purchase Negotiations," *Journal of Applied Psychology*, 72 (August), 351-358.

_____ and Julie L. Ozanne (1985), "Influences on Exchange Processes:Buyers' Preconceptions of a Seller's Trustworthiness and Bargaining Toughness," *Journal of Consumer Research*, 11 (March), 939-53.

Siegel, Sidney and Lawrence E. Fouraker (1960), *Bargaining and Group Decision Making*, New York: McGraw-Hill.

To Buy or Not to Buy? That is Not the Question: Female Ritual in Home Shopping Parties

Brenda Gainer, York University
Eileen Fischer, York University

ABSTRACT

A participant observation study of home shopping parties was undertaken to explore the seemingly irrational and coercive aspects of party purchasing. Consideration of the meanings with which party shopping and buying are invested by female shoppers suggests these activities must be viewed in a much broader context than that of simple economic transactions. Shopping parties offer unusual opportunities to foster personal relationships among segregated individuals in an atomized society through participation in the rituals of a moral economy. At the same time, the parties play a part in the cultural definition of female roles and the very construct of "femininity" itself.

Interest in the experience of shopping and the meaning it holds for consumers has grown among researchers in recent years (Belk, Sherry and Wallendorf 1988; Rook 1987; Sherry and McGrath 1989). In fact, companies which market goods through home shopping parties have long recognized that shopping can be more than a search for product attributes: a tacit understanding of the social and recreational facets of shopping itself has helped them to structure social situations which facilitate sales. Recently, investigators have begun to explore how interpersonal influences are tapped to stimulate effective party selling (Prus and Frisby 1989) and how the act of buying (vs. the objects purchased) leads to social utility (Frenzen and Davis 1990). These studies have provided valuable contributions to our awareness of the connection between buyer-seller relationships and the purchase decision. They provide limited insight, however, into the particularly female nature of the party shopping experience. This study examines the meanings that participation in home shopping parties holds for the women who attend them, and explores how the experience draws on and preserves gender role stereotypes. The study thus helps to account for some of the success of party shopping as well to increase our understanding of the meaning and use of shopping by women more generally.

THE NATURE OF HOME SHOPPING PARTIES

Home shopping parties depend on a dealer, most often a woman, finding another woman to host a party to which she invites her friends to shop for a specific product. Products marketed in this way range from plastic housewares through children's toys, craft items, copperware, crystal and cosmetics to seductive lingerie and kinky sex aids. The hostess of a party typically receives a reward for her "work" in finding purchasers; the size of this reward depends on the quantity of goods her friends buy. The hostess also receives rewards based on the number of her guests who agree to host further parties or become dealers. The dealer receives a commission on the sales made at her parties, as well as a royalty on all sales made by dealers she has recruited. Thus, from the dealer's point of view, the product being sold is as much future party dates or potential dealerships (i.e. the party plan) as the goods being demonstrated (Biggart 1989).

Two observations about these parties form the point of departure for this study. First, despite the vast array of goods sold this way, and despite the fact that lucrative possibilities might exist if men's social networks were tapped, these parties are almost exclusively attended by women. Second, research indicates that guests are often buying out of a sense of obligation to either the hostess or dealer as well as, or instead of, out of a desire to obtain a needed good (Frenzen and Davis 1990; Prus and Frisby 1989).

How can we explain the observations that women make the majority of home party purchases, and do not behave like a prototypical "economic man" engaged in a classical search process for desirable product attributes when they do so? One cultural notion, perpetuated in popular literature, jokes and comic strips, is that women are irrational creatures, completely unable to control themselves in the face of consumer temptation. Women are colloquially characterized as hopelessly susceptible to the buying impulse, as described by Rook (1987). We can dismiss this interpretation on several counts. Attending a home party is a planned, not an impulsive, behavior. Moreover, not every woman who is invited to a party attends it. In order to make sense of why women (and only women) participate as they do in home shopping, and thus offer a superior interpretation of their behavior, it was necessary to find a means of understanding their experiences from their own points of view.

METHODOLOGY

The method chosen for this study was participant observation. Numerous recent articles have appeared in consumer behavior advocating the use of methods like participant observation to develop deep understandings of consumer phenomena in consumers' own terms (Belk, Sherry and Wallendorf 1988; Hirschman 1986; Sherry and McGrath 1989; Thompson, Locander and Pollio 1989). Interpretive methods are particularly useful in probing socio-cultural factors involved in shopping which may be impossible to capture through the use of more typical instruments of marketing research.

A factor which confirmed our decision to use the participant observation method was that, although we had attended shopping parties as "lay people" and found them not altogether unpleasant, coercive events, preliminary interviews we undertook with party shoppers revealed a tendency for informants to emphasize the unpleasant, coercive aspects of party shopping. Published research has also described the resentment party shoppers feel at "having to" attend parties (and hence buy products) because they were asked by people who were expecting them to (Prus and Frisby 1989). This reported resentment contrasted not only with our personal observations as members of seemingly happy party shopping groups, but also with the statistical evidence that this shopping channel is extremely successful. We speculate that party shoppers are embarrassed to talk about buying things that they don't strictly "need" in front of people whom they perceive as educated consumer "experts" and are therefore more likely to emphasize the coercive aspects of party shopping over the pleasure they provide when they are overtly questioned. In any event, we felt that the typical marketing research survey or even depth interviews might not provide sufficient insight into women's reasons for participating in home shopping parties, and the meanings these parties hold.

Accordingly, we adopted the technique of participant observation as a means of gaining insight into the seeming paradox of resentment of shopping being coupled with frequent and often enthusiastic attendance and purchasing. It must be emphasized that this initial study is deliberately narrowly focussed to achieve depth at the expense of breadth, and we make no pretense to "representativeness" or "generalizability". The project was conceived as an attempt to develop an ethnographic record and an interpretive framework that could lead to broader theoretical investigation in the future.

Our data were collected through attendance at five home shopping parties, three for Tupperware plastic houseware, which is one of the original party products, and two for Discovery Toys, a relative newcomer to the party shopping scene. For both companies, we contacted a dealer, explained our research interests, and asked if they would be willing to arrange for us to attend several of their parties. We attended the parties individually, in order to minimize our intrusion into a small gathering of people, most of whom were well-known to one another. The dealers checked with their hostesses to make sure we would be welcome, and apparently none of the hostesses showed any reluctance to have us attend their parties. The dealers explained to the hostesses that we were a student and a professor of marketing "interested in home shopping." None of the hostesses passed this information on to their guests. Most of the guests initially assumed we were with the dealer, either to help her or to receive training as novice dealers ourselves. During conversation with the guests we made no attempt to hide the fact that we were doing research in order to write an article about party shopping, but none of the guests to whom this was stated showed any interest in this fact or seemed to become self-conscious or change their behavior in any way. We both made a point of participating in any games that were held at our parties, joining in conversation and buying products; one of us went so far as to attend the toy parties with a small baby. In order to minimize the intrusive effect of our attendance we did not take notes at the parties or tape record any of the proceedings. Instead we relied on very extensive field notes which we wrote immediately after leaving the parties. We supplemented these notes by lengthy conversations with the dealers in which we checked some of our perceptions as well as factual information regarding individual purchases and sales totals.

Across the parties attended, guests and party hostesses with a broad range of ages and social classes were observed. The youngest guest (excluding the children of guests and hostesses) was in her early twenties; the eldest was in her sixties. At one party, the hostess and guests in attendance all appeared to be of the lower to lower middle social class; at others, the hostesses and guests could be classified as middle to upper middle class.

THE MORAL ECONOMY OF HOME SHOPPING PARTIES

One of the most striking features of all the parties we attended was that nearly everyone in attendance bought something, or at least promised to do so in a few days. This near-universality of purchase is in marked contrast to shopping behavior in stores or other direct sales channels such as catalogues. While purchasing something was the norm for parties in which we participated, however, we observed several distinct types of purchase behavior.

The most numerous shoppers were the "enthusiasts"; these were people who purchased at least one major item quickly and spent upwards of $30.00 easily. These people usually discussed the products knowledgeably, and had been to other shopping parties for the product before, often with many of the same people. A second small groups of shoppers made what clearly seemed to be token purchases. Interestingly enough, each of them bought two small items and not just one, thus raising their total purchase to between $15 and $20 even though there were small single items available for under $10. These shoppers appeared to be indecisive about their orders, and often were among the last guests to go up to the dealer with their order form. We noted that the women who made such token purchases appeared least integrated into the group and had the weakest social or familial connection with the hostess.

Violations to the norm of purchasing did occur. At one party, the woman who appeared to be least integrated purchased nothing: it became evident towards the end of the party that she was out of work. The dealer confided later that non-purchasing was unusual behavior and attributed it to the fact that the woman couldn't afford to buy. We observed, however, that another woman at the same party was also out of work and did make a token purchase. The unemployed woman who made no purchase had never met the hostess prior to the party and attended because a friend of the hostess had invited her; the unemployed woman who made a token purchase had a strong social connection to the hostess. Only four other people were observed to buy nothing at the parties; in two cases they were close relatives of the hostess (a sister and a sister-in-law). The other two gave elaborate explanations to the hostess, indicating that they had to check with their husbands, but would certainly call her with their order in a few days. Finally, during each party we attended it became evident that some people had been invited who had either refused or left some ambiguity about their possible attendance and in the end didn't appear.

Some of these observations confirm the findings of Prus and Frisby that, in general, women do not attend home shopping parties unless they are prepared to make purchases. The "norm of purchasing" seemed to be widely accepted given that most people who had little desire for the products still felt compelled to either buy some small items or offer repeated excuses as to why they were not. Other people had seemingly elected not to accept the invitation, "probably because [they] didn't need any toys now," as one guest put it. The only exceptions to participation in the ritual of compulsory purchase (or excuses and apologies) was one woman who was not connected to the hostess, and who was experiencing financial difficulties, and two who were close relatives of the hostess. At the same time, it seemed quite obvious that not all of the women who were making purchases wanted the goods they were buying. Some of them proclaimed this fact quite openly, as in the case of one woman who conscripted the researcher to help her choose her goods "because [she] already had all this stuff, but [she] *had* to buy *something*!" In fact, she purchased over $60 worth of merchandise.

Why do women who are not interested in buying the goods offered at such parties, or who can purchase comparable products in stores if they are interested, attend parties and accept their coercive aspects? Prus and Frisby report that some subjects say they *have* to attend them because they're asked, but that they resent it. Yet if resentment is the main outcome of attending shopping parties, why do so many women continue to attend so many different parties? And, more puzzling still, why do hostesses continue to invite guests and therefore presumably endanger their friendship ties?

Based on our observations and analyses, we suggest that party shopping has thrived and continues to thrive because parties foster, rather than threaten, friendship ties. In effect, they support a "moral economy" based primarily upon social exchanges rather than exchanges of goods or money. Cheal (1989) argues that the reciprocal nature of gift giving is a means of ritually constructing social worlds through economically redundant transactions. Public gift-giving allows people to give social recognition to relationships; reciprocal giving facilitates the reinforcement of relationships over a span of time (Cheal 1989). The purchase of unnecessary or unwanted articles is not, then, so much an irrational "waste" of money as a "gift" given to the hostess. Obviously the goods purchased are not themselves gifts, for both their economic value and practical use remains with the guest, not the hostess. However the hostess does receive material benefit as a result of the guest's purchase, namely credit towards free merchandise. The hostess is well aware of the value of each person's "gift" to her, because the goods for all her guests are delivered to her and she distributes the orders to her friends (and in some cases even collects the payment for them). Thus, the guests purchases are analogous to flowers or a bottle of wine one might offer the host or hostess of a dinner party.

Frenzen and Davis (1990) report that the strength of social ties binding buyers to hostesses and dealers has a positive impact on the likelihood of purchase at home shopping parties. We, however, observed that while women with lesser social connections might fail to purchase, they felt they had to justify this behavior; those with closer ties were able to refrain from purchasing without explanation. This observation helped us to deal with an aspect of our interpretation which remained perplexing: if party purchases actually constitute a gift to the hostess, why is it that women involved in this moral economy do not simply buy their plastics or toys at a store when they need them, and give their hostess a conventional gift on more generally recognized ritual occasions such as Christmas and birthdays? Upon reflection, we realized that while Christmas (and other more traditional gift giving occasions, like birthdays) provide a forum for recognizing and reinforcing the closest family ties (Caplow 1982), such events as home shopping parties create a less common opportunity for publicly recognizing more distant family and social relationships as well. Particularly for women, to whom the work of fostering the extended network of social relationships often falls, home shopping parties provide an opportunity to engage in the gift-giving rituals of the moral economy with non-kin who are often excluded from Christmas or other major rituals.

This interpretation suggests that although women may emphasize the coercive aspects of shopping parties when questioned directly, they experience home shopping parties as an opportunity to construct the personal relationships which constitute their "small world." They "have to" say yes to invitations because their social relationships are important and they tacitly recognize the value of opportunities to maintain them. Close relatives (who have the opportunity to engage in ritual gift-giving with kin on festive occasions) or people with little connection to the hostess (who presumably construct their small worlds elsewhere) are the only people likely to attend a party and not buy. This does not suggest that none of the other shoppers are interested in purchasing the goods offered for sale at home parties, of course. Often the buyers are enthusiastic users, some even collectors, of the products. The idea of the gift, however, explains why people who want the product would choose to purchase it in the more expensive forum of a friend's party than in a store, and also explains why people who don't want the product would attend a party and buy it. It also explains why a hostess would ask her friends to spend their money in this way. She is, in fact, not coercing them but providing them with an opportunity to interact with her by providing her with "redundant" goods that she could afford to purchase on her own if she wished. It is likely that, in her turn, she will attend parties they host and make purchases. Though inefficient from an economic perspective, this pattern of behavior does allow the women to maintain something of value to them: their social ties with others.

What of the women who refused to attend or did not show? Did they sever relationships within their social networks? This remains unclear, since we did not talk to non-attenders or hear them talked much about. However, we speculate, based on conversations about other parties which many shoppers had attended, that there is sufficient redundancy in the chains of parties that individuals who maintain their small worlds in this manner may miss some parties so long as they attend others.

FEMALE WORK AND FEMALE RITUAL

A second aspect of home shopping parties which we sought to explain is their overwhelmingly feminine nature. Although men may be involved in the higher management and ownership levels of companies which specialize in home shopping parties, the dealers, hostesses and guests are overwhelmingly female. It was suggested above that one of the reasons women are more involved in party shopping than men is because women are socialized to do more of the "relationship work" in society. This does not seem to offer a full explanation of the lack of male customers at shopping parties or the dearth of male-oriented products marketed in this way, however: while men may be *less* involved in major gift-giving rituals such as Christmas and birthdays, they never the less participate extensively in the gift economy.

The sexual division of labour in contemporary society suggests that attendance at home shopping parties is almost exclusively female because shopping is one of the household tasks traditionally allocated to women. Certainly a number of women we observed seemed to consider their attendance to be part of their domestic burden. This often became apparent when husbands' whereabouts were discussed. For example, women at all the parties that were not attended by children were heard to explain that their husbands had agreed to baby-sit because, as one woman expressed it, "he knows I have to do the shopping." One young woman, a new mother, was out for the first time without the baby; she explained that the child was being cared for by her husband who, she said, did not consider baby-sitting to be his job. Apparently he had agreed to care for their child and allow her to shop only for the minimum amount of time in which one could conceivably buy plastics; she (and two other young women at the same party whose husbands were baby-sitting) left early. Interestingly, at three parties the women who seemed most concerned about having to justify their attendance to their husbands were the most formally attired. While their husbands accepted shopping parties as "housework," their clothing seemed appropriate for the leisure and entertainment provided by a party. Perhaps these women experienced greater tension because their husbands, observing these clothes, sensed the social aspect of the shopping party, and were less accepting of this form of shopping as part of their wives' normal duties. As one reviewer noted, shopping parties may function as an inexpensive "girls' night out," and in some social strata, few acceptable venues for such exclusively female evening social activities exist.

A number of women seemed to use the performance of their task of nurturing and caring for other family members to justify their expenditures. The woman with the largest total bill at any of the parties we attended ($127.00) announced each item she was purchasing to another shopper and prefaced each remark with a phrase like "my kids can make hamburgers more easily with this press," "my kids love salads," or "my husband needs this when he barbecues." Another woman purchasing a large set of cupboard organizers stated that her husband hated messy cupboards. At the toy parties, several of the women buying the most costly items agreed that they were extravagant but "really educational." These attempts to justify large expenditures appeared to be quite effective. The "big spenders" did not seem to feel guilty or worried about their purchases; in fact, most of the shoppers who bought anything but the smallest amounts seemed excited and pleased about buying the merchandise.

Overall, it appeared that many women viewed party shopping and buying as a justifiable part of their domestic work; at the same time, they took pleasure in the activity. Concepts developed by Valadez and Clignet (1984) help to explain these observations. These authors suggested that domestic work is a cultural ordeal of both civility and conviviality. By an ordeal of civility, they mean a recurring test of who "passes" as a member of a certain cultural group; by an ordeal of conviviality, they mean a symbolic demonstration of signs of fraternity (or, in this case, sorority). These ideas help make sense of the emphasis some shoppers placed on characterizing shopping as a means of caring for their families, and of some of the pleasure they took in the event.

It is a type of ordeal of civility, or effort to signal membership in the social category of "good wife and mother," to stress that products are purchased judiciously in the interests of the family. We observed that women who appeared to have a more "modern" conception of women's roles engaged in this behavior to the same extent as more "traditional" women: the only difference we found between seemingly traditional and seemingly modern women was in their product focus and thus the particular aspect of domestic work they emphasized. For example, the most traditional women we observed were at a party in a middle class Italian suburb of a major eastern city. Despite the women's range of ages, marital statuses and working statuses, their emphasis was on how the plastic housewares facilitated family food preparation. A great deal of talk concerned the relationship between the individual products offered for sale and caring for specific family members and their individual tastes and needs. These women showed very little interest in the toys or the decorator items offered for sale. The most modern women we observed were attending a toy party in a middle class neighborhood in a major western city. These women were college educated professionals; a lawyer, a college professor and an engineer were among the guests, and all of the women at the party were combining motherhood with full-time careers. Their conversation was exclusively devoted to their children's development, or their family plans for Christmas or Hanukkah celebrations. A third party, held in an upper-middle class Jewish suburb of a major eastern city, was attended by college-educated women who were almost all full-time homemakers. These women concentrated on the plastic decorator and organizational items and their discussion centered on homes and their relative features such as closets, cupboards and basements.

Despite the array of personal styles and subjects of conversation described here, topics discussed at all the parties we attended were the traditional female tasks of cooking, decorating, household management and child-rearing. Moreover, although the shoppers at each party shared most of the same domestic tasks, there seemed to be an awareness of varying degrees of skill on the part of the shoppers with regard to the performance of them. On the one hand, the group seemed to provide help and reassurance for the insecure or inexpert shoppers. At all of the parties, some women were clearly seeking advice from others. One woman remarked to the researcher that she shopped at parties because she found the advice and experience of the other shoppers beneficial. This woman described herself as not being a very "smart" shopper, unlike some of the others whom she pointed out as being quite "smart." Another woman asked the researcher for help "because [she] always went home with a lot of junk [she] didn't want." At the same time as some women were asking for help with their purchases, others were offering advice. At one party in particular, one of the women who clearly had a great deal of experience with the product made a point of telling the other guests what they should get after quickly putting in a large order herself. At all of the parties the women discussed not only their purchases, but their reasons for making them.

Thus it seems that one of the purposes home shopping parties serve is as a showcase for women's membership in the "wife/mother" role and their relative skill at performing the shopping aspect of this role. In this situation, "success" did not seem to be judged on the basis of finding bargains or unique or unusual items. Instead, success seemed to be judged by how well the purchase represented an act of caring for the family or home. The parties served to confirm the image of the secure, self-confident shoppers as successful homemakers, wives and mothers. The insecure, nervous shoppers received encouragement and reassurance from the "experts" that their purchases also enabled them to "pass" the requirements for inclusion among the good wives and mothers. Thus party shopping seems to serve as a symbolic opportunity for women to take and pass the "test" for demonstrating characteristics traditionally prescribed for women in North American society, namely those associated with domesticity and nurturing.

At the same time as there seemed to be a recognition that some people were "better" shoppers than others, there seemed to be a general spirit of cooperation at all the parties. For all that shopping seemed to serve as a symbolic test of fit within socially prescribed female roles, the party guests appeared eager to ensure that everyone ultimately "passed." At one party a particularly indecisive woman was unable to place her order even when all the other guests had made theirs; at this point they all joined in helping her, discussing all the possible pros and cons of each of the products she was considering and asking detailed questions about her family and house. No one showed signs of impatience at the length of this discussion.

This behavior has led us to characterize the shopping party as not only an "ordeal of civility" but also as an "ordeal of conviviality". Parties serve both as a means of displaying distinctly feminine characteristics and as a forum to reaffirm and strengthen the bonds of sorority. This interpretation is supported and extended by our observations concerning what happened when men interrupted parties.

Generally, the parties had much of the flavor of a bridal shower, a sorority meeting, or even an adolescent girl's pajama party: the sense of a private ritual being performed away from men was marked. At one party, for example, when asked where her husband was, the hostess said "I sent him away." When he returned later, while the party was still in full swing, conversation immediately broke off and the guests became self-conscious and began to make moves to leave. Many of the women present knew this man well as a neighbor and friend, and some stayed to chat with him and his wife about neighborhood affairs in the kitchen. The atmosphere had subtly changed when he arrived, however, and the dealer began to pack up while the women started to talk about other things than shopping. Another party which was held after dinner in a distant suburb of a major eastern city began with children present. After half an hour several husbands showed up on their way home from work to take the children home to baby-sit. As each man invaded the party there was a great deal of giggling and teasing while some women simply looked embarrassed. Even at the two parties we attended in very large houses with several separate living areas, the husbands were not simply banished from the room in which the party was held but sent out of the house altogether.

Smith-Rosenberg suggests that rigid gender-role differentiation within the family and within society generally led to the emotional segregation of men and women in the 18th and 19th centuries and that as a result women formed their close emotional ties with other women with whom they shared a "female world" of mutual support, caring and ritual (1975). She relies on an understanding of 19th century North American culture to explain the female emotional bonds and rituals of Victorian times, and suggests that weddings have persisted as one of the last female rituals remaining in twentieth-century America. While perhaps not so rigid, gender-role differentiation is still prevalent in contemporary society, and we suggest that home shopping parties constitute another particularly female ritual of the twentieth century in which women gather to celebrate and cooperate in the traditional female task of shopping. Interestingly, the shopping party seems to transcend the divisions of social class, education and ethnicity: they appear to have become a ritual female activity in North America used in the social construction of femininity itself.

CONCLUSION

This study has attempted to make sense of the success of the home shopping parties in the face of the reportedly coercive element underlying party attendance and the seemingly irrational nature of party purchasing. An interpretation of party shopping behaviors which focuses on the moral economy which party purchases support, and on the way shopping serves to establish and reinforce women's roles, helps to explain the party shopping phenomenon.

Further, although this study was undertaken in the limited site of the home shopping party, some of the ritual aspects of the consumer behavior observed here occur in a less obvious form in other retail settings. Women seem to shop together more than men do, for example, and frequently discuss shopping trips and purchases with each other. The social and cultural phenomena which we have described here can provide a basis for further investigation of the culturally rich and meaningful world of women's shopping.

REFERENCES

Belk, Russell, John Sherry and Melanie Wallendorf (1988), "A Naturalistic Inquiry into Buyer and Seller Behavior at a Swap Meet," *Journal of Consumer Research*, 14 (4): 449-470.

Biggart, Nicole (1989), *Charismatic Capitalists*, Chicago: University of Chicago Press.

Caplow, Theodore (1982), "Christmas Gifts and Kin Networks," *American Sociological Review*, 89 (6): 1306-1323.

Cheal, David (1989), *The Gift Economy*, New York: Routledge.

Frenzen, Jonathan and Harry L. Davis (1990), "Purchasing Behavior in Embedded Markets," *Journal of Consumer Research*, 17 (1), 1-12.

Hirschman, Elizabeth (1986), "Humanistic Inquiry in Marketing Research: Philosophy, Method, and Criteria," *Journal of Marketing Research*, 23 (August): 237-249.

Prus, Robert and Wendy Frisby (1989), "Persuasion as Practical Accomplishment: Tactical Manoeuverings at Home Party Plans," in Helena Znaniecki Lopata (ed.) *Current Research on Occupations and Professions: Societal Influences* Greenwich, Connecticut: Jai Press.

Rook, Dennis (1987), "The Buying Impulse," *Journal of Consumer Research*, 14 (2), 189-199.

Sherry, John and Mary Ann McGrath (1989), "Unpacking the Holiday Presence: A Comparative Ethnography of the Gift Store" in Elizabeth Hirschman, ed. *Interpretive Consumer Research* Provo, Utah: Association for Consumer Research.

Smith-Rosenberg, Carroll (1975), "The Female World of Love and Ritual: Relations between Women in Nineteenth-Century America," *Signs: Journal of Women in Culture and Society* 1 (1): 1-29.

Thompson, Craig, William Locander and Howard Pollio (1989), "Putting Consumer Experience Back into Consumer Research: The Philosophy and Method of Existential Philosophy," *Journal of Consumer Research*, 16 (2), 133-146.

Valadez, Joseph J. and Remi Clignet (1984), "Household Work as an Ordeal: Culture of Standards versus Standardization of Culture," *American Journal of Sociology*, 89 (4): 812-835.

Service Satisfaction: An Exploratory Investigation of Three Models

Rama Jayanti, Louisiana State University
Anita Jackson, Louisiana State University

ABSTRACT

While researchers have focused on determinants of satisfaction for products, very little research has been done on determinants of satisfaction for services. This paper examines three models of satisfaction as applied to services. Disconfirmation, performance, and individual difference models are examined and compared in the context of hairstyling services. In an exploratory study comparing these three models, it was found that the individual difference model performed best, the disconfirmation model performed second best, and the performance model performed the worst.

INTRODUCTION

Consumer satisfaction is recognized as a key variable in models of consumer behavior and occupies a central position in the marketing concept. Several authors have conceptualized and operationalized satisfaction with products (Churchill and Suprenant 1982; Oliver 1980; Tse and Wilton 1988) but generalizations to services are rare (Hill 1986; Lietchty and Churchill 1979; Smith and Houston 1983; Parasuraman et al 1986).

Due to the increasing importance of services to the economy, processes underlying service satisfaction need to be explored further. This paper examines three theoretical perspectives from which service satisfaction can be explained using a causal modeling approach.

THE DISCONFIRMATION PARADIGM

The disconfirmation model of satisfaction has achieved wide acceptance with products. Briefly, the disconfirmation model holds that satisfaction is related to the size and direction of the disconfirmation experience, where disconfirmation is defined as the difference between the individual's initial expectations and the actual performance of the product/service. A person's expectations are (1) confirmed when a product/service conforms to expectations, (2) negatively disconfirmed when the product/service does not perform as well as expected, and (3) positively disconfirmed when the product/service performs better than expected (Churchill and Suprenant 1982). Thus, the disconfirmation model is hypothesized to be a function of expectations, performance, disconfirmation, and satisfaction.

The disconfirmation model theorizes that expectations are crucial in the formation of satisfaction judgments. Perceived performance is usually depicted as a standard of comparison by which to arrive at disconfirmation. As the model proposes satisfaction to be a function of the discrepancy between expectations and performance, enhanced levels of performance should logically lead to enhanced satisfaction. Disconfirmation is treated both as an intervening variable and an independent variable in the satisfaction literature. Oliver (1980) maintains that it is important to measure disconfirmation independently of expectations and performance as it exerts an independent effect on satisfaction judgments. Satisfaction on the other hand, is conceptualized as a post purchase attitude resulting from the consumer's comparison of the rewards and costs of the purchase. Satisfaction is operationalized as the sum of satisfactions with the different attributes of the product or service and is measured as the difference between expectations and performance. Thus, satisfaction is not measured directly but only as a subtractive function of expectations and performance.

Churchill and Surprenant (1982) have included four constructs (expectations, performance, disconfirmation and satisfaction) in a structural model and assessed the effects of each variable. They found inconsistent results among durable and non durable products. The disconfirmation model performed better for the non durable product whereas the performance model provided a parsimonious explanation of variance for the durable product. Churchill and Suprenant argue that when involvement is high as in the case of the durable good (as also in services, especially experiential services) performance overrides all other considerations.

PERFORMANCE MODEL OF SATISFACTION

Oliver (1980) suggests that when performance judgments tend to be subjective (as in services due to intangibility) expectations may play only a minor role in the formation of satisfaction. Although some authors (Hill 1984; Smith and Houston 1983) have suggested the disconfirmation model to be appropriate for services, empirical evidence has yet to be found for this proposition. In light of the argument of Oliver (1980) regarding the weak performance of the disconfirmation model when satisfaction judgments tend to be subjective and the empirical evidence provided by Churchill and Surprenant (1982) with high involvement products, it is reasonable to assume that satisfaction judgments with services may be a function of performance alone. The performance model suggests that performance alone explains a major portion of variance in satisfaction judgments. Due to the peculiar characteristics of services (intangibility, heterogeneity, inseparability and perishability) performance may become the only tangible evidence on which to base consumer evaluations of services. Moreover, lack of pre-purchase information in most services forces the consumer to form very few if any, expectations regarding the service to be encountered (Zeithaml 1981) and place even less confidence in those expectations. Even if we assume consumer expertise in a particular category of service, the high variability in the service provided from encounter to encounter creates uncertainty which inhibits formation of pre-purchase expectations.

The above discussion suggests that the disconfirmation model of satisfaction may perform poorly in case of services and that the performance model could better explain satisfaction in services.

INDIVIDUAL DIFFERENCES MODEL

Consumer participation in the production of services is another distinguishing feature of services as compared to goods (Chase 1978; Mills and Morris 1986; Bowen and Jones 1986). For those services which require a substantial input from consumers, usually in the form of information (as in the case of physicians and hair dressers) individual differences would make a major contribution to satisfaction judgments. Again, keeping in view the intangible nature of services, three individual difference variables, perceived risk, involvement and innovativeness are hypothesized to exert substantial influence on satisfaction judgments.

Theoretical justification for the inclusion of these three individual difference variables and their relationship to satisfaction are discussed in the following paragraphs.

Perceived Risk

Perceived risk has been studied in goods literature (Bauer 1960; Bettman 1973) extensively. However, it has received less attention in services literature (see Cox and Rich 1964 and George, Weinberger and Kelley 1986 for exceptions). Zeithaml (1981) suggests that consumers perceive higher risk compared to goods in a service encounter. She attributes this disparity to the peculiar characteristics of services, the limited number of cues available to evaluate services and to the lack of guarantees and warranties associated with services. Gummesson (1981) proposes that consumers lower their demands on the service providers in an effort to reduce their risk perceptions. This in turn, increases the probability of maximizing their chances of getting expected results.

The above discussion suggests that perceived risk and satisfaction are negatively related with the increased level of risk associated with lower levels of satisfaction.

Involvement

Closely related to the concept of perceived risk is that of involvement with the service category. Perceived risk has been characterized as an empirical definition of involvement. There is general agreement in the literature that involvement is the degree to which an object is central to an individual's ego structure, or his general interest level in an object (Engel and Blackwell 1982; Zaichkowsky 1985). Richins and Bloch (1986) differentiate situational involvement from that of enduring involvement and demonstrate the temporal stability of enduring involvement. One problem with the research on the concept of involvement is that various authors have conceptualized it in different ways. Zaichkowsky's (1985) definition of involvement is thought to be relevant to a service situation and is adapted here with minor modifications. She defines involvement as a "person's perceived relevance of the object (service) based on inherent needs, values and interests". Perceived relevance based on inherent needs, values and interests is especially appropriate to services which are people based and should be delivered on a person to person basis. However, Zaichkowsky (1985) conceptualizes involvement as a function of importance, risk and pleasure. Given the importance of perceived risk in a service situation, it is incorporated into our model as an exogenous variable. Consequently, involvement in this study may be thought of as a function of importance and pleasure only.

Literature suggests that level of involvement mediates consumer information acquisition behavior (Bettman 1979; Engel and Blackwell 1982). Highly involved consumers are motivated to acquire more information about the service, as a result of which their expectations may be well within realistic levels. Thus, involvement is hypothesized to be positively related to satisfaction with high involvement consumers being more satisfied with the service compared to their less involved counterparts. Although there may be differences in satisfaction judgements due to enduring as opposed to situational involvement, we postpone the study of this distinction to a later date due to space limitations.

Consumer Innovativeness

Midgley (1977) implies that innovativeness is an innate expression of a person's psychological or sociological characteristic. Service innovation may be thought of as a function of psychological processes due to the difficulties involved in communicating new services. As a psychological characteristic service innovation may exert considerable influence on consumer evaluation processes. Midgley and Dowling (1978) define innovativeness as the degree to which an individual makes innovation decisions independently of the communicated experience of others. This implies that innovators have greater confidence in their evaluative judgements compared to non innovators. Consistent with this idea, Green, Langeard and Favell (1974) found opinion leadership to be significantly related to innovativeness in retail services. Higher confidence in turn, may lead to higher expectations thus enhancing the level of satisfaction. Thus, innovativeness is hypothesized to be positively related to satisfaction.

Although we treat all three individual difference variables as exogenous to our model we do recognize the theoretical relationships among these three variables. The relationship between risk and involvement as well as risk, innovativeness and involvement are well established in the literature. A replication of these linkages is not attempted in this paper since our main concern is to study satisfaction processes.

In summary, the above discussion suggests that satisfaction with services can be a function of (1) mutual interdependency between service provider and customer (disconfirmation model) (2) service provider alone (performance model) or (3) consumer alone (individual differences model). There are two types of hypotheses germane to our model. First, each linkage proposed in the model represents a hypothesis. Second, as the purpose of our research is to evaluate the explanatory ability of the three models, the following hypotheses are proposed:

H1: Satisfaction with services is a function of the discrepancy between expectations and perceived performance.

H2: Satisfaction with services is a function of perceived performance alone.

H3: Satisfaction with services is a function of individual differences (perceived risk, involvement and innovativeness) among consumers.

METHOD

Subjects

The data was gathered by surveying 175 undergraduate students of a large south-eastern university. The service category chosen was the services of hairstylists. This choice was prompted by several considerations. First, this service category is high on experiential qualities (Zeithaml 1981) and the service itself involves high interaction between service provider and customer. Second, the participation level of consumers in the service act is high, as the hairstylist directly works on the information provided by the customer. Third, substantial heterogeneity in this service class creates uncertainty at every encounter which in turn impacts consumer satisfaction. And finally, the service class is one used by most college students.

Construct Measurement

A questionnaire was designed to capture the various constructs represented in the model. The SERVQUAL scale (Parasuraman et al 1988) was modified to fit the specific service category under investigation. To assess the appropriateness of SERVQUAL scale to study hairstyling services we subjected all items to scale purification and validation through factor analysis and internal consistency tests. Specifically, expectations, performance and disconfirmation were measured with the help of ten items each, constructed by modifying the Servqual scale. Seventeen items were constructed to tap the domain of satisfaction with the service. Consistent with Churchill and Surprenant (1982) satisfaction was assessed as a function of various attributes of the service and overall satisfaction. Perceived risk was measured as a function of uncertainty and consequences (Cunningham 1967). Eleven items were used to tap the perceived risk construct. Fifteen items were constructed to measure the construct of involvement and nine items were constructed to measure innovativeness. As suggested earlier, involvement was measured as a function of personal importance and pleasure. A Likert scale was used for all measures except disconfirmation which was measured as a function of expectations (better than expected/just as expected/worse than expected). All items were derived from an intense search of past research and scale verification. One hundred and fifty usable questionnaires were returned giving a response rate of 86%.

Before calculating the parameter estimates of the models the measures were analyzed for reliability and nomological validity using factor analyses and Cronbach alphas. As recommended by Anderson and Gerbing (1988) a factor analysis was used to eliminate the redundancy in the measures and to confirm the measurement model prior to the simultaneous estimation of the structural and measurement models by LISREL. This procedure is believed to eliminate the redundancy in the measures. Only those items with acceptable Cronbach alphas were used as indicators of the latent constructs. Satisfaction was measured by four variables with a Cronbach alpha of .90; Performance was measured by four variables with a Cronbach alpha of .89; Expectations were measured by three variables with a Cronbach alpha of .82; Disconfirmation was measured by three variables with a Cronbach alpha of .52; Involvement was measured by five variables with a Cronbach alpha of .85; Risk was measured by five variables with a Cronbach alpha of .82; and Innovativeness was measured by three variables with a Cronbach alpha of .85. As shown by the data above the reliability and nomological validity of the measures was confirmed before the analysis was conducted as recommended by Bagozzi (1981). These measures were confirmed in the analysis by high coefficients of determination for the X and Y variables (.85 for X and .97 for Y). Table I provides the sample items used in the study along with scale reliabilities.

LISREL Analysis and Results

LISREL VII (Joreskog and Sorbom 1989) was used to analyze the data and derive the parameter estimates. Overall fit statistics are based upon analysis of the correlation matrices. Figures 1a, 1b and 1c show the Disconfirmation model (DC model), Performance model (PR model) and Individual differences model (ID model) respectively, with all the relationships and parameter estimates.

The first model is a full model with all four constructs of expectations, performance, disconfirmation and satisfaction. Expectations are hypothesized to impact performance, disconfirmation and satisfaction. Performance exerts an independent effect on both disconfirmation and satisfaction. Disconfirmation influences satisfaction. The strongest relationship is between performance and satisfaction (Beta 3,1=.57). This

TABLE I

Variable/Sample Item	No. of Items	Cronbach's Alpha
Expectations		
The hairstylist should be helpful	3	.82
Perceived Performance		
The hairstylist was knowledgeable	4	.89
Disconfirmation		
My expectation regarding the politeness of the hairstylist was:	3	.52
Satisfaction		
The hairstylist understood my needs	4	.90
Perceived Risk		
I hate to go around with a bad hair cut	5	.82
Involvement		
My hairstyle is important to me	5	.85
Innovativeness		
I look at fashion magazines to know about new hairstyles	3	.85

would suggest that performance is significantly related to satisfaction. The chi square with 61 df for this model is 350.16, the GFI is .795, and the AGFI is .647.

Comparing the disconfirmation model to the performance model specified in Figure 1b, there is a strong relationship between performance and satisfaction (Beta 1,1=.56). The performance model has a chi square of 224.91 with 20 df, a GFI of .740 and AGFI of .532. As can be seen the performance model did not perform as well as the disconfirmation model. The individual difference model (Figure 1c) takes into account the impact of individual differences on satisfaction judgments. Involvement and innovativeness are positively related to satisfaction whereas risk is negatively related to satisfaction. Involvement seems to have the strongest impact on satisfaction lending support to our initial argument that the highly involved consumers, due to their propensity to acquire more information tend to experience higher levels of satisfaction. This model has a chi square of 203.10 with 104 df a GFI of .869 and an AGFI of .808. These statistics indicate that the individual difference model performed better than either the disconfirmation or performance models. This suggests that in services the individual consumers' characteristics play an important role in satisfaction judgments. Table II summarizes the various statistics for all three models.

DISCUSSION

Comparing the three models by comparing the chi square/df (Carmines and McIver 1981) and the goodness of fit indices, it becomes apparent that the individual differences model performs the best compared to the other two. This suggests that, at least in those categories of services where experience qualities are high, consumers input into the service may be significant.

In most instances, consumers attribute the failure of service to themselves rather than to the service provider, due to the importance of information the consumer has to provide to the service provider (Zeithaml 1981). Accordingly it is not surprising that Individual differences make a strong impact on satisfaction judgments. Although Chase (1978) has questioned the role of consumers

FIGURE 1A
The DC Model

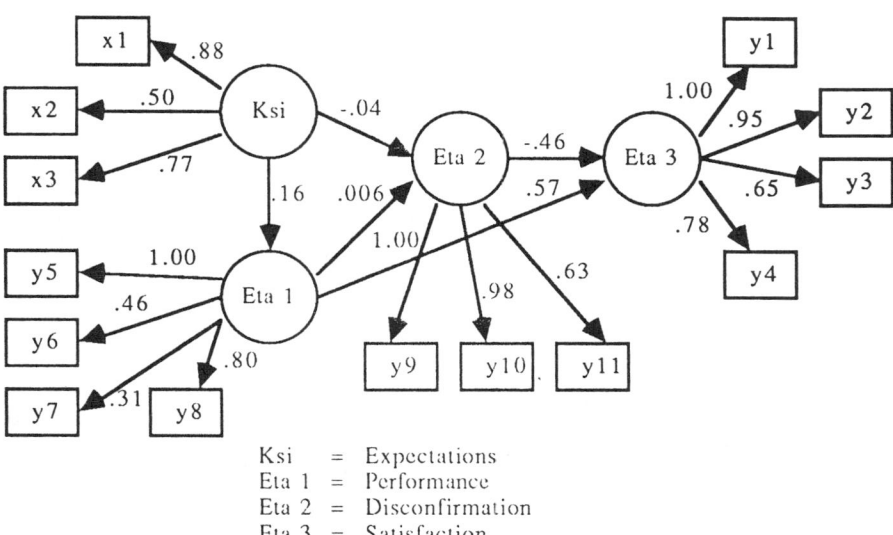

Ksi = Expectations
Eta 1 = Performance
Eta 2 = Disconfirmation
Eta 3 = Satisfaction

FIGURE 1B
The PR Model

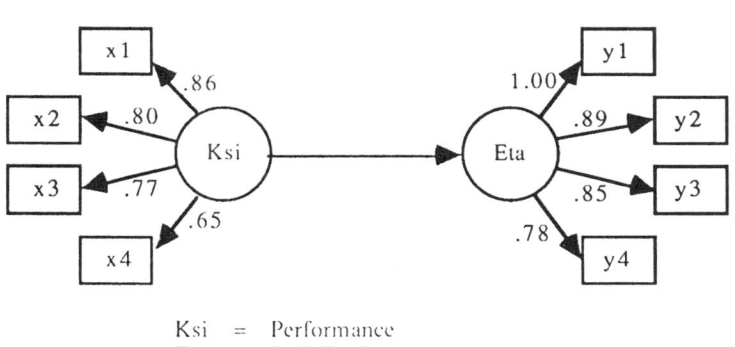

Ksi = Performance
Eta = Satisfaction

in the service exchange, researchers have not considered the important role played by individual differences on service evaluations. Our data suggests that we need to take individual differences into account when attempting to explain satisfaction with services.

Our study also suggests that neither the disconfirmation model, nor the performance model by itself explain satisfaction parsimoniously. Due to the peculiar nature of services and also the high level of participation of consumers in the service encounter, satisfaction processes in services may differ substantially from satisfaction processes in products. Hence researchers need to exercise caution in unambiguously accepting the proposition to embrace the disconfirmation paradigm to service industries.

Limitations and Future Research Directions

The impact of demographic variables, in particular sex, may be substantial given the type of service category we have chosen. Unfortunately our model as constructed does not allow us to study this discrimination. Future research needs to consider this important variable in studies of consumer evaluation processes.

The low reliability of the disconfirmation measure is of particular concern in this study. Coupled with some inherent problems with LISREL

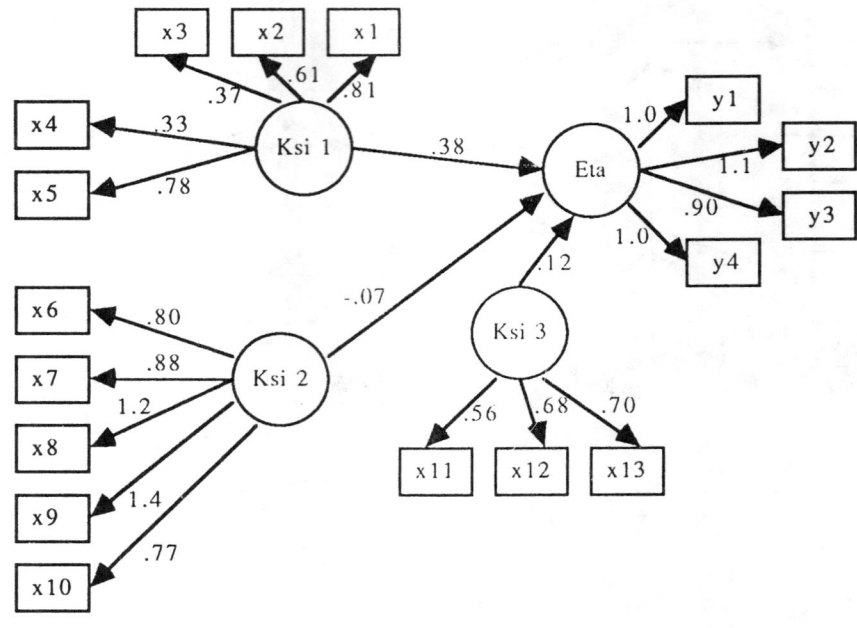

FIGURE 1C
The ID Model

Ksi 1 = Involvement
Ksi 2 = Perceived Risk
Ksi 3 = Innovativeness
Eta = Satisfaction

TABLE II

	DC Model	PR Model	ID Model
Chi-Square	350.16	224.91	203.10
df	61	20	104
P value	.000	.000	.000
GFI	.795	.740	.869
AGFI	.647	.532	.808
RMSR	.150	.155	.066
Chi-Square/df	5.74	11.25	1.95

analysis such as the sensitive nature of Chi-square test our conclusions are tentative at best.

Another interpretation of our data may be that a purely cognitive model of satisfaction as applied to goods may not be appropriate for services. Services involve affective processes toward the service provider which may play an important role in satisfaction judgments. Future research needs to take affective responses into consideration to expand our knowledge about satisfaction processes.

To improve the generalizability of the conclusions, researchers need to investigate the relationships examined here in other contexts and in other categories of services. We would also like to suggest that instead of focusing on the service provider exclusively the consumer should also be considered as an important element in models of service satisfaction.

REFERENCES

Anderson, James C. and David W. Gerbing (1988), "Structural Equation Modeling in Practice: A Review and Recommended Two-Step Approach," *Psychological Bulletin*, Vol.103, 3, 411-423.

Bagozzi, Richard (1981), *"Causal Models in Marketing"*, New York, John Wiley & Sons, Inc.

Bauer, Raymond A. (1960), " Consumer Behavior as Risk Taking", in *Dynamic Marketing for a Changing World*, Robert S. Hancock (ed) Chicago AMA, 389-98.

Bettman, James R. (1979), *"An Information Processing Theory of Consumer Choice"*, Reading, MA: Addison-Wesley.

Bowen, David E. and Gareth R. Jones (1986), "Transaction Cost Analysis of Service Organization-Customer Exchange", *Academy of Management Review*, Vol 11, 2, 428-441.

Carmines and McIver (1981), " Techniques for Estimating Measurement Models " in *Social Measurement: Current Issues"* Bohrnstedt and Borgatta (eds), Sage Publications, London.

Chase, R. B. (1978), " Where Does the Customer Fit in a Service Operation?", *Harvard Business Review*, 56(6), 137-42.

Churchill, Gilbert A. and Carol Suprenant (1982), " An Investigation into the Determinants of Customer Satisfaction", *Journal Of Marketing Research*, 19, 491-504.

Cox, Donald F. and Stuart U. Rich (1964), "Perceived Risk and Consumer Decision Making-The Case of Telephone Shopping", *Journal of Marketing Research*, 1,(Nov) 32-39.

Cunningham, S.M. (1967), "Perceived Risk in Information Communications" in *Risk Taking and Information Handling in Consumer Behavior*, D.F. Cox, ed; Boston, MA; Division of Research, Harvard University.

Engel, James F. and Roger D. Blackwell (1982), *Consumer Behavior*, New York, Dryden Press.

George, William, Marc Weinberger and patrick T. Kelley (1986), "Consumer Risk Perceptions: Managerial Tool for the Service Encounter", in *The Service Encounter*, Czepial, Solomon and Suprenant (Eds), Lexington, MA: Heath and Company, 83-101.

Green, Robert T., Eric Langeard and Alice C. Favell (1974), "Innovation in the Service Sector: Some Empirical Findings," *Journal of Marketing Research*, Vol.11, Aug, 323-326.

Gross, Neal C. (1942), *The Diffusion of a Culture Trait in Two Iowa Townships*, M.S. Thesis. Ames: Iowa State University.

Gummesson, Evert (1981)," The Marketing of Professional Services-25 Propositions", in *Marketing Of Services*, James H. Donnelly and William R. George (eds)., Chicago: AMA.

Hill, Donna J.(1986)," Satisfaction and Consumer Services", in *Advances In Consumer Research*, Vol.13, 311-315.

Joreskog and Sorbom (1989), *"Lisrel 7: A Guide to the Program and Applications"*, SPSS Inc. Chicago, Illinois.

Liechty, Margaret G. and Gilbert A. Churchill jr.(1979), "Conceptual Insights into Consumer Satisfaction with Services", *AMA Educators Conference Proceedings*, Chicago: American Marketing Association, 509-515.

Midgley, David F. (1977), *Innovation and New Product Marketing*, New York: Halsted Press.

Midgley, David F. and Graham Dowling (1978), "Innovativeness: The Concept and Its Measurement," *Journal of Consumer Research*, 4, 229-42.

Mills Peter K. and James H. Morris (1986), " Clients as Partial Employees of Service Organizations: Role Development in Client Participation", *Academy of Management Review*, 11, 4, 726-735.

Oliver, Richard (1980)," A Cognitive Model of the Antecedents and Consequences of Satisfaction Decisions", *Journal Of Marketing Research*, 17 (Nov) 460-9.

Parasuraman, A., Valarie Zeithaml, and Leonard Berry (1986), "A Conceptual Model of Service Quality and its Implications for Future Research", *Journal Of Marketing*, 49, no. 4 , (fall), 41-50.

Parasuraman, A., Valarie Zeithaml, and Leonard Berry (1988), "SERVQUAL: A Multi-Item Scale for Measuring Customer Perceptions of Service Quality," *Journal of Retailing*, 64, (Spring), 12-40.

Richins, Marsha L. and Peter H. Bloch (1986), "After the New Wears Off: The Temporal Context of Product Involvement", *Journal of Consumer Research*, Vol 13,(Sept), 280-85.

Smith, Ruth and Michael Houston (1983), " Script-Based Evaluations of Satisfaction with Services" in *Emerging Perspectives in Services Marketing*, Leonard L. Berry, Lynn Shostack and gregory D. Upah, (Eds) AMA, Chicago, 59-62.

Tse, David K. and Peter c. Wilton (1988), " Models of Consumer Satisfaction Formation : An Extension", *Journal of Marketing Research*, Vol.XXV (May) 204-12.

Zaichkowsky, Judith L.(1985), "Measuring the Involvement Construct", *Journal of Consumer Research*, Vol 12, (Dec), 341-52.

Zeithaml, Valarie A. (1981)," How Consumer Evaluation Processes Differ Between Goods and Services", in *Marketing Of Services*, Eds.,James H.Donnelly and William R.George,Chicago:AMA. 186-190.

Mutual Understanding Between Customers and Employees In Service Encounters

Lois A. Mohr, Arizona State University
Mary Jo Bitner, Arizona State University

ABSTRACT

Through re-analysis of critical incident data (Bitner, Booms and Tetreault 1990; Bitner, Booms and Mohr in progress), the construct "mutual understanding" between customers and employees emerges as an important underlying factor in determining customer satisfaction in service encounters. It is hypothesized that mutual understanding results when the customer and employee are cognitively similar and/or when their role taking accuracy is high. Role and script theory are relied on to suggest hypotheses for when these conditions leading to mutual understanding are most likely to occur.

INTRODUCTION

While a growing number of firms are realizing the importance of making customer satisfaction a priority (see, for example, Phillips, et al. 1990; Webster 1988), many do not fully comprehend all that it takes to achieve high levels of satisfaction. In service encounters, where interactions between employees and the customer often become part of the service itself in the customer's mind, not only the service outcome but also the manner in which the service is delivered is important to the customer (Parasuraman, Zeithaml, and Berry 1985). This paper looks at the results of two studies of memorable service encounters in three service industries (Bitner, Booms, and Mohr in progress; Bitner, Booms, and Tetreault 1990) to gain an understanding of the interactions between contact employees and customers that lead customers to distinguish very satisfactory services from very dissatisfactory ones. Based on these studies, it is proposed that mutual understanding between the customer and employee is a major factor influencing customer satisfaction in service encounters. The construct "mutual understanding" is defined; then role and script theory are used to generate hypotheses about when mutual understanding is more or less likely to occur.

CRITICAL INCIDENT RESEARCH AND MUTUAL UNDERSTANDING

In two studies, data were collected on service encounters that are particularly memorable because they are highly satisfying or dissatisfying to customers. Both employees (Bitner, Booms, and Mohr in progress) and frequent customers (Bitner, Booms, and Tetreault 1990) of the hotel, restaurant, and airline industries were asked to describe the circumstances, employee behaviors, and results of the encounters. Employees were asked to put themselves in the customer's shoes and describe incidents that they believed were memorable to the customer, while customers were asked to describe incidents memorable to themselves. A total of 699 customer and 774 employee incidents (approximately half satisfactory and half dissatisfactory in each group) were analyzed.

Throughout the authors' reading of these accounts, one recurring factor that seemed clearly related to customer satisfaction was mutual understanding between the contact employee and the customer. For example, one restaurant customer described an incident involving an extremely long wait for service as highly *satisfactory* because the waitress apologized profusely and compensated the customer for the bill. In this situation the employee understood how negatively the customer was feeling about the speed of service (even though the customer did not specifically complain), and she acted to change that reaction. In contrast, another restaurant customer recounted a dissatisfactory incident where the waitress refused to move him from a window table on a hot day because there was no table left in *her* section. Here the employee either failed to understand how uncomfortable the customer was or she failed to act on that understanding. In addition, she did not give the customer an adequate reason for her refusal to comply with his request to be moved, i.e., she was unable to get the customer to understand and accept her point of view.

The connection between mutual understanding and customer satisfaction is also evident in the comparison of customer and employee results. The incidents gathered from customers (Bitner, Booms, and Tetreault 1990) were classified into three major groups that could account for all satisfactory and dissatisfactory incidents: (1) employee response to service delivery system failures, (2) employee response to customer needs and requests, and (3) unprompted and unsolicited employee actions. When attempting to use the same classification system for the incidents gathered from employees (Bitner, Booms, and Mohr in progress), it was discovered that 86 encounters (11.1%) did not fit into any of the three groups. These 86 incidents were categorized into one group labeled "problematic customer behavior." In each of these incidents employees perceived the *customer's* own behavior (such as drunkenness, verbal abuse of employees, breaking laws, and uncooperativeness) to be the source of dis/satisfaction. Of these 86 encounters, 83 (96.5%) were dissatisfactory.

Interestingly, in our sample, customers *never* mentioned such incidents, indicating that they either are unable to see that their behavior is sometimes the cause of a dissatisfactory service encounter (i.e., they lack understanding of the employee or firm's point of view) or they are unwilling to admit such embarrassing incidents to an interviewer. Although these two explanations cannot be sorted out with these data, a reading of the incidents in this group leads us to believe that lack of mutual understanding does play a part. To illustrate, 42 incidents (49% of the problem customer group) were categorized in the subgroup called "pigheaded"/ uncooperative customer. Here the customer is generally rude and uncooperative or extremely demanding; all efforts made by the employee to compensate for a perceived service failure are rejected. These are situations where the employees do more for the customers than could be reasonably expected, yet the customers still are not satisfied. For example, one couple in a restaurant was served their entrees undercooked. The waitress apologized and offered them a new meal plus free drinks and free dessert. The manager also tried to appease the couple, but they left the restaurant angrily. Another example involves a flight where the airline ran out of meals. As a result, there was no dinner for one businessman sitting in the back of the plane. The flight attendant apologized and offered him one of the crew meals. When he refused the crew meal, she offered him a $25 certificate towards another flight. Though he did accept that offer, he continued to complain and behave in an agitated manner toward the flight attendant. It is unlikely that such customers understand the perspectives of the employee or the firm in these encounters.

We conclude, then, from these two studies of critical incidents, that customer satisfaction can be adversely affected if the employee does not understand the customer or if the customer does not understand the employee. Because the understanding of both parties to the encounter is important, we suggest that mutual understanding positively affects the encounter. On these grounds, the following hypothesis is proposed:

H1: The greater the mutual understanding between service employees and customers during the service encounter, the higher the customer satisfaction with the service will be.

It is important to clarify that this hypothesis is intended to convey one factor that may affect satisfaction. Other constructs, such as the amount of effort exerted by the employee and the employee's adaptiveness to the customer's needs, were also apparent in the data. In this paper, however, we explore mutual understanding.

As an additional caveat, we are not arguing that a service delivery factor such as mutual understanding would necessarily overpower service outcome factors. For example, when the service is clearly bad (e.g., the restaurant's food is poorly prepared), employee-customer agreement about the low quality is unlikely to result in a satisfied customer. But mutual recognition of the problem may lead the customer to view the encounter more favorably than were the employee oblivious to his perceptions. On the positive side, mutual understanding between participants may enable the employee to fine tune a successful encounter to further please an already satisfied customer. Such service extras could be a basis for competitive advantage.

The next step in this paper is to define the concept of mutual understanding and explore conditions that make its occurrence more likely.

MUTUAL UNDERSTANDING

By mutual understanding we mean that, between two people, the messages received equal the messages sent, with no distortion. Messages can be sent verbally or through gestures and demeanor, and they can be sent and received more or less consciously. It is obvious that perfect mutual understanding is unattainable, but a high level of understanding is desirable if people are to successfully communicate. Miscommunication (i.e., low or zero mutual understanding) is to be avoided because it generally prevents the parties of an interaction from achieving their goals or, at the very least, it increases the costs of interacting. In the service context, Parasuraman, Zeithaml, and Berry (1985) propose that management misunderstanding of consumer expectations (Gap 1) diminishes the customer's evaluation of service quality.

Given that mutual understanding is a desirable goal for service encounters, how do we go about achieving it? A review of the social psychology literature suggests two concepts that help explain mutual understanding: role taking and cognitive similarity. These are two distinct concepts which are, however, strongly interrelated. Each concept is discussed below.

Role Taking

Drawing on the work of George Herbert Mead, Schwalbe (1988) defines role taking as entering the perspective of the other. We use Schwalbe's work to define role taking as understanding the other's imagery of the external world. This cognitive process of role taking is clearly related to mutual understanding for, if one understands how another person sees an event, one is more likely to understand that person's communications about the event. Schwalbe (1988) asserts that role taking is essential for establishing stable patterns of interaction. Furthermore, when habitualized interaction is not working, role taking is necessary for realigning behavior. Some of the research on role taking shows that this factor leads to more successful negotiation of arbitration disputes (Neale and Bazerman 1983), to building positive counseling relationships (Gladstein 1983), and to satisfaction in romantic relationships (Davis and Oathout 1987).

Role taking captures the idea of customers and contact personnel understanding each other's perspectives even when their own perspectives may be different. Brown and Swartz (1989) conducted research that supports the idea that accuracy of role taking influences customer satisfaction. They gathered data on patient experiences with their physicians and compared them to the physician's perceptions of their patients' experiences. Thirty-three items (e.g., "My doctor hears what I have to say.", "My doctor prescribes drugs and pills too often.") were used to measure perceptions. The differences between physician and patient perceptions were rather large, and the size of the differences was significantly related to overall patient satisfaction. Based on this discussion, the following hypothesis is proposed:

H2: Increased accuracy in cognitive role taking leads to a higher level of mutual understanding between encounter participants.

Cognitive Similarity

There are a number of studies showing that cognitive similarity leads to more effective communication. Argyle, Furnham, and Graham (1981) review some of this research. Typical of the writers in communication, Rommetveit (1974) discusses commonality of cognitive categorization as a prerequisite for mutual understanding and communication. There are, however, several types of cognitive similarity. One type involves two people utilizing the same underlying attribute or dimension in forming judgments of people or events. In a service encounter this might mean that both the employee and customer judge the encounter's quality primarily by the employee's responsiveness to the customer's needs. Runkel (1956) and Triandis (1960) found such similarity related to communication effectiveness, while Landfield and Nawas (1964) found it related to client improvement in psychotherapy.

A different type of cognitive similarity, one which is a major focus of this paper, is role and script congruence. Solomon et al. (1985) argue persuasively that discrepancies between an employee's and customer's role conceptions or scripts for the service encounter can reduce customer satisfaction. For example, if the employee and customer have different ideas of what each other's behavior in the encounter should be, problems in communicating and understanding each other are very likely to arise. Based on this discussion the following hypothesis is proposed:

H3: Cognitive similarity leads to greater mutual understanding between encounter participants.

Relationships Between Role Taking and Cognitive Similarity

Before discussing the concepts of role and script congruence in more depth, we will suggest several ways in which role taking and cognitive similarity are interrelated. First, the more cognitively similar two actors are, the more accurate their cognitive role taking is likely to be (Hickson 1985). The idea here is that role taking is more difficult when the actors use different attributes for evaluating an encounter or when they have incompatible expectations. For example, if a hotel clerk in a preindustrialized country thinks he is providing superb service, he may have difficulty seeing that his relatively wealthy customer from a highly industrialized country is regarding his hotel stay as a gruelling experience. However, if both participants are from the same society and view the encounter similarly, the clerk will be more likely to understand the customer's evaluation of the service. Evidence for this is provided by Biddle (1986), who reviews research that finds role taking positively associated with similarity in the background, training, and outlook of people.

Second, it is also probable that role taking accuracy in an encounter will lead to similarity of cognitive structures relevant to the encounter. In the course of an interaction it is not unusual for people to be influenced by each other. The understanding of another's views often leads us to change our own perspective or interpretation of events. This idea is encapsulated in Deutsch and Gerard's (1955) concept of informational social influence, whereby we accept information obtained from another as evidence about reality. Based on this discussion, we hypothesize a relationship with no dominant causal direction between role taking and cognitive similarity:

H4: Cognitive similarity and role taking accuracy during a service encounter will be positively correlated.

In summary, we suggest that customer satisfaction is positively influenced by mutual understanding which, in turn, depends on role taking accuracy and cognitive similarity. We also propose that the concepts of role taking and cognitive similarity are connected by reciprocal on-going relationships during the interaction that takes place in a service encounter. These relationships, along with those discussed throughout the remainder of the paper, are diagrammed in the Figure.

The next step in this paper is to explore the perspectives of role and script theory for insight on when mutual understanding in the service encounter is more or less likely. Hypotheses for future research on the service encounter will be generated from these analyses.

PREDICTING MUTUAL UNDERSTANDING THROUGH ROLE AND SCRIPT THEORY

Roles and Scripts

According to Biddle (1986), role theory focuses on three major concepts: (1) role behavior, the patterned and characteristic activities of a person occupying a particular position, (2) social position, the part or identity that is assumed by social participants, and (3) role expectation, the standards for role behavior that are understood by everyone and generally adhered to by role performers. In this paper, the term role will be used to encompass all three of these concepts -- behavior, position, and expectations.

FIGURE
Summary of Hypothesized Relationships

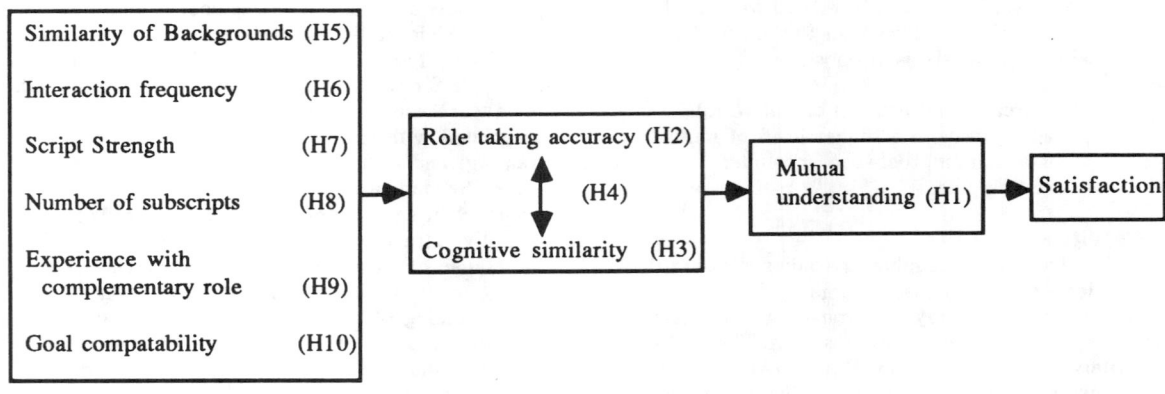

Role expectations are connected to specific positions, not to the people themselves; one person can occupy any number of social positions over time, and behavior will be expected to change accordingly (Sarbin and Allen 1968). Inherent in the concept of roles is the notion of complementarity; that is, a role only exists in relation to other, complementary roles (e.g., father and daughter, physician and patient, customer and sales clerk). The occupants of roles that are directly associated with a focal person's role are called that person's role-set. (Katz and Kahn 1978). For example, a waiter's role-set would include his customers, coworkers, and boss.

The fact that each role implies other related roles is an important one, for it means that people who are enacting roles are interdependent. Such interdependency implies that, for successful role enactment, people need to be able to predict how other role players will behave (Solomon, et al. 1985). To help ensure that role occupants will behave properly, role expectations are often communicated, or sent, from role-set members to the focal person. The acts that make up role-sending are both informational and attempts at influence. These acts need not be continuous, however, because role occupants have often been previously socialized into their roles (Katz and Kahn 1978).

Abelson (1981) defines a script as a hypothesized cognitive structure that, when activated, organizes one's comprehension of event-based situations. Scripts without sequence information are called weak scripts, while those that include learned associations between prior and consequent events are called strong scripts. Each script includes a number of roles. A strong script, then, is a structure that describes appropriate sequences of role behaviors in a particular context (Schank and Abelson 1977). Scripts are assumed to define expectations that function both as behavioral guides and as norms for the evaluation of people's performances (Smith and Houston 1983).

According to Schank and Abelson (1977), strong scripts generally handle stylized situations, situations that are largely predetermined and stereotyped. Many service encounters, such as those between bank teller or hotel desk clerk and customer, have strong scripts. In standardized situations scripts specify behavior very clearly. Yet, if it is elaborate enough, a script can also handle interferences, events that prevent normal script enactment. Schank and Abelson describe two types of interferences: (1) obstacles, which occur when an enabling condition is missing, and (2) errors, which occur when the action is completed with the wrong result. An example of encountering an *obstacle* would be arriving at a restaurant hoping to begin a dining-out script and learning that there are no available tables. It would be an *error* if the waiter brought a different entree than the one ordered. There are often role prescriptions for overcoming obstacles or for correcting errors, but sometimes an actor will give up and leave the scene instead of completing the scripted performance. Scripts grow by adding prescriptions to overcome obstacles and errors. Occupational role members generally need elaborate scripts to successfully perform their roles. Since customers add variability, the service provider who interacts with customers frequently needs particularly elaborate scripts.

Predicting Mutual Understanding Through Roles and Scripts

With this foundation in mind, we now turn to the question of how these role and script concepts can be used to examine the amount of mutual understanding between service providers and customers. In the following sections the term mutual understanding encompasses role taking accuracy, cognitive similarity, and their reciprocal connections, as discussed above. Research on role taking has found both similarity of backgrounds and frequency of interactions positively related to role taking accuracy (Biddle, 1986; Hickson 1985). It is also a straightforward assumption that for two people, background similarity and interaction frequency increase their cognitive similarity (e.g., Triandis 1960). Similarity of background can be along lines such as home country, social class, educational level, subculture, age, gender, etc. People with similar backgrounds tend to have experiences that lead to a high level of role and script agreement. In addition, when people have interacted frequently in the past, they are likely to have established mutually acceptable reciprocal role behaviors. In both these situations, where there is a high level of pre-established role agreement, there is less need for role expectations to be communicated. Therefore there is less chance for miscommunication than when backgrounds are different and the role occupants have not interacted before. The following hypotheses are therefore proposed:

H5: The more similar the backgrounds of the service provider and customer are, the greater their mutual understanding about the service encounter will be.

H6: The more frequently the service provider and the customer interact, the greater their mutual understanding about the service encounter will be.

Because role behaviors are interdependent, their successful enactment requires that the people involved have similar expectations of what the appropriate role behaviors are. Strong scripts provide detailed information about what behaviors should occur and when they should be enacted. A person with a strong script is what Katz and Kahn (1978) would call a "self-sender," that is, a role-sender to himself. Since strong scripts arise for situations that are largely predetermined, there is more role agreement and less need for role-sending between participants than when scripts are weak. This leads to the following hypothesis:

H7: Mutual understanding in service encounters will be greater when both customers and employees hold strong scripts.

Scripts can vary in complexity in addition to strength. One of the ways scripts increase in complexity is by including prescriptions, or subscripts, for handling interferences. Experience is a factor here, for role participants that are highly experienced have more elaborately developed scripts. They are prepared to reach their scripted goals in spite of errors or obstacles. The ability to enact subscripts to overcome interferences should make mutual understanding more likely. Indirect evidence is provided by Leong, Busch, and John's (1989) research showing that effective salespeople have more elaborate, sophisticated sales scripts than less effective salespeople. The following hypothesis is therefore proposed:

H8: Mutual understanding in service encounters will increase when participants have a greater number of strong subscripts for handling obstacles and errors.

Because the roles in a script are complementary rather than the same, role expectations can at times lead to misunderstanding. This is because a role sensitizes its participant to features of the environment that are important for successful role behavior (Leigh and Rethans 1984), and different roles require different behavior. For example, a waitress needs to attend to some details of the environment, such as signals from the cook and other customers waiting to be served, that the customer safely ignores. In the process, she may miss gestures of disapproval that a customer makes as she delivers the order to the table.

Because a script is a cognitive structure, there will inevitably be some differences between all people's scripts; but differences are likely to be larger between those who occupy different roles. As evidence, Katz and Kahn (1978) cite a number of studies showing a relationship between role occupancy and attitudes, values, behaviors, and perceptions. So we would expect two waitresses to have more similar restaurant scripts than a waitress and a customer would have. Following from this, we would also expect that experience with the complementary roles of a script would increase the mutual understanding of the role occupants. For example, the waiter who often eats out himself would be likely to view the restaurant encounter more similarly to his customers than a waiter who always eats at home. This effect would be strongest for the waiter who does not let his occupational identity be known to the restaurant's employees when eating out; such a person will be treated like "an ordinary customer" and experience more fully the complementary role. This leads to the following hypothesis:

H9: Amount of experience with the complementary role of the service encounter is positively related to mutual understanding about the service encounter.

An additional way that misunderstandings may arise stems from role conflicts between the participants in a scripted encounter. Although the roles of a script are basically complementary, the cooperation that this implies is rarely perfect. There may, in fact, be situations where the role occupants work against each other. An example of this is the struggle for control that can occur even within scripted events. In her study of supermarket cashiers, Rafaeli (1989) found both customers and cashiers vying for control of the check-out process. Customers believed that they had some right to control the speed and accuracy of the process since they were paying for the service, while cashiers felt they needed to retain control to do their jobs properly. A more extreme example is the situation created when management rewards employees for the number of customers processed while customers want more time and attention from employees.

Zeithaml, Berry, and Parasuraman (1988) discuss management commitment to service quality as a major factor influencing customer perceptions of service quality. Firms that emphasize cost reduction and short-term profit over customer service set up systems where employee and customer goals will surely conflict. In this sort of situation where there is competition between the participants, one would expect misunderstandings and miscommunications between employees and customers to flourish. Evidence is provided by Shaw and Costanzo (1970), who cite several studies finding greater communication difficulties in competitive than in cooperative groups. The following hypothesis can be drawn from this:

H10: The level of goal compatibility between customers and employees is positively related to mutual understanding about the service encounter.

In summary, roles and scripts exert a powerful force towards standardizing expectations, behavior, and perceptions of behavior. To the extent that all goes smoothly in a service encounter, the employee and customer are thought to be reading from a common script (Solomon et al. 1985), and the customer is likely to evaluate the encounter positively. But roles and scripts also allow for divergence in perspectives. To the degree that a customer's expectations in an encounter are not met and role-sending communications do not correct the situation, the customer is likely to view the service as a failure. Employee factors such as lack of experience on the job, lack of experience with the customer, and goals that are not customer-oriented can lead to misunderstanding and low customer satisfaction. Customer factors such as lack of script knowledge or inflated role expectations can produce the same negative results.

CONTRIBUTIONS AND LIMITATIONS

From a theory-development point of view the hypotheses suggested above contribute to our basic understanding of consumer behavior, particularly for consumption situations such as service encounters, where social interaction plays a part in product evaluation. In such situations the outcome of the consumption experience is highly dependent on human behaviors, and customers will evaluate not only the final outcome, but also the process by which the outcome was delivered. It is suggested here that the process and outcome of service delivery (and thus, satisfaction) will be enhanced through mutual understanding. Role and script theories provide a strong theoretical base for predicting mutual understanding. It is likely that the mutual understanding construct would apply to satisfaction in other consumption situations beyond the service encounter, as for example, in sales situations.

In addition to contributing to theory development in consumer behavior, the hypotheses in this paper all have practical implications for managing service encounters. For example, if support is found for the hypothesis that similarity of backgrounds is positively related to mutual understanding, this would lead to the recommendation that firms recruit contact personnel whose backgrounds match those of their customers or target markets. To the extent that this is not possible, training whereby employees are exposed to detailed descriptions of the ways their customers think about service encounters in their industry could help bridge the gap. If support is found for the hypothesis that frequency of interactions between encounter participants is positively related to mutual understanding, then managers would be advised to set up systems for allowing repeat customers to deal with the same employee whenever possible. If it is found that strong, complex scripts facilitate mutual understanding, then service firms might invest in training and communications to strengthen the scripts of their employees and potential customers, and to help them develop subscripts for dealing with obstacles and errors. If experience with the complementary role is important, then perhaps employees should be asked, as part of their ongoing training, to play the role of a customer periodically. Finally, if goal compatibility is important, then managers should examine carefully what they are asking of their employees and how employee rewards are structured, to see whether these are in line with customer goals.

The above discussion is clearly limited by lack of empirical data from service encounter contexts. While the critical incident data suggest the general importance of mutual understanding, the specific hypotheses have not been tested. This is clearly the next, necessary step.

In addition, the hypotheses presented are based on previous research in a variety of contexts. The same results cannot be automatically assumed for service encounters, however. It could be argued, for example, that most service encounters are low involvement settings where mutual understanding has relatively little impact on customer satisfaction. Since critical incident research samples memorable encounters, such research may tap those encounters where involvement is exceptionally high. For this reason, the hypotheses suggested here should be tested in the more typical service encounter context.

REFERENCES

Abelson, Robert P. (1981), "Psychological Status of the Script Concept," *American Psychologist*, 36 (July), 715-729.

Argyle, Michael, Adrian Furnham, and Jean Ann Graham (1981), *Social Situations*. Cambridge: Cambridge University Press.

Biddle, B. J. (1986), "Recent Developments in Role Theory," *Annual Review of Sociology*, 12, 67-92.

Bitner, Mary Jo, Bernard H. Booms, and Lois A. Mohr, "Views of Service Encounters by Customers and Employees," in progress.

_____, _____, and Mary Stanfield Tetreault (1990), "The Service Encounter: Diagnosing Favorable and Unfavorable Incidents," *Journal of Marketing*, 54 (January), 71-84.

Brown, Stephen W. and Teresa A. Swartz, (1989) "A Gap Analysis of Professional Service Quality," *Journal of Marketing*, 53 (April), 92-98.

Davis, Mark H. and H. Alan Oathout (1987), "Maintenance of Satisfaction in Romantic Relationships: Empathy and Relational Competence," *Journal of Personality and Social Psychology*, 53 (August), 397-410.

Deutsch, Morton and Harold B. Gerard (1955), "A Study of Normative and Informational Social Influences Upon Individual Judgment," *Journal of Abnormal and Social Psychology*, 51 (November), 629-636.

Gladstein, Gerald A. (1983), "Understanding Empathy: Integrating Counseling, Developmental, and Social Psychology Perspectives," *Journal of Counseling Psychology*, 30 (October), 467-482.

Hickson, Joyce (1985), "Psychological Research on Empathy: In Search of an Elusive Phenomenon," *Psychological Reports*, 57 (August), 91-94.

Katz, Daniel and Robert L. Kahn (1978), *The Social Psychology of Organizations*, NY: John Wiley and Sons.

Landfield, A. W. and M. M. Nawas (1964), "Psychotherapeutic Improvement as a Function of Communication and Adoption of Therapist's Values," *Journal of Counseling Psychology, 11 (Winter), 336-341.*

Leigh, Thomas W. and Arno J. Rethans (1984), "A Script-theoretic Analysis of Industrial Purchasing Behavior," *Journal of Marketing*, 48 (Fall), 22-32.

Leong, Siew Meng, Paul S. Busch, and Deborah Roedder John (1989), "Knowledge Bases and Salesperson Effectiveness: A Script-Theoretic Analysis," *Journal of Marketing Research*, 26 (May), 164-178.

Neale, Margaret A. and Max H. Bazerman (1983), "The Role of Perspective-Taking Ability in Negotiating Under Different Forms of Arbitration," *Industrial and Labor Relations Review*, 36 (April), 378-388.

Parasuraman, A., Valarie A. Zeithaml, and Leonard L. Berry (1985), "A Conceptual Model of Service Quality and Its Implications for Future Research," *Journal of Marketing*, 49 (Fall), 41-50.

Phillips, Stephen, Amy Dunkin, James B. Treece, and Keith H. Hammonds (1990), "King Customer," *Business Week*, (March 12), 88-91+.

Rafaeli, Anat (1989), "When Cashiers Meet Customers: An Analysis of the Role of Supermarket Cashiers," *Academy of Management Journal*, 32 (June), 245-273.

Rommetveit, R. (1974), *On Message Structure*, London: John Wiley and Sons.

Runkel, Philip J. (1956), "Cognitive Similarity in Facilitating Communication," *Sociometry*, 19 (September), 178-191.

Sarbin, Theodore R. and Vernon L. Allen (1968), "Role Theory," in *The Handbook of Social Psychology*, 2nd ed., Vol. I, eds. Gardner Lindzey and Elliot Aronson, Reading, MA: Addison-Wesley Publishing Co., 488-567.

Schank, Roger C. and Robert P. Abelson (1977), *Scripts, Plans, Goals and Understanding*, NY: John Wiley and Sons.

Schwalbe, Michael L. (1988), "Role Taking Reconsidered: Linking Competence and Performance to Social Structure," *Journal for the Theory of Social Behaviour*, 18 (December), 411-436.

Shaw, Marvin E. and Philip R. Costanzo (1970), *Theories of Social Psychology*, NY: McGraw-Hill.

Smith, Ruth A. and Michael J. Houston (1983), "Script-Based Evaluations of Satisfaction With Services," in *Emerging Perspectives on Services Marketing*, eds. Leonard L. Berry, G. Lynn Shostack, and Gregory D. Upah, Chicago: American Marketing Association, 59-62.

Solomon, Michael R., Carol Surprenant, John A. Czepiel, and Evelyn G. Gutman (1985), "A Role Theory Perspective on Dyadic Interactions: The Service Encounter," *Journal of Marketing*, 49 (Winter), 99-111.

Triandis, Harry C. (1960), "Cognitive Similarity and Communication in a Dyad," *Human Relations*, 13 (May), 175-183.

Webster, Frederick E., Jr. (1988), "The Rediscovery of the Marketing Concept," *Business Horizons*, 31 (May-June), 29-39.

Zeithaml, Valarie A., Leonard L. Berry, and A. Parasuraman (1988), "Communication and Control Processes in the Delivery of Service Quality," *Journal of Marketing*, 52 (April), 35-48.

Gender Representation in Advertising
Nancy Artz, University of Southern Maine
Alladi Venkatesh, University of California, Irvine

OBJECTIVE OF THE SESSION

The objective of this session is to discuss how practitioners and academics have approached the study of gender representation in advertising and to consider alternative ways to advance future research in this area. The session is designed to bring together practitioners and academics who share a common interest in the topic but whose perspectives (both between and within these two groups) may be different. For example, some focus on gender as an operational aspect of advertising, some are more concerned with the theoretical construction of gender, and others are interested in media images of sex-role stereotypes. By bringing together different perspectives, we hope to sensitize consumer researchers to the full range of possibilities in gender research in advertising and encourage fruitful discussions on the representations of men and women in advertisements.

BACKGROUND

The history of the modern "Women's movement" is short but dramatic. The movement is widely acknowledged to be one of the most important social developments in the second half of the twentieth century. In recognition of the significance of the movement, the year 1975 was declared "International Women's Year". This social and intellectual movement, which began in the 1960's, is still evolving and giving rise to new vocabulary and discourse. The term "gender" itself, which has undergone much intellectual scrutiny in the recent years, does not even appear in the now famous 1964 issue of Daedalus examining "The Women of America". The term "women's movement" has become anachronistic and is slowly being replaced by other terminology. As expected with an important social movement, its basic ideas have cast their long shadow on the theory and practice of marketing and advertising. It is to this topic that we shall return in this paper.

Studies on gender and advertising are of a recent origin (dating back to the early seventies) and cut across a variety of disciplines including mass communications (Busby 1975), sociology (Goffman 1976), critical theory/social criticism (Williamson 1978), feminist theory (Barthel 1988), marketing/consumer research (Courtney and Lockeretz 1971, Courtney and Whipple 1983, Belkaoui and Belkaoui 1976, Lundstrom and Siglimplaglia 1977, Venkatesan and Losco 1975, Wagner and Banos 1973) and international marketing (Gilly 1988, Lysonski 1985). In the field of marketing/consumer research (represented by the authors of this paper), a recent book by Courtney and Whipple (1983) provides a comprehensive summary of the discussion and debates on this topic. In addition to the academic publications just cited, there have been some important contributions from practicing marketing professionals. Of these, the work by Bartos (1982) is particularly noteworthy.

If we go beyond advertising to broader issues concerning gender and marketing, there is a much larger body of work from the seventies. A special issue of the *Journal of Marketing* (July 1977) was devoted to the changing roles of women and their implications for marketing theory and practice. This was followed by Venkatesh's (1985) work based on his dissertation. Some of the many marketing scholars who have worked in this area include Roberts, Wortzel, Gentry, Iyer, Debevec, Strober, Douglas, McCall.

After an initial burst of research activity in the seventies and early eighties, there has been a general deceleration of published research in this area. Does it mean there are no more new questions, or that the old questions have all been answered adequately? We would have to respond 'no' to both. In our opinion, the questions have become more complex, the issues are much more nuanced, and there is scope for both exciting and sustained scholarship. In a modest way, we explore these issues in this session.

AN ANALYSIS OF PAST APPROACHES

In considering the past approaches to the study of gender in marketing, or more specifically, gender in advertising, we begin by highlighting positive contributions and then provide a critique and suggestions for future research.

The positive contributions of researchers within the marketing/consumer behavior discipline can be summarized as follows: the discipline has responded to the shifts in gender-based roles by readjusting its intellectual focus, by developing analytical strategies, and by fostering sensitivity to the causes and consequences of momentous changes in the social arena. Marketing practice has similarly undergone some fundamental shifts in response to the actual and potential impact of sex-role changes on consumption patterns. The profession as a whole has come to the realization that these changes are not limited to a particular situation or context, but have had a lasting impact on consumers in their capacity as individuals and as members of households, work groups, and other institutional settings. Consumer behavior text books have legitimated the subject by devoting entire chapters to this topic.

It is ironic that the academic research effort on this topic has slowed now that the topic is accepted as legitimate. This decline in attention, however, is not reflected in marketing practice or in the general media attention to women's issues. One has only to visit a neighborhood book store to find numerous books and magazines devoted to gender and its many forms. We find it significant that there is a lack of attention to this topic among marketing scholars given the simultaneous explosion of media attention. We now examine these and other related issues by way of a critique.

Single Issue Research

One criticism of the past approaches to the study of gender issues in marketing and advertising is that there has been a preoccupation with a single theme, sexual-stereotyping. (There are some interesting exceptions - see for example, Alreck, Settle and Belch 1982, Gentry, Doering, and O'Brien l978). The number of articles on this single issue is staggering. We feel that the endless repetition of content-analyses on this narrow theme has finally produced a state of analytical exhaustion. The problem is that the content analyses are limited to frequency counts of role portrayals that yield rather superficial and somewhat self-evident inferences (see Ferguson, Kreshel and Tinkham 1990 for an attempt to expand the approach). The result of this narrow focus on content analyses of role portrayals has trivialized the fundamental issue of gender representation by ignoring other richer dimensions.

A related criticism involves the discipline's preoccupation with the representation of women and subsequent lack of focus on the representation of men. This exclusion of male representation is an obvious illustration of how gender is more comprehensive than its construction in this research stream. A final criticism is that the research has tended to describe sex-role portrayal but has not fully examined the persuasive implications of gender representation.

Limited Perspectives of Advertising Practice

The advertising industry, like the academic community, has also had a narrow perspective. Rather than view the women's movement as an opportunity to reconceptualize marketing practice, the advertising industry has had a single response to changing sex-roles. That response has been to de-emphasize traditional role portrayals and emphasize role portrayals that conform to modernistic/egalitarian norms. Some critics charge that the industry's response is self-serving and demonstrates that the industry has misunderstood the true nature of the women's movement. In this view, superficial changes in role portrayals are simply a way of exploiting or taking advantage of the women's movement rather than a way of promoting emancipation. In all, the marketing approach has been unimaginative and driven by narrow concerns of the bottom line.

A Lack of Theory

Because the marketing literature was produced in response to a contemporary social movement, there was not sufficient time or attention paid to theoretical issues. Such a theoretical vacuum is not uncommon to problems of this sort, and some parallels can be found in other instances - consumer movement, oil crisis, ghetto marketing, etc. In all these cases, marketing studies were generated within the specific context of a movement without any conceptual or theoretical foundations to guide a sustained discourse.

Inadequate Distinction Between Sex, Gender and Sexuality

Past study of gender representation can be termed simplistic for not examining the rich multi-dimensionality of related concepts. " Gender" needs to be understood as a culturally constructed category which goes beyond but encompasses the biological category of sex, the social-psychological category of sex role, the psychological category of masculine/feminine identity, and the psycho-behavioral category of sexuality. In the marketing literature there has been a tendency to confuse these categories and a failure to appreciate their theoretical underpinnings.

A Lack of Critical Approach and A Lost Opportunity

The academic work in marketing has typically and rather uncritically sided with the practitioner perspective subscribing to the view that the "women's movement" offers one more opportunity to effectively create a marketing niche for various products and services. There is thus a lost opportunity to meaningfully address a rich array of issues concerning aesthetics, politics of advertising, symbolic aspects of gender representation, production and reproduction of cultural imagery, and the like.

The above represent some of the more important reasons why fruitful research in "gender and advertising" has stagnated. We would now like to offer a few suggestions for reviving and advancing research interest in this area.

HOW CAN GENDER RESEARCH BE ENRICHED?

Gender research should move beyond the sex-role stereotyping framework. We do not recommend that the sex-role framework be completely abandoned. We see some possible extensions here. For example, the intersection of gender and other demographic characteristics is relatively unexplored in the marketing literature. How do sex-role issues pertain to children, teenagers, and ethnic minorities? Marketing scholars and practitioners might want to examine Goffman (l976) for a brilliant analysis of roles and ritual practices.

Alternative frameworks to the study of gender in advertising can be developed by systematically examining the theoretical ideas enunciated in different disciplines. Disciplines that can provide valuable foundations for future gender studies in marketing include the fields of literary theory, intellectual history, philosophy, phenomenology, linguistics, and cultural studies. (We refer to Venkatesh's paper in this session for a representative account of the ideas from these disciplines.)

Gender research must be grounded in both theory and practice. In terms of theory, gender must be evaluated not only in terms of sex-roles (a loosely constructed social-psychological concept that describes sexual division of labor), but in terms of psycho-social and psycho-analytical terms. Concepts such as identity, subjectivity, sexuality can describe gender from a multi-dimensional perspective. (The session on sexuality at this conference chaired by Gould is an interesting start in this direction). Research should address both intra-gender and inter-gender dynamics. Consideration should be given to underlying social-structural issues, power relationships between gender categories, and mythological and metaphorical issues as well.

The study of gender representation in advertising must be grounded in theories of representation applied to other cultural settings like literature, art, film, etc. Gender representation must be studied not only psychologistically (e.g., subjectivity, identity) but anthropologistically (relationships to the human environment). Gender can also be studied semiotically as a signification process (We refer to Artz's paper on this panel). While psychological approaches deal with internal representations of the "being", semiotic processes deal with symbolic configurations and the communication of meaning.

In terms of grounding the research in practice we propose the following. We should continue to study the persuasive implication of gender dimensions in advertising (We refer to the Bartos and McManamon and Whipple papers in this session) and begin to study advertising practice, itself, as it relates to gender. Specifically, we should consider the underlying production processes in advertising and institutional practices that lead to particular constructions of gender and gender representations. Thus one can study where the ideas for gender representation come from, who the cultural and corporate elites are, and what the social apparatuses are that determine how and what gender-based advertising should be. To gain a further understanding of the prevailing cultural norms and the practices, advertising professionals must be interviewed along with models and characters who figure in advertising copy or commercials. We believe advertising should be studied in naturalistic settings. That is, advertising practices must be systematically deconstructed by a comprehensive analysis of the commercials, the people, and the media.

The above are but a few suggestions to expand the scope and enhance the quality of research on gender in advertising. We shall now turn our attention to the papers in this special topic session.

INTRODUCTION TO SPECIAL SESSION PAPERS

The session represents a new consciousness in gender research and opens the door to future possibilities for research. The papers represent a first glimpse at some new directions. We hope that our comments above and the ideas expressed by the paper presenters will help consumer researchers initiate new studies and find fresh sources of ideas for their research.

Paper 1 by Rena Bartos: This paper presents the perspective of a practitioner who has been a pioneer in the analysis of gender in advertising. Her approach to the study of gender is analytical and based on years of experience in the field. She argues that sex-role stereotypes have had a limiting effect on marketing strategy and she urges practitioners to assess consumers' attitudinal response to gender imagery as part of their standard copy testing procedure.

Paper 2 by Mary K. McManamon and Thomas W. Whipple: This paper uses an experimental approach to study the persuasive effect of gender in advertising. Four gender-related variables in advertising are examined: the sex of the spokesperson, the sex of the announcer, the gender of the product, and the sex of the target audience. As is typical of experimental research, gender is viewed in a relatively simple categorical sense. The focus is less on the complexities of gender as a construct and more on how gender as an operational variable influences consumer response to advertising.

Paper 3 by Nancy Artz: This paper examines the portrayal of women in advertising. An attempt is made to describe gender portrayal in rich, contextual terms rather than narrowly focus on sex-role stereotypes using simplistic terms (e.g., traditional versus non-traditional occupations). Semiotic analysis is used to show how subtle executional elements influence gender portrayal and the viewer's evaluation of that portrayal.

Paper 4 by Alladi Venkatesh: This conceptual paper reviews feminist theory to provide a deeper understanding of gender as a construct. The goal is to show that gender can be viewed in ways other than as simple sex-role stereotypes or as a simple classification of consumers and products as masculine or feminine. The paper argues for a sophisticated construction of gender as the basis for analyzing gender representation in media practices. Many of the arguments in this paper are derived from social criticism, literary theory, critical theory and philosophy, and postmodernism.

As a final remark, this session makes a contribution by beginning to sensitize practitioners and academics to the full-range of gender construction. By juxtaposing different approaches to the study of the representation of gender in advertising, we hope to have made a meaningful start. More detailed abstracts of the individual papers are presented next.

OBSERVATIONS ON GENDER IN ADVERTISING

Rena Bartos, Rena Bartos Company

This talk provides observations on gender and advertising garnered from twenty years of industry experiences. Throughout her career, the author has analyzed the women's market, sex-role stereotypes, and how to communicate with women consumers through the media.

The paper outlines the author's approach to the study of gender and draws from the work described in *The Moving Target* (1982) and *Marketing to Women Around the World* (1989). The relationship between gender portrayal and advertising effectiveness is considered. The author recommends that advertisers study consumer reaction to sex-role portrayal as part of their standard copy testing procedure. In the author's experience the like/dislike reaction of consumers to advertising is a good way to capture the emotional and attitudinal responses of consumers to gender imagery. Recent research indicates that the like/dislike scale is a better predictor of sales than other copy testing methods.

ASSESSING THE EFFECTS OF SPOKESPERSON AND ANNOUNCER GENDER ON THE COMMUNICATION EFFECTIVENESS OF ADVERTISEMENTS
Mary K. McManamon and Thomas W. Whipple, Cleveland State University

A controlled, experiment was used to investigate audience reaction to male and female spokespersons and announcers in advertising messages. Based on the results of content analyses and the predominant use of men as commercial announcers, it was hypothesized that male voices would be more effective than female voices in advertisements for both gender-specific and non-gender specific products.

Audio portions of commercials for four products (two gender specific and two non-gender specific) were heard by 473 respondents. Announcer gender and spokesperson gender were manipulated in each commercial. Respondents evaluated one commercial for each product using a series of ten items tapping cognitive, conative, and affective dimensions. Based on the results of a factor analysis, the ten items were used to form two variables labeled "effectiveness" and "irritation." These variables were used as dependent measures in a MANOVA with independent variables of the gender of the target audience, the spokesperson, and the announcer.

For non-gender specific products, the target audiences found male and female voices equally "effective" as announcers and the female voice more "effective" than the male as a spokesperson. For gender-specific products, respondents rated the same-sexed spokespersons and opposite-sexed announcers as more "effective." With respect to "irritation" level of the commercials, male respondents found male spokespersons to be less "irritating." Female respondents, on the other hand, found a spokesperson less "irritating" if he or she was the opposite sex of the user of the gender-specific product.

The study showed that women are equally "effective," and in some cases, more "effective" and "less irritating" than men both as spokespersons and announcers in commercials.

AUTHORIAL PERSPECTIVE IN ADVERTISING: A CASE STUDY OF THE PORTRAYAL OF WOMEN
Nancy Artz, University of Southern Maine

This paper introduces a new approach to the study of gender representation. With the exception of visual imagery research (Goffman 1976, Kilbourne 1987), content analyses of advertising have focused on easily quantified, well-defined sex-role stereotypes (c.f., Courtney and Whipple 1983). In the simplest case, sex-role portrayal has been categorized as traditional or modern. This simplistic view of sex-role portrayal has been a useful start, but is limiting. For example, why are consumers with traditional sex-role orientations sometimes the most enthusiastic supporters of advertisements depicting non-traditional occupations? Clearly consumers respond to the attitudes and emotions symbolized in an advertisement and not just to the depicted occupations (Bartos 1982). We can go beyond simple categorizations of portrayed sex-roles by using the approach of the structural semiotician, Boris Uspensky (1973). Uspensky states that the viewer uses the structural elements of an artistic composition (the ad) to interpret the ideological perspective of the author (the advertiser). The author's ideological perspective or world view includes the author's attitudes toward men and women. The author's perspective may or may not be similar to the sex-role orientation of the focal character. To the extent that viewers respond to the ideological perspective of the author and not just the literal image of a focal character, it is important that we look at the totality of the advertisement and not just at the occupation of focal character when studying the portrayal of gender in advertisements.

Uspensky has outlined a detailed, technical approach to analyzing the author's perspective. This paper introduces this structural approach and shows how this approach provides a richer characterization of gender portrayal. Propositions are offered about the types of executional factors that contribute to gender portrayals.

FOR A CRITIQUE OF THE SOCIAL CONSTRUCTION OF GENDER IN ADVERTISING
Alladi Venkatesh, University of California, Irvine

Background

During the period dating from the mid-70's to early 80's, consumer researchers began to respond to the changing demographic forces by initiating some early studies on the role portrayals of women in advertising. The work of Courtney, Whipple, Belkaoui, and Wortzel, to mention a few, were primarily focused in this direction. A more generalized version of this theme (the changing roles of women) came under a broader inquiry within the field of marketing (not just advertising), as reflected in the works of Bartos, Debevec, Gentry, Iyer, Roberts, Venkatesh, McCall, Douglas and a few others. A major part of this work was motivated by the changing consciousness embedded in the social/political activism of the "women's movement." Although this was a vigorous start and promised to be an ongoing research stream, one of the shortcomings of the marketers' approach to the whole issue was that there was no particular theoretical framework driving their empirical work, nor did the results of their empirical work produce any noteworthy theoretical ideas for others to follow. Consequently, much of the work came to a halt, so to speak. The blame should not be attributed to marketers alone since the women's movement itself was first a social movement rather than an intellectual movement, and was very similar in its genesis and development to other movements such as consumerism, which also suffered a similar fate after the initial activism had died down. As Epstein (forthcoming) has noted, "The fact that the movement's appeal is based more on the strength of its own vision than any direct link to the daily concerns of existing communities gives it a certain fragility. A movement constructed almost entirely on the process of political action can easily dissolve."

A related aspect to this lack of theory in marketing literature, which limited genuine intellectual dialogue was the fact that the approach employed by consumer researchers was essentially based on an analytical-functional framework rather than a critical one. For example, it was argued that the best way to deal with the changing demographic scene was to coopt the essentials of the change tendencies into appropriately altered media representations and marketing practices. The sooner it was done, the argument went, the more effective the response. This, according to the critics, resulted in the problem of quickly turning an underdeveloped and underinvestigated concept into a questionable "praxis." (I use the term praxis in the Aristotelean sense of human conduct which has both practical and ethical implications, rather than in a Marxian sense of a synthesis between theory and practice.) The reason why this is termed a questionable practice is that if indeed one of the goals of the women's movement was (and still is) both freedom from media exploitation and true emancipation, the media, instead of participating in this process, raised the exploitation to another notch or moved it to a different arena. In other words, it was exploitation in a new form, or as Peggy Lee's sardonic ballad of disappointment asked the question, "Is that all there is?"

Much has been said and written in the last ten or fifteen years, and we are in a better position to understand the true nuances of women's movement and feminist ethos. We, as consumer researchers, can both look back and think forward in our analysis of the underlying issues, and this is really what this paper will attempt to accomplish.

Present Study

The purpose of this proposed paper is to describe feminist theory and its different interpretations in critical-historical terms, and use them as the basis for analyzing gender representation in media practices. Attention will be paid to different schools of feminism, which is not a monolithic concept. These schools can be classified as liberal, marxist, radical, psychoanalytic, historical, cultural/structural, existentialist, and postmodern. While there is some common agreement among different schools regarding the goals of the feminist movement, and some schools are closer to others in their overall configuration, there are differences in approaches and philosophical assumptions on gender construction and representation. Because of space limitations, the paper will not attempt an exhaustive account of the various developments in feminist theory, but will highlight important trends. I shall rely on representative contributions for elaborating various ideas. These will include the ideas of Mill, Friedan and Steinem (Liberal School), Boserup, Davis, MacKinnon (Marxist school), Dworkin, Jaggar, Millett, Rich (Radical school), Chodorow, Gilligan (Psychoanalytical school), Scott (Historical school), Ortner, Rosaldo (Cultural/Structural school), De Beauvoir (Existentialist school), Cixous, Fraser, Irigary, Kristeva (Postmodern school). For the purpose of this paper advertising is viewed here primarily as a representational system, a discursive practice, and a cultural discourse -- and only secondarily as an economic institution.

Some Basic Arguments

Recent developments in feminist theory have provided us with important distinctions between various terms such as, sex, sexuality, sex roles and gender. In the now famous 1964 issue of Daedalus, the term "gender" does not even appear in the index. But today, it is an all-encompassing term. Only a quarter of century ago both gender and sex were treated almost synonymously to signify the biological differences between men and women. In contemporary discourse, gender is understood as a cultural category which goes beyond the biologically based distinction between masculine and feminine, and refers to the social organization of the relationship between sexes in personal, institutional and socio-cultural terms. A discussion on gender cannot escape reference to such varied theoretical categories as sex (referring to a biological category), sexuality (referring to power relationships based on body as the focal socio-cultural category), sex-roles (referring to the social-psychologically based patterns of identity), mothering (referring to the psychoanalytical dimensions of reproduction and domesticity), division of labor (referring to the social-economic dimensions of work.) In sum, gender is a complex construction of the social system that defines the relationship between the two sexes. It must be understood in its historically rooted and culturally constructed context and not in the simplistic terms that consumer researchers have incorporated it into their work.

By providing a deeper understanding of gender construction, I hope to initiate a fruitful discussion on advertising images of both men and women in a critical/constructivist manner.

REFERENCES

Alreck, Pamela L., Robert E. Settle, Michael A. Belch (1982) "Who Responds to 'Gendered' Ads and How?", *Journal of Advertising*, Vol 2(2), April 25-32.

Barthel, Diane (1988), *Putting on Appearances: Gender and Advertising*, Temple University Press.

Bartos, Rena (1989), *Marketing to Women Around the World*, Boston: Harvard Business School Press.

_____ (1982), *The Moving Target*, NY: The Free Press.

Belkaoui, Ahmed, and Janice M. Belkaoui (1976), "A Comparative Analysis of the Roles Portrayed by Women in Print Advertisements: 1958, 1970, 1972," *Journal of Marketing Research*, Vol XIII, May, 168-172.

Courtney, Alice E. and Sarah W. Lockeretz (1971), "A Woman's Place: An Analysis of the Roles Portrayed by Women in Magazine Advertisements," *Journal of Marketing Research*, Vol 8, February, 92-95.

Courtney, Alice and Thomas Whipple (1983), *Sex Stereotyping in Advertising*, Lexington MA, Lexington Books.

Ferguson, Jill Hicks, Peggy J. Kreshel, Spencer F. Tinkham (1990), "In The Pages of Ms.: Sex Role Portrayals of Women in Advertising," *Journal of Advertising*, Vol 19(1), 40-51.

Gentry, James W., Mildred Doering, and Terrence V. O'Brien (1978), "Masculinity and Femininity Factors in Product Perception and Self Image," *Advances in Consumer Research*, Vol. 5, ed. H. Keith Hunt, Ann Arbor, MI: Association for Consumer Research, 326-332.

Gilly, Mary (1988), "Sex Roles in Advertising," *Journal of Marketing*, Vol 52, April, 75-85.

Goffman, Erving (1976), *Gender Advertisements*, NY: Harper/Colophon Books (Harper and Row Publishers).

Gould, Stephen J. (1990), "Sexual Significations and Consumer Lovemaps: New Directions in Improving Our Understanding of the Relationship Between Sexuality and Consumption," a special session at the 1990 Conference of the Association for Consumer Research, conference chairs: R.H. Holman and M. R. Soloman, October 1990, New York.

Kilbourne, Jeanne (1987), *Still Killing Us Softly*, Film. Available from J. Kilbourne, P.O. Box 385, Cambridge, Mass.

Lundstrom, William J., and Donald Siglimplaglia (1977), "Sex Role Portrayals in Advertising," *Journal of Marketing*, Vol 14, July, 72-79.

Lysonski, Steven (1985), "Role Portrayals in British Magazine Advertisements," *European Journal of Marketing*, Vol 19(7), 37-55.

Uspensky, Boris (1973), *A Poetics of Composition: The Structure of the Artistic Text and Typology of a Compositional Form*, translated by Valentina Zavarin and Susan Wittig, Berkeley: University of California Press.

Venkatesan, M. and Jean Losco (1975), "Women in Magazine Ads: 1959-71," *Journal of Advertising Research*, Vol 15, October, 51.

Venkatesh, Alladi (1985) *The Significance of the Women's Movement to Marketing*, NY: Praeger Publishers.

Wagner, Lowis and Janis B. Banos (1973), "A Woman's Place: Follow-up Analysis of the Roles Portrayed by Women in Magazine Advertisements," *Journal of Marketing Research*, Vol 10, May, 213-214.

Williamson, Judith (1978), *Decoding Advertisements*, London, Marian Boyars, Ch 2.

Affect and Consumer Behavior: Examining the Role of Emotions on Consumers' Actions and Perceptions

Mary T. Curren, California State University, Northridge
Ronald C. Goodstein, University of California, Los Angeles

ABSTRACT

The purpose of this paper is to provide a summary of a special topic session organized to address recent developments in affect research in consumer behavior.

OVERVIEW

Recent research in consumer behavior has illustrated that cognitive reactions alone cannot account for the total variance we find in response to marketing stimuli. Zajonc and Markus (1982), for instance, caution us that in attitude formation there is a significant interaction of both affective and cognitive reactions. From an applied perspective, several studies in the advertising area reveal that affective reactions play as large a role as cognitive reactions in determining advertising effectiveness. Therefore, it is important that marketers both understand and consider affective reactions in their strategic planning. This session extended the study of affect's influence on consumer behavior by examining its effects across several domains.

Four papers were presented in this session that examined the role affect plays with respect to consumers' attitudes and actions. The first two of these papers were extensions of prior research concerning affect and advertising effectiveness. They explored the issues of the contextual and temporal influences of affect on ad attitudes and recall, respectively. The third paper also examined a temporal issue, this one dealing with inconsistencies between expected and actual outcomes and how such inconsistencies influence the intensity of consumers' affective reactions. Finally, the fourth paper addressed affect's role within a specific behavioral domain; variety-seeking.

By way of a more detailed overview, the paper by Kamins, Sanft, and Kiesler explores how the affect one brings to an ad exposure influences recall and attitudes subsequent to that exposure. Contextual affective states, they find, are especially important when advertisers' goals are to change consumers' brand attitudes. The paper by Edell and Moore addresses how feelings might be cued at the point of purchase so that consumers can (re)form brand attitudes in the store. They compare these attitudes with those formed immediately after ad exposure and find that the intensity of one's emotional experience will dictate the degree to which the attitude can be recreated at a later point in time. The Meyers-Levy and Maheswaran paper looks at affect as a dependent variable. They examine how involvement and temporal distance will influence the degree of affective reactions to gaps between expected and actual outcomes. The last paper in this session, by Isen and Kahn, studies how positive affect encourages consumers to process incoming information with greater cognitive flexibility. This results in positive affect leading to subsequently higher variety-seeking behavior in non-risky choice scenarios and to lower levels of variety-seeking in the realm of risky choices. Taken together, these works explore and extend the role of affect in consumers' attitude formation, persuasion, and behaviors. More detailed abstracts of the papers provided by the authors are presented next.

ABSTRACTS

Context-Induced Mood Effects in Advertising
Michael A. Kamins, Henrianne Sanft, and Tina Kiesler
University of Southern California

The influence of consumers' moods upon their thoughts, memory and actions has recently become a topic of interest to consumer researchers. In Gardner's (1985) review of the literature in this area, she suggests that mood induced by media context may affect behavioral responses to advertising. Certainly this is a belief that is held by companies, as indicated by Coca Cola's corporate policy not to advertise on TV news because "there's going to be some bad news in there and Coke is an upbeat, fun product" (*Advertising Age* 1980).

The purpose of this study was to examine the influence of mood upon consumers' responses to an advertisement for a new product. Mood was induced by the editorial context (happy stories versus sad stories) that preceded a print ad. It was hypothesized that the feeling state of the consumers prior to exposure to the advertisement would influence their cognitive responses, attitudes toward the ad and the brand, and memory. Consumers who read happy stories were expected to feel happier (be in better moods) than those who read sad stories. It was expected that this would result in the recall of more favorable information when in a happy as opposed to a sad mood as well as in more positive cognition and more favorable ad and brand attitudes.

Results indicate that consumers do affectively respond to advertisements and the advertised brand in a manner consistent with their context-induced mood. However, consumers' mood at the time they observed the ad did not significantly influence the information that was remembered from the ad.

Emotional Intensity and Cue Type as Moderators of the Effect of Ad-Induced Emotions on Ad and Brand Evaluation
Julie A. Edell and Marian Chapman Moore
Fuqua School of Business, Duke University

In most advertising studies that investigate the effect of emotions on advertising effectiveness, subjects provide their reactions to ads immediately after seeing the ad. Even if the subject was in a delayed measurement condition, providing reactions up to a month after the initial exposure to the ad, the subject sees the ad again during the measurement setting. Consumers do not always form ad or brand evaluations immediately upon seeing an ad, however. Furthermore, in the "real" purchase or decision environment, the ad is not usually present to act as an explicit cue for the consumer. Research in other areas (Lichtenstein and Srull 1985) has shown that evaluations that are formed shortly after viewing a stimulus differ from those formed two days after viewing the stimulus.

It is important, therefore, to determine if the effect of emotions differs based on when the ad and brand evaluations are made. This study will investigate that issue. We expect that the intensity with which feelings are experienced during ad exposure will influence the nature of the impact of those feelings on ad and brand evaluations that are taken three or five days subsequent to viewing the ad. Further, we expect that the intensity of the feelings will be a function of ad characteristics that determine the relevance of the ad for the subject. These characteristics include features that determine how much the subject identifies with the ad features such as the characters in the ad, the setting of the ad, the music in the ad, the slice of life that is depicted in the ad, and so forth.

The experiment will also manipulate the type of cue that is used to retrieve previously experienced feelings. Keller (1987) has explored the role of cues in recall of brand information but the relationship between cues and feelings was not investigated. In this study we will use three types of cues that come from the ad: a picture of the product, a complete scene from the ad (which will be tested to assure that it captures the essence of the ad with respect to the characteristics that we think will affect the intensity of feelings), and the entire ad. We expect that the intensity of the previously experienced feelings will moderate the ability of the cue to bring the feelings "back to life." The results of this study will have important implications for the design of the purchase environment as well as for understanding how feelings influence choice. For instance, if the scene from the ad is better at eliciting previously experienced feelings than the picture of the product, then it might be effective to use the scene as an on-package cue, in a free-standing insert coupon, or as part of an in-store display.

Consumers' Emotional Responses to Unrealized Expectations and Variations in Temporal Distance
Joan Meyers-Levy, University of Chicago
Durairaj Maheswaran, New York University

Consumers often face inconsistencies between their expectations and reality. While the majority of the literature has focused on how such mismatches influence consumers' cognitive and memory related activities (Houston, Childers, and Heckler 1987; Meyers-Levy and Tybout 1989; Sujan 1985), such inconsistencies are also likely to engender fairly pronounced emotional reactions. For example, the time that separates expected outcomes and reality may influence the perception of the mismatch, as well as the magnitude of emotional responses.

Consider a man who, in honor of his anniversary, rushes at the last minute to buy a necklace his spouse has admired, only to discover that the necklace was sold a month ago. This consumer would likely have an emotional reaction to not being able to complete his planned purchase. Now compare his likely reaction to that of another man in a similar situation whose attempt to purchase the necklace is thwarted by a purchase only five minutes (versus the month) earlier. Research by Kahneman and Tversky (1982) and Miller and McFarland (1987) implies that the shorter, five minute temporal distance separating expectations and reality is likely to be perceived by most people as more extraordinary, incongruent, and unfortunate than the one month temporal distance. Thus, although both individuals may emotionally respond to their unexpectedly interrupted purchases, the latter individual may have a stronger reaction.

The purpose of this study was to determine why, how, and when variations in the temporal distance separating expectations and reality can affect consumers' affective or emotional responses. Subjects received a message that solicited funds for a charity and described a situation illustrating how the charity attempted to assist two needy children. All subjects received the same message except that in one condition, a short temporal distance separated the expected outcome from reality (e.g., a plan developed by the charity to help the children was invalidated just one day before it was to be enacted), whereas in a second condition, a long temporal distance separated expectations and reality (e.g., the plan was invalidated nine months before it was to be enacted).

Results revealed that when involvement with the message issue was low, subjects exhibited heightened emotional responses and were more persuaded to contribute funds to the charity when a short, rather than a long, temporal distance separated expectations and reality. However, when message involvement was high, subjects' emotional responses and persuasion were constant, regardless of variations in the temporal distance between expectations and reality. Cognitive response and recall measures provided support for the process hypothesized to mediate these findings.

Effects of Positive Affect on Variety-Seeking Behavior
Alice M. Isen, Cornell University
Barbara E. Kahn, University of Pennsylvania

The purpose of this research is to understand the influence of positive affect on variety-seeking in choice behavior. We define affect as feelings induced by commonplace events or circumstances rather than intense focused emotions; examples would include the kinds of things one feels as one goes about the activities of the day -- listening to music, receiving a compliment, finding a quarter in a phone booth. We define variety-seeking behavior as the deliberate tendency to switch away from the brand chosen on the last one or more occasions; thus, more switching in a choice history indicates more variety seeking.

Past research has shown that relative to subjects in control conditions, those in positive affect states notice more features of objects and are more flexible in the way they think about and organize information in non-risky situations. However, in risky situations in which the potential for real, meaningful loss is salient, subjects in positive affect conditions are more conservative in behavior or more averse to risk than control subjects.

We propose that positive affect influences brand choice behavior in an analogous way. In non-risky choice situations, where brands are familiar, subjects in positive affect conditions should notice and think about more features of each brand. The more features that are identified, the more stimulating a brand would seem and the more appropriate it would seem to be for different contexts. Thus, consumers in positive affect conditions should be more likely to switch among brands over time, or exhibit more variety-seeking behavior, than control subjects.

On the other hand, if a consumer's choice set includes some brands for which the consumer is uncertain about the quality, then subjects in positive affect conditions would become more risk averse and less likely to switch among brands than would subjects in control conditions. Thus, their behavior would appear more brand loyal than the behavior in the control conditions.

We conducted computer-based experiments which supported these hypotheses. In follow-up experiments, we investigate how these results are affected by strength of brand names and by the degree of prototypicality of the brands within the product category.

ACKNOWLEDGEMENT

The session coordinators thank Alice M. Isen of Cornell University for providing valuable comments as discussant.

REFERENCES

Gardner, Meryl Paula (1985), "Mood States and Consumer Behavior: A Critical Review," *Journal of Consumer Research*, 12 (December), 281-300.

Houston, Michael J., Terry L. Childers and Susan E. Heckler (1987), "Picture-Word Consistency and the Elaborative Processing of Advertisements," *Journal of Marketing Research*, 24 (November), 359-369.

Kahneman, Daniel and Amos Tversky (1982), "The Simulation Heuristic," in *Judgment Under Uncertainty: Heuristics and Biases*, eds. Daniel Kahneman, Paul Slovic and Amos Tversky, Cambridge: Cambridge University Press, 201-208.

Keller, Kevin Lane (1987), "Memory Factors in Advertising: The Effect of Advertising Retrieval Cues on Brand Evaluations," *Journal of Consumer Research*, 14 (December), 316-333.

Lichtenstein, Meryl and Thomas K. Srull (1985), "Conceptual and Methodological Issues in Examining the Relationship Between Consumer Memory and Judgment," in L. F. Alwitt and A. A. Mitchell (eds.), *Psychological Processes and Advertising Effects: Theory, Research, and Application*, Hillsdale, NJ: Erlbaum.

Meyers-Levy, Joan and Alice M. Tybout (1989), "Schema Congruity as a Basis for Product Evaluation," *Journal of Consumer Research*, 16 (June), 39-54.

Miller, Dale T. and Cathy McFarland (1986), "Counterfactual Thinking and Victim Compensation: A Test of Norm Theory," *Personality and Social Psychology Bulletin*, 12 (December), 513-519.

Sujan, Mita (1985), "Consumer Knowledge: Effects on Evaluation Strategies Mediating Consumer Judgments," *Journal of Consumer Research*, 12 (June), 31-46.

Zajonc, Robert B. and Hazel Markus (1982), "Affective and Cognitive Factors in Preferences," *Journal of Consumer Research*, 9 (September), 123-131.

Extending Innovation Characteristic Perception To Diffusion Channel Intermediaries and Aesthetic Products

A. Richard Petrosky, University of Arizona

ABSTRACT

An extension of Rogers' innovation characteristic framework is proposed that applies to aesthetic rather than utilitarian products as perceived by facilitators rather than consumers. Aesthetic products are defined as works of art, music, and fashion. Facilitators are defined as actors intermediate to producers and consumers in the diffusion channel who perform the functions of criticism and interpretation of the product. Facilitator-level evaluations of jazz and clothing fashion are examined, resulting in the discovery of supplementary categories: 1) legitimacy, defined as an assessment of the innovation with respect to the conventions of the product category, and 2) potential genrefication, defined as an assessment of the innovation in terms of ability to foster a genre within the broader domain of styles in the product category. Roger's complexity is reconsidered as having a curvilinear effect on adoption.

INTRODUCTION

Diffusion theory has garnered much attention in the consumer behavior literature and continues to be the focus of considerable research in the marketing discipline (Mahajan, et al. 1990). One area of diffusion research which has recently received less consideration by consumer researchers despite its obvious importance is the study of perceived innovation characteristics.

In their review of diffusion literature, Gatignon and Robertson (1985) find most of the innovation characteristics research either utilizing or confirming the taxonomy developed by Rogers (1962) relating relative advantage, compatibility, complexity, divisibility, and communicability of the product to its adoption. Rogers and Shoemaker (1971) compile the results of numerous studies which support the applicability of this taxonomy to a wide assortment of products, such as agricultural chemicals and commercial fertilizer, contraceptives, televisions, and new food products. But, as Gatignon and Robertson point out, little effort has been directed toward the establishment of a comprehensive classification scheme for innovations. Until this is accomplished it may be premature to call Rogers' scheme comprehensive.

Despite the enormous range of cases to which the Rogers scheme has been applied, the vast majority of perceptions analyzed have the final users of the innovation as their source, and innovations that are utilitarian as their object. One way to examine the comprehensiveness of the Rogers taxonomy is to apply the scheme to sources of perceptions other than final users and to objects of perception that are not utilitarian. This study explores the applicability of the Rogers taxonomy in this manner using two unusual sources of secondary data.

Commentary on jazz constitutes the first source, and clothing fashion commentary constitutes the second. These sources are used to ask two questions of Rogers' framework. First, can the framework account for the manner by which intermediary consumers -- critics and other information disseminators (e.g. "market mavens," Feick and Price 1987) - perceive innovations? Second, does the framework, presently applied only to utilitarian products, perform equally well with aesthetic innovations as the object of inquiry? The answer to these questions is a qualified "yes," provided modifications of the framework outlined in the later sections of this paper are undertaken.

In the following section, the available literature is briefly reviewed regarding a) innovation perception among non-consumers, and b) differences between aesthetic and utilitarian innovations. This is followed by a brief description of the method of the analysis, the resultant conceptual framework developed in the analysis, a comparison of the emergent scheme with the Rogers framework, and general conclusions for the present study.

Non-consumer perceptions. Mansfield (1967) investigates diffusion of innovations among producers, and elaborates a perception set not unlike what rogers has developed for end-consumers. Other literature indicates, however, that groups intermediate to producers and final users may have unique perceptions which will require new or modified taxonomies. Hirsch (1972) maintains that the invention and ultimate adoption stages have been the primary focus of diffusion researchers, while the influence of intermediaries is generally disregarded. This focus results in inadequate appraisal of the "throughput" sector, which is comprised of influential individuals and/or organizations which "filter the overflow of information and materials intended for consumers." For many members of this throughput sector, adoption (or non-adoption) is not necessarily an end state; instead they may seek to influence or facilitate the adoption decisions of others. Given this basic difference, the throughput sector may present an interesting opportunity to consider a class of innovation perceptions that cannot be comfortably accommodated by the Rogers taxonomy.

Aesthetic Innovations. A second class of innovation perceptions that may require further accommodations are perceptions of aesthetic, rather than utilitarian innovations. Aesthetic innovations can be defined as new products or product extensions in product categories which emphasize artistic value, such as art, music and fashion. Hirschman (1980) suggests that for many product classes, "objective, tangible attributes which a product possesses are dominated by the subjective, intangible attributes associated with it (p.11)." The existence of such product differences are well documented: Hirsch

(1972) explains that some products "serve an esthetic or expressive function" while others serve a "clearly utilitarian function". That there are particular products more likely to be experienced for their aesthetic rather than their utilitarian content - such as "Beverly Sills performances, Picasso paintings, Shakespearean sonnets, and Paul Desmond recordings" (Holbrook 1980, p.37)- has been noted in the consumer behavior literature (Holbrook and Hirschman 1982).

Moreover, the systems within which aesthetic products are propagated provide an example of a dense, dynamic throughput sector, as well as provide focal products which may differ from the utilitarian products evaluated in Rogers and Shoemaker. Becker (1982) identifies aesthetic systems as comprising many levels, including the producer and other influencer groups whose influence is felt well before the final user consumes. As Becker (1976) maintains, an inquiry into this area necessarily includes all who contribute to the end result:

> The people who conceive the idea of the work (e.g. composers or playwrights); people who execute it (musicians or actors); people who provide the necessary equipment and material (e.g. musical instrument makers); and people who make up the audience (playgoers, critics and so on)...(p.703-4)

All those described here - except for the playgoers - are members of the throughput sector. For the purpose of clarity, those who play any of these throughput roles will henceforth be referred to as *facilitators*. McCracken (1986) echoes the influential nature of these facilitators in his examination of the fashion system:

> It must be admitted that everyone in the diffusion chain plays a gatekeeping role and helps to influence the tastes of individuals looking for opinion leadership (p.77).

In sum, this study examines whether modifications to the scheme are required. The present research proceeds from the notions that 1) aesthetic content may so strongly influence the perceptions of some products that it may also significantly influence the way they are diffused, and 2) the different goals of facilitators relative to consumers or producers will influence the way they perceive innovations.

METHOD

As mentioned above, two sets of data were used for this study. The first of these was a collection of a recurring feature called "The Blindfold Test," which appeared in *downbeat* magazine, which primarily features articles on jazz. In each of these features, a well-known player of jazz is selected by critic Leonard Feather. This guest critic then listens to a number of jazz recordings selected by Feather, and comments on them without having been given any information on their source, hence the term "blindfold." The responses revolve solely around the recordings and generally include some type of rating and an attempt by the guest critic to identify the players. Along with the test responses, each article included a brief biography of the guest critic, communicating the "school" of jazz with which he/she was primarily identified. Approximately 200 articles were selected from the period of 1958-61; this period was selected for its relatively high incidence of innovative styles, which was reflected in the recordings chosen for the feature.

To extend and refine the concepts developed from the jazz data set, another data set was investigated - one containing evaluative responses to a different type of aesthetic product. In the spirit of purposive sampling (Lincoln and Guba, 1985), the choice of the second data set was made in order to achieve maximum variation sampling. The aesthetic product category chosen was clothing fashion, a category that is perceptibly different from jazz on a number of dimensions.

Clothing fashion and jazz are both product categories where taste and the discrimination of relative beauty bear greatly on perceptions. An alteration in design, an added feature, or the augmentation of an attribute in a refrigerator or a sewing machine will produce a predictable response: a more energy efficient design or enhanced capability in such a product will elicit a generally positive reaction. An augmentation in style, a revolution in presentation in music or fashion cannot hope to win such a universal badge of approval: while one sector may enthusiastically sing the praises of the latest modal musical transmogrification or laud the chic of a well-turned *chapeau*, there likely lies in wait another group to slander those same sounds and vilify the visor in vogue. By their nature, aesthetic products contain an element of mystery driven by the elusiveness of a generally acceptable criterion of beauty.

Yet there are differences between jazz and clothing fashion. The greatest of these differences is the physical limitation of innovation. Musical styles can and have varied wildly, constrained only by the imagination of their creators. Clothing fashion, on the other hand, must ultimately return to a particular function or purpose: covering and/or adorning the human body. Music has no restricting arms to ensleeve, no modesty to shield, few functional expectations. To the musical innovator, the "new" is virtually infinite; to the fashion designer, the available direction for flights of fantasy is noticeably finite.

The fashion data set includes approximately 100 articles drawn primarily from 1989 issues of *Women's Wear Daily*; in addition, all installments of the feature called "Designers on Designing" from its inception in January 1986 until May 1989 were included. Of the articles included, all contain evaluative comment from facilitators, some in the form of reviews of fashion shows, and some in the designer's own words.

As with utilitarian products, the definition of what constitutes an innovative aesthetic product is problematic. Degree of continuity - for new music as well as new culinary devices - is a socially negotiated quality. For both sets of data, an innovation is considered as a deviation at the stylistic level, as identified by the facilitators.

The research proceeded along the guidelines of the qualitative method of generating theory grounded in data as detailed by Glaser and Strauss (1967). Data were analyzed using the constant comparative method, identifying consistencies and divergences in the data, and developing categories to explain these. The analysis focused on the passages within the data set which involved perceptions of the characteristics and peculiarities of an innovation as perceived by the facilitator. Marginal notes were made on the language contained in the relevant passages, and content generalities were developed from these. From this point a pattern coding was developed using the data set. These codes expressed the major themes/categories contained in the facilitators' perceptions of innovation characteristics. With the coding complete, further comparison and contrast of items of particular code were done to reduce the large number of themes into a more focused, well-defined description of relevant categories. These hypothesized categories were then combined into a workable scheme.

This process was first applied to the jazz data set. The investigation continued until a set of categories which could account for the responses made with respect to the innovative compositions was developed. The process was then repeated with the fashion data set, with particular emphasis placed on determining the existence of the emergent categories and Rogers' categories within the responses, though remaining open to the possibility of discovering supplementary or competing categories.

ANALYSIS

Categories revealed in both sets of data. The following categories of innovation characteristics were identified in the jazz and fashion data sets:

1) Complexity -is the degree to which the style is difficult to understand or to execute.

Jazz data. Examples of commentary employing this characteristic include:

- They never got off the ground. But before I criticize any more, if I had to play it, I don't think I could play it either.
- I'm interested in execution of ideas as well as inspiration. And until such time as he gets his own playing and his group organized, then I can't take him very seriously.

In addition to comments regarding specific instances of style difficulty or the difficulty of understanding what the performer was attempting with the selection, there were other responses that suggested some selections were too simple:

- [Part] One sounded simple, kind of basic - you know,"two changes and everybody will remember it" kind of thing. I liked the second part- it swung.

The definition of complexity therefore requires further delineation with regards to a certain threshold level having been attained. Berlyne (1960) suggests there is an interaction of positive and negative aspects of complexity which leads to an inverted-U relationship between complexity and positive evaluation. Zuckerman (1979) reiterates this point and notes several studies which ascribe complexity preference to creative persons. Given this, a simple linear relationship between this "complexity" and adoption facilitation cannot be drawn.

Fashion data. As with the jazz data, the complexity of the particular style introduced in fashion contains an essential duality - something which is judged "too simple" can be regarded as uninteresting. At the same time, simplicity of an innovation can be seen as a virtue. The exact threshold at which simplicity transforms from bane to boon is indiscernible in the responses. Separate evaluations of the same innovation were not available to discern whether the judgment of the positivity or negativity of simplicity remained consistent across responses.

- Something that is simple is often successful because it appears that there are no problems involved. The surface may seem facile and spontaneous when, in fact, complex labor lies beneath it. The end result, however, looks like it just happened.
- All that richness is exactly what our customer will love - and there is the striking simplicity of the black statement.
- But when things get too flamboyant, it's like a drag show.
- He has already proved he's a surehanded designer, but he's strongest when he stays simple.
- Nice, but too many tricks.

2a) Legitimate Style Mechanics-is the degree to which the execution is done according to established tenets.

2b) Legitimate Style Derivation-is the degree to which the new style is derived from a legitimate precursor.

Jazz data. The following responses conform to the legitimate style mechanics characteristic category:

- The clarinet player got a good legitimate sound.
- It's most probably a classical player with a good feeling for jazz.

For the jazz data set, this refers to the actual playing of the instrument. Comments in this category often revolve around speculation on the extent and type of training the player(s) received, and whether that training conforms to what the guest reviewer deems as appropriate. Often a player was 'illegitimate' by not having mastered the subtler nuances of the instrument in a jazz sense: perhaps a young player who had not yet 'paid his dues,' or a crossover talent who had established a personal style in a non-jazz idiom. Responses which conform to the second category of legitimate style derivation include the following:

- Though it's a legitimate piece, it's somebody who has his roots in jazz who wrote this thing.
- It certainly isn't jazz. Is it supposed to be jazz?
- I don't believe *jazz* will move in the direction of the last record, but I believe people may be led to believe that kind of music is jazz.

This concept could also be seen as a preoccupation with classification:

- ...kind of West Coast sounding.
- It sounds New Yorkish to me.

This refers primarily to the composition, rather than the playing. As in the legitimate style mechanics section, there is concern with respect to the source of inspiration: is the composition jazz-inspired, or structured like a non-jazz musical idiom. A great deal of these comments center on a selection's adherence to core attributes of jazz, namely improvisational content and 'swinging' feel. Problems arise due to the inexact nature of these attributes' definition. As some performances become standard in a once-improvisational format, or as band size necessitates more rigid compositional structure, it becomes more and more difficult to delineate improvisational from non-improvisational (Berendt, 1975). Likewise, though swinging feel is often achieved by particular placement of emphasis on certain beats in a measure, there may be alternative means to develop this attribute. Thus the guest reviewer may also incorporate non-attribute comparison bases, by likening it holistically to 'successful' forerunner styles, or other current schools.

Fashion data. Legitimacy aspects of clothing fashion tend to cluster around two main themes: fashion is discussed in terms of where its inspiration is derived, and the manner in which the design is executed. These two themes map well onto the style derivation and style mechanics concepts, respectively, derived for the jazz response data. However, while these themes are prevalent in a wide variety of contexts, they are not consistently positively or negatively related to adoption or potential for diffusion. For example, while one designer may launch into a discourse on the legitimacy of adopting a current theme - from existing themes in fashion, previously popular themes in fashion, or themes taken from other aesthetic product categories - another may disfavor the use of thematic departure altogether. *Inspiration* was a strong theme throughout, and the source of the given inspiration was often outside the fashion world; for fashion innovation, this extends the perceived legitimacy of the precursor for the specific aesthetic product category to the general realm of aesthetic products.

- There's so much hype in the fashion industry today that anyone can come in off the street, pour 20 million into a company and call herself a designer. But those designers are a quick fix, a short-term thing. The companies which have longevity are those like Liz Claiborne that take a pragmatic approach to the industry.
- I don't work within themes. It's not like I go to a Picasso exhibit and then show a 'Calvin interprets Picasso collection.' I'm not designing costumes. I'm doing very real clothes for the modern woman.
- I think clothes have to have a sense of tradition. I don't design clothes to be thrown out after each season.
- ...there are times when ideas flow - inspired by magazines, movies, or as with last fall's silver collection, by an aluminum trash can...
- Sometimes I get on a theme kick. I'll base a group or a collection on a country I've been to or an exhibit I've seen. But the themes are for my benefit - you can't tell looking at the clothes what the theme was.

3) *Potential "Genre-fication"* -is the degree to which the style is not self-limiting and contributes to a broader domain of styles.

Jazz data. Unlike the legitimacy constructs, genrefication statements in the jazz data set do not center on the "jazziness" of the style, but rather on the potential contribution it can make to jazz as a broader domain of styles, how well it extends the overall constraints of the jazz idiom.

- I don't dig it myself, it doesn't sound good to me. I can't say anymore. It's an experiment to see how many changes in key they can get and how many odd progressions. Nothing happens, no rating.
- The style in playing is extreme, but it does show that there is more freedom to be taken advantage of than is as a rule. I think that in time to come there will be more freedom to be taken advantage of, but it will be used more musically.
- I have no objection to the harmonica in jazz - at least the way he plays it, it has very good potential.

- That internal doubling is good for some
  effects, but all the way through, it's not
  very effective. There's so much meat in his
  work, and he's definitely a shepherd.

These comments generally focus on whether the selection is an experiment too narrowly defined, or has genuinely interesting and variably replicable elements. For example, the building of a selection around an exotic time signature could be viewed as a 'trick,' something which would create one interesting piece of music but which would become too repetitious and uninteresting in subsequent use. On the other hand, composition with non-chromatic scales may be embraced as a variant on the usual method with the potential to be repeatedly used as a mechanism to create a body of related - but not overly similar - work.

Fashion data. As was the case in the jazz data set, the potential of an innovation to exist in many subtly different constructions is strong in the clothing fashion data set. Just as the jazz producer was concerned with the limitation of compositions that could flow from a particular style innovation, so is the clothing fashion designer concerned with the collection that derives from the innovation. A sidelight of this concept is the prevalent theme of editing in the fashion response set. Editing here refers to the process of delineating the final content of the collection: the collection is viewed as a coherent whole, and seems to have a traditional restriction on size, though this restriction is by no means well defined. Anything that detracts from this coherence or inflates it beyond traditional size must be extracted. From the responses, it seems very important that the collection stem from a core idea and the correctness of editing the collection reflects this.

- The funny thing is when I look back to the
  first complete collection I made, it was
  well thought out, it was right.
- There were some very good numbers here,
  but they got lost in a collection that veered
  in too many directions.
- I don't think the concept ever grew.
  Sprouse was doing the day-glo sixties the
  first time and he did the same thing the
  second time.
- I'm designing one wardrobe. Whether you're
  talking about a sable coat or a pair of
  jeans, it's one mindset.

In the same way that the jazz facilitator is aware of an innovation's latent potential to transcend its 'trick' and become the basis of a style, the fashion facilitator looks for the fashion innovation which does more than just solve a single problem in a particular collection. In the fashion set this potential is recognized in two ways: as the innovation's contribution to the coherence of one collection, as well as its ability to sustain nonrepetitive variations across successive collections.

Additional categories revealed in the fashion data set. Unlike the jazz data set, the fashion responses contained many instances of responses which could easily be categorized using some of the Rogers characteristics.

Relative Advantage- Designers and reviewers alike compared the functional aspects of using an alternative fabric and other similar advantage-based notions.

- I'm crazy about cold-weather quilting. It's
  the new answer to fur.

Compatibility- Designers spoke of appealing to a presiding taste among a particular audience, as well as a buyer who wanted to buy piece by piece to match their existing wardrobe. This is also seen in the incorporation of accessories.

- Once the collection has begun to take
  shape, her employees visit accessory
  showrooms to see what is available that
  season. "I will adapt the accessories for
  my collection," says Herrera, who buys the
  accessories used in her show.
- I don't do hosiery colors, or anything else,
  to complement other people's clothes.

Divisibility characteristics were not discovered in either set of data. Likewise, observability issues were not evident, potentially due to a high degree of observability common for all items in the product category.

DISCUSSION

The concepts developed for the jazz data are combined as a taxonomy of innovation characteristics for aesthetic innovations, and their suggested effect on facilitators' expedition of the adoption process. This model is represented by the single-lined boxes of the *Figure*. The additional categories from the Rogers' scheme which were necessary to complete the perceived characteristic set for the fashion data are represented by double-lined boxes.

Comparing the set of concepts to the generalized set of characteristics of Rogers (1962), it may be possible to find areas of agreement and isolate areas of extension for the aesthetic products which in turn could be tested on other aesthetic products for generalizability. Initially it should be recognized that the Rogers characteristic categories and those revealed from the analysis of the jazz data will necessarily influence different areas within the diffusion process. As Rogers' categories focus on the characteristics from the ultimate adopters' perspective, the categories are positioned as directly influential on adoption; the revealed categories, however, focus on the facilitator perspective and therefore the endpoint which is being influenced by the innovation characteristics is the facilitation of the process - interpretation, sponsorship, or whatever means available to the given facilitator -

FIGURE
INNOVATION CHARACTERISTICS FOR AESTHETIC PRODUCTS *

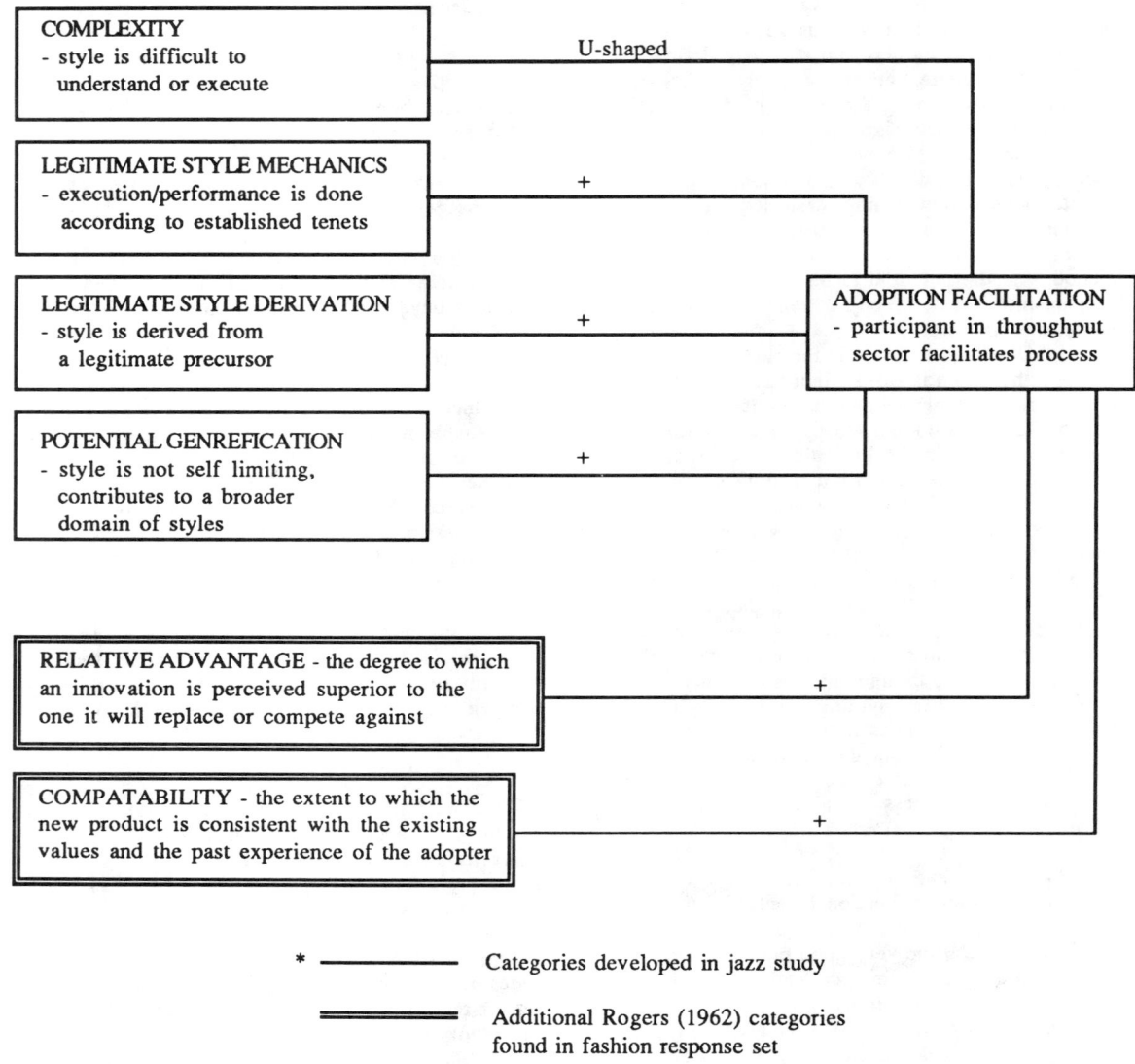

* ———— Categories developed in jazz study

═══ Additional Rogers (1962) categories found in fashion response set

rather than actual adoption. So while comparisons may be drawn between the two sets, such comparison should be done with the knowledge that the described effects of the characteristics are not precisely the same.

First of all, while the concept of complexity occurs in both schemes, a closer look reveals a potential difference. The relationship between complexity and facilitation in the revealed scheme does not appear to be a linear one, as is the case in the Rogers' scheme. It may very well be that a certain level of complexity is required by the facilitator, below which the innovation is uninteresting, but beyond which complexity has a negative correlation with the decision to facilitate adoption. Wallendorf, et al.(1980) suggest a similar relationship between complexity of fiction passages and enjoyment (positive evaluation).

Legitimacy seems to define much of the same territory as compatibility and the competition aspect of relative advantage, in so far as it places importance on adhering to existing principles and coexisting with other styles, respectively. But legitimacy evaluations are more likely to be subject to the associations and predilections of the particular facilitator - given there may be many facilitators with competing legitimacy rationales - while compatibility is a more physical/tangible property. Likewise, the superiority aspect of relative advantage would seem to map on that of genrefication in a very superficial way, since a negatively-evaluated genrefication potential would limit acceptability as a style of play. But genrefication evaluations highlight the potential of the innovation beyond its current incarnation, an aspect not incorporated in measures of relative advantage. Both legitimacy and potential genrefication operate at a more specific level than these Rogers scheme counterparts, and therefore contribute over and above what similarities they share with compatibility and relative advantage, respectively.

Furthermore, evidence of Rogers' trialability and observability is absent in the responses of both data sets. For trialability, the absence is of no concern since all samples were essentially triable in that they are available recordings or designs; likewise, observability has no alternate levels since consumption here is all public. So, while there is no evidence of either, this could be due to the collection method. Additionally, trialability may be a moot issue due to the level of those doing the assessment: facilitators are not necessarily adopters, and trialability may ultimately be tied to an adoption risk to which facilitators are not exposed.

CONCLUSION

The characteristic categories of complexity, legitimacy, and genrefication developed for the jazz data set were not sufficient for explaining what evaluations took place for the clothing fashion set; this second set required additional categories borrowed from the conventional characteristics described by Rogers (1962). It may be reasonable to assume that some mixture of the two category sets reflects a mixture of aesthetic and utilitarian elements. The first category of jazz could be classified as largely aesthetic, with little utilitarian content; the second aesthetic product category of clothing, while definitely incorporating an aesthetic element, could be regarded as a product category which exhibits significant functional/utilitarian aspects as well.

One outcome of this study is the notion that the perceived presence of aesthetic and utilitarian content in a given product category may be responsible for the type of evaluations to which it is subjected. Given this finding, it may be interesting to reevaluate the work of Tornatsky and Klein (1982), who, in their meta-analysis of innovation characteristic research, found significant relationships for complexity, relative advantage, and compatibility, but none with any consistency for trialability or observability. Likewise, Midgley (1987) reports largely insignificant findings across numerous innovation characteristic studies, and suggests further exploration of possible moderating factors between the characteristics and adoption. Perhaps these inconsistencies could be accounted for if the different products studied could be partitioned by their relative aesthetic and utilitarian content. As with the present study, the salience of the trialability and observability categories may be diminished for the highly aesthetic products.

One problem in drawing distinctions between products of primarily aesthetic nature and those of a functional nature is that of overemphasizing the difference. Technological advances, for example, may seem on the surface to be more easily and forthrightly evaluated than aesthetic innovations: a refrigerator with an ice-cube maker, for example, is an obvious improvement over one without, whereas a cubist painting has no obvious advantage over an impressionist one. This distinction, however, is a false one - the relative ease of evaluation in the first case is an artifact of the acceptance of the more-is-better orientation in modern Western societies (Veblen 1899). If we account for cultures who value simplicity and tradition, the evaluation of the technological advance is no more obvious than that for the aesthetic change.

The essential difference, then, is one of scale. The preference for change over tradition (or stagnation, depending on your point of view) tends to pervade at a societal level, whereas aesthetic choices exist at a more intimate level. Adherents to particular modes of aesthetic expression swim in schools: a romantic school, an impressionist school, a revisionist school, a neo-classicist school, ad infinitum. These schools will never develop the mass appeal of a societal norm such as the acceptance of technological change. Where Rogers is safe in predicting the positive and negative relationships of his innovation characteristics on adoption, he does so in describing the tendency of a *society* - the relationships may not be universally true, but their scope is large. For aesthetic innovations, the operative level is likely to be much smaller. The strongest adherents to school-specific views may more likely be found in the throughput sector than in the consumer sector, which necessitates further research into the impact of facilitator groups on diffusion.

In sum, there would seem to be promise in drawing aesthetic/utilitarian and facilitator/consumer partitions in the study of the diffusion of innovations. Further research should be done to distinguish the individual impact of aesthetic innovations as product category and facilitators as the perceiving group, which are confounded in the present study.

REFERENCES

Becker, Howard S. (1976), "Art Worlds and Social Types," *American Behavioral Scientist*, 19:6, pp.703-719.

———— (1982), *Art Worlds*, Berkeley: University of California Press.

Berendt, Joachim (1975), *The Jazz Book*, Westport, Connecticut: Lawrence Hill and Co.

Berlyne, D.E. (1960), *Conflict, Arousal, and Curiosity*. New York: McGraw-Hill Book Company, Inc.

Feick, Lawrence F. and Linda L. Price (1987), "The Market Maven: A Diffuser of Marketplace Information," *Journal of Marketing*, 51 (January), pp.83-97.

Gatignon, Hubert and Thomas S. Robertson (1985),"A Propositional Inventory for New Diffusion Research," *Journal of Consumer Research*, 11 (March), pp.849-867.

Glaser, Barney and Anselm L. Strauss (1967), *The Discovery of Grounded Theory :Strategies for Qualitative Research*, Chicago: Aldine.

Hirsch, Paul M. (1972), "Processing Fads and Fashions: An Organization-Set Analysis of Cultural Industry Systems," *American Journal of Sociology*, 77 (January), 639-659.

Hirschman, Elisabeth C. (1980), "Attributes of Attributes and Layers of Meaning," in Kent Monroe (ed.) *Advances in Consumer Research*, Vol. 7, Ann Arbor, MI: Association for Consumer Research.

Holbrook, Morris B. (1980), "Introduction: The Esthetic Imperative in Consumer Behavior," in *Symbolic Consumer Behavior*, E.C. Hirschman and M.B. Holbrook (eds.). Ann Arbor: Association for Consumer Research.

——— and Elizabeth C. Hirschman (1982), "The Experiential Aspects of Consumption: Consumer Fantasies, Feelings, and Fun," *Journal of Consumer Research*, 9 (September), pp.132-140.

Lincoln, Yvonna S. and Egon Guba (1985), *Naturalistic Inquiry*. Beverly Hills: Sage Publications.

Mahajan, Vijay, Eitan Muller and Frank M. Bass (1990), "New Product Diffusion Models in Marketing: A Review and Directions for Research," *Journal of Marketing*, 54 (January), pp.1-26.

Mansfield, Edwin (1967), *The Economics of Technological Change*, New York, NY: W.W. Norton and Co.

McCracken, Grant (1986),"Culture and Consumption: A Theoretical Account of the Structure and Movement of the Cultural Meaning of Consumer Goods," *Journal of Consumer Research*, 13 (June), pp.71-84.

Midgley, David (1987), "A Meta-Analysis of the Diffusion of Innovations Literature," in M. Wallendorf and P. Anderson (eds.) *Advances in Consumer Research*, Vol. 14, Provo, UT: Assoc. for Consumer Research.

Rogers, Everett M. (1962), *Diffusion of Innovations*, New York: The Free Press.

———, and Shoemaker, Floyd F. (1971), *Communication of Innovations*, New York: The Free Press.

Tornatsky, L. G. and R. J. Klein (1982), "Innovation Characteristics and Innovation Adoption-Implementation: A Meta-Analysis of Findings." *IEEE Transactions on Engineering Management*, EM-29, pp.28-45.

Veblen, Thorstein (1899,1931), *The Theory of the Leisure Class*, New York, NY: The Modern Library.

Wallendorf, Melanie, George Zinkhan, and Lydia Zinkhan (1980),"Cognitive Complexity and Aesthetic Preference," *Proceedings of the Conference on Consumer Esthetics and Symbolic Consumption*, E.C. Hirschman and M.B. Holbrook,eds.; Ann Arbor: Association for Consumer Research.

Zuckerman, Marvin (1979). *Sensation Seeking: Beyond the Optimal Level of Arousal*. Hillsdale, NJ: Lawrence Erlbaum Associates, Publishers.

The Nature of Communication Networks Between Organizations Involved in the Diffusion of Technological Innovations

David F. Midgley, Australian Graduate School of Management
Pamela D. Morrison, Australian Graduate School of Management
John H. Roberts, Australian Graduate School of Management

ABSTRACT

This paper examines the nature of the communication networks that exist between organizations involved in the adoption of technological innovations. We investigate the impact of differing network topologies and alternative models of social contagion on observed adoption patterns. We do this both by means of an empirical field study and a simulation model. The preliminary evidence given here supports the work of previous authors in suggesting that departures from commonly held assumptions about network structure may be the rule, rather than the exception. Our findings from the simulations suggest that such departures can have a substantial effect on the shape of the diffusion curve and supplier strategies to influence it.

INTRODUCTION

The networks of interpersonal communications that link organizations adopting technological innovations are of considerable economic and social importance. The operation of these networks can have a significant impact on observed adoption patterns - even to the extent of determining the success or failure of an innovation. This applies particularly to industrial markets where mass marketing techniques are less prevalent and often substantial technical information is necessary to evaluate the benefit of an innovation. Network communications leading to contagion effects in industrial marketing include requests for advice, site visits, and casual conversations. Despite the importance of such communications there have been few recent studies of industrial networks, and moreover the literature that does address this topic does not reflect current thinking on innovation.

The purpose of this paper is twofold. First, we contrast current thinking on the diffusion of innovations with a seminal paper on industrial networks. We use this contrast to suggest an agenda of three research questions regarding network process and structure. Second, we present preliminary findings from two pilot studies. The first is a field study of communication networks within one industry - designed to establish whether the phenomena we discuss do exist. The second study is a simulation model which allows us to assess the impact of these phenomena on adoption patterns.

THE NATURE OF INNOVATION NETWORKS

The marketing discipline has long recognized the significant role of interpersonal communication in the diffusion of innovations. In their recent review of diffusion, Gatignon and Robertson (1985) advance interpersonal communication networks as one of the key elements of the diffusion process. Despite recognition of its importance little research effort has been devoted to investigating interpersonal communication - particularly with respect to the structure of communication networks (one exception being Reingen et al 1984). Equally, most of this prior research is concerned with innovations in consumer products rather than industrial innovations. Indeed, since the pioneering work of Czepiel in the 1970's almost no effort appears to have been devoted to industrial networks.

Czepiel (1975) studied interpersonal communication networks relating to the adoption of continuous casting techniques within the US steel industry. Using sociometric techniques he found some support for his hypothesis that this industry formed an identifiable social community. Contrasting Czepiel's methods with the conceptual developments that have occurred since 1975 suggests at least three areas where there is potential for more sophisticated research approaches.

First, Czepiel's network maps were constructed on the basis of respondents nominating other organizations with which they had "regular advice/opinion relationships". Such a definition narrows our view with respect to the messages concerning a specific innovation, implying a rigid and deterministic view of the diffusion process which has been questioned in subsequent years (Gatignon and Robertson 1985). A potential adopter may only activate a small part of his regular (pre-existing) network and may also perceive a need to create new links to other members of the population with whom he or she has no regular contacts. The possible linkages between two organizations in a network are detailed in Table 1.

Second, and in common with much of the marketing and diffusion literature, Czepiel assumes that interpersonal influence is transmitted directly by communication between adopters and potential adopters. While this is a commonsense assumption, it has subsequently been brought into question by the debate over the "cohesion" and "structural equivalence" models in the sociological literature. The cohesion model makes the traditional assumption that influence is passed directly from adopters to potential adopters during discussions on the merits of the innovation. On the other hand the structural equivalence model stresses competition between people of similar status and roles within a social structure. That is, the more attractive the adoption of an innovation makes one person to the rest of their social contacts, the more likely is a person of similar status also to adopt. Awareness is spread via third parties or by observation. In his re-

TABLE 1
Possible Links Between Two Organisations with Respect to Adoption of A Specific Innovation

		Are Existing General Network Links in Place?	
		YES	NO
Is there communication for the specific innovation?	YES	Activating The General Network	Generating New Links
	NO	Area of No Perceived Relevance	Disconnected Population

TABLE 2
NETWORK POSSIBILITIES

	Mainly Inter-Industry	Mainly Intra-Industry
Regular Communication Network	General Structural Equivalence	General Social Cohesion
Innovation Specific Network	Idiosyncratic Structural Equivalence	Idiosyncratic Social Cohesion

analysis of the classic Coleman, Katz and Menzel (1957) study Burt (1987) found more support for the structural equivalence model than for the cohesion model.

In many ways the structural equivalence model seems more relevant to a competitive industrial setting than the more commonly assumed cohesion model. In such a setting there may be strong norms restricting direct communication, particularly if the innovation provides a significant competitive advantage to the adopter. Czepiel took the social cohesion view of diffusion and therefore concentrated only on communication links between companies within the industry. While this view may have been legitimate for an innovation such as continuous casting, many innovations have wider relevance and cross industry boundaries; for example, personal computers, facsimile machines, and cellular telephones. For these innovations messages may not be confined to sources originating within the industry and may well come from a variety of sources outside the industry. Equally the more competitive an industry the more likely are members of it to turn to outside sources. Examples of structural equivalence communications in the industrial setting would include information from (and to) suppliers, customers, consultants or industry groups. These communications might be formal advice, casual conversations or direct observations. Such indirect communications would be emphasized under the structural equivalence view of the process rather than under the social cohesion perspective. Table 2 illustrates the possible extremes of structural equivalence/social cohesion models and regular network / innovation specific network structures. A continuum of possibilities along either axis is possible.

The nature of these links is important both from the perspective of modelers who wish to write equations describing the dynamics of diffusion, and from the perspective of marketing strategists who wish to target promotional campaigns in an effective manner. Most existing diffusion models assume direct contact between "innovators" and "imitators" and homogeneous mixing of the population. This corresponds to a special case of the General Social Cohesion cell in Table 2. This model is also the one assumed by Czepiel (1975). For marketing strategists structural equivalence implies more subtle social cues to adoption behavior and therefore more sophisticated promotional campaigns.

Essentially all the research questions raised so far are also bound up with the topology of the communication network for a specific innovation. This being the case it is instructive both to outline Czepiel's findings with respect to topologies and to make some suggestions about future research.

Czepiel (1975, p15) identified two cliques which had significantly different firm characteristics but were connected through a small number of links or "bridges". The implication of findings such as these is that we cannot automatically assume perfect mixing of the population in a given diffusion situation. A network with two cliques linked through a small number of organizations may well display different patterns of diffusion to one in which all members are linked to all other members, as is assumed by most quantitative diffusion modelers.

In summary we have raised three research questions which we consider important to the way in which network structure could impact upon the industrial innovation diffusion process, namely:

* Do messages about the innovation flow primarily through the regular communication channels or through networks specific to individual innovations?

* Is cohesion (direct communication with adopters) or structural equivalence (influence inferred via indirect relationships to others) a better explanation of observed adoption patterns?

* What impact do different network topologies have on the rate and patterns of diffusion?

Given the scarcity of marketing network studies this is a difficult research agenda. Here we report the findings from two pilot studies which point to the extent of problems of the dominant perfect mixing paradigm and suggest ways in which they can be addressed. With these two studies we essentially first ask whether the conditions of social cohesion, regular network structures and absence of cliques assumed by most diffusion modelers do actually pertain in a real setting. We then assess the implications of departures from these three assumptions on a typical model of industrial diffusion.

EMPIRICAL METHODOLOGY

To examine the prevalence of different types of network structure and process we selected the Australian life insurance industry. With 32 major companies this industry is large enough to provide for interesting network topologies and the companies are easily identifiable for research purposes. The innovation we chose to investigate was facsimile machines; a technology which has primarily been adopted in the last 3 years. The respondent was the senior manager in charge of communications and the questionnaire was administered by mail with a telephone follow-up. Respondents were first asked to name all those organizations with which they had regular discussions regarding telecommunications technology, and to indicate the organization type of each contact. Each respondent was also asked a similar question but in the context of communications specially concerning facsimile.

STUDY ONE: EMPIRICAL NETWORKS

Survey Response

17 out of 32 major life insurance companies responded to our survey. As this sample represents over 80% of industry turnover and the vast majority of industry potential for facsimile machines we feel that it is adequate for our purposes here.

Structure of the Intra-Industry Network

In Figure 1 we present a network diagram of all the regular communication links between the 17 life insurance companies in our sample (including links to companies not included in the survey). In the diagram the companies are arrayed around the circumference of the circle and the nominated communication links are represented by the connecting lines. As can be seen in Figure 1, there are three companies (nodes) who had more extensive links to other organizations (A, B and C). However, the general pattern is for most life insurance organizations to have relatively few links to other members of the industry. Indeed while each company could have links to all others (the 32 top companies were listed, together with an "other" category), the average in this industry is 5.2 (or 3.1 excluding the three major nodes), representing a 16% connected network.

Also of note in Figure 1 is that the three major nodes are linked to each other, and that most other organizations are linked to at least two of these nodes. In contrast to Czepiel's findings for the US steel industry there is little evidence of a clique structure in the Australian life insurance industry. Rather we have a pattern of strong opinion leadership. So, like Czepiel, we can not support the assumption of a completely connected network.

General Versus Innovation Specific Networks.

In Table 3 we present an analysis of the communication links that assisted the diffusion of facsimile machines. As can be seen in the table both regular and new links were activated during the diffusion of facsimile machines. Across the sample about 60% of the pre-existing or regular links were activated for this innovation (17.4% out of 29.2%). However, new links equivalent in number to about 40% of the regular links were also established (6.9% versus 17.4%). Overall we can see that, at least for this industry and innovation, communications were transmitted through both regular and innovation specific links.

In addition to their general communication links with other insurance companies, respondents were also asked to list links with other organizations (including outside companies, consultants, suppliers, overseas companies, and

FIGURE 1
Intra-Industry Networks

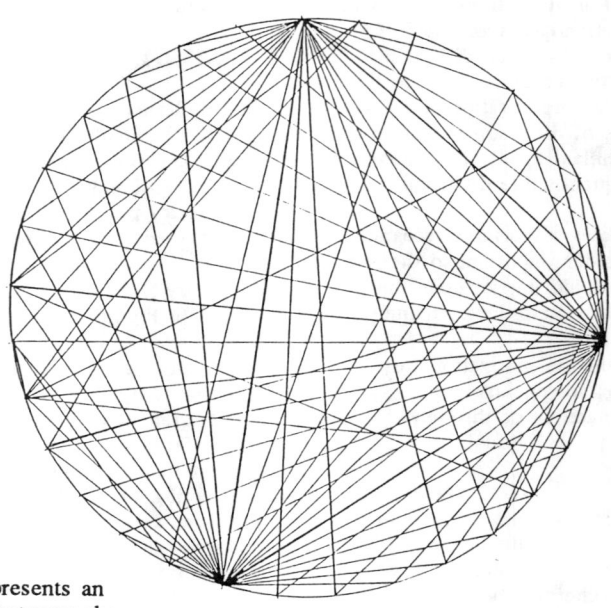

Each point on the circle represents an insurance company. Lines between the points represent regular communication links between two organizations.

TABLE 3
NETWORK LINKS

	Linked For General Communication	Not Linked For General Communication
Links Used For Facsimile	17.4%	6.9%
Links Not Used For Facsimile	11.8%	63.9%

government and professional bodies). Preliminary qualitative research showed that customers (insurance brokers) were not a source of information about telecommunications innovations, nor did they arise during the survey. In the general communication networks there were 90 links between respondents and other insurance companies, while there were 56 with organizations external to the industry. That is, approximately one third of the companies' links are of a structural equivalence type and two thirds are of a social cohesion type.

However, those statistics relating to regular networks understate the role of outside companies in the communication process with respect to the facsimile innovation. Many of the new links formed are external to the industry, while of the pre-existing, intraindustry links only a minority are activated. Table 4 presents a breakdown of network links used by the 17 respondents, both internal and external to the life insurance industry. (Suppliers have been omitted from the table as outside organizations because all respondents reported seeking advice from them. To include them would

TABLE 4
LINKS USED BY RESPONDENTS FOR FACSIMILE EVALUATION

		Intra-Industry Links Used?		
		YES	NO	TOTAL
Links External to the Industry Used (excluding suppliers)?	YES	3	7	10
	NO	1	6	7
	TOTAL	4	13	17

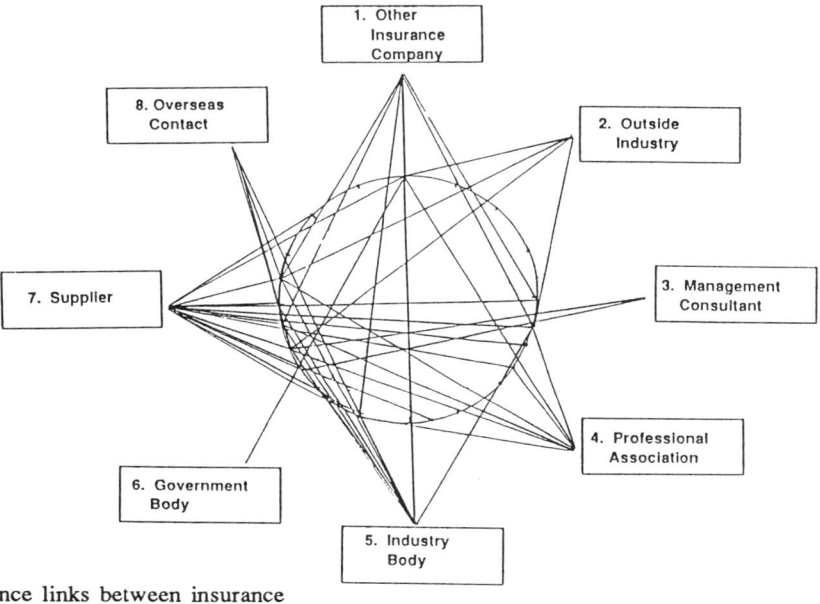

FIGURE 2
General Networks

Structural equivalence links between insurance companies (on large circle) and outside organizations for regular communications

further reinforce the role of external organizations.) It may be seen that network links external to the industry are employed by 10 of the 17 respondents, while internal links are used by only 4. Only one respondent relied solely on word of mouth from within the industry. However, we do see both forms of communications in evidence. It is therefore possible that both the structural equivalence and social cohesion processes were operative during the diffusion of this innovation.

In Figures 2 and 3 we display the details of these external links in the form of inter-industry network diagrams (links between insurance companies not being shown). In the diagrams we can see the heavy reliance on suppliers, removed from Table 4. Presumably suppliers are a primary but biased source of product information while the other companies are less biased but not as informed.

THE SIMULATION MODEL

To examine the effect of departures from perfect mixing on the diffusion curve we developed a model of industrial diffusion which we could adjust to reflect these changes. With a product category such as facsimile machines we have a diffusion process within the organization. That is, the organization initially adopts a few machines and progressively buys more until it reaches some saturation level. This intra-organizational diffusion process is occurring at one level. At another level there is a related inter-organizational diffusion process whereby the adoption of facsimile technology by one company leads to its adoption by others. We can use simulation to study the effects of different network structures on both diffusion processes.

The model we use for intra-organizational diffusion is the same as that applied by Bass (1969) although our interpretation is somewhat different.

FIGURE 3
Networks Used for Adoption of Facsimile

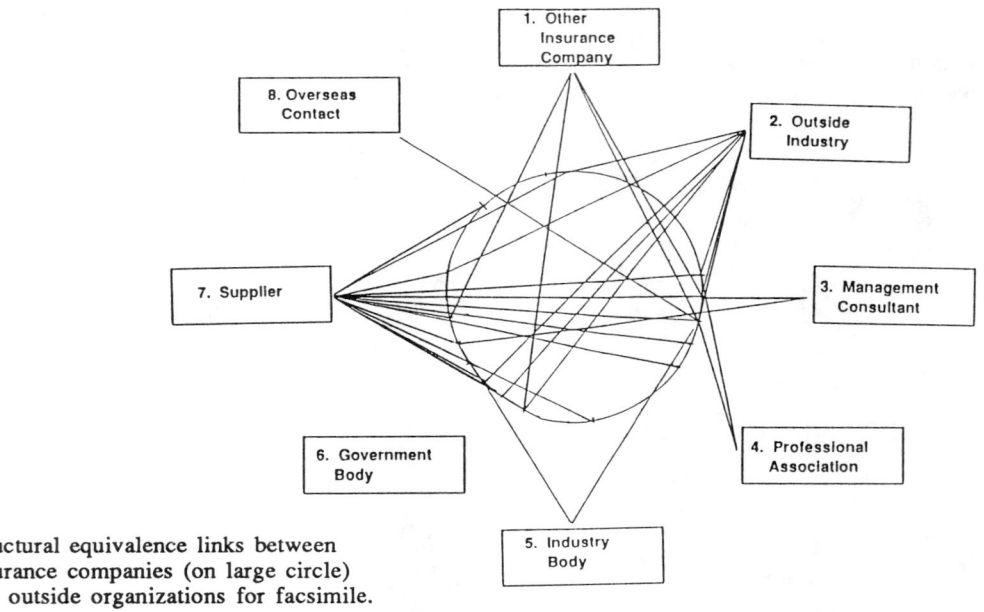

Structural equivalence links between insurance companies (on large circle) and outside organizations for facsimile.

We regard the individual organization i as the population throughout which facsimiles are diffusing. The change in penetration during time t, S_{it}, is given by

$$S_{it} = (p_{it} + q_i * Y_{i,t-1}/m_i) * (m_i - Y_{i,t-1}) \quad \text{for } t > t_{i0}$$
$$= 0 \quad \text{for } t < t_{i0}$$

where Y_{it} = level of cumulative sales to organization i
p_{it} = coefficient of external influence
q_i = coefficient of internal influence
m_i = organizational potential for innovation
t_{i0} = Time of initial adoption

The coefficient of external influence, p_{it}, will depend on the organization's environment and its connectedness to that environment, as well as organizational traits unrelated to its current level of adoption. Under the cohesion model it will vary directly with the penetration of the innovation in other organizations, while under the structural equivalence model it will depend on communications with bodies related to the industry who in turn will draw their information from early adopters in this and other industries. Under both scenarios, as the external environment adopts the innovation the pressure on organization i will increase, so p_{it} will be monotonic increasing in the penetration levels of the various other companies within the market. At time $t=t_{i0}$ (when $Y_{it}=0$) $p_{it_{i0}} * m_i$ gives the level of trial at the time of adoption. The degree of lead, t_{i0}, enters the market penetration equation not only in determining how soon an organization becomes an adopter and thus starts purchasing, but also in generating inter-organizational influences through the network.

The coefficient of external influence may be modeled as a function of the cumulative penetration of other organizations within the industry. Thus we may write:

$$p_{it} = p'_{it} + p''_{it} * \Sigma (d_{ij} * e_{ij} * Y_{j,t-1})$$

where p'_{it} = coefficient of influence external to industry
p''_{it} = coefficient of industry influence
d_{ij} = 1 if i and j are linked in the network, 0 otherwise
e_{ij} = effectiveness of the link between i and j

p'_{it} will change with communication levels about the innovation from outside the industry. In general it will initially increase as consultants and suppliers, for example, move to exploit the growing industry market. p''_{it}, the effect of intra-industry word of mouth may also be dynamic. It is

FIGURE 4
The Effect of Communication Links

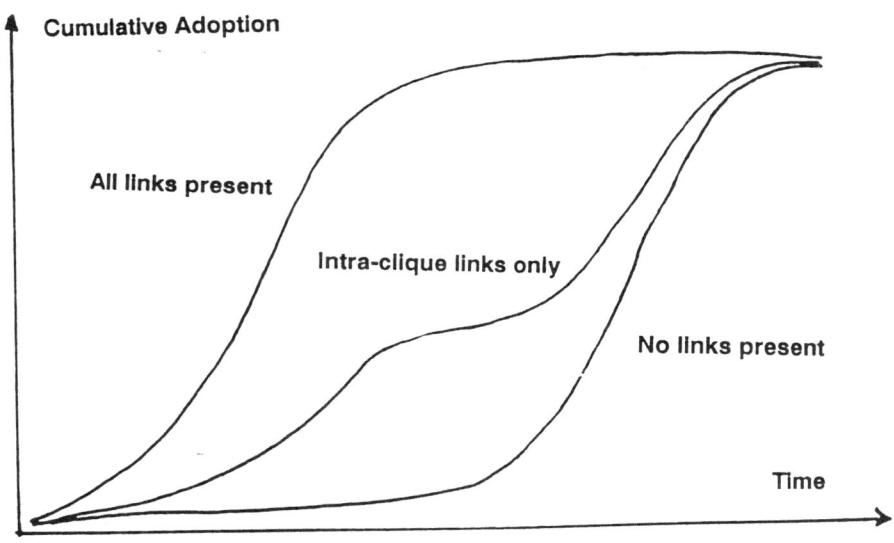

interesting to examine the implications of regular versus innovation-specific links and social cohesion versus structural equivalence on the above model of intra- and inter-organizational diffusion. This we do by changing the assumptions and model structure to match each hypothesis. For example, if communication links are enduring across innovations then we would expect exchanges of information to occur soon after organizations gain experience. If they are innovation-specific then we would expect to see a lag in the establishment of the link. That is, if organizations i and j have no regular communications it is reasonable to surmise that it will take i longer to realize that he has something to learn from j. Under the model of social cohesion we would expect influence external to the industry (p'_{it}) to be small relative to influence internal to the industry (p''_{it}). Under the model of structural equivalence we would expect (p'_{it}) to be large relative to (p''_{it}).

STUDY TWO: SIMULATION RESULTS

In this section we look at standard network topologies and process assumptions to see if the simulation model can shed insight into the effect of differing innovation networks on the diffusion of innovation. We start with 30 firms in a hypothetical industry. We assume them to be of equal size and distributed equally amongst three cliques. In each simulation we assume that there is one innovator in this market. This firm has a 10% penetration of the innovation at the beginning of the simulation but in every other respect all firms are equal. This limited scenario allows us to contrast the results of different network structures on aggregate diffusion patterns. A more complete set of network structures would allow a correspondingly richer set of diffusion patterns.

The Envelope of Diffusion Feasibility

In the first scenario we assume no communication between organizations. For all but the seeded firm (firm 1 in clique 1) penetration is slow and in fact would not occur if we did not include a small time trend in the coefficient of innovation external to the industry (p'_{it}), representing increasing pressure from suppliers and other related organizations. The aggregate result of this "no links present" scenario is shown in Figure 4. This can be contrasted with the second scenario where all members of all cliques communicate with each other (a complete network, shown as "all links present"). Because the lower curve represents the minimum rate of diffusion (associated with no communication) and the upper curve represents the maximum rate (with total communication), any intermediate (incomplete) network structure will lead to a diffusion pattern falling within the area bounded by these two curves. Thus we call the area the envelope of diffusion feasibility. Also included in Figure 4 (as "links within cliques only") is the diffusion curve associated with a network in which there is intra-clique communication, but no inter-clique communication. Although we do not show this here a link between, say, a member of clique 1

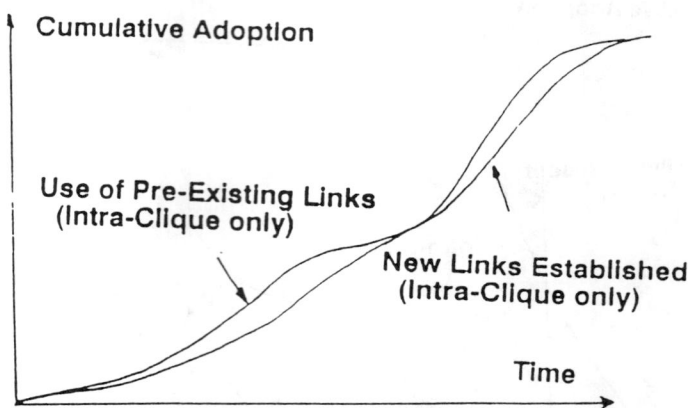

FIGURE 5A
Effect of Lags in the Communication Process
(Existing Versus New Links)

and clique 2 greatly accelerates the penetration rate of clique 2, leaving clique 3 being slow to start. Multiple links between cliques obviously speed the innovation process further and can change the trajectory of penetration at the aggregate level. A more detailed description of these simulations and an introduction to the concept of network efficiency may be found in Midgley, Morrison and Roberts (1990).

To examine the effect of establishing new links for a specific innovation relative to using pre-existing ones we can introduce a lag into the communication system, representing the time that it takes to establish a link specifically for that innovation. If we look at the resultant diffusion pattern relative to the previous simulations we see that the lag in hearing about the lead of another firm and the delay in establishing links with it, slow down the diffusion process considerably, both in the penetration of clique 1 and then later in the penetration of cliques 2 and 3. This is shown in Figure 5a.

Social Cohesion Versus Structural Equivalence

To compare the social cohesion models we have examined so far to a structural equivalence model we assume there are no intra- or inter-clique links. Rather there are links to a new group of outside organizations (consultants, suppliers, or other groups external to the industry) and that these feed information back into the industry. We also assume that links from industry organizations to these third parties are less effective than intra-industry links, since they describe an environment in which organizations try to protect knowledge about the competitive advantage of an innovation. Links from third parties to other firms within the industry are assumed to be highly efficient because third party organizations have a vested interest in promoting the information they have managed to acquire, either because it will aid in their sales (suppliers) or because that is their function (consultants). If we contrast this network to one with a series of weak inter-organizational links (a complete network) we can see that for networks that are of the same average effectiveness the social cohesion network is more effective early in the diffusion process, while the structural equivalence model gives stronger communication support after the point of inflection. These results are shown in Figure 5b.

SUMMARY AND FINDINGS

The results which we have presented have implications for researchers studying the diffusion process and for managers attempting to direct it. For researchers, the simulations we present above indicate that network structure can have a significant impact on the diffusion process. Of particular relevance here are our findings on the impact of (i) lags in establishing network links, and (ii) asymmetrical effectiveness in network links to third parties. Lags may not only slow down the diffusion curve but also alter the rate at which the innovation is adopted by various cliques. Asymmetrically effective network links can lead to a slower take-off but faster finish to the diffusion process. Such asymmetries would be expected under the structural equivalence model rather than the social cohesion model.

The preliminary evidence from our empirical pilot study suggests that such innovation specific and structural equivalence effects may well arise. We found clear evidence of organizations establishing new (innovation specific) links as well as organizations activating pre-existing links. A substantial proportion of these links were to organizations outside the life insurance industry. For managers, networks with cliques or highly

FIGURE 5B
Societal Cohesion Versus Structural Equivalence

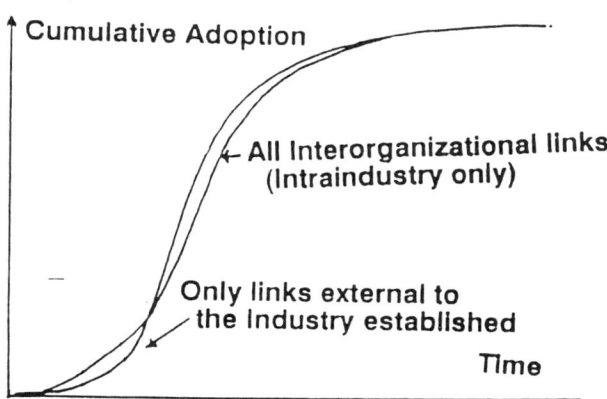

connected opinion leaders call for directed targeting strategies to ensure that there are not pockets of laggards due to communications isolation and communication occurs as rapidly as possible. The value of seeding individual organizations can be estimated using this modeling approach (see Midgley, Morrison and Roberts 1990 for details).

In conclusion, we have suggested that the effects discussed in this paper can have an important impact on the diffusion process. By our pilot study (as well as drawing on the work of others) we have provided evidence that these effects exist in some situations. In the future we would hope that diffusion researchers will at least test for the presence or absence of clique structures, innovation specific links and influence via structural equivalence before assuming perfect mixing. Alternatively, they should test the sensitivity of their models to such phenomena.

REFERENCES

Bass, Frank M. (1969), "A New Product Growth Model for Consumer Durables," *Management Science*, 15 (5), 215-227.

Burt, Ronald S. (1987), "Social Contagion and Innovation: Cohesion versus Structural Equivalence," *American Journal of Sociology*, 92 (May), 1287-1335.

Coleman, James S., Elihu Katz and Herbert Menzel (1957), "The Diffusion of an Innovation Among Physicians," *Sociometry*, 20 (December), 253-270.

Czepiel, John A. (1975), "Patterns of Interorganizational Communications and the Diffusion of a Major Technological Innovation in a Competitive Industrial Community," *Academy of Management Journal*, 18, 1(March), 6-24.

Gatignon, Hubert and Thomas S. Robertson (1985), "A Propositional Inventory for New Diffusion Research," *Journal of Consumer Research*, 11 (March), 849-867.

Midgley, David F., Pamela D. Morrison and John H. Roberts (1990), "The Effect of Network Structure in Industrial Diffusion Processes," Working Paper Number 90-019, Australian Graduate School of Management, University of New South Wales, Kensington, NSW

Reingen, Peter H., Brian L. Foster, Jacqueline Johnson Brown and Stephen B. Seidman (1984), "Brand Congruence in Interpersonal Relations: A Social Network Analysis," *Journal of Consumer Research*, 11 (December), 771-783.

The Use of Diffusion Theory in Marketing: A Qualitative Approach to Innovative Consumer Behavior

Tina M. Lowrey, University of Illinois

ABSTRACT

This paper offers preliminary findings from a qualitative study of owners of compact disc players. The focus of the research was to explore consumers' reasons for purchasing particular products, their reasons for postponing purchase decisions, and their reasons for resisting other product purchases. The underlying framework for this research is that of diffusion of innovation, particularly as it is used by consumer behavior researchers. This paper argues for a new approach to the study of consumer innovativeness.

INTRODUCTION

The theory of diffusion of innovation has developed across many fields of research over the past several decades (Rogers 1983). While the study of diffusion originated in sociology and anthropology, marketing and consumer behavior theorists have adopted the general paradigm for use in their fields to explain new product acceptance and diffusion over time. Intuitively, it is obvious that there are inherent differences between sociological or cultural innovations and the introduction of new consumer products. However, for the most part, the marketing tradition of diffusion research has accepted the general theory without questioning many of its underlying assumptions (Gatignon and Robertson 1985). Very few studies exist in the consumer diffusion literature which challenge the basic conceptual framework. Criticisms of diffusion research are outlined clearly by Rogers (1983), particularly the pro-innovation bias of most diffusion researchers.

The pro-innovation bias is defined by Rogers as "... the implication of most diffusion research that an innovation should be diffused and adopted by all members of a social system, that it should be diffused more rapidly, and that the innovation should be neither re-invented nor rejected (p. 92)." Causes of this bias include the funding of the research by the change agencies themselves and a focus on studying only successful innovations (after completion of the diffusion process). Although the concept of the pro-innovation bias is much more complex than this brief discussion implies, it is clear that this bias affects two diffusion research areas in particular. The first is the categorization of individuals into adopter categories based on innovativeness and the subsequent attempt to assign personality characteristics to members of each adopter category. The second is the study of characteristics of innovations themselves.

ADOPTER CATEGORIES

Rogers (1983) identified five adopter categories of innovativeness. These categories fall along the normal frequency distribution curve. In simple terms, the first 2.5% of a given social system to adopt a particular innovation are labeled as innovators. The next 13.5% who adopt are considered early adopters. The third category, the early majority, constitute 34% of the population under study, followed by a group of the same size (34%) known as the late majority. The final category is made up of the last 16% to adopt (and also, presumably, non-adopters). The individuals in this category are known as laggards.

Rogers describes dominant characteristics of each of these categories briefly, as follows: innovators are venturesome, early adopters are respectable, the early majority are deliberate, the late majority are skeptical, and laggards are traditional. In addition, socioeconomic characteristics, personality variables, and communication behaviors are analyzed across adopter categories in an attempt to further define the individuals from each category. The use of this categorization scheme presents two specific problems for marketing researchers. One critical observation which can be made is the general lack of necessity implicit in the majority of consumer offerings. Given this fact, the classification of non-adopters (or slow adopters) into the laggard category (with the negative attitude implied by the label) leads to an incorrect placement of blame. Assumptions are made regarding the personality characteristics of a non-adopter, such as lack of rationality and/or aversion to risk. What is not discussed is the fact that many consumer products simply do not fit all individuals' needs. Rogers (1983) explains this quite succinctly, "...we have often assumed that all adopters perceive an innovation in a positive light, as we ourselves may perceive it. Now we need to question this assumption of the innovation's advantage for adopters (p. 100)."

A second question for consumer behavior researchers to ask is how valid a categorization scheme based on innovativeness can be when individuals are not consistently innovative. Again, this problem emerges due to the vast amount of products available which are not necessities. To claim that innovators are venturesome while laggards are traditional overlooks the fact that the same individual can be placed in either category depending on the product under study. Robertson (1971) follows this line of thought by asking whether or not a general innovator may exist, concluding, "...consistency of innovativeness cannot be expected across product categories, but can be expected within product categories and, sometimes, between related product categories (p. 111)."

Although recently Feick and Price (1987) have defined "market mavens" as individuals who possess information about many types of products and the marketplace in general, their focus is on common household products. When shifting attention toward innovative consumer technologies, such as compact disc players, VCR's, and personal computers, it becomes more difficult to find such generally information-rich individuals. Although there are some "technologically advanced" consumers who embrace each new innovation that comes along, there is an innate amount of specialization in this more complex area of technological products. Thus, you are more likely to find audiophiles, PC buffs, etc. who have a great amount of information about one specific product category. This fits well with Robertson's theory of innovation within a product category. However, a problem emerges with Robertson's theory when focusing on consumer technology innovations. When one uses product category as a unit for differentiation among innovators, the definition of a product category becomes critical. For example, if the product category is too broad, i.e., sound reproduction equipment, than individuals will not be likely to adopt within the category. This is due to the duplicate technologies which are offered to consumers. An innovator within such a category may adopt one particular technology and reject all others.

INNOVATION CHARACTERISTICS

This leads to the second major area of diffusion research which is impacted by the pro-innovation bias, the objective characteristics of the innovation itself. Rogers (1983) outlines five factors: relative advantage, compatibility, complexity, trialability, and observability. Quite briefly, relative advantage refers to the innovation's superiority to existing products or methods. Compatibility is the degree to which an innovation fits with existing values, needs, and ideas. Complexity refers to the fact that an innovation may be difficult to understand or use. Trialability is the ability to experiment with the innovation before total commitment is made (a form of risk-reduction). Observability refers to the visibility to others of the results of adopting a given innovation. These characteristics tend to become oversimplifications when applied to specific innovations, particularly in consumer behavior and marketing. Several researchers have identified additional ways to characterize innovations. For example, Fliegel and Kivlin (1966) argued for innovation-specific attribute characterization due to the difficulty in accurately defining and comparing attributes across disciplines. Their agricultural emphasis utilized 15 variables, some of which are identical to Rogers' classification scheme. For instance, divisibility for trial is comparable to trialability, and complexity appears in both. However, Fliegel and Kivlin include such factors as initial cost, continuing cost, and pervasiveness (which pertains to the innovation's contribution to additional changes).

Perhaps one of the most valuable additions to diffusion theory in this area for marketing purposes has been Robertson's (1971) simple innovation continuum. Innovations may be either continuous (resulting in little or no behavioral change), discontinuous (requiring major change), or may fall anywhere between these two endpoints. This basic theory has been extended by Heany (1983), whose continuum begins with style changes, progresses through product improvements, and ends with new products for new (undefined/undimensioned) markets. What each of these approaches suggest is that, in the area of consumer products, a minor innovation will have associated with it a different set of salient attributes than those associated with a major innovation. The difficulties which arise in trying to apply traditional innovation attributes to consumer products in general become increasingly problematic when focusing on new consumer technologies.

These technologies have additional factors which simply are not adequately addressed by existing diffusion theory. Several consumer researchers have begun to tackle the issues which are encountered when studying such discontinuous technologies. One interesting area which has been addressed by behavioral researchers is the impact of consumers' perceptions of innovation attributes and the subsequent effect on consumer expectations. While traditional diffusion research focuses on objective descriptions of innovations, this line of inquiry isolates the consumers' subjective perceptions as one of the most important determinants of successful diffusion.

Fliegel and Kivlin's (1966) study was one of the first to attempt to measure the individual perceptions of (in their case) farmers rather than relying on an objective listing of attributes by the researchers themselves. The study successfully obtained individual perceptions using attribute scales, which were then pooled over the sample to estimate shared community perceptions. They found that, as expected, those innovations perceived as least risky and most rewarding had the highest chance of successful adoption.

In the two decades since this study very few perceptual research designs have been incorporated into marketing diffusion research. The few that have all contributed greatly to our understanding of the very complex interaction between consumer perceptions and successful innovations. Ostlund (1974) found that perceptual variables were much more successful at predicting purchase outcome for low-risk innovations than were respondent characteristics. In a more recent study, Wilton and Pessemier (1981) investigated the importance of consumer perceptions in acceptance of a major, discontinuous innovation, finding that changes in perception which occur as product information is received are directly related to successful diffusion of innovations. In another study of a highly discontinuous technology, Dickerson and Gentry (1983) compared demographic, psychographic, and technical product experience variables of adopters and non-adopters. They argue that the differences between their profile and Rogers' original adopter categorization stem from the nature of the innovation, "We suggest that the nature of the adopter of an innovation is partially a function of the characteristics of the innovation itself (p. 233)." This points directly to the complex interaction of adopter categories and innovation characteristics to which this paper previously alluded.

A key characteristic which the majority of innovative consumer technologies share is the increasingly rapid rate of introduction of improvements and/or replacements. This factor differentiates this particular area of diffusion research from many others. Norton and Bass (1987) incorporated this factor into a diffusion model. In particular, they argue that substitution effects will impact the diffusion of an earlier technology. For example, customers who have not yet adopted a given innovation will instead adopt the newer, displacement technology. Additionally, adopters of the prior technology may "reject" and shift to the newer innovation. This will not completely halt the diffusion of the earlier innovation but will, of course, significantly affect it. Holak, Lehmann, and Sultan (1987) also address this issue, focusing on its relation to consumer perceptions and expectations. They hypothesized that consumers incorporate expectations of technological improvements and price reductions into their purchase decisions which results in purposeful delay of purchase. The results of their study showed a positive relationship between technological improvement expectations and delayed intention to purchase. Price reduction expectations were not shown to be related to intention.

One area of study which has been overlooked is how individuals themselves would describe the decision-making process they may utilize when adopting innovative consumer technologies. The focus of the research reported in this paper was to explore consumers' purchase behaviors by allowing each informant to explain in detail the decision-making process which was followed prior to adoption of a range of innovative consumer technologies, as well as their reasons for postponing or even resisting other product purchases. What are the actual decision-making stages experienced by consumers, in their own words? Are these decisions purposive and rational, particularly decisions to delay purchase? Can consumers be easily placed into a specific adopter category and thus be presumed to exhibit particular personality characteristics (which will predict attitudes toward other innovations)? What are the attributes of innovative consumer technologies which appear to be most salient in this process? To increase understanding of this complex phenomenon, a qualitative approach was taken to ensure that the everyday life experiences, attitudes, and perceptions of these individuals would be captured while attempting to minimize researcher bias.

METHOD

Data were collected through depth interviews of nine informants, all of whom had purchased their own compact disc player. The findings being reported here are based on 17 hours of interviews with individuals who responded voluntarily to a study request placed in record stores throughout the community. Although no attempt was made to select informants based on any demographic criteria, the volunteers were all males, ranging in age from late teens to early forties, and included college students (both undergraduate and graduate), local businessmen, and self-employed individuals. In addition, informants differed in how long they had owned compact disc players, ranging from several years to only a few months.

At the request of each informant the interviews were conducted in the researcher's office. Two separate hour-long sessions were held per informant, with the exception of one individual who preferred to complete both interviews in a single session. Although ownership of a compact disc player was a prerequisite for participation in the study, the interviews included detailed discussion of an entire range of innovative consumer technologies. This enabled the researcher to examine commonalities and/or contrasts in decision-making behavior across products and product categories. The specific products discussed are listed below:

- CD players, portable disc players, portable cassette players/recorders, stereos/stereo components, digital audio tape players, and electronic musical instruments
- personal computers, modems, and printers
- televisions, VCR's, laser disc players, video games, and HDTV
- answering machines, cordless phones, and car phones
- disc cameras and camcorders

The purpose for including such a varied array of products was to see if individuals followed different processes for products from different categories, and also to enable informants to focus on products which were of particular importance to them personally.

In the first session, each informant discussed in detail the process they went through before purchasing their compact disc player and another appropriate product of their choice. Discussion was guided by a structured but open-ended interview schedule. However, the informants themselves were more responsible than the interviewer for the products discussed, the major focus, and direction of the interviews. The second session focused entirely on products which the informants did not own. These were divided into those which were not desired at all versus those which were desired in varying degrees. Again, the informants were responsible for categorization of these products rather than the interviewer. Depth probing was utilized to examine the reasons for an individual's lack of desire for a product and/or delay of purchase.

Although this study is quite limited in its scope and is not an example of naturalistic inquiry, data analysis was guided by techniques outlined by

Glaser and Strauss (1967), Miles and Huberman (1984), and Lincoln and Guba (1985), including the constant comparative method for establishing categories and the search for emergent overall themes. What is reported here are the preliminary findings of the analysis of over 300 pages of transcripts from 16 60-minute microcassette audiotaped interviews and one 60-minute videotaped interview.

THEMATIC FINDINGS

Three overall guiding categories which shaped the analysis of this data were the purchasing process these individuals described for the two owned products discussed, the reasons for delaying purchase of desired items, and the attitudes and perceptions of items which were not desired. By investigating the categories which emerged from the interviews it was then possible to see themes which apply to the two underlying concepts which spurred this research: adopter categories and innovation characteristics.

The Decision-Making Process

It was evident that all informants were very cognizant of how they went about searching for information, which external forces were influential during the process, and how they came to a final purchase decision. Indeed, most informants were very aware of "mistakes" they had made in the past and how they would avoid repeating these mistakes in the future.

> "I bought what I thought had good specifications for the money. Which I don't think is the way to go about finding stereo equipment. But I didn't know too much then."

> "And I just listened to what the salesperson said and bought it there. I mean, but now I would know better."

The majority reported a very independent process with little external influence on actual purchase.

> "My friend reinforced what I already felt about it. The decision to buy was totally mine."

External influence tended to manifest itself during the search process. Many reported relying on experience with a friend's product prior to deciding to purchase one for themselves. Additionally, many reported utilizing existing literature as a reference guide before entering a store to get hands-on experience. Few reported relying on in-store help for advice. Rather, the in-store advice which was received was discounted as biased by most of the informants. In fact, one reported utilizing stores merely to see and hear the actual products prior to purchasing through a discount mail-order catalog.

> "I had a chance to play around with his CD player a little bit before I was really even in the market."

> "I talked to several of my friends who had computers, some who just use them and a couple of them who are actually in computer science."

> "No, in fact, if the store's advice had influenced my decision, it would have influenced it negatively."

> "I try to find as much information as I can before I even get ready to purchase - along with that I'll go to the stores just to look and get a feel for the things. But when I finally get ready to buy, I order through the mail because you can get things so much cheaper."

Although final purchases were sometimes described as impulsive, none omitted a fairly lengthy search process.

> "I'd been thinking about getting a boom box for a long time and had been looking, but I wasn't sure when I should get it. And I thought - well, I'm going to need one for the summer - and I need one right now - so I ran out to the store and got one."

> "I got to the point where I just said - all right, I'm going to make myself buy a TV. I'm going to do it."

> "I agonized and agonized over spending the money. And I finally just said to myself - just do it. So, I did."

Indeed, there was a great deal of similarity in the process across informants and across products. Each informant searched for information, either through literature or one's peers, followed by in-store experience with the product, with a final decision to purchase. This seems to be an effort on the individuals' part to achieve trialability, albeit somewhat limited, before committing to the purchase of basically high-expense, high-risk items. Delays can occur at any point, most often due to a lack of available funds, a lack of need at a given point in time, or an expectation of a future sale or promotion.

Cost-Benefit Analysis

Another interesting, yet not surprising, cause of purchase delay was the search for particular features. Most of the informants reported that there were features which were absolutely essential before they would commit to a purchase. This most often resulted in sacrificing features of lesser importance. This willingness to give up some relatively unimportant features also manifested itself in financial terms.

> "I had to have a tape counter that read out in real time. My old deck had that and I loved it. I figured any replacement I got would

have to have that - there were two or three things I gave up that were really minor."

"It had to have random shuffle play. Absolutely. I had to sacrifice some other things in order to get that."

"I'd been shopping around a little bit and looking at different places to get the best price - or, rather, to get the best price with the best features that I wanted."

This cost-benefit analysis approach was also a determinant of purchase delay of desired items. In fact, most informants would initially give strictly financial reasons for waiting to buy particular products. Common initial reasons were that the products were "too expensive", that the individual "couldn't afford them" or "didn't have that kind of money right now". However, the informants themselves would talk their way out of the easy answer into a more complex decision to wait.

"See, it's funny, because, to tell you the truth - any of these things I really wanted to buy right now - if I really wanted to, I could."

"I would use it so infrequently that it just isn't worth the money. If they came down in price, but I still didn't have time to use it, I guess I'd wait. But if I had the time and they were still expensive, I'd definitely buy one."

The majority of informants realized through discussion that there were deeper, underlying reasons why they were waiting until a future point in time to purchase these items.

Future Expectations
One major reason given for a purchase delay was an expectation of something occurring in the future which would make the purchase more satisfactory. This expectation often regarded the informant himself. Many were waiting for a new phase of life before purchasing new or additional equipment.

"Because the thing that I'd be waiting for is getting my own apartment. You know, after I graduate and get myself established I'll start, you know, stocking up."

"Once I move up out of the student level of society into the working force - that's when all that will happen."

"I might move and find a room that a portable TV would be handy in, I don't know. Same for a cordless phone."

"Maybe when I am gone alot, and I plan to be, then it would be different and I'd need an answering machine - they're so convenient. But right now it just wouldn't make any sense."

"I want a VCR, but I'm just trying to save my money to make it last as long as I can so I can finish my novel. Because, to me, having time to work on my novel is more important right now than having the choice of watching movies or any of that kind of stuff."

Another way future expectations played a part in the decision-making process was related to the products. As previously mentioned, Holak, Lehmann, and Sultan (1987) found that expectations of technological improvement were positively related to delayed intention to purchase, but did not find such a relationship with price reduction expectations. However, these individuals mentioned both types of expectations quite frequently.

"HDTV isn't available yet, but when it is it's going to be really expensive. I'm probably going to go for it, though, when it's within reach - although I'll want to wait for companies to introduce new features to it. I definitely won't buy the first generation HDTV."

"And there were a couple of things that made me wait. One, I was waiting for the prices to come down. Two, with any new technology you don't want to buy the first thing that comes out because there are certain bugs and certain other features that are added, and so forth."

Finally, the necessity for packaged or linked product purchases, and the price and availability of related software were also factors in delay of purchase.

"The laser discs themselves are really expensive too."

"If I bought a TV it would be with the laser disc player. But laser discs are still a somewhat new format and there's nowhere near the selection of movies like with videos. But, you know, once the technology's caught on and the price comes down and they come out with more movies, then that would look more desirable."

"When the time comes and I do get a computer I'll definitely get a modem for it, because we've got one at the office and I've found it to be real handy."

Alternative Technologies
One remaining reason many informants gave for waiting was the current existence of cheaper alternatives, or access to a product without self-purchase.

"But the fact that I'm waiting until my first one completely conks tells you something. I'll probably end up buying one, but not until I have to."

"A laser disc player would be nice, but since I have a VCR I don't know how much use I'd really have for that."

"There's always a computer I can use somewhere. Either at a business, or at school, or anything like that."

This existence of alternatives seems to point to Rogers' innovation characteristic called relative advantage. Another reoccurring characteristic is compatability with existing needs.

Non-Adoption

The previously discussed cost-benefit analysis approach is particularly obvious in discussion of products which are not desired at all. Many responses to depth probes regarding the reason one did not desire a product could be traced back to some type of cost-benefit analysis on the part of the informant. It was a perceived lack of benefits which was the main contributor to lack of desire.

"I just couldn't bring myself to spend the kind of money they wanted for the quality of sound that they deliver."

"The only benefit I can see for a car phone is for someone to get ahold of me in some work-related capacity. And to be honest with you, I'd rather not be bothered."

"Video game players are really novel at first, but then you get bored with them. After you've figured them out. Alot of electronic products are like that. They're fun to work with at first, and then . . ."

"I guess I don't have enough uses for a computer to make it worth the money."

Philosophical Opposition

Other reasons given for not wanting particular products had an underlying philosophy attached to them.

"I just don't like to get in the habit of watching TV. I was kind of raised that way."

"I'd become a couch potato - and one day you wake up and you're 60 years old and what have you done with your life?"

"So many people have the stupid things now. I mean, eventually, people are never going to have two-way conversations on the phone anymore."

"I object to (boom boxes) aesthetically - I guess I view it kind of like an invasion of my privacy. I guess I just object to them in principle."

"I don't take snapshots because I just think it's dumb to try to preserve the past."

"I just don't get into listening to music while I'm walking around outside. I like to know what's going on around me."

"I am philosophically opposed to these for two reasons. One, they're unsafe. And two, it's sort of like a technological version of walking around with your nose up in the air. I don't like them, I hate them, they bother me."

These are examples of a lack of compatability with existing values.

Poor Quality

One final, very simple reason given for lack of desire for a given product was a perceived lack of quality.

"I don't like boom boxes. They're just an abomination."

"My parents had a cordless phone and it never worked very well."

Given the tendency to pin non-adoption on personality characteristics, this is particularly important. Marketers must come to terms with the fact that some products do not meet the *standards* of consumers, even if they do fit their values or needs.

CONCLUSION

To summarize, the overriding characteristics of innovations which seemed to shape the decision-making processes of these nine individuals differed depending on the decision outcome. For actual purchases, trialability seemed to be the most salient part of the overall process. All of the informants attempted product trial either through in-store searching or experience with a friend's acquisition. Delay of purchase, however, tended to be caused mainly by a lack of compatibility with existing needs or a lack of relative advantage over some alternative product, with future expectations playing a major role in the process. For product non-adoption, compatibility with existing values was a key factor, along with a simple lack of quality of the product. Across each of the three decision-making categories was a very clear-cut, rational cost-benefit analysis. At no point in any of the interviews was observability or complexity mentioned as contributing to a decision. This does not mean that they are not factors in the decision-making process. Rather, it means either that these individuals did not consider them to be of much importance in their decisions, or chose not to share them as important factors.

These individuals were, admittedly, a non-randomized group consisting of fairly enthusiastic volunteers. An obvious extension of this research would be to conduct additional interviews with a more average type of consumer. However, the very fact that these informants were somewhat specialized in their product experience leads to the conclusion that categorizing individuals' innovativeness based on adoption of a single product is overly simplified. Although these informants had similar underlying decision-making processes, they differed drastically in which products applied to the three categories. In other words, one informant would never consider purchasing digital audio tape while another listed that as his next purchase priority. Similarly, one individual hated answering machines while another had one and loved it. The point is that predicting attitudes and perceptions based on ownership of a given product, or membership within a traditional adopter category would seem to be difficult.

It is necessary for diffusion researchers to begin defining individuals' innovativeness based on ownership of and attitudes towards a range of products. The previously described body of research which focuses on subjective perceptions of innovations is an essential step in this effort. Researchers have realized for a long time that the study of consumer behavior is difficult. The interviews reported in this paper represent only a scratch on the surface of the complex interaction between the personalities of individuals, their perceptions of the products, and the decision of whether or not to adopt a given innovation. Continued research which focuses on this interaction is essential for a deeper understanding of the diffusion process.

REFERENCES

Dickerson, Mary Dee and James W. Gentry (1983), "Characteristics of Adopters and Non-Adopters of Home Computers," *Journal of Consumer Research*, 10 (September), 225-235.

Feick, Lawrence F. and Linda L. Price (1987), "The Market Maven: A Diffuser of Marketplace Information," *Journal of Marketing*, 51 (January), 83-97.

Fliegel, Frederick C. and Joseph E. Kivlin (1966), "Attributes of Innovations as Factors in Diffusion," *American Journal of Sociology*, 72, 235-248.

Gatignon, Hubert and Thomas S. Robertson (1985), "A Propositional Inventory for New Diffusion Research," *Journal of Consumer Research*, 11 (March), 849-867.

Glaser, Barney G. and Anselm L. Strauss (1967), *The Discovery of Grounded Theory: Strategies for Qualitative Research*, Chicago: Aldine.

Heany, Donald F. (1983), "Degrees of Product Innovation," *Journal of Business Strategy*, 3 (Spring), 3-14.

Holak, Susan L., Donald R. Lehmann, and Fareena Sultan (1987), "The Role of Expectations in the Adoption of Innovative Consumer Durables: Some Preliminary Evidence," *Journal of Retailing*, 63 (3), 243-259.

Lincoln, Yvonna S. and Egon G. Guba (1985), *Naturalistic Inquiry*, Beverly Hills, CA: Sage.

Miles, Matthew B. and A. Michael Huberman (1984), *Qualitative Data Analysis: A Sourcebook for New Methods*, Beverly Hills, CA: Sage.

Norton, John A. and Frank M. Bass (1987), "A Diffusion Theory Model of Adoption and Substitution for Successive Generations of High-Technology Products," *Management Science*, 33 (9), 1069-1086.

Ostlund, Lyman E. (1974), "Perceived Innovation Attributes as Predictors of Innovativeness," *Journal of Consumer Research*, 1 (September), 23-29.

Robertson, Thomas S. (1971), *Innovative Behavior and Communication*, New York: Holt, Rinehart & Winston.

Rogers, Everett M. (1983), *Diffusion of Innovations*, New York: The Free Press.

Wilton, Peter C. and Edgar A. Pessemier (1981), "Forecasting the Ultimate Acceptance of an Innovation: the Effects of Information," *Journal of Consumer Research*, 8 (September), 162-171.

The Role of Love, Affection, and Intimacy in Family Decision Research

Jong-Hee Park, Washington State University
Patriya S. Tansuhaj, Washington State University
Richard H. Kolbe, Washington State University

ABSTRACT

Consumer behavior research has given little credence to the affective component present in family decision making. This paper suggests there is a need to recognize the salience of love, affection, and intimacy as important sources of the individual goals and desires that influence joint decisions in families. Basic concepts of family are discussed, including definitions of "family" and how it functions differently than other formal groups, such as businesses or social organizations. The paper also describes how the affectional dimensions fit within the existing family decision research paradigm. Suggestions for future research are provided.

INTRODUCTION

"Home is the place where, when you have to go there, they have to let you in."
Robert Frost, *Death of the Hired Man*

Frost's statement exemplifies the special role of home and family in human interactions. The relationships between family members which create notions of hearth and home are centered on the deep-seated affection members have for one another. The implications of such interpersonal affection pervades all family decisions.

The significance of the affection component is not lost on marketers. Television or magazine advertisements frequently depict a couple's deep emotional relationship and their feelings of love, affection, and intimacy. In advertisements for baby products, we often see expressions of love, affection, and caring for children used in compelling and heartwarming appeals. Thus, advertising practitioners apparently recognize the viability of the love, affection, and intimacy present in a family setting as an advertising method. However, previous family research has given little attention to these factors, focusing instead on the power/conflict dimensions of family interactions.

Family decision research has generally attempted to understand which family members influence one another in terms of family or household purchases. The research which has examined the issues of who is influential in purchasing decisions led consumer behavior scholars to focus on power relations and conflict in family decision making situations. Even though this approach yields results which offer a rich understanding of family decision processes, the scope of this research can be broadened. There is a need to examine other aspects of family relationships that affect the decision making process.

In this article, we explore the potential of affective dimensions in family decision research. Specifically, consideration is given to how affection or the desire to maintain intimate relationships affect family decision making. Following Davis' (1976) urge, introduction of the affectional dimension leads to a research focus on the family decision process, rather than the decision outcomes.

The initial discussion of the affectional components in family decision making necessitates some consideration of the definitions of relevant terms. The concepts of love and affection have been described as:

> Words used more or less interchangeably to designate warm, positive feelings directed to individuals. The difference between love and affection can be made. Love usually implies more intense feeling than affection, or love may be restricted to feelings with a strong sexual component and affection to those supposedly free of it. (Sills 1968, p. 121)

Concerning intimacy, Sternberg (1986) presented it as one of three major components of love; the other two are passion and commitment. It refers to "sharing that which is inmost with others" (McAdams 1988, p. 18). Helgeson, Shaver and Dyer (1987) found that people perceive intimacy as feelings and expressions of closeness, appreciation, and affection. McAdams (1982, p. 19) defined the intimacy motive as "a recurrent preference or readiness for experiences of warm, close, and communicative interaction with others -- interpersonal exchange perceived as an end in itself rather than a means to another end." In summary, it is clear that affection for family members is a deep-seated emotion, represented by intimate, long-term relationships which are unique in comparison to other social relationships. In the remainder of the paper, the aforementioned concepts will be referred to as *affection*.

Consumer researchers have used theoretical constructs drawn from several disciplines in an attempt to explain the phenomenon of family decision behavior. However, the concepts and theories borrowed from other paradigms must be used with consideration of the underlying contexts, assumptions, and the conceptual relationships established by each research discipline. The research in family decision making has taken concepts from political science, sociology, and other disciplines as explanatory paradigms for this group behavior. The concepts of power or bargaining in a political setting or a more formal organization have been applied in family studies. As an example, Gupta, Hagerty, and Myers (1983) used game theory in formulating their family decision-making model. According to this theory, each of the group members is motivated to obtain the best payoff in a joint decision process. However, if we consider affection as a component of familial interactions, the self-interest motives in game theory may well miss the subtle aspects present in family settings. Thus, consideration needs to be given to the major and minor differences between the family and other group decisions to provide a more sensitive measure and appraisal of family decision behavior.

In a family structure, the linkage among members can generally be characterized by levels of intimacy and affection. It would seem reasonable that family decisions take into consideration the affectional, highly personal aspects which are present in these interactions.

DEFINITIONS AND FUNCTIONS OF THE FAMILY

To provide a more complete picture of family characteristics, the definition and functional values of the family will be discussed from an affectional perspective. A comparison between the family and other groups will be made to better isolate the differentiating characteristics of the family. Assuming that affection is an important construct that influences family decisions, we will explore how the construct fits the definition and functions of the family.

Definitions of the Family

A clear definition helps focus on or isolate key questions and issues. Some examples of family definitions are provided and critiqued. Officially, the U.S. Census Bureau (1978, p. 20) defines a family as "a group of two persons or more related by blood, marriage, or adoption and residing together." This definition describes membership of the family structurally rather than functionally, quite likely useful for census purposes but lacking insight for research purposes.

Reiss (1965) refers to the family in terms of an institution, based on socially defined norms and relationships that family members come to understand in the process of socialization. The family here is characterized as a socially derived and maintained entity. However, it says little about the roles of individuals within the family structure.

A more detailed definition based on an anthropological view was provided by Coser (1974). She defined the family as "a group manifesting the following organization attributes: it finds its origin in marriage; it consists of husband, wife, and children born in their wedlock,...the group is united by...sexual rights and prohibitions as well as such socially patterned feelings as *love, attraction, piety,* and *awe*" (Coser 1974, p. xvi). The emotional aspect and care-taking function of the family, which have been ignored in other definitions, are included here, although it does exclude a group formed by informal marriage (living together). However, such contemporization of the definition has little effect on the general notion of family presented here.

The implications of the definitions of family and its components are considerable. In total, the entity called 'the family' is a complex union of individuals. The structure of a family and the roles of its membership are learned from social norms and family members. Uniting forces for a family include the individual's needs for and feelings of love, affection, and attraction to one another. From this perspective, these forces are likely to mediate many decisions made by a family. Thus, consideration of these affectional factors may be important in understanding the dynamics present in the processes of family decision making.

Functions of the Family

To further understand the family, it is important to consider its various functions. In sociology, Murdock (1949) proposes that the family had four essential functions: (1) socialization, (2) economic cooperation, (3) reproduction, and (4) sexual relations. Among these functions, Reiss (1965) found that socialization is the most prevalent function in the nuclear family. While the concept of consumer socialization has been well researched, the integration of this concept into the family decision framework and the affectional aspects of family interactions may provide additional insight into this phenomenon.

Hoffman and Manis (1979) reported that the most important value of having children in a family in the United States is to maintain primary group ties characterized by face to face contact, smallness of size, frequent and intense contact, and affection (love, companionship, and giving love). For many children, most of the needs for love, affection, and intimacy are met by family units. The family is the group where we can potentially find intimacy, nurturing, and a sense of loving and being loved by someone.

To further describe the uniqueness of the family and the necessity for including the affectional dimensions in family decision research, it may be worthwhile to compare functional characteristics of the family to those of other groups. It is reasonable to assume that an individual behaves differently when he or she interacts with different groups of people. For example, a person may behave differently in a family setting than when s/he is in a business meeting. Therefore, the identification of relative differences between the family and other groups is a critical first step in determining whether there is a need to consider family decision processes as uniquely different from other formal group decisions. The existence of differences would suggest a need to propose alternative explanations for the family decision process. The relative differences between families and other groups are offered in the Table.

As previously defined, the family is formed by formal or informal marriage, and birth, while other groups are established by various methods differing from family. The formation of family leads to more permanent relationships, both physically and psychologically. For example, children are

TABLE
RELATIVE DIFFERENCES BETWEEN FAMILIES AND OTHER GROUPS

	Family	Other Groups
(1)	Formation by Marriage or Birth	Formation by Job or Task
(2)	More Permanent Relationship	More Contractual Relationship
(3)	More Interpersonal Relations Oriented	More Goal Oriented
(4)	More Emotional Ties	More Rational Oriented Ties
(5)	More Intrinsic Value Seeking	More Extrinsic Value Seeking
(6)	Group Oriented (cooperative)	Self Oriented (competitive)

nurtured and are closely associated with their parents, usually for many years. Thus, most people have their longest and most intimate contacts with others in the family setting. Strong affectional ties (both positive and negative) within the family generally result from this long and close relationship.

The strong emotional ties in return may not be dissolved at the individual's will, unlike relationships in other groups. Families are motivated to maintain the intimate emotional relationships by protecting the family and by maintaining the harmony of the home which has intrinsic value. In this family setting, it is reasonable to assume that the affective factors (love, affection and intimacy) are important in the family decision making process. It may not be as likely that individuals develop as intimate a relationship in other groups as would be present in family membership. Further, in general, rational factors and/or utilitarian factors (e.g., cost and benefit analysis) are more important in the group decision making process than for the family. In addition, the members in other groups tend to pursue their own self-interest or seek extrinsic values (e.g., pay and promotion). This self-interest and extrinsic value seeking behavior leads more readily to conflict situations, encouraging individual members to exert power over others. While self-interest certainly is present in family decisions, the complexity and affectional aspects of the family place different parameters on the process.

ORIENTATION OF PREVIOUS FAMILY RESEARCH

The previous literature can be loosely categorized into two types of studies: (1) determination of who influences and/or makes decisions in the family and what differences in family decision making can be explained by socio-demographic and psychographic variables and (2) the investigation of the family decision making process.

Previous family decision research has attempted to understand and describe how family members interact and influence one another in terms of family or household purchases. The family decision-making literature has focused mainly on who is influential (Cosenza and Davis 1981; Davis 1970; Ekstrom, Tansuhaj, and Foxman 1987; Filiatrault and Ritchie 1980; Foxman, Tansuhaj, and Ekstrom 1989; Gupta et al. 1983; Kelly and Egan 1969; O'Connor, Sullivan, and Pogorzelski 1985; Qualls 1982; 1984; Woodside 1975), and who makes the decisions about purchases within families (Brinberg and Schwenk 1985; Davis 1971; Green and Cunningham 1975; Imperia, O'Guinn, and MacAdams 1985; Munsinger, Weber, and Hansen 1975; Sharp and Mott 1956; Wilkes 1975; Wolgast 1958).

Other research has used individual factors to predict and show differences between groups of decision makers/influencers. These factors are called "background factors" and include demographic and socioeconomic characteristics, family group factors, and cultural factors among others. The determinants (independent variables) that previous research have investigated are mainly demographic and socioeconomic factors: *income* (Davis 1976; Green and Cunningham 1975; Munsinger et al. 1975; Sharp and Mott 1956), *age* (Green and Cunningham 1975; Munsinger et al. 1975; Sharp and Mott 1956; Wolgast 1958), *job status* (Wolgast 1958; Woodside 1975), *education* (Munsinger et al. 1975; Woodside

1975), *years of marriage* (Cox 1975; Munsinger et al. 1975), *opinion leadership* (Woodside 1975), and *marital role* (Brinberg and Schwenk 1985; Buss and Schaninger 1983; Kelly and Egan 1969; O'Connor et al. 1985; Qualls 1982, 1984; Sharp and Mott 1956; Wolgast 1958). These background factors have been shown to effectively discriminate between groups of decision makers.

In total, these studies have provided information about the decision outcomes and the individuals who make and are involved in these decisions. Both groups of studies, however, do little to address the process of family decision making, focusing only on the outcome of the decisions. In other words, the research has provided a clear picture of who participates and decides in family decisions and offers a description of these individuals' characteristics, but does not address the dynamics of the personal interactions which are involved in the decision process (Davis 1976).

To advance our knowledge of family decisions, we need to address process and the factors which influence the process more broadly. A number of models have been proposed which attempt to describe the family decision process -- that is, how individuals interact and what factors (i.e., individual, interpersonal dynamics, product-related, and group factors) influence each decision process. In general, a key assumption made in previous studies of the family decision process has been that each family member has different motives, and these unilateral motives lead to conflict and negotiations in a joint decision process (Moore and Wilkie 1988). These notions have led family decision researchers to focus on conflict situations. The conflict literature can be characterized by research in two areas: (1) conflict avoidance and (2) conflict resolution. Within conflict avoidance we have the behaviors of abrogation of rights, decision specialization, withdrawal, and routinization of decisions resulting from having made multiples of these decisions (Blood and Wolfe 1960). Individuals may resolve conflicts by bargaining a compromise solution, trading off a loss for future considerations, using persuasive techniques, seeking mediation by a third party, and using problem solving skills and techniques (Sheth and Cosmas 1975).

THE ROLE OF AFFECTION IN FAMILY DECISION PROCESSES

To more fully understand the family decision process and its dynamics, there needs to be some consideration of the personal relationships based on love and affection. Knowledge of the role of affection on family decisions will enhance the existing literature based on power (i.e., it helps us understand how power is used and conflicts are resolved more clearly). Buss and Schaninger (1983), Corfman and Lehmann (1987), Gupta et al. (1983), and Sheth (1974) all include model components which relate factors which influence what an individual brings to the decision process. These factors influence the manner in which the participants in the decision process interact. If love and affection are at the base of the family structure, then individuals in the process should include these factors in their interactions. Thus, in addition to the use of factors such as sex roles, power relationships, spousal responsibilities, and level of interest in the decision, the affectional dimensions should be considered as components of the interpersonal dynamics in the family decision process.

The role of affection in family decision making will be manifest in a number of different ways. Research on the affectional component may well address such areas based on the following propositions:

P1: Affectional bonds may inhibit hard-line, uncompromising, self-interest positions as members are cognizant and have a desire to maintain their long-term affective relationship. A willingness to acquiesce to members' desires follows.

P2: The greater an individual member's requirements/need for intimate relationships with family members the greater will be the use of conflict avoidance strategies.

P3: The intimacy of family members affect the means for solving conflict. Highly intimate members may resolve conflict in more cooperative manners such as bargaining, trading, logical persuasion, and problem-solving (Sheth and Cosmas 1975). Conversely, low intimacy families may make greater use of coercion, authority, formal authority and the like.

P4: Greater intimacy of families may result in greater incidence of joint decision-making as opposed to single member decision-making dominance.

P5: The impact of the affection component in family decision-making may differ by product class and type. Products that involve the entire family by means of joint usage, involvement, or interest will likely reflect more affectional elements than those which are used exclusively by only one member of the family.

P6: Similarity of goals and values among members may reduce family decision conflict levels.

Measurement Issues

Affection in the family decision making process can be measured by a number of scales available in the literature. For example, intimacy of spouses can be examined by using the Personal Assessment of Intimacy in Relationships Scale (Schaefer and Olson 1980). This scale examines five types of intimacy: emotional, social, sexual, intellectual, and recreational. In research applications, the level of intimacy ascertained by the scale was positively related to satisfaction with the marital union, cohesiveness of the family, and negatively related to conflict arousal and willingness to control the spouse. Rubin's (1970) scale also may be used in this research stream. Here, love is measured to include three components: (1) affiliative and dependent needs; (2) predisposition to help; and (3) orientation of exclusiveness from and absorption in another person.

The ability to measure affection levels within the individual and between individuals is integral to the study of the role of affection in family decision making. The development of affection specific scales for family decisions would be a necessary second step. The mediating influence of affection on the decision process can be assessed by examining family decisions and the differences between high and low affection family units. Simulated as well as actual buying situations may be used in making this measurement.

One of the outcomes of this affection orientation is that the decision process need not focus solely on who influences/dominates in a situation typically characterized by conflict. Rather, such an orientation will necessitate a broader approach to the entire family decision process and require that more interpersonal factors be examined in the research. This further necessitates that scholars distinguish family decision making from other group decisions, creating models which include dimensions unique to this process. Dimensions such as affection among decision participants likely provides great insights into the decision process.

CONCLUSION AND SUGGESTIONS FOR FUTURE RESEARCH

To more fully understand family decision making phenomena, researchers need to pay more attention to family decision processes. The shift from looking narrowly at the decision outcomes has been encouraged for over a decade by Davis' (1976) critical review of this research area. In this article, we discussed definitions and functions of the family, and offer the affectional concepts to help develop an understanding and interpretation of family interactions and family dynamics. The affective dimensions can be combined with issues of power and conflict resolution, thereby helping to broaden the domain of family decision research. To explore how the affectional dimensions fit within the existing 'power' paradigm in family research, researchers are encouraged to investigate interactions between effects of power and of affection in the decision process, instead of studying each in isolation.

Cross-cultural family studies could also benefit from the inclusion of affectional influences on how families in diverse societies make purchase decisions. For example, do these variables have less effect on family decision outcomes in cultures where such feelings are not explicitly expressed. Are the affective dimensions more important in explaining family decisions and behaviors in modern, materialistic, or advanced societies than in other societies?

In conclusion, love, affection, and intimacy are basic human emotions. The inclusion of these dimensions in the family decision making process helps to establish these emotional components as important explanatory factors. The richness of their inclusion in models of family decision making should yield greater insights into the interpersonal dynamics of the process. It is hoped their inclusion will foster a new and broadened perspective in our efforts to examine and explain the family decision making process.

REFERENCES

Blood, Robert O., Jr. and Donald M. Wolfe (1960), *Husbands and Wives*, New York: Free Press.

Brinberg, David and Nancy Schwenk (1985), "Husband-Wife Decision Making: An Exploratory Study of the Interaction Process," in *Advances In Consumer Research*, Vol. 12, ed. Elizabeth C. Hirschman and Morris B. Holbrook, Provo, UT: Association for Consumer Research, 487-491.

Buss, W. Christian, and Charles M. Schaniger (1983), "The Influence of Sex Roles on Family Decision Processes and Outcomes," in *Advances in Consumer Research*, Vol. 10, eds. Richard P. Bagozzi and Alice M. Tybout, Ann Arbor, MI: Association for Consumer Research, 439-444.

Corfman, Kim P. and Donald R. Lehmann (1987), "Models of Cooperative Group Decision-Making and Relative Influence: An Experimental Investigation of Family Purchase Decisions," *Journal of Consumer Research*, 14 (June), 1-13.

Cosenza, Robert M. and Duane L. Davis (1981), "Family Vacation Decision Making Over The Family Life Cycle", *Journal of Travel Research*, 20 (Fall), 17-23.

Coser, Rose Laub (1974), *The Family: Its Structures & Functions*, New York: St. Martin's Press.

Cox, Eli P. III (1975), "Family Purchase Decision Making and the Process of Adjustment," *Journal of Marketing Research*, 12 (May), 189-95.

Davis, Harry L. (1970), "Dimensions of Marital Roles in Consumer Decision Making," *Journal of Marketing Research*, 7 (May), 168-177.

_____ (1971), "Measurement of Husband-Wife Influence in Consumer Purchase Decisions," *Journal of Marketing Research*, 8 (August), 305-312.

_____ (1976), "Decision Making Within the Household," *Journal of Consumer Research*, 2 (March), 241-260.

Ekstrom, Karin M., Patriya S. Tansuhaj, and Ellen R. Foxman (1987), "Children's Influence in Family Decision and Consumer Socialization: A Reciprocal View," in *Advances in Consumer Research*, Vol. 14, eds. Melanie Wallendorf and Paul Anderson, Provo, UT: Association for Consumer Research, 283-287.

Filiatrault, Pierre and J. R. Brent Ritchie (1980), "Joint Purchasing Decisions: A Comparison of Influence Structure in Family and Couple Decision-Making Units," *Journal of Consumer Research*, 7 (September), 131-140.

Foxman, Ellen R., Patriya S. Tansuhaj, and Karin Ekstrom (1989), "Family Members' Perceptions of Adolescents' Influence in Family Decision Making," *Journal of Consumer Research*, 15 (March), 482-491.

Green, Robert T. and Isabella C. M. Cunningham (1975), "Feminine Role Perception and Family Purchasing Decisions," *Journal of Marketing Research*, 12 (August), 325-332.

Gupta, Sunil, Michael R. Hagerty, and John G. Myers (1983), "New Directions in Family Decision Making Research," in *Advances in Consumer Research*, Vol. 10, eds. Richard P. Bagozzi and Alice M. Tybout, Ann Arbor, MI: Association for Consumer Research, 445-450.

Helgeson, Vicki S., Phillip Shaver, and Margaret Dyer (1987), "Prototypes of Intimacy and Distance in Same-Sex and Opposite-Sex Relationships," *Journal of Social and Personal Relationships*, 4, 195-233.

Hoffman, Lois Wladis and Jean Denby Manis (1978), "Influences of Children on Marital Interaction and Parental Satisfaction and Dissatisfaction, in *Child Influences on Marital and Family Interaction*, eds. Richard H. Lerner and Graham B. Spanier, New York: Academic Press, 165-212.

Imperia, Giovanna, Thomas C. O'Guinn, and Elizabeth A. MacAdams (1985), "Family Decision Making Role Perceptions Among Mexican-American and Anglo Wives: A Cross Cultural Comparison," in *Advances in Consumer Research*, Vol. 12, eds. Elizabeth C. Hirschman and Morris B. Holbrook, Provo, UT: Association for Consumer Research, 71-74.

Kelly, Robert F. and Michael B. Egan (1969), "Husband and Wife Interaction in a Consumer Decision Process," in *Marketing Involvement in Society and The Economy*, Chicago: American Marketing Association, 250-258.

McAdams, Dan P. (1982), "Intimacy Motivation," in *Motivation and Society*, ed. A. J. Stewart, San Francisco: Jossey-Bass, 133-171.

_____ Personal Relationships," in *Handbook of Personal Relationships*, ed. Steve Duck, New York: John Wiley and Sons.

Moore-Shay, Elizabeth and William L. Wilkie (1988), "Recent Developments in Research on Family Decisions," in *Advances in Consumer Research*, Vol. 15, ed. Michael J. Houston, Provo, UT: Association of Consumer Research, 454-460.

Munsinger, Gary M., Jean E. Weber, and Richard W. Hansen (1975), "Joint Home Purchasing Decisions by Husbands and Wives," *Journal of Consumer Research*, 1 (March), 60-66.

Murdock, George P. (1949), *Social Structure*, New York: The MacMillan Co.

O'Connor, P. J., Gary L. Sullivan, and Dana A. Pogorzelski (1985), "Cross Cultural Family Purchasing Decisions: A Literature Review," in *Advances in Consumer Research*, Vol 12, eds. Elizabeth C. Hirschman and Morris B. Holbrook, Provo, UT: Association for Consumer Research, 59-64.

Qualls, William J. (1982), "Changing Sex Roles: The Impact upon Family Decision Making," in *Advances in Consumer Research*, Vol. 12, eds. Elizabeth C. Hirschman and Morris B. Holbrook, Provo, UT: Association for Consumer Research, 267-270.

_____ (1984), "Sex Roles, Husband-Wife Influence, and Family Decision Behavior," in *Advances in Consumer Research*, Vol. 11, ed. Thomas C. Kinnear, Provo, UT: Association for Consumer Research, 270-275.

Reiss, Ira L. (1965) "The Universality of the Family: A Conceptual Analysis, *Journal of Marriage and The Family*, 27, 443-453.

Rubin, Zick (1970), "Measurement of Romantic Love," *Journal of Personality and Social Psychology*, Vol. 16, 2, 265-273.

Schaefer, Mark T. and David H. Olson (1981), "Assessing Intimacy: The Pair Inventory," *Journal of Marital and Family Therapy*, (January), 47-60.

Sharp, Harry and Paul Mott (1956), "Consumer Decisions in the Metropolitan Family", *Journal of Marketing*, 21 (October), 149-156.

Sheth, Jagdish N. (1974), "A Theory of Family Buying decisions," in *Models of Buyer Behavior*, ed. Jagdish N. Sheth, New York: Harper & Row.

Sheth, Jagdish and S. Cosmas (1975), "Tactics of Conflict Resolution in Family Buying Behavior," paper presented at American Psychological Meetings.

Sills, David L. (1968), *International Encyclopedia of the Social Sciences*, New York: The MacMillan Company and The Free Press.

Sternberg, Robert J. (1986), "A Triangular Theory of Love," *Psychological Review*, 93 (2), 119-135.

U. S. Bureau of Census (1978), "Population Profile in the United States," U.S. Series P-20, No. 324, Washington, DC: U.S. Government Printing Office.

Wilkes, Robert E. (1975), "Husband-Wife Influence in Purchase Decisions -- A Confirmation and Extension," *Journal of Marketing Research*, 12 (May), 224-227.

Wolgast, Elizabeth H. (1958), "Do Husbands or Wives Make the Purchasing Decisions?" *Journal of Marketing*, 23 (October), 151-158.

Woodside, Arch G. (1975), "Effects of Prior Decision-Making, Demographics, and Psychographics on Marital Roles for Purchasing Durables," in *Advances in Consumer Behavior Research*, Vol 2, ed. M. Schlinger, Chicago: Association for Consumer Research, 81-91.

Financial Decision Making of Babyboomer Couples

Amardeep Assar, State University of New York at Binghamton
George S. Bobinski, Jr., State University of New York at Binghamton

ABSTRACT

Financial management practices of babyboomer couples are examined based on a mail survey, with wives and husbands responding separately. The prevalence of budgeting, individual ownership of checking accounts, savings accounts, and credit cards and joint ownership of investments were found to be related to family income, individual income, presence of children, sex role attitudes, and locus of control. The patterns of relative influence for these types of financial services were also related to many of these factors as well as to ages of children and perceived role overload.

INTRODUCTION

Family financial management practices have received an increasing amount of attention from consumer researchers in recent years. These practices are significant because they affect decisions about savings and investments as well as the purchases of products and services. As a result, an improved understanding of the underlying factors can benefit both consumers and marketers.

Although recent studies have examined the relationships between sociodemographic and attitudinal factors, and family financial management practices, there are many unresolved issues (Moore-Shay and Wilkie 1988). These include identifying the factors related to the use and ownership of particular financial services, the prevalence of budgeting, and the patterns of relative influence in financial decisions. We chose to study married babyboomers, that is, those people born between 1946 and 1964. This group is important because it makes up a very large percentage of all married couples. Approximately 24 million married couples are in the 25-44 year age group, accounting for 47% of all married couples. They have a spending power in excess of $850 billion annually (Their median family incomes can be estimated at approximately $37,000 for 1987, based on Waldrop 1989). In addition, these couples are at the stage where major financial decisions are typically being made, such as buying homes, deciding on family size, and investing for the future. This makes them an important segment for marketers of financial services and other products.

The conceptual framework for the study was a general model of family decision making (Buss and Schaninger 1983). This study relates financial management practices to such factors as household and individual incomes, family life cycle, sex role attitudes, locus of control, and perceptions of role overload. As suggested by those authors and others (Scanzoni 1977, Rosen and Granbois 1983), the relationships were tested using both spouses as respondents in an exploratory survey.

The next section presents the conceptual model. After that, the literature is reviewed to identify factors that have been found to be important in earlier studies of family decision-making. These factors are then related to individual ownership of some types of financial services, and also to patterns of relative influence for other decisions where a greater degree of joint decision-making is expected. Hypotheses for empirical study are then developed.

LITERATURE REVIEW

One of the goals of this paper is to examine whether different demographic and attitudinal factors are related to wives and husbands decisions about a variety of financial services. Buss and Schaninger (1983) presented a general model of family decision making, to serve as a "mid-range theoretical structure" in studying the husband-wife dyad. Their model consists of antecedent conditions, individual attitudes, situational factors, and process factors that affect process outcomes. Examples of antecedent conditions provided by the authors include demographic characteristics of respondents and the allocation of tasks by the spouses. Individual attitudes include sex-role norms and life style values. Decisions may also be influenced by situational factors such as the number of alternatives and the risk of the decision. Finally, their model includes aspects of the decision making process such as the strategies used by spouses in managing conflict. Examples of process outcomes included in the model are patterns of consumption, decision behavior, and marital satisfaction.

In relation to the Buss and Schaninger model, the antecedent conditions in this study included a set of demographic variables--family and individual incomes, presence or absence of children, and family life cycle. The attitudinal variables included sex role attitudes and locus of control. Perceived role overload was used as a situational factor, while the process aspect of conflict was not examined. This study examined process outcomes relating to financial decisions.

One important outcome of family decision-making is the decision to own or purchase a particular product or service. Certain financial services can be purchased and owned by one spouse, independent of the other, or else by both of them jointly. These include checking accounts, savings accounts, major credit cards (e.g., VISA, MasterCard, American Express), and retail store cards. The paper examines individual ownership of these financial products separately for wives and husbands.

In addition to ownership, numerous studies have examined the relative influence of wives and husbands. The extent of influence may vary by (1) type of product, (2) stage in the decision process, (3) type of decision (e.g., budgeting, purchase or brand choice) and (4) family characteristics. According to Davis and Rigaux (1974), family decisions may be wife-dominated (e.g., for food, kitchenware and children's clothing), husband-dominated (e.g., life insurance, cars) or syncratic (e.g., housing, vacations). Finally, autonomic decisions are made by the individual (e.g., husband's clothing). The paper examines relative influence patterns for financial decisions, including budgeting, investments, and jointly held checking and savings accounts.

Variables in Family Decision Making

A large number of variables have been studied in the context of family decision making. One of these variables is sex role attitude which can be thought of as ranging from the traditional to the modern. For example, this variable has been used to study home-buying (Qualls 1987) and also relative influence in making financial decisions and implementing them via day to day responsibilities (Rosen and Granbois 1983). The decision-making of traditional wives and husbands is expected to be consistent with distinct areas of responsibility and expertise, while more modern individuals will tend to be more joint in their decisions (Cunningham and Green 1974). Sex role moderns may be expected to act in a manner that runs counter to the traditional mold. For products and services that are traditionally jointly owned, they may assert their independence and also want to purchase services for themselves.

Another important variable that has been studied in the context of joint decision making is family life cycle stage. As a family moves through the life cycle, there may be less joint decision making (Wolgast 1958; Ferber and Lee 1974). Over time, wives and husbands may specialize in some areas. If this occurs, they may make fewer joint decisions and more specialized ones (Kenkel 1961).

An individual's view of the world may also have a bearing on family decisions. Locus of control has been defined as the extent to which people perceive rewards and reinforcements as being contingent on their own behavior or independent of it (Rotter 1966). Persons with an internal locus of control will perceive that events are contingent on their own behavior. Consistent with this, internals are expected to attribute more importance to decisions, and thus be more likely to make decisions jointly. In contrast, those with an external locus of control may be perfunctory in doing these tasks (Rosen and Granbois 1983).

The concept of wife's role overload was introduced in consumer research by Reilly (1982). Role overload arises when a person faces excessive demands on available time and effort. A spouse who is not overloaded is expected to take up tasks that the overloaded spouse is unable to handle. In that study, wives' role overload had only a weak positive relationship with family ownership of durables and use of convenience foods. Foxman and Burns (1987) extended this idea and proposed that husbands may also be overloaded. This was empirically supported and perceived husband role load and perceived wife role load were found to be independent dimensions.

HYPOTHESES

Budgeting Decisions

A family's pattern of budgeting can intuitively be expected to play a major role in its purchase and investment decisions. A number of researchers have studied whether families make budgets. This is studied here under ownership in the sense that couples "buy" the idea of making budgets. About two-thirds of families have been found to do some advance planning for spending their income (Beutler and Sahlberg 1980) or prepare written or non-written budgets (Granbois, Rosen, and Acito 1986).

Families are more likely to budget when they face extra demands on their resources, such as at early stages of the family life cycle or because of the presence of children (Beutler and Sahlberg 1980; Granbois, Rosen, and Acito 1986). Education has been found to be positively related to budgeting and planning (Beutler and Sahlberg 1980), but household income has not been found to predict formal planning, or at most has been only weakly related (Granbois, Rosen, and Acito 1986). Considering those families that do budget, husbands with higher incomes may have more relative influence in the budgeting decision. Sex role attitudes have been found to be related to how families budget and to relative influence in this process. When wives are traditional, they are more likely to plan the use of surplus funds, but the sex roles of husbands are not related to this practice (Granbois, Rosen, and Acito 1986). In making savings decisions and handling expenses, more modern sex roles are associated with sharing of responsibility (Kim and Lee 1989; Schaninger, Buss, and Grover 1982).

Deacon and Firebaugh (1975) proposed that people with a more positive outlook on life may be more likely to plan in order to have more control over the future. Based on this, Beutler and Sahlberg (1980) tested how outlook on life might relate to formal planning and budgeting by families. They found that optimists were more likely to do formal financial planning. In addition, locus of control has been found to be related to the incidence of budgeting, even though results were conflicting. In families that used special accounts for budgeting, wives were more external while husbands were more internal (Granbois, Rosen, and Acito 1986; Rosen and Granbois 1983). Since sex role has already been extensively studied, we chose to examine whether locus of control is related to the likelihood that a family budgets, and to the relative influence in this decision. Based on this, we propose the following conceptual hypotheses:

- Families that have children are more likely to use budgets compared to those that do not have children.

- Families are more likely to budget when wives have a more external locus of control, or when husbands have a more internal locus of control.

- In families that budget, relative influence will be greater for wives with a more external locus of control, and for husbands with a more internal locus of control.

- In families that budget, relative influence will be greater for husbands with higher individual income, and for wives whose husbands have lower individual income.

Checking and Savings Accounts

A wife's decision to open her own checking or savings account may be related to her own attitudes and to family characteristics like household income, i.e. her decision is largely autonomous. But for accounts that are jointly held, the wife may report her husband has more relative influence, because he typically earns the bulk of the family income. Thus, different factors may underlie decisions about individual versus jointly-owned accounts.

In the absence of any reports in the literature, we propose that individual ownership of these types of financial services by a spouse will be more likely when that person is sex role modern. Further, wives will be more likely to have these accounts in their own names when they have higher individual incomes. Husbands or wives that work for pay will likely have a checking account for day to day transactions, or use a savings account as a place for extra funds.

Turning to joint accounts, the factors affecting choice of institution may be somewhat different. Since participation in the paid workforce for men in the 25-44 year age group is very widespread, they are likely to be earning an income that provides for a major part of family earnings in many families. Thus, the husband's individual income may give him more relative influence in decisions involving joint accounts. Also, the husband's sex role attitude may be an important variable. When the husband is more traditional he will be more likely to retain influence, but when he is more modern the couple's pattern of influence will be more joint.

The choice of institution for checking and savings accounts is a one-time decision, analogous to brand choice. Since these services are comparable across institutions, this choice does not involve particularly large consequences. Foxman and Burns (1987) propose that overloaded spouses may be more involved in major decisions (e.g., budget allocation) but less involved in the less important choices like generic product choice and least of all in specific brand or variant selection. Based on this, if the wife is overloaded, she may leave the decision about choice of institution to the husband. When she is not facing any role overload, she may have more relative influence. The following conceptual hypotheses are proposed:

- Individual ownership of checking and savings accounts by wives will be more likely when they have more modern sex role attitudes, higher family incomes, and higher individual incomes. It will be more likely for husbands when the latter have more modern sex role attitudes and higher household incomes.

- In the choice of financial institution for joint accounts, wives will have more relative influence when they do not feel high role overload or when their husbands have lower incomes. Husbands will have more relative influence when they have higher incomes or have more traditional sex role attitudes.

Investments

A family can be expected to own joint investments provided it has surplus household income. Turning to decisions about when to invest, the type of investment, and how much to invest, the extent of relative influence of each spouse may be driven by different factors. The traditional husband may dominate in these decisions, which have typically been the responsibility of the husband, or because he happens to earn a major part of the family income. For sex-role modern couples, the detailed decisions may be made jointly. The wife may not want much involvement, perhaps because she is preoccupied with the demands of child-raising. But life-cycle aspects must also be considered. There is likely to be role specialization as couples move into later years of the family life cycle (FLC).

- The ownership of joint investments will be positively related to total family income.

- For details of investment decisions, such as when to invest, type of investment, and how much to invest, relative influence for wives will be negatively related to presence and ages of children. For the husband, his relative influence will be greater when his sex role attitude is more traditional, and also when he has higher individual income.

Credit Cards

Credit card ownership and usage has been studied from economic and behavioral perspectives. Previous research includes relating demand to finance charges (Garcia 1980), attitudes towards credit (Awh and Waters 1974), and impact on spending (Feinberg 1986; Hirschman 1979). In comparing credit card owners to non-owners, the former are more likely to be older and have higher levels of income, education, and socioeconomic status (Kinsey 1981, Mandell 1973).

An early study found that men were more likely to own travel and entertainment cards (e.g.,

American Express) and bank cards (e.g., VISA), while women were more likely to own retail store cards (Adcock et al 1977). Hirschman (1979) proposed that credit card ownership may be partially explained by traditional sex role attitudes. She attributed differences by sex to the traditional family roles of the man as "provider" and the woman as homemaker and "purchasing agent." The author further suggested that the increased "blurring" of sex role differences could be expected to alter these patterns.

This paper examines the extent to which wives and husbands own credit cards in their own names. The factors relating to individual ownership may differ from those affecting joint ownership. Further, the distinction needs to be made between major credit cards and retail store cards. Marketers of major credit cards require substantial incomes, while the income standards used by retailers are not as strict. For wives, individual ownership of major credit cards can be expected to depend on their sex role attitudes and their own incomes, in addition to family income. For husbands, we would expect sex role moderns to be more likely to have their own retail cards. Based on this, the following conceptual hypotheses are proposed:

- Individual ownership of major credit cards by wives will be more likely when they have more modern sex role attitudes, higher family incomes, and higher individual incomes. Turning to husbands, individual ownership of major credit cards will be more likely when they have more modern sex role attitudes and higher household incomes.

- Individual ownership of retail credit cards by wives will not vary by sex role attitude. For husbands, individual ownership of retail credit cards will be more likely for sex role moderns.

METHODOLOGY

The data used in this study were obtained through a mail survey conducted in a medium-sized northeastern city. To obtain participants, a judgement sample of civic organizations and churches was contacted. These organizations were asked to provide the names of couples where at least one member of the couple might be between the ages of 25 and 44. Approximately 30 percent of the contacted organizations agreed to cooperate. The couples were asked if they would be willing to participate in a study of financial decision making. They were also screened to ensure that at least one member of the couple was a babyboomer. To encourage participation, the couples were informed that a cash donation would be made to a charity of their choice once the completed questionnaires were received. In addition the couples were given a chance to win one of four prizes consisting of U.S. savings bonds.

A packet which included a cover letter, two surveys, and two return envelopes was mailed to the couples. The instructions explicitly stated that each member of the couple was to work independently. Approximately three-quarters of those volunteering actually participated. One hundred and sixty-eight completed questionnaires were received. In two cases, the spouse did not respond resulting in responses from 83 couples. The mean age for the wives was 35 years and that for the husbands was 36.3 years. The median family income for the participants was $46,500 in 1989. As stated earlier we estimated that the median family income estimated for the entire 25-44 year age group was $37,000 in 1987.

There were five parts to the questionnaire. The first section asked about ownership of financial services and the relative influence of the two spouses in financial decisions. A five-point scale was used to measure relative influence (1=me, 2=me more than my spouse, 3=shared equally, 4=my spouse more than me, and 5=my spouse). Before doing the analysis, husbands' answers were recoded so that for all respondents a high number indicated high husband influence and a low number indicated high wife influence.

In the second section, the participants' locus of control was measured using a scale developed by Rotter (1966). The sex role attitudes of the participants were measured in the third section using Osmond and Martin's (1975) Sex Role Attitude Scale. This scale was modified by dropping some items. The first group consisted of stereotypes of male/female nature and behaviors, e.g. women are as capable as men of enjoying a full sex life. We also dropped four items that dealt with social change as related to sex roles, e.g. men's clubs and lodges should be required to admit women. It was felt that the items omitted would have little relationship to family financial decision making. Reilly's (1982) scale was used to measure role overload in the fourth section. The final section measured various demographic characteristics including income, and number and ages of children.

ANALYSIS AND RESULTS

For the prevalence of budgeting and the ownership of specific financial services, separate discriminant analyses were performed using the hypothesized independent variables. These results are summarized in Table 1. The hypotheses about the relative influence of the spouses in joint decision making were tested by performing analyses of variance separately for the wife and husband. These findings are summarized in Table 2.

Budgeting

As hypothesized, wives' responses indicated that the family was more likely to budget if it included children ($p < .004$). However, the wife's locus of control did not differentiate between families that budget and those that did not. The husbands' responses also indicated that families that included children were more likely to budget ($p<.03$).

Figure 1
Wives' Responses on Decision to Budget

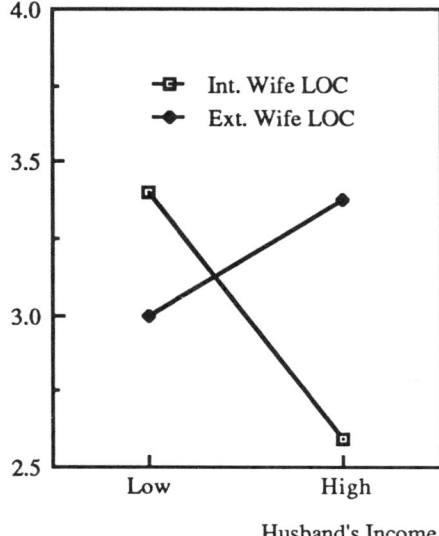

Figure 2
Husbands' Responses on Decision to Budget

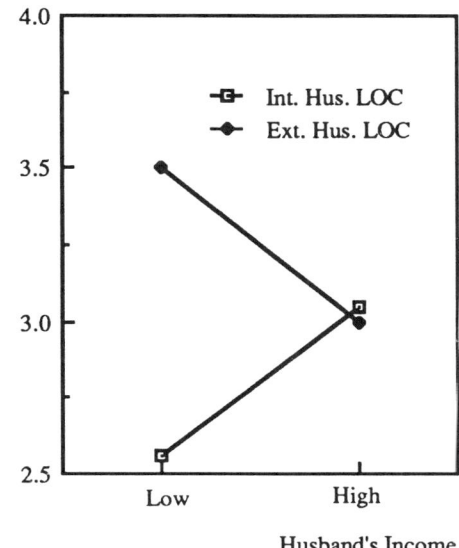

In addition, as hypothesized those families that budgeted were more likely to have husbands with a more internal locus of control ($p < .04$).

For the wife's rating of her relative influence in the decision to make a budget, there was an interaction of husband's income and her locus of control (see Figure 1). The wife dominated the process when her husband had a high income and she had an internal locus of control. The husband dominated when he had a low income and she had an internal locus of control, and also when he had a high income and she had an external locus of control. When the husband had a low income and she had an external locus of control, the process was joint.

For the husband's rating of his relative influence in the decision to make a budget, there was an interaction of husband's income and his locus of control (see Figure 2). When the husband had a high income the task was joint. In contrast, when he had a low income, the task was husband dominated if he had an external locus of control and wife dominated if he had an internal locus of control.

Checking and Savings Accounts

As hypothesized, women with more modern sex role attitudes were more likely to have their own checking account ($p < .05$) and their own savings account ($p < .04$). Women with higher household incomes were more likely to have individual savings accounts ($p < .03$), but no more likely to have their own checking accounts. In addition, wife's income was not related to individual ownership of either type of account.

Husbands' ownership of individual checking accounts was more likely when family income was higher as hypothesized ($p < .004$), but this was not the case for individual savings accounts. Turning to sex role attitudes, traditional husbands were more likely to have individual checking accounts ($p < .006$) and those with more modern sex role attitudes were more likely to have individual savings accounts. The latter relationship was only marginally significant ($p < .09$). In hindsight, if we consider that traditional husbands may have more control over their families' finances, it is reasonable to expect them to express this control through individual ownership of checking accounts.

Wives' rated their relative influence to be higher in the selection of joint checking ($p < .005$) and joint savings accounts ($p < .05$) when their husbands had low incomes. However, note that there was also a significant interaction between wife's role overload and husband's income for both joint checking accounts ($p < .02$) and joint saving accounts ($p < .008$). These interactions are shown in Figures 3 and 4. When the wife had high role overload the decisions were somewhat husband dominated and relatively unaffected by husband's income. There was a different pattern if the wife had low role overload. In this case, if the husband had a high income, he dominated the decision and if he had a low income, the decisions were somewhat wife dominated.

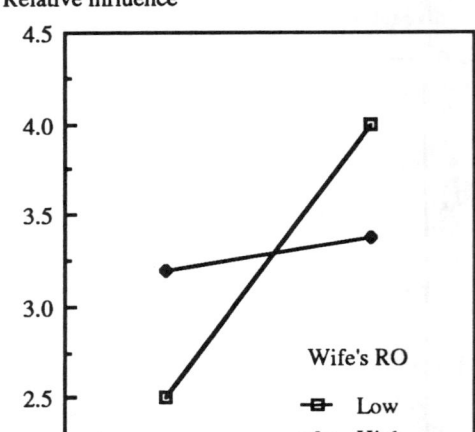

Figure 3
Wife's Rel. Influence in Selection - Checking

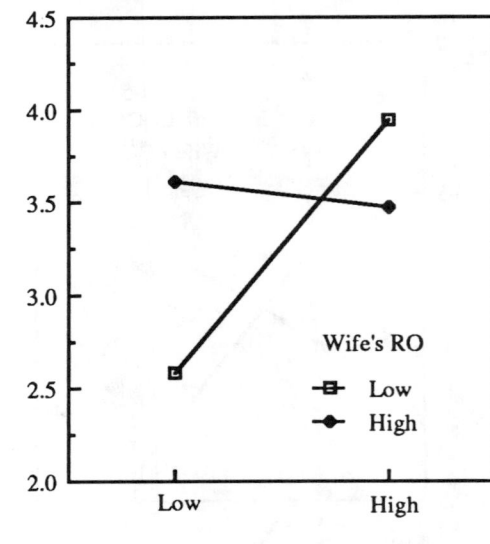

Figure 4
Wife's Rel. Influence in Selection - Savings

As hypothesized, husbands perceived they had more relative influence in selecting joint checking ($p < .003$) and savings institutions ($p < .005$) when they had high incomes. Traditional husbands rated their influence as higher in selection of the joint checking account ($p = .05$) although the same was not true for joint savings.

Investments

Couples with higher incomes were more likely to have joint investments as indicated by the responses of the wives ($p < .002$) and husbands ($p < .09$). For husbands, this relationship was only marginally significant. The wife's estimate of her influence on when to invest, what type of investment to make, and how much to invest were all related to the family life cycle ($p < .02$, $p < .02$, $p < .005$). For all three decisions the wife's influence was greatest for couples that had no children, intermediate for those couples with at least one child under six years old, and lower for those couples with older children.

As hypothesized, husbands with traditional sex role attitudes estimated they had more influence on the joint investment activities. This effect was significant for when to invest ($p < .02$), type of investment ($p < .05$), and how much to invest ($p < .05$). In addition, husbands with high individual incomes had more influence over when to invest ($p < .04$).

Credit Cards

As hypothesized, women who had major credit cards in their own name had more modern sex role attitudes ($p < .02$), higher household incomes ($p < .01$), and higher individual incomes ($p < .02$). Wife's sex role attitude was not related to ownership of retail credit cards as predicted.

Husbands with higher incomes were more likely to have a major credit card in their own name as expected ($p < .000$). Sex role attitude was not related to ownership of major credit cards, however husbands with more modern sex role attitudes were found to be more likely to own their own retail credit cards ($p = .05$).

Discussion and Future Research

Before discussing the findings of the study we would like to provide some caveats. While we contacted a wide variety of civic and church organizations to elicit respondents, certain types of respondents may be under or over represented. There is also the potential for nonresponse biases. For example, respondents in previous studies of family decision making have typically had high levels of income and education. Since a mail survey was used, it is difficult to rule out the possibility that spouses may have influenced each other's responses. However, there is little indication of this. First, as instructed, all spouses used separate envelopes to return their surveys. In many cases these envelopes had different postmarks. Finally, the spouses answers to both factual and attitudinal items were different in many cases.

This study provides strong support for using the general model of family decision making proposed by Buss and Schaninger (1983). Many of the conceptual hypotheses were in terms of

TABLE 1
Discriminant Analysis Differentiating Owners and Non-owners for the following Financial Decisions

Dependent variable	Independent var.	p	Group means Own / Not own	
Budget (wife's response)	Kids	.004	.87	.57
	Wife's LOC	n.s.		
Budget (husband's response)	Kids	.03	.87	.65
	Husband's LOC	.04	.34	.40
Wife's individual checking account	Wife's SRA	.05	2.24	2.44
	Household income	n.s.		
	Wife's income	n.s.		
Husband's individual checking account	Husband's SRA	.006	2.58	2.53
	Household income	.004	10.3	8.1
Wife's individual savings account	Wife's SRA	.04	2.27	2.47
	Household income	.03	9.05	7.74
	Wife's income	n.s.		
Husband's individual savings account	Husband's SRA	.09	2.41	2.59
	Household income	n.s.		
Investments (wife's resp.)	Household income	.002	8.63	6.10
Investments (husband's resp.)	Household income	.09	8.58	7.25
Wife's individual major credit card	Wife's SRA	.02	2.23	2.46
	Household income	.01	9.30	7.85
	Wife's income	.02	4.15	2.56
Husband's individual major credit card	Husband's SRA	n.s.		
	Household income	.000	9.53	7.53
Wife's individual retail credit card	Wife's SRA	n.s.		
Husband's individual retail credit card	Husband's SRA	.05	2.42	2.59

antecedent demographic factors (e.g., family and individual income and family life cycle), and attitudinal variables such as sex role attitudes and locus of control. Wife's perceived role overload, a situational variable, had an interesting interaction with husband's income for relative influence in choosing the institution for checking and savings accounts.

The study looked at patterns of ownership and relative influence across a range of financial decisions, including budgeting. It covered checking and savings accounts, investments, and credit cards. Many of the specific predictions were borne out. In addition to income, family life cycle, the presence/absence of children, and sex role attitude entered many of the relationships examined, for wives and husbands. Interestingly, husbands' individual income was often related to wives' perceptions of relative influence.

A variety of financial services were examined here, e.g., major vs. retail credit cards, checking and savings accounts, and investments. Further, the study focused on babyboomers, a very important group from a managerial perspective. While the findings should be interpreted with caution, the use of a mid-range theoretical structure can help managers better understand how demographic as well as attitudinal variables relate to consumer behavior for financial services. This can help in designing marketing strategy (e.g., segmentation and positioning decisions), as well as designing service attributes and promotion appeals (message content). The sample was small, but compares with those in other studies of family decision-making where both spouses have been surveyed. Subsequent studies should examine these and related issues with larger samples.

TABLE 2
Analysis of Variance for Relative Influence in Financial Decision Making

Wives' responses

Dependent variable	Independent var.	p	Group means
Decide to budget	Husband's income	n.s.	
	Wife's LOC	n.s.	
	Hus. inc.x wife LOC	.03	see figure 1
Selected joint checking	Husband's income	.005	<40K=2.91; ≥40K=3.71
	Wife role overload	n.s.	
	Hus. inc x wife RO	.02	see figure 3
Selected joint savings	Husband's income	.05	<40K=3.20; ≥40K=3.74
	Wife role overload	n.s.	
	Hus. inc x wife RO	.008	see figure 4
When to invest	FLC	.02	N*=3.07; Y=3.72; O=4.11
Type of investment	FLC	.02	N=3.20; Y=3.63; O=4.22
How much to invest	FLC	.005	N=3.00; Y=3.60; O=4.11

*Note: For FLC, N = no children, Y= at least one child under six years, O = children over six years old

Husbands' responses

Dependent variable	Independent var.	p	Group means
Decide to budget	Husband's income	n.s.	
	Husband's LOC	n.s.	
	Hus. inc.x hus. LOC	.10	see figure 2
Selected joint checking	Husband's income	.003	<40K=3.21; ≥40K=4.00
	Husband's SRA	.05	Modern=3.36 Trad.=3.89
Selected joint savings	Husband's income	.005	<40K=3.32; ≥40K=4.03
	Husband's SRA	n.s.	
When to invest	Husband's income	.04	<40K=3.36; ≥40K=3.90
	Husband's SRA	.02	Modern=3.35 Trad.=3.95
Type of investment	Husband's income	n.s.	
	Husband's SRA	.05	Modern=3.55 Trad.=4.03
How much to invest	Husband's income	n.s.	
	Husband's SRA	.05	Modern=3.39 Trad.=3.85

An important methodological issue in family and group studies is whether to use one or more respondent. This study suggests that both spouses should be studied in order to capture the differences between the factors that may influence their behaviors, even if there is agreement on the outcomes.

Three areas for future research appear promising. First, it will be useful to examine the extent of agreement between wives and husbands on relative influence for financial decisions. It is possible that groups may be identified that differ on this dimension. Future research can address what factors underlie the extent of agreement. Second, there were interesting interactions of income with locus of control for budgeting decisions, and with role overload for choice of checking and savings institutions. These interactions can be examined in greater detail to identify whether there are any other contextual factors (e.g., sex of respondent, for locus of control) that will add to our understanding.

Finally, sex roles and the other attitudinal variables can be studied in the context of other aspects of financial decisions not reported here, such as jointly-owned credit cards and insurance decisions. Some of these aspects form part of our continuing research program.

REFERENCES

Adcock, William O., Elizabeth C. Hirschman, and Jac L. Goldstucker (1977), "Bank Card Users: An Updated Profile," *Advances in Consumer Research*, 4, William D. Perreault, Jr. ed., Atlanta, Georgia: Association for Consumer Research, 236-241.

Awh, Robert and Don Waters (1974), "A Discriminant Analysis of Economic, Demographic, and Attitudinal Characteristics of Bank Charge-Card Holders: A Case Study," *Journal of Finance*, 29 (June), 973-980.

Beutler, Ivan F. and Kristine M. Sahlberg (1980), "Spending Plans and the Managerial Decision Process", *Advances in Consumer Research*, 7, 480-485.

Buss, Christian W. and Charles M. Schaninger (1983), "The Influence of Sex Roles on Family Decision Processes and Outcomes," *Advances in Consumer Research*, 10, R. P. Bagozzi and A. M. Tybout eds., Ann Arbor, MI: Association for Consumer Research, 439-444.

Cunningham, Isabella C. M. and Robert T. Green (1974), "Purchasing Roles in the U.S. Family, 1955 and 1973," *Journal of Marketing*, 38 (October), 61-64.

Davis, Harry L. and Benny P. Rigaux (1974), "Perception of Marital Roles in Decision Processes," *Journal of Consumer Research*, 1 (June), 51-62.

Deacon, R.E. and F.M. Firebaugh (1975), *Home Management Context and Concepts*, Boston: Houghton-Mifflin.

Feinberg, Richard A. (1986), "Credit Cards as Spending Facilitating Stimuli: A Conditioning Interpretation," *Journal of Consumer Research*, 13 (December), 348-356.

Ferber, Robert and Lucy Chao Lee (1974), "Husband-Wife Influence in Family Purchasing Behavior," *Journal of Consumer Research*, 1 (June), 43-50.

Foxman, Ellen and Alvin C. Burns (1987), "Role Load in the Household," *Advances in Consumer Research*, 14, Melanie Wallendorf and Paul Anderson eds., Provo, Utah: Association for Consumer Research, 458-462.

Garcia, Gillian (1980), "Credit Cards: An Interdisciplinary Survey," *Journal of Consumer Research*, 6 (March), 327-337.

Granbois, Donald H., Dennis L. Rosen and Franklin Acito (1986), "A Developmental Study of Family Financial Management Practices," *Advances in Consumer Research*, 13, Richard J, Lutz ed., Provo, Utah: Association for Consumer Research, 170-174.

Hirschman, Elizabeth C. (1979), "Differences in Consumer Purchase Behavior by Credit Card Payment System," *Journal of Consumer Research*, 6 (June), 58-66.

Kenkel, William F. (1961), "Family Interaction in Decision-Making on Spending," in Nelson Foote, ed., *Household Decision-Making* (New York: New York University Press) 140-164.

Kim, Chankon and Hanjoon Lee (1989), "Sex Role Attitudes of Spouses and Task Sharing Behavior," *Advances in Consumer Research*, 16, 671-679.

Kinsey, Jean (1981), "Determinants of Credit Card Accounts: An Application of Tobit Analysis," *Journal of Consumer Research*, 8 (September), 172-182.

Mandell, Lewis (1972), *Credit Card Use in the United States*, Ann Arbor, MI: Institute for Social Research, University of Michigan.

Moore-Shay, Elizabeth S. and William L. Wilkie (1988), "Recent Developments in Research in Family Decisions," *Advances in Consumer Research*, 15, Michael J. Houston ed., Provo, UT: Association for Consumer Research, 454-460.

Osmond, Marie W. and Patricia Y. Martin (1975), "Sex and Sexism: A Comparison of Male and Female Sex-Role Attitudes," *Journal of Marriage and Family*, 37 (November), 744-758.

Qualls, J. William (1987), "Household Decision Behavior: The Impact of Husbands' and Wives' Sex Role Orientation," *Journal of Consumer Research*, 14 (September), 264-279.

Reilly, M.D. (1982), "Working Wives and Convenience Consumption," *Journal of Consumer Research*, 8 (March), 407-418.

Rosen, Dennis L. and Donald H. Granbois (1983), "Determinants of Role Structure in Family Financial Management," *Journal of Consumer Research*, 10 (September), 253-258.

Rotter, Julian B. (1966), "Generalized Expectancies for Internal Versus External Control of Reinforcement," *Psychological Monographs*, 80(1), Whole No. 609.

Scanzoni, John (1977), "Changing Sex Roles and Emerging Directions in Family Decision Making," *Journal of Consumer Research*, 4 (December), 185-188.

Schaninger, Charles M., W. Christian Buss and Rajiv Grover (1982), "The Effect of Sex Roles on Family Finance Handling and Decision Influence." *An Assessment of Marketing Thought and Practice*, 1982 Educator's Conference Proceedings, Bruce J. Walker, William O. Bearden, William R. Darden, Patrick E. Murphy, John R. Nevin, Jerry C. Olson and Barton A. Weitz eds., Chicago: American Marketing Association, 43-47.

Waldrop, Judith (1989), "Inside America's Households," *American Demographics*, (March), 20-27.

Wolgast, Elizabeth H. (1958), "Do Husbands of Wives Make the Purchasing Decisions?" *Journal of Marketing*, 22 (October), 151-158.

An Investigation of a Role/Goal Model of Wives' Role Overload Reduction Strategies

Shreekant G. Joag, St. John's University
James W. Gentry, University of Nebraska-Lincoln
Karin Ekstrom, University of Goteborg

ABSTRACT

Joag, Gentry, and Hopper (1984) proposed a model to explain the manner in which the wife's work status and her work goals affect her consumption behavior. This paper suggests several refinements in the model and presents a revised model that could explain behavioral differences in several aspects of the wife's life style. The paper also reports a test of the model, which yields a somewhat inconsistent pattern of results, indicating that complex relationships exist between a wife's goals and work roles and her perception of role overload.

INTRODUCTION

The large increase in the number of females in the work force has provided incentive for marketers to study differences in the buyer behavior of working and nonworking women. The basic premise of most of the research is that role overload occurs among working women, resulting in more convenience-oriented consumption behavior than for nonworking females. That is, the wife's employment would take away a share of her time and energy from home production activities and, thus, result in increased purchase of time-saving goods and services.

Support for this premise has been mixed. Working wives have been found to spend less time in supermarkets (Hacklander 1978), to make fewer shopping trips (Anderson 1972; Douglas 1976; McCall 1977), and to spend fewer hours on housework (Nickols and Fox 1983; Reynolds, Crask, and Wells 1977). Conflicting findings have emerged regarding the purchasing of more convenience-related items among working women. A few studies support this idea (Rizek and Peterkin 1980; Vickery 1979; Waldman and Jacobs 1978), while the majority of studies fail to find strong evidence that working wives purchase more convenience products (Anderson 1972; Douglas 1976; Reynolds, Crask, and Wells 1977; Strober and Weinberg 1977, 1980; Weinberg and Winer 1983). In fact, Bryant (1988) found that wives' employment was inversely related to the purchase of durables. Realizing that work status alone is somewhat limited (and, apparently, somewhat insufficient) as a predictor of household purchase behavior, researchers have begun to look for additional constructs to explain the differences in the consumption behaviors of working and nonworking wives. Reilly (1982) discussed the concept of role overload, which is the role conflict that occurs when demands from the family and the job position of the working wife exceed the amount of time and energy available to her. Role overload was hypothesized to lead to more convenience-oriented consumption. Although his findings indicated a causal link between role overload and the purchase of time-saving durables, the amount of variance explained was very small.

A second extension was the three-way occupational status scheme introduced by Schaninger and Allen (1981). Their approach is based upon the Rappoports' (1971) distinction between dual income and dual career families. The three categories of occupational status used in this scheme are nonworking wife, low-occupational status working wife, and high-occupational status working wife. The researchers hypothesized that the high-occupational status working wife would experience the greatest overload due to her dedication to her career, and they used the Hollingshead Index of Social Position (Hollingshead and Redlich 1958) to categorize wives according to their work status. Other studies (Joag, Gentry, and Hopper 1984; Nickols and Fox 1983) have also used a similar approach. In general, some differences in purchase behavior have been explained with the three-way classification system, but other variables seem to do just as well, if not better. For example, Nickols and Fox (1983) found income to be a better explanatory variable of purchase behavior than the occupational status of the wife.

Some variables appear to be missing in these efforts to explain overload. In our research we examine critically several current assumptions regarding role overload and suggest other variables that can explain the phenomenon. Moreover, we will investigate the convenience consumption patterns resulting from different levels of role overload. We also propose a role/goal model and test it empirically.

THE COMPLEX NATURE OF ROLE OVERLOAD

The nature of role overload is complex. The addition of a job does not necessarily create time and energy demands beyond the wife's capacity. Sieber (1974) suggested that additional responsibilities (i.e., a job outside the home) may involve positive outcomes such as role privilege, status, security, status enhancement, and personality involvement which outweigh the additional role overload. Consequently, a wife's total available amount of energy may expand to handle the additional load. Gove and his colleagues (Gove and Geerken 1977; Gove and Tudor 1973) developed an even stronger proposition in their Role-Stress Theory. They argue that employed women will be LESS psychologically distressed than housewives because they have two sources of potential gratification (work and family). To the extent that the wives want to be in the work force, we would concur with the predictions of Role-Stress Theory. Thus, investigation of the wife's work goals and her motivation to achieve them is critical in the assessment of her perceived role overload.

Reilly (1982) argues that the wife's role overload is created by her total position set (home, work, social, etc.) and the nature of responsibilities involved, an argument which was supported empirically by Foxman and Burns (1986). Marks (1977) argued that an individual's commitment to each responsibility within a set determines the amount of energy required to fulfill the complete set. Tradeoffs within the total role set may result in little increase in objective role load.

Deci and Ryan (1990) distinguish between "self" and "skin" in terms of the motivation for intentional behavior. Those activities undertaken willingly are associated with "self," while those undertaken out of obligation ("I have to" rather than "I want to") are associated with the "skin" but not the "self." Both job and home responsibilities may be associated with intrinsic motivation for some individuals, while others may handle both sets out of obligation. The subjective perception of the responsibilities determines role overload, and not the objective role loads themselves.

Wives may reduce perceived role overload in a number of ways. Most studies in consumer research have focused on the purchase of time-saving durables (Anderson 1972; Reilly 1982; Strober and Weinberg 1977, 1980; Weinberg and Winer 1983), and the purchase of convenience goods (Anderson 1972; Douglas 1976; McCall 1977; Reilly 1982; Schaninger and Allen 1981). A smaller number of studies has investigated time economizing with the use of convenience services (Bellante and Foster 1984; Joag, Gentry and Hopper 1984; Nickols and Fox 1983), the use of substitute labor of family members for housework, the application of efficient management practices, and reduced leisure activities (Nickols and Fox 1983). All these strategies could be employed by wives to reduce their perceived role overload.

This discussion suggests that measurement of role overload is a complex task. However, studies have typically used occupational status or role overload to investigate consumption differences in working and nonworking wives. Recently, Joag, Gentry, and Hopper (1984) proposed a model that integrated the wife's work role with the wife's work goal (or work motivation) in an attempt to explain purchase behavior.

THE ROLE/GOAL MODEL

Joag, Gentry, and Hopper (1985) proposed that role overload is not just a function of the demands of a total position set as suggested by Reilly (1982), but rather a function of the match (or mismatch) between the wife's goals (which define her desired state) and her roles (which define her actual state). Together, these two constructs determine her motivation and her capacity to carry out the various roles and, thus, her perceived role overload. This perceived role overload, in turn, impacts her consumption behavior. The model proposed that a wife with career as her goal may perceive role overload in housework, while one with being a homemaker as her goal may perceive role overload in her job. Therefore, the actions taken by the two in reducing their perceived overload may be totally different, with one trying to minimize her commitments at home and the other her commitments at work.

One major shortcoming of the model is the assumption of a clear dichotomy of the wife's goals into career versus being a homemaker. While any wife may be able to rank her goals in order of priority, the assumption of the model that she would ultimately choose one over the other is questionable. On the contrary, many wives may like to pursue several goals simultaneously to varying degrees. Therefore, the wife's goals must be considered as a multidimensional variable. Each dimension of her goals, in combination with her role set in the related sphere of activities, would influence her behavior. The need for such independent treatment of various goal dimensions is further supported by the premise that the perception of role overload depends upon the perceived demands on the wife's time and energy, and upon her perceived total capacity to meet such demands. Thus, a wife who does not consider being homemaker as an important goal may perceive role overload in her family role even if she does not work outside the home.

The revised model suggests that the wife's worlds inside the home and outside the home can be considered independently. Concerning the wife's position as a homemaker, the model classifies wives by their possible goals as "personalizer," "provider," and "avoider." A "personalizer" considers herself the primary person responsible for carrying out household tasks, and these need to be done with a personal touch in order to bond the family. A "provider" still considers the household tasks as primarily her responsibility; however, any means are justified so long as the job is done. Her personal involvement in doing everything is not necessary. She may, for example, accept help from family members or buy convenience-related goods or services. Finally, an "avoider" feels little, if any, primary or special responsibility for the household tasks, and she believes that other family members have at least equal responsibility for carrying out household tasks.

Similarly, in the outside world, the wife's goals can be defined as "no-desire-to-work," "just-a-job," and "career." In some respects this classification resembles several existing motivation-based classifications. Bartos (1977) discusses a Yankelovich survey that asked working women: "Do you consider work you do 'just a job' or a 'career'?" In her own research, Bartos (1977, 1978) defined four groups of women: stay at home, plan to work, just a job, and career-oriented. Zeithaml (1985) used this definition of work motivation (calling it "female working status") and found significant differences among groups for the number of supermarkets shopped, the amount of pretrip

FIGURE 1
Role Goal Interaction Model to Explain Differences in Wives' Consumption Behavior

	Role Set Demands on Time and Energy		
Roles	Low	Medium	High
Goals			
Figure 1a: Home			
Personalizer	A1 Harmony	A2 Lo Ovld Home	A3 Hi Ovld Home
Provider	B1 Lo Ovld Home	B2 Harmony	B3 Hi Ovld Home
Avoider	C1 Lo Ovld Home	C2 Hi Ovld Home	C3 Harmony
Figure 1b: Outside Home			
No-Desire-to-Work	D1 Satisfaction	D2 Lo Ovld Job	D3 Hi Ovld Job
Just-a-Job	E1 Dissatisfaction	E2 Satisfaction	E3 Lo Ovld Job
Career	F1 Dissatisfaction	F2 Dissatisfaction	F3 Satisfaction

planning done, the amount of money spent, and the attitudes towards grocery shopping.

Wives' roles in the revised role/goal model are defined similarly to the those in the previous model (Joag, Gentry, and Hopper 1984): "nonworking," "stagnant job" (just a job), and "career." The new model, shown in Figure 1, extends the previous model and provides a basis for investigating how the match or mismatch of roles and goals will affect the wife's behavioral patterns in related spheres of life.

The top part of Figure 1 presents the model for the wife's world inside the home. In her role as a homemaker, the wife with her goal as a "personalizer" probably avoids purchasing home-oriented convenience products because her self concept depends upon providing products and services with a personal touch. Thus, other things being equal, this segment more likely purchases products that enhance the personal touch in homemaking: cookbooks, serving materials, more traditional household appliances, and fewer convenience goods. However, if a "personalizer" is employed in a stagnant job or in a career, she experiences role overload in her work and purchases job-related convenience products: a new car, a home close to the place of work, a job close to home, or a less demanding job. Such overload may also force her to use some household-related convenience products, though only to the extent absolutely necessary.

The "provider" will feel high home overload if she is working because she still perceives the household as her primary responsibility. She can be characterized as using convenience consumption patterns to reduce her overload. However, the extent will depend on other ways to reduce overload, e.g. how much help she gets from other family members since she willingly accepts help from others. A non-working provider will feel a low amount of home overload since she does not consider being a homemaker as her top priority in comparison to the personalizer. She will, therefore, use convenience consumption patterns.

A wife whose goal can be described as being an "avoider" will perceive role overload in her role as a homemaker irrespective of her work status. Such a wife would be a heavy user of convenience goods and time- and effort-saving strategies. Given employment outside the home, these women perceive even higher levels of overload at home and explore all possible avenues to rid themselves of the household tasks.

The bottom part of Figure 1 presents the model for the wife's world outside the home. A wife who has "no-desire-to-work" will feel satisfied when not employed outside the home. If she for whatever reason (financial, status, etc.) has to work, the model predicts that she will feel low job overload in a stagnant job and high job overload in a career. As her feeling of job overload increases, her usage of job-related convenience products such as a new car or a computer will also increase. She may also search for a less demanding job, fewer hours of work, or a job closer to home.

The model predicts that a "just-a-job" wife would feel dissatisfied if she were not employed outside the home. She would feel harmony if she had a stagnant job. If placed in a career-oriented position, she would feel job overload in the job, and thus would likely use some job-related convenience products.

Finally, a career wife will feel dissatisfied unless employed in a career job. Her dissatisfaction will lead to the use of job training products and services to a great extent. The use of these products and services will most likely be higher for a non-working career wife than for a stagnant job wife.

In summary, the wives falling in the cells D1, E2, and F3 along the diagonal will experience greater harmony and satisfaction since their actual and desired work status match. The use of job-related convenience products will increase to the right of the diagonal (cells D2, D3, E3). The cells to the left of the diagonal describe situations where individuals want to secure a job (cells E1 and F1) or a career employment (cell F2). Wives in these categories are likely to be heavy consumers of job training products and services.

METHOD

Wives in Madison, Wisconsin, were contacted at their residences, and asked to complete a ten-page questionnaire and to mail it back to the investigators. If the female contacted was not currently married, the interviewer thanked her and went to the next household. Several neighborhoods were sampled in order to provide a mix of socio-economic backgrounds. Most of the contacts were made during the early evening or on weekends. A total of 185 responses were received, out of the 230 which were distributed. No financial incentive was provided the respondents. Refusals to participate were infrequent (less than 20), but households that could not be contacted in two visits were plentiful. Sixty-two of the wives in the sample did not work, while the other 123 did.

Dependent Measures. The questionnaire asked the respondents about their perceived role overload and their usage of strategies to reduce that overload. Perceived role overload was measured as a summation of the items listed in Appendix 1, where the overload reduction strategies are also listed. The Cronbach alpha for the perceived role overload measures was .63. Consumption-related strategies were investigated further by including items concerning ownership of time-saving durables, their use of time-saving services, and their time allocations to various household and leisure activities.

Independent Variables. For the Goal constructs, three levels for both the Home Goal and for the Job Goal were proposed. Three questions were used to measure the Home Goal, one for each level (Personalizer, Provider, and Avoider). Several questions were used to measure the Job Goal and its three levels (Home-Oriented, Just-a-Job, and Career-Oriented). However, for both constructs, there was not a clean separation for the three levels. In both cases, the items measuring the first two levels (Personalizer/Provider and Home-Oriented/Just-a-Job) were highly positively correlated with each other and highly negatively correlated with the third level. Indices for both goal variables were created by summing those items associated with the first levels and subtracting those items associated with the third levels. Cronbach alphas for the Home Goal and the Job Goal were .53 and .80, respectively.

The Role variable was operationalized through the use of the occupational status of the respondent. This status was determined using the Hollingshead (Hollingshead and Redlich 1958) index as was done in previous research (Joag, Gentry, and Hopper 1984; Nickols and Fox 1983; Schaninger and Allen 1981). For our sample, 62 were non-working, 30 lower social status (LSS), and 93 higher social status (HSS).

The Role variables and the Goal variables were related to perceived role overload and the overload reduction strategies, holding constant the effects of wife's income, total household income, wife's age, and the presence of children in the home.

RESULTS

Pearson Product Moment Correlations

The first look at the direct relationships between roles and goals and perceived role overload was obtained through the use of the Pearson product moment correlations. [Given space constraints, the tables will not be included here but can be obtained from the authors.] One's home goal is inversely related to one's job goal and to the amount of time spent on the job. All three are positively related to perceived role overload, although the job goal is not related significantly. All three are related strongly to the wife's age; older wives worked less, had weaker career goals but stronger home goals. The age relationship explains the somewhat counter-intuitive relationship between the presence of children (and of young children) in those households working more, with strong job goals, and with weaker home goals. The wife's income was related positively to the amount worked and to one's job goal (and inversely to one's home goal), but the total household income was not significantly related to either hours worked by the wife nor to one's home goal. The wife's education was inversely related to her home goal and positively related to her job goal.

Partial Correlations

A second investigation of the relationships between the role and goals and perceived role overload and possible overload reduction strategies was made by looking at partial correlations, holding the wife's income, age, and education as well the presence of children and total household income constant. Both the home goal and the job goal were positively related to the level of perceived role overload, although job goal was not significantly related in most cases. Similarly, there was a direct relation between the number of hours worked and role overload except when age is held constant.

A strong job goal is related positively to postponing home responsibilities but inversely to buying time-saving products; apparently career-oriented wives are more interested in avoiding household tasks rather than doing them more quickly. They are interested in minimizing travel time to the job, but not in minimizing time on the job. They are not more likely to ask family members to help out. They are likely to discuss the pressures they face with close friends, but not necessarily with their husbands.

On the other hand, those with strong home goals were less likely to ask family members to help with household tasks and to postpone household activities. They are more likely to buy time-saving products. Like those with strong job goals, they are likely to discuss the pressures faced with close friends but not with their husbands. In both cases, though, this relationship does not hold when age is held constant. Neither one's job role nor one's home goal was related to the use of external help in the household.

Those working more hours per week were more likely to ask family members for help and to buy time-saving products, but less interested in minimizing time spent on the job. They were not more likely to seek external help, minimize travel time, or postpone home responsibilities. They were more likely to discuss pressures with close friends than those working less.

Given the relationships found above, we investigated further by looking at issues such as meals eaten out, meal preparation, home time allocation, and leisure time allocation. One's job goal is not related to the number of meals eaten out, once the effects of income, children, and age are held constant. However, there is evidence that those with stronger job goals are likely to prepare fewer meals at home and to wash fewer loads of laundry per week. On the other hand, those with strong home goals are less likely to eat breakfast out (but not lunch or dinner), to eat at pizza restaurants, and to have food delivered. They are likely to eat at elegant restaurants more frequently, prepare more meals at home each week, have more items per meal, and do more loads of laundry per week. Those working more hours per week are more likely to have food delivered and to eat at a pizza restaurant. They are likely to cook fewer meals, to have fewer items per meal, and to do fewer loads of laundry each week. Also, they are less likely to eat at elegant restaurants.

Husbands of wives with strong home goals spent less time with housework and child care, but more time with family finances. However, the wife's job goal was a stronger determinant of the husband's participation in housework, as husbands of wives with strong job goals spent more time in housework and in caring for children. Also, husbands wives with stronger job goals spent less time with the family finances. Thus the strong job goal apparently results in each spouse taking on responsibilities that were formerly those of the other spouse. The wife's job goal was a stronger influence on the husband's allocation of time than was the amount of hours worked, except for family finances.

On the other hand, the wife's job goal had little relationship with the allocation of her own time once income, age, and children were held constant. The wife's home goal was related strongly to her allocation of time to housework. However, the best explanatory variable for the wife's household time allocation was the number of hours worked per week. Those working more outside the home allocated less time to housework, to child care, to the family finances, to watching the children's leisure activities, and to watching the husband's leisure activities. Thus, the wife's job goal has major influence on the husband's household time allocation, while the amount of time worked by the wife is the major influence of her own household time. Surprisingly, the more the wife works, the less time each spouse spends on the family finances. Maybe the added income reduces the financial burden to the extent that neither spouse views finances as a worry.

In terms of leisure activities, there is a tendency for those working more to spend less time watching TV, interacting socially, and doing volunteer work. Those with strong job goals watch less TV, but the goals were unrelated to any other leisure time allocations. Those with strong home goals watch more TV and spend more time in volunteer work.

The job goal has little effect on one's shopping for groceries, clothes, or appliances. Those who work more grocery shop less frequently, but the amount worked is not related to clothes shopping frequency nor to appliance shopping. Those with stronger home goals are likely to grocery shop more frequently, to shop for clothes for oneself more frequently, and to shop for clothes for other family members more frequently.

Wife's Occupational Status

The wife's Role as measured by her occupational status (non-working, low social status, and high social status) was not included in the previous analyses due to its categorical nature. It was analyzed separately using ANCOVA, with the wife's income, age, and education, the household income, the presence of children, and the presence of a child under five as the covariates. There are no differences in the perceived role overload across the three occupational groups. There were some differences in the use of the strategies to reduce role overload, as those from the low social status group were the most likely to ask other family members to help with housework, while those non-working were the least likely to ask. Those non-working indicated that they would be more likely to minimize the time on the job if they were working than those currently working. Those from the higher social status group were more likely to eat dinner out, to eat pizza and hamburgers out, to have food delivered, and to prepare fewer meals at home each week than were the members of the other two groups. They also spent less time with housework, child care, the family finances, and watching TV. Those non-working spent more time in social interactions, while those in low social status occupations spent the least. The LSS group also spent more time each month shopping for clothes for other family members.

DISCUSSION

The study investigated the impact of the wife's Home and Job Goals and her Work Role on perceived role overload and on the strategies used to reduce that role overload. The wife's job and home goals and her work roles explain some differences in role overload and in the use of overload reduction strategies, but the relationships, while statistically significant, are not large (most of the partial correlations were in the range of .2 to .3) and are somewhat sparse. The overall pattern of results indicates that the influence of goals and work roles is not consistent across overload reduction strategies; simple notions such as working wives seeking to purchase time-saving products are not supported. In fact, our results indicate that strong job goals and heavier work roles are not related to the purchase of time-saving products, once variables such as age and income are controlled. Instead, wives with strong home goals are more likely to purchase time-saving products.

The results provide support for the contention that goals should be investigated as well as work roles. For example, the amount of time which the wife spends at work had the major influence on her allocation of time to various household activities, while her job goal had the strongest relative influence on the husband's household time allocations. A strong job goal leads the wife to seek help with housework from other family members, while a strong home goal has just the opposite influence.

REFERENCES

Anderson, Beverlee B. (1972), "Working Women Versus Nonworking Women: A Comparison of Shopping Behavior," in 1972 Combined *Proceeding*, eds. Boris W. Becker and Helmut Becker, Chicago: American Marketing Association, 335-359.

Bartos, Rena (1978), "What Every Marketer Should Know About Women," *Harvard Business Review*, 56, 73-85.

Bellante, Don and Ann C. Foster (1984), "Working Wives and Expenditure on Services," *Journal of Consumer Research*, 11 (September), 700-707.

Bryant, W. Keith (1988), "Durables and Wives' Employment Yet Again," *Journal of Consumer Research*, 15 (June), 37-47.

Davis, Harry L., Stephen J. Hoch, and E. K. Easton Ragsdale (1986), "An Anchoring and Adjustment Model of Spousal Predictions," *Journal of Consumer Research*, 13 (June), 25-37.

Deci, Edward L. and Richard M. Ryan (1990), "Integration in Personality: A Motivational View of Self," in Richard A. Dienstbier (Ed.), *Nebraska Symposium on Motivation: Perspectives in Motivation*, Vol. 38, Lincoln, NE: University of Nebraska Press, forthcoming.

Douglas, Susan P. (1976), "Working Wife vs. Nonworking Wife Families: A Basis for Segmenting Markets?", *Advances in Consumer Research*, 3, 191-198.

Foxman, Ellen and Alvin C. Burns (1987), "Role Load in the Household," *Advances in Consumer Research*, 14, 458-462.

Gove, Walter R. and Michael R. Geerken (1977), "The Effect of Children and Employment on the Mental Health of Married Men and Women," *Social Forces*, 56, 66-76.

Gove, Walter R. and Jeannette Tudor (1973), "Adult Sex Roles and Mental Illness," *American Journal of Sociology*, 78, 812-835.

Hacklander, Effie H. (1978), "Do Working Wives Shop Differently for Food?", *National Food Review*, 2 (April), 14-22.

Hollingshead, August B. and Frederick C. Redlich (1958), *Social Class and Mental Illness*, New York: John Wiley and Sons.

Joag, Shreekant G., James W. Gentry, and JoAnne Hopper (1984), "Explaining Differences in Consumption by Working and Nonworking Wives," *Advances in Consumer Research*, 11, 582-585.

Marks, Stephen R. (1977), "Multiple Roles and Role Strain: Some Notes on Human Energy, Time, and Commitment," *American Sociological Review*, 42, 921-936.

McCall, Suzanne H. (1977), "Meet the Workwife," *Journal of Marketing*, 41 (July), 55-65.

Nickols, Sharon Y. and Karen O. Fox (1983), "Buying Time and Saving Time: Strategies for Managing Household Production," *Journal of Consumer Research*, 10 (September), 197-208.

Rappoport, Rhona and Robert N. Rappoport (1971), "Further Considerations on the Dual Career Family," *Human Relations*, 24, 519-533.

Reilly, Michael D. (1982), "Working Wives and Convenience Consumption," *Journal of Consumer Research*, 8 (March), 407-418.

Reynolds, Fred D., Melvin R. Crask, and William D. Wells (1977), "The Modern Feminine Life Style," *Journal of Marketing*, 41 (No. 3, July), 38-45.

Rizek, Robert L. and Betty B. Peterkin (1980), "Food Costs and Practices of Households with Working Women and Elderly Persons," *Family Economics Review*, Winter, 13-17.

Schaninger, Charles M. and Chris T. Allen (1981), "Wife's Occupational Status as a Consumer Behavior Construct," *Journal of Consumer Research*, 8 (September), 189-196.

Sieber, Sam D. (1974), "Towards a Theory of Role Accumulation," *American Sociological Review*, 39, 567-578.

Strober, Myra H. and Charles B. Weinberg (1977), "Working Wives and Major Family Expenditures," *Journal of Consumer Research*, 4, 141-147.

Vickery, Clair (1979), "Women's Economic Contribution to the Family," in *The Subtle Revolution: Women at Work*, ed. Ralph E. Smith, Washington, D.C.: The Urban Institute, 159-200.

Waldman, Elizabeth and Eva E. Jacobs (1978), "Working Wives and Family Expenditures," in *Proceedings of the American Statistical Association Annual Meeting*, Washington, D.C.:American Statistical Association, 41-49.

Weinberg, Charles B. and Russell S. Winer (1983), "Working Wives and Major Family Expenditures: Replication and Extension," *Journal of Consumer Research*, 10 (September), 259-263.

Zeithaml, Valarie A. (1985), "The New Demographics and Market Fragmentation," *Journal of Marketing*, 49 (Summer), 64-75.

The Influence of Information Source on Brand Loyalty and Consumer Sex Roles of the Elderly

Ruth Belk Smith, University of Baltimore

Although experience is important in the marketplace, elderly consumers continue to be socialized by different agents and states of being such as advertising and social class. This study investigates the influence of some antecendent states and socialization agents on brand loyalty and the extent of traditional consumer sex roles among the elderly. Findings suggest that reliance on family and salespeople for information and social class are related to both brand loyalty and traditional consumer sex role perceptions.

It has long been noted by marketers that certain behavior patterns change over the life cycle (Engel, Blackwell, and Miniard 1986; Wells and Gubar 1966). Retirement and old age are dramatized by the relinquishment of certain consumption categories (consumer durables, children's education expenses, etc.) and the assumption of others (health care, securities and investments, travel), within the context of the role shift. Retirees who are financially independent are expected to have self-gratification consumption goals; those who are not are expected to be frugal; and both groups are expected to be independent (Ahammer 1969). In order to keep pace with the changing marketplace, the elderly consumer must continuously learn, forming new attitudes and skills and changing old ones (Mauldin 1976). Therefore, in much of the same way socialization applies to adult learning in a general context, it should also apply to the development and change of elderly consumers' cognition, attitudes, and behavior toward marketing stimuli (e.g., Smith and Moschis 1985). For example, as people grow older they tend to interact differently with various sources of consumer information, particularly in their increased exposure to the mass media (Real, Anderson, and Harrington 1980). The criteria for media use preference also seems to change with age (Bernhardt and Kinnear 1976, Hendricks and Hendricks 1977, Phillips and Sternthal 1977).

Individuals proceeding through the middle and later years must continually learn to play new or altered roles and to relinquish old ones. Moreover, with the secular trend toward increased longevity, more mature people will be called upon to play a variety of roles in the social structure (Riley el al 1969). Thus, there is a continuous need for socialization through adulthood and old age (Albrecht and Gift 1975, Smith and Moschis 1983 and 1990).

Although some studies have focused on specific information sources used by elderly consumers (e.g., Klippel and Sweeny 1974, Schiffman 1971), research has not considered the influence of the various sources on elderly consumer behavior. Given the growing interest in the areas of the elderly consumer and of consumer socialization as well the lack of systematic research on both topics (e.g., Meadow, Cosmas and Plotkin 1980, Ward 1974), this study (1) offers a general conceptual framework that is useful in organizing and conceptualizing variables for the study of the influence of various information sources on the elderly consumer, (2) applies the general theoretical and conceptual notions of socialization to the specific context of elderly consumer socialization, and (3) provides empirical data which may be useful in future research in the area. The findings should prove useful in answering some questions relating to mass media and interpersonal influence on elderly consumer behavior.

CONCEPTUAL FRAMEWORK

Consumer socialization research is based primarily on two models of human learning. The cognitive development model essentially views learning as a cognitive psychological process of adjustment to one's environment. Socialization is viewed as a function of qualitative changes (stages) in cognitive structures the individual can use in perceiving and dealing with the environment. As a person "moves" from one stage to another, he or she is assumed to be developing various learning properties. The social learning model, on the other had, seeks explanations for the formation of various cognitions and behaviors from environmental forces acting upon the individual--commonly known as "socialization agents" with which the individual interacts in various social settings. Socialization agents are directly involved in socialization because of their frequency of contact with the individual, primacy over the individual, and control over rewards and punishments given to the individual (Brim 1966).

Previous consumer socialization studies have used a conceptual framework of consumer socialization based upon the two main socialization theories (Moschis and Moore 1978 and 1979, Moschis and Churchill 1978, Churchill and Moschis 1979, Smith and Moschis 1985). The conceptual model incorporates five different types of variables: learning properties (criterion variables); age or life cycle and social structural variables (antecedents); and agents and learning processes, both combined to form specific socialization processes (Moschis and Churchill 1978). Socialization theory and research also suggest linkages between specific types of variables. Generally, socialization processes are conceived as having direct influence on criterion variables, while the influence of antecedent variables can both direct and indirect by impact upon socialization processes (see Figure 1). "Socialization takes place through interaction of the person and various agents in specific social settings" (McLeod and O'Keefe 1972, p. 135).

FIGURE 1
Model of Consumer Socialization

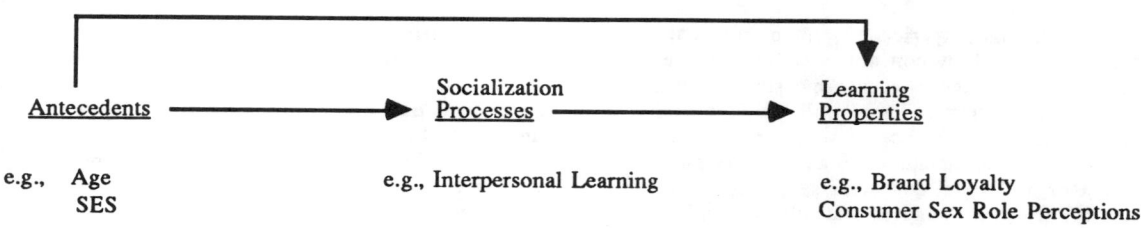

Source: Adapted from Churchill and Moschis (1978).

These agents may change as new ones are added when older ones are displaced, but they continue to influence the individual through a series of "self-other" interaction systems. The result of these interactions is that the individual is oriented to the evaluations and prescriptions of significant others (Cooley 1912). The specific socialization agents examined in this study are mass media advertising, family, peers, and salespeople, while antecedents variables used are age, sex, and social class. The outcomes of consumer socialization are neither specific nor invariant (Ward 1974). This study considers brand loyalty and consumer sex role perceptions, in line with previous consumer socialization research (e.g., Moschis and Moore 1979). The selection of these properties was guided by 1) relevance to issues of interest to marketers and consumer researchers 2) lack of (or inadequate) previous investigation.

Brand Loyalty

According to a review of the literature by Phillips and Sternthal (1977), the elderly process information less efficiently than younger people in that they require more time for decision making, slower pacing of stimuli, and fewer distracting influences. One means of alleviating stress related to choice making is simply to routinize responses to the decision situation, consistently adhering to the same decision criteria and preference rankings (Howard and Sheth 1968). Consumers have been reported to evidence more brand loyalty as they age (Guest 1942, 1955, 1964; Miller 1955). Thus brand loyalty may be one way in which the elderly compensate for information integration deficits, using experience and personally important sources of information.

Consumer Sex Role Perceptions

Both social psychological literature (e.g., Hess 1975, Lipman 1961, Neugarten 1968) and biological literature (e.g., Boulière 1963, Finch and Hayflick 1977) suggest that sex differences decrease with age. Neugarten (1968) notes that aging men become more affiliative and aging women more aggressive, so that there is more egalitarianism in decision making. This may be based partly on social reasons, such as the loss of the male's employment role upon retirement, and the relatively unchanged role status of the traditionally unemployed elderly woman. It may also be based partly on physiological changes (Finch and Hayflick 1977). Hormonal changes associated with aging include less production of male testosterone and female estrogen so that the small amounts of androgens ("other sex" hormones) normally found in humans have noticeable effects on the individual. Thus sex roles, including consumer sex roles, may change as a result of both interpersonal (sociopsychological) and intrapersonal (developmental) variables. (Smith, Moschis, and Moore 1987).

Mass Media.

Several researchers have found the elderly to be heavy users of mass media (e.g., Real, Anderson, and Harrington 1980; Samli 1967, Smith et al 1987). Samli and Palunbiskas (1972) reported that the elderly rely heavily on mass media sources of information, while others indicate that the elderly learn appropriate behavior for the later years through observation of the mass media (e.g., as a "retiree"). Schramm (1969) suggested that the elderly use the mass media to combat social disengagement. It has been noted that increased use of mass media influences perceptions and attitudes (e.g., Gerbner et al 1980) and, since nationally advertised brands are typically the recipients of brand preference and loyalty, greater use of the mass media by the elderly consumer is expected to be related to a greater level of brand loyalty.

Personal Source of Consumer Information

Peers and family have been identified as important sources of primary relationships in later life and are thought to be major agents of elderly socialization (Rosow 1974; Riley et al 1969; Reisman, Glazer and Denny 1950; Smith and Moschis 1985) while friends, relatives, and salespeople are reported to be important sources of consumer information for the elderly (Schiffman 1971, Klippel and Sweeny 1974). Some research (e.g., Gelb 1978, Lambert 1979) has found dissatisfaction with treatment given older shoppers by salespeople, although little is known about the influence of interaction with various sources of information, or socialization agents, on the elderly's consumer behavior. Some previous research has shown that social interaction affects the behavior of the elderly in general (e.g., Lemmon et al. 1972) and that social interaction may affect brand loyalty of consumer (Engel, Blackwell and Miniard 1986).

Antecedent Variables

Age, sex, and social class have been identified as important antecedent variables concerning the elderly in general (e.g., Rosow 1974, Neugarten 1968, Hess 1972, Dowd 1980), and consumers in particular (e.g., Moschis and Churchill 1978, Moschis and Moore 1979, Churchill and Moschis 1979). Empirical studies suggest that as consumers age they interact with fewer personal sources of consumer information and more mass media (e.g., Phillips and Sternthal 1977; LaForge, French and Crask 1981, Smith and Moschis 1985, Smith et al 1987). The elderly are reported to utilize fewer information cues than younger consumers (Schaninger and Sciglimpaglia 1981), to evidence less deliberation in purchase decision (Katona and Mueller 1955), to rely more upon personal experience (Schiffman 1971), and to be more brand loyal (Guest 1942; LaForge, French and Crask 1981).

A positive relationship has been noted between social class and social interaction among consumers in general (Engle, Blackwell and Miniard 1986), and among the elderly (Rosow 1974). Clark (1956) notes a negative relationship between social class and mass media exposure among the elderly, as do Schreiber and Boyd (1980). Although many researchers agree that socioeconomic status of the aged is a powerful predictor of knowledge, attitudes and behavior (e.g., Rosow 1974, Dowd 1980), little empirical research is found on the effects of social class on elderly consumer socialization processes, (specifically, the extent to which those of differing SES use particular consumer information sources.)

In previous consumer socialization studies, sex has been used as an antecedent to socialization processes (e.g., Churchill and Moschis 1978, Smith and Moschis 1985). Sex differences have been noted by several researchers to decrease with age due both to developmental (biological) factors (Finch and Hayflick 1975) and interpersonal factors (e.g., retirement) (Neugarten, 1968). Thus the influence of gender is explored to reveal whether any *difference* is observed. The previous discussion suggests the following set of hypotheses:

1. Age is positively associated with
   a. brand loyalty
   b. reliance on mass media advertising

2. Age is negatively associated with
   a. "traditional" consumer sex role perceptions
   b. reliance on friends, family, and salespeople (personal information sources)

3. Social class is
   a. positively related to reliance on personal sources of consumer information
   b. negatively related to reliance on mass media advertising

4. Greater reliance on mass media advertising is positively related to brand loyalty.

5. There will be no difference due to gender on intervening or outcome variables.

METHODOLOGY

Sample

Self-administered questionnaires were completed by 286 elderly respondents representing diverse social classes, races, and ethnicity and ranging in age from 55 to 89 years. The questionnaires were personally administred, and the nonresponse rate was less than 10%. The instrument had been pretested on thirty-eight elderly respondents in order to resolve any problems with length, ambiguous wording, and clarity of questions. The self-administration technique may cause some bias toward those respondents who are not perceptually or educationally impaired. This problem is naturally more prevalent in gerontological research than in studies of other age groups because of the perceptual declines accompanying advancing age and the lower overall educational level of the elderly as a group (Botwinick 1978). The sample is compared to U.S. Census data in Table 1.

As the table shows, the sample is fairly representative of both local and national elderly demographic characteristics. Approximately sixty percent of the sample was obtained at senior citizen centers and forty percent from other senior groups, such as the Retired Teachers Association and the Retired Business Persons Association, thus possible bias exists in that elderly who belong to these centers or groups have different social characteristics from those who do not. Burton and Hennon (1980), however, did not find different consumer concerns expressed by members of senior citizen centers vs other elderly groups.

Definition and Measurement of the Variables

Brand Loyalty is operationally defined as whether or not the respondent indicates loyalty to a specific brand. It was measured by summing responses to items indicating whether the respondent would, if s/he found his/her store to "be out of your favorite brand, wait until it was stocked, buy another brand, or go to another store for my brand". Cronbach's α for the brand loyalty scale was .96. Twelve products/services from each of the

TABLE 1
Comparison of Sample With Census Data

	Mean Age	%Black	%White	%Female	Income
Local Est*	71.3 years	23.1	77.3	62.0	$9,247
U.S. Est.*	70.9	12.5%	81.5	70.0	10,140
Sample	71.9	19.8	78.5	68.5	8,200

*Source: U.S. Bureau of the Census, *Current Population Reports*, Series P-25, 311, 519, 614, 643, 704, 870, and 875.

TABLE 2
Correlation Matrix of Variables

		(1)	(2)	(3)	(4)	(5)	(6)	(7)	(8)	(9)
(1)	Reliance on Mass Media Advertising	1								
(2)	Reliance on Family	.24[a]	1							
(3)	Reliance on Friends	.26[a]	.44[a]	1						
(4)	Reliance on Salespeople	.50[a]	.32[a]	.44[a]	1					
(5)	Age	[-08]	[.26][a]	[-20][a]	[-.19][a]	1				
(6)	Social Class	[.18][b]	[.34][a]	[.39][a]	[.37][a]	-.23[a]	1			
(7)	Sex	-02	.12[c]	.13[b]	.12[c]	-.10[c]	.17	1		
(8)	Brand Loyalty	[.15]	.3[a]	.25[a]	.28	[-.17][b]	.33	.05	1	
(9)	Consumer Sex Role Perceptions	.12[b]	.26[a]	.26[a]	.25	[-.18][b]	.32	.02	.48	1

a $p \leq .001$
b $p \leq .01$
c $p \leq .05$
[ ] Hypothesized

Bureau of Labor Statistics' major expenditure categories were used. To avoid low product salience, products/service in each category were selected which had greater than average use among people over 65.

Consumer Sex Role Perception refers to cognitive orientations related to the appropriateness of one-spouse domination of certain consuming decisions (Herbst 1952). It was measured in line with previous studies (e.g., Moschis and Moore 1979) by a 0-to-12 point index of degree of egalitarianism, using the same twelve product/services in items such as "who should decide what car to buy." Responses were "husband", "wife", or "both". The Cronbach α was .95.

Reliance on mass media advertising was measured by asking respondents to indicate whether, before buying a new brand of each of the twelve items, they would "rely upon television, radio, newspaper, and magazine advertisements for information and advice" (e.g., Smith, Moschis and Moore 1981). The reliability coefficient was .90.

Reliance on family members for information on consumption matters was measured by asking respondents to indicate whether they rely upon relatives for consumption-related advice before buying a new brand of each of the twelve products. The α coefficient was .93.

Reliance on peers for consumer information was measured by respondents' indicating whether they rely on their friends for consumption-related advice before buying a new brand of each of the twelve products (e.g., Smith, Moschis and Moore 1981). The Cronbach α was .91. *Reliance upon salespeople* was similarly measured with an α coefficient of .90. *Socioeconomic* status was measured using Duncan's (1976) SES index, and sex was a dichotomous variable (1=male, 2=female).

RESULTS

Table 2 shows the correlation matrix of variables. Hypothesized relationships are shown in brackets. As the matrix shows, age is associated

TABLE 3
Relationships Between Explanatory Variables and Outcomes

Dependent variables	Independent Variables				Age	SES	Sex	R2
	Reliance on mass media Advertising	Reliance on family	Reliance on Peers	Reliance on Salespeople				
Brand Loyalty	.02	.33[a]	-.02	.11[c]	.03	.18[b]	.03	.23[a]
Consumer Sex Role Perceptions	.02	.11[c]	.07	.09[c]	-.13[b]	.21[a]	-.04	.15[b]

Note: Table entries are standardized regression coefficients
a p .001
b p .01
c p .05

with lower levels of reliance upon all consumer information sources, while social class is related to higher overall levels of reliance. Females appear to rely more on personal sources than males. Both brand loyalty and consumer sex role perceptions are shown to be positively associated with reliance on all sources and with social class. Age is negatively associated with brand loyalty and traditional consumer sex role perceptions.

Relative Influence of Independent Variables

In order to assess the relative influence of the explanatory variables on each dependent variable, multiple regression was performed. This allowed separation of influences of antecedent and intervening variables on the outcomes. Such investigation also seems useful in providing answers to empirical questions regarding the processes by which the elderly receive and evaluate commercial information and in accumulating research findings that could be useful in advancing theory in the area. Two dominant features of social phenomena are 1) the lack of agreement as to what variables are important, and 2) the large number of subtle and interrelated causal relationships that influence most events (Duncan 1975). An approach which combines the theoretical derivation of hypotheses and the search for modifications necessary for theory building is called "a more efficient overall procedure [which] simultaneously provide [s] a more accurate representation of the process that actually occurs in building scientific knowledge" (Duncan 1975, p. 154). Thus it was expected that an assessment of the relative effects of the explanatory variables on the outcome variables would be fruitful.

The major limitation in using multiple regression to assess the relative effects of the explanatory variables is the possibility of intercorrelations among them which would result in arbitrary allocation of variance among variables in the equation. As Table 2 shows, the relationships among information sources are fairly high, thus caution is advised in interpreting the results, although the purpose is to show the effects of each agent. Table 3 shows relationships between explanatory variables and each dependent variable.

Brand Loyalty

The strongest predicator of brand loyalty was family communication about consumption (b=.33, p< .000). Thus, greater brand loyalty is found to be one result of family communication about consumption. This may be partly explained by the nature of family decision making where the individual who determines brand choice also establishes the most important evaluative criteria and influences other family members' evaluations by choosing brands most closely adhering to the family's needs. It may also be partly due to the cohesiveness of small groups which Stafford (1966) found exerts influence toward conformity on member brand preferences. Another strong predictor of brand loyalty is social class (b=.18, p<.01). This relationship suggests that the elderly consumer is more apt to remain brand loyal to the extent allowed by disposal income, not because of age itself. Reliance on salespeople was positively related, but reliance on mass media advertising was not associated with greater levels of brand loyalty. There was no sex difference in degree of brand loyalty, as expected.

Consumer Sex Role Perceptions. Social class and reliance on family for consumer information were the strongest predictors of traditional sex role perceptions. The social classes represented were lower and middle, thus the relationship between social class and traditional sex role perceptions is in line with previous research findings (e.g., Davis and Rigaux 1974) for this sample of elderly consumers.

Reliance on salespeople was also significantly related to traditional consumer sex role perceptions (b=.09, p<.05).

The correlation matrix shows that reliance on mass media advertising is associated with both brand loyalty and consumer sex role perceptions, however in the analysis of relative effects these relationships lost significance. The relationships between reliance on both family members and salespeople with the two outcome variables remain significantly positive. Given the fairly high zero-order correlation coefficients between reliance on mass media and the various personal sources of consumer information, a possible explanation is that interaction with personal sources intervenes between interaction with mass media advertising and the outcome. This is consistent with the agenda-setting hypothesis (Katz and Lazarsfield 1955), and has been reported in previous consumer socialization studies (e.g., Churchill and Moschis 1978). Thus, although mass media advertising may appear to have a socializing effect on certain types of elderly consumer behavior, these effects may be mitigated by interaction with personal sources of consumer information. The implication is that personal sources are stronger socialization agents for the elderly than mass media. Therefore mass media advertising directed toward the elderly should stimulate positive word of mouth among the target audience and their family members, and friends as these are found to be important sources of consumer information and perhaps influence other elderly consumer behavior, as well as brand loyalty. The moderating effect of both intervening variables on the outcomes studied supports the conceptual framework of consumer socialization used here. It also suggests that researchers consider how many times age may have simply served as a proxy variable for any number of other explantory variables upon the dependent variables under study, be they sociological, psychological, biological, even spiritual.

It may also be that social class is a more powerful predicator of elderly consumer behavior than age. Middle class elderly consumers may rely more on all sources of information than those in the lower class. They may also be more brand loyal and hold more traditional consumer sex role perceptions, thus different marketing efforts may be required for the lower and middle class elderly consumer. Females may rely more upon personal sources than males; (a well-known sociological concept) however, there seem to be no other differences due to gender.

These findings show that age itself is not related to greater levels of brand loyalty as previous studies have indicated (e.g., Guest 1955). Increasing age does appear to be associated with more egalitarian consumer sex role perceptions, thus the older a marketer's target market, the less appropriate traditional sex role prescriptions may be. Future research should seek to further separate the different socialization influences on elderly consumers, with causal modeling approaches and with longitudinal analyses.

REFERENCES

Ahammer, Inge (1969), "Social Learning Theory as a Framework for the Study of Adult Personality Development", in D.A. Goslin (ed.), *Handbook of Socialization Theory and Research*, Chicago:Rand McNally and Company, 253-284.

Albrecht, G. and H. Gift (1975), "Adult Socialization:Ambiguity and Adult Life Crises," in N. Catan and L. Ginsburg (eds.), *Life-Span Developmental Psychology:Normative Life Crises*, New York:Academic Press.

Bernhardt, K. and T. Kinnear (1976), "Profiling the Senior Citzen Market" in (ed.) B. Anderson, *Advances in Consumer Research*. Vol. 3.

Botwinick, Jack (1978), *Aging and Behavior:A Comprehensive Integration of Research Findings*, (2nd edition), New York Springer.

Boulière, F. (1963), "Assessing Biological Age" in R.H. Williams, C. Tibbits, and W. Donahue (eds), *Processes of Aging:Sociological Perspectives*, Vol, 1, New York:Atherton Press.

Brim, O.G. (1966), "Socialization Through the Life Cycle, "in O.G. Brim and S. Wheeler (eds.), *Socialization After Childhood:Two Essay*, New York: Wiley.

Burton, J.R. and C.B. Hennon (1980), "Consumer Concerns of Senior Citizen Center Participants," *Journal of Consumer Affairs*, 14(2), 366-382.

Churchill, G. and G.P. Moschis (1979), "Television and Interpersonal Influences on Adolescent Consumer Learning," *Journal of Consumer Research*, 6,23-35.

Clark, A.C. (1956), "The Use of Leisure and Its Relation to Levels of Occupational Prestige," *American Sociological Review*, 21.

Cooley, C.H. (1912), *Social Organization*, New York:Scribners.

Davis, H.L. and B. Rigaux (1974), "Perception of Marital Roles in Decision Processes," *Journal of Consumer Research*, 1, (June), 51-61.

Dowd, J. (1980), *Stratification Among the Aged*, Montery,CA:Brooks/Cole Publishing Co.

Duncan, O.D. (1975), *Introduction to Structural Equation Models*, New York Academic Press.

Engle, J.F., R.D. Blackwell, and P.W. in Miniard (1986), *Consumer Behavior* (5th ed.), Chicago:The Dryden Press.

Finch, C. L. Hayflick (eds.) (1977), *Handbook of the Biology of Aging*, New York: Van Nostrand.

Gelb, B. (1978), "Exploring the Gray Market Segment", *MSU Business Topics*, 26 (Spring), 41-46.

Guest, L. (1942), "The Genesis of Brand Awareness," *Journal of Communication*, 24, 88-96.

_____ (1955), "Brand Loyalty:Twelve Years Later," *Journal of Applied Psychology*, 39 (December),405-408.

_____ (1964), "Brand Loyalty Revisited:A Twenty-Year Report", *Journal of Applied Psychology*, 48 (April), 93-97.

Gerbner, G.L., Gross, N. Signorielli, and M. Morgan (1980), "Aging With Television: Images on Television Drama and Conception of Social Reality", *Journal of Communication*, 30, 37-47.

Hendricks, J. and C. Hendricks (1977), *Aging in Mass Society:Myths and Realities*, Cambridge, MS: Winthrop.

Herbst, P.G. (952), "The Measurement of Family Relationship," *Human Relations*, 5, 3-35.

Hess, B. (1972), "Friendship," in M. Riley, M. Johnson, and A Foner (eds.) *Aging and Society*, Vol 13, New York: Russell Sage Foundation.

Howard, J. and J. Sheth (1969), *The Theory of Buyer Behavior*, New York: John Wiley and Sons.

Katona, J. and E. Mueller (1955), *Consumer Behavior*, New York:New York University Press.

Katz, E. and P.L. Lazarsfield (1955), *Personal Influence*, Glencoe, IL:The Free Press.

Klippel, E., and J. Sweeney (1974), "Use of Information Source by the Aged Consumer," *Gerontologist*, 14, 163-166.

LaForge, M.W., W. French, and M. Crask (1981), Segmenting the Elderly Market", Paper presented to the Association for Decision Science, (December).

Lambert, Z. (1979), "An Investigation of Older Consumers' Unmet Needs and Wants at the Retail Level." *Journal of Retailing* 55 (Winter), 35-57.

Lemmon, Bruce W., Vern Bengson, and James Peterson (1972), "An Exploration of the Activity Theory of Aging: Activity Types of Life Satisfaction Among In-Movers to a Retirement Comunity," *Journal of Gerontology*, 27, (4), 511-523.

Lipman, A. (1961), "Role Perceptions and Morale of Couples in Retirement," *Journal of Gerontology*, 16,167-271.

Mauldin, C. (1976), "Communication and the Aging Consumer," in H.J. Oyer and E. J. Oyer (eds.), *Aging and Communication*, Baltimore: University Park Press.

McLeod, J. and G. O'Keefe, Jr. (1972), "The Socialization Perspective and Communication Behavior," in G. Kline and P. Tichenor (ed.) *Current Perspectives in Mass Communication Research*, Beverly Hills: Sage.

Meadow, H.L., S. Cosmas, and A. Plotkin (1980), "The Elderly Consumers:Past, Present, and Future," In K. Monroe (ed.), *Advances in Consumer Research*, 8, Association for Consumer Research, 742-747.

Miller, D.L. (1953), "The Life Cycle and the Impact of Advertising, in (ed.) L.W. Clark, *The Life Cycle and Consumer Behavior*, New York: New York University, Press, 61-65.

Moschis, George P. and Gilbert A. Churchill, Jr. (1978), "Consumer Socialization: A Theoretical and Empirical Analysis," *Journal of Marketing Research*, 15, 599-611.

_____ and Roy L. Moore, (1978), "An Analysis of the Acquisition of Some Consumer Competencies Among Adolescents," *Journal of Consumer Affairs*, 12 (Winter) 277-291.

_____ and _____ (1979), "Decision Making Among The Young:A Socialization Perspective," *Journal of Consumer Research*, 6 (September), 101-112.

Neugarten, B. (1968), *Middle Age and Aging: A Reader in Social Psychology*, Chicago: University of Chicago Press.

Phillips, L. and B. Sternthal (1977), "Age Differences in Information Processing:A Perspective on the Aged Consumer," *Journal of Marketing Research*, 14, 444-457.

Real, M.R., N. Anderson and M. Harrington (1980), "Television Access for Older Adults," *Journal of Communication*, 30, 74-76.

Reisman, D., N. Glazer, and R. Denny (1950), *The Lonely Crowd*, New Haven:Yale University Press.

Riley, M.W., Anne Foner, Beth Hess, and Marcia L. Toby (1969), "Socialization of the Middle and Later Years," in D.A. Goslin (ed.), *Handbook of Socialization Theory and Research*, Chicago:Rand McNally & Co., 951-981.

Rosow, Irving (1974), *Socialization to Old Age*, Berkeley, CA: University of California Press.

Samli, A.C. (1967), "The Elusive Senior Citizen Market," *Dimensions*, 7-16.

Schaninger, C. and O. Sciglimpaglia (1981), "The Influence of Cognitive Personality Traits and Demographics on Consumer Information Acquisition. "*Journal of Consumer Research*, 8 (September), 208-216.

_____ and F. Palubinskas (1972, "Some Lesser Known Aspects of the Senior Citizen Market - A California Study," *Akron Business Review*, 3, 47-55.

Schiffman, L.G. (1971), "Sources of Information for the Elderly," *Journal of Advertising Research*, 11, 33-37.

Schramm, W. (1969), "Aging and Mass Communication," in *Aging and Society, Vol 2, Aging and the Professions*, M. Riley and M. Johnson, eds. New York: Russell Sage.

Schrieber, E. and D. Boyd (1980), "How do Elderly Perceive Television Commercials," *Journal of Communication*, 61-69.

Smith, R.B. and G.P. Moschis (1983), "Consumer Socialization of the Elderly:An Exploratory Study," in T. Kinnear (ed.) *Advances in Consumer Research*, Vol. 11, Ann Arbor:Association for Consumer Research.

_____ and _____ (1985), "Socialization Explanations of Some Consumer Orientations of the Elderly," *Journal of Consumer Affairs*, 19 (1), 74-95.

_____ and _____ (1990), "The Socialization Approach to the Study of the Elderly Consumer" in V. Ziethaml (ed), *Review in Marketing 1990*, Chicago: American Marketing Association, in press.

_____ , _____ , and R.L. Moore (1981), "The Impact of Mass Communication on Consumer Decision Making Among the Elderly," presented to the Association for Education in Journalism Annual Convention, Mass Communication and society Division, East Lansing, Mich.

_____, _____, and _____ (1987), "Social Effects of Advertising and Personal Communication on the Elderly Consumer, in P.N. Bloom (ed.), *Advances in Marketing and Public Policy*, Vol. 1, JAI Press, 65-92.

Stafford, James E. (1966), "Effect of Group Influences on Consumer Brand Preferences," *Journal of Marketing Research*, 3 (February), 68-7.

Ward, Scott (1974), "Consumer Socialization," *Journal of Consumer Research*, 2, 1-16.

Wells, W. and J. Gubar (1966), "The Life Cycle Concept in Marketing Research," *Journal of Marketing Research*, 3, 355-363.

On Golden Pond: Elderly Couples and Consumer Decision Making

Louise A. Heslop, Carleton University
Judith Marshall, Carleton University

ABSTRACT

A review of studies on husband-wife decision making would tend to suggest that marriages end at about the age of 50. Demographic statistics certainly suggest otherwise. The fastest growing age groups in North America are those over 45, and with increasing longevity, more couples are surviving intact well beyond retirement.

Two areas of research will be brought together in this paper -- research on the consumer behaviour of the elderly and research on husband-wife decision making. The paper will then draw from the literature to develop propositions for research and a framework. The framework recognizes that retirement and aging are separate processes affecting decision making of couples directly and indirectly through effects on resources and needed goals.

"Grow old along with me,
The best is yet to be,..."
Rabbi Ben Izra, Robert Browning

INTRODUCTION

A review of studies on husband-wife decision making would tend to suggest that marriages end at about the age of 50. Demographic statistics certainly suggest otherwise. The fastest growing age groups in North America are those over 45, and with increasing longevity, more couples are surviving intact well beyond retirement. Eighty-three percent (83.4%) of total households composed of people aged 55-64, and 72% of households in the 65-74 year old group are couple households (Statistics Canada 1986). So the consumer behaviour literature contains a great gap in information about the decision processes of these consumer dyads. This gap must be filled if marketing managers are to successfully reach the seniors market -- *the* fastest growing market in terms of both numbers and disposable income (Cymbal 1987; Gelb 1982; Langer 1982).

The purpose of this paper is to propose a model of husband-wife decision making among elderly couples. Background for the model will be presented briefly, followed by a discussion of the model and related propositions.

Model Background (Context)

We are focusing on consumer couples 50 years of age and older recognizing that this is by no means a homogeneous group (Weeks 1986). This age group is the market being cited in the popular business press by business leaders as the fastest growing crucial market for the future. As well, the lower age limit of 50 years was chosen because the movement into the 5th decade of life often marks the beginning of serious planning for retirement and a recognition of the end of youth. (Atchley 1979; Keating, and Marshall 1980)

The model attempts to marry ideas from two very separate and distinct literature - husband-wife consumer decision making and consumer behaviour of the elderly. A detailed review of each of these streams of research is beyond the scope of this paper and a complete review is published elsewhere. (A major table summarizing selected research and consumer behaviour among the elderly is availabale from the second author.) However, a few comments will help place our model in context.

First, it is important to note that in the base of general research on consumer behaviour, the elderly are under-represented and the focus has been on individual consumers - not couples.

Secondly, although there is a relatively large set of studies on husband-wife consumer decision-making, virtually nothing is known about the process when elderly couples are involved (one notable exception is a recent study by Elbeck (1989) focusing on vacation decisions).

Within the limited age ranges analyzed in most husband-wife decision-making studies, joint consumer decision making has been found to decline with age and stage of the family life cycle. The reasons usually suggested for this finding are that spouses learn the preference patterns of each other and can take them into account without direct input from the spouse, or that decision specialists emerge over time in a marriage (McGhee 1983), or that time is too limited once children are around to permit as much joint husband-wife decision-making as there was shortly after the marriage (Burns and Hopper 1985). However, there are many reasons why the relationship between joint decision making and age would be curvilinear rather than linear, as will be discussed below.

The literature shows very little overlap between the two research streams. Research on the elderly has not looked at husband-wife consumer decision making. Research on husband-wife consumer decision-making has not looked at the elderly. The proposed framework attempts to address this gap.

A FRAMEWORK FOR STUDY

Figure 1 presents a model of factors affecting husband-wife decision-making of the elderly. The model combines two major processes - retirement (which is essentially an administrative category), and aging (a natural process). They are separate entities since retirement comes at no necessarily fixed time in the aging process and does not directly affect the rate or the process of aging.

A basic assumption of the model is that most consumption is a means to an end, rather than an end in itself. Therefore, consumer decision making processes are seen as a consequence of two central

FIGURE I
A Proposed Model of Factors Affecting Husband-Wife Decision Making of the Elderly

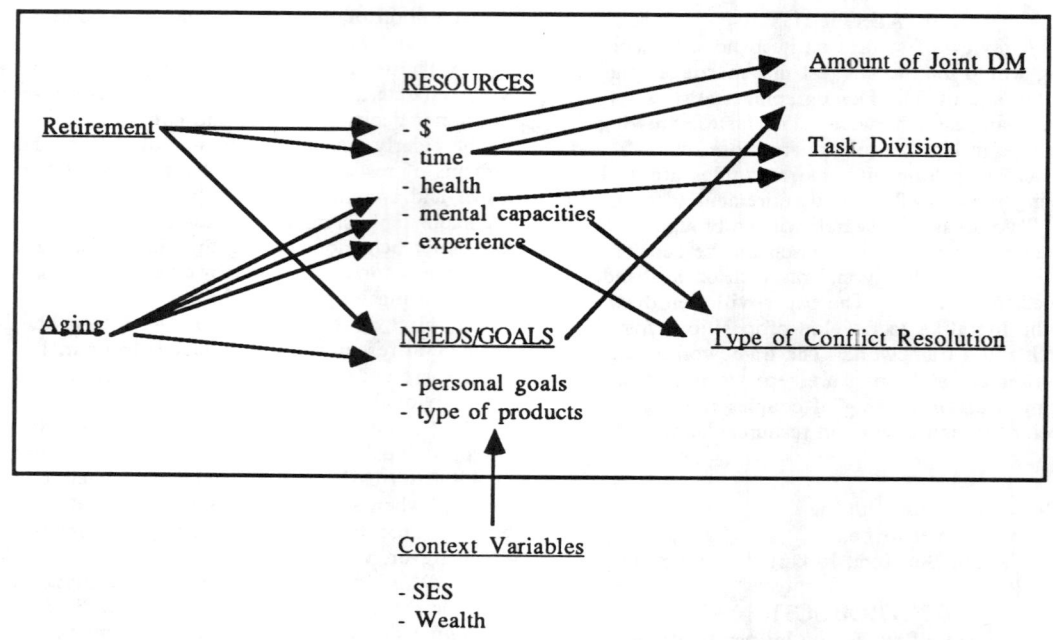

controlling factors -- the needs/goals, and the resources of the individuals separately and the couple as a unit. The major resources available to the couple include time, money and capital, physical health and vigour, mental capacities, and stored knowledge from experiences. These resources and needs/goals are both affected by the two process of aging and retirement (Lumpkin 1984; Moschis 1987).

Using the model as a framework for discussion, the effects of both retirement and aging on resources and needs/goals will be discussed below. Then the outcome variables - amount of joint decision-making, and the type of task division and conflict resolution - will be discussed. A summary of the model's interrelationships and several research propositions derived from the model will conclude the paper.

THE EFFECT OF RETIREMENT

Retirement and Resources

Retirement is most likely to have immediate effects on resources by increasing the time available to couples to pursue goals and spend resources but at the same time reducing the money flows available to pursue the goals. Two problems repeatedly faced by retirees is how to spend the 1/3 of their day that had previously been devoted to paid work and how to do so on the limited money now available (Howard et al 1982). In fact, there is a very wide range of income levels among the elderly. The distribution within this range tends to be bi-modal rather than normal (Heslop 1985; Mertz and Stephens 1986; Moschis 1987). There is a large group of elderly households which live on incomes at or below the poverty line. These households usually consist of widows living alone receiving only any guaranteed government assistance for seniors. The upper income ranges usually consist of couples and either both are receiving the basic government support plus some private or government contribution-based pension, or one of the members of the couple is still in the labor force. They typically own their own home free of a mortgage. So they have considerable discretionary income.

The time available for consumption and consumption-related activities increases after retirement. Many seniors find that shopping becomes a major recreational activity (Howard et al 1982; Keating 1980; Lumpkin 1984; Moschis 1987; Schewe 1985). This increased emphasis on shopping as a recreational activity is likely to increase the amount of joint decision making.

Finally it should be taken into consideration that the relative resource-based power of husbands and wives is likely to shift with retirement. The employed husband with an unemployed wife often controls more resources and has more power in decision making because he brings more monetary resources into the household (Atchley 1979; Blood and Wolfe 1960). However, with retirement his financial contribution usually declines. In addition, the wife may begin to receive, for the first time, her own income from universal pension plans. So the relative financial contribution of each spouse to the household becomes much more equal, reducing any resource-based power discrepancies and increasing the incidence of joint decision making (Atchley 1979; Blood and Wolfe 1960; Smith and Moschis 1985).

Retirement and Needs/Goals

At retirement many employment-related needs are reduced, such as contributions to pension plans, health care plans, union dues, etc. and costs of clothing and transportation. Also, the goals of individuals and the couple may shift from those appropriate to workers -- doing a good job and serving the employer -- to those more concerned with personal self-expression, freedom and service to family and the broader community (Andreasen 1984; Howard et al. 1982; Keating 1980; Keating and Marshall 1980). So the types of products bought will shift to products and services concerned with personal pleasure and experiences, e.g., travel and hobbies. Spending on others in gifts of money, time or in kind may increase (Fareed and Riggs 1982; Heslop 1985). For many, the emphasis will shift away from time-saving products to time-using ones -- gourmet cooking, taking the scenic route while out driving rather than the expressway.

Also, retirement involves such a major change for people that they frequently re-assess priorities and are encouraged by retirement planners to set new goals. These goal shifts may mean significant changes in the types of products and services desired and the allocation of spending.

THE EFFECT OF AGING

Aging and Resources

The aging process will also affect the resources and the needs/goals of individuals and couples. There are well-documented impacts of aging on health and body functions (Mertz and Stephens 1986). However, there are tremendous variations in the extent of these effects and the point at which they interfere with normal functioning (Capon et al. 1981). Generally, between the ages of 65 and 75 most people do not suffer from medical conditions that seriously restrict their activity. However, after age 75 such restrictions and a general slowing down are more obvious, although most people still can function quite well into their 80's.

The effects of aging on mental capacities are more controversial. Some decreases in information processing abilities and memory have been noted by some researchers (McGhee 1982 Phillips and Sternthall 1977; Ross 1981; Zeithaml and Fuerst 1983). However, others argue that the results observed are mainly the result of the testing methods applied and/or that speed of processing but not ability to process information is decreased (Roedder-John and Cole 1986; Cole and Houston 1987). Others suggest that training and aids to help seniors sort out important from unimportant information can eliminate any differences seen in decision making and information processing between young and old adults (Roedder-John and Cole 1986).

One very important resource that the elderly have to draw on that has not been dealt with in research to date is their set of experiences or knowledge store. The elderly have a lifetime of experiences as consumers which can assist them in many ways (Moschis 1987; Ross 1981). They have seen producers and retailers come and go. They have experienced the emergence of entire new forms of retailing, of consumer protection measures, of buyer-seller communication. Through the years they have had many opportunities to learn what to expect from retailer services, product warranties, advertising claims, and product performance for many durable and non-durable goods. Most have relatively realistic expectations of what the marketplace can provide. Also, elderly couples share this knowledge store through their joint experiences. Therefore, they can likely draw on it with quick reference to previous situations (e.g., "Remember when we bought that sofa and what happened to the material....").

Of course, some of this experience and knowledge storehouse of the elderly couple contains inappropriate information. New advances in materials and products, high technology processes, and international market developments bring continuing and rapid changes to product origins, compositions and performance levels. The elderly are less likely to have had experience with highly technical and sophisticated electronic products and services such as VCRs, microwave ovens, automated banking machines. So their knowledge store will be much less useful to them in these situations. Moreover, there is evidence that the elderly avoid the use of such products and services, perhaps because they are not prepared to invest the effort to acquire the knowledge necessary to use the new technologies (Gilly and Zeithame 1985; Marshall and Heslop 1988). So their experience advantage is specific to a large but limited set of products and services, and retailing innovations (Marshall and Heslop 1988).

Aging and Needs/Goals

The effects of aging on needs/goals may be similar to those caused by retirement. The changes in life associated with aging milestones may lead to reassessment of what is important and sought after in life. Aging also may affect relationships with the spouse. Many couples report a new closeness as the busy time of raising children is over and there is more time to devote to each other (Spiro 1983). Personal goals may be submerged, if necessary, to care for a spouse whose health is deteriorating.

Many changes in consumer processes, such as resource allocations and spending patterns, do not occur with retirement, but seem more closely associated with aging. The major shifts actually occur not at age 65, but rather around age 75. This latter age has often been designated the beginning of old-old age or late senescence. After age 75 there are often major shifts in expenditure patterns. There is less spending on food, smoking and alcoholic beverages, travel and transportation, security and taxes, but higher expenditures on gifts and contributions (Heslop 1985).

THE MODEL'S OUTCOME VARIABLES

Amount of Joint Decision Making

Previous research has extensively documented that the extent of joint decision making depends on the products or services being purchased. Durable goods, and products and services central to the goals of the household or with major onsequences for family security and well-being will involve much joint decision making. Such products and services include major household appliances, cars, insurance, and vacations. The purchasing of many of these products and services is much more limited among the elderly than among younger couples (Fareed and Riggs 1982; Heslop 1985). In more recent years, the consumption of cars by the elderly, especially couples, has moved closer to that of younger consumers. However, cars owned by the elderly still face much lower replacement rates because of lower average mileage. Vacation services use of the elderly is increasing rapidly, however. Elbeck's (1989) study of elderly couples purchasing vacations indicates high levels of joint decision making and he proposes that this is because the consumption area is one which involves well-being. Elderly couples who are well-off financially also engage in more recreational activities and often do so jointly, increasing the amount of joint decision making.

Task Division

Joint decision making is likely to increase post retirement for non-durable items, such as food, as mentioned earlier. There is more time for shopping by the husband who may "tag along" for something to do (Zbytniewski 1985). So it is likely that retired couples will spend more time than non-retired couples in shopping activities. Once at the store and pushing the cart, husbands usually wish to have some input to the decisions. Since they are no longer making decisions in the work domain, they can find some outlet in family purchasing. If the couple has faced major declines in income with retirement, the food dollar may have to be allocated very carefully. So shopping for food involves significant consumer choices in which both partners become involved.

Joint decision making takes more time. The only major time saving likely to occur when there is more than one decision maker is if the overall job can be broken into tasks which are assigned to individuals in the group. Elbeck (1989) suggests that for vacation services task division is not the norm, rather joint activities are more likely to characterize all stages of the decision process for elderly couples. Since elderly couples tend to have more time available for consumption activities, they may find that joint decision making has many advantages as a user of time and a way to share daily activities generally.

If decision making tasks are divided, what will be the pattern of such a division? Previous research on husband/wife decision making has found that the bases for division are usually related to who has, or is assumed to have expertise, in the area. (Buss and Schaninger 1983; Rosen and Granbois 1983; Spiro 1983). The elderly couples of today grew up and formed gender stereotype attitudes during a more traditional era and are likely to retain these attitudes rather than to make radical shifts with age. Therefore, where task division occurs, it is likely to be along traditional role definition lines.

Another determinant of task division has been relative interest in the product. The spouse who will use the product the most, or who for some reason feels the product is more important to her/him will take over the major tasks, especially the final choice. On this basis, wives were found to have more control and performed more activities related to decisions regarding goods purchased for home and family use. (Davis and Rigaux 1974). In the traditional family structure, this home domain and the social well-being of the family were more central to her role. The husband's role was more external to the family and involved securing the family's economic well-being. So he took primary responsibility for purchasing insurance and investing in the home. Otherwise he exercised his decision making authority outside the home on the job. With retirement that domain for decision making vanishes. The husband may try to transfer his decision making skills and the accompanying desire for control to the household. His areas of interest have been redefined as the work-related interests disappear. As a result, the wife may find that her husband wishes to take control at least partially over decisions she has been making independently for years (Keating 1980). Undoubtedly, some period of transition, adjustment, renegotiation and strife can be expected. So the initial post-retirement period will require more discussions not only to make the decisions but also to decide how the decisions will be made. (Howard, Marshall, Rechnitzer, Cunningham and Donner 1982). This takes time-- which the couple now has. It can result in a new closeness or a new strain in the marital relationship.

The task division will also depend on the mental and physical health of the partners. If one partner faces significant restrictions in mobility or mental capabilities, the other spouse will need to take over most or all of the consumer decisions, even in areas not traditionally theirs. For example, many husbands find that when their wife is ill they suddenly face the unfamiliar supermarket aisles for the first time. Many wives, used to leaving financial matters to their husbands, may be overwhelmed if he can no longer manage the affairs and she must deal with the bank, trust company, lawyers, accountants, insurance agents, etc. As well, since older couples are likely to experience higher incidences of health problems, it is likely that they will spend less time in shopping activities than younger retired couples. To repeat, the elderly of today are more likely to have families with these traditional role divisions, unlike the more egalitarian marriages of more recent years in which more decisions are jointly made. (Qualls 1982). So significant learning and re-adjustment will be required if sudden deteriorations in the health of one partner occur.

Type of Conflict Resolution

Spiro (1983) has found that there is less effort to affect the decision of the other spouse in husband-wife decision making by couples who had been married longer. However, her sample did not include elderly couples. Such a shift over time might be expected to continue as the couple reaches senior citizen status. Also, as discussed earlier, the couple may seek more interaction and harmony and may be able to attain it now that the children have left home.

Knowledge of the needs, interest, and desires of the spouse are likely to be greater among elderly couples who have had a lifetime of living together and consuming products and services to gain specific insight to selection criteria. Indeed Elbeck (1989) found that there was significant congruity in answers given by senior husbands and wives separately to questions about consumer decision making control. Research by Davis (1971) on younger couples did not find such agreement. Therefore, it is expected that older couples will make fewer attempts to influence each other in decision making than younger couples.

RESEARCH PROPOSITIONS AND SUMMARY OF EFFECTS

It is likely that joint husband-wife decision making will be altered with retirement and old age (Lumpkin 1984; Moschis 1987). As the literature reviewed above suggests, shifts are likely to occur in the amount of joint decision making, the way in which decision tasks are divided, and the type of conflict resolution techniques used by husbands and wives. Two key propositions have been developed from the model - these propositions summarize the effects discussed in earlier sections of this paper.

Proposition 1 Retired couples will:
(i) make more joint consumer decisions than non-retired couples,
(ii) do more joint information seeking than non-retired couples,
(iii) spend more time in shopping activities and enjoy shopping more than non-retired couples,
(iv) do more joint shopping than non-retired couples,
(v) seek consensus rather than "single winner" decisions.

Proposition 2 Elderly couples will:
(i) make more joint consumer decisions than younger couples,
(ii) shift decision making control to the "well" spouse if the health of one spouse deteriorates,
(iii) spend less time in shopping activities than younger retired couples but more time than younger non-retired couples,
(iv) have greater knowledge of the preferences of the spouse for products, and for the relative importance of decision criteria,
(v) make fewer attempts to influence each other in decision making,
(vi) seek more consensus decisions than younger couples.

Proposition one sets out five effects that retirement (an administrative category) is likely to have on husband-wife decision making, while proposition two focuses on the effects of aging (a 'natural' process). Several of the proposed relationships are overlapping because both retirement and aging are likely to affect outcomes. In other cases, the proposed relationships recognize that the main effects are likely to flow mainly from one of the two events (either retirement or aging). Elderly couples with one spouse still in the labor force can be expected to behave differently from elderly couples with neither spouse working. Also, retired couples who are under 65 years of age, 65-75, and 75 and over will generally be found to behave differently. (Atchley 1979; Capon, Kuhn and Gurucharri 1981; Lumpkin 1984. (Both 'aging' and 'wellness' are of course continuous variables which will have to be operationally defined in future research).

The propositions deal specifically with the outcomes of the model rather than the intermediate relationships. These relationships do need further research but in the context of being intermediate rather than outcome variables. The outcome variables are of direct interest to those who study consumer behaviour decisions. It is also important to note that the entire model recognizes the overall influences of the broad context variables of socio-economic status and wealth. Care needs to be taken when devising research projects to measure and/or control for these variables. Large effects of these variables on variables and relationships in the model can be expected and a lack of concern for and control of them will likely muddy research results.

The amount of joint decision making will have to be studied in the context of the type of product being consumed and the time available for the decision. Given earlier research on husband-wife decision making in general and considering the areas of consumption experience most central to the elderly, it can be suggested that certain product categories bear special consideration. Housing is an obvious example because of the large expenditures involved and the centrality of the product to family life and well-being. Often the elderly face major relocation decisions and, therefore, study of these decisions is feasible and would be of utmost importance to marketers and public policy makers in the housing industry.

Leisure and recreation decisions become far more important to the elderly couple and again are important to well-being. Because of the rapidly growing importance of the elderly consumer in this market, marketers in leisure and recreation oriented businesses would benefit especially from research in this product domain. Therefore, they should be an important focus for research.

Food takes such a large share of expenditures for seniors and so much of their shopping time that it is a significant area for study. It also is an area where major adjustments are likely to be made by couples, providing a fruitful field for studying these adjustment processes.

CONCLUSION

"We all of us in Marketing are now aware that the over - 50 population is the single, largest consumer group in the history of marketing! ... We all know the potential of this market. But what we don't always know is the 'how-to'. How to approach this market" (Kaye 1989). As this quote from the publisher of one of the recent newsletters that have sprung up to assist managers in approaching the senior market suggests, the senior market has great potential. However, lack of understanding of this market is hindering our effectiveness in reaching it.

The purpose of this paper is to draw attention to the gap in research on husband-wife consumer decision making by elderly couples - a key part of the seniors market. Given the importance of this component of the senior market, the authors have attempted to increase understanding of husband-wife consumer decision making among the elderly by proposing a model (see Figure 1) of factors affecting husband-wife decision making of the elderly was proposed - along with several propositions for future research.

Since the field of study of husband-wife decision making among elderly couples has received virtually no attention, there is much that can be done. The authors will be using the model and the resulting propositions to guide the selection of variables for study and the development of data collection instruments and would hope other researchers will also do so.

REFERENCES

Andreasen, A.R. (1984), "Life Status Changes and Changes in Consumer Preferences and Satisfaction," *Journal of Consumer Research*, 11, December, 784-794.

Atchley, R.C. (1979), "Issues in Retirement Research," *The Gerontologist*, 19, 44-54.

Blood, R.O. and D.M. Wolfe (1960), *Husbands, Wives: The Dynamics of Married Living*, Glencoes, Ill: Free Press.

Burns A.C. and J. Hopper (1985), "An Analysis of the Presence, Stability, and Antecedents of Husband and Wife Purchase Decision Making Influence Assessment Agreement and Disagreement," in Richard Lutz (ed.) *Advances in Consumer Research*, XII, Provo, UT: Association for Consumer Research, 175-180.

Buss, Christian W. and C.M. Schaninger (1983), "The Influence of Sex Roles on Family Decision Processes and Outcomes," in *Advances in Consumer Research*, Vol. 10, eds. Richard P. Bagozzi and Alice M. Tybout, 439-444.

Capon, Noel, Deanna Kuhn and M.E. Gurucharri (1981), "Consumer Information Processing Strategies in Middle and Late Adulthood," *Journal of Applied Developmental Psychology*, 2, 1, 1-12.

Cole, Catherine and Michael J. Houston (1987), "Encoding and Media Effects on Consumer Learning Deficiencies in the Elderly," *Journal of Marketing Research*, XXIV, Feb., 55-63.

Cymbal, M. (1987), "The Other 'Grey Market'," *Canadian Traveller*, 108, 3, 34.

Davis H.L. (1971), "Measurement of Husband-Wife Influence in Consumer Purchase Decisions," *Journal of Marketing Research*, 8, Aug., 305-312.

Davis H.L. and B.P. Rigaux (1974), "Perceptions of Marital Roles in Decision Processes", *Journal of Consumer Research*, 1, June, 51-61.

Elbeck, Matt (1989), "Marketing Vacations to Elderly Couples: Aspects of Marital Role Specialization in the Decision Process," in A. D'Astous (ed.) *Administrative Sciences Association of Canada Proceedings - Marketing Division*, Montreal.

Fareed, A.E. and G.D. Riggs (1982), "Old-Young Differences in Consumer Expenditure Patterns," *Journal of Consumer Affairs*, 16, Summer, 152-160.

Gelb, B.D. (1982), "Discovering the 65+ Consumer," *Business Horizons*, May-June, 42-46.

Gilly, M.C. and V.A. Zeithame (1985) "The Elderly Consumer and Adoption of Technologies", *Journal of Consumer Research*, 12(3) 353-357.

Heslop, L.A. (1985), *Expenditure Patterns of Elderly Women: An Analysis of Expenditure Patterns of the Elderly*. Research Paper No. 19, Social and Economic Studies Division, Statistics Canada.

Heslop, Louise A. (1985), *Cohorts Going Through Life Together: An Analysis of Expenditure Patterns of the Elderly*. Research Paper No. 13a, Statistics Canada.

Howard, J.H., J.J. Marshall, P.A. Rechnitzer, D.A. Cunningham, and A. Donner (1982), "Adapting to Retirement," *Journal of the American Geriatrics Society*, 30, 8, 488-500.

Kaye, E.M. (1989), "From the Publisher", *Senior Market Report*, Senior Market Report, Dec., New York, New York.

Keating, N. (1980), "What Do I Do With Him 24 Hours a Day? Changes in the Housewife Role At Retirement," *The Gerontologist*, 20, 4, 437-443.

Keating, N., and J.J. Marshall (1980), "The Process of Retirement: The Rural Self Employed," *The Gerontologist*, 20, 4, 437-448.

Langer, Judith (1982), "The 50-Plus Market: Who Says I'm Old," in *Consumers in Transition In-Depth Investigations of Changing Lifestyles*, American Marketing Association Publications Division.

Lumpkin, J.R. (1984), "The Effect of Retirement Versus Age on the Shopping Orientations of the Older Consumer," *The Gerontologist*, 24, 6, 622-627.

Marshall, Judith and Heslop, Louise A. (1988), "Technology Acceptance in Canadian Retail Banking: A Study of Consumer Motivations and Use of ATM's," *International Journal of Bank Marketing*, 6, 4, 31-42.

McGhee, Jerrie L. (1982), "Elderly Consumer Decisional Processes and Public Policy," *Journal of Consumer Studies and Home Economics*, 6, 47-62.

McGhee, J.L. (1983), "The Vulnerability of Elderly Consumers," *International Journal of Aging and Human Development*, 17, 3, 223-246.

Mertz, B. and N. Stephens (1986), "Marketing to Older American Consumers," *International Journal of Aging and Human Development*, 23, 1, 47-58.

Moschis, G.P. (1987), *Consumer Socialization: A Life Cycle Perspective*, Lexington Books, D.C. Heath & Co., Toronto.

Phillips, Lyn W. and Brian Sternthal (1977), "Age Differences in Information Processing: A Perspective on the Aged Consumer", *Journal of Marketing Research*, XIV, 744-757.

William J. Qualls (1982), "Changing Sex Roles: Its Impact Upon Family Decision Making", in Andrew Mitchell (ed.) *Advances in Consumer Research*, 9, Ann Arbor, MI: Association for Consumer Research, 267-270.

Roedder-John, Deborah and Catherine C. Cole (1986), "Age Differences in Information Processing: Understanding Deficits in Young and Elderly Consumers," *Journal of Consumer Research*, 13, 3, December, 297-315.

Rosen, Dennis L. and Donald H. Granbois (1983), "Determinants of Role Structure in Family Financial Management," *Journal of Consumer Research*, 10 (September), 253-285.

Ross, Ivan (1981), "Information Processing and the Older Consumer: Marketing and Public Policy Implications," in Kent B. Monroe (ed.) *Advances in Consumer Research*, IX, Ann Arbor, MI: Association for Consumer Research, 31-39.

Schewe, C.D. (1985), "Gray America Goes to Market," *Business*, April-June, 3-9.

Smith, Ruth Belk and George P. Moschis (1985), "A Socialization Perspective on Selected Consumer Characteristics of the Elderly," *Journal of Consumer Affairs*, 19, 1, Summer, 74-95.

Spiro, R.L. (1983), "Persuasion in Family Decision Making," *Journal of Consumer Research*, 9, March, 393-402.

Statistics Canada (1986), *Census Families*, Catalogue No. 93-106, Table 7-2.

Weeks, William A. (1986), "Applying Disengagement Theory From Social Gerontology to Predict and Explain Segments Within the Senior Market," in Melanie Wallendorf and Paul Anderson (eds.) *Advances in Consumer Research*, XIII, Provo, Utah: Association for Consumer Research.

Zbytniewski, Jo-Ann (1985), "The Older Shopper: Over 65 and Overlooked?" Reprinted in *The Elderly Market: Selected Readings*, Compiled by Charles D. Schewe, 83-85.

Zeithaml, Valerie A. and William L. Fuerst (1983), "Age Differences in Response to Grocery Store Price Information," *Journal of Consumer Affairs*, Winter 1983, 17, 2, 402-420.

Toward a New Understanding of the Effects of Advertising: A Look at Implicit Memorial Processes

Ida E. Berger, University of Toronto[1]

This paper summarizes the contents of a special topic session (session 9.1) held on Sunday, October 7'th. Papers were presented by Susan E. Heckler, Christopher P. Puto and Francoise Jaffe (University of Michigan); Carol Pluzinski (New York University); Douglas M. Stayman (Cornell University) and Frank R. Kardes (University of Cincinatti); and Ida E. Berger and Karen Finlay (University of Toronto). The session was chaired by Ida E. Berger with Larry Percy (LINTAS: USA) serving as a discussant.

SESSION OVERVIEW

Within the last few years several consumer behaviour researchers have been investigating the role of implicit memorial processes in persuasion. Working independently, these investigators have developed analytical frameworks and research methodologies to test several interesting and new hypotheses regarding the impact of non-conscious, spontaneous or implicit responses to advertising. The fundamental goal of this session was to bring these researchers together to share with each other and other ACR participants the results of their pioneering work. Taken together this body of research represents a new perspective on advertising effects.

Historically, advertising effects have been studied within the context of attitude-change paradigms. The underlying assumption of most advertising studies has been that an advertisement (or its repetition) must change attitudes in order to be effective. Much effort has consequently been expended in understanding what executional, repetition or situational variables lead to the encoding/retrieval of desired information and the formation of positive attitudes. Similarly, we have seen much progress in the development of measures of advertising effectiveness that test the conscious, controlled or explicit effects of advertising exposure (i.e. Day after Recall and Persuasion scores). While the limitations of this perspective and these measures have been discussed before, no integrated new perspective has appeared. The four papers presented in this special session did not, in and of themselves, *define* a new perspective, but they raised some important issues and pointed out some interesting new research directions.

---

[1] The author thanks Karen Finlay for her contribution to this summary paper and gratefully acknowledges the financial support of the Social Sciences and Humanities Research Council of Canada, Grant # 410-90-1431.

THE FOUR PAPERS

The Impact of Non-conscious Processing: Immediate vs. Time-Delayed Measurement of Automatic Processing Effects

The session began with a paper by Heckler, Puto and Jaffe. Heckler laid the foundation for the empirical work by pointing out the potential of recent developments in the investigation of non-conscious and automatic information processing in psychology (cf. Hasher and Zacks 1979, 1984; Zajonc 1980; Zajonc and Markus 1982; Lewicki 1986). Non-conscious information processing refers to human activities which are based on a complicated set of rules that are (1) not acquired through the mediation of consciousness, (2) not operating at the level of consciousness and (3) not consciously available (Lewicki 1986). Examples from everyday life include speech production, recognition of faces, judging beauty, etc.

Heckler pointed out that the outcome of such processes may be the development of memorial associations which are utilized in subsequent conscious and unconscious processing activities. Studying these processes is not seen as an alternative to the examination of consciously controlled mental activities, but rather, as a potentially important part of a general effort to understand consumer information processing and behaviour. For example, consumers may process and acquire product information without being aware of it, or decision rules and shopping procedures may utilize algorithms or memory traces acquired non-consciously.

Research in cognitive psychology (e.g., Hasher and Zacks 1979; 1984) and social cognition (e.g., Lewicki 1986; Zajonc 1980) has recently examined the effects of non-conscious processes on higher level cognitive operations such as the formation of memory traces and the development of preferences. One particularly interesting series of studies (Lewicki 1986) demonstrated support for the learning of covariation information (e.g., that short haired women were "kind" and long haired women were "capable"), despite subjects' inabilities to identify such covariation when consciously evaluating the stimuli. Another set of studies showed that in the absence of memorial or other externally available information, such non-consciously acquired associations may be utilized in forming preferences or making judgments regarding similar stimulus objects. Once again, subjects were unable to consciously access the covariation information which appeared to have influenced the subsequent judgments.

In a study that carefully mirrored Lewicki's (1986) methodology but used marketing oriented stimuli, Heckler and Puto (1987) showed that memory traces which linked packaging information with product attributes (for example, tall, slender shampoo bottles with "economical" shampoos and short, rounded bottles with "conditioning" shampoos) could be non-consciously acquired. Two questions not addressed in any of Lewicki's experiments nor in the Heckler and Puto research are (1) the potential decay over time of memory traces acquired through non-conscious mechanisms and (2) the effects of "noise" on these non-conscious processes. Each of these issues is especially relevant to a consumer behaviour environment. The strength of the associations over time must be examined because some research has suggested that processes"... may not last long enough for the person who views an advertisement on television, say, to get to the grocery store (Kihlstrom 1987, p. 1449). Additionally, in most consumer goods categories few associations are completely consistent (i.e., not all shampoos of a certain bottle shape share the same positioning strategy).

Accordingly, Puto then presented new empirical work utilizing the experimental techniques and measures developed by Lewicki and extended by Heckler and Puto (1987). Specifically, he presented the results of two studies, one which measured the impact of the non-conscious information acquisition immediately after exposure and after a 4-7 day delay and a second that added new non-conforming attribute information ("noise") to the product descriptions.

The results showed that covariation information acquired non-consciously was accessible to influence subsequent processing even after a 4-7 day delay. However, noise present at the time of processing rendered the target covariation information inaccessible. These results demonstrated that in noise free circumstances, the effect of non-consciously acquired information on judgements is robust and impervious to the effects of time delays. The results provide insight for advertising theoreticians and practitioners regarding the way in which non-conscious information processing might affect memory and judgements of marketing stimuli.

Automatic processes in Consumer Response to Advertising

The second paper in the session continued the "non-conscious processing" theme by exploring the notion of "partial activation". Reporting on work from her dissertation (Pluzinski 1990), Carol Pluzinski discussed the fact that current recall based measures of advertising effectiveness assume that access to information about a brand name is an all or nothing process. In other words, it is assumed that either a brand name is activated in memory or it is not. Yet consumers may have vague, transient or even feeling oriented reactions to ads that cannot be verbalized and thus cannot be captured by simple recall based responses. Contrary to existing frameworks, Pluzinski introduced the idea that there exist various *levels* of activation of a concept in memory and suggested that information that is only "*partially activated*" may have systematic effects on consumers' impressions/reactions to brands.

Partial activation refers to a state in which a concept (i.e., idea, thought, judgment, evaluation) is not fully activated in memory; it is the state in which a concept is activated, but below the threshold of conscious awareness. Pluzinski argued that partial activation may be an important element in either the process of encoding (people may not always fully attend to ads) or the process of retrieval (people do not always fully remember ads). Her study examined how certain consumer responses to advertisements, while inaccessible to conscious awareness, might still be activated (partially), and thus be accessible for non-conscious, automatic processing. Hence, a finer grained representation of reactions to advertising was provided.

Using existing advertising slogans as primes, Pluzinski's study created conditions of both full and partial activation of a brand name, and then compared the effects on subsequent processing of that brand, including evaluations. The findings showed that full activation of a brand name (correct recall following the slogan prime) facilitated subsequent processing and lead to more favourable evaluations. Partial activation, by contrast, was associated with interference, inhibition and evaluations that were based on very subjective feelings, (meta-cognitions such as strong feelings of knowing). She concluded that advertisers should not assume that a brand name below a recall threshold will not be activated at all. In fact it may be partially activated and thereby may influence subsequent judgements. However, she cautioned that unless the brand is consciously processed (ie. totally activated), its *evaluation* will not be automatically activated.

Effects of Inference Generation and Utilization on Attitude Accessibility

The third paper (prepared by Doug Stayman and Frank Kardes and presented by Frank Kardes) focused on individual differences that lead to the formation of strong brand attitudes. The paper was based on recent findings indicating that omitting explicit conclusions from advertisements and thereby inducing consumers to infer their own conclusions facilitates the development of strong brand attitudes (Kardes 1988; Sawyer 1988). Kardes argued that this subtle indirect approach to persuasion offers many advantages over more traditional approaches. For example, with indirect persuasion: (a) counter-arguing is minimized, (b) reactance is avoided, (c) self-generated arguments are more credible and memorable than explicit arguments, and (d) attitudes based on self-generated inferences are accessible, confidently held, and exert a strong influence on subsequent judgments and decisions (for a review, see Kardes forthcoming).

Stayman and Kardes extended previous approaches by examining the role of two key inference processes in persuasion: inference generation and inference utilization. They predicted that any variable that influences the extent to which consumers elaborate on the contents of a persuasive text should affect inference generation. Following Kardes (1988), a mock ad was created and response latencies to inferential and attitudinal inquiries were used to test this hypothesis. As expected, the likelihood of spontaneous inference generation was greater for high (as opposed to low) need for cognition individuals (Experiment 1) and in high (as opposed to low) involvement conditions (Experiment 2).

Kardes further argued that consumers who generate inferences do not necessarily use these inferences as inputs for brand attitude formation in all cases. Indeed, high need for cognition individuals engage in elaborate processing simply because they enjoy the process of thinking, not because they are motivated to satisfy some extrinsic goal. However, individuals who are attuned to internal, self-generated information - such as attitudes, opinions, and inferential beliefs - are likely to use inferences in brand attitude formation, given that inferences had been formed spontaneously and are available for use. Hence, he predicted that inference utilization would be more likely for low (as opposed to high self-monitoring individuals). Consistent with this prediction, more extreme, more confidently held, and more accessible brand attitudes were formed when consumers were likely to both generate (i.e., high need for cognition individuals) and use (i.e., low self-monitoring individuals) inferences as inputs in brand attitude formation.

The experimental results were consistent with a two-stage inference process model in which variables that influence elaborate processing also affect inference generation, and variables that influence sensitivity to self-generated information also affect inference utilization. Extreme, confidently held, and accessible judgments are formed when consumers are likely to generate and utilize inferences derived from explicit product information. Kardes concluded by emphasizing the important insights that an understanding of processing effects can yield. In the Stayman and Kardes study for instance, the strategic deletion of portions of a persuasive message created a more effective and compelling message, that lead to stronger brand attitudes for some individuals in some situations.

The Role of Attitude Confidence and Attitude Accessibility in the Process by which Attitudes Guide Behaviour

The last paper in this session was prepared by Berger and Finlay. Berger began the presentation by pointing out that psychological and consumer behaviour researchers are exhibiting growing interest in the notion that attitudes have at least two dimensions: valence and strength. Furthermore, recent evidence in the advertising repetition area (Berger and Mitchell 1989) indicates that advertising exposures can have a strong impact on at least two aspects of attitude strength (attitude accessibility and confidence) and thereby on attitude-behaviour consistency. Berger and Finlay's paper introduced a Two-Stage model of how attitudes guide behaviour. The model disentangles the determinants, memorial processes and behavioral consequences of high attitude confidence and high attitude accessibility.

Berger argued that in order for a previously formed attitude to guide a subsequent decision, two processes must occur. First, the attitude must be activated from memory. This may happen in a controlled fashion, as when an individual tries to consciously "remember" how they feel about an object, or in a spontaneous fashion, as when their feelings simply "pop" into their consciousness in the presence of the object. Second, the activated attitude must be accepted as a piece of information upon which a decision can be based. An individual who has active an attitude that s/he finds "unacceptable" may not behave in accordance with this attitude. Rather, under some circumstances, the behavioral implications of the previously formed attitude may be overwhelmed by new information available in the situation.

Attitude accessibility and attitude confidence may play distinct roles in this "Two-Stage attitude-to-behaviour process". Attitude accessibility may influence the likelihood of spontaneous activation of the attitude and thereby may influence the first stage of the process. Attitude confidence, on the other hand, may influence the likelihood that an attitude is considered acceptable or relevant to the decision and thereby may influence the second stage of the process. Berger pointed out that this Two-Stage model assumes that attitude accessibility and attitude confidence represent distinct psychological constructs accomplishing unique functions in the a-b process. Furthermore, the model suggests that under some behavioral circumstances, an attitude that is highly accessible, but held with low levels of confidence, will not be very predictive of subsequent behaviour.

These propositions were tested in a laboratory experiment that used repeated attitudinal expression and advertising repetition to independently manipulate attitude accessibility and attitude confidence, respectively. The results indicated that attitudes that were repeatedly expressed were indeed more accessible from memory, but were held with no more confidence. Attitudes that were based on multiple ad exposures were indeed held with more confidence, but were no more accessible from memory. In other words, the factors expected to influence the constructs uniquely, did so, and importantly, under these circumstances, the constructs exhibited no inter-relationship. Furthermore, in a behavioral situation in which subjects had the opportunity to reconsider their attitudes, attitude-behaviour consistency was moderated only by attitude confidence. There was no evidence of any influence due to accessibility.

Not only were these results consistent with the predictions of the Two-Stage model, but, as Berger pointed out, the results have direct implications for advertisers. Research on advertising has assumed that the effects of exposure can be completely captured in an ad's effect on a brand's evaluation. By contrast, this study showed that under some circumstances advertising does not influence brand attitudes but rather influences how accessible attitudes are from memory or how confidently they are held. Therefore, via its influence on attitude strength (accessibility or confidence) advertising can influence the strength of the relationship between attitudes and behaviour.

THE DISCUSSANT'S COMMENTS

The discussant for this special session, Larry Percy from Lintas: USA, commented on the applicability of the work to advertisers and advertising agencies. Although he indicated that it was interesting and important to understand advertising effects in terms of implicit memorial processes, he argued that researchers' consideration of some real-world constraints might provide more immediate utility to advertisers. In particular, he pointed out that most of the processes advertisers deal with are visually driven (eg. recognition of product in the purchase situation), so that verbal recall of brands and brand information may not be all that relevant. On the other hand, the results might be more exciting if the measures could be extended to include non-verbal stimuli and responses.

Secondly, since consumers often make purchases in a stimulus-based situation, recognition may be a better measure of advertising effectiveness than recall, particularly for low involvement products. In fact partial activation may be an indicator that a brand will likely be recognized in a purchase situation. This may be an interesting area for future research.

Thirdly, as interesting as the study of the effects of individual difference variables on processing is, if those kinds of individuals can't be isolated in the population, the results do not have immediate applicability. Direct matching of target demographics just does not seem to be affordable in today's media buying situations. From a managerial perspective, greater attention to variables that have a more "general" effect on processing might be more attractive.

Finally, Percy questioned the relevance of attitude confidence in low involvement purchase situations, but acknowledged that for high involvement products, it may make sense to use advertising frequency to drive up attitude confidence.

CONCLUSIONS

By way of conclusion it might be useful to highlight the *three* dominant themes addressed in these papers. First, all four papers focused on the accessibility, as opposed to the content of information in memory. Previous models have given advertisers the tools to influence the content of memory (attitude valence, specific beliefs) but these papers pointed out that with a better understanding of accessibility, advertisers could actually influence what associations (Heckler, Puto and Jaffe), brand names (Pluzinski), inferences (Stayman and Kardes), or attitudes (Berger and Finlay) are activated in a behavioral situation.

Secondly, all four papers concentrated on the process by which memorial information is activated or utilized. The dominant question in these papers was not whether a memorial concept was available for retrieval (ie. covariation information following non-conscious learning, Heckler, Puto and Jaffe; brand names following a slogan prime, Pluzinski; inferences following conclusion omission, Stayman and Kardes; attitudes following advertising expression, Berger and Finlay) but whether and how this memorial information might influence subsequent processing. By understanding the variables that influence these processes, advertisers will be better equipped to influence market outcomes.

Finally, all four papers grappled with the possibility that the processes being investigated are at least partially spontaneous. Traditional advertising researchers have shed considerable light on the nature of controlled, conscious information processes, while recognizing that not all processes are of this kind. The papers in this session (particularly Heckler, Puto and Jaffe and Pluzinski) tried to understand, or model processes that occur outside of conscious awareness, that cannot be articulated and often can only be inferred from resulting psychological or behavioral states. These spontaneous, implicit, uncontrolled processes represent a part of the 'black box' that advertisers are just beginning to explore.

The perspective advocated by all presenters in this session moved well beyond traditional attitude-change paradigms. According to these researchers, even without changing brand evaluations, advertising that induces non-conscious learning, or only partially activates memorial information, or induces self-generated inferences or creates confidently held attitudes can be very effective. The methods developed in these studies and the results presented should contribute to a new understanding of the effects of advertising.

REFERENCES

Berger, Ida E. and Andrew A. Mitchell, (1989) "The Effect of Advertising on Attitude Accessibility, Attitude Confidence and the Attitude-Behaviour Relationship", *Journal of Consumer Research*, 16 (December) 269-279.

Hasher, Lynn and Rose T. Zacks (1979), "Automatic and Effortful Processing in Memory", *Journal of Experimental Psychology:General*, 108, 356-388.

Hasher, Lynn and Rose T. Zacks (1984) "Automatic Processing of Fundamental Information," *American Psychologist*, 39 (December), 1372-1388.

Heckler, Susan E. and Christopher P. Puto (1987) "Unseen Effects of Advertising:Non-conscious Consumer Information Processing", presented at the Annual Conference of the Association for Consumer Research, Cambridge, Massachusetts.

Kardes, Frank R. (1988), "Spontaneous Inference Processes in Advertising: The Effects of Conclusion Omission and Involvement on Persuasion", *Journal of Consumer Research*, 15 (September), 225-233.

Kardes, Frank R. (forthcoming) "Consumer Inferences: Determinants, Consequences and Implications for Advertising", in *Advertising, Exposure, Memory and Choice*, ed. Andrew A. Mitchell, Hillsdale, NJ:Erlbaum, in press.

Kihlstrom, John F. (1987) "The Cognitive Unconscious", *Science*, 237.

Lewicki, Pawel (1986), *Non-conscious Social Information Processing*, Orlando, FL: Academic Press, Inc.

Pluzinski, Carol (1990) *Automatic Processes in Consumer Response to Advertising*, Unpublished Doctoral Dissertation, University of Michigan, Ann Arbor.

Sawyer, Alan G. (1988) "Can There Be Effective Advertising Without Explicit Conclusions? Decide for Yourself," in Nonverbal Communication in Advertising, eds. Sidney Hecker and David W. Stewart, Lexington, MA:Lexington, 159-184.

Zajonc, Robert B. (1980) "Feeling and Thinking:Preferences Need No Inferences," *American Psychologist*, 35 (February), 151-175.

Zajonc, Robert B. and Hazel Markus (1982), "Affective and Cognitive Factors in Preferences," *Journal of Consumer Research*, 9 (September), 123-131.

Consumer Responses to Environmentally Based Product Claims

T.J. Olney, Western Washington University
Wendy Bryce, Western Washington University

ABSTRACT

Recent increases in public awareness of environmental problems have lead many manufactures to position their offerings as environmentally friendly. Some practices have lead to substantial confusion about what it means to be environmentally aware and caring. This paper focuses a critical eye on the kinds of practices followed "because that's what the customer wants" which have the long term effect of eroding consumers' confidence in companies which say they encourage environmentally sound consumption. Several cases are used to illustrate some of the problem areas which have evolved. A research agenda is developed for delineating the critical areas for consumer research relating to this phenomenon.

INTRODUCTION

During the late 1980's and into 1990, consumers have received formidable input through the media about what constitutes environmentally sound behavior. Marketers, ever alert to trends and fads, have been quick to pick up on environmental concerns and to tailor product offerings to be more environmentally palatable. This strategy, which leads to greater consumption of the more palatable alternative, unfolds in one of two ways. First, companies can and do find ways to make their offerings have less deleterious impact on the environment. Second, companies create ways to reposition offerings by playing up some attributes and minimizing other attributes of the offering. Both methods seek to arrive at a perception of environmentally friendly companies producing environmentally benign products to the end of solving an environmental crisis.

Just what is this environmental crisis, what passes for environmentally friendly, and what makes a product environmentally benign? To attempt answers to these questions is to enter into a world of semantic land mines, where scientific researchers are loathe to tread. In fact, whether for this reason, or others, little scientific research to date has examined the role of environmental issues in shaping consumer behavior, in spite of calls for both causal and descriptive research of social marketing problems as early as 1974 (Wright 1974). This paper then seeks to define some of the areas where the expertise of consumer researchers can be brought to bear on these problems. Several anecdotal cases serve to illustrate these research arenas.

Definitions

The language of the "Green" movement provides a starting ground for discourse. At the heart of the environmental movement lies the issue of collectively poisoning ourselves through our consumption. The analogy has been made to the lives of yeast in a wine fermentation process. Here, the fermentation proceeds until the yeast essentially pollutes itself to death in a sea of alcohol. The creation, sale, and ultimate disposal of a product, seen from this perspective, can be more or less deleterious to the long term survival of the human species or for that matter to the long term survival of the majority of species on earth. The issues involve the release of toxic wastes into our air, our water supply, and our food production systems. This release may occur at any stage of the process from sourcing of raw materials, through manufacture to distribution, acquisition, use, and finally to disposal. The complexity of environmental issues arising out of the interplay between elements and subsystems of the earth's ecosystem make simple analyses of actual effects next to impossible. Ecological experts faced with the same data on existing conditions often reach highly divergent predictions of consequences. By reason of this uncertainty, environmental defenders would have us take a conservative approach to environmental effects. A conservative approach (not to be confused with the political terms conservative and liberal, which have long strayed from their original meanings) views any action as deleterious until proven benign. This conservative view takes a rather hard line on how we can recognize a product as environmentally benign: "It is not obnoxiously frivolous, like the new electric pepper mill. It releases no toxins into the environment during production, use, or disposal. It is made from recycled material or renewable resources extracted in a way that does not damage the environment. It is durable and reusable first, or recyclable or truly biodegradable next. It is responsibly and minimally packaged. It includes information on manufacturing, such as location, labor practices, animal testing, and the manufacturer's other business" (Dadd and Carothers, 1990). Passing our daily consumption items through such a sieve would force most of us into a life of voluntary simplicity. Certain keywords in the above definition, however, hint toward actions that people might take to lessen their own personal measure of environmental guilt. These same keywords have been appropriated by astute marketers to tout the benefits of certain attributes of their products. Herein lies the rub.

Keywords

Recyclable, reusable, durable, biodegradable, ozone friendly, and environmentally friendly apply to products in varying degrees. Like food labels such as "jumbo" they are meaningless out of context. As there is no standard definition for recyclability, biodegradability, or environmentally friendly, manufacturers have considerable latitude when applying the terms to their particular offering. Additionally, the application of one term to a product might mask serious problems on some other dimension of potential harm to the environment. These considerations lead to the potential for the erosion of an already fragile trust which consumers place in corporate America. Furthermore, consumers' awareness of environmental issues, and their confidence in their own ability to make environmentally sound purchase decisions, (assuming as the polls tell us that they are motivated to make such decisions if possible) vary vastly from individual to individual. This variability and the generally low level of environmental expertise leave consumers vulnerable to exploitation by unscrupulous business practitioners in much the same way that health claims for food products might. In turn, the well intentioned business will suffer additional marketing costs in order to communicate that it is indeed one of the good guys. The claim of being a good guy, however, will not go unquestioned by an already wary public.

SAMPLE PROBLEMS

In order to illustrate the complexity of the situation facing consumers who would do right by the environment, let's look at a few of the more salient environmental problems.

Landfills

First, landfills are filling up. It is a fact. They are filling up with municipal solid waste consisting of 40-50% paper, less than 1% disposable diapers, less than 1/10 of one percent fast food packaging, 13% plastics (Rathje 1989). The general public has become aware of this situation as municipalities across the country struggle with problems of solid waste disposal. Marketers, sensing a need to be filled, make claims about their products which imply that using their products will help solve the problem. Two product attributes, which appear to assuage the problem are recyclability and biodegradability. The unfortunate reality appears that most materials in landfills don't biodegrade anyway (Rathje 1989) and that for much of what is theoretically recyclable, the infrastructure doesn't exist to carry our the recycling. In spite of these realities, marketers have created products and made claims concerning degradability and recyclability of products.

In one case involving degradability , Mobil Chemical, manufacturer of Hefty plastic garbage bags, changed its product with an additive which accelerates deterioration of bags when exposed to wind, rain, and sunlight. A prominent advertising claim on packages was that the bags were degradable. Mobil faced charges by a group of state attorneys general for making allegedly false advertising claims concerning environmental benefits of the bags (Smith 1990b). Other companies have added a starch to plastic, which can be eaten by microorganisms, causing the plastic to disintegrate into microscopic pieces. Unfortunately, there is no guarantee that in the landfill, this will happen, further, it still leaves behind the 94% plastic in a potentially more dangerous powdered form (Rathje 1989).

Disposable diapers, whose salient benefits include dryer babies and convenience for diaper changers, have come under fire for the sheer bulk they represent in the landfill. To counter this criticism, brands have been developed which claim to be biodegradable. The problem is the same. If left in a home compost pile and turned every week, they might biodegrade, but in modern landfills the claim is meaningless. Hence one brand, Bunnies, has come under federal scrutiny for its claims (Lipman 1990).

Plastics are not alone with these biodegradable problems, finding company with paper products. Many paper manufactures have added claims for biodegradability to their products and or paper packaging. The FTC has begun investigating claims made for paper products which infer that the products will help solve landfill and disposal problems because they are biodegradable (Smith 1990c). As previously noted, when these paper products find their way to a landfill, they do not degrade.

The other landfill oriented response involves recycling and the concept of recyclability. Consensus exists on the value of recycling as a means of conserving scarce resources and as a means of keeping disposed items out of landfills. Thus, companies have been quick to ad cheerful admonitions on packages that they be properly recycled. This practice has seen at least two types of abuse to date. The first consists of labeling as recyclable products which cannot be recycled. MacDonald's found itself doing that with coated paper hash-brown containers but has discontinued the practice (Holusha 1990b). The second abuse occurs with plastics, which are indeed recyclable, but for which no infrastructure as yet exists to recycle them (Sherman 1989). Heinz created a large public relations effort surrounding the change of its squeezable ketchup bottle from a seven layer system which contained adhesives to a five layer system containing only two types of plastic, both of which can be recycled (Holusha 1990a). Unfortunately, the layering system prevents it from being purely PET (polyethylene terephthalate) one of the high value plastics for which a recycling infrastructure has already developed (although it is 98.5% PET). Instead, the squeeze bottle must bear a recycling classification of 7 for "other" indicating that it cannot be recycled as PET.

Another marketing action to promote the recycling attribute, has been the emphasis of the fact that some things are actually made from recycled material. The deception here lies in the knowledge gap between what the public thinks recycled means, and what is required by the FTC to use the label recycled. Paper may be labeled recycled if it contains only a fraction of recycled fibers, and even if the "recycled" fibers are only the mill ends created in the manufacture of some finished paper product.

Air Pollution

Air pollution in general and the ozone layer in particular, combine to form a second major area of public concern about the environment. Using this concern as a point of departure, companies have begun to label products as "ozone friendly". Two examples of this are White Rain styling mousse by Gillette and Alberto VO5 hair spray by Alberto-Culver (Smith 1990a). The criticism here stems from the vagueness of the claims, and from the fact that even though the cloroflourocarbon propellant has been changed to a hydrocarbon propellant, hydrocarbons are potent greenhouse gasses and therefore not environmentally benign.

Non-renewable Resources

A third area where environmental claims have started to appear might be called non-renewable resources claims. In particular, the nuclear power industry has been promoting nuclear power as the environmentally safe alternative to the use of fossil fuels. This flies in the face of the extreme toxicity and disposal problems encountered with byproducts of nuclear power generation. It also ignores the potential for extremely hazardous accidents on the scale of Chernobyl or worse.

THE ROLE OF CONSUMER RESEARCH

So the problem with the environment is that collectively, we need to clean up our act. We need to buy only benign products that we really need and dispose of them in the most environmentally conscious manner possible, right? So why don't we, the consumers, do all of these things? Is it lack of knowledge on the part of consumers? Is it lack of good will on the part of consumers or firms? Is it technologically unfeasible? Is it economically unfeasible? Clearly each of these are part of the overall problem. What then is the role of the consumer researcher in addressing these questions?

The role of the consumer researcher can be viewed from a process point of view or from a focus point of view. Process here indicates the stage of a consumer in a consumption process which might be acquisition, use, or disposal. Focus here indicates the level of analysis to be used in a particular study from a personal orientation, to an interpersonal orientation and finally through a cultural or cross-cultural orientation. Each cell in the resultant framework holds potential as a research area to further our understanding of consumer behavior in general and our understanding of the special cases surrounding issues of environmental impact.

At the Personal level of focus, we might study the antecedents of decisions to live lives of voluntary simplicity. We might investigate how conservation behavior has been learned. We might investigate the kinds of trade-offs that people might make in acquiring products vis a vis environmental concerns. A particularly promising area for research involves the types and sizes of incentives which might be provided to encourage environmentally benign behavior. The personal characteristics and habits surrounding the purchase and use of previously used goods, or the continual re-use of goods which others might use only once provide additional areas for study. Disposal patterns might be investigated, in search of key characteristics of people or products which lead to less impactful disposal. Here we can investigate the issue of credibility. In a media environment rife with strident critics, what kinds of claims do people believe?

At the Interpersonal level models of social influence might be applied to these environmentally related behaviors at any level of the acquisition-use-disposal process. Sharing behavior might be a fruitful area of investigation, to determine conditions under which people can be encouraged to adopt such resource conserving behaviors as passing along magazines and sharing tools. At this level we might look at the signaling ability of the various "green seals" which have come into being and the effects that these signals have on consumers attitudes and behaviors. At this level investigations of community based recycling efforts might focus, asking what works, what doesn't work and why?

Cultural and cross-cultural focuses serve as additional windows onto the problem. Here the roles of regulations and tax policies can be investigated both in terms of their effectiveness in changing behavior, and in terms of their effect on consumers' attitudes toward the behaviors, toward the firms, and toward the government itself. Cultural barriers to behavior might be investigated... Is it "tacky" to sort through your trash? The mythologies surrounding environmental issues need investigation. What are the cultural values? How do they change over time? What mechanism(s) cause the changes? Do any of the lessons learned at the personal level about voluntary simplicity have implications for how some of these values might be transmitted to a culture hooked on consumption? How can people be persuaded to purchase more ecologically sound transportation? A last area which needs addressing and which has alarming implications to dedicated environmentalists is the possibility that the current interest in environmental issues is a fad. A European poll by *The Economist* showed that "the proportion of voters listing the environment as one of the most important political issues fell by half between July 1989 and February 1990." If the United States follows Europe on this as it has on other trends regarding the environment, all of this current interest might just degrade.

In many ways, environmentally friendly consumption is a generalization of the special case of energy conservation which received considerable attention during the late 1970's and early 1980's (see for example Anderson and Claxton 1982) and smaller, but steady stream of attention through the 1980's. As such, we can look to that literature to find examples of research procedures which might generalize to the broader arena covering all aspects of environmental impact.

The study of the interface between consumer behavior and the environment should prove both exciting and fruitful. Problems of eroding consumer trust through abuse will doubtless prove to be a minor area of interest. We will find ourselves humbled as we explore methods of applying our theories and knowledge of consumer behavior to areas of intimidating global significance.

REFERENCES

Anderson, C. Dennis and John D. Claxton (1982), "Barriers to Consumer Choice of Energy Efficient Products," *Journal of Consumer Research*, 9 (September),163-170.

Dadd, Debra Lynn and Andre Carothers (1990), "A Bill of Goods?" *GreenPeace* 15(3) 8-12.

Holusha, John (1990a), "New Plastic in Heinz Bottles to Make Recycling Easier," *The New York Times*, April 10.

Holusha, John (1990b), "Some Smog In Pledges to Help Environment," *The New York Times*, April 19.

Lipman, Joanne (1990), "Trendy Environmental Themes Hit Sour Notes Among Public," *The Wall Street Journal*, May 3, p.B7.

Rathje, William L. (1989), "Rubbish!," *The Atlantic Monthly*, December 99-109.

Sherman, Stratford P. (1989) "Trashing A $150 Billion Business," *Fortune*, August 28, 90-90.

Smith, Randolph B. (1990a), "Environmentalists, State Officers See Red As Firms Rush to Market 'Green' Products," *The Wall Street Journal*, March 13.

Smith, Randolph B. (1990b), "Mobil Unit Said to Face Suit on Hefty Bags," *The Wall Street Journal*, June 12, p. B1.

Smith, Randolph B. (1990c), "Ecology Claims May Just Look Good on Paper," *The Wall Street Journal*, September 13, p. B1.

Wright, Peter (1974), "On the Application of Persuasion Theory in Social Marketing," in *Marketing Analysis for Societal Problems*, ed. Jagdesh Sheth and Peter Wright.

The Effects of Incentives on Environment-Friendly Behaviors: A Case Study

R. Bruce Hutton, University of Denver
Frank Markley, University of Denver

ABSTRACT

The use of incentives to encourage social change behaviors has received a good deal of attention in past years, primarily from a conservation perspective. This paper reports the results of a financial incentive program to reduce air pollution. Almost 9% of the 6500 employees of a large public utility participated in the program by changing their commute mode from driving alone to carpooling, vanpooling, or taking a bus.

INTRODUCTION

The year 1990 has become a pivotal year for assessing society's response to the host of environmental issues that have arisen in the past two decades. In 1970, environmental concerns were focused by the first grass roots organized Earth Day and the passage of the National Environmental Policy Act. Concerns about the state of the environment were further expanded by the 1973 Arab oil embargo which introduced the importance of political and economic factors in developing environmental policy.

Today, concern for the environment may be at an all time high. Over the past twenty years, recurring problems and serious incidents - Love Canal, Times Beach, PCBs, dioxin, vinyl chloride, contaminated groundwater, air pollution, acid rain, asbestos, radon gas, nuclear waste, Exxon Valdez, global warming, rainforest destruction, Bhopal - have continued to keep the environment at the front of the public consciousness, prominent in the media, and magnified by worldwide environmental groups. And, the current Middle East crisis vividly points out the continued importance of environmental resources in shaping political and economic policies around the world.

Over the past twenty years governnment policies have emerged (e.g., Clean Air Act, 1970; Environmental Education Act, 1970; Energy Policy and Conservation Act, 1975) and technological solutions developed (e.g., nuclear power, solar power, fuel efficiency standards). In both cases and with varying degrees of success, strategies and programs designed to encourage public acceptance of these policies and technologies have also been introduced. While the values expressed by society strongly support protecting the environment, many behaviors simply do not. For example, in 1989, 80% of the sample in a national poll agreed with the statement, "Protecting the environment is so important that requirements and standards cannot be too high, and continuing environmental improvements must be made regardless of cost" (Ruckelshaus 1989). And yet, in the past twenty years, public transportation use has plummeted 50% and net energy demand in the United States is on the rise (Udall 1989). The struggle to establish what Robert Cahn (1988) refers to as an "environmental ethic" or the Science Council of Canada (1976) describes as a "conserver society" may have been explained best by Benjamin Franklin in 1781:

> "To get the bad customs of country changed and new ones thought to be better introduced, it is necessary first to remove the prejudices of the people, enlighten their ignorance, and convince them that their interests will be promoted by the proposed changes; and this is not the work of a day."

One of the ways that has shown some promise in encouraging behavior change is the use of incentives. This article describes the results of a pilot program to encourage employees of a large public utility to change their commute mode in order to reduce air pollution. The program was voluntary, and it used a financial incentive to motivate commuters to change from commuting in single occupied vehicles to an alternative form of transportation that would result in less air pollution (e.g., carpool, bus, vanpool, bicycle, walk).

THE VALUE OF INCENTIVES IN SOCIAL CHANGE PROGRAMS

The concept of incentives has long been used by both the public and private sectors to encourage behavior change among targeted audiences. The typical goals for incentive programs are to generate repeat purchase, influence sampling, and motivate consumers to read product or program advertising (Advertising Age 1978).

Winett and Kagel (1984) note that it is an accepted practice to categorize behavioral procedures as antecedent and consequence strategies. Antecedents are defined as stimuli that precede a desired behavior and are designed to elicit or modify the behavior (e.g., advertising, educational materials). Consequence strategies, on the other hand, are stimuli that follow the presence or absence of a behavior and are designed to increase or decrease the frequency of the behavior (e.g., feedback, tax credits, rebates). Incentives are usually classified as a consequence strategy.

One of the most fertile areas in which the value of incentives has been explored is energy conservation. Of course, from a transportation perspective, the strategies to conserve fuel or reduce air pollution are very similar (i.e., reduce the number of miles driven). Ritchie and McDougall (1985) provide a broad overview of conservation strategies, including financial incentives. Nemetz and Hankey (1984) provide the most comprehensive review of economic incentives to encourage conservation. Hutton and McNeill (1981) provide an example of the impact of incentives that are not financial in nature.

Financial incentives are typically divided into positive and negative types (Nemetz and Hankey 1984):

Incentives	
Positive	Negative
• Tax incentives (credits, deductions, rebates, exemptions)	• Taxes
	• Fines
	• Special charges/ rates
• Grants	
• Loans	• Price increases
• Subsidies	

Of the 71 energy conservation incentive programs compiled by Nemetz & Hankey (1984), 22 are transportation related. One category of programs focused on reducing energy use in the automobile sector by providing positive incentives for vanpooling or carpooling, providing tax deductions for fuel-conserving devices, and lowering automobile registration fees for energy efficient cars. Negative incentives within the automobile sector included taxing gasoline, parking spaces, highway access, and "gas guzzler" automobiles. Programs targeting urban transportation, commuting, and intercity passenger travel almost exclusively utilized employee or public subsidization and fare reductions for mass transportation programs.

Ritchie and McDougall (1984) reached the following conclusions regarding the use of financial incentives:

- Cash incentives combined with feedback on electricity use reduced energy consumption, in some cases, only in the short-term.

- The cost of previous incentive or rebate programs has far outweighed the resultant benefits.

- Consumers are more receptive to better public transporation services than to reduced fares.

Ritchie and McDougall (1984) also cite three major problems when considering incentives to encourage curtailment behaviors. These include:

- Curtailment behaviors usually offer substantially lower energy savings than do efficiency behaviors.

- Visualization of how a rebate program based on reduced energy use could be implemented on a large scale is difficult.

- The long-term effects of incentives on curtailment behaviors are unknown and there may be a "wear-out" effect which occurs over time.

After examining hundreds of economic incentive programs, Nemetz and Hankey (1984) identify nine common elements essential to successful programs and four reasons for program failure:

Factors Leading to:

Success
Ease of participation
Significant monetary incentives
Extensive information diffusion
Consultation and participation of industry and community leaders
Ease of enforcement
High coverage and impact
Need for mandatory elements
Need for follow-up monitoring
Need for quality control

Failure
Inadequate monetary incentives
Inadequate prior consultation
Poor information dissemination
Poor targeting of program

PROGRAM BACKGROUND

In 1984, the combined problems of carbon monoxide and particulate pollution had moved Denver, Colorado into a tie with Los Angeles, California as the two cities with the worst air pollution problems in the United States. The primary culprit was tail pipe emissions. Vehicle miles traveled in Denver had risen from 15 million per day in 1971 to 32 million in 1985. Further, it was projected that, by the turn of the century, travel would more than double to 65 miles million per day.

In response, the State Department of Health in conjunction with the Environmental Protection Agency implemented the Better Air Campaign, a voluntary driving reduction program targeted at individual drivers in the metro area during a three month "high pollution" season. It utilized a variety of antecedent type strategies anchored by a mass media advertising and public relations campaign.

Over a five year period, the program evolved to include not only voluntary driving reduction components but also mandatory use of oxygenated fuels and wood burning bans on extreme pollution days. Results of the program were mixed. Both mandatory components, wood burning bans and oxygenated fuels use, achieved policy stated goals. The voluntary driving reduction component produced positive results for early consumer response levels (e.g., awareness, attitudes, intentions) but statistically insignificant reductions in vehicle miles traveled. For a complete evaluation of the program, see Hutton and Ahtola (1990).

A number of important lessons were learned from the program. It was clear that mass media oriented programs targeting a total community cannot build significant behavior changes, even over time. It was recommended that future driving reduction programs be targeted to specific segments utilizing a more "grass roots" oriented strategy to produce needed behavior change.

In 1988, taking a more targeted approach, the governor created the Corporate Alliance for Better

Air as a way to involve the business community directly in the air pollution battle. In response to recommendations from the Better Air Campaign evaluation, the State Department of Health and the Alliance developed the Clean Air Colorado program in 1989. The goals of the program were threefold:

- Develop a series of individualized pilot programs for business, government, and education to reduce pollution and waste.

- Implement the pilot programs during the 1989-90 high pollution season.

- Disseminate the lessons learned from the case studies to other organizations and communities through personal consultation and an Air Quality Workbook which could be used as a guide for organizations wishing to start their own program.

In the first year of this new initiative, 13 pilot programs were designed and implemented. The following describes the results of one company's efforts to motivate its employees to change their commute mode buy offering financial incentives.

THE CLEAN AIR CAMPAIGN

Public Service Company of Colorado is the state's largest public utility, with over 6500 employees statewide. The primary purpose of the program was to encourage employees not to drive to work alone. A variety of antecedent and consequence strategies were utilized, including:

- *Cash Incentives.* Each employee received one dollar for each day he or she did not drive alone to and from work between November 1, 1989 and January 31, 1990.

- *Clean Air Day.* This day was designed to thank employees for participating. There was a breakfast for employees at various locations statewide.

- *Expanded Van Pool Program.* Additional commuter vans and routes were added.

- *Discount Appliance Booklets.* The booklet contained coupons for discounts on natural gas products to encourage conversion of woodburning fireplaces.

- *Information Campaign.* Displays and other information were made available to employees stressing the importance of clean air and how to participate.

METHODOLOGY

The most visible and innovative component of the program was the cash incentive. A dollar a day incentive was offered to each employee who commuted to and from work in some way other than driving alone. Alternative methods to driving alone had to be used at least five days a month to qualify. To keep track of participation, each employee was provided a calendar to record the day, mode of transportation used, mileage to and from work, commute time, and other employee information. The calendar was turned in at the end of each month, and the money earned was recorded and applied to the following month's paycheck.

In order to determine program acceptance a telephone survey was conducted of both participants (defined as any person who turned in at least one calendar) and non-participants (employees who did not turn in a calendar). A random sample of 250 employees from each category was taken.

RESULTS

Three groups of employees are relevant for discussion: (1) participants who normally drive alone to work; (2) participants who normally commute in some way other than driving alone; and (3) non-participants.

Table 1 shows that regardless of whether employees participated, they viewed the incentive program favorably. Even among non-participants (primarily drive alone commuters) 45% indicated some likelihood of participating next year.

There was strong indication that the multidimensional nature of the program did not come through. Less than 50% of any group cited awareness of the other program components. Further indication that the program may have suffered from a lack of cohesive presentation is found in the 2-5% of respondents who indicated the program was disorganized.

Interestingly, the educational value of the program was the second most mentioned positive program perception. This is consistent with other research that has shown an incentive alone is not likely to drive significant behavior change among certain groups.

Table 2 provides participation figures. Percentages have been weighted proportional to the total employee base. Overall, 22.2% of employees turned in at least one calendar. Of those, 3.3% were normally drive alone commuters and 18.9% were already commuting in some way other than driving alone. Interestingly, 5.5% of the nonparticipants (i.e., drive alones who did not turn in a calendar) reported changing their commute mode enough to qualify for the incentive, but they did not turn in a calendar. Primary reasons cited for not turning in a calendar were: (1) too much trouble (46%) or (2) forgot (10%). Consequently, the incremental gain from the program was 8.8%.

Table 2 also shows the differences between the normal drive alones and those who normally commute by some means other than driving alone. Only 37% of drive alones participated all three months compared to 84% of the other group. Additionally, 98% of the other group has continued their ridesharing mode compared to 26% of the normal drive-alones.

TABLE 1
Attitudes and Perceptions Toward the Program

Perception	Participants		Non-Participants (n=250)
	Drive Alone (n=42)	Other (n=208)	
Favorable attitude[1]	98%	97%	95%
Liklihood of participating next year[2]	79	97	45
Awareness of program components besides incentive	36	44	28
Positive program characteristics			
$1/day incentive	33	61	38
Educational value	21	15	17
Reduced pollution	14	13	7
Negative perceptions			
None	81	71	76
Size of incentive	4	2	2
Disorganized	5	2	3

[1] Subjects responded to a 4 point scale. The percentages reported combine "very favorable and "somewhat favorable" responses.

[2] Subjects responded to a 4 point scale. The percentages reported combine "very likely" and "somewhat likely" responses.

TABLE 2
Participation

	Participants		Non-Participants (n=250)
	Drive Alones (n=42)	Other (n=208)	
Altered commute mode on at least 5 working days but did not turn in a calendar[1]	NA	NA	5.5%
Turned in at least 1 calendar[1]	3.3%	18.9%	NA
Months participated			NA
One	42	9	
Two	20	7	
Three	37	84	
Continued with new commute method post-incentive	26	98	
Same frequency of use	82	99	NA

[1] Percentages are weighted proportional to their representation in the total population of employees.

When non-participants were asked why they were unable to participate, primary reasons given were:

- No one to carpool with   41%
- Variable work hours   28
- No bus in area   19
- Need car in job   15

These responses indicate the primary barriers to participation to be either job related (e.g., work hours) or a perceived lack of alternatives (e.g., no bus).

In an open-ended question, all respondents were asked how they would improve next year's program. The most frequently mentioned recommendations were:

- Increase incentive   20%
- More information/better communication   14
- Increased vanpool routes   8
- Discount bus passes   5
- Flextime/4 day weeks   5

Finally, in order to better understand differences, participants and non-participants were examined along several classification questions. Participants were more likely to hold a non-management position. While over 50% of support and operations respondents surveyed turned in at least one calendar, only 42% of managers did so. Further, managers were much more likely to report driving alone to work (65% vs. 56%). Not surprisingly participants were also more likely to be younger and to have worked for the company fewer years.

CONCLUSIONS AND RECOMMENDATIONS

In its first year as a pilot program, Public Service Company's Clean Air Campaign achieved modest success. Almost 9% of the employee workforce who normally drive alone to work participated in the incentive program. Overall, 18.9% of participants reported not driving alone to work as their normal commute pattern. For this group the average number of days they did not drive alone during the three month period was 16.2. The average number of trip miles saved per day was 507. The number of days and trip miles saved per day by the employees who changed because of the program was 11.9 and 291 respectively. Consequently, the incentive program reduced miles driven by 43% from normal.

An examination of the program in the context of Nemetz and Hankey's elements of success for incentive programs provides valuable insight into what was right about the program and what could be improved to ensure greater success in the next phase.

Ease of participation. The pilot program received mixed reviews in this area. Providing each employee with a calendar that could be filled out and turned in to the payroll department appeared to be an easy way for employees to document their participation. In fact, it was viewed by many as cumbersome and too much trouble to fill out. Even a percentage of those who were already doing the "right" commute modes to qualify chose not to fill out the calendars in some cases. It appears the program would benefit from a more streamlined self-report instrument in the future.

Also, while some attempts were made to expand the options for employees (e.g., increased vanpools), little, if anything, was done to help organize the options for employees. One recommendation in this area is to organize a within company carpool/vanpool matching service. Also, providing options for four day work weeks and flextime scheduling were employee recommendations.

These recommendations are consistent with reasons given by non-participants for not taking advantage of the program. Essentially, their reasons fall into two categories: (1) work related barriers such as variable work hours which prohibit caropooling and busing and (2) lack of available options such as not having a bus in their area or no one to share driving with.

Significant monetary incentives. In this case, the cost/benefit trade-off is difficut. The company spent approximately $50,000 in incentives plus time. The reward was an incremental 9% participation rate and an average of 798 miles saved per work day. The real value of the investment depends on the goals of the program and the follow-up impact in the second year's efforts. In some respects the money can be viewed as an investment in future returns.

From the employees standpoint, a dollar a day is not too significant. However, the value of the incentive should not only be measured in terms of absolute monetary value. The incentive also provides a positive message to employees from top management that speaks to the company's commitment to clean air and the importance of reducing pollution.

Extensive information diffusion. Based on employee feedback and the overall lack of awareness of program components, it is clear that campaign communications should be improved. First, a more coordinated effort to tie all components together should increase interest and visibility. Second, more information besides the incentive program should have been emphasized. Employees report valuing the educational component of the program. This could be expanded. For example, multiple benefits could be stressed. It was reported that the primary reason current ridesharers commute the way they do is convenience, economics or to avoid stress. These attributes could be highlighted along with the environmental benefits.

Consultation. Company officials did work with health department officials in program design and evaluation. However, the program started too late for any substantial changes to be made.

Enforcement. The program was voluntary in nature. Therefore, enforcement had only to do with the accounting and payroll procedures used to audit days participated and to pay accordingly.

Coverage and impact. There was little feedback given during the program in terms of impact. This lack of feedback is likely to have dampened the initial enthusiasm of some new participants as well as failed to encourage later adoptors.

Mandatory elements. The only mandatory element present was in the rules of the program. That is, an employee had to participate five days a month and change the commute both ways before he or she was eligible. Participation was strictly voluntary.

Follow-up monitoring. Some self-report data was available regarding continued ridesharing following the program. But it has not been extensive. Evaluation in the second year will provide additional information.

Quality control. Policing was done in two ways. Random samples were taken over the course of the campaign to determine if reported ridesharing was, in fact, occuring. And, on every calendar another person had to be given as a reference (e.g., vanpool driver). Also, each calendar was checked for inconsistencies.

In summary, this first year pilot program did have some success, but much was learned about how to improve performance to gain additional participation in following years. The value of the financial incentive is still open to question. One key to the next iteration may well be to target the program to more specifically meet the needs of the current drive alone segment. For example, providing an at work carpool for managers who need a car in their job would alleviate the need to commute in a single occupied vehicle. After all, the purpose of a grass roots campaign is to tailor the program to those specific smaller constituencies.

REFERENCES

Advertising Age (1978), "Premiums and Incentives," Special Report.

Cahn, Robert (1988), "What is an Environmental Ethic ?," *EPA Journal*, (July/August), 2-4.

Clean Air Act (1970), Public Law 91-604.

Energy Policy and Conservation Act (1975), Public Law 94-163.

Environmental Education Act (1970), Public Law 91-516.

Hutton, R. Bruce and Olli T. Ahtola (1990), "Consumer Response to a Five Year Campaign to Combat Air Pollution," Working Paper, University of Denver, Denver, Colorado.

_____ and Dennis L. McNeill (1981), "The Value of Incentives in Stimulating Energy Conservation," *Journal of Consumer Research*, 8 (December), 291-298.

National Environmental Policy Act (1970), Public Law 91-190.

Nemetz, Peter N. and Marilyn Hankey (1984), *Economic Incentives For Energy Conservation*, New York, NY: John Wiley & Sons.

Ritchie, J.R. Brent and Gordon H.G. McDougall (1985), "Designing and Marketing Consumer Energy Conservation Policies and Programs : Implications From a Decade of Research," *Journal of Public Policy & Marketing*, 4 , 14-32.

Ruchelshaus, William D. (1989), "Toward a Sustainable World," *Scientific American*, (September), 166-174.

The Conserver Society (1979), American Marketing Association, Proceedings Series, Karl E. Henion and Thomas C. Kinnear (eds), Chicago, Illinois.

Udall, James R (1989), "Turning Down the Heat," *Sierra*, (July/August) 26-39.

Winett, Richard A. and John H. Kagel (1984), "Effects of Information Presentation Format on Resource Use in Field Settings," *Journal of Consumer Research*, 2 (December), 655-667.

Recent Studies of Time in Consumer Behavior
Ziv Carmon, University of California at Berkeley[1]

ABSTRACT

This paper summarizes the special session "New Directions in Time Research in Consumer Behavior." Four papers were presented in the session:

* "The Effects of Visual Cues on Consumers' Preferences for Single and Multiple Queuing Systems" (Bernd Schmitt, Columbia University; Laurette Dube, University of Montreal; and France Leclerc, Massachusetts Institute of Technology).
* "Situational Determinants of Consumers' Dissatisfaction with Waiting" (Ziv Carmon, University of California at Berkeley).
* "Contextual Issues in Time Perception and Orientation" (Jacob Hornik, Tel-Aviv University).
* "Preferences Toward Temporally Separated Outcome Sequences" (George Loewenstein, Carnegie Mellon University; and Drazen Prelec, Harvard University).

The session reviewed recent developments in time research, focusing on three interrelated topics: perception of time (Hornik), consumers' preferences and attitudes towards queues (Carmon, and Schmitt, Dube and Leclerc) and intertemporal choice (Loewenstein and Prelec).

We briefly consider time research and its relationship to consumer behavior. A summary of the papers follows.

BACKGROUND

Many people seem to be increasingly pressed for time in spite of the evolving leisure society in the U.S. Consequently, there is an intensifying awareness of the temporal expenditures that are involved in purchase situations (Schary 1971). It is predicted that this trend will continue, and the consumer of the nineties will be more concerned than ever with temporal expenditures (see, for example, Miller 1988). Hence, it is surprising that although consumers typically spend both time and money to acquire goods and services, monetary expenditures have been studied extensively, while temporal expenditures received relatively little attention.

The dimension of time has played a major function in several research disciplines that are closely related to consumer behavior. The role of time has been particularly emphasized in economics (e.g., Stigler 1961, and Becker 1965), sociology (e.g., De Grazia 1961, Robinson 1967, and Hall and Schroeder 1970), operations research (e.g., Erlang 1917, Little 1961, and Buffa 1983), and psychology (e.g., Gulliksen 1927, and Fraisse 1963, 1984).

The importance of time as a major variable of interest to consumer behavior theory had already been recognized in the early stages of consumer research (Nicosia 1966, Howard and Sheth 1969, and Engel et al. 1973). Over the past twenty years, several research streams concerning time have evolved within the consumer behavior literature. These included the effects of time pressure on consumer decision making (e.g., Howard and Sheth 1969, Wright 1974, and Johnson and Payne 1985), people's allocation of their time (e.g., Marby 1970, Feldman and Hornik 1981, and Holbrook and Lehman 1981), and perception of time (e.g., Hornik 1984, Feinberg and Smith 1989, Dube-Rioux et al. 1989, and Carmon 1990). Several interdisciplinary reviews also appeared in the marketing literature (e.g., Jacoby et al. 1976, Feldman and Hornik 1981, and Gross 1987).

Recently, there has been a growing interest in time related research, focusing primarily on three interrelated topics: preferences and attitudes towards queues, time perception, and intertemporal judgement and choice. Accordingly, the papers presented in the session represent these three topics.

PREFERENCES AND ATTITUDES TOWARDS QUEUES

Operations Research has dominated both research and applications related to queues. For decades, researchers in this field have studied queuing systems and methods for improving their efficiency. This research has advanced our understanding of the relationship between characteristics of queuing systems (e.g., service rate, customers' arrival rate and number of servers in the system) and their performance (e.g., average queue length and average waiting time per customer). Although it has led to substantial improvements in the service consumers received, this approach has been rather narrow as it focused exclusively on physical aspects of the queuing system. In taking this perspective, O.R. has failed to consider other perceptual factors that may affect consumers' *attitudes and preferences* regarding queues. The first two papers (Carmon, and Schmitt, Dube and Leclerc) address this issue. Both papers examine contextual factors that affect consumers' perceptions of queuing systems, demonstrating the potential contribution of consumer research in this area when a psychological framework is applied.

Carmon considers factors that affect consumers' attitudes toward the time they spend waiting for service. Within the context of his studies, he shows that providing information about the expected waiting duration or about the causes of the delay, can reduce dissatisfaction with waiting

---

[1] I would like to thank Eric Johnson for volunteering his wit and wisdom as the session's discussant.

whether or not this information can lead to alternative utilization of the time. Moreover, what may appear to be minor differences in the format in which the information is provided, affect its impact on consumers' satisfaction. He also shows that the dis/satisfaction depends on consumers' prior expectations. However, contrary to the common interpretation of Prospect Theory, in the case of temporal expenditures, gains loom larger than losses. Finally, subjects' dissatisfaction with waiting is affected by the availability of alternative activities while waiting, as well as by the value of the service. He concludes by examining possible reasons for the effectiveness of these factors and proposing applications of the findings.

Schmitt, Dube and Leclerc investigate whether consumers prefer single queuing lines or multiple lines when they wait for services. More specifically, they focus on the effect of visual cues on consumers' preferences for queuing systems. Normative theories in Operations Research seem to suggest that consumers should prefer single lines since these theories predict that, on average, the waiting time in single waiting lines will be shorter. This prediction was contrasted with the fact that people often employ visual cues in their duration estimates (e.g., the longer the line, the longer the service time) which would favor a system with multiple lines. It was found that when subjects, who were familiar with O.R. queuing theories, examined a visual representation of these queuing systems, they preferred systems with multiple lines over single line systems. These subjects also estimated single line systems to have shorter waiting times relative to systems with multiple lines, based on the visual cue. However, when they were asked to consider which one they thought was better, in the absence of the visual cue, they chose single line systems over systems with multiple lines.

TIME PERCEPTION

People are frequently influenced by situational conditions when making judgements about time (see for example Fraisse 1963, 1984). Indeed, recent research has demonstrated that certain momentary conditions, like mood, play a critical role in the process of time use and allocation. Little attention has been paid, however, to the way in which a consumer's affective state alters his or her evaluation of time and temporal orientation (-- the relative dominance of the past, present or future in a person's thoughts).

Hornik presents studies on the influence of different mood states on the way people estimate the duration of recent events as well as on their stated temporal orientation. He suggests that positive and negative emotions result in underestimation and overestimation of duration, respectively. He further suggests that people in a positive mood tend to be future oriented, while people in a negative mood have more of a present orientation. Two experiments using two different mood-inducing manipulations support his suggestions revealing strong mood effects on subjects' time perception and orientation.

INTERTEMPORAL CHOICE

Another time related research topic which is currently receiving considerable attention is intertemporal choice, a term that refers to decisions concerning cases in which costs and benefits are spread over time. Understanding choice between sequences of temporally separated outcomes is important because most intertemporal decision making involves choices between sequences, rather than between simple outcomes. Choices involving activities that take up time -- e.g., school, work, vacations, eating chores -- always involve choosing between sequences since single events cannot generally be rescheduled without changing the timing of other activities.

Additively separable formulations of intertemporal choice, such as the discounted utility (DU) model, imply that the overall value of a sequence can be determined directly from the values of its component prospects. Loewenstein and Prelec suggest that consumers' choice patterns can be explained by the operation of two motives not incorporated in conventional models: a preference for improvement over time and a desire to spread outcomes over time. The authors present a model of intertemporal choice applicable to sequences, discuss experiments designed to test the model and compare its explanatory power to that of the DU model.

They demonstrate that an individual's valuation of a complex outcome sequence may not be well predicted by his valuation of the component outcomes. Although most people *do* discount simple prospects in a conventional manner, their choices between sequences reveal surprising patterns that are not compatible with conventional discounting. For example, they find a common tendency to prefer sequences that are back- rather than front-loaded, and a desire for U-shaped sequences which provide high levels of utility up front and at the end.

SUMMARY

The objective of the session was to focus attention on the major role of time in consumer behavior theory. In spite of the major role of this construct, to date it has clearly been under-studied. The richness of issues that can be investigated and the wide variety of approaches that can be taken to studying time-related issues were demonstrated. Hopefully, the research presented in this session as well as additional current time related research (e.g., Varey and Kahneman 1990, Ross and Simonson 1990, Goodwin and Smith 1990, and Hui and Bateson 1990) will motivate much needed, further research on time in consumer behavior.

REFERENCES

Becker, Gary S., (1965), "A Theory of the Allocation of Time,"*The Economic Journal*, 75 (September), 493-517.

Bell, Daniel, (1973), The Coming of Post-Industrial Society; A Venture in Social Forecasting, New York, NY: Basic Books.

Berry, Leonard L., (1979), "The Time Buying Consumer," *Journal of Retailing*, 55 (Winter), 58-59.

Buffa, E. S., (1983), "*Modern Production/Operations Management*," New York, NY: John Wiley.

Carmon, Ziv, (1990), "Situational Determinants of Consumers' Dissatisfaction with Waiting," Working Paper, Haas School of Business, University of California, Berkeley, CA, 94720.

De Grazia, S., (1961), " The uses of Time," in *Aging and Leisure: A Research Perspective into the Meaningful Use of Time*," ed. Kleemeier, R. W, New York, NY: Oxford Univ. Press, 113-153.

Dube-Rioux, Laurette, Bernd Schmitt, and France Leclerc, (1989), "Consumers' Reactions to Waiting: When Delays Affect the Perception of Service Quality," in *Advances in Consumer Research*, Vol. 16, ed. Thomas K. Srull, Provo UT: Association of Consumer Research, 59-63.

Engel, James F., David T. Kollat, and Roger D. Blackwell, (1973), *Consumer Behavior*, Hisdale, IL: Dryden.

Erlang, A. K., (1917), "The Solution of Some Problems of Significance in Automatic Telephone Exchanges," *P. O. Electric Engineering Journal*, 189.

Feinberg, Richard A., and Peter Smith, (1989), "Misperceptions of Time in the Sales Transaction," in *Advances in Consumer Research*, Vol. 16, ed. Thomas K. Srull, Provo UT: Association of Consumer Research, 56-58.

Feldman, Laurence P., and Jacob Hornik, (1981), "The Use of Time: An Integrated Conceptual Model," *Journal of Consumer Research*, 7 (March), 407-419.

Fraisse, Paul, (1963), *The Psychology of Time*, Greenwood Press: Westport, CT.

_____ , (1984), "Perception and Estimation of Time," *Annual Review of Psychology*, 35, 1-36.

Goodwin, Cathy, and Kelley L. Smith (1990), "An Equity Theory Perspective of Service Quality Evaluation," Paper presented at the Association of Consumer Research Conference, New York, NY.

Gorss, B., (1987), "Time Scarcity: Interdisciplinary Perspectives and Implications for Consumer Behavior," in *Research in Consumer Behavior: A Research Annual*, eds. J. Sheth and E. Hirschman, Vol. 2, 1-54.

Gulliksen, Harold, (1927), "The Influence of Occupation upon the Perception of Time," *Journal of Experimental Psychology*, 52-59.

Hall, F. T., and Schroeder, M. P., (1970), "Effects of Family and Housing Characteristics on Time Spent on Household Tasks," *Journal of Home Economics*, 62 (January), 23-29.

Hornik, Jacob, (1981), "Time Cue and Time Perception Effect on Response to Mail Surveys," *Journal of Marketing Research*, 18 (May), 243-249.

_____ , (1984), "Subjective vs. Objective Time Measures: A Note on the Perception of Time in Consumer Behavior," *Journal of Consumer Research*, 11 (June), 615-618.

Howard, John A., and Jadish N. Sheth, (1969), "*The Theory of Buyer Behavior*," New York, NY: Wiley.

Holbrook, Morris B., and Donald R. Lehman, (1981), "Allocating Discretionary Time: Complementarity Among Activities," *Journal of Consumer Research*, 7 (March), 395-406.

Hui, Michael, and John Bateson, (1990), "How Perceptions of Perceived Control Can Contribute to Evaluation of the Service Encounter," Paper presented at the Association of Consumer Research Conference, New York, NY.

Jacoby, Jacob, George J. Szybillo, and Carol K. Bering, (1976), "Time and Consumer Behavior: An Interdisciplinary Overview," *Journal of Consumer Research*, 2 (March), 320-339.

Johnson, Eric J. and John W. Payne (1985), "Effort and Accuracy in Choice," *Management Science*, 31 (April), 395- 414.

Lee, Lucy C., and Robert Ferber (1977), "Use of Time as a Determinant of Family Market Behavior," *Journal of Business Research*," 5, 75-91.

Little, John D. C., (1961), "A Proof for the Queuing Formula: $L=\lambda W$," *Operations Research*, 9, Is. 3, 383-387.

Miller, Thomas A. W., (1988), "31 Major Trends Shaping the Future of American Business," *The Public Pulse*, Vol. 2, Is. 1.

Nicosia, Franco M., (1966), *Consumer Decision Processes: Marketing and Advertising Implications*, Engelwood Cliffs, NJ: Prentice-Hall.

Robinson, John P., (1967), "Social Change as Measured by Time Budgets," ASA Proceedings, SF.

Ross, William T., and Itamar Simonson (1990), "Evaluations of Purchase and Consumption Experiences: A Preference for Happy Endings," Working Paper, Wharton School of Business Administration, Philadelphia, PA.

Schary, Philip B., (1971), "Consumption and the Problem of Time," *Journal of Marketing*," 35 (April), 50-55.

Stigler, George J., (1961), "The Economics of Information," *Journal of Political Economy*, 59 (June), 213-225.

Varey, Carol, and Daniel Kahneman, (1990), "Experiences Extended across Time: Evaluation of Moments and Episodes," Working Paper, Psychology Department, University of California, Berkeley, CA 94720.

Wright, Peter, (1974), "The Harassed Decision Maker: Time Pressures, Distractions, and the Use of Evidence," *Journal of Applied Psychology*, 59 (October), 555-561.

Evaluating the Impact of Alcohol Warning Labels

Robert N. Mayer, University of Utah
Ken R. Smith, University of Utah
Debra L. Scammon, University of Utah[1]

ABSTRACT

This paper describes the rationale, methodology, data collection, and preliminary results of a study to evaluate the impact of recently mandated warning labels on alcohol beverage containers. Data collection began in April 1989 and has proceeded at three-month intervals through July 1990. The results reported here involve three data points in each of the pre- and post-warning periods. The study also takes advantage of a non-exposed, non-equivalent comparison group to identify the independent effect, if any, of the labels. The results suggest that the warnings have achieved a considerable level of public awareness, with the admonition against drinking during pregnancy being the most memorable portion of the warning. But there is no evidence yet that the labels have affected knowledge of the health and safety risks associated with alcohol or self-reported alcohol consumption.

INTRODUCTION

Warnings are one of the most common and politically palatable forms of information disclosure to consumers. Federally- or state-mandated warnings exist for cigarettes and smokeless tobacco, saccharin, tampons, aspirin used by children, an anti-acne drug, power lawnmowers, all-terrain vehicles, pressurized cans, and, as of November 1989, alcoholic beverages.

In sharp contrast to the ubiquity of product warnings is the small number of rigorous evaluation studies of their effects, especially studies carried out under real world conditions. And even when resources have been devoted to evaluation research, as in the case of cigarette warnings, it has proven difficult to single out the independent effects of a warning from other contemporaneous events and interventions.

This paper reports the preliminary results of a study designed to evaluate the impact of a newly required warning label for alcoholic beverage containers. All such containers shipped after November 19, 1989 are required to bear the following message:

Government Warning: (1) According to the Surgeon General, women should not drink alcoholic beverages during pregnancy because of the risks of birth defects. (2) The consumption of alcoholic beverages impairs your ability to drive a car or operate machinery, and may cause health problems.

The study reported here is based on data collected over a 15 month period. Three surveys were conducted before implementation of the warning, and three were conducted after; each involved a statewide random sample of adults. The primary outcome measures of interest are awareness of the new labels and their content, knowledge of the risks associated with alcohol consumption, and self-reported frequency and location of alcohol consumption. The study also takes advantage of the characteristics of a single state, Utah, to create a comparison group of devout Mormons who are virtually unexposed to the new warnings. The responses of the devout Mormons are intended to detect the impact of non-warning factors on knowledge of the health and safety risks of alcohol consumption.

RELEVANT RESEARCH

Warnings are an appealing policy tool because of their relatively low cost (both in administration and compliance) and their consistency with individual freedom of choice. Despite the advantages of warnings and their frequent use by policy makers, there is only limited evidence that warnings are effective in altering individual behavior. Warnings may fail for any number of reasons. An individual warning may be hard to read, difficult to comprehend, or stated too generally. Even a well crafted warning may go unnoticed if it exists in an environment full of other warnings. Referring to this possible saturation effect, Paul Schlemm, chairman of Vintners International Inc., predicted that the new alcohol warning labels would be ineffective because "the public has become completely immune to warning labels" (Freedman 1989).

The warning policy that has been most extensively researched (and which is most akin to the case of alcohol) concerns cigarette warnings. Starting in 1965, the federal government has imposed ever stronger and more conspicuous warnings in an effort to reduce cigarette consumption, and indeed cigarette consumption has declined in the United States over this period. But there is no strong evidence that the warnings reduced consumption (FTC 1969; McAuliffe 1988; Murphy 1980; US DHHS, 1987a). Besides concerns that the cigarette warnings are unreadable or go unread (Davis and Kendrick 1989; Fischer et al. 1989; Myers et al. 1981), the fundamental problem is separating the possible effects of the warning from contemporaneous events (e.g., the release of reports by the Surgeon General or the death of a celebrity from lung cancer) or general trends (e.g., increased health awareness) that might also discourage

---

[1] Support for data collection for this project was provided by the College of Social and Behavioral Science, the University of Utah Research Committee, and the Division of Substance Abuse of the Utah State Department of Social Services.

cigarette consumption. A 1989 report by the Surgeon General (US DHHS 1989) found that "there are no controlled studies to permit a definitive assessment of the independent impact of cigarette warnings on knowledge, beliefs, attitudes, or smoking behavior" (pp.478-9).

There have been several *laboratory* studies of the effectiveness of alternative label formats (Karnes and Leonard 1986; Morris 1980; Viscusi and Magat 1987), but a recent review of research on the impact of health warnings concluded that no *field* study to date has used a pre- and post-test design with matched treatment and controlled groups (US DHHS 1987a). In the absence of matched treatment and control groups, evaluation research on the actual impact of product warnings has relied on statistical control of other potential influences. In an interrupted times series design, researchers compare trends before and after policy implementation, controlling for other factors that might affect the criterion variable under investigation. For example, in examining the impact of the saccharin warning label on the consumption of diet drinks, Schucker et al. (1983) controlled for advertising expenditures and prices for diet and non-diet drinks as well as for media coverage of the risks associated with saccharin. The value of interrupted time series designs is directly dependent on the researcher's ability to identify and accurately measure all the non-warning factors that might serve as competing explanations for any shifts in policy-relevant variables.

Sales or consumption data are usually the outcome measure used in interrupted time series designs. The main advantage of this type of data is that it is relatively free from measurement error, but it has several limitations as well. For one, there is usually a serious delay between policy implementation and accumulation of sufficient sales and consumption data to evaluate a policy; as a result, no short-run policy adjustments can be based on these evaluations. More important, using sales or consumption data to evaluate the impact of a warning ignores the possibility that a warning can be effective without changing aggregate data (e.g., by reinforcing "safe" behavior or shifting behavior from a less safe to a more safe setting).

Given the limits of interrupted times series studies, some researchers have used cognitive outcome measures and/or alternative methods of isolating the independent impact of a warning label. To evaluate the effectiveness of cigarette package warnings, for example, the Federal Trade Commission conducted a survey of consumer awareness and knowledge of the health hazards of smoking cigarettes (Myers et al. 1981). There are obvious problems in trying to draw conclusions from a cross-sectional study conducted after a policy has been in place; baseline data are needed.

In a 1978 study by the Swedish National Smoking and Health Association, nationally representative samples of adults were interviewed both before and after the 1977 implementation of rotating cigarette warnings. In addition to measuring knowledge of the health hazards covered by the warnings, respondents were queried about health hazards *not* covered by the rotating labels. The purpose of the latter questions was to measure background factors that might account for any effect of the new cigarette labels. Then, any effect attributed to the labels would need to be discounted by any increases in awareness of the non-covered health hazards. While this approach is ingenious, the possibility also exists that increased awareness of risks not covered in the labels might be an indirect or "spillover" effect of the labels.

The Swedish study attempted to isolate the effects of the cigarette warnings in a second way. The study approximated treatment and control groups by defining smokers as having been exposed to the labels, and nonsmokers as not having been exposed. Besides relying on self-reports of smoking behavior, the main problem with this approach is that it creates experimental groups based on one of the supposed effects of the treatment. If the labels worked as intended and caused people to switch from being smokers to nonsmokers, then the latter group might show larger increases in risk knowledge--the exact opposite of what was predicted. Stated more generally, differential increases in knowledge of health hazards between smokers and nonsmokers could reflect sample selection (i.e., the changing composition of the smoker group) as opposed to the impact of the labels.

In sum, evaluation studies require the external validity that is offered by field settings, but research designs that are feasible in the field pose threats to internal validity. Even when adequate data are collected in the pre-policy period, there is no single way of fully isolating the independent effects of a product warning. The identification of these effects remains a major challenge in conducting real world evaluations of the impact of product warnings.

METHODS

Research Design

In the absence of a control group unexposed to the warning, the best research design for studying the impact of a nationwide product warning is usually an interrupted time series design. As mentioned above, however, a warning must be in place for several years before an interrupted time series analysis can be carried out. Moreover, the sales and consumption data typically used in interrupted time series analyses may not be the most appropriate measure of a warning's impact.

The project described here attempts to blend some of the advantages of an interrupted times series design with the advantages of cognitive outcome measures collected directly from individuals. The study reported here has five key features:

1. data collected from statewide samples at multiple points both before and after the appearance of the alcohol warning labels;

2. multiple, cognitive outcome measures;

TABLE 1
Schematic of Study Design

	Data Collection Periods					
	Pre-Warning (1989)			Post-Warning (1990)		
Measures:	April	July	October	Jan.	April	July
Awareness						
Labels	X	X	X	X	X	X
Restaurant Signs	X	X	X	X	X	X
Content of new label			X	X	X	X
Attributable Risk						
Driving accidents	X	X	X	X	X	X
Birth defects	X	X	X	X	X	X
Cirrhosis of liver	-	X	X	X	X	X
Leukemia	-	X	X	X	X	X
Alcohol Behavior						
Monthly frequency	X	X	X	X	X	X
Home/Away from home	X	-	X	X	X	X

3. questions on risks *not* covered in the warnings;

4. a naturally occurring comparison group of people (devout Mormons) unexposed to the warning; and

5. a setting that minimizes the possibility of new, anti-alcohol interventions during the study period.

Samples and Data Collection

Data collection for this project took place at three month intervals beginning in April 1989. Questions were attached to an ongoing omnibus statewide survey. There were three waves of data collection before implementation of the new alcohol warning labels (April, July, and October of 1989). To date, there have been three waves of data collection after the warnings began to appear in November 1989 (January, April, and July 1990). For all six waves, data were collected from a representative, statewide sample of at least 400 Utah households. Within each household, data were gathered from a randomly selected person aged 18 or older.

Data collection was conducted by interviewers from a University-based survey research center via computer-assisted telephone techniques. The cooperation rate (the number of known eligible respondents completing the survey divided by the number of eligible households reached) across the six surveys was 81%.

Measures

Ultimately, the impact of the alcohol warning labels should be gauged in terms of the number of traffic fatalities and birth defects it prevents. As a proxy, alcohol sales or consumption data might also be used. In the short run, however, cognition-based outcome measures are both more feasible and appropriate. If the labels are going to affect behavior, first they must be noticed and change consumer perceptions of the risks of alcohol consumption. Accordingly, this study uses a combination of awareness, knowledge, and self-reported behavioral items to measure the possible impact of the alcohol warning labels. Table 1 shows the measures used in each of the six surveys.

The awareness measures are straightforward; they ask respondents whether alcohol warnings appear on beverage containers and in establishments that serve alcohol. The inclusion of a measure gauging perception of the risks associated with alcohol consumption is suggested by several theories of behavioral change (e.g., health belief model). Respondents can be asked to rate the degree of danger or harm associated with a particular object or activity. An attributable risk perception measure was chosen for this study because it has an obective referent and can therefore be used as an indicator of knowledge. The attributable risk question posed to respondents took the following form: What would be your best estimate of the percentage of traffic deaths in Utah that are related in some way to the consumption of alcohol? (For the sake of comparison, a relative risk measure was also used, but the results are not reported here.)

It is important to note that the attributable risk measures refer both to risks covered on the labels (drinking when driving or when pregnant) and risks not covered on them (cirrhosis of the liver and leukemia). There is a strong and well-known relationship between alcohol consumption and cirrhosis of the liver. If some non-warning factor or event heightens public perception of alcohol-related risks in general, this should be reflected in the cirrhosis measures in addition to the two risks listed on the warning labels. Perceptions of alcohol's role in causing leukemia (for which there is no scientific evidence) are used to control for the effects of social desirability in social surveys (i.e., the tendency to alter answers in line with what a respondent believes is expected or most acceptable).

Utah-Specific Characteristics of the Study

The study attempts to take advantage of the unique characteristics of a Utah sample. Whereas Utah's low level of alcohol consumption makes it an unlikely candidate for an evaluation study of alcohol warning labels, Utah's devout Mormons constitute the closest group possible to a *naturally occurring, non-exposed, non-equivalent comparison group* (Phillips and Calder 1980).

All states have people who abstain from alcohol, but even such abstainers may come into contact with the new labels in grocery stores or at social gatherings. In contrast, many Utahns are devout Mormons who not only abstain from the consumption of alcoholic beverages but are extremely unlikely to have first-hand contact with the new warning labels. (Alcoholic beverages in Utah, with the exception of reduced-alcohol beer, can only be purchased in state-owned liquor stores.) Thus, like a true control group, devout Mormons in Utah are highly unlikely to be exposed to the experimental stimulus (i.e., the warning labels). Unlike a true control group, however, they may differ from other study participants who may be exposed to the new labels. The inclusion of devout Mormons in the study not only makes the results representative of the entire state but, more importantly, helps identify non-label influences on public awareness and knowledge.

A Utah-based study has one final advantage. Unlike other states in which warning posters for alcohol have recently been required in establishments that sell alcohol (e.g., California), Utah's posting requirement has been in place since 1978. One does not have to worry, therefore, that the effects of the new warning labels might be confounded by the introduction of new warning requirements for establishments that sell alcoholic beverages.

RESULTS

Before examining the data for possible changes between the pre- and post-warning periods, it is necessary to examine changes within these two periods. In addition, the accuracy of the responses can be assessed, and the responses of study subgroups can be compared.

Differences Among Groups in the Pre-Warning Period

In this study, religion (including religiosity) was used to differentiate the sample by degree of potential exposure to the alcohol warning labels. Using religion is preferable to using self-reported alcohol consumption because the latter can be influenced by exposure to the warning labels. That is, if the warning has the desired effect of changing drinking behavior, the composition of the experimental groups will change as well.

Using information on religion and the frequency of church attendance, the respondents can be divided into three groups: devout Mormons (50.7% of all subjects), less-devout Mormons (19.2%), and non-Mormons (30.1%). Devout Mormons attend church at least once a week. Less-devout Mormons attend church less often than once a week.

Table 2 shows that the three study groups differ from one another. Not surprisingly, self-reported alcohol consumption varies substantially, with devout Mormons reporting almost total abstention. More interesting is the fact that devout Mormons consistently attribute a greater role to alcohol in causing health and safety problems than do the non-Mormons. The attributions of less-devout Mormons generally fall between the other two groups.

Accuracy of Responses

Table 2 also reveals several important inaccuracies in respondent awareness of alcohol warnings and knowledge regarding the health and safety risks of alcohol consumption. A substantial number of people in the pre-warning surveys incorrectly reported that the alcohol warning labels existed when they did not. Post-warning estimates of label awareness need to be discounted by the amount of these "false positives."

Respondents, regardless of religion, tended to overestimate the role of alcohol in causing various health and safety problems, especially in the case of birth defects. Scientific estimates of the role of alcohol in causing traffic fatalites, birth defects, cirrhosis of the liver, and leukemia vary. Using national data, the best estimates seem to be 40% for traffic fatalities (NHTSA 1988a, 1988b), 5% for birth defects (US DHHS 1987b), at least 50% for cirrhosis of the liver (*Alcohol and Health* 1987), and 0% for leukemia. Because of Utah's low level of alcohol consumption, these figures would be somewhat lower in Utah.

The self-reported items on alcohol consumption raise a final issue regarding accuracy. Self-report items are always suspect, especially when they involve socially stigmatized behavior. In this study, 73.4% of respondent said that they consumed alcohol less than one time per month or not at all. A 1985 study conducted in Utah reported that 69.3% of adults described themselves as nondrinkers (Smith et al. 1990). In addition to these similar results, a 21-state study found that self-reported alcohol consumption is highly correlated ($r = 0.81$) with per capita sales of alcoholic beverages.

Stability of the Data

The stability of the data within the pre- and post-warning periods has both substantive and methodological implications. Substantively, it is important to know whether the outcome variables were changing even before implementation of the warning. If they were, an observed pre-post change

TABLE 2
Differences Within and Across Study Periods by Religious Groups

Non-Mormons

	Pre-Warning				Post-Warning				Pre/Post	
	4/89	7/89	10/89	p	1/90	4/90	7/90	p	p±	p*
Awareness										
Warning Labels (% Yes)	14.3	13.7	9.7	.50	26.8	30.5	34.9	.43	.00	.00
Restaurant Signs (% Yes)	25.5	22.6	21.2	.74	23.7	23.1	27.6	.69	.60	.58
Alcohol Consumption										
Frequency										
< 1 day/month	51.0	50.8	57.9		42.5	53.6	54.2			
2-4 days/month	25.5	29.4	28.9		30.6	33.0	24.9			
4+ days/month	23.5	19.8	13.2		26.9	13.5	20.9			
				.35				.07	.75	.79
Location										
% home > away	52.9	-	62.3	.30	58.2	53.0	58.6	.72	.96	.97
Attributable Risk (%)										
Traffic Fatalities	47.7	43.6	44.1	.25	48.1	43.1	42.2	.10	.78	.78
Birth Defects	29.3	33.9	24.8	.03	23.8	24.7	29.7	.13	.05	.04
Leukemia	-	10.9	11.1	.94	9.4	12.0	11.6	.59	.99	.96
Cirrhosis of Liver	-	55.6	57.0	.74	64.9	62.3	57.5	.20	.04	.03

Less-Devout Mormons

	Pre-Warning				Post-Warning				Pre/Post	
	4/89	7/89	10/89	p	1/90	4/90	7/90	p	p±	p*
Awareness										
Warning Labels (% Yes)	10.1	6.1	10.1	.61	15.3	16.5	21.7	.56	.01	.01
Restaurant Signs (% Yes)	17.0	22.8	9.0	.06	29.4	16.6	24.5	.17	.04	.04
Alcohol Consumption										
Frequency										
< 1 day/month	63.4	61.1	65.5		67.4	77.3	65.6			
2-4 days/month	27.9	30.0	24.2		20.0	13.3	24.5			
4+ days/month	8.7	8.9	10.4		12.6	9.4	9.8			
				.44				.74	.12	.54
Location										
% home > away	71.4	-	68.9	.83	56.9	44.6	48.6	.61	.01	.01
Attributable Risk (%)										
Traffic Fatalities	45.6	46.4	45.4	.96	49.1	43.5	44.9	.21	.96	.49
Birth Defects	34.0	38.1	33.2	.57	27.8	29.1	29.5	.91	.02	.02
Leukemia	-	14.9	16.1	.77	17.5	17.5	15.6	.91	.65	.69
Cirrhosis of Liver	-	56.8	62.1	.26	60.8	54.4	59.1	.46	.58	.60

TABLE 2 (CONTINUED)

Devout Mormons

	Pre-Warning				Post-Warning				Pre/Post	
	4/89	7/89	10/89	p	1/90	4/90	7/90	p	p+	p*
Awareness										
Warning Labels (% Yes)	6.9	5.3	7.3	.70	11.7	8.6	13.0	.32	.01	.01
Restaurant Signs (% Yes)	11.6	12.5	14.4	.69	15.6	18.1	11.1	.11	.34	.39
Alcohol Consumption										
Frequency										
< 1 day/month	98.4	98.4	96.9		100.0	99.6	98.9			
2-4 days/month	1.2	1.2	2.2		0.0	0.4	0.0			
4+ days/month	0.4	0.5	0.9	.84	0.0	0.0	1.1	-	-	-
Location										
% home > away	82.2	-	53.8	.34	0.0	39.6	36.5	.63	.11	.24
Attributable Risk (%)										
Traffic Fatalities	51.0	51.5	49.5	.57	50.7	49.5	50.5	.79	.73	.88
Birth Defects	38.2	40.0	31.4	.00	30.9	33.4	36.3	.06	.07	.16
Leukemia	-	19.0	18.0	.75	20.5	18.6	20.5	.64	.46	.31
Cirrhosis of Liver	-	61.4	64.9	.23	64.7	62.6	64.5	.70	.78	.88

Notes:

1. "p" refers to tests for stability within periods based on chi-square (awareness and alcohol consumption) and F-tests from one-way anovas (attributable risk).
2. "p+" refers to tests for pre-post differences collapsing within periods and not controlling for other variables. Again, the p+ values are based on chi-square and F-tests.
3. "p*" refers to tests for pre-post differences collapsing with periods and controlling for age, sex, education, and urbanicity. The p* values are based on logistic regressions for the categorical variables (awareness and alcohol consumption) and ordinary least squares for the continuous variables (attributable risk).

---

might simply be the function of long-term trends rather than the warning label itself. Similarly, the shape of the post-warning curve needs to be known to see whether any effects increase, decrease, or remain constant over time. From a methodological point of view, the stability of the pre- and post-warning data influences the methods of data analysis used. If, for example, the data are stable within both periods, the results of different surveys can be combined and the data analysis can be greatly simplified.

Table 2 shows that the outcome measures were extremely stable within the pre- and post-warning periods. Within the pre-warning period, there were only two measures whose value changed using a statistical significance level of $p < .05$. Among both non-Mormons and devout Mormons, the perceived role of alcohol in causing birth defects declined in the final pre-warning survey. While the reason for this decline is not known, one can at least rule out the possibility that some non-warning factor was operating to *increase* sensitivity to the connection between alcohol and birth defects. For the post-warning period alone, none of the measures changed within any of the three subgroups.

Pre-Post Differences

The stability of the data within the pre- and post-warning periods permits one to collapse within the two periods and compare across them. Awareness of the warning labels increased between the two periods, but surprisingly, it did so in all three groups, including the devout Mormons. This suggests that awareness of the warning, even among potential drinkers, might be partly attributable to factors such as media coverage of the labels. The researchers monitored television and newspaper coverage during November 1989. Interestingly, coverage in the media owned by the Mormon Church (KSL-TV and the *Deseret News*) was virtually non-existent. While many devout Mormons are exposed to media other than these two, the increased awareness among devout Mormons could be due to some other unidentified factor.

Given the increased awareness of the new warning labels, what individual characteristics

TABLE 3
Logit Analysis of Warning Label Awareness for Merged Post-Warning Surveys

Variable	Beta	Stan. Error	Chi-Sq. p value
Age	-.013	.005	.008
Sex			
Female (=1)	-.098	.155	.521
(Male Omitted)			
Education			
Less than High School (=1)	-.012	.395	.976
Greater than High School (=1)	-.117	.167	.484
(High School Omitted)			
Area of Residence			
Urban (=1)	-.081	.174	.644
Rural (=1)	-.140	.213	.510
(Suburban Omitted)			
Religion			
Non-Mormon (=1)	1.127	.178	.000
Less-Devout Mormon (=1)	.453	.222	.042
(Devout Mormon Omitted)			
Intercept	-1.326	.296	.000

Dependent Variable:
1 = Yes, Warnings Appear on Labels
0 = No, Warnings Do Not Appear/Don't Know

Goodness of Fit:
Change in Chi-Square = 61.9
Change in Degrees of Freedom = 8
p = .000

---

predict the likelihood that a person will report awareness? Table 3 presents the results of a logistical regression based on the three post-warning surveys. The analysis separates people who reported awareness of the warning labels from all other respondents (i.e., people who didn't know whether the labels existed are combined with those who incorrectly said that the labels did not exist).

The results indicate that awareness was related to a respondent's age and religious group. Older respondents and devout Mormons were least likely to report awareness of the new labels. Educational attainment, sex, and area of residence were not related to warning label awareness. Additional analyses included a sex by age interaction term and attributable risk responses (as a measure of possible predisposition to the warning label) but yielded the same results. The key finding is that younger people (18-30 years old in this survey), who are at greatest risk of driving under the influence of alcohol or drinking while pregnant, were most aware of the warning label.

Among the attributable risk measures, there were some pre-post differences, most of which are difficult to explain. Counter to what might have been expected as a result of the warning labels, the perceived role of alcohol in causing birth defects declined between the pre- and post-warning periods. Among non-Mormons only, perceptions of the role of alcohol in causing cirrhosis of the liver increased. There were no changes among the three groups in attributions involving traffic fatalities or leukemia.

Among less-devout Mormons, awareness of warnings posted in establishments that sell alcohol increased between the two study periods. If the new labels somehow heightened awareness of already existing posted warnings, why would this effect not be equally pronounced among non-Mormons? A final anomalous finding is that among less-devout Mormons who report drinking, the percentage of those who drink primarily at home decreased between the pre- and post-warning periods. This change cannot be explained in terms of seasonal changes (i.e., the Christmas drinking season).

A final set of findings, not shown in the tables, is potentially quite important. In the three post-warning surveys only, people who answered "yes" to the question of whether warning labels appear on beverage containers were asked follow-up questions. First, they were asked whether they had actually seen the labels. If they had, they were asked in four separate questions whether the label contained information about the role of alcohol in traffic fatalities, birth defects, leukemia, and cirrhosis of the liver. Combining the three post-warning surveys, the most readily recalled part of the warning was the message about birth defects, with 66% of the relevant respondents correctly noting the inclusion of this information in the labels. In comparison, only 54% of the respondents correctly recalled the label's caution against drinking and driving. Small percentages of respondents incorrectly stated that the labels mentioned cirrhosis of the liver (14%) and leukemia (4%).

In light of the fact that alcohol accounts for a far greater percentage of traffic fatalities than birth defects, it is striking that a larger percentage of respondents remembered that the labels contained information about birth defects than about traffic fatalities. One possible explanation is that the labels explicitly mention birth defects while traffic fatalities are only alluded to with the phrase "consumption of alcoholic beverages impairs your ability to drive a car." A second possibility is that the link between alcohol and traffic fatalities is common knowledge, but the link between alcohol and birth defects has only recently become a matter of scientific consensus. The connection between alcohol and birth defects still has the quality of "news," and seeing it on government mandated labels may, for the moment at least, be capable of catching a person's attention.

DISCUSSION AND CONCLUSIONS

Given the limitations of the present study as well as the fact that additional post-warning data remains to be collected, what can be said about the success or failure of the alcohol warning labels? From the point of view of public health promotion, there are three positive points. First, the new labels have been noticed by all population subgroups. Among non-Mormons, awareness of the new labels already exceeds awareness of the warning posters that have been required in Utah for 12 years! Second, awareness of the labels is greatest among young people, that is, among the group at highest risk of driving under the influence of alcohol (young males) or drinking during pregnancy (young females). Third, public recall of label content is quite accurate; moreover, information about birth defects seems to be particularly memorable, probably due to its quality as new information.

The results of this study are very similar to those reported by Mazis, Morris, and Swasy (1991). Comparing results from two national surveys conducted in May 1989 and May 1990, they found increased label awareness across time, with awareness being greatest among younger respondents. (They also reported substantial numbers of false positives in the pre-warning survey.) The major difference between the findings of Mazis et al. and this study concerns risk perception. While we found no evidence to this point that the labels have affected knowledge and perception of the role of alcohol in causing health and safety problems, Mazis and his colleagues found a small but statistically significant increase in the number of people who described alcohol as "very harmful." (There was no significant change between their two surveys, however, when "very harmful" and "somewhat harmful" responses were combined.)

While the absence of a clear impact on risk perception and knowledge may be disappointing to public health professionals, perhaps this was to be expected. Consider that the labeling requirement has been in effect for less than a year. With the exception of beer, alcoholic beverages continue to be sold in containers that were shipped prior to the time of the warning requirement. In addition, many of the early warning labels suffered from problems of noticeability and legibility, resulting in new requirements beginning in November 1990. Finally, research on other forms of consumer information disclosure suggests that cognitive changes (awareness and knowledge), precede changes in affect, which, in turn, precede changes in behavior.

Other methodological approaches might also yield more positive assessments of the alcohol warning label's effects. Clearly, data collection needs to continue beyond the first few months of the post-warning period. Eventually, however, one runs into the problem of differentiating the warning from other historical factors. Another step might be to focus exclusively on high risk populations (e.g., young people or Native Americans). A final approach would be to use a panel design rather than a trend design. In a panel design, one can directly observe individual change. In a trend design, one can only measure net change across the population.

Even with other approaches, one might still conclude that the alcohol warning label, even in its revised form, has not been and will not be successful. If so, one should start with the content of the label for an explanation. The label states the obvious with respect to drinking and driving, while remaining vague about the health risks of alcohol consumption (other than during pregnancy). In contrast to the weak content of the warning labels, the current legislative proposal to require rotating warnings in advertising is very hardhitting. One of the warnings would state that "alcohol is a drug and may be addictive." Another would say that "the consumption of this product, which contains alcohol, can increase the risk of developing hypertension, liver disease, and some cancers." Judging from the results of this study, a warning will be effective to the extent that it contains specific information that is not already widely known. Without such information, one should not be surprised if people ignore labels and rationalize their content.

REFERENCES

Alcohol and Health. Seventh Special Report to the U.S. Congress from the Secretary of Health and Human Services. Rockville, MD: National Institute on Alcohol Abuse and Alcoholism, 1990.

Davis, R.M. and Kendrick, J.S. (1989), "The Surgeon General's Warnings in Outdoor Cigarette Advertising," *Journal of the American Medical Association*, 261, pp. 90-94.

Federal Trade Commission (1969). *Report to Congress Pursuant to the Federal Cigarette Labeling and Advertising Act*. Washington, D.C.: Federal Trade Commission.

Fischer, P.M., Richards, J.W., Jr., Berman, E.J., and Krugman, D.M. (1989), "Recall and Eye Tracking Study of Adolescents Viewing Tobacco Advertisements," *Journal of the American Medical Association* 261, 1989, pp. 84-89.

Freedman, A.M. (1989), "Rebelling Against Alcohol, Tobacco Ads," *Wall Street Journal*, November 14, 1989, p.B1.

Karnes, E.W. and Leonard, S.D. (1986), "Consumer Product Warnings: Reception and Understanding of Warning Information by Final Users." In: Karwowski, W., ed., *Trends in Ergonomics/Human Factors III*. Holland: Elsevier, pp. 995-1003.

Kruger, Elizabeth L. (1988), "Mitigating Alcohol Health Hazards Through Health Warning Labels and Public Education," *Washington Law Review* 63, pp. 979-996.

Mazis, Michael B., Louis A. Morris, and John L. Swasy (1991), "An Evaluation of the Alcohol Warning Label: Initial Survey Results," *Journal of Public Policy and Marketing* 10, No.1, in press.

McAuliffe, Robert E. (1988), "The FTC and the Effectiveness of Cigarette Advertising Regulations," *Journal of Public Policy and Marketing* 7, pp. 49-64.

Myers, M.L., Iscoe, C., Jennings, C., Lennox, W., Minsty E. and Sacks, A. (1981). *Staff Report on the Cigarette Advertising Investigation*. Washington, D.C.: Federal Trade Commission.

Morris, L.A. (1980), "Estrogenic Drugs--Patient Package Inserts." In: Morris, L.A., Mazis, M. and Barofsky, I., eds., *Product Labeling and Health Risks--Banbury Report 6*. Cold Spring Harbor, NY: 1980, pp. 23-36.

Murphy, R.D. (1980), "Consumer Responses to Cigarette Health Warnings." In: Morris, L.A., Mazis, M. and Barofsky, I., eds., *Product Labeling and Health Risks--Banbury Report 6*. Cold Spring Harbor, NY: 1980, pp. 13-21.

National Highway Traffic Safety Administration (1988a). *Alcohol Involvement in Fatal Crashes 1986*. Report No. DOT HS 807 268. Washington, DC: NHTSA.

_____ , National Center for Statistics and Analysis (1988b). *Drunk Driving Facts*. Washington, DC: NHTSA.

Phillips, L.W. and Calder, B.J. (1980), "Evaluating Consumer Protection Programs: II. Promising Methods," *Journal of Consumer Affairs* 14, pp. 9-36.

Schucker, R.E., Stokes, R.C., Steward, M.L., and Henderson, D.P. (1983), "Impact of the Saccharin Warning Label on Sales of Diet Soft Drinks in Supermarkets," *Journal of Public Policy and Marketing*, Volume 2, 46-56.

Smith, Perry F., Patrick L. Remington, David F. Williamson, and Robert F. Anda (1990), "A Comparison of Alcohol Sales Data with Survey Data on Self Reported Alcohol Use in 21 States," *American Journal of Public Health*, 80 (March), 309-12.

Swedish National Smoking and Health Association Study of Sweden's rotational label system (1978). Described in U.S. Department of Health and Human Services, 1987a.

U.S. Department of Health and Human Services (1987a). *Review of the Research on the Effects of Health Warning Labels: A Report to the United States Congress*. U.S. Department of Health and Human Services.

U.S. Department of Health and Human Services (1987b). *Program Strategies for Preventing Fetal Alcohol Syndrome and Alcohol-Related Birth Defects*. Rockville, MD:: National Institute on Alcohol Abuse and Alcoholism.

U.S. Department of Heath and Human Services (1989). *Reducing the Health Consequences of Smoking: 25 Years of Progress. A Report of the Surgeon General*. Rockville, MD: U.S. Department of Health and Human Services, Public Health Service, Centers for Disease Control, Center for Chronic Disease Prevention and Health Promotion, Office on Smoking and Health.

Viscusi, W.K. and Magat, W.A. (1987). *Learning About Risk*. Cambridge, MA: Harvard University Press.

Political Advertising in the 1990s: Expected Strategies, Voter Responses, and Public Policy Implications

Ronald Paul Hill, Villanova University

ABSTRACT

This paper examines current and predicted advertising practices of political campaign strategists as well as potential voter responses. Both the trade and academic literatures in advertising suggest that negative advertisements, while *generally* ineffective, will continue to be used widely in national and local elections in the 1990s. Public policy directions are discussed, and future research necessary to provide appropriate guidance in the development of such policy is suggested.

INTRODUCTION

During the first debate of the 1988 presidential election, Michael Dukakis and George Bush were asked by representatives of the media to discuss important national issues such as abortion, drug abuse, and the growing federal deficit. However, ensuing media attention to these matters faded quickly, and was replaced with a concentration on the advertising tactics and strategies of the candidates (Colford 1988). Most of this attention focused upon the use of negative advertising in an attempt to degrade the opponent. For example, Dukakis used four advertisements titled "The Packaging of George Bush," that show Bush's "image-makers" in a conference setting searching for ways to gloss over their candidate's liabilities. These media advisors go back and forth looking for the right "sales" gimmick, and their conversation "reeks of contempt for voters and cynicism over the electoral process" (Garfield 1988, p. 76). In a consistent fashion, Bush utilized a number of different negative ads that focus on the past policies of his opponent. One ad, titled "The Dukakis Furlough Program," suggests that Dukakis pursues a liberal policy towards criminals in his state that has led to increased violent crimes such as rape and murder. Kathleen Jamieson (1988), author of *Packaging the President*, sums up this situation:

> Never before in a presidential campaign have television ads sponsored by a major party candidate lied so blatantly as in the campaign of '88 (p. C1).

This approach was not limited to the presidential contest in 1988. For example, in a New Jersey senate race, the Democratic incumbent and the Republican challenger denigrated each other for months with negative television commercials, spending a record $16 million (Joseph Sullivan 1988). Also, in a Florida senate race, the Republican incumbent scorned his Democratic opponent with a barrage of 10-second TV ads that conclude, "Hey Buddy, you're liberal!" (Rosenbaum 1988). However, the "archetypal" negative political ad comes from the 1988 Israeli elections (Brinkley 1988). One (of many) television advertisements showed the Labor Party leader as a friend and ally of Yasir Arafat, chairman of the Palestine Liberation Organization. Included in this ad is an old film clip revealing a grinning Mr. Arafat pointing a rifle and saying, "Through this barrel, we can get everything we want."

What conditions in the political campaign environment have led to such a reliance on these tactics? Is this approach to political advertising expected to continue? How do voters respond to the use of negative ads? What responses can we expect in the future? Furthermore, given the current and future tactics as well as voter responses, what are the public policy implications? These questions will be addressed in the following sections, and research opportunities will be delineated.

CURRENT AND FUTURE PRACTICES AMONG POLITICAL ADVERTISERS

The use of negative ads during the 1988 elections was anticipated by members of the advertising profession. For example, during a 1987 *Advertising Age* roundtable, five leading political consultants for both Democrats and Republicans predicted that use of this practice would increase from the 1986 campaigns where $190 million was spent predominately "on 30-second, mainly negative, mainly corrosive, mainly disruptive, television commercials" (Honomichl 1988, p. 3). Further, George Will (1988) speculated that the preferred style of political campaigns - "going negative" - would dominate the media during the 1988 elections.

Why have campaign consultants and politicians relied so heavily on such tactics? In a humorous way, George Will (1988) provides three reasons for the continued use of negative advertising:

(1) The other guy started it.
(2) I'm not being negative, I'm just alerting the electorate to my loathsome opponent's squalid record.
(3) Negative campaigning is as American as apple pie - and, by the way, did I mention that my opponent hates apple pie? (p. 66).

Regardless, widespread usage of negative ads in recent political campaigns has been due to the perception that they influence voters (Axelrod 1988). Furthermore, advertisers speculated that the failure of both presidential candidates in the 1988 election to outline their positions on important issues led to the proliferation of negative advertisements (Horton and Chase 1988). Former Arizona Governor Bruce Babbitt, who ran unsuccessfully for president in the Democratic primaries, agreed and stated that:

> The negative tenor is caused by the absence of thematics, the absence of issues. It [advertising] fills the vacuum created by the candidates' tacit agreement not to discuss the issues (p. 66).

Therefore, instead of clearly establishing his position, each candidate tried to cast his opponent's views on these issues in an unfavorable light. This set of circumstances may have been the case for many of the 1988 political election races, leading to similar approaches (Hill 1989).

In general, these tactics have disturbed advertisers, and caused the American Association of Advertising Agencies to monitor political ads during the 1984 elections (Stiansen 1984). Nevertheless, the 1988 campaigns received even worse reviews by the advertising community. Executives attending the American Association of Advertising Agencies' western region conference characterized these campaigns with adjectives such as "cutthroat" and "huckstering" (Horton and Chase 1988). Further, Bob Garfield, in his weekly *Advertising Age* column, was critical of the negative ads of the Dukakis campaign and stated that:

> If the presidential election hinges on advertising - and, my friends, I believe it does - Michael Dukakis, a man of substance and vision, will be the next governor of Massachusetts.

However, while *generally* opposed to such an approach, many advertising strategists suggest that negative advertisements may be effective if used judiciously and/or if certain conditions exist. According to Axelrod (1988):

> ... negative advertising has its dangers. Like radiation therapy, the right amount of negative advertising can prove very effective. A few rads over the line, however, and attack ads can sometimes prove fatal to the candidate who engages in them (p. 88).

Further, consider the situation where a lesser known opponent is challenging a better known incumbent. Given this condition, a negative approach may be an effective challenger strategy if it is focused on a weakness of the incumbent that is widely believed by the electorate (Honomichl 1988). On the other hand, it may be an effective incumbent (or leader) strategy when the opponent is a relatively unknown quantity. Here, negative information is provided by the leader in an attempt to get voters to base their early (and often lasting) impressions of the opposition on negative information (see Taylor 1989).

Many political consultants speculate that negative advertisements will be used with even greater frequency in the 1990s. There are several reasons for this prediction. First, the American Association of Political Consultants (AAPC) has yet to take disciplinary action against a single member for violation of its Code of Ethics, which forbids members to intentionally disseminate "false or misleading information" and/or to indulge "in any activity which corrupts or degrades the practice of political campaigning" (Broder 1989a, p. A22). Second, the media relies heavily upon consultants to provide newsworthy information on campaigns, and this "symbiotic relationship" may reduce the ability of the press to objectively and critically evaluate political advertising tactics (Broader 1989b). Finally, and (perhaps) most importantly, many candidates and their consultants believe that they are faced with the "prisoner's dilemma." Democratic pollster Paul Maslin stated:

> "The techniques have gotten so refined, the weapons so powerful, that if you don't use them, you will lose them, because the other side will use them on you" (Taylor 1989, p. A14).

VOTER REACTIONS TO POLITICAL ADVERTISEMENTS

In contrast to current and (predicted) future practice in political campaigning, there is evidence that suggests negative advertising may not be effective. For example, in 1986, Republicans outspent Democrats in 23 of 34 senate races, concentrating most of the $122 million spent on negative television advertisements (Will 1988). Nonetheless, the Democrats won 20 of the 34 senate seats. Some industry experts believe that these outcomes demonstrate that voters view negative ads critically, and subsequently become cynical about the entire political process (Grove 1989; Honomichl 1988; Taylor 1989).

Few would disagree that American voters tend to deplore politics and politicians. However, the 1988 races produced more negative feelings than previous elections (Oreskes 1988). According to a *Wall Street Journal*/NBC poll, a sense of skepticism or cynicism was prevalent among voters prior to the 1988 elections, with nearly 6 out of 10 members of the electorate wishing they had other choices (Hume and Jaroslovsky 1988). Further, only 50.16% of eligible voters went to the polls, the lowest percentage since 1924 and lower than any other industrial democracy (Berke 1988; Taylor 1989).

In order to investigate reactions to political ads, Hill (1989) exposed potential voters in the 1988 presidential election to one of three types of advertisement for either the Democratic or Republican presidential candidate, and subsequently asked them to respond with written protocols and to complete attitude toward the ad (A_{ad}) measures. These three types of ad were labeled "sponsor-positive," "opponent-negative," and "comparative." Based on the work of Merritt (1984), they are defined as follows: Sponsor-positive (or competitive) ads describe positive attributes of the sponsor and implicitly suggest an absence of these attributes in the competitor. Opponent-negative ads (the classic "negative" political advertisement) and comparative ads are both variants of the same approach. Both name or identify the competitor; however, comparative advertising identifies a competitor for the purpose of claiming superiority while opponent-negative ads identify a competitor for the purpose of imputing inferiority (see Prasad 1976). Further, unlike comparative advertisements, opponent-negative ads do not mention the sponsoring candidate's attributes, and, therefore, intend to move voters away from the opponent rather than towards the sponsor (see Colford 1987; Honomichl 1988).

Results from this investigation show that voters' overall reactions as well as their reactions toward the ad sponsor are more positive for sponsor-positive than for comparative or opponent-negative political advertisements. Further, these responses do not vary significantly between comparative and opponent-negative ads, and responses directed toward the opponent of the ad sponsor remain constant across all three types of advertisement. Interestingly, only one of these mean response measures is positive, suggesting that the widespread voter disenchantment with the 1988 presidential campaign may have been captured by this study.

The measures of A_{ad}, however, produced different results. These data indicate that voters have more favorable A_{ad} for comparative and opponent-negative than for sponsor-positive political advertisements (no differences were found between the comparative and opponent-negative ads). According to Hill (1989), one possible interpretation of the seeming inconsistency between the reactions to the ad sponsor and the ads themselves is that the negative tenor of these ads is compatible with voters' perceptions of this political campaign (see Hume and Jaroslovsky 1988). Therefore, the data should not be interpreted to indicate *preference* but may signify some form of cognitive *consistency* (Aaker and Myers 1987). Another interpretation suggests that this form of "confrontainment" is entertaining to the American public, and *The New York Times* provides anecdotal evidence that nastiness has become a popular commodity (Williams 1988). However, this is not a positive outcome from the perspective of typical advertising objectives.

Hill (1989) interprets the results of this study as suggesting that the use of comparative or opponent-negative political advertisements may produce negative reactions from voters, may reflect negatively on the ad sponsor, and may have little impact upon the opposing candidate when compared to sponsor-positive ads. Further, data from the attitude toward the ad measures imply that comparative or opponent-negative advertisements may convey an image of the political process that is consistent with voters' negative perceptions (which they also may find entertaining).

These data and recent polls suggest that a widespread negative approach may reduce both candidates in the estimation of the electorate and may cause a reduction in their believability across all issues. Although some analysts believe that Bush won the 1988 presidential election because of "superior marketing skills" (Hiam 1988; Stringer 1988), he only received votes from 26.77% of eligible voters - hardly a mandate (Berke 1988). Thus, Bush's victory may have been a function of Dukakis's inability to establish a positive image for himself among voters (John Sullivan 1988; McCabe 1988; Toner 1988). Further, those who voted for Bush may have done so because of his close relationship to Ronald Reagan rather than his ability to establish an acceptable image through advertising (Lister 1988; Plattner 1988). This conclusion explains why Bush was often greeted with chants of "four more years" as he campaigned around the country (Boyd 1988).

Many informed sources expect the future to bring increasingly negative responses and even greater voter apathy (see Grove 1989; Taylor 1989). For instance, reliance on graphic and memorable negative images (e.g., the advertisement depicting Willie Horton, the Massachusetts' prisoner furloughed by Dukakis who committed assault and rape) are predicted to continue in national elections, and also may be used with increasing frequency in local elections. Thus, voters will be inundated with negative stimuli, resulting in a highly reinforced negative image of the entire electoral process (Hill 1989). Further, the "baby boomer" generation, a 75 million persons segment of the eligible voting population, increasingly will control electoral contests. Because of their higher levels of education and their emphasis on quality goods and services (see Wilkie 1986), this group should demand *more* rather than *less* information regarding the positions of candidates on relevant issues. Consequently, voters in future elections may be less receptive to campaigns focussed on a predominately negative approach that provide little, if any, credible information from an obviously self-serving sponsor (see Gorn and Weinberg 1984; Swinyard 1981).

PUBLIC POLICY IMPLICATIONS

The preceding discussion suggests that advertisers, candidates, and voters all share a *negative* attitude toward the use of negative advertising. This situation has led some experts to suggest that the privately financed Fair Campaign Practices Commission (FCPC) be revived to arbitrate disputes involving political ads. However, as a tax-exempt organization, the FCPC was prevented from taking any actions that might be construed as intervening on behalf of a particular candidate (Broder 1989a). To overcome this obstacle, Maloney (1989) recommends the establishment of a bipartisan presidential commission containing former members of the Federal Trade Commission, present members of the National Advertising Review Board, the American Association of Advertising Agencies and the Association of National Advertisers, and network, advertising agency and media representatives. Such a commission would be asked to use its collective experience and wisdom as a basis for judging the suitability of individual political ads. However, due to the First Amendment right of free speech, political consultants could still air advertisements deemed unsuitable by the commission. Nonetheless, the "unsuitable" rating and moral suasion that followed the ad may act to limit their use (see Maloney 1990 for more details).

Preferred method notwithstanding, most individuals associated with the advertising profession feel that some form of regulation will be necessary unless the candidates themselves practice self-restraint (Caywood 1989) - an unlikely scenario given the current belief in the effectiveness of negative political advertising campaigns. Thus, some politicians support legislation limiting ads to the "talking head" variety as a way to encourage reasoned discourse over visual demagoguery, requiring the sponsoring candidate to appear at the end of their ads to vouch for their veracity, and providing free response time to the targets of negative ads (Taylor 1990). According to a spokesperson for Senator John Danforth, the Missouri Republican who has included the "enhanced disclosure" rule in his package of legislation called the Clean Campaign Act, "It would be a pretty potent deterrent to the type of advertising your parents would be ashamed of you running" (Rothenberg 1990, p. E4). However, the constitutionality of such a measure is questionable. Thus, Senator David L. Boren of Oklahoma would condition the provision on the candidate's voluntary acceptance of public financing. Here, the First Amendment issues become unclear (see Rothenberg for more details).

Before such a body convenes, more research in the consumer behavior tradition is necessary to improve our understanding of this phenomenon and to help determine the appropriate public policy direction(s). First, future investigations should use more than one issue to explore whether responses are consistent across voter concerns. In the 1988 presidential election, topics such as abortion, defense spending, AIDS, super-power relationships, and the homeless would have provided appropriate choices. Results may show that for some issues (e.g., abortion) a simple statement of position contained within a comparative or opponent-negative ad may be perceived as useful by voters. However, for more complex or less clear-cut issues (e.g., the homeless), the tendency to mislead may be greater and simple statements may not capture the essential character of an opponent's position.

Second, test ads need to be examined to determine whether voters' perceptions are consistent with advertisers' intentions. For example, do voters feel that sponsor-positive ads implicitly criticize the opponent? Do they feel that ad sponsors who disparage opponents in comparative or opponent-negative ads remain credible? Investigations of these questions will help determine whether such an approach has the *potential* to deceive voters.

Third, the use of traditional two-sided messages (i.e., pros and cons of the sponsor's positions on major issues in relation to the opponent) should be tested. Swinyard (1981) found the use of such messages in a comparative format increased the credibility of the sponsor significantly. Thus, these ads may serve a useful purpose consistent with the original position of the FTC regarding comparative ads (Wilkie and Farris 1975).

Fourth, stimulus ads should be developed using both print and broadcast media, and should emphasize pictorial versus verbal/written information or a combination of both to determine whether these factors impact the effectiveness of political ads. For example, in a review of the literature Lang and Lanfear (1990) found that negative political ads are more effective when embedded in a strong visual image. On the other hand, they concluded that positive ads can be presented either visually or verbally and still be effective.

Fifth, variations in the sponsor of the advertisement may impact their effectiveness. Garramone and Smith (1984, p. 771) state that:

> Experimental research indicates that independently-sponsored political commercials are more effective than those sponsored by a candidate. Specifically, independently-sponsored *negative* advertising attacking a targeted candidate results in a more negative perception of that candidate's image than negative ads sponsored by the opposing candidate.

Finally, behavioral intentions to vote for a particular candidate need to be included as a dependent variable because of their ultimate importance to political elections. In order for ads to have an effect on this variable, several exposures to stimulus ads may be required. Further, a special emphasis on less-committed or uncommitted voters is needed because of their significance in close elections, and an attempt should be made to recruit study subjects from diverse social and economic backgrounds including young voters, the elderly, and the disadvantaged who traditionally have been the focus of FTC actions.

REFERENCES

Aaker, David A. and John G. Myers (1987), *Advertising Management*, Englewood Cliffs, NJ: Prentice-Hall, Inc.

Axelrod, David (1988), "Broadcast Views," *Advertising Age*, 59 (48), 88, 91-92.

Berke, Richard L. (1988), "50.16% Voter Turnout Was Lowest Since 1924," *The New York Times*, (December 18), 36.

Boyd, Robert S. (1988), "Emotional Issues Helped Move Bush Into the White House," *The Philadelphia Enquirer*, (November 13), 4-E.

Brinkley, Joel (1988), "Israeli TV Political Ads Lowering the Low Road," *The New York Times*, (October 9), 18.

Broder, David S. (1989a), "Politicians, Advisers Agonize Over Negative Campaigning," *The Washington Post*, A1, A22.

Broder, David S. (1989b), "Should News Media Police the Accuracy of Ads?," *The Washington Post*, (January 19), A22.

Caywood, Clark (1989), "Political Ads in Jeopardy," *Advertising Age*, 60 (6), 20.

Colford, Steven W. (1988), "Campaign Flak Flies: Pols' Ads Have Negative Charge," *Advertising Age*, 59 (46), 4.

Colford, Steven W. (1987), "Political Advertisers Veer from Smear," *Advertising Age*, 58 (50), 53.

Garfield, Bob (1988), "With Ads Like These, Duke's Going Home," *Advertising Age*, 59 (43), 76.

Garramone, Gina M. and Sandra J. Smith (1984), "Reactions to Political Advertising: Clarifying Sponsor Effects," *Journalism Quarterly*, 61 (4), 771-775.

Gorn, Gerald J. and Charles B. Weinberg (1984), "The Impact of Comparative Advertising on Perception and Attitude: Some Positive Findings," *Journal of Consumer Research*, 11 (3), 717-727.

Grove, Lloyd (1989), "How Experts Fueled a Race with Vitriol," *The Washington Post*, (January 18), A1, A14.

Hiam, Alex (1988), "Presidential Campaign: A Triumph of Marketing," *Marketing News*, (December 19), 4.

Hill, Ronald Paul (1989), "An Exploration of Voter Responses to Political Advertisements," *Journal of Advertising*, 18 (4), 14-22.

Honomichl, Jack, (1988), "Negative Spots Likely to Return in Election '88," *Advertising Age*, 58 (3), 3, 70, 72.

Horton, Cleveland and Dennis Chase (1988), "Agency Execs Rap Candidates on Ad Tactics," *Advertising Age*, 59 (44), 1, 66.

Hume, Ellen and Rich Jaroslovsky (1988), "New Poll Finds Voters Broadly Dislike Choice in Presidential Race," *The Wall Street Journal*, (October 28), A1, A6.

Jamieson, Kathleen Hall (1988), "For Televised Mendacity, This Year is the Worst Ever," *The Washington Post*, (October 30), C1-C2.

Lang, Annie and Patrick Lanfear (1990), "The Information Processing of Televised Political Advertising: Using Theory to Maximize Recall," in *Advances in Consumer Research*, Vol 17, ed. Marvin Goldberg, Gerry Gorn, and Rick Pollay, Provo, UT: Association for Consumer Research, 149-158.

Lister, John (1988), "George Bush, Line Extension," *Advertising Age*, 59 (51), 17.

Maloney, John F. (1989), "For a Gentler Election Campaign," *Advertising Age*, 60 (6), 20.

McCabe, Ed (1988), "The Campaign You Never Saw," *New York*, (December 12), 32-48.

Merritt, Sharyne (1984), "Negative Political Advertising: Some Empirical Findings," *Journal of Advertising*, 13 (3), 27-38.

Oreskes, Michael (1988), "Negative Ads About Negative Ads: Final Pitches to an Electorate Grown Cold," *The New York Times*, (October 23), Section 4, 1-2.

Plattner, Andy (1988), "An End and a Beginning," *U.S. News & World Report*, (November 14), 21.

Prasad, V. Kanti (1976), "Communications-Effectiveness of Comparative Advertising: A Laboratory Analysis," *Journal of Marketing Research*, 13 (2), 128-137.

Rosenbaum, David E. (1988), "Florida Senate Contest Turns on Performance," *The New York Times*, (October 23), 26.

Rothenberg, Randall (1990), "Politics on TV: Too Fast, Too Loose?," *The Washington Post*, (July 15), E1, E4.

Stiansen, Sarah (1984), "Ads Fuel the Trench Warfare of Politics," *Advertising Age*, 55 (75), 82.

Stringer, Howard (1988), "Party is Over; Myth Returns," *Advertising Age*, 59 (51), 17.

Sullivan, John Fox (1988), "The Unselling of a Candidate," *Advertising Age*, 59 (46), 20.

Sullivan, Joseph F. (1988), "Negative Ads in Senate Race Are Putting Off Many Voters," *The New York Times*, (October 16), 1, 7.

Swinyard, William R. (1981), "The Interaction between Comparative Advertising and Copy Claim Variation," *Journal of Marketing Research*, 18 (2), 175-186.

Taylor, Paul (1990), "Political Pitches Called Insulting to Advertising," *The Washington Post*, (March 25), A1, A20-A21.

Taylor, Paul (1989), "Consultants Rise Via the Low Road," *The Washington Post*, (January 17), A1, A14.

Toner, Robin (1989), "Campaign Flawed, Dukakis Aide Agrees," *The New York Times*, (January 22), 22.

Wilkie, William L. (1986), *Consumer Behavior*, New York, NY: John Wiley & Sons, Inc.

Wilkie, William L. and Paul Farris (1975), "Comparison Advertising: Problems and Potential," *Journal of Marketing*, 39 (4), 7-15.

Will, George F. (1988), "The Other Guy Started It," *Advertising Age*, 59 (66), 66-67.

Williams, Lena (1988), "It Was a Year When Civility Really Took It on the Chin," *The New York Times*, (December 18), 1, 38.

An Empirical Test of a Model of Consumer Ethical Dilemmas
Lawrence J. Marks, Kent State University
Michael A. Mayo, Kent State University

ABSTRACT

The present study introduces and develops the concept of consumer ethical dilemmas. Hunt and Vitell's (1986) general theory of marketing ethics is used to describe how consumers might resolve their ethical dilemmas. Results indicate that consumers do encounter ethical dilemmas and that the Hunt and Vitell model captures some of the decision making processes consumer may use. A modified version of the Hunt and Vitell model which considers teleological evaluations for the decision maker separately is presented. Additionally, the study investigates how consumers feel during and after the resolution of their dilemma. The concept of consumer ethical decision making is discussed as a future direction for buyer behavior research for the 1990s.

INTRODUCTION

In the decade of the 1980's, researchers have become concerned with the issue of marketing-related ethics. This concern can be seen in a variety of areas, such as the ethics of personal selling (e.g., Kramer 1980), the ethics involved in marketing research (e.g., Akaah and Riordan 1989), and the ethics of creating a product for sale (e.g., Benton 1985). However, given that the field of marketing purports to have a consumer orientation, it is rather interesting to note that the focus of "marketing ethics" has been on the firm and management rather than on the consumer.

This managerial focus is exemplified by Hunt and Vitell's (1986) approach in creating a "General Theory of Marketing Ethics." They model the factors which are thought to influence the *manager's* decision process for evaluating and solving ethical problems. While their application of elements of moral philosophy to a business perspective is useful, their approach does not explicitly consider the ethical decision making problems which consumers may encounter in marketing-related situations.

The need to consider the consumer's perspective has been recognized by Mowen (1990) who suggests several areas in which consumers may encounter ethical issues and provides a set of normative guidelines for ethical consumer behavior. The concerns Mowen discusses are important, however much work remains to be done in understanding how consumers resolve their ethical dilemmas.

In general, there has been little overlap between the philosophers ideas of ethical behavior and the decisions of the buying public (Katz and Barbash 1982). For example, in the domain of environmental concerns, Katz and Barbash (1982) found that while philosophers have created models based on ethical interests which "transcend the human community ... consumers are still debating among (and within!) themselves the significance of their own competing interests" (p.154). This clearly suggests the need to study the ethical dilemmas with which consumers must contend.

The purpose of this paper is to introduce and define the concept of consumer ethical dilemmas and to test an initial model of consumer ethical decision making. From the perspective taken here, consumer ethical dilemmas are a special type of consumer problem requiring a decision process which is different from that typically used in choosing among products. Certainly, it is commonly accepted that consumers often deal with "problems" in the purchase and consumption process. For example, models of consumer decision making (e.g., Bettman 1979; Engel, Kollat, and Miniard 1990) have always recognized that consumers have problems regarding *whether* to purchase a product, *which brand* of a product to purchase, whether to pay *cash or use credit*, and so on. Such problems, however, are not *dilemmas* as they do not normally have an ethical or moral dimension. Ethical dilemmas are not specifically covered by existing consumer behavior models. We suggest, then, that "consumer ethical dilemmas" are an interesting and important type of dilemma, which have not been explicitly considered or adequately modeled.

CONSUMER ETHICAL DILEMMAS

A moral dilemma occurs when (a) at least two actions form a conflict, that is, when one action may harm (conflict with) the actions, interests, values of others (or one's self), and (b) "the negative (unintended) consequences of *one* action are *logically* implied in positive (intended) consequences of the *other* action, and *vice versa*" (Villenave-Cremer and Eckensberger 1985, p.180). If such actions are in the domain of a purchase or consumption situation, then a "consumer ethical dilemma" exists.

An example may help clarify this concept. A consumer wants to buy a foreign-made car. The *intended* consequence of this action is that the consumer will receive a high status and high quality means of transportation, which will fulfill the consumer's personal values related to quality and personal reward. Purchasing a foreign car, however, has the *unintended* consequences of contributing to the imbalance of trade and perhaps putting U.S. laborers out of work. Putting American workers out of work and contributing to the trade imbalance both run counter to this consumer's personal values of what is "right," "correct," or "moral" behavior.

On the other hand, while buying the American car results in the intended consequences of helping American workers and not contributing to the national trade imbalance, it also creates unintended consequences because the consumer will not get the desired quality or status which violates the consumer's personal values. This situation is clearly a "consumer ethical dilemma" (it fulfills the definition of a moral dilemma and is domain of purchase and/or consumption). As in most dilemmas, the decision to satisfy one's own desires runs counter to the interests of others, and vice versa. Clearly, marketers (both foreign and domestic, in this case) have an interest in the way in which such dilemmas are resolved.

RESOLVING CONSUMER ETHICAL DILEMMAS

In their general theory of marketing ethics, Hunt and Vitell (1986) summarize an extensive philosophy literature which deals with how people resolve moral dilemmas. Briefly, the model indicates that marketing managers make judgments about ethical problems by applying both deontological norms (i.e., personal values about "right" and "wrong") and teleological principles (i.e., the consideration of what consequences are likely to occur and how good or bad the consequences will be for relevant stakeholders) to the situation. The exogenous variables to the process include the cultural environment, the industry environment, the organization environment, and personal experiences. There is some evidence that this model may adequately represent marketers' ethical decision making processes (Mayo and Marks 1990).

MODELS OF CONSUMER ETHICAL DECISION MAKING

It seems possible that managers and consumers may resolve ethical dilemmas using similar processes. Like managers, consumers are likely to combine both a deontological and a teleological evaluation to derive a final judgment about an ethical problem. The exogenous variables influencing the consumer, however, are likely to differ from those affecting marketing managers. Thus, the Figure presents a somewhat modified version of Hunt and Vitell's (1986) general theory of marketing ethics. The exogenous variables include the consumer's cultural environment (which encompasses the consumer's subculture and social class), their reference groups (i.e., family, friends, and relevant others), and their past personal experiences.

Except for the suggested revisions in the exogenous variables, the revised model is identical to Hunt and Vitell's original work. It retains the concepts of perceived ethical problem, perceived alternatives, and perceived consequences. The deontological norm construct represents the personal values of the consumer which are used in the deontological evaluation of the dilemma. As in the original model, the consumer is hypothesized to base teleological evaluations on an estimation of the probability of the consequences which will occur from selecting any course of action, the desirability of those consequences to the stakeholders, and the importance of those stakeholders to the consumer.

The ethical judgment of the alternative is then a function of the consumer's deontological and teleological evaluations, and it, in turn, influences the consumer's behavioral intentions. Finally, the actual consequences of the consumer's behavior will become part of the consumers' learning experiences.

Of course, people do not always take the most ethical action. Hunt and Vitell suggest people may intend to choose a less ethical alternative when it leads to a preferred consequence. For example, the less ethical alternative may result in some personal gain. In such a case, the person's intention is affected independently by the teleological evaluation of the alternatives. This suggests that the decision processes which lead to ethical and unethical behavior may be different. Additionally, Hunt and Vitell note that actual behavior may not be consistent with the most ethical choice because of situational conditions which consumers may perceive as "enabling" them to engage in unethical behaviors.

When people choose an unethical alternative they may have guilt feelings (Hunt and Vitell 1986). Relatively little research in the consumer behavior domain has attempted to investigate consumer guilt (see Ghingold 1981). This affective state is interesting in the context of consumer ethical decision making because it may influence the consumer's future behavior.

While the just described model of consumer ethical decision making is quite consistent with the Hunt and Vitell model, there is an interesting question regarding the teleological process. It seems quite likely that consumers will always consider themselves as relevant stakeholders in the decision. If true, it would be important to make a distinction between consequences which result for one's self and those which result for others (e.g., Miniard and Cohen 1983) especially in a dilemma situation. Thus, an alternative way to model the teleological evaluative process would be to consider the consequences for one's self separately from the consequences for others.

THE RESEARCH QUESTIONS

This research was developed to investigate four major questions. First, can (and will) consumers identify and report "consumer ethical dilemmas?" If the first question is answered in the affirmative, the next questions become relevant. Second, how well do the decision processes proposed in Hunt and Vitell's (1986) general theory of marketing ethics explain the resolution of consumer ethical dilemmas? Third, is it necessary to separate the teleological evaluative process into the consequences for self and the consequences for others? Finally, do consumers who choose less ethical alternatives use different decision processes and/or feel more guilt than those who choose more ethical alternatives?

FIGURE
A MODEL OF CONSUMER ETHICAL DECISION MAKING
Adapted from Hunt, Shelby and Scott Vitell (1986), "A General Theory of Marketing Ethics," *Journal of Macromarketing*, (Spring), 8

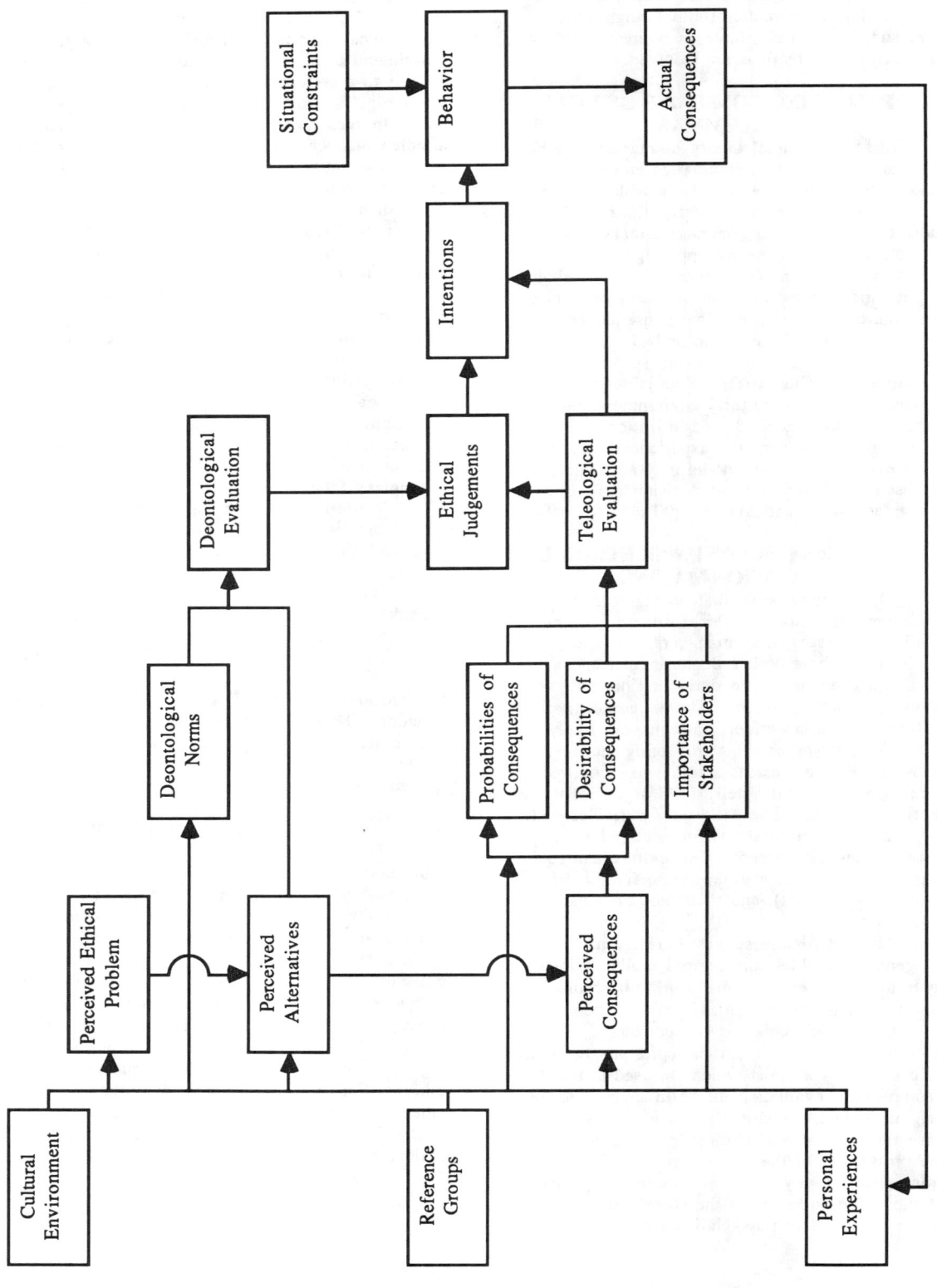

METHODOLOGY

The Sample

A self-administered questionnaire was developed and made available to undergraduate (juniors and seniors) students taking a marketing course at a Midwest university. Those who desired extra credit in the course were required to fill out the questionnaire and to recruit two non-student adults (over 21 years old) to respond as well. Fifty-five students decided to participate, creating a convenience sample of 165. As will been described in the following section, the questionnaire was long, detailed, and time consuming. Thus, it was not surprising to find that only 47 (28%) of the instruments that were returned were usable. The age of the respondents ranged from 20 to 73 years old, with the average for students being 23.6, while the average for the non-students was 36.5 (sample mean=31.1). Overall, 60% of the respondents were female. In terms of education, none of the students had completed college, while approximately 3% of the non-students had some high school, 15% had completed high school, 44% had some college, 26% had a college degree, and 11% had a graduate degree. Finally, 46% of the non-students reported total household income of under $50,000 per year while 54% reported income of $50,000 or more.

Two observations can be made about this sample. The first is that it is an improvement over the "usual" convenience sample consisting solely of undergraduate students, which is often used for this type of research. Unlike the typical undergraduate convenience sample, this sample has a wide range in all of the demographic variables. The second is that those who provided usable surveys were somewhat unusual. They not only understood the concept of consumer ethical dilemma and were willing to report their experiences, but they were willing to answer a detailed questionnaire that took approximately one hour to complete.

It should be noted that care was taken to assure anonymity to both the students and the non-students who were asked to participate. While each person was required to sign and return a consent form, this form was detached from the questionnaire before it was returned. No other identifying marks were placed on the questionnaires. Additionally, each questionnaire was returned in a sealed envelope, so that neither the (student) administrator nor the researchers could identify the respondents. Given the potentially sensitive nature of consumer ethical dilemmas, this guaranteed anonymity seemed critical.

The Questionnaire/Measures

General Instructions. The first page of the questionnaire explained that not all purchases consumers make are simple, and that at times "we are faced with decisions in which any alternative we select goes against some personal value we hold" (i.e., we have a consumer ethical dilemma). Next, a hypothetical example of such a dilemma was provided. It involved the question of whether to buy a diamond ring which was desired, when the diamond was known to be from South Africa. Buying the ring would provide personal pleasure, but it would, in some sense, support the racial policies of the South African government. The respondents were asked to think of and report a consumer ethical dilemma which they had encountered recently. This data collection strategy was preferred over providing a standard set of scenarios to each respondent as typically found in the ethics literature. The scenario approach has been criticized for both failing to create substantial subject involvement and not tapping a "deeper level of psychological processing" (Smith, Winer, and George 1983). Verbal reports of actual consumer experiences may overcome these deficiencies and provide accurate information (Beniot and Beniot 1984).

To ensure that the situations reported by respondents were truly consumer ethical dilemmas, they were asked to apply the following three criteria: "(1) Was there a DILEMMA? Did you actually consider more than one alternative? (2) Did you feel some discomfort as you thought about your decision? Did thinking about one of the choices make you feel unethical, dishonest, etc? (3) Would you judge at least one of the alternatives you actually considered to be relatively ethical, and at least one to be relatively unethical?" If the respondent could answer "Yes" to these questions, then they were told that their situation was probably an appropriate "consumer ethical dilemma."

These three criteria captured the basic elements of the definition of consumer ethical dilemmas provided earlier. In pre-tests we found that respondents listed as "consumer ethical dilemmas" a variety of inappropriate situations. In some cases, the consumer clearly knew from the start what the "right" thing to do was, and intended to do it. In other cases, the consumer had no initial feelings that they were considering doing something "wrong." From the start, they had rationalized their decision and, even though they did the unethical thing, they did not feel uncomfortable about it (e.g., "the store personnel had treated me badly, and so I felt that it was okay to take the blouse.") Finally, some consumers only listed alternatives which they felt were ethical ones. None of these situations adequately fits the definition of "consumer ethical dilemmas" and it was felt that the application of the three criteria would reduce the number of inappropriate responses.

The Dilemma and Alternatives. In the next section, the respondent was asked to provide a complete description of their consumer ethical dilemma and then to list the alternatives that they were trying to choose among. A measure of the impact of the dilemma on the respondent was obtained through seven semantic differential-type scales (7-point scales, anchored with Anxious/Content, Innocent/Guilty, Nervous/Calm, Remorseful/Not Remorseful, Not Embarrassed/Embarrassed, Shameful/Proud, and

Ethical/Unethical). These seven items were suggested by pretest results. Respondents were next asked to think back to how it felt as the decision was being made, and to use the scales to rate how they felt as they were making their final decision. After the rating task, the respondents indicated what alternative they actually selected and provided the reason for that choice.

It should be noted that much research into ethical decision making has used a scenario approach (e.g., Hunt and Vitell 1986), in which all respondents rate situations which are created by the researcher. Allowing the subjects to describe and use their own consumer ethical dilemmas assures a degree of realism and involvement which would be hard to achieve with scenarios. Also, this approach provides insight into the types of ethical dilemmas which consumers encounter. However, a this approach does create problems. Even though the respondents were given the criteria to apply to determine whether their situation was a consumer ethical dilemma, many of the completed questionnaires were rejected because the situations described did not fulfill the criteria.

Deontological Evaluations. To investigate the deontological evaluative process which the respondents may have used, they were next asked to list ALL the personal values (i.e., deontological norms) that they considered in resolving the alternative, relevant to both the selected and rejected alternatives. They then indicated how strongly each of these values would have been reflected by each of the alternatives they were considering (+2, strongly agree that the alternative reflects the personal value; -2, strongly disagree). The summation of these ratings reflects a deontological evaluation of each alternative considered.

Teleological Evaluations. The teleological evaluative process was measured by having the respondents first list the people whose opinion or welfare they considered as they thought about each alternative (including themselves). Then for each alternative considered, they provided the major consequences that would have resulted for the stakeholders which were relevant to this alternative. The consequences were rated in terms of their probability of occurring (5=Very Likely, 1=Very Unlikely) and their desirability for the party involved (+2=Very Desirable, -2=Very Undesirable). Finally, the importance of the party to the respondent was rated (5=Very Important, 1=Very Unimportant).

For each stakeholder the product of these three variables (probability x desirability x importance) was divided by the number of consequences considered for that stakeholder. The sum of these scores for all the stakeholders considered for a given alternative provided a measure of the subject's teleological evaluation of that alternative. This teleological score was easily separated into "self" versus "others.

Ethical Judgment. Each alternative considered was rated in terms of how ethical the respondent perceived it to be (5=Very Ethical, 3=Neither Ethical nor Unethical, 1=Very Unethical), providing an overall measure reflecting the consumer's ethical judgment of the alternatives.

This measure also was an important check used to determine the appropriateness of the situation and the alternatives. As previously noted, to be included in the study, at least one alternative had to be rated as "Ethical" (i.e., a 4 or 5) and at least one alternative had to be rated "Unethical" (i.e., a 1 or a 2).

Post-decision Feelings. The last measurement taken, excluding the demographics, asked the respondents to think how they felt *after* they made their final decision, and to rate their feeling on the same seven semantic-type scales described previously.

RESULTS

Consumers' Ability to Report Ethical Dilemmas

Although the rate of successful completion of the questionnaire was not especially high, it is clear that the first research question can be answered in the affirmative (i.e., people can and will report their "consumer ethical dilemmas"). The questionnaires included in the analysis met the three criteria described earlier. First, they all listed more than one alternative. Second, as Table 1 shows, these respondents felt quite uncomfortable as they were deciding what to do about their dilemma (coefficient alpha=.79 for the 7 items while making the decision, and .91 after making the decision). All of the scale items were directionally appropriate, and all the measures except for "embarrassed" were significantly different from the scale midpoint ($p \leq .01$, one-tailed t-tests). Third, the subjects all rated at least one alternative as relatively ethical, and one as relatively unethical. The mean ethicalness rating of the least ethical alternatives was 1.89, while it was 4.57 for the most ethical alternatives. Thus, respondents can and will report situations which appear to be consumer ethical dilemmas.

The Applicability of the Models

This allows investigation of the question regarding how well the processes described in the Hunt and Vitell model explain the resolution of consumer ethical dilemmas. Table 2 presents the results, using the consumers' judgment of the ethicalness of the selected alternative as the dependent variable. Looking at the full set of subjects, the model based on Hunt and Vitell does not do as well as the model which differentiates between self and others in the teleological evaluative process. In the first case, the model accounts for 11% of the variance (based on the adjusted r-square) in the ethicalness of the selected alternative. Within this model, the teleological evaluative process has a higher beta weight than does the deontological evaluation, and only the former is statistically significant. However, when the teleological process involving self is separated

TABLE 1
MEANS AND STANDARD DEVIATIONS OF SEMANTIC SCALES

While making decision

VARIABLE	All Subjects (n=47)		"Unethical" (n=20)		"Ethical" (n=27)	
	Mean	S.D.	Mean	S.D.	Mean	S.D.
Anxious	2.72	1.15	2.65	1.27	2.78	1.09
Guilty	2.47	1.33	2.40	1.14	2.52	1.48
Nervous	3.08	1.57	2.90	1.59	3.22	1.60
Remorseful	3.55	1.31	3.60	1.50	3.58	1.17
Embarrassed	3.79	1.52	3.45	1.47	4.04	1.53
Shameful	3.11	1.13	2.85	1.09	3.30	1.14
Unethical	2.89	1.15	2.60	.68	3.11	1.37
Total	21.67	6.16	20.45	6.29	22.61	6.01

After making decision

VARIABLE	All Subjects (n=47)		"Unethical" (n=20)		"Ethical" (n=27)	
	Mean	S.D.	Mean	S.D.	Mean	S.D.
Anxious	5.02	2.06	3.90	2.17	5.85	1.54
Guilty	4.00	1.93	2.60	.99	5.04	1.81
Nervous	4.87	1.79	3.80	1.70	5.67	1.41
Remorseful	4.83	1.82	3.75	1.55	5.65	1.57
Embarrassed	4.74	1.86	3.80	1.36	5.44	1.89
Shameful	4.53	1.84	3.40	1.23	5.37	1.78
Unethical	4.40	1.80	3.15	1.09	5.33	1.66
Total	32.50	10.55	24.40	6.68	38.73	8.58

TABLE 2
Regression Analysis for the Selected Alternatives

	All Subjects		Unethical		Ethical	
	Standardized Beta Weights	Adjusted r-square	Standardized Beta Weights	Adjusted r-square	Standardized Beta Weights	Adjusted r-square
Model 1						
Deon. Eval	.14		-.19		.44[b]	
Tele. Eval	.37[b]	.11[b]	.43[c]	.12	.14	.13[c]
Model 2						
Deon. Eval	.14		-.16		.46[a]	
Tele. Self	.42[a]		-.12		.56[a]	
Tele. Other	.04	.15[b]	.55[b]	.16	-.32[c]	.35[a]

[a] $p \leq .01$
[b] $p \leq .05$
[c] $p \leq .10$

from that involving others, it can be seen that the model accounts for 15% of the variance. In this model, the highest beta weight (and the only one reaching statistical significance) is for the teleological processes involving one's self. This suggests it may be important to create a distinction between the self and other stakeholders when modeling the teleological process.

The Process for Ethical versus Unethical Decisions

An interesting question involves consumers who choose an unethical alternative compared to those who do not. In general, it seems likely that people who choose alternatives which they perceive to be unethical go through a different decision process than those who choose either a neutral alternative or an ethical alternative. Consumers who select unethical alternatives must face their own guilt and possibly social criticism which would not apply to those choosing alternatives which are neutral or ethical. Based on this assumption, Table 2 presents the results of consumers who selected unethical alternatives (rated as 2 or less) and those who chose neutral or ethical alternatives (rated as 3 or more).

As Table 2 shows, for both groups the model which separates the self from the others in the teleological evaluation explains more of the variance (16% for the unethical group, 35% for the neutral/ethical group) than the model which does not separate these two constructs (12% and 13%).

Looking at the model based on Hunt and Vitell, teleological processes appear to be more important than deontological processes for the unethical group (although neither reaches a .05 level of significance). Interestingly, this pattern is reversed for the subjects who selected a neutral to ethical alternative. In this case, the personal values represented in the deontological evaluative process is more important (and is significant at the .05 level).

The model which separates the teleological evaluative process into self and others provides some useful insights. First, for both the neutral/ethical and the unethical groups, the standardized beta weights for the deontological evaluative process and the teleological/self process have the same signs and are the *opposite* of that for the teleological/other evaluative process. This is consistent with what would be expected to occur in an ethical dilemma situation. A dilemma exists largely because what is good for one's self is not good for other people. These results reflect that notion. Second, consumers who choose an alternative which they personally consider to be unethical appear to do so because it has positive consequences for other important stakeholders (however, not positive for themselves). Third, consumers who select the ethical alternative, do so because it supports their personal values (deontological evaluation) and because it provides positive consequences for themselves, even though others may suffer.

Resolution of the Dilemma and Feelings of Guilt

Examination of the means in Table 1 for the consumers choosing a neutral/ethical versus an unethical alternative reveals that there were no significant differences in their reported feelings *while* they were making their decision. This result is interesting because it suggests that, despite the potential biases involved in retrospective evaluations of decision processes, the subjects apparently were able to "role play" their decision processes without having their actual final decision unduly bias their reported feelings. If there were strong biases created by this retrospective reporting, one would expect to find differences in the reported feelings of the "ethical" and "unethical" subjects before, as well as after, the decision was made. Such differences would be expected as consumers rationalize their decisions after the fact.

However, after the dilemma is resolved, the consumers who selected an alternative which they considered unethical reported feeling significantly more anxious, guilty, nervous, remorseful, embarrassed, shameful, and unethical than did the subjects selecting an ethical alternative (all $p \leq .001$).

DISCUSSION

The present study broadens the domain of ethical decision making in marketing to include consumers in addition to its past focus on management. Results indicated that consumers do encounter ethical dilemmas when purchasing goods and services. Additionally, it appears that consumers are able to report in detail the nature of these dilemmas and how they are resolved.

The general theory of marketing ethics proposed by Hunt and Vitell (1986) proved to be a useful model to describe how consumers resolved ethical dilemmas. The present studied modified this model by dividing the teleological process into two parts: consideration of consequences that occurred to the decision maker and those that befell other stakeholders. This division provided additional insights into how the consumers resolved their ethical dilemmas. Initially it appeared that consumers arrived at their ethical judgments of the selected alternatives by teleological (rather than deontological) considerations. Upon further analysis, however, only a subset of teleological considerations (those that directly impacted the decision maker) was an important determinant of subsequent ethical judgments. From this analysis, it appears that consumers may attempt to resolve ethical dilemmas by promoting their greatest self-interest (ethical egoism).

However, this is not always the case. This study shows that, at times, consumers choose alternatives which they consider to be unethical and which may run counter to their own best interests, because of consequences (i.e., benefits) to other people. These results support Hunt and Vitell's (1986, p.10) assertion that people may choose an alternative which is not judged as the most ethical because of certain "preferred consequences."

These results suggest that consumers and marketing managers resolve ethical dilemmas in similar ways. For example, consumers who did not resolve dilemmas in an unethical manner tended to rely on personal values and how their choice would impact themselves as the major determinants of ethical judgment. Consumers, in this respect, are similar to managers who act from ethical principles (rather than majority opinion) and exhibit more consistency between moral judgment and moral action (cf. Trevino 1986). On the other hand, consumers who chose an unethical means to resolve their moral dilemma tended to rely on how their choice would impact other stakeholders as the major determinant of ethical judgment. In this respect, consumers are similar to marketing managers for whom the beliefs of significant others may have a greater impact on ethical decision making than personal beliefs and values (cf. Ferrell, Gresham, and Fraedrich 1989).

The concept of "consumer ethical dilemmas" has implications for marketing practitioners in the 1990's. Because marketing managers whose customers consider the ethical implications of their purchases (e.g., buying foreign automobile, buying non-union products, etc.) have a vested interest in how consumers resolve moral dilemmas, they may want to influence how consumers resolve such dilemmas. The results of this study tentatively suggest that marketing managers might be able to influence consumers to act ethically by emphasizing the consequences to the decision maker themselves. Some support for this notion is found in several contemporary advertising campaigns, such as "Buy U.S.A." and "Buy Union-Made," which emphasize the quality and value that such purchases will bring the consumer.

However, researchers need to develop the concept of consumer ethical dilemmas and ethical decision making further before marketing practitioners can use the concept to revise and plan marketing strategies. Several research questions remain. First, further research needs to determine what kind of purchases are likely to present consumers with ethical dilemmas. Bearden and Etzel's (1982) work on how reference groups influence brand and product choices may be a useful typology to identify purchases likely to have ethical implications for consumers. The results from the present study suggest that reference groups (i.e., teleological considerations that effect other stakeholders) impact unethical choice. Using Bearden and Etzel's work as a base, it could be hypothesized that significant others may exert the strongest influence on ethical choices that involve the purchase of public luxuries (e.g., fur coats). Second, researchers should determine if the consumer's level of moral development (Kohlberg 1981) influences how they resolve ethical dilemmas. In a managerial context, ethical decision making is guided more by ethical principles than group consensus as managers operate at higher levels of moral development (cf. Trevino 1986). It is unknown if this finding can be generalized to consumers. Third, further investigation should be done to determine the personal and situational factors which influence the consumers' selection of an ethical or unethical alternative. For example, the intensity of the clarity of the dilemma may influence consumers' resolution of the dilemma.

LIMITATIONS

The findings of this study are subject to several limitations. First, the variables measured were suggested by a particular theoretical model. In as much as these variables accounted for as little as 11% of the variance in the consumers' ethical judgments, it seems likely that other unmeasured variables have an influence. Thus, the results are limited by the set of variables investigated. For example, the approach taken here focuses on a cognitive evaluation. However, some researchers have suggested that ethical decisions may be influenced by affective processes as well (Villenave-Cremer and Eckensberger 1985). Second, the causal relationships being tested were measured retrospectively. It is certain that the retrospective ratings acquired contain some degree of bias due to the consumers' rationalizations and coping strategies. While it would be quite difficult to obtain measures of the decision process while the dilemma was actually being encountered, such an approach would be an improvement over the methodology used here. Third, while the subjects used in this study represent an improvement over the use of exclusively undergraduate students, it is still a convenience sample and so contains unknown biases which may have influenced the results. Finally, over 70% of the returned questionnaires had to be rejected for reasons including noncompletion or failure to provide an appropriate consumer ethical dilemma. It is unclear how this affects the generalizability of the results.

REFERENCES

Akaah, Ishmael P. Edward A. Riordan (1989) "Judgments of Marketing Professionals About Ethical Issues in Marketing Research: A Replication and Extension", *Journal of Marketing Research*, 26(February), 112-120.

Bearden, William O. and Michael J. Etzel (1982) "Reference Group Influence on Product and Brand Purchase Decisions," *Journal of Consumer Research*, 9(Sept) 185-194.

Benoit, Pamela J. and William L. Beniot (1986) "Consciousness: The Mindlessness/Mindfulness and Verbal Report Controversies," *Western Journal of Speech Communication*, 50(1), 41-63.

Benton, Raymond Jr. (1985), "Alternative Approaches to Consumer Behavior," in Nikhilkesh Dholakia and Johan Arndt (eds.), *Widening Marketing Theory, Research in Marketing, Supplement 2*, 197-218.

Bettman, James (1979), *An Information Processing Theory of Consumer Choice*, Reading, Mass.: Addison-Wesley Publishing Co.

Engel, James F., Roger D. Blackwell, and Paul W. Miniard (1990), *Consumer Behavior*, 6th edition, Chicago: The Dryden Press.

Ferrell, O.C., Larry G. Gresham, and John Fraedrich (1989) "A Synthesis of Ethical Decision Models for Marketing", *Journal of Macromarketing*, (Fall), 55 - 64.

Ghingold, Morry (1981), "Guilt Arousing Marketing Communications: An Unexplored Variable," in *Advances in Consumer Research*, Volume 8, Kent Monroe (ed), 442 - 448.

Hunt, Shelby D. and Scott Vitell (1986) "A General Theory of Marketing Ethics", *Journal of Macromarketing*, 6 (Spring), 5 - 16.

Katz and Barbash (1982), "Environmental Ethics and Consumer Choice: A Conceptual Case Study," *Humboldt Journal of Social Relations*, 9(Spring/Summer), 143-159.

Kohlberg, Lawrence (1981), *Essays on Moral Development, Volume One: The Philosophy of Moral Development*, San Francisco: Harper and Row.

Kramer, Hugh E. (1980) "The Moral Dilemma of Salesmanship: Sources, Modes and Moral Hierarchies of Purposeful Communication", in *Academy of Marketing Science Monograph Series*, Harold W. Berkman and Jane K. Fenyo, eds., 1 - 20.

Mayo, Michael A. and Lawrence J. Marks (1990) "A Empirical Investigation of a General Theory of Marketing Ethics", *Journal of the Academy of Marketing Science*, 163-171.

Miniard, Paul W. and Joel B. Cohen (1983) "Modeling Personal and Normative Influences on Behavior", *Journal of Consumer Research*, 10 (September), 169-180.

Mowen, John C. (1990), *Consumer Behavior*, 2nd edition, New York: MacMillian Publishing Company.

Smith, H. Wayne, Jane L. Winer, and Clay E. George (1983) "The Relative Efficacy of Simulation Experiments," *Journal of Vocational Behavior*, 22(Feb), 94-104.

Trevino, Linda Klebe (1986) "Ethical Decision Making in Organizations: A Person-Situation Interactionist Model", *Academy of Management Review*, 11 (3), 601 - 617.

Villenave-Cremer, Susanne and Lutz H. Eckensberger (1986) "The Role of Affective Processes in Moral Judgment Performance" in *Moral Education: Theory and Application*, Marvin W. Berkowitz and Fritz Oser, eds., Hillsdale, NJ: Lawrence Erlbaum Associates, 175 - 194.

Elements of Experiential Consumption: An Exploratory Study
Brian Lofman, University of Connecticut[1]

An exploratory study was undertaken to uncover the elements of experiential consumption. Content analysis of respondent protocols indicates that there are six primary elements: setting, sensation, thought, feeling, activity, and evaluation. These inductively generated elements are similar to the deductive constructs in Hirschman and Holbrook's (1986) Thought-Emotion-Activity-Value (TEAV) Model. Differences in experiential consumption are highlighted by comparing the salience of factors in instrumental and hedonic consumption experiences. The results suggest that, in contrast to instrumental consumption, hedonic consumption involves relatively greater emotional processing and more activity and evaluation, but comparatively less overall cognitive processing and sensory stimulation.

Experience is the best teacher.
- Unknown

INTRODUCTION

Researchers are increasingly finding and acknowledging that there is a broad range of consumption beyond brand choice and purchase behavior. Such recognition better reflects the fact that the verb, "to consume," can be defined in many ways: to use up; to squander, spend wastefully; to eat up, devour; to absorb the attention of, engross; to absorb the mental or emotional faculties; to take to oneself, receive into one's system, incorporate; to penetrate deeply; to possess entirely. These distinctions give a flavor for the varied nature of consumption and collectively point to the need to examine more broadly the realm of experiential consumption: the experiences consumers have while using, consuming, and possessing market offerings (e.g., see Belk 1988; Thompson, Locander, and Pollio 1989).

Studies based on assumptions implicit in the experiential perspective (Holbrook and Hirschman 1982) have emphasized esthetic products and emotional processing. Havlena and Holbrook (1986) studied eight broad types of human experience, only some of which involved market offerings. Additionally, in order to contrast two major typologies of emotion (Mehrabian and Russell 1974; Plutchik 1980), their research focused on experiences evoking strong feelings and emotions. Scholars need to gain a broader understanding of the differences in experiential consumption across the market offering spectrum.

The purpose of this research is twofold. The first objective is to identify inductively the elements of experiential consumption. The second objective is to compare the salience of these elements across consumption experiences reflecting differing value orientations. Research is conducted on consumption experiences involving extrinsically valued and intrinsically valued market offerings. The distinction between extrinsic and intrinsic values is reflected in two different types of consumption: instrumental consumption and hedonic consumption.

BACKGROUND

Psychological Theories

The instrumental/hedonic distinction in the consumer behavior literature is based on psychological theories, particularly those from the phenomenological or humanistic school that theorize a dichotomy in sensory perceptual states. As originally formulated by Koch (1956), behavior may be extrinsically motivated or intrinsically motivated. Whereas extrinsic motivation underlies consumption as a means toward an end (utilitarian or instrumental consumption), intrinsic motivation underlies consumption as an end in itself (hedonic consumption).

Schachtel (1959) contrasted two modes of perception, secondary autocentricity and allocentricity. In secondary autocentricity, the perceiver views objects in terms of the needs or uses they may serve, thereby engaging in problem solving and approach-avoidance behavior. In allocentric perception, the perceiver is completely absorbed in the object.

Maslow (1962) compared two types of cognitive activity, cognition and b-cognition. Cognition involves comparing, judging, and evaluating; b-cognition involves experiencing the object as a whole, apart from any particular purpose. Maslow's "being-psychology" is oriented to ends as opposed to means, such as end-experiences (pp. 73-74).

In a review of psychological literature, Tellegen (1981) proposed fundamental differences between what he termed the instrumental and experiential sets. The instrumental set refers to "a state of readiness to engage in active, realistic, voluntary, and relatively effortful planning, decision making, and goal-directed behavior," whereas the experiential set represents "a state of receptivity or openness ... to undergo whatever experiential events, sensory or imaginal, that may occur, with a tendency to dwell on, rather than go beyond, the experiences themselves and the objects they represent" (p. 222).

Consumer Research

In the early 1980s, theorists began to question the assumption of the rational consumer and postulate that consumers engage in both cognitive and emotional processing (Zajonc 1980; Zajonc and Markus 1982). Researchers have made a

---

[1]The author gratefully acknowledges the support and invaluable assistance of Susan Spiggle and Robin Higie.

conceptual distinction between behavior based on utilitarian or instrumental values and behavior based on pleasure seeking or hedonic values (e.g., see Tse, Belk, and Zhou 1989). Additionally, scholars have focused increasingly on hedonic consumption as a distinct area of study (Ahtola 1985; Hirschman and Holbrook 1982; Holbrook et al. 1984).

Holbrook and Hirschman (1982) proposed an experiential perspective of consumer behavior as an alternative to the information processing and purchase decision making approach. Subsequently, they developed a framework that included value (Holbrook and Corfman 1985), cognition (Hirschman 1985a), emotion (Holbrook 1986), and holistic-intuitive consciousness (Hirschman 1985b) in experiential consumption. Hirschman and Holbrook (1986) proposed the Thought-Emotion-Activity-Value (TEAV) Model, suggesting that it encompasses all forms of consumption, including those implicit in the Cognition-Affect-Behavior-Satisfaction (CABS) Model (Engel, Kollat, and Blackwell 1968; Howard and Sheth 1969; Nicosia 1966). Each of the four constructs in TEAV is a broadened conceptualization of the respective constructs in CABS. In addition to cognition, "Thought" includes dreaming, imagining, and fantasizing. "Emotion" involves diverse types of feelings, expressive behaviors, and physiological responses. "Activity" includes physical and mental events relating to both action and reaction. "Value" pertains to evaluative judgments in consumption. TEAV assumes that consumption experiences are complex processes and suggests interdependencies among its constructs and hence nonlinearity.

In sum, researchers have painted two contrasting, though not necessarily opposing, pictures of the consumer. One stream of research -- the instrumentally oriented -- assumes a rational, information processing problem solver who follows a purchase decision making strategy to fulfill a specific need. A second stream -- the hedonic orientation -- assumes an experiential being who consumes for enjoyment. Collectively, theory and research indicates that the consumer is both instrumentally and hedonically oriented, suggesting that experiential consumption may be classified as primarily hedonic, primarily instrumental, or some mix of the two.

AN EXPLORATORY STUDY

The purpose of the present study is to uncover elements in experiential consumption and to contrast the salience of these elements in instrumental consumption (IC) and hedonic consumption (HC). The research requires respondents to report on experiences involving extrinsically and intrinsically valued market offerings.

Method and Measurement

One hundred and four undergraduate students at a northeastern university responded to a pencil and paper questionnaire. The instructions used to elicit an IC experience read "Some market offerings are sought, acquired, and/or consumed for their use in achieving some goal or end state. That is, they are means to some other end, not intrinsically valued for themselves." The instructions used to elicit an HC experience read "Other market offerings are sought, acquired, and/or consumed for the experiences they provide. That is, the experiences during consumption represent ends in themselves". After reading the definitions, subjects responded to: "Think of a market offering that fits into the [first/second] category. Please make a list of the images, associations, and words which reflect what you think and how you feel when you recall your most recent experience in using or consuming that market offering. Number each item on the list. Each item may be a single word, a phrase, or more." This open end approach was used to elicit verbal statements reflecting feelings, perceptions, desired states, and so on which relate to the experiential domain (Fennell 1985, p. 548). No time limit was set for protocol completion, but most subjects completed both protocols within fifteen minutes. One hundred and two protocols were generated for each type of consumption experience.

Content Analysis

Subsets of the protocols were content analyzed to determine the appropriate classification scheme. Category development progressed through several stages; the number of categories increased over the iterative coding process. After the categories had been developed inductively, they were collapsed into a smaller number of categories representing the elements of experiential consumption, including Setting, Sensation, Thought, Feeling, Activity, and Evaluation. The operationalization for each category is provided in the Appendix. Two judges other than the author independently coded the protocols. The interjudge reliability (percentage of agreement) for all responses is 93 percent, ranging from 84 percent to 98 percent for the categories and subcategories. A third judge resolved all disagreements.

Comparison with TEAV Model Constructs

The Thought, Feeling, Activity, and Evaluation elements derived in this empirical study are similar to the respective constructs in Hirschman and Holbrook's (1986) TEAV Model. "Thought" encompasses not only cognitive processing regarding the market offering itself, but also imaginal processing as reflected in associations made during consumption. "Feeling" in this research is equivalent to "Emotion," but better represents protocol responses such as "makes me feel happy" and "feeling thirsty." "Activity" in this study is the same as its counterpart in TEAV. "Evaluation" is a more appropriate term than the broader conceptualization "Value." In this research, evaluative responses reflected self-oriented (economic, hedonic) value but not other-oriented value, which is more likely to be evident in human relational experiences rather than market offering consumption. "Setting" in this study is related to "Environment (Information)" -- an input to the

TABLE 1
Instrumental and Hedonic Market Offerings

Market Offering Category	Instrumental	Hedonic
Appliance/Automobile	14	0
Beauty/Health/Hygiene	42	4
Cassette/CD/Radio	0	24
Clothing	4	13
Concert/Sporting Event	0	5
Food/Alcohol/Restaurant	9	30
Miscellaneous Nondurable	7	2
Movie/TV	0	19
Participatory Game/Vacation	1	5
Service	25	0
All	102	102

consumption process in TEAV -- in that objects in the immediate environment serve as sources of information for the consumer.

There are two minor differences between the inductively generated elements in this research and the deductively generated constructs in TEAV. First, whereas functional and psychosocial benefits are included within "Thought" in this study, they appear to correspond to the reasons, motives, wants, and wishes treated within the "Person (Motivation)" construct, another input to the consumption process in TEAV. Functional and psychosocial benefits as well as concrete and abstract attributes are links in a means-end chain, which is a hierarchical knowledge structure containing attributes, consequences (benefits), and values (Gutman 1982; Peter and Olson 1989). Beyond its use in understanding product knowledge, then, the means-end chain may be useful in understanding experiential consumption.

Second, since sensory imagery is a mental event, it could be considered a part of "Thought" as it is in TEAV (see Hirschman 1985a; Hirschman and Holbrook 1982). However, "Sensation" is treated as a distinct element in this study to reflect the importance of the translation or interpretation of the market offering during consumption and to emphasize the distinction between sensory processing and cognitive processing.

Both the elements in this research and the constructs in TEAV dovetail with the conceptual approach of Richardson (1984), who defines experience as "an event to be described in terms of a sensory, imaginal and affective complex" (p. 195). Interestingly, Richardson advocates incorporating the experiential dimension along with the oft-studied behavioral and physiological dimensions of psychology, just as some consumer researchers have begun to consider experiential consumption in addition to information processing and other cognitive oriented approaches to consumer behavior.

Distribution of Market Offerings

The market offerings are categorized in Table 1 according to whether they were perceived as instrumental (extrinsically valued) or hedonic (intrinsically valued) by the respondents. There was considerable agreement among respondents. Appliances, automobiles, and a variety of services (e.g., college, haircutting, travel agency) were viewed as instrumental market offerings and valued extrinsically. Music related products, live events, and movies and television programs were perceived as hedonic market offerings and valued intrinsically. However, some of the market offerings (e.g., clothing) were seen as instrumental by some respondents but as hedonic by others, indicating that at least some market offerings may be valued both extrinsically and intrinsically.

Distribution of Protocol Responses

The total number of responses for the 102 IC experiences was 506, each protocol averaging 5.0 responses. The total number of responses for the 102 HC experiences was 521, or 5.1 responses per protocol. The range in the number of responses was two to thirteen for each type of consumption experience.

The percentages of responses falling into the elements by consumption type are reported in Table 2. The results of the difference between proportions significance tests indicate significant differences in the relative salience of elements in IC and HC. Thought is clearly the most salient element for both IC and HC: it accounts for over three-fifths of IC responses, but less than one-half of HC responses. However, significant differences exist only for the Benefits category and its Functional and Psychosocial subcategories: Benefits represent over one-third of IC responses, but less than one-sixth of HC responses. Sensation also accounts for a significantly larger percentage of IC responses than HC responses.

The percentages corresponding to Feeling, Activity, and Evaluation are greater for HC than IC.

TABLE 2
Percentage of Total Responses for Elements of Instrumental and Hedonic Consumption

Element	Instrumental	Hedonic	(t-value)*
A1. Setting	5.7%	7.7%	(-1.26)
B2. Sensation	9.3%	4.8%	(2.80)++
C. Thought	62.6%	48.0%	(4.63)+++
C3. Attributes	14.6%	19.2%	(-1.94)
C3a. Concrete	4.9%	5.8%	(-0.63)
C3b. Abstract	9.7%	13.4%	(-1.82)
C4. Benefits	35.6%	15.7%	(7.21)+++
C4a. Functional	23.9%	9.4%	(6.17)+++
C4b. Psychosocial	11.7%	6.3%	(2.98)++
C5. Associations	12.5%	13.1%	(-0.28)
D. Feeling	13.4%	20.3%	(-2.91)++
D6. Emotion/Mood	9.1%	15.0%	(-2.86)++
D7. Physiological	4.3%	5.4%	(-0.80)
E8. Activity	4.0%	7.7%	(-2.50)+
F9. Evaluation	2.6%	9.2%	(-4.43)+++
10. Miscellaneous	2.4%	2.3%	(0.11)
Total (A1,B2,C,D,E8,F9,10)	100.0%	100.0%	

*Significance tests for differences between IC and HC proportions:
    +p<0.05 for a two-tailed test.
    ++p<0.01 for a two-tailed test.
    +++p<0.001 for a two-tailed test.

Although Feeling encompasses a larger percentage of HC responses than IC responses, a significant difference exists only for Emotion/Mood. The percentage of responses falling into Setting are not significantly different for IC and HC.

Discussion

The results of this study suggest that instrumental consumption is grounded in the consumer's immediate experiential world, particularly the consumer's narrow relationship with the market offering. Relative to hedonic consumption, the consumer is more likely to link the market offering with both functional and psychosocial needs, perhaps through structured thought and logical reasoning. Hedonic consumption involves experiences which seem to diffuse through the consumer's extended experiential world. Relative to instrumental consumption, the consumer is more likely to experience emotional reactions and to be actively involved in the experience. The differences between hedonic and instrumental consumption appear to relate to the type of market offering (Table 1), suggesting the possibility of placing market offerings on an instrumental/hedonic scale.

These empirical findings support a broadened definition of thought in experiential consumption (Hirschman 1985a). Further, the results and the implications derived from them support the conceptual importance which has been placed on emotion in hedonic consumption (Holbrook and Hirschman 1982; Holbrook 1986). Finally, the findings demonstrate the importance of studying instrumental consumption experiences in addition to continuing research to better understand hedonics (Hirschman and Holbrook 1982).

MEASUREMENT ISSUES

A weakness of this study relates to the limitations of consumer self-report. Although there is considerable controversy regarding the extent of self-report problems in consumer research, it is widely acknowledged that such problems exist to some degree (e.g., see Nisbett and Wilson 1977). The present study may suffer from inaccuracy as it relates to incompleteness of information (Rip 1980). As defined by Hirschman and Holbrook (1986, p. 219), the consumption experience is "an emergent property that results from a complex system of mutually overlapping interrelationships in constant reciprocal interaction with personal, environmental, and situational inputs." The many interactions inherent in the TEAV Model reflect the assumption that the whole of the experience is different than the mere sum of its constituent parts. Therefore, words can probably never adequately describe a consumption experience; in particular, having subjects provide a list of words, associations, and images is a fairly crude method of conveying the experience of consumption. Whereas complete descriptions of phenomenological consumption experiences undoubtedly would have provided richer qualitative data, the analysis of such gestalts would have required methods (e.g., see Geertz 1973) beyond the exploratory scope of this study.

A second problem relates to the fact that responses were summed across all respondents for each type of consumption experience, as opposed to treating each experience individually. Thus, the results of this study can not be applied to each and every case of experiential consumption. For example, it would be incorrect to posit that every experience of hedonic consumption involves relatively more feeling than every experience of instrumental consumption.

A third issue concerns the scope of this exploratory study, which is limited to examining various aspects of consumption within the context of the experience itself. Further research might contrast instrumental and hedonic consumption more systematically by controlling for type of market offering and personal and situational factors. The conceptual distinction suggests that, for instance, hedonically oriented eating experiences involve more emotion and less cognition than instrumentally oriented eating experiences.

CONCLUSION

The findings of this exploratory study indicate that researchers investigating experiential consumption need to be concerned with a number of factors, including the environmental context or situation (Setting), various factors relating to the consumer (Thought, Feeling, Activity, Evaluation), and the consumer's stimulation through sensory modalities (Sensation). Scholars should additionally be aware of possible variations in experiential consumption arising from differences in consumer orientation, specifically, extrinsic versus intrinsic value orientations. The study suggests that, in comparison with instrumental consumption, hedonic consumption involves relatively greater emotional processing and more activity and evaluation, but relatively less overall cognitive processing and sensory stimulation. Whereas instrumental consumption may be grounded in the consumer's immediate experiential world, hedonic consumption may diffuse through the consumer's extended experiential world.

Consumer researchers clearly need to continue striving for a broader and deeper understanding of the consumer-market offering dyad than can be understood in the limited context of behaviors such as information search and purchase. This will require "a full investigation of the relationship between people and objects" (Csikszentmihalyi and Rochberg-Halton 1981, p. 173), may involve the introduction of radically new concepts, and should -- at the very least -- provide scholars with interesting perspectives on consumption.

REFERENCES

Ahtola, Olli T. (1985), "Hedonic and Utilitarian Aspects of Behavior: An Attitudinal Perspective," in *Advances in Consumer Research*, Vol. 5, eds. Elizabeth C. Hirschman and Morris B. Holbrook, Provo, UT: Association for Consumer Research, 7-10.

Belk, Russell W. (1988), "Possessions and the Extended Self," *Journal of Consumer Research*, 15 (September), 139-168.

Csikszentmihalyi, Mihaly and Eugene Rochberg-Halton (1981), *The Meaning of Things: Domestic Symbols and the Self*, Cambridge: Cambridge University Press.

Engel, James F., David T. Kollat, and Roger D. Blackwell (1968), *Consumer Behavior*, New York: Holt, Rinehart and Winston.

Fennell, Geraldine (1985), "Things of Heaven and Earth: Phenomenology, Marketing, and Consumer Research," in *Advances in Consumer Research*, Vol. 12, eds. Elizabeth C. Hirschman and Morris B. Holbrook, Provo, UT: Association for Consumer Research, 544-549.

Geertz, Clifford (1973), *The Interpretation of Cultures: Selected Essays by Clifford Geertz*, New York: Basic Books.

Gutman, Jonathan (1982), "A Means-End Chain Model Based on Consumer Categorization Processes," *Journal of Marketing*, 46 (Spring), 60-72.

Havlena, William J. and Morris B. Holbrook (1986), "The Varieties of Consumption Experience: Comparing Two Typologies of Emotion in Consumer Behavior," *Journal of Consumer Research*, 13 (December), 394-404.

Hirschman, Elizabeth C. (1985a), "Cognitive Processes in Experiential Consumer Behavior," in *Research in Consumer Behavior: A Research Annual*, Vol. 1, ed. Jagdish N. Sheth, Greenwich, CT: JAI Press, 67-102.

_____ (1985b), "Dual Consciousness and Altered States: Implications for Consumer Research," *Journal of Business Research*, 13 (June), 223-234.

_____ and Morris B. Holbrook (1982), "Hedonic Consumption: Emerging Concepts, Methods and Propositions," *Journal of Marketing*, 46 (Summer), 92-101.

APPENDIX
Coding Scheme

This coding scheme represents the resultant framework of the iterative coding process. The inductively derived elements of consumption are indicated by capital letters, categories by numbers, and subcategories by small letters. Note that some elements are also coding categories, as indicated by a number next to the capital letter. For example, "Setting" is category "1" in addition to representing element "A".

A1. Setting (or experiential input) -- refers to objects and people in the immediate physical environment as well as atmospheric and other environmental intangibles which help describe the time and place of the experience. For example, "scissors," "beach," and "friends" are physical elements in experiential settings. "Spring," "dark theater," and "romantic dinner" are environmental intangibles.

B2. Sensation (or sensory stimulation) -- refers to the consumer's translation of the market offering through sensory processes/modalities. Hearing, seeing, tasting, smelling, and touching are various sensory modalities. "Minty" and "smells like papaya" are sensations or sensory imagery.

C. Thought -- refers to attributes, benefits, and associations in consumption.
    3. Attributes -- relate to how various aspects of the market offering are perceived.
        3a. Concrete Attributes -- refer to the physical elements and qualities or sensory descriptions associated with a specific market offering. "Tiny," "thick," and "$14" are concrete attributes.
        3b. Abstract Attributes -- refer to the nonphysical qualities associated with a specific market offering. "Good quality," "long-lasting," "reliable," and "good service" are abstract attributes.
    4. Benefits (or Disadvantages) -- relate to how the market offering may satisfy (or fail to satisfy) the consumer's personal needs and desires.
        4a. Functional Benefits (or Disadvantages) -- refer to the instrumental or special purpose needs which may be satisfied (or fail to be satisfied) through consumption of the particular market offering. Typically, these benefits relate to physiological or other life sustaining and maintenance needs. "Prevents wrinkles," "decreases use of hairspray," "gets telephone messages when not home," and "makes me thin" are functional benefits.
        4b. Psychosocial Benefits (or Disadvantages) -- refer to the psychological or social needs which may be satisfied (or fail to be satisfied) through consumption of the particular market offering. Typically, such benefits relate to self-esteem, status, or self-actualization. "Others notice it," "pleasing parents," and "broadening horizons" are psychosocial benefits.
    5. Associations -- refer to thoughts linking the consumed market offering to other market offerings, objects, symbols, concepts, people, places, or events beyond the consumption experience itself. "Victoria Principal," "the characters are similar to people I know," and "thought of good old days of high school" are examples of associational imagery.

D. Feeling -- refers to affective responses in consumption, including diverse types of feelings that consumption may bring about in the consumer or that the consumer may bring to the consumption experience.
    6. Emotion and Mood State -- refer to the relatively intense feelings the consumer experiences in consumption, or to the relatively diffuse, prolonged states of feeling which may accompany consumption. "Mad," "sad," "fear," "pride," and "envy" are emotions. "Curiosity," "mischievous," "devious," "passionate," and "adventuresome" are moods.
    7. Physiological Feeling -- refers to organically derived or organically related feelings (bodily states) in consumption. "Hungry," "thirsty," "hot," "tired," and "nauseated" are organically derived feelings. "Makes me energetic," "stimulated," and "relaxed" are organically related feelings.

E8. Activity -- relates to behaviorally related events that occur during consumption. Mental activity refers to internal dialogue consisting of a running commentary or narrative as though the consumer is relating the event to another person. "Thinking about the other person I'm talking to" and "Choosing from the best available items" are mental activities. Motor activity refers to physical movement during consumption. "Swimming in the ocean," "getting dressed up," and "made believe I played guitar and sang to it" are motor activities.

F9. Evaluation (or experiential output) -- refers to an overall appraisal of a market offering in the context of the particular consumption experience. Evaluative responses may relate to market offering use, such as "satisfied," "pleased with results," or "happy with the purchase." Also, evaluative responses may relate to market offering appreciation, such as "fulfilling," "fun," "entertaining," or "incredible."

10. Miscellaneous -- responses which do not fit into the categories and subcategories defined above.

_____ and Morris B. Holbrook (1986), "Expanding the Ontology and Methodology of Research on the Consumption Experience," in *Perspectives on Methodology in Consumer Research*, eds. David Brinberg and Richard J. Lutz, New York: Springer-Verlag, 213-251.

Holbrook, Morris B. (1986), "Emotion in the Consumption Experience: Toward a New Model of the Human Consumer," in *The Role of Affect in Consumer Behavior: Emerging Theories and Applications*, eds. Robert A. Peterson, Wayne D. Hoyer, and William R. Wilson, Lexington, MA: D.C. Heath.

_____, Robert W. Chestnut, Terence A. Oliva, and Eric A. Greenleaf (1984), "Play as a Consumption Experience: The Roles of Emotions, Performance, and Personality in the Enjoyment of Games," *Journal of Consumer Research*, 11 (September), 728-739.

_____ and Kim P. Corfman (1985), "Quality and Value in the Consumption Experience: Phaedrus Rides Again," in *Perceived Quality: How Consumers View Stores and Merchandise*, eds. Jacob Jacoby and Jerry C. Olson, Lexington, MA: D.C. Heath, 31-57.

_____ and Elizabeth C. Hirschman (1982), "The Experiential Aspects of Consumption: Consumer Fantasies, Feelings, and Fun," *Journal of Consumer Research*, 9 (September), 132-140.

Howard, John A. and Jagdish N. Sheth (1969), *The Theory of Buyer Behavior*, New York: John Wiley & Sons.

Koch, Sigmund (1956), "Behavior as 'Intrinsically' Regulated: Work Notes Towards A Pre-Theory of Phenomena Called 'Motivational'," in *Nebraska Symposium on Motivation*, ed. Marshall R. Jones, Lincoln, NE: University of Nebraska Press, 42-87.

Maslow, Abraham H. (1962), *Toward a Psychology of Being*, Princeton, NJ: D. Van Nostrand.

Mehrabian, Albert and James A. Russell (1974), *An Approach to Environmental Psychology*, Cambridge, MA: MIT Press.

Nicosia, Francesco M. (1966), *Consumer Decision Processes*, Englewood Cliffs, NJ: Prentice-Hall.

Nisbett, Richard and Timothy D. Wilson (1977), "Telling More Than We Know: Verbal Reports on Mental Processes," *Psychological Review*, 84, 231-259.

Peter, J. Paul and Jerry C. Olson (1989), *Consumer Behavior: Marketing Strategy Perspectives*, Homewood, IL: Irwin.

Plutchik, Robert (1980), *Emotion: A Psychoevolutionary Synthesis*, New York: Harper & Row.

Richardson, Alan (1984), *The Experiential Dimension of Psychology*, Queensland: University of Queensland Press.

Rip, Peter (1980), "The Informational Basis of Self-Reports: A Preliminary Report," in *Advances in Consumer Research*, Vol. 7, ed. Jerry C. Olson, Ann Arbor, MI: Association for Consumer Research, 140-145.

Schachtel, Ernest G. (1959), *Metamorphosis: On the Development of Affect, Perception, Attention, and Memory*, New York: Basic.

Tellegen, Auke (1981), "Practicing the Two Disciplines for Relaxation and Enlightenment: Comment on 'Role of the Feedback Signal in Electromyograph Biofeedback: The Relevance of Attention' by Qualls and Sheehan," *Journal of Experimental Psychology*, 110 (June), 217-226.

Thompson, Craig J., William B. Locander, and Howard R. Pollio (1989), "Putting Consumer Experience Back into Consumer Research: The Philosophy and Method of Existential-Phenomenology," *Journal of Consumer Research*, 16 (September), 133-146.

Tse, David K., Russell W. Belk, and Nan Zhou (1989), "Becoming a Consumer Society: A Longitudinal and Cross-Cultural Content Analysis of Print Ads from Hong Kong, the People's Republic of China, and Taiwan," *Journal of Consumer Research*, 15 (March), 457-472.

Zajonc, Robert B. (1982), "Feeling and Thinking: Preferences Need No Inferences," *American Psychologist*, 35 (February), 151-175.

_____ and Hazel Markus (1982), "Affective and Cognitive Factors in Preferences," *Journal of Consumer Research*, 9 (September), 123-131.

A Meaning-Based Framework for the Study of Consumer-Object Relations

Susan Fournier, University of Florida

ABSTRACT

This paper proposes a typology for the categorization of consumption objects that builds upon learning in two emergent areas of consumer research -- namely, consumer-object attachments and the semiotic motive. The conceptual scheme is based on the view that three underlying dimensions of psychological meaning [i.e. (1) objective versus symbolic center of meaning, (2) shared versus personalized source of meaning, and (3) high versus low emotional response] interact to determine the roles played by various consumption objects in the lives of their users. The eight categories of objects resulting from this 2x2x2 model are described and research implications of adopting the meaning-based framework are discussed.

INTRODUCTION

The concept of consumer behavior has been broadened greatly in the past decade to accommodate extensions suggested in the experiential view of consumption (Hirschman and Holbrook 1982; Holbrook and Hirschman 1982) and to incorporate insights generated through alternative disciplinary perspectives and paradigms (Csikszentmihalyi and Rochberg-Halton 1981; McCracken 1986; Mick 1986). This broadened view has sparked a renewed interest in the subjective and emotive aspects of consumption. Of particular interest are studies of the concept of product meaning (Friedman 1986; Hirschman 1980; Kleine and Kernan 1988; McCracken 1986; Mick 1986) and investigations into the various emotional and functional roles played by consumption objects (Belk 1988; Furby 1978; Holman 1986; Myers 1985; Prentice 1987; Shimp and Madden 1988; Solomon 1983, 1988; Wallendorf and Arnould 1988).

Existing product classification schemes and typologies can be enriched by considering the experiential/symbolic perspective and applying the learning generated in the above-mentioned streams of research. Consideration of theories of product meaning and consumer-object attachment can yield a revised classification scheme that is not only anchored in important consumer behavior constructs, but also exhibits increased consumer relevance and more extensive coverage of the range of possible consumer-object relations.

In the sections to follow, the theoretical foundation for a meaning-based framework for the categorization of consumption objects is developed. First, existing schemes for the classification of consumer products are reviewed and findings concerning product roles and functions are synthesized. Theories concerning the psychological bases of product meaning are then incorporated as a means of identifying the dimensions that underlie the various product roles and functions. A typology of consumer-object relationships that builds from these foundational components is then presented. Benefits of the framework and implications of adopting the revised perspective are discussed in a concluding section.

PRODUCT TYPOLOGIES AND CLASSIFICATION SCHEMES

As consumer research has evolved from an emphasis on the objective and functional to a consideration of the subjective, the emotive and the symbolic, so too has the study of the product classification issue. Table 1 summarizes some of the major product classification approaches and schemes that have been advanced in the marketing literature.

Original classification schemes (Copeland 1923; Kotler 1984) and their more recent extensions (Holbrook and Howard 1977; Murphy and Enis 1986) are particularly functional and descriptive in their orientation. They adhere to an objective conceptualization of the product as a "bundle of attributes and benefits." Generally, products are grouped in terms of underlying effort and risk dimensions reflective of consumer-perceived product importance. While these initial schemes indeed have their uses, they are limited by their driving strategic objectives and by their foundational conceptions of the product as a "bundle of utility."

A needed breakthrough in perspective is provided in the hedonic, experiential view of consumption. Those adopting this perspective stress that consumer objects may be grouped according to the nature of the consumption experience (Hirschman and Holbrook 1982; Holbrook and Hirschman 1982; MacInnis and Jaworski 1989). It is acknowledged that all products contain degrees of both hedonic and utilitarian elements, which allows for the placement of objects along a hedonic/utilitarian continuum.

Holman (1986) proposes a typology of products that captures the exact nature and character of these emotional experiences. Arrayed along a continuum reflecting the intensity and centrality of the emotional experience, she goes beyond the utilitarian/ experiential dichotomy to present five categories of products that range from background props to sources of emotions.

Another way to qualify the hedonic/utilitarian continuum is to focus on kind rather than degree, more fully explicating the specific symbolic, experiential and utilitarian needs that are served by the product. A call for categorization schemes that consider such needs and value expressions has in fact been put forth in the literature (Sheth 1980; Upah and Sudman 1979). Studies of consumer-object relations specifically address this objective. Although these investigations have been undertaken from diverse research perspectives, there exists a great deal of agreement regarding the primary roles played by products in consumer's lives.

TABLE 1
A Synthesis of Product Classification Approaches Presented in the Literature

View of Product: Functional -- Symbolic

Product Grouping Basis:	Benefits Provided	Cost (Risk, Effort)	Usage Experience	Functions Served
Classification Schemes:	Product Class Definition (ex. cleaners)	Convenience Preference Shopping Speciality	Utilitarian Hedonic/ Experiential	<u>Functional</u> Control Transitional Developmental Need-Based
		Convenience Package Goods Services Durables	Background Mediators Enhancers Self-Expressions Emotion Objects	<u>Expressive</u> Self, Family, Group, Role Identity <u>Experiential</u> Arousal Mood Management
Sources:	Kotler (1984)	Copeland (1923) Holbrook and Howard (1977) Murphy and Enis (1986)	Hirschman and Holbrook (1982) Holbrook and Hirschman (1982) Holman (1986)	Belk (1988) Csikszentmihalyi and Rochberg-Halton (1981) Furby (1978) MacInnis and Jaworski (1988) Myers (1985) Park et al (1986) Prentice (1987) Settle and Alreck (1989) Solomon (1985, 1988) Wallendorf and Arnould (1988)

The purely *functional* role served by many consumer objects is widely acknowledged (Csikszentmihalyi and Rochberg-Halton 1981; Furby 1978; Holbrook and Hirschman 1982; Holman 1980; MacInnis and Jaworski 1989; Park et al 1986; Prentice 1987). Products play a functional role in the life of the consumer by fulfilling necessary functions, permitting control of the environment and allowing the solution of externally-imposed problems.

Other products and services play a predominantly *experiential* role in the everyday life of the consumer. Such consumer objects provide sensory pleasure, aesthetic enjoyment, entertainment and generalized emotional arousal (Csikszentmihalyi and Rochberg-Halton 1981; Hirschman and Holbrook 1982; MacInnis and Jaworski 1989; Myers 1985; Park et al 1986; Prentice 1987; Settle and Alreck 1989; Wallendorf and Arnould 1988). They may also play the role of pacifiers and comforters (Furby 1978; Myers 1985), providing the user with a sense of security and feelings of warmth.

A third role consistently uncovered for consumer products concerns the function of *identity*. Products perform an identity function at the individual level by serving as expressions of self-concept and individuality (Belk 1988; Csikszentmihalyi and Rochberg-Halton 1981; Furby 1978; Holman 1985; MacInnis and Jaworski 1989; Myers 1985; Settle and Alreck 1989), by providing linkages with childhood and family (Belk 1988; Csikszentmihalyi and Rochberg-Halton 1981), by tangibilizing past experiences and relationships (Prentice 1987; Wallendorf and Arnould 1988) and by acting as extensions of self (Belk 1988). Products can help in the creation and management of identities at the group and society levels as well by serving as unambiguous announcements of role and position (Prentice 1987; Solomon 1985, 1988).

For consumer research and advertising practice, perhaps the most useful and insightful of the product classification schemes are those anchored in constructs of product role and psychological meaning. Such frameworks reveal the essence of the connection between the consumer and the product. They capture the "key consumer insights" that make for great advertising. Typologies that explicitly recognize the functional, experiential and identity functions served by products move us closer to our general goal as consumer researchers; namely, to understand the meaning of the product in relation to the lives of its users (Levy, 1981).

The research on consumer-object relations reported above, while addressing this objective, lacks a wholistic character. Studies tend to focus exclusively on one function or one need (e.g., role facilitators) or are concerned only with a sub-segment of possessions (e.g., "favorite things"). An integration and synthesis of this research can yield a more comprehensive typology of consumption objects that directly considers the nature of the consumer-object interaction.

To be truly useful and insightful, however, the typology should go beyond a simple categorization of the roles and functions served by consumer objects to consider the dynamics that give rise to the overall structure of consumer-object relations. What drives the nature of the consumer-object interaction? What are the fundamental components of the various consumer-object relations? How do these different dimensions interact to determine the quality of the consumer-object experience? Questions such as these can be addressed through the literature on the nature and structure of product meaning.

DIMENSIONS OF MEANING

Research highlights three dimensions that collectively characterize the meaning of a given object: tangibility, commonality and emotionality. After each of these dimensions is described in terms of function and dynamics, their joint determination of the various categories of consumer-object interaction is illustrated.

Tangibility: The Attribute Basis of Product Meaning

A primary dimension of meaning discussed in the literature is tangibility (Friedman 1986; Hirschman 1980; Holbrook et al 1986). This concerns whether the attribute basis of meaning is primarily objective, tangible and verifiable through the senses or whether it is primarily subjective, interpreted through experience and dependent upon associations. While it is recognized that all objects will have both subjective and objective components of meaning, it is felt that one or the other of these components will be particularly salient such that classification of objects as utilitarian or symbolic becomes meaningful.

Tangibility refers to the object's primary center of meaning. Specifically, it concerns whether meaning is resident in the object itself or in the mind of the user. Systematic differences in process dynamics and consumer response will be evidenced for objects that are objective and tangible versus those that are subjective and symbolic. The reader is referred to writings on experiential and hedonic consumption for a thorough discussion of these distinctions and manifestations (Hirschman and Holbrook 1982; Holbrook and Hirschman 1982).

The Emotional Dimension of Product Meaning

Since Osgood's (1952) original formulation, it has been accepted that meaning is comprised of "a bundle of components" including experiences, images and feelings in addition to information. These components are so infused with affect that the emotional component has come to represent a vital and integral portion of the meaning of an object (Hirschman 1980). In fact, research attempts to disentangle the emotional side of product meaning from its objective counterparts have been criticized for their artificiality and lack of validity (Hirschman 1980).

Literature that has considered the emotional component of the consumer-object interaction suggests that "emotion" includes aspects of arousal and felt experience (Hirschman and Holbrook 1982; Holbrook and Hirschman 1982) as well as investment or degree of emotional attachment (Holman 1986; Shimp and Madden 1988). Consumption objects can thus be arrayed along a continuum of generalized emotional response that ranges from low to high intensity. Systematic differences in process will be exhibited by low versus high response objects.

High intensity objects will generally be associated with identified and labelled emotional experiences such as enjoyment, serenity or excitement. These emotional experiences are not merely consequences of consumption; they are the ends sought in consumption. The emotional experiences associated with low intensity objects, on the other hand, may be better characterized as the simple affective reactions captured in constructs of attitude and preference. The consumption experiences for high versus low intensity objects may also require different types and levels of mental activity (e.g., fantasy, imagery, right-brain processing) (Hirschman and Holbrook 1982).

The Commonality Dimension of Product Meaning

A third dimension of meaning discussed in the literature is that of commonality, the degree to which meaning possesses a shared versus individualized character. To allow for effective communications and to serve the function of integration into society, meaning must be shared by members of the culture at some basic level (Blumer 1969; McCracken 1986). Theoreticians also stress the personalized aspects of meaning, however, recognizing that meaning is created by the user through experience and interaction (Blumer 1969; Hirschman 1986). Through various rituals in which consumers interact with the products of culture, meaning is granted a unique, individual character

(Belk 1988; McCracken 1986). In this manner, the equally-valued function of differentiation from society is performed. As with tangibility, it can be speculated that one or the other of these components will be particularly salient such that meaning becomes primarily shared or individualized.

With respect to consumer objects, commonality refers to the source that is most responsible for the assignment of meaning to the object. This source may be cultural (e.g., advertising, fashion systems) or personal (e.g., historical experience and reflection). The dynamics of meaning creation and the processes of consumer-object interaction may vary systematically as a function of these different sources.

Meaning transfer from the product to the consumer is likely to be a more reinforcing and on-going process for personalized objects than it will be for cultural objects. The temporal quality exhibited by many objects with personalized sources of meaning (e.g., the favorite sweatshirt from college, the china that Grandmother used, the ring received on wedding day) encourages on-going reflection by the owner/user, resulting in knowledge structures that are more dynamic and evolutionary.

The forces that drive the meaning creation process may also differ by source of meaning. Advertiser-constructed messages may be more dominant in the creation of meaning for objects with a cultural center while empathic responses and the generation of self-referent ties may be more likely to govern the creation of personalized meaning. Because of these ties with the self, objects with personalized meaning centers may enjoy higher levels of enduring involvement, greater salience and evocation potential, and stronger motivations for processing and elaboration.

Interactions between people and objects in the form of consumption rituals (McCracken 1986) may also vary as a function of meaning source. First, the goals of rituals for personalized and cultural consumer objects may differ. With personalized objects, the objective may be to supercharge the good through the process of reflection while with cultural objects, the objective may be to supercharge the owner through the usage experience. Moreover, the nature of possession rituals (McCracken 1986) may differ by meaning source. With personalized objects, private encounters will likely dominate, as with cleaning and periods of contemplation. With cultural objects, the ritual may be more public, involving display and overt comparison.

A MEANING-BASED FRAMEWORK FOR CONSUMER-OBJECT RELATIONS

Eight categories of consumption objects can readily be identified in terms of these primary dimensions of meaning such that each exhibits a characteristic pattern of tangibility, commonality and emotionality (See Figure I). It is important to remember that in reality, the eight categories represent positions on the set of three continuous dimensions rather than eight distinctive *types* of consumer objects. However, as a necessary simplification for presentational and managerial purposes, the continuous dimensions are represented as binary components, yielding a 2x2x2 matrix.

These eight categories are elaborated in terms of content, role and function below. It is important to recognize that the proposed typology is consumer-dependent, not product-driven. As such, the categories are not static in terms of their specific product members. Individual variation in terms of cultural background and experience (Hirschman 1979), the polysemic character of the meaning of objects and the context-dependency of interpretation preclude the absolute assignment of individual objects to categories. Product examples are included only for heuristic purposes.

Objects of Utility. The significance of objects of utility is intimately tied to characteristic attributes and benefits and the inherent need satisfaction these provide. Product usage is often driven by externally-generated problems in need of a solution. Examples include necessities (e.g., blankets) and objects that allow manipulation and control of the environment (e.g., can openers and air conditioners).

Objects of Action. In contrast, the value of these objects lies not in the products themselves, but in the experiences and emotions they allow. The primary function of objects of action is to provide the user with stimulation, excitement and arousal. Included in the category are objects that can create moods (e.g., stereos), provide escapes (e.g., sports cars) and invite fantasies (e.g. romance novels).

Objects of Appreciation. These objects are experienced and appreciated as a whole. As with objects of action, the goal of their consumption is to provide the user with a quality emotional experience. The experience, however, is primarily one of enjoyment or pleasure, rather than general arousal. Moreover, the object is pivotal and central to that experience; it is not simply instrumental to that experience. Examples include the performing arts, household decorative items and fine wines.

Objects of Transition. These items provide their users with feelings of serenity, security, warmth and comfort in times of change. While encountered most frequently in childhood, these objects appear periodically throughout the life cycle to help their users negotiate various role transitions (Myers 1985). Representative objects include role facilitators (eg. the business suit) and steadfast reminders of happy times (eg. old college sweatshirts).

Objects of Childhood. A special category is included for objects that were once used during childhood and are picked up again in later years. These objects are broadly reminiscent of the childhood period, having served a function as background objects during that time. They are not tied to specific memories of people and events, nor are they regarded as purposive transitional objects.

FIGURE 1
A Meaning-Based Framework of Consumer-Object Relations

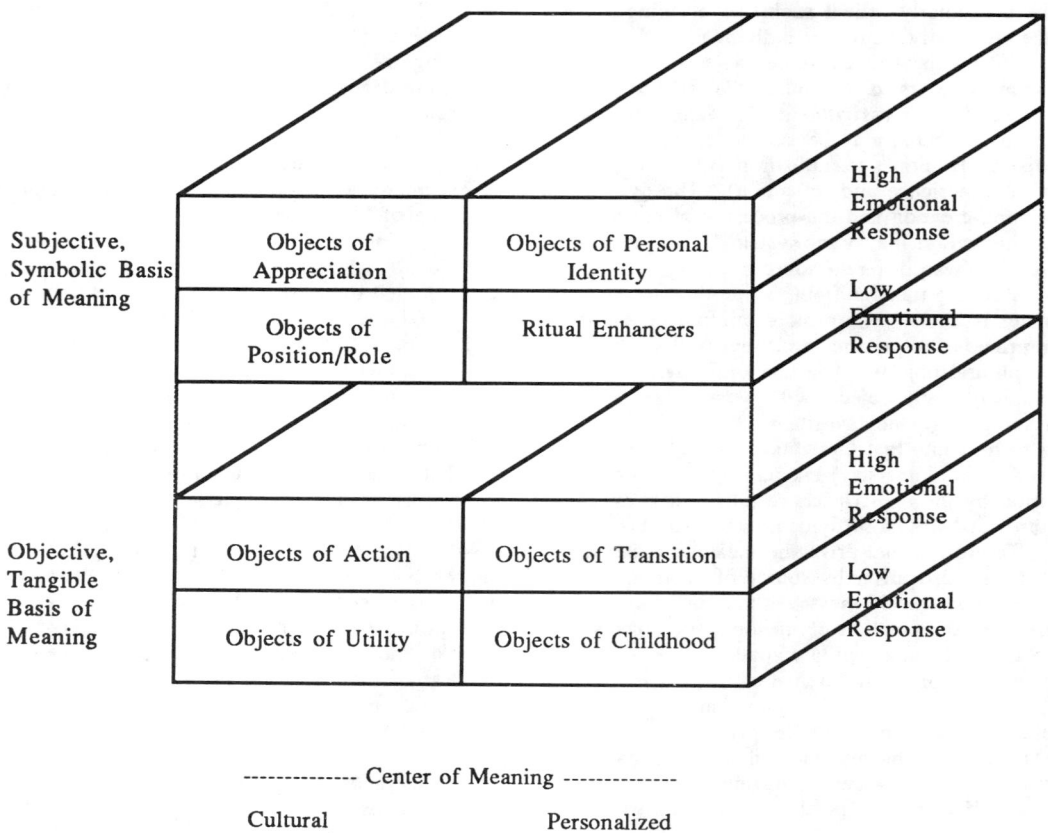

They are simply imbued with feelings of familiarity and, as a consequence, enjoy a favorable predisposition for response. Examples include "the brand that mom always used" and TV shows enjoyed as a kid.

Ritual Enhancers. These objects are associated with habituated behaviors and personal rituals, serving as mediators of valued personal experiences. The meaning of ritual enhancers is highly dependent on context; apart from the ritual, the object has little or no significance to the user. The meaning is also highly subjective, derived from the totality of props present in the situation and symbolic of the ritual that is being enacted. An example is the cup of coffee or newspaper consumed as part of the morning wake-up ritual. Apart from this setting, the coffee and paper hold little meaning for the user. Within the setting however, the objects are highly personal and symbolic.

Objects of Personal Identity. Objects of personal identity make statements about the actual or ideal self and telegraph the values that are centrally held by the individual. Their use and display serves the function of individuation within society. Tangible records of accomplishments (eg. diplomas), reflections of goals and interests (eg. bicycling gear), creative outlets (eg. woodworking tools), and symbols of aspiration (eg. books on sailing) are primary examples of these expressive products. Other objects of personal identity serve a more contemplative function. These objects are tangible representations of meaningful and influential events, relationships and experiences past. The objects per se have little inherent meaning; their value lies in the rich storehouses of emotions, feelings and knowledge that are associated with them. Examples are gifts, photos and family heirlooms.

Objects of Position and Role. These objects make statements regarding self at the cultural level, serving the function of integration into society. Included are status symbols (eg. travel experiences) and role-related product clusters (Solomon 1988) such as those employed in enactment of the "Yuppie" role.

BENEFITS AND EXTENSIONS OF THE PROPOSED FRAMEWORK

The proposed typology offers several advantages over existing frameworks. First, it goes further in explaining the meaning of consumer objects than does a single continuum of experience or a scheme based on functional product attributes by better capturing the essence of the consumer-object interaction. In doing so, the scheme also offers greater consumer relevance. Both of these advantages support increased utility as a strategy development tool for the advertising practitioner.

The proposed typology also offers benefits of broader coverage. In identifying eight qualitatively-different object categories, it goes beyond existing schemes to cover a broader range of possible consumer-object relations. Moreover, it highlights for study object categories that have previously been ignored in the literature (e.g., objects of childhood and ritual enhancers).

The level of analysis of the proposed framework also offers benefits over existing approaches. While the meanings assigned to products may in fact vary across individuals and product categories, the emotions and values to which these meanings are connected are likely to be more stable and enduring. The proposed categories should be more productive of generalizable knowledge regarding product roles than are categories defined on artificial, objective bases.

The framework also offers general benefits versus the simple continuum approach to the product categorization issue. In general, typologies are useful for theory building in that they highlight similarities and differences among phenomena that are useful in selecting elements for a model. They also are useful in their integration and summary functions, providing valuable guidance for future research efforts.

Lastly, the framework serves to suggest several interesting areas for future research. The framework could be used to study the ways in which consumers use products to structure their realities. Personal and household product inventories could be analyzed for their "mix" of object categories to identify a typology of "consumption lifestyles" (Sheth 1980; Upah and Sudman 1979). Changes in portfolio mixes over time could also be studied for an interesting developmental perspective on the roles and functions of product inventories. Relationships among portfolio mixes, personalities, functional attitudes and instrumental values could also be examined for insight into the ways that these constructed realities reflect and shape general perceptual and psychological processes.

The consumer-dependent quality of the framework also suggests a new approach to segmentation issues. "Meaning-based" segments, i.e. groups based on agreements regarding the roles and functions served by products, could be identified. Because of their consideration of idiosyncracies in processes of perception and interpretation, these segments may perhaps be more reliable and valid than those based on simple usage habits.

These are the types of questions that could be pursued as we probe further into the relationships consumers have with the products they own and use. While the proposed framework offers but one approach to this important and complex issue, it does appear to offer some insight. To this extent, it may indeed prove a useful tool for research.

REFERENCES

Belk, Russell (1988), "Possessions and the Extended Self," *Journal of Consumer Research*, 15 (September), 139-168

Blumer, Herbert (1969), *Symbolic Interactionism: Perspectives and Method*, Englewood Cliffs, NJ: Prentice-Hall

Copeland, Melvin (1923), "The Relation of Consumer's Buying Habits to Marketing Methods," *Harvard Business Review*, 1 (April), 282-289

Csikszentmihalyi, Mihalyi and Eugene Rochberg-Halton (1981), *The Meaning of Things: Domestic Symbols and the Self*, London: Cambridge University Press

Friedman, Roberto (1986), "Psychological Meaning of Products: Identification and Marketing Applications," *Psychology and Marketing*, 3 (Spring), 1-15

Furby, Lita (1978), "Possessions: Toward a Theory of their Meaning and Function throughout the Life Cycle," in *Life Span Development and Behavior*, P. Baltes (ed), New York: Academic Press, 297-336

Hirschman, Elizabeth (1980), "Attributes of Attributes and Layers of Meaning," in *Advances in Consumer Research, Volume 7*, Jerry Olson (ed), Ann Arbor, MI: Association for Consumer Research, 7-11

Hirschman, Elizabeth (1986), "The Creation of Product Symbolism," in *Advances in Consumer Research, Volume 13*, Rich Lutz (ed), Provo, UT: Association for Consumer Research, 327-331

Hirschman, Elizabeth and M. Holbrook (1982) "Hedonic Consumption: Emerging Concepts, Methods and Propositions," *Journal of Marketing*, 46(3), 92-101

Holbrook, Morris and E. Hirschman (1982), "The Experiential Aspects of Consumptions: Fantasies, Feelings and Fun," *Journal of Consumer Research*, 9 (September), 132-140

Holbrook, Morris and John Howard (1977), "Frequently Purchased Non-Durable Goods and Services," in *Selected Aspects of Consumer Behavior*, R. Ferber (ed), Washington DC: National Science Foundation, 189-222

Holman, Rebecca (1986), "Advertising and Emotionality," in *The Role of Affect in Consumer Behavior*, R. Peterson, W. Hoyer and W. Wilson (eds), Lexington: D.C. Heath and Co, 119-140

Kleine, Robert and J. Kernan (1988), "Measuring the Meaning of Consumption Objects: An Empirical Investigation," in *Advances in Consumer Research, Volume 15*, M. Houston (ed), Provo, UT: Association for Consumer Research, 498-504

Kotler, Phillip (1984), *Marketing Management: A Planning Approach*, Englewood Cliffs, NJ: Prentice-Hall

Levy, Sidney (1981), "Interpreting Consumer Mythology: A Structural Approach to Consumer Behavior," *Journal of Marketing*, 45 (Summer), 49-61

MacInnis, Deborah and Bernard Jaworski (1988), "Information Processing from Advertisements: Toward an Integrative Framework," *Journal of Marketing*, 53 (October), 1-23

McCracken, G. (1986), "Culture and Consumption: A Theoretical Account of the Structure and Movement of Cultural Meaning of Consumer Goods," *Journal of Consumer Research*, 13 (June), 71-84

Mick, David Glen (1986), "Consumer Research and Semiotics: Exploring the Morphology of Signs, Symbols and Significance," *Journal of Consumer Research*, 13 (Sept), 196-213

Murphy, Patrick and Ben Enis (1986), "Classifying Products Strategically," *Journal of Marketing*, 50 (July), 24-42

Myers, E. (1985), "Phenomenological Analysis of the Importance of Special Possessions: An Exploratory Study," in *Advances in Consumer Research, Volume 12*, E. Hirschman and M. Holbrook (eds), Provo, Utah: Association for Consumer Research, 560-565

Osgood, C.E. (1952), "The Nature and Measurement of Meaning," *Psychology Bulletin*, 49, 197-237

Park, C. Whan, Bernard Jaworski and Deborah MacInnis (1986), "Strategic Brand Concept-Image Management," *Journal of Marketing*, 50 (October), 135-145

Prentice, D. (1987), "Psychological Correspondence of Possessions, Attitudes and Values," *Journal of Personality and Social Psychology*, 53(6), 993-1003

Settle, Robert and Pamela Alreck (1989), *Why They Buy*, New York: John Wiley & Sons

Sheth, Jagdish (1980), "The Surpluses and Shortages in Consumer Behavior Research," *Journal of the Academy of Marketing Science*, 7 (Fall), 414-427

Shimp, Terence and Thomas Madden (1988), "Consumer-Object Relations: A Conceptual Framework Based Analogously on Sternberg's Triangular Theory of Love," in *Advances in Consumer Research, Volume 15*, M. Houston (ed), Provo, UT: Association for Consumer Research, 163-168

Solomon, M. (1983), "The Role of Products as Social Stimuli: A Symbolic Interactionism Perspective," *Journal of Consumer Research*, 10 (December), 319-329

Solomon, Michael (1988), "Mapping Product Constellations: A Social Categorization Approach to Consumption Symbolism," *Psychology and Marketing*, 5 (Fall), 233-258

Upah, Gregory and Seymour Sudman (1979), "The Consumer Expenditure Survey: Prospects for Consumer Research," *Advances in Consumer Research, Volume 6*, William Wilkie (ed), Ann Arbor: Association for Consumer Research, 262-266

Wallendorf, M. and E. Arnould (1988), "My Favorite Things: A Cross-Cultural Inquiry into Object Attachment, Possessiveness, and Social Linkage," *Journal of Consumer Research*, 14 (March), 531-547

Jungian Analysis and Psychological Types: An Interpretive Approach to Consumer Choice Behavior

Stephen J. Gould, Rutgers University

Further development with respect to personality in consumer behavior may depend on the better understanding of holistic psychological types. This paper discusses how Jung's (1971) typology of psychological types can be helpful in this regard. Two important dimensions of this typology for choice behavior are considered extensively: (1) sensing-intuiting which relates to perception and information processing and (2) thinking-feeling which relates to how an individual makes choices and decisions. The analysis shows how the psychological type of the consumer can play a determinant role in his or her everyday decision making.

An individual's behavior is a function both of his or her individual personal characteristics (P) and the surrounding environment (E), B = f(P,E), as Lewin (1935) formulated the equation. Personality as a key element of P does not seem to have been a rewarding area of investigation for consumer researchers. Kassarjian (1971) is often cited in this regard. But Kassarjian (p. 416) made an interesting point supporting further personality research, which seems to have been overlooked, i.e. "We seem to feel that the only function of science and research is to predict rather than to understand, to persuade rather than to appreciate." His words, which indicate a need for a change in attitude toward the goals of personality research rather than an abandonment of it, seem prophetic today in light of the recent movement toward interpretive approaches in consumer research. Personality as a key and highly individual construct needs to be reconsidered theoretically and in a more holistic fashion in light of these new approaches.

One important beginning in this direction was made by Albanese (1987). According to him, personality is a key factor in understanding the economic behavior of individual consumers. He demonstrated how personality development is related to ordinal utility theory in that, "The highest position along the personality continuum strikingly supports ordinal utility theory; i.e., the economic postulate of rationality, which requires consistent consumption behavior, is supported by this position on the personality continuum" (Albanese 1987, p. 14). Consumer behavior at the intermediate range of personality development is viewed by Albanese as unstable and inconsistent and at the lowest ranges, as irrational. In terms of integrating personality and consumer preference, this approach serves as a departure for the further consideration of a personality approach to consumer preferences, namely a Jungian approach.

While as suggested by Albanese, consumers will differ in terms of metapreferences on the basis of their development, there are further elements of differentiation which need to be accounted for. For example, two people at about the same level of personality development in Albanese's conception may still differ, radically, in terms of their metapreferences and also in terms of manifest behavior. These individual differences reflect a person's psychological type (Jung 1971). It has been suggested in a number of contexts that a person's type may influence his preferences and decision-making style (Hirschman 1985; Nutt 1986). The purpose of this paper is to consider theoretically how psychological type plays an important role in determining consumer preference structure.

THE THEORY OF PSYCHOLOGICAL TYPES

Modern psychological type theory is derived from Jung and largely follows the format established in the Myers-Briggs type indicator (Myers 1980; Myers and McCaulley 1985). The Myers-Briggs typology identifies four important dimensions of personality which determine a person's response to the world: (1) sensing-intuiting, (2) thinking-feeling, (3) extroversion-introversion, and (4) judging-perceiving. According to Myers (1980), the first dimension reflects the individual's way of finding out about the world (information processing) while the second represents his or her decision style. Generally, an individual has a preference for one or the other of each the opposing poles of each dimension. For example, a person will prefer to use either sensing or else intuiting in processing information about the world.

Sensing (S) and intuiting (N) relate to how a person finds out about the world. A sensing person is more oriented to sensory information and prefers to process information in that way. The intuitive person, on the other hand, tends to prefer using his or her intuition and inspiration in developing informational input. The sensing type is practical, good with detail and numbers, and likes tangible objects; the intuitive type finds patterns and trends in things and is quite at home with intangibles.

Thinking (T) and feeling (F) are opposite ways of making decisions. Thinking is based on logic and leaves less room for human emotion. The feeling type makes decisions not so much on logic as on what is important to oneself, that is matters which reflect personal values and also consideration of significant others. The thinking type is 'objective' and the feeling type is 'subjective.' It should be noted that feeling in Jungian (1971) terms involves a valuation process of acceptance (liking) or rejection (disliking) apart from our usual understanding of feeling as affect. Jung (1971, p. 435) designates affect as something different from feeling. He calls it "feeling-sensation" in which both feeling and sensation are combined.

Another dimension relates to the individual's orientation to the world- whether he is more extroverted (E) or introverted (I). The extroverted person is oriented to the external world of people and objects while the introvert is generally more comfortable with the internal world of his or her own mind. The final dimension of the typology relates to how a person views the outside world- whether in a judging (J) or perceiving (P) mode. Judging individuals want to control and regulate life based on their judgements as to how it should be. Perceiving individuals, on the other hand, are relatively flexible and want more to adapt to life and understand it rather than control it.

These four dimensions of personality are integrated into a personality typology of sixteen psychological types. Thus for example, an individual may be an ESTJ (extroverted, sensing, thinking and judging). This individual would be a down to earth, realist type. On the other hand, an INFP, is more adaptive, flexible, and intuitive in his or her approach to the world. The most common way to measure these types has been to use the Myers-Briggs Type Indicator which has been found by some to be valid and reliable (Carlyn 1977; Nutt 1986), although consumer research need not necessarily be restricted to that particular scale. It is beyond our scope here to discuss each of the sixteen subtypes in detail but instead we shall draw on this typology more parsimoniously in showing how consumers manifest different tastes. Thus, the remainder of this paper will focus on the subset of dimensions which are most relevant to the economic dimensions of consumer behavior theory, i.e. processing of information (sensing-intuiting) and decision-making (thinking-feeling). Jung (1971) considered these dimensions to be the basic psychological functions of the individual. Myers also considered these to be the most important dimensions by which to group individuals (Myers and McCaulley 1985) and there is a great deal of precedent for considering them based on previous research (e.g. Hirschman 1985; Mitroff and Kilmann 1975).

PSYCHOLOGICAL TYPE AND THE DEVELOPMENT OF PREFERENCES

A typology of psychological type, based on sensing-intuiting and thinking-feeling, consists of four groups of individuals: (1) sensing-thinking (STs), (2) sensing-feeling (SFs), (3) intuiting-thinking (NTs), and (4) intuiting-feeling (NFs). The ST is perhaps the epitome of the individual consumer whom classical and neo-classical economists have theorized about. In fact, it could be argued that as they are most probably STs themselves (based on Mitroff and Kilmann's (1975) and Hirschman's (1985) studies of researchers), they have projected their own behavior onto other personality types. The ST comes closest to their assumptions about rational, economic man in that he or she does try to logically and empirically make rational decisions. Of the four types considered here, the ST will weigh economic considerations most heavily in making a purchase decision and thus will tend to be more price sensitive than others especially in light of his or her tendency toward the quantitative side of things. The ST is also the epitome of the problem solving cognitive man who goes through a chain of search and information processing in order to arrive at a solution. The ST has been found in a management setting to be quite risk averse and averse to acting in making a decision (Henderson and Nutt 1980). STs will identify with material objects and in that sense, may be said to be highly materialistic.

As an economic decision maker, the SF is also quite empirical and data oriented. However, the SF differs from the ST in that he or she make decisions more subjectively, based on things that matter in the sense of personal values as opposed to logic (Myers 1980). The SF is more person oriented than the ST and is more likely to include consideration of others in his or her decisions. He or she may tend to share risk with others (Henderson and Nutt 1980). The SF, as the ST, identifies with material objects but is more likely to be conscious of how they influence his or her relations with others and even to be status conscious.

The NT tends to be holistic in orientation, that is to take a broad view of their particular situation (Mitroff and Kilmann 1975). While intuitive and relying on imagination, they tend to use logic in their decision making. They can be quite theoretical and even speculative (Mitroff and Kilmann 1975; Myers 1980). Mitroff and Kilmann suggest that NTs have extended time horizons while STs and SFs have short ones. We would also expect that both NTs and NFs are more likely to use mental imagery than STs and SFs who would tend to rely on concrete imagery which can they tangibly see. In making consumer decisions, the NT is likely to consider a wide range of possibilities, largely through imagination and then, as a thinking type, to logically weigh them in his or her mind. Thus, material objects become more props or doors to the individual's own imagination rather than as ends in themselves. Furthermore, the material object is seen in a broad, holistic context which may exist only in the individual's mind.

The NF is the total opposite of the ST. Like the NT, the NF considers a great range of possibilities and operates in a holistic manner (Mitroff and Kilmann 1975; Myers 1980). They tend to have an indefinite time horizon and to be people oriented (Mitroff and Kilmann 1975). As consumers, the NF considers a large range of possibilities, as do NTs, but are more likely to involve others in their decisions. Both NTs and NFs are more likely to be risk oriented than sensing types and are therefore also more likely to consider new products for which there is little or no data or past experience. This suggests that intuiting types are more likely to be both product innovators and novelty seekers. As does the NT, the NF weaves the outer material into his or her own inner network of imagination; however, the NF, as a feeling type, is more likely to imagine what others would feel about these dreamed of possibilities as well and also to want to share them.

DISCUSSION AND IMPLICATIONS

Personality differences are likely to help explain a great deal of economic phenomena and consumer behavior. Behavioral economists must consider the interaction of personality with environment in order to more fully understand individual behavior. Jungian theory offers us a way to go beyond merely recognizing that there are individual differences to systematically understanding and assessing those differences on a theoretical basis. In the remainder of the paper, we will consider how this theory might apply in the following key areas of consumer psychology and behavior: (1) utility theory, (2) information processing, (3) decision making, (4) the notion of the consumer as a 'naive' scientist, and (5) rationality.

Utility Theory

While economists often speak of individual tastes, choices and utility, they usually tend to form their theories more with an environmental (situational) perspective, assuming personal factors away, by simply ignoring them or by treating them as random noise or as constant. For example, expected utility theory (Von Neumann and Morgenstern (1947) tends to look at the distribution of individuals' situational behavior as a situational phenomenon rather than examining the basic structure of personality which might help explain individual differences. Theories such as prospect theory (Kahneman and Tversky (1979) and anticipated utility (Quiggin 1982) involve approaches which move away from traditional expected utility and which compel researchers to face the fact that people do not operate within the strict bounds of previously modeled rationality. Yet, while these approaches embrace cognitive psychological insights, they still have tended not to examine individual differences except as relative aberrations.

The understanding and investigation of psychological type can help us to understand the origins of people's tastes from a more biological perspective and see how those manifest within the constraints of cultural norms as suggested by Frank (1986). Individuals of each psychological type will develop tastes consistent with their natural orientation to the world. Sensing types, particularly STs, will probably tend to conform more with the expected utility, rational man approach in the development of their utility functions. Intuitive types, on the other hand, will draw more on intuition and imagination in forming their utility functions. Of the four types, NFs are probably the furthest removed from the standard economic model in that they operate primarily in the worlds of intuition and feeling, the opposites of sensing and thinking, which are generally more compatible with traditional economic theory and the rational calculus of choice. Interestingly, intuition has been a topic of interest to researchers who have considered the use of intuitive and other heuristics in the face of uncertainty (e.g. Tversky and Kahneman 1983). But, no one has used the psychological type approach in determining which individuals are comfortable with and/or better at intuitive information processing and which are not. For a better understanding of the entire utility process, researchers need to consider how different types function under different conditions.

Furthermore, as (Frank 1986) points out in discussing seemingly inconsistent behavior, such behavior may appear to be inconsistent because it is examined within too narrow a context. We would contend here in agreement, that much present utility and judgement research, particularly that in very restricted or hypothetical experiments, forces people into very constrained situations. Though these situations are of intrinsic interest, many of them may have relatively little to do with how individuals function in most everyday situations and also in their evolving choice behavior over time. In fact, individuals of a specific type may be forced to act in experimental settings in a way contrary to how they would normally function. For example, a sensing type may be forced to use intuition in an experiment which calls for it and react in an artificial way, as required by the experiment, rather than as he or she would normally, such as seeking more information or even withdrawing from the situation if no more information is available. It also may be that some individual differences get submerged or are ignored because a sample may be biased in terms of the psychological types it contains (e.g. a study of business school students is likely to contain many STs) and also because the overall population has more of certain types, especially sensing than intuitive types (e.g. Thorne, Fyfe, and Carskadon 1987). In other words, some individual differences may be written off as random noise rather than as systematic variance.

As one solution to these problems, we need to look more between-subjects, particularly on the basis of psychological types, as well as within-subjects, in empirical research in this area. In addition, we should consider that choices do not occur merely as single discrete events but that they also occur as part of the context of an individuals' whole life. Both intransitivities and seemingly irrational behavior may take on 'rationality' when viewed in the context of the gestalt of an individuals' social and psychological needs, especially as they interact with his or her psychological type and utility determining style. Thus, these problems of both methodological and theoretical validity suggest that future research and theory development not only needs to incorporate psychological type as a metapreferential orientation in forming preferences, but also a greater recognition of lived everyday experience- something urged by Holbrook and Hirschman (1982) in a different context, as well.

Information Processing

One of the two personality dimensions which we have considered in detail was that of sensing-intuiting which relates to how a person processes information. The sensing person will consider the world as it appears to the senses as a concrete, present reality while the intuiting person will be more likely to rely on his or her imagination, to perceive the gestalt of a situation, and to consider how the world could or might be (Hirschman 1985; Mitroff and Kilmann 1975). The sensing person is likely to be more literal in his or her interpretation of the world than the intuiting type who will view it more in terms of connotation and inference. At present, most information processing research has seemed to focus on what appears to be the sensing type in that it has dealt with denotative meaning and less with connotative, experiential, imaginative, or gestalt perspectives (cf. Hirschman 1985; Holbrook and Hirschman 1982; Thompson, Locander, and Pollio 1989). Some research has focused on right-brain/left brain differences in processing with the view that the right brain is more holistic and intuitive and the left brain more cognitive (Myers-Levy 1989). There needs to be more research along these lines, especially that which considers psychological type in relation to preferred brain processing patterns. From the environment side, a better understanding can be developed of which information providing stimuli and messages (e.g. emotional versus informational advertising appeals) are most effective in communicating choice-relevant information to each psychological type.

Decision Making

Decision making in the Jungian framework is a function of the thinking-feeling dimension of personality. Feeling types are more likely to make decisions with consideration of significant others, than are thinking types. In one sense, this dichotomous construct of personal decision making may correspond to the attitude-norm dichotomy of the much used attitude model of Ajzen and Fishbein (1980), in that feeling as a decision process takes into account others (the social norm), while thinking tends to be more internalized and self-reliant in scope (one's own attitude) - the extroversion/introversion trait is also likely to play a role. Feeling types tend to personalize and thinking types tend to depersonalize decisions. Thus, the two types will form their behavioral intentions and engage in their ultimate behaviors on the basis of different attitude formation processes. Viewing decision making from this perspective allows us to bring individual differences into decision making theory which has largely emphasized general rules and/or situational exigencies in the past.

Consumer as 'Naive' Scientist

Kelley (1973, p. 109) developed the notion of the lay person as a 'naive' scientist who "uses a naive version of the method used in science." Related research has examined such matters as lay persons' sensitivity to statistical information (Kruglanski, Friedland, and Farkash 1984) and the "scientific health consumer's" evaluation of scientific and medical information (Gould 1988, p. 115). The idea of the lay person as naive scientist, as adapted here, incorporates both information processing and decision making, and is an important one as consumers, who themselves are becoming better educated, are at the same time, increasingly called upon to evaluate scientific evidence, as well as to act upon it in making everyday rational choices. All types of people are generally forced to act upon incomplete evidence as Kelley suggests, but they still tend to differ from one another in the way they act. From the perspective of psychological types, it can be hypothesized that sensing types would tend to evaluate risk on the basis of what has already been proven or shown to be the case. On the other hand, intuiting types would tend to read into the evidence and go beyond what is 'definitely proven.'

For example, consider the statement that 'acid rain might possibly be harmful on the basis of early study although in need of further corroborating research.' Such a statement would tend to give sensing types less motivation to act than intuiting types who might imagine that the course of future research evidence will bear out the earlier findings, and thus conclude that the early work represents enough evidence for taking remedial action. Therefore, we suspect that most intuiting types are likely to go beyond 'definitely proven' evidence in the direction of greater perceived risk. Thus, many environmentalists, who tend to use such evidence, are likely to be intuitives. On the other hand, many individuals on the opposite side of the debate are likely to be sensing types. Interestingly, some who profess to find no risk in situations where the scientific evidence appears overwhelming may also operate intuitively. For example, some continue to eat a great deal of cholesterol rich foods in the face of evidence about the cholesterol-heart disease link. These individuals hold the belief, based on their own self-intuited evidence, that 'nothing will happen to me.'

Financial investment decisions may also be viewed from the perspective of the 'naive' scientific consumer and psychological type. For example, in making stock purchase decisions, sensing types will carefully weigh balance sheets and financial record information to get the objective facts. STs may make their own decisions and even use discount brokers while SFs will want to include the recommendations of others as part of their data. Others will buy on an intuitive hunch. NFs may buy stock on the basis of what they heard at a cocktail party. These examples illustrate how consumer economic decision makers evaluate evidence and make decisions in their roles as 'naive' scientists.

Rationality

Jung (1921/71) saw rationality as a reasoning process which may manifest as either thinking or feeling (it is important to recall here that feeling for Jung represents a valuation process as opposed to affect). Both thinking and feeling are directed or motivated functions which are rational when they are concerned with the "rational choice of objects, or with the qualities and interrelations of objects" (Jung 1921/71, p. 455). They can lose their rationality due to the incidental and unintended intercession in the mind of the perception of the flux of events, either intuitive or sensational. Such states represent a lack of rational direction. Thus for Jung, rationality is intentional in directing the individual's behavior, but it is also limited in being only a part of the psychology of the individual- a thought echoed from a different perspective by Etzioni (1986) who found rationality to be only a part of all cognitive activity. Considering the Jungian view of rationality, we can see that different individuals will approach rationality and reason in different ways and look for different evidence to support their perspectives. The logical-thinking person is clearly different from the feeling type in how he or she directs his or her own decision-making.

Returning to the perspective of Albanese (1987), we find that he related rationality to a pattern of stable and consistent consumption behavior as opposed to one which is alternating and contradictory. From the perspective of psychological types, this view poses two interesting considerations. First, the stable and consistent pattern of the individual may appear to be totally irrational to another type of individual. Second, inconsistency may be relative and even 'rational' to some types of individuals. For example, intuitive types may appear inconsistent to sensing types because they change quite a bit in pursuing and materializing a wide range of possibilities. Feeling types may appear inconsistent to thinking types in that they may sway in their consistency with popular feeling. It should be noted that the same problems arise whether it is individual consumers or researchers who assess the degree of rationality, since both groups operate from the perspective of their own psychological type. Thus, rationality from this perspective should be viewed as a being a reflection of an individual's psychological type. On the other hand, since Jung (1971) suggested that a psychologically healthy person would integrate the various dimensions of personality, rationality might be viewed in terms of the degree to which an individual was able to do so and thus, make decisions by using the information processing and decision making personality modalities required by the particular situation (e.g. using sensing when there is good available data and intuiting when there is not). In any case, given a Jungian perspective, we can well understand how one person's rationality is another's irrationality and how different people all seeing themselves as 'rational' might reach different conclusions when confronting the same situation or scenario.

CONCLUSION

In this paper, we have discussed how important psychological type might be in determining a wide variety of consumer behavior. Future research relating this construct to various demographics, personality traits, and person-situation interactions may prove useful in predicting behavior better than other personality constructs have because of its powerful combination of holism and dimensionality. Moreover, research with this construct may be especially intriguing for interpretive researchers who might otherwise shy away from personality research, but who in this case could use phenomenological (Thompson et al. 1989) and other interpretive methodologies in conjunction with this construct, as did Hirschman (1985). Such research might proceed in two ways: (1) by first measuring psychological types using Myers-Briggs and then applying interpretive methodologies and assessing the results across psychological type, or (2) by developing new ways of assessing psychological type and related behaviors which are totally rooted in interpretive methodology. In conclusion, this paper represents but a first step in encouraging research which more deeply probes the phenomenology of personality in consumer behavior.

REFERENCES

Albanese, Paul J. (1987), "The Nature of Preferences: An Exploration of the Relationship between Economics and Psychology," *Journal of Economic Psychology*, 8 (March), 3-18.

Ajzen, Icek and Martin Fishbein (1980), *Understanding Attitudes and Predicting Social Behavior*, Englewood Cliffs, NJ: Prentice-Hall.

Carlyn, Marcia (1977), "An Assessment of the Myers-Briggs Type Indicator," *Journal of Personality Assessment* 41 (October), 461-473.

Etzioni, Amitai (1986), "Rationality is Anti-Entropic," *Journal of Economic Psychology* 7, 17-36.

Frank, Robert J. (1986), "The Nature of the Utility Function" in *Economic Psychology: Interactions in Theory and Application*, eds. Alan J. MacFadyen and Heather W. MacFadyen, North-Holland: Elsevier, 113-132.

Gould, Stephen J. (1988), "Consumer Attitudes Toward Health and Health Care," *Journal of Consumer Affairs* 22 (Summer), 96-118.

Henderson, John C. and Paul C. Nutt (1980), "The Influence of Decision Style on Decision Behavior," *Management Science*, 26 (April), 371-386.

Hirschman, Elizabeth C. (1985), "Scientific Style and the Conduct of Consumer Research," *Journal of Consumer Research*, 12 (September), 225-239.

Holbrook, Morris B. and Elizabeth C. Hirschman (1982), "The Experiential Aspects of Consumption: Consumer Fantasies, Feelings, and Fun," *Journal of Consumer Research*, 9 (September), 132-140.

Jung, Carl G. (1921/71), *Collected Works, Volume 6: Psychological Types*, Princeton, NJ: Princeton University Press.

Kahneman, Daniel and Amos Tversky (1979), "Prospect Theory: An Analysis of Decision under Risk," *Econometrica* 47 (March), 263-291.

Kassarjian, Harold H. (1971), Personality and Consumer Behavior: A Review," *Journal of Marketing Research*, 8 (November), 409-418.

Kelley, Harold H. (1973), "The Processes of Causal Attribution," *American Psychologist*, 28 (February), 107-128.

Kruglanski, Arie W., Nehemia Friedland, and Ettie Farkash (1984), "Lay Person's Sensitivity to Statistical Information: The Case of High Perceived Applicability," *Journal of Personality and Social Psychology*, 46 (March), 503-518.

Lewin, Kurt (1935), *A Dynamic Theory of Personality: Selected Papers*, New York: McGraw-Hill.

Mitroff, Ian I. and Robert H. Kilmann (1975), "On Evaluating Scientific Research: The Contribution of the Psychology of Science," *Technological Forecasting and Social Change*, 8 (2), 163-174.

Myers, Isabel B. (1980), *Introduction to Type*, Palo Alto, CA: Consulting Psychologists Press.

Myers, Isabel B. and Mary H. McCaulley (1985), *Manual: a Guide to the Development and Use of the Myers-Briggs Type Indicator*, Palo Alto, CA: Consulting Psychologists Press.

Myers-Levy, Joan (1989), "The Influence of a Brand Name's Association Set Size and Word Frequency on Brand Memory," *Journal of Consumer Research*, 16 (September), 197-207.

Nutt, Paul C. (1986), "Decision Style and Its Impact on Managers and Management," *Technological Forecasting and Social Change* 29 (July), 341-366.

Quiggin, John (1982), "A Theory of Anticipated Utility," *Journal of Economic Behavior and Organization*, 3 (September), 323-343.

Thompson, Craig J., William B. Locander, and Howard W. Pollio (1989), "Putting Consumer Experience Back into Consumer Research: The Philosophy and Method of Existential-Phenomenology," *Journal of Consumer Research*, 16 (September), 133-146.

Thorne, B. Michael, Julia H. Fyfe and Thomas G. Carskadon, (1987), "The Myers-Briggs Type Indicator and Coronary Heart Disease," *Journal of Personality Assessment*, 51 (Winter), 545-554.

Tversky, Amos and Daniel Kahneman (1983), "Extensional versus Intuitive Reasoning: The Conjunction Fallacy in Probability Judgement," *Psychological Review*, 90 (October), 293-315.

Von Neumann, John and Oskar Morgenstern (1947), *Theory of Games and Economic Behavior, Second Edition*, Princeton, NJ: Princeton University Press.

Measurement Techniques Assessing Learning Processes Across Alternative Outdoor Advertising Executions

Joan Treistman, Treistman and Stark Marketing, Inc.

This paper describes two different behavioral research methodologies we at Treistman and Stark Marketing use to assess consumer reaction to outdoor advertising. One approach incorporates eye tracking; the other utilizes the tachistoscope. There are unique circumstances which suggest the use of one or the other and I will describe them.

First, I will present a context for considering outdoor advertising research. Next, I will present circumstances and objectives related to eye tracking methodology for outdoor research. Then I will describe the research procedure. This paper additionally addresses the same issues related to using the Tachistoscope.

CONTEXT

Outdoor advertising effectiveness is dependent on drivers riding past billboards. Specifically, effective outdoor advertising requires:

o Attention to the board
o Involvement with key components
o Registration of desired information
o Positive imagery
o Persuasiveness

Effectiveness can be enhanced by repeat exposure to the advertisement. Consequently, advertisers often invest in multiple locations and extended periods of time which allow for repeat exposure. These efforts are intended to increase the opportunity of an advertisement to be seen at least once and hopefully, more than once.

In this context of outdoor advertising, it is important to realize that the advertiser is buying space, not time. The passerby is in control of the time given the board. Thus, it is a combination of the board's position, size, environment and execution which generates attention. Eye tracking research provides a means to document the attention getting ability of outdoor advertising. Continued involvement is dependent on other variables. Therefore, to ensure that the desired communication occurs, depends on an execution which quickly and accurately conveys the intended message and associates it with the brand, product or service. This is the issue addressed with the Tachistoscope. To simplify and differentiate - eye tracking deals with attention, the Tachistoscope focuses on communication.

EYE TRACKING

I'd like to briefly describe the eye tracking process. There are two options for presenting the stimuli - either in the form of a photograph, i.e. 35 mm slide or a video. In both cases they deliver to the respondent a depiction of a drive along the highway with billboards and the surrounding environment. This makes it possible for the outdoor advertising to be missed, as well as seen -- an important dimension if attention is to be measured. As the person views the slide or video image, eye movements are recorded. A beam of light reflected off the participant's eye is captured to document precisely what he or she is looking at.

A record of where the person is looking is recorded onto a computer at the rate of 60 times a second. Each component of the stimulus is accounted for so that the following measures can be made:

% seeing the board
% of time spent with the board
% noting executional elements, such as
    brand name
    illustration
    people
    logo
    product
% reading copy
re-examination

The research procedure is typically as follows:

1. Respondents are screened for qualifying characteristics, such as, demographics, product and brand usage.

2. Each participant is seated at a screen and asked to view a drive sequence. Timing is controlled to simulate an appropriate speed for highway or inner city driving. As the individual views the screen, eye movements are recorded.

3. Typically, after the drive sequence is viewed, an interview is administered. This usually includes recall questions, and interest in purchasing the products advertised.

If more than one brand is tested, the questions are kept brief. If the study is focused on one brand, the interview may be more comprehensive to assess the communications value of the test execution.

In essence, we learn from this what opportunity has been created to communicate information on the billboard. From an industry perspective we have been able to understand the influences of variables such as, board size, position, type of board, (poster, bulletin, etc.) and the use of devices such as extenders.

Further, the accumulation of such data across industries has provided insights regarding the unique ability of various product and service categories to maximize attention to outdoor advertising.

TABLE 1
Outdoor Advertising Attention by Category
(Eye Tracking)

	Category			
	A	B	C	D
Average # of times board noted	4.2	3.8	3.7	3.6
Percent of time spent on board	43%	37%	35%	35%
Saw advertiser's name	79%	40%	54%	58%
Read copy	55%	68%	68%	65%

This table indicates that the attention drivers give to outdoor advertising can vary by category. This may at times reflect creative approaches used in the advertisements. For example, if the brand names in one category, such as "A," are always large and well situated on the boards, they are likely to generate attention. If the name is small in size, it is more likely to be missed. Category "B," exemplifies that, with less than half the respondents seeing advertisers' names.

Of course, this data is typically complemented by additional information yielded by verbal interviews conducted among the same respondents. Consequently, relationships between attention and the building of awareness have been examined. Further, the influence of the boards on brand perceptions and attitudes toward usage are explored through follow-up interviews.

The analysis of the data focuses on strengths and weaknesses of the boards in generating desired attention as well as registering brand identification and conveying a positive image. So it is possible with this approach to provide detail about one execution as well as examine the results of pre-defined billboard types or a category of products or services. Consequently, advertisers can determine which alternatives direct consumer attention as desired. Further, adjustments can be made to increase attention to elements of the ad which are important to the overall strategy.

For advertisers this is a useful tool in planning for better utilization of outdoor advertising. What this means to the company is a greater return on the advertising investment dollar.

TACHISTOSCOPE

As I mentioned at the outset, the tachistoscope focuses on communication. Given the potential of extremely brief viewing intervals when the outdoor board is placed on the highway, advertisers need to know if their executions have the ability to communicate quickly.

The Tachistoscope is a device which allows us to control the amount of time the stimulus is seen. There are two options in developing the research procedure. One option is to keep the distance and size of the outdoor board constant and vary the time intervals. The other is to vary the distances from which the board is photographed and keep the time interval constant. Since there is less control over board placement vis a vis consumer attention, we typically show the board from one distance and lengthen the interval of time it is seen over three exposures.

The research procedure is usually as follows:

1. Respondents are screened for qualifications (product and/or brand usage plus driver's license).

2. Seated at a screen they view a projection of an outdoor board unrelated to the study to educate them to the tachistoscope process. The slide is seen for three brief intervals and the participant is asked to describe everything she/he sees or reads after each exposure.

3. Next, the respondent sees the test slide for three brief exposures. Again, after each viewing, which is typically a fraction of a second up to 1 second, the respondent is asked to describe everything she or he has seen or read on the board.

4. Typically, an interview is administered after the T-scope procedure. The questionnaire is designed to elicit consumer reactions to aesthetics of the board and the product as presented by the execution in terms of image and stimulation of purchase interest.

The cumulative effect of three viewings demonstrates the ease or difficulty for the execution in conveying its information. In addition, it displays the learning process as it occurs as a consequence of repeat exposures. Further, the responses uncover elements which may be dominant or weak. Hence, we are able to develop insights for modification which will assist the board in improving its communication value. For the advertiser this can ensure a greater return on the advertising investment.

TABLE 2
Speed of Communication
(T-Scope)

	Outdoor Advertisement			
	Proposed	Previously Tested		
	A	B	C	D
Base:	(150)	(100)	(100)	(100)
	%	%	%	%
Brand Name				
1/30"	45	81	62	20
1/4"	73	92	80	55
1/2"	97	98	95	80
Product Type				
1/30"	14	10	5	15
1/4"	41	21	11	33
1/2"	64	34	20	50
Key Illustration				
1/30"	34	13	9	2
1/4"	63	39	20	6
1/2"	95	72	39	20

Proposed ad "A" communicates the brand name significantly slower than ads "B" and "C," achieving parity only at final viewing (1/2"). However, brand communication is significantly faster than for ad "D."

For product identification, ad "A" significantly exceeds each of the previously tested boards. A difference such as this, we have found, can be attributable to a board's simplicity, that is, the presence of fewer elements for the respondent to actually register.

Similarly, the key illustration for ad "A" is a salient element in comparison to prior boards.

These results suggest a need to improve brand name communication for ad "A." However, the trade-off vis a vis product identification may be palatable for the advertiser so that the ultimate outcome of the research requires a dialogue with brand management.

CONCLUSION

The evaluation of outdoor advertising executions may require an assessment of attention dynamics and evidence of desired communication. Eye tracking research permits the documentation of attention and involvement with outdoor ad components. Results from Tachistoscope procedures determine speed and accuracy of conveying desired information.

When these techniques are incorporated in a research methodology, they permit direct access to consumer behavior, allowing advertisers to optimize their use of outdoor advertising by increasing the opportunity to be seen, read and understood.

"Headlines make ads work" (Caples 1979): New Evidence
Highlights of the Special Topic Session:
Jacqueline Hitchon, University of Wisconsin-Madison

SUMMARY

"All messages have headlines. In TV, it's the start of the commercial. In radio, the first few words. In a letter the first paragraph. Even a telephone call has a headline. Come up with a good headline, and you are almost sure to have a good ad. But even the greatest writer can not save an ad with a poor headline." (Caples 1979)

In the context of print advertising, the headline has long been considered of great, if not greatest, importance by advertising practitioners and academicians alike (e.g., Caples 1975, Cohen 1988, Ogilvy 1964, Malickson and Nasan 1982, Rothschild 1987, Ziegler and Johnson 1981). And yet this key component has been the focus of relatively few investigations (Assael et al. 1967, Beltramini and Blasko 1986, Hanssens and Weitz 1980, Holbrook and Lehmann 1980, Myers and Haug 1967, Soley and Reid 1983). In most cases, and despite industry intuition to the contrary, research studies have failed to demonstrate a relationship between the headline and the overall successful performance of industrial and consumer print ads. This failure has been attributed to, among other factors, inadequate sampling of existing print ads and limitations in the dependent variables, usually standardized readership scores such as Starch scores (Beltramini and Blasko 1986, Mandell 1984).

It is noteworthy that disappointing research findings have not resulted in disillusionment with the central role of the headline, but rather in general confusion on the subject (Business Marketing 1987). The industry remains convinced of the headline's importance on two counts. First, it is often the only part of the ad to be read. In fact, Ogilvy's (1963) much-quoted estimate that five times as many people read the headline as the body copy has recently been inflated to seven times (Communication Briefings 1984). Second, it is thought to be mainly because the headline invites further perusal of the ad that the entire copy does get read in some cases.

Given these concerns, this special session had a twofold purpose. Our first objective was to present fruitful tests of long-held and influential assumptions with regard to the types of headline that are most effective (Papers 1 and 2). Our second objective was to extend our understanding of the central role of the headline beyond the domain of print advertising. Since, to quote Caples, "all messages have headlines" advertisements must survive in an editorial and programming environment where non-advertising headlines influence their effectiveness. Paper 3 investigates the effects of TV news headlines on the reception of subsequent commercials.

A brief description of the content of each paper is given below.

PAPER 1: WILLIAMS MILBRATH AND ESTHER THORSON
"A Test of Ogilvy's Conceptualization of Advertising Effectiveness for Print Headlines"

This paper compared the effectiveness of three kinds of headlines: News, Benefit and Curiosity. News headlines announce that the product or service has something new to provide the consumer; Benefit headlines emphasize what the product will do for the consumer; Curiosity headlines attempt to intrigue the reader by means of ambiguity, to the extent that the headline may not even indicate the nature of the product or brand. Industry wisdom holds that Curiosity headlines are less effective than the other two major types. Testing this general proposition was the objective of this research, and our findings relating to persuasion were reported in the session.

In brief, specific hypotheses were tested in a 3(Headline Type: News vs. Benefit vs. Curiosity) x 9(Product Type) split plot design. Pooling across products, a signficant main effect of Headline Type was found with respect to attitude toward the brand and purchase intention. Contrary to industry wisdom, Curiosity headlines led to the most favorable attitudinal responses.

PAPER 2: JACQUELINE HITCHON
"Effects of Metaphorical vs. Literal Headlines on Advertising Persuasion"

Since a metaphor and its literal counterpart can never be equated exactly, their comparison is philosophically unacceptable in some fields of study. In advertising, however, the persuasive efficacy of a metaphorical product claim versus its more mundane (i.e., literal) alternative is an important practical issue in copywriting. In the context of headlines, where metaphors are considered a special case of Curiosity headlines, the use of metaphor is widely disparaged. Moreover, an initial study designed to test the persuasive effects of metaphorical vs. literal processing in advertising copy foundered through the use of a "dead," i.e., cliched, metaphor (Jaffe 1986). Industry cynicism regarding the use of metaphorical language is surprising, however, given the substantial literature base in such diverse areas as psychology, anthropology, semeiotics and literary criticism that testifies to the persuasive function of metaphor. this paper forms part of a more extensive research project that tests a theoretically-driven model of metaphorical processing. Novel metaphors (novel 'A is B' statements) all hypothesized to result in reconstruction of the cognitive representation of A, leading under certain conditions to more favorable evaluations of A. In this research, A is operationalized as the product or service being advertised. Since any single metaphor and its literal counterpart can never be equated in any exact sense, it was believed important to sum across a number of metaphors and their literal equivalents. Four products and two services, and a total of twelve metaphors and their literal counterparts were featured in two experiments.

The results provide support for the model. Both studies found more favorable brand attitudes as a result of novel metaphorical headlines, relative to equivalent literal headlines. In addition, equating a product with a negatively-valenced entity in a metaphorical headline was found to result in more favorable attitudes, ruling out affect transfer as an explanation for the psychological process of equation in metaphor. Consistent with the model, attitude change was mediated by a reconstruction process that, in part, involved a significant increase in the perceived importance of the product characteristic shared by A and B.

As psychological theory and industry wisdom suggest, the effects of metaphor on attitude toward the advertisement itself were moderated by product tangibility and the salience of the product characteristic shared by A and B.

PAPER 3: JOAN SCHLUEDER
"How Viewers Use News Teaser Headlines to Process Commercial Information More Efficiently"

Commercials in most television programming come as a surprise "break." In the news, they are announced with what the broadcast industry calls teasers. The purpose of a teaser is to keep viewers from switching channels during the commercial breaks with phrases such as "A little girl in trouble and the town that rallied to help--after these messages." This study examined how news teasers influence the moment-to-moment processing of the commercials they precede.

These specific questions were addressed: (1) Do the presence of teasers facilitate attention to commercials and enhance the viewer's ability to remember the commercial message? (2) Are the effects of teasers on attention to and memory for commercials affected by whether the persuasive appeal is emotional or neutral? (3) Does the serial position of commercials within a pod interact with the presence of teasers?

The cognitive processing theories that most closely address these questions offer alternative predictions and explanations for the effect that teasers have on attention, visual memory and verbal memory. News teasers may have PROACTIVE INTERFERENCE EFFECTS on subsequent processing; the teasers may also stimulate greater overall COGNITIVE CAPACITY; and viewers may engage in SEGMENTATION of the ongoing flow of the news and commercial information such that the teasers signal the viewer that one viewing unit is complete and another is about to begin.

A three factor repeated measures experiment was designed to see which theoretical approach best explained teaser effects. The teaser factor had two conditions: presence of teasers vs. absence of teasers. The emotion factor also had two conditions: emotion vs. neutral appeal. The serial order of the commercials within a pod had three conditions: first, second and third. Three types of counterbalancing were used so that serial order effects observed would be due to the commercial position and not to an idiosyncratic characteristic of a commercial or a particular teaser-commercial combination. Teasers and commercials were embedded in simulated 20-minute newscasts that were created for each network--ABC, CBS and NBC. Two commercial pods were included in each newscast, one was preceded by teasers and one was not. Finally, attention was measured while subjects viewed the commercials. The secondary task reaction time method was used as an indicator of how intensely viewers paid attention to the commercials.

Viewers allocated more attention to commercials following teasers than to commercials that did not follow teasers, but there was no main effect for memory. The presence of teasers and emotional appeal interacted to affect both visual and verbal memory. Subject's visual memory scores were highest when they viewed emotional commercials that were not preceded by teasers. Teasers and serial order of commercials interacted to affect viewer attention. When commercials were not preceded by teasers, the first and last commercials in a pod elicited the most attention. In the presence of teasers, the middle commercial elicited the most attention. The pattern of results for visual memory and verbal memory was the same as that found for attention. In sum, none of three cognitive processing theories outlined in the paper explain all of the results, but the segmentation theory predictions were supported by the majority of the findings.

The three papers were critically appraised in detail by Martin Horn, Vice President and Associate Director of Marketing Decision Systems, a division of the Marketing Research Department at DDB-Needham in Chicago. Highlights of his discussion included a plea for more research on the effectiveness of print, advertising. He noted that the findings of the first two papers would delight many people working on the creative side of advertising. More difficult to persuade would be clients who are wary of curiosity headlines and of metaphorical language, in particular. Furthermore, Marty pointed out the value of research on context effects, as exemplified by Paper 3. Although advertisers do not currently have control over the type of news headline that their commercial follows, it is important to understand the relationship between the advertising environment and advertising effectiveness. Without such research, advertisers cannot negotiate with the media for greater control over placement in situations where control is feasible.

REFERENCES

Assael, Henry, John H. Kofron, and Walter Burgi (1967), "Advertising Performance as a Function of Print Ad Characteristics," *Journal of Advertising Research*, 7, 2, 20-26.

Baltramini, Richard F. and Vincent J. Blasklo (1986), "An Analysis of Award-Winning Advertising Headlines," *Journal of Advertising Research*, April/May, 47-52.

Business Marketing (1987), "Heads Screwed on Right," July, 97-100.

Caples, John (1975), "Fifty Things I Have Learned in Fifty Years in Advertising," *Advertising Age*, September 22, 47.

Caples, John (1979), "Caples on Copy," series in the *Wall Street Journal*.

Cohen, Dorothy (1988), *Advertising*, Scott, Foresman and Company.

Communication Briefings (1984), "Advertising Research Findings That May Surprise-Even Stratle-You," August, Vol. 3, No. 10, 8a-8d.

Malickson, David L. and John W. Nason (1982), *Advertising: How to Write the Kind that Works*, Rev. ed. New York: Charles Scribner's Sons.

Mandell, Maurice I. (1984), *Advertising*, Englewood Cliffs: Prentice-Hall, Inc.

Myers, James H. and Arne F. Haug (1967), "Declarative vs. Interrogative Advertisement Headlines," *Journal of Advertising Research*, 7, 3, 41-44.

Ogilvy, David (1963), *Confessions of an Advertising Man*, New York: Dell Publishing Co.

Rothschild, Michael (1987), *Advertising: From Fundamentals to Strategies*, D. C. Heath and Co.

Soley, Lawrence C. and Leonard N. Reid (1983), "Industrial Ad, Readerships as a Function of Headline Type," *Journal of Advertising*, 12, 2, 34-38.

Zeigler, Sherolyn K. and Douglas J. Johnson (1981), *Creative Strategy and Tactics in Advertising*, Columbus, Ohio: Grid Publishing Co.

Processes and Effects in the Construction of Normative Consumer Beliefs: The Role of Television

L. J. Shrum, University of Illinois
Thomas C. O'Guinn, University of Illinois
Richard J. Semenik, University of Utah
Ronald J. Faber, University of Minnesota

ABSTRACT

The knowledge that individuals use to make decisions and judgments comes from both direct and indirect experience. Such information may result from participation, from social networks, or via more indirect routes such as mass media. With respect to mass media, consumer researchers have been concerned predominantly with the effects of advertising. It is the contention of this paper that the programs between the ads also convey a wealth of information with respect to consumption, and may very well influence the decision making process. This paper presents studies which attempt to assess this influence. Survey and reaction time data serve to address both process and effects in discerning how individuals go about constructing their concepts of the social reality of consumption. The results support the notion that heavy television viewing influences consumption perceptions such that they more closely resemble the "reality" of the television world.

INTRODUCTION

We know that consumers are influenced by perceptions of what others have and do. Some of these perceptions are determined via direct experience, others through less direct representations. Unfortunately, models of social influence in the field of consumer behavior have not taken account of how or how much the institutionalization of television in American homes has impacted this process. When most extant social influence models were forged, television was still a relative novelty. Today the average household watches over seven hours of it every day (Nielsen Television Index 1990). Further exacerbating this situation is that as a field, consumer behavior tends to think of mass communication narrowly as advertising. The things between the ads (a.k.a. programs) are rarely if ever studied as having any consumption related influence. This is unfortunate, because these programs provide overt and implied information about consumption norms and behavior. The manner in which this material is acquired, processed and utilized may yield significant theoretical and methodological implications for both consumer socialization and social cognition.

This paper argues and presents data in support of the belief that television programming is a significant and overlooked source of consumption related perceptions. This effect should be stronger among those who watch more television than those who watch comparatively less. In other words, we believe that people who watch more television have consumption related normative beliefs which more resemble the world as portrayed on television than those who watch less television. Furthermore, we believe that these beliefs are more accessible in memory among those who view more frequently.

THEORY

Antecedent to many attitudes and behaviors are normative beliefs, or beliefs about what is average or modal. The influence of normative beliefs are thought to extend to a wide range of processes and outcomes, from basic perception to overt behavior. Further, we have no reason to suspect that this is any less the case in the domain of consumer behavior. What we believe others possess, use, desire and value are subject to the same processes of social construction as any other normative belief. Yet, there has been little research in the pursuit of a more complete understanding of the acquisition and maintenance of normative economic and consumption related social beliefs. This seems particularly surprising in the field of consumer behavior, since so many ads, designed to attract attention and influence behavior, work on the basis of creating a positive perception for the targeted reference group member (i.e., housewife, business executive, teenager, happy family). From the 1920's on, this has been the essential premise of "reason why" and "slice of life" advertising (Fox 1984; Liess, Kline and Jhally 1988). These ads depended on the creation of the perception of the average person with an average problem, (then halitosis, now gingivitis), that only the advertised good or service could remedy.

From a social science perspective, it is also essential to understand that life on television significantly differs from life directly experienced. Many things are over-represented (i.e., wealthy people), others under-represented (i.e., minorities). Television producers have over time decided what best fits the medium, and have structured portrayals accordingly. In the McLuhan (1964) sense of the medium being the message, this is reflected in things from the purely fictional portrayals of family life in the average situation comedy, to what is selected as news and how it is structured to best fit the demands and constraints of the medium. This disparity does, however, provide the researcher with a unique opportunity, the context for differentiating things learned via television versus more direct experience.

Cultivation

One of the more enduring, provocative and controversial contributions of mass communication research to social science has been in the area of social reality effects. Collectively, this research has demonstrated modest yet consistent associations between exposure to television and individuals' beliefs about various aspects of their social environment. Most commonly associated with Gerbner's cultivation theory (Gerbner et al. 1977, 1980), research in this area has now extended beyond the bounds of that particular theory and constitutes a somewhat broader area of inquiry in mass communication known as social reality research (Hawkins and Pingree 1982). Still, both the general theoretical and methodological orientation of contemporary work in this area remains largely consistent with Gerbner's original conceptualizations. While there are some legitimate and well documented methodological criticisms of this research (Hirsch 1980, 1981), its intuitive appeal has kept it alive. It has most recently been bolstered by supportive work in social psychology (Tyler 1980, 1984), and consumer behavior (O'Guinn et al. 1989; O'Guinn and Shrum 1990; Shrum, O'Guinn and Faber 1990).

The theory of cultivation holds that television viewing significantly assists in creating or cultivating a view of reality which is biased toward the highly formulaic and stylized narrative content of television. The more one views, the greater the effect. Cultivation research examines not the conscious acquisition and rational utilization of information, but rather the mere absorption of it. Summary beliefs about our social environment are built or "constructed" a la Berger and Luckman (1967), with bits of information from a number of sources, and these sources differ significantly in their properties. Television is a largely narrative, dramatic medium in which individual viewers willfully "suspend their disbelief," often in a very passive cognitive state (Ray 1973), for an average of four hours per day (NTI 1990). It therefore seems quite reasonable to cultivation theorists that television figures prominently in the individual's construction or summary beliefs about the nature of social things.

Psychologically, cultivation is a black box theory. It posits no explicit psychological dynamic. It offers instead a somewhat vague sort of socialization theory based on notions of frequency and passivity of viewing. Other theories may, however, contribute to understanding the cultivation effect, and assist in modifying and extending related social reality research. One is the work of decision scientists Kahneman and Tversky (1982; Tversky and Kahneman 1973) on the availability heuristic. The basic premise of this work is that the things more easily retrieved from memory are more accessible or more "available", and are thus disproportionately represented in judgments regarding the occurrence of events or the frequency of things. An heuristic is said to be most typically employed in low involvement situations or in simplifying complex tasks (see Folkes 1988). It could be that when television viewers are asked to estimate the incidence of something like the likelihood of being the victim of a violent crime, they rely on an heuristic in which mass media portrayals are simply more accessible. A finding supportive of this notion has been reported in at least one study. Lichtenstein et al. (1978) found that mass media exposure was positively correlated with overestimating the frequency of certain lethal events prominently displayed in the media.

The work of Tyler (Tyler 1984; Tyler and Cook 1984) is also important in this context. He and his colleagues have offered support for the belief that direct and indirect experience yield very different outcomes. Essentially, he argues that direct experience influences personal risk assessment, but not estimates of societal risk, and that indirect experience does just the opposite, influences environmental estimates, but not personal risk. So, for example, if a man was mugged in his neighborhood, this direct experience would lead him to believe that he is more at risk of violence and thus personal risk would be adjusted. However, seeing violent television programming will lead him to believe that the world in general is more violent, but have no impact on personal risk assessments. This may help to explain some of the inconsistencies in other social reality researchers' works, and may help predict precisely what will be more accessible in memory given the question posed by the research. This effect would also be consistent with most modern models of memory. Perhaps simply due to the higher probability of recently encountering a televised portrayal, such portrayals are more frequently represented, making their retrieval more probable.

One particular criticism of social reality research is that people know that television is not real, and therefore tend not to use the information gleaned from television. Indeed, some social reality research looks specifically at those viewers who tend to indicate that they believe the world of television to be real (termed "perceived reality", Potter 1986). However, such an assumption is not totally consistent with the person memory literature. In fact, many models of social cognition assume that subjects do not make an exhaustive search of memory for information bearing on a particular proposition, but instead search memory and use the first relevant piece of information encountered, which may or may not be initially perceived as real (see Wyer and Srull 1989; Sherman and Corty 1984). Furthermore, Wyer and Hartwick (1980) demonstrated that amount of processing influences both recall and judgments, showing that subjects remembered implausible arguments better than plausible ones, and were more apt to use these more easily recalled arguments as a basis for judgment. Thus, more accessible information, even though it is not necessarily more believable, may be used as a basis for judgment.

Social Reality and Consumption

A growing number of researchers interested in consumer behavior have written about the role of advertisements in creating symbolic and cultural beliefs in consumers (Mick 1986; McCracken 1986;

Levy 1959). However, advertising represents only a small portion of media content. Furthermore, symbolic meaning is only one aspect of social reality. Perhaps even more fundamental, exposure to the "world" as portrayed on television has the potential to influence our perceptions of the very existence or incidence of things. If unchallenged, these perceptions become part of enduring cognitive structures. We begin to believe the world, or at least part of it, exists as it is constituted on television. Again, it is important to remember that these beliefs may not exist in a logical, rational or elaborated sense. It may, in fact, be the uncritical and vague way in which they are encoded and stored that gives them much of their power.

Very few studies have been published which have directly investigated consumer cultivation. Fox and Philliber (1978) examined the impact of television viewing on perceptions of affluence in the U.S. They found a significant relationship between amount of viewing and perceptions of affluence, but this relationship disappeared when control variables were applied. (Weimann 1984) conducted a study of Israeli viewers of American programs in Israel, and found that heavy viewers overestimated the percentage of Americans owning various household items as well as the average earnings of American families, relative to light viewers. Additionally, by testing different causal models, Weimann found that the data were best explained by a model in which control variables influence amount of viewing, but not cultivation effects directly, thus indicating that amount of viewing does have a direct effect on cultivation. However, the control variables did not include any measure of direct experience with American households. Lee (1988) and Lee and O'Guinn (1990) have studied cultivation among Taiwanese immigrants to the United States. By taking measures in Taiwan and at several levels of years lived within the United States, these researchers were able to use a cross-sectional design to study the process by which immigrants learned about the role and value of consumption objects. In Taiwan, respondents greatly overestimated material abundance in the United States, and this relationship was significantly explained by exposure to U.S. television programming. They also found that exposure to television remained a very strong predictor of beliefs concerning consumption behavior in Taiwanese immigrants, even after several years in the U.S.

It may also be important to consider the way consumer decision making is portrayed on television. Research has shown that decisions on television tend to infrequently consider important purchase decisions such as available finances and alternative choices (Faber 1978; Way 1982). Additionally, few sources of information are considered and decisions are made within a very short time frame (typically within one day) on television. Therefore, we may find that heavy viewers believe the average person to be less deliberate and thorough in their purchase decision making.

In sum, these studies support the basic cultivation hypothesis, but are also subject to the standard criticisms and limitations leveled at such work. With the above mentioned studies in mind, this paper presents the results of three studies which seek to extend mass-mediated social reality research into the domain of consumer behavior and to explore the psychological process which may account for these effects. In the first study a general population survey was administered. Given the variance in life experience in different demographic groups, it was deemed vital to collect data from widely divergent groups. Since we were also interested in process, a series of quasi-experiments were conducted. We will present the preliminary results of the survey and the results of the two quasi-experimental reaction time studies.

STUDY 1 (ILLINOIS GENERAL POPULATION SURVEY)

Method

Sample and Procedure. An extensive survey was prepared and mailed to approximately 2800 members of the adult Illinois population. The sample was selected via a standard systematic procedure using city directories. The sample was designed to best represent the adult population of Illinois. As of the writing of this paper, approximately 800 completed surveys had been returned.

The questionnaire attempted to assess the respondents' perceptions of the incidence of ownership, use or participation in consumption related behaviors, as well as their perceptions of income distributions. There were 42 such items, 30 of which were purely consumption oriented, and another 12 which were broader societal level questions concerning handguns, violence, AIDS, etc. Following each question respondents were also asked about direct experience. An example of the format is:

What percentage of American households have a convertible automobile? _____
Do you currently have a convertible?
Yes_____ No_____
If not, have you had one in the past five years? Yes_____ No_____

Other examples of incidence measures were jacuzzis, maids or servants, the percentage of adult Americans suffering from gingivitis or athlete's foot, the percent who are millionaires, comparison shop while making a purchase, suffer from high blood pressure and have dandruff. The items chosen were ones which were deemed to be over-represented on television (as compared to real life), either via program depictions or in commercials. Respondents were also asked to complete the 24 item Belk materialism scale (Belk 1985), as well as a full set of demographic measures.

TABLE 1
Third Order Partials Between TV and Perception Measures
(controlling for age, income and education)

(TV Movies / Males Only / n=121)

Perception Measures	r, significance
% households w/ private tennis court	.36, p < .001
% households w/ convertible automobile	.16, p < .05
% households w/ maids or servants	.22, p < .005
% households w/ swimming pool	.23, p < .01
% households w/ a car telephone	.26, p < .005
% Americans who suffer from gingivitis	.31, p < .001
% households w/ income < $15,000	.23, p < .01
% households who belong to private gym or spa	.21, p < .05
% Americans who are millionaires	.23, p < .01
% Americans who are currently addicted to crack or cocaine	.20, p < .05
% Americans who have had cosmetic surgery	.31, p < .001
% adult Americans who have called a 900 number dating or companion service	.16, p < .05
% of Americans w/ bladder control problems	.20, p < .05
% of Americans w/ dandruff problems	.30, p < .001

(Soap Opera / Males Only / n=121)

Perception Measures	r, significance
% Americans w/ an alcohol dependency problem	.29, p < .001
% American males who regularly use a condom while having sex	.21, p < .05
% American high school students who regularly use illegal drugs	.72, p < .001
% Americans who have visited a friend or relative in the hospital in the last month	.64, p < .001
% Americans who have had cosmetic surgery	.29, p < .001
% Americans who are millionaires	.17, p < .05
% Americans who suffer from athlete's foot	.63, p < .001
% Americans who suffer from hemorrhoids	.17, p < .05

Television viewing was assessed in two ways. First, we had respondents estimate the number of hours they watched television in an average week during specific dayparts or time periods (6:00am - noon), (noon - 7:00pm), (7:00pm - 10:00pm), (10:00pm - 6:00am). Secondly, we asked them to estimate the weekly hours spent watching specific types or genres of shows: soap operas, action/adventure, drama, etc.

Analysis

As of the writing of this paper, only 240 cases of the incoming data had been input and analyzed. Simple frequencies indicate sample statistics being very close to known population parameters in Illinois and the U.S, including the amount of television viewed. For example, the average person reported watching 3.9 hours of television per day in our survey compared to Nielsen's 4.1 (NTI 1990).

Three demographic measures were found to covary with many of the dependent measures and amount of television viewed. For example, TV viewing covaried with age ($r = +.24$, $p < .001$); education ($r = -.27$, $p < .0001$); and income ($r = -.19$, $p < .01$). Therefore, these demographic measures were used as control variables. Materialism did not covary with these variables and therefore was not used as a control variable. Zero through third order partial correlations were calculated between viewing hours for each program type and the normative perception measures. Analyses were also nested within gender. This procedure was considered necessary because of observed differences in viewing by gender (NTI 1990; Shrum, O'Guinn and Faber 1990) and the likelihood that direct experience with many dependent variables would also vary by gender.

Results

The general hypothesis, that heavier television viewers would have significantly higher estimates on the perception measures, was supported. Simple and partial correlations between the consumption related percentage estimates and the total hours of television viewing per week provided strong support for the general hypothesis. Most of the dependent measures were correlated in the .2 to .3 range ($p < .05$). However, stronger results were found when correlations were computed within genre or type of television show.

Length restrictions and the sheer volume of correlations preclude us reporting more results. Table 1 does, however, offer some illustrative findings. Shown are third order partial correlations for males who watch two different popular television genres: movies and soap operas. Higher levels of movie viewing among males were associated with higher estimates of the percentages of American households with private tennis courts (r= .36), convertible automobiles (r=.16), car telephones (r=.26), maids or servants (r=.22) and swimming pools (r=.23). Movie viewing among males was also positively associated with estimates of the number of people suffering from gingivitis (r=.31), having annual incomes of less than $15,000 (r=.23), belonging to a private spa or gym (r=.21), who are millionaires (r=.23), who are currently addicted to crack or cocaine (r=.20), suffering from bladder control problems (r=.20), having dandruff problems (r=.30), who have had cosmetic surgery (r=.31), and who have called a 900 number dating or companion service (r=.16).

Interesting and fairly substantial third order partials were also observed when looking at soap opera viewing among men. Heavier television viewing correlated positively with higher levels of estimates of the percentage of adult Americans who suffer from hemorrhoids (r=.17), percent of American high school students regularly using illegal drugs (r=.72), percent of adult Americans suffering from athlete's foot (r=.63), percent of Americans who have had cosmetic surgery (.29), and the percent of adult Americans who have visited a friend or relative in the hospital in the last month (r=.64). These activities and advertising related health problems are common soap opera fare.

Several things remain to be done with respect to the survey data. One of the more pressing is to analyze the data while controlling for direct experience. This may allow us to get at some of the theoretical issues raised by Tyler (1984) and others. Also, once more of the data is in, we will be able to perform more comprehensive and sophisticated multi-factor analyses to determine viewing patterns as well as perception factors or clusters.

STUDY 2A AND 2B (REACTION TIME STUDIES)

In order to address the issues of process in making the perceptual estimates, a reaction time methodology was employed. Two specific hypotheses were tested: 1) heavy television viewers would give estimates which more resembled television portrayals relative to light television viewers, and 2) heavy television viewers would make these inferences quicker, thus showing faster response latencies. It is our contention that those who tend to watch more television should have a greater number of informational bits stored in memory. Television moves much faster than real life, consequently leading to numerous impressions about world beliefs. When asked to make an inference, subjects tend to use the information most accessible. This may take the form of a previously constructed belief. If this is the case, then subjects will most likely retrieve that judgment and terminate the search. Alternatively, if no previously constructed belief exists, then subjects will search for relevant information to use in making a probabilistic inference. In either case, if increased television viewing results in greater quantities of relevant information being deposited in memory, then it is quite probable that these television-originated bits of information will be used to make a judgment or indicate the likelihood of the occurrence of a particular event. Furthermore, if such information is over-represented in memory, then it would be more accessible, resulting in shorter response latencies.

Method

Samples and Procedures. Study 2a and 2b consisted of two separate but methodologically similar quasi experiments conducted during the 1989-1990 academic year. Because a prior study (Shrum, O'Guinn and Faber 1990) had indicated gender differences on the perception measures, Study 2a consisted of 55 undergraduate males in an introductory advertising class at a large midwestern university. Study 2b used the same subject pool, but consisted of 130 subjects, all of whom were women. Subjects in both studies performed the exercise on a microcomputer. Following established procedures for most reaction time studies (see Fazio 1990 for a review), subjects were instructed to be both quick and accurate. Upon directions to start the exercise, subjects were instructed via computer screen to press the space bar in order to receive a question. When the space bar was pressed, the first question appeared. Because the particular reaction time program employed did not allow for anything other than single digit responses, subjects indicated their response by pressing a key labeled from 0 to 9. These integers corresponded to an intuitive scale encompassing percentages from 0% to 99% (i.e., 0 = 0 - 9%, 1 = 10 - 19%, 4 = 40 - 49%, and so on). As soon as a key was pressed, the question disappeared and the subject received a prompt to press the space bar for the next question. An internal clock recorded the time between when the space bar was pressed (causing the question to appear) and when the response was entered.

The single digit response scale was somewhat problematic due to the subjects' constraints on differentiation. Consequently, Study 2b attempted to overcome this problem by having subjects record via pencil and paper the precise number they were thinking of when they entered the scaled value on the computer. After each answer was recorded on the microcomputer, subjects were instructed to immediately write down their answers onto a questionnaire. These measures, rather than the computer recorded values, are reported.

Subjects were taken through several practice questions. After beginning, the first three items they encountered were also treated as practice questions. In order to rule out the possibility that reaction time results may be confounded because high television watchers, for whatever reasons, may be faster at responding on the computer, two measures were used to establish baseline reaction time. These items were chosen because they represented questions which should take virtually no time to compute. The two items were "Half of 100 is what?" and "How old are you?", and were the fourth and fifth items encountered. The reaction times for these two items were averaged for each person to create a baseline index. All reaction times were then transformed by subtracting the baseline index from the raw reaction time for each response. Such a transformation should theoretically yield a reaction time measure which only measures the time needed to develop an answer, thus eliminating individual differences in reading speed and dexterity. Although the raw reaction times of the baseline questions were not faster for high television viewers, indicating that high television viewers do not respond faster for dexterity reasons, the transformation was still used in order to remove variance due to individual response times apart from the decision making process.

Subjects were asked to indicate hours of viewing by daypart and by genre. The results presented for both studies represent a combination of hours of prime time viewing and afternoon viewing. These time periods were considered to give robust portrayals of consumption related phenomena. The low viewership within each daypart precluded individual analyses of each daypart alone, so the categories were collapsed. Subjects were divided into either high or low television viewing based on a median split of total weekly viewing hours. The median for the collapsed category for both studies was 8 hours per week.

Dependent Measures. The questions were much the same as those used in Study 1, i.e., "What percentage of Americans drive a convertible?", "What percentage of American households have a Mercedes?", etc. Study 2a used 60 measures and Study 2b used 42 measures. Only a portion of the questions pertained to consumer behavior issues, and only these are reported.

Results

The results of the two studies are shown in Table 2, and lend partial support for our hypotheses. In the first study, the reaction times tended to be significantly faster for the high television viewers, while the perception measures were significant for only 3 of the 7 measures, though all in the right direction. The dependent measures which yielded the most promising results tended to be fairly specific questions about ownership: % American households which have a private plane was significant for both reaction time and perception; % American households with a sports car was significant for reaction time. Two more general questions showed some significant differences between high and low viewers: % Americans who cheat on their taxes was significant for reaction time and perception; % of American households which live beyond their means was significant for reaction time. In the second study, the perception measures tended to show differences, while the reaction times showed significant differences in only 1 of 4 instances, but again, all in the predicted direction. % Americans who have at one time or another used the services of a prostitute was significant for reaction time and perception; % of Americans who comparison shop was significant for perception, but in this case high TV viewers underestimated relative to low viewers, a finding consistent with television portrayals; the % of American high school students who regularly use illegal drugs and % American households with an annual income of less than $15,000 were significant for perception, consistent with the findings in Study 1; % of adult Americans who have called a 900 number dating or companion service was only significant for reaction time.

Similar results were obtained on the non-consumer behavior perception questions. The data in total showed that virtually all of the reaction time measures were in the predicted direction (56 of 60 in Study 2a, 37 of 42 in Study 2b), with high television viewers responding faster. Approximately 70% of the perception measures were in the predicted direction.

DISCUSSION

Both the Illinois general population survey in Study 1 and the reaction time studies in Study 2a and 2b yield results consistent with our general hypotheses and theory. The data indicate that the more people watch television, the higher they estimate the incidence of product ownership and wealth, relative to low television viewers. In addition, consistent with the notion that television portrays a world of extremes, high television viewers gave higher estimates for both the number of households making less than $15,000 as well as the number of millionaires. As expected, stronger associations were demonstrated in the general population survey, since college students watch decidedly less television than the general population, and also have more similar experiences. Thus, one should not be surprised to find weaker effects among students.

The perception measures also indicated enough differences to encourage further exploration into this phenomenon. However, more work needs to be done in refining both the measurement instrument and the measurement method. A closer analysis of the television message may elicit more thoughtful and meaningful questions. A more detailed look at viewing patterns, or analyses within genre, would seem to be promising, since studies have shown that different genres do indeed convey qualitatively different messages (Greenberg 1980; Potter and Ware 1987). It should also be noted that the analyses within genre are very basic. More sophisticated analyses of isolating effects from specific types of programs are planned.

The attempts to address psychological process through the reaction time measures seem especially promising. Given the exceedingly large number of results in the predicted direction (90%

TABLE 2
Perception and Reaction Time Differences (Studies 2a and 2b)

Study 2a (Prime Time and Afternoon / Males Only)

Dependent Measures	Reaction Time		Mean Perception	
	high	low	high	low
% households w/ a private plane	1.19	1.73	1.70	0
	p < .01		p < .03	
% Americans who are lawyers	1.97	2.50	11.8	10.8
	p < .01		n.s.	
% households w/ a sports car	1.60	2.07	27.8	23.2
	p < .05		n.s.	
% households w/ a vacation home	1.54	1.99	17.5	9.6
	p < .06		p < .03	
% households which live beyond their means	1.82	2.62	40.4	38.4
	p < .01		n.s.	
% Americans who cheat on their taxes	1.44	1.82	27.9	14.4
	p < .05		p < .02	
% households w/ a Mercedes	1.40	1.94	11.4	7.2
	p < .03		n.s.	

Study 2b (Prime Time and Afternoon / Females Only)

Dependent Measures	Reaction Time		Mean Perception	
	high	low	high	low
% American households w/ annual income < $15,000	3.69	3.86	30.6	24.6
	n.s.		p < .02	
% adult Americans who have used the services of a prostitute	2.39	3.44	22.3	16.5
	p < .01		p < .01	
% of Americans who comparison shop	2.56	2.59	46.8	52.2
	n.s.		p < .12	
% of American high school students who regularly use illegal drugs	2.75	3.25	40.3	33.0
	n.s.		p < .05	
% of adult Americans who have called a 900 number dating or companion service	3.19	3.92	21.7	20.6
	p < .08		n.s.	

over the two studies), it would seem that this is something more than mere chance or an easily detected third variable. Still, methodological concerns remain. For example, the response scale is by most standards much too long (Fazio 1990). A "Yes-No" or "True-False" format may help to reduce the variances in the response times. Not only would such a format make the physical act of responding easier, but the time needed to formulate an answer would be shorter.

While the reaction time results from student samples were quite promising, the perception differences were less impressive. As mentioned above, collecting data from non-students, who typically have a far broader range of television viewing and life experiences, may show greater cultivation effects. We are currently in the process of analyzing reaction time data collected from a non-student sample. Hopefully, such refinements of measures and techniques will prove helpful in teasing out the subtleties involved.

The effects of television programming have been of interest for some time to those in the field of mass communication. It seems that consumer researchers would also be interested in the effects of such a ubiquitous source of consumption information. Furthermore, the availability of this naturally occurring, and passively viewed background source, seems particularly attractive in its implications for social cognition.

REFERENCES

Belk, Russell (1985), "Materialism: Trait Aspects of Living in the Material World," *Journal of Consumer Research*, 12, 265-280.

Berger, P. L. and T. Luckman (1967), *The Social Construction of Reality: A Treatise in the Sociology of Knowledge*, Garden City, NY: Doubleday.

Faber, Ronald J. (1978), "Decision Making on Television: A Content Analysis," unpublished manuscript, University of Wisconsin.

Fazio, Russell H. (1990), "A Practical Guide to the Use of Response Latency in Social Psychology Research," in *Review of Personality and Social Psychology*, Vol. 11, ed. Ladd Wheeler, Beverly Hills: Sage.

Folkes, Valerie (1988), "The Availability Heuristic and Perceived Risk," *Journal of Consumer Research*, 15, 1 (June), 113-123.

Fox, Stephen R. (1984), *The Mirror Makers: A History of Advertising and its Creators*, New York: Random House.

Fox, Stephen and William Philliber (1978), "Television Viewing and the Perception of Affluence," *Sociological Quarterly*, 19, 103-112.

Gerbner, George, Michael Eleey, Marilyn Jackson-Beeck, Suzanne Jeffries-Fox, and Nancy Signorielli (1977), "TV Violence Profile No. 8: the Highlights," *Journal of Communication*, Vol. 27, 171-180.

_____ , Larry Gross, Michael Morgan and Nancy Signorielli (1980), "The 'Mainstreaming' of America: Violence Profile No. 11," *Journal of Communication*, 30, 10-27.

Greenberg, Bradley S. (1980), *Life on Television: Content Analyses of U.S. TV Drama*, Norwood, NJ: Ablex.

Hawkins, Robert, and Suzanne Pingree (1982), "Television's Influence on Constructions of Social Reality," in *Television and Behavior: Ten Years of Scientific Progress and Implications for the Eighties*, eds. D. Pearl, L. Bouthilet, and J. Lazar, Technical Reports, Washington: U.S. Government Printing Office, 224-247.

Hirsch, Paul (1980), "The Scary World of the Nonviewer and Other Anomalies: A Reanalysis of Gerbner et al.'s Findings on Cultivation Analysis," *Communication Research*, 7 (4), 403-456.

_____ (1981), "On Not Learning From One's Own Mistakes: A Reanalysis of Gerbner et al.'s Findings on Cultivation Analysis," *Communication Research*, 8, 3-37.

Kahneman, D. and Amos Tversky (1982), *Judgment Under Uncertainty: Heuristics and Biases*, New York: Cambridge University Press.

Lee, Wei-Na (1988), *Becoming an American Consumer: A Cross-Cultural Study of Consumer Acculturation Among Taiwanese, Taiwanese in the U.S. and Americans*, unpublished doctoral dissertation, University of Illinois.

_____ and Thomas C. O'Guinn (1990), "The Consumer Acculturation of Taiwanese Immigrants," Working Paper, University of Texas.

Levy, Sidney (1959), "Symbols for Sale," *Harvard Business Review*, 37, 117-124.

Lichtenstein, Sarah, Paul Slovic, Garuch Fischhoff, Mark Layman and Barbara Combs (1978), "Judged Frequency of Lethal Events," *Journal of Experimental Psychology: Human Learning and Memory*, 6 (November), 551-578.

Liess, William, Stephen Kline and Sut Jhally (1988), "The Modern Advertising Industry," in *Social Communication in Advertising: Persons, Products and Images of Well Being*, New York: Methuen, 127-145.

McCracken, Grant (1986), "Culture and Consumption: A Theoretical Account of the Structure and Movement of the Cultural Meaning of Consumer Goods," *Journal of Consumer Research*, 13, 71-84.

McLuhan, Marshall (1964), *Understanding Media: The Extensions of Man*, New York: McGraw Hill.

Mick, David G. (1986), "Consumer Research and Semiotics: Exploring the Morphology of Signs, Symbols and Significance," *Journal of Consumer Research*, 13, 196-213.

Nielsen Television Index (1990), *Nielsen National TV Ratings*, New York: A.C. Nielsen Company.

O'Guinn, Thomas C., Ronald J. Faber, Nadine J. J. Curias and Kay Schmitt (1989), "The Cultivation of Consumer Norms," in *Advances in Consumer Research*, Vol. 16, ed. Thomas K. Srull, Provo, Utah: Association for Consumer Research.

_____ and L. J. Shrum (1990), "The Psychology of Normative Economic Beliefs: Mass Mediated Processes and Effects in Consumer Socialization," in *Applied Economic Psychology in the 1990's*, eds. Stephen Lea, Paul Webley and Brian Young, Exeter, England: International Association for Research in Economic Psychology.

Potter, W. James (1986), "Perceived Reality and the Cultivation Hypothesis," *Journal of Broadcasting and Electronic Media*, 2 (Spring), 159-174.

_____ and W. Ware (1987), "An Analyses of the Contexts of Anti-social Acts on Prime Time Television," *Communication Research*, 14, 664-686.

Ray, Michael L. (1973), "Marketing Communication and the Hierarchy-of-Effects," in *New Models for Mass Communication Research*, ed. P. Clarke, Beverly Hills: Sage, 147-176.

Sherman, Steven J. and E. Corty (1984), "Cognitive Heuristics," in *Handbook of Social Cognition*, Vol. 1, eds. Robert S. Wyer and Thomas K. Srull, Hillsdale, NJ: Lawrence Erlbaum Associates.

Shrum, L. J., Thomas C. O'Guinn and Ronald J. Faber (1990), "Television and the Social Construction of Reality," paper presented at the International Communication Association conference, Dublin, Ireland.

Tversky, Amos and D. Kahneman (1973), "Availability: A Heuristic for Judging Frequency and Probability," *Cognitive Psychology*, 5 (September), 207-232.

Tyler, Tom R. (1980), "Impact of Directly and Indirectly Experienced Events: The Origin of Crime-Related Judgments and Behaviors," *Journal of Personality and Social Psychology*, 39 (1), 13-28.

⎯⎯⎯⎯ (1984), "Assessing the Risk of Crime Victimization: The Integration of Personal Victimization Experience and Socially Transmitted Information," *Journal of Social Issues*, 40;1, 27-38.

⎯⎯⎯⎯ and Fay L. Cook (1984), "The Mass Media and Judgments of Risk: Distinguishing Impact on Personal and Social Level Judgments," *Journal of Personality and Social Psychology*, 47 (4), 693-708.

Way, Wendy (1982), "The Consumer Content of Prime-Time Television: Implications for Consumer Educators," paper presented to the American Council on Consumer Interests.

Weimann, Gabriel (1984), "Images of Life in America: The Impact of American T.V. In Israel," *International Journal of Intercultural Relations*, 8, 185-197.

Wyer, Robert S. and Jon Hartwick (1980), "The Role of Information Retrieval and Conditional Inference Processes in Belief Formation and Change," *Advances in Experimental Social Psychology*, Vol. 13, ed. Leonard Berkowitz, New York: Academic Press.

⎯⎯⎯⎯ and Thomas K. Srull (1989), *Memory and Cognition in its Social Context*, Hillsdale, NJ: Lawrence Erlbaum.

Processing Conditional Relations as Biconditionals: Some Poor Consequences and Rich Opportunities

Thomas K. Srull, University of Illinois at Urbana-Champaign

ABSTRACT

When A implies B, it does not follow that B implies A; yet people usually assume that it must. One thesis of the present paper is that processing conditional relations as biconditionals is logically fallacious, but psychologically irresistible. It is argued that this tendency can account for both the counterfactual reasoning results reported by Folkes and Lassar and the construction-of-reality results reported by Shrum, O'Guinn, Semenik, and Faber. More generally, the case is made that processing conditional relations as biconditionals is at least partially responsible for the following heuristics: availability, representativeness, time estimation, mental simulation, beliefs in a just work, similarity and attraction, and salience and perceptions of influence.

My fascination with cognitive psychology just never seems to go away. It is an insightful and quickly advancing discipline, and I believe it has much to offer to consumer researchers of all disciplinary backgrounds and theoretical perspectives.

Contemporary cognitive psychology continues to be dominated by the information processing model. People are said to represent the present in perception, the past in memory, and the future in goals, plans, and intentions. To put it another way, people are said to represent *the subjective reality of* the present in perception, *the subjective reality of* the past in memory, and *the subjective reality of* the future in goals, plans, and intentions.

Among other things, the preceding papers illuminate three points that cognitive psychologists occasionally acknowledge, but rarely address explicitly. First, representations of reality are often constructed, sometimes haphazardly, and rarely stored as coherent entities that are simply retrieved and activated into consciousness. The system is flexible and adaptable, and the software is just as important as the hardware.

The second point is that a representation of reality is constructed for a purpose. In other words, there are *functional* determinants of information processing. In the present context, representations of reality are constructed so that one can reason about them. It is clear that such reasoning can occur both forward and backward in time. In the "forward" case people ask themselves such questions as: what would it be like to get married and have children, what will my colleague say when I tell her that I lost the manuscript, or would I enjoy working on the client side? In the "backward" case, people ask such questions as: would I have been happier if I hadn't passed up that fellowship, would my colleague be friendlier if I already finished that last draft, or what could I have bought with the money if I hadn't lost it at the race track? As one can see, however, the boundary between backward and forward processing sometimes becomes blurry.

The third point flows naturally from the fact that people reason both forward and backward in time. Specifically, once a representation of reality is constructed to reason with, it is often compared to imagined alternatives. These alternative constructions of reality may be placed in the past (what if he hadn't said that), the future (what will I do if he says this), or the present (what does it mean if he is mad rather than just busy).

To see the value of an information processing perspective, let us begin by considering two basic effects that have been reported in the preceding papers. Then I will attempt to take a little closer look at each of them.

Folkes and Lassar have reported some very intriguing effects of counterfactual reasoning. Their basic effect is that consumers experience greater anger when a product breaks down shortly after a warranty expires. Their interpretation is that such an event makes it very easy to engage in counterfactual reasoning. Specifically, because the product failure occurred so close in time to the expiration date of the warranty, it is (relatively) easy to imagine oneself using the product in such a way that the failure would have occurred while it was still covered by the warranty. They have provided an important and ingenious way to examine counterfactual reasoning within the domain of consumer behavior and experience. Counterfactual reasoning is a special case of Kahneman and Tversky's (1982) simulation heuristic in which reactions to an event are determined by the way in which people construct different ways in which the event might have played out.

Shrum, O'Guinn, Semenik, and Faber have also examined the construction of reality. But they have used a different domain and a very different set of methodologies. Their basic effect is that estimates of frequency or the probability of various key events is influenced by the amount of television to which one is exposed. More specifically, events that are often depicted on television receive from heavy viewers higher estimates of frequency for the general population. Their interpretation is that this is based on an availability heuristic. Because heavy viewers of television find it very easy to retrieve specific instances of key events (such as having a maid), they give higher estimates of frequency than do light viewers of television.

Although these are quite distinct streams of research, and both the phenomena and interpretations vary considerably, I believe there is a set of very basic psychological mechanisms that plays a role in each of them. Moreover, these mechanisms are so basic and so ubiquitous that they play a role in many other areas of consumer research as well. To the degree my claims are true, they allow (and, I would argue, demand) the construction of more general theories of consumer behavior, ones that will bring coherence to what have historically been considered quite disparate areas of research. In the following section, I will try to make the case that we are much closer to this state of affairs than generally recognized.

REASONING WITH BICONDITIONALS

Many judgements and inferences, especially those made in the context of consumer behavior, are made in terms of conditionals. When one states, for example, that Japanese cars are better than American cars, this is just a shorthand way of saying that the probability that a car is high in quality is greater if it was built in Japan than if it was built in the United States. The same is true whenever we infer that an object has a particular feature (e.g., low price) because it belongs to a particular category (e.g., country-of-origin).

The likelihood (or conditional probability) that an object belongs to a category if it has a particular feature is *not* logically the same as the likelihood (or conditional probability) that the object has the feature if it belongs to a particular category. Generating a few extreme examples that have very small base rates is the easiest way to see the fallacy in such logic. For example, the probability that one is rich given that one drives a Maserati is quite high. At the same time, however, the probability that one drives a Maserati given that one is rich is quite low. Similarly, the probability that one is a man given that one smokes cigars is high; the probability that one smokes cigars given that one is a man is low.

Although logically such inferences are not justified, psychologically they appear to be compelling. I believe that conditional relations are typically processed as biconditionals, even though they should not be from a rational perspective. In other words, people believe that if A implies B, then B must imply A as well. This very basic tendency can, in my view, account for several of the effects reported in the preceding papers, as well as for most examples of heuristic processing that have been portrayed in the literature. Heuristics, of course, are generalized rules that people use to simplify very difficult judgments. Such rules do not always produce correct judgments, but they require far less extensive processing than would be needed to arrive at a judgment through more algorithmic means. A few examples of how many of the heuristics that have been reported result from processing conditional relations as biconditionals will help to illustrate just how important these low-level cognitive mechanisms are in everyday life.

AVAILABILITY

The results reported by Shrum and his colleagues ultimately rest upon the use of an availability heuristic. Most people believe that if a particular event occurs frequently, it will be easy to remember. Based on this belief, they assume that if something is easy to remember, it is likely to have occurred frequently. Consequently, they infer the frequency with which events have occurred from the ease with which instances of them come to mind. This rule, denoted by Tversky and Kahneman (1973) as the availability heuristic, has been demonstrated in numerous areas of research (for a review, see Sherman & Corty, 1984). For example, people infer that more English words begin with the letter k than have k as the third letter, although the reverse is actually true. This occurs because it is easier to generate words that begin with k. To use an example that is closer to the effects of the mass media, 80% of subjects infer that death is more likely to occur from an accident than from a stroke. In reality, however, strokes cause far more deaths than do accidents (Lichtenstein, Slovic, Fischoff, Layman, & Combs, 1978). Consistent with the work of Shrum et al., however, accidents are often written up in very vivid detail in newspapers and are portrayed more often on television. Thus, instances of them come to mind more easily.

REPRESENTATIVENESS

People often believe that members of a given category have particular attributes. Consequently they often infer that objects that have the attribute must belong to the category. In one study, for example, subjects were randomly assigned to play the roles of quizmaster and contestant in a game. The quizmaster was asked to generate questions that would stump the contestant and, because each person has available a huge storehouse of rather esoteric information, this was easily done. Afterwards, both observers and the participants themselves rated the quizmaster as smarter. Because people believe that smart people are able to stump others, they also inferred that one who stumps others must be smart. Similarly, because dull people are believed to be incapable of answering many questions, people infer that one who cannot answer questions is likely to be dull (see Kahneman & Tversky, 1971 for other examples).

TIME ESTIMATION

People typically believe that events are easier to remember in detail if they have occurred more recently. Consequently, they often infer that an event has occurred more recently if they can recall a lot about it. The use of this heuristic was demonstrated by Brown, Rips, and Shevell (1985) who found that subjects' judgments of the temporal order of events depicted by the mass media (e.g., the death of John Lennon vs. the eruption of Mt. St. Helens) were predictable from the relative amounts of knowledge they could retrieve about the events in question.

MENTAL SIMULATION

The results reported by Folkes and Lassar appear to be due to some type of mental simulation process. People generally believe that events are easier to imagine if they are likely to occur than if they are improbable. Consequently, they infer that events are more likely to occur if they are easy to imagine. Many demonstrations of the use of this simulation heuristic have been reported by Kahneman and Tversky (1982). It was found in one study, for example, that people believe a disease with easy-to-imagine symptoms is more likely to affect them than an equally prevalent disease with difficult-to-imagine symptoms (Sherman, Cialdini, Schwartzman, & Reynolds, 1982).

The effects of generating explanations of an event on predictions of its occurrence provide an additional example. In several studies, for instance, subjects were asked to explain a hypothetical event involving either themselves or another, and then to predict the actual likelihood of its occurrence. The process of generating an explanation for the hypothetical event presumably made the occurrence of the event easier for subjects to imagine, and this increased their predictions of its likelihood (Ross, Lepper, Strack, & Steinmetz, 1977; Sherman, Skov, Hervitz, & Stock, 1981).

Folkes and Lassar have extended this principle by further assuming that people will be more upset by the occurrence of an undesirable event if they can easily imagine how it might have been avoided (making it seem more likely that it *could* have been avoided) than if they cannot. This also appears to be a general principle. In another study, for example, subjects were asked to consider two persons who are caught in a traffic jam and arrive at the airport thirty minutes late for their scheduled departure. One person finds that his flight left on time, while the other learns that his flight was delayed by twenty-five minutes, and only left five minutes beforehand. Which man is more upset at having missed his flight? It is easier to imagine how five minutes could have been saved (by not stopping to buy a paper, by not having a second cup of coffee, etc.) than to imagine how thirty minutes could have been saved. Consequently, the second passenger is more likely to believe that he could have made his flight, and so he is more disappointed by failing to do so (Kahneman & Tversky, 1982). In an analysis that has much to do with issues such as product usage, Gleicher, Kost, Baker, Strathman, Richman, and Sherman (1990) have recently examined the separate effects of imagining alternative actions (e.g., performing a maintenance procedure) as opposed to inactions (e.g., not performing a maintenance procedure). Once again, however, the use of the simulation heuristic ultimately depends on processing conditional relations as biconditionals.

BELIEFS IN A JUST WORLD

As a result of personal experience, parental upbringing, reading Horatio Alger, or religious training, people often believe that persons will be punished or experience adversity if they are bad, but that they will experience joy and success if they are virtuous. As a result, there is a tendency to infer that people are bad if something terrible happens to them but are virtuous if they experience joy and success. This is the root of blaming the victim and the principle was first proposed by Lerner and Simmons (1966) as the "just world" hypothesis. As an example, subjects who witness someone experience pain (for reasons that are ostensibly beyond the person's control) evaluate the person more negatively if they believe that the pain will continue than if they believe the pain will be terminated or offset by a positive experience (Lerner & Simmons, 1966). More generally, subjects' disparagement of a sufferer is directly proportional to the amount of pain they believe he or she must endure.

SIMILARITY AND ATTRACTION

People usually learn from experience that individuals like one another if they have similar attitudes or interests. Treating this conditional relation as a biconditional, they infer that people have similar attitudes or interests if they like one another. The reverse is also true. Because people believe that individuals dislike one another if they have dissimilar attitudes, they infer that people must have dissimilar attitudes if they dislike each other (see Insko, 1984; Rosenbaum, 1986; Wyer, 1974).

SALIENCE AND PERCEPTION OF INFLUENCE

Finally, people discover from experience that they pay more attention to participants in a social interaction, and have better memory for what they say and look like, if the participants are influential, or if they otherwise dominate the interaction, than if they do not. As a result, people infer that a participant has been more dominant of influential if they recall having paid more attention to that participant, or if they have a more vivid memory of what the person looked like. Experiments using quite different paradigms have supported this conclusion. For example, in a study by Taylor, Fiske, Close, Anderson, and Ruderman (1974), subjects observed a group discussion in which one person was rendered unique by virtue of his or her gender, race, or clothing. The unique participant was later judged to be more influential in the group discussion than persons who were similar to one another in these respects. Other studies show that subjects attribute more responsibility in conversations to people who are in their real or imagined line of vision as they observe the conversation (Regan & Totten, 1975; Storms, 1973). These studies converge on the conclusion that salient aspects of a person, which may have nothing to do with the person's actual responsibility for what occurred in a situation, are likely to capture subjects' attention and, therefore, to be contained in the representation of the situation that is stored in memory. Consequently, the person is likely to be attributed influence and responsibility for what went on in the situation when this representation is retrieved and used as a basis for judgments.

CONCLUSIONS

I have tried to show in this paper that the processing of conditional relations as biconditionals is a ubiquitous phenomenon. There is a difference between logic and psychologic and, as a result of such processing, many erroneous judgments and inferences are made. I also believe, however, that the information processing model offers the most useful perspective for understanding the causes, correlates, and consequences of such processing. In all of these areas, work has just begun.

Consumer behavior is obviously a domain in which conditional relations play a central role. Consumers actively infer one attribute from another, and understanding how and when they do so is critical for a more complete understanding of both prepurchase and postpurchase activities. Very little is understood about these matters however. I have tried in the present paper to place this issue in the larger context of information processing, and I hope that my comments will further stimulate researchers to examine the cognitive psychology of consumer behavior and consumer experience.

REFERENCES

Brown, N.R., Rips, L.J., & Shevell, S.K. (1985). The subjective dates of natural events in very-long-term memory. *Cognitive Psychology, 17,* 139-177.

Gleicher, F., Kost, K.S., Baker, S.M., Strathman, A.J., Richman, S.A., & Sherman, S.J. (1990). The role of counterfactual thinking in judgments of affect. *Personality and Social Psychology Bulletin, 16,* 284-295.

Insko, C.A. (1984). Balance theory, the Jordan paradigm, and the Wiest tetrahedron. In L.Berkowitz (Ed.), *Advances in experimental social psychology* (Vol. 18). New York: Academic Press.

Kahneman, D., & Tversky, A. (1971). Subjective probability: A judgment of representativeness. *Cognitive Psychology, 3,* 430-454.

Kahneman, D., & Tversky, A. (1982). The simulation heuristic. In D. Kahneman, P. Slovic, & A. Tversky (Eds.), *Judgments under uncertainty: Heuristics and biases.* New York: Cambridge University Press.

Lerner, M.J., & Simmons, C.H. (1966). Observers' reaction to the "innocent victim": Compassion or rejection? *Journal of Personality and Social Psychology, 4,* 203-210.

Lichtenstein, S., Slovic, P., Fischoff, B., Layman, M., & Combs, B. (1978). Judged frequency of lethal events. *Journal of Experimental Psychology: Human Learning and Memory, 4,* 551-578.

Regan, D., & Totten, J. (1975). Empathy and attribution: Turning observers into actors. *Journal of Personality and Social Psychology, 32,* 850-856.

Rosenbaum, M.E. (1986). The repulsion hypotheses: On the nondevelopment of relationships. *Journal of Personality and Social Psychology, 51,* 1156-1166.

Ross, L., Lepper, M.R., Strack, F., & Steinmetz, J. (1977). Social explanation and social expectation: Effects of real and hypothetical explanations on subjective likelihood. *Journal of Personality and Social Psychology, 35,* 817-829.

Sherman, S.J., Cialdini, R.B., Schwartzman, D.F., & Reynolds, K.D. (1982). *Imagining can heighten or lower the perceived likelihood of contracting a disease: The mediating effect of ease of imagery.* Unpublished manuscript, Arizona State University, Tempe, AZ.

Sherman, S.J., & Corty, E. (1984). Cognitive heuristics. In R.S. Wyer & T.K. Srull (Eds.), *Handbook of social cognition* (Vol. 1), (pp. 189-286). Hillsdale, N.J.: Erlbaum.

Sherman, S.J., Skov, R.B., Hervitz, E.F., & Stock, C.B. (1981). The effects of explaining hypothetical future events: From possibility to probability to actuality and beyond. *Journal of Experimental Social Psychology, 17,* 142-158.

Storms, M. (1973). Videotape and the attribution process: Reversing actors' and observers' point of view. *Journal of Personality and Social Psychology, 27,* 165-175.

Taylor, S.E., Fiske, S.T., Close, M.M., Anderson, C.E., & Ruderman, A. (1974). *Solo status as a psychological variable.* Unpublished manuscript, University of California, Los Angeles, CA.

Tversky, A., & Kahneman, D. (1973). Availability: A heuristic for judging frequency and availability. *Cognitive Psychology, 5,* 207-323.

Wyer, R.S. (1974). *Cognitive organization and change: An information processing approach.* Potomac, Md.: Erlbaum.

How Entrants Affect Multiple Brands: A Dual Attraction Mechanism
Timothy B. Heath, University of Pittsburgh
Subimal Chatterjee, University of Pittsburgh[1]

Past research has demonstrated that adding an asymmetrically dominated alternative to choice sets generally increases the share of the dominating (target) brand. The present paper demonstrates that such attraction effects do not always occur. In particular, it is argued that entrants can enhance the attractiveness of nontarget as well as target brands. In such situations, the dual attraction effects nullify each other. Thus, although asymmetrically dominated, the entrant has little effect on market share.

Understanding the effect of new entrants on existing markets is important for understanding consumer choice processes and devising marketing strategies (for some strategic issues see Hauser and Shugan 1983). For example, one fundamental assumption underlying most mathematical choice models is regularity (Luce 1959): Introducing a new brand cannot increase the market share of an original brand. Yet violations of regularity are well documented. Entrants often increase the share of superior brands to which they are similar (e.g., Huber, Payne, and Puto 1982). This has been dubbed the *attraction effect* since an entrant similar to a target brand seems to attract consumers to the target.

The current paper addresses the possibility that asymmetrically dominated alternatives will increase the share of the target brand in some instances but not others. The lack of market share effects is predicted and empirically demonstrated in those instances where a single entrant is expected to enhance the attractiveness of multiple brands simultaneously. It will be argued that such dual attraction effects offset one another such that the entrant has little effect on market shares.

Prior Research and Theory on Attraction

The attraction effect is best understood by referring to Brands A, B, and E summarized in Table 1 and Figure A. Neither A nor B dominates the other since each is superior on at least one attribute. Entrant E, however, is dominated by B but not by A. Thus, E is said to be asymmetrically dominated. In Figure A, the region of such asymmetrically dominated entrants is shown by the rectangular shaded area. Relative to the market consisting of only Brands A and B, adding asymmetrically dominated entrants like C and E generally increases the probability of choosing the dominating brand B (Huber, Payne, and Puto 1982; Huber and Puto 1983; Ratneshwar, Shocker, and Stewart 1987; Simonson 1989).

The middle shaded region of Figure A consists of relatively inferior alternatives. Entrants from this region (e.g., Brand D) are always more similar (closer) to B than to A, irrespective of the attribute weights or the distance metric used. Huber and Puto (1983) found that some entrants from this region reduced B's share by stealing from B (substitution effect), but that other entrants increased B's share by moving consumers from A to B (attraction effect).

Several explanations have been put forth for the attraction effect (see Ratneshwar et al. 1987 for a review). These can be broken down into (1) perceptual mechanisms, (2) choice heuristics, and (3) moderating influences.

Perceptual Mechanisms. Huber et al. (1982) suggested that range and frequency effects (Helson 1964) may be involved in attraction. Entrant D (Table 1 and Figure A) increases the quality range from 10 to 15 and thereby makes A's 10-point quality advantage over B seem smaller. On the other hand, increasing the number (frequency) of brands along the dimension on which the target (dominating brand) dominates may draw more attention to that dimension (e.g., price). Thus, Entrant E may enhance the salience of B's price advantage since B now dominates two brands on price. Although such perceptual mechanisms may be involved in attraction effects, attraction effects have been found that cannot be explained in these terms (Huber et al. 1982; Huber and Puto 1983).

Choice Heuristics. Choice heuristics have been suggested as explanations for attraction effects (Huber et al. 1982; Huber and Puto 1983). One heuristic consists of comparing all brands on all attributes and counting the "number of wins." Another related process is referred to as *relative attribute comparisons* (Huber and Puto 1983). Consumers use one brand, for example Entrant D in Figure A, as an anchor. They then evaluate the attribute tradeoffs when switching from the anchor to the other brands. Switching from D to A costs 75 cents but gains 15 quality points. Each added quality point costs 5 cents. But switching from D to B costs 5 cents and gains 5 quality points, such that each added quality point costs only 1 cent. Thus, B looks better than A when comparing relative attributes. While one of two studies using concurrent verbalizations reported some evidence of such heuristic processing (Simonson 1989), the other did not (Ratneshwar et al. 1987).

Moderating Influences. Three variables have been suggested as moderators of attraction effects: (1) familiarity, (2) meaningfulness, and (3) accountability. Ratneshwar et al. (1987) argued that the attraction effect could be due to the lack of familiarity and meaningfulness of stimuli typically used in experimental choice tasks. They found only directional evidence of familiarity effects. However, using elaborated attribute descriptions to increase

---

[1]The authors wish to thank Mike Rich and Bob Soergel for their help in data collection.

TABLE 1
Example Choice Sets

Brand	Price	Quality	Value (quality/price)
A	$4.95	75	15.15
B	$4.25	65	15.29
(Entrant) D	$4.20	60	14.29
(Entrant) E	$4.30	65	15.12
(Entrant) J	$4.85	65	13.40

NOTE: Only one entrant would be added to the original A-B set at a time.

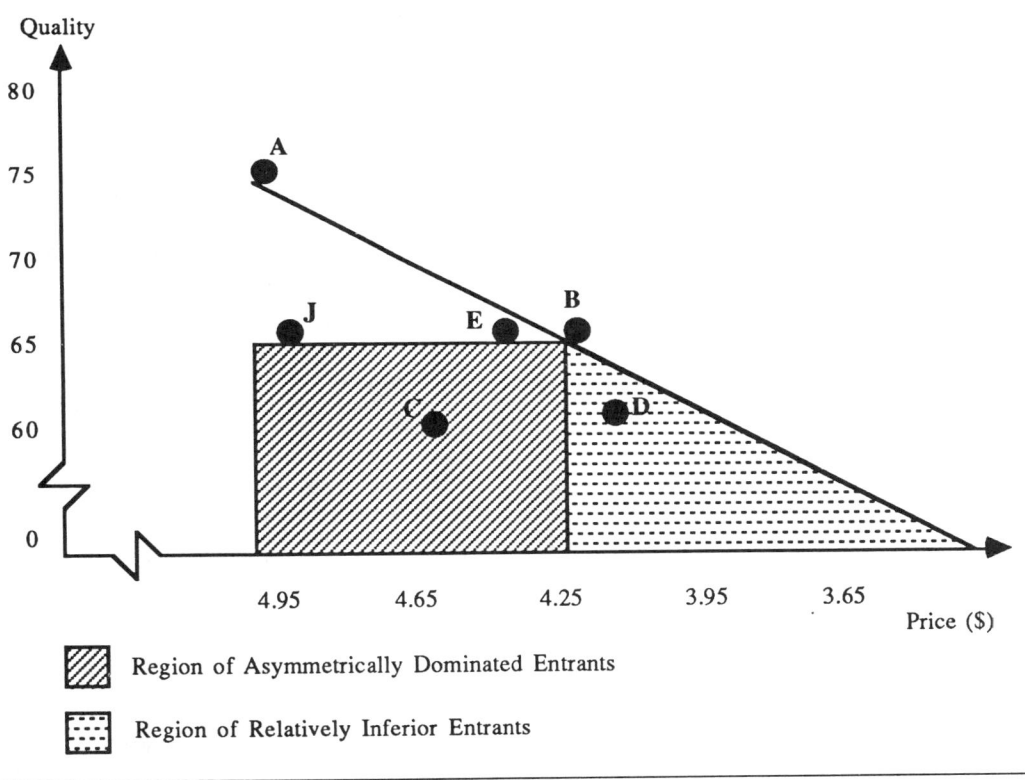

FIGURE A
Positioning of Asymmetrically Dominated and Relatively Inferior Entrants

the meaningfulness of the stimuli reduced the size of attraction effects. While meaningfulness may moderate entrant effects, it cannot explain all attraction effects since attraction occurred even with the more meaningful stimuli.

Simonson (1989) hypothesized that people seek reasons for their choices, particularly when expecting to justify their selections to others. He found that attraction effects were stronger when subjects believed they would be held accountable for their choices. Although it may be easier to justify decisions when asymmetric dominance exists, the mechanisms underlying this ease are probably some combination of those discussed earlier (e.g., relative attribute comparisons).

An Added Mechanism for Asymmetric Dominance

Failure of Relative Attribute Comparisons. As noted above, the relative-attribute-comparison heuristic can account for attraction effects when entrants are relatively inferior (e.g., Brand D in Figure A). However, it does not always work with asymmetrically dominated entrants. For example, if the consumer anchors on E in Table 1 (also Figure A), switching to B saves 5 cents and has no effect on quality. Switching to A costs 65 cents and gains 10 quality points such that each quality point costs 6.5 cents. Whether A or B looks more appealing according to relative attribute comparisons is not clear. Yet attraction effects are commonly reported with such entrants (e.g., Simonson 1989).

Considering Entrant J in Table 1 further demonstrates the difficulty that the relative-attribute-comparison heuristic has predicting the effects of some asymmetrically dominated entrants. Switching to B saves 60 cents and loses no quality, whereas switching to A costs 10 cents but gains 10 quality. Again, relative attribute comparisons do not clearly favor A or B. Further, and more importantly, the relative-attribute-comparison heuristic does not predict different effects from Entrants E and J. But as discussed next, there is ample reason to expect that Entrant E will increase B's share more than will Entrant J.

Salience of Value Differences. Relative attribute comparisons based on anchor brands are likely whenever entrants differ from both brands on both attributes. However, for the reasons just discussed, attraction effects due to entrants that differ from existing brands on only one attribute are difficult to explain in terms of relative attribute comparisons. An additional process seems to be at work in such instances. Instead of treating one brand as an anchor, we propose that consumers focus on any obvious differences in value (quality/price).[2] Given the mental arithmetic necessary to calculate and compare values, value differences that are not obvious are expected to be ignored.

The differential salience of value comparisons can be illustrated with Brands A, B, and E in Table 1 (also Figure A). If consumers were to calculate the values of each brand, then Entrant E would make both A and B look better since its value of 15.12 is lower than that of A (15.15) and B (15.29). But since such calculations can be mentally taxing, consumers may recognize only the obvious value difference. The B-E value difference is obvious since B has the same quality as E but a lower price. B's advantage can then be discerned simply by noting its lower price. On the other hand, the A-E value difference is not so obvious since A costs more but

offers more quality than E. To appreciate A's advantage over E, consumers would have to calculate and then compare the values of A and E (i.e., price and quality would have to be traded off carefully). Hence, this heuristic suggests that Entrant E will increase B's market share because consumers focus on the salient B-E value advantage and essentially ignore the less salient A-E advantage.

In contrast to the relative-attribute-comparison heuristic, the salience heuristic predicts different effects of Entrants E and J in Table 1. As just noted, Entrant E is expected to increase B's market share since B's value advantage over E is much more salient than A's. But the salience hypothesis also predicts that A's advantage over an entrant will become more salient as the entrant's price increases and approaches that of A (i.e., the entrant's value decreases). For example, A's value advantage over Entrant J should be fairly obvious since A has about the same price as J but higher quality. Unlike Entrant E, Entrant J is expected to enhance the attractiveness of both B *and* A. This leads us to what on the surface is a counterintuitive proposition: B's market share should improve more when the entrant is stronger (e.g., E) than when it is weaker (e.g., J). This nonmonotonic relationship between the entrant's appeal and the target's (B's) market share is captured in the following hypothesis:

H1: Adding an asymmetrically dominated entrant similar to the target will increase the target's market share (attraction effect). But as the entrant becomes weaker and increasingly similar to the nontarget brand, the improvement in the target's market share should become less.

In prior research, changes in a brand's market share were used to infer changes in the brand's attractiveness. However, if an entrant can influence multiple brands, then market share may not measure an entrant's effect on a brand's attractiveness. Market shares may remain constant when an entrant improves the attractiveness of A and B comparably. Readers should be alerted to the fact that the phrase *dual attraction* does not imply increased market shares of multiple brands. Instead, the phrase *dual attraction* means that an entrant makes both brands appear more attractive which, due to offsetting effects, has little impact on market share.

STUDY OVERVIEW

Hypothesis 1 was tested in an experiment. The entrant's price was held constant while its quality was varied. For theoretical reasons, the current study used various entrant versions. To keep the size of the study manageable, a single product class was used. Fortunately, this does not pose a serious problem for the current study since the generalizability of attraction effects is well established. Attraction has been demonstrated in such varied product categories as beer, cars, light

---

[2] Although the term value connotes quality per price, in the present context it is not restricted to situations where price is an attribute. For example, Simonson (1989) examined cars differing in their gas mileage and ride quality. In this instance, value could be defined as either mileage/ride quality or as ride quality/mileage.

TABLE 2
The Effect of an Entrant's Quality On Brand A's Market Share

Entrant's Quality	A's Control Share (n)	A's Experimental Share (n)	p
72	49.0% (51)	80.8% (46)	.001
67	49.0% (51)	72.3% (47)	.015
65	49.0% (51)	61.5% (52)	n.s.

NOTE: The entrant's price was constant at $4.95.

bulbs, barbeque grills, restaurants, lotteries, film, televisions, calculators, and mouthwashes. To enhance generalizability as much as possible, we selected the one product category from Ratneshwar et al.'s (1987) study that was completely unaffected by stimulus meaningfulness (i.e., beer).

EXPERIMENT

Subjects

One-hundred-and-ninety-six undergraduate and masters level business students from three large eastern universities voluntarily served as subjects.

Design and Procedure

A one-way between-subjects experiment consisting of four conditions was used. Subjects were told to imagine being in the market for a six-pack of beer. The control group was asked to choose from a market consisting of two brands: Brand A was priced at $4.95 and had a quality rating of 75 (1-100 scale). Brand B was priced at $4.25 and had a quality rating of 65. The experimental groups chose between the same two brands, although an out-of-stock entrant was added.

The entrant's price was held constant across groups at $4.95 (A's price). Its quality was then varied systemtatically to assess attraction effects on Brand A. Three levels of the entrant's quality were used: 72, 67, and 65. An entrant with quality of 72 was expected to enhance the attractiveness of only Brand A and thereby increase Brand A's share. However, this improvement was expected to be less when the entrant's quality was at 67 since the entrant was then somewhat similar to B and expected to simultaneously enhance the attractiveness of A and B. When the entrant's quality was further lowered to 65, the entrant was expected to have little effect on market shares since it was expected to enhance the attractiveness of A and B comparably.

Subjects in the experimental groups were told that the entrant was out of stock and that they had to confine their choices to Brands A and B. Excluding the entrant from choice consideration eliminated any possibility of substituting the entrant for A or B. Substitution effects are relatively unlikely when entrants are clearly dominated. However, unavailable brands were used in this study in part to make it comparable to a parallel study currently underway.

Results

In keeping with previous attraction studies (e.g., Huber and Puto 1983), between-group differences were assessed with Fisher's Exact Test of Independence (Cox 1989). The Exact Test is used in place of Chi^2 tests when sample sizes are small and the normal approximation to the binomial distribution is not valid. The Exact Test restores the power that would otherwise be lost. A separate 2 X 2 contingency table was formed for each pairwise comparison between control and experimental group.

Brand A's share in the control group was 49%. It was hypothesized that adding an entrant at $4.95 and 72 quality would increase A's share, but that this increase would become smaller as the entrant's quality was reduced to 67 and then to 65. Table 2 summarizes the results.

Consistent with Hypothesis 1, adding an entrant with a quality rating of 72 significantly increased A's share from 49% to to 80.8% (p = .001). This replicates the attraction effects reported in other studies.

Making the entrant even weaker by decreasing its quality to 67 *de*creased A's share to 72.3%, and further decreasing the entrant's quality to 65 further decreased A's share to 61.5%. The difference between the quality-72 and quality-67 conditions was not statistically significant, nor was that between the quality-67 and quality-65 conditions. However, both the quality-72 and quality-67 groups differed significantly from the control group while the quality-65 group did not. Further, the quality-72 group differed significantly from the quality-65 group (p = .029).

The steady reduction in A's share as the entrant became weaker cannot be accounted for by relative attribute comparisons, range effects, or frequency effects. However, the trend is consistent with Hypothesis 1's salience-based dual-attraction mechanism. As the entrant's quality approached that of B, the entrant increasingly enhanced the attractivenss of B which then offset the simultaneous attraction effect on A.

GENERAL DISCUSSION

The critical finding in the present study is that decreasing an entrant's attractiveness increases a target's share only to a point, beyond which decreasing entrant attractiveness actually reduces the target's share. Decreasing entrant attractiveness eventually leads to an attraction effect toward the nontarget brand which then nullifies the simultaneous attraction effect on the target. This apparent dual attraction can be accounted for only by appealing to the salience of value differences between different brands. Neither relative attribute comparisons, nor range effects, nor frequency effects can account for these findings.

It is important to note, however, that the choice of a heuristic may depend on the configuration of brands in the market. For example, value salience should play a role when Entrant X below is introduced since X is easily compared with A on value. However, Entrant Y below is not as easily compared with A or B. Therefore, consumers may not focus on value salience when Y is introduced, and instead may use relative attribute comparisons.

Brand	Price	Quality	Value (quality/price)
A	$4.95	75	15.15
B	$4.25	65	15.29
Entrant X	$4.85	60	12.37
Entrant Y	$4.65	70	15.05

Two recent studies using concurrent verbalizations are consistent with the expectation that market configurations can lead to different heuristics. Using entrants that differed from targets on only one attribute, Simonson (1989, Experiment 3) found evidence of pairwise comparisons. In contrast, Ratneshwar et al. (1987, Experiment 4) used entrants that differed from targets on both attributes and found no evidence of pairwise comparisons.

Although different heuristics may be used in different markets, scenarios can be devised where either heuristic might be used. For example, a model based on relative attribute comparisons predicts that Entrant X above will enhance B's attractiveness and thereby increase B's share. In contrast, since A's value advantage over X is fairly salient, the salience hypothesis predicts that Entrant X will additionally increase the attractiveness of A and potentially nullify the attraction effect on B. So called "strong tests" between competing mechanisms should help researchers hone in on consumer choice processes.

The current study suffered from shortcomings that future research needs to address. First, only one product class was used which may threaten the generalizability of the findings. However, this concern is partially mitigated by the fact that attraction effects have been found repeatedly in many product classes. Second, choice sets consisted of only three brands. Future research needs to address scenarios that more closely approximate the multiple-brand markets of the real world.

Third, entrants in the current study differed from targets on only one attribute. Although we have noted that relative attribute comparisons cannot explain the effects of such entrants, relative attribute comparisons probably exist when entrants differ from other brands on multiple attributes as noted earlier.

Fourth, the current study inferred dual attraction effects based on choice data that were consistent with an underlying theory. However, a more direct test of dual attraction would be to test the effects of various entrants on the liking for the two brands. For example, if the dual attraction mechanism is at work, Entrant E in Table 1 should elevate only liking for Brand B, whereas Entrant J should elevate liking for both A and B.

REFERENCES

Cox, David R., and E. J. Snell (1989), *Analysis of Binary Data*, Monographs on Statistics and Applied Probability, No. 32, New York: Chapman and Hall.

Hauser, John R., and Steven M. Shugan (1983), "Defensive Marketing Strategies," *Marketing Science*, 4 (Fall), 319-360.

Helson, Harry (1964), *Adaptation-Level Theory: An Experimental and Systematic Approach to Behavior*," New York: Harper and Row.

Huber, Joel, John W. Payne, and Christopher Puto (1982), "Adding Asymmetrically Dominated Alternative: Violations of Regularity and the Similarity Hypothesis," *Journal of Consumer Research*, 9 (June), 90-98).

_____ and Christopher Puto (1983), "Market Boundaries and Product Choice: Illustrating Attraction and Substitution Effects," *Journal of Consumer Research*, 10 (June), 31-44.

Luce, R. Duncan (1959), *Individual Choice Behavior*, New York: Wiley.

Ratneshwar, Srinivasan, Allan D. Shocker, and David W. Stewart (1987), "Toward Understanding the Attraction Effect: The Implications of Product Stimulus Meaningfulness and Familiarity," *Journal of Consumer Research*, 13 (March), 520-533.

Simonson, Itamar (1989), "Choice Based on Reasons: The Case of Attraction and Compromise Effects," *Journal of Consumer Research*, 16 (September), 158-174.

Tversky, Amos (1972), "Elimination by Aspects: A Theory of Choice," *Psychological Review*, 79 (July), 281-299.

An Exploratory Study Comparing Amount-of-Search Measures to Consumers' Reliance on Each Source of Information

Jeff Blodgett, Indiana University
Donna Hill, Bradley University

Researchers measure external information search by counting the number of times each particular behavior was undertaken. For example, respondents are asked how many stores were visited, how many friends one talked to about the product, etc. A serious limitation of this type of measure is that it provides only limited information as to how much each consumer relied on a particular source of information when making the purchase decision; i.e. their search strategy. This paper introduces a new measure (instrumentality) of consumers' reliance on each source of information, and suggest that this measure can complement the traditional amount-of-search measures. By relating the antecedents of search to the instrumentality measures researchers can gain more insight into consumers' search strategies.

Researchers investigating the external information search process have made much progress in the past decade. For example, Kiel and Layton (1981) identified several different dimensions of external search, while Furse, Punj, and Stewart (1984) created a topology of individual search strategies. Punj and Stewart (1983) and Duncan and Olshavsky (1982) investigated the effects of several different determinants of external search on a measure of total search. Beatty and Smith (1987) expanded upon these studies by investigating the effects of purchase involvement, ego involvement, time availability, and product class knowledge across the different dimensions of search (identified by Kiel and Layton 1981). This latter approach - investigating the effects of individual and environmental differences across the different types of search - is particularly informative.

Despite these conceptual and methodological advances, researchers have yet to explain much of the variance of external information search. One reason for this empirical shortcoming has been noted by Bloch, Sherrell, and Ridgway (1986). They noted that much search activity is understated because it is part of an ongoing search process, therefore, most studies - which focus on prepurchase information search - actually measure only a subset of consumers' total search activity. This paper argues that another factor limiting our understanding of the search process lies in the definition of external search; these studies define external search solely as amount-of-search. The problem with this definition (and measurement) is that it does not take into account the extent to which an individual *relied* on a particular source of information. Because one of the main goals of research on the external search process has been to do just that (i.e. to explain why different individuals rely on different search strategies) this issue is important. The purpose of this paper is to elaborate on this problem and to offer a new measure of search as a possible solution. An exploratory study was undertaken to provide a first step towards validating this new measure of search.

LIMITATIONS OF CURRENT MEASURES

Researchers have measured the different types of search (e.g. in-store search, interpersonal search, neutral source search, etc.) by asking the respondent to recall the number of times each particular behavior was undertaken. For example, respondents are asked how many stores were visited, how many friends one talked to about the product, how many buying guides were read, etc. (see Kiel and Layton 1981; Duncan and Olshavsky 1982; Punj and Staelin 1983; Furse, Punj, and Stewart 1984; Bloch, Sherrell, and Ridgway 1986; Beatty and Smith 1987). As just mentioned, a serious limitation of this type of measure is that it provides only limited insight as to how much each consumer relied on a particular source of information when making the purchase decision. For example, imagine two consumers who both consult one issue of *Consumer Reports* during the search process: one consumer studies this buying guide in detail and relies solely on this information when making the purchase decision, while the other consumer also looks at this buying guide but discounts the information and instead relies on another source of information. In this situation it is quite obvious that the search behavior of these two consumers differed significantly (with respect to the buying guide), however, studies using amount-of-search as the dependent measure would not make this distinction. This shortcoming holds true across the other dimensions of external search also: number of friends talked to, number of retailers visited, etc. In other words, amount-of-search measures do not always accurately reflect individual consumers' search strategies.

Engel, Kollat, and Blackwell (1968) recognized long ago that amount-of-search - or *exposure* to an information source - is not necessarily the same as the importance of an information source. They state that (p. 404):

> One way of expressing the importance of an information source is in terms of *exposure*. For example, an information source could be judged more important than other sources in that a greater percentage of consumers report being exposed to it. ... *There are, however, fundamental problems involved in using exposure in this manner* [italics added]. Consumers can be exposed to information sources without using them or finding them helpful in making purchasing decisions. As a consequence, there may be a significant

difference between *exposure* and *effectiveness*, and an information source that is most important in terms of exposure may be of lesser importance when the criterion of effectiveness is employed.

Indeed, Engel et al. (1968) list several studies which found that consumers often relied more heavily on low-exposure information sources than on high-exposure information sources when making their purchase decisions (see LeGrand and Udell 1964; Sargent 1959; Katz and Lazersfeld 1955). Despite these findings, recent studies have relied solely on exposure to measure external search.

This paper argues that external search can be better understood by measuring what we will call the *instrumentality* of the information source (i.e. effectiveness), in addition to amount-of-search. The causal effects of the determinants of search could then be compared across these two measures, thus providing more insight into individuals' search strategies. Used in this manner, the instrumentality measures could be a useful complement to the traditional measures of external search. Before the instrumentality measures can be considered to have any practical importance, however, they must first be shown - empirically - to be somewhat different than their respective amount-of-search measures. The purpose of this pilot study, then, is to study the relationship between these two measures of external search to determine whether the instrumentality argument is valid. At issue is: first, how to measure instrumentality and second, whether or not measures of instrumentality will differ from measures of exposure (or amount-of-search). Thus, this paper is an attempt to develop a reliable measure of instrumentality and to take a preliminary step toward establishing the validity of this measure.

MEASURES

Amount-of-Search

This study will measure five different dimensions of search (see Duncan and Olshavsky 1982; Kiel and Layton 1981; Bennett and Mandell 1969). These five dimensions, and their traditional amount-of-search measures, are: 1) in-store search, which is measured by the number of stores visited and the number of models examined; 2) interpersonal search is a measure of how many friends, relatives, and/or neighbors who were consulted; 3) an unsponsored (neutral) sources factor is a measure of how many buying guides (such as *Consumer Reports*) the consumer read; 4) a fourth factor reflects the number of salespeople or other store employees who the consumer talked to; and 5) a media factor measures the number of TV, radio, magazine, and newspaper advertisements seen, heard, or read. The Furse et al. (1984) study provides support for these five dimensions. This classification is more precise than Kiel and Layton's (1981) in that it explicitly includes a salesperson dimension. Previous research (Olshavsky 1973) has shown that salespeople can be important sources of information. Like Beatty and Smith (1986), it also separates the media and neutral sources dimensions.

Instrumentality of the Information Source

In addition to the amount-of-search measures, we will also assess the instrumentality of each dimension of search. Again, we intend for the instrumentality construct to reflect the degree to which the consumer *relied* on a particular source of information when making the purchase decision. As such, the domain of this construct might also encompass the relative helpfulness, usefulness, and importance of the particular source of information.

In order to develop a reliable measure of instrumentality multiple items are needed (Churchill 1979). Therefore, we measure each of the instrumentality constructs with three 7-point interval scales, using agree/disagree, not at all useful/extremely useful, and did not rely on at all/I relied most heavily (on this information) as scale endpoints. Examples of items (one for each dimension of search) that were used include:

To what extent did you rely on the advice of your friends, relatives, or neighbors, etc., in making this purchase decision?

I found consumer rating guides, such as *Consumer Reports*, or hobbyist magazines, such as *Modern Photography* to be very useful when deciding which brand to buy.

To what extent did you rely on the advice of the different salespeople, or other store employees, who you talked to?

When deciding which brand to buy, I found advertisements in newspapers or magazines, and/or on TV or the radio, to be very useful.

Compared to these other strategies, when deciding which brand to buy to what extent did you rely on just visiting different stores and comparing the various brands that were available?

METHOD

The data for this study was collected as part of another study being conducted by the authors. A convenience sample of 114 adults participated in the study; 64% were white-collar workers enrolled in evening MBA courses, while 36% were staff employees (mainly secretaries and clerks) at a midwestern university. Forty-four percent were male while 56% were female. Respondents were provided with a list of major durable products and asked which ones they had purchased within the last twelve months. This list included VCR's, stereo equipment, camera equipment, televisions, and personal computers (this product group is similar to that used by Beatty and Smith 1987). They were then asked to use the product they purchased most recently (from among this list) as the focal point of this

TABLE 1

Type of Search	Amount-of-Search*		Instrumentality**	
	Mean	S.Dev	Mean	S.Dev
In-store	5.99*	2.43	4.36	1.57
Interpersonal	2.19	1.73	3.79	1.71
Neutral Sources	.62	1.12	2.20	1.72
Salespersons	1.67	1.63	3.10	1.49
Media (ads)	3.41	3.74	2.87	1.62

* refers to number of sources consulted
** a 1 indicates no reliance while a 7 indicates heavy reliance

study. To avoid problems of recall among subjects who had purchased the particular product before only responses from first time purchasers were utilized. As recommended by Feldman and Lynch (1988), the 15 instrumentality items and the amount-of-search items were spread throughout the questionnaire, with reverse wording on many of the instrumentality items. This practice reduces subjects' propensity to retrieve one response as the basis for another, thus providing a more stringent test of reliability.

RESULTS

The means and standard deviations of both types of measures are shown in Table 1. Respondents, on average, visited 3.11 stores and considered 2.88 brands, for an in-store mean of 5.99. They asked for advice from 2.19 friends, or relatives, on average, and from 1.67 salespeople. Only .62 neutral sources were used, on average, while respondents obtained product information from an average of 3.41 radio, television, newspaper, and/or magazine ads. Respondents relied most heavily on in-store search, followed by interpersonal sources and information from salespeople. Surprisingly, respondents did not rely very heavily upon neutral sources.

Reliability of the Instrumentality Measures

Before proceeding to empirically assess the discriminant validity of the instrumentality measures, one should first check to see whether these measures are reliable (Churchill 1979). Coefficient alpha is the most common indicator of reliability, and was computed for each of the instrumentality measures. In addition to being reliable, the three items measuring each dimension of search should load together, with each set of three items loading on separate factors (Schwab 1986). A principal components factor analysis was performed. The factor loadings, and the reliability (Cronbach's alpha) of each measure, are shown in Table 2.

The items measuring each dimension of search load cleanly on separate factors. The factor loadings are all high (above .80), and the cross loadings are all small (none over .35). These results surpass the standards suggested by Nunnally (1978) for criterion validity. In addition, each instrumentality measure is fairly reliable (the lowest alpha is .78 and the highest is .94), surpassing the standard for reliability suggested by Nunnally (1978) for exploratory research. Overall, the results indicate that we have indeed measured what we set out to measure - instrumentality, or one's reliance on a particular source of information. With this assurance in mind, we can now set out to compare the instrumentality measures to the amount-of-search scores.

Correlations

The correlations within the amount-of-search measures and within the instrumentality measures can be seen in Table 3. An interesting finding is that all of the significant amount-of-search correlations are positive while two of the instrumentality correlations are negative. The latter findings imply that, for many people, interpersonal and neutral sources information are substitutes for in-store information, while the correlations for the amount-of-search measures imply that consumers who undertake greater amounts of in-store search also undertake greater amounts of all other types of search. Although it is a bit difficult at this point to reconcile these findings, it is important to note that these findings are not necessarily contradictive. Rather, these findings lend credibility to the argument that the information gained from using the instrumentality measures might complement that gained from the traditional amount-of-search measures. Future studies that investigate the causal effects of the determinants of search might be able to use these findings to better explain consumers' search strategies.

Table 4 shows the correlations between the amount-of-search scores and the instrumentality scores. In order to convincingly argue that the instru-mentality measures might complement the amount-of-search measures these two types of measures should not be too highly correlated with one another. The correlations are low enough to suggest that the instrumentality measures are related, but not identical, to the amount-of-search measures.

TABLE 2
Factor Analysis Loadings and Reliability

	IN STORE	INTER PERSONAL	MEDIA (ADS)	SALES PERSON	NEUTRAL SOURCES	CRONBACH'S ALPHA
		Factor loading below .35 not shown				
STORE 1	.90					
STORE 2	.81					.78
STORE 3	.80					
INTER 1		.91				
INTER 2		.86				.85
INTER 3		.81				
MEDIA 1			.90			
MEDIA 2			.84			.84
MEDIA 3			.81			
SPERSON 1				.85		
SPERSON 2				.82		.81
SPERSON 3				.81		
NEUTRAL 1					.94	
NEUTRAL 2					.91	.94
NEUTRAL 3					.91	

TABLE 3

Amount-of-Search Correlations

	Store	Inter	S/P	Ntrl
Interpersonal	ns			
Salesperson	.42*	.23		
Neutral Sources	.24*	.18	ns	
Media (ads)	.27*	.29*	ns	.22

Instrumentality Correlations

	Store	Inter	S/P	Ntrl
Interpersonal	-.27			
Salesperson	ns	.19		
Neutral Sources	-.20	ns	ns	
Media (ads)	ns	ns	ns	ns

* $p < .01$; other correlations are significant at $p < .05$

Therefore, the instrumentality measures might indeed provide researchers with additional information.

DISCUSSION

One of the goals of previous researchers has been to explain what causes different consumers to undertake different types of search. To do so, researchers have tried to model the effects of various antecedents of search on the different dimensions of search (see Beatty and Smith 1987). Having established that the instrumentality and amount-of-search measures are somewhat different, it is argued that researchers might find some interesting results when they compare the effects of the various determinants of search across these two types of measures (i.e. across the different dimensions). That is, our interpretation of the causal effects of the various determinants of search might well depend on which type of dependent measure is used. Consider again two fictitious consumers: consumer number one is highly confident in her ability to judge new cars (i.e product class, or subjective knowledge) and

TABLE 4

Correlations Between Amount-of-Search and Instrumentality of the Information Source

In-Store	.40
Interpersonal	.60
Salesperson	.54
Neutral Sources	.74
Media (ads)	.59

all correlations significant at $p < .01$

undertakes an extensive search process. In addition, she asks for advice from *one* friend, but does not rely on this advice when deciding which brand to buy. Consumer number two, who has little confidence in his ability to judge new cars, undertakes very little search and instead relies entirely on the advice of *one* relative. In this situation because both consumers undertook the same amount of interpersonal search it would not appear that product class knowledge had any effect upon search when regressed upon this measure. However, while it would be correct to say that this variable had no effect on the *amount* of interpersonal search, it would not be correct to say that this determinant had no effect on these two consumers' search strategies. Obviously, researchers would reach different conclusions regarding the effect of product class knowledge depending on whether the amount-of-search or the instrumentality measure is used. Again, we do not suggest that one measure is better than the other, rather, we feel that the information gained from using the instrumentality measures would certainly complement that from the amount-of-search measures.

To illustrate the potential contribution of the instrumentality measures, Beatty and Smith (1987) were able to explain only 15%, 7%, and 5% of the variance of the amount of interpersonal, media, and neutral sources search, respectively. Because the instrumentality measures appear to better reflect consumers' search strategies, we feel that researchers who use these measures will be able to explain a significantly greater percent of the variance of external search. For example, Beatty and Smith (1987) found the effects of time availability and ego involvement to be .17 and .14 when regressed on the amount of neutral source measure. Again, these two determinants (plus purchase involvement and subjective product class knowledge) explained only 5% of the variance of this type of search. Going back to the example cited earlier in this paper (regarding *Consumer Reports*), researchers might find these determinants to have a much greater effect on one's reliance on these sources. In addition, other variables that had no effect on the amount of neutral search - such as product importance - might have a significant effect when instrumentality is used as the dependent variable.

A related area of research where it might pay to use the instrumentality measures concerns the stages of the decision process. It has generally been considered that different types of information sources will be used at different stages of the decision process. For example, when consumers are in the early stages of the decision process (problem recognition and refinement) they tend to seek information from the various media sources (Mowen 1987). During the purchase specification stage consumers turn to friends, relatives, and neutral sources such as *Consumer Reports*. As the consumer enters the purchase respecification stage and begins to visit different stores he or she is more likely to seek information from a salesperson. If the in-store and salesperson information confirms the consumer's prior beliefs he/she may decide not to seek any more information (Wilkie and Dickson 1985) and to make the purchase. By examining the sequence of search, and by determining consumers' reliance upon different types of information at these different stages, we can better understand the effects of the various individual and situational determinants of search. With this information we can create more precise profiles of consumers' search strategies.

FUTURE RESEARCH - A COMPREHENSIVE MODEL OF SEARCH

Future research should focus on the relationships between the antecedents of search, the instrumentality of search sources and the amount of search. Figure 1 provides a conceptual diagram of such a model. Rather than aggregating the various measures of search it is proposed that in-store search, media search, interpersonal search, neutral sources search, and salespersons' advice search all be treated as separate dependent variables. The rationale for treating each dimension of search separately is that when all of the different measures of search are aggregated many interesting effects are averaged out. For example, one consumer might undertake a high amount of retailer search and very little media and neutral source (buying guide) search while another consumer does the exact opposite. Although these two consumers undertook different types of search an aggregate measure would reflect only the amount of search undertaken, obscuring the

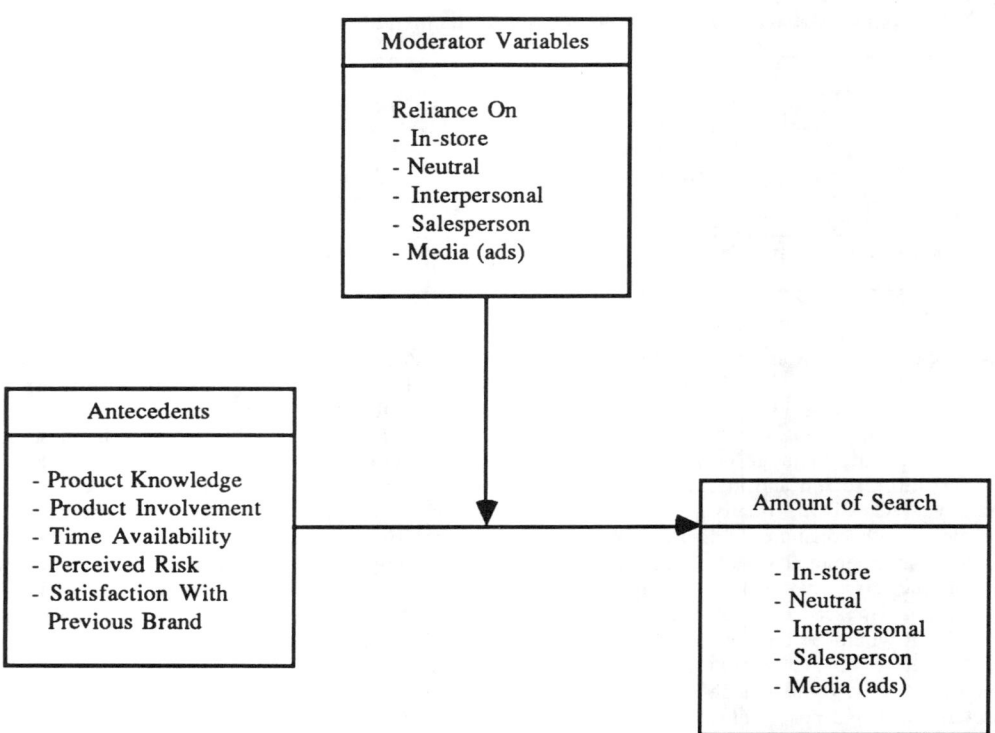

FIGURE 1
Comprehensive Model of Search

independent-dependent variable relationship. Data regarding the *type* of search undertaken is much more interesting and informative than data regarding *how much* search occurred overall.

By introducing the instrumentality measures into the model the researcher will have information on the extent to which the consumer relied on each source of information. It is hypothesized that each of the antecedent variables will have a different impact on the type of sources consulted for additional information. For example, higher levels of subjective knowledge (and ability to judge) should lead to less reliance on interpersonal sources and more reliance on retailer/in-store information (Selnes and Gronhaug 1986; Duncan and Olshavsky 1982). Higher levels of satisfaction with previous brands might lead to less dealer and media search while not having a significant effect on the other types of search (Kiel and Layton 1981; Katona and Mueller 1955; Newman and Staelin 1972). If little time is available the consumer might rely heavily on interpersonal sources and salespersons' information, and undertake little retailer search.

Although the effects on retailer search and interpersonal search seem fairly straightforward the same is not true of the other dimensions of search. Overall, it is difficult to go beyond generalizations at this point; there are too few empirical studies and little theory to rely upon to develop specific hypotheses. Nonetheless, one of the purposes of model building is to develop realistic pictures of the world, with or without adequate theoretical justification.

SUMMARY

The purpose of this paper has been to propose that our knowledge of the external information search process can be better understood by taking into account the instrumentality of the various sources of information. In the future, we plan to compare the causal effects of several determinants of search across these two different measures of search. Only then can the validity of these measures accurately be assessed. The current study is encouraging in that it provides a strong justification for this type of inquiry. Again, we believe that researchers will be better able to interpret the effects of the various determinants when the instrumentality measures are used, thus enhancing our knowledge of consumers' search strategies.

REFERENCE LIST

Beatty, S.E. & Smith, S.M. (1987). "External Search Effort: An Investigation Across Several Product Categories," *Journal of Consumer Research*, 14 (June), 83-95.

Bennett, J.H. & Mandell, R.M. (1969). "Prepurchase Information Seeking Behavior of New Car Purchasers - The Learning Hypothesis," *Journal of Marketing Research*, 6 (November), 430-33.

Bloch, P.H., Sherrell, D.L. & Ridgway, N.M. (1986). "Consumer Search: An Extended Framework," *Journal of Consumer Research*, 13 (June), 119-126.

Churchill, G. (1979). "A Paradigm for Developing Better Measures of Marketing Constructs," *Journal of Marketing Research*, 16 (February), 64-73

Duncan, C.P. & Olshavsky, R.W. (1982). "External Search: The Role of Consumer Beliefs," *Journal of Marketing Research*, 19 (February), 32-43.

Engel, Kollat, & Blackwell (1968). *Consumer Behavior*, Chicago, Il.: Holt, Rinehart, and Winston, Inc.

Feldman, J.M. & Lynch, J.G. (1988). "Self-Generated Validity and Other Effects of Measurement on Belief, Attitude, Intention, and Behavior," *Journal of Applied Psychology*, 73, no. 3, 421-435.

Furse, D.H., Punj, G.N. & Stewart, D.W. (1984). "A Topology of Individual Search Strategies Among Purchasers of New Automobiles," *Journal of Consumer Research*, 10 (March), 417-31.

Katona, G. & Mueller, U. (1955). "A Study of Purchasing Decisions," in *Consumer Behavior: The Dynamics of Consumer Reaction*, L. H. Clark (ed.), New York, NY: New York University Press, 30-87.

Katz, E. & Lazersfeld, P. (1955). "*Personal Influence*, New York, NY.: The Free Press of Glencoe.

Kiel, G.C. & Layton, R.A. (1981). "Dimensions of Consumer Information Seeking Behavior," *Journal of Marketing Research*, 18 (May), 233-39.

LeGrand, B. & Udell, J.G. (1964). "Consumer Behavior in the Market Place," *Journal of Retailing*, Fall, 32-40, 47-48.

Mowen, J. (1987), *Consumer Behavior*, New York: Macmillan Publishing Company.

Newman, J.W. & Staelin, R. (1972). "Prepurchase Information Seeking for New Cars and Major Household Appliances," *Journal of Marketing Research*, 17 (November), 460-69.

Nunnally, J.C. (1978). *Psychometric Theory*, New York: McGraw Hill Book Co.

Olshavsky, R.W. (1973). "Customer-Salesman Interaction in Appliance Retailing," *Journal of Marketing Research*, (May) 10, 208-212.

Punj, G.N. & Staelin, R. (1983). "A Model of Consumer Information Search Behavior for New Automobiles," *Journal of Consumer Research*, 9 (March), 366-380.

Punj, G. and W. Stewart (1983), "An Interaction Framework of Consumer Decision Making," *Journal of Consumer Research*, 10 (September), 181-196.

Sargent, H.W. (1959). "*Consumer Product Rating Publications and Buying Behavior*, Urbana, Il.: University of Illinois Bureau of Economic and Business Research.

Schwab, D.P. (1986). "Construct Validation in Organizational Behavior," in L.L. Cummings and B. Staw, eds., *Research in Organizational Behavior*, 12, Greenwich, CT: JAI Press, 41-50.

Selnes, F. & Gronhaug, K. (1986). "Subjective and Objective Measures of Product Knowledge Contrasted," in R. Lutz (ed.) *Advances in Consumer Research*, 13, Provo, Utah: ACR, 61-71.

Wilkie, W. and P. Dickson (1985), "Shopping For Appliances: Consumers' Strategies and Patterns of Information Search," Report No. 85-108, Cambridge Mass: Marketing Science Institute.

An Information Theoretic Approach to Understanding the Consideration Set/Awareness Set Proportion

Ayn E. Crowley, Washington State University
John H. Williams, Texas Southern University

ABSTRACT

This paper investigates the consideration set/awareness set proportion and proposes an information theoretic model which identifies a 63:37 proportion as "optimal". This proportion may lead to efficiencies in information processing and has been found in various types of evaluative judgments in prior research. This information theoretic model is applied to two product categories and results support the hypothesized relationships. The depth with which consumers process product category information is identified as a possible boundary condition for this phenomenon.

INTRODUCTION

Before purchasing a product, consumers must first be aware of the product and believe that the product will meet their needs. Indeed, this act of purchase is often conceptualized as a *process* (cf. Nicosia 1966, Howard and Sheth 1969). In the marketing literature the concepts of *awareness set* and *consideration set* are used to help describe one of the basic processes which leads to purchase of a product (Nedungadi 1987). Consumers may eliminate some brands which they are aware of from further consideration in order to reduce the complexity of the decision process.

Marketers attempt to gain entry into the consumer's awareness set through promotional efforts. Many steps are also taken to help ensure that consumers will perceive the product positively and will include the product among those considered for purchase.

The size of the awareness set is fairly large for some product categories. For example, Campbell (1969) reported a mean awareness set size of 15.2 brands of dishwashing liquid. For cake mixes, Jacoby and Olson (1970) found an average of 7.8 brands in the awareness set. The consideration set is a subset of the awareness set, consisting of brands the consumer considers relevant for the purchase occasion (Alba and Chattopadhyay 1985). This approach to consumer decision making is often described as a simplifying heuristic (Hauser and Wernerfelt 1990), or "funneling" process (Howard and Sheth 1969). Several researchers believe that there may be an upper bound on the size of the consideration set (e.g., Alba and Hutchinson 1987).

The relative sizes of the awareness and consideration sets have been discussed in the marketing literature (Brown and Wildt 1987, Campbell 1969, Jarvis and Wilcox 1973, Narayana and Markin 1975, Ostlund 1973). Yet, the consideration set/awareness set ratio has not been examined. In particular, the *proportion* of brands in the awareness set which are included in the consideration set has received little investigation. In the present paper, an information theoretic model is used to predict the tendency of this particular proportion. The consideration set is viewed in this context as the brands in the awareness set that are *evaluated positively*. Those brands which the consumer is aware of but does not include in the consideration set are viewed as *negatively evaluated* brands.

Information theory suggests a positive:negative proportion which may offer several information processing efficiencies. This proportion has been found repeatedly in empirical tests of positive:negative evaluations of persons (Benjafield and Adams-Webber 1976, Rigdon and Epting 1982), words (Adams-Webber 1978), and objects (Crowley 1990). The major contribution of this paper is the identification of a consistent proportional tendency between positive and negative brand evaluations within a product category.

The inclusion of the concept of a consideration set in quantitative models has been shown to improve the predictive ability of several of these models (e.g., Hauser and Gaskins 1984, Louviere 1988, Silk and Urban 1978). The consideration set, however, is very dynamic and may vary from one point in time to another due to the influence of internally and externally generated retrieval cues (Nedungadi 1987). Also, the measurements of consideration set size and composition may be susceptible to the influence of methodological factors that may produce results that are an artifact of the methods employed rather than valid measures of the consideration set.

The awareness set, on the other hand, is less susceptible to influence from these factors. Therefore, if it can be established that there is a relatively stable relationship between the sizes of the awareness and consideration sets, more reliable estimates of the size of the consideration set may be available to researchers and marketing practitioners. Similarly, the proportion could be considered as the *probability* that a new product will achieve inclusion in the consumer's consideration set.

In the present study, it is postulated that the information theoretic proportion (i.e., 63:37) will be found in the consideration set/awareness set relationship. The information theoretic rationale for the hypothesized relationsip is described below. This is followed by a brief summary of the related psychological literature and a discussion of the possible boundary conditions for the phenomenon. Related findings from the marketing literature are then discussed. Subsequently, a study used to investigate the hypothesized relationships is reported.

INFORMATION THEORY APPLIED TO THE POSITIVE:NEGATIVE DICHOTOMY

"Information" is an important concept in many disciplines including psychology, communication, and marketing. Information theory offers an approach to quantifying the amount of information contained in a message. Information theoretic concepts were developed within the field of communciation by Shannon and Weaver (1949) and Weiner (1948). This research, along with the work of Miller (1956), is now viewed as the precursor of the cognitive approach within psychology.

The concept of *uncertainty* (often termed entropy) is central to understanding "information" in this quantitative context, as will be explained in detail below. Uncertainty is quite analogous to "surprise". In information theory, the reduction in uncertainty is quantified as *information*.

The amount of information received, on the average, is dependent upon two factors. First, the *number* of possible alternative symbols (n) which can be "sent" affects average information. Secondly, the *probability* (p_i; i=1 to n) associated with each alternative symbol being sent is used to calculate average information. With a given number of alternative symbols, the information quantity is maximized when the alternatives are equiprobable (Young 1971).

In communication theory, information is usually measured in *bits*, or binary digits. If the alternative messages are equiprobable, the amount of information is:

$$I = \log_2 n$$

Often, the alternatives are not equiprobable. The general formula used to calculate entropy is (cf. Garner 1962, Pierce 1961):

$$H = -\sum_{i=1}^{n} p_i \log_2 p_i = \sum_{i=1}^{n} p_i \log_2(1/p_i)$$

where:

H = average information per symbol sent by a source (expressed in bits).

p_i = the proportion of total symbols sent by a source which are symbol *i* specifically.

n = the number of possible alternative symbols which the source can send.

The behavior of the information theoretic function over various values of p_i for a dichotomy is illustrated in Figure 1.

Several aspects of the application of the entropy formula to psychological processes are discussed by Berlyne (1971). Berlyne conceptualizes the contribution to average information as an index of the *strikingness* or "salience" of the information. This measure of "strikingness" is postulated to reflect the psychological impact of an element or signal. Therefore, a low probability event could carry a great deal of information, as would be reflected in the events' contribution to the H function.

To understand the information theoretic predictions described by Berlyne (1971), it is necessary to examine the behavior of *part* of the entropy formula. In the present application, this would represent one of the two possible affective categories (positive and negative). The form of the function for the contribution of one category to average information is depicted in Figure 2. As noted by Berlyne (1971, p. 231), the maximum contribution to average information occurs at about .37 or 1/e. This is the point at which the minor category represents about 37 percent of the total. At this point, the contribution to total information is .53. When 1-p = .63 (i.e., 1-.37), the value of $(1-p)\log_2\{1/(1-p)\}$ is .43. Thus, average information per evaluation in this case is .53 + .43 or .96 bits. At the 63:37 proportion, the minor category contributes the maximum possible amount to total information. In essence, there is maximum "contrast" between the minor category (or foreground) against the background of the major category.

The average information obtained at the 63:37 proportion is about 4 percent less (i.e., 1.00-.96) than the maximum possible information abtained in the equiprobable case. Thus, the decrement in information which would be obtained from evaluations is very small compared to the gains, such as increased salience for one category of information.

Based on the rationale described above, it is posited that the human affective system would gradually evolve through natural selection toward the information theoretic processing proportion. This proportion may contribute to an organism's chances of survival due to the *efficiency* it contributes to affective processing. For example, maximizing the "strikingness" of negative information (Berlyne 1971) may imply that this information can be processed *faster*. A speed of processing advantage of even a fraction of a second could lead to evolutionary tendencies toward the information theoretic ratio for evaluative judgments. If this rationale is correct, the information theoretic phenomenon should be a robust one. Indeed, empirical evidence suggests that this processing proportion has been found in a variety of psychological contexts, as described subsequently.

PSYCHOLOGICAL RESEARCH

Evaluative Judgments

The 63:37 information theoretic proportion has been found in human affective functioning, and in evaluative judgments specifically. The term "golden section proportion" is often used in the psychology literature, reflecting the special geometric properties of a related 62:38 proportion (Crowley 1990). Due to the large amount of prior

FIGURE 1
Uncertainty of dichotomous distributions with probabilities p and $1-p$.

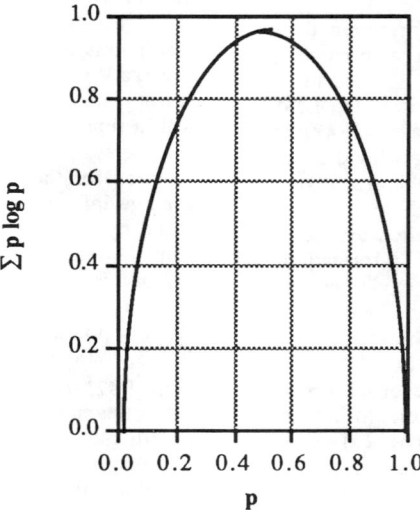

FIGURE 2
Values of $-p \log p$ as a function of p.

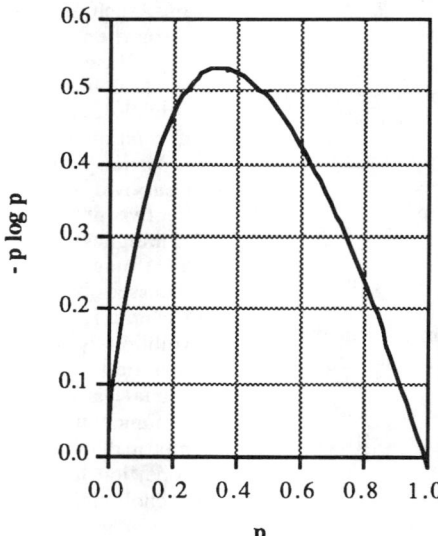

research on this topic all relevant findings cannot be presented. Thus, only those findings which directly impact hypothesis development are reported.

The first known psychological application of this information theoretic concept occurred in the field of experimental aesthetics. Several investigators (see Huntley 1970) have found that subjects tend to prefer rectangles based on the proportion. For example, McManus (1980) found evidence for preference for rectangles based on proportions near 63:37.

Research by Frank (1959, 1964) and Berlyne (1971) has been especially important in applying the information theoretic proportion in experimental aesthetics. Frank (cited in Berlyne 1971) performed experiments in which subjects were asked to select squares from a collection offering many squares in several colors and to arrange these squares so as to make one color as "striking" as possible. The subjects used the "striking" color, on the average, between 37 and 38 percent of the time, using various other colors to form the "background" for the striking color.

More recently, Benjafield and Adams-Webber (1976) reported data from five experiments in which subjects made dichotomous judgments of acquaintances (e.g., pleasant:unpleasant). Subjects were asked to rate the acquaintances on several semantic differential dimensions. The hypothesis tested in each study was that, when subjects make dichotomous judgments about a series of acquaintances in terms of bipolar dimensions, they will tend to make these judgments in proportions which approximate the information theoretic/golden section ratio, using positive adjectives 62 percent of the time and negative adjectives 38 percent of the time. The aggregate level results of each of these five studies were within 0.01 of the hypothesized proportion.

An important extension of the information theoretic/golden section hypothesis resulted from the work of Rigdon and Epting (1982). In their experiment, subjects were asked to generate their own construct dimensions, rather than using a set of provided dimensions. Rating acquaintances on these elicited constructs, the proportion of positive judgments was .63, which did not differ significantly from the predicted proportion of .62.

Perhaps most importantly, Rigdon and Epting asked subjects to rate the usefulness of the constructs in terms of "how useful you feel each construct-contrast pair is to you in accurately describing and characterizing people." Their hypothesis that subjects would rate the constructs which they had used in the information theoretic/golden section proportion as more useful than constructs used in other positive/negative proportions was supported: subjects rated constructs which they had used in this proportion as more useful in describing and characterizing people.

In summary, evidence has been accumulated which indicates that some human attitude structures are constructed in approximately the 63:37 proportion. Information theory provides a mathematical rationale indicating that this particular proportion may offer processing efficiencies by maximizing the contribution of the minor category to total information.

A Test of the Information Theoretic Hypothesis in a Marketing Context

One study has examined proportional relationships in consumers' perceptions of a marketing stimulus (Crowley 1990). Subjects in this study rated a retail store environment on twenty semantic differential scales. Responses at the midpoint of these scales were considered affectively neutral and were eliminated from the analysis.

Results of the Crowley (1990) study indicated that subjects' ratings of the store environment followed a 63:37 positive:negative proportion, with the major category being negative evaluations. In addition, responses were factor analyzed and the 63:37 proportion was found within each major factor comprising the overall judgments of the stimulus. The existence of these relationships within these orthogonal factors comprising more "global" judgments may be considered a form of "nesting" of these proportions.

Summary

Evidence supporting the information theoretic proportion in evaluative judgments is far from conclusive. Yet, the evidence is strong enough to warrant further research and application of this concept. The broadest implication of the research summarized in this brief review of the literature is that the proportion may be operative in many types of affective judgments. This may include affective judgments made in a marketing context. Affective processes have been the subject of increasing research interest in marketing. Understanding of the processes has added richness and validity to models of consumer decision making. The information theoretic proportion, if it is found to apply to marketing-related affective judgments, can represent a stride forward in gaining deeper insight into the processes underlying these judgments.

Awareness and Consideration Set Findings

The awareness set for a particular product class can be viewed as a cognitive structure held in long-term memory. This structure consists of brand names, information about brands, attributes, and perhaps even decision criteria for evaluating the brands. When a brand choice decision is made, the individual obtains brand information from the external environment and/or retrieves information from long-term memory. Both positively and negatively perceived brands along with neutral brands may be considered by the consumer. The size and composition of the set of brands considered by the individual may be influenced by the accessibility of brand information contained in the cognitive structure for the product class and the particular retrieval cues available at the time the brand choice decision is being made.

Howard and Sheth (1969) hypothesized that the number of brands of a product that a consumer considers for purchase bears some relationship to the number of brands that s(he) is aware of. Several consumer researchers have examined this relationship. The results of these studies are summarized in Table 1. The mean size of the awareness sets for the various products ranged from 3.5 for mouthwash to 19.3 for laundry detergent. The mean size of the consideration sets ranged from 1.3 for mouthwash to 5.6 for dishwashing liquid. The ratio of the mean consideration set size to the mean awareness set size ranged from .27 for laundry detergent to .64 for table napkins with a mean proportion of .39 across all product categories. Variation in consideration set proportions may have

TABLE 1
Awareness and Consideration Set Sizes[a]

Source	Product Category	Awareness Set Mean (S.D.)	Consideration Set Mean (S.D.)	Consideration Set Proportion
Campbell 1969	Laundry detergent	19.3(3.0)	5.0(2.9)	.26
	Toothpaste	10.4(2.2)	3.1(2.1)	.30
Jacoby & Olson 1970	Cake mix	7.8(na)	3.2(na)	.41
Jarvis & Wilcox 1973	Coffee	10.2(1.3)	4.2(2.2)	.41
	Dishwashing liquid	15.2(3.2)	5.6(3.6)	.37
	Table napkins	7.3(1.6)	5.0(1.9)	.64
Narayana & Markin 1975	Toothpaste	6.5(1.33)[b]	2.0(0.50)[b]	.31
	Mouthwash	3.5(0.83)[b]	1.3(0.50)[b]	.37
	Deodorant	6.0(1.67)[b]	1.6(0.67)[b]	.27
	Beer	10.6(3.50)[b]	3.5(2.17)[b]	.33
Prasad 1975	Hair shampoo	5.1(2.67)[b]	2.1(2.17)[b]	.41
	Headache remedies	4.3(1.83)[b]	2.2(1.83)[b]	.51
	Toothpaste	5.6(2.83)[b]	2.3(2.50)[b]	.41
Church et al. 1985	Color television	13.06(na)	5.16(2.06)	.40
Brown & Wildt 1987	Fast food restaurants	11.78(4.24)	5.39(2.90)	.46
	Gasoline	6.72(2.33)	2.98(1.45)	.44
	Soft drinks	14.32(4.06)	5.06(2.51)	.35

[a]In most of these studies, the term "evoked set" was used and was operationally defined in different ways (e.g., the set of brands a consumer "would consider buying", "finds acceptable", "is "willing to buy").

[b]Estimate of standard deviation was obtained by assuming a normal distribution and dividing the range by 6.

resulted from product category and research design differences.

The sizes of both the awareness and consideration sets were larger when aided rather than unaided recall was used. However, the mean size of the consideration set relative to the mean size of the awareness set was not significantly different for the two approaches. The average consideration set proportion was .40 when aided recall was used and .39 when unaided recall was used.

HYPOTHESIZED RELATIONSHIPS

As described above, it is hypothesized that the 63:37 proportion will be found in the consideration set/awareness set relationship within product categories. This is reflected in Hypothesis 1A:

H1A: Among the brands a consumer is aware of, the consumer will tend to include either 37 percent or 63 percent of these brands in the consideration set.

This hypothesis is based upon the fact that these product judgments are evaluative, and may be governed by the information processing bias found in several psychological studies described previously.

Further, it is hypothesized that the 63 percent versus 37 percent distinction will be a function of the size of the awareness set. This view posits that the consumer is often an "efficient" information processor who will only want to consider a few brands in depth (Bettman 1986). Thus, the consumer who is aware of many brands in a particular product category may consider a relatively small proportion of this plethora of brands. This could reflect a tradeoff between decision making effort (costs) and the desire to make an optimal decision, as described by Hauser and Wernerfelt (1990). Conversely, the consumer is likely to be aware of only a few brands in certain product categories. We might expect a larger proportion of these brands to be considered, as this would still imply a relatively small consideration set. Hypothesis 1B also reflects the idea that there are limits on the amount of information that can be processed at any given time (Miller 1956). This tendency is also reflected by direct empirical evidence regarding typical sizes of consideration sets (see Hauser and Wernerfelt 1990).

> H1B: The consideration set/awareness set ratio will be a function of the size of the awareness set. With a larger awareness set, there will be a tendency for 37 percent of the brands to be included in the consideration set. With a smaller awareness set, there will be a tendency for 63 percent of the brands to be included in the consideration set.

Hypothesis 2 represents an attempt to investigate the boundary conditions of the information theoretic proportion. A review of related studies in the psychology literature indicated that the 63:37 proportion was found when subjects gave *in-depth* consideration to categories such as acquaintances. This concept is quite analogous to the *degree of analysis* described by Alba and Hutchinson (1987). Degree of analysis is a continuum and "refers to the extent to which consumers access all and only the information that is relevant and/or important for a particular task" (Alba and Hutchinson 1987, p. 417). With more analytic or "in-depth" processing, information search is effortful and extends beyond the most accessible information.

Hypothesis 2 is based upon the rationale that the 63:37 proportion is more likely to be found when subjects access their product category knowledge and affective structure more *completely*. Thus, cues will be presented to some subjects prior to the experimental task which may facilitate retrieval of this information. As described by Biehal and Chakravarti (1983, p. 4), "The retrieval of information from memory is known to be cue-dependent, i.e., the cues available at retrieval influence whether or not previously stored information can be accessed from memory."

In the present study, some subjects will consider the product category in-depth, while others will not. This will allow an initial glimpse at a possible boundary condition for the information theoretic proportion. Hypothesis 2 addresses the question: Is in-depth processing a necessary condition for finding the 63:37 proportion in attitude structures?

> H2: The 63:37 relationship will only be found when subjects engage in in-depth processing of product category information.

METHODOLOGY

Subjects
A total of 139 juniors and seniors from an upper-level business class participated in the study. These subjects received extra credit in return for their participation.

Independent Variable
The consideration set/awareness set ratio was examined in this study for two products: automobiles and television sets. Automobiles were selected to represent a product category for which consumers' awareness sets would tend to be relatively large, while it was expected that awareness sets for TVs would be relatively small.

The independent variable was designed to manipulate the depth with which subjects processed their knowledge of the product category. Before completing the dependent measures (awareness set and consideration set size), subjects completed detailed questionnaires about a product category. In this initial task, subjects were asked to rate the importance of several attributes of a product class in terms of the attributes' influence on their decision about which brand to buy. Attribute importance was assessed with a five-point scale anchored by "extremely important influence" and "not an important influence". Next, subjects were asked to rate each attribute in terms of perceived differences among brands using a five-point scale anchored by "extreme differences" and "no differences" (Alpert 1971).

Dependent Variables
The attribute questionnaires were followed by a page which asked, "Please list every (product) manufacturer you are aware of" and, "Of those brands you listed above, which would you consider purchasing if you were going to buy a (product)?" The number of manufacturers listed by the subject represented the dependent measures.

Procedure
The product category asked about in the initial questionnaires was either the same as that used for the consideration set/awareness set questioning ("match") or represented a different product category ("mismatch"). For example, a subject in the "match" condition of the automobile experiment would be asked questions about automobile attributes, and subsequently asked to list every automobile manufacturer s(he) could think of. In the "mismatch" condition, subjects were asked attribute questions about an unrelated product category (radio/alarm clocks).

Subjects completed the questionnaires for the study in a classroom environment at their own pace. They were told that their input was needed for developing advertisements for a research study. Subjects were debriefed during a later class period.

TABLE 2
Findings of Study

Awareness Set Questioning	Attribute Questioning	Mean Proportion*
Automobile (n = 66)	Automobile (match) n = 43	.38
	Clock (mismatch) n = 23	.30
Television (n = 73)	Television (match) n = 48	.60
	Clock (mismatch) n = 25	.47

*Proportion = consideration set size/awareness set size

RESULTS AND DISCUSSION

The mean consideration set/awareness set proportions for the four groups of subjects are shown in Table 2. The matched conditions did not differ significantly from the hypothesized proportion of .37 for automobiles (t = .32) and .63 for TVs (t = -.81). There was a significant difference between the information theoretic proportion and the actual proportion in the unmatched conditions for both the automobile (t = -2.52) and the television (t = -2.93). These results provide support for Hypotheses 1A and 2.

Hypothesis 1B posited that the 63 percent versus 37 tendency would be a function of awareness set size. The mean awareness set size for automobile manufacturers was 15.23 (matched) and 17.86 (unmatched); for television sets the mean was 6.54 (matched) and 6.88 (unmatched). Thus, Hypothesis 1B was also supported.

These results may indicate that consumers are "efficient" information processors in terms of the information theoretic model described in this paper. When information is processed in sufficient depth, the consideration set/awareness set relationship was found to approximate the 63:37 information theoretic or "golden section" proportion. The division of the awareness set into brands which are considered vs. not considered for purchase is viewed in this context as a division of brands into "positive affect" and "negative affect" subsets. According to the information theoretic model, this proportional division may offer efficiency in terms of speed of processing or maximum "contrast" between these two subsets of the awareness set.

The present study represents a first step in applying this information theoretic model to purchase decisions. This study is limited in the sense that only two product categories were examined among a relatively small number of subjects. Because of this, the depth of processing, or "degree of analysis" is confounded with product class in the research design. A more extensive study utilizing a variety of product classes could provide more conclusive results.

If the 63:37 tendency is indeed operative in consumers' consideration set/awareness set proportions, several additional avenues for research are suggested. For example, the consumer's degree of expertise regarding a product category may be reflected in a relatively large awareness set. Does the consideration set expand correspondingly? Future research could also investigate these proportional relationships for the brand loyal versus variety seeking consumer within various product categories. Studies such as these would help to clarify the boundary conditions for the 63:37 information theoretic proportion.

In a broader context, the proportion may have implications for many other aspects of consumer behavior studied under the current information-processing paradigm. Examples of key areas of marketing inquiry in which related research may prove fruitful include information search, product pricing and positioning, consumer satisfaction, package design, inference formation, categorization phenomena and category-based processing, and attitude change.

BIBLIOGRAPHY

Adams-Webber, J. (1978), "A Further Test of the Golden Section Hypothesis," *British Journal of Psychology*, 69, 439-442.

Alba, Joseph W. and Chattopadhyay, Amitava (1985), "Effect of Context and Part-Category Cues on Recall of Competing Brands," *Journal of Marketing Research*, 22 (August), 340-349.

_____ and Hutchinson, J. Wesley (1987),"Dimensions of Consumer Expertise," *Journal of Consumer Research*, 13 (March), 411-454.

Alpert, Mark I. (1971), "Identification of Determinant Attributes: A Comparison of Methods," *Journal of Marketing Research*, 8 (May), 184-191.

Benjafield, John and Adams-Webber, J. (1976), "The Golden Section Hypothesis," *British Journal of Psychology*, 1, 11-15.

Berlyne, D. E. (1971), *Aesthetics and Psychobiology*, New York: Meredith Corporation.

Bettman, James R. (1986), "Consumer Psychology," *Annual Review of Psychology*, 37, 257-289.

Biehal, Gabriel and Chakravarti, Dipankar (1983), "Information Accessibility as a Moderator of Consumer Choice," *Journal of Consumer Research*, 10 (June), 1-14.

Brown, Juanita J. and Wildt, Albert R. (1987), "Factors Influencing Evoked Set Size", working paper, University of Missouri-Columbia.

Campbell, Brian M. (1969), *The Existence of Evoked Set and Determinants of Its Magnitude in Brand Choice Behavior*, unpublished Ph.D. Dissertation, Columbia University.

Church, Nancy J., Laroche, Michel, and Rosenblatt, Jerry A. (1985), "Consumer Brand Categorization for Durables with Limited Problem Solving: An Empirical Test and Proposed Extension of the Brisoux-Laroche Model, *Journal of Economic Psychology*, 6, 231-253.

Crowley, Ayn E. (1990), "The Golden Section: The First Universal Law in Marketing?" *Psychology and Marketing*, in press.

Frank, H. (1959), *Grundlagunprobleme der Informationsasthetik und erste Anwendung auf die mime pure*, Quickborn: Schnelle.

_____ (1964), *Kybernetische Analysen sebjektiver Scachverhalte*, Quickborne: Schnelle.

Garner, Wendell R. (1962), *Uncertainty and Structure as Psychological Concepts*, New York: John Wiley and Sons.

Hauser, John R. and Gaskin, Steven P. (1984), "Applications of the 'Defender' Consumer Model," *Marketing Science*, 3 (Fall), 327-351.

Hauser, John R. and Wernerfelt, Birger (1990), "An Evaluation Cost Model of Consideration Sets," *Journal of Consumer Research*, 16 (March), 393-408.

Howard, John A. and Sheth, Jagdish N. (1969), *The Theory of Buyer Behavior*, New York: Wiley.

Huntley, E. H. (1970), *The Divine Proportion*, New York: Dover.

Jacoby, J. and Olson, J. C. (1970), "An Attitudinal Model of Brand Loyalty: Conceptual Underpinnings and Instrumentation Research," paper presented at the Conference on Attitude Research and Consumer Behavior (Urbana: University of Illinois, December 5-6, 1970).

Jarvis, Lance P. and Wilcox, James B. (1973), "Evoked Set Size - Some Theoretical Foundations and Empirical Evidence," *Combined Proceedings*, Thomas V. Greer, ed., Chicago: American Marketing Association, No. 35, 236-240.

Louviere, Jordan J. (1988), "On the Consequences of Misspecifying Consumers' Choice Sets in Multinomial Logit Choice Models," working paper, University of Alberta, Edmonton, Alberta, Canada T6G 1S2.

McManus, I. C. (1980), "The Aesthetics of Simple Figures," *British Journal of Psycholgy*, 71, 505-524.

Miller, George A. (1956), "The Magical Number Seven, Plus or Minus Two: Some Limits on Our Capacity for Processing Information," *The Psychological Review*, 63 (March), 81-97.

Narayana, Chem and Markin, Rom J. (1975), "Consumer Behavior and Product Performance: An Alternative Conceptualization," *Journal of Marketing*, 39, 1-6.

Nedungadi, Prakash (1987), *Formation and Use of A Consideration Set: Implications for Marketing and Research on Consumer Choice*, unpublished Ph.D. Dissertation, University of Florida.

Nicosia, Franceso M. (1966), *Consumer Decision Processes: Marketing and Advertising Implications*, Englewood Cliffs, NJ: Prentice-Hall.

Ostlund, Lyman E. (1973), "Evoked Set Size: Some Empirical Results," in Thomas V. Greer, ed., *Combined Proceedings*, Chicago: American Marketing Association, No. 35, 226-230.

Pierce, John R. (1961), *Symbols, Signals and Noise: The Nature and Process of Communication*, New York: Harper.

Prasad, V. Kanti (1975), "Evoked Set Size - Personality Correlates and Mediating Variables," *Journal of Academy of Marketing Science*, 3, 272-279.

Rigdon, Michael A. and Epting, Franz R. (1982), "A Test of the Golden Section Hypothesis With Elicited Constructs," *Journal of Personality and Social Psychology*, 43, 1080-1087.

Shannon, C. E. and Weaver W. (1949), *The Mathematical Theory of Communication*, Urbana: University of Illinois Press.

Silk, Alvin J. and Urban, Glen L. (1978), "Pre-Test Market Evaluation of New Packaged Goods: A Model and Measurement Methodology," *Journal of Marketing Research*, 15 (May), 171-191.

Weiner, N. (1948), *Cybernetics*, New York: Wiley.

Young, John F. (1971), *Information Theory*, New York: Wiley.

Perceived Price Fairness and Dual Entitlement
Rosemary Kalapurakal, Ohio State University
Peter R. Dickson, Ohio State University
Joel E. Urbany, University of South Carolina

ABSTRACT

A principle of price fairness called "Dual Entitlement" proposes that it is fair for sellers to pursue a pricing rule of raising prices when their costs increase, but not reduce their prices when costs decrease. In this study the fairness of this rule is tested against an alternative cost-plus rule and a buffer rule, both of which were observed to be more fair than the rule derived from the Dual Entitlement principle. Situational effects are also demonstrated which raise questions as to whether any general norms of fairness exist in pricing decisions.

INTRODUCTION

Traditional price research has focused on economic determinants of price-setting. However, in recent years, many researchers in economics and other fields have attempted to enrich the model of the agent by including "nonrational" motives. This paper examines one stream of research focusing on consumers' judgments of price fairness: whether and how subjective preferences for 'equitable,' 'just' or 'fair' prices influence behavior.

Price Fairness

Research in the area of price-perceptions has many diverse branches, some of which will be examined briefly in this section. In Marketing, the relevant stream of research has focused on the 'psychophysics of price,' building up conceptual and empirical support for the effect of various price perceptions on determinants of price acceptability, including price fairness (Kamen and Toman 1970), price-quality perceptions (Monroe 1973) and reference prices (Klein and Oglethorpe 1987). Although Kamen and Toman (1970) find support for the proposition that "consumers have some preconceived ideas about what is a fair price for a given item and are (only) willing to pay this price or below...," they do not examine the notion of what constitutes a 'fair' price to consumers. In Economics, researchers have included fairness in the consumer's objective function for a variety of economic reasons, including anticipation of hostile consumer reaction to unfair treatment (Okun 1981) and concerns about building up trust and goodwill over time (Akerlof 1970; Arrow 1973).

The immediate impetus for the present work comes from two recent papers which put forward two important claims: (1) that community norms of what constitutes a fair price may influence the pricing behavior of firms and (2) that a 'Dual Entitlement' principle (hereafter referred to as the "DE" principle) determines such norms (Kahneman, Knetsch and Thaler 1986 a; 1986 b). According to these scholars, a supplier may examine the fairness of its intended pricing tactic as judged by community standards. If it is not fair, the supplier will be less likely to go ahead with its planned pricing tactic. Moreover, these researchers propose that the constraining motive could be primarily moral, and at times, dominate the purely economic motives of avoiding loss of customer goodwill and jeopardizing long-term profits.

Few would argue that ethics do not influence human behavior, including economic behavior. Business enterprises often sacrifice their economic interest in many unheralded ways through charitable donations, special consideration of employees and community services. What is controversial is the claim that the incorporation of norms of price fairness into the traditional economic theory of buyer and seller behavior results in a parsimonious extension of the theory, whereby it can correctly specify when and how norms of fairness will modify the basic model of these economic agents (Kahneman, Knetsch and Thaler 1986a, p. s299).

The Dual Entitlement Principle. Kahneman et al demonstrate that consumers do form subjective judgments about the fairness of various prices (1986a; 1986b). In addition, their experimental research (1986a) indicates a willingness on the part of subjects to "punish" unfair pricing behavior, even at some cost to themselves. However, the present focus is on their findings regarding the conceptualization of the "community norms" of fairness. On the basis of their survey findings, they concluded that standards of fairness are based neither on a strict cost-plus rule (output price should be related to input costs) nor on the "law" of supply and demand (charging what the market will bear). Rather, it is suggested that they are governed by a 'Dual Entitlement' principle. This principle proposes that sellers and buyers are entitled to the profit and price terms, respectively, of a "reference" transaction. Possible reference points may include the most recent transaction or an 'average' transaction (see Klein and Oglethorpe 1987). The reference transaction serves as a yardstick against which the terms (price and profit) of the current transaction are compared, in arriving at judgments of fairness. The DE principle implies that it is not fair for sellers to increase the price to the buyer in order to exploit increased market power (such as when demand increases). Similarly, if there is increased supply, it is not fair for prices to be lower to the consumer because it would violate the terms of the reference transaction.

However, the most intriguing aspect of the proposed formulation is its claim that the seller's profit entitlement takes precedence over the buyer's price entitlement whenever both are threatened. This implies that it is consistent with community norms of fairness for cost increases to be passed on to consumers in the form of higher prices, in order to protect the seller's reference profit. Moreover, the DE principle effectively implies that the supplier is allowed to increase its profits when there are cost reductions. The buyer is only entitled to the current reference price and not to a share of the cost savings in the form of a lower price. If, over time, such increased profits become the 'expected' level of seller profits, they are further protected when costs increase. In short, it is fair for prices and profits to only ever increase, because it is consistent with this norm of fairness for sellers to pass on cost increases and not cost decreases.

We agree with Kahneman et al that "rules" of fairness in the domain of supplier pricing behavior should not be intuited or inferred from conventional economic theory (Kahneman, Knetsch and Thaler 1986a, p s299-300) but should be empirically established. If the DE principle is indeed a principle (i.e. a basic truth, law or doctrine that embodies community norms of fairness), then its discovery is an important advance in economic ethics and political economy. It merits further examination because it favors the supplier and argues that aspects of the standard free-market clearance mechanisms are unfair.

Context and the robustness of the DE principle. The context in which decision problems are presented can give rise to different preferences, even if the objective information remains invariant (Kahneman and Tversky 1984). Examples of framing biases in perceptual judgment issues are common and have been raised in the well-known work on prospect theory (Tversky and Kahneman 1986). A way to explore the robustness of the Dual Entitlement principle therefore, is to examine the effects of different perspectives on subjective perceptions of fairness. Indeed, Kahneman et al themselves conclude that "...judgments of fairness are susceptible to substantial framing effects" (1986b, p. 740). What we demonstrate is that the judged fairness of pricing rules are indeed subject to some important contextual effects. The consideration of these effects leads to some different conclusions about fairness, as well as about the robustness and generalizability of the DE principle.

Research Issues

The present research questions the empirical evidence supporting the DE principle and attempts to examine further the determinants of judgments about fairness. Specifically:

(1) The initial experimental scenarios were designed to replicate the findings that the DE principle embodies a "community" norm of fairness. The DE implication that cost-based price increases are more justified than exploitation of market power was also examined.

(2) Following from our discussion of the fairness of alternative pricing strategies, the next set of experimental scenarios focused on whether the DE rule is, in fact, considered to be more fair than (a) a cost-plus rule (b) a brokerage rule and (c) a "buffer" rule (where the seller does not pass on cost increases).

(3) Finally, other contextual factors were examined in order to determine how sensitive judgments of fairness are to situational elements. Such factors include information about the seller's past pricing strategies and whether the passing on of a cost increase was initiated by the seller or was a competitive response. Additional contextual factors include personal relevance (in terms of economic consequences) of the proposed action and the identity of the actor (seller or buyer).

METHODOLOGY AND RESULTS

The robustness of the DE rule was tested empirically by placing the reported pricing behavior of the firm within different contexts or frames. A set of four pricing scenarios were presented to a sample of 189 business students. Two earlier studies of business students (sample size 105 and 78 respectively) were also undertaken, which helped in the preparation of the final experimental scenarios. These studies produced a similar pattern of results and hence the details are not reported.

In each scenario, the context was systematically manipulated by presenting different scenarios describing a seller's pricing decision to subjects in different treatment conditions. All manipulations were between subject. Subjects read the scenario and then responded to a series of scales about the perceived fairness of the pricing action taken by the seller. The order of presentation of the four cases was also manipulated and had no effect on the subjects' responses.

Our examination of the research issues detailed above is presented in the following sections. A description of the scenarios in each instance is provided, along with the results and a discussion of the implications of each.

The Effect of Illustrating the Complete Rule on Fairness. Our concerns over potential framing biases can best be illustrated by using the following question, the answers to which have been pivotal in the research supporting the DE principle:

> "My first questions are about the behavior of people in business. Suppose a factory produces a particular table, which it sells to wholesalers. The factory has been selling all of the tables it can produce for $150 each. Suppose that the factory has now found a supplier who charges $20 less for the materials needed to make each table. Does fairness require the factory to change its price from $150 in this case?" (Respondents who answered yes were then asked what is a fair price that it could charge to the wholesalers).(Kahneman et al 1986a, p.s293)

The first issue is that the above scenario cannot be regarded as a complete test of either the cost-plus *or* the competing DE rule because it does not describe the history of the application of the rule; in particular, it does not describe what the factory would do if faced with a $20 *increase* in its cost of raw materials. The fairness of the cost-plus rule may well depend on a give-and-take sharing norm. In fact, Kahneman et al suggest that "...it remains possible that respondents might follow a cost-plus rule if asked to consider together the appropriate price response to increases and to reductions of costs" (Kahneman, Knetsch and Thaler 1986a, s295). The absence of information explaining what the factory did when it last faced a cost increase of $20 may, therefore, have biased responses in the Kahneman et al study; it is plausible that some percentage of subjects may have assumed that the firm would absorb any cost increase that might occur as well. Therefore, this effectively tests the application of only half the rule, the perceived fairness of which may depend critically on how the other half of the rule was executed.

To explore this issue, the above scenario was contrasted with two others, which provided a historical context on how the manufacturer had handled a past cost increase. A "buffer rule" version included the following information prior to the description of the critical pricing situation: "...Recently it absorbed this cost increase and did not raise it selling price." A final (Dual Entitlement) version stated: "...Recently the factory experienced an increase of $20 in its cost of materials. It raised its selling price by $20 to $170 each." Subjects were required to evaluate the fairness of maintaining the price at $170 when input costs fell by $20, a condition consistent with the fairness implications of the DE rule.

Of the subjects responding to the original scenario 65% (41/63) indicated that it was quite fair for the factory to keep charging $150, a result consistent with the findings of Kahneman et al. Moreover, this figure jumped to 91% (58/64) when they were informed that the seller had "buffered" the cost increase in the past. However, the effect of the historical information in the third scenario (the complete DE rule) was dramatic: now only 63.5% (33/52) thought it was fair to continue charging $170 in the face of a cost decrease of $20 ($p<0.0001$).

Viewed one way, it can be argued that this result provides support for the fairness of the DE principle. More than half the subjects perceived the application of the complete DE rule to be fair. Moreover, on average, it was felt that only $8.64 of the $20 saving needed to be passed on to the shopper (the average fair price suggested by this group was $161.36). From another perspective however, these findings suggest that the proposition that the DE rule represents the community norm of fairness is somewhat misleading; the buffer rule was considered by a much higher percentage of subjects to be fair compared to the DE rule (91% vs. 65%, $p < 0.001$).

Testing the complete rule appears to be especially important when we consider the possibility that regular customers' perceptions of the fairness of a firm's pricing behavior may well be based on the history of its behavior rather than on a single incident. In particular, industrial consumers, who are likely to be aware of changes in input prices, will judge the fairness of a firm's pricing policy not just on its last behavior but also on its consistent application of a pricing rule over time. Pricing decision-makers should accordingly, be more interested in consumers' perceptions of the application of the complete DE price-rule.

Fairness and Consistent Treatment of Cost Changes. In examining the robustness of the DE principle, a factor to be considered in the formation of judgments about fairness is whether or not the seller behaves in a consistent manner with respect to price increases and decreases. To study this issue further, subjects were presented with the following scenario:

A department store has been buying an oriental floor rug for $100. The standard pricing practice used by department stores is to price floor rugs at double their cost so the selling price of the rug is $200. This covers all the selling costs, overheads and includes profit. The department store can sell all of the rugs that it can buy. Suppose because of exchange rate changes the cost of the rug rises from $100 to $120 and the selling price is increased to $220. As a result of another change in currency exchange rates, the cost of the rug falls by $20 back to $100. The department store continues to sell the rug for $220.

As seen here, fluctuating exchange rates was cited as the reason for both an initial increase in cost and a subsequent decrease in cost of the rugs. It has been observed that changes in currency values are a nice test of the DE principle because it can be observed that resulting cost increases are passed on quickly but resulting cost decreases tend not to be passed on (see Kahneman, Knetsch and Thaler, 1986a, p. 739). This scenario is a direct test of the full DE principle i.e. an initial cost-plus price increase -no subsequent price decrease rule is described. In this scenario, the mean rating of the above pricing behavior that fully describes the application of the DE principle was -0.4 (-3: extremely unfair; +3: extremely fair).

In contrast to the DE formulation, two more price-behavior scenarios were presented, which described the *consistent* application of a cost-plus or brokerage rule to both the price increase and decrease. In the first (cost-plus) scenario, the price was increased (decreased) by $20 when the cost increased (decreased) by $20. In the brokerage scenario, when the cost increased (decreased) by $20, the store increased (decreased) the price by $40. Although the average rated fairness in the cost-plus and brokerage conditions were not significantly different from each other (+2.3 and +2.2 respectively), the behavior consistent with the full DE principle was rated as being significantly less fair than behavior describing the consistent application of the cost-plus rule or the brokerage rule (+2.3 versus -0.4, +2.2 versus -0.4, $p < 0.0001$ in the respective contrast tests).

This test thus provides further support for our claims that judgments of fairness are based on a historical perspective rather than on the present situation alone. The *consistent* application of the cost-plus or brokerage rules to both cost increases and decreases is considered much more fair than a rule which only applies to cost increases and hence favors the supplier (i.e. the DE rule). This suggests therefore, that sellers may be able to pursue a pricing policy consistent with the DE principle, not because it reflects community norms of fairness but because of information asymmetry between supplier and consumer: buyers may not have enough information about a firm's pricing practices, and in particular, may not know about the cost decreases that have not been passed on to them.

The Effect of Cost Increase Justification on Fairness Ratings. As proposed by Kahneman et al, a theory of fairness governed by the provisions of the reference transaction implies that cost-induced price increases will be assessed by consumers as being fair whereas price increases resulting from a shortage in supply and exercise of market power by a seller will not be perceived as fair: the latter violates the buyer's entitlement to the reference price even in the absence of a threat to the seller's reference profits. These propositions were tested and confirmed in the present study.

Subjects were presented with two scenarios describing a local shortage of lettuce and the pricing responses of sellers. In the first situation, a wholesaler responds by increasing the price of lettuce by 30 cents a head to a retailer (grocer) who passes on this cost increase to his customers. Although this is a straightforward test of the fairness of cost-induced price increases, it is interesting to note that it is the wholesaler's exercise of market power that produced the 30 cent price increase. To check on whether respondents object to a supplier directly taking advantage of the forces of supply and demand, a second group of subjects was informed that the grocer "grows his own lettuce rather than buy from wholesalers," implying that his costs would be unaffected by the wholesale price increase. This grocer also responds by increasing the price of lettuce by 30 cents a head.

Our results show that while the action of the grocer in raising the price of lettuce to match the wholesale cost increase was still considered fair on average, it was significantly less so than in the situation where the price increase is cost-induced at the retail level (+2.3 versus +0.8, $p < 0.0001$). This supports the proposition that the use of a market clearance pricing rule is not considered as fair as a cost-plus rule. It also suggests that the price increase is considered more justifiable when it is initiated by some unknown channel intermediary rather than the retailer because the latter is seen has having no option but to pass on costs. This issue is examined in greater detail in the next section.

Is Initiating a Price Increase Less Fair than Following? Another factor that may moderate judgments of fairness of various price-setting behaviors by a party is information as to who initiates the price increase. In order to test the significance of this factor, the previous "lettuce" price-setting scenario also included conditions in which information was provided as to whether the price increase *at the retail level* was initiated by the grocer or by a competitor. The question of interest is whether the supplier's pricing behavior will be considered less fair if it initiates the price increase in contrast to a situation where it is a tactical response to a price change by a competitor, regardless of the price justification. The answer is a marginal yes; when the grocer initiated the price increase in response to a cost increase, the price increase was still considered fair but, as predicted, significantly less so than when competitors raised their prices and the grocer followed (average rating +1.06 vs. +1.61, $p < 0.05$: one-tailed test).

The Effect of Personal Relevance on Perceived Fairness. Underpinning the DE principle is the concept of an ethical "community" norm. However, if self-interest is a motivating factor, then the individual buyer's perspective does matter. It was expected that the behavior of the seller might be rated less fair when it was likely to have a direct adverse effect on the judge. A possible explanation for any difference in evaluations would therefore be that economic self-interest is an important antecedent of buyers' fairness judgments; the latter are not driven purely by moral issues.

The significance of this factor was studied using the first pricing behavior scenario (the manufacturer of the table) described earlier. Half the respondents were asked to imagine that they themselves were the customer ("Imagine you are a customer wanting to buy such a table.") This manipulation of orientation had no statistically significant effect on the rated fairness of the manufacturer's pricing behavior. In retrospect, perhaps this is not surprising, as such role playing is a rather weak manipulation of personal relevance.

Is Fair Buyer Behavior Rated Unfair When Sellers Do It? The research undertaken by Kahneman et al found that price increases related to excess demand are generally considered to be unfair. A related issue of interest is whether the relative fairness of the exercise of market power depends on whether it is the supplier or the buyer who exercises market power. Assuming that student subjects will be inclined to identify with the buyer (as members of the consuming public themselves), it was expected that it would be considered more acceptable for a buyer to exploit market conditions than for a seller to do so. This was tested in the following way. Subjects were asked to rate one of the following two scenarios:

A car dealer has in stock the last of an exclusive automobile for which he has several potential customers. He contacts the customers and plays them off each other to obtain the highest price for the car. (Average rated fairness: +0.85)

A new car buyer visits several dealers who stock a particular model he wishes to buy. He plays them off against each other to obtain the lowest price for the model that he wants to buy. (Average rated fairness: +2.9).

The results indicate that adopting the perspective of one or other party in the exercise of market power has a significant influence on perceptions of fairness; it was considered more fair for the buyer to exploit market power than for the seller to do so ($p < 0.0001$). Even in a scenario where the buyer was described as resorting to deceit (exaggeration of the lowest price offered by other dealers), it was still perceived to be at least marginally fair (average rating: +0.7). It is clear that a different standard of fair play is applied to buyers than is applied to sellers and that it favors the buyer, at least for respondents who identify with the buyer rather than with the seller.

DISCUSSION

The present set of experiments raise a number of issues which modify and extend the interesting and original work of Kahneman et al. Consistent with the first issue, our findings replicate the previous research in that we find strong evidence that respondents can and do make evaluations of fairness that are significantly influenced by various economic and non-economic factors. We find some support for the suggestion made by Kahneman et al (1986a; 1986b) that pricing behavior favoring the supplier is, on average, considered fair. Its implications in terms of differential evaluations of fairness of cost-based versus market-based responses are also supported here. Moreover, this research indicates that the reference transaction plays an extremely important role in shaping such perceptions.

However, there are additional interesting findings in the present work that are worthy of further discussion. One major finding is that the case for the Dual Entitlement principle may not be as strong as argued by Kahneman et al. Our research suggests that a buffer rule (absorbing cost increases and decreases) or a cost-plus rule applied consistently to cost increases and decreases is considered to be more fair than the DE rule.

A second important implication is that situation norms determine what is judged to be fair or unfair pricing behavior. Inasmuch as perceptions about the situation depend greatly on the level of knowledge or ignorance of the judge, we might expect considerable variance in how buyers and the community view the fairness of a supplier's behavior. In addition, the efforts of the supplier to cast its behavior in a more favorable light and the efforts of its competitors to expose the same behavior as "selfish opportunism" will increase the uncertainty and variance in perceptions of the fairness of a supplier's action. This conclusion may need to be modified even further as a result of future studies which consider an increasing number of situational factors. The motivation behind such studies is the need to develop the theory of the subjective perceptions of price fairness. An important and related issue is whether issues of fairness really do influence buyer and seller behavior over and beyond the long-term economic interest of the buyer and seller.

Limitations and Issues for Further Research

The present study suffers from a number of limitations. From a methodological viewpoint, it was necessary to test our propositions using scenarios rather than a behavioral format. Each subject was allowed to arrive at his/her own definition of "fairness:" no definition was provided by the researchers, and this may have increased the random variance. Moreover, a single-item scale was used to measure subjects' perceptions of fairness. A multi-item scale would have been a more appropriate measurement procedure, given the subjective nature of the construct. The "community" norms of fairness examined here may not be generalizable to sections of society other than students (although the initial findings are consistent with the Kahneman et al surveys of the general public). Finally, subjects' perceptions of fairness were explicitly solicited. An attempt to assess the importance of "nonrational" issues such as fairness perceptions in buyer-seller interactions would have greater validity if such judgments were unsolicited, occurring 'naturally' in response to the description of a seller's pricing decision. As such, we do not test the relative importance of subjective considerations such as fairness against the more objective economic factors in the formation of purchase and consumption decisions.

In the present research, we studied the fairness perceptions of business students, acting as consumers. However, this stream of research clearly has important implications for *seller* pricing perceptions as well. In fact, if sellers do not ever consider community norms of fairness in making pricing decisions or are unaware what these norms are, then the whole issue is rather academic. It is possible that sellers apply industry-specific norms of fairness, if they apply them at all. Community norms pertaining pricing practices have a variety of antecedents, of which we focus only on the ethical one. It is left to future research to determine what other antecedents may be relevant. Moreover, it may prove useful to determine what subjects consider to be fair in more detail, and study how they arrived at that determination.

In conclusion, we suggest that (1) since fairness evaluations appear sensitive to situational factors and information available, there may be no simple robust principles that govern norms of what is fair or unfair pricing behavior (2) such contextual factors include, amongst other things, the judge's self-interest and involvement in the transaction, knowledge about a supplier's initial costs and profit margins and information about a supplier's past pricing behavior and competitors' behavior. Both the conceptual and empirical explorations in the present study indicate limits to the generalizability of the Dual Entitlement principle. Our empirical results show that, given sufficient information, other pricing rules are perceived to be more fair. However, on the basis of our findings, no specific rule can be claimed to embody community norms of fairness.

REFERENCES

Akerlof, G (1979), "The Case Against Conservative Macroeconomics: An Inaugural Lecture," *Economica*, 46 (August), 219-237.

Arrow, Kenneth (1973), "Social Responsibility and Economic Efficiency," *Public Policy*, 21 (Summer), 303-317.

Kahneman, Daniel, Jack L. Knetsch and Richard H. Thaler (1986a), "Fairness and the Assumptions of Economics," *Journal of Business*, 59(4), pt.2, s285-300.

_____ , Jack L. Knetsch and Richard H. Thaler (1986b), "Fairness as a Constraint on Profit Seeking: Entitlements in the Market," *American Economic Review*, 76(4) (September), 728-741.

Kahneman, Daniel and Amos Tversky (1984), "Choices, Values and Frames," *American Psychologist*, 39(4), (April), 341-350.

Kamen, J.M. and R.J. Toman (1970), "Psychophysics of Prices," *Journal of Marketing Research*, 7 (February), 27-35.

Klein, Noreen M. and Janet E. Oglethorpe (1987), "Cognitive Reference Points in Consumer Decision-Making," in *Advances in Consumer Research*, Volume 14, eds. Melanie Wallendorf and Paul Anderson, Provo, UT: Association for Consumer Research, 183-187.

Monroe, Kent B. (1973), "Buyers' Subjective Perceptions of Price," *Journal of Marketing Research*, 10, (February), 70-80.

Okun, Arthur (1981, *Prices and Quantities: A Macroeconomic Analysis*, Washington: The Brookings Institute.

Tversky, Amos and Daniel Kahneman (1986), "Rational Choice and the Framing of Decisions," *Journal of Business*, 59(4), pt.2, s251-278.

Symbolic Meanings of a Price Ending
Robert M. Schindler, Rutgers University - Camden

ABSTRACT

This paper discusses the possibility that the rightmost digits, or ending, of a price can carry connotations about various attributes of a product or retailer. A survey of hypothesized price-ending meanings is presented, and two types of causes of these meanings are proposed. A review of the empirical evidence supporting the role of these meanings suggests that it may be desirable for retailers to be more deliberate in their decisions concerning which price endings to use.

INTRODUCTION

There is a general awareness within marketing that price can serve an informational as well as allocative function (Rao 1984). However, virtually all of the research attention on price as an information cue has focused on what the price *level* can communicate about a product or retail outlet (e.g., Monroe and Krishnan 1985; Lichtenstein and Burton 1989; Oxenfeldt 1966, pp. 54-55; Scitovsky 1945).

What has not been adequately addressed is whether a price *ending* can also serve as a cue which communicates information about a product or retail outlet. A price's ending consists of one or all of the rightmost digits of a price and can be manipulated more or less independently of the level of the price. For example, the prices, $29.95 and $30.00, have different endings, but are at virtually the same level.

The goal of this paper is to describe more clearly how a price's ending may serve as a second means by which a price communicates information, and to summarize the existing thinking and research on the topic. First, price-ending meanings will be distinguished from other aspects of price endings which may affect the consumer, and the possibility of meaning effects will be placed into a theoretical context. Then the price-ending meanings which have been proposed will be reviewed, and possible causes of such meanings will be discussed. The paper will conclude with a brief summary of the empirical research which has been conducted on this issue to date.

SYMBOLIC MEANINGS ARE DISTINGUISHABLE FROM OTHER EFFECTS OF PRICE ENDINGS

In this review, a price ending will be said to have a meaning if it brings to the consumer's mind information or thoughts about the price or about a non-price attribute of the product or retailer. The primary concern here is meanings which are "symbolic," or context-independent. Thus, for example, the 99 ending of $49.99 may connote a discount, the 00 ending of $200 may connote high quality, and a 63 ending of $7.63 may connote a carefully determined price. In each case, the rightmost digits can be considered a separate unit of meaning which can be used strategically, in a wide variety of situations, to create an impression. In designing a price advertisement, a manager might use a meaningful price ending in the same way he or she might use any meaningful element of verbal copy.

The symbolic meaning of a price ending can be distinguished from any effect a price ending may have on the consumer's perception of the *level* of the price. In particular, it has often been hypothesized that "odd prices," or prices which are just below a round number (e.g., $49.88, $49.95, and $49.99 are just below $50.00), are encoded by the consumer into a form which represents a lower price (e.g., Georgoff 1972, pp. 4-6; Lambert 1975; Schindler and Warren 1988; Simon 1989, p. 183). For example, consumers might think of the just-below price of $49.99 as "forty and some change," "forty-something," or even "around forty." This perceptual underestimation may be only fleeting, but sufficient to serve the purpose of attracting the consumer's attention to an advertisement (Whalen 1980), or it may occur only later when the price is recalled (Brenner and Brenner 1982; Schindler and Wiman 1989). But the various forms of this "underestimation hypothesis" have in common the postulation of an effect of price ending on the perceived *level* of a price.

Distinguishing meaning effects from underestimation effects raises the question of how the two types of price-ending effects may be related. They are not so closely related that they will necessarily occur together. For example, a consumer may take pains to avoid encoding $49.99 as "forty and something" and attend carefully to each of the digits, but may still have the connotations of "sale price" come to mind. And, it should be noted that the two types of effects are likely to have some very different causal factors, and thus may need to be managed very differently. But, as will be discussed below, it is likely that an effect of a price ending on the perceived level of the price will play a role in causing that ending to have a meaning to consumers, and thus there may be a tendency for the two effects to co-occur.

The symbolic meaning of a price ending can also be distinguished from effects of price ending which are dependent on a particular price or advertisement. For example, it appears from the use of prices such as $66.66 and $333 in price advertising that retailers may use the rightmost digits of a price to emphasize, and perhaps call attention to, the leftmost digit. While it is plausible that the rightmost digits may add some emphasis, this would not be considered a meaning effect since the effect of the rightmost digits would be dependent on their following certain leftmost digits and would not occur out of that context.

The price-ending meanings which are the concern of this paper are those which are understood by the consumer. It has been reported (e.g., Calogero 1982) that retailers will sometimes use price endings as a means of coding information such as whether the item is a special purchase which is not reorderable or is from a regular vendor. In such cases, price endings have meanings which are interpretable within the retailing organization, but which are almost certain to be impenetrable to the consumer.

IMPORTANCE OF PRICE-ENDING MEANINGS

Convincing evidence that price endings have meanings which affect consumer behavior would contribute to our understanding of how the consumer responds to price. It would tell us that the informational function of price involves more than just the level of a price, and would bear on the nature of those inevitable wrinkles in demand curves known as "price points." In addition, it would tell us that concepts such as region of indifference, latitude of acceptance, and just noticeable difference (e.g., Monroe and Petroshius 1981) are of limited value in assessing price response. If a price change which is well within consumers' region of indifference happens to change the price ending to one of a very different meaning, then a sales change could in fact result.

It is of course likely that the size of a sales change resulting from a change in the meaning of a price ending alone would rarely be more than modest. But even if careful management of price-ending meanings results in a sales increase as small as one percent, this could still represent an important opportunity for the retailer. Such a small increase in sales could have a much greater effect on profits, especially since the costs of managing price endings are likely to be quite low and the effects of identifying the best meanings for the situations which usually occur are likely to be long-lasting.

PRICE-ENDING MEANINGS WHICH HAVE BEEN PROPOSED

The compilation of price-ending meanings which is presented below is based on a survey of published materials and on informal conversations with a wide variety of retailers and consumers. What is recorded here are hypotheses, speculations, and opinions about the meanings that price endings may have. These proposed meanings can be divided into two broad categories: (1) those concerning price, and (2) those concerning non-price attributes of the product or retail outlet.

Meanings Concerning Price

It has often been hypothesized that a just-below price ending connotes that the price is low (Bliss 1952; Dodds and Monroe 1985). The consumer might interpret this as low relative to competition (i.e., the "lowest price around"), or low with respect to costs (i.e., "lowest price possible"; Mason and Mayer 1990, p. 443). These low-price connotations of advertised products might also give the impression that the retail outlet in general is low-priced (Nagle 1987, p. 249).

Two related price-ending meanings which have been hypothesized for just-below price endings concern how the price may have changed recently. The first is the frequent proposal that just-below pricing suggests that the price has been reduced, perhaps from the next higher round-number price (Alpert 1971, p. 112; Beckman and Davidson 1967, p. 501; Friedman 1967; Knauth 1949; Kreul 1982). The second is the possibility that a just-below price connotes one which has not been recently increased (Schindler 1984).

It is commonly suggested that a just-below price ending connotes a sale or discount price (Berman and Evans 1986, p. 453; Kotler 1988, p. 211; Kreul 1982; Nagle 1987, p. 249; Raphel 1968; Simon 1989, p. 183). A sale or discount price would differ from other recently decreased prices in that the price is expected to be temporary, either because the price will later be returned to its pre-discount level, or because the product will no longer be available at that retail outlet. Although it is usually suggested that all just-below price endings may carry the connotation of being a sale price, some authors (Alpert 1971, pp. 112-3; Lewison and DeLozier 1986, p. 591) have implied that prices which end in the digits 3 or 7 are more strongly associated with discounts (or suggest larger discounts) than prices which end in the digits 5, 8, and 9. The ad in the Figure appears to have been designed with this possibility in mind.

As one would expect, the hypotheses that just-below price endings connote low, decreased, or discount prices also suggest that round-number prices (i.e., primarily prices with one or more 0's in the rightmost digits) may connote that the price is high, recently increased, or is the full, "regular" price. It has even been suggested that just-below prices have become so common that some consumers may interpret a round-number price as involving, say, a 5-cent "surcharge" over the corresponding 95-ending price (Whalen 1980).

It is sometimes believed that the use of price endings which appear random are interpreted by consumers as the result of a more precise and careful pricing process. For example, Sears has recently been advertising prices with a mixture of unusual endings such as 17, 67, 82, and 31 in order to give consumers the impression of "having priced more sharply" (i.e., having reduced the price as much as possible). Also, since wholesale prices use a wider mix of endings than retail prices (Friedman 1967), unusual endings may also be used to support the claim that a retailer's prices are fair because they result from a fixed markup on costs or to support a claim that a retailer is offering certain items at wholesale prices.

Consistent with this is the possibility that round-number prices may give the impressions that they are the result of a quick and somewhat careless

FIGURE
Example of an Advertisement Where Price Endings Change with Level of Discount

SAVE AN EXTRA 20% STOREWIDE

On already marked down items and special purchase merchandise with price endings of 99 cents.

Here's how it works: ▶

*$79.00 and $99.00 women's down coats excluded from this event.

STARTS TODAY

THREE DAYS ONLY
FRIDAY
SATURDAY
SUNDAY

Look for the red sale signs throughout the entire store. That's where your extra 20% special savings begin.

The extra savings are not marked on merchandise. We take off the additional 20% when we ring in your purchase.

FILENE'S
FOR EXAMPLE:
ORIGINAL PRICE
40.00
MARKED DOWN PRICE
24.99
THREE DAYS ONLY AFTER-INVENTORY PRICE
19.97

pricing process. This may lead consumers to believe the stated price is only a starting price and that it can be negotiated downward. On the other hand, this connotation of round-number prices could support the claim that the retailer has slashed prices impulsively and with abandon in his or her impatience to get rid of the product, and thus the prices represent unusually good values.

The last two price-ending meanings which communicate information about the price concern the commonness of prices ending in 95 and 99 cents. The first is that these endings have become synonymous with the higher even-dollar amount, and thus will be less effective in connoting a low price than the less common endings of 96 and 97. The second is that consumers tend to see prices using these common endings as "correct" and therefore more desirable (Gabor and Granger, 1964; Monroe 1990, p. 48).

Meanings Concerning Non-Price Attributes of the Product or Retailer

It has been hypothesized that just-below price endings carry connotations of low quality (Kreul 1982). These connotations may correspond to the types of low quality that consumers believe goes along with low or discount prices (such as being leftovers or out-of-date items), or may simply involve an impression of the features that are normally used to judge products in that category. It has also been suggested that if a retailer's use of just-below pricing is not limited to sale items, that the low-quality connotations of these prices may affect consumer expectations about the quality of all of the items available from that retail outlet.

It is also possible that at least some consumers interpret just-below prices as an attempt by the retailer to be sneaky, slick, or simply not willing to "play it straight" (Calogero 1982). One related possibility is that they consider just-below prices a sign of tackiness or lack of sophistication. A second related possibility is that the consistent use of any single price ending (other than 00) might suggest to the consumer that the marketer is using price ending as an influence tool and thus arouse some suspicion.

As one might expect from the hypothesis that just-below prices may connote low quality, round-number price endings have been hypothesized to indicate high quality (Wingate, Schaller, and Miller 1972, p. 122). Consumers may attribute this higher quality to only those items advertised with a round-number price, or they may attribute it to all of the items offered by the retail outlet (Nagle 1987, p. 249).

It has often been hypothesized that prices with round-number endings contribute to giving a store or product an image of classiness (Spohn and Allen 1977, p. 188), sophistication (Raphel 1968), prestige (Alpert 1971, p. 112), or "a touch of dignity" (Feinberg 1962). Such meanings may be communicated in prices under $100 simply by leaving out the cents digits entirely. This might lead the consumer to infer that the store, and the customers who shop there, are above even *thinking* about pennies. For fashion products such as clothing or perfume, round-number endings might also communicate a high-fashion image (Bolen 1982, p. 228; Whalen 1980).

It is also possible that a particular price ending may become associated with a particular retail outlet so that its use enhances the retailer's distinctiveness in the minds of consumers. Such a "signature" price ending may be whimsical in origin; for example, for many years the Lechmere stores in the Boston area used 88 endings in their price advertising simply because the flagship store had the address "88 1st Street." Or, the price ending may be consistent with the store's theme, such as with the Dollar General chain's distinctive use of even-dollar prices (Bolen 1982, p. 228).

Finally, it may be possible to use price endings to communicate a "fun" image. For example, the repeated use of a very unusual ending such as 71 might suggest a certain playfulness on the part of the retailer. Or, a flyer from a charity which talks about its ambitious goals for 1989, and then asks for a contribution of $19.89 may communicate a high-spiritedness that many consumers could find attractive.

Summary of Hypothesized Price-Ending Meanings

This survey of hypothesized price-ending meanings has generated the fourteen possibilities described above. These are summarized in Table 1. Rather than an exhaustive list, this collection of possible meanings should be considered as a starting point for future research on the topic. The focus of this work should be on the investigation of the factors which may cause price endings to have meaning to the consumer and the empirical determination of whether each of these meanings indeed exists and what effect it may have on consumer decision making.

POSSIBLE CAUSES OF PRICE-ENDING MEANING

Consideration of these fourteen hypothesized price-ending meanings suggests two general types of causal mechanisms which may be involved. Each carries somewhat different implications about what meanings to look for among a particular group of consumers at a particular time or place, how to test for these meanings, and how these meaningful price endings may be used to communicate with consumers.

The first type of causal mechanism is simple association. For example, if the lower prices in a market are indeed more likely to have just-below endings than the higher prices, then one would expect consumers to learn this correlation over the course of their shopping experience. The results of at least one price survey (see Table 2) suggest that such correlations may in fact exist (Hawkins, Best, and Coney 1989, p. 576).

TABLE 1
Summary of Hypothesized Price-Ending Meanings

Meanings Concerning Price

1. The price is low
2. Price has been reduced
3. Price has not been increased recently
4. Discount or sale price
5. Price results from a careful and precise process
6. Price is negotiable
7. Price is synonymous with even-dollar amount
8. Price is the "correct" price

Meanings Concerning Non-Price Attributes of the Product or Retailer

1. Low quality merchandise
2. Retailer is sneaky, slick, or doesn't "play it straight"
3. High quality merchandise
4. Classiness, sophistication, or prestige
5. Distinctive signature of retailer
6. Playfulness

TABLE 2
Results of a Price Survey of Five Toy Brands in Tucson, Arizona

Product	Market Prices	
	Lowest	Highest
Play Family Sesame Street	$12.97	$27.50
Magic Jewel	10.44	26.50
Weeble Treasure Island	12.99	24.00
Monopoly	3.88	9.00
The Six-Million Dollar Man	10.99	18.95

Source: Hawkins, Best, and Coney (1989), p. 576

Since the learning of such correlations may well be "incidental" or low-involvement learning, it may never produce clearly formulated beliefs which the consumer could retrieve from memory. Thus, the possibility of such a mechanism suggests that measurement of price-ending meanings not rely solely on asking consumers what a particular price ending means to them. Rather, research should also include designing a set of price ads or displays which differ only in price ending and then questioning separate sets of consumers about each one.

If such learning of price-ending correlations is an important determinant of price-ending meanings, then one would expect that changes over time in the way a price ending is used would result in changes in the meanings which consumers perceive that price ending to have. Consistent with this is the observation that the meanings of just-below price endings to American consumers have changed over the last 100 years (Georgoff 1972, pp. 14-15). In the 19th Century, just-below price endings symbolized high quality, since such endings were used most often for imported goods, which were typically of higher quality than domestically made items. By the 1930's, these endings were most often used in low or discount prices, and thus began to be associated with such prices and the retailers who tended to offer them.

Of course, considering the correlation between a certain type of price ending and a certain type of price or product as a cause of price-ending meaning begs the question of more basic cause: what are the factors that cause the correlation to occur in the first place? In the case of the correlation between just-below endings and low or discount prices, it is likely that retailers' beliefs (whether true or not) that consumers will underestimate the levels of just-below prices caused them to choose these endings in situations where a low price or a discount was an important selling point. In this sense, the possibility that consumers may underestimate just-below prices can be said to be a cause of just-below price endings connoting low or discount prices. And this interrelation would explain why both meaning and underestimation explanations of hypothesized price-ending effects often predict similar effects.

The second type of mechanism which may cause price endings to acquire meaning is that consumers may develop "schemer schemas" (Wright 1986), or intuitive theories, about why particular price endings are used. For example, consumer curiosity about why a price ending such as 31 is used could lead to the schema or theory that price endings which seem random must result from a very careful and precise price-setting process and that the retailer takes the trouble to be so careful in order to give the consumer the lowest price possible.

Schemer schemas might well enrich the meanings of price endings which have acquired meanings through the associational mechanism. For instance, if just-below endings have come, through association, to mean low prices, the schema that low price can be offered only at the expense of quality could lead just-below endings to develop a low-quality meaning also. However, schemer schemas might be particularly likely to be important determinants of price-ending meaning for endings which are unusual or for which there are no obvious meanings. It is these which are most likely to arouse consumers' theorizing about the price-setter's motivations.

In contrast to the associational mechanism, the schemer-schema mechanism of meaning development would respond to a more direct means of measurement. Rather than comparing the responses of different consumers to the same price with different endings, consumers' intuitive theories could best be investigated by showing consumers a variety of price endings and directly questioning them about their theories concerning the reasons why each price ending is used.

Price-ending meanings acquired through incidental learning of correlations which occur in the marketplace are likely to be more difficult to change than meanings acquired through schemer schemas. To change consumers' associations would require providing long-term repeated exposure to price endings in the context of the to-be-learned price, product, or store attributes. By contrast, it may be possible to change consumers' intuitive theories by persuasively suggesting alternative explanations, or "undermines" (Kirmani and Wright 1989), in advertising copy. For example, the claim that a retailer can offer high quality at low prices because of volume buying may lead consumers to modify the schema that low price must be an indication of low quality.

EMPIRICAL EVIDENCE FOR THE EXISTENCE OF PRICE-ENDING MEANINGS

Considering the amount of speculation concerning price-ending meanings which has reached print, it is surprising that there is so little published empirical investigation of whether or not such meanings exist in the minds of consumers. One of the first detailed report of evidence that price endings can have meanings to consumers came out of a study of whether or not price ending affects the ability of consumers to recognize whether a price has recently been increased (Schindler 1984). It was found that consumers' overall recognition accuracy was lower when prices were presented with 99 or 98 endings than when they were presented with 00 endings. But it was also found that subjects showed a bias toward judging that the prices with the just-below endings were ones which had *not* been increased. This suggests that, when memory failed to provide the needed information, the subjects' responses were guided by an impression that prices with 99 or 98 endings are the type of prices which are less likely to have been recently increased.

Dodds and Monroe (1985) reported a more direct test of meaning effects of just-below pricing. They provided subjects with a description of a portable cassette player which either did or did not include a brand name, and which was displayed with either a high, medium, or low price which had either a 95 or round-number ending. They found no effect of price ending on perceived quality of the product. However, they reported evidence that, for the situation when the price was at the middle level and no brand identity was provided, the just-below ending caused the product to be perceived as a better value. Since value is a function of price as well as quality, this result may have been due to low-price connotations of the 95 ending of the price.

Schindler and Kibarian (1989) tested for meaning effects of just-below pricing in a situation similar to that in which Dodds and Monroe found evidence of some effect. They selected price advertisements from out-of-town newspapers and altered the ads so that one version showed prices with 99 endings and the other version showed the corresponding 00-ending prices. Because the subjects were unfamiliar with the stores in the out-of-town ads and because the prices were kept very close to the original prices in the ad, the conditions of this experiment approximated Dodds and Monroe's no-brand-information, middle price-level condition.

Schindler and Kibarian found that the just-below price ending increased consumers' likelihood of judging that the advertised prices were the lowest prices around and increased their likelihood of judging that the prices had not recently been increased. Thus, they confirmed the findings of the two previous studies. Further, they found that the prices with 99 endings were more likely to be judged as sale prices than the prices with 00 endings, and that the 00 endings increased their likelihood of rating the quality of the items advertised as "above average."

A fourth study (Schindler 1989) differs from the previous three in that it tested the effect of price endings on actual sales rather than consumers' responses to questionnaire items. A split-run test was conducted with the 24-page winter sale catalog of a direct-mail women's clothing retailer. A randomly selected sample of thirty thousand customers received a version of the catalog printed with all prices ending in the digits 00. A second sample of thirty thousand customers received a version of the catalog printed with all prices ending with the digits 99. A third sample of thirty thousand customers received a version of the catalog printed with all prices ending with the digits 88. After three months, the gross dollar sales for the 99-ending catalog was 10% higher than that for the 00-ending catalog. However, the business generated by the 88-ending catalog was virtually the same as that of the 00-ending catalog (even though each price was 12 cents lower!).

The important result of this study is not to provide evidence for any particular set of price-ending meanings, but to support the general idea that price-ending meanings can affect sales. Meaning effects clearly *could* have caused the obtained pattern of results; for example, the 00-ending catalog may have suggested regular prices, the 88-ending catalog may have suggested low prices without being on sale (and thus low quality could be inferred), and the 99 endings may have connoted a genuine sale. In contrast, it is difficult to imagine how this pattern of results could have been produced by underestimation effects alone. If the 99-ending prices performed better than the 00-ending prices because the consumers dropped off one or more of the rightmost digits and thus underestimated the levels of these prices, then one would expect them to have also done so with the 88-ending prices. Thus this study, while remaining mute on the specific meanings involved, does provide empirical support for the idea that price-ending meanings can affect consumer response.

CONCLUSIONS

The symbolic meaning which a price ending may evoke in the minds of consumers is a possible cause of price-ending effects, and is one which is distinguishable from any tendency consumers may have to underestimate the level of just-below prices. Although a rich array of price-ending meanings have been hypothesized, the process of systematically testing for the presence of these meanings has only just begun. However, the initial results are promising, and suggest that managerial decisions about price endings need not be governed solely by intuition, tradition, or imitation of competitors. With the benefits of further research, all marketers may be able to use price endings in a more deliberate way, as a versatile tool to more effectively communicate with consumers.

REFERENCES

Alpert, Mark I. (1971), *Pricing Decisions*, Glenview, IL: Scott, Foresman and Company.

Beckman, Theodore N. and William R. Davidson (1967), *Marketing*, 8th edition, New York, NY: Ronald Press.

Berman, Barry and Joel R. Evans (1986), *Retail Management: A Strategic Approach*, 3rd edition, New York, NY: Macmillan Publishing Company.

Bliss, Perry (1952), "Price Determination at the Department Store Level," *Journal of Marketing*, 17 (July), 37-46.

Bolen, William H. (1982), *Contemporary Retailing*, 2nd edition, Englewood Cliffs, NJ: Prentice-Hall.

Brenner, Gabrielle A. and Reuven Brenner (1982), "Memory and Markets, or Why Are You Paying $2.99 for a Widget?" *Journal of Business*, 55, 147-158.

Calogero, Jim (1982), "Some Odd Ways in Setting Price," *Boston Globe*, (November 8), 42, 44.

Dodds, William B. and Kent B. Monroe (1985), "The Effect of Brand and Price Information on Subjective Product Evaluation," in *Advances in Consumer Research*, Vol. 12, eds. Elizabeth C. Hirschman and Morris B. Holbrook, Provo, UT: Association for Consumer Research, 85-90.

Feinberg, Samuel (1962), "Quiet Defiance of Psychological Pricing," *Women's Wear Daily*, 104 (March 11), 10.

Friedman, Lawrence (1967), "Psychological Pricing in the Food Industry," in *Prices: Issues in Theory, Practice, and Public Policy*, eds., Almarin Phillips and Oliver E. Williamson, Philadelphia: University of Pennsylvania Press, 187-201.

Gabor, Andre and C. W. J. Granger (1964), "Price Sensitivity of the Consumer," *Journal of Advertising Research*, 4 (December), 40-44.

Georgoff, David M. (1972), *Odd-Even Retail Price Endings*, East Lansing, MI: Michigan State University.

Hawkins, Del I., Roger J. Best, and Kenneth A. Coney (1989), *Consumer Behavior: Implications for Marketing Strategy*, 4th edition, Homewood, IL: BPI/Irwin.

Kirmani, Amna and Peter Wright (1989), "Money Talks: Perceived Advertising Expense and Expected Product Quality," *Journal of Consumer Research*, 16 (December), 344-353.

Knauth, Oswald (1949), "Considerations in Setting Retail Prices," *Journal of Marketing*, 14 (July), 1-12.

Kotler, Philip (1988), *Marketing Management: Analysis, Planning, Implementation, and Control*, 6th edition, Englewood Cliffs, NJ: Prentice-Hall.

Kreul, Lee M. (1982), "Magic Numbers: Psychological Aspects of Menu Pricing," *The Cornell Hotel and Restaurant Administration Quarterly*, 23 (August), 70-75.

Lambert, Zarrel V. (1975), "Perceived Prices as Related to Odd and Even Price Endings," *Journal of Retailing*, 51 (Fall), 13-22, 78.

Lewison, Dale M. and M. Wayne DeLozier (1986), *Retailing*, 2nd edition, Columbus, Ohio: Merrill Publishing Company.

Lichtenstein, Donald R. and Scot Burton (1989), "The Relationship Between Perceived and Objective Price-Quality," *Journal of Marketing Research*, 26 (November), 429-443.

Mason, J. Barry and Morris L. Mayer (1990), *Modern Retailing: Theory and Practice*, 5th edition, Homewood, IL: BPI/Irwin.

Monroe, Kent B. (1990), *Pricing: Making Profitable Decisions*, 2nd edition, New York, NY: McGraw-Hill Publishing Company.

_____ and R. Krishnan (1985), "The Effect of Price on Subjective Product Evaluations," in *Perceived Quality: How Consumers View Stores and Merchandise*, eds., Jacob Jacoby and Jerry C. Olson, Lexington, MA: Lexington Books.

_____ and Susan M. Petroshius (1981), "Buyers' Perceptions of Price: An Update of the Evidence," in *Perspectives in Consumer Behavior*, 3rd edition, eds., Harold H. Kassarjian and Thomas S. Robertson, Glenview, IL: Scott, Foresman and Company, 43-55.

Nagle, Thomas (1987), *The Strategy and Tactics of Pricing: A Guide to Profitable Decision Making*, Englewood Cliffs, NJ: Prentice-Hall.

Oxenfeldt, Alfred R. (1966), *Executive Action in Marketing*, Belmont, CA: Wadsworth Publishing Co.

Rao, Vithala R. (1984), "Pricing Research in Marketing: The State of the Art," *Journal of Business*, 57 (January), S39-S60.

Raphel, Murray (1968), "Is 99 Sense More Than a Dollar?" *Direct Marketing*, (October), 76.

Schindler, Robert M. (1984), "Consumer Recognition of Increases in Odd and Even Prices," in *Advances in Consumer Research*, Vol. 11, ed. Thomas C. Kinnear, Provo, UT: Association for Consumer Research, 459-462.

_____ (1989), "A Field Test of the Effects of Price Ending on Sales," Working paper, School of Business, Rutgers University - Camden, Camden, NJ.

_____ and Thomas Kibarian (1989), "The Image Effects of Odd Pricing," Working paper, School of Business, Rutgers University - Camden, Camden, NJ.

_____ and Lori S. Warren (1988), "Effect of Odd Pricing on Choice of Items from a Menu," in *Advances in Consumer Research*, Vol. 15, ed. Michael J. Houston, Provo, UT: Association for Consumer Research, 348-353.

_____ and Alan R. Wiman (1989), "Effect of Odd Pricing on Price Recall," *Journal of Business Research*, 19 (November), 165-177.

Scitovsky, Tibor (1945), "Some Consequences of the Habit of Judging Quality by Price," *Review of Economic Studies*, 12(2), 100-105.

Simon, Hermann (1989), *Price Management*, Amsterdam, The Netherlands: Elsevier Science Publishers.

Spohn, Robert F. and Robert Y. Allen (1977), *Retailing*, Englewood Cliffs, NJ: Prentice-Hall.

Whalen, Bernard F. (1980), "Strategic Mix of Odd, Even Prices Can Lead to Increased Retail Profits," *Marketing News*, 13 (March 7), 24.

Wingate, John W., Elmer O. Schaller, and F. Leonard Miller (1972), *Retail Merchandise Management*, Englewood Cliffs, NJ: Prentice-Hall.

Wright, Peter (1986), "Schemer Schema: Consumers' Intuitive Theories About Marketers' Influence Tactics," in *Advances in Consumer Research*, Vol. 13, ed. Richard J. Lutz, Provo UT: Association for Consumer Research, 1-3.

Individual Differences in Latitude of Acceptable Prices

Patricia Sorce, Rochester Institute of Technology
Stanley M. Widrick, Rochester Institute of Technology

ABSTRACT

This research tested the impact of individual differences on consumers' latitude of acceptable price and on actual price paid for durable goods. The width of the latitude was positively correlated with perceived brand differentiation but not with price consciousness. The magnitude of the upper threshold of latitude was found to be the best predictor of actual price paid.

How do buyers use price in making a purchase decision? Price information is encoded and interpreted by the consumer within a frame of reference of acceptable prices (Monroe 1973; Jacoby and Olson 1977; Dodds and Monroe 1985; Winer 1986; Lichtenstein, Bloch and Black 1988; Zeithaml 1988; Lattin and Bucklin 1989). Price acceptability is the judgment of price of a product as acceptable or unacceptable based on the comparison of the price cue in the environment to a *range* of acceptable prices stored in memory (Lichtenstein, Bloch & Black 1988). Consumers encode price information by comparing prices against their internal range of acceptable prices; the degree of discrepancy between the actual price and the acceptable price range results in a judgement of acceptable or unacceptable, which affects the probability of purchase (Winer, 1986).

The existence of latitude of acceptable prices has been well-documented (Gabor and Granger 1964; Monroe 1971; Lichtenstein, Bloch and Black 1988). It is the goal of the present research to extend our understanding of the impact of individual differences on latitude of acceptable prices for a wide range of durable goods.

Theoretical Foundations and Development of Hypotheses

The notion of an internal reference point such as the latitude of acceptable prices is an extension of Helson's adaptation level theory (1964). The adaptation process describes how a consumer will respond to an external stimulus. The encoding of the stimulus depends on an adaptation level which can be viewed as a continuum of acceptance and rejection, with a wide neutral zone where uncertainty prevails.

Adaptation level is formed through prior experiences (Sherif 1963; Della Bitta and Monroe 1973) and is influenced by individual differences. One important area of individual difference in buyer behavior is involvement. Sherif and Hovland (1961) theorized that involvement with an issue was associated with narrower latitudes of acceptance. This can be interpreted to mean that high involvement with price in terms of its financial sacrifice (price consciousness) should be negatively correlated with latitude of acceptable price. Lichtenstein, Bloch & Black (1988) found support for this hypothesis where price consciousness (defined as involvement with price in terms of its sacrifice) was negatively correlated with latitude of acceptable prices for running shoes. The present study was designed to extend our understanding of the impact on price consciousness on latitude acceptable prices by measuring its effects across a wide range of products rather than a single product.

In addition, the study assessed the impact of a second individual difference variable, perceived brand differentiation, on latitude of price acceptability. Lichtenstein, Bloch, and Black (1988) found that perception of quality variations between a low and high priced running shoes was positively correlated with price acceptability (measured by a point estimate), but was not related to the width of the *latitude* of acceptable prices. Possibly, differences in brand differentiation affects both the upper and lower price acceptability thresholds an equivalent amount, resulting in latitudes of similar magnitude for both high and low differentiation subjects. In order to better understand the relationship between perceived brand differentiation and price acceptability, the present study measured the upper and lower thresholds of the latitude of acceptable price as separate dependent variables. This was warranted since Gabor and Granger (1964) found individual difference variables affected the upper and lower thresholds independently.

Lastly, the study examined the association between price acceptability and buyer behavior. Berkowitz and Walton (1980) found that price acceptability was positively correlated with willingness to buy (as measured by purchase intention). In more recent research, the magnitude of the discrepancy between actual retail price and the consumer's reference price was related to purchase probability: the greater the discrepancy, the lower the probability of purchase (Winer 1986; Lattin and Bucklin 1989). In most prior research, the dependent variable price was operationalized by stating a purchase intention or by a self report of price paid on a recent purchase. The present study was designed to test the impact of price acceptability on the observed price paid.

In sum, the research was designed to extend previous research on latitude of acceptable prices by examining the impact of individual difference variables on latitude of price acceptability. The major contributions of the present study will be the inclusion of a wide range of durable goods in the data collection, the isolation of the upper and lower thresholds in the measures of latitude, and the inclusion of observed price paid as a dependent variable.

METHOD

The method used was to intercept and interview customers immediately following their purchase. A total of 323 customers of 16 durable product lines were interviewed and asked questions about their product purchase.

The interviews were completed during January and February 1989 in 30 different durable goods retailers (including chain department stores, appliance specialty stores, and off-price appliance retailers) in Monroe County, New York. At each store, all customers within the time period sampled were intercepted immediately after they paid for one of the 16 product categories (87% of those approached agreed to cooperate).

The variables collected on each subject were defined and operationalized as follows:

Independent Variables:
Price consciousness -- relative importance of price in the selection of the durable good; measured on a scale of 1 - 6 where 6 = most important and 1 = least important.

Perceived brand differentiation--customer perceived similarity of choices available, measured on a five point scale where 1 = all choices the same and 5 = all very different.

Dependent Variables: All dependent variables were transformed into index scores (referenced to the product category prices) due to the wide range of products, and hence prices, used in the study.

Price paid (indexed to SKU range) - this decimal measured the observed price consumers paid in relation to the SKU prices available at that retailer for the product category where the purchase was made, and was calculated using:
Paid = Actual price paid by the customer
High = Highest priced SKU for that product category at that retailer
Low = Lowest priced SKU for that product category at that retailer

$$\text{Price paid index} = \frac{\text{Paid - Low}}{\text{High - Low}}$$

Lower threshold - this decimal number measured the customer's lower acceptable price threshold within the range of prices available at retail for that product category. This variable required the High and Low SKU values discussed above in addition to Least:
Least = Lowest price the customer actually considered paying

$$\text{Lower Threshold} = \frac{\text{Least - Low}}{\text{High - Low}}$$

Upper threshold - this decimal number measured the customer's upper acceptable price threshold within the range of prices available at retail for that product category. This variable required the High and Low SKU values discussed above in addition to Most:
Most = Highest price the customer actually considered paying

$$\text{Upper Threshold} = \frac{\text{Most - Low}}{\text{High - Low}}$$

Latitude of acceptable price--the difference between the lowest price and the highest price they considered paying for the product category, indexed to the price range.

Latitude = Upper threshold - Lower threshold

See Table 1 for the list of products used in the study and the absolute values of the SKU ranges and latitudes of acceptable prices.

RESULTS

Table 2 presents correlation matrix for the variables used in the study. The first hypothesis tested the relationship between price consciousness and the width of the latitude of acceptable prices. From Table 2, latitude was not found to be significantly correlated with price consciousness. However, price consciousness was negatively correlated with both the upper and lower thresholds ($r = -.113$ and $-.102$ respectively) and price paid ($r = -.145$). Consumers who were very price conscious had lower values of the upper and lower thresholds (and paid lower prices) for durable goods than those who were less price consciousness.

The second hypothesis tested the relationship between perceived brand differentiation and price acceptability. Table 2 again presents the results, where all four dependent variables were significantly correlated with brand differentiation. Consumers who perceived a wide variation among brands had wider latitudes, higher upper thresholds, higher lower thresholds, and paid more for their durable goods than consumers who perceived brands as all the same.

To determine the relative impact of each of the independent variables on the four dependent variables, four step-wise regressions were computed, with price consciousness, brand differentiation, and their interaction, as the independent variables. Brand differentiation was the first to enter the three equations for latitude (beta = .19), upper threshold (beta = .225), and price paid (beta = .205) dependent variables. Price consciousness was the first to enter the equation predicting the lower threshold (beta = .178). The interaction effect was not significant in any of the analyses.

Lastly, the relationship among the dependent variables was explored. If price acceptability is a useful construct, it should be positively related to the price paid. A regression analysis using upper and lower thresholds as independent variables predicted 62% of the variance in price paid. Moreover, the upper threshold explained more

TABLE 1
Product Profile, Average Price Paid, Latitude of Acceptable Price and Retail SKU Price Range

Product category	#	Average price	Latitude of acceptable price	Retail SKU price range
Televisions	60	$398	$207	$1585
Auto tires	44	81	43	118
Washing machines	31	411	154	388
VCRs	29	307	159	491
Microwaves	25	239	120	390
Vacuum cleaners	24	138	125	308
Kitchen stoves	18	620	254	674
Refrigerators	17	683	272	1158
Auto batteries	13	50	32	68
Clothing dryer	11	354	143	255
Telephones	10	89	63	159
Humidifier	9	61	39	75
CD players	9	223	102	412
Dishwashers	8	355	137	372
Portable heaters	8	76	37	84
Auto stereos	7	224	124	387
totals	323			

TABLE 2
Correlation Matrix

	Price Paid	Latitude	Upper Threshold	Lower Threshold
Price Consciousness	-.145	ns	-.113*	-.102*
Brand Differentiation	.235	.191	.223	.172

All correlations are signficant at the .01 level, except when noted with an asterix, which indicates significance at the .05 level.

---

variance in price paid ($R^2 = .54$) than the lower threshold ($R^2 = .06$).

DISCUSSION

The present study extends previous research by documenting the correlates of price acceptability across a wide range of durable goods. Price consciousness was found to be negatively correlated with the upper and lower thresholds of price acceptability, but not with the width of the latitude. In essence, the width of the latitude remained the same for high versus low price conscious consumers, but the upper and lower thresholds were lower for the high price conscious versus low price consciousness consumer. This finding is contrary to that of Lichtenstein, Bloch and Black (1988), who found a significant negative correlation between price consciousness and width of the latitude. The failure to replicate the price consciousness/latitude correlation could be explained by a number of factors, ranging from the nature of the products under study to the nature of the measures of price consciousness. Further investigation of the relationship between these variables is warranted.

Latitude of acceptable prices was positively related to perceived brand differentiation, where consumers who perceived many differences among brands had wider latitudes than consumers who perceived fewer differences. The wider latitude was a function of the higher upper threshold for consumers who perceived a large variation between brands. The present results contrast with previous results of

Lichtenstein, Bloch and Black (1988) who found significant correlations between brand differentiation and the point estimate of price acceptability but not with the width of the latitude. Again, further research into these relationships is warranted.

Lastly, the predictive validity of price acceptability on buyer behavior was tested by the regression analysis between the upper and lower thresholds and actual price paid. The results showed that the magnitude of the upper threshold explained more variation in price paid than the lower threshold. This result suggests the powerful role that price acceptability has on buyer behavior. Moreover, it reinforces the notion that upper and lower thresholds are important dependent variables to include in further studies in price acceptability.

REFERENCES

Berkowitz, Eric and John Walton (1980), "Contextual Influences on Consumer Price Responses: An Experimental Analysis," *Journal of Marketing Research*, 17 (August) 349 - 58.

Della Bitta, Albert and Kent B. Monroe (1973), "The Influence of Adaptation Levels on Subjective Price Perceptions," *Advances in Consumer Research* S. Ward and P. Wright (eds), Volume 1, (Urbana, Ill: Association for Consumer Research) 359 - 369.

Dodds, William and Kent Monroe (1985), "The Effect of Brand and Price Information on Subjective Product Evaluations", *Advances in Consumer Research* Elizabeth Hirschman and Morris Holbrook,eds. Provo, Utah: Association for Consumer Research, 85-90.

Gabor, Andre and Clive Granger (1964) "Price Sensitivity of the Consumer" *Journal of Advertising Research*, 4 (December) 40-44.

Helson, Harry (1964). *Adaptation -Level Theory*. New York: Harper and Row.

Jacoby, Jacob and Jerry Olson (1971) ,"Consumer Response to Price: An Attitudinal, Information Processing Perspective," *Moving Ahead with Attitude Research*, Yoram Wind and Marshall Greenberg eds, Chicago, IL: American Marketing Association, 73-86.

Lattin, James M. and Randolph E. Bucklin (1989) "Reference Effects of Price and Promotion on Brand Choice Behavior" *Journal of Marketing Research*, (August) 299-310.

Lichtenstein,Donald R., Peter H. Bloch and William C. Black (1988) "Correlates of Price Acceptability" *Journal of Consumer Research*, 15 (September) 243-252.

Monroe, Kent B. (1971), "Measuring Price Thresholds by Psychophysics and Latitudes of Acceptance," *Journal of Marketing Research*, 8 (November) 460-464.

Monroe, Kent B. (1973), "Buyers' Subjective Perceptions of Price" *Journal of Marketing Research*, 10 (February) 70-80.

Monroe, Kent B and Susan Petroshius (1981), "Buyers' Perceptions of Price: An Update of the Evidence," *Perspectives in Consumer Behavior* Harold H. Kassarjian and Thomas S. Robertson (eds) (Glenview, Illinois: Scott, Foresman) 43-55.

Sherif, Carolyn (1963), "Social Categorization as a Function of Latitude of Acceptance and Series Range," *Journal of Abnormal Psychology*, 67 (August) 148-156.

Sherif, Muzafer and Carl Hovland (1961). *Social Judgment: Assimilation and Contrast Effects in Communication and Attitude Change*. New Haven: Yale University Press.

Winer, Russell S. (1986), "A Reference Price Model of Brand Choice for Frequently Purchased Products," *Journal of Consumer Research*, 13 (September) 250-256.

Zeithaml, Valerie A. (1988), "Consumer Perceptions of Price, Quality, and Value: A Means-End Model and Synthesis of Evidence" *Journal of Marketing*, (July) 2-22.

Measuring Communication-Evoked Imagery Processing

Pam Scholder Ellen, Georgia State University
Paula Fitzgerald Bone, West Virginia University

ABSTRACT

During the 1980s, interest among consumer researchers in imagery processing increased. In order for this line of research to continue to be productive, it is important that a measure of imagery processing which is evoked by a particular communication be made available. This paper details the initial stages of the development of a multi-item imagery scale which appears to be a reliable and valid scale of communication-evoked imagery.

INTRODUCTION

During the 1980's, consumer researchers became more and more interested in imagery processing and its relative merits over purely discursive processing. Imagery processing is defined as the representation of any sensory experience in working memory (MacInnis and Price 1987). While most empirical work in imagery processing has focused solely on visual imagery, imagery processing may be any multi-sensory experience (i.e., sight, taste, sound, smell, or touch) evoked by a message (MacInnis and Price 1987; Childers and Houston 1982). Of specific interest in this research is memory imagery, or imagery recalled or created in the absence of the actual sensory stimulus (Richardson 1969).

Consumer researchers have examined the effects of imagery-inducing strategies on various consumption-related outcomes such as brand name recall, information search, behavioral intentions, and to a limited extent, attitudes. (See MacInnis and Price 1987 for a review). In doing so, imagery processing is often treated as a distinct process from discursive processing although the researchers acknowledge that the two processes coexist. Additionally, few of these studies have actually assessed the form of processing. Instead most studies have inferred that imagery processing, as opposed to verbal processing, occurred by examining observed differences in these consumption-related variables.

For these reasons, it seems appropriate to develop indicators of the extent or degree of imagery processing evoked by a communication. The purpose of this research is to describe the initial development of such measures which may be used across studies. Reliable indicators with evidence of validity may be useful either as manipulation checks, criterion or predictor variables in subsequent imagery research. In the following section, we review existing imagery measures and describe the proposed measures.

MEASUREMENT OF IMAGERY PROCESSING

A number of scales currently exist to measure individual differences in imagery processing abilities and preferences (see MacInnis 1986 for a review). Some of the measures assess a person's ability to engage in imagery (e.g. Betts' Questionaire Upon Mental Imagery (Betts 1909; Sheehan 1967)) while others assess individual differences in preferred processing style (e.g. Style of Processing Questionnaire (Childers, Houston and Heckler 1985)). These scales were designed to measure general traits rather than imagery states induced by a communication. "The use of these [trait] scales to predict *specific* consumer behaviors requires careful consideration" (MacInnis 1986, p.92). As MacInnis (1986) points out, one individual may have a greater score on an imagery ability or preference scale, yet another individual may experience more imagery because of greater knowledge or familiarity with a specific domain. Thus, the imagery evoked by a specific communication is a function of both one's ability and the stimulus itself and is not adequately captured by the trait scale.

A few researchers have attempted to assess the effects of imagery-inducing strategies on actual processing. Lutz and Lutz (1977) used a self-report to assess whether subjects used visual or verbal processing. While this type of measure provides an indication of the type of processing, there is no indication of the extent of imagery processing. In addition, this measure is limited to visual imagery. Smith, Houston and Childers (1983) and McGill and Anand (1989) attempted to measure the extent of imagery processing by asking subjects to provide written protocols as they considered a situation. Smith, Houston and Childers (1983) also asked subjects to indicate whether each activity described was visualized or verbalized and if visualized, how vivid or clear the images were. The primary disadvantage of such measures is that they require the subjects to translate sensory experiences into verbal protocols. Morris and Hampson (1983) argue that sensory experiences may be difficult to verbalize. Note that these measures are also limited to visual imagery and exclude the other senses. Thus, it appears that there is a need for a measure of the extent of imagery processing evoked by a communication which can be used across studies, can incorporate visual as well as other sensory experiences, and does not depend on the subject's ability to verbalize the imagery content.

The first step in developing such a measure was to examine the existing imagery literature to identify possible dimensions of communication-evoked imagery. The following section addresses that issue. Next, a multi-item scale developed to tap the various dimensions is introduced. Then, empirical work which investigates the dimensionality, internal consistency, sensitivity to processing differences, and discriminant validity is presented.

POTENTIAL INDICATORS OF COMMUNICATION-EVOKED IMAGERY

Imagery-evoked by a communication may be reflected in several different dimensions. The dimensions discussed here are the vividness and/or clarity, quantity, ease, and links experienced as a result of the message.

Morris and Hampson (1983) identify vividness as the major dimension of imagery. While vividness is by far the more prevalent characteristic ascribed to differences in imagery processing (Betts 1909; Cartwright et al. 1978; MacInnis and Price 1987, Marks 1973), assessing the vividness of evoked images assumes that the vividness of images varies and indicates the quality of the imagery (Morris and Hampson 1983). However, attempts to measure vividness are often confounded with measures of other dimensions, especially clarity. While they are likely related dimensions, clarity refers to the detail of the images while vividness is more closely associated the intensity of the images. Morris and Hampson (1983) argue that there is not sufficient empirical or theoretical support for the assumption that these dimensions are the same therefore it is important to consider these descriptors as separate initially.

While vividness and clarity tap qualitative aspects of evoked-imagery, Smith, Houston and Childers (1983) suggest that there may also be quantitative differences in imagery processing. McGill and Anand (1989) found that the use of imagery instructions resulted in a greater number of evoked scenes and a greater number of inferred attributes. The quantity or number of different images created may or may not be related to the vividness or clarity of the images. One person may evoke a single, very vivid image while another may experience numerous images which may be much less vivid.

Ease of imagining has been suggested by several researchers as an important aspect of imagery processing (Anderson 1983; Paivio 1968; Sherman et al. 1983). The more available that information is concerning the subject to be imagined, the easier it should be for the individual to engage in imagery processing. For instance, much of the discussion of effects of concrete words and sentences on recall are attributed to the ease with which associated images can be elicited.

The final dimension of imagery is imagery links (Kisielius and Sternthal 1986; Lord 1980; MacInnis and Price 1987). One of the touted advantages of imagery processing over verbal processing is its greater ability to link or activate other information in long term memory. This activation occurs because imagery processing allows activation of stored information through a number of means (i.e., sensory experiences) other than simply semantic links. Such links should ultimately result in greater elaboration and therefore greater availability of the information at judgment or decision-making time.

In sum, there have been at least five dimensions of imagery processing discussed in the literature. In the next section, we present a set of measures developed to measure these dimensions: vividness, clarity, quantity, ease and links.

PROPOSED INDICATORS OF COMMUNICATION-EVOKED IMAGERY

To develop the items to measure each of the dimensions, we first examined the approaches used in previous research to describe aspects of imagery and measure imagery processing abilities. We developed a list of items or descriptors used in previous research (c.f., Paivio 1968) as well as synonyms. For vividness, consistent with Morris and Hampson (1983), we included descriptors assessing both intensity and clarity in these measures.

In sum, nineteen items were developed to assess communication-evoked imagery: eleven vividness/clarity items, three quantity items, three ease items and two link items. The items are presented in Table 1. Given differences in item scaling (5-point vs. 9-point), all items were standardized prior to any analysis. We now turn our attention to determining whether these are indeed separate dimensions.

METHOD

The data from two separate studies were used to assess the proposed measures. College students (n=179 for Study 1 and n=144 for Study 2) were processed individually in an audio-visual lab, and each subject was randomly assigned to one of the seven professionally-produced advertisements for a fictitious brand of popcorn, a product selected for its high sensory attributes. In each study, subjects listened to either one of several high-imagery radio advertisements or a low-imagery control ad. Participants listened to the ad twice to allow adequate time for creating images as well as comprehending the message.

All six high-imagery ads used concrete words, actionable sentences, present tense, and instructions to imagine in order to facilitate imagery processing in general (Sherman et al. 1983; Paivio 1976; Alesandrini and Sheikh 1983; Carroll 1978). The ads contained no music or sound effects, and all were similar in that different types of sensory experiences were described in each: sights, sounds, aromas, tastes, and body movement. The character and situation imagined differed in the ads; however, these differences are unimportant for this discussion and are not addressed here.

In addition to the high-imagery ads, one low-imagery control ad was used. The ad was for the same product and contained the same number of mentions of brand name as the high-imagery ads, however, the advertisement contained no instructions to imagine and no concrete words or sensory descriptions. After listening to the ad, subjects completed the measures of communication-evoked imagery and the short version of Betts' Questionnaire upon Mental Imagery (QMI) (Sheehan 1967; Betts 1909).

TABLE 1
Measures of Communication-Evoked Imagery Processing

QUANTITY

As you listened to the ad, to what extent did any images come to mind?
(To a very small extent....To a very great extent)

While listening to the ad, I experienced (Lots of images....Few or no images)

All sorts of pictures, sounds, tastes and/or smells came to my mind while I listened to the ad. (Strongly Agree....Strongly Disagree)

EASE

How difficult or easy were the images to create? (Extremely Easy....Extremely Difficult)

How quickly were the images aroused?(Very Quickly....Not quickly at all)

I had no difficulty imagining the scene in my head.(Strongly Agree....Strongly Disagree)

VIVIDNESS

The imagery which occurred while I listened to the ad was:(Does not Describe at All....Describes Perfectly)

Clear	Intense
Pale	Vague
Fuzzy	Lifelike
Detailed	Sharp
Weak	Well-Defined
Vivid	

LINKS

The ad reminded me of other times in my life. (Strongly Agree....Strongly Disagree)

The ad brought back memories of events that happened to me in the past.(Strongly Agree... Strongly Disagree

---

ASSESSING THE DIMENSIONALITY OF THE INDICATORS

The nineteen items were subjected to confirmatory factor analysis using three, four and five factor solutions. It was expected that there would be one factor each for quantity, ease and links and either one vividness factor or separate vividness and clarity factors. Results for both studies are presented in Table 2.

The results from the two studies are remarkably similar. In both cases, the most interpretable solution was a four factor solution. The solution for both studies indicated a joint quantity and ease factor, a vividness factor, a paleness factor and a links factor. Although the X^2 for all three models was significant, the four factor solution was significantly better than the three factor (one dimension for both vivid and pale) with a X^2 difference of 124.46 (df=16, p<.01) and 255.09 (df=16, p<.01) for Study 1 and 2, respectively. The four factors accounted for 62.2% and 62.4% of the variance, respectively. In each case, there is a quantity/ease factor, explaining 29.9% and 18.9% of the variance, respectively, in the imagery measures. There are two separate factors accounting for the vividness/clarity items. The first factor, vividness, explains 19.9% (Study 1) and 30.9% (Study 2) of the variance. The second factor includes items indicating the paleness (or lack of clarity) in the imagery, explaining 7.6% and 7.8% of the variance in the two studies. The final factor, the links items, explain 5.7% and 4.8% of the variance in the two datasets.

The factor loadings in each case were quite clear and very similar. Specifically, factor loadings for the individual items exceeded 0.50 on the appropriate factor in all but one case (vivid on the vividness factor in Study 1). In every case, the loading was significantly larger on one factor than on the remaining three.

The results indicated that the number of images imagined and the ease with which they are

TABLE 2
FACTOR ANALYSIS RESULTS

Measure	STUDY 1				STUDY 2			
	Quan/Ease	Vivid	Pale	Links	Quan/Ease	Vivid	Pale	Links
Quan1	.65	.42	.21	.16	.60	.30	.39	.07
Quan2	.57	.22	.11	.08	.68	.26	.11	.11
Quan3	.65	.17	.11	.25	.63	.17	.11	.22
Ease1	.74	.20	.24	.12	.83	.18	.22	.15
Ease2	.78	.11	.15	.10	.83	.19	.13	.08
Ease3	.63	.23	.30	.07	.73	.27	.22	.09
Clear	.26	.63	.31	.16	.42	.58	.33	.10
Detailed	.12	.69	.25	.01	.09	.63	.19	.26
Vivid	.30	.48	.34	.12	.31	.57	.28	.00
Intense	.29	.52	.14	.15	.22	.40	.13	.13
Lifelike	.30	.57	.21	.18	.32	.64	.21	.23
Sharp	.23	.80	.14	.16	.32	.61	.37	.09
Well-Defined	.11	.82	.30	.12	.18	.81	.19	.20
Pale	.26	.21	.72	.09	.24	.10	.79	.05
Fuzzy	.16	.26	.77	.02	.22	.24	.73	.10
Weak	.19	.31	.73	.15	.16	.30	.55	.05
Vague	.23	.28	.71	.16	.09	.33	.66	.15
Link1	.21	.21	.12	.95	.22	.25	.19	.81
Link2	.23	.17	.14	.77	.20	.25	.05	.94
Eigenvalue	5.69	3.6	1.44	1.08	3.59	5.87	1.47	.92
Variance(%)	29.90	19.90	7.60	5.70	18.90	30.90	7.80	4.80

imagined are highly correlated and in this case are captured by one factor. (The correlation between the separate summated indicators of the quantity and ease items is .71 and .74 in the two studies.) Vividness and paleness appear best handled as separate dimensions. The three factor solution results in a single dimension for all eleven items but the fit is substantially worse for that model. Finally, the links factor, while explaining the least amount of variance, still represents a significant and potentially important indicator of overall imagery processing. The factor analysis provided some evidence of the unidimensionality of the different measures.

The next step in the validation of these measure was to look at their reliability. Coefficient alpha was used for the quantity/ease measure and the vividness and paleness measures, while Pearson product moment correlation was used to assess the internal consistency of the link items. The reliabilities for each dimension are high--all exceed 0.83. For the quantity/ease dimension, coefficient alphas are 0.88 and 0.91 for Study 1 and Study 2, respectively. The reliabilities for vividness are 0.88 (Study 1) and 0.87 (Study 2) and for paleness are 0.89 and 0.84. The correlation between the two link measures is 0.91 for Study 1 and 0.93 for Study 2. One should note that the reliability indicators are quite similar between the two studies. Thus, the empirical evidence supports the claim that the four indicators of message-evoked imagery dimensions are internally consistent.

ASSESSING THE VALIDITY OF THE INDICATORS

Once dimensionality and reliability were assessed, we turned our attention to validity issues. We examined validity in two ways. The first was to assess whether the proposed measure is sensitive to processing differences and the second was to determine whether the measure differs from trait measures of imagery, specifically one's intrinsic ability to engage in imagery processing.

When assessing whether this measure is sensitive to differences in processing style, we relied heavily on the imagery literature in developing an advertisement which should evoke greater imagery and one which should evoke less imagery processing. Thus, the high-imagery ad used concrete words (Sherman et al. 1983; Paivio 1976), active voice (Alesandrini and Sheikh 1983), instructions to imagine (Carroll 1978; Paivio 1976) and interaction with the product (Alesandrini and Sheikh 1983), while the low-imagery ad did not contain these elements.

To assess whether the measures reflect differences in imagery-evoking strategies, we compared responses on each dimension for a high-imagery ad group and a low imagery ad group from each study. A MANOVA model was used to address

TABLE 3
CORRELATIONS FOR ASSESSING DISCRIMINANT VALIDITY

Study 1

	Pale	Vivid	Quan/Ease	Links
Vivid	-.61			
Quantity/Ease	-.52	.58		
Links	-.34	.43	.43	
Betts'	-.11	.20	.22	.11

Study 2

	Pale	Vivid	Quan/Ease	Links
Vivid	-.59			
Quantity/Ease	-.48	.63		
Links	-.30	.50	.41	
Betts'	-.18	.23	.23	.23

the question at hand. The high vs. low imagery advertisement served as the independent variable and the four summated indicators of imagery processing (quantity/ease, vividness, paleness and links) served as the dependent variables. The Wilks' lambda for Study 1 was significant (lambda= 0.72, F=4.44, p<0.01). Individual ANOVAs indicated that statistically significant differences existed between the two advertisements for the quantity/ease factor (F=17.06, p<0.01) and the vividness factor (F=9.57, p<0.01). The paleness factor was not significant (F=2.68, p=11) while the links factor was only marginally significant (F=3.11; p=0.08). Examination of the means indicated that the high-imagery ad resulted in greater quantity, easier imaging and more vivid images.

Similar results are found for the Study 2. The overall Wilks' lambda was marginally significant (lambda= 0.78, F=2.45, p=.06). Differences were found between the two groups for the quantity/ease factor (F=7.23, p<0.05) and the vividness factor (F=5.42, p<0.05) but not for the paleness factor (F=1.5, p=.23) or the links factor (F=0.12, p=0.74).

This analysis suggests that the quantity/ease factors and the vividness factors are working as expected, but that the paleness and links factors are not. It appears that more research of these factors are needed. It may be that these inconclusive results are an artifact of the specific message content.

ASSESSING DISCRIMINANT VALIDITY

A critical issue in developing this measure is to determine whether the measure is sensitive to a particular communication or is simply measuring a person's innate ability to imagine. It must be shown that the measure of communication-evoked imagery does not duplicate measures of imaging ability, otherwise it provides no additional value beyond what is currently available.

Two methods of addressing the discriminant validity of the proposed message-evoked communication measure were used. First, we examined the correlations between the shortened version of Betts' QMI (Sheehan 1967) and the communication-evoked imagery measures. Second, we examined whether the proposed measure of communication-evoked imagery accounted for differences between high and low imagery ad groups once the effects of an individual's ability to imagine were accounted for.

Correlational Results. One would expect that the ability to imagine and the amount of imagery evoked by a particular communication to be positively correlated, but only slightly so since the degree of imagery evoked by a message is also a function of the individual's familiarity and knowledge with the message content as well as imagining ability. On the other hand, one would expect stronger correlations among the different indicators of communication-evoked imagery processing. Table 3 shows the correlational results for the full datasets of both studies. As can be seen in Table 3, the correlations among the imagery measures were stronger than the measures' correlation with the QMI scale.

With respect to Study 1, we found that the correlations between the Betts' QMI (the measure of innate ability to imagine) ranged from -0.11 to 0.22

with the different indicators of communication-evoked imagery, while the correlations between the four measures were stronger, ranging in absolute terms from 0.34 to 0.61. The same pattern appeared when Study 2 is analyzed. Specifically, correlations between Betts' QMI and the indicators of communication-evoked imagery ranged from -0.18 to 0.23 and the correlations among the communication-evoked imagery measures ranged in absolute terms from 0.30 to 0.63. This analysis supports the contention that the communication-evoked imagery measure is tapping something different than simple ability to imagine.

Experimental Results. The MANOVA model used in the previous section was re-run with the addition of the Betts' QMI as a covariate. For Study 1 (n=51), the Betts' covariate was not significant ($F=.63$, $p=.65$). After the covariate was factored out, the Wilks' lambda remained significant (lambda=0.71, $F=4.66$, $p<0.01$). Significant differences were found between the high and low-imagery groups on the quantity/ease factor ($F=18.07$, $p<0.01$) and the vividness factor ($F=10.00$, $p<0.01$). The paleness factor again was not significant ($F=2.86$, $p=.10$). The links factor, as before, was marginally significant ($F=3.34$, $p=0.07$).

For Study 2 (n=41), the Betts' covariate was significant ($F=2.90$, $p<0.05$). Once this influence was taken into account, the overall MANOVA model was still significant (lambda=0.76, $F=2.75$, $p<0.05$). In addition, the quantity/ease factor still showed differences between the two groups ($F=8.90$, $p<0.01$) as did the vividness factor ($F=6.69$; $p<0.01$). Neither the paleness nor links factor were significant ($F=2.17$, $p=.15$; $F=0.22$, $p=0.64$, respectively). Again, these results are similar to those found when the Betts' covariate was not included.

In sum, it appears that these indicators, especially the quantity/ease and vividness dimensions, are more than a measure of one's ability to engage in imagery processing. While they are positively related to the ability to imagine, they are also sensitive to the content or message elements.

DISCUSSION AND IMPLICATIONS

This article describes the development of a set of reliable indicators of the imagery-evoked by a message such as an advertisement. These measures would provide researchers with items which can be used as indicators of the effects of different strategies designed to induce imagery processing. In addition, they may serve as manipulation checks for experimental research investigating imagery effects on consumption-related outcomes.

The results suggest that the self-report measures are reliable indicators of several different aspects of imagery processing. Factor analysis results indicated stable loadings of the items on four dimensions across the two studies. In addition, there is evidence that these measures have some validity in terms of their sensitivity to different imagery-inducing strategies. Finally, these indicators seem to be related to, but different from, indicators of imagery processing abilities.

Additional work still needs to be done to validate these items. Obviously many of the criticisms of self-report measures are applicable here. For instance, Morris and Hampson (1983) suggest that such measures may suffer from social desirability bias. There are the associated difficulties of tapping unobservable activities through any type of obtrusive verbal measure. These measures rely on the subject's awareness of his/her internal processes to reply. Certain physiological approaches may hold promise as alternative indicators of these internal processes. For example, Cacioppo, Petty and Tassinary (1989) have used surface electromyographic response to examine differences in subjects performing an activity and those simply imagining it for evidence of differences in cognitive and affective activity. While physiological measures may be preferable in some cases and may be useful for validating the indicators proposed here, in general, physiological measurement is often not practical as a regular means of imagery processing assessment. Thus, the self-report measures proposed have definite advantages over physiological measures in imagery research.

Tests of convergent and discriminant validity also should include other measures of imaging ability as well as preferences. Specifically, such tests should include assessing differences in processing preferences using the revised Style of Processing Scale (Childers, Houston and Heckler 1985).

Finally, differences in knowledge and familiarity with the products, scenes, schemas described in a message should be examined to determine their relative effects on the imagery-induced as measured by the indicators described here. In particular, these variables may significantly affect the paleness and links dimensions. For instance, one would expect greater knowledge of a subject to evoke more links with existing information in long term memory. Since the procedures we used did not manipulate or control for knowledge, this could explain why we found no differences on the paleness and links factors.

As with all initial studies, the generalizability of this investigation is unknown. Future research should include different imagery-induction techniques, different subjects and different media. However, the indicators described here can provide researchers with a valuable tool for such assessments.

REFERENCES

Alesandrini, Kathy Lutz and Anees A. Sheikh (1983), "Research on Imagery: Implications for Advertising," in A.A. Sheikh (Ed.) *Imagery: Current Theory, Research and Application*, New York: John Wiley & Sons, 535-56.

Anderson, Craig A. (1983), "Imagination and Expectation: The Effect of Imagining Behavioral Scripts on Personal Intentions," *Journal of Personality and Social Psychology*, 45, 2, 293-305.

Betts, G. H. (1909), *The Distribution and Functions of Mental Imagery*, Teachers College, Columbia University, New York, New York.

Cacioppo, John T., Richard E. Petty and Louis H. Tassinary (1989), "Social Psychophysiology: A New Look," *Advances in Experimental Social Psychology*, 22, 39-91.

Carroll, John (1978), "The Effect of Imagining an Event on Expectations for the Event: An Interpretation in Terms of the Availability Heuristic," *Journal of Experimental Social Psychology*, 14, 88-96.

Cartwright, Desmond S., Mary E. Marks, and John H. Durrett, Jr. (1978), "Definition and Measurement of Three Processes of Imagery Representation: Exploratory Studies of Verbally Stimulated Imagery," *Multivariate Behavioral Research*, 13, (October) 449-473.

Childers, Terry L. and Michael Houston (1982), "Imagery Paradigms for Consumer Research: Alternative Perspectives from Cognitive Psychology," *Advances in Consumer Research*, 10, 59-64.

____ , Michael Houston and Susan Heckler (1985), "Measurement of Individual Differences in Visual vs. Verbal Information Processing," *Journal of Consumer Research*, 12 (September), 125-134.

Kisielius, Jolita and Brian Sternthal (1986), "Examining the Vividness Controversy: An Availability-Valence Interpretation," *Journal of Consumer Research*, 12 (March), 418-31.

Lord, Charles G. (1980), "Schemas and Images as Memory Aids: Two Modes of Processing Social Information," *Journal of Personality and Social Psychology*, 38 (2), 357-69.

Lutz, Kathy and Richard J. Lutz (1977), "Effects of Interactive Imagery on Learning: Application to Advertising," *Journal of Applied Psychology*, 62 (4), 493-98.

MacInnis, Deborah J. (1986), "Constructs and Measures of Individual Differences in Imagery Processing: A Review," *Advances in Consumer Research*, 14, 88-92.

____ and Linda L. Price (1987), "The Role of Imagery in Information Processing: Review and Extensions," *Journal of Consumer Research*, 13 (March), 473-91.

McGill, Ann L. and Punam Anand (1989), "The Effect of Imagery on Information Processing Strategy in a Multiattribute Choice Task," *Marketing Letters*, 1 (1), 7-16.

Marks, David F. (1973), "Visual Imagery Differences in the Recall of Pictures," *British Journal of Psychology*, 64, 17-24.

Morris, Peter E. and Peter J. Hampson (1983), *Imagery and Consciousness*, London: Academic Press.

Paivio, Allan (1968), "A Factor-Analytic Study of Word Attributes and Verbal Learning," *Journal of Verbal Learning and Verbal Behavior*, 7, 41-49.

Paivio, Allan (1976), "Imagery in Recall and Recognition," in John Brown (Ed.) *Recall and Recognition*, London: John Wiley & Sons, 103-129.

Richardson, A. (1969), *Mental Imagery*, New York: Springer 1969.

Sheehan, Peter (1967), "A Shortened Form of Betts' Questionnaire Upon Mental Imagery," *Journal of Clinical Psychology*, 23, 386-389.

Sherman, Steven, Kim S. Zehmer, James Johnson, and Edward R. Hirt (1983), "Social Explanation: The Role of Timing, Set and Recall on Subjective Likelihood Estimates," *Journal of Personality and Social Psychology*, 44, 1127-43.

Smith, Ruth Ann, Michael J. Houston and Terry L. Childers (1983), "Verbal Versus Visual Processing Modes: An Empirical Test of the Cyclical Processing Hypothesis," *Advances in Consumer Research*, 11, 75-80.

Humor In Television Advertising: The Effects of Repetition and Social Setting

Yong Zhang, University of Houston
George M. Zinkhan, University of Houston

ABSTRACT

This study investigates the effect of humor in advertising on three dependent measures of advertising effectiveness: perceived humor, attitude toward the brand, and ad recall. Also examined are the effects of multiple exposures and the effects of social setting (size of the audience). Humor is found to influence consumers' brand attitude and their brand information recall. Perceived humor appears to be affected by social setting, but unaffected by another mediating factor: frequency of exposure.

INTRODUCTION

Humor has been used extensively in consumer product advertising on TV, radio, and in print media. Estimates of its usage range from 15% to over 40% (Kelly and Solomon 1975; Markiewicz 1974). Implicit in such practice is the rooted belief that humor produces desirable effects in persuading consumers to adopt products. Understandably, a considerable amount of effort has been spent on investigating the relationship between humor and a diverse array of response variables.

Among these variables are the humor perceived by the consumer when viewing or hearing the ads, brand attitude, and ad recall. It has been proposed that the effect of humorous ads passes beyond temporary amusement and influences message recall (Gelb and Zinkhan 1986). Eventually, as a result of this process, consumers in the target audience form positive brand attitudes toward the product. These hypothesized humor effects may be mitigated by a variety of other factors such as the number of exposures which the target audience experiences and the social context in which the humorous message is viewed or heard. In this study, perceived humor, recall and brand attitude constitute the three dependent variables of interest. These variables are expected to be related. The two key independent variables are repetition and social setting. The major research question is: to what extent do repetition and social setting influence perceived humor, memory, and attitude?

HUMOR AND REPETITION

Several authors have studied the effect of repetition and humor in advertising. Belch (1982) found that consumers' cognitive responses follow separate patterns depending on the number of repetitions. Positive responses do not decline over repetitions as has been predicted by the two-factor theoretical repetition effect model (Berlyne 1970). According to this model, the effect of repetition is determined by two opposing psychological factors: positive habituation and tedium. As the number of exposures increases, the domination of the first factor declines and that of the second factor increases, causing the deterioration of the ad's persuasive power. Further, Belch and Belch (1984) demonstrated in a later study that unaided recall and intention to use Federal Express, designed as a measure of persuasion, did not reveal any significant effect of humor, number of exposures, and the interactions between the two. These results however are contradicted by another study (Gelb and Zinkhan 1985) which found that humor can be used to improve commercial effectiveness and that perceived humor significantly declines as the number of repetitions increases.

THE INFLUENCE OF SOCIAL SETTING

A second mitigating factor of humor effect is social setting. Humor and the intimately related result it elicits, laughter, have long been considered to be a social phenomenon. They are expected to occur within patterns of social interactions, and are regulated by society in much the same way as other social-physiological reactions such as yawning (Coser 1959). Humor and laughter are often shared, and they are defined as part of the interactive process of social life. In this regard, laughter is often thought to be contagious; but most humor-related consumer behavior studies have ignored this social dimension to humor.

Repetition causes wear-out of humor. The wear-out of humor refers to the phenomenon that humorous ads lose their humor after a number of re-runs. It indeed may cause adverse responses, such as irritation, on the part of the viewer or listener. According to a proposed theory, this wear-out effect can be mitigated by social setting. Zinkhan and Gelb (1990) argue that humor has a social dimension and that if the audience listening to or watching a commercial consists of more than one person, then the social setting dimension increases the likelihood that a message will be perceived as humorous, even after repetition. Their proposition is based on the findings of several studies in this area (see Butcher and Whissell 1984; Aiello et al. 1983; Brown et al. 1982).

HUMOR AND ADVERTISING EFFECTIVENESS

While few researchers argue about the attention-grabbing quality of humorous ads, whether or not humorous ads are a more effective means of persuasion than serious ads remains the focal point of argument. Scott et al. (1990) argue for the view that, to be effective, commercials should: a) contribute to the main point of the message and b) pertain to an advertised product which is appropriate for the use of levity. They showed that such promotional messages can have a positive effect both on enjoyment and behavior (i.e., attendance of social events). Osterhouse and Brock (1970) demonstrated that humor distracts an audience during a persuasive communication. Such distraction leads to decreased levels of counterargumentation and, therefore, to an increase in message reception and persuasion.

Duncan and Nelson (1985) and Madden and Weinberger (1984), among others, concede that humor increases commercial effectiveness by drawing more attention from consumers. But they think it is less appropriate in gaining higher levels of comprehension and persuasion. Their results appear to support the view that despite the fact that humor improves attention, it may inhibit message comprehension and reception. Based on the same argument, it has been suggested that attitude as a measure of persuasion be included in experiments studying humor effects (Sternthal and Craig 1973).

This study intends to further investigate the plausible relationships between humor and measures of advertising effectiveness operationalized here as message recall and brand attitude. The above discussion suggests the following three hypotheses:

H1: Humorous message has a positive effect on message recall, attitude towards the advertised brand, and therefore, the effectiveness of the ad.

H2: Multiple exposures of TV audiences to the same humorous message diminishes the perceived humor of ads, and therefore, advertising effectiveness.

H3: Social setting influences the degree of perceived humor. That is, as the number of people in the audience increases perceived humor increases.

METHOD

An experiment was conducted using 216 student subjects, all of whom were undergraduate business majors in a large urban university. Just under 40% of the subjects were females. The stimulus TV ads were for soft drinks and had been previously aired on network television. As a guise, subjects were told that they would be watching some music videos and would be later asked to indicate their musical preferences.

Three variables were manipulated in the experiment: humor in the ads (Message), number of ad exposures (Repeat), and the size of the audience exposed to the ads (Size). Humor in the ads had two levels: an ad that contained humor and an ad that had no humor. The ads were pretested to ensure the effectiveness of the humor manipulation.

Half of the subjects were exposed to the humorous ad, the remaining subjects were exposed to the non-humorous ad. Both versions of the ad contained similar information about the product, but differed concerning the inclusion of the humor stimulus. The commercials were imbedded in 30 minutes of prerecorded music videos. The stimulus video programs contained three different numbers of exposures of the ads. The numbers of ad exposures varied from one to three to five repetitions. The placement of the ads were approximately at equal intervals at breaks between music excerpts in an effort to minimize potential confounding due to unequal spacing. The size of the audience had three levels: one-person audience, three-person audience, and six-person audience. The experimental surroundings where the subjects received the stimuli for the different conditions were made identical.

Thus, this study had a factorial design with all the factors completely crossed. With this design, it was possible to investigate the main effect of the factors and the interaction effects among them. The study had a balanced design with twelve subjects in each condition. All subjects were assigned to the conditions in a randomized fashion.

After the subjects were exposed to the commercials, they were requested to complete a questionnaire containing the three dependent measures: brand attitude (Attitude), perceived humor (Humor), and ad recall (Recall). Both perceived humor and brand attitude were measured using six-point Likert-type scales anchored by the words "strongly disagree" and "strongly agree". The third scale (Recall) was a composite score which was calculated by summing the number of correct answers to ten questions about information contained in the ad. The minimum possible score was zero while the maximum score was ten on this true-false recall test.

The three dependent variables represent three components in a much investigated theoretical framework, which specifies that high levels of perceived humor lead to better recall, which in turn contributes to the formation of positive attitude towards the advertised brand (Gelb and Zinkhan 1986). This kind of hierarchical model is amenable to a multivariate approach for the analysis of the experimental data since the dependent variables are expected to be related in the sense that they may be regarded as different facets of the overall measure of the "effectiveness" of the ads. Therefore, MANOVA technique was used to assess the humor effect in this analysis.

MANOVA has advantages over ANOVA with a series of individual F-tests in this situation (Hair et al. 1987). The individual F-tests in ANOVA result in an inflated Type One Error which may cause false positive, and render significant tests spurious and irreplicatable (Haase and Ellis 1987). MANOVA provides a single overall test of group differences at a specified alpha level, thus avoiding the multiple F-tests and the resulting Type One Error inflation problem. MANOVA also enables us to test the linear combination of the dependent variables that provides the strongest evidence of overall group differences. Such evidence is not provided by the univariate tests.

RESULTS

The MANOVA results are summarized in Table 1. All the interaction effects are insignificant at 0.05 significance level. This result helps to reduce the uncertainty associated with the interpretation of the main effect results. The first hypothesis

TABLE 1
MANOVA Results of the Main Effects and the Interaction Effects*

Effect	F-Value	Pr <
Message	19.78	0.0001
Repeat	1.63	n.s.
Size	1.29	n.s.
Message * Repeat	1.44	n.s.
Message * Size	1.19	n.s.
Repeat * Size	0.62	n.s.
Message * Repeat * Size	0.65	n.s.

* F-values are based on Wilks' Lambda

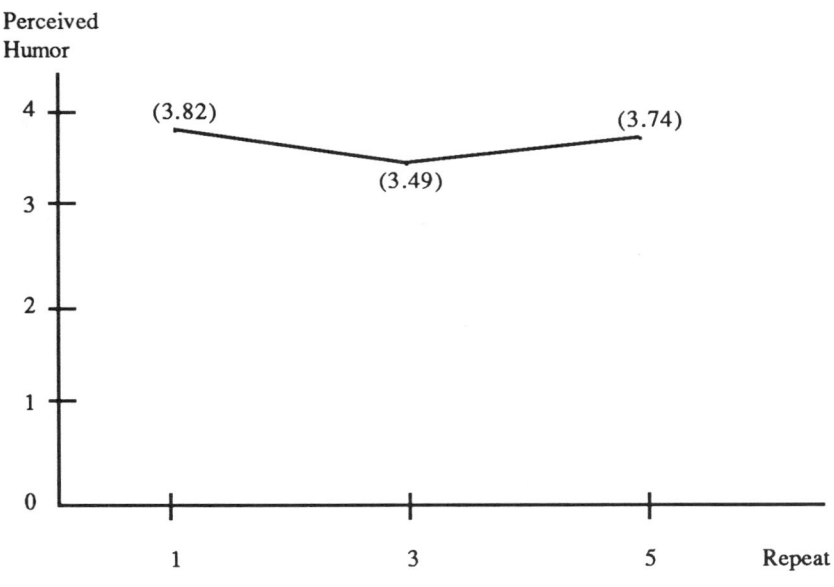

FIGURE 1
Mean Difference on Perceived Humor for Each Level of Repetition

concerns the effect of humor on brand attitude and recall. This hypothesis is supported by the Message main effect results (F = 19.78, p < 0.0001).

The second hypothesis was not supported by the MANOVA main effect results (F = 1.63 for Repeat, n.s.). This finding is echoed by a plot of the mean differences in perceived humor over the treatment. As illustrated in Figure 1, the mean perceived humor scores (3.82, 3.49, 3.74) do not vary much across the repetition levels.

Another MANOVA was performed with respect to the social and repetition factors on subjects' responses to the humorous treatment. The results are presented in Table 2. Audience size had a significant influence on the dependent variables. Univariate follow-up indicated that the source of the variation resulted from the mean differences of perceived humor over the audience size levels (see Figure 2). When the audience consisted of more than one person, mean scores of perceived humor considerably increased. Therefore, the third hypothesis that social setting positively influences perceived humor was supported by the results of this study. As is shown in Table 2, the repetition effect was again not significant.

The significant omnibus MANOVA result on the Message factor (see Table 1) shows that there is an overall group difference caused by the two levels of the Message factor across the three dependent measures. It would be of interest to find out which measures represent the difference. Therefore, three post hoc tests were subsequently carried out using

TABLE 2
Two-Way MANOVA Results on Humorous Ad

Effect	F-Value	Pr <
Repeat	0.50	n.s.
Size	2.32	0.05
Repeat * Size	0.65	n.s.

* F-values are based on Wilks' Lambda

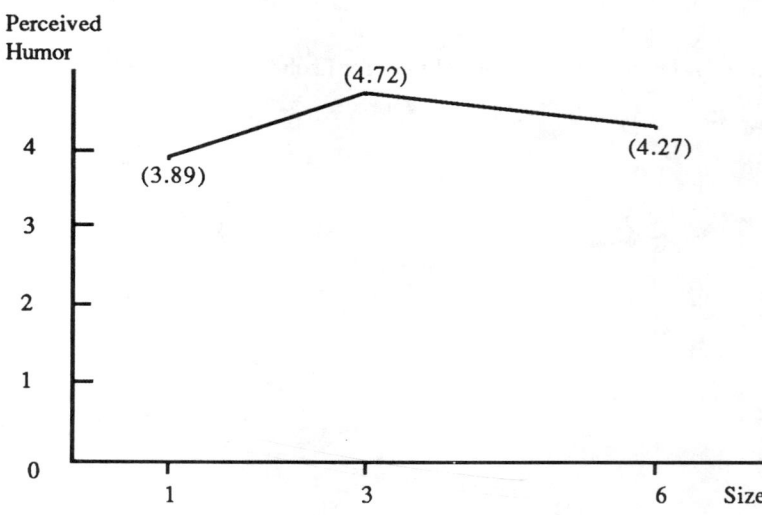

FIGURE 2
Perceived Humor Scores for the Humorous Ad across Each Level of Audience Size

TABLE 3
Post hoc 3-Way Factorial ANOVA Test Results Following a Significant MANOVA on the Factor Message

| | Message Mean Scores | | 3-Way ANOVA | |
Variable	Non-humor Ad	Humor Ad	F-value	Pr <
Attitude	3.62	4.80	3.09	0.0001
Humor	3.06	4.30	3.48	0.0001
Recall	4.06	6.16	2.13	0.01

univariate factorial ANOVA. Attitude, Humor and Recall were used separately as the dependent variable in the ANOVA procedures, and the results are presented in Table 3. Again, significant results are obtained for Attitude and Recall. There are significant mean differences over the levels of Message. Thus, the hypothesis that humorous ads have a positive effect on message recall and brand attitude is fully supported by this study.

The univariate results on the dependent measure Humor is also significant with regard to Message, further confirming the existence of the main effect of the humor manipulation. One interesting finding is that the interaction effect of Message and Repeat on the dependent variable Humor is significant at $p < 0.05$. This suggests that the effect of ad type (Message) is not the same across the levels of repetition (Repeat). Given the fact that the repetition main effect is non-significant over all dependent variables, as is shown by the MANOVA results, one might suspect that this interaction is caused by the strong effect of Message factor. Another speculation is that the omnibus test by MANOVA did not provide enough power to discern the interaction in the multivariate analysis. MANOVA has been shown to be extremely conservative (Hummel and Sligo 1971). Although the MANOVA tests failed to support the hypothesized effect of repetition, this significant interaction points the way for a follow-up study of the effect of ad type across levels of repetition --- one of the enduring themes of research in this area.

DISCUSSION

This study is supportive of a theoretical model which specifies that humorous ads tend to produce higher levels of perceived humor, positive brand attitude, and brand information recall. The results of this study differ from findings by Belch and Belch (1984) who found humor did not affect recall levels. But similar results are obtained regarding the repetition effect on perceived humor and brand attitude. Based on this sample, humorous ads have more persuasive power than serious ads possibly through a third mediating process such as the reduction of counterargumentation. And humor is perceived to be funnier when someone else is present. The findings here also indicate that repetition does not influence perceived humor and the overall effectiveness measure of advertising. This is inconsistent with the theoretical propositions and empirical results of several studies. As is suggested by the significant Message and Repeat interaction in the univariate procedure, the pattern of wear-out of humor as a function of repeated exposure clearly deserves further investigation.

Several cautions should be heeded when interpreting the results of this study. First, the contrived experimental settings may not have fully induced the social effect of humor. For example, a more realistic and interactive audience composed of friends or family members may produce more marked results. This may be an important area for future research, as social effects on humor may vary depending upon the composition of the audience watching or hearing the advertising message. When all of the members of an audience are friends, or family members, messages may be perceived as more humorous than in instances where a group of relative strangers are exposed to the same message.

Second, the strong Message effect which we observed might be dampened if a less homogeneous sample were tested. Education level of the subjects is a factor which may influence perceived humor, and it has been shown that more highly educated people are more sensitive to humor (Brooker 1981).

Third, repetition typically refers to the frequency of viewing a message over a period of time (weeks, months). Here, we completed all repetitions within a 30 minute period. It is also quite common for audience members to be exposed to the same commercial several times during a short period of time (e.g. one hour viewing session) in the natural environment. However, some of the theoretical work on repetition has specified that effects over time (e.g., forgetting) may play an important role in determining commercial effectiveness particularly over a longer period of time. Repetition effect of humor over longer periods of time should also be studied.

Beyond these three caveats, there may be other reasons for concerns. For example, there may be other (unmeasured) variables which could play important moderating roles. Involvement may be one such variable. Under conditions of high involvement, the presence of humor may lead to reduced comprehension; and this effect may be reversed under low involvement conditions. Alternatively, there may be important, non-linear effects over both social and repetition conditions which should be investigated in later studies.

CONCLUSION

Given these cautions, this study offers another piece of empirical evidence in the quest for a better understanding of humor in advertising. The results suggest that humor increases ad information recall and positively affects brand attitude. This process may be positively moderated by social setting. Due to its potential usefulness, humor and its role in commercial advertising will continue to interest researchers and practitioners alike. The social aspect of humor appreciation deserves further investigation. Those conducting future research may wish to focus on alternative social factors, beyond size of the audience. Despite the fact that social effects have been widely studied concerning other aspects of buyer behavior (e.g., attitude formation), it is only rarely that we have considered laughter and humor to be inextricably linked to patterns of social exchange. Without a social context, there is little grounds for judging a potentially humorous message as funny or not.

REFERENCES

Aiello, John R., Donna E. Thompson, and D. M. Brodzinsky (1983), "How Funny is Crowding Anyway? Effects of Room Size, Group Size, and the Introduction of Humor," *Basic and Applied Social Psychology*, 4 (No. 2), 193-207.

Appel, Valentine (1971), "On Advertising Wear Out," *Journal of Advertising Research*, 11, 11-13.

Belch, E. (1982), "The Effects of Television Commercial Repetition on Cognitive Response and Message Acceptance," *Journal of Consumer Research*, 9 (June), 56-65.

Belch, George E. and M. A. Belch (1984), "An Investigation of the Effects of Repetition on Cognitive and Affective Reactions to Humorous and Serious TV Commercials," *Advances in Consumer Research*, 11, 4-10.

Berlyne, D. E. (1970), "Novelty, Complexity, and Hedonic Value," *Perception and Psychophysics*, 8, 279-286.

Brooker, George (1981), "A Comparison of the Persuasive Effects of Mild Humor and Mild Fear Appeals," *Journal of Advertising*, 10, 29-40.

Brown, Gary E., Paul A. Dixon, and D. Hudson (1982), "Effect of Peer Pressure on Imitation of Humor Response in College Students," *Psychological Reports*, 51, 1111-1117.

Butcher, Jennifer and Cynthia Whissell (1984), "Laughter as a Function of Audience Size, Sex of the Audience and Segments of the Short Film 'Duck Soup'," *Perceptual and Motor Skills*, 59, 949-950.

Calder, Bobby J. and Brian Sternthal (1980), "Television Commercial Wearout: An Information Processing View," *Journal of Marketing Research*, 17 (May), 173-186.

Chattopadhyay, Amitava and Junal Basu (1989), "Prior Brand Evaluation as a Moderator of the Effects of Humor in Advertising," Paper under reviewing.

Coser, Rose L. (1959), "Some Social Functions of Laughter," *Human Relations*, 12, 171-182.

Craig, C. Samuel, B. Sternthal and C. Leavitt (1976), "Advertising Wearout: An Experimental Analysis," *Journal of Marketing Research*, 13 (November), 365-372.

Duncan, Calvin P., and Janes E. Nelson (1985), "Effects of Humor in a Radio Advertising Experiment," *Journal of Advertising*, 14, 33-40, 64.

Gelb, Betsy D. and George M. Zinkhan (1986), "Humor and Advertising Effectiveness After Repeated Exposures to a Radio Commercial," *Journal of Advertising*, 15 (No. 2), 15-20, 34.

Hair, Jr., J. F., Rolph E. Anderson and Ronald L. Tatham (1987). *Multivariate Data Analysis*, 2nd ed., Macmillan Publishing Company, New York.

Haase, Richard F. and Michael V. Ellis (1987), "Multivariate Analysis of Variance," *Journal of Counseling Psychology*, 34 (No. 4), 404-413.

Hummel, Thomas and Joseph Sligo (1971), 'Empirical Comparison of Univariate and Multivariate Analysis of Variance Procedures," *Psychological Bulletin*, 76 (No. 1), 49-57.

Kelly, J. P. and P. J. Solomon (1975), "Humor in Television Advertising," *Journal of Advertising*, 4, 33-35.

Madden, Thomas J. and Marc G. Weinberger, (1984), 'Humor in Adverting: A Practitioner View," *Journal of Advertising Research*, 24, 23-29.

Osterhouse, Robert and Timothy Brock (1970), "Distraction Increases Yielding to Propaganda by Inhibiting Counterarguing," *Journal of Personality and Social Psychology*, 15 (August), 344-358.

Scott, Cliff, David M. Klein, and Jennings Bryant (1990), "Consumer Response to Humor in Advertising: A Series of Field Studies Using Behavioral Observation," *Journal of Consumer Research*, 16, 498-501.

Sternthal, Brian and Sanmuel Craig (1973), "Humor in Advertising," *Journal of Marketing*, 37, 12-13.

Zinkhan, George M. and Betsy D. Gelb (1985), "The Effect of Repetition on Humor in a Radio Advertising Study," *Journal of Advertising*, 14, 13-20, 68.

Zinkhan, George M. and Betsy D. Gelb (1990), "Humor, Repetition, and Advertising Effectiveness," *Advances in Consumers Research* Vol. 17, 438-441.

Cue Modality: Video and Audio Effects on Recall

Carolyn L. Costley, Texas A & M University
Duane DeWald, Texas A & M University

ABSTRACT

We present theoretical justification for a cue modality hypothesis. The hypothesis asserts that the sensory mode of retrieval cues triggers recall for same-modality information. Results from an experiment using video and audio presentations suggest that cue modality does influence recall for video material but not for audio. Pictures, furthermore, were recalled better than words regardless of cue. We suggest implications for marketing communications and recommend that future studies address other modalities and other attention conditions.

Most communicators want their audiences to remember the material they presented. What one remembers from a communication, however, may be context-dependent. We argue that the modality[1] of a cue is one context factor that influences retrieval processes and potentially affects what one remembers. In other words, pictures trigger memory for pictures, sounds trigger memory for sounds, etc. We review research that led to this cue modality hypothesis, present test results, and discuss communication implications.

Modality effects can be particularly important to advertisers who regularly communicate via multiple modalities (primarily audio and visual, but also tactile and olfactory (scratch-and-sniff)). Advertisers desire that their audiences remember information such as brand name and product attributes, especially at decision times such as point-of-purchase or exposure to a competitor's ad (a preliminary decision).

Understanding memory-related factors can be important for designing and for evaluating marketing communications. It is essential to study and understand things that affect consumers' memories because what they remember can be critical to their decisions. While advertisements provide much information about different brands, rarely do consumers remember everything when they choose a brand. Marketing scholars have posited an influential role for memory in consumer decision processes and have called for more research on this aspect of consumer decision making (Bettman, 1986; Lynch & Srull, 1982).

We propose that the sensory mode of communication devices such as advertisements can influence consumers' memory for them. The modality of an initial stimulus (such as an ad) and the modality of a subsequent cue (such as another ad) may interactively affect memory accessibility. The reported research investigated visual and audio modes inherent in video communications. The following sections describe retrieval cue effects, perceptual processing modes and the cue modality hypothesis.

RETRIEVAL CUE EFFECTS

Encoding and retrieval are mental processes important to any discussion of memory accessibility. Information, from an ad for instance, goes into memory via encoding and is remembered via retrieval. Between encoding and retrieving, information is stored in memory. Storage form and structure and the encoding and retrieval processes interact to affect what people remember. Either encoding or retrieval processes can affect information accessibility in the memory store. A great deal of empirical evidence supports the notion that retrieval is cue-dependent. This section reviews the principle literature on retrieval cue effects.

Tulving and Pearlstone (1966) distinguished between "available" memory information and "accessible" memory information. All events and information that have ever been encoded are available for recall in the memory store (Lachman, Lachman, & Butterfield, 1979). When it is hard for a person to find (access) certain information, forgetting results. Accessibility depends both on availability and on retrieval cues. Retrieval cues can affect the *amount* of information recalled by affecting information accessibility. That is, cued recall often is better than uncued recall (Tulving & Pearlstone, 1966; Tulving & Psotka, 1971).

Retrieval cues not only facilitate the level of recall but also can affect recall *content*. This may occur in either of two ways. Retrieval cues may bias recall content by facilitating access to information associated with the cue (Anderson & Pichert, 1978). Alternatively, retrieval cues may bias recall content by inhibiting access to other items (Rundus, 1973). The second is known as the part-list cuing effect (Slamecka, 1968, 1969).

Encoding Specificity Hypothesis

The encoding specificity hypothesis asserts that retrieval probability depends on the compatibility between stored information and information in the retrieval environment (i.e., cues) (Tulving, 1983). The hypothesis is based on the notion that a memory trace and the retrieval environment interact to influence retrieval (Tulving & Thomson, 1973). Hard-to-recall information often becomes accessible in the appropriate retrieval environment (Tulving & Pearlstone, 1966). Furthermore, according to the hypothesis, associations between the retrieval environment and the encoding environment facilitate retrieval *only* if information was encoded with respect to that association.

Godden and Baddeley (1975) examined the interaction between encoding and retrieval environments, extending investigations to the

---

[1] Modality refers to any sensory mode: visual, audio, olfactory, tactile, or taste.

surrounding context. They studied under sea and dry land environments. Recall was better when the encoding and retrieval environments were the same. This research is particularly interesting because it suggests that people encode the contextual environment and that a similar retrieval environment affects recall.

Little is known about the perceptual system's role in information storage and retrieval (Tulving, 1972). There is evidence that modality information is encoded (Lehman, 1982) suggesting that modality context or modality specific processes in the encoding and retrieval environments may affect recall. The next section focuses on modality issues.

PERCEPTUAL PROCESSING MODES

There is evidence that people use unique mental processing modes for encoding and retrieving different sensory types of information (Brooks, 1968; Segal & Fusella, 1970; Glenberg, 1984). That is, visual, audio, tactile, taste, and olfactory information may be processed through different mental systems.

Brooks (1968) observed that people took longer to complete multiple process tasks that involved the same modality than they did mixed modality tasks. Brooks speculated that this indicated competition for modality specific processing capacity. Such competition supports the existence of modality specific information processing systems.

Segal and Fusella (1970) also found support for distinct processing modes corresponding to perceptual processes. Subjects first participated in a signal detection task. They indicated whether the signal was a sound, a picture, or nothing. Then subjects imagined either a visual image (e.g., a volcano) or an auditory image (e.g., the sound of a typewriter). A signal (a sound, a picture, or nothing) was presented while they were imaging. Detection of the signal was poorer when the image and the signal were in the same sensory mode than when they differed. The results indicate that imagery and perception are similar processes and that distinct processing modes may correspond to perceptual processes.

Greater competition for processing capacity between same-modality stimuli than between different-modality stimuli (demonstrated by the above two studies) suggests that unique processing systems exist and correspond to perceptual systems. Applying the encoding specificity hypothesis to this phenomenon we speculate that the processing systems employed in the encoding and retrieval contexts will interact to affect recall. That is, information encoded by one system may be retrieved better by the same system than by another.

Encoding

Modality of encoded information can also influence its accessibility. Paivio (1979) augmented the multiple processing systems idea when he proposed similar multiple storage codes[2]. He specifically dealt with a visual code and a linguistic code. His theory suggests that the form of a stimulus (e.g., pictorial or verbal) triggers a processing system which stores information in a corresponding unique code. Paivio's dual-code theory maintains that the storage code for picture stimuli is relatively more accessible than the storage code for verbal stimuli. The empirical evidence that people remember pictures better than words (Edell & Staelin, 1983; Childers & Houston, 1984 are examples in marketing literature) is commonly referred to as a picture superiority effect.

Other researchers insist that a single storage code can accommodate the data explained by dual codes (Anderson, 1976, 1978). If memory networks use a single code, then modality information may reside in an associated node. A single code system is consistent with our cue modality hypothesis provided that people encode modality information.

Research results attest that information about presentation modality is processed, stored, and available in memory (Lehman, 1982; Lehman & Mellinger, 1984; Lehman, Mikesell, & Doherty, 1985; Murdock & Walker, 1969; Nilsson, 1973). Lehman and her colleagues provide evidence that modality processing is automatic according to specified criteria (Hasher & Zacks, 1979). Other research indicates that modality information may be useful during retrieval (Murdock & Walker, 1969; Nilsson, 1973).

Hasher and Zacks (1979) contend that automatically encoded information's cognitive function is to guide retrieval. If so then information modality may guide retrieval. Modality, however, may be a useful guide only under special circumstances. Nilsson (1973) found that people can organize recall by modality when instructed to do so and that they will spontaneously organize recall by modality when no other organizational basis exists.

CUE MODALITY HYPOTHESIS

The encoding specificity hypothesis and the existence of multiple processing modes, taken together, suggest a processing modality effect on recall. If context includes the operative processing mode, then recall should be better when the retrieval mode is the same as the encoding mode than when they differ.

The cue modality hypothesis posits that the perceptual mode of new information triggers a corresponding processing system and that information originally encoded through that same system will be more accessible than information encoded via another mode. It asserts, for example, that a visual retrieval cue stimulates the visual processing system, instigating quicker access to visually processed material (picture memories) than to audio material. In this case, an individual would

---

[2]Code refers to the symbolic representation of a sensory modality.

more likely recall a picture stimulus than an auditory stimulus, or would recall it faster.

AN EXPERIMENT

We tested the cue-modality hypothesis using visual and audio stimuli presented on video tape. We hypothesized that people would more likely remember pictured items when presented with picture cues than when presented with spoken cues. Similarly, we hypothesized that people would more likely remember spoken items when presented with spoken cues than when presented with picture cues. We also tested for picture superiority, hypothesizing that pictorial information would be recalled better regardless of cue modality.

Pretests were necessary to determine category membership for the target-cue pairs, picture recognizability and naming, and encoding task. Category membership was pretested because items from the same category as target items were thought to be appropriate cues via associated links in memory (Glass and Holyoak 1986). We selected 25 categories from Battig and Montague (1969) and generated more following their procedures[3].

Of the two items selected from each category, the *most* representative was assigned to the cue list. We did not want a high ranking target item to be recalled because it was strongly associated with the category instead of remembered from the target list. Furthermore, higher ranking items should stimulate the category node in memory and be more likely to cue other category members.

Having selected target and cue category representatives, we collected the items and videotaped them individually against the same background. Thirty-six people viewed the tape and named the items. We used the items that consistently received the same name and we used that name for the spoken stimuli.

Finally, we pretested incidental and intentional encoding task conditions. We opted for the intentional condition ("try to remember each item") because recall exhibited neither a lower bound (i.e., recall was significantly different from zero) nor an upper bound.

FIGURE A
Experimental Design

Target	Cue video	Cue audio
video	1	2
audio	3	4

---

[3]The final list of categories and items is available from the authors.

Experimental Design

Target (2) and cue (2) modalities created the within-subject conditions. Using videotaped lists of familiar items (e.g., farm animals, furniture, fruit), we presented two codes (video and audio) of memory information and two codes of cue information. Each subject received all four modality conditions (see Figure A for the within-subject design). List *content* was counter-balanced across experimental conditions making four *between*-subject conditions. The cow/horse pair, for example, was picture-picture, picture-word, word-picture, and word-word for *different* subjects. Each subject was exposed to "cow" and "horse" only once.

Randomly ordered target lists contained 34 items while each cue list contained 28 items[4], half pictures and half words, 7 items in each treatment condition. The first and last items were not treatment items. They were used to absorb primacy and recency effects and to illustrate category membership in the recall instructions. Video items remained on the screen for about 5 seconds, audio items for as long as it took to speak the word. Five seconds between each item resulted in an even-paced presentation.

Recall was the dependent variable. If recall for the video-video pairs and for the audio-audio pairs exceeded recall for the mixed target-cue pairs (video-audio pairs and audio-video pairs) the cue modality hypothesis would be supported. We expected some interaction between cue modality effects on recall and picture superiority effects on recall. Referring to the cells in Figure A, we expected recall performance to be ordered: 1 - 2 - 4 (or 4 - 2) - 3. Video recall given a video cue was expected to be better than recall in any of the other conditions. Audio recall given a video cue was expected to be worse than recall in any of the other conditions.

One hundred and one students used the 5-second intervals to "learn and remember" each item in the target list. About an hour later the students viewed the cue items. They wrote down the name of the item from the first tape that was most similar to each item on the second tape. There were about 5 seconds in which to respond between items.

Analysis and Results

Multivariate, repeated measures analysis of variance was performed on the data. The multivariate procedure is recommended by LaTour and Miniard (1983) because it produces accurate estimates of Type I error (the probability of rejecting a true null hypothesis). The dependent variables in the model were recall totals (ranging from 0-7) for each of the within subject treatments.

---

[4]Only 28 categories met all of our pretest criteria. Desiring to compare recall to the similar Costley and Brucks study (1990), we included 34 items in the target list so that recall would be from the same sized set as in their study.

TABLE 1
Recall Means in Each Within Subject Treatment Condition

Target Modality	Cue Modality	
	video	audio
video	3.20	2.41
audio	1.61	1.80

Respondents recalled between 0 and 6 of the 7 possible items in each of the video target conditions and between 0 and 5 items in each of the audio target conditions. Table 1 displays mean recall scores for each treatment condition.

Not only are the recall means in the predicted order, but both the cue modality and the picture superiority effects are significant. Figure B graphically depicts the results. The multivariate test criteria (Wilks' criterion, Pillai's trace, Hotelling-Lawley trace, and Roy's maximum root criterion) indicated that modality match between target and cue significantly affected recall ($F_{(1,97)} = 16.08$, $p = .0001$). The slope of the lines in the graph represent the cue modality effect. We observed a picture superiority effect ($F_{(1,97)} = 102.43$, $p = .0001$) clearly indicated by the distance between the lines in the figure. Video representations in the target list were recalled better than audio regardless of the cue.

The interaction (target modality x modality *match*), however, is also significant ($F_{(1,97)} = 5.32$, $p = .0232$). One can see in the graph that the cue modality effect is "steeper" for video material than for audio material (indicated by the slope of the lines). Indeed audio-audio recall was not significantly different from audio-video recall ($p = .2089$).

DISCUSSION

Since we observed a "cue modality effect" in one modality but not in the other, we can not claim support for the processing modality theory. Figure C may help us speculate about explanations. Recallability of a target item is a function of its accessibility via memory links. Regardless of its modality, the cue item provides the link to the category label (B). Links A and B were pretested and held constant. Differences in recallability, therefore, are functions of link C. We hypothesized that link C would be strengthened when the target item was pictured (picture superiority) and when the target and the cue were of the same modality. Support required that *both* modalities exhibit modality-match enhanced recall.

What we observed was a synergy between pictorial stimuli, i.e., enhanced recallability when the target item was pictured and further enhancement when the cue was also pictured. One explanation is that category membership (links A and B) provides a sufficient organizational basis for recall and that pictorial cues carry the same kind of recall-enhancing traits as do pictorial targets (picture superiority of retrieval *and* encoding). The characteristic (saliency, amount of information) that causes the effect is unclear.

It is interesting to compare these results to a nearly identical study that used print stimuli (Costley and Brucks 1990). The earlier study did not find a statistically significant cue modality effect. Mean recall in each treatment condition was almost the same between studies. The only difference is that recall was *better* in our video-video condition than in the former study's picture-picture condition. This suggests that some quality of video presentation (e.g., spatial information or color) enhances recall compared to line drawings. It further suggests that audio presentations do not provide a similar benefit over printed words.

If our results are due to picture saliency (retrieval cue picture superiority) then we should have observed enhanced recall for words given a video cue. We did not. If, however, *both* retrieval cue picture superiority and our hypothesized target-cue modality match acted to enhance recall then we would get results similar to those observed. While an audio cue may have enhanced audio recall, if a video cue also enhanced audio recall, then there might be no statistically significant difference between audio recall conditions. One must use a third modality cue and a no cue control group in order to test this.

Alternative explanations are that video provides better category information than audio (link B) or that video processing is holistic and faster than audio processing. The audio cue may have indeed triggered associated processing modes but video processing may be faster than audio processing. Our recall time constraint may have capped any audio-audio enhancement over audio-video recall. It may be worth replicating this study with longer exposures.

Finally, this study was conducted under high involvement conditions. Respondents' attention to the stimuli was high because they were specifically asked to try to learn and remember the list items. Cue modality may influence recall even more when

FIGURE B
Recall Results as a Function of Target and Cue Modalities

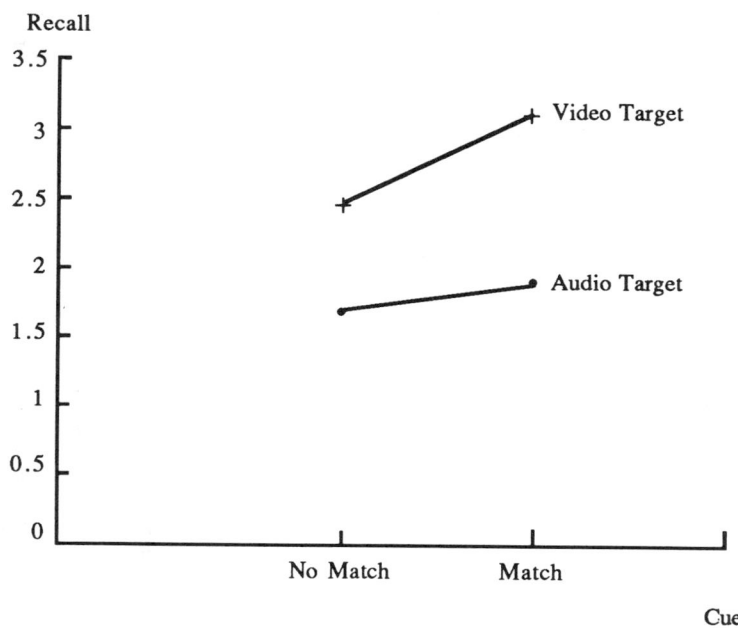

FIGURE C
Conceptual Model

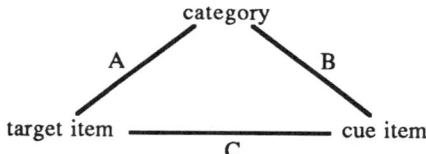

there are fewer other influences. Lower involvement conditions that are typically associated with television viewing may be riper for cue modality influence and remain untested.

Implications

Current results are not directly generalizable to consumer behavior applications. However, these results build theoretical support for an ongoing stream of research that has implications for planning and evaluating marketing communications. Our cue modality effects suggest developing promotional campaigns as cohesive packages. Greater effectiveness may be achieved when both the original processing and cuing modalities are considered. For example, when point-of-purchase displays are used to cue prior television ads (similar to Keller 1987), pictures should elicit better video recall than plain text or audio.

Cue modality may also be relevant for evaluating ad effectiveness and misleading potential. If retrieval cue modality indeed biases recall, then cue modality must be considered in the evaluation and control functions. An ad may be memorable in some contexts but not in others. Similarly, failure to recall key points may ultimately be misleading.

SUMMARY

In this article, we presented theoretical justification for a cue modality hypothesis. A preliminary study did not confirm it, but lends it merit and we recommend additional research. The hypothesis asserts that the sensory mode of retrieval cues triggers recall for same-modality information.

If true, then sounds in the retrieval environment (i.e., audio cues) will trigger recall for audio ads more so than for pictorial ads and vice versa. We observed that video cues enhanced recall for video targets compared to audio cues. We failed to observe a similar modality match effect for audio targets. The findings provide the theoretical foundation for continued research on marketing stimuli and consumer behavior.

REFERENCES

Anderson, John R. (1976), *Language, Memory, and Thought*, Hillsdale, NJ: Erlbaum.

Anderson, John R. (1978), "Arguments Concerning Representations for Mental Imagery," *Psychological Review*, 85, 249-277.

Anderson, Richard C. and James W. Pichert (1978), "Recall of Previously Unrecallable Information Following a Shift in Perspective," *Journal of Verbal Learning and Verbal Behavior*, 17, 1-12.

Battig, William F. and William E. Montague (1969), "Category Norms for Verbal Items in 56 Categories: A Replication and Extension of the Connecticut Category Norms," *Journal of Experimental Psychology Monograph*, 80 (3), Part 2, 1-46.

Bettman, James R. (1986), "Consumer Psychology," *Annual Review of Psychology*, 37, 257-289.

Brooks, Lee R. (1968), "Spatial and Verbal Components of the Act of Recall," *Canadian Journal of Psychology*, 22, 349-368.

Childers, Terry L. and Michael J. Houston (1984), "Conditions for a Picture-Superiority Effect on Consumer Memory," *Journal of Consumer Research*, 11 (September), 643-654.

Childers, Terry L., Michael J. Houston, and Susan E. Heckler (1985), "Measurement of Individual Differences in Visual Versus Verbal Information Processing," *Journal of Consumer Research*, 12 (September), 125-134.

Costley, Carolyn L. and Merrie Brucks (1990), "Perceptual Processing Modes and Advertising Effectiveness," working paper, Marketing Department, Texas A&M University, College Station, TX 77843-4112.

Edell, Julie A. and Richard Staelin (1983), "The Information Processing of Pictures in Print Advertisements," *Journal of Consumer Research*, 10, 45-61.

Glenberg, Arthur M. (1984), "A Retrieval Account of the Long-Term Modality Effect," *Journal of Experimental Psychology: Learning, Memory and Cognition*, 10 (1), 16-31.

Godden, D.R. and A.D. Baddeley (1975), "Context-Dependent Memory in Two Natural Environments: On Land and Underwater," *British Journal of Psychology*, 66, 325-332.

Hasher, Lynn and Rose T. Zacks (1979), "Automatic and Effortful Processes in Memory," *Journal of Experimental Psychology: General*, 108 (3), 356-388.

Houston, Michael J., Terry L. Childers, and Susan E. Heckler (1987), "Picture-Word Consistency and the Elaborative Processing of Advertisements," *Journal of Marketing Research*, 24, 359-369.

Keller, Kevin Lane (1987), "Memory Factors in Advertising: The Effect of Advertising Retrieval Cues on Brand Evaluations," *Journal of Consumer Research*, 14 (December), 316-333.

Lachman, Roy, Janet L. Lachman, and Earl C. Butterfield (1979), *Cognitive Psychology and Information Processing*, Hillsdale, NJ: Erlbaum.

LaTour, Stephen A. and Paul W. Miniard (1983), "The Misuse of Repeated Measures Analysis in Marketing Research," *Journal of Marketing Research*, 20 (February), 45-57.

Lehman, Elyse Brauch (1982), "Memory for Modality: Evidence for an Automatic Process," *Memory & Cognition*, 10, 554-564.

Lehman, Elyse Brauch and Jeanne C. Mellinger (1984), "Effects of Aging on Memory for Presentation Modality," *Developmental Psychology*, 20 (6), 1210-1217.

Lehman, Elyse Brauch, James W. Mikesell, and Suzanne C. Doherty (1985), "Long-Term Retention of Information about Presentation Modality by Children and Adults," *Memory & Cognition*, 13, 21-28.

Lynch, John G. and Thomas K. Srull (1982), "Memory and Attentional Factors in Consumer Choice: Concepts and Research Methods," *Journal of Consumer Research*, 9, 13-37.

Murdock, Bennet B. and Keith D. Walker (1969), "Modality Effects in Free Recall," *Journal of Verbal Learning and Verbal Behavior*, 8, 665-676.

Nilsson, Lars-Goran (1973), "Organization by Modality in Short-Term Memory," *Journal of Experimental Psychology*, 100, 246-253.

Paivio, Allan (1979), *Imagery and Verbal Processes*, Hillsdale, NJ: Erlbaum.

Rundus, Dewey (1973), "Negative Effects of Using List Items as Recall Cues," *Journal of Verbal Learning and Verbal Behavior*, 12, 43-50.

Segal, Sydney Joelson and Vincent Fusella (1970), "Influence of Imaged Pictures and Sounds on Detection of Visual and Auditory Signals," *Journal of Experimental Psychology*, 83, 458-464.

Slamecka, Norman J. (1968), "An Examination of Trace Storage in Free Recall," *Journal of Experimental Psychology*, 76, 504-513.

Slamecka, Norman J. (1969), "Testing for Associative Storage in Multitrial Free Recall," *Journal of Experimental Psychology*, 81, 557-560.

Tulving, Endel (1972), "Episodic and Semantic Memory" in Endel Tulving and Wayne Donaldson (eds.) *Organization of Memory*, New York: Academic Press, 4-48.

Tulving, Endel (1983), *Elements of Episodic Memory*, New York: Oxford University Press.

Tulving, Endel and Zena Pearlstone (1966), "Availability Versus Accessibility of Information in Memory for Words," *Journal of Verbal Learning and Verbal Behavior*, 5, 381-391.

Tulving, Endel and Joseph Psotka (1971), "Retroactive Inhibition in Free Recall: Inaccessibility of Information Available in the Memory Store," *Journal of Experimental Psychology*, 87 (1), 108.

Tulving, Endel and Donald M. Thomson (1973), "Encoding Specificity and Retrieval Processes in Episodic Memory," *Psychological Review*, 80, 352-373.

AUTHOR INDEX

Aaker, Jennifer 462
Adelman, Mara B. 532
Allen, Chris T. 392
Alpert, Judy I. 232
Alpert, Mark I. 232
Alwitt, Linda F. 550
Anderson, Helen H. 342
Anderson, Laurel 129
Andrews, J. Craig 194
Anglin, Kenneth A. 434
Anglin, Linda K. 296
Arnthorsson, Arni 217
Artz, Nancy 618
Assar, Amardeep 657
Attaway, Jill S. 334
Babin, Barry J. 334
Baer, Robert 310
Bagozzi, Richard P. 24
Bahn, Kenneth D. 586
Baumgartner, Hans 24
Belk, Russell W. 521
Berger, Ida E. 688
Bernard, Aaron 532
Berry, Wendall E. 217
Bitner, Mary Jo 611
Bloch, Peter H. 445
Blodgett, Jeff 773
Bloom, Paul N. 255
Bobinski, George S., Jr. 657
Beller, Gregory W. 172
Belton, Ruth N. 558
Bone, Paula Fitzgerald 806
Brennan, Ian 586
Broach, V. Carter 94
Brucks, Merrie 591
Bryce, Wendy 693
Buckley, Patrick G. 491
Burnkrant, Robert E. 28
Burton, Scot 501
Carmon, Ziv 703
Celuch, Kevin G. 284
Chatterjee, Subimal 768
Cherian, Joseph 77
Cole, Catherine A. 515
Colombo, R. 576
Coon, Gregory S. 521
Cooper-Martin, Elizabeth 372
Costley, Carolyn L. 819
Court, Kym 84
Crowley, Ayn E. 780
Curren, Mary T. 624
Darley, William K. 303
DeWald, Duane 819
Dickson, Peter R. 788
Dinkel, M. 528
Doherty, Peter A. 453
Dröge, Cornelia 210
Dubé, Laurette 52
Durvasula, Srinivas 194
Ekstrom, Karin 666
Ellen, Pam Scholder 806
Englis, Basil G. 111

Faber, Ronald J. 755
Fazio, Russell H. 30
Feick, Lawrence F. 187
Feinberg, Richard A. 426, 441
Fennell, Geraldine 262, 271
Finn, David W. 483
Firat, A. Fuat 70
Fischer, Eileen 597
Flynn, J. H. "Mike" 280
Fournier, Susan 736
Freitas, T. 528
Gainer, Brenda 597
Gardner, Meryl P. 94, 249
Gentry, James W. 135, 434, 666
Goodstein, Ronald C. 624
Gopal, Yasmin 143
Gould, Stephen J. 381, 743
Green, Paul E. 476
Greenleaf, Eric 470
Griffin, Mitch 334
Grønhaug, Kjell 566
Halstead, Diane 210
Harrigan, Judy A. 11
Havlena, William J. 323
Heath, Timothy B. 768
Heide, Morten 566
Herr, Paul M. 30, 90
Heslop, Louise A. 681
Hess, Mike 540
Higie, Robin A. 187
Hill, Donna 773
Hill, Ronald Paul 715
Hirschman, Elizabeth C. 1
Hitchon, Jacqueline 752
Holak, Susan L. 323
Holbrook, Morris B. 330
Holt, Douglas B. 57
Hong, Jae W. 348
Hui, Michael 150
Hunt, H. Keith 7
Hutton, R. Bruce 697
Hyatt, Carole 18
Innis, Daniel E. 317
Jackson, Anita 603
Jayanti, Rama 603
Joag, Shreekant G. 666
Joy, Annamma 150
Kalapurakal, Rosemary 788
Kamins, Michael A. 176
Kardes, Frank R. 90, 392
Kassarjian, Harold H. 5
Kellaris, James J. 243
Kent, Robert J. 243
Kim, Chankon 150
Kim, John 90
Kirmani, Amna 414
Kivel, S. 528
Ko, Gary 135
Kolbe, Richard H. 651
Kosenko, Rustan 310
Krugman, Dean M. 143
Kulikowski, Judith E.P. 453

Lamb, Jr., Charles W.	483
Langmeyer, Lynn	364
Langrehr, Frederick W.	428
Laroche, Michel	150
Lascu, Dana-Nicoleta	290
Leckliter, L.	528
Lehmann, Donald	470
Lepisto, Lawrence R.	296
Lichtenstein, Donald R.	501
Lim, Jeen-Su	303
Lofman, Brian	729
Loken, Barbara	84
Lowrey, Tina M.	644
Malhotra, Naresh K.	583
Manrai, Lalita A.	249
Markley, Frank	697
Marks, Lawrence J.	720
Marshall, Judith	681
Martin, Ingrid	225
Mayer, Robert N.	706
Mayo, Michael A.	720
McAlexander, James H.	43
Melnick, E. L.	576
Melnick, K. R.	576
Meoli, Jennifer	426, 441
Midgley, David F.	635
Milne, George R.	255
Mita, Charise	23
Mohr, Lois A.	611
Morrison, Pamela D.	635
Moschis, George P.	517
Murry, John P., Jr.	120
Muthukrishnan, A. V.	407
Nelson, James E.	445
Netemeyer, Richard G.	501
O'Guinn, Thomas C.	755
Olney, T.J.	693
Olson, Jerry C.	172
Owen, Robert S.	552
Page, Thomas J., Jr.	28
Park, Jong-Hee	651
Pavelchak, Mark A.	94
Peracchio, Laura A.	23
Percy, Larry	100
Petrosky, A. Richard	627
Phelps, Joseph	202
Piron, Francis	509
Polsfuss, Mark	540
Prato, H.	528
Price, Linda L.	187
Ridgway, Nancy M.	445
Roberts, John H.	635
Roberts, Scott D.	40
Robinson, Michael	545
Romeo, Jean B.	399
Rossiter, John R.	100
Rucker, Margaret	528
Rust, Langbourne	18
Saegert, Joel	262
Saunders, Don	84
Scammon, Debra L.	706
Schaffer, Catherine M.	476
Schindler, Robert M.	330, 794
Schmitt, Bernd H.	52
Schouten, John W.	49
Schroeder, Jonathan E.	532
Schurr, Paul H.	591
Scott, Linda M.	355
Semenik, Richard J.	755
Shimp, Terence A.	158
Showers, Linda S.	284
Shrum, L. J.	755
Smith, Ken R.	706
Smith, Ruth Ann	379
Smith, Ruth Belk	673
Sorce, Patricia	802
Srull, Thomas K.	764
Stern, Barbara B.	164, 384
Stewart, David W.	176, 179
Stoltman, Jeffrey J.	434
Strate, Lance	115
Stuenkel, J. Kathleen	296
Tansuhaj, Patriya S.	651
Tashjian, R.	576
Tax, Steve	84
Thompson, Craig J.	63
Thorson, Esther	202, 538
Treistman, Joan	749
Unnava, H. Rao	28, 317
Urbany, Joel E.	217, 788
Venkatesh, Alladi	618
Wadkins, Marsha	129
Walker, Beth A.	342
Walker, Mary	364
Wallace, Wanda T.	239
Ward, James	84
Weitz, Barton A.	407
Westgate, Lori	441
Widrick, Stanley M.	802
Williams, John H.	780
Witkowski, Terrence H.	123
Wynes, M.	528
Yamamoto, Yoshito	123
Yi, Youjae	24, 414, 417
Young, Charles E.	545
Young, Melissa Martin	33
Zaltman, Gerald	8
Zhang, Yong	813
Zinkhan, George M.	348, 813